TEXTBOOK OF PHARMACOLOGY
(For Pharmacy Students)

A man would do nothing,
if he waited until he could do it so well
that no one would find fault
with what he has done

—Cardinal Newman

TEXTBOOK OF PHARMACOLOGY

(For Pharmacy Students)

F.S.K. Barar
M.Sc. (Med.), M.D. (Pharmacol.)
Former Senior Professor and Head
Department of Pharmacology
S.M.S. Medical College, Jaipur
&
Former Associate Director (*Pharmacy*)
Lachoo Memorial College of Science & Technology, Jodhpur

S. Chand And Company Limited
(ISO 9001 Certified Company)

S. Chand And Company Limited

(ISO 9001 Certified Company)

Head Office: D-92, Sector–2, Noida – 201301, U.P. (India), Ph. 91-120-4682700

Registered Office: A-27, 2nd Floor, Mohan Co-operative Industrial Estate, New Delhi – 110 044, Phone: 011-49731800

www.**schandpublishing.com**; e-mail: **info@schandpublishing.com**

Marketing Offices:

Chennai	:	Ph: 23632120; chennai@schandpublishing.com
Guwahati	:	Ph: 2738811, 2735640; guwahati@schandpublishing.com
Hyderabad	:	Ph: 40186018; hyderabad@schandpublishing.com
Jalandhar	:	Ph: 4645630; jalandhar@schandpublishing.com
Kolkata	:	Ph: 23357458, 23353914; kolkata@schandpublishing.com
Lucknow	:	Ph: 4003633; lucknow@schandpublishing.com
Mumbai	:	Ph: 25000297; mumbai@schandpublishing.com
Patna	:	Ph: 2260011; patna@schandpublishing.com

First Edition 2013

Reprints 2014, 2020, 2022 (Twice)

Reprint 2025

ISBN: 978-81-219-4080-1

Product Code: H3PHR63PHRM10ENAA13R

PRINTED IN INDIA

By Vikas Publishing House Private Limited, Plot 20/4, Site-IV, Industrial Area Sahibabad, Ghaziabad – 201 010 and Published by S Chand And Company Limited, A-27, 2nd Floor, Mohan Co-operative Industrial Estate, New Delhi – 110 044.

Dedicated to

My wife, and my children

and

my students

PREFACE

"Science cannot grow by routine work alone, it cannot even live, because, like a tree if it is not growing it is dying. If routine gets the upper hand science becomes fossilized into formulae and rules. once these become rigid they become fallacious, reflecting the errors and limitations of those who originated them in their once living form".

— A.D. Ritchie, 1950

Paleopharmacological studies bear evidence to the use of medicinal plants in the treatment of disease even in the pre-historic era. In ancient **Egypt** pharmacological knowledge was recorded in various papyri like the **Ebers Papyrus** of 1550 BC, and the **Edwin Smith Papyrus** of the 16th century BC. **Aesculapius** whose descent was traced by the ancient Greeks directly from Apollo was considered to be the Greek God of Medicine. **Hippocrates** (born about 460 BC), renowned as the *"Father of Medicine"* , was the embodiment of the highest ideals in medical ethics. His famous *"Hippocratic Oath"* continues to be an everlasting memorial to his greatness. He eschewed 'superstition' and brought in scientific methods into the domain of healing. The name of **Chang Ching Chung** known as the "Hippocrates of China" occupies a prominent place in the history of Chinese medicine. His famous "Treatise of Fevers" dates back to about 170 AD. The greatest name in Roman medicine was **Claudius Galen** (130-c.200). Galen was educated in the Alexandrian School where Anatomy was taught at advanced levels. He worked on the nervous system and settled in Rome in the year 161, and wrote over 200 treatises. In the Middle East **Rhazes** (865-915AD) promoted the use of chemicals in the treatment of disease.

Ancient Indian Medicine was also very advanced comparable to the Greeks. The earliest compilation of medicinal substances was the **Sushruta Samhita**, an Indian Ayurvedic treatise attributed to the great philosopher **Sushruta Muni**, dating back to the 6th century BC. Two ancient preserved texts date back to the 3rd or 4th century AD: the **Charaka Samhita**, attributed to Charaka Muni, the renowned physician of ancient Indian medicine; and the Sharngadara Samhita attributed to Sharngadara Muni. These compilations form the foundation of the *Indian Ayurvedic System of medicine.*

Historically, pharmacy as an independent science is relatively young. Its origin dates back to early 19th century. As a discipline pharmacy has always been connected to the practice of medicine. Advances in the Middle East in botany and chemistry led to the development of pharmacy.

Rhazes (850-932 AD), promoted the medicinal uses of chemicals, and **Abulcasis** (936-1013 AD) started preparing medicines by *sublimation* and *distillation*. Later, **Al-Biruni** (973-1050 AD) wrote a valuable book on pharmacology titled *Kitab al-Saydalah* (*The Book of Drugs*) detailing properties of drugs, outlining the role of pharmacy, and duties of a pharmacist. **Avicenna** (980-1037 AD), Persian physician and philosopher, was known for his *Canon of Medicine* (describing about 700 preparations, with their mode of action, properties and uses). It was a standard medical textbook used in Europe until the 17th century. In Europe pharmacy developed as a science from the 13th century onwards in the reign of Emperor Fredric II.

In the 1990s *clinical pharmacy* as an important branch of pharmacy came up, which involves pharmacists and pharmacoeconomists responsible for optimizing the use of medication to promote health and prevent disease in hospitals, nursing homes and clinics. They work in unison with physicians, and health professionals. Now disease that struck down thousands of suffering humans can now be treated by drugs.

The text has 17 main chapters, followed by 3 appendices, and an index for rapid consultation and revision. Relevant basic information related to the use of drugs has been provided in each chapter. The subject material covers the current syllabus prescribed for pharmacy students. In addition, the *"Newer Drug's Digest"* provides information on drugs in the process of research and development. Any suggestions from readers are solicited.

Last but not the least, I offer profound thanks to editorial and management team at S. Chand & Company Ltd., New Delhi for their efficient and prompt cooperation towards the printing and publication of this work.

A tribute to Researchers Anonymous

"If you take a prescription to a drugstore today, the chances are overwhelming that the pharmacist will have to use at least one wonder drug to fill it. Yet 90 percent of the prescriptions written by doctors today could not have been filled in 1935, because one or more of the prescribed drugs was then unknown".

— Donald G. Cooley, 1954

F.S.K. Barar
bararfsk@gmail.com

CONTENTS

ABBREVIATIONS

ACh	Acetylcholine
AChE	Acetylcholinesterase
ACTH	Adrenocorticotrophic hormone, Corticotrophin
ADH	Antidiuretic hormone
ADP	Adenosine diphosphate
AIDS	Acquired Immunodeficiency Syndrome
ANS	Autonomic nervous system
ATP	Adenosine triphosphate
AV	Atrioventricular
BP	Blood pressure
c-AMP	Cyclic adenosine 3′, 5′ monophosphate
ChE	Cholinesterase
CNS	Central nervous system
CoA	Coenzyme A
COMT	Catechol-O-methyltransferase
CSF	Cerebrospinill fluid
CtZ	Chemoreceptor trigger zone
CVP	Central venous pressure
DNA	Deoxyribonucleic acid
DOPA	Dihydroxyphenylalanine
ECF	Extracellular fluid
ECG	Electrocardiogram
ECT	Electroconvulsive therapy
EEG	Electroencephillogram
FFA	Free fatty acid
FSH	Follicle stimulating hormone
g	Gram
GABA	Gamma-aminobutyric acid
GFR	Glomerular filtration rate
GH	Growth hormone
c-GMP	Cyclic guanosine 3′, 5′ monophosphate
G-6-PD	Glucose-6-phosphate dehydrogenase
GTP	Guanosine triphosphate
HCG	Human chorionic gonadotrophin
HMG	Human menopausal gonadotrophin
5-HT	5-Hydroxytryptamine
HVA	Homovanillic acid
Hz	Hertz (1 Hertz is 1 cycle per second)
Ig	Immunoglobulin
IM	Intramuscular
IV	Intravenous
l	Litre
LH	Luteinizing hormone
log	Logarithm
LSD	Lysergic acid diethylamide
M	Molar
MAO	Monoamine oxidase
MAOI	Monoamine oxidase inhibitor
mcg	Microgram
mg	Milligram
MIC	Minimal inhibitory concentration
min	Minute
mol	Mole (gram molecular weight)
mRNA	messenger ribonucleic acid
Na	Noradrenaline
NADP	Nicotinamide adenine dinucleotide phosphate
NADPH	Nicotinamide adenine dinucleotide phosphate (reduced)
ng	Nanogram
PABA	Para-aminobenzoic acid
PG	Prostaglandlin
pH	Negative log of hydrogen ion concentration
pKa	Negative log of dissociation constant
P450	Cytochrome with maximum absorption at wavelength 450 nm.
RNA	Ribonucleic acid
SA	Sinoatrial
SC	Subcutaneous
SRS-A	Slow reacting substance of anaphylaxis
$t_{1/2}$	Half life
THC	Tetrahydrocannabinol
tRNA	Transfer RNA
TSH	Thyroid stimulating hormone, Thyrotrophin
v/v	Volume per unit volume
WHO	Wold Health Organisation
w/v	Weight per unit volume
w/w	Weight per unit Weight

1

GENERAL PARMACOLOGY

1.1 SCOPE OF PHARMACOLOGY

Definitions

Pharmacology, Pharmacognosy, Pharmacy, Pharmacokinetics, Pharmacodynamics, Pharmacotherapeutics, Therapeutics, Toxicology, Pharmacogenetics, Clinical Pharmacology

Historical Development
Drug Information Sources
The Pharmacopoeias, etc.

Pharmacology is the study of drugs. Drugs are chemicals that produce therapeutically useful effects. They modify functions of living organisms, and are generally given to **prevent**, **diagnose**, or **cure** disease processes. Pharmacology has a wide scope, and derives from various other disciplines like physiology, microbiology, pathology, biochemistry and various clinical specialities.

DEFINITIONS

Pharmacology is defined as the science of drugs. The term is derived from the Greek words *pharmakon*, meaning a drug, and *logos*, meaning a study. Pharmacology has the following major subdivisions:

Pharmacognosy (Greek *gnosis*, knowledge) is the study of the sources of drugs derived from plants and animals, and of the physical and chemical properties of such substances.

Pharmacy is the study of the preparation, compounding and dispensing of medicines. It is the science and art of preparing a drug or drug combination, in a suitable dosage form, fit for administration to the patient. The **pharmacist** is concerned primarily with preparing, compounding and dispensing medicines upon the written order of a licensed medical practitioner.

Pharmacokinetics (Greek *kinesis*, movement) is the study of the fate of drugs in body, right from the time they (drugs) enter the body until they, or their by-products, are eliminated from the body, *i.e.*, the movement of drugs in the body. In short, this includes absorption, distribution, metabolism and excretion of drugs.

Pharmacodynamics (Greek *dynamis*, force) is the experimental study of actions of drugs on the living organism, including their mode or mechanism of action.

Pharmacotherapeutics (Greek *therapeia*, medical treatment) is the treatment of disease by means of drugs. It utilizes information on drugs obtained by pharmacodynamic studies.

Therapeutics (Greek *therapeutike*, medical practice) is the practical branch of medicine dealing with the science and art of the treatment of disease.

Chemotherapy according to the definition proposed by Paul Ehrlich, deals with the use of drugs capable of inhibiting or destroying invading microbes, parasites, or cancer cells; while having minimal effect on healthy living tissues.

Toxicology (Greek *toxikon*, poison) is the science of poisons—their source, chemical composition, action, tests for detection and antidotes. **Clinical toxicology** deals with the detection, diagnosis and treatment of poisoning. **Toxicodynamics** describes the harmful effects that the poison produces on the body. **Toxicokinetics** encompasses the absorption, distribution, biotransformation and elimination of the poison.

Pharmacogenetics is a relatively new field, and deals with the study of genetically determined variations in drugs response.

Clinical pharmacology is the division which deals with the pharmacologic effects of drugs in man. It provides information about the usefulness, potency and toxicity of new drugs in humans.

Historical Development

Earliest prescriptions are recorded in a Sumerian tablet of 2100 B.C. describing ointments and medicines containing asafoetida, thyme (source of Thymol), sodium chloride and potassium nitrate. The **Ebers Papyrus** written in 1550 B.C. contains prescriptions of castor oil, opium, colchicum and other drugs. Perhaps, Chinese Medicine was about the earliest, dated at about 2500 B.C. Ephedra or *Ma huang* was used even in those early days. **Ayurveda** or *Indian Medicine* is about equally ancient, and it has given some useful remedies to modern medicine.

Some giants in the history of medicine were *Hippocrates, Aristotle, Theophrastus, Pliny, Dioscorides* and *Galen*. **Hippocrates** (460-370 B.C.) is referred to as the "father of medicine", and many of his writings dealt with anatomy and physiology. The "Hippocratic Oath" of modern day medicine reflects the high esteem with which this Greek physician is regarded. Hippocrates was the first to recognize disease as an abnormal reaction of the body rather than as a visitation from the Gods. **Aristotle** (384-322 B.C.), a student of Plato, is considered to be the most influential Greek Philosopher. He attempted to separate superstition from fact. **Theophrastus** (370-287 B.C.), a student of Aristotle, utilized his teacher's scientific reasoning, and applied it to the plant kingdom. **Dioscorides,** a Greek physician of the first century B.C. described several plants of medicinal value. Later, **Pliny** (23-70 A.D.) compiled 37 volumes of natural history, which served as reference data for many years. The Hippocratic concept of disease was then lost and did not reappear until the Renaissance (15th Century A.D. marking the transition from the Middle Ages to the modern world). During this dark period the concept of **Galen** (131-201 A.D.) and his dogmatic system of polypharmacy prevailed. Galen, a Greek pharmacist physician, who lived in Rome, described many formulae containing plant and animal drugs. He compiled this knowledge in 20 books. Galen's name is retained in the term "galenical" pharmacy, which includes preparation of crude vegetable drugs.

Paracelsus (1493-1541 A.D.), an outstanding leader of the Renaissance, reintroduced free thought and critical enquiry. He attacked the Galenic system of polypharmacy, and introduced the use of simple chemicals for treating disease. He introduced mercurials in the treatment of syphilis. During his time the first official pharmacopoeia was printed.

Experimental medicine and therapeutics had to wait long for the advances in physiology, which during the decade (1850-1860) became an experimental science. **Virchow**, the German physiologist in 1855 propounded the concept of "all cells from cells". Later, with advances in the knowledge of the physiology of circulation, central nervous system, the hormones and enzymes in the body, the study of pharmacology and therapeutics was stabilized. *In fact, pharmacology originated as a branch of physiology*. The application of scientific method to studies on drugs was generated in France by **Francois Megendie** (1783-1855), and was expanded by **Claude Bernard** (1813-1878), who came to be known as the "father of experimental medicine". The name of **Oswald Schmiedeberg** (1838-1921) is associated with the development of experimental pharmacology in Germany, and **John Jacob Abel** (1857-1938) played a similar role in the United States of America. in India **Sir Ram Nath Chopra** (1882-1973) was responsible for the development of pharmacology as a well defined discipline. He was the Founder Director of the Drug Research Laboratory which is now known as the Regional Research Laboratory of the Council of Scientific and Industrial Research (CSIR), located at Jammu-Tawi. Sir Chopra has been widely acclaimed as the Father of Indian Pharmacology, because of his investigations on Indian indigenous drugs. The growth of pharmacology was further stimulated by the development of synthetic organic chemistry, which has provided many new therapeutic agents.

The Pharmacopoeias

The term *pharmacopoeia* is derived from the Greek words *pharmakon*, meaning "drug", and *poiein*, meaning "make". The term was first used in 1580 for a book of drug standards in Bergame, Italy. The pharmacopoeias are a class of drug compendia, and its main body contains monographs on drugs and ancillary substances. A pharmacopoeia is periodically revised and kept up-to-date. The **National Formulary** is a smaller and much more handy book containing formulations of therapeutic value. Drugs and substances which are included in the current edition of a pharmacopoeia are designated as *official*.

In England the first **British Pharmacopoeia** (BP) was published in 1864. In the USA Dr. Lyman Spalding planned a national pharmacopeia, and in the year 1820 the first **United States Pharmacopeia** (USP) was published. The **European Pharmacopoeia** (Vol. I, 1969; Vol. II, 1971) was published by the Public Health Committee and the European Pharmacopoeia Commission.

The **International Pharmacopoeia** is published by the World Health Organization (WHO). It is published in many languages (English, French, Russian, Spanish). This pharmacopoeia is meant for use and adoption all over the world. Some of the drug compendia are detailed below:

India

1. *Pharmacopoeia of India* (The Indian Pharmacopoeia), Sixth Edition, Two Volumes. Government of India, Ministry of Health & Family Welfare, New Delhi, 2010.
2. *National Formulary of India* (NFI), 4th Edition, Formulated by the Indian Pharmacopoeia Commission (IPC), New Delhi, 2010.
3. *Monthly Index of Medical Specialities, MIMS, INDIA*, Editor, Gulhati, C.M. (published every month).
4. *Drugs Bulletin*, Editor, P. Pandhi, Department of

Pharmacology, PGIMER, Chandigarh (published quarterly).

Great Britain

1. *British Pharmacopoeia* (*BP*), Six Volumes. Her Majesty's Stationary Office (HMSO), London, 2011.
2. *The* (*British*) *Pharmaceutical Codex* (*BPC*), 12th Edition; The Pharmaceutical Press, London, 1994.
3. *British National Formulary* (*BNF*), Number 61, Joint publication of the British Medical Association and the Pharmaceutical Society of Great Britain, London, 2011.
4. *The Extra Pharmacopoeia* (*Martindale*), 29th Edition, Editor, Sweetman, S.C. The Pharmaceutical Press, 2011.

U.S.A.

1. *The United States Pharmacopeia* (*USP*), 34th edition, and The *National Formulary* (NF), 29th Edition, United States Pharmacopeial Convention Inc. Rockville, MD, 2011.
2. *American Drug Index* (*ADI*), 55th Edition, Editors Billups, N.F. and Billups, S.M., Published by Facts and Comparison JB Lippincott Co., Philadelphia, 2011.
3. *Physicians' Desk Reference* (*PDR*), published by Medical Economics Inc. Oradell, N.J., U.S.A. 65th edition, 2011. (published every year).
4. *AMA Drug Evaluations*, 5th Edition; prepared by the AMA Division of Drugs with the American Society for Clinical Pharmacology and Therapeutics, WB Saunders Co., Philadelphia, 1986.
5. *Drug Facts and Comparisons*, 65th Edition; JB Lippincott Co., Philadelphia, 2011.

Some hospitals maintain their own special formularies and handbooks for the drugs and formulations frequently prescribed in their institutions.

1.2 SOURCES, NATURE AND NOMENCLATURE OF DRUGS

The term "drug" is derived from the French word "drogue" meaning a dry herb. A *drug* is defined as a substance used for the **diagnosis, prevention, treatment** or **palliation** (relief from symptoms) of disease. A fifth category of drug usage is for prevention of pregnancy, i.e., contraception; a non-disease condition. Sixthly, drugs may also be used for maintenance of optimal health.

Sources of Drugs

Drugs are derived from four main sources: (*i*) *plants*; (*ii*) *animals*; (*iii*) *minerals* or *mineral products*; and (*iv*) *synthetic* chemicals made in the laboratory. Drugs have also been obtained from micro-organisms, and their growth products include antibiotics like *bacitracin*; enzymes like *streptokinase*; and today genetically modified *E. coli* produce *human insulin*, a hormone.

Plant drugs: The roots, leaves and barks of plants were used to treat disease till the beginning of this century. Later, the active principles were extracted and used in modern medicine. Plant products like **quinine, morphine, ephedrine** and **digoxin**, continue to be important drugs. **Antibiotics** produced by living bacteria, yeasts and moulds are valuable in the treatment of infectious disease. **Penicillin, streptomycin, chloramphenicol** and the **tetracyclines** are some useful antibiotics.

Animal drugs: Animal products are: **insulin**, extracted from pork and beef pancreas, is used for diabetes mellitus; **thyroid powder** for hypothyroidism; **heparin** as an anticoagulant; and different hormones for various endocrinal diseases.

Mineral drugs: Minerals as simple elements or their salts provide useful drugs, like *ferrous sulphate* for anaemia, *magnesium trisilicate* for hyperacidity and peptic ulcer. Radioactive isotopes of Iodine, Phosphorus and Gold are also used in modern medicine.

Synthetic drugs: Majority of drugs in use today are prepared synthetically from chemical substances. Semisynthetic drugs are naturally occurring substances that have been chemically altered. Some examples are: **sulphonamides, thiazide diuretics, oral antidiabetics, synthetic corticosteroids, sympathomimetics** and other autonomic agents.

Recombinant DNA technology: This innovative technology is now being used for production of *human insulin* by introducing coded DNA into harmless strains of *Escherichia coli*. The amino acid sequence of human insulin thus produced is identical to endogenous human insulin. Synthetic **human growth hormone** is also being prepared by recombinant DNA technology. This technology in the future would be successfully used for producing many drugs which are presently derived solely from animal or human sources.

Nature of Drugs

Plants and animals yield a large number of drugs. They can be grouped according to their physical and chemical properties into one of the following :

1. **Alkaloids.** Alkaloids (alkali-like) are compounds composed of carbon, hydrogen, nitrogen and oxygen. They have a bitter taste, and are often poisonous. The name of an alkaloid ends in "ine", e.g., **caffeine, atropine** and **morphine**. Alkaloids are basic substances, and combine with an acid to form a salt. These salts of alkaloids are used in medicine in preference to pure alkaloids, as they are more soluble, e.g., atropine sulphate or morphine sulphate. Increased solubility makes administration by injection possible. A number of alkaloids have been chemically synthesized in the laboratory. Both alkaloids and their salts are precipitated by **tannic acid**, and oxidized by **potassium permanganate**. Hence these substances can be used as antidotes for poisoning from alkaloids.
2. **Glycosides.** They are ether-like combinations of sugars with other organic substances found in plants. Glycosides are referred to as **glucosides** if the sugar in combination is glucose. The carbohydrate molecule is usually not essential for the action of the glycoside, and in the body it may be removed to liberate the active **aglycone** or **genin**. The pharmacological action of the

glycoside is due to the aglycone component, and the sugar modifies the solubility, penetration, reactivity, distribution and duration of action of the glycoside. Important examples are the cardiac glycosides found in digitalis leaf. Out of them **digoxin** and **digitoxin** are mostly used.

3. **Oils.** The term oil is applied to a large number of liquids which are insoluble in water and highly viscous. Their greasy feel is the result of these properties. Oils are of two kinds: **Volatile *oils*** and **Fixed *oils*.**

   Volatile oils are liquids that impart an aroma to a plant, and are volatilized by heat. They evaporate and leave no greasy stain. Because of their pleasant odour and taste they are frequently used as **flavouring agents**. Examples are **peppermint**, **spearmint** and **clove oil**. Oil of **Wintergreen** is almost pure methyl salicylate used locally for relief of muscle and joint pains.

   Fixed oils are the glycerides of oleic, palmitic and stearic acids. They are greasy and do not evaporate readily. They are extracted chiefly from the seeds, occurring within the cells as droplets or crystals. Fixed oils do not exert marked pharmacological activity. *Olive oil* and **cotton seed oil** are used as food of high calorific value. Fixed oils of vegetable origin include olive oil, castor oil, croton oil and peanut oil. Fixed oils of animal origin are cod liver oil, shark liver oil, lard and butter. **Fats** are fixed oils which remain solid at ordinary temperature. **Waxes** are composed of fatty acids combined with monohydric alcohol. They are more firm with a higher melting point and are mostly used as ointment bases. The term **lipids** includes fixed oils, fats and waxes.

   Mineral oils are mixture of hydrocarbons of the methane and related aliphatic series, obtained from petroleum by fractional distillation. They are produced in various consistencies - **hard paraffin**, **soft paraffin** and **liquid paraffin**. The first two are used as ointment bases, and liquid paraffin is used as a laxative.

4. **Tannins.** They are non-nitrogenous plant constituents, and have an astringent action. They are of two types: the **pyrogallol tannins** which are glycosides of glucose and occur in oak galls; and the **pyrocatechol tannins** which are sugar-free derivatives of catechol and occur in catechu and eucalyptus. Tannin for medicinal use is obtained from oak galls, and known as **tannic acid**. Tannins are used for treating burns and diarrhoea.

5. **Gums.** They are exudates from plants. Chemically they are **polysaccharides**, and on hydrolysis yield simple sugars. Upon addition of water some of them swell up and form adhesive mucilaginous masses; and some remain unchanged. In the gut they act as hydrophillic (water-loving) colloids and function as bulk laxatives, e.g., agar and psyllium seeds. Synthetic hydrophilic colloids like **methylcellulose** and **sodium carboxymethyl cellulose** have replaced the natural gums as laxatives. **Tragacanth** gum in the from of an emulsion is used for chapped skin. **Acacia** is used as a suspending agent in making emulsions and mixtures like Bismuth-Kaolin Mixture for diarrhoea.

6. **Resins.** They are ill-defined solid substances found in plants, and are produced by oxidation and polymerization of volatile oils. The rosin used by violinists is an example of a solid resin. They are insoluble in water, but soluble in alcohol, ether and chloroform. Resins are of many types: **oleoresins** (aspidium); **gum-resins** (asafoetida); **oleo-gum-resin** (myrrh); **balsams** (benzoin, tolu, Peru). Balsams are used in the treatment of cough and bronchitis for their antiseptic and protective properties. **Podophyllum** resin is an irritant purgative.

7. **Antibiotics.** They are chemical substances produced or derived from living cells which have a lethal (bactericidal) or inhibitory (bacteriostatic) action on micro-organisms. The main sources of antibiotics are moulds, yeasts and bacteria.

8. **Hormones.** They are specialized chemicals generally derived from animal endocrine glands. Hormones are largely used in medicine as substitution therapy. They vary in their chemical structure, e.g., **insulin** is a polypeptide; **sex hormones** and **corticosteroids** are steroids; **thyroxine** is an iodine derivative of the amino acid tyrosine.

Drug Nomenclature

Drugs may be conveniently divided into two main groups: (*i*) **non-prescription drugs**, which may be sold "over-the-counter" (OTC) since they are judged to be safe for use without medical supervision; and (*ii*) **prescription drugs**, which are considered to be unsafe for use except under medical supervision, therefore, they are dispensed only on a physician's prescription.

Every drug has three names: (*i*) the **chemical name**; (*ii*) the **approved** name (*non-proprietary*); and (*iii*) the **trade** (*proprietary, brand, registered*) name. The **chemical name** gives the chemical constitution of the drug, indicating the precise arrangement of atoms and atomic groups in the molecule. For example, the chemical name of the antianxiety drug **diazepam** is 7-chloro-2-methylamino-

5-phenyl-3H1, 4-benzodiazepine-4-oxide. Thus chemical names are too complex to be widely used.

There are two classes of **non-proprietary names**: (*i*) the **Official** name, which is used in the official book like the Indian, British, United States or the International pharmacopoeia. This name may be identical with the generic name; and (*ii*) the **Approved** name, same as adopted or generic name. This is the name which may or may not be included in the pharmacopoeia, but alternatively is the adopted name given by bodies like the United States Adopted Names (USAN) Council. This is an agency which adopts appropriate non-proprietary names for all new drugs, and was formed in 1964. The USAN Council coordinates with the pharmaceutical firms and other agencies like the World Health Organization (WHO), and helps in adopting and standardizing the non-proprietary nomenclature for drugs as far as possible.

The **proprietary** ("brand" or "registered" or "trade") name is the exclusive property of the pharmaceutical firm which sells the drug, although it may not have made the drug itself. Thus a single drug may be sold under many proprietary names by different firms, but regardless of this there is only one generic or official name in each country. For example, take the oral antidiabetic drug chlorpropamide:

Chemical name	:	1-(4-chlorobenzenesulphonyl)-3-propylurea
Official name	:	Chlorpropamide
Generic name	:	Chlorpropamide
Trade name	:	Diabinese

Thus to simplify, each drug has a **non-proprietary** (generic or official) and a **proprietary** (brand, trade or registered) name, apart from the rarely used **chemical** name. The clinicians usually prescribe drugs by their brand names. The use of many names for the same drug can be a cause for confusion. Hence, there is a line of thinking which supports prescribing of drugs by their *generic* name. The debate continues.

Drug Classification

Drugs may be classified according to any one or more of the following ways: (*i*) their **anatomical site of action**; (*ii*) their **therapeutic activity**; (*iii*) their **mode of action**; and (*iv*) their **origin**. The central nervous system (CNS) depressant phenobarbitone sodium can be classified respectively as (*i*) a drug acting on the CNS, (*ii*) a sedative-hypnotic, (*iii*) a CNS depressant, and (*iv*) a derivative of barbituric acid.

1.3 DOSAGE FORMS AND ROUTES OF DRUG ADMINISTRATION

A **dosage form** of a drug is a product suited for administration to the patient by various routes for diagnosis or treatment of disease. **Pharmaceutical preparations** are recognized by the pharmacopoeias and other official and non-official compendia. The term dosage form is replacing the expression pharmaceutical preparation.

Suitable dosage forms are needed for the following reasons: (*i*) for protection of the drug from destructive influences of the atmospheric oxygen or moisture (coated tablets, sealed ampules); (*ii*) for protection of drug from destruction by gastric acid on oral administration (enteric coated tablets); (*iii*) to mask the bitter taste or foul odour of the drug (capsules, coated tablets, flavoured syrups); (*iv*) to provide liquid preparations of substances which are insoluble or unstable in the desired vehicle (suspensions); (*v*) to provide extended drug action through controlled release mechanisms (retarded release tablets, spansules or suspensions); (*vi*) to provide optimal drug action on topical administration (ointments, creams, eye/ear/nasal drops); (*vii*) to provide for drug administration by insertion into body orifices (rectal or vaginal suppositories); (*viii*) to provide for placement of drugs within body tissues (injections); (*ix*) to provide for liquid dosage forms of soluble substances in the desired vehicle (solutions); and (*x*) to provide for drug action through inhalation (aerosols). In addition many dosage forms permit drug identification through distinctive colour, shape or markings.

Vehicles

Vehicles or solvents are used to dissolve or suspend drugs. **Waters** are solutions of volatile oils or other aromatic substances in distilled water, e.g., Peppermint, Cinnamon and Anise waters. They are used to mask the bad taste of drugs. *Syrups* are solutions of flavouring or medicinal substances in an almost saturated solution of sugar (sucrose) in water. *Simple syrup* is a saturated solution of sugar in water, which is used to make other syrups. Some *flavoured syrups* used to mask the bad taste are Cherry, Orange and Raspberry syrups. An example of a *medicated syrup* is Ipecac syrup. **Elixirs** are sweetened, pleasantly flavoured hydroalcoholic solutions of medicinal substances. *Simple elixir* or orange elixir is a popular solvent. It contains about 22 percent alcohol. *Medicated elixirs* include Phenobarbitone, Terpin hydrate and Codeine elixirs.

Colouring Agents

Colouring agents are harmless substances used for lending colour to drugs to make them more acceptable to patients. The quantity to be added is fixed within safe limits. **Amaranth Solution** colours red; **Caramel** (burnt sugar) colours brown; **Cochineal** colours bright red.

Sweetening Agents

Solid sweetening agents usually employed are : (*i*) **Sucrose** or cane sugar for syrups and elixirs; (*ii*) **Saccharin**, which is about 500 times sweeter than sugar. It is a non-caloric sweetener and may be used by diabetics or obese patients to restrict their carbohydrate intake. Lately, there is suspicion that saccharin is carcinogenic; and (*iii*) **Aspartame** is 200 times sweeter than sugar and has been cleared as a safe sugar substitute. It does not have a metallic after-taste like saccharin. Aspartame is metabolized in the body like proteins. It loses its sweetness under heat, making it unsuitable for sweetening baked confectionary.

Flavouring Agents

The term flavour refers to a mixed sensation of taste, touch, smell, sight and sound, all combining to produce different grades of perception of a substance. The four primary tastes are: *sweet*, *bitter*, *sour* and *saline*. Proper selection of flavour has to be made to mask nauseating medicines: bitter taste by Cocoa or Raspberry syrup; sour taste by Raspberry or Acacia syrup; saline taste by Cinnamon or Orange syrup; and oily taste by Compound Sarsaparilla syrup.

Aqueous Solutions

Aqueous solutions contain one or more drugs dissolved in water. They are of two categories: (*i*) **Solutions for oral use**, e.g., Strong iodine solution; and (*ii*) **Solutions for injection**, which are sterile liquids or suspensions, packaged in suitable containers to maintain sterility, and are intended for parenteral use. The aqueous vehicles mostly used for preparing injections are: Water for Injection and Sodium Chloride Injection. Injections are available in sealed glass ampules or vials. **Ampules** are sealed glass containers and usually contain one dose of the drug, e.g., Neostigmine (Prostigmin) Injection, Nalorphine hydrochloride (Nalline) Injection etc. **Vials** are glass containers with hermetically (airtight) sealed rubber stoppers, and usually contain multiple doses of the drug, e.g., Insulin Injection; Isophane Insulin Suspension etc. A sterile hypodermic needle is inserted through the rubber stopper to withdraw a measured dose from the vial. The pharmacopoeias document specific requirements for **sterility** and **absence of pyrogens** for all injections.

Aqueous Suspensions

Aqueous suspensions contain one or more chemical substances dispersed in water by means of harmless suspending agents. They are preparations of finely divided, undissolved drugs dispersed in liquids. Suspensions meant for parenteral use (injections) have already been detailed above under aqueous solution. Suspensions for oral use are as under:

Emulsions are suspensions of fats or oils in water with the aid of an emulsifying agent (gum acacia). The oil particles are coated with gum so that they do not coalesce as the interfacial tension between the oil and water is lowered. Thus a stable suspension is produced. Emulsified oils are more palatable and more easily digested than undispersed oils. *Examples*: Cod Liver Oil Emulsion, Castor Oil Emulsion.

Gels are colloidal aqueous suspensions of hydrated inorganic substances. *Example*: Aluminium Hydroxide Gel.

Magmas are bulky suspensions of poorly soluble substances in water. They are also called *milks* as they are white liquids. Magmas and gels are similar except that the particles suspended in a magma are larger. Thus magmas tend to separate on standing and require a "shake well" label. *Example*: Milk of Magnesia or Magnesium Hydroxide Mixture.

Mixtures are preparations where the drug or drugs are in solution or suspension meant for oral administration. An example of a mixture with a suspension of a solid substance in water is Bismuth-Kaolin Mixture.

Alcoholic Solutions

Spirits or **Essences** are concentrated alcoholic solutions of volatile substances. The dissolved substance may be solid, liquid, or gaseous. Most spirits contain 5 to 20 percent of the active material. Spirits containing volatile oils are prepared by diluting 10 volumes of oil with 90 volumes of alcohol, and colouring material may also be added. Many spirits are used as flavouring agents. Alcohol serves both as a preservative and solvent. *Examples*: Peppermint Spirit, Lemon Spirit, Compound Orange Spirit, Aromatic Ammonia Spirit.

Extractive Preparations

Extractive preparations are made from vegetable drugs and contain the active principles in a hydroalcoholic solvent called the *menstruum*. They are made by two processes: (*i*) **Maceration**, in which the coarsely divided drug is mixed and frequently shaken with solvent, and after 3 or 4 days the solution is filtered, e.g., Compound Benzoin Tincture; and (*ii*) **Percolation** in which the solvent trickles through a column of coarsely divided drug, and thus the active substances are extracted. Various classes of extractive preparations are as under:

Tinctures are alcoholic or hydroalcoholic preparations of vegetable drugs, usually prepared in 10 percent strength for potent drugs. **Examples:** Belladonna Tincture, Digitalis Tincture. For nonpotent substances the strength is between 20 and 50 percent. Such tinctures are used as flavouring agents. **Examples:** Lemon Tincture, Sweet Orange Peel Tincture, Vanilla Tincture. Hydroalcoholic solutions of inorganic or organic agents are used as antiseptics. Examples: Tincture Iodine, Nitromersol Tincture.

Fluid extracts are alcoholic or hydroalcoholic extracts of vegetable drugs which are highly concentrated (about 10 times stronger than the usual tinctures). **Example:** Aromatic Cascara Sagrada Fluid Extract.

Extracts are concentrated, solid or semisolid preparations made by percolation and evaporation of the percolate. They may also be obtained by evaporating the solvent from tinctures or fluid extracts. **Examples:** Belladonna Extract, Cascara Sagrada Extract.

Solid Dosage Forms

Many drugs are more conveniently marketed and administered in their powdered or crystalline form. Some commonly used solid dosage forms are as under:

Powders are medicinal substances in a dried and finely divided form. They may be **simple** (one active ingredient), or **compound** (more than one active ingredient). Powders are used internally or externally. Effervescent powders like **Seidlitz powder** when dissolved in water liberate carbon dioxide, which makes the preparation more palatable.

Capsules are small containers usually made of gelatin and may be **hard** or **soft**, depending on the amount of glycerine in the gelatin. Sizes of capsules range from 5 (small) to 000 (big), available in different colours. Capsules are one of the most popular dosage forms for oral administration of **powders, oils** and **liquids**. They dissolve readily in the stomach and make the contents available for absorption. **Examples:** Sodium Amobarbital capsules, Halibut liver oil capsules. Capsules may be coated with substances that resist the action of gastric juice, and do not disintegrate in the stomach, but on reaching the intestines they dissolve in alkaline juices and release the drug, called **enteric coated capsules**. On occasions capsules may be administered rectally or vaginally.

Spansules are delayed action capsules prepared by variably coating the drug particles with material that permits gradual release of the drug in the gut. Such a measure provides for a long period of uniform medication. On ingestion some particles disintegrate immediately, others after 2 to 4 hours, and still others after 6 to 8 hours. Thus medication over a period of 10 to 12 hours is possible on one time administration. **Example:** Spansule Dexedrine Sulphate.

Tablets are solid dosage forms containing granulated or powdered drugs that are compressed or moulded into round or discoid shapes. They may be made with or without a diluent (dextrose, lactose, starch), and may differ greatly in size, shape and weight. Some tablets are *scored* (marked with an indented line across the surface) so that they may be easily divided if smaller doses are required.

Compressed tablets contain solid drugs (mostly in granulated form) subjected to great mechanical pressure and pressed into tablets. These tablets usually contain in addition to the drug a **diluent**, a **binder**, a **disintegrator**, and a **lubricant**. Diluents are used when the amount of the active ingredient is small, and the lubricant keeps the tablet from sticking to the machines. A disintegrator like starch helps the tablet to split readily in the stomach, as starch swells up on contact with moisture. Tablets may be coated with sugar or chocolate to enhance their palatability. They may be *enteric coated* to protect the drug from the effect of gastric secretions, or to prevent drug irritation of the gastric mucosa. Compressed tablets are administered orally. **Examples:** Aspirin Tablets, Erythromycin Tablets.

Moulded tablets or tablet triturates are prepared by mixing the moistened powdered drug with sugar, milk sugar or some other inert diluent. The resulting plastic mass is then moulded into discoid forms and dried. Most tablet triturates weigh about 60 mg. They may be used for oral, sublingual or buccal administration (sublingual or buccal tablets). **Examples:** Ergotamine Tartrate Tablets, Nitroglycerin Tablets.

Hypodermic tablets are compressed or moulded tablets that dissolve completely in water, making a solution suitable for injection. These tablets are dissolved in water for injection under aseptic conditions just before administration. **Examples:** Atropine Sulphate Hypodermic Tablets, Morphine sulphate Hypodermic Tablets.

Pellets are sterile spheres formed by compression of certain steroid hormones. They are suitably implanted subcutaneously and form a depot from which the hormone is slowly released. Pellets are marketed in sterile vials. **Examples:** Desoxycorticosterone Acetate Pellets, Testosterone Pellets.

Pills are powdered drugs mixed with adhesive substances like honey or glucose. This adhesive mass is moulded into globular, oval or flattened bodies convenient for swallowing. Pills are unsuitable for injection. The disadvantage with pills is that they become hard on drying and may not dissolve in the gut. The term *pill* is at times used for tablets or capsules in general, but strictly speaking it is a misuse of the term. In fact, pills now have been gradually replaced by tablets and capsules.

Troches or *lozenges* are flat, round or rectangular preparations that are kept in the mouth till they dissolve, liberating the drug or drugs they contain. In addition to the drug they usually contain water, sugar and mucilage. Troches temporarily produce a high concentration of the drug in the oral cavity, and are used to treat local conditions in the mouth and throat.

Dosage Forms for External Administration

Liniments are liquid suspensions or dispersions, applied to the skin by inunction or rubbing. They contain one or more active ingredients in a liniment base of a fixed oil, soap or alcohol. Liniments usually contain an anodyne (to relieve pain) or a *rubifacient* (to redden the skin). They relieve pain and swelling by counter-irritation and improvement in circulation. *Example:* Camphor Liniment.

Lotions are liquid preparations, applied to the skin without rubbing. Their base is usually aqueous. Glycerine and suspending agents are sometimes required for suspensions or dispersions. Lotions can be protective, emollient, cooling, cleansing, astringent or antipruritic depending on their content. **Example:** Calamine Lotion.

Ointments are semisolid greasy substances intended for local application to the skin or mucous membranes. The usual ointment has a petrolatum base (petroleum jelly or mineral oil), emulsifying agents and thickening substances. The base helps to keep the medicinal substance in prolonged contact with skin. Some ointment bases are miscible with water. Ointments serve as soothing agents, astringents, and antiseptics. **Examples:** Zinc Oxide Ointment, Sulphur Ointment, Bacitracin Ointment.

Ophthalmic ointments are sterile medicated ointments for use in the eye. The ointment base selected must be non-irritating to the eye, must permit free diffusion of the drug, and must not destroy the drug which it contains. **Examples:** Chloramphenicol Ophthalmic Ointment, Oxytetracycline Ophthalmic Ointment.

Pastes are ointment-like preparations of one or more medicaments and some adhesive material. They are applied to oozing surfaces, and afford greater protection and more absorptive action than ointments. **Example:** Zinc Oxide Paste.

Suppositories are mixtures of drugs with a firm base that can be moulded in shapes suitable for insertion into a body cavity or orifice. The base usually is glycerinated gelatin, hard soap or cocoa butter. They melt at body temperature, releasing the drug to come in contact with mucous membrane to produce a local or systemic effect. *Rectal* suppositories are conical or bullet shaped; *vaginal* suppositories are conical or spherical; and *urethral* suppositories are pencil-shaped. Suppositories should be stored preferably in a refrigerator, as they have low melting point ingredients.

Plasters are solid adhesive preparations, applied to the skin to protect, support, soothe and lessen pain. Substances having adhesive properties are spread evenly on a suitable fabric which may or may not be coated with a water repellent film. **Examples:** Zinc Oxide Plaster, Mustard Plaster.

Transdermal system is a unique and new drug delivery method applied through the skin. It provides for a prolonged and uniform release of a drug like **scopolamine** or **nitroglycerin**. The adhesive matrix contains a mineral oil and polyisobutylene.

Ophthalmic solutions (Collyria) are sterile, usually isotonic, buffered solutions for instillation in the eye. To prevent irritation, solutions used in the eyes should be isotonic. **Example:** Sliver Nitrate Ophthalmic Solution.

Sprays are solutions of one or more drugs in oil or water, administered by atomizers. Air forced through the atomizer by squeezing the rubber bulb carries with it a coarse liquid spray containing the drug into the nose or throat. *Example*: Tyrothricin Spray.

Inhalants are drugs which because of their high vapour pressure can be carried into the nasal passages with the inhaled air. They are available in portable inhalers. *Example*: Propylhexedrine Inhalant.

Inhalations (Aerosols) are stable suspensions of extremely small liquid or solid particles (0.5 to 5 microns) in a medium such as air or oxygen. They are produced and administered by **nebulizers**. The nebulized mist reaches the bronchi or even the alveoli. Aerosol-producing devices are employed in respiratory therapy.

Routes of Drug Administration

Route of administration of a drug is determined by its **physical** and **chemical properties**, **patient characteristics**, and the **rapidity** of response desired. The major routes are **oral**, **parenteral**, and **topical**. Each has advantages, disadvantages, indications for use, and special techniques of administration. For systemic effects the oral, or a parenteral route is employed.

Oral Route

The oral (enteral) route of administration is the safest, most economical, and the most convenient way of giving medicines. Therefore, medications should be given orally unless some distinct advantage is to be gained by using another route. The dosage forms for oral route include **tablets, capsules, powders, mixtures, emulsions** and **gels.** Drugs in solution are more quickly absorbed than solids. If a rapid effect is desired, the substance should be diluted and given with water **before meals**, as they are rapidly absorbed from an empty stomach. If the drug is likely to cause gastrointestinal irritation, it is given with or immediately **after meals**. If a medication such as a cough syrup is to be given for a local effect on the throat mucosa, it should not be diluted or followed by water. Most drugs are absorbed from the small intestines; some are absorbed from the stomach and colon.

On oral administration, drug action has a **slower onset** and **more prolonged** but **less potent effect** than when drugs are given parenterally. This is the result of: (*i*) **variation in absorption** due to food content, gastric or intestinal pH or motility, and pathology within the gut; or (*ii*) **alteration of the drug** due to its inactivation or partial destruction by the liver as it traverses via the hepatic circulation before entering systemic circulation.

Drugs may also be given through tubes placed in the gastrointestinal tract, like the **nasogastric** or **gastrostomy** tubes. In patients who cannot take drugs orally, this route is usually preferable to injections.

Disadvantages of oral administration of certain drugs are: (*i*) an objectionable odour or taste; (*ii*) damage or discolouration of teeth; (*iii*) irritation of the gastric mucosa, causing nausea and vomiting; (*iv*) aspiration into the lungs in seriously ill or uncooperative patients; and (*v*) they may be destroyed by digestive enzymes.

Sublingual. Some drugs like isoprenaline and nitroglycerin may be given sublingually by placing them under the patient's tongue, where they are retained until dissolved and absorbed, or the desired effect is produced. The thin epithelium and the rich capillary network under the tongue permit rapid absorption and drug action. In addition the drug is saved from hepatic inactivation, and destruction by digestive enzymes, as it reaches the general circulation without traversing through the liver. A drug may be applied against the mucosa of the cheek for *buccal* absorption. Patients must be instructed not to swallow the tablet, and water should not be taken immediately after the tablet to ensure proper sublingual or buccal absorption.

Rectal. Rectal administration can be used advantageously when the stomach is non-retentive due to vomiting; when the drug has an objectionable taste or odour; or when it can be destroyed by digestive enzymes. It is a reasonably convenient and safe method of giving drugs when the oral method is unsuitable, as when the patient is unconscious. Drugs like **paraldehyde, aminophylline** or **prochlorperazine** may be administered rectally. For rectal administration the suppository is far superior to the retention enema. An evacuant enema prior to administration of medication is usually advisable.

Parenteral Routes

The term parenteral route refers to any route other than gastrointestinal (enteral), but is commonly used to indicate **subcutaneous, intramuscular**, and **intravenous** injections. These routes may be selected when the drug is **poorly absorbed** from the gut; or **inactivated** by digestive enzymes; or **metabolized during its first passage** through the liver; or if the patient is **unable to take or tolerate** oral medication; or if a **rapid effect** is desired.

Aseptic technique must be employed when the drug is given parenterally. Although the skin cannot be made absolutely sterile, it must be as clean as possible. A cotton pledget soaked in a germicidal solution (or rectified spirit) is applied at the site of injection in a circular motion, moving from the centre outwards. All equipment used for giving an injection **must be sterile**, and handled in a manner as to maintain sterility. Poor technique may cause infection at the site of injection, or systemic infection may occur on intravenous administration. Knowledge of the anatomy of the area is essential. The technique has to be learnt and practised to avoid unintentional puncturing of vessels, undue pain, or injury to nerves. Injections require special drug preparations and equipment.

Drugs for injection. Parenteral drugs must be packaged, prepared and administered in a manner which maintains sterility. **Multiple-dose** vials can be reused if sterility is maintained. Remaining medication of once broken ampules must be discarded, as it no longer remains sterile and cannot be reused. When vials or ampules contain the drug in powder form, sterile water for injection or sodium chloride injection must be added and the drug dissolved prior to withdrawal. **Tubexes** are a brand of glass tubes of medication solutions with attached needles. They are inserted into specially designed holders and used like other syringe-needle units.

Syringes and Needles

Drugs in solution are administered parenterally by means of a **syringe-needle unit** or an **intravenous infusion set**. The common syringe is made of glass and consists of a **plunger** and a **barrel**. The needle is attached to the thin neck of the barrel. Some syringes have a metal tip. The Luer-Lock syringe has the advantage of locking the needle in position so that it is not dislodged when pressure is applied to the plunger, or the syringe is withdrawn from the injection site.

Syringes are available in various size – 1, 2, 5, 10, 20 and 50 ml. There are specialized insulin and tuberculin syringes. An **insulin syringe** may be marked so that there are 40 calibrations per 1 ml or 80 calibrations per 1 ml. The U 40 syringes are usually marked in *red*, while the U 80 syringes are marked in *green*. Double scale syringes are also available. The **tuberculin** syringe has a capacity of 1 ml, and calibrated in 0.01 ml markings. It is a syringe of choice for administration of very small volumes. Lately, sterile **disposable syringes** and **needles**, individually packed, have been made available. The advantages are assurance of sterility, the convenience, and a sharp needle, although at a higher cost.

Needles, precisely called *hypodermic needles*, are made of high quality stainless steel, which is strong, flexible and rust resistant. The needle size is designated by two numbers, **the gauge and the shaft length**. The gauge numbers run from 27 (finest) to 13 (thickest). The shaft is measured from the junction of the hub to the tip of the point. The tip of the needle is bevelled to different grades (regular, short or very short bevel). Choice of the needle gauge and length depends on the route of administration; the viscosity of the solution; and the size of the patient. Usually, a 25-gauge, 5/8 inch needle is used for **subcutaneous** injections, and a 22 or 20 gauge, 1.5 inch needle is used for **intramuscular** or **intravenous** injections. For "drawing up" of a dose from an ampule, the ampule is clean broken at the constricted portion by applying lateral pressure following gentle filing by a **serrated** metal file. For "drawing up" of a dose from a rubber stoppered vial, a hypodermic needle is inserted into the vial and some air is injected first to facilitate withdrawal of the liquid medication. Then the vial is inverted to withdraw the desired amount of the material.

Jet injection syringe (hypospray) is a devise for administration of a drug parenterally without a needle. It resembles a flash light. It forces a fine jet of the medicament of almost microscopic size, under high pressure through the skin into the tissues. The procedure is almost painless, and the efficacy equals that of subcutaneous injection. It is mostly employed in mass immunization programmes for diphtheria, tetanus, typhoid and cholera. Injections may be given at a rate of upto 1000 per hour by hypospray.

The various types of injections for parenteral administration of drugs are: **intradermal, subcutaneous** (SC), **intramuscular** (IM), **intravenous** (IV), **intramedullary, intraarterial, intrathecal, epidural, intracardiac, intraarticular** and **intraperitoneal.**

Intradermal (intracutaneous) injection. The drug is injected into the outer layers of the skin. The amount of drug given is small and absorption is slow. The medial surface of the forearm is the site frequently used. This injection is best made with a fine (26 gauge), short needle and a *tuberculin syringe*. This route is mainly used for diagnostic tests like Schick test for diphtheria, Dick test for scarlet fever and the Tuberculin test. It is also used for injecting BCG vaccine. Local anaesthetics are first injected intradermally, and then further deeper injections are made through the superficially anaesthetized tissues. Also used for *allergic sensitization testing* in patients.

Subcutaneous (hypodermic) injection (SC). The injection is made into the loose subcutaneous tissue under the skin. Common sites for SC injections are the **outer surface of the upper arm, abdomen, and front of the thigh.** This route is used to inject a small amount of the drug (2 ml or lesser). Drug absorption is slower, and drug action is longer with SC injections than with intravenous or intramuscular injections. SC injections are not advised in shock states because the reduced peripheral circulation may decrease the absorption rate. Irritant drugs should not be given subcutaneously, as they are painful and may cause tissue necrosis and sterile abscess formation. The piston of the syringe should be withdrawn slightly before injecting the drug to make sure that a blood vessel has not been entered. The angle of insertion should be 45 to 60 degrees. Drugs like **adrenaline, morphine** and **insulin** are usually administered subcutaneously.

Hypodermoclysis is a form of SC injection that permits the slow administration of large amounts (500 to 1000 ml in adults) of fluid such as **isotonic saline** or glucose solution. A large bore needle is inserted into the loose subcutaneous tissue over the anterior aspect of the thigh, or elsewhere, and the fluid is slowly infused. Occasionally the spread of such locally injected fluid is facilitated by adding the enzyme **hyaluronidase** to the solution, which temporarily decreases the viscosity of the ground substance in connective tissues. This aids the dispersal of the fluid from the injection site, and thus lessens painful tissue tension. Hypodermoclysis is particularly useful in infants and young children to counteract dehydration. Care is required to avoid too rapid an absorption resulting in a circulatory overload on the heart.

Intramuscular injection (IM). The injection is given with a longer and heavier needle that penetrates the subcutaneous tissues, and the drug is deposited deep between the layers of the muscle mass. This route is suitable for administration of **solutions** or **suspensions**. The muscle is more vascular and less sensitive than subcutaneous tissue, hence irritant solutions or suspensions are better tolerated when given intramusculary. Absorption from the site is more rapid than from subcutaneous injection sites. Small volumes (upto 3 ml) are injected in the **deltoid muscle**. Small or large volumes (upto 10 ml) are injected into the **gluteal mass** underlying the upper and outer quadrant of the left or right buttock. The **vastus muscle** underlying the lateral surface of the thigh is an alternate area. Needles from 1 to 3 inches in length (gauge 19 to 22) are used for IM injections. Drug suspensions form a "pool" in the muscle, causing slow absorption and a prolonged duration of action. The use of *waxes* or *oils* is permissible along with the drug to delay absorption and prolong action (depot preparations). A precaution is that after the needle is inserted (at almost a 90 degree angle) the plunger should be slightly withdrawn to make certain that the needle is not in a blood vessel. Although this problem seldom occurs when the injection site is properly selected, this precaution must always be taken. Choice of the site of IM injection depends on the amount and type of drug, the age, and built of the person receiving the injection. To sum up, IM injections may be made in the **dorsogluteal** area (upper outer quadrant of the buttock in the gluteus maximus muscle); **ventrolateral gluteal area** (when the patient's conditions does not permit change of position); **laterofemoral area** (outer, lateral surface of the thigh); and the **deltoid area** (lateral aspect of the upper arm into the body of the deltoid muscle). Care is required to avoid injury to nerves. The needle is held perpendicular to the skin, and the inserting movement should be quick and smooth to prevent undue discomfort to the patient.

The IM route is used for administering long-acting **esters of sex hormones, corticosteroids,** or poorly soluble salts like **benzathine penicillin G or procaine penicillin G.**

Intravenous injection (IV). When an immediate drug effect is desired, or when for any reason the drug cannot be injected into other tissues, or when absorption may be inhibited by poor circulation, it may be introduced directly into a vein as an **injection** or **infusion**. The **cubital vein** at the bend of the elbow is selected, although any other suitable vein or even the **superior longitudinal sinus** in children may be selected. This technique requires skill and asepsis, and the drug must be soluble and capable of withstanding sterilization. The IV injection is of great value in emergencies. The dose has to be determined accurately, as the drug directly reaches the blood stream, and there is no recall. From this standpoint it is one of the least safe methods of administration. The IV injections generally should be made slowly, and caution must be observed to avoid leakage of the drug solution into the surrounding tissue. Sloughing of tissues can occur if vasoconstrictors like noradrenaline are extravasated.

Intravenous injection of a comparatively small amount of solution, referred to as a *bolus*, are given by means of a syringe. The drug is dissolved in a suitable amount of normal (physiologic) saline or some isotonic solution. Factors that determine the choice of a vein are related to the thickness of the skin over the vein, the closeness of the vein to the surface, and the presence of a firm support (bone) under the vein. The veins in the antecubital fossa, though readily accessible, are uncomfortable sites for the patient requiring long-term IV therapy. They are frequently reserved for obtaining samples of blood. A vein that is distended with blood is much easier to enter than a collapsed vein. If an arm vein has been chosen, a tourniquet is applied tightly around the middle of the upper arm to distend the vein, the air is expelled from the syringe, and the needle (20 to 22 gauge) is introduced quickly and forcefully pointing upwards towards the heart. A few drops of blood aspirated into the syringe indicate that the needle is in the vein; the tourniquet is then removed; and the solution is injected slowly and steadily. Drugs should not be injected rapidly intravenously, because high concentrations of any compound perfusing the heart, regardless of its pharmacological properties, can cause cardiac arrhythmias.

An **infusion** is the intravenous administration of larger amounts of fluid, varying from 1 to 2 litres, and the method somewhat differs. The solution flows by gravity from a graduated glass bottle or plastic bag through a drip-set (a system of sterile tubes consisting of a drip chamber and tubing inserted above into a bottle/bag of infusion fluid and below through a connecting tip into the needle or catheter placed in the vein). Such a set up provides for a continuous slow administration of fluid into the body at a uniform rate. Infusions are mostly given to relieve tissue dehydration, to restore depleted blood volume, to dilute toxic substances in the blood and tissues, to supply electrolytes, drugs and foods. The fluid is given slowly to prevent fluid overload, which may impair cardio-pulmonary function. Ordinarily 3 to 4 hours are required for every 1000 ml of fluid, depending on the condition of the patient, the nature of the solution, and the purpose of administration. For children the rate is slower and is determined by age, weight and urinary output.

Insoluble drugs, oily substances, or drugs in suspension, or markedly acid or alkaline salts incompatible with blood should never be administered by the IV route. Limitations of IV injections are that: overdosage can lead to immediate toxicity; drug is excreted rapidly and the duration of action is shortened; leakage into the surrounding tissue may cause tissue damage; special skill and aseptic precautions are required; and accidents like air embolism, thrombophlebitis and venothrombosis may occur.

Intramedullary injection. This route is also designated as **bone marrow injection**, and the material is injected into the bone marrow of the **sternum** or **tibia**. Rapidity of drug effect is comparable with IV injection. This route is used when the veins are not available, specially in children, and a special needle is used. **Whole blood, normal saline** or **glucose** may be administered by this route.

Some injection routes are used to achieve high local concentrations of certain drugs, while minimizing their systemic absorption and ill effects. The following are some examples:

Intra-arterial injection. In this highly specialized procedure the needle is placed in an artery, through which an arterial blood sample may be withdrawn for blood gas studies, or a radio-opaque substance may be injected to make arteries of the part visible on an X-ray film (arteriography). Certain *cytotoxic drugs* may be perfused through the artery for treating specific areas, specially in cases of malignancy involving the limbs (regional perfusion).

Intrathecal (Intraspinal) injection. By this method a drug is injected into the subarachnoid space. These injections are made by inserting the needle through the **vertebral interspinous** spaces into the spinal fluid, usually by lumbar puncture. This route is used to produce intense action of drugs on the cerebrospinal system while treating infectious types of meaningitis or to produce **spinal anaesthesia**, or for introduction of radio-opaque contrast media into the subarachnoid space to visualize the spinal cord (**myelography**).

Epidural injection. By this method the drug is deposited through a vertebral interspace between the dura of the spinal cord and the periosteal lining of the spinal canal (also known as peridural or extradural injection). It is used to produce epidural nerve block by depositing the local anaesthetic solution in the space where the spinal nerves emerge from the dural membrane and enter the intervertebral foramina.

Intracardiac injection. In some emergencies like **sudden cardiac arrest** of an otherwise normal heart (as happens during anaesthesia, electrocution or drowning), injection of **adrenaline** directly into the heart may restart the heart beat. The injection is given by a long needle in the left fourth intercostal space close to the sternum.

Intra-articular injection. The drug (usually a glucocorticoid) is injected into the joint space to attain high local concentrations within the inflamed joint, without much danger of systemic steroid toxicity. Strict asepsis must be maintained. Patients are advised not to overuse the injected joint when the pain is relieved, as such strain may damage the joint further.

Intraperitoneal injection. A needle or trocar is inserted into the peritoneal space, and a special fluid is cyclically circulated through the space for *removal of toxins* or *drugs* in case of acute poisoning. This route is mostly used for *peritoneal dialysis*, which is a life saving procedure in cases of *acute poisoning*, and in *renal failure*.

INHALATION

Two classes of substances may be administered by inhalation – **volatile** and **non-volatile**. Volatile substances like gaseous **anaesthetics; vapour of liquid anaesthetics**; gases like **oxygen and carbon dioxide**; and drugs like **amyl nitrite** produce rapid effects when inhaled. Non-volatile substances have to be broken down into small particles, and inhaled as **aerosols**. Aerosols are liquid or solid particles, so small that they remain suspended in air for a long time instead of settling down rapidly due to gravity. Smaller the particle size, deeper it would reach in the respiratory passages. The particle size also influences the rate of absorption through the alveoli, i.e., smaller the particle size, greater amounts reach the alveoli and are absorbed. Common aerosol-producing devices are: **vaporizers, humidifiers, atomizers, nebulizers, inhalers** and **spinhalers**. Bronchodilators like adrenaline, isoprenaline and salbutamol may be administered by inhalation for prompt action.

Dermal Application

Drugs are not ordinarily absorbed through the skin. The dosage forms applied topically (locally) to the skin are **powders, lotions, liniments, ointments, creams, pastes** and **jellies**. These preparations are used mostly for their local antiseptic, antipruritic, analgesic, emollient and healing effects.

Absorption of drugs through the skin is proportional to their lipid solubility, as the *epidermis* acts like a lipid membrane barrier. The **dermis** is freely permeable to many fluids. Absorption through the skin may be enhanced by: (*i*) suspending the drug in an oily vehicle (ointment), and rubbing it into the skin, known as **inunction**; and (*ii*) **iontophoresis** (Greek *phorein* = to carry) in which the absorption rate of lipid insoluble ions is enhanced by the passage of a galvanic current through a solution of the drug applied to the skin in contact with an electrode. The other electrode is placed elsewhere on the body.

Mucosal Application

Local application is often used in the nose, throat, rectum or vagina to produce systemic effects, because of the good absorption through the highly vascularized mucosa of these areas. Dosage forms for mucosal application include **lozenges, sublingual tablets, buccal tablets, suppositories, otic solutions, aerosols, nasal solution,** and **ophthalmic solutions. Demulcents**, i.e., substances which protect and soothe the mucous membranes from irritation are also applied locally. The various routes of drug administration and primary dosage forms applied are summarized in **Table 1.3-1**.

Thus, there are enteral and parenteral routes of drug administration. The enteral method includes sublingual, oral and rectal routes. The parenteral method includes injections, inhalation and application to the skin and mucous membrane.

Table 1.3-1. Routes of drug administration and primary dosage forms applied

Route of Administration	*Site*	*Primary Dosage Forms*
Oral (enteral)	Mouth Gastrointestinal tract via mouth	Tablets, capsules, solutions, syrups, elixirs, suspensions, magmas, gels, powders
Sublingual	Under the tongue	Tablets, troches or lozenges
Parenteral	Other than gastrointestinal tract (various types of injections)	Solutions, suspensions
Topical	Skin surface	Ointments, creams, pastes, plasters, powders, lotions, solutions.
Conjunctival	Conjunctiva	Ointments
Intraocular	Eye	Solutions, suspensions
Intraaural	Ear	Solutions, suspensions
Intranasal	Nose	Solutions, sprays, inhalants, ointments
Intrarespiratory	Lung	Aerosols
Rectal	Rectum	Solutions, ointments, suppositories
Vaginal	Vagina	Solutions, ointments, emulsion foams, tablets, suppositories
Urethral	Urethra	Solutions, suppositories

1.4 FACTORS INFLUENCING DOSAGE AND DRUG ACTION

Age and Body Weight
Sex Factors
Time and Place Factors
Physiological Factors
Pathological Factors
Pharmacogenetic Factors (Idiosyncrasy)
Immunologic Factors (Drug allergy)
Psychological and Environmental Factors
Tolerance
- **Congenital Tolerance**
- **Acquired Tolerance**
- **Tachyphylaxis (Acute tolerance)**
- **Cross Tolerance**

Cumulation
Pharmacokinetic Factors: Half-life ($t_{1/2}$)
- **Loading and Maintenance Dose**

Combination of Drugs: Addition, Potentiation, Synergism, Antagonism, Drug Interactions

A **dose** (Greek, *dosis*) is the amount of the medicament to be administered to the patient, as directed by the physician. It is expressed in terms of **weight** (g, mg, mcg), **volume** (ml), or **in standard units**. The official doses mentioned in the pharmacopoeias are **oral doses** for adults, unless mentioned otherwise. The change in the activity of the cell or tissue produced by the drug is called the **response**. Both, the dose and the response are closely related, termed as the **dose-response relationship**. Thus, the factors which modify the dose, also in turn modify the response to a drug.

Drugs should be administered in a dose that produces the desired response, without producing adverse effects. Many patient factors affect drug action qualitatively and quantitatively. Thus there is no fixed dose for a drug, and within a certain **safe dose range** most patients suitably respond. Idealy, the dosage should be adjusted to suit the individual patient. Factors influencing the dose and the response to drugs are discussed hereunder.

AGE AND BODY WEIGHT

The age of the patient often affects his response to drugs, specially at the extremes of life, i.e., the newborn infant and the elderly. Intense effect of drugs at extremes of age can be due to deficiencies in their ability to biotransform (detoxify) drugs to inactive metabolites.

Many formulae are available to calculate the dose to be administered to children, who obviously require smaller doses of drugs than adults. These rules are based on *age, weight* or *body surface area* of the child.

1. **Young's Rule.** This is used for children from 2 to 12 years of age.

$$\text{Child's Dose} = \frac{\text{Age in years} \times \text{Adult dose}}{\text{Age} + 12}$$

Example. To calculate the dose of paracetamol (Official adult dose 500 mg orally) for a 3 years old child substitute:

$$\text{Child's Dose} = \frac{3 \times 500}{3 + 12} = 100 \text{ mg}$$

2. **Clark's Rule.** This is based on proportional body weight as related to an average adult weighing 150 pounds.

$$\text{Child's Dose} = \frac{\text{Weight in Pounds} \times \text{Adult dose}}{150}$$

Example. To calculate the dose of paracetamol (adult dose 500 mg orally) for a child weighing 30 pounds substitute:

$$\text{Child's Dose} = \frac{30 \times 150}{150} = 100 \text{ mg}$$

3. **Hamburger's Rule.** This is based on body weight as related to an average adult weighing 70 kilograms.

$$\text{Child's Dose} = \frac{\text{Weight in kg} \times \text{Adult dose}}{70}$$

Example. To calculate the dose of paracetamol (adult dose 500 mg orally) for a child weighing 14 kg substitute:

$$\text{Child's Dose} = \frac{14 \times 500}{70} = 100 \text{ mg}$$

4. **Body Surface Area Rule.** Although calculations based on body weight are more accurate than those based on age, there may be marked variations in weight at any given age. A more accurate method for calculating the dose for children or adults is to determine the **body surface area** (BSA). **Nomograms** are available for determining the BSA of infants, children and adults from the patient's weight and height. On obtaining the BSA use the following formula:

$$\text{Child's Dose} = \frac{\text{BSA in } M^2 \text{ of Child} \times \text{Adult dose}}{1.7}$$

M^2 = Square metres of BSA

1.7 = Average BSA in an adult

(Same formula is applied for adult dosage)

Example. To calculate the dose for a child weighing 50 pounds (height 47 inches), and the adult dose of the drug is 60 mg, determine the BSA from the nomogram (BSA from nomograms is 0.86 M^2). Then substitute:

$$\text{Child's Dose} = \frac{0.86 \times 60}{1.7} = \frac{51.6}{1.7} = 30 \text{ mg}$$

All the above formulae provide a **first approximation** only, which has to be further adjusted for the individual patient. For patients over 70 years of age the first approximation is obtained by reduction of the dose to three-quarters of the adult dose. No formula can be absolutely relied upon for calculating dosage for premature infants and full-term neonates less than a week old.

Age is an important factor in determining drug action, e.g., young infants lack the liver enzyme breaking down **chloramphenicol**, and very small doses can cause serious toxicity. Children tolerate larger doses of *atropine* than adults, whereas they tolerate less of *morphine*. Elderly patients are more susceptible to *digoxin toxicity*.

Sex Factors

Drug responses in women and men are not always similar, for which satisfactory explanations are not available. Women require smaller doses of drugs, probably due to their lesser body weight. Drugs must be used with special care during pregnancy as they may have a **teratogenic** (embryopathic) effect on the foetus. Purgatives must be avoided during pregnancy and menstruation. During lactation many drugs are excreted in the milk, and such bitter drugs discourage breast feeding. Drugs in breast milk may have their own unwanted effects on the infant. **Morphine** may produce more excitation prior to sedation in women. **Ephedrine** more frequently produces excitation and tremors in women than in men.

Time and Place Factors

Presence of food in the stomach and intestines delays absorption of drugs, whereas when the stomach is empty, the absorption of the drug is faster. It is known that **alcohol** produces a far more rapid and intensified action on the central nervous system when taken before a meal, rather than when taken after a meal. Administration of a drug with food may be taken advantage of to reduce its irritant action on the gut.

Diarrhoea is associated with gastrointestinal hypermotility, and as such the absorption of the ingested drug is reduced. **Emotional states** may produce a pyloric spasm, and the ingested drug is held up in the stomach leading to a delayed absorption.

The time of the day affects drug action. Daylight is a stimulant and enhances the effect of **stimulant drugs,** while the action of **hypnotics** is diminished. On the other hand, darkness is a sedative, and hypnotics are more effective at night. Certain place factors like **high altitudes** (low barometric pessure) diminish the capacity of the body to oxidize drugs. Hence, the usual dose may produce toxicity.

Physiological Factors

The physiological state of the cells and tissues is an important factor in determining the dose of the drug. Hormones like **ACTH** and **cortisol** exhibit a cyclic 24-hour rhythm (diurnal or circadian rhythm). This knowledge is applied to administer glucocorticoids only when the glandular cells are least sensitive to damage, i.e., as a single early morning dose, or as alternate day therapy for chronic diseases. Such measures minimize adrenocortical insuffi- ciency which is a serious hazard of **long-term steroid therapy**.

The response of patients to drugs is often different when physiological factors like acid-base and water or electrolyte balance is distorted. **Acetazolamide** diuresis is diminished by metabolic acidosis due to excessive loss of bicarbonate and sodium ions.

Pathological Factors

Diseases of the liver and kidney interfere with the detoxification and excretion of drugs, and usual doses can accumulate to toxic levels in the body. **Thiopental**, an ultrashort acting barbiturate, may cause an unexpectedly deep and prolonged unconsciousness or death due to respiratory failure in patients with hepatic insufficiency. In patients with impaired renal function, drugs like **streptomycin**, **gentamicin** and **kanamycin** may accumulate to toxic levels causing serious eighth cranial nerve damage, as they are not adequately excreted via the kidneys. Special tables based on creatinine clearance values, are available which give correction factors for drug doses to be administered to patients with renal insufficiency.

Patients with **hyperthyroidism** are excessively sensitive to **adrenaline** and other **sympathomimetics,** and relatively resistant to **digitalis** and **morphine**. Patients with **hypothyroidism** respond to these drugs in the opposite way.

Pharmacogenetic Factors

Genetic factors sometimes account for differences in the response of patients receiving similar doses of the same drug. For example some people are **rapid inactivators** of **isoniazid**, while others are **slow inactivators**. The latter are more likely to suffer the ill effects óf isoniazid like polyneuritis. This ability to inactivate isoniazid by acetylation is genetically determined. Similarly there are other examples involving drugs like **succinylcholine, primaquine, halothane** and **warfarin**, where the atypical response is genetically determined.

Idiosyncrasy is an old term and stood for an extraordinary and peculiar response to a drug which was different from its **pharmacologic** response. The majority of these idiosyncratic responses could not be attributed to drug allergy. Lately, with the development of **pharmacogenetics**, most idiosyncratic reactions to drugs are now being attributed to genetically determined defects, particularly in certain enzyme systems.

Immunologic Factors (Drug Allergy)

Immunologic factors cause some patients to react in a totally different way than a majority of others. The first (primary) exposure of the patient to the drug stimulates the immunologic mechanisms to produce antibodies. Later when the patient receives the same drug again, a reaction may occur which manifests in different ways, ranging from a breathing difficulty to skin, joint and blood disorders. Such manifestations are due to **drug allergy** or **hypersensitivity**. History of allergy to a certain drug in a patient is an **absolute contraindication** for the use of that drug.

Psychological and Environmental Factors

Nonpharmacologic factors also often play an important part in the way people respond to drugs. Some patients even respond to administration of a pharmacologically inert material, or **placebo** (Latin, I shall please). Placebos are inactive dosage forms, usually tablets or capsules containing sucrose or lactose. A placebo administration by a physician in whom the patient has confidence, may act upon suggestion by the prescriber, and may result in improvement in sleep, appetite, bowel habits and general well being. It has been worked out that the administration of a placebo produces a variety of positive responses in about 30 to 35 per cent of patients classified as "**placebo responders**". Thus, placebos have a difinite place in therapeutics.

Responses to active drugs are also influenced by the underlying personality structure of the patients, which is more true for drugs that affect the mood and thought process, i.e., **psychotropic drugs**. Environmental factors influence effects of drugs of abuse like *alcohol*, *Cannabis*, and *LSD*, i.e., it depends on the *set* and *setting*.

Tolerance

Tolerance is a condition of *decreased responsiveness* developed after prior or repeated exposure to a given drug or to a closely allied drug which resembles the former in its pharmacologic activity. Tolerance is said to develop if the effect of a drug diminishes when it is given repeatedly, so that larger doses are required to produce the same therapeutic effect. Tolerance may be natural or existing from birth, which is called **congenital**, or it may be **acquired** later in life by constant use of a drug.

Congenital tolerance. Certain species of animals like rabbits are tolerant to large doses of **atropine**, due to the presence of atropine esterase in the liver which destroys atropine fast. In humans the Negroes are tolerant to the mydriatic action of sympathomimetics like **ephedrine**.

Acquired tolerance. This form of tolerance is produced by drugs like **cocaine, heroin, morphine, alcohol, nicotine, barbiturates, amphetamine** and **nitrites**. The tolerance developed to drugs that affect mood and behaviour is frequently associated with either **psychological** or **physical dependence**, or both.

The factors responsible for acquired tolerance are: (*i*) **Poor absorption** of the drug from the gut, whereby it is excreted before sufficient quantities reach the site of action. Such a tolerance is labelled as **pseudotolerance**. Chronic alcoholics who develop a thickened gut mucosa can tolerate large amounts of alcohol, as it is not effectively absorbed; (*ii*) Rapid excretion of the drug before it is absorbed may occur in patients suffering from persistent diarrhoea or dysentery. This is also a type of **pseudotolerance**, but it is transient; (*iii*) **Rapid detoxification** of the drug occurs in the body. This capacity may be congenital or acquired. Habitual barbiturate users develop the capacity to detoxify barbiturates at a faster rate, and this leads to an acquired **true tolerance**; and (*iv*) **Acclamatization** of the target tissues may occur to the presence of the drug in the system. At the cellular level there is a reduction in the normal reactivity of the **receptors**. Such cellular acclamatization is also a type of **true tolerance**. This usually occurs to **psychotropic drugs** like the **minor tranquillizers**, **morphine** and **nicotine**. Due to such cellular tolerance heroin addicts are capable of taking heroin in doses many times that would kill a non-tolerant person. **Physical dependence** is a phenomenon which often accompanies the development of tolerance. Tolerance to a drug is gradually lost if its intake is discontinued. In short, factors (*i*), (*ii*) and (*iii*) decrease the effective concentration of the drug at the site of action, and may be grouped under **drug-disposition tolerance**; and factor (*iv*) is responsible for the reduction in the normal reactivity of the cellular receptors, and may be called **pharmacodynamic tolerance**.

Tachyphylaxis (*acute tolerance*). It is an acute development of tolerance to the rapid and repeated administration of a drug. This phenomenon probably occurs due to a transient saturation of the cell receptors with the drug. **Ephedrine** on repeated intravenous doses at short intervals elicits smaller and smaller hypertensive responses on the blood pressure in an anaesthetized animal (dog). If an adequate time interval is allowed tachyphylaxis does not occur with ephedrine. Tachyphylaxis also occurs to the hypertensive action of *tyramine*. Tachyphylaxis develops rapidly in contrast to tolerance. Moreover, in tolerance the original effect can be obtained by increasing the dose, which is not possible in tachyphylaxis.

Cross tolerance. This is a type of acquired tolerance developed as a result of repeated use of a drug, and which is manifested also towards other drugs closely related chemically or related in their pharmacological action.

Persons tolerant to the vasodilator effect of **nitroglycerin** are also resistant to other nitrates and nitrites. Heroin addicts are tolerant to the action of morphine and other opiates. Chronic alcoholics are resistant to the action of general anaesthetics like ether.

CUMULATION

Cumulation occurs when the rate of removal or inactivation of a drug is slower than the rate of administration. Such a phenomenon can lead to dangerous overdosage or toxicity, and is more likely when the drug has a long half-life ($t_{1/2}$) in the body. A drug is cumulative when its elimination and/or detoxification are slow, and the full effect is only produced by two or more doses. Digitoxin is a cumulative drug.

PHARMACOKINETIC FACTORS

Aim of drug therapy is to attain an effective concentration of the drug in the reactive tissues, and then to maintain this level by repeating the drug dosage at appropriate intervals. This goal is approached by applying the knowledge of pharmacokinetics of the particular drug.

Half-life ($t_{1/2}$). With most drugs the rate of elimination is proportional to the amount in the body, i.e., the amount of drug eliminated is not constant, but is a **constant fraction** of the total amount in the body at any one time. The time a drug takes to reach an **effective concentration** or **steady-state** level depends upon its rate of elimination from the body. This is expressed in terms of the drug's **biological half-life** or $t_{1/2}$ i.e., the time it takes for the amount of drug in the body to decrease to one-half of the peak previously attained. This index for different drugs varies widely. **Penicillin G** has a short half-life (less than 1 hr), as it is rapidly excreted by the kidneys. **Digoxin**, a cardiotonic drug has a long half-life (about 1 week). The anticoagulant **dicoumarol** has a half-life (about 24 hours), because it is slowly released from its plasma protein binding sites. Thus, to avoid toxicity it must be ascertained that the detoxification/elimination routes for the drug are optimally functioning. Presence of liver or kidney damage in the patient completely alters the dosage schedule.

Loading and maintenance doses. In emergencies, it is often necessary to raise the drug concentration rapidly to an effective level. For this, the drug is given initially in doses that exceed their elimination rate from the body. Such a **loading dose** is usually administered within a short period of time in several small doses, and the patient's response to each fraction is carefully monitored. On attainment of a steady-state level, the dose is reduced which is intended to make up for the portion of the drug metabolized or eliminated from the body each day. This is the **maintenance dose**. For example, the initial digitalizing (loading) dose of **digoxin** is 1.0 to 1.5 mg orally and the daily maintenance dose is 0.25 to 0.75 mg orally.

COMBINATION OF DRUGS

When one drug is given together with a second drug, the effects produced by the first drug may either be **increased** or **decreased** by the concurrent administration of the second drug. The terms usually employed to describe the combined effects of drugs are **addition, potentiation** and **antagonism**. At times these terms are used loosely, but such a practice must be avoided.

Addition or Summation. The combined effect of the two drugs is equal to the algebraic sum of their independent effects (2 + 2 = 4). Strictly speaking, when the two drugs act by the same mechanism (receptors), the combined effect is an **additive effect**, e.g., **aspirin** and **paracetamol** exemplify **addition**. In contrast, when the two act by different mechanisms (receptors) producing the same response, the combined effect is **summation**, e.g., **aspirin** and **codeine** produce analgesia by summation as they act by different mechanisms.

Potentiation or Synergism. The combined effect of the two drugs is greater than the algebraic sum of the independent effects of each drug (2 + 2 = 5).

Potentiation describes combined drug action by two drugs, only one of which produces a particular effect, while the other is inactive in that respect, e.g., **physostigmine** potentiates acetylcholine action by saving acetylcholine from destruction by the enzyme cholinesterase.

Synergism is seen when two drugs produce the same **type of effect**, but by acting at **different sites** and by **different mechanisms**, e.g., combination of **hydrochlorothiazide with methyldopa** in the treatment of essential hypertension. At times the terms potentiation and synergism are loosely used interchangeably. It may be pointed out that slightly varying definitions of these terms are found in different reference texts.

Antagonism. The combined effect of two drugs is *lesser* than the algebraic sum of the individual effects of each drug (2 + 2 = 1). The opposing action of certain drugs has been utilized in **toxicology** in the treatment of poisoning as **antidotes** or antagonists. In short, an **agonist** is an agent which is capable of producing a response by stimulating a *receptor*, at times playing a physiological role like **acetylcholine** and **noradrenaline**. The **antagonist** is a drug which prevents the action of an agonist, and may be used as an *antidote* to reduce or abolish the poisonous effect of an overdose of the agonist. There are **four** mechanisms by which one drug may oppose the action of another. Thus, there are four types of antagonism: **pharmacologic**; **physiologic**; **biochemical**; and **chemical antagonism**.

Pharmacologic antagonism is observed when an antagonist reduces or blocks the effect of the **agonist** by preventing the latter from combining with its **receptor**. Pharmacologic antagonism is competitive when the antagonist combines reversibly with the same receptor sites as the agonist, and can be displaced from these sites by an excess of the agonist, e.g., **diphenhydramine and histamine; atropine and acetylcholine.** Pharmacologic antagonism is **non-competitive** when the antagonist combines irreversibly with same receptor sites as the agonist, but it cannot be displaced from these sites by an excess of the agonist, e.g., **phenoxybenzamine and noradrenaline.**

Physiologic antagonism is observed, when two agonists, acting at different sites, counterbalance each other by producing opposite effects on the same physiologic function, e.g., **acetylcholine** induced contraction of the isolated intestine or uterus is antagonized by **adrenaline**; bronchoconstriction produced by **histamine** is antagonised by **adrenaline**; hypotension induced by **histamine** is antagonized by **noradrenaline**.

Biochemical antagonism is observed when one drug indirectly decreases the amount of the second drug that would otherwise be available to its site of action in the absence of the first drug (antagonist). This type of antagonism is the **opposite of synergism**, e.g., **phenobarbitone** induces the hepatic microsomal enzyme activity and increases the rate of metabolism of drugs like **phenytoin, warfarin, dicoumarol, griseofulvin** and **digitoxin**, whereby their availability at the site of action and the effect is indirectly decreased by phenobarbitone.

Chemical antagonism is simply the reaction between an agonist and an antagonist to form an inactive product. The agonist is inactivated in direct proportion to the extent of chemical interaction with the antagonist, e.g., the anticoagulant effect of **heparin** which is negatively charged, is antagonized by the strongly basic dye **toluidine blue** or the basic protein **protamine**; neutralization of excess gastric hydrochloric acid by antacids like **aluminium hydroxide** or **sodium bicarbonate**; weak **potassium permanganate** solution oxidizes drugs like **morphine, strychnine** and **picrotoxin.**

Lastly, the complex **drug interactions** which occur within the human body influence drug effects and may cause unanticipated toxicity.

1.5 ABSORPTION, DISTRIBUTION, METABOLISM AND EXCRETION OF DRUGS (DRUG DISPOSITION AND PHARMACOKINETICS)

In order to achieve its effect, a drug must first be **administered** in a suitable dosage form at an appropriate site. It must then be **absorbed** effectively from the site of administration, and **distributed** in the body to reach its site of action. After its action, for the termination of its effect, the drug must be **metabolized**, and the metabolites **excreted** from the body **(Fig. 1.5.1)**.

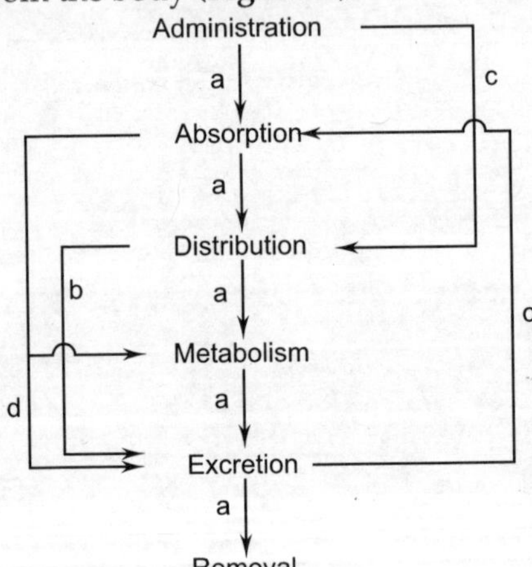

Fig. 1.5.1: Relationship between the various events involved in drug absortion, distribution, metabolism and excretion of drugs (see text).

Absorption and distribution comprise the **disposition** of a drug, i.e., its placement in the body. Metabolism and excretion comprise the **fate** of a drug.

Most commonly drugs are administered orally, and their pathway involves absorption, distribution, metabolism and excretion of both the unchanged drug and its metabolites (pathway a). A drug that is excreted in its unchanged form will bypass metabolism (pathway b). An intravenously administered drug undergoes no absorption (pathway c). An oral dose can be rapidly metabolized in the portal circulation and excreted in the bile before distribution in the body (pathway d). Lastly, excretion products in the intestine can be reabsorbed (pathway e).

Simply speaking, **absorption** is the entry of the drug molecules into the blood via the mucous membranes of the alimentary or respiratory tracts, or from the site of injection. **Distribution** is the movement of the drug molecules between the water, lipid and protein constituents of the body. **Metabolism** or **biotransformation** is the process of alteration in the structure of the drug molecule in the body, specially the liver, and excretion is the removal of the original drug molecule, or its metabolites from the body. Collectively, the term **elimination** is used for the process of metabolism and excretion of a drug.

The above mentioned four processes (absorption, distribution, metabolism, excretion) are studied quantitatively in the mathematical science of **pharmacokinetics**, and together they determine the concentration of drug molecules at the site of action.

Drugs and Cell Membranes

The processes of absorption, distribution, biotransformation and excretion require the **passage of the drug across cell membranes.** These membranes consist of a bimolecular layer of lipid molecules, coated with a protein layer on each surface **(Fig. 1.5.2)**. The cell membrane also has small "pores" and active transport systems. The ability of the drug to cross this membrane depends on its chemical and physical properties.

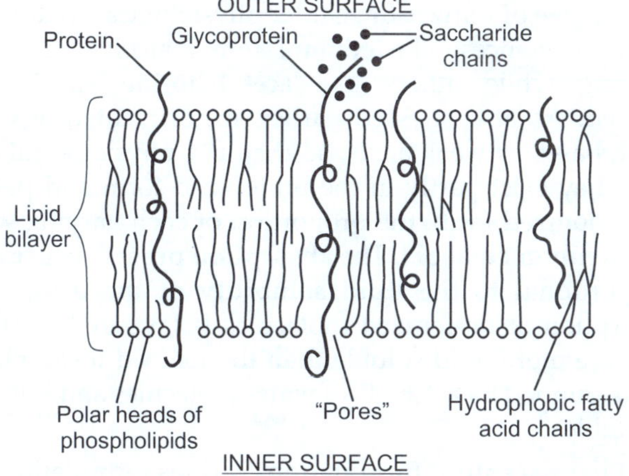

Fig. 1.5.2: Major features of a lipid bilayer cell membrane.

The chemical structure of a drug determines whether a drug will be more fat-soluble or water-soluble. In addition certain reactive portions of the molecule, or **functional groups** are responsible for the interaction of the drug with the tissue receptors.

Drugs may cross body membranes by the following mechanisms:

1. **Passive Transfer**
   Simple diffusion
   Filtration
2. **Specialized Transport**
   Active transport
   Facilitated diffusion
   Pinocytosis

Passive Transfer

The term *passive transfer* means that a drug or substance is taken up across a membrane without the need for energy. **Simple diffusion** requires no energy, and depends on the difference in concentration of the drug on either side of the membrane. Both fat-soluble and water-soluble molecules of small size may cross the membrane by simple diffusion. The term **filtration** is used when a porous membrane exists which allows the flow of substances of a certain size only, with the larger molecular sizes being blocked. The glomerular membrane of the kidney is an example of a filtering membrane.

Most drugs are weak *organic acids* or *bases*, and at the physiological pH of body fluids (7.35 to 7.45), drug molecules exist as a mixture of the *non-ionized* or uncharged molecular form and the *ionized* or charged form. In general, it is observed that drugs are more lipid-soluble (fat-soluble) and less water-soluble when they are non-ionized; whereas, ionized molecules are less lipid-soluble and more water souble. The principle is that: **Cell membranes are more permeable to the non-ionized form of a drug than to an ionized form.** The basis of this is the greater lipid-solubility of the non-ionized form in the cell membrane. The **degree of ionization** of a given drug depends on two factors: the pKa of the drug, and the surrounding pH. The pKa value is defined as the pH at which the drug is half ionized and half non-ionized. For example, **acidic drugs** like **phenobarbital** (pKa = 7.4) and **aspirin** (pKa = 3.5) are present predominently in the un-ionized form in areas of low pH like the stomach (pH = 1-3). Hence, these drugs are significantly absorbed from this site. **Basic drugs**, in contrast, like **morphine** (pKa = 7.9) and **amphetamine** (pKa = 9.8) would be largely ionized at the pH of the stomach and not well absorbed. As these drugs move down the intestinal tract, the pH increases and acidic drugs become more ionized, whereas basic drugs are less ionized. Therefore, the absorption of **basic** drugs (morphine, amphetamine) increases as the molecules move through the intestines. The concept of pKa is derived from the Henderson-Hasselbalch equation:

$$pKa = pH + \log \frac{(\text{conc. non-ionized drug})}{(\text{conc. of ionized drug})} \quad \text{(acids)}$$

$$pKa = pH + \log \frac{(\text{conc. ionized drug})}{(\text{conc. of non-ionized drug})} \quad \text{(bases)}$$

It follows from these equations that, when a substance is half ionized and half non-ionized at a certain pH, its pKa is equal to the pH. In other words, a substance is half ionized at a pH equal to its pKa. The following examples would further substantiate the concept of pKa, and the influence of the pH on the degree of ionization.

Salicylic acid (pKa = 3)		*Quinine (base) (pKa = 8.4)*	
pH = 2	9% ionized	pH = 7.4	91% ionized
pH = 3	50% ionized	pH = 8.4	50% ionized
pH = 4	91% ionized	pH = 9.4	9% ionized

Specialized Transport

Active transport of a drug refers to a situation when the drug is moved against a concentration gradient, by the use of energy. **Facilitated diffusion** is a unique form of transport in which the drug attaches to a special "carrier" which facilitates the diffusion of the drug across the membrane, and then releases the drug. In this process the drug is not chemically altered, and the carrier is again free to facilitate further drug transfer. This process does not require energy as in the case of active transport. Further, facilitated diffusion differs from active transport in that it **can only work in the presence of an appropriate concentration gradient,** i.e., it can only move drugs into the cell provided that their extracellular concentration is higher than their intracellular concentration. An example is the uptake of glucose by cells. **Pinocytosis** describes the ability of cells to surround and engulf small droplets. This process is of importance in the uptake of large molecules.

It is important to remember that the cell plasma membrane is not a fixed structure, but a **dynamic** one in which the various components are mobile. It contains membrane-bound water that interacts with ionized groups, and thus forms a barrier to the diffusion of water-soluble agents.The membrane is asymmetrical both structurally and electrically; it contains "pores" formed both within the membrane of a single cell and between the membranes of adjacent cells. Drugs with a molecular weight not exceeding 100 daltons are able to diffuse freely across the membrane through the polar pores. The pore size differs in the cell membrane of different tissues. The pores in the capillaries and the renal glomeruli are probably the largest (50-100 nm diameter) and offer greater ease of passage of substances compared to those in other tissues. The external surface of the membrane also contains pharmacological receptors (described later). These receptors are linked with intracellular mechanisms that can be switched on or off by the interaction of specific drug molecules with the membrane receptor.

A drug is unlikely to be absorbed unless it goes into **solution,** e.g., barium ions are very poisonous but **barium sulphate** can be safely used in radiology as a contrast agent as it is **highly insoluble.**

Drug Absorption

Drugs may act at the site of drug administration, or more commonly at some distant part of the body. Most drugs are given orally, and they must pass through the gut wall to enter the blood stream. Whether a drug is applied locally, or is administered systemically, there are five main factors which determine its fate in the body: (*i*) **molecular weight;** (*ii*) **chemical stability;** (*iii*) **lipid solubility;** (*iv*) **degree of ionization;** and (*v*) **pharmaceutical formulation of the drug.** Each drug has its own characteristic physico-chemical **profile** which governs its fate in the body.

Molecular weight. Substances with a high molecular weight are not usually absorbed intact except in minute quantities. They may also be altered by enzymatic action, e.g., on oral administration **proteins** will be broken down to their constituent amino acids. Thus, insulin undergoes enzymatic breakdown in the gut, and for practical purposes is not effectively absorbed.

Chemical stability. Unstable drugs are inactivated in the gastrointestinal tract. **Benzylpenicillin** is unstable in an acid medium, and cannot be relied upon to produce satisfactory results on oral administration, because a high proportion of the drug is inactivated by the acid in the stomach. In contrast, **phenoxymethylpenicillin** is more stable in an acid medium than benzylpenicillin, and adequate oral doses are therapeutically effective.

Lipid solubility. If a drug is to be absorbed from any part of the gastrointestinal tract, including the mouth, it is necessary for it to pass through cell membranes. Thus it must first pass through the cells of the mucous membrane of the gut, and then into the circulation either directly via the capillaries or indirectly via the lymphatic channels. As cell membranes are lipid in nature, the degree and rate of penetration of the drug through them is dependent to a large extent on the **lipid solubility of the drug.**

Degree of ionization. Under physiological conditions some substances, like **ethanol** (ethyl alcohol) are un-ionized, while others like **acetylcholine** are highly ionized. As also stressed earlier, majority of drugs are weak bases or weak acids, so that at a physiological pH (7.4) they exist partly in the un-ionized form and partly in the ionized form, the proportion of each varying with the environmental pH. The **absorption process is usually proportional to the lipid solubility of the drug.** The absorption of un-ionized molecules is favoured because they are more lipid-soluble than the ionized form which is surrounded by a "shell" of water molecules and is lipid-insoluble.

Pharmaceutical formulation. Various formulations of a drug can greatly influence the *amount* and *rate* at which it is absorbed, e.g., effervescent aspirin (0.6 g orally) produced more than double the plasma level produced by an equivalent dose of ordinary aspirin (both measured after 30 minutes). However, when the same dose of ordinary aspirin was given in hot water it resulted in a plasma concentration almost as high as that attained with the effervescent preparation. Sometimes tablets or capsules may fail to disintegrate in the gut so that absorption does not take place. The absence of a therapeutic effect may be wrongly labelled to other factors such as too small a dose, or failure of the patient to take the medicine.

Absorption via Gastrointestinal Tract

Absorption of nearly all drugs from any site in the gastrointestinal tract is by **passive diffusion.** For most drugs, the **proximal small intestine** with its **large surface** area is the major site of absorption. Although **acidic drugs** such as aspirin and barbiturates can be absorbed from the stomach, they are usually absorbed faster when they reach the duodenum. **Basic drugs** including antipsychotics, anticholinergics, narcotics and sympathomimetics are usually absorbed only in the intestine. Their absorption is delayed if taken with food and trapped in the stomach until the pyloric sphincter opens.

First-pass metabolism refers to the biotransformation of drugs during absorption through the intestine and their transport through the liver in the portal circulation. It can significantly reduce the percentage of an oral dose that reaches systemic circulation. Drugs like **propranolol** are extensively metabolized as they pass through the liver—the **"first-pass effect". Sublingual** administration may be an alternative to the oral route if a drug is either destroyed in the gastrointestinal tract or **completely inactivated** as it passes through the liver for the first time, e.g., **isoprenaline** and **nitroglycerin,** respectively. Nitrates, such as **nitroglycerin** and **isosorbide dinitrate** are more effective when given sublingually. Drugs may also be considered for sublingual administration, if the patient is vomiting. Sublingual *ergotamine* can be used to terminate migraine headaches in the nauseated and vomiting patient. Drugs administered sublingually must be non-irritating and absorbed quickly to avoid being swallowed in saliva. Few drugs fulfil both these criteria. Absorption of drugs through the buccal mucosa is limited by its *small surface area, palatibility* of the drug, and the extent to which it is ionized.

On *oral* administration *three* processes precede absorption: (*i*) **Disintegration** of the solid dosage form (tablet or capsule) into **granules.** The **disintegration rate** (in terms of time) is dependent on the dosage form. **Compressed tablets** take some time to break up in the stomach, and sometimes disintegration may be very slow, which delays absorption. Disintegration is deliberately delayed in **enteric coated tablets,** by a special acid-resistant coating material which is soluble only at a higher pH in the intestine. In general, both the *rate* and *extent* to which a drug is absorbed are greatest when the drug is administered in *solution* form and decreases in the mentioned sequence—solution, suspension, capsule, tablet, enteric coated tablet; (*ii*) **Deaggregation** of the granules forms *fine particles;* and (*iii*) **Dissolution** of the active material form fine particles into a *solution.* The *dissolution rate* depends on the particle size, the drug material, and the surrounding pH. On these three processes **(Fig. 1.5.3)** depends the ultimate absorption and **bioavailability** of the drug. With certain drugs none of the three processes is complete and thus their bioavailability is reduced. In contrast, with certain formulations the tablet or its granules may directly undergo dissolution to form a solution, thus increasing **drug bioavailability.**

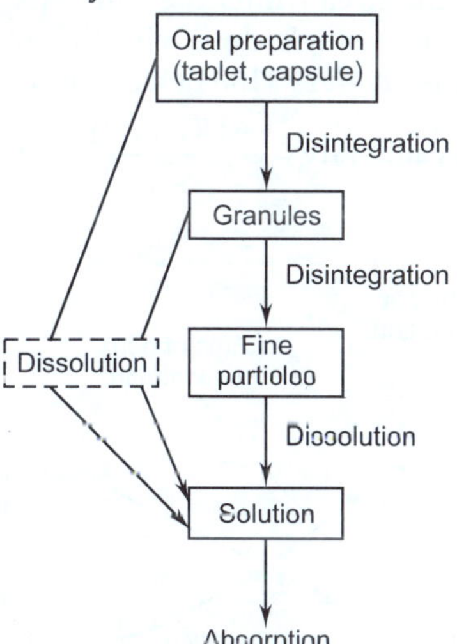

Fig. 1.5.3: Diagrammatic representation of the fate of oral preparations in the gut (see text).

Optimal absorption of drugs from the gut cannot occur unless they are in solution by the time they reach the intestine. **Drug formulation** is one of the major factors determining the rate and extent of absorption. Variation between different "brands" of the same drug in their rate of dissolution produces major differences in the total amount of the drug reaching the site of action through systemic circulation (bioavailability). For drugs like **digoxin, phenytoin, tolbutamide** and **griseofulvin** the dissolution rate is an important factor regulating their absorption. The binding of drugs in the gastrointestinal lumen also decreases the rate and extent of their absorption. One drug may decrease the absorption of another drug, e.g., **tetracyclines** have **chelating** properties and form insoluble complexes with bivalent and trivalent cations in **antacids** and in **iron salts. Liquid paraffin** reduces the absorption of **lipid-soluble drugs and vitamins.**

Other factors which govern drug absorption from the gut are: (*i*) **Surface area of absorption;** (*ii*) **Gastric emptying speed;** (*iii*) **Motility of the gut;** (*iv*) **Splanchnic blood flow;** (*v*) **Contents of the gut,** like food and other substances in the gut may delay absorption by binding or diluting drugs; (*vi*) **Certain disease states** involving the gut; and (*vii*) **pH within the gut.**

Briefly stated, the absorption of drugs from the gastrointestinal tract is mainly by **passive diffusion** through the lipid sheet, and few drugs are small enough to diffuse through the **pores** in the cell membrane. Uptake of sugar and other nutrients is by **active transport systems.** The gut membrane is more permeable to **non-ionized** lipid-soluble forms of drugs, and less permeable to the **ionized** form.

Absorption via Parenteral Sites

Drugs when injected intravenously (IV) are rapidly distributed, as they reach the blood stream directly without crossing any membranes. The factors which influence the rate of absorption from intramuscular (IM) and subcutaneous (SC) injection sites are: (*i*) **Drug concentration;** (*ii*) **Solubility of the drug;** and (*iii*) **Local blood flow.** Absorption following IM and SC injections usually occurs by **simple diffusion** in the direction of the concentration gradient from the injection site to the plasma or lymph. The most important factors controlling absorption from SC or IM sites are the **area of the absorbing capillary membranes,** and the **solubility of the drug** in the interstitial fluid. **Filtration** through channels in the endothelial capillary membrane is also very efficient, as these channels are relatively large and can allow passage of most lipid-insoluble drugs.

The dosage **formulation** can also affect absorption from parenteral sites, e.g., drugs in aqueous *solutions* are usually absorbed more rapidly than drugs in *suspension,* e.g., benzathine penicillin with procaine penicillin G. Often drugs are suspended in certain vehicles, like oil, to reduce their rate of absorption and provide a prolonged action, e.g., long-acting hormone preparations.

Absorption of drugs from IM sites is usually more rapid than from SC sites, because of the higher vascularity of the muscle compared to subcutaneous tissue. Decreased peripheral blood flow in conditions of "shock" significantly reduces the rate of absorption of injected drugs. Blood flow to an area can be increased and absorption enhanced by application of heat, local vasodilators and massage. In contrast, the absorption can be delayed by application of cold, a tourniquet, or vasoconstrictors. All the above mentioned factors have a profound effect on the **onset** and **duration** of action of a drug.

Absorption via Lungs (Inhalation)

Drugs presented in the correct form to the trachea and lungs are absorbed by **simple diffusion.** However, lipid-soluble compounds diffuse most readily. The correct form is a **vapour,** an **aqueous solution,** or a **suspension** of particles small enough to be evenly distributed over the mucous membrane. Examples of agents which diffuse rapidly through the respiratory mucosa include **nicotine, volatile anaesthetics** and **disodium cromoglycate.**

Absorption via Topical Sites

Drugs are usually applied to the skin for their topical (local) effects. Absorption of most drugs through the intact skin is poor, as the keratinized **epidermis** behaves like a barrier. However, the underlying **dermis** is quite permeable to many drugs, and significant absorption can occur if the skin is abraded or denuded. The extent of absorption through the skin is proportional to the lipid solubility of the drug and the surface area to which the drug is applied. Absorption can be enhanced by dissolving the drug in an **oily base, vigorous massaging of the area, occlusive dressing,** or simultaneously applying a keratin softening agent like **salicylic acid.**

Lately, drugs intended for systemic action are being formulated in a way that topical application is utilized as the route of administration. For example, the **nitroglycerin transdermal system patch (Chap. 1.3).** This drug-impregnated patch is applied to the skin of the upper torso in patients of angina pectoris. Nitroglycerin is slowly absorbed through the skin to provide consistent and effective plasma levels for 12 to 24 hours. **Transdermal** patches of **scopolamine** and **clonidine** are now also available for control of motion sickness and hypertension respectively.

Absorption of most drugs through mucous membranes is usually very rapid, mainly due to the thin and highly vascular absorbing surface. However, drugs applied to mucous membranes are generally used for their local action, e.g., nasal decongestants or vaginal anti-infectives. Rather their systemic absorption may result in unwanted side effects. Some drugs like **ergotamine** and **vasopressin** may be applied to mucous membranes to facilitate their systemic absorption.

Bioavailability

The term **bioavailability** has been used to describe a number of concepts associated with the effect of administration of a drug preparation, namely, **its extent of absorption, its availability at receptor sites,** and **its therapeutic effectiveness.** However, at a simplified level, it is used to describe the biological availability of a drug from a preparation, and is quantified in terms of the **amount** and the **rate** of appearance of the drug in the blood. There has been much interest currently in the observation that various preparations of the same drug administered orally may give different serum concentrations.

Bioavailability has been defined as the relative absorption *efficiency* of a test dosage form compared to a standard preparation. Thus, bioavailability of a drug is the percentage of a dose that reaches the systemic circulation after administration via a stated route. The application of this concept of bioavailability to the comparison of various formulations of the same drug is referred to as *bioequivalence.*

The bioavailability of any drug after IV administration is 100 percent, and is usually assumed to be close to this value when given IM or SC. However, some highly insoluble drugs like **phenytoin, digoxin** and **diazepam** partly precipitate at the site of injection, and then are slowly absorbed. The bioavailability of drugs after oral administration is frequently less than 100 per cent. In view of this, problems regarding drug bioavailability usually refer to the oral administration of drugs.

In short, bioavailability describes the *extent* and the *rate* of drug absorption from a dosage form as reflected by the **serum concentration-time curve.** This curve is obtained by plotting serum concentration of the drug versus time **(Fig. 1.5.4).**

Bioavaliability of an oral dosage form is determined by comparing the **Area Under the Curve** (AUC) after oral administration of a single dose with that obtained when the same dose is given IV (100 percent absorption):

$$\text{Drug bioavailability} = \frac{\text{AUC (oral)}}{\text{AUC (IV)}} \times 100$$

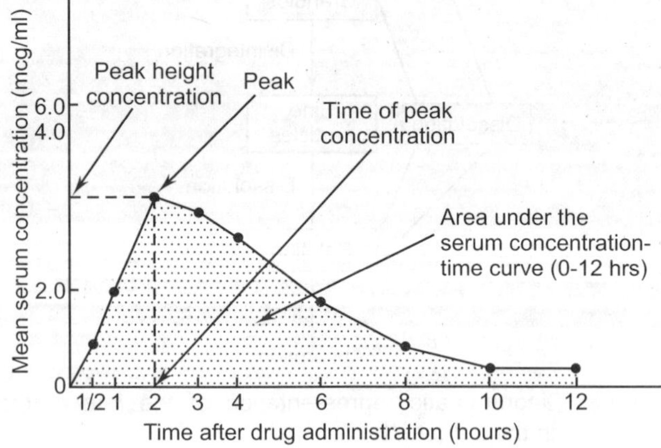

Fig. 1.5.4: Serum concentration-time curve for a hypothetical drug showing peak height concentration, time of peak concentration, and area under the curve (AUC).

If all the drug that is absorbed is excreted unchanged in the *urine,* then a similar determination can be carried out using the **urine concentration versus time curve.** But if the drug is metabolized in the body, as usually happens, the metabolites as well as the parent drug must be measured. The bioavailability can also be determined after chronic administration of a drug, and there is usually good agreement between the results obtained by a single and multiple dose studies.

The main factors determining bioavailability of an orally administered drug include: (*i*) **Drug formulation;** (*ii*) **Inactivation in gut lumen, bowel wall and liver;** (*iii*) **Interactions in gut lumen;** (*iv*) **pH within the gut;** (*v*) **Gastric emptying time and gut motility;** and (*vi*) **Certain disease states involving the gut.** The relevant details have already been discussed under the head-Absorption via gastrointestinal tract (refer back).

Bioequivalence

Bioequivalence is said to exist when the bioavailability of a drug from different formulations is the same. But manufacturers do not always use identical processes and formulae in tablet production of a drug, so that **disintegration** and **dissolution** rates may very. Such variations often lead to differences in drug bioavailability from tablets of identical stated potency prepared by different manufacturers. Such **bio-inequivalence** has been found to exist in different preparations of a number of drugs like **digoxin, tetracyclines, aspirin, phenytoin, theophylline** and **warfarin.** The clinical significance of bio-inequivalence of some dosage forms is greatest for drugs with a low therapeutic index, where the drug effect is closely related to their plasma concentration, and the margin of safety is narrow, e.g., **warfarin, digoxin, phenytoin, oral hypoglycaemics** and **cytotoxic drugs.** Bio-inequivalence of different formulations of the same drug has been widely publicised by the pharmaceutical industry as a rational argument in favour of prescribing drugs by their **proprietary** or **brand names** rather than their **generic names.**

Prodrugs

An approach to improve bioavailability is to modify the drug molecule chemically to form a better absorbed compound, which liberates the active drug after absorption. Such modified drugs are known as *prodrugs.*

Table 1.5-1. *Prodrugs and their active metabolites*

Prodrug	*Active metabolite*
Dipivalyladrenaline	Adrenaline
Ibuterol	Terbutaline
Indanyl Carbenicillin	Carbenicillin
Pivampicillin	Ampicillin
Talampicillin	Ampicillin
Prazepam	Desmethyldiazepam
Clorazepate	Desmethyldiazepam

For example, **dipivalyladrenaline** is a prodrug of adrenaline, and is enzymatically converted to adrenaline after instillation in the eye. As dipivalyladrenaline is better absorbed, less drug is required and side effects are minimized. Similarly, carbenicillin is poorly absorbed from the gut, but its ester **indanyl carbenicillin** is much better absorbed, and on absorption is hydrolysed to carbenicillin **(Table 1.5-1).**

Drug Distribution

After a drug has been absorbed into the circulatory system, its distribution in the dody is governed by a number of factors. Drug distribution describes the process which transports a drug to its site of action, to other storage sites in the body, and to organs of metabolism and excretion **(Fig. 1.5.5).** The movement of drug molecules in these areas determines its **effectiveness, its duration of action,** its mode of **metabolism,** and its rate of **excretion.** As the distribution pattern of a drug is ultimately dependent on its ability to cross cellular membranes, the principles governing

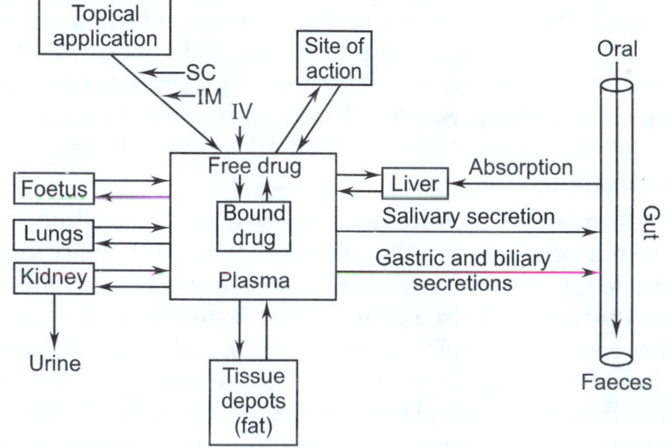

Fig. 1.5.5: Basic model of pathways of drug movement (pharmacokinetics) in the body. Bidirectional arrows denote that a drug and/or its metabolites move in both directions between the indicated points. (SC = Subcutaneous; IM = Intramuscular; IV = Intravenous).

membrane transport of drugs, discussed earlier in this Chapter, also apply here. Thus, **lipid-soluble** drugs tend to distribute more widely in the body compared to *lipid insoluble* drugs, as they cross cellular membranes more readily. Considering the highly permeable nature of the capillary endothelium (except brain capillaries), almost all organs (except CNS) can be affected by any given drug. Initial distribution of a drug is primarily dependent on the **cardiac output** and the **local blood flow** in various body organs. Thus, highly perfused organs like the **heart, liver, kideny** and **brain** receive the largest amount of drug immediately after absorption. Subsequently, other factors come into play that govern the **final distribution pattern of a drug.**

The main factors which govern distribution are:

1. Physicochemical characteristics of the drug.
2. Route of drug administration.
3. Binding to plasma proteins.

4. Regional blood flow.
5. The availability of active transport systems.
6. Special compartments and barriers.

All these factors are interdependent, and are considered briefly below:

Physicochemical characteristics. Drugs reach the extracellular space by **passive diffusion** through junctions or "pores" between the endothelial cells, except in the brain which has tight junctions between these cells. Only lipid soluble drugs cross cell membranes effectively to an extent which depends on their pKa and the pH of the surrounding medium as discussed earlier. Lipid-soluble compounds like **lignocaine, propranolol,** and **tricyclic antidepressants** are widely distributed in tissues like the brain, liver and lung. In contrast, **heparin** is confined to the plasma because of its high molecular weight and ionization.

Route of administration. Drugs given intravenously are preferentially distributed in organs with a high regional blood flow. In contrast, drugs which are well absorbed from the gut are extracted and concentrated in the liver during their "first-pass", e.g., **propranolol** and **tricyclic antidepressants.** Their distribution pattern and metabolic fate is different when administered orally and intravenously.

Binding to proteins. Drugs may bind either to plasma proteins, usually albumin, or to proteins of cells (nucleoproteins). Drugs bound to plasma protein are in equilibrium with free drug in the plasma water, but only the **free drug** exerts a pharmacological effect. Plasma protein binding of a drug slows the disappearance of the drug from the plasma, limits its access to its site of action, and prolongs the time the drug remains in the body by slowing its renal filtration. Most of the drugs bind to plasma albumin because of its high concentration providing a large total surface area. Only a few drugs are appreciably bound to other proteins, e.g., steroid hormones and thyroxine to alpha-globulins; fat soluble vitamins to alpha- and beta-globulins. The importance of protein binding is illustrated in the use of **diazoxide,** an antihypertensive drug used to treat acute hypertensive crisis. The speed of intravenous injection is critical to its intensity and duration of action. If it is injected slowly over minutes, its antihypertensive effect is not pronounced. When it is injected rapidly (10 seconds), its intensity of action and duration of effect is pronounced, as the drug in this case exists in much greater quantity in the "free" or unbound form. Therefore its access to its site of action in the blood vessels is enhanced. On slower injection, nearly all the drug becomes protein bound, and its effectiveness is reduced. Thus, diazoxide is administered intravenously as a rapid "bolus" injection for its optimal effect.

The total amount of drug bound in the plasma depends on: (*i*) its **plasma concentration;** (*ii*) **affinity for binding sites on albumin;** and (*iii*) **the total number of available protein binding sites.** The binding is usually reversible and an equilibrium exists between the **free** and **bound** forms of a drug, expressed as:

$$\text{Free Drug} + \underset{\text{(albumin)}}{\text{Plasma protein}} \underset{k_2}{\overset{k_1}{\rightleftharpoons}} \text{Drug:Protein complex}$$

here k_1 reflects the rate at which the drug *binds* to plasma proteins, and k_2 is the rate of *dissociation* of drug from plasma proteins. The processes of *association* and *dissociation* are very rapid and are measured in milliseconds only. Since it is only the **free drug** that is capable of crossing membranes, protein binding interferes with the access of a drug to its site of action. In addition, as binding slows excretion, a "reservoir" of the drug develops in the plasma. As free drug leaves the plasma by excretion, metabolism, or diffusion into other tissues, the drug-protein complex dissociates to supply more free drug. Conversely, as the drug concentration increases in the plasma, more free drug becomes bound. As the binding capacity of plasma proteins is limited, a point of saturation can be reached. Once the protein-binding sites are completely occupied, further administration of the drug results in toxic reactions due to the large amount of the drug remaining non-protein-bound. Many different kinds of drugs are protein bound, and simultaneous administration of two or more of these drugs can result in competition for available sites on the binding proteins, and displacement of active drug may result in enhanced or toxic drug effects. This aspect is further discussed in **Chap. 1.8.** There are a large number of drugs which are more than 90 percent bound to plasma albumin at therapeutic blood concentrations, e.g., **doxycycline, nalidixic acid, warfarin, sulphinpyrazone, indomethacin, chlorothiazide, propranolol, diazoxide, chlorpropamide, imipramine, amitriptyline,** and **phenytoin.** The distribution and efficacy of drugs which are highly bound to plasma proteins can be influenced by disease, e.g., in *hypoalbuminaemia* due to hepatic cirrhosis or nephrotic syndrome.

Regional blood flow. Blood flow markedly varies from tissue to tissue. The brain, endocrine glands, the heart, kidneys, liver and the lung are *well* perfused. Muscle and skin are **moderately** perfused, whereas adipose tissue (fat) is *poorly* perfused, and the bones and teeth receive the least blood supply. Tissues with a good regional flow equilibrate rapidly with the drug present in the blood, i.e., the skeletal muscle equilibrates more slowly than the heart and brain, but faster than adipose tissue. Drug distribution is grossly altered when tissue perfusion is reduced like in **heart failure, cardiogenic shock** or **hypothyroidism.**

Availability of active transport systems. Some drugs are concentrated in certain tissues as a result of uptake by selective active transport systems, e.g., the adrenergic neurone blocker (guanethidine) into the adrenergic nerve terminal; iodine is actively concentrated into the thyroid cells. In contrast, the blood-brain barrier prevents many drugs from entering the central nervous system (CNS).

Special Compartments and Barriers

The plasma space. Drugs leave the plasma by diffusing across the capillary membrane which has the characteristics of a lipid membrane. In contrast to other membranes there are relatively large "pores" in capillary membranes that allow unrestricted diffusion of water-soluble drugs of molecular weight (MW) upto 5000, and relatively unrestricted diffusion upto MW 69000. Thus all drugs other than those that are proteins can readily diffuse into the extracellular space. The protein bound fraction of drugs cannot diffuse out of the plasma, hence cannot reach receptor sites. The capillaries of the hepatic sinusoids, and those of the gut have larger "pores" than elsewhere, and this accounts for the fact that some highly protein-bound drugs can be taken up rapidly by the liver.

Blood-brain barrier. Anatomically there is a dual barrier in the CNS—the blood-brain barrier and the blood-CSF (cerebrospinal fluid) barrier. The dye **trypan blue** given IV does not stain the brain, but the brain is stained after its intrathecal administration. It is established that some drugs enter the CNS with relative ease, while others do not enter at all. This is because the endothelial cells of brain capillaries differ from most other capillaries, as they are very tightly joined together and lack intercellular "pores" and pinocytotic vesicles. In addition, brain capillary cells are enveloped by less permeable cells, known as the **pericapillary glial cells.** Thus, drug molecules have not only to diffuse across the tightly packed endothelial cells, but also must cross the poorly permeable glial cells to enter the CNS. It must be stressed that this is *not an absolute barrier,* but there is a measurable difference in the permeability of CNS capillaries to various drugs compared to other capillaries. To cross the blood-brain barrier more easily, a drug should possess the following qualities:

(*i*) Low ionization at plasma pH;

(*ii*) High lipid-solubility of the non-ionized form of the drug; and

(*iii*) Minimal plasma protein binding.

Thus, a highly lipid-soluble barbiturate like thiopentone readily enters the CNS and exerts almost an immediate depressive effect on the CNS. Whereas, drugs which are highly ionized like most **penicillins** and **gentamicin** penetrate very slowly. On inflammation of the meninges (meningitis or encephalitis) the permeability of the blood-brain barrier is greatly increased, and many drugs previously excluded from the CNS are able to cross the barrier.

Placental barrier. The structure of the placenta is well suited for exchange of materials. The passage of most drugs from the maternal to foetal circulation occurs quite easily. Thus the term *barrier* is inappropriate as applied to the placenta. The placenta membrane is **lipid in nature,** and readily allows the transfer of **non-ionized, lipid-soluble** drugs by **simple diffusion** down a concentration gradient. Thus, most drugs that are well absorbed orally can easily enter the foetal circulation. Only other drugs that are highly ionized or have a molecular weight above 1000 find it difficult to cross the placental membrane. Lipid-soluble drugs like **paraldehyde, chlorpromazine, gaseous anaesthetics, sulphonamides, barbiturates, morphine, pethidine, heroin** and **alcohol** readily cross the placental membrane.

Placental transfer of drugs is responsible for many untoward effects on the foetus that result from use of drugs by the mother. Moreover, many drugs have the potential to cause physical defects in the growing foetus, specially if given during the first trimester of pregnancy. These are labelled as **teratogenic effects,** and have been found to be associated with the use of **phenytoin, cortisone, streptomycin** and many **antineoplastic drugs.**

Eye. The conjunctiva, sclera, iris and the ciliary muscle receive moderate blood supply (cornea and lens are avascular). Lipid-soluble drugs can penetrate and reach these structures and the aqueous humour from the conjunctival sac, e.g., **prednisolone sodium phosphate, atropine, chloramphenicol** and **cocaine.** The choroid and retina are moderately vascular but the vitreous humour is avascular. These structures are not reached by medication via the conjunctival sac, but only from systemic circulation.

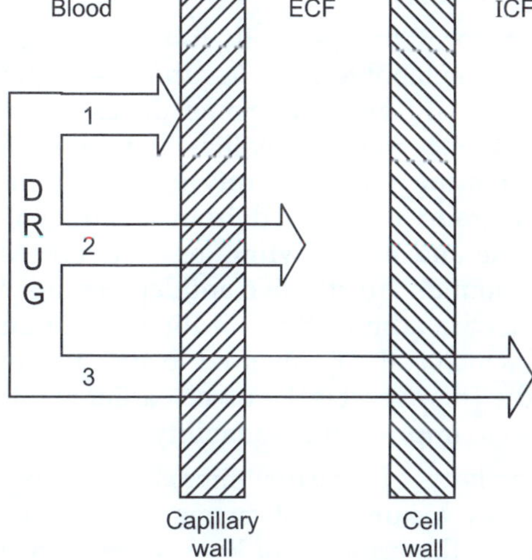

Fig. 1.5.6: Differential drug distribution: After absorption drug is bound to plasma protein (1); water-soluble drugs may either penetrate fully (3) or be confined to the ECF (2); lipid-soluble drugs readily penetrate into the ICF (3). Important membrane barriers are the blood-brain barrier, placenta, eye, intestinal mucosa and the kidney. ECF = extracellular fluid; ICF = intracellular fluid.

To sum up, after absorption drugs are distributed like nutrients by the blood stream. A variable amount of the drug is bound to plasma proteins and tissues, and is rendered temporarily inactive. Because of special characteristics of the capillaries in the brain, placenta, eye, intestinal mucosa and kidneys there is a **differential distribution** of drugs which is dependent on their physicochemical properties **(Fig. 1.5.6).**

Drug Metabolism (Biotransformation)

Termination of drug effect, also termed as **drug elimination,** involves two processes: (*i*) **metabolism,** mainly in the liver and kidney; and (*ii*) **excretion** of the unchanged drug and/or its metabolites by the kidneys, gut, lungs, sweat glands, breasts and salivary glands. Some drugs (general anaesthetics) are excreted from the body unchanged, but the majority of them are metabolized in the body. The metabolic conversions, **firstly,** render the compound more suitable for excretion by the liver and kidney, and **secondly,** play a role in determining the effective concentration of the drug in the body. The term **biotransformation** may be used interchangeably with **metabolism** of drugs.

Drug metabolism occurs predominently in the liver by way of **hepatic microsomal enzyme systems.** These consist of a group of enzymes located on the **smooth endoplasmic reticulum** of liver cells. The endoplasmic reticulum resembles a series of canals that are continuous with the cell membrane and the membrane of the nucleus. Lipid-soluble drugs easily gain access to these metabolizing enzymes in liver cells. The microsomal enzymes catalyze several important reactions involved in drug metabolism, notably **oxidation** and **conjugation.** Other reactions like **hydrolysis** and **reduction** may be catalyzed both by microsomal and non-microsomal enzymes (see later).

Biotransformation generally results in the conversion of a drug to a metabolite that is *less active,* less lipid-soluble, and hence easily excreted. Some drugs are converted by liver enzymes into metabolites that are *equally active,* e.g., **imipramine** and **amitriptyline** are N-methylated (a methyl group is removed from a nitrogen) to form **desipramine** and **nortriptyline,** respectively. All four of these compounds are effective antidepressants. Whereas, some drugs are administered in the form of an inactive **prodrug,** which is then converted to an active metabolite in the body. This aspect is discussed earlier in this Chapter as a means to improve bioavailability.

The activity of **hepatic microsomal enzymes** can be altered by a number of factors. Enzymatic function is reduced in the presence of **liver diseases or impaired circulation.** Drugs like monoamine oxidase inhibitors (MAOIs) and organophosphorus insecticides also adversely affect the liver microsomal enzyme system. Decreased enzymatic activity results in slowed metabolism of drugs, leading to **cumulation** and **toxicity.**

Microsomal enzyme function can also be increased by a number of drugs, and is termed as **enzyme induction.** Prolonged administration of **barbiturates, phenytoin, carbamazepine, ethanol** and a number of other drugs results in an accelerated metabolism of drugs by the hepatic microsomal system. This effect is responsible for the development of *tolerance* to the action of those drugs which are metabolized in the liver because of the presence of an enzyme inducer.

In the liver biatransformation of drugs usually occurs in two phases : (*i*) *Phase I reactions;* and (*ii*) *Phase II reactions* **(Table 1.5-2).**

Phase I reactions. These **preconjugation** reactions produce a chemical change in the drug molecule. Such reactions include oxidation (e.g., hydroxylation; dealkylation; deamination; sulfoxide formation); *reduction* (e.g., azo dye reduction; nitro-reduction; dehalogenation); and *hydrolysis* (e.g., cleavage of ester and amide bonds). The concerned enzymes require the presence of cytochrome P450, NADPH (reduced nicotinamide adenine dinucleotide phosphate) and molecular oxygen, which are localized mainly in the microsomal fraction of the liver cell. Phase I reactions are non-synthetic in nature, and generally produce a more water soluble and less active metabolite. The majority of phase I metabolites are generated by a common hydroxylating enzyme system known as cytochrome P450.

Phase II reactions. These **conjugation** or **synthetic** reactions inivolve the coupling of the drug or its metabolites formed in phase I to another chemical group (e.g., sulphate, acetate), or substrate (carbohydrate, amino acid). The end products formed are more water soluble and can be eliminated in bile or urine. Phase II reactions

Table 1.5-2. *Phase I and Phase II reactions involved in drug metabolism*

Phase	*Reaction*	*Enzyme*	*Typical Examples*
I	*Oxidation* of aliphatic and aromatic groups	Cytochrome P450	Meprobamate, Barbiturates, Phenytoin, Phenothiazines, Antihistamines, Steroids, Chlordiazepoxide, Diazoxide
I	*Reduction* of azo	Flavin	Chloramphenicol
	and nitro groups	enzymes	Chloral hydrate
I	*Hydrolysis*	Esterases	Procaine
		Amidases	Lignocaine, Indomethacin
II	*Glucuronide synthesis*	Glucuronyl transferase	Paracetamol, Chloramphenicol
II	*Methylation*	Catechol-O-methyl transferase	Isoprenaline
II	*Acetylation*	*N-acetyl transferase*	*Isoniazid, Sulphonamides*

can also occur without prior phase I reactions (oxidation, reduction or hydrolysis) if suitable groupings pre-exist on the molecule. The outline of processes involved in biotransformation is given in **Fig. 1.5.7.**

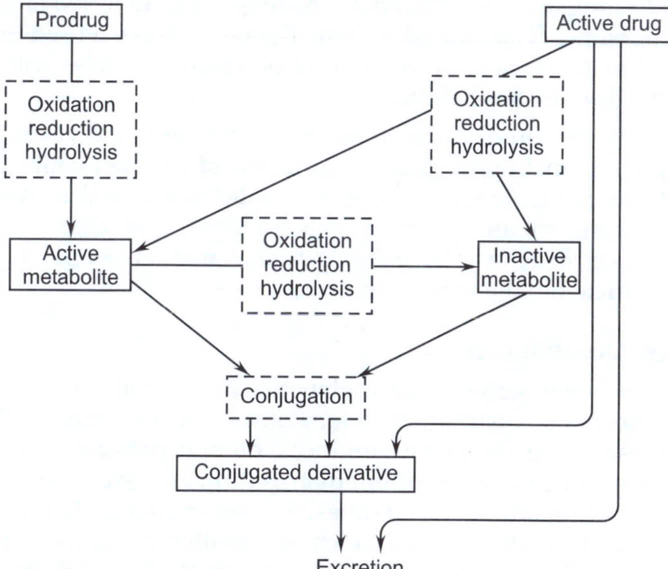

Fig. 1.5.7. Flow chart of reactions involved in biotransformation of drugs. Active drugs may be conjugated or excreted without undergoing metabolism (right).

Hepatic non-microsomal drug metabolism. Apart from the hepatic celllular microsomes, the *cell sap* is another site in the liver where phase II reactions can take place. An important enzyme located in the cell sap is N-acetyltransferase which is responsible for **acetylation** of **isoniazid, hydralazine, sulphonamides** and **procainamide.**

Although the liver is the main site for metabolism of the majority of drugs, several other organs also contain drug-metabolizing enzymes and biotransform drugs. These important sites are the **kidney, lung, intestinal mucosa, plasma,** and **nerve endings.**

There may be considerable variation in the rate at which different individuals metabolize drugs. Some of the important factors are: (*i*) **Associated liver diseases;** (*ii*) **Age;** (*iii*) Presence of other drugs like barbiturates, pesticides and dyes which cause microsomal enzyme induction; and (*iv*) **Genetically determined differences in metabolic activity, which may explain hypersensitivity, drug resistance or tolerance in certain subjects.**

Drug Excretion

Drugs can be excreted in their **unchanged** form or as metabolites by several routes including the **kidney, lungs** and **intestine,** and to a lesser extent by the **sweat, salivary** and **mammary glands.** Among these, the most important excretion channel for the majority of drugs is the kidney. In general, the more water-soluble a drug or a metabolite, the more efficiently it is eliminated from the body.

Renal Excretion

Three major processes are involved in the excretion of drugs by the kidneys: (*i*) **Glomerular filtration;** (*ii*) **Tubular secretion;** and (*iii*) **Tubular reabsorption.** The first two processes remove drugs from the plasma, whereas the third process retains drugs in the body by returning them to the plasma **(Fig. 1.5.8).** The *net excretion* of a drug therefore, depends on the sum total of the three processes.

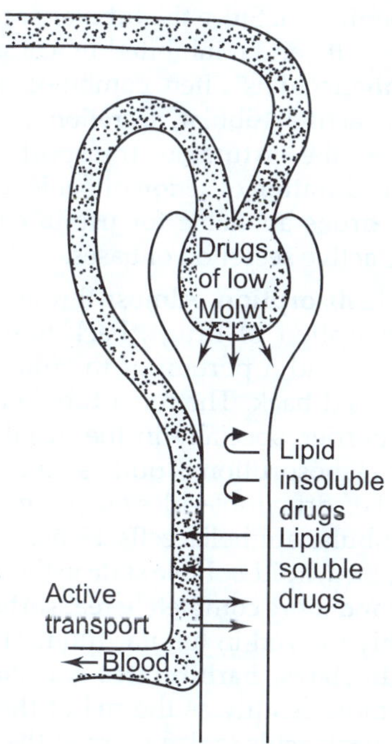

Fig. 1.5.8: Excretion of drugs by the kidney (diagrammatic)

Glomerular filtration. By this process drug molecules diffuse out of the blood perfusing the glomeruli of the nephron, and pass into the tubules of the kidney. The capillaries of the glomerulus are similar to those elsewhere allowing unimpeded diffusion of drugs with a molecular weight (MW) 5000 or less, and partially impeded diffusion of drugs between 5000-69000 MW. Thus, all drugs that are not protein bound appear in the glomerular filtrate. The glomerular filtrate is about 120 litres/day, but the daily urine volume is only 1-2 per cent of this volume. Drugs which are highly protein bound (phenobarbitone, warfarin, diazepam, digoxin) are excreted slowly, as the amount of free drug available for filtration is low. The drug which is passed into the glomerular filtrate may either be reabosorbed into the blood at various segments of the tubule, or excreted into the urine. Thus, several factors influence renal excretion by glomerular filtration: (*i*) **Molecular size,** as smaller molecules are more readily filtered; (*ii*) **Plasma protein binding,** as only free drug can be filtered by the kidney, and protein binding decreases renal excretion; and (*iii*) **Renal blood flow** and **volume of filtrate,** as greater the glomerular perfusion, larger is the volume of fluid filtered leading to faster drug removal from the plasma.

Tubular secretion. The proximal renal tubule can actively secrete certain drugs, transporting them from the blood stream into the tubular fluid. This is an energy requiring or carrier-mediated process, and is not significantly affected by protein-binding as long as the binding is reversible. Active secretory mechanisms exist for both acidic (e.g., salicylates, sulphonamides, thiazide diuretics, penicillins, cephalosporins) and basic (e.g., adrenaline, noradrenaline, dopamine, neostigmine, hydralazine, morphine, procaine, quinine) drugs. Many drugs that are secreted by the tubule are also filtered by the glomeruli, and thus have a very short duration of action, e.g., **penicillin.** Since the tubular secretion process requires energy, it can be inhibited by certain drugs. For example, **probenecid** is often combined with *penicillin* to inhibit the active tubular secretion of penicillin by competing for the saturable transport system, thus prolonging the duration of action of penicillin in the body. There are no drugs available for use in clinical practice that block the active secretion of bases.

Tubular reabsorption. Almost throughout the renal tubules, reabsorption of drugs, back into the capillary network occurs, and a portion of the filtered fraction of a drug is retained back. The renal tubule behaves like a typical lipid barrier, specially in the distal region. Thus, renal tubular reabosorption is quite similar to absorption from the gut, i.e., drug molecules are *passively* transported through the tubular epithelial cells. Hence, a drug existing in the non-ionized, lipid-soluble state in the tubular fluid is more rapidly and more completely reabsorbed than a drug which is highly ionized in tubular fluid. Therefore, weak acids like **salicylates, barbiturates** and **sulphonamides** are excreted more readily as the pH of the tubular fluid increases, as weak acids ionize more as the urine is made more basic. In contrast, weak bases like **amphetamines, ephedrine** and **pethidine** are best excreted in an acid urine, as they are largely ionized at low pH. Acidification or alkalization of urine with drugs like ascorbic acid or sodium bicarbonate, respectively, may be employed to hasten excretion of certain drugs in cases of overdosage or poisoning. For example, phenobarbital or salicylate intoxication may be managed in part by administration of sodium bicarbonate (forced alkaline diuresis) to raise the urine pH, thus promoting ionization of the drug. Less frequently forced acid diuresis may be used to enhance the excretion of amphetamines, strychnine and quinidine.

Biliary Excretion

Excretion in the bile is a relatively minor route of elimination of unmetabolized drugs, but it is a *major* route of elimination of drug metabolites, particularly water-soluble conjugates like glucuronides. Drugs like **ampicillin, tetracycline and rifampicin** are actively secreted in the bile, and passed into the intestines, from where they may be either reabsorbed or lost in the faeces. Drugs that are unabsorbed from the gut, or secreted into the gastrointestinal tract by the bile, salivary glands and digestive glands are excreted in the faeces.

Pulmonary Excretion

This route of excretion is important primarily for *gaseous* and **volatile liquid general anaesthetics**, which can be excreted from the blood stream across the alveolar membrane into *the expired air. Many other volatile substances like ethyl* **alcohol, paraldehyde** and oils can appear in the expired air in small amounts. Enough ethyl alcohol can be eliminated unchanged by the lungs to be detected and measured. This procedure (breathometer) is often used to estimate the blood level of alcohol which correlates with the degree of intoxication.

Excretion of drugs in **sweat, saliva, milk** and **gastric juice** is mainly by passive diffusion of the non-ionized form. Some drugs are reported to be transferred to the suckling infant in breast milk in significant amounts. Hence, drug use by a *breast feeding* mother should be restricted to the minimum.

Pharmacokinetics

In a broad sense pharmacokinetics is the study of drug absorption, distribution, metabolism and excretion. All these factors interact to produce a definite pattern for the time course of **absorption, distribution** and **excretion** of each drug and its metabolites. Strictly speaking pharmacokinetics is the science which uses mathematical models to describe and quantify processes which determine the time course of drug action. It is a complex science, hence only basic considerations are included in this text.

Drug plasma concentration. The speed of onset, intensity and duration of drug effects are determined by the drug concentration at its site or sites of action. In most cases, it is impossible to obtain this measurement. Thus, an assumption is made that the time course of drug concentration at its site of action is determined by that in the plasma.

If a drug is administered intravenously, it enters the blood and is rapidly distributed to the tissues. By taking repeated blood samples, the fall in **plasma concentration** of the drug as related to **time** can be measured, i.e. the **rate of drug elimination.** Often the concentration falls rapidly at first, and then the rate of fall progressively decreases. If this fall is plotted against time, the resultant curve is **exponential,** i.e. at any given time a **constant fraction** of the drug is eliminated in unit time. This is called **first-order kinetics** of drug elimination **(Fig. 1.5.9)** Most drugs follow the first-order kinetics. If any enzyme system responsible for drug metabolism becomes *saturated* then the elimination kinetics changes to **zero-order kinetics,** i.e., the rate of elimination proceeds at a **constant rate** and is unaffected by the level of concentration of the drug (e.g., ethanol, phenytoin).

Volume of distribution (Vd). This is the *apparent* volume into which the drug is distributed on intravenous administration. Vd can be calculated by the following equation:

$$\text{Vd (in litres)} = \frac{\text{Amount of drug in the body (dose in mg)}}{\text{Concentration of drug in plasma (mg/l)}}$$

A value of Vd <5 litres implies that the drug is retained within the vascular compartment. A value of < 15 litres suggests that the drug is restricted to the extracellular fluid, while large volumes of distribution (Vd > 15 litres) indicates distribution throughout the total body water or concentration in certain tissues. The Vd can be used to calculate the clearance of the drug.

Clearance. This represents another estimate of the body's efficiency to remove a drug. Clearance is analogous to renal clearance, i.e., the total volume of plasma from which the drug has been removed per unit time. It can be calculated from the equation:

$$\text{Clearance (Clp)} = \frac{\text{Vd} \times 0.693}{\text{half–life } (t_{1/2})}$$

The whole body clearance of a drug is the volume of plasma "cleared" of the drug per minute, regardless of the means by which it is cleared or removed from the plasma. Thus, Clp = Clm (metabolic clearance) + Clr (renal excretion). In fact, it is clearance and not half-life ($t_{1/2}$) which provides an indication of the ability of the liver and kidney to dispose of drugs.

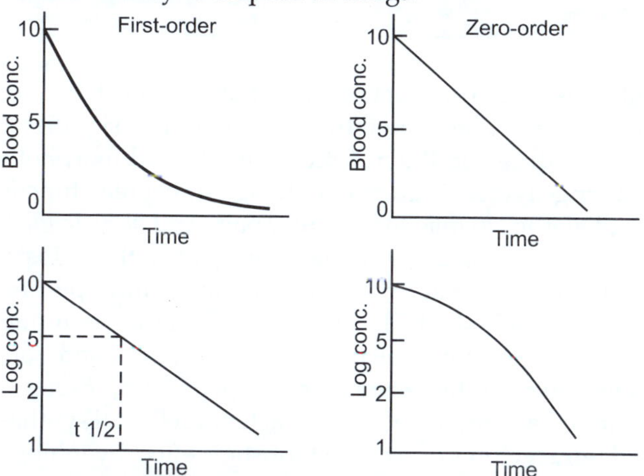

Fig. 1.5.9: The relationship between drug concentration and time with first order and zero-order elimination processes (see text).

Half-life ($t_{1/2}$). It is the time taken for the concentration of a drug in the plasma to fall by half of its original value. The **plasma half-life** is the most used measure, and is closely related to the concentration of the drug at the site of action. It is comparatively easily measured, and is influenced by the route of administration, diffusion into tissues, plasma protein and tissue binding, metabolism and renal excretion. Further, plasma $t_{1/2}$ determines the time taken to achieve a steady-state or an equilibrium condition with any constant dose rate. In practice a useful estimate of time required to reach a steady-state is obtained by the equation:

Time to 95% steady-state = 4.3 × $t_{1/2}$

As a working rule it is followed that it will take five half-lives to reach a steady-state on regular dosing. A caution is that if a *loading dose* is given the time taken to reach a steady-state is reduced.

Drug dosage. The clearance values of drugs can be used to plan dosage regimens. Ideally, in drug treatment, a **steady-state plasma concentration** is required within a known *safe* and *effective therapeutic range.* It is important to maintain the blood concentration of a drug within the therapeutic range for an optimal effect, as at a lower level it would be ineffective, and higher levels would lead to overdosage toxicity **(Fig. 1.5.10).** This steady-state will be achieved when the rate of drug entering the systemic circulation (dosage rate) equals the rate of elimination.

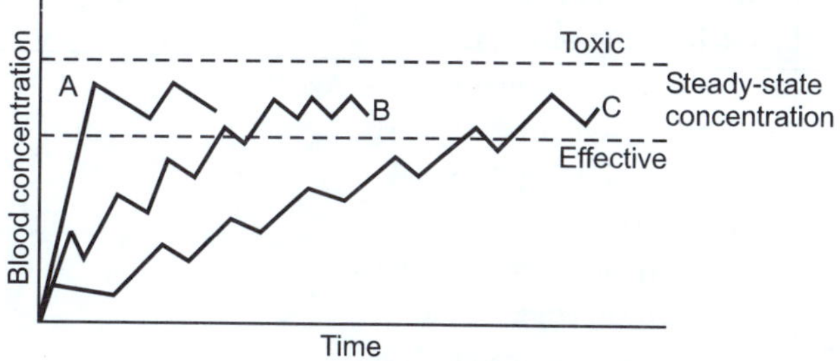

Fig. 1.5.10: Drug concentration profiles on repetitive dosing. A: drug with a long plasma $t_{1/2}$ given in an initial loading dose followed by constant maintenance doses; B: drug with a short plasma $t_{1/2}$ given in constant repetitive dosage; and C; drug with a long plasma $t_{1/2}$ given in constant repetitive dosage. Steady-state concentrations can be maintained on repetitive dosing in all three cases.

Therapeutic Drug Monitoring (TDM)

There is at times marked variability between patients in their pharmacokinetic parameters and in drug responsiveness. This renders the concept of generally accepted `therapeutic dose' rather inaccurate and invalid. An alternative would be to monitor and maintain drug plasma concentrations at a level which is necessary to produce a therapeutic effect. Such a procedure is designated as **therapeutic drug monitoring** (*TDM*). Some commonly monitored drugs are **carbamazepine, digoxin, lithium, phenytoin, sodium valproate and theophylline.**

Situations in which monitoring of drug plasma concentration is useful are as under:

1. Drugs which have a **narrow therapeutic index**, e.g., **digoxin, gentamicin, lithium** and **procainamide** should be desirably monitored by determination of their plasma concentrations. This reduces the liability of overdose effects.
2. In **renal failure**, when it is necessary to use drugs mostly excreted in the urine, e.g. **gentamicin, rifampicin, digoxin, doxycycline, tetracycline** and others. The half-lives of these drugs are appreciably prolonged in renal failure, and the dosage has to be accordingly reduced.
3. To establish **patient compliance**, i.e., whether the patient is following the doctors' instructions or not. Poor patient compliance is the single most important factor accounting for treatment failure and/or a high incidence of **adverse drug reactions** (*ADRs*).
4. In the management of **drug overdose poisoning** repeated estimations of drug levels are helpful in determining the severity of poisoning and response to therapy.

Basic knowledge about **drug disposition** and **pharmacokinetics** is essential for rational and safe drug therapy.

1.6 MECHANISMS OF DRUG ACTION (PHARMACODYNAMICS)

Pharmacodynamics forms a major part of classical pharmacology, and is concerned with the **actions, interactions** and the **mechanism (mode) of action** of drugs. When a drug produces an effect on a tissue, it is the end result of an interaction between its molecules and some part of the tissue cells. In some cases, this interaction is highly **specific,** whereas in others some **nonspecific** chemical or physical properties of the drug account for the observed effects. In fact, on this basis drugs can be divided into *two* major categories: those acting on **pharmacological receptors** situated on or within the cells, and those in which the **receptors are not involved.**

Drugs which **act via receptors:** (*i*) act at *low* concentrations; (*ii*) react with *specific receptors;* (*iii*) show *structure-activity relationhips;* and (*iv*) can be antagonized by specific *antagonists.* Examples are *acetylcholine, adrenaline, noradrenaline* and *histamine.*

In contrast, drugs which do **not act via receptors:** (*i*) act at *higher* concentrations; (*ii*) do *not* react with specific receptors; (*iii*) *tend not* to show structure-activity relationships; and (*iv*) *do not* have specific antagonists. Examples are general anaesthetics like *diethyl ether* and *halothane; diuretics* like the *thiazides;* and *detergents* which non-specifically destroy cell membranes.

Basis of Drug Action

Drugs do not create new functions. They can only *modify* the inherent functions of the tissues or the cells concerned. Hence, drugs act by stimulating or depressing cellular activity; replacing deficient substances; causing irritation; or by killing or weakening the invading foreign organisms. Considering these processes briefly: **stimulation** is an increase in the rate of the functional activity of a cell or tissue, e.g., *caffeine* and *amphetamine* stimulate the CNS; **depression** denotes a reduction in such activity, e.g., *barbiturates, alcohol* and *trimethadione* depress CNS; *replacement* is done for conditions associated with the underproduction of a natural substance, e.g., *insulin* for diabetes mellitus; and **irritation** signifies the effect of drugs on the nutrition, growth and morphology of living tissues, inducing a change in cellular function, e.g., *liniments* to relieve muscular pain, and *phenolphthalein* which functions as an irritant purgative. **Bacteriostatic** (inhibition of bacterial growth and multiplication) and **bactericidal** (death of bacteria) activity is induced by complex mechanisms by **antibiotics** and other **chemotherapeutic drugs,** e.g., **penicillin** exerts its bactericidal effect by blocking bacterial cell wall synthesis, and **tetracyclines** exert a bacteriostatic effect by inhibiting protein synthesis in bacterial ribosomes.

Though the precise mechanism of action of many drugs remains to be established, it is convenient to recognise *five* patterns of action:

1. Drug-receptor interactions (specific interactions).
2. Drugs acting on enzymes (partially specific interactions).
3. Non-receptor mechanisms (non-specific interactions)
   (*i*) Antimetabolites.
   (*ii*) Chelation.
   (*iii*) Drugs affecting the permeability of cell membranes
   (*iv*) Drugs acting by their physical or chemical action.
   (*v*) Drugs acting as antiseptics.
4. Drugs acting through antibodies.
5. Placebo effects.

Drug-Receptor Interactions

Historically, the concept of receptors grew out of the work of **Paul Ehrlich** (*1854-1915*). He believed that living matter was composed of large protoplasmic molecules that possess 'side-chains', and developed the side-chain theory of immunity, enzyme action and drug action. The proposal that drugs may act upon special sites or receptive substances was made in 1905 by *J.N. Langley (1852-1925).* Over the following 75 years, evidence for the existence of 'receptive substances' grew steadily which are now renamed as 'pharmacological receptors'. Mathematical theories to explain the relationship between the *dose* of a drug and its *response* were developed by other workers, specially **A.J. Clark** *(1885-1941),* and also by **J.H. Gaddum, H.O. Schild** and **E.J. Ariens.** More recently with new techniques, attempts have been made to visualize and isolate receptors. The development of various binding techniques has made it possible to map out and to measure the **density of receptors** for drugs, hormones and neurotransmitters on various tissues, and also the changes that take place during disease states.

Receptor Theory of Drug Action

Paul Ehrlich was greatly impressed by the high degree of antibody specificity against the antigenic substance that stimulated their production, and he imagined a stereospecific **lock-and-key** fit between them. He also carried this idea into *chemotherapy.* Using this lock-and-key analogy, the site is the receptor or "lock", for which the drug is the specific "key". The structure of the *drug* is related to the correlative structure of the **receptor,** and as just one key can fit in one lock, so also one drug is specific for one receptor type. The three essential components for explaining drug action on this basis are: (*i*) the drug has to *reach* the receptor in optimal amounts; (*ii*) the drug is *specific* to its matching receptor; and (*iii*) this specificity is based on the **chemical structure** of the drug, which is termed as the structure-activity-relationship (SAR) of the drug **(Fig. 1.6.1).** Implicit in the "**receptor concept**" of drug action is the understanding that drugs exert a **quantitative,** and not a qualitative effect at receptor sites, i.e., a drug is capable of altering the rate of an ongoing process, but cannot create a new function for a cell.

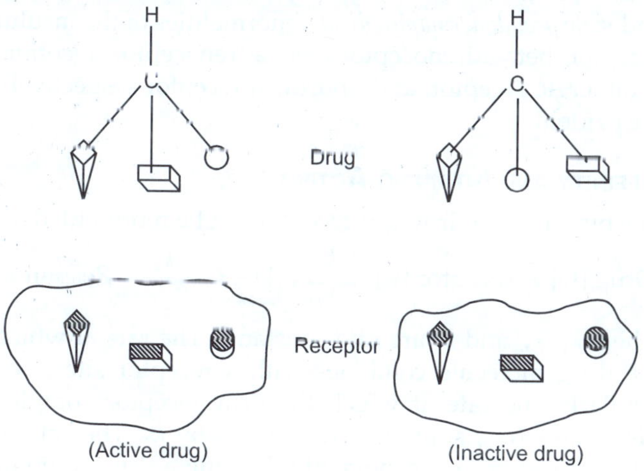

Fig. 1.6.1: The receptor concept.

Terminology. A pharmacological *receptor* is a macromolecule with special sites to which *specific substances,* i.e., drugs (sometimes called ligands) bind. Drug-receptor (ligand-receptor) binding leads to a change in the macromolecule, which in turn triggers a sequence of events resulting in a *response* of the tissue or organ, e.g., *acetylcholine* induces contraction of intestinal smooth muscle, secretion of exocrine glands and inhibition of the myocardial muscle. In this context some important terms related to drugs and receptors must be defined.

An **agonist** is a drug (or hormone, or neurotransmitter) which combines with its *specific receptor,* activates it, and initiates a response, e.g., **acetylcholine** and **noradrenaline** activate cholinoceptors and adrenoceptors, respectively.

An **antagonist** is a drug which binds to the receptor, but does not activate it. Moreover, it prevents the action of the agonist by rendering the receptor unavailable for interaction with the agonist, e.g., **atropine** antagonizes acetylcholine, and **phentolamine,** antagonizes noradrenaline. A **pure antagonist** has no action of its own, but acts only by interfering with the action of an agonist, e.g., the opioid antagonist **naloxone.**

A **partial agonist** binds to the receptor, but activates it weakly and prevents the action of a full agonist. In fact, it is a drug that acts on a receptor with **an intrinsic activity** or **efficacy** of less than 1 (see later). Practically, an activity of 1 means the ability of a drug to elicit a maximal response. Thus it follows that the largest response obtainable from a partial agonist is less than the maximum that can be achieved by a full agonist acting on the same receptor. The term **partial agonist** is a comparative one, i.e., the degree of agonism is measured by comparing the maximum responses obtainable from a whole series of compounds acting on the same receptor. The one that produces the largest response is said to have an **intrinsic activity** or efficacy of 1 [the symbol α (alpha) is used for this so that in this case $\alpha = 1$], and the other compounds are ranked in descending order.

A **mixed agonist-antagonist** is a relatively new term, and is frequently confused with the term partial agonist. A mixed agonist-antagonist is a drug that acts simultaneously on a mixed group of receptors with an *agonist action* on one set, and with an *antagonist action* on another set. Examples are found among the *opioids.*

Thus, at any receptor *four* types of drugs may act (agonists, antagonists, partial agonists, mixed agonist-antagonists) by attachment to receptor site, and may either *produce* or *prevent* a response. For a drug to attach to a reactive area, forces must be present to attract and hold the drug molecule to the receptor site. These **binding forces** in drug receptor interactions include **covalent bonds** (usually the strongest, producing almost irreversible effects), **ionic bonds, hydrogen bonds** and **van der Waals forces** (weakest attractive bonds producing a readily reversible effect).

The *pharmacological receptors* are named according to either, (*a*) the principal endogenous agonist that activates them (*adrenoceptors, cholinoceptors, glucocorticoid receptors,* etc.), or (*b*) the first *exogenous* agonist found to activate them (*opioid receptors, benzodiazepine receptors*) whether or not an endogeneous agonist is discovered later.

Location of Drug Receptors

The *sites* in which drug receptors are found are as under:

1. **On or within cell membranes:** These may be of two types: (*i*) those that act on membrane permeability to alter it with a very fast response time (*in milliseconds*), such as produced by the *nicotinic acetylcholine receptor,* or (*ii*) those that act on intracellular *second messenger* with a fast response time (*in seconds or minutes*), such as is produced by *adrenaline* or *noradrenaline.*
2. **Inside the cells:** The *cytoplasmic glucocorticoid receptors* alter DNA transcription with a slow response time (*in hours*), such as produced by *corticosteroids.*

From the above it is evident that there is a cascade of events that links the interaction of an *agonist* with its *receptor* leading to the ultimate biological response. In a way this multi-stage system is analogous to an *amplifier* in that the initial molecular interaction leads to progressively larger number of interactions at each stage. Thus, just as a small signal from a microphone can be amplified in stages so that the output is capable of driving many powerful loudspeakers, so also small molecules of acetylcholine acting upon the muscle endplate can ultimately result in a powerful contraction of a large skeletal muscle. As discussed earlier, theoretically the complexity of the receptor-response mechanisms is very great, and the number of mechanisms can be limited to **three** as follows: (*i*) **Receptor-ion channel coupling** in which the interaction between the agonist and receptor causes a conformational change in the cell membrane with the result that an ion channel opens to allow the passage of a particular ion, e.g., action of *acetylcholine* on nicotinic cholinoceptors results in influx of sodium ions. This leads to depolarization of the muscle endplate, which triggers off an action potential. This brings about a release of calcium ions, which in turn lead to a contraction of muscle fibres; (*ii*) **Receptor-enzyme coupling** in which the interaction between the agonist and receptor leads to a conformational change in the enzyme, e.g., activation of β-adrenoceptors that are coupled to the enzyme adenylate cyclase in the cell membrane. Activation of this enzyme leads to the formation of cyclic-AMP, which then phosphorylates a protein kinase, which in turn phosphorylates intracellular proteins modifying the activity of the cell; and (*iii*) **Intracellular steroid receptor-protein synthesis coupling** in which steroid hormones which are highly lipid-soluble penetrate the cell membrane with ease and combine with specific receptor-binding proteins in the cytosol. The hormone-receptor complex then enters the cell nucleus, and triggers changes that are transcribed into messenger RNAs. These in turn signal the synthesis of specific proteins which then modify cellular activity.

Receptor Regulation

There is evidence that neither the density nor the affinity of receptors remains fixed. Tissues innervated by the autonomic nervous system, for example, the vascular smooth muscle, after *sympathetic denervation* shows *supersensitivity* to the catecholamines, noradrenaline and adrenaline. This phenomenon is known as the **Cannon's Law of Denervation.** The use of modern techniques has shown that the *density* and *affinity* of receptors are in a *dynamic state,* depending on various physiological and pathological factors. Thus, alterations in the receptors will modify the effects produced by agonists (drugs, neurotransmitters, hormones) acting on these receptors, and may play an important role in the pathology of various diseases and in their therapy. **Table 1.6-1** lists some factors regulating alpha - and beta-adrenoceptors.

Table 1.6-1. *Factors regulating alpha- and beta-adrenoceptors*

Regulatory agent or condition	*Effect on number of receptors*
Alpha-adrenoceptors	
Alpha-adrenergic catecholamines	Decrease
Denervation	Increase
Hyperthyroidism	Decrease
Beta-adrenoceptors	
Beta-adrenergic catecholamines	Decrease
Denervation	Increase
Hyperthyroidism	Increase
Hypothyroidism	Decrease
Propranolol	Increase

In addition, there are certain diseases in which receptor abnormalities have been demonstrated, e.g., in *diabetes mellitus, bronchial asthma, hypothyroidism, myasthenia gravis,* and *male pseudohermaphrodism* abnormalities of the insulin receptor, beta-adrenoceptor, beta-adrenoceptor, nicotinic cholinergic receptor, and androgen receptor respectively are evident.

Affinity and Intrinsic Activity

The binding of a drug to a receptor can be represented as:

$$\text{Drug [D]} + \text{Receptor [R]} \underset{k_2}{\overset{k_1}{\rightleftharpoons}} \underset{\text{Complex}}{\text{D}-\text{R}} \xrightarrow{k_3} \text{Response}$$

where k_1, k_2, and k_3 are rate constants. The rate at which the drug molecule combines with a receptor site is k_1. Similarly, the rate at which the drug-receptor complex dissociates (i.e., splits apart) is given by k_2. The rate at which a response is generated following a drug-receptor interaction is given by rate constant k_3. These constants are used to define some basic concepts related to drug-receptor interactions.

The term **affinity** describes the ability of a drug to form and subsequently maintain a complex with a receptor site. It is quantitatively expressed as k_1/k_2, i.e., the rate at which the complex forms compared to the rate at which the complex dissociates. The term **intrinsic activity** describes the ability of a drug to evoke a pharmacologic response on combining with a receptor, and can be measured by k_3. Thus, *agonists* possess both affinity and intrinsic activity, whereas antagonists display only affinity, i.e., the k_3 for antagonists is zero. For example, *acetylcholine* acts as a cholinergic agonist, but its effects are inhibited by *atropine*, a cholinergic antagonist, capable of occupying the same receptor sites but possessing no intrinsic cholinergic activity of its own. In contrast, a **partial agonist** possesses less intrinsic activity than a full agonist, but may have equal affinity. Thus, the presence of a partial agonist can reduce the effects of a full agonist by competing with the available receptor sites. However, if the partial agonist is present alone, an agonistic action will be observed.

Intensity of Drug Response

Simply speaking, an **agonist** is a drug capable of interacting with a receptor to produce a response. When an **antagonist** attaches itself to the receptor, no response is produced, and in the presence of an antagonist, the normally elicited response by the agonist is diminished or totally blocked. In most instances a specific chemical structure is required for a drug to act as an agonist or an antagonist **(Fig. 1.6.2)**.

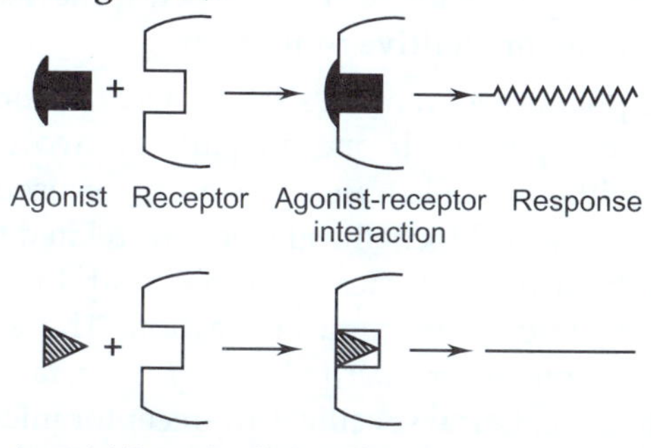

Fig. 1.6.2: Drug-receptor interactions. The agonist neatly fits and interacts with the receptor site to produce a pharmacologic response. Whereas, the antagonist only partially fits the receptor site, hence it is unable to produce a response itself, and prevents the agonist from combining with the receptor.

The magnitude of the response elicited by a drug-receptor interaction can vary widely. Currently *three* theories attempt to explain the nature of drug-receptor interactions and their relationship to the response produced: (*i*) the **receptor occupation theory;** (*ii*) the **rate theory;** and (*iii*) theories involving drug-induced protein changes at receptor site.

The **receptor occupation theory** postulates that the magnitude of the response produced by a drug is directly proportional to the number of receptors occupied. A maximal drug effect occurs when all the receptors are occupied. This is an oversimplified view, as it does not account for differences in absolute milligram potencies among drugs.

The **rate theory** postulates that the intrinsic activity of the drug is related to the rate of complex formation (k_1), and the rate of complex breakdown (k_2), which are in turn the measures of association and dissociation of the drug with the receptor. The **agonists** have high rate of association and dissociation, and it is this **"turnover number"** which decides the magnitude of the response. In contrast, the *antagonists* produce a stable complex with the receptor that does not readily breakdown, thereby preventing the interaction of an agonist with the receptor. **Agonists have a high rate of dissociation, while antagonists have a slow rate, with partial agonists in between.** This theory explains many aspects of the time course of drug effects. A typical curve illustrating the intensity of a drug effect with increasing dosage (conventionally plotted as log dose) is shown in **(Fig. 1.6.3)**.

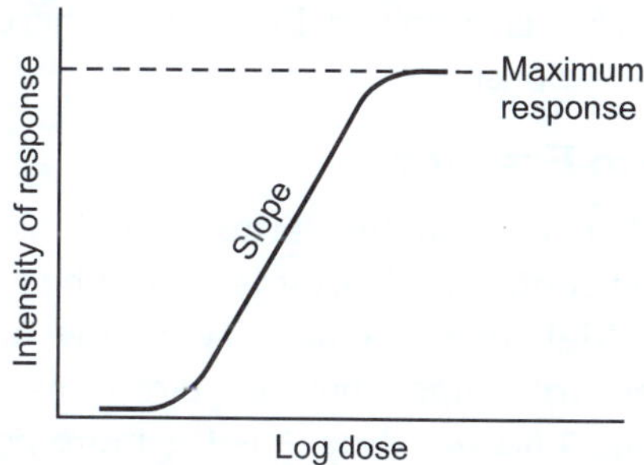

Fig. 1.6.3: A typical log dose-response curve for a drug.

The slope of the upward part of the curve is of therapeutic significance in assessing the relative safety of the drug. For example, many CNS depressants have a *steep* dose-response curve, indicating a narrow margin between the dose that produces sedation and the dose that is potentially toxic which produces coma. Therefore, the more shallow the slope of the dose-response curve, the greater is the safety margin of the drug **(Fig. 1.6.4)**.

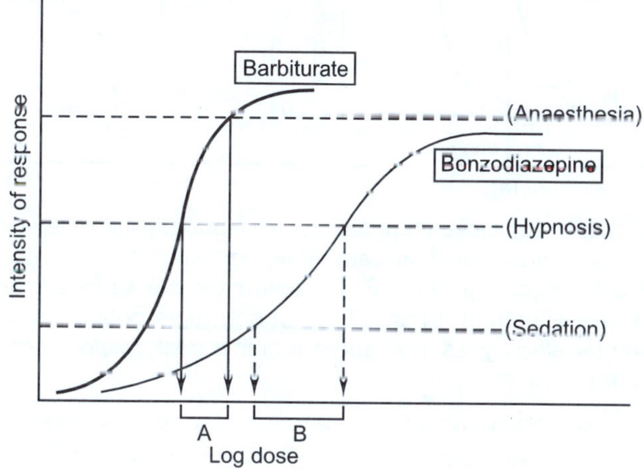

Fig. 1.6.4: Log dose-response curves for a barbiturate and a benzodiazepine, illustrating the greater margin between the sedative and hypnotic doses of a benzodiazepine (B) compared to a barbiturate (A).

Thus, the main advantage of the benzodiazepine group of antianxiety drugs, such as diazepam or oxazepam over the barbiturates for the relief of anxiety is their much *shallower dose-response curve,* indicating a wider margin of safety of the benzodiazepines.

Certain theories suggest that the *agonist* exerts its action by inducing some **temporary structural changes in the protein constituents at the receptor site.** Such structural alterations modify the permeability of cell membranes and produce a response. Possibly antagonists produce structural changes that prevent the formation of an agonist-receptor complex.

Strictly speaking, a lot remains to be known about drug-receptor interactions producing a response. Some hormones (glucagon, antidiuretic hormone, adrenaline) stimulate the membrane enzyme adenylcyclase. This in turn promotes the local formation of cyclic-adenosine monophosphate (c-AMP), which functions as a "second messenger" and is involved in cellular energy transfer producing a response.

Potency and Efficacy

Potency and **efficacy** are two terms related to drug action that are often confused. A drug is said to be *potent* when it possesses **high intrinsic activity at low unit weight doses.** Of the two drugs whose dose-response curves are plotted in **Fig. 1.6.5 (*a*),** drug A is the more potent drug, since it produces the intensity of response as drug *B* at much smaller doses. However, the maximal response with each drug is similar.

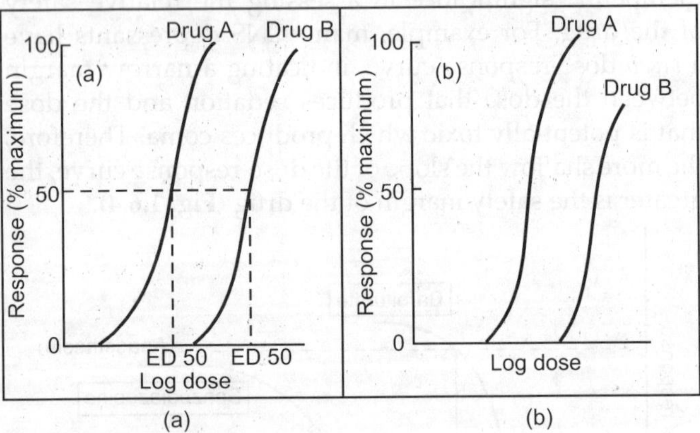

Fig. 1.6.5: Log dose-response curves showing the difference between potency and efficacy (diagrammatic). In (a) drug A is more potent than drug, B, but both have the same efficacy (maximal effect). In (b) drug A is not only more potent but has a greater efficacy, as it produces a higher peak response than drug B (see text).

Thus, potencies are comparisons based on doses that elicit the same intensity of effect. Knowledge of a drug's potency is important for finding out the appropriate dosage level to be administered, but is relatively unimportant in deciding which of the two drugs exhibiting the same maximal effect should be preferred. It makes little difference if the dose of a drug is 5 mg or 500 mg as long as the dosage can be conveniently administered. It is not rational to believe that the more potent drug is the clinically preferred drug, as is sometimes stressed and implied in drug advertising.

Efficacy, in contrast refers to the *maximal* or *peak* response produced by a drug, and is an important determinant in the drug selection process. In **Fig. 1.6.5 (*b*),** drug A is not only more potent, it also exhibits greater efficacy, since the maximal effect obtainable with drug *A* is greater than that obtainable with drug *B*. For example, oral administration of 4 mg of hydromorphone results in much greater pain relief than 65 mg of propoxyphene. Thus, hydromorphone is both more potent and more efficacious than propoxyphene.

Drugs Acting on Enzymes

Many drugs inhibit the action of membrane bound or intracellular enzymes. Some drugs compete with the normal substrate at the active site of the enzyme, preventing its metabolism. This competition may be *reversible,* as with the xanthine oxidase inhibitor *allopurinol,* or with the anticholinesterase *physostigmine.* Such a mechanism is termed as **competitive inhibition.** Some drugs may exert an *irreversible* action, as with the organophosphorus anticholinesterase *diisopropyl fluorophosphate (DFP),* which phosphorylates the active site of the enzyme cholinesterase. Such a mechanism is termed as **non-competitive inhibition.**

In the phenomenon of *substrate competition* either two substrates compete with one enzyme, or two enzymes compete with one substrate. This term is used rather loosely for all those biochemical reactions related to drugs in which the drug competes with the natural metabolite for entering into a biochemical reaction. The effects of drugs on enzymes are *partially specific* interactions, in contrast to the classical specific drug-receptor interactions discussed above.

Non-Receptor Mechanisms

Some drugs do not act by combining with receptor sites. For example, *gastric antacids* act by neutralizing the hydrochloric acid secreted by parietal cells in the stomach. **Osmotic diuretics,** like mannitol, remove excess of fluid from the body by increasing the osmolarity of plasma and the glomerular filtrate resulting in diuresis. Certain **antimetabolites,** like *structural analogues of purines* and *pyramidines* can be incorporated into nucleic acids disrupting their functioning. These antimetabolites are used in treating many types of cancers. **Volatile general anaesthetics** produce anaesthesia without directly involving receptors. **Metal chelating agents,** like EDTA, are employed in the treatment of poisoning by heavy metals. In addition, certain *antiseptics* act as *protoplasmic* *poisons* by non-specifically acting on cells with which they come in contact. The **vaccines** produce their effects by stimulating the defence mechanisms in the body, and induce production of antibodies (e.g., vaccine against poliomyelitis, rabies, smallpox, typhoid and cholera); while *antisera* contain antibodies which neutralize toxins in the body (e.g., antisera against diphtheria, tetanus and gas gangrene).

Placebo Effects

A *placebo* (means, I shall please) is an inactive substance given to satisfy the patient's demand for medicine. Many diseases which are chronic in nature have a substantial subjective (psychogenic) element, in addition to the somatic element. Studies have shown that inert medicines (placebos) can lead to improvement in more than one-third of all patients (about 35 per cent). This is termed as a placebo response. Sometimes doctors use the placebo response to reinforce the effects of treatment.

Therapeutic Index

An "ideal" drug should cure all patients in a dose that kills none. The therapeutic index gives a measure of the safety margin of a drug, although it does not take into account the possible occurrence of an abnormal response, like an allergic or hypersensitivity reaction

The dose of a drug necessary to produce the desired effect in one half of all patients is known as the **median effective dose,** or ED_{50}. Similarly, the dose of a drug that exhibits an undesirable toxic reaction in one half of all patients is termed the **median toxic dose,** or TD_{50}. In toxicity studies in laboratory animals, the toxic end-point frequently used is death, and is referred to as the **median lethal dose,** or LD_{50}. Clinical studies for obvious reasons, do not attempt to determine the LD_{50} of a drug. Thus, in a clinical situation, the larger the difference between the TD_{50} and the ED_{50}, the greater is the safety margin of the drug. The therapeutic index is **defined** as the ratio of the TD_{50} to the ED_{50}, as expressed under:

$$\text{Therapeutic Index (TI)} = TD_{50}/ED_{50}$$

The greater the ratio, i.e., the lower the ED_{50} or the higher the TD_{50}, the greater is the safety of the drug. Drugs do not have a single TI, since the TD_{50} and ED_{50} values are dependent on the particular end-points chosen. It is important to remember that the TI is simply a measure of the drug's safety and has no bearing on the drug's efficacy. The TI must be viewed as a general index, as some patients may display extreme sensitivity to certain drugs, e.g., aspirin is a very safe drug in therapeutic doses in the majority of persons, however, severe hypersensitivity reactions to small doses of aspirin may occur in some patients.

In acute toxicity studies done on animals, the end-point is taken as the dose which kills 50 per cent of all animals, i.e., LD_{50}. Hence, the TI is expressed as under:

$$\text{Therapeutic Index (TI)} = LD_{50}/ED_{50}$$

When it is proposed to prescribe any drug, its toxicity must always be taken into consideration, and the risk of treatment weighed against the risk of the disease (risk: benefit ratio). An example of the application of this principle in practice is the use of highly toxic drugs for the treatment of cancer.

Repeated Dosage

The frequency and duration of drug dosing can influence the safety and efficacy of therapy. The plasma concentration of a systemically administered drug must attain a certain level so that enough drug can be distributed to the site of action. Therefore, the plasma level is an often employed parameter for measuring drug efficacy, and the dosage of many drugs is adjusted so as to maintain the plasma concentration within a certain range. If the plasma level falls below the lower limit of the desired range, effectiveness is reduced or abolished, conversely, an increase in plasma concentration above the upper limit of the desired range is frequently associated with untoward reactions. A typical plasma concentration curve for a single dose of an orally administered drug is shown in **(Fig. 1.6.6).**

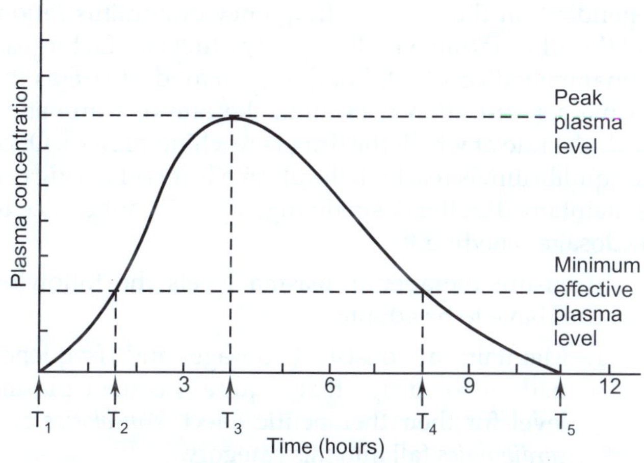

Fig. 1.6.6: A typical plasma-concentration curve for a single dose of an orally administered drug. T_1 = Time of administration; T_1-T_2 =Time of onset of action (1½ hours); T_1-T_3 =Time of attainment of peak plasma concentration (4 hours), T_2-T_4 = Duration of effective plasma concentration (6½ hours); T_1-T_5 = Time of complete removal of drug from the plasma (11 hours).

The **time of onset of action** is the time necessary for the drug to be absorbed to an extent that the effective plasma level is reached, and the drug is distributed to its site of action in sufficient quantity to produce a response. As more drug is absorbed, the plasma level rises, more drug reaches the site of action, and the response increases reflecting the attainment of the **peak** or **maximum plasma level** possible with the particular dose. As the drug is circulating in plasma, elimination begins, either of the unchanged drug molecules or its metabolites. The plasma level begins to decline and the effect of the drug decreases.

Once the plasma concentration falls below the minimal level, drug action ceases, even though some drug still remains in the plasma. Therefore, the **duration of action** of the drug corresponds to the length of time that the drug is present in the plasma in concentrations enough to produce the desired response.

The **elimination half-life** ($t_{1/2}$) is the time required for the plasma level of a drug to be reduced by one half of the initial level. Approximately 95 per cent of a dose of a drug is eliminated in four half-lives. Knowledge of half-life of a drug serves as an indicator of how frequently a drug is to be administered to ensure maintenance of effective plasma concentrations. Thus, a drug with a half-life of 4 to 5 hours needs to be given every 4 hours to maintain its effectiveness, while a drug with a half-life of 10 to 12 hours may only require twice-daily administration.

When a drug is administered repeatedly, the absorbed fraction of each dose is added to the amount remaining in the plasma at the particular time. Thus, the *maximum* and *minimum* plasma levels slowly rise until the rate of elimination *equals* the rate of administration. At this point, assuming that the drug is being given in fixed dosage at constant time intervals, a steady-state plasma range is attained, and the concentration of the drug in the plasma reaches a **plateau**. The plateau concentration of a drug is dependent on the *dose*, the **frequency** of administration, and the **elimination half-life** $t_{1/2}$. The first two factors can be maintained constant, but the $t_{1/2}$ may decrease as the plasma concentration rises, until the rate of elimination *equals* the rate at which the drug is reaching plasma. Once the equilibrium is reached, the plasma levels of a drug can be maintained in the desired range by strict adherence to the dosage schedule.

To ensure therapeutic plasma levels the following measures have to be adopted:

1. Maintain a consistent dosage and frequency pattern for drugs that require a certain plasma level for their therapeutic effect. *Antibiotics* and *cardiotonics* fall into this category.
2. Plasma levels of drugs are reliable only if the blood is drawn at the correct time interval after dose administration, e.g., *lithium* blood levels should be sampled just prior to the subsequent dose, i.e., approximately 8 to 12 hours following the previous dose.
3. *Loading doses* of drugs may be given to facilitate rapid attainment of therapeutic plasma levels. In this type of dosing also the dose and frequency schedule should be strictly followed.

Combined Effects of Drugs

The combined effects of drugs are discussed in **Chap. 1.4** as they influence dosage. They are briefed here as they also influence drug action.

Synergism

Two drugs are said to have a *synergistic* action when the therapeutic effects of the drug combination are *greater* than those elicited by either drug alone. Two types of synergism—*addition* and *potentiation*—are recognized:

Addition. When the net effect of two drugs used together is *equal* to the *algebraic sum* of the individual drug actions, the drugs are said to have an *additive effect*, i.e., if the dose of each were reduced by one half, the resultant effect would be equal to the effect observed with either drug used at full dosage.

Potentiation. When the net effect of two drugs given together is *greater* than the algebraic sum of the individual drug effects, the term *potentiation* is frequently used. Potentiation is usually seen where the two drugs elicit the same clinical effect by different mechanisms, e.g., the combined antihypertensive effect of *hydrochlorothiazide*, a diuretic, and *propranolol*, a beta-blocker.

Antagonism

The effects of one drug can be *reduced* or *abolished* by the presence of a second drug, and this effect is termed *antagonism*. Antagonism is mainly of two types: *competitive* and *non-competitive* antagonism.

Competitive antagonism. In this situation the antagonist reacts *reversibly* with the same receptor as the agonist, i.e., the antagonist and agonist compete for occupation of the same receptor. The relative effectiveness of the agonist or antagonist depends on their relative affinity for the receptor and their concentration, i.e., there is a dynamic equilibrium between the two. An increase in the effective concentration of either of the competing molecules will displace the other from the receptor. Such an antagonist causes a parallel displacement of the log dose-response curve to the right, and there is no change in its shape, slope or maximum response **(Fig. 1.6.7).**

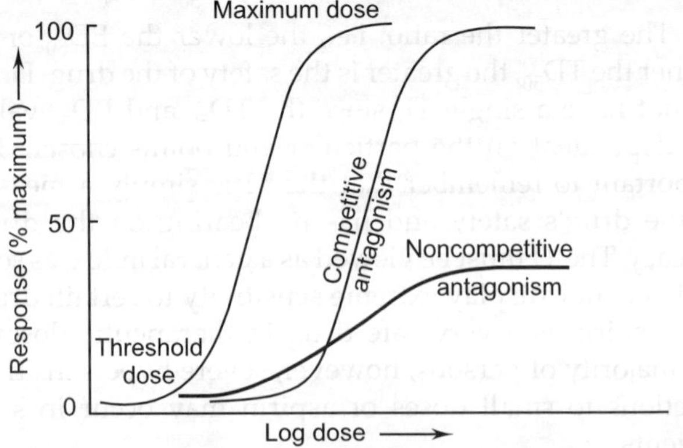

Fig. 1.6.7: A typical log dose-response curve for an agonist (extreme left), and the effect of a competitive and a non-competitive antagonist on this relationship (see text).

This antagonism is **competitive or surmountable,** e.g., acetylcholine-atropine; acetylcholine-tubocurarine; noradrenaline-phentolamine; isoprenaline-propranolol; histamine-diphenhydramine and others.

Non-competitive antagonism. In this situation the antagonist forms a more stable bond (covalent bonding) with its receptor, which is irreversible or at least long lasting. The antagonist is not displaced by a high concentration of the agonist, thus the log dose-response curve would be displaced to the right, but its slope and maximum response would be decreased **(Fig. 1.6.7)**. Such an antagonism is **non-competitive** or **unsurmountable,** e.g., between noradrenaline and phenoxybenzamine; and between organophosphorus anticholinesterase (DFP) and cholinesterase.

In addition, two other types of antagonism are also recognized, namely—*physiologic* and *chemical* antagonism. In **physiologic antagonism** the agonist and antagonist have different cellular sites of action, but the responses elicited are opposed, e.g., histamine-noradrenaline on blood pressure and anaphylaxis. In **chemical antagonism** the chemical reactions between the two drugs take place within the body, and the biologic activity of the offending drug is abolished, e.g., heparin versus protamine; and mercury or arsenic versus dimercaprol.

1.7 ADVERSE DRUG REACTIONS AND TREATMENT OF POISONING

When a drug is administered to a patient, essentially two types of reactions can occur, **desired** effects and the **undesired** effects. The desired drug effects are those clinically beneficial actions for which the drug has been prescribed. On the other hand, undesired drug effects are pharmacologic actions which are not sought for. These are further divided into those that are **innocuous**, and those that are **harmful** to the patient. The latter group is commonly referred to as **adverse drug reactions** or **untoward reactions.**

In this era of **drug explosion** many potent drugs are available, and the incidence of adverse drug reactions (ADRs) is appreciable. Sometimes even the physician is responsible for certain drug-induced diseases (iatrogenic diseases). ADRs have increased in number and severity due to: (*i*) increased availability of potent drugs; (*ii*) availability of dangerous drugs without prescription; (*iii*) exposure of man to drugs/chemicals used in industry and agriculture, and *via* the polluted environment; (*iv*) **polypharmacy**, i.e., irrational use of many drugs together; and (*v*) **self-medication** for minor ailments. **Lasagna** has pointed out that in drug reactions often a clear cause-and-effect relationship cannot be established. **Sir William Osler** has correctly said, "one of the duties of the physicians is to educate the masses not to take medicines".

Terms frequently used but often wrongly interchanged are *side effects* and *adverse reactions*. The term **side effects** should be restricted to therapeutically undesirable but unavoidable effects of drugs, even when they are used in their therapeutic doses. They are often anticipated and mild in nature. *Examples* of side effects include anorexia, cramps, mild diarrhoea, dizziness, drowsiness, euphoria, fatigue, glossitis, headache, hiccups, nausea, mild skin rash, vertigo, weakness and xerostomia.

Major **adverse drug reactions** can involve many organs and include addiction, allergic reactions, anaphylactic shock, blood dyscrasias (agranulocytosis, thrombocytopenia), cardiac arrhythmias, coma, congestive heart failure, convulsions, diabetes mellitus, encephalopathy, deafness, haemorrhage, hypotension, hypertension, kidney or liver dysfunction, mental depression, neoplasia, ocular damage, pancreatitis, paralysis, photosensitivity, psychoses, respiratory depression, superinfections and skin reactions.

Changing the dose, dosage form, route of administration or diet can often reduce or abolish many side effects. Major adverse drug reactions, however, are frequently dose and dosage form independent. Drugs causing a high degree of adverse effects should never be used for minor ailments, e.g., **chloramphenicol**, a highly toxic antibacterial agent, is acceptable for the treatment of salmonella or meningeal infections, but the drug should not be used for uncomplicated respiratory tract infections. **Corticosteroids** are useful anti-inflammatory agents but should not be routinely used for minor ailments.

DEFINITION

An adverse drug reaction (ADR) is any response to a drug which is noxious (injurious) and unintended, and which occurs at doses used in man for prophylaxis, diagnosis or therapy of disease. Strictly speaking, ADRs exclude therapeutic failures, and consequences of administration of the wrong drug, to the wrong patient, in a wrong dosage, at the wrong time or for the wrong disease. Any single "wrong" may result in unwanted effect or cause a reaction.

Adverse drug reactions can be logically separated into two types, those which are normal but *augmented* (Type A), and those which are totally abnormal or *bizarre* (Type B) effects:

Type A (augmented) ADRs are the result of an augmented pharmacological action of a drug when given in usual therapeutic doses, e.g., **bradycardia** with beta-blockers; **haemorrhage** with anticoagulants; **drowsiness** with benzodiazepines. Type A reactions are **predictable** and **dose-dependent**. Their incidence and morbidity is often high, but the mortality is low.

Type B (bizarre) ADRs are totally abnormal and are not expected on the basis of the known pharmacology of the drug when given in usual therapeutic doses, e.g., **malignant hyperthermia** of anaesthesia, **porphyria**, and many immunological **reactions**. They are **unpredictable** and are usually not observed during conventional toxicological screening. Their incidence and morbidity is usually low, but the mortality may be high.

CLASSIFICATION OF ADRs

Adverse drug reactions may be classified as under :

1. **Pharmacologic ADRs**

(i) Extension of therapeutic effect
(ii) Nontherapeutic adverse effects

2. **Non-pharmacologic ADRs**
(i) Hypersensitivity (drug allergy)
(ii) Idiosyncrasy (pharmacogenetics)
(iii) Photosensitivity

3. **Disease-related ADRs**
4. **Multiple-drug reactions**
5. **Miscellaneous ADRs**
(i) Carcinogenicity
(ii) Teratogenicity (dysmorphogenesis)
(iii) Drug dependence
(iv) Overdosage (relative and absolute)
(v) Drug-induced sexual dysfunction

PHARMACOLOGIC ADRs

Many ADRs are the result of a greater than desired pharmacologic action of the drug, or one or more "secondary" drug effects in addition to the "primary" or intended drug effect.

Extension of therapeutic effects. Overdosage with a drug usually elicits an excessive reaction to the *primary* effect of the drug, e.g., *tranquillizers* used as daytime sedatives in excessive doses will usually produce drowsiness and hypnosis; haemorrhage occurs on overdosage of *anticoagulants;* water and electrolyte depletion can occur on overdosage of *diuretics*.

Nontherapeutic adverse effects. Drugs seldom exhibit a single pharmacologic effect, and some adverse effects caused by drug administration are the result of one or more *secondary* effects produced by a drug. In some cases the secondary effects can be minimized or eliminated by adjusting the dose, however, many times these adverse reactions are inescapable, e.g., therapeutic doses of many *antihistamines* cause profound drowsiness; *anticholinergics* used as spasmolytics produce xerostomia (dry mouth), blurring of vision, and some degree of urinary retention and constipation; *narcotic analgesics* cause constipation; *diuretics* produce hypokalaemia and hyperuricaemia; *broad spectrum antibiotics* and *cytotoxic drugs* induce vitamin deficiency and superinfection; and *antipsychotics* produce postural hypotension.

The secondary effects of a drug usually cannot be controlled by dosage adjustment, however, the effect can be reduced by substituting or adding other drugs to the regimen, e.g., the drowsiness with some antihistamines can be minimized by using *caffeine*, or by switching to an antihistamine with minimal CNS depressant actions like *terfenadine*; the hypokalaemia with thiazide diuretics can be minimized by *potassium supplementation*.

Potentially dangerous secondary effects of drugs include the possibility of thrombotic complications with *oral contraceptives;* cardiac arrhythmias with *digitalis;* and gastrointestinal bleeding and ulceration with *aspirin* and related drugs. Most pharmacologic adverse reactions are well documented. Thus, in assessing the suitability of a particular drug regimen, the predictable risk involved should be weighed agaisnt the beneficial effects (risk : benefit ratio).

NON-PHARMACOLOGIC ADRs

This group of ADRs has little relationship with the pharmacologic effects of a drug. They occur as a result of an abnormal sensitivity or reactivity of the individual to a chemical substance. Such reactions are *not* predictable on the basis of the pharmacologic profile of the drug, and occur in a small but significant proportion of patients.

HYPERSENSITIVITY (DRUG ALLERGY)

This is the largest single group of untoward drug effects. Allergic reactions are usually *not* dose related and independent of the pharmacologic properties of the drug molecule. They are associated with an altered reactivity or sensitization of the patient resulting from prior exposure to a drug or chemical that behaves like an allergen. Macromolecules (proteins, peptides) can act as *complete antigens*, but most drugs are small molecules and do not stimulate antibody production. They combine with other carrier macromolecules and function as *haptens* or *partial antigens*, activating the reticuloendothelial system, resulting in production of antibodies to the drug molecule. A subsequent exposure to the same drug elicits an antigen-antibody reaction that produces symptoms like itching, oedema, congestion and wheezing. Allergic drug reactions are either **immediate** (anaphylaxis, urticaria) or **delayed** (serum sickness).

Immediate hypersensitivity develops within minutes of drug exposure. This involves formation of specific antibodies called reagins that belong to the IgE class. Upon re-exposure, the antigen combines with the antibodies on the target tissue, and certain natural substances like *histamine, 5-hydroxytryptamine, slow-reacting substance (SRS-A), bradykinin* and *prostaglandins are liberated.* These substances react with the smooth muscles of many tissues (bronchioles, blood vessels, GI tract) to produce characteristic signs of the allergic reaction like bronchoconstriction and vasodilation. The symptoms may be very mild (rash, itching, urticaria) or serious (respiratory distress, severe hypotension—termed as *anaphylactic shock*) which require immediate attention to prevent death. Immediate immune reactions like anaphylactic shock, asthma, rhinitis and angioneurotic oedema occur within a few minutes of re-exposure, e.g., penicillin allergy.

Delayed hypersensitivity reactions develop slowly following drug challenge. The allergen reacts with preformed antibodies that are bound to sensitized lymphocytes. The clinical picture of delayed hypersensitivity includes a diffuse rash, fever, angioedema, swollen lymph nodes, and stiff joints. This syndrome is referred to as *serum sickness*. This name is derived from the fact that the allergic response results from damage produced by the *circulating immune complexes* that may lodge in small vessels. Sometimes the liver, kidney and bone marrow may also be damaged.

Idiosyncrasy (Pharmacogenetics)

Strictly speaking, idiosyncrasy refers to a peculiarity of bodily function that causes an individual to react in an abnormal manner to a drug. These reactions are not caused by formation of an antigen-antibody complex but result from a genetically determined defect in the patients' ability to handle a particular drug. Idiosyncrasy today is a term of the past.

A specialized field of study termed **pharmacogenetics** deals with those altered drug responses that are under hereditary control. With the increasing knowledge of pharmacogenetics most idiosyncratic drug reactions are now recognized as being genetically determined, and related to a relative or total deficiency of a particular enzyme, e.g., in glucose-6 phosphate dehydrogenase (G-6-PD) deficiency a usual dose of *primaquine* may cause *haemolytic anaemia*; in individuals who lack normal plasma cholinesterase activity *suxamethonium* may cause *prolonged apnoea;* slow acetylators are more likely to develop polyneuritis with *isoniazid* or systemic lupus erythematosus with *hydralazine*, whereas fast acetylators may show drug resistance or failure of response. Other pharmacogenetic abnormalities include resistance to *coumarin anticoagulants*; resistance to *vitamin D; malignant hyperthermia* induced by the general anaesthetic *halothane;* hereditary methaemoglobinaemia; and acute intermittent porphyria induced by barbiturates, sulphonamides, pentazocine, tolbutamide, methyldopa, chlordiazepoxide and oral contraceptives.

Photosensitivity

A unique type of skin hypersensitivity reaction following use of many drugs is observed on exposure to sunlight, and is termed **photosensitization**. Two types of reactions can occur in people whose skin has been sensitized by topical or internal use of photosensitizing drugs; (*i*) a **photoallergic reaction** is a papular eruption on sun-exposed areas similar to that resulting from contact dermatitis. It is probably due to the photosensitizing drug forming an antigen by absorption of sunlight and combination with skin protein. The resultant antibody formation sensitizes the patient to further sun-exposure; and (*ii*) a **phototoxic** *reaction*, in contrast, is characterized by a severe sunburn, and as such is not always viewed as a hypersensitivity reaction. It is probably the result of a photosensitizing chemical absorbing *ultraviolet radiations* to such an extent that it becomes toxic to epidermal cells. *Examples* of photosensitizing drugs include amitriptyline, antimalarials, barbiturates, carbamazepine, chlordiazepoxide, chlorthalidone, clindamycin, contraceptives (oral), cyproheptadine, diethylstilbestrol, 5-fluorouracil, frusemide, griseofulvin, haloperidol, imipramine, lincomycin, nalidixic acid, phenothiazines, phenytoin, salicylates, sulpho- nyluneas, tetracyclines, thiazide diuretics, triamterence and trimethadione.

Disease-Related ADRs

The pathophysiologic state of the patient is a major factor determining the potential for a drug to cause adverse effects. Some common abnormalities are described below:

Hepatic disease. Since the liver plays a major role in metabolism of many drugs, impaired liver function may result in abnormally high plasma levels of drugs for a long period of time. If normal dosage schedules are followed, accumulation of drug in the body can occur, resulting in symptoms of overdosage.

Renal disease. The presence of renal disease can lead to adverse reactions with those drugs that are largely eliminated from the body via the kidneys. In renal disease, doses of drugs excreted by the kidney need to be reduced to avoid accumulation and toxicity, e.g., most aminoglycoside antibiotics are excreted by glomerular filtration in an unchanged form. Thus, these drugs are potentially quite toxic even in normal doses in patients with impaired renal function, as their excretion is slowed and the serum half-life is prolonged. In progressive renal failure, plasma albumin stores are likely to be decreased, which can reduce the plasma protein binding of many drugs, resulting in exaggeration of their effects.

Emotional disorders. Mentally unstable patients should not be allowed to monitor their own drug therapy. Often they do not follow proper dosage schedules, and this can lead to overdosage with dangerous drugs like antipsychotics, antidepressants, or hypnotics.

Other disease states. Existence of certain diseases increases the likelihood of an ADR to a particular drug. Patients with bronchial asthma must use nonselective beta-blockers (*nadolol, propranolol*) with caution, since their bronchospastic action can worsen ventilatory function. Similarly, beta-blockers and the calcium channel blocker *verapamil* should not be given to patients with heart block as they further slow atrioventricular conduction. Patients with a healed duodenal ulcer are likely to suffer from increased bleeding if given non-steroidal anit-inflammatory agents like indomethacin, naproxen or sulindac.

Multiple-Drug Reactions

The presence of a second drug may modify the actions of a simultaneously administered drug. Sometimes drugs are used together (drug combinations) to obtain a better clinical response than either drug could achieve alone. In contrast, indiscriminate multiple drug use can be hazardous. This domain of drug interactions would be covered in **Chapter 1.8**.

Miscellaneous ADRs

There are various other ADRs which are not covered within one of the above groups.

Carcinogenicity

Many drugs have been implicated as potential cancer-inducing agents. Under current drug regulations, screening of a drug's cancer-inducing potential is an essential part of preclinical testing of new drugs which are to be used in man. Of course the long-term risk is impossible to evaluate under laboratory conditions.

Some drugs generally recognized as being potentially carcinogenic are : androgens, antineoplastic agents, busulphan, carbon tetrachloride, clofibrate, corticosteroids, cyclamates, griseofulvin, metronidazole, oestrogens, and tobacco smoke.

Teratogenicity (Dysmorphogenesis)

The term "teratogenic" means monstor-producing (*teratos* = monstor), and similarly "dysmorphogenic" means causing a derangement in form. Administration of certain drugs to pregnant women, specially during the first trimester of pregnancy, has resulted in foetal deformities. Such drugs are said to be teratogenic. In the early 1960s the teratogenic effects of *thalidomide*, a sedative-hypnotic used primarily in Germany, came to be known. Although this drug proved safe in adults, with a low incidence of side effects. Further, animal experimentation is not always able to predict the teratogenic potential of a drug. The Food and Drug Administration (FDA) of USA has established certain categories indicating the potential for a drug to cause birth defects. It should be stressed that the *risk: benefit ratio* must be assessed in *each* particular case, and then a decision taken, e.g., *phenytoin*, an antiepileptic drug used to treat grand mal epilepsy, has been associated with foetal abnormalities like cleft palate. However, the risk to the foetus from a generalized maternal seizure on withdrawal of the drug may be far greater than the risk of developing a congenital abnormality. Similarly, discontinuation of the antineoplastic drug *methotrexate* may have more serious consequences for the mother compared to the risk of foetal damage associated with its use.

Drugs with known teratogenic effects include antiepileptics (phenytoin, phenobarbitone); antithyroid drugs (carbimazole); antineoplastics (methotrexate, cyclophosphamide, busulphan, chlorambucil); sex hormones (androgens, progestogens); corticosteroids; sulphonylureas; ethyl alcohol and tobacco smoke.

In general, no drug (including alcohol and nicotine) should be used during the *first trimester* of pregnancy, unless very necessary. Only then after a careful assessment of the risk: benefit ratio a decision should be taken. Foetal damage usually does not occur when drugs are administered late in pregnancy, but complications like neonatal bleeding, respiratory depression and drug addiction in the foetus are likely.

Drug Dependence

An "ideal" drug should be one that has a single pharmacologic action, exhibits no adverse effects, does not interact with other drugs, and is inexpensive. Such drugs do not exist, and a drug molecule has both beneficial and deleterious effects. The use of drugs particularly those acting on the central nervous system, for "non-medical" or "recreational" purposes is becoming increasingly common, specially among the youth. The tendency of a drug to produce dependence is determined not only by its chemical and pharmacologic properties, but more importantly by the emotional make up of the drug taker (**Chapter 2.10**).

Overdosage

With overdosage ill effects occur in direct relation to the total amount of drug present in the body. The term **toxicity** is often used for these undesired and detrimental effects of a drug. All drugs are toxic to all individuals, and *toxic* effects occur when the therapeutic dose is exceeded. Toxic reactions can be subdivided into *two* categories : (*i*) those arising from the normal pharmacology of the drug. These are an extension of the pharmacological actions of the drug, but not necessarily its main action. Their severity depends on the dose; and (*ii*) those arising out of an abnormality in the individual. Such responses include *drug allergy, pharmacogenetic abnormality*, and reactions for which the mechanism is yet unknown. Overdosage may be *absolute* due to an acute excess of accumulation of the drug in the body; or *relative* due to an underlying abnormality in the patient, e.g., in renal failure the usual dose of a drug like streptomycin may cause severe unwanted reactions.

Drug-induced Sexual Dysfunction

A wide variety of drugs have been implicated as causing sexual dysfunction. Most of the drug effects on sexual function are *Type A* effects, and they are predictable on the basis of the known pharmacology of the drug, and they are *dose-related*. Drugs may cause sexual dysfunction by affecting the autonomic nervous system, by causing CNS depression, or by altering endocrine function. The effects of various drugs on *libido* (sex drive), *potency* (erection), and *ejaculation* are summarized in **Table 1.7-1** on next page.

Drugs can also produce infertility either by a direct effect on the gonads (e.g., cytotoxics, sulphasalazine, antimicrobials, anticonvulsants), or indirectly by inhibiting secretion of pituitary gonadotrophins (e.g., steroid hormones, cimetidine, alcohol, cannabis, smoking).

Acute Poisoning

A *poison* is a substance which when consumed endangers life due to derangement of certain vital physiological functions. The study of the poisonous effects of drugs and other chemical substances in known as *toxicology*.

Acute poisoning in adults is usually deliberate and self-inflicted. Drugs employed include *hyptnotics*, *anxiolytics*, *antidepressants*, and *analgesics*. In children acute poisoning is usually accidental due to the natural instinct of the infant for oral exploration and the substances include anything ranging from insecticides to weed-killers, contraceptive pills or whatever is available around. The general principles of treatment are discussed in this Chapter:

Diagnosis. Some drug poisonings produce characteristic physical signs. However, a large number of patients are brought to the hospital in a comatosed state, and sometimes even a history is not available from the attendants or relatives.

A conscious patient may be able to give a history. Thus, in practice mostly emergency treatment of acute poisoning is symptomatic. If facilities exist, the *Poison Control Centre* or the hospital emergency department must be promptly informed.

For the treatment of poisoning a selective antagonist i.e., an *antidote* may be available for use, e.g., *nalorphine* and *naloxone* against morphine-like drugs, *atropine* against cholinergic agents, and *pralidoxime* against anticholinesterases **(Table 1.7-2).**

Table 1.7-1. *Adverse effects of drugs on ejaculation, potency and libido*

Drugs	*Inhibition of ejaculation*	*Impotence*	*Decreased libido*
Alcohol	X	X	
Amphetamines	X		
Anorectics		X	
Anticholinergics	X	X	
Barbiturates	X	X	X
Benzodiazepines	X	X	
Bethanidine	X	X	
Butyrophenones		X	X
Cannabis		X	
Cocaine	X		
Chlorthalidone		X	X
Cimetidine		X	X
Clofibrate		X	
Clonidine		X	X
Digoxin		X	X
Disopyramide		X	
Glutethimide	X	X	X
Guanethidine	X	X	
Hydrochlorothiazide		X	
Hydralazine		X	
Indomethacin		X	
Lithium	X	X	
Methyldopa	X	X	X
Methysergide		X	
Metoclopramide		X	
Metronidazole			X
MAOIs	X		
Nicotine		X	
Opiates	X	X	X
Phenothiazines	X	X	X
Phentolamine	X		
Phenoxybenzamine	X		
Prazosin	X		
Propranolol		X	
Spironolactone		X	X
Thioxanthines	X	X	X
Tricyclic antidepressants	X	X	X

General Principles of Management of Poisoning

The following measures should be adopted to treat a poisoning case:

1. **Identify the poison.** Use of a selective antagonist may be helpful.
2. **Ensure and maintain a clear airway.** Remove debris (vomitus, mucus, dentures), suck away secretions. Consider endotracheal intubation or tracheostomy, if necessary.
3. **Ensure adequate ventilation.** Underventilation leads to hypoxaemia, and overventilation may cause alkalosis and hypotension.
4. **Suppress convulsions.** If convulsions provoked by the poison are not controlled by adequate ventilation, diazepam 10 mg IV should be administered in adults. Barbiturates must be avoided.
5. **Fluid and electrolyte therapy.** The aim is expansion of circulating blood volume and restoration of venous return and cardiac output. For this, *isotonic saline* (0.9% w/v), or *isotonic glucose* (5% w/v), or *plasma* may be used. In general, 1 litre of isotonic saline plus 1 litre of isotonic glucose solution per day must be administered. The urine volume and fluid balance should be recorded to aovid or manage renal failure.

Table 1.7-2. *Some antidotes used against drug overdosage (poisoning)*

Drug in overdose	*Antidote*	*Mechanism*
Narcotic analgesics (morphine, pethidine, pentazocine)	Nalorphine Naloxone	Partial agonist Antagonist
Iron salts	Desferrioxamine (deferoxamine)	Chelation
Lead salts	Penicillamine	Chelation
Mercury salts	Dimercaprol	Chelation
Paracetamol	Acetylcysteine	Reduction of oxidized glutathione
Anticholinesterases (physostigmine, neostigmine)	Atropine	ACh antagonist
Organophosphorus anticholinesterases	Pralidoxime	Cholinesterase reactivation

6. **Decontamination.** The stomach should be emptied by **gastric lavage** in a conscious patient. Vomiting may be induced by *apomorphine* or *syrup of ipecac* (15-20 ml orally). *Gastric lavage* and *induction of vomiting are contraindicated* if the patient is drowsy or unconscious. Induction of vomiting is also contraindicated if a caustic alkali or corrosive mineral acid has been ingested. **Activated charcoal** 10-30 g suspended in 100 to 200 ml of water may be introduced in the stomach to *bind* the unabsorbed drug. **Universal antidote** (or burnt toast) 2 parts; magnesium oxide (milk of magnesia) 1 part; and tannic acid (or strong tea) 1 part mixed together may be administered orally.
7. **Specific antidotes.** These antagonists may be administered with advantage. They are listed in **(Table 1.7-2)**
8. **Non-specific pharmacological antidotes** like *anticonvulsants* in convulsant; and *analeptics* in narcotic poisoning may be employed. Analeptics (respiratory stimulants) have no place if a mechanical respirator facility is available.
9. **Promote elimination of the drug.** Forced diuresis (fluid load and diuretic) reduces the transit time through the nephron and lessens reabsorption of drugs. Ionization of the drug also reduces reabsoption, and increasing the pH of urine by sodium bicarbonate or THAM favours ionization of acidic drugs (phenobarbital, salicylates, probenecid), whereas, reducing the urine pH favours ionization of bases (amphetamine, pethidine, chloroquine).
10. **Haemodialysis or peritoneal dialysis may be instituted.** These specialized techniques are more effective than diuresis. Dialysis is indicated when the patient's condition deteriorates in spite of conventional treatment; or oliguria/anuria supervenes; or in the presence of very high blood concentrations of drugs like *aspirin* or *phenobarbital*. Haemodialysis is 5 to 10 times more effective than peritoneal dialysis, but peritoneal dialysis is a much easier technique, whereas haemodialysis can only be done in bigger hospitals or special centres. Some dialysable drug intoxicants are: *amphetamines, barbiturates, phenytoin, diphenhydramine, methaqualone, MAOIs, propoxyphene and tricyclic antidepressants.*
11. **General supportive and nursing measures** have to be simultaneously instituted, specially in the comatosed or semicomatosed patient. The general principles of management of drug poisoning are summarized in **(Table 1.7-3)**.

Table 1.7-3. *The principles of management of drug poisoning*

Maintenance of vital functions	Airway Circulation Fluid and electrolytes Hypothermia (gradual rewarming if rectal temperature low)
Elimination of drug	Induced vomiting/gastric lavage* Other techniques—Forced diuresis, dialysis
Antidotes	Specific Pharmacological (symptomatic treatment)

* Never done when corrosive agents have been ingested; never done in unconscious patients, unless cuffed endotracheal tube in position.

1.8 DRUG INTERACTIONS

Drug interactions occur on simultaneous use of two or more drugs. When two drugs are administered in close sequence to each other, they may interact either to *enhance* or *diminish* the intended effect of one or both drugs, or they may produce an unintended and potentially harmful reaction.

DEFINITIONS

The term **drug interaction** is defined as an alteration in the *duration* or *magnitude* (or both) of the pharmacological effect of one drug produced by another drug. When more than one drug is administered simultaneously the combined effect may be **antagonistic** or **synergistic**. In **antagonism** the effect of one drug is reduced or abolished by the other, whereas, in synergism the effects may be **additive** or **supra-additive** (potentiation). The incidence of such reactions has increased mainly due to three factors (*i*) *drug explosion*; (*ii*) availability of *potent drugs*; and (*iii*) *irrational polypharmacy*, i.e., indiscriminate prescribing of combined preparations by the clinician (iatrogenic or doctor-induced diseases).

The term **polypharmacy** covers the practice of multiple drug therapy in the management of disease. Judicious use of drug combinations (**rational polypharmacy**) can be of considerable benefit to the patient for the following reasons:

1. To produce a **synergistic** effect which is not obtained by one drug alone, e.g., *hydrochlorothiazide* plus *hydralazine* plus *propranolol* in severe hypertension; combination of *isoniazid*, *rifampicin* and *ethambutol* in tuberculosis.
2. To **minimize side effects of drugs**, e.g., potassium supplementation or *potassium sparing diuretics* in patients on potent diuretic and digitalis therapy; addition of a diuretic to overcome salt and water retention caused by methyldopa.
3. Several **diseases may coexist**, specially in the elderly, and each requires treatment, e.g., association of *hypertension*, *coronary artery disease*, *diabetes mellitus* and *arthritis*. Therapy has to be judiciously chalked out to minimize untoward effects. The benefit-to-risk ratio is of critical importance in such cases.

It must be stressed that multiple drug therapy can be very useful, but the risks involved in the treatment increase. Greater the number of drugs used together, greater the risk of serious adverse reactions.

FACTORS PREDISPOSING TO DRUG INTERACTIONS

Many adverse drug interactions can be avoided if the following predisposing factors are kept in mind:

1. **Insufficient knowledge.** Effective and safe combination drug therapy requires adequate understanding of the pharmacokinetics and pharmacodynamics of the drug.
2. **Dietary factors.** Constituents of an individual's diet can interact with certain drugs, e.g., MAOIs interact with tyramine-containing foodstuffs inducing a hypertensive crisis; green leafy vegetables decrease the anticoagulant response of coumarin anticoagulants as they contain vitamin K. Some drug-food interactions are summarized in **Table 1.8-1**.

Table 1.8-1. *Some important drug-food interactions*

Drug	*Food Item*	*Effect*
Anticoagulants	Food rich in vitamin K (e.g., egg yolk, citrus fruits, green leafy vegetables)	Decreased anticoagulant response due to enhaced hepatic synthesis of clotting factors.
Antihypertensives, diuretics	Licorice (glycyrrhizic acid)	Causes hypokalaemia, sodium retension, elevated blood pressure
Digoxin	Milk products	Slowed gastric absorption and decreased therapeutic effect
Erythromycin	Acidic fruit juices	Decompose the drug and reduce effect
Griseofulvin	High fat content	Increased absorption rate

Table 1.8-1. Contd...

Drug	*Food Item*	*Effect*
MAOIs (pargyline, phenelzine)	Food rich in tyramine (e.g., cheese, red wine, chicken liver)	Hypertensive crisis
Paracetamol	Carbohydrates	Slow drug absorption and therapeutic effect
Quinidine	Basic foods (e.g., milk, nuts, most vegetables)	Decreased renal clearance due to increased urine alkalinity, toxic reaction may occur
Tetracycline	Milk products containing Ca^{++}	Decreased gastrointestinal absorption and drug inactivation

3. **Physiology of the individual.** Factors such as age, sex, weight and genetic abnormalities influnece the occurrence of drug interactions. These factors have been discussed in **Chapter 1.4 and 1.7.**
4. **Presence of disease states.** Pathologic conditions like liver diseases, kidney damage, or altered enzyme systems may affect the handling of drugs by the body. This can lead to adverse drug reactions **(Chap. 1.7).**
5. **Patient behaviour.** The common practice of consulting more than one physician at a time can increase the risk of drug interactions, if each prescriber is not fully aware of the drugs being taken by the patient. **Self-medication** is also responsible for a number of drug interactions, and can be avoided by proper counselling. Similarly, the large number of over-the-counter (OTC) preparations can interact with prescription drugs. **Table 1.8-2** lists some OTCs which can interact with prescribed drugs. In addition, certain factors like poor *compliance* (failure to take the medication as directed); *smoking* (increases metabolism of many drugs); *excessive alcohol consumption* (altered drug metabolism and potentiation of the action of CNS depressants); and use of *dependence producing drugs* are examples of human behaviour which may lead to drug interactions.

Table 1.8-2 *Some over-the-counter (OTC) medicaments that can interact with prescription drugs*

OTC medicaments	*Major interactants*
Analgesics	
Paracetamol	Increased hepatotoxicity of other drugs that also damage the liver
Salicylates (aspirin)	Increased bleeding with anticoagulants and other platelet inhibitors; increased GI ulceration with other gastric irritants (corticosteroids, anti-inflammatory agents); potentiation of oral antidiabetics, barbiturates, phenytoin, and sulphonamides by displacing them from protein binding; decreased effectiveness of vitamin C by increasing its excretion
Antacids	Impaired absorption of many drugs
Anticholinergics (atropine, scopolamine)	Increased side effects (dry mouth, blurred vision, constipation) of other drugs having anticholinergic activity (antihistamines, tricyclic antidepressants, carbamazepine, disopyramide)
Antidiarrhoeals	Decreased absorption of many drugs by slowing GI motility
Antihistamines	Increased sedative effect of CNS depressants; increased anticholinergic effects of other anticholinergics
Bronchodilators (adrenaline, ephedrine)	Increased hypertensive effect of pressor agents; decreased effect of oral antidiabetics; increased toxicity of digitalis
Decongestants (Phenylephrine, pseudoephedrine)	Decreased effectiveness of antihypertensives; increased danger of hypertension with MAOIs, other vasopressors and CNS stimultants like amphetamine
Expectorants (guaifensin)	Increased risk of haemorrhage with heparin
Vitamin B_6 (Pyridoxine)	Decreased effectiveness of levodopa
Vitamin B Complex	Increased risk of bleeding by increasing prothrombin time
Vitamin C	Decreased excretion of weak acids (barbiturates,, salicylates, sulphonamides); increased excretion of weak bases (amphetamine, atropine, quinidine)

6. **Enviromental factors.** Small amounts of insecticides, fungicides, or industrial wastes can markedly alter the effect of certain drugs, e.g., chlorinated insecticides stimultate drug metabolism by liver enzymes; some pesticides are cholinesterase inhibitors and serious toxicity (respiratory distress, skeletal muscle weakness, convulsions) can occur in cases of poisoning by another cholinergic drug.
7. **Dosage form factors.** Incompatibility of different dosage forms may result in drug interactions at either a *physical* or a *chemical* level. Generally, the main factor in this regard is of *bioavailability*, i.e., what fraction of the dose is available through absorption at the site of action. Of particular concern in this regard are the many "long-acting" or "sustained-release" dosage forms currently available. Many of these products are tablets or capsules that dissolve slowly over many hours, providing a sustained release of medication for a certain period of time, and fairly stable plasma levels are maintained. This steady-state plasma concentration can be upset by the presence of another drug which increases gastrointestinal motility and peristalsis. As a result the sustained-release dosage form traverses the intestine too quickly to provide for a prolonged drug effect.

Some over 1600 potential drug interactions have been described in man. Many of them are of great clinical significance. It is impossible to remember them, but ready information is available in pocket books, manuals on drug interactions, drug interaction discs, slide rules or from hospital drug information centres. Harmful interactions can occur between **drug-drug; drug-patient-drug;** and **drug-foodstuffs**.

Classification and Mechanisms of Drug Interactions

Drug interactions may occur outside the body (*in vitro*) or inside the body (*in vivo*):

I. **Outside the body (in vitro)**
   1. Physical
   2. Chemical

II. **Inside the body (in vivo)**
   1. Pharmacokinetic interactions
   2. Pharmacodynamic interactions

Outside the Body

These interactions may occur during formulation and mixing of drugs, and the term *incompatibility* is often used to designate these *in vitro* interactions.

1. **Physical interactions.** This term applies when the physical state of either drug is altered when the chemicals are mixed e.g., *amphotericin* precipitates if mixed with normal saline instead of 5 percent dextrose; the anticoagulant effect of *heparin*, a negatively charged acid is antagonized by protamine, a positively charged base.
2. **Chemical interactions.** This term applies when the components of a drug mixture interact to form chemically altered products, e.g., drugs mentioned below are chemically incompatible in solution: methicillin and kanamycin; aminophylline and chlorpromazine; dopamine and sodium bicarbonate; furosemide and ascorbic acid. In most cases chemical incompatibilities are manifested by precipitation or colour change.

General guidelines to avoid such interactions occurring *in vitro*: (*i*) Do not add drugs to blood or amino acid solutions; (*ii*) In the absence of special knowledge, a drug should only be added to simple solutions (normal saline, dextrose, dextro-saline). It should be remembered that these solutions have very little buffering capacity; (*iii*) Interactions may occur without any visible changes in the solution; (*iv*) Drugs should be mixed with the infusion fluid immediately before use; (*v*) Single drug additions to simple solutions are likely to be safe, while two or more drugs are likely to interact; and (*vi*) Drug firm package inserts should be consulted, as they contain useful information on likely drug interactions.

Inside the Body

Most of the drug interactions occurring inside the body can be categorized as either *pharmacokinetic* or *pharmacodynamic* interactions.

Pharmacokinetic Interactions

In this category the change in response to the first drug is the result of an alteration in the concentration of the drug at the receptor site, and is produced by differences in drug *absorption, distribution, metabolism* and *excretion.*

Interactions During Gastrointestinal Absorption

Many factors influence drug absorption from the digestive tract, which include **dissolution rate** of the ingested drug, **gastric emptying time, gut motility** and **blood flow.** Drugs are absorbed mainly in their non-ionized form from the gut. Many drugs are weak acids or weak bases, and the proportion of ionized to non-ionized drug is dependent on the pKa value of the drug and surrounding pH **(Chap. 1.5)**.

Decreased gut motility by anticholinergic agents like *atropine* increases the total absorption of drugs which are otherwise slowly and incompletely absorbed. The *purgatives* decrease drug absorption by speeding the passage of material through the intestine.

Antacids that contain calcium, magnesium or aluminium (polyvalent cations), interfere with the

Table 1.8-3. *Drug interactions which result in altered absorption from the gastrointestinal tract*

	Interacting drugs	*Result of interaction*
1.	Antacids with anticoagulants like dicoumarol and warfarin	Antacids interfere with the absorption resulting in the antagonism of anticoagulant action
2.	Antacids with certain anti-infective agents like sulphonamides, nalidixic acid and nitrofurantoin	Antacids interfere with absorption of these weakly acid agents resulting in a reduction of their activity
3.	Antacids (and milk) with tetracycline	Calcium, magnesium and aluminium ions tend to bind tetracyclines in poorly absorbable complexes
4.	Mineral oils and fat soluble vitamins (A, D, E, K)	Mineral oil reduces the absorption of fat-soluble vitamins
5.	Cholestyramine with vitamins A, D and K; also anticoagulants; possibly other weakly acid drugs like chlorothiazide and phenylbutazone	Cholestyramine (anion exchange resin) has a strong affinity for acidic substances. Binding of these drugs results in their faecal excretion and poor systemic absorption

absorption of tetracycline which forms a chelate with these metals. Some important interactions are summarized in **Table 1.8-3**.

Interactions During Distribution

Plasma Protein Binding

When certain drugs are absorbed into the blood stream, most of their molecules attach themselves to plasma proteins. The portion of the drug which is being transported in the *bound* form is pharmacologically inactive, and only the *free* molecules that diffuse into the tissue exert their effect. The presence of a second drug with a *higher affinity* for protein, competes with the first drug for protein binding sites, and displaces the first drug, producing serious toxicity, e.g., *warfarin* is 98 per cent protein bound, and only 2 per cent is free in the plasma which is the active fraction. If another drug like *phenytoin* is given, competition for the binding sites occurs and warfarin is displaced. If the binding of warfarin is reduced to 96 percent, it would lead to doubling (2% unbound to 4% unbound) of the free concentration of the drug leading to toxicity. Certain drugs which have a higher binding affinity to plasma proteins displace agents with lower binding affinities **(Table 1.8-4)**.

Table 1.8-4. *Displacement of drugs from plasma protein binding sites*

Drug displaced (lower binding affinity)	*Displacing agent (higher binding affinity)*
Acetaminophen	Phenylbutazone, clofibrate, phenytoin, salicylates
Methotrexate	Salicylates, sulphonamides
Pamaquine	Quinacrine
Sulphonamides	Phenylbutazone, oxyphenbutazone, warfarin, salicylates, tolbutamide
Warfarin	Phenylbutazone, oxyphenbutazone, clofibrate, salicylates, phenytoin, sulphinpyrazone

Interactions During Biotransformation

The process of conversion of drugs to their respective metabolites is termed as **biotransformation** and it usually occurs in the liver **(Chap. 1.5)**. These reactions are generally mediated by enzymes, so that drugs capable of altering the enzymatic processes involved in drug metabolism can lead to drug interactions.

Enzyme induction. Liver microsomal enzymes involved in drug metabolism can be stimulated by drugs including barbiturates, hydantoins, griseofulvin, chlorinated hydrocarbon insecticides and many others. This is termed as **enzyme induction** and results in a reduced therapeutic response to those drugs that are metabolized by microsomal enzymes **(Table 1.8-5)**.

Table 1.8-5. *Drugs that induce the metabolism of other drugs*

Inducer	*Drugs affected*
Alcohol	Tolbutamide
Chloral hydrate	Bishydroxycoumarin, warfarin
Chlorcyclizine	Steroid hormones
Haloperidol	Warfarin
Phenobarbital	Adriamycin, barbiturates, bishydroxycoumarin, chloramphenicol, cortisol, cyclophosphamide, digitoxin, griseofulvin, phenylbutazone, phenytoin, progesterone, testosterone, thyroxine, warfarin
Phenylbutazone	Steroid hormones
Phenytoin	Steroid hormones
DDT	Steroid hormones

Enzyme induction can be utilized for its beneficial effects also, e.g., *phenobarbitone* is used in the treatment of *neonatal hyperbilirubinaemia*, because it accelerates the metabolism of bilirubin to more readily excreted compounds. Enzyme induction may be responsible for development of *tolerance*, as some drugs stimulate their own liver metabolism, e.g., phenobarbitone, meprobamate, orphenadrine, phenylbutazone.

Enzyme inhibition. Compounds that interfere with the activity of inactivating enzymes can potentiate the action of other drugs or endogenous substances, e.g., *monoamine oxidase inhibitors* (MAOIs) inhibit the normal functioning of the endogenous enzyme monoamine oxidase (MAO), elevate levels of biogenic amines and may produce a hypertensive crisis in the presence of pressor amines; *allopurinol*, a xanthine oxidase inhibitor, increases plasma levels of mercaptopurine by blocking its breakdown; and *physostigmine* and *neostigmine*, cholinesterase inhibitors, block the degradation of choline esters, and can enhance the effects of *acetylcholine*, other cholinergic drugs and *succinylcholine*. These increased levels can result in toxicity **(Table 1.8-6)**.

Table 1.8-6 *Inhibition of drug metabolism*

Drug	*Metabolic inhibitor*
Bishydroxycoumarin	Chloramphenicol, oxyphenbutazone, phenylbutazone
Cyclophosphamide	Chloramphenicol
Hexobarbital	Metyrapone, p-aminosalicylate, norethynodrel, progesterone
6-Mercaptopurine	Allopurinol
Nortriptyline	Hydrocortisone
Pethidine	Oral contraceptives
Phenytoin	Bishydroxycoumarin, p-aminosalicylate, chloramphenicol, cycloserine, isoniazid, methylphenidate
Tolbutamide	Alcohol, chloramphenicol, phenylbutazone, monoamine oxidase inhibitors, salicylates, probenecid

A therapeutically useful interaction based on enzyme inhibition is the combination of *carbidopa* with *levodopa*. Carbidopa competitively inhibits the enzyme dopa decarboxylase peripherally (outside the brain). Thus, peripheral dopa decarboxylase inhibition permits a greater fraction of the dose of levodopa to enter the brain, leading to increased formation of dopamine to replace the deficient stores of dopamine and relieve symptoms of parkinsonism.

Interactions During Excretion

Interactions occurring during excretion of drugs may involve any of the renal excretory processes, i.e., glomerular filtration, tubular reabsorption, or active tubular secretion. Most important drug interactions occur as a result of either *changes in urinary pH* which alters the fraction of reabsorbed drug, or through *competition for active tubular mechanisms.*

Changes in urinary pH. Acidification of the urine with agents like *ammonium chloride* results in reduced effectiveness of basic drugs (amphetamine, quinidine), as they will be largely ionized in acidic pH and readily excreted. In contrast, renal excretion of acidic drugs (salicylates, barbiturates, anticoagulants) will be accelerated by alkalinization of urine with *sodium bicarbonate, acetazolamide* or *potassium citrate.*

Urinary pH also influences the solubility of drug molecules in tubular fluid, e.g., *sulphonamides* are poorly soluble in acidic urine and may precipitate in the renal tubules causing crystalluria and obstruction. Alkalinization of the urine facilitates the excretion of sulphonamides.

Competition for tubular mechanisms. Many drugs and metabolites are *actively* secreted from renal blood vessels into the tubules and subsequently eliminated. Interactions may occur when any *two actively secreted drugs are used together, due to competition for the active secretory mechanisms.* Drugs which may interact by this means, resulting in prolonged therapeutic effects are *salicylates, sulphonamides, penicillins, probenecid, thiazides, dicumarol, indomethacin, oral hypoglycaemics, acetazolamide, methotrexate* and *diazoxide*. Small doses of aspirin impair the uricosuric action of probenecid by interfering with the active secretion of uric acid into the renal tubules. Competition for active tubular secretion can be used therapeutically as well, e.g., use of *probenecid* with *pencillin* to delay the rapid excretion of the penicillin molecule, leading to a significantly prolonged effective duration of action of penicillin.

Changes in fluid and electrolyte levels induced by certain drugs can affect the therapeutic effectiveness and toxicity of other drugs, specially those acting on the heart, kidney and skeletal muscles. *Hypokalaemia* produced by diuretics and corticosteroids increases the likelihood of *digitalis toxicity*, and can *antagonize* the antiarrhythmic activity of quinidine, lidocaine, procainamide, phenytoin and disoyramide. Drugs that cause excessive diuresis (high-ceiling diuretics) may potentiate the hypotensive effects of antihypertensive drugs.

Pharmacodynamic Interactions

Pharmacodynamic interactions occur at the site of drug action. They usually lead to an altered sensitivity of the affected organ. Mostly drug effects are the result of binding of the drug to specialized areas on or within the cells, known as **receptor sites**. The magnitude of the effect depends on the **concentration of the free drug** at its receptor site. As already discussed in **Chapter 1.5,** the **free drug** or an active metabolite concentration at the receptor site depends on the amount of drug in the body, which in turn is regulated by: (*i*) physical and chemical properties of the drug; (*ii*) altered gastrointestinal absorption or competition for protein binding sites or receptor sites; (*iii*) altered drug metabolism; (*iv*) changes in acid-base

Table 1.8-7 *Interactions occurring at receptor site.*

Drug A + Receptor ⟶ Drug A: Receptor complex ⟶ Response
Drug B + Receptor ⟶ Drug B: Receptor complex ⟶ No response (blockade)

Receptor/site	*A-type drugs*	*B-type drugs*
Vessel alpha-receptor	Noradrenaline	Phentolamine, phenoxybenzamine, imipramine, phenothiazines
Vessel beta-receptor	Isoprenaline	Propranolol
Cardiac sino-atrial node	Acetylcholine	Atropine, antihistamines, imipramine, phenothiazines
Neuromuscular junction	Acetylcholine	d-Tubocurarine
Adrenergic neurone	Noradrenaline	Guanethidine, amphetamine, tricyclic antidepressants, phenothiazines
Liver cell	Vitamin K	Salicylates, propylthiouracil, anabolic steroids, chloramphenicol

equilibrium; and (*v*) alterations of haemodynamic or renal tubular function influencing renal drug clearance. The quantity of drug associated with receptor sites depends on the amount of drug in the body; its accessibility to the receptor; and the affinity constant of the drug for the receptor, i.e., the ratio of association to dissociation constants of the drug for the receptor. Further details of drug-receptor interactions are covered in **Chapter 1.6**. Some basic and clinically important pharmacodynamic interactions may be considered under the following heads:

Interactions at adrenergic nerve terminals. These interactions may be at times severe and life threatening. They are of two major types : (*i*) those between monoamine oxidase inhibitors (MAOIs) and foodstuffs/ drugs; and (*ii*) those between tricyclic antidepressants and catecholamines/ hypotensive drugs.

The MAOIs inhibit intraneuronal MAO, and the sensitivity to infused or injected indirectly acting sympathomimetics (amphetamines) is increased. Any foodstuff or beverage which contains significant amounts of tyramine may cause the release of accumulated noradrenaline from the adrenergic nerve terminals causing a hypertensive crisis. The substances which can interact with MAOIs are : **foodstuffs**—cheese, yoghourt, yeast extract, liver, broad beans; **beverages**—sherry, chianti, beer; and **drugs**—levodopa, tricyclic antidepressants.

Interactions in the CNS. The aminoglycoside antibiotics (streptomycin, kanamycin, gentamycin) and the potent loop diuretic frusemide when used concurrently may cause severe ototoxicity. The aminoglycosides also increase and prolong the action of skeletal muscle relaxants.

Interactions in the bronchial tree. Bronchial relaxation depends upon the formation of cyclic 3′5′-AMP (c-AMP). The formation of this "second messenger" is increased when adenylcyclase in stimulated by **catecholamines**. Alternatively, the breakdown of c-AMP can be inhibited by **aminophylline**. Thus the combination of the two may be useful in the treatment of bronchial asthma.

Receptor blockade. The development of drugs that selectively block receptors, particularly those of the automonic nervous system, has led to several important interactions, e.g., *alpha-adrenoceptor blockade* with phenoxybenzamine prevents the action of noradrenaline and other alpha-sympathomimetics; *beta-blockade* with propranolol reduces or abolishes the cardiac stimulating activity of adrenaline and isoprenaline. Some important interactions at the receptor site are listed in **Table 1.8-7**.

Interactions in the heart. Interactions at this site mainly involve the *beta-adrenoceptor blockers* and *cardiac glycosides*. The beta-blockers can produce a profound bradycardia, and delayed auriculoventricular conduction. These actions are mainly due to the unopposed action of the vagus nerve, and can be overcome by administering atropine concurrently.

The cardiotoxicity of *cardiac glycosides* increases to 3-fold by hypokalaemia induced by diuretics.

Adverse Drug Interactions

The number of potential drug interactions is large, but those which are more important involve drugs with a narrow margin between their therapeutic and toxic doses (low therapeutic index). Caution must be exercised whenever such drugs are prescribed concurrently with *digitalis glycosides, anticonvulsants, oral anticoagulants, oral hypoglycaemics, cytotoxic agents, hypotensives and MAOIs*. Some life-threatening interactions are listed in **Table 1.8-8**.

Table 1.8-8 *Some clinically observed adverse drug interactions*

Major Symptoms	*Interacting drugs*
Hypertensive crisis	MAOI + Tyramine (cheese)
	MAOI + methamphetamine
Haemorrhagic episodes	Warfarin + phenylbutazone
	Warfarin + sulphinpyrazone
Hypoglycaemic reaction	Tolbutamide + phenylbutazone
	Tolbutamide + sulfisoxazole
Cardiac arrhythmias	Digitalis + chlorothiazide
	Digitalis + reserpine
Respiratory paralysis	Neomycin + succinylcholine
	Neomycin + ether

Prevention of Adverse Drug Interactions

The truism "the harder you look, the more you find" is best exemplified in the area of drug interactions. Life-threatening emergencies like haemorrhage, hypoglycaemic coma, cardiac arrhythmias, convulsions or a hypertensive crisis may occur. It is important to recognize and prevent such catastrophies, for which certain guidelines would be helpful:

1. The more potent the drug, higher is the risk of toxicity.
2. When it is essential to use combinations of drugs that are highly protein bound, adjustment of dosage is required for proper and safe control.
3. Any drug that is lipid-soluble at physiological pH should be considered a candidate for its enzyme inducing capability, and the dosage should be appropriately adjusted.
4. Authentic manuals on drug interactions must be readily available for consultation.
5. Maintain a detailed drug history and medical record of the patient.
6. Avoid irrational polypharmacy.

Combinations of drugs are employed in therapy to enhance effects and to prevent adverse reactions. **Beneficial drug interactions** have a special place in the treatment of diseases, like **essential hypertension, tuberculosis** and **cancer**. Here mention must also be made about **fixed-dose combination products** available in the market. Some fixed-dose combinations are rational, e.g., combination of a local anaesthetic with adrenaline to provide more effective and prolonged anaesthesia. However, the majority of **fixed-dose combinations** have certain **disadvantages:** (*i*) the dosage of individual ingredients cannot be adjusted; (*ii*) half-lives of individual agents may be different leading to accumulation of agents with longer half-lives on repeated dosing at a particular dose interval; (*iii*) there is a likelihood of some ingredients being administered unnecessarily to the patient; (*iv*) there is a possibility of increased toxicity and allergenicity; and (*v*) the higher cost of the product.

There are, however, certain **advantages** of fixed-dose combinations, like: (*i*) the *synergistic* effect of aspirin with codeine for analgesia; and (*ii*) *improved compliance* by the patient, as the number of medicaments to be taken is reduced.

1.9 BIOLOGICAL ASSAY OF DRUGS (BIOASSAY)

Biological standardization or **bioassay** of drugs is defined as the assessment of the activity of a preparation by measuring its effect on *living animals* or *tissues*. It is essential that the amount of the active principle in a *dose* be uniform and of known potency. This enables the clinician to prescribe a dose that will always, as nearly as possible, induce the same magnitude of action. **Thus, bioassay is a procedure for determining the quantitative relationship between the dose (or concentration) of a drug and the magnitude of response it evokes.** Such procedures utilize intact animals, isolated living tissues, animal preparations or micro-organisms.

Selection of the Method

The quantitative estimation of a drug may be done by physical, physico-chemical or biological methods. In **physical methods**, a physical property of the drug like colour, fluorescence or irradiation is used; in **physico-chemical methods**, a combination of a physical property and a chemical reaction is used, e.g., changing the colour by a chemical reaction and then measuring the intensity of the colour; and in **biological methods** some biological property is used to estimate activity. Whatever method is chosen, it should fulfil the criteria for *reliability*, i.e., it should be *sensitive*, *specific* and *accurate*; with *practicability*, i.e., it should be *simple*, *quick* and *cheap*. Based on these criteria the physical and physico-chemical methods are usually superior to biological methods. However, the biological methods for assay of drugs are still used to measure the potency of substances for which physical or physico-chemical methods are not available. If for a certain drug both physico-chemical and bioassay methods are available, the former are preferred as they are more accurate, less time consuming and convenient to follow.

Bioassay methods are usually required for substances derived from plant or animal sources. Synthetic drugs do not require bioassay for standardization, as they fulfil the purity criteria, mere weighing or measuring is a reliable gauge of their activity.

The foremost principle of bioassay is to compare quantitatively the effect of the preparation under **test** (sample) with that of **standard** preparation. The *accuracy* and *reliability* of these assays depends on : (*i*) specially trained staff; (*ii*) details of the procedure as described in the official compendia (pharmacopoeias); and (*iii*) proper selection of the animals and the test procedure.

The details of bioassay methods to be followed are given in the pharmacopoeias (IP, BP etc.). For many drugs there are more than one bioassay methods. The assay parameters recorded for some drugs are given below :

Adrenaline. Blood pressure raising effect in the cat or dog.

Noradrenaline. Rise of blood pressure in the spinal cat.

Histamine. Contraction of the isolated guinea pig ileum.

Insulin. Hypoglycaemic convulsions in mice.

Acetylcholine. Contraction of the frog's rectus adbominis muscle.

d-Tubocurarine. Rabbit head drop due to paralysis of neck muscles.

Androgen. Growth of the capon's comb.

Oestrogen. Cornification of the vagina in rats.

Digitalis. Death due to cardiac arrest in systole in the guinea pig.

Application of Bioassay Methods

The various applications of bioassay methods are:

(*i*) **Standardization of drugs** of natural origin.

(*ii*) **Estimation of biologically active substances** like acetylcholine, adrenaline, noradrenaline and serotonin in body fluids or tissue extracts.

(*iii*) **Screening of new compounds** for biological activity. Even synthetic products are subjected to these methods, as chemical structure does not truly predict pharmaco- logical activity.

(*iv*) Bioassay is employed if the drug is composed of a **complex mixture of substances** of varying structure and activity, e.g., digitalis, posterior pituitary.

(*v*) **Diagnosis and research.** The concentration of gonadotrophins in the blood or urine may be estimated by injecting these fluids in animals (chemical methods may be employed, if available).

(*vi*) **Estimation of the dose** of a drug required to produce a therapeutic or toxic response, e.g., ED_{50} (effective dose 50) or LD_{50} (lethal dose 50).

When results of biological and chemical methods for the assay of an active substance disagree widely, the bioassay result is upheld.

Principles of Bioassay of Drugs

Burn and Dale have enunciated certain principles for the conduction of bioassay procedures. These *must* be followed for obtaining valid results.

Principle 1. All bioassays (laboratory studies, toxicity studies, clinical trials) must be comparative against a standard drug or preparation. This is one way of minimizing error in bioassays due to biological variation (see later), as the new sample is simultaneously compared with the standard preparation.

Standard preparations (Reference Standards). A standard preparation is a selected representative of the substance which serves as a basis for the comparative measurement of activity. These standard preparations are distributed to experts, pharmaceutical firms and research laboratories to standardize new batches of their preparations.

In India these Reference Standards are maintained and distributed by the *Central Drug Research Laboratory, Calcutta*, and the *Central Research Institute, Kasauli*. In USA they are maintained by the *US Pharmacopeial Authorities*, and in Great Britain by the *National Institute of Medical Research, London*. The *Expert Committee on Biological Standardization* of the WHO also maintains and distributes these preparations to various laboratories.

A **Unit** is defined as a definite weight of one of these Standard Preparations which produces a certain effect in terms of the preparation under test.

Principle 2. The Standard and the new drug should be, as far as possible identical to each other. If it is so, their dose-response curves will have the same *slope* and would be parallel, i.e., the *potency ratio* would be constant all along the response levels. However, if the curves are not parallel, this statement is invalid.

Principle 3. The method for comparing the unknown and the standard drug should preferably (but not essentially) test the therapeutic property of the drug. Ideally an *analgesic* should be tested for analgesic activity, and an *anticonvulsant* for anticonvulsant activity. However, it is not always possible to do so, e.g., for insulin lowering of blood glucose would be the ideal potency index, but the commonly used method is the *mouse convulsion method*, in which the percentage of mice developing convulsions with the standard and new insulin is compared.

Principle 4. The method should estimate, as far as possible, and allow an estimate of the error due to biological variation in different animals/persons at any one time, and in the same animal/person at different times. The precautions to be taken to minimize error due to biological variation are: (*i*) the experimental conditions must be kept constant; (*ii*) the biological response (indicator) should be sensitive to the drug; (*iii*) the *indicator* should be insensitive to other drugs; (*iv*) the indicator should be capable of giving constant and reproducible results; (*v*) a preparation of known concentration (standard) must be available to compare the response; (*vi*) the number of experiments should be sufficiently large, and the assay designed to minimize biological variation; and (*vii*) the animals should be of the *same species and strain* (preferably litter mates), of similar *age, weight and sex*, kept on similar diet and housed under similar conditions. In certain bioassay designs cross-over of animals receiving the *sample* and the *standard* is possible.

In short, the sources of error in bioassays are mainly of two types. Firstly, errors *due to biological variation*; and secondly errors due to *faulty methodology*.

Biological Variation

Individuals and animals show marked variability in their response to a drug. The response of any drug even in a fixed dose in a most carefully selected group of animals is variable, due to the law of biological variation. If such an experiment is conducted on a large number of animals, and the frequency of the response (vertical axis) is plotted against the dose (horizontal axis), one obtains the **normal frequency distribution curve (Fig. 1.9.1).** The features of the normal distribution curve are that it is bell shaped, symmetrical, with two tails which never actually touch the horizontal axis, although they continuously approach it, and the mean lies at the peak of the curve i.e., the highest frequency.

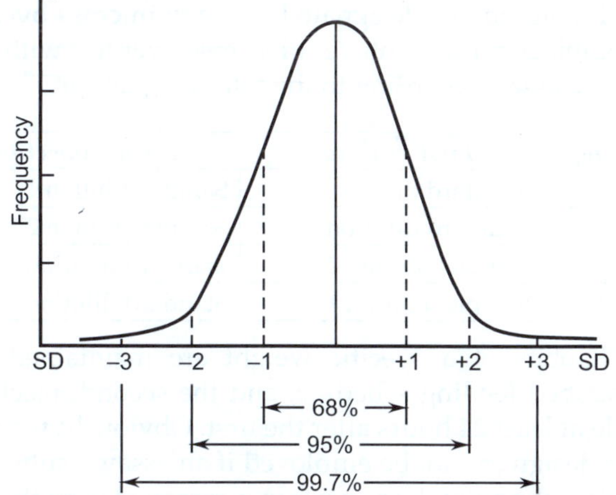

Fig. 1.9.1: Normal frequency distribution curve (Gaussian Curve). $\bar{X}$ = mean; SD = standard deviation.

The normal distribution curve has a symmetrical shape, but the exact location and scale of distribution depends on two constants, namely the *mean* and the *standard deviation* (see later). The normal distribution curve indicates that a majority of the animals show a particular degree of response, but there are animals which are *hyporeactors* (left half of the curve), and others are *hyper-reactors* (right half of the curve). The mean indicates the average response in that group of animals.

To assess the extent of biological variation, the extent of **spread of responses** (scatter) is to be indicated by calculating the **Standard Deviation** (SD). The SD may be geometrically described as the distance from the mean to the steepest part of the normal distribution curve vertically (dotted line), and this is an excellent measure of variability. An analysis of the normal distribution curve **(Fig. 1.9.1)** shows that mean ± 1 SD includes about 68% of animals showing responses within this range. Mean ± 2 SD includes about 95% of the animals, and Mean ± 3 SD includes about 99.7% of the animal responses. The wider the base of this curve, the greater the variability. The maximum frequency is midway between the highest (+) and the lowest (–) point on the horizontal axis i.e., at the mean value.

The method of expressing the error due to biological variation, in the form of standard deviation or standard error of the mean value, or the significance of the difference between two means is described in the section on "biostatistics" in this Chapter. In expressing the limits of error of biological assays the term "limits of error (P = 0.99)" is used. This statement is based on the convention that for practical purposes, a probability of 0.99 is equivalent to certainty, i.e., the result of the assay will be within the stated limits 99 times out of 100 times that the assay is made.

Methods of Bioassay

Four methods are usually employed for interpreting results of biological assay.

Method 1. Threshold dose measured on each animal (Direct end-point assays). In this type of assay the threshold dose is measured for obtaining a specific biologic end-point in each animal. In these assays the drug (standard or test sample) is administered slowly to the animal until some sharply observable effect (end-point) is produced. The amount of the drug or the time for reaching the end-point is then noted. For example, the assay of **digitalis** in cats is carried out by infusing the extract containing digitalis into a vein at the rate of 1 ml per minute till the heart stops and the blood pressure falls to zero. The volume of the fluid passed into the vein (threshold dose) is noted in each animal. This is the minimal lethal dose of digitalis in cats. Two series of experiments are done with the standard preparation and the unknown preparation, and the potency ratio is calculated. Direct end-point assays are applicable when an end-point can be reached in each animal; the drug effect appears rapidly; and the drug effect is directly proportional to the dose.

Method 2. Responses recorded or measured (Graded response assays). At times the effect of the drug can be observed repeatedly on the same tissue. The standard preparation and the test sample are administered alternately, and the doses adjusted until they give equal effects. Precisely, a fixed dose of the standard is matched against varying doses of the test sample, the object being to find out equivalent doses of the two. The concentration of the standard being known, the concentration of the unknown is easily found out. This technique is known as **matching assay**. The assay of histamine on the isolated guinea pig ileum is an example of matching assay methodology. Very small quantities of histamine can only be assayed biologically. Similar methodology can be used for the bioassay of the **posterior pituitary extract, adrenaline** and **acetylcholine.**

Many of the vitamins and hormones can be assayed by obtaining their graded responses. One randomly selected group of animals receives doses of the standard preparation, and the other similar group receives doses of the unknown preparation to be tested. The experiment is repeated measuring the response (e.g., liver glycogen content in mice for glucocorticoids; percent fall in blood sugar for insulin in rabbits) at two or three dose levels, separately for the standard and the unknown preparation and the mean response at the various dose levels is obtained. The relationship between the dose and the response is plotted on a graph paper to give the **dose-response curve** which is not a straight line as on the ordinary arithmetic scale the doses are not equally spaced. But if the response (y-axis) is plotted against the log dose (x-axis) a straight line is obtained, as the logarithm of the dose is linearly related to the response. This is termed as the *log dose-response curve* **(See Chap. 1.6)**. Thus two or more fixed doses of both *standard* and *unknown* are used, and the responses to each measured in an adequate number of animals. Depending on the number of doses (two or three) of the standard and unknown used, the assay is known as a 2 × 2 or 3 × 3 assay.

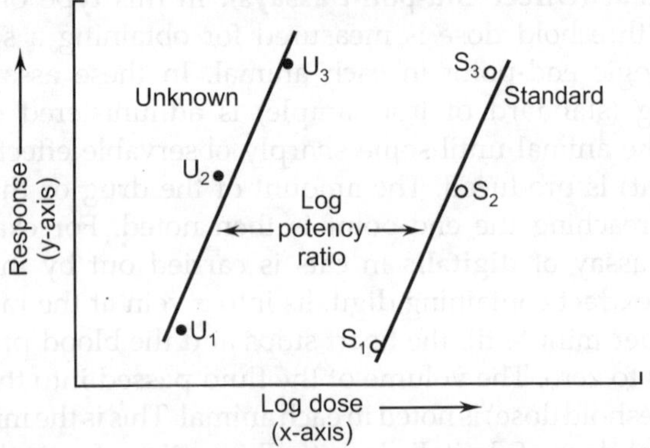

Fig. 1.9.2: A typical 3 × 3 graded response assay (diagrammatic). The log dose-response curves are parallel. The unknown preparation is more active than the reference standard by a factor which is given by the antilogarithm of the horizontal distance between the two lines. Confidence limits can be calculated from the scatter of the experimental points around the fitted parallel lines.

From the results, log dose-response curves are constructed **(Fig. 1.9.2)**, and the potency of the unknown sample relative to the reference standard is estimated by fitting parallel lines to the data statistically and by calculating the horizontal distance between the two lines. This gives the logarithm of the relative potency. Such assays are only applicable and valid if the two log dose-response lines are parallel, i.e., when the potency ratio is constant with both low and high doses. For this reason a statistical test for parallelism is included in the routine analysis of such assays. Non-parallelism indicates that the potency ratio is not constant, and the active components are not present in the same proportion in the standard and the unknown preparation, or may be the unknown preparation has an interfering compound which makes its mechanism of action different from that of the standard preparation. The statistical calculations involved are complex and have been excluded.

Cross-over test. When the effect of the drug can be observed and measured more than once in the same animal, the accuracy is greatly increased by arranging the experiment according to the cross-over design. On the first day one group of animals receives the standard drug and another similar group receives the unknown preparation and the effects are measured; on another day the standard and unknown are crossed over, so that the first group receives the unknown preparation and the second group receives the standard. The average effect of each preparation, for both stages of the experiment is then calculated, and the results interpreted by the method of drawing **log dose-response curves** as already discussed. The advantage of this arrangement is that it eliminates errors between one animal and another, since both the standard and the unknown are tested on the same animal.

This experimental design is used for the assays of insulin on rabbits, designated as the **twin cross-over test**. It combines the advantages of a cross-over test with those of 2 × 2 assay, according to the following design :

Group	*First injection*	*Second injection*
1	Standard dilution 2	Sample dilution 1
2	Standard dilution 1	Sample dilution 2
3	Sample dilution 2	Standard dilution 1
4	Sample dilution 1	Standard dilution 2

Rabbits of a specific weight are maintained on a prescribed feeding schedule, and the second injection is made at least 24 hours after the first. Obviously, the cross-over design cannot be employed if an assay results in the death of the animal, or an organ is removed from the body in the test procedure.

Method 3. Percentage of positive effects measured (Quantal assays or All-or-none assays). A quantal response is obtained and the percentage of positive effects at each dose is computed. The unknown is then compared with a standard with respect to potency in causing the quantal effects. However, the most familiar example of quantal assays is in toxicity testing e.g., LD_{50} determinations.

The **median lethal dose** (LD_{50}) is that dose of the drug/poison which kills 50 per cent of a test population of animals. For the determination of LD_{50} the drug/poison in different doses is injected into groups of animals, and the percentage mortality determined. This percent mortality is plotted against the dose, and a curve is drawn through the plotted points. This curve is *sigmoid* or S-shaped, as in low doses all animals live, and in higher doses all animals die **(Fig. 1.9.3)**.

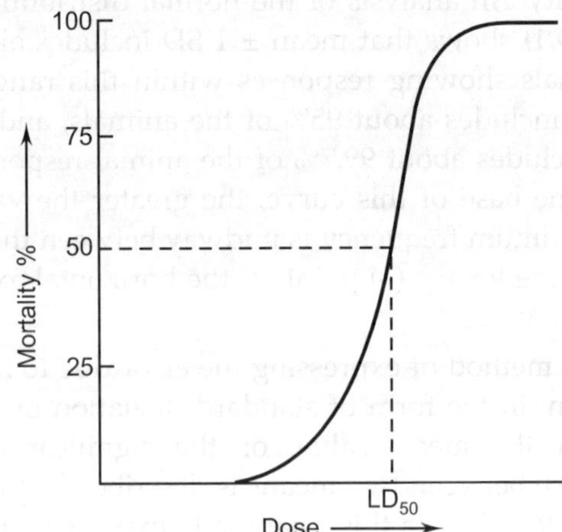

Fig. 1.9.3: Determination of LD_{50} of a drug/poison (diagrammatic). The per cent mortality is plotted against the different doses injected into animals (rats/mice); and the dose estimated which killed 50 per cent of the animals (dotted line).

Such quantal assay methods can also be employed for the bioassay of *insulin*, where the presence or absence of hypoglycaemic convulsions (in mice) at the doses tried is taken as an indicator. The curves for the unknown insulin and standard insulin are compared with respect to potency.

Method 4. Microbiological assays. These methods are used for assaying antibiotics. The test preparation is compared with the standard preparation for its inhibitory effect on particular organisms, sensitive to the agent.

BIOSTATISTICS

Statistics is defined as the science which deals with **collection, presentation** and **analysis** of data, and the **interpretation** of results obtained, with an aim to draw an inference. According to R.A. Fisher statistics essentially is a branch of applied mathematics, and may be regarded as mathematics applied to observational data. **Biostatistics** is statistics applied to biological sciences and to medicine. Whatever the definition, statistics is the science of information presentation in a numerical form which enables us to maximize our understanding of such information. Biostatistics has two sub-divisions.

(*a*) **Descriptive Statistics.** This deals with methods of describing and presenting a large mass of data, with the help of tables, graphs, histograms, pictograms, piecharts, bar charts, statistical maps, multiple bar charts and others.

(*b*) **Analytical Statistics.** This deals with methods that enable us to draw a conclusion from the data obtained, with the help of significance tests, correlation, regression and other methods.

Biological responses are variable, as already discussed in the section on biological variation in this Chapter. Thus it is essential that drug action should be studied in a large **population**. Usually a few individuals/animals are selected from the population at **random**, forming the *sample*, which for all practical purposes represents the population. All experimental designs must include proper groups of subjects/animals, which serve as **control** groups. These control groups are exposed to all conditions and procedures except the drug treatment the effect of which is under study. The results obtained from the **treatment group** are then compared with the **control group**. To understand statistics one should be familiar with the following terms:

PROBABILITY

Many statistical calculations aim to establish whether the observed differences between two sets of observations could have occurred just by *chance*. If the calculations indicate a low probability of a *chance* occurrence then the observed differences are said to be *statistically* significant.

CENTRAL TENDENCY

Biological data have a central tendency of occurrence, i.e., the maximum frequency of occurrence is placed centrally in the *normal frequency distribution curve* **(Fig. 1.9.1)**. The other observations are distributed evenly around it, giving the curve a symmetrical bell shape. The three common measures of location are the arithmetic mean, median and mode.

Arithmetic mean. All the readings/values are added up, and divided by the total number of observations, giving the mean value (average). This value can be used in further statistical calculations.

Median. It is the central value of all the observations arranged from the lowest to highest (arrayed), i.e., half of the observations exceed the median value, and half are below it. This measure is not amenable to further statistical treatment.

Mode. It is the most frequently occurring value in a series of observations. The limitations of this measure are that there may be more than one mode in a single set of data, and the mode cannot be used in further statistical calculations.

MEASURES OF VARIATION

These measures give an idea about the variation or spread of observations around the mean, i.e., whether the scatter of observations (indirectly the degree of biological variation) is great or small. The commonly used measures are, the range and the standard deviation.

Range. It is the interval between the lowest and the highest values in the set of observations, and is the simplest measure of variation. It does not indicate the distribution of values in between, and is greatly influenced by the extreme values.

Standard deviation (SD). This measure is universally used to show the scatter of individual measurements around the mean in a given distribution. Mathematically it is the square root of the average of the squared deviations of the measurements from their mean, and is calculated as under:

(*a*) First find out the **mean** of the observations.

(*b*) Then find out the **deviation** (d) of each value from the mean.

(*c*) Each value of 'd' is then squared and the values of d^2 are added up.

(*d*) This total is then divided by the number of observations minus one to obtain the "variance" and its square root is called **Standard deviation** (Σ denotes summation). SD is calculated by the formula :

$$\text{Variance} = \frac{\Sigma d^2}{n-1}$$

$$\text{Standard Deviation (SD)} = \sqrt{\frac{\Sigma d^2}{n(n-1)}}$$

where Σd^2 is the sum of the square of the deviations, and n is the number of observations.

Standard Error of the Mean (SE or SEM). The arithmetic mean is merely an approximation of the "true mean" of the whole population, and thus is subject to error. The SE is the value which allows one to find out the range in which the true mean would lie. Thus, SE is a measure of the scatter of the mean value. It can be calculated as under:

$$\text{Standard Error (SE)} = \frac{\text{SD of the Sample}}{\sqrt{\text{Sample size}}} = \frac{\text{SD}}{\sqrt{n}}$$

or, in a single step (without first calculating the SD) it can be calculated as:

$$SE = \sqrt{\frac{\Sigma d^2}{n(n-1)}}$$

Tests of Significance (t-test)

The Student's t-test is applied to assess the statistical significance of difference between two independent means (unpaired means), obtained from two series of data. The essential assumptions for the application of the t-test are that the two means are from two normally distributed populations, with approximately equal variances. The value of 't' is determined by the formula:

$$t = \frac{m_1 - m_2}{\sqrt{(SE_1)^2 + (SE_2)^2}} \quad \text{(for equal sample sizes)}$$

where $m_1 - m_2$ is the difference between the two means, while SE_1 and SE_2 are the standard errors of the two means. Higher the value of t, lesser is the probability (p), that the difference between the means is due to chance variation.

When the number in the two independent samples (n_1 and n_2) is unequal, there is a likelihood that the variance of the two means (m_1 and m_2) also is unequal. Hence, the above formula is unsuitable. In such a case the data are corrected for unequal variance by applying the following formula:

$$t = \frac{m_1 - m_2}{\sqrt{\frac{(n_1-1)S_1^2 + (n_2-1)S_2^2}{n_1+n_2-2}}} \times \sqrt{\frac{n_1 \, n_2}{n_1+n_2}}$$

where $m_1 - m_2$ is the difference between the two means, while S_1 and S_2 are the standard deviations of the two means, and n_1 and n_2 are the number of observations in the two samples.

Books on Statistics or Statistical Tables give the "t-distribution table", from which the value of p (probability) may be ascertained if the value of t and the number of observations in the two groups (n_1 and n_2) are known. From the number of observations the number expressing the degrees of freedom (df) for unpaired means is computed as $df = n_1 + n_2 - 2$. Enter the t-table horizontally at the particular df, and if the value of t exceeds the value mentioned in the 0.05 column of values, then the p is less than 0.05 ($p < 0.05$). This indicates that the difference between the two means is **statistically significant**, and not due to chance (its probability of having occurred just by chance is only 5 times out of 100 times or 1 chance in 20). The level of significance for biological data is usually chosen as 95% or p = or < 0.05 ($p \le 0.05$). Precisely the p value is a fraction which expresses the probability by which the difference between the two means could be due to chance variation, e.g., $p = 0.05$ means 1 chance is 20; $p = 0.01$ means 1 chance in 100; $p = 0.001$ means 1 chance in 1000, and so on.

The t-test is still used very frequently, although the necessary assumptions are more limiting (normal distribution, approximately equal variability of the two samples) and the tables are more extensive. It is currently recommended that the t-test be replaced by the *z-test* for n greater than 30, and the *Wilcoxon test* for n less than 30. For the latter two tests no particular assumptions are needed.

To assess the significance of difference between two means obtained as "before" and "after" values (paired means) the following formula is applied:

$$t_{n-1} = \frac{\bar{d}}{SE\,\bar{d}}$$

where d is the mean difference between the "before" and "after" values taken in the same direction, and $SE\bar{d}$ is the standard error of the mean difference. The t-distribution table is consulted for the determination of the p value as described above, except that the number expressing the degrees of freedom for paired means is computed as $df = n - 1$, where n stands for the number of pairs of observations.

Probit Transformation

This is often employed in bioassay procedures for the transformation of percentage data. The "probit" is best defined in terms of the **normal equivalent deviation** (NED). The NED corresponding to any given percentage is calculated from the shape of the normal curve whose standard deviation is one. The NED is the deviation (from the mean) equivalent to the given percentage of the area of the curve. The *probit* is equal to the NED plus 5.

Broadly speaking, biostatistics is used in pharmacological studies for the following :

(*a*) to consolidate and present experimental data;

(*b*) to analyse the data, and assess the significance of results obtained on comparison of the effects of two or more drugs, with an aim to draw conclusions; and

(*c*) for bioassay of drugs in animals or in human beings (clinical trials).

Chemical Assay Methods

About 2 decades ago chemical assay methods were rather too insensitive to be of much value in pharmacology. However, now there are several analytical methods whose *sensitivity* and *specificity* match or even exceed that of bioassays. Some important chemical assay techniques are:

1. Radioimmunoassay (RIA).
2. Gas chromatography and mass spectrometry (GCMS).
3. High performance liquid chromatography (HPLC).
4. Spectrophotometry and fluorimetry.

Radioimmunoassay (RIA)

RIA was first developed in 1960 for the assay of insulin. In principle the requirements are: (*i*) an **antibody** which combines specifically with high affinity with the substance to be assayed; (*ii*) a **radioactively labelled form** of the substance to be assayed; and (*iii*) a **method for separating** antibody-bound form from free material in the solution.

Enzyme-linked immunoassay (EIA) is a variant of RIA in which the label used is an enzyme rather than a radioisotope.

Some important drugs measurable by radioimmunoassay are: adriamycin, carbamazepine, chlorpromazine, diazepam, digitoxin, digoxin, lignocaine, morphine, pethidine, nortriptyline, phenobarbitone, phenytoin, procainamide, propranolol and quinidine. In general, the *sensitivity* of immunoassays is high, because *antibody affinity* is usually sufficiently high that effective competition between *standard* and *sample* occurs at very low concentrations, and also because radioactivity can be measured with very high sensitivity.

Chromatographic Techniques

Chromatography provides a good battery of techniques for separation of different chemical substances. Combined with a *detector* of sufficient sensitivity, chromatography provides the basis for many useful assays.

The basic principle by which chemical separation is achieved is common to all types of chromatography. The **stationary phase** consists of particles of a substance such as resin, cellulose or alumina packed into a tube through which the **mobile phase** flows. The mobile phase is a liquid (usually an aqueous solution) or a gas, into which is introduced the sample containing the substance(s) to be separated. Separation occurs because the stationary phase either binds, or selectively excludes, substances present in the sample. The more the substance is bound to the stationary phase the longer it will take to emerge through the column. The main drawback of conventional **liquid chromatography** as an assay method is its slowness. Two advanced techniques, namely *gas chromatography* and *high performance liquid chromatography* have reduced the *run time* from hours to minutes, greatly increasing the usefulness of the method for routine assays.

Gas Chromatography (GC)

The rate of diffusion of molecules in a gaseous in contrast to a liquid medium is much higher, particularly if the temperature is increased. Hence the **column flow rate** can be greatly increased, allowing for separation in a few minutes. The drawback is that the test substance must be volatile, which most drugs are not. However, they can often be converted to volatile derivatives by reactions like esterification, or by controlled thermal decomposition (pyrolysis). GC is now widely used to measure concentration of drugs and their metabolites in body fluids for pharmacokinetic studies.

High Performance Liquid Chromatography (HPLC)

This is a technical advancement of conventional liquid chromatography in which by reducing particle size of the stationary phase to 5-20 μm, the **diffusion distance** is reduced, and hence equilibration of the test molecules between the two phases is speeded up. To achieve adequate *flow rates* through such tightly packed columns high pressures, plumbing, pumps and injection devices of high precision are required. HPLC has overcome many drawbacks of GC, and it has a wider applicability in pharmacology. HPLC can be used for many routine analytical procedures.

Mass Spectrometry (MS)

In a mass spectrometer the substance is converted to a volatile form, introduced into an evacuated chamber, and then ionized. The resulting ions are accelerated in an electric field, as a beam, which is deflected by applying a transverse magnetic field. The degree of deflection of individual ions depends on the ratio of their mass to their charge (m/e ratio), those with the largest m/e ratio being deflected the least. At the far end of the instrument is a narrow slit through which a slice of the *ion beam* passes to a detector which measures its intensity. The strength of the magnetic field is varied in a scanning fashion, so that the beam of ions separated according to their m/e ratios sweeps across the detector slit in a sequence.

For most biological estimations the sample is first put through a GC column, the outlet of which is connected directly to the inlet of the mass spectrometer. This combined GCMS technique provides for a highly purified sample being subjected to MS analysis. Accurate assays of *acetylcholine* can be done by using the GCMS technique. Limitations of the technique are the high cost of equipment and the complex and time-consuming procedure.

Spectrophotometry and Fluorimetry

The property that molecules can *absorb* energy from *photons* provides the basis for analytical techniques that have many pharmacological applications.

In **absorption spectrophotometry** the amount of light emerging after passing through a standard sized cell containing a chemical solution is measured. The fraction of light absorbed is estimated by comparing the intensity of the **emergent** beam with that of the **incident** beam, and depends on : (*i*) the nature of the absorbing compound; (*ii*) its concentration and the length of the light path through the solution, and (*iii*) the wavelength of the light. Because of the wavelength specificity of particular chemical groups, substances can be distinguished by differing shapes of their absorption spectrum, and this can be used to distinguish changes in a particular chemical component in a mixture. The simplicity of absorption spectrophotometry is a great advantage, and the technique is widely used. For many drugs the concentration which gives a satisfactory signal for assay purposes ranges between 1-10 mcg/ml.

In **fluorescence spectrophotometry** (fluorimetry) the principle is that when a molecule absorbs a *photon*, the energy causes one of its electrons to move into an unstable higher energy state. This excited state persists for a very brief time (10^{-8} to 10^{-7} sec) and the molecule recovers by releasing the energy in the form of another photon, of lower energy, i.e., of a longer wavelength than the one that was absorbed. These emitted photons can be detected as fluorescence by a sensitive wavelength selective photomultiplier tube. **Fluorimetry is both more sensitive and more selective** than absorption spectrophotometry. The solvent, pH, and the presence of other substances dissolved in it can affect the fluorescence signal, but the technique is very sensitive and versatile. Fluorescence assays are widely used for measuring the catecholamine **(dopamine, noradrenaline, adrenaline)** content of tissues and body fluids. Histamine and serotonin can also be assayed fluorimetrically.

1.10 DISCOVERY AND DEVELOPMENT OF NEW DRUGS

In ancient times, most drugs used in the treatment of disease were derived from naturally-occurring substances of plant origin, e.g., **opium** from poppy, **quinine** from cinchona, and **digitalis** from foxglove. Presently, the majority of new therapeutic agents are **synthetic** in nature. Every year about 20 to 25 new chemicals are marketed as *drugs* to be used in the treatment of disease. In the UK the total cost of discovering, developing and marketing a new drug which is therapeutically innovative ranges between 30-50 million Pounds. That is why new drugs are costly. During the "patent" period the pharmaceutical companies make all efforts to sell their drugs through various marketing promotion techniques, like advertising and gifting through aggressive drug representatives. This money is to recoup the company's investment and make a profit, and some of it is re-invested into research and development of another drug. When the drugs' patent expires, and competitors market other formulations the price of the drug falls.

Drug Discovery

The starting point for the discovery of a new drug may be reached in several ways. The genesis of a research programme in pharmaceutical establishments, from where most of the drugs came today, is mainly by the following *five* procedures:

(*i*) **Random screening.** In this procedure new chemical entities are subjected to a battery of screening tests designed to determine different types of biological activity. Such tests include studies on animal behaviour, isolated tissues, intact animals, and sometimes even animal models of disease. It is a sort of "blind hitting to hit a nail head". Such studies are time consuming, expensive and have a low yield. It has been estimated that only *one* in every 4000 to 5000 new chemical entities screened is marketed. It is possible that the new drug thus found may ultimately turn out to be similar in its action to already existing drugs, with no added advantage. Such "me too drugs" add to the existing *drug explosion*.

(*ii*) **Molecular manipulation.** In this procedure chemical analogues of existing drugs are synthesized and tested for their biological activity. This is a more logical approach, and may yield new compounds with certain advantages like better absorption, greater potency, more selective action, and fewer side effects, e.g., hydrogenation of the parent thiazide diuretic **chlorothiazide** has increased the sodium losing, and decreased the potassium losing potential of the resultant compounds, thereby raising their potency and lessening side effects. The **thiazides** and the oral hypoglycaemic **sulphonylureas** represent slight modifications of the old antibacterial drug, sulphanilamide. Many **synthetic penicillins** and **cephalosporins** have been developed in this manner.

(*iii*) **Molecular designing.** This is the most rational form of drug research and development. It aims at designing of substances to fulfil a specific biological task. In its simplest form this may involve the synthesis of a naturally occurring substance, a hormone, a vitamin, or a precursor of a neurotransmitter, e.g., **dopamine** for cardiogenic shock; **lovodopa** for parkinsonism; **allopurinol**, an analogue of xanthine, preventing synthesis of uric acid by inhibiting xanthine oxidase, used in gout.

(*iv*) **Metabolites of drugs.** Sometimes active metabolites of drugs are found to possess therapeutic

Table 1.10-1 *Some side effects of drugs which were used with advantage therapeutically*

Drug	*Original proposed use*	*Side effect*	*Derived use*
Merbaphen	Antitreponemal	Diuresis	Mercurial diuretics
Sulphanilamide	Antibacterial	Hypoglycaemia	Sulphonylureas
		Diuresis	Carbonic anhydrase inhibitors, Thiazides Thiouracils
		Thyroid inhibition	
Amphetamine	CNS stimulant	Appetite loss	Anorexiants
Iproniazid	Antituberculosis	Euphoria	Antidepressants (MAOIs)
Chlorpromazine	Antihistamine	Sedation	Phenothiazine antipsychotics
Reserpine	Antihypertensive	Sedation	Antipsychotic
Nalorphine	Narcotic antagonist	Analgesia	Agonist-antagonist analgesics
Diazoxide	Antihypertensive	Hyperglycaemia	Hyperglycaemic agent

advantages over the parent compound, e.g., **paracetamol** is a metabolite of phenacetin and is effective as an analgesic, but does not cause renal damage; **chlordiazepoxide** is metabolized to other active benzodiazepines which have a shorter action, and this has led to the introduction of drugs like **oxazepam**; the active metabolite of procainamide, **N-acetyl-procainamide**, is an effective antiarrhythmic drug, but does not cause a lupus-like syndrome that can occur with procainamide; **sulphasalazine** is metabolized to 5-aminosalicylic acid and sulphapyridine, the former has therapeutic activity and the latter (sulphapyridine) causes adverse effects—thus 5-aminosalicylic acid is now being used to treat ulcerative colitis.

(*v*) **Serendipity.** It means "happy observation by chance" and has led to the introduction of many useful remedies in the past, e.g., use of *organomercurials* for cardiac oedema; *penicillin* as an antibacterial agent; *lignocaine* and *phenytoin* as antiarrhythmics, *amphetamines* to control hyperkinetic behaviour in children; *methotrexate* for severe psoriasis; *cyclophosphamide* and *azathioprine* to prevent tissue rejection in kidney transplants, and to treat autoimmune diseases. Thus new uses are found for old drugs and the side effects find therapeutic applications **(Table 1.10-1)**.

Drug Development

Once a new chemical entity is discovered it has to be subjected to the developmental process. Chemical synthetic activity is mostly carried out in the Research and Development (R and D) divisions of pharmaceutical laboratories by the **synthetic chemist**. The structure-activity relationships (SAR) are determined. After synthesis the structure of the new compound and its purity is determined and confirmed by the **analytical chemist**. Further, the study of a promising compound can be divided into two stages: (*i*) **Preclinical pharmacology** (animal studies); and (*ii*) **Clinical pharmacology** (human studies). The new candidate drug is passed on to **basic pharmacologists**, who work out the pharmacological actions and toxicity of the compound. Detailed toxicological (acute, subacute and chronic toxicity), and metabolic studies are carried out.

These preclinical data are scrupulously screened and analysed by the Drug Control Authority of the country, and if considered safe, permission for human trials is granted. The drug is then subjected to a **clinical trial** under the guidance and supervision of a **clinical pharmacologist** and a specialist **clinician**. The candidate drug has thus to pass through a strict evaluation channel from the laboratory to the market for use in man for the treatment of disease.

To summarize, the following steps are involved in the development of a new drug:

1. Preliminary synthesis and physico-chemical analysis.
2. Preliminary biological evaluation.
3. Secondary and specific biological evaluation.
4. Range-finding toxicological studies.
5. Target organ toxicological studies.
6. Acute and subacute toxicological studies.
7. Metabolic studies.
8. Synthesis and quality control of bulk material.
9. **Phase I Clinical Evaluation** (human toxicity and metabolic studies).
10. Final formulation, and final physico-chemical analysis.
11. **Phase II Clinical evaluation** (dose titration and limited efficacy studies).
12. **Phase III Clinical Evaluation** (Broad efficacy and tolerance studies in a large population of patients; chronic, toxicological studies).
13. **Phase IV Clinical Evaluation** (Surveillance during general clinical use).

Setps 1 to 8 and 10 involve *medicinal chemistry* and *pharmaceutics*. Steps 2 to 7 are covered by *preclinical pharmacological evaluation* of the drug in animals. Steps 9, 11 and 12 are in the domain of *clinical pharmacological evaluation* of the drug in humans. Step 13 is an ongoing process of surveillance to ensure safe use of the drug. If all these steps are satisfactorily passed by the candidate drug, it is granted *registration as a new drug* for use in man.

Preclinical Evaluation (Animal Studies)

The candidate drug is subjected to extensive pharmacological testing in vivo in animals, and on in vitro preparations. In addition, its pharmacokinetics is studied in animals. Acute and chronic toxicity testing in animals is also initiated. This gives some idea about the likely therapeutic application of the drug and its dose-related adverse effects. Based on these studies specific screening for antibacterial, analgesic, anti-inflammatory, anticonvulsant, antiarrhythmic, muscle relaxant, antidepressive or tranquillizing properties of the drug are undertaken. The experimental animals used include mice, rats, guinea pigs, dogs and sometimes monkeys.

The three major areas of preclinical evaluation are:

1. Acute, subacute and chronic toxicity studies (toxicity profile).
2. Therapeutic index (safety and efficacy evaluation).
3. Absorption, distribution and elimination studies (pharmacokinetics).

Acute, Subacute and Chronic Toxicity

In **acute toxicity** studies most commonly the median lethal dose (LD_{50}) is determined. The drug is given in graded doses to groups of animals by the oral or intraperitoneal or intravenous route, and the percentage of animals dying in each group within a specific period of time (usually 24 hours) is plotted against the dose. From this curve the dose that kills 50 per cent of the animals is estimated and is called LD_{50}. This particular dose mortality figure is chosen as the curve approaches a straight line in this region. To minimize biological variation, care is taken to have all the groups of animals as similar to each other as possible regarding their age, species, sex and weight. Conventionally at least *three* different animal species (rats, mice and rabbits) are used for acute toxicity testing. Other toxic symptoms (convulsions, stupor, tremors, hyperactivity) suffered by the animals are also recorded.

In **subacute toxicity** studies usually the drug is administered orally. Several doses are used, some within the range of the estimated human dose, and others that produce toxic reactions. The animals are carefully observed, and a number of laboratory studies including **haematologic** examinations, **renal** and **hepatic function tests** are carried out. More than one animal species are employed. The animals are maintained at the maximum tolerated dose for 2 to 3 weeks to allow for the development of pathological changes, if any, and then killed and subjected to a complete *histopathological examination*.

In **chronic toxicity** studies, usually two species of animals, one rodent (rat) and one non-rodent (dog or monkey) are used. The drug is administered for many months, usually over a major portion of the animals expected life span. Detailed **biochemical** and **histological** measurements are made. The animals are killed periodically for **histopathological** studies of various organs.

Today, toxicological studies with all new drugs for their effect on reproduction and development have become mandatory. These studies have assumed prime importance after the "thalidomide disaster" of the late 1950's which left more than 10,000 infants congenitally deformed and crippled. The tests carried out are:

(*a*) **Tests for fertility and reproductive performance** are usually carried out in rats, treated with the new drug before and after the mating period. The effects on the early and late stages of embryonic and foetal development, and lactation are studied.

(*b*) **Teratological studies** are usually carried out in two animal species to assess the effects of the drug on organogenesis. The drug is given after "mating" during the period of organogenesis. Foetuses are carefully examined for visceral and skeletal abnormalities; the number of live and dead foetuses is recorded; and resorption sites in the uteri and corpora lutea are examined.

(*c*) **Study of the adverse effects on the mother and offsprings** in the perinatal and postnatal period is carried out by administering the new drug during the last third of pregnancy upto weaning. Observations are made for adverse effects on labour, lactation and direct toxic effects on the newborn.

In all these tests "control" groups of untreated animals in sufficient numbers must be studied to assess the drug effects, if any, accurately.

Therapeutic Index

Therapeutic index refers to the relative **margin of safety** of a drug. As described above the **median lethal dose** (LD_{50}) for the drug, which is lethal to 50 per cent of the test population of *animals* is determined. Then the dose which is effective in 50 per cent of the test population, termed as the **median effective dose** (ED_{50}) is estimated. The ratio of the LD_{50} to the ED_{50} is the therapeutic index (TI):

$$\text{Therapeutic Index (TI)} = \frac{LD_{50}}{ED_{50}}$$

The TI indicates how close the effective dose is to the lethal dose for 50 percent of the test population. Thus it gives an idea about the margin of safety **(Fig. 1.10.1)**. As the ED_{50} approaches the LD_{50}, the danger of drug toxicity increases significantly. If the LD_{50} is 9 grams, and the ED_{50} is 1 gram, the TI is 9; but if the LD_{50} is 6 grams and the ED_{50} is 4 grams, the TI would be 1.5. The TI of *penicillin* is 100, indicating that the drug is relatively safe in terms of toxic effects of overdosage. On the contrary, digoxin has a rather low TI of 1.5 to 2.0 and the margin of safety is narrow.

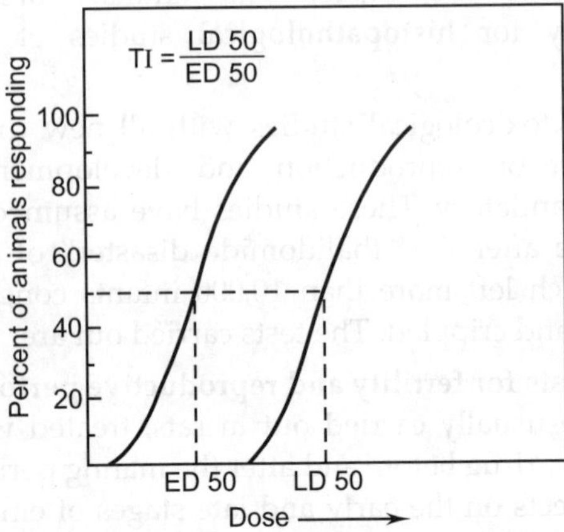

Fig. 1.10.1: Concept of the therapeutic index (TI) in animals, indicating the effective dose (ED_{50}) and the lethal dose (LD_{50}) for 50 percent of test population (diagrammatic).

In animals a modification of this concept can be applied. The *therapeutic index* can be calculated as:

$$TI = \frac{\text{Plasma concentration causing adverse effect}}{\text{Plasma concentration causing therapeutic effect}}$$

The objective is to get some idea of the *benefit: risk ratio*.

In clinical medicine the **therapeutic index** based on LD_{50} and ED_{50} is not valid. Instead, in the clinic a dose that has some unwanted effect in 50 percent of humans (e.g., a specified increase in heart rate in case of an adrenoceptor agonist) can be related to that dose which is effective 50 percent of patients of bronchial asthma (e.g., a specified decrease in airway resistance). In man the TI data are not available for many drugs, however, this concept provides a sensible way of comparing the usefulness of one drug with another, i.e., *safety* in relation to *efficacy*.

Thus, the therapeutic index is of little value as a measure of clinical usefulness of a drug. It is often pointed out that digoxin is a very useful drug in spite of its low TI. The **benzodiazepines** have replaced **barbiturates** as hypnotic drugs, because their TI is very high compared to the barbiturates. To sum up, the TI provides a valid general concept, but it provides no measure of the actual usefulness of a drug.

Absorption, Distribution and Elimination (Pharmacokinetics)

All promising new compounds are subjected to pharmacokinetic studies in several species of animals, usually, rats, dogs and sometimes monkeys. These studies should establish the relative **bioavailability** of the compound on oral or parenteral administration. The rate of excretion can be expressed as **elimination half-life** ($t_{1/2}$), i.e., the time required for one-half of the drug to be excreted **(Chap. 1.5)**. Such information is useful in estimating optimal dosage intervals. Data obtained on animals *must* be applied to humans very cautiously. This information from animals is at best useful for the initiation of human studies.

Clinical Evaluation (Human Studies)

Preclinical data obtained from animal studies provide a **general pharmacological, toxicological** and **pharmacokinetic profile** of the new drug. These data are scrutinized by Expert Government Bodies in each country, with the aim that clinical drug trials should be undertaken with great care and meticulous planning of the methodology adopted. The New Drug Application in the prescribed format, with all relevant literature and preclinical data must be submitted to the Drug Control Authority for scrutiny, and sanction obtained before clinical evaluation studies are initiated.

In U.K. the introduction of new drugs is regulated by the Committee on Safety of Medicines (CSM); and in the USA by the Food and Drug Administration (FDA). In India the Drug Controller, Government of India, based in New Delhi is responsible for the organisation of this system. Only when approval is given by this body, the drug can be administered to man for clinical evaluation.

Clinical Pharmacology

In short, clinical pharmacology deals with the effect of drugs on the body, and the effect of the body on drugs in man, i.e., the **pharmacodynamic** and **pharmacokinetic** studies respectively in man. In its modern form this discipline began in the 1950's when it was recognized to have made a distinct contribution to the safe practice of medicine. It has *three* distinct parts: (*i*) **Confirmatory Pharmacology** in which studies are carried out in healthy volunteers to confirm animal pharmacology; (*ii*) **Human Biotransformation Studies** about the absorption, distribution and elimination of the drug carried out in volunteers; and (*iii*) **Clinical Trials** or drug trials.

Sir Bradford Hill (1966) defined a clinical trial as "a carefully and ethically designed human experiment with the aim of answering some precisely framed questions". This definition is valid even today.

Clinical Trials

To design a perfect clinical trial a lot of thought and expertise is needed, and a perfect team work is involved. Some salient guidelines are:

(*i*) **Ethics and patient selection.** The **Declaration of Helsinki** of the World Medical Association (1964) codifies recommendations for guidance of doctors in clinical research. These must be followed by investigators working on patients or healthy volunteers. **Informed consent** must be obtained in writing from subjects (patients or volunteers), or their guardians if the patient is incapable of giving consent. The subject must be informed that a new drug is being tried which may be beneficial, however, a calculated risk is involved. The new treatment is compared with the known conventional treatment. Use of "placebo controls" is unethical and is not permissible if an effective remedy is available for the disease. Criteria for *selection of patients* should be well thought out and defined. Special care must be taken if more than one doctor is involved in the selection of patients in the trial, specially in multicentric trials.

(*ii*) **Response measurements.** The end-points should be clearly defined. It is useful to even define *non-responders*. Side effects should be carefully observed and recorded.

(*iii*) **Experimental design.** The design of the trial must be statistically sound, for which preferably a biostatistician should be consulted. In general, **controlled clinical trials** must include four safeguards against bias: (*a*) **double-blind** technique; (*b*) **randomization** of treatment; (*c*) **matching** of patients; and (*d*) **cross-over** technique.

The final stage of a clinical trial is the **statistical analysis** of data obtained. Relatively simple tests like the Student's t-test or the **Chi-square** test may be sufficient to determine the **significance** of results. Complex statistical methods include **non-parametric tests, analysis of variance, covariance, dispersion** and **sequential techniques.**

Phases of a Clinical Trial

Phase I: Clinical Pharmacologic Evaluation

Phase I studies are usually carried out on 20-50 healthy volunteers or patients, depending on the class of drug and its safety. These studies are mainly concerned with **human toxicity, tolerated dosage range, pharmacological actions** and **pharmacokinetics of the drug.**

Phase II: Controlled Clinical Evaluation

Phase II studies are carried out on 50-300 patients. In fact they are extensions of Phase I studies, and are carried out by a larger number of investigators with a greater range of assessments. These studies mainly aim to ascertain the *safety* and *efficacy* of the new drug, and are strictly controlled. Late Phase II studies are done in a **controlled double-blind manner**, and at the conclusion of these studies one should be convinced about the therapeutic usefulness of the drug. Drug *toxicity* and *interactions*, if any, are carefully recorded.

Phase III: Extended Clinical Evaluation

These are formal therapeutic trials carried out preferably in a **double-blind controlled** manner in 250-1000 patients. A large number of investigators are involved to familiarize them with the use of the new drug. **Efficacy** and **safety** of the new drug is evaluated, and even comparison with other drugs is undertaken. If after Phase III studies both the sponsor and the Drug Control Authority are satisfied about the safety and efficacy of the drug, a "package insert" is prepared by the sponsor, which has to be approved by the Drug Control Authority. After this the drug is marketed for general use.

Phase IV: Surveillance during Post-marketing General Clinical Use

After the drug is released for general clinical use, certain unusual type of adverse reactions may be observed even after years of clinical usage. Thus, an **adverse reaction monitoring** is carried out in Phase IV evaluation, and this continues till the drug is used.

To summarize, based on the data obtained during the preclinical development phase of the new drug, approval is obtained from the regulatory authority for undertaking a *clinical trial*. The basis upon which new treatments are evaluated involves comparison with either an existing treatment or a placebo. The sequence of executing such a *controlled clinical trial* is shown in **(Fig. 1.10.2).**

Scientific personnel participating in the development of new drugs include the **medicinal chemist**, the **experimental pharmacologist**, the **toxicologist**, sometimes **vaterinarians**, the **clinical pharmacologist**, the **clinical investigator**, and the **biostatistician**. Thus, the development of new drugs requires skill and team effort from a number of disciplines. **During its life history a drug travels through the laboratory to the clinic and the population of patients during which it must be continuously monitored for its efficacy and safety.**

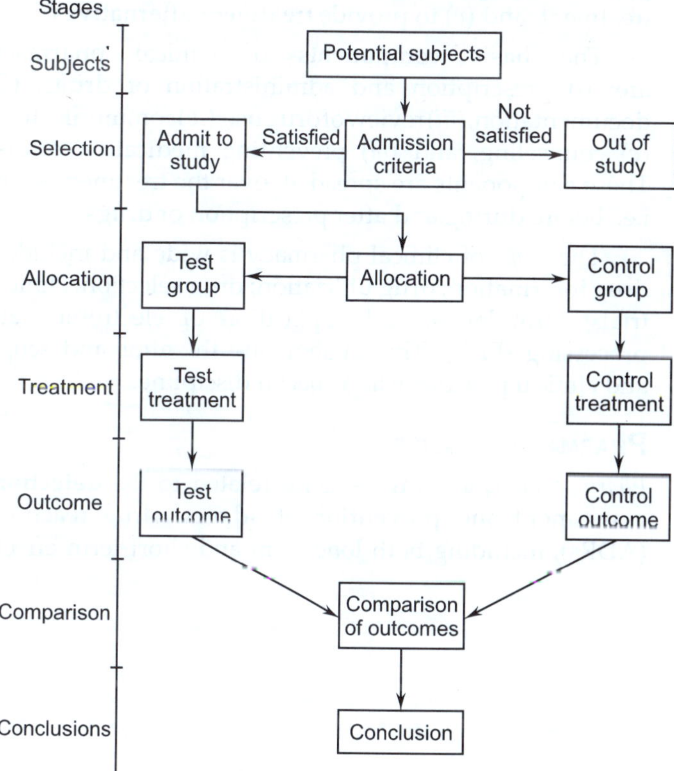

Fig. 1.10.2: A typical flow chart of a controlled clinical trial.

1.11 CLINICAL PHARMACY AND GENERAL PRINCIPLES OF DRUG THERAPY

Clinical Pharmacy
Pharmacovigilance
General Principles of Drug Therapy

Drug therapy involves the use of drugs to *prevent* or *treat* diseases. The goal of drug therapy is to *maximize* the beneficial effects, and to *minimize* their adverse effects. *Clinical pharmacy* and *pharmacovigilance* are measures to ensure *effective*, *economical*, *appropriate* and *safe* use of medication avoiding adverse drug reactions (ADRs).

CLINICAL PHARMACY

Clinical pharmacy is defined as that area of pharmacy concerned with the science and practice of rational medication use. It is the branch of pharmacy where pharmacists and pharmacoeconomists provide patient care and optimize the use of medicines to promote health and prevent disease. They care for patients in all health care settings like **nursing homes, clinics,** and **hospitals**. Clinical pharmacists have extensive education in **biomedical, pharmaceutical,** and **clinical sciences**. They provide scientifically valid information about appropriate, safe and cost-effective use of medications.

The **overall goal** of clinical pharmacy is to promote appropriate use of medicines and devices involved in patient care. The main aims are: (*i*) **maximizing** the clinical effect of medicines; (*ii*) **minimizing** the risk of adverse drug reactions; (*iii*) **monitoring** the therapy; ensuring patient's compliance; (*iv*) **minimizing** expenditure on treatment; and (*v*) to provide **treatment alternatives**.

The **basic components** of clinical pharmacy are: (*i*) prescription and administration of drugs; (*ii*) documentation; (*iii*) review of drug use; (*iv*) communication; (*v*) counseling; and (*vi*) preventing medication errors. These components are spread all over the treatment span, i.e., before during and after prescription of drugs.

The *scope* of clinical pharmacy is wide and includes; drug information; drug utilization; drug selection; clinical trials; formularies; and application of electronic data processing (EDP). This in short are the aims and scope and clinical pharmacy as a special discipline.

PHARMACOVIGILANCE

Pharmacovigilance is the science related to the **detection, assessment** and **prevention** of adverse drug reactions (ADRs), including both long-term and short-term effects of medication. This term comes from *pharmakon* (Greek), "drug", and *vigilare* (latin), "to keep watch". It involves **collecting, analyzing, assessing,** and **monitoring** of adverse effects of medication, revealing new information about ADRs, and prevention of harm to the patient.

The aims of pharmacovigilance are: (*i*) **identification** and quantification of unrecognized ADRs, (*ii*) finding **subgroups of patients** at high risk of ADRs; (*iii*) continued monitoring of **safety** of a product; (*iv*) **comparative ADR** *profile* of products within the same class of drugs; (*v*) detection of **inappropriate prescribing** and administration of drugs; (*vi*) further elucidation of the drug's **pharmacological** and **toxicological profile;** and (*vii*) detection of **drug-drug interactions** hitherto unknown. Pharmacovigilance is an important parameter counting towards safe use of medication in treatment of diseasee.

GENERAL PRINCIPLES OF DRUG THERAPY

The following principles must be followed to obtain maximal benefit out of the drugs administered:

1. Drug therapy should be **patient centered** and **individualised**.
2. Minimize the number of drugs to be taken by the patient. This would improve *compliance*. Multiple drug therapy is recommended in certain conditions like **essential hypertension** and **tuberculosis**.
3. **Fixed-dose combinations** of drugs should be avoided.
4. **Recommended dosage schedules** should be adopted, with due regard to the patient's condition.
5. Drug therapy during **pregnancy** and **lactation** needs special care.
6. In **paediatric drug therapy** appropriate doses must be calculated as a fraction of the adult dose.
7. In **geriatric drug therapy** generally smaller doses than doses for young adults are needed due to the physiologic changes in the elderly with ageing.

2

DRUGS ACTING ON THE CENTRAL NERVOUS SYSTEM

2.1 GENERAL CONSIDERATION

The human nervous system is an extremely complex structure, having more than 12 billion nerve cells or **neurones.** Together with the **endocrine system,** it coordinates and regulates the functioning of all body organs. Transmission of information in the endocrine system is by circulating **hormones,** and this provides for a slowly developing but long-lasting control, i.e., it functions as a **slow communication system.** In contrast, the **nervous system** can evoke rapid changes in body function as transmission of information is through **electrical** conduction of impulses along nerve fibres, and chemical transmission of impulses by **neurotransmitters** between nerve fibres, resulting in a moment-to-moment control, i.e., it functions as a **rapid communication system.**

Divisions of the Nervous System

The basic organization of the nervous system is as under:

1. **Central Nervous System**
   - (*i*) Brain
   - (*ii*) Spinal cord
2. **Peripheral Nervous System**
   - (*i*) Somatic system
   - (*ii*) Autonomic system
     - (*a*) Parasympathetic division
     - (*b*) Sympathetic division

The central nervous system (CNS) consists of the brain and spinal cord, and serves to coordinate and direct all body functions. It is only this control which enables the organism to adapt to a constantly changing environment, thereby maintaining **homeostasis. Fig. 2.1.1** diagrammatically shows the functional aspects of the CNS and the peripheral nervous system.

Impulses to the brain (afferent) from sensory receptors, and from the brain (efferent) to the skeletal muscle are conveyed by a sequence of electrical and chemical means **(Chap. 3.7).** The sensory and motor branches in combination comprise the somatic system, and the nature of the response is **voluntary.** This somatic system does not have synapses outside the spinal cord before reaching the muscle, or the sensory receptor site. In contract, there are ganglionic synapses in both the divisions of the autonomic nervous system (ANS). These additional synapses in the ANS offer potential sites for drug effects apart from the terminal neuroeffector sites. The ANS is **involuntary** in nature and controls the vegetative functions in the body. Its two divisions maintain a balance of opposing effects on the body's smooth muscle, myocardium, viscera and glands **(Chap. 3.1).**

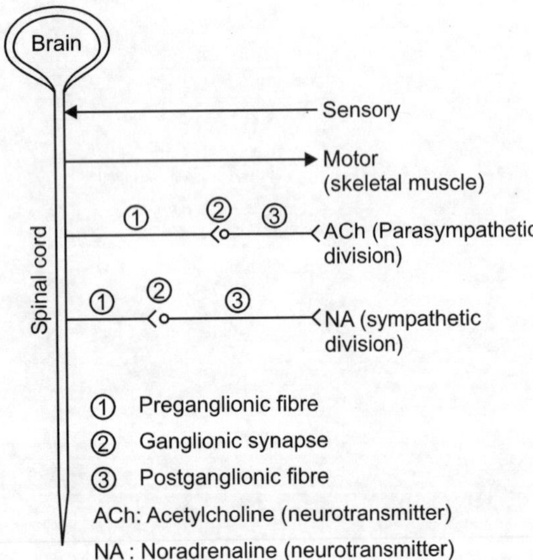

Fig. 2.1.1: Functional diagram of the central and peripheral nervous system showing the somatic branches (sensory, motor) and the autonomic divisions (parasympathetic, sympathetic), their synapses and neurotransmitters.

The various functions regulated by the CNS can be illustrated by outlining the major anatomical subdivisions of the brain and the main **physiological functions** controlled by each area. The brain may be roughly divided into *five* sub-divisions, based on embryological terminology. They are the **telencephalon, diencephalon, mesencephalon, metencephalon** and **myelencephalon (Fig. 2.1.2).**

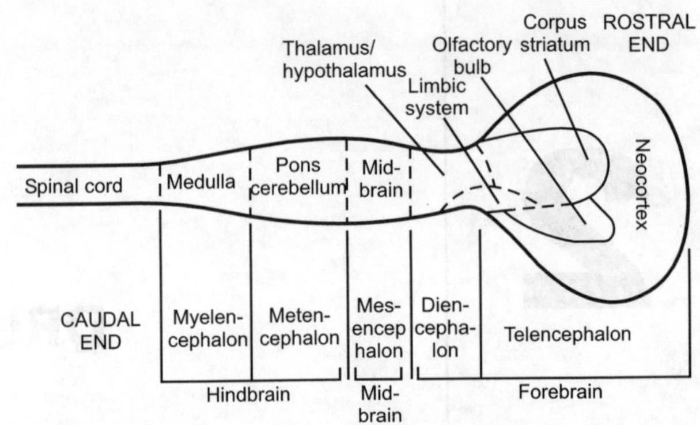

Fig. 2.1.2: A diagrammatic sketch of the major sub-divisions of the mammalian brain (see text).

The functions regulated by the various brain sub-divisions are as under :

I. FOREBRAIN

1. **Telencephalon**
   (*a*) **Cerebral cortex**
   Analysis of sensory input (primary sensory areas).
   Memory development (temporal lobe).
   Storage of short-term information (temporal and frontal lobe).
   Analysis and control of muscle coordination (superior temporal gyrus and frontal lobe).
   Speech (temporal lobe).
   Hearing (superior temporal lobe).
   Vision (occipital lobe).
   (*b*) **Corpus striatum**
   (Caudate nucleus, putamen, globus pallidus)
   Planning, programming, and modulation of motor movement.
   Control of muscle tone.
   (*c*) **Corpus callosum**
   Interconnects the two hemispheres of the cerebral cortex, providing functional integration.
2. **Diencephalon**
   (*a*) **Thalamus**
   Relay centre of discrimination of incoming sensory stimuli (pain, temperature, touch).
   Modulation of motor impulses from cerebral cortex.
   Integration of emotional behaviour.
   (*b*) **Hypothalamus**
   Regulation of cardiovascular function.
   Regulation of electrolytes and body water.
   Regulation of temperature.

Regulation of food intake and satiety.

Control of endocrine function.

Control of sleep-wake mechanisms.

Modification of behaviour.

II. MIDBRAIN

1. **Mesencephalon**

(*a*) **Corpora quadrigemina** (superior and inferior colliculus)

Relay centres for hearing and visual reflexes.

(*b*) **Cerebral peduncles**

Control of motor coordination and postural reflexes.

(*c*) **Red nucleus**

Regulation of motor functioning.

(*d*) **Substantia nigra**

Regulation of motor functioning.

III. HINDBRAIN

1. **Metencephalon**

(*a*) **Cerebellum**

Coordination of muscle activity (synergia).

Maintenance of posture and equilibrium.

(*b*) **Pons**

Relay centre for impulses from medulla to higher cortical centres.

Regulation of respiration.

2. **Myelencephalon**

(*a*) **Medulla Oblongata**

Control of respiration and cardiovascular function.

Regulation of some reflex activities (salivation, swallowing, vomiting).

Modulation of gastrointestinal function.

To sum up, the brain has three major divisions – the **hindbrain** (myelencephalon, metencephalon), the **midbrain** (mesencephalon), and the **forebrain** (diencephalon, telencephalon). The hindbrain runs from the top of the spinal cord into the midbrain, and includes the **medulla oblongata** and the **pons** (the most primitive part of the brain). These form the **brainstem** on which the **cerebrum** seems to be balanced. Above and behind the brainstem is the **cerebellum.**

Functions of the CNS

Cerebral Cortex

The cerebral cortex contains sensory, motor and association areas that receive information, which is processed and signals are transmitted to appropriate parts of the body along effector neurones. The **association areas** are the most highly evolved and sophisticated areas of the cerebral cortex. They establish relationship among the many sensory inputs the cortex collects, interpret and integrate information from all other parts of the CNS. As outlined earlier, the **association areas** are responsible for the highest mental activities, namely, **memory, reasoning, judgement** and **imagination.** The cerebral cortex is also responsible for the integration of the autonomic nervous system, and provides a link between the somatic and vegetative functions of the body, including the cardiovascular and gastrointestinal systems.

Basal Ganglia

The *basal ganglia* comprise three areas in the forebrain – the *caudate nucleus, putamen,* and *globus pallidus* – as well as several areas in the midbrain, such as the *substantia nigra, red nucleus, and subthalamic nucleus.* These structures are responsible for the integration and regulation of locomotor activity and postural reflexes. Pathologic changes in these gangila result in the appearance of many movement disorders like **parkinsonism,** in which there is a marked deficiency of dopamine in the basal ganglia.

Limbic System

The main group of brain structures controlling emotional behaviour is collectively termed as the *limbic system.* It consists of several subcortical areas **(thalamus, hypothalamus, olfactory** and **pyriform lobes, hippocampus, amygdala, septum, preoptic area, portions of the basal ganglia),** and a surrounding ring of cortical tissue on the medial and ventral surfaces of each cerebral hemisphere **(Fig. 2.1.3).** The limbic system regulates many aspects of behaviour, like feelings of *pleasure, anger, rage and fear.* It also regulates *biological rhythms, sexual activity, feeding* and *learning.*

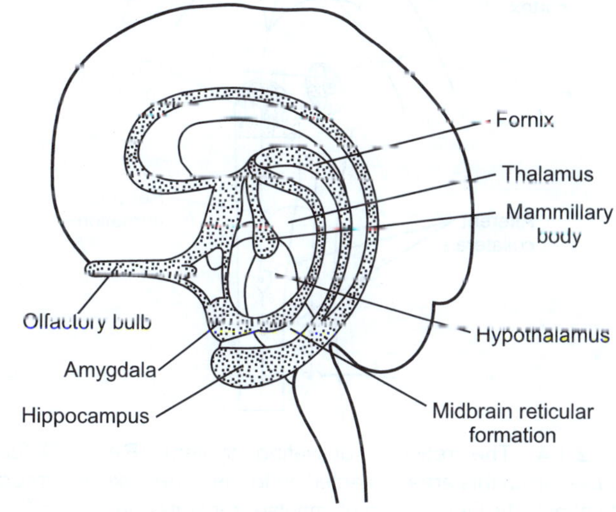

Fig. 2.1.3: The limbic system (see text).

Drugs used in the treatment of emotional disorders (antipsychotics, antidepressants, anxiolytics, antimanics) exert at least a part of their action on the components of the limbic system.

Reticular Formation

The *reticular formation* is a diffuse network of cells and nuclei scattered throughout the brainstem and extending upwards into the midbrain. The mesencephalon, pons and medulla oblongata connect the cerebral hemispheres and thalamus-hypothalamus to the spinal cord. These *bridge portions* of the CNS contain most of the nuclei of the cranial nerves, as well as the inflow and outflow tracts from the cortices and the spinal cord. The term ascending **reticular activating system** (RAS) is often used with reference to these structures. It is believed that information from effector organs is transmitted via the *spinothalamic tract* to thalamic nuclei, and then to the cortex. At the same time signals are relayed via afferent collaterals to the reticular formation, and then to thalamic relay nuclei, and ultimately to the cortex **(Fig. 2.1.4).** The RAS possibly provides the *missing link* between the classical sensory pathways of the brain, and many nonspecific behavioural phenomena like alertness, arousal, sleep and attention.

Functionally, the RAS serves to arouse the cortex, and maintain a state of *alertness or arousal.* Depression of the RAS results in sedation and loss of consciousness, and deep irreversible coma results from injury or destruction of the RAS. The function of the RAS is very susceptible to many classes of drugs like **barbiturates, anaesthetics** and **antipsychotics.**

Thus, the *basal ganglia, limbic system* and the *reticular formation* function as integrated systems to control certain aspects of behaviours.

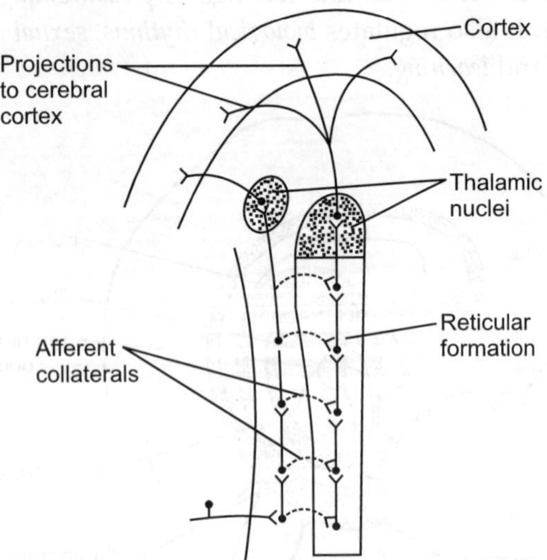

Fig. 2.1.4: The reticular activating system (RAS). Diffuse impulses from this area projected on to the cortex excite cerebral cortical activity. Depression of impulse transmission via the RAS reduces alertness and wakefulness (see text).

Electroencephalogram (EEG)

The EEG is a tracing of changes in voltage that are generated by the brain. Many studies of the effect of drugs on the CNS have made use of the EEG, and in man it is often the only method available for monitoring the level of excitation of the brain. To record the EEG, electrodes are placed over various areas of the scalp, and activity of the underlying region of the cortex is recorded. These cortical tracings also reflect activity in subcortical structures, which is however modified by the activity of the cortex. By means of electrodes implanted subcortically, recordings can be made from specific sites within the CNS. Recording from single neural units in the brains of animals is possible by means of **microelectrode techniques.**

Basic Neuroscience

The functional unit of the CNS is the **neurone.** CNS neurones, like those in the periphery, are capable of receiving and transmitting information from other neurones, and peripheral end organs like muscle cells, glandular cells, and specialized receptors involved with proprioception and temperature sensing.

The **depolarization** associated with an action potential causes the release of a specific chemical substance at the **synapse** between two neurones. This chemical substance *(neurotransmitter)* on release, diffuses across the **synaptic cleft,** and causes a change in the ionic composition of the second neurone. This change in ionic composition results in a local altered potential difference in the second neurone, and is known as the **postsynaptic potential.** The direction of the potential change may be either *depolarizing* or *hyperpolarizing.* A depolarizing postsynaptic potential is called an **excitatory postsynaptic potential** (EPSP), and if its magnitude is great enough, an action potential is produced in the second neurone, which is then transmitted in an all-or-none manner through the neurone and its processes. On the other hand, a hyperpolarizing postsynaptic potential is known as an **inhibitory postsynaptic potential** (IPSP), and it inhibits the production of a depolarizing action potential in the second neurone.

It is generally accepted that the **synaptic vesicles** serve as storage sites for transmitter substances, and that each neurone releases only one neurotransmitter. However, recent evidence indicates that many neurones may release more than one transmitter.

Synaptic transmission between neurones can be affected by altering the levels of the neurotransmitter in the presynaptic neurone. This can be achieved by agents which: *(i)* **block or enhance the biosynthesis** of the neurotransmitter; *(ii)* **block or enhance the metabolic degradation** of the neurotransmitter; or *(iii)* **alter the re-uptake and re-utilization** of the neurotransmitter in the presynaptic terminals. In some cases it is possible to alter the neurotransmitter release by activating **presynaptic receptors** (autoreceptors) which are located on the presynaptic membrane of the synapses **(Chap. 3.1).**

CNS NEUROTRANSMITTERS

The accepted criteria that a substance must fulfil before it can be designated as a *neurotransmitter* substance are :

1. The transmitter substance must be present in the presynaptic terminals.
2. It must be released into the synaptic cleft when the nerve is stimulated.
3. At the postsynaptic membrane the transmitter must cause a local depolarization (excitation), or hyperpolarization (inhibition).
4. Direct application of the transmitter to the neurone must mimic the effect of nerve stimulation.
5. There must be a mechanism present at site for the synthesis, and removal or inactivation of the transmitter.
6. Specific antagonists must block the synaptic action.

A large number of CNS neurotransmitters have been either tentatively or positively identified. They may be considered under two main heads :

I. Fast Point-to-point Signalling

(*i*) **Acetylcholine** (nicotinic effects)

(*ii*) **Amino acids**

(*a*) Glutamate

(*b*) Aspartate

(*c*) Gamma-aminobutyric acid (GABA)

(*d*) Glycine

II. Slow Diffuse Regulatory Signalling

(*i*) **Neuropeptides**

(*a*) Substance P

(*b*) Met-enkephalin

(*c*) Leu-enkephalin

(*d*) Angiotensin II

(*e*) Somatostatin

(*f*) Leuteinizing hormone releasing hormone (LHRH)

(*g*) Calcitonin gene-related peptide (CGRP) and others

(*ii*) **Monoamines**

(*a*) Dopamine

(*b*) Noradrenaline

(*c*) Adrenaline

(*d*) Serotonin (5-HT)

(*iii*) **Acetylcholine** (muscarinic effects)

(*iv*) **Histamine**

Acetylcholine (ACh) is mainly excitatory in the brain. It was the first compound to be identified as a transmitter in the CNS. Eccles in the early 1950s showed that excitation of **Renshaw cells** by motor axon collaterals in the spinal cord was blocked by nicotinic antagonists. Further, these Renshaw cells were extremely sensitive to nicotinic agonists. This is the best example of a central nicotinic synapse. The excitatory effects of ACh on central neurones are usually mediated via muscarinic receptors and may involve suppression of a voltage-sensitive K-conductance. This inhibition increases the excitability of the cell.

Cholinergic neurones are particularly abundant in the basal ganglia, and others are involved in cortical **arousal** responses and in **memory.** Hence, atropine-like drugs can impair memory, and this action is made use of in *anaesthetic premedication.* They are also used for their central actions in **motion sickness** and **parkinsonism.** It has been found that presenile dementia of the Alzheimer type is associated with selective loss of cholinergic neurones.

AMINO ACIDS

Glutamate and Aspartate excite almost all central neurones. Possibly some neurones use glutamate and others aspartate. Currently some experimental glutamate antagonists are being studied. No therapeutic agent is known so far to produce its effect by acting at excitatory amino acid synapses.

Gamma-aminobutyric acid (GABA) is present in all areas of the CNS, mainly in local inhibitory interneurones. It promptly inhibits central neurones when applied locally by iontophoresis. The response is mediated by receptors, which are blocked by **bicuculline** and are called $GABA_A$ receptors. Some GABA receptors ($GABA_B$) are not blocked by bicuculline, but are stimulated by the antispastic drug *baclofen.* The physiological function of $GABA_B$ receptors is unclear.

A neuronal GABA receptor has been identified, and when coupled with GABA, induces a shift in membrane permeability, primarily to chloride, causing a *hyperpolarization* of the neurone.

Drugs which are thought to act by modifying GABAergic synaptic transmission include the **benzodiazepines, barbiturates, beta-carbolines, alcohols, valproate** and **general anaesthetics.** Several CNS convulsants like bicuculline, picrotoxin and pentylenetetrazol are antagonists at the GABA receptor. GABA agonists include muscimol, isoguvacine and THIP. At present, these compounds have found no clinical use.

Glycine is another inhibitory CNS neurotransmitter. Whereas, GABA is primarily located in the brain, glycine is found predominantly in spinal interneurones (ventral horn). Glycine is antagonized by **strychnine,** and its release is prevented by **tetanus toxin,** thereby both substances cause convulsions.

Neuropeptides appear to possess the essential characteristics of neurotransmitters, i.e., their release in Ca^{2+} dependent; they are localized in specific neurones; and their release induces changes in the postsynaptic neuronal systems.

The most widely studied of these putative peptide neurotransmitters (or neuromodulators) are the **endorphins** which exhibit pharmacological properties similar to morphine, and can bind to "morphine receptors" in the brain. There are several endogenous peptides that occur naturally in the brain, and mimic the properties of morphine, but the most prominent of them are **met-enkephalin, leu-enkephalin, beta-endorphin,** and **dynorphin**.

Other peptides present in the brain, and the gut as well also appear to possess neurotransmitter properties, e.g., **vasoactive intestinal peptide** (VIP), **cholecystokinin** (CCK) and **gastrin.** Evidence is accumulating that substances termed as hypothalamic-releasing hormones are actually functioning as neurotransmitters.

MONOAMINES

The **catecholamines** generally have **inhibitory** effects when applied locally onto central neurones.

Dopamine among the catecholamines, is the most important neurotransmitter in the CNS, while noradrenaline and adrenaline are important biogenic amine neurotransmitters in the peripheral sympathetic nervous system. Dopamine pathways project from the **substantia nigra** in the midbrain to the **basal ganglia,** and from the midbrain to the **limbic cortex** and other limbic structures. A third, **tuberoinfundibular** pathway is involved in the regulation of prolactin secretion. The **nigrostriatal pathway** is concerned with modulating the control of voluntary movement and its degeneration results in *parkinsonism.* The **mesolimbic pathway** is "overactive" in *schizophrenia* but the reason is unclear. *Dopamine agonists* are used in the treatment of parkinsonism **(Chap. 2.11),** and *antagonists* or *neuroleptics* are used in schizophrenia **(Chap. 2.8).**

Noradrenaline containing cell bodies are located in the brainstem. Most central noradrenergic neurones are located in the nucleus *locus coeruleus* of the pons and in the *reticular formation.* Fibres from these nuclei innervate a large number of cortical, subcortical and spinomedullary areas. Functions ascribed to noradrenergic neurones include learning and memory, sleep-wake cycle and a role in affective disorders. Impairment of noradrenergic function is associated with depression **(Chap. 2.8).** Noradrenaline and dopamine in the limbic forebrain are involved in an ascending 'reward' system.

Adrenaline is found only in very low concentration in the mammalian CNS. It is of minor importance in the brain, but innervation of the nucleus *tractus solitarius* may play an important role in central *blood pressure control.*

Serotonin (5-hydroxytryptamine) is localized in the **raphe nuclei,** and considerable amounts are also present in the **hypothalamus,** the **limbic system,** the **brainstem,** and the **pituitary gland.** In humans, about 90 percent of the total serotonin in the body is in **enterochromaffin cells** in the gut, and the remaining 10 percent is primarily in the platelets and brain. Current evidence indicates that serotonin is involved in the regulation of several aspects of behaviour, sleep/wake cycle, temperature control, pain perception, depression, sexual activity, aggressiveness, and hypothalamic control of the release of pituitary hormones.

Histamine occurs in the brain, particularly in certain **hypothalamic neurones,** and evidence is strong that histamine is a neurotransmitter. Depolarization of hypothalamic slices causes a calcium-dependent release of histamine. There is uneven distribution of **histamine,** its synthetic enzyme **histidine decarboxylase,** and its major brain metabolite **methyl histamine.** A possible role of histamine in regulation of food and water intake, thermoregulation, and hormone release has been suggested.

BLOOD-BRAIN BARRIER

It has been long known that not all substances present in the bloodstream can readily gain entry into the brain. Organic dyes injected intravenously into animals, could stain all tissues except the brain, which remained *schneeweiss* (snow-white). However, this apparent barrier to drugs is *relative* rather than *absolute.*

The term **blood-brain barrier** (BBB) is usually applied to the lack of passage of certian drugs, or other exogenously administered chemicals into the brain. The brain capillaries differ in several respects from capillaries in other body locations: (*i*) the endothelial cells of brain capillaries are so closely joined to each other that passage of substances does not readily occur through intercellular clefts; (*ii*) brain capillaries have fewer fenestrae (pores); (*iii*) brain capillaries possess very few pinocytotic vesicles (these vesicles play a role in the transport of large molecules through capillary walls); and (*iv*) brain capillaries contain many more mitochondria compared to other capillaries. These mitochondria supply energy for active transport of water-soluble nutrients into the brain like glucose, amino acids, and purines.

An important property which determines the entry of substances from systemic circulation to the brain is the **molecular weight.** Compounds with molecular weights of 60,000 and above tend to remain outside the brain. Furthermore, agents that are *lipid-soluble,* and *unionized* at physiologic pH, and *bind poorly to plasma proteins,* diffuse more readily across the BBB. The BBB serves primarily to preserve the internal environment of the brain and prevent sudden increase in concentration of a variety of water-soluble ionized substances. In the human foetus and newborn, the barrier is not as well developed as in later life.

Broadly speaking, drugs acting on the CNS may be classified as: (*i*) **General depressants** which are capable of depressing the entire nervous tissue, e.g., *general anaesthetics, sedatives* and *hypnotics;* (*ii*) **Selective depressants** which alter certain specific central functions when given in doses that do not cause general depressions of the CNS, e.g., *anticonvulsants, narcotic analgesics, major tranquillizers, anxiolytics, antiparkinsonian drugs* and *analgesic-antipyretics;* and (*iii*) **CNS stimultants** which increase the general excitability of the CNS, e.g., *amphetamines, caffeine, analeptics* like *pentylenetetrazol* and *nikethamide* (which act directly), and *monoamine oxidase inhibitors* (MAOIs) and tricyclic antidepressants (which act indirectly).

2.2 ALCOHOL AND ALCOHOLISM

Production of alcohol needs only a few basic ingredients: these are **sugar, water, yeast** and a **warm atmosphere.** In fact, alcohol is produced by fermentation of almost anything with a high carbohydrate content. It is formed naturally by yeast fermentation of starch and sugar in fruits, grains, potatoes or sugarcane, and in many countries the law only permits naturally formed alcohol to be used for human consumption. **Ethanol** (ethyl alcohol, grain alcohol) for industrial use is produced mainly by organic synthesis from ethylene. **Alcoholic beverages** have been used as nutritious foods, medicines and sacred liquids for religious ceremonies. Alcohol drinkers can be divided into three groups: (*i*) **Social drinkers** who consume a limited amount only at social functions, and generally do not become intoxicated; (*ii*) **Social heavy drinkers** who drink in excess at social functions and commonly become intoxicated. About one-half of such drinkers become alcoholics; and (*iii*) **Alcoholics** who drink in excess habitually to the detriment of their health, and their socioeconomic situation.

Alcohols and Alcoholic Beverages

All alcohols have the general formula (R-OH). The hydroxyl (-OH) group is responsible for the characteristic properties of the alcohol family. The R-group determines the rate at which the alcohol undergoes certain reactions, and at times also the type of reactions that occur. The **aliphatic** alcohols form a homologous series beginning with **methanol** (methyl alcohol); **ethanol** (ethyl alcohol); **n-propanol; isopropanol** etc. The first three are readily soluble in water in all proportions, but as the carbon chain length increases, water solubility decreases, and *octanol* (8 carbons) is almost insoluble. In ethanol the hydroxyl and ethyl moieties confer both **hydrophilic** and **lipophilic** properties to the molecule. Thus, ethanol is an **amphophile,** a property important to its pharmacological activity. The higher alcohols and methanol are mainly used in industry. The general term *alcohol* is used in chemistry to designate a class of compounds that are hydroxy derivatives of aliphatic hydrocarbons. However, in this Chapter when the term *alcohol* is used without additional qualification, it indicates ethyl alcohol (ethanol).

Alcoholic beverages mainly contain ethanol (concentration varies with the type of preparation), used for human consumption. Traces of higher alcohols, aldehydes, and esters are also present, which lend different alcoholic beverages their distinctive tastes and aromas. The terms *beverage* stands for a liquor for drinking. All alcoholic beverages are produced by the process of fermentation. This process of fermentation stops when alcohol concentration is high enough to inhibit yeast. In the presence of water, yeasts convert the sugar (glucose) of plants into alcohol as under:

$$\underset{\text{(Glucose)}}{C_6H_{12}O_6} + \xrightarrow{\text{Yeast}} \underset{\text{(Ethanol)}}{2C_2H_5OH} + \underset{\text{(Carbon dioxide)}}{2CO_2}$$

Distillation can further increase the alcohol concentration greatly, and the law sets limits on the content which may be sold. The "Proof" figure expresses the standard of strength for alcoholic content of distilled beverages (Whisky, Rum, Vodka) and is almost twice the percentage of alcohol by volume, e.g., 100 *proof* whisky contains 50 percent v/v alcohol by volume **(Table 2.2-1)**

Table 2.2-1 *Alcohol content of alcoholic beverages*

BEVERAGE (type or source)	*PERCENT ALCOHOL by volume (V/V)*	*PROOF*
Neutral spirits	90 – 95	180 – 190
Vodka (from neutral spirits)	40 – 55	80 – 110
Gin (from neutral spirits)	40 – 45	80 – 110
Whisky (from cereal grains)	40 – 45	80 – 110
Rum (from molasses)	40 – 55	80 – 110
Brandy (from wine)	40 – 55	80 – 110
Wine (table, light)	10 – 12	–
Wine (dessert)	15 – 22	–
Cider (hard)	8 – 12	–
Ale	6 – 8	–
Beer (light)	3 – 6	–

Ethanol (Ethyl Alcohol)

Pharmacokinetics

Absorption

Ethanol (CH_3CH_2OH) is a water soluble molecule, and is rapidly and almost completely absorbed throughout the gastrointestinal tract. About 80 percent is absorbed from the small intestine. The rate of absorption is determined by the quantity of ethanol consumed, the concentration of ethanol in the beverage, the rate of consumption, and the composition of the gastric contents. On an empty stomach, most of the ingested alcohol is absorbed into the blood within 30-60 minutes. On oral administration alcohol can be detected within 5 minutes in the blood, and peak levels are attained within half to 2 hours. Individuals show great variation in the speed of absorption, and those habituated to alcohol show a steeper and higher peak.

Distribution

The **distribution** of alcohol is throughout the body water. The rate of distribution to specific parts depends on the degree of vascularization. In organs of high blood flow, like the **brain, liver, lungs** and **kidneys,** equilibrium occurs rapidly. The uniform distribution of alcohol throughout the body is of practical legal importance. Tests for drunkenness generally involve an analysis of blood, the *expired air* or the urine for their alcohol content. At equilibrium, the blood ethanol is about 77 percent of that of urine, and about 2000 times that of expired air. Generally, a blood alcohol concentration of 0.10 percent (100 mg%, 100 mg per 100 ml of blood) is considered the level at which the person is *legally drunk.* Alcohol readily crosses the placental barrier.

Metabolism

Over 90 percent of the alcohol consumed is completely oxidized in the liver, the remainder being eliminated through the lungs and in small amounts in the urine. Unlike most other substances, the rate of oxidation of alcohol follows **zero-order kinetics,** which means that a constant amount of alcohol is metabolized irrespective of time and the concentration of the drug. The *average* rate at which alcohol is metabolized is about 10 ml/hour, but this rate can vary, depending on body weight, the presence of liver dysfunction, or metabolizing enzyme alterations.

The alcohol breakdown reaction in the liver consists of three steps:

(*i*) **Hepatic oxidation of alcohol to acetaldehyde.** The major pathway is *rate limited by cytoplasmic alcohol dehydrogenase* (a zinc-containing enzyme), using the hydrogen acceptor nicotinamide adenine dinucleotide (NAD) as coenzyme. This reaction is slow and determines the speed at which alcohol is removed from the body, and is termed as the **rate limiting step.** In addition, alcohol is metabolized to acetaldehyde by the *microsomal enzymes* using NADPH as cofactor, and a minor pathway involving *catalase* which oxidises ethanol in the presence of a hydrogen peroxide generating system **(Fig. 2.2.1).**

(*ii*) **Conversion of acetaldehyde to acetate** is catalysed by the enzyme *aldehyde dehydrogenase.*

(*iii*) The acetate formed enters the **Kreb's tricarboxylic acid cycle** producing energy (7 KCal per gram of ethanol). Later, it is converted to carbon dioxide and water. Carbon dioxide leaves the body in the exhaled air.

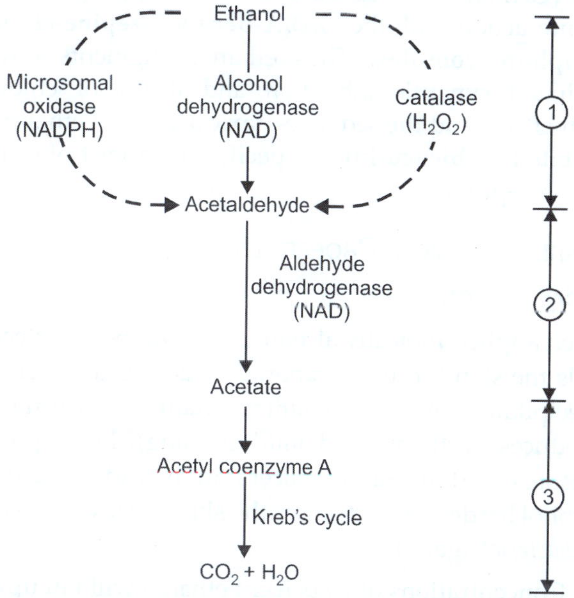

Fig. 2.2.1: Metabolic pathways of ethanol oxidation.

Certain findings suggest that the rate of enthanol elimination exhibits a circadian rhythm, being lowest around 8 a.m. and fastest at about 9 p.m. (the 'cocktail hour'). An increase in alcohol oxidation is observed in chronic alcoholics due to an **induction** of microsomal ethanol oxidation activity.

Excretion

Normally, 90 to 98 percent of an ingested dose of ethanol is metabolized by the liver. Most of the remaining 2 to 10 percent is excreted unchanged in the urine and exhaled air. The ethanol content in the urine is about 130 percent of the blood concentration, and the expired air contains about 0.05 percent of the blood ethanol level, and both these levels are fairly constant. As mentioned earlier, measurement of ethanol in the breath is used in law for ascertaining the degree of drunkenness.

Mode of Action

Ethanol probably exerts its action on the brain by dissolving in **neuronal plasma membranes,** rather than by acting on a specific receptor. Ethanol, because of its **amphophilic** (having both hydrophilic and lipophilic activity) properties can readily partition into lipids despite its high aqueous slubility. This property ethanol shares with many volatile anaesthetic agents, and is referred to as the **membrane-fluidizing effect.** Once ethanol dissolves in lipid membranes, it disturbs the function of ion channels and other proteins embedded therein. This disrupts important cellular functions. Ethanol appears to block the normal movement of *sodium* and *calcium* ions. They are responsible for the generation of electrical impulses and the release of neurotransmitters. The movement of *chloride* ions, specially that stimulated by gamma-aminobutyric acid (GABA), is enhanced by ethanol, and this involves its interaction with the **GABA-benzodiazepine-chloride ionophore complex.** Thus ethanol augments GABA-mediated synaptic inhibition and fluxes of chloride. Such effects and the sedative-ataxic actions of ethanol are inhibited by **bicuculline,** a specific antagonist of GABA-ergic receptors.

Pharmacological Properties

Local Actions

When applied topically alcohol has a number of effects. It cools the skin through evaporation; acts as an astringent (precipitates protein), **counterirritant,** or **rubifacient** (produces erythema and mild burning); helps prevent bedsores and decubitus ulcers in bedridden patients (alcohol hardens and cleanses the skin; serves as a general *antibacterial* agent.)

Concentrations of 70 percent ethanol will kill upto 90 percent of surface bacteria within 2 minutes if the area is kept moist. When injected around a nerve, ethanol can cause neuritis and **nerve degeneration.** Such a procedure can be employed to treat severe pain of **trigeminal neuralgia.**

Systemic Actions

Central nervous system. Alcohol is primarily a CNS depressant, and the degree of depression is directly proportional to the quantity of ethanol consumed. The "stimulation" which is frequently noted in the initial stages of alcohol consumption is the result of a depression of the brain areas which ordinarily exert inhibitory control over psychomotor activity and behaviour. This stimulation is expressed as decreased social and psychological inhibitions in the person. As blood ethanol levels increase, behavioural activation, characterized by **euphoria, talkativeness, aggressiveness** and a loss of behavioural control occur. Progressive depressant effects of alcohol range from sedation and decreased anxiety to ataxia, slurred speech, altered judgement, coma and death **(Table 2.2-2).**

Table 2.2-2. *Behavioural effects of ethanol associated with increasing blood ethanol concentrations*

Blood concentration	*Nature of effect*
<50 mg/dl	Increased sociability; euphoria
50-100 mg/dl	Disturbances in gait
	Lack of concentration
	Increased reaction time
100-150 mg/dl	Ataxia
	Impaired mental and motor skills
	Impaired short-term memory (STM)
	Slurred speech
200 mg/dl	No response to sensory stimuli
250 mg/dl	Coma
500 mg/dl	Death

Chronic ingestion of alcohol may lead to serious neurological disorders ranging from memory loss, reduced perceptual activity, emotional and sleep disorders to psychotic behaviour (Korsakoff's psychosis).

Cardiovascular system. In moderate amounts, alcohol causes vasodilation, specially of the cutaneous vessels, probably due to a mild central vasomotor depression. Myocardial contractility is reduced, and excessive ingestion can lead to **congestive heart failure.** Cardiotoxic effects are in part due to accompanying nutritional deficiencies and acetaldehyde. **Elevated triglyceride levels** are noted in chronic alcoholics, however, small to moderate amounts can elevate the levels of high-density lipoproteins (HDL), which have a protective action by aiding in the clearance of cholesterol.

Gastrointestinal system. Small amounts of alcohol stimulate secretion of gastric juice and hydrochloric acid. High concentration of alcohol on prolonged consumption results in inflammation of the gastric mucosa and development of *gastritis.* Gastrointestinal bleeding can lead to blood loss and anaemia. Impaired absorption of nutrients and vitamins (specially water-soluble vitamins) can lead to *malnutrition* and vitamin deficiencies. Chronic alcohol ingestion increases the risk of *pancreatitis.* Chronic alcohol ingestion also leads to accumulation of fat in hepatic parenchymal cells, hepatitis and ultimately *cirrhosis.* Malnutrition and vitamin deficiencies also contribute to **alcoholic liver damage.**

Endocrine system. Gynaecomastica and testicular atrophy have been noted in alcoholics. It is a popular belief that alcohol is an *aphrodisiac.* Aggressive sexual behaviour is often evident after alcohol, as a result of loss of inhibition and restraint. However, objective measurements reveal that alcohol significantly decreases sexual responsiveness in both men and women. **Impotence** and **sterility** are potential consequences of prolonged alcohol consumption.

Musculoskeletal system. Alcohol significantly **impairs psychomotor performance** and **blunts reflex motor activity.** Ethanol is a smooth muscle relaxant, and its myometrial relaxant action may be used to suppress *premature labour.*

Other systems. Alcohol has a diuretic effect, proportional to the blood alcohol level, and presumably due to inhibition of release of the antidiuretic hormone (ADH) from the posterior pituitary.

Chronic alcohol ingestion increases the risk of certain types of cancer, notably oropharyngeal, laryngeal, oesophageal, hepatic and possibly pancreatic.

Excessive alcohol consumption during pregnancy, specially during the first trimester, can lead to foetal abnormalities (teratogenesis), the so-called **foetal alcohol syndrome.**

Therapeutic Uses

Ethanol has little therapeutic value, although it has been suggested as being useful in the treatment of many ailments.

External uses. Application of alcohol to the skin has a cooling effect with evaporation, and alocohol sponges are sometimes used to **lower fever.** Alcohol solutions may be used as rubbing agents to prevent **decubitus ulcers** in bedridden patients, although such treatment is currently discouraged, as it leads to drying and scaling of the skin; as **skin disinfectant** prior to injection, blood sampling and other invasive needle procedures (optimal strength for this purpose is 70 percent by volume); as an ingredient of **anhidrotic** and **astringent** lotions to decrease sweating.

Local uses. Injection of dehydrated alcohol around the nerves or ganglia is used for relief of chronic, intractable pain e.g., pain of **trigeminal neuralgia,** or **inoperable carcinoma.** Inhalation of **ethanol mist** has been used as an **antifoaming** agent to collapse the foam obstructing the tracheobronchial tree in **acute pulmonary oedema** secondary to **left heart failure**.

Systemic uses. Ingestion of alcohol has limited application as a **sedative, hypnotic, analgesic, antipyretic** or even as a stomachic to act as an **appetizer.**

Drug Interactions

Ethanol can interact with other drugs in four distinct ways: (*i*) produce **additive** pharmacological action, e.g., CNS depression; (*ii*) **inhibit the metabolism** of another coadministered drug; (*iii*) have its own metabolism inhibited by a coadministered compound; and (*iv*) induce a **cross tolerance** with other drugs, specially after chronic use. A list of drugs that can interact with alcohol is presented in **Table 2.2-3.**

Adverse Reactions

Acute Ethanol Intoxication

Patients with severe intoxication present disturbances of the sensorium in degrees which vary with the blood alcohol levels. Most patients recover with only residual **hangover.** An additional feature of intoxication is **hypothermia,** specially in the elderly. If the coma continues for 8 to 10 hours hypostatic pneumonia or increased intracranial pressure may occur. The skin is cold and clammy, pupils normal or dilated, and the respiration is depressed and noisy.

Treatment. The treatment is essentially *supportive* and consists of maintaining respiration; blood pressure and body temperature until the ethanol has been

Table 2.2-3. *Drug-Alcohol interactions*

Drug	*Effects of simultaneous use of alcohol*
Anticoagulants	Increased likelihood of bleeding
Anticonvulsants	Decreased anticonvulsive effectiveness
Antidepressants	Decreased antidepressant action; raised blood pressure
Antihistamines	Increased drowsiness
Antihypertensives	Increased blood pressure lowering action; reduced drug effectiveness in chronic alcoholics
Diuretics	Increased hypotension and diuresis
CNS Stimulants (e.g., caffeine)	Reduced stimulatory effect
Hypoglycaemics	Interference with control of diabetes; increased hypoglycaemia
Narcotic analgesics	Increased drowsiness, respiratory depression, and motor impairment
Sedative-hypnotics	Increased CNS depression
Salicylates and other anti-inflammatory drugs	Increased gastrointestinal distress and bleeding
Vitamins	Decreased utilization of most vitamins

removed by metabolism or by **haemodialysis.** There is no effective remedy for hangover. Administer **hypertonic mannitol** solution intravenously, if intracranial pressure is raised. Regulate **fluid** and **electrolye balance.** The **phenothiazines** or **butyrophenones** may be needed to control psychotic behaviour.

CHRONIC ETHANOL ABUSE

Alcoholism is among the major health problems in many countries. Why alcoholism develops readily in some individuals than in others is not known. There is evidence that alcoholism may be, partly, genetically determined.

Chronic alcoholism produces tolerance and ultimately dependence. **Tolerance** with repeated use is a complex process, involving several mechanisms like *accelerated metabolism*, and central **neuronal receptor adaptation** to the continued presence of alcohol. Both, **psychological** and **physical dependence** can occur. On reduction in the amount consumed, or sudden cessation of drinking, a characteristic **withdrawal syndrome** may begin within 6 to 8 hours. The withdrawal progresses through several stages, as under :

Stage I: Onset of nausea, vomiting, sweating, tremors and hyperactivity.

Stage II: Increased severity of above *with* auditory or visual hallucinations and seizures (grand mal, nonfocal).

Stage III: Delirium tremens (DTs), profound confusion, disorientation and extreme autonomic hyperactivity.

A number of organs are affected adversely by chronic ethanol use as a result of a **direct cytotoxic action.** Hepatic fatty infiltration and **cirrhosis** are common in alcoholics; cancer may develop in advanced stages of hepatic disease. Progressive malnutrition and vitamin deficiency occur, and may contribute to cirrhosis. **Alcoholic cardiomyopathy** has been reported with nonspecific ECG abnormalities, cardiomegaly, biventricular heart failure, and associated mural thrombi. Ethanol causes **chronic gastritis** and **constipation.** Other pathological findings include **pancreatitis, peripheral neuropathy,** and **gonadal failure** in both men and women, accompanied by low blood levels of sex hormones.

The CNS involvement includes **Wernicke's encephalopathy** and **Korsakoff's psychosis.** The encephalopathy is characterized by mental confusion, ataxia and polyneuropathy as a result of thiamine dificiency. Thiamine treatment reverses the disorder. Patients with Korsakoff's phsychosis have learning and memory disabilities. Ethanol readily passes across the placenta causing the **foetal alcohol syndrome** with microcephaly, prenatal growth deficiency and short palpebral fissures.

Treatment of alcoholism. The immediate concern is often *detoxification* and management of the *withdrawal syndrome.* **Multivitamin supplements** are helpful in combating dietary deficiencies. **Benzodiazepines** are the drugs of choice for suppressing the withdrawal syndrome. Additional treatment requires complete **abstinence, psychiatric treatment** and support from organization like the **Alcoholics Anonymous** (AA).

ALCOHOL DETERRENT DRUGS

Both the deterrent drugs – *disulfiram* and *citrated calcium carbimide* – are used in the *aversion therapy* of alcoholism, as adjuncts to supportive emotional rehabilitation.

DISULFIRAM

Disulfiram (tetraethylthiuram disulphide) is an antioxidant which blocks the oxidative metabolism of ethanol at the acetaldehyde stage **(see Fig. 2.2.1).** In fact, it **interferes with the metabolism of acetaldehyde by inhibiting aldehyde dehydrogenase.** Thus when ethanol is ingested even in small amounts by an individual who has previously taken disfulfiram, there is a 5- to 10-fold increase in blood acetaldehyde levels, and this leads to unpleasant symptoms known as the **disulfiram reaction** or **acetylaldehyde syndrome** or **mal rouge.** It is a classic example of a drug interaction employed for the management of properly motivated chronic alcoholics who desire to free themselves from the abuse. The disulfiram-alcohol reaction consists of flushing, nausea, sweating, thirst, throbbing in the head, dyspnoea, weakness, vertigo, blurred vision, confusion and syncope. With large amounts of alcohol serious adverse reactions like congestive heart failure, arrhythmias, respiratory depression, convulsions and even death can occur. A similar sensitization to alcohol is produced by the hypoglycaemic **sulphonylureas, metronidazole, griseofulvin, phenothiazines** and **animal charcoal.** In the absence of alcohol, disulfiram produces virtually no effects.

Pharmacokinetics. Disulfiram is rapidly and completely absorbed from the gut. Optimal effects appear within 8 to 12 hours, and persist upto 2 weeks on withdrawal of medication, as the drug is highly lipid-soluble and localizes in fatty tissue. The elimination is slow, and the drug is excreted in the urine.

Therapeutic use. Disulfiram is used in the adjunctive treatment of **chronic alcoholism** with proper motivation and behavioural therapy.

Dosage. Administered orally in a single daily dose of 500 mg for 1 to 2 weeks. Once the patient has fully recovered, a maintenance dose of 125 to 500 mg per day may be used until the patient feels no compulsion to drink.

Adverse reactions. Usual side effect encountered in the absence of alcohol is transient drowsiness. Other adverse effects include headache, restlessness, skin eruptions, optic or peripheral neuritis, metallic taste, impotence, fatigue, tremor and occasionally psychosis.

Contraindications and interactions. Disulfiram is absolutely contraindicated in the presence of severe myocardial disease, coronary occlusion, psychoses, and pregnancy. **Caution** should be observed in patients with diabetes, hypothyroidism, cirrhosis, nephritis, epilepsy or cerebral damage. Notable interactions are: disulfiram potentiates the effects of diazepam, chlordiazepoxide, oral anticoagulants and phenytoin; with **metronidazole** and **isoniazid** behavioural changes and psychotic reactions can occur; **paraldehyde** is partially metabolized to acetaldehyde and may add to the toxic reactions produced.

Citrated Calcium Carbimide (Abstem)

It is a mixture of 1 part of calcium carbimide, and 2 parts of citric acid. It has similar actions to disulfiram, although milder and of a shorter duration. Alcohol deterrents are dangerous drugs, and should be used with extreme caution and under strict supervision.

Methanol

Methanol (methyl alcohol, wood alcohol, CH_3OH) is the simplest aliphatic alcohol. It has no therapeutic use, but is widely used commercially as an industrial *solvent*, as an ethanol **denaturant,** and as a **fuel.** Methanol has pharmacological properties similar to ethanol. It is sometimes consumed accidentally or as a substitute for ethanol, often with disastrous results (blindness, coma and death).

Methanol is readily absorbed and distributed throughout the body. It is metabolized at about one-seventh the rate of ethanol and is largely oxidized to *formic acid.* In humans, methanol is predominantly metabolized by **alcohol dehydrogenase.** Methanol toxicity appears to be primarily due to the formation of *formic acid,* and direct toxic action of **formaldehyde.**

Methanol is a generalized CNS depressant, but less potent than ethanol. After an initial acute intoxication, there is a period of 8 to 36 hours in which the patient is asymptomatic A severe **acidosis** then develops, and is followed by optic damage that can lead to partial or total blindness.

Treatment of methanol poisoning involves counteracting the **acidosis** by **infusion of sodium bicarbonate** (about 3 gm/hr) until the urine pH reaches 7.5. Although acidosis itself is not responsible for retinal damage, it is likely that retinal damage and bindness are caused by a product of methanol metabolism, probably formic acid. Since ethanol and methanol are metabolized by the same enzyme (alcohol dehydrogenase), and toxicity of methanol is related to its metabolites, ethanol administration has been used in the treatment of methanol poisoning. Ethanol has a higher affinity for alcohol dehydrogenase than does methanol, and is preferentially metabolized by the enzyme. This reaction prevents the formation of the toxic metabolites of methanol, thereby allowing time for methanol to be excreted unchanged.

Isopropanol and Other Alcohols

Isopropanol (isopropyl alcohol) is used as a rubbing alcohol. Higher-chain alcohols like **butanols** and **pentanols** are more toxic than ethanol, but are rarely involved in poisoning.

The **dihydroxyalcohols** (glycols) like **propylene glycol** are used as solvents for many drugs and cosmetics. **Ethylene glycol** was formerly used as a solvent for drugs, but caused several deaths. Hence it is not employed medicinally. Deaths have also occurred from ingestion of antifreeze mixture containing ethylene glycol.

2.3 GENERAL ANAESTHETICS

- **Objectives of General Anaesthesia**
- **Stages of General Anaesthesia**
- **Mechanisms of General Anaesthesia**
- **Adjunctive Anaesthetic Medication**
  - **Preanaesthetic Medication**
  - **Medication during Anaesthesia**
  - **Postoperative Medication**
- **Classification**
  - **Inhalation Anaesthetics**
    - **Gases: Nitrous Oxide, Cyclopropane, Ethylene**
    - **Volatile Liquids: Ether, Halothane, Enflurane, Isoflurane, Methoxyflurane**
  - **Intravenous Anaesthetics**
    - **Ultrashort-acting Barbiturates: Thiopental, Methohexital, Thiamylal**
    - **Non-barbiturate Hypnotic: Etomidate**
    - **Dissociative Agents: Ketamine, Fentanyl/Droperidol (Neuroleptanalgesia, Neuroleptanaesthesia)**

Alcohols and opiates were used for centuries to suppress the pain of surgical procedures. It was in the middle of 1800s that the first demonstrations of drug-induced general anaesthesia using volatile liquids **chloroform** and **diethyl ether** were reported. Later, the anaesthetic properties of *nitrous oxide gas,* originally suggested by Priestley in 1776, were revealed. However, the modern age of anaesthesia began with the introduction of the intravenous barbiturate, **thiopental** in the 1930s, and the skeletal muscle relaxant **d-tubocurarine** about a decade later. The term **"balanced anaesthesia"** is applied to the practice of using two or more anaesthetics together with other ancillary medications (e.g., anticholinergics, muscle relaxants, anxiolytics) to provide smooth induction, sufficient depth and duration, adequate muscle relaxation, decreased tracheobronchial secretions, and minimal danger to vital body systems.

Objectives of General Anaesthesia

General anaesthetics are CNS depressants that are used to bring about a **reversible loss of pain sensation and consciousness.** The goals of general anaesthesia are: (*i*) **analgesia;** (*ii*) **loss of consciousness,** in which the patient is unaware of what is going on, and is later totally unable to recall what took place, i.e., **amnesia;** (*iii*) **loss of reflexes** to minimize laryngospasm, cardiac arrhythmias, salivation, vomiting, and postoperative abdominal distension; and (*iv*) **skeletal muscle relaxation,** which is often desirable during abdominal surgery.

Stages of General Anaesthesia

As the degree of general anaesthesia deepens, a series of physiologic changes occur, which provide an indication of the depth of depression of the CNS. Traditionally, these changes have been categorized into **four** stages. This classical pattern described by Guedel in 1920 applies to *diethyl ether,* a drug having a slow onset of action, and thus exhibiting a distinct separation between the various stages. In modern anaesthesiology, however, the distinctive signs of each stage are frequently obscured, because many newer agents have a very *rapid onset of action* and quickly bypass the early stages.

Stage I: Analgesia

Stage I lasts until consciousness is lost. The *analgesia* produced persists postoperatively as ether is lipid-soluble, and continues to be released slowly from tissue stores. With supplemental muscle relaxation surgery can be done in such a relatively awake patient under "ether analgesia".

Stage II: Excitement

Stage II begins with the loss of consciousness, and ends with the beginning of rhythmical respiration, i.e., surgical anaesthesia. This stage is most difficult to manage, since the patient may move, vocalize, salivate, cough, retch, and vomit. Modern drugs allow patients to pass through this stage rapidly, reducing these hazards.

Stage III: Surgical Anaesthesia

Stage III is further divided into *four* planes, and begins with the appearance of rhythmical respiration and ends with apnoea (cessation of respiration).

Plane 1. It begins with reappearance of regular respiration. Patient behaviour is characterized by loss of automatic eyelid closure, and loss of reflex closure of eyelids upon conjunctival stimulation. Most muscular and airway reflexes are obtunded. This plane ends with cessation of eye movement.

Plane 2. This plane begins with the cessation of eye movement, and ends with the beginning of paralysis of the respiratory muscles, excluding the diaphragm.

Plane 3. This plane begins with increased abdominal excursions, and ends with paralysis of all respiratory muscles, except the diaphragm.

Plane 4. This plane begins with the cessation of intercostal muscle movements, and ends with diaphragmatic paralysis.

Stage IV: Apnoea

Stage IV begins with complete respiratory paralysis and ends with failure of circulation. It is considered as the stage of overdosage, and the medullary centres are completely paralyzed. The heart and circulation fail, and the amplitude of the EEG waves becomes smaller, and eventually all electrical activity disappears. Vigorous and prompt resuscitative measures, and administration of oxygen by mechanical means may help revive the patient.

During **recovery** from deep anaesthesia, the patients reflexes return in reverse order from that in which they were lost.

Mechanisms of General Anaesthesia

The general anaesthetics produce a *progressive depression* of the CNS. The degree of depression depends on the concentration of the drug in the CNS.

An important site of action of general anaesthetics is the reticular formation in the brainstem. They preferentially depress the **ascending reticular activating system** (RAS), which is concerned in maintaining alertness and wakefulness. These drugs progressively **reduce sensory awareness,** and when a sufficient concentration of the anaesthetic is reached, consciousness is lost.

Several theories have been provided to explain the mechanism of action of general anaesthetics, but no single theory adequately explains the effects observed with diverse agents. General anaesthetics do not have a specific receptor to act upon as is true for many other drugs. In short, the **conformational distortion theory** postulates that the physical presence of the anaesthetic molecules within the nerve membrane distorts the conformation of the membrane and impedes ionic flow through the channels. The **decrease in sodium influx reduces neuronal excitability and slows the rate of rise of the nerve action potential.** The **Meyer-Overton theory** correlates the potency of a general anaesthetic with its lipid-solubility, i.e., the more lipid-soluble a drug is, the greater is its anaesthetic potency.

The **hydrate or water crystal theory** was proposed in early 1960s, and states that the anaesthetic agent reacts with the water in brain tissue to form hydrates or **microcrystals of ice** which inhibit nerve cell functioning, probably by coating the neuronal membrane and impeding ion exchange. A number of **biochemical theories** have been advanced, like inhibition of glucose metabolism in brain cells, to block production of high-energy phosphate compound (ATP), and to impair oxygen utilization and cellular respiration. Therefore, the precise mechanism as to how general anaesthetics act still remains unknown.

Adjunctive Anaesthetic Medication

Production of safe and efficient general anaesthesia depends to a great extent on the proper preparation of the patient.

Preanaesthetic Medication. Premedication is defined as the administration of drugs before the anaesthetic is given. The main aims are: (*i*) **Relief of anxiety** (anxiolytics, e.g., diazepam, midazolam); (*ii*) **Reduction in salivary and mucous secretions** (anticholinergics, e.g., atropine, hyoscine, glycopyrrolate); and (*iii*) **Inhibition of undesirable side effects** (e.g., bradycardia and muscle spasms) occurring reflexly in response to the anaesthetic agent. **Anti-infective agents** like cefazolin or metronidazole may be administered before and for a short period after certain types of surgery, e.g., vaginal hysterectomy and cesarean section.

Medication during anaesthesia. Drugs given during the surgical procedure depend upon the type and length of the operation, and the condition of the patient. **Neuromuscular blocking agents** are administered during the operation while the patient is still at a light level of anaesthesia. Muscle relaxants like **succinylcholine, pancuronium,** and **gallamine** are given to provide an additional degree of skeletal muscle relaxation, and thereby allow a lower dose of the general anaesthetic to be used, reducing the incidence of adverse reactions.

Postoperative medication. The main indications for the use of drugs postoperatively are to relieve: (*i*) nausea and vomiting by **antiemetics** (e.g. prochlorperazine); (*ii*) abdominal distention and urinary retention by **cholinergics** (e.g. bethanechol); (*iii*) pain by analgesics (e.g., pethidine) and (*iv*) constipation by **laxatives** and stool softeners (e.g., docusate, bisacodyl). **Anticholinesterase drugs** may be used postoperatively to antagonize neuromuscular blockade **induced by drugs like d-tubocurarine.**

Judicious use of **anxiolytics, anticholinergics, skeletal neuromuscular relaxants** and **antiemetics** can greatly facilitate induction and maintenance of anaesthesia, and an uneventful recovery with minimal adverse effects.

Classification

The general anaesthetics may be classified as under:

I. Inhalation anaesthetics

(*a*) *Gases* (Nitrous oxide, Cyclopropane, Ethylene)

(*b*) *Volatile liquids* (Ether, Halothane, Enflurane, Isoflurane, Methoxyflurane)

II. Intravenous anaesthetics

(*a*) *Ultrashort-acting barbiturates* (Thiopental, Methohexital, Thiamylal)

(*b*) *Non barbiturate hypnotic* (Etomidate)

(*c*) *Dissociative agents* (Ketamine, Fentanyl/ Droperidol)

Inhalation Anaesthetics

The properties of an *ideal* inhalation anaesthetic are that: (*i*) it should be free from toxic effects, with a wide margin of safety; (*ii*) it should be nonirritant, free from unpleasant taste and smell, act rapidly and produce pleasant induction with smooth recovery without unpleasant symptoms of nausea and hangover; (*iii*) the potency should be high so that adequate amounts of oxygen can be administered with the anaesthetic; (*iv*) for control of depth of anaesthesia, the agent should be rapidly acting and rapidly eliminated from the body; (*v*) from the surgeon's viewpoint the agent should produce complete muscle relaxation and should not increase capillary bleeding; and (*vi*) the agent should be cheap and stable on storage. A typical anaesthetic sequence for major surgery is: induction with a basal anaesthetic like **thiopental,** maintenance of unconsciousness with an inhalation anaesthetic like **nitrous oxide with oxygen,** and production of muscle relaxation with a neuromuscular blocker like **d-tubocurarine.**

The inhalation anaesthetics include *gases* and *volatile* liquids. Both types enter the circulation rapidly on absorption from the alveoli of the lungs. From the blood the agent is transferred to the brain. Eventually most inhalation agents are returned to the lungs and excreted in exhaled air mostly unchanged. However, halothane and methoxyflurane are metabolized in the liver to a significant extent. The factors that determine the rapidity and efficiency of this transfer are the *lipid-solubility* of the drug, its *concentration* in inspired air, the pulmonary *ventilation rate* and *blood flow,* and the *blood gas partition* coefficient. As it is not possible to measure the anaesthetic concentration in the brain tissue directly, *a frequently used measure of anaesthetic potency is the minimum alveolar concentration (MAC).* It is *defined* as the concentration of anaesthetic in the pulmonary alveoli which prevents response to painful stimuli (e.g., incision) in 50 percent of patients. The lower the MAC, the more potent is the anaesthetic drug. Simultaneous use of sedatives or other preanaesthetic medications lowers the effective MAC **(Table 2.3-1).** In general, most surgery is performed between 0.8 and 1.2 times the MAC. A potential danger with most of the potent, lipid-soluble inhalation anaesthetics is **malignant hyperthermia,** an acute condition characterized by a sudden, drastic elevation of body temperature that is often fatal unless treated promptly and vigorously.

Gases

Three gases (nitrous oxide, eyclopropane, ethylene) are available for use, and of these nitrous oxide is used most extensively. A total anaesthetic regimen includes *other anaesthetics, sedatives, narcotics, anxiolytics* and *muscle relaxants.* Such a regimen, termed **balanced anaesthesia,** produces rapid induction with minimal adverse effects.

Nitrous Oxide (N_2O)

Nitrous oxide (laughing gas) is an inorganic general anaesthetic commonly used as a component of "balanced anaesthesia" and as a supplement to more potent inhalational anaesthetics. It is a nonexplosive inert gas that supports combustion, displays a *rapid onset* of action and a *short duration* of action. It is a *poor muscle relaxant,* and due to its lack of potency, can induce only a very light plane of anaesthesia. It cannot elicit sufficient depth of anaesthesia to allow surgical procedures when used alone. *Hypoxia* results if concentration of nitrous oxide is greater than 80 percent. So at least 20 percent oxygen has to be provided whenever nitrous oxide is used.

Uses. Nitrous oxide is used for: (*i*) *Induction* of anaesthesia; (*ii*) *Supplemental maintenance* of general anaesthesia; and (*iii*) *Production of analgesia* for minor surgical or dental procedures.

Administration. It is given by inhalation, in oxygen mixture. For *analgesia,* 20 to 50 percent of N_2O is used in brief surgical or dental procedures, or in obstetrics. For rapid induction of anaesthesia, concentrations of 80 percent or occasionally higher may be given for short periods of time.

Table 2.3-1. *Salient characteristics of inhalational anaesthetics*

Drug	*Minimum alveolar concentration (MAC)* %*	*Onset of anaesthesia*	*Muscle relaxation*
Gases			
Nitrous oxide	>100**	Rapid	Fair
Cyclopropane	10	Rapid	Fair
Ethylene	80	Rapid	Poor
Volatile Liquids			
Halothane	0.75	Rapid	Fair
Enflurane	1.68	Rapid	Good
Isoflurane	1.2	Rapid	Good
Methoxyflurane	0.16	Slow	Fair/Good
Ether	2.0	Slow	Excellent

* MAC = Minimum alveolar concentration of anaesthetic agent (in percent) that prevents a response to surgical incision in 50 percent of patients; serves as a measure for comparison of potency among general anaesthetics; lower the MAC, the more potent the drug.

** MAC of greater than 100 percent indicates that not even one MAC can be attained at normal barometric pressure; thus nitrous oxide is the least potent general anaesthetic.

Fate. Onset of anaesthesia is rapid, duration of action is short. Excretion is almost entirely by exhalation.

Adverse reactions. Patients may experience dizziness, vivid dreams, and hallucinations. Serious hypoxia, cyanosis, convulsions and bone marrow depression may occur. High concentrations of N_2O may result in vomiting, myocardial and respiratory depression, and death. Diffusion hypoxia can occur at the termination of N_2O anaesthesia if the patient abruptly begins to breathe room air. This problem can be avoided by administration of 100 percent oxygen for a short period on termination of N_2O anaesthesia. Because of its high partial pressure in blood and its low blood gas partition coefficient, N_2O diffuses into air-containing body cavities. This can lead to distension of the gut, expansion or rupture of pulmonary cysts, and pneumoencephalus.

Cyclopropane

Cyclopropane is an anaesthetic gas which has a *rapid* onset of action and a wide margin of safety. It produces *satisfactory analgesia* and *skeletal muscle relaxation* in full anaesthetic doses. Due to its explosive nature, it must be administered in a **closed rebreathing system** with oxygen. Respiratory irritation is minimal, occasionally laryngospasm may occur, and blood pressure is well maintained during anaesthesia. Cyclopropane sensitizes the myocardium to the arrhythmogenic effects of catecholamines, and this may cause sudden death. Postoperative nausea, vomiting and headaches occur frequently. **Malignant hyperthermia** has been associated with cyclopropane. This drug is *obsolete* today.

Ethylene

Ethylene is a highly volatile gas, produces rapid induction and recovery, exhibits low toxicity, and possesses a wide margin of safety. It is slightly more potent than nitrous oxide, but unlike N_2O, it is highly explosive, and has an unpleasant odour. As more potent and less hazardous general anaesthetics are available today, the use of ethylene has been given up.

Volatile Liquids

They are administered by *inhalation of the vapours* given off by the liquid, along with adequate amounts of oxygen. The *depth* of *anaesthesia* can be controlled fairly well by varying the concentration, as these agents are generally short acting.

The first volatile liquid to be used was *diethyl ether,* and for many years it was the preferred inhalational anaesthetic. Currently, however, *ether is obsolete,* as more potent, more rapid acting, and safer anaesthetics are available.

Ether (Diethyl Ether)

It has a good safety margin, excellent skeletal muscle relaxing ability, minimal effects on the cardiovascular system, and substantial analgesic effect. Its **disadvantages** included noxious odour, slow and unpleasant induction, respiratory irritation, prolonged emergence, extreme flammability, increased salivary and bronchial secretions. There is a high incidence of postoperative nausea and vomiting. As the disadvantages outweigh the advantages ether is rarely used currently.

Ether is occasionally used where sophisticated patient-monitoring equipment is not available. The various stages of ether anaesthesia **(Table 2.3-1)** are well delineated. Concentrations of 5 to 10 percent are used to induce anaesthesia, and maintenance is possible with 3 to 5 percent concentration.

Halothane

Halothane is a potent, non-flammable, pleasant smelling volatile liquid anaesthetic, and is one of the most widely used anaesthetics. It is non-irritating to the lungs, dilates the bronchioles, and does not increase salivary or bronchial secretions. Skeletal muscle relaxation is only fair, and as such an additional skeletal muscle relaxant is almost always used. **Nitrous oxide** is often used concomitantly to reduce the concentration of halothane needed. Halothane is a myocardial depressant, and cardiac output, contractile force, and blood pressure are decreased. Furthermore, halothane sensitizes the myocardium to the arrhythmogenic effects of catecholamines. Respiratory depression, apnoea, hypoxia and acidosis may develop during deep anaesthesia, requiring controlled ventilation. Postanaesthetic nausea and vomiting are rare.

Uses. Induction and maintenance of general anaesthesia.

Dosage. Halothane is commonly administered for induction and maintenance of general anaesthesia by closed, inhalation, with either oxygen or a mixture of nitrous oxide and oxygen. The concentration for induction is 1 to 4 percent, and for maintenance it is 0.5 to 1.5 percent.

Fate. Induction and recovery are rapid. Elimination is primarily via the lungs.

Adverse reactions. Halothane produces rapid, shallow respiration, slight fall in blood pressure and transient bradycardia. *Cardiac arrhythmias* can be precipitated in the presence of catecholamines. *Hepatitis* is a rare but potential complication, possibly due to a hypersensitivity reaction due to one of the metabolites of halothane. **Malignant hyperthermia** occurs rarely with halothane use.

Precautions. Halothane should not be used for obstetrical anaesthesia, because it is a potent uterine relaxant. Other *contraindications* are active hepatic and biliary disease, and its combination with catecholamines.

Interactions. Halothane potentiates the action of non-depolarizing skeletal muscle relaxants (gallamine, pancuronium) and also ganglionic blockers. It prevents the uterine response to oxytocics like ergometrine and oxytocin.

ENFLURANE

Enflurane is a potent anaesthetic, widely used today for many surgical procedures. Induction and recovery are rapid, and the drug is non-flammable. Salivary and bronchial secretions are increased. Enflurane produces better muscle relaxation, and less myocardial sensitization to catecholamines than halothane. It causes profound respiratory depression. Liver damage has been reported.

Uses. Induction and maintenance of general anaesthesia, usually in combination with nitrous oxide and/or minimal amounts of skeletal muscle relaxants.

Dosage. For *induction* concentrations of 2 to 4.5 percent for 7 to 10 minutes is adequate. Surgical levels of anaesthesia are maintained with concentrations between 0.5 to 3 percent.

Fate. It is excreted largely (85 to 90%) through the lungs, the remainder is metabolized by the liver and excreted via the kidney.

Adverse reactions. Slight hypotension may occur, and shivering can occur during emergence. CNS stimulation can occur with prolonged use, resulting in spasms, tremors and convulsions.

Precautions. Enflurane should be used with caution in patients with impaired renal function, epilepsy and cardiac arrhythmias. *Interactions* are of a similar nature as observed with halothane.

ISOFLURANE

Isoflurane is structurally similar to enflurane, but with several advantages. It has a rapid onset and quick recovery. It **does not sensitize the heart to catecholamines and produces good muscle relaxation.** CNS excitation is minimal, but respiratory depression may be significant. The blood pressure progressively decreases with depth of anaesthesia.

Isoflurane is used for the induction and maintenance of general anaesthesia. *Dosage:* Induction 1.5 to 3 percent for 5 to 10 minutes; maintenance 1.0 to 2.5 percent with nitrous oxide. **Fate:** Induction and recovery are rapid; less than 1 percent is metabolized; primarily excreted through the lungs.

Adverse reactions. Mild hypotension is occasionally noted during administration. Other untoward reactions include respiratory depression, tachycardia, and rarely malignant hyperthermia. Isoflurane should be administered *cautiously* in patients with respiratory or cardiac failure.

METHOXYFLURANE

With a MAC of 0.16 percent, methoxyflurane is the most potent anaesthetic available. It has a slow onset and recovery, and produces fair muscle relaxation and significant analgesia at light levels of anaesthesia. It induces minimal sensitization of myocardium to catecholamines and the incidence of arrhythmias is low. The drug is associated with liver and specially kidney damage due to the accumulation of free fluoride ion as a metabolic byproduct of methoxyflurane.

Uses. For *maintenance* of surgical anaesthesia of less than 4-hour duration, usually with nitrous oxide and oxygen. Also for *production of analgesia* in obstetrics and minor surgical procedures.

Dosage. To provide analgesia for minor surgical procedures, concentrations of 0.3 to 0.8 percent are given by inhalation. To *induce* anaesthesia concentrations upto 2 percent for 2-5 minutes are administered. Lower levels (0.1 to 2%) are then used to *maintain* anaesthesia, together with oxygen and 50 percent nitrous oxide.

Fate. Onset is slow, but analyesia occurs rapidly. Emergence is prolonged. Excretion is primarily through the lungs, but in the liver some metabolism occurs yielding free fluoride ions, which are nephrotoxic.

Adverse reactions. Slight hypotension, nausea and postoperative drowsiness occur. Respiratory depression, delirium, hepatic dysfunction, malignant hyperthermia, renal dysfunction and failure may occur. The potential **nephrotoxicity** is the major reason for the rather limited usage of methoxyflurane.

INTRAVENOUS ANAESTHETICS

The general anaesthetics administered IV include: (*i*) three **ultrashort-acting barbiturates** (methohexital, thiamylal, thiopental), mainly used for *induction* of anaesthesia and as sole anaesthetics for *short surgical procedures,* and to supplement other anaesthetic agents during longer procedures; (*ii*) a **rapid-acting non-barbiturate hypnotic,** *etomidate* used for induction and for supplementing other anaesthetics like nitrous oxide; (*iii*) two **dissociative anaesthetics** which can be administered IV or IM to induce a *neuroleptic-like* state, characterized by analgesia, quietude, and detachment from the environment without loss of consciousness. These two drugs, **ketamine,** and a combination of the narcotic **fentanyl** and the neuroleptic **droperidol** differ slightly in some of their properties, as discussed below.

ULTRASHORT-ACTING BARBITURATES

The **major advantages** of the IV barbiturates compared to inhalation anaesthetics are: (*i*) the rapidity and smoothness of onset; (*ii*) absence of salivation; greater patient acceptance, as there is no occlusive face mask; (*iii*) short duration of action, allowing better control; (*iv*) speedy recovery; (*v*) non-flammability; (*vi*) absence of bronchial irritation; and (*vii*) little danger of cardiac arrhythmias.

The **disadvantages** of IV barbiturates include: (*i*) higher incidence of respiratory and circulatory depression; (*ii*) laryngospasm; (*iii*) bronchospasm; (*iv*) the danger of tissue necrosis if leakage occurs; and (*v*) prolonged or repeated administration may result in cumulative toxicity as the drugs are eliminated slowly from the body. As there are many similarities among the *three* anaesthetic barbiturates they are discussed as a group.

Thiopental/Methohexital/Thiamylal

The IV barbiturates depress the CNS, producing hypnosis and anaesthesia without analgesia. Muscle relaxation is inadequate, even with deep anaesthesia. They cause a dose-dependent respiratory depression. Large doses directly depress the myocardium, decrease cardiac output and lower blood pressure. Hepatic blood flow and glomerular filtration rates are temporarily decreased.

Uses. The main uses are: (*i*) induction of anaesthesia; (*ii*) supplementation of other general anaesthetics; (*iii*) production of anaesthesia for short surgical procedures with minimal pain; (*iv*) induction of hypnosis; (*v*) control of convulsive state during and following general or local anaesthesia; and (*vi*) for **narcoanalysis** and **narcosynthesis** in psychiatric disorders (thiopental).

Fate. Induction is smooth and rapid. Onset occurs within 30-60 seconds of IV injection. They quickly cross the blood-brain barrier, and are then rapidly redistributed to other parts of the body, first to highly vascular organs and then to fatty tissue, where they are stored.

Adverse reactions. A dose-dependent respiratory depression occurs. Other side effects are laryngospasm, coughing, and yawning. Other unwanted reactions include myocardial and circulatory depression, thrombophlebitis, bronchospasm, headache, delirium, nausea, vomiting, allergic reactions, shivering and muscle twitchings.

Precautions. Absolute contraindications include latent or manifest porphyria, and absence of suitable veins for IV administration. Thiopental is contraindicated in status asthmaticus. *Caution* is to be observed in the presence of cardiovascular disease, bronchial asthma, hypotension, shock, hepatic and renal dysfunction, myxoedema, severe anaemia, increased intracranial pressure, and myasthenia gravis.

Nonbarbiturate Hypnotics

Etomidate

Etomidate produces rapid hypnosis following IV injection, but is not an analgesic. Its haemodynamic effects resemble those of thiopental, but the drug has little effect on heart rate, cardiac output, and peripheral circulation. Cerebral blood flow is slightly reduced. The intracranial and intraocular pressures fall. Respiratory depression is minimal.

Uses. Etomidate is used for induction of general anaesthesia; supplemental anaesthesia during short operations; and for prolonged sedation of critically ill patients.

Dosage. For induction 0.2 to 0.6 mg/kg IV over 30-60 seconds; *maintenance* 0.1 to 0.3 mg/kg IV in combination with nitrous oxide and oxygen.

Fate. Onset is within 1 minute, and effect persists for 3 to 5 minutes. It is rapidly metabolized in the liver and primarily excreted by the kidneys.

Adverse reactions. Hypotension, tachycardia, cardiac arrhythmias, laryngospasm, hiccups, postoperative nausea and vomiting can occur. Common side effects are venous pain, myoclonic skeletal muscle movements, tonic muscle acitivity and eye movements. Etomidate has embryocidal activity.

Dissociative Agents

Two drugs, **ketamine** and **fentanyl/droperidol** (Innovar) are used in certain situations when an anaesthesia-like state is desired, but unconsciousness would be disadvantageous. They differ in their actions and thus would be discussed separately.

Ketamine

Dissociative anaesthesia is a state in which the anaesthetized patient feels totally dissociated from the surroundings. Ketamine is a rapid-acting anaesthetic producing a state of **dissociation,** with profound analgesia, normal skeletal muscle tone and laryngeal reflexes, and variable cardiovascular and respiratory reflexes. The patient appears to be awake, but does not respond to pain and does not recall the experience on recovery (amnesia). The actions of ketamine are presumed to result from an **interruption of association pathways** in the brain. Ketamine has a *wide margin of safety* and is compatible with commonly used local and general anaesthetics. Emergence is prolonged and marked by psychological manifestations ranging from pleasant (dream-like state, vivid imagery) to disagreeable (nightmares, hallucinations).

Uses. Diagnostic and short surgical procedures not requiring muscle relaxation, e.g., treatment of burns. For *induction* of anaesthesia, and supplementation of low potency agents like nitrous oxide.

Dosage. Ketamine is available in three strengths (10 mg/ml, 50 mg/ml, 100 mg/ml) for IV and IM injection. For *induction,* doses are 1 to 4.5 mg/kg IV given over 60 seconds, or 6.5 to 13 mg/kg IM. To *maintain* anaesthesia one-half of the induction dose is repeated as needed.

Adverse reactions. Ketamine can cause numerous untoward reactions, and close patient monitoring is essential. Emergence reactions (detailed above) can be minimized by giving diazepam or a short-acting barbiturate.

FENTANYL/DROPERIDOL (INNOVAR)

Innovar is a drug combination containing a **narcotic analgesic** fentanyl, and a **neuroleptic** droperidol. The two are often used together to produce **neuroleptanalgesia,** a state in which consciousness is not lost, but the anxiety of the patient is allayed, and the ability to perceive pain is reduced or abolished. The addition of nitrous oxide to this combination produces **neuroleptanaesthesia.** Hypotension and bradycardia can occur.

Uses: Innovar is used for: (*i*) production of tranquillization and analgesia for diagnostic and minor surgical procedures; (*ii*) anaesthetic premedication and induction of anaesthesia; and (*iii*) adjunct for general anaesthesia in combination with nitrous oxide and oxygen.

Dosage. Innovar (1 ml contains 0.05 mg fentanyl and 2.5 mg droperidol).

Premedication: 0.5 to 2.0 ml IM 45 to 60 minutes before surgery; *Induction;* 1 ml/20-25 lb. body weight by slow IV injections; *Diagnostic:* 0.5 to 2.0 ml IM 45 to 60 minutes before the procedure.

Adverse reactions. Muscle rigidity, hypotension, slight respiratory depression and drowsiness have been reported following Innovar use. Delirium, hallucinations, laryngospasm, and bronchospasm may occur. The neuroleptic droperidol can induce extrapyramidal reactions.

2.4 SEDATIVE-HYPNOTICS AND ANXIOLYTIC DRUGS

The primary use of **sedative-hypnotics** and **anxiolytics** is to induce calmness (anxiolytics or sedatives), or to produce sleep (sedative-hypnotics). **Insomnia** is a common problem. It includes a wide variety of sleep disturbances, like difficulty in falling asleep, early or frequent awakenings, and remaining unrefreshed after sleep.

The **ideal** anxiolytic drug should calm the patient without causing too much daytime sedation and drowsiness, and should not produce psychological or physical dependence. Similarly, the **ideal** hypnotic drug should initiate and maintain sleep of sufficient duration and optimal quality so that the patient awakes refreshed without a "hangover". Ideal agents are not available as they have varying degrees of drawbacks.

Sleep Patterns

Normal sleep consists of two major phases, REM (rapid eye movement) and non-REM sleep, which occur cyclically over an interval of about 80 to 90 minutes **(Fig. 2.4.1)**. REM sleep covers about 20 to 25 percent of total sleep time, and during this most dreaming occurs. The REM phase is associated with rapid movement of the eyeballs, increased heart rate, irregular breathing, and other autonomic manifestations, e.g., increased secretions, and penile erection.

Non-REM sleep comprises 75 to 80 percent of total sleep time, and progresses through four stages (1-4), as the level of sleep deepens. The greatest proportion of sleep time (50-55%) is spent in stage 2, with only about 20 percent of sleep being spent in stages 3 and 4, where the brain waves (EEG) show their greatest amplitude and slowest frequency. The deeper phases of sleep occupy more of the early sleep cycles, whereas lighter sleep and REM sleep are more evident in the later sleep cycles. Children spend more time than adults in deep sleep, whereas the elderly spend relatively little time in deep sleep.

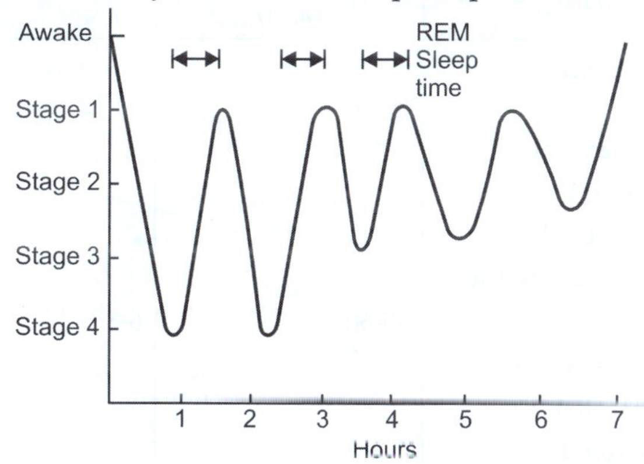

Fig. 2.4.1: Normal sleep cycles and the stages of sleep.

Many different drugs are capable of causing a dose-dependent CNS depression. In this Chapter we shall discuss the *sedative-hypnotics*, and the *antianxiety* drugs, which are mainly used in the management of insomnia and anxiety.

Sedative-hypnotics

The sedative-hypnotics are generally classified into two broad groups: **barbiturates**, derivatives of barbituric acid; and **non-barbiturates**, a group of drugs structurally unrelated to barbituric acid, but having many actions of barbiturates. The relative safety of the various sedative-hypnotics depends on the *slope* of their representative dose response curves. A **steep curve** indicates a narrow margin of safety, whereas a **shallower curve** indicates a wider margin of safety, i.e., there is a wider separation between the hypnotic and the toxic dose.

Barbiturates

Barbiturates are derivatives of malonylurea (barbituric acid), which is a condensation product of urea and malonic acid. Barbituric acid itself has no depressant action on the CNS. Changes in chemical structure that increase lipid-solubility speed up the onset of action, shorten the duration of action, and increase the hypnotic potency of the compound. When oxygen at C-2 position of oxybarbiturates is replaced with sulphur, it becomes a **thiobarbiturate,** a compound with enhanced lipid-solubility.

Barbiturates are valuable as **anaesthetics** and **anticonvulsants**. However, the **benzo-diazepines** have replaced the barbiturates as hypnotics, sedatives and anxiolytics. This is because the barbiturates are more hazardous; the hazards are proneness to dependence, frequency of death from overdose, and interactions with many other drugs.

Classification

Barbiturates have been traditionally classified, based on their duration of action as **long-acting, intermediate-acting, short-acting** and **ultrashort-acting** compounds **(Table 2.4-1)**.

The ultrashort-acting barbiturates are primarily used as intravenous general anaesthetics **(Chapter. 2.3)**. The remaining barbiturates have some minor pharmacokinetic differences, but possess essentially similar pharmacologic and toxicologic profiles. Their main actions are collectively reviewed below.

Pharmacological Actions

The barbiturates were used extensively in the past as sedative-hypnotic drugs, but currently except for a few specialized uses, they have been replaced by the *benzodiazepines,* which are much safer agents (see later).

1. **Sedation:** In low doses, barbiturates produce mild drowsiness, accompanied by decreased motor activity and a sense of well-being. This sedative action results primarily from a non-specific depression of the **reticular activating system** (RAS) in the brainstem. The level of sensory awareness of higher brain centres is governed by the RAS, and depression of RAS functioning by the barbiturates results in reduced alertness and blunted reaction to environmental stimuli, e.g., light, sound and touch.

Table 2.4-1 *Classification of barbiturates*

Drug	*Onset of action (min)*	*Peak effect (hrs)*	*Elimination Half-life (hrs)*	*Adult Oral Dose (mg)*	
				Sedative	*Hypnotic*
Long-acting					
	60-90	10-12	60-120*		
Mephobarbital					
Metharbital					
Phenobarbital				15-30 bid/tid	100-200
Intermediate-acting					
	45-60	6-8	15-40**		
Amobarbital				15-50 bid/tid	100-200
Aprobarbital				40 tid	40-160
Butabarbital				7-60 tid/qid	100-200
Talbutal				30 bid/tid	120
Short-acting					
	10-15	3-4	18-42		
Pentobarbital				20 tid/qid	100
Secobarbital				30-50 tid/qid	100
Ultrashort-acting					
	0-1	3-5 min	3-8	For IV general anaesthesia	
Methohexital				–	–
Thiamylal				–	–
Thiopental				–	–

* Values are for phenobarbital only.

** Values are for amobarbital, aprobarbital, and talbutal. Half-life for butabarbital is 3-5 days.

2. **Hypnosis:** An indication for most barbiturates is the relief of **temporary insomnia.** They induce sleep in a dose 3 to 4 times higher than the sedative dose. Sleep induced by barbiturates resembles normal stage 2 sleep in many ways: there is reduction in heart rate, blood pressure, respiratory rate, body temperature, basal metabolic rate, CNS activity and skeletal muscle tone. The *latency* of sleep onset is reduced, i.e., sleep occurs quickly, the duration of stage 2 sleep is increased, and REM sleep time is shortened. Deprivation of normal REM sleep is probably responsible for behavioural changes in chronic barbiturate users. Barbiturate withdrawal exhibits an increase in REM sleep time. This *REM rebound* results in nightmares and poor quality of sleep. Barbiturate use also has "hangover" effects such as daytime drowsiness, psychomotor impairment and depression. Thus, barbiturates are only indicated for **short-term relief of insomnia.**
3. **Anaesthesia:** The highly lipid-soluble, rapid-acting derivatives (methohexital, thiamylal, thiopental) are administered IV for induction of anaesthesia **(Chapter 2.3).** These agents quickly equilibrate into the brain, because it is highly vascular, and thereby induce a rapid loss of consciousness.
4. **Anticonvulsant activity:** The three long-acting compounds, **phenobarbital, mephobarbital** and **metharbital** are indicated in the therapy of **grand mal epilepsy** and **cortical focal seizures.** These drugs appear to have selective anticonvulsant activity, not present in other barbiturates, in doses which minimally affect the RAS. Phenobarbital is the preferred anticonvulsant.
5. **Respiratory depression:** Barbiturates exert a dose-dependent respiratory depression. Both, the respiratory drive and the rhythmic mechanisms are depressed. Large doses can severely depress the medullary respiratory centre.
6. **Enzyme induction:** Barbiturates, specially phenobarbital, can accelerate the functioning of hepatic microsomal enzymes, a process called *enzyme induction.* This results in increased metabolism, and hence decreased effectiveness of many drugs. Barbiturates, in fact, accelerate their own metabolism, and thus tolerance develops.

Other actions: Barbiturates selectively *depress transmission in sympathetic ganglia* producing hypotension. Amnesia (forgetfulness) may follow barbiturate use. *Aggressive behaviour* is sometimes observed in barbiturate abusers. The pharmacologic basis for the clinical uses of barbiturates is summarized in **Table 2.4-2.**

Mode of Action

Barbiturates depress the sensory cortex, reduce motor activity, and in higher doses, impair respiration and vasomotor function in the brainstem. The most sensitive area of the CNS to the action of the barbiturates is the **midbrain reticular formation,** where they elevate the threshold for electrical stimulation. This action depresses the firing rate of the neurones and cortical activation is decreased, leading to sedation and hypnosis. Neuronal activity in the limbic system and hypothalamus is also reduced by barbiturates. Facilitation of GABA (gamma-aminobutyric acid) activity in the brain, has been observed with barbiturates. At low doses, barbiturates either have a GABA-like action or enhance the effects of GABA. Barbiturates are less selective than benzodiazepines, which also have GABA-like actions (see later).

Table 2.4-2. *The pharmacologic basis for the clinical uses of barbiturates*

Pharmacological Actions	*Therapeutic Uses*	*Preferred Barbiturates*
Sedation	Anxiety states themselves and organic conditions involving other organ systems like the cardiovascular and gastrointestinal system	Amobarbital, butabarbital, pentobarbital, phenobarbital
Hypnosis	Insomnia; preanaesthetic medication (intermediate-acting agents at bedtime; short-acting drugs 1 hour prior to surgery)	Amobarbital, butabarbital, pentobarbital, secobarbital
Anticonvulsant activity	Grand mal epilepsy (long-acting drugs); control of acute convulsions in eclampsia, tetanus and overdoses of convulsant poisons (short-acting drugs)	Phenobarbital, mephobarbital, metharbital (long- acting), thiopental, pentobarbital, amobarbital (short-acting)
Anaesthesia (basal and general)	Rapid and pleasant induction of anaesthesia prior to other general anaesthetics; or a sole anaesthetic in short surgical operations and manipulative procedures	Thiopental, thiamylal, methohexital, hexobarbital
Analgesia	Combined with salicylates and other analgesics (not used alone)	Amobarbital, butabarbital, pentobarbital
Amnesia	In obstetrics to reduce memory of delivery pain	Pentobarbital
Disinhibition	In psychiatry, for narcoanalysis, narcosuggestion; narcosynthesis and narcotherapy	Thiopental, secobarbital, pentobarbital

Pharmacokinetics

Barbiturates are absorbed to varying degrees from the stomach, small intestine, rectum and IM sites. Absorption depends on factors like pH, presence of food, and the chemical form of the drug (acid or sodium salt). They readily cross the placental barrier, and concentrations in the foetal blood approach those in maternal blood. The duration of action of a barbiturate depends on: (*i*) its rate of hepatic degradation; (*ii*) its degree of lipid-solubility; and (*iii*) the degree of binding to serum proteins, which reduces renal clearance.

Long-acting barbiturates are metabolized mainly in the liver, by a slow oxidation of radicals at the C-5 position, producing more polar derivatives with low lipid-solubility. **Ultrashort-acting barbiturates** are highly lipid-soluble and have a rapid onset and short duration of action.

Barbiturates and their metabolites are mainly excreted via the kidneys. Alkalinization of the urine expedites the excretion of barbiturates with lower lipid-solubility like phenobarbital.

Therapeutic Uses

1. Infrequently used as **sedative** and **hypnotic** agents. Barbiturates have been replaced for this purpose by the benzodiazepines (see later).
2. Short-term treatment of insomnia (maximum 2 weeks).
3. Control of **acute convulsive states** (IV or IM). But in status epilepticus in adults the benzodiazepines are the drugs of choice.
4. Treatment of **grand mal epilepsy** (phenobarbital).
5. **Pre- and postoperative sedation.** Used infrequently as the benzodiazepines have replaced them.
6. Induction of anaesthesia, and brief minor surgical procedures (ultrashort-acting barbiturates).
7. Aid in psychoanalysis.
8. Management of **ketatonic** and **manic reactions.**
9. **Kernicterus.** Barbiturates raise bilirubin binding Y protein. Phenobarbital has been used in hyperbilirubinaemia and kernicterus.

Adverse Reactions

1. **Hangover** and drowsiness occur in the morning after barbiturate use, due to residual depression of the CNS.
2. **Effect on sleep.** Therapeutic doses produce satisfactory sleep for the first one or two weeks. Thereafter because of habituation, sleep is not readily induced and may result in insomnia and excessive dreaming. Barbiturates suppress REM sleep, and on withdrawal an **REM rebound** may occur.
3. **Respiratory depression** occurs with about 10 times the hypnotic dose.
4. **Paradoxical excitement.** In some patients (particularly in the elderly and debilitated) barbiturates produce restlessness, excitement and delirium paradoxically.
5. **Drug automatism.** It is a state of amnesia in which the patient takes repeated doses of barbiturates until *acute barbiturate poisoning* occurs.
6. **Hypersensitivity reactions** like asthma, urticaria, angioedema may occur sometimes.
7. **Barbiturate dependence.** On chronic use psychological and physical dependence can occur.
8. **Acute barbiturate overdosage.** Toxic doses of barbiturates vary considerably, and may be as low as 2 g. Acute poisoning results in marked respiratory depression (Cheyne-Stokes breathing), lowered body temperature, tachycardia, hypotension, oliguria, circulatory collapse and coma. **Treatment** consists of supporting respiration and circulation. With longer-acting barbiturates, **alkalinizing** the urine promotes excretion of the drug and diuresis. **Haemodialysis** or **peritoneal dialysis** is often needed. **Fluid replacement** should be undertaken. Emesis should only be induced in conscious patients; otherwise **gastric lavage** with **activated charcoal** may be attempted.

Contraindications

Barbiturates should be given cautiously in the presence of hepatic and pulmonary insufficiency. They are *contraindicated* in patients with chronic emphysema, cor pulmonale, myxoedema, renal failure, senile dementia, intermittent porphyria, and in patients with suicidal tendencies and predilection to drug abuse.

Drug Interactions

Barbiturates cause induction of the hepatic microsomal enzymes **(Chapter 1.8).** Thus they increase their own metabolism leading to *tolerance*. Additionally, there is an increased metabolism of drugs like *corticosteroids, oral anticoagulants, digitoxin, doxycycline, oral contraceptives, phenytoin, testosterone,* and many other drugs. Barbiturates potentiate the CNS depressant effects of alcohol, narcotic analgesics, antihistamines, anaesthetics, anxiolytics, central muscle relaxants and other sedative-hypnotics.

Nonbarbiturate Sedative-Hypnotics

The nonbarbiturates are a heterogenous group of drugs which are capable of producing sedation and sleep. The *benzodiazepine hypnotics* have several advantages over barbiturates, like absence of enzyme induction, little effect on REM sleep, and small abuse potential, and thus have become the most widely prescribed hypnotics.

Classification

Classification of nonbarbiturate sedative-hypnotics is difficult, as they have varied chemical structures. However, all agents possess the ability to produce a dose-dependent depression of the CNS. They can be listed as under:

1. *Benzodiazepine Hypnotics*
   Flurazepam, Temazepam, Triazolam
2. Chloral hydrate
3. Paraldehyde
4. Ethchlorovynol
5. Propriomazine

Benzodiazepine Hypnotics
Flurazepam
Temazepam
Triazolam

The three benzodiazepines, namely, **flurazepam, temazepam,** and **triazolam** are solely used for the short-term management of insomnia, and termed as *benzodiazepine hypnotics.* These three agents are seldom employed as daytime sedatives.

The **benzodiazepine hypnotics** and the barbiturates are equally effective for short-term treatment of insomnia. In contrast to the barbiturates and other nonbarbiturate hypnotics, the benzodiazepine hypnotics have several **advantages:** (*i*) wider margin of safety (shallower dose response curve); (*ii*) minimal REM sleep time reducing effect; and (*iii*) absence of enzyme-inducing effects. Thus, the benzodiazepines are the preferred hypnotics in most patients. However, the incidence of **psychological dependence** on benzodiazepines is increasing with their rising usage.

The benzodiazepine hypnotics differ in their pharmacokinetic properties **(Table 2.4-3).** Following withdrawal of these drugs after prolonged use rebound insomnia can occur.

Mode of Action

The basic mode of action of benzodiazepines is **facilitation** of the action of the inhibitory neurotransmitter GABA. The precise mechanism involved is not known, but the membrane permeability to chloride is increased leading to **hyperpolarization** (see later). The binding of GABA to its receptors is also enhanced by benzodiazepines. The site of action in the CNS appears to be **limbic system, thalamus,** and the **midbrain reticular formation.** This is in contrast to the barbiturates which act on higher cortical areas.

Use

Short-term (maximum 4 weeks) treatment of *insomnia.*

Pharmacokinetics

The oral absorption of all the three hypnotic benzodiazepines is good; sleep usually occurs within 15 to 45 minutes. Flurazepam has the fastest onset of action. It is converted to an active metabolite (N-desalkyl-flurazepam) with a half-life of 50 to 100 hours. Thus, it has the longest duration of action, and can produce a prolonged "hangover" effect. The drugs and their metabolites are mainly excreted in the urine.

Dosage

The usual dosages are presented in **Table 2.4-4.**

Adverse Reactions

Hypnotic doses of benzodiazepines frequently cause daytime drowsiness, lightheadedness, headache, dizziness, ataxia, and slight motor incoordination. Flurazepam causes "hangover" on repeated administration, and interferes with psychomotor performance like driving. Serious adverse reactions are rare, but include disorientation, slurred speech, memory impairment and depression. **Paradoxical reactions** like nervousness, irritability, tachycardia, sweating and nightmares have been recorded. **Tolerance** can occur. Benzodiazepine **dependence** is less severe than with barbiturates, but the withdrawal symptoms are similar to those noted with barbiturates and alcohol. Benzodiazepines are contraindicated in pregnant women as foetal damage has been reported with their use in early pregnancy.

Chloral Hydrate

Chloral hydrate is used as a mild sedative-hypnotic. It exerts a depressant action on the CNS with little involvement of the lower brain centres regulating respiration and blood pressure. The drug has negligible effects on REM sleep, and "hangover" effects are minimal.

Table 2.4-3. *Pharmacokinetic characteristics of benzodiazepine hypnotics*

Drug	*Onset of Sleep (min)*	*Elimination Half-life (hrs)*	*Protein Binding (%)*	*Active Metabolites*
Flurazepam	15-20	50-100*	97	Yes
Temazepam	30-45	8-12	98	No
Triazolam	15-30	2-4	90	No

* includes half-life of active metabolite.)

Table 2.4-4. *Dosage and characteristics of benzodiazepine hypnotics*

Drug	*Preparation*	*Adult Dosage Range (Oral)*	*Clinical Characteristics*
Flurazepam	Capsules-15, 30 mg	15-30 mg at bedtime	*Longest-acting benzodiazepine;* residual effects persist for days after stoppage, not recommended for children under 15 years.
Temazepam	Capsules-15, 30 mg	15-30 mg at bedtime	*Intermediate acting benzodiapine;* transient sleep disturbances after discontinuation; not recommended in children under age 18 years.
Triazolam	Tablets-0.125, 0.25, 0.5 mg	0.25 to 0.5 mg at bedtime	*Short-acting hypnotic;* minimal hangover; not recommended in children under age 18 years; rebound insomnia may occur.

Chloral hydrate is used in the treatment of **insomnia,** and for **preoperative** and **postoperative sedation.** It is available as capsules (250, 500 mg), syrup (250 mg/5 ml, 500 mg/5ml) and suppositories (324, 500, 648 mg). Capsules are given with a glass of water and should not be chewed or broken. The *hypnotic dose* in adults is 500 mg to 1 g 30 minutes before bedtime. In children 50 mg/kg upto 1 g is given in a single dose. One-half of the hypnotic dose is used for sedation.

Chloral hydrate is rapidly absorbed from the gut and converted to **trichloroethanol,** the active metabolite with a half-life of 4 to 12 hours. Trichloroethanol is converted in the liver and kidney to trichloracetic acid, which is highly protein bound, and slowly excreted in the urine.

Adverse reactions include gastric upset, unpleasant taste, lightheadedness, motor incoordination, and allergic skin reactions. Rarely the drug causes leucopenia, eosinophilia, delirium, confusion, nightmares and hallucinations. Chronic use can lead to *habituation* and *dependence.* Chloral hydrate is contraindicated in the presence of hepatic or renal impairment, and in women in labour as trichloracetic acid frees bilirubin from plasma albumin-binding sites, leading to *kernicterus.*

PARALDEHYDE

Paraldehyde is a polymer of acetaldehyde which causes a nonselective, reversible CNS depression. It is a rapid-acting hypnotic which is used IM or IV in a hospital setting for the emergency treatment of *convulsive states.* In therapeutic doses it has slight effect on respiration and blood pressure. It has no analgesic activity, and may elicit CNS excitation in the presence of pain.

It is used: (*i*) as a mild sedative and hypnotic; (*ii*) for emergency control of convulsions, associated with tetanus, eclampsia, status epilepticus, and poisoning by convulsant drugs; and (*iii*) for inducing sleep in children to facilitate EEG studies.

Dosage. Paraldehyde is available as a liquid for *oral* or *rectal* use, and for IM or IV injection as 1 g/ml. The recommended doses are as under :

Adults

Oral : 4 to 8 ml in milk or fruit juice.

Rectal : 10-20 ml with one to two parts of olive oil or isotonic saline.

IM, IV:

Hypnosis: 10 ml IM in 2 divided doses or 10 ml IV diluted with 200 ml 0.9 percent sodium chloride injection at a rate not exceeding 1 ml/min.

Sedation : 2-5 ml IM or 5 ml IV diluted with 100 ml of 0.9 percent sodium chloride injection at a rate not exceeding 1 ml/min.

Children

Hypnosis: 0.3 ml/kg IM.

Sedation: 0.15 ml/kg IM.

Adverse reactions. Oral paraldehyde has a disagreeable taste and a strong aromatic odour. Rectal administration may cause mucosal irritation. Other adverse reactions include skin rash, swelling and pain at injection site, nerve damage and metabolic acidosis. Prolonged use may result in addiction, which resembles alcoholism. It is **contraindicated** in patients with bronchopulmonary disease, hepatic insufficiency and severe GI ulceration. Parenteral doses should be drawn in a glass syringe as paraldehyde is incompatible with most plastics.

ETHCHLORVYNOL

Ethchlorvynol is a tertiary alcohol. In addition to its sedative-hypnotic properties, it possesses muscle relaxant and anticonvulsant activity. Its mechanism of action is not completely known, but it elicits an EEG pattern similar to that seen with barbiturates. The safety margin with ethchlorvynol is the same as with barbiturates. **Habituation** and **psychologic dependence** are frequent on chronic use. It is absorbed rapidly from the gut, with an onset of action in 30 minutes and a duration of action of 5 hours.

Ethchlorvynol is used for the short-term treatment of insomnia. It is given orally, as capsules (200, 500, 750 mg). The usual dose is 500 to 750 mg at bed time.

Propriomazine

Propriomazine is a phenothiazine derivative having sedative, antihistaminic and antiemetic effects. It is occasionally used as IV or IM in a hospital setting as a sedative to relieve preoperative anxiety, and as an adjunct to analgesics during labour. *Dosage* generally ranges from 20 to 40 mg, and is frequently combined with 50 mg of pethidine.

Antianxiety Drugs

Antianxiety drugs or *anxiolytics* are agents used to relieve stress, tension and anxiety, generated by the complex and hectic modern daily life. *Anxiety* is defined as an exaggerated feeling of apprehension, uncertainty, and fear. It is an unpleasant state of tension with an anticipation of imminent danger. The *Cannon's hypothesis* is still widely held, and anxiety is perceived as a threat arising primarily from within, triggering somatic and visceral responses through the **autonomic nervous system** (ANS), and the **hypothalamo-pituitary-endocrine system.** *Acute anxiety* is generally transient, but may reappear with appropriate stimuli. The *somatic* manifestations of anxiety include fatigue, dizziness, palpitation, indigestion, headache, muscle aches, insomnia, and excessive perspiration. Anxiety is associated with almost all emotional disorders, and frequently with physical illnesses. It is often the presenting symptom of serious emotional disorders like depression and schizophrenia. The continuing search for the "ideal" anxiety-relieving drug in the late 1950s led to the development of **chlordiazepoxide,** the first *benzodiazepine* anxiolytic drug.

The antianxiety drugs are sometimes referred to as **minor tranquillizers** (an unsatisfactory term) to distinguish them from the more toxic antipsychotic drugs, or the **major tranquillizers** (also an inappropriate term). These terms are seldom used today. Most antianxiety drugs have significant **anticonvulsant activity.** Their main advantage over the barbiturates is their significantly **higher sedative-to-hypnotic ratio,** i.e., the margin between their calmness producing dose and the hypnotic dose is much greater than that of the barbiturates. The benzodiazepines have a *shallow* dose-response curve, whereas, the barbiturates have a *steep* dose-response curve **(Chapter 1.6; Fig. 1.6.4).**

Classification

The currently available antianxiety drugs can be classified into three groups:

1. **Benzodiazepines:** Chlordiazepoxide, Diazepam, Clorazepate, Alprazolam, Halazepam, Lorazepam, Midazolam, Oxazepam, Prazepam
2. **Carbamates:** Meprobamate
3. **Miscellaneous:** Buspirone, Hydroxyzine, Propranolol, Chlormezanone.

Benzodiazepines

The benzodiazepines are the most commonly prescribed antianxiety agents. The benzodiazepines discussed are primarily used for relief of *situational anxiety,* with the exception of midazolam, a short-acting agent used parenterally for preoperative and postoperative sedation.

Pharmacological Actions

All of them have qualitatively similar actions, but there are quantitative differences. These agents produce **sedation, hypnosis, anxiolytic activity, skeletal muscle relaxation** and **anticonvulsant activity.**

Antianxiety effects. The benzodiazepines exert a specific effect on the limbic system, and therefore reduce anxiety in doses which do not produce drowsiness or sleep. However, larger doses are sedative, and ultimately produce sleep. The benzodiazepines and meprobamate diminish aggressive behaviour in animals without causing impairment of neurological function.

Anticonvulsant effects. The benzodiazepines raise the threshold for electrically-induced seizures, and fits due to pentylenetetrazol in experimental animals. Clinically, *diazepam, clonazepam, lorazepam* and *nitrazepam* are used as antiepileptics **(Chapter 2.5).**

Skeletal muscle relaxant effect. The benzodiazepines induce voluntary muscle relaxation (hypotonia) without affecting normal locomotion in therapeutic doses. They decrease decerebrate rigidity in cats and rigidity in patients with cerebral palsy. In therapeutic doses neuromuscular transmission is not affected, **but an inhibition of polysynaptic reflexes within the spinal cord occurs.** It is suggested that muscle relaxation could be due to stimulation of inhibitory *glycine receptors* in the spinal cord.

Hypnotic effect. The benzodiazepines can be used as hypnotics, and in therapeutic doses they do not suppress REM sleep, but markedly suppress stage 4 sleep. Most benzodiazepines decrease sleep latency, and reduce the number of awakenings, and time spent in stage of wakefulness. Despite the shortening of stage 4 sleep, the net effect is an increase in total sleep time.

Cardiovascular system. The cardiovascular effects are minor, except in severe intoxication in which the blood pressure falls.

Analgesic action. Diazepam causes transient analgesia in man on intravenous administration. Other benzodiazepines have no analgesic effect.

Mode of Action

The benzodiazepines act selectively on the polysynaptic neuronal pathways throughout the CNS. Their main site of action is the **midbrain reticular formation,** which is the region responsible for maintenance of wakefulness. In short, the benzodiazepines facilitate the action of gamma-aminobutyric acid (GABA).

In detail, the benzodiazepines bind with high affinity to specific macromolecules within the CNS. These **benzodiazepine receptors** are closely associated with the receptors for GABA, which is the major inhibitory neurotransmitter in the brain **(Fig. 2.4.2)**. Experimental evidence suggests that benzodiazepines potentiate GABAergic neurotransmission in all areas of the CNS, and this is thought to occur *indirectly* at the postsynaptic GABA receptor complex.

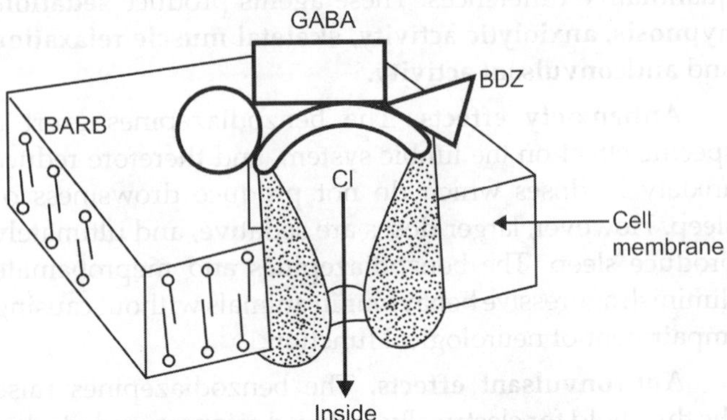

Fig. 2.4.2: A model of the GABA-chloride ionophore. GABA binding to its receptor (GABA) activates and opens the chloride channel, increasing the inward flux of chloride ions. Benzodiazepines bind to specific receptors (BDZ) and promote the effect of GABA on the chloride channel. Barbiturates bind to their receptors (BARB) and prolong the GABA-induced opening of the chloride channel. Barbiturates in high dose may directly open the chloride channel.

The functional significance of this drug-receptor interaction is that the receptor complex regulates the entrance of chloride into the postsynaptic cells. The increase in chloride conductance mediated by GABA is intensified by the benzodiazepines **(Fig. 2.4.2)**. This facilitation of GABA-induced chloride conductance results in a relatively greater **hyperpolarization** of these cells and leads to diminished synaptic transmission. The *barbiturates* also bind to receptors associated with the GABA-chloride ionophore, but these drugs prolong rather than intensify GABA effects.

In addition to the clinically useful benzodiazepines which act as **agonists** at the benzodiazepine receptor, there are two types of ligands which also interact with this binding site. These are the benzodiazepine receptor **antagonists** and the **inverse agonists.** The receptor antagonist, **flumazenil,** selectively blocks the effects of other benzodiazepines at the binding sites. Flumazenil has potential clinical application in the treatment of benzodiazepine overdose. The *inverse agonists* interact with benzodiazepine receptors, and decrease GABA-mediated changes. These also can antagonize the effects of benzodiazepine agonists, but when administered alone, they can be **anxiogenic** and **proconvulsant.** Experimentation is continuing in this field.

PHARMACOKINETICS

Benzodiazepines are generally well absorbed orally, but the rates differ widely. Thus, there is variability in the onset of action following a single dose **(Table 2.4-5).** IM absorption of **lorazepam** is rapid and complete, but that of chlordiazepoxide and diazepam is erratic.

The benzodiazepines are quite lipid-soluble and distribute widely throughout the body. Protein binding is high (80%-99%). Most drugs (except oxazepam and lorazepam) have long elimination half-lives, as their metabolites are also active. **Prazepam** and **chlorazepam** are inactive themselves, but are metabolized to **desmethyldiazepam,** an active metabolite. These drugs are mainly metabolized in the liver and excreted as both unchanged drug and metabolites, largely through the urine **(Fig. 2.4.3).**

Table 2.4-5. *The pharmacokinetic parameters and dosage of some selected benzodiazepines*

Drug	*Daily Dosage Range (mg)*	*Onset of Action (Oral)*	*Peak Plasma Levels (hrs)*	*Activity of Metabolites*	*Elimination Half-life (hrs)*
Alprazolam	0.75-3.0	Fast	1-2	Active*	12-15
Chlordiazepoxide	15-100	Moderate	0.5-4	Active	5-30
Chlorazepate	15-60	Fast	1-2	Active	30-90
Diazepam	4-40	Very fast	0.5-1.5	Active	20-50
Halazepam	60-160	Fast	1-3	Active	12-15
Lorazepam	2-8	Moderate	1-4	Inactive	10-15
Nitrazepam	5-10	Moderate	1-3	Inactive	18-28
Oxazepam	30-120	Slow	1-4	Inactive	5-15
Prazepam	20-60	Slow	2-6	Active	30-100

*Alprazolam has two metabolites, one of which is inactive.

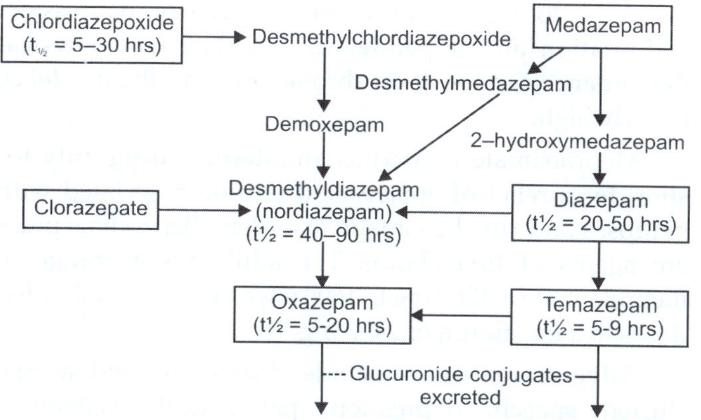

Fig. 2.4.3. The metabolic interrelationship of some benzodiazepines. Each compound is pharmacologically active; and the boxed compounds are marketed for clinical use. The conjugated products are excreted via the urine.

The central and important position of desmethyldiazepam (nordiazepam) must be appreciated, as it has a very long $t_{1/2}$ (90 hours), and at steady-state its levels exceed those of its parent substances. This accumulation may therefore explain the frequently observed "hangover" effects of continued use of benzodiazepines like *diazepam* **(Fig. 2.4.4).** In contrast, *temazepam* which does not form this metabolite, and is largely excreted unchanged as glucuronide, has a shorter $t_{1/2}$ (5-9 hours), produces much less sedation and hangover.

Metabolism of benzodiazepines is stimulated by DDT, phenobarbital, spironolactone and lynoestrol by enzyme induction. Benzodiazepines themselves are very weak inducers of microsomal enzymes.

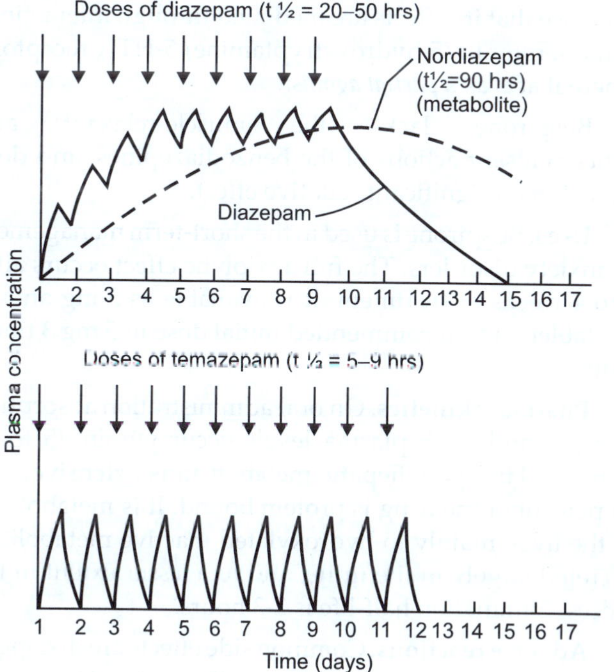

Fig. 2.4.4. Diagrammatic illustration of plasma concentrations following daily dosage of diazepam (accumulation), and temazepam (no accumulation). Hangover is appreciable with the former, and negligible with the latter (see text).

Therapeutic Uses

The benzodiazepines are widely used drugs, and quite often overused. Their main uses are detailed below:

1. **Symptomatic relief of anxiety,** tension and irritability associated with neuroses, depression, psychoneuroses, and psychosomatic disorders. *Diazepam, chlordiazepoxide, oxazepam* and *lorazepam* are used as anxiolytics, preferably on a short-term basis, not exceeding 4 months.
2. **Insomnia.** For this condition *nitrazepam, flurazepam* and *temazepam* are used.
3. **Epilepsy.** The agents *clonazepam* and *diazepam* are very useful in *status epilepticus.* Clonazepam has proved of value in petit mal and akinetic attacks.
4. **Preoperative sedation.** Midazolam, a short-acting agent is used parenterally for pre- and perioperative sedation.
5. **Spasticity.** Diazepam reduces spasticity associated with upper motor neurone lesions.
6. **Muscle spasm** due to pain or anxiety and tension states is reduced by diazepam.
7. **Tetanus.** A continuous IV infusion of diazepam 3-10 mg/kg/24 hours, or intermittent IV doses of 0.1-0.3 mg/kg may be used to control spasms.
8. **Alcohol withdrawal** manifestations are best controlled by *diazepam* or *chlordiazepoxide.*
9. Adjunctive treatment prior to cardioversion or endoscopic procedures to lessen anxiety and reduce recall (diazepam or lorazepam used IV or IM).
10. **Miscellaneous.** Used for relieving anxiety in disorders like peptic ulcer, hypertension, angina pectoris, and rheumatic disorders. Benzodiazepines have also been experimentally tried to control nocturnal enuresis and "night terrors".

Adverse Reactions

Transient drowsiness, ataxia, confusion, fatigue and lethargy occur in the initial phase of therapy. Other adverse reactions are less commonly seen during short-term therapy, but their incidence increases with prolonged usage. Adverse effects are grouped below according to the system involved.

CNS. Confusion, disorientation, agitation, slurred speech, headache, syncope, vertigo, depression, tremors, paradoxical excitement, (hostility, rage, irritability, vivid dreams, euphoria, hallucinations, insomnia) can occur specially in psychotic patients.

Gastrointestinal/Urinary. Dry mouth, constipation, nausea, anorexia, vomiting, urinary retention, incontinence.

Cardiovascular/Haematologic. Bradycardia, hypotension, palpitation, oedema, weight gain, cardiovascular collapse, agranulocytosis, neutropenia.

Hypersensitivity. Skin rash, urticaria, angioneurotic oedema, bronchial spasm.

Miscellaneous. Changes in libido, menstrual irregularities, nasal congestion, hiccups, diplopia, nystagmus, hepatic dysfunction, thrombophlebitis on IV injection, pain on IM injection. Drug dependence can occur, although the liability is much less compared to barbiturates.

Overdosage with benzodiazepines alone is seldom fatal. Symptoms include drowsiness, confusion, ataxia, and hypotension, but rarely significant circulatory or respiratory depression is seen. *Treatment* is mainly supportive, and includes IV fluids, pressor agents and osmotic diuretics. As protein binding is considerable haemodialysis does not accelerate plasma clearance, but haemoperfusion through an activated charcoal column may be useful.

Drug Interactions

1. Benzodiazepines enhance CNS-depressant effects of *alcohol, barbiturates, antihistamines, phenothiazines, opiates* and others.
2. The effects of *phenytoin* may be potentiated by benzodiazepines.
3. The effects of *levodopa* may be antagonized by benzodiazepines.
4. The effects of benzodiazepines are lessened in individuals who smoke.
5. Increased muscle relaxant effect can occur on combination with other centrally or peripherally acting muscle relaxants.
6. *Oral contraceptives* and valproic acid reduce the metabolism of diazepam.

Carbamates

This class of antianxiety drugs is presently represented by only one agent, *meprobamate.*

Meprobamate

Meprobamate acts at several levels of the CNS, including the limbic system, thalamus, and spinal cord. It does not appear to have a specific depressant action on the reticular activating system (RAS), but it has mild to moderate **tranquillizing, anticonvulsant,** and **skeletal muscle relaxing** activity. Unlike the benzodiazepines, meprobamate does not interact with the inhibitory neurotransmitter GABA, but it **inhibits multineuronal spinal reflexes.** Meprobamate reduces REM sleep time, as with barbiturates, and also causes **hepatic enzyme induction** on prolonged administration. High doses can lead to significant cardio-respiratory depression. **Habituation** and **dependence,** including **true physical dependence** can result on chronic use, and the incidence is fairly high.

Meprobamate is used as an **alternate drug only** for **short-term** relief of anxiety and tension associated with neuroses and psychosomatic disorders. Benzodiazepines are agents of first choice. The adult dosage range of meprobamate is 1200 mg to 1600 mg a day in 3 or 4 divided doses to a maximum of 2400 mg/day.

Adverse reactions include drowsiness and ataxia, slurred speech, depression, paradoxical excitement, euphoria, and hyperactivity. Hypersensitivity reactions may occur. Leucopenia, agranulocytosis, thrombocytopenia, aplastic anaemia and pancytopenia have been reported. Meprobamate may increase the incidence of grand mal attacks. It is contraindicated in acute intermittent porphyria.

Miscellaneous Antianxiety Drugs

Buspirone

Buspirone is the first member of a new class (azapirones) of anxiolytic agents that can relieve symptoms of anxiety in doses that do not cause sedation. It is structurally unrelated to the existing psychotropic drugs. The *mode of action* of buspirone is not completely established, but it appears to have an affinity for certain *serotonin* and *dopamine receptors.* Unlike the benzodiazepines it does not interact with the GABA, nor bind to benzodiazepine receptors. There is evidence that its effects are mediated through interactions at the serotonin (5-hydroxytryptamine) 5-HT_{1A} receptors, where it acts as a *partial agonist.*

Buspirone lacks the muscle-relaxant and anticonvulsant actions of the benzodiazepines, and does not exhibit a significant sedative effect.

Uses. Buspirone is used in the short-term management of anxiety disorders. The full anxiolytic effect occurs after 2 to 4 weeks of treatment. It is available as 5 mg and 10 mg tablets. The recommended initial dose in 5 mg 3 times daily.

Pharmacokinetics. On oral administration absorption is rapid and peak plasma levels occur within 45 to 90 minutes. First-pass hepatic metabolism is extensive, and 95 percent of the drug is protein bound. It is metabolized in the liver, mainly to hydroxylated inactive metabolities excreted largely in the urine, and to a lesser extent in the faeces. Elimination half-life is 2-3 hours.

Adverse reactions. Common side effects are dizziness, headache, nervousness, fatigue, excitement and insomnia. Abuse, dependence, and withdrawal symptoms have not been reported, and buspirone does not produce cross-tolerance with benzodiazepines.

Hydroxyzine

Hydroxyzine is an antihistamine (H_1-receptor antagonist) that exhibits a mild CNS-depressant action, exerted at subcortical brain levels. It possesses a number of other pharmacologic actions like **anticholinergic, bronchodilator, analgesic, antispasmodic, antiemetic** and **skeletal muscle relaxant activity.** This drug displays a good safety margin.

Mode of action is incompletely known. It suppresses neuronal activity at subcortical levels. It interferes with the action of histamine, acetylcholine, and possibly serotonin.

Uses. Hydroxyzine has many uses: (*i*) Symptomatic treatment of *psychoneurotic states;* (*ii*) To relieve symptoms of *anxiety* associated with digestive disorders, allergic conditions, senility, menopause, alcoholism, and behavioural problems in children; (*iii*) Management of **pruritus,** associated with dermatoses and other histamine-mediated conditions; (*iv*) Adjunctive treatment of alcohol withdrawal or delirium tremens; and (*v*) Pre- and postoperative sedation. The usual dosage for adults is 50 to 100 mg orally 3 to 4 times daily. For pre- and postoperative sedation the dose is 25 to 100 mg IM. Hydroxyzine is available in tablet, capsule, syrup and suspension form.

Some other H_1-receptor antagonists (diphenhydramine, promethazine) can also be used as sedative-hypnotics.

Propranolol

The beta-blocker propranolol has been widely used in the treatment of cardiovascular diseases. It is also useful in some forms of anxiety, particularly characterized by somatic symptoms or by performance anxiety (stage fright). Propranolol may be used in a dose of 80-120 mg daily in divided doses for relief of stress-related somatic manifestations of anxiety.

Chlormezanone

Chlormezanone is infrequently used for the treatment of anxiety and tension states. Its dosage is 100-200 mg 3 to 4 times daily. It has no advantage over other antianxiety drugs.

Antipsychotic drugs like **chlorpromazine** and the tricyclic antidepressants, **amitryptyline** are reserved drugs for the treatment of some selected patients of anxiety.

None of the drugs available is an "ideal" antianxiety drug. The **benzodiazepines** approach closest to the ideal, and hence their wide popularity.

2.5 ANTIEPILEPTICS

Epilepsy is a chronic disorder of the central nervous system (CNS), with a prevalence rate between 3 and 6 per thousand population. The term **primary** or **idiopathic epilepsy** includes those cases where no cause for the seizure can be identified. **Secondary** or **symptomatic epilepsy** designates the disorder when factors like trauma, neoplasm, infection, poisoning, fever, developmental abnormalities, cerebrovascular disease, withdrawal of certain drugs, or various metabolic disorders contribute as a cause of the disease.

Classification of Epileptic Seizures

The term "epilepsy" is used to describe a number of conditions having in common the occurrence of sudden, recurring discharges from abnormally functioning brain cells, leading to the appearance of *motor, sensory, autonomic,* and *psychic* manifestations. Such abnormal brain discharges are called seizures.

Seizures can be broadly categorized into **generalized** and **partial** (localized) types. The more common generalized seizures are: (*i*) tonic-clonic convulsions or **grand mal epilepsy;** (*ii*) simple absence seizures or **petit mal epilepsy;** (*iii*) **myoclonic jerking;** (*iv*) **atonic/akinetic;** and (*v*) **infantile spasms** (hypsarrhythmia). Generalized seizures are bialateral and symmetric, and do not have a specific locus of onset in the CNS. *Partial seizures* originate in a specific part of the brain. A simplified classification of the common epilepsies is presented in **Table 2.5-1.** The epileptic seizures are the result of an uncontrolled discharge from an area of abnormally functioning CNS tissue, termed the **focal lesion** or **seizure focus.**

The older terms major and minor epilepsy have been discarded. Traditionally, from the clinical standpoint, important subdivisions of epileptic seizures are **grand mal, petit mal, psychomotor, focal** or **Jacksonian seizures** and **status epilepticus.** Recording of the electrical activity of the brain by placing electrodes on the scalp (EEG) is a standard diagnostic procedure, and is specially useful in the evaluation of the patient.

Guidelines for Drug Therapy

The following guidelines are applicable for effective drug control of epilepsy:

1. Before commencement of drug therapy, attempts must be made to ascertain the cause of seizures. Some seizures are successfully treated surgically. The choice of the drug depends on the *benefit-risk ratio* of the antiepileptic.
2. Control should initially be attempted using a single drug (monotherapy), chosen according to the type of epilepsy. The dose is increased until either the seizures cease, or toxicity appears. On combining antiepileptic drugs in most cases effects are *additive.*
3. Anticonvulsant drug dosage must be *individualized* to avoid serious adverse reactions. Whenever possible, *plasma drug concentrations* must be monitored.
4. All changes in drug therapy should be made as gradually as possible.
5. Trauma or emotional **stress** may increase dosage requirement.
6. A great majority of petit mal seizures are limited to childhood, and with age spontaneous remissions may occur.
7. Possible drug interactions must be kept in mind.
8. Once a suitable drug regimen is established, it should be maintained until there is *complete freedom from fits for at least 3 years* with 3 consecutive normal EEGs recorded at 3 to 4 months intervals.

9. A large number of *treatment failures* result from *non-compliance* of prescribed drug regimen.
10. Patients affected by drowsiness due to antiepileptics should not drive a car, or operate machinery.
11. **Haemopoietic depression** and renal damage are common toxic effects of anticonvulsants. Blood counts and urine analysis should be done at regular intervals.
12. If it is decided to withdraw an antiepileptic drug, the withdrawal should be done gradually over a period of months.
13. Psychomotor stimulants like dextroamphetamine (Dexedrine), methamphetamine (Desoxyn), and methylphenidate (Ritalin) may be used to counteract excessive drowsiness caused by antiepileptic agents.

Classification of Antiepileptics

The antiepileptic (anticonvulsant) drugs may be conveniently classified according to their chemical structure as under:

1. **Anticonvulsant Barbiturates:** *Phenobarbital,* mephobarbital, metharbital.
2. **Hydantoins:** *Phenytoin,* ethotoin, mephenytoin.
3. **Oxazlidinediones:** *Trimethadione,* paramethadione.
4. **Succinimides:** *Ethosuximide,* methsuximide, phensuximide.
5. **Iminostilbines:** *Carbamazepine.*
6. **Benzodiazepines:** *Clonazepam, diazepam,* clorazepate, nitrazepam.
7. **Valproic acid derivatives:** *Valproic acid,* valproate sodium, divalproex sodium.
8. **Chemically unrelated anticonvulsants:** Acetazolamide, primidone, progabide, phenacemide, paraldehyde, lidocaine, magnesium sulphate.

Table 2.5-1. *Classification of seizures, their characteristics, and drugs employed in management*

Seizure Type	*Seizure Characteristics*	*Effective Drugs*
I. Generalized		
Tonic-clonic (Grand mal)	Tonic rigidity of extremities followed by massive clonic jerking for several minutes; urinary incontinence; stupor follows; onset at any age.	Phenytoin, Phenobarbital, Primidone, Carbamazepine
Simple absence (Petit mal)	Sudden loss of consciousness upto 30 seconds can occur hundreds of times a day; characteristics 3/sec spike-wave EEG pattern; clonic jerking of eyelids but no motor activity; onset between 3-10 years of age; rare in the adult.	Ethosuximide, Trimethadione, Clonazepam, Valproic acid
Myoclonic jerking	Sudden, violent contractions of extremities, with or without loss of consciousness; often occurs after awakening or before retiring, often in combination with other seizure types; age of onset 5-20 years.	Phenobarbital, Clonazepam, Valproic acid
Atonic/Akinetic	Sudden loss of muscle tone lasting 10-60 seconds; EEG shows a slow spike-wave pattern; often due to organic brain disease; age of onset 1-5 years.	Diazepam, Clonazepam
Infantile spasms (hypsarrhythmia)	Brief, recurrent myoclonic jerks with abrupt flexion/extension of limbs or whole body; patients mostly mentally retarded; high voltage, slow waves are predominant in EEG; age of onset under 1 year.	Diazepam, Clonazepam, Phenobarbital Corticotrophin
II. Partial		
Simple seizure (focal or Jacksonian seizures)	Manifestations variable depending on site of lesion; convulsions confined to a single limb or muscle group; no impairment of consciousness; sensory disturbances occur; EEG shows spiking at the site of the focus; onset at any age.	Primidone, Clorazepate, Carbamazepine (?); Valproic acid(?)
Complex partial seizures (Psychomotor epilepsy)	Confused behaviour, with involuntary, purposeless, repetitive motor activity; accompanied by autonomic manifestations and loss of consciousness; seizures last several minutes, but patients have no recall of attacks; EEG spiking is present in the temporal lobe; control is difficult; onset at any age.	Carbamazepine, Primidone, Phenytoin, Phenacemide

Anticonvulsant Barbiturates

Phenobarbital, Mephobarbital, Metharbital

The *three* long-acting barbiturates - **phenobarbital, mephobarbital, metharbital** - are effective antiepileptics at **subhypnotic** doses. They exert a prolonged action, and are reasonably well tolerated. **Phenobarbital** is the most commonly used compound, although it is claimed that mephobarbital produces fewer side effects.

Mode of action. The antiepileptic activity of barbiturates probably involves several mechanisms: (*i*) the excitability of the nerve cells is reduced due to their **increased firing threshold;** (*ii*) **decreased neuronal excitability** limits the spread of the abnormal discharge; and (*iii*) active transport of ions across the neuronal membranes is impaired, which lowers their firing rate. The exact role of gamma-aminobutyric acid (GABA) is unclear, but **potentiation of GABA-ergic activity** is associated with barbiturate-induced hypnosis, and may also be playing a role in their anticonvulsant action.

Pharmacokinetics. The antiepileptic barbiturates are well absorbed orally, specially on an empty stomach. Onset of action ranges between 30 minutes to 2 hours, and effects persist for 8-12 hours. These drugs are widely distributed in the body; metabolized by the hepatic microsomal enzyme system; unchanged drug and the metabolic products are excreted in the urine.

Therapeutic Uses

1. Treatment of **grand mal seizures;** used alone in infants and children, and usually in combination with phenytoin in adults.
2. Generalized **myoclonic jerks** and **cortical focal seizures.**
3. Complex **absence seizures** with autonomic manifestations.
4. Adjunctive treatment of **infantile spasms** (efficacy not established).
5. Control of **status epilepticus** (IV phenobarbital used).

The preparations and dosage schedules are presented in **Table 2.5-2.**

Adverse reactions. Drowsiness, lethargy and dizzines are the most frequently noted side effects. Less common adverse reactions are bradycardia, hypotension, hypoventilation, bronchospasm, laryngospasm, apnoea, skin rash, confusion, ataxia, hallucinations, and aggressive behaviour. Chronic *phenobarbital* therapy may result in megaloblastic anaemia and liver damage.

Hydantoins

Phenytoin, Ethotoin, Mephenytoin

The hydantoins are the most effective drugs for the treatment of **grand mal** seizures, and can also be used to control **psychomotor epilepsy.** Unlike barbiturates, these drugs are not CNS depressants, and do not interfere with sensory function. *Phenytoin* is the most frequently prescribed drug out of the hydantoins.

Mode of action. The hydantoins **inhibit the spread** of seizure activity to neurones surrounding the seizure focus. The **motor cortex** is the primary site of action. These drugs produce a **stabilization of the neuronal membrane,** i.e., the threshold of excitability is increased and the **duration of after-discharge** is reduced. Perhaps by increasing Na^+ – K^+ adenosine triphosphatase (ATPase) activity, sodium efflux from neuronal cells is stimulated, **blocking post-tetanic potentiation** (PTP). This prevents focal seizure activity to spread to adjacent areas. Increased release or activity of GABA has been postulated as an additional possible mechanism of action.

Table 2.5-2. *Preparations and dosage(s) of anticonvulsant barbiturates, hydantoins, oxazolidinediones, and succinimides*

Drugs	*Preparations*	*Dosage Range*	*Comments*
Anticonvulsant barbiturates			
Phenobarbital	*Tablets* - 8, 16, 32, 65, 100 mg	*Oral* Adults: 50-100 mg bid or tid	Drowsiness is common in early stages of therapy, then diminishes with continued use. Used IM/IV for status epilepticus and other acute convulsive states
	Capsules - 16 mg *Elixir* - 15 mg/ml, 20 mg/5 ml	Children: Initially 3-5 mg/kg/day for 7 days, later adjust to blood level of 10-15 mcg/ml *IM, IV*	
	Injection - 30, 60 65, 130 mg/ml	Adults: 200-300 mg, repeat in 6 hours Children IV: 20 mg/kg initially then 6 mg/kg every 20 minutes as needed	
Mephobarbital	*Tablets* - 32, 50, 100 mg	Adults: 400-600 mg/day Children: 32-64 mg tid or qid. Under 5 yrs 6-32 mg tid or qid	Similar to phenobarbital in most respects,, but producing somewhat less sedation. Largely converted to phenobarbital in the body

(Contd.)

Table 2.5-2 contd...

Drugs	*Preparations*	*Dosage Range*	*Comments*
Metharbital	*Tablets* - 100 mg	Adults: Initially 100 mg OD to tid, adjust to optimal dose Children: 5-15 mg/kg/day	Less effective than phenobarbital, but possesses somewhat greater sedative action
Hydantoins			
Phenytoin	*Chewable tablets* 50 mg *Suspension* - 30, 125 mg/5 ml *Capsules* - 30, 100 mg *Injection* - 50 mg/ml	*Oral* Adults: Initially 100 mg tid; range 300-400 mg/day Children: Initially 5 mg/kg/day bid or tid *Parenteral (IV)* Status epilepticus- 150-250 mg, repeat in 30 min, with 100-150 mg, if necessary *Arrhythmias* - 100 mg every 5 min till arrhythmia is abolished (maximum 1000 mg)	Do not administer IM in status epilepticus, as adequate plasma levels cannot be attained
Ethotoin	*Tablets* - 250, 500 mg	Adults: 250 mg qid initially, increase to optimal levels usually 2-3 g/day Children: 750 mg/day initially, maintenance 500-1000 mg/day	Less effective than phenytoin, but somewhat less toxic; not used as an antiarrhythmic
Mephenytoin	*Tablets* - 100 mg	Adults: Initially 50-100 mg per day, increase to optimal levels (range 200-600 mg/day)	Most toxic of the hydantoins; use reserved for refractory patients; possesses strong sedative action
Oxazolidinediones			
Trimethadione	*Chewable Tablets* - 150 mg *Capsules* - 300 mg *Solution* - 40 mg/ml	Adults: Initially 300 mg tid, usual maintenance dose 900-2400 mg/day in divided doses	Plasma levels of dimethadione (the active metabolite) used as dosage guide and maintained at 700 mcg/ml for optimal control of petit mal attacks
Paramethadione	*Capsules* - 150, 300 mg *Solution* - 300 mg/ml	Adults: 300-600 mg tid or qid Children: 300-900 mg tid or qid	Less effective but slightly less toxic than trimethadione, no myasthenia-like reaction but sedation is common
Succinimides			
Ethosuximide	*Capsules* - 250 mg *Syrup* - 250 mg/5 ml	Adults: Initially 500 mg/day; increase by 250 mg every 4 to 7 days till control achieved (maximum 1500 mg per day) Children: 250 mg/day, increased slowly to optimal level	This drug may colour the urine pink to reddish brown; administer with meals to reduce GI upset, long half life, therefore do not exceed recommended dosage as cumulation occurs
Methsuximide	*Capsule* - 150, 300 mg	Initially 300 mg/day for 1 week, may be increased by 300 mg weekly to a maximum of 1200 mg	Equally effective in petit mal as ethosuximide, but more toxic specially to the CNS
Phensuximide	*Capsules* - 500 mg	Adults: 500-1000 mg bid or tid (range 1-3 g/day) Children: 600-1200 mg bid or tid	Slightly less effective and less toxic than other succinimides

Pharmacokinetics. Phenytoin is slowly absorbed from the small intestines, and the extent of absorption varies widely among different preparations, the sodium salt being the best absorbed. Bioavailability differs widely (20% to 90%) among products of different manufacturers. Peak serum levels are attained in 2 to 3 hours. Phenytoin is erratically absorbed on IM injection. It is metabolized in the liver, and excreted largely as conjugated metabolities in urine. The elimination half-life is dose-dependent and ranges from 8 to 60 hours (average 20-30 hours). Steady-state levels are attained within 7 to 10 days.

Therapeutic Uses

1. Control of **grand mal seizures** (phenytoin may be used alone, or in combination with phenobarbital, primidone, or carbamazepine).
2. Treatment of **psychomotor epilepsy.**
3. Adjunctive treatment of **trigeminal neuralgia,** and **alcohol withdrawal syndrome.**
4. Control of **status epilepticus,** and seizures occurring during neurosurgery (IV phenytoin).
5. Elementary (focal) or Jacksonian seizures (mephenytoin only).
6. Termination of digitalis-induced cardiac arrhythmias (IV phenytoin).

The preparations and dosage schedules are presented in **Table 2.5-2.**

Adverse reactions. Frequent side effects are sluggishness, ataxia, slurred speech, nystagmus and confusion. Other adverse reactions include:

GI - nausea, vomiting, dysphagia; **CNS** - headache, tremors, behavioural disturbances; **Dermatologic** - skin rashes, urticaria, Stevens-Johnson syndrome, hirsutism, lupus erythematosus, exfoliative dermatitis (rarely); **Haematopoietic** - blood dyscrasias, megaloblastic anaemia, bone marrow depression; *Others* - **Gingival hyperplasia** (20-30% incidence), periodontal infection polyarthropathy, hepatitis, hyperglycaemia, pulmonary fibrosis and osteomalasia. IV phenytoin may result in hypotension, cardiac arrhythmias and cardiovascular collapse. Abrupt withdrawal of the drug may result in **status epilepticus.** Phenytoin may increase the effects of oral anticoagulants, antihypertensives, sedatives and hypnotics, propranolol and methotrexate.

Oxazolidinediones

Trimethadione, Paramethadione

The oxazolidinediones are effective drugs for the control of simple absence (petit mal) seizures, but the incidence of adverse reactions is high.

Mode of action. Repetitive discharges in the thalamocortical systems are responsible for absence (petit mal) seizures, and the oxazolidinediones prolong the recovery period of the postsynaptic neurones in these systems, thereby exerting an antiseizure effect. They **elevate the seizure threshold** in the thalamus, and interfere with the propagation of seizure activity.

Pharmacokinetics. Oxazolidinediones are readily absorbed from the GI tract, and peak plasma concentrations occur in 30-60 minutes. They are widely distributed in the body, and are not protein bound. Both compounds are metabolized in the liver to an active metabolite, which is slowly excreted by the kidneys. The plasma half-life of the parent compounds is 12-24 hours, whereas the active metabolite has a half-life of 6 to 12 days.

Therapeutic use. Simple *absence (petit mal) seizures* refractory to other drugs. Dosage: See **Table 2.5-2.**

Adverse reactions. Common side effects are drowsiness, GI distress, hiccups and photophobia. Other adverse effects are: **GI** nausea, vomiting, anorexia; **CNS** - vertigo, irritability, personality changes, precipitation of grand mal seizures; **Ocular** - diplopia, scotomata, hemaralopia (day blindness), retinal haemorrhage; **Haematologic** - epistaxis, mucosal bleeding, neutropenia; **Others** - skin rashes, exfoliative dermatitis, albuminuria, alopecia, lymphadenopathy, myasthenia-like reaction, nephrosis and hepatitis. Foetal malformations occur during oxazolidinedione therapy, and these drugs should not be used during pregnancy.

Succinimides

Ethosuximide, Methsuximide, Phensuximide

The succinimides are the *drugs of choice* for the treatment of absence (petit mal) seizures. They are *not* more effective than the oxazolidinediones, but are less toxic compared to other alternative drugs (oxazolidinediones, valproic acid, clonazepam). The three succinimides currently available have little differences amongst them, and are discussed together.

Mode of action. The succinimides resemble the oxazolidinediones in that they suppress the 3/sec spike-wave EEG pattern characteristic of absence seizures. They have a depressant effect on the motor cortex, and *elevate the firing threshold* of cortical neurones.

Pharmacokinetics. Succinimides are well absorbed orally, and peak serum levels are attained in 2-4 hours. They are *not* bound to plasma proteins, and have a short half-life (2-4 hours), except ethosuximide (30-60 hours). They are metabolized in the liver, and both active and inactive metabolites are excreted in the urine.

Therapeutic use. They are drugs of choice for *simple absence (petit mal) seizures,* and also used as adjunctive treatment of psychomotor and other minor motor seizures (methsuximide). The preparations and dosages are presented in **Table 2.5-2.**

Adverse reactions. Common side effects are GI distress, drowsiness, ataxia and dizziness. Other adverse effects include: **CNS** - nervousness, euphoria, hyperactivity, aggressiveness, confusion, depression, night terrors, sleep disturbances; *Ocular* - myopia, blurred vision, photophobia, periorbital oedema; **Haematologic** - blood dyscrasias; **Dermatologic** - urticaria, systemic lupus erythematosus, Stevens-Johnson syndrome;

Genitourinary - urinary frequency, albuminuria, haematuria, renal damage; **Others** - alopecia, vaginal bleeding, hirsutism and swelling of the tongue. Increased libido results if ethosuximide is combined with other anticonvulsants.

Iminostilbines

Carbamazepine

Carbamazepine is structurally related to tricyclic antidepressants, and has actions similar to phenytoin.

Mode of action. Carbamazepine increases latency, decreases responsivity, and suppresses after-discharges in polysynaptic pathways associated with cortical and limbic function. It also reduces post-tetanic potentiation. In addition, carbamazepine has anticholinergic, antidepressant, and muscle-relaxant actions.

Pharmacokinetics. Oral absorption is slow but complete, peak plasma levels are attained in 4 to 6 hours; widely distributed and highly protein bound (75%); and serum half-life is 12 to 20 hours. It is metabolized in the liver, and metabolites together with unchanged drug are excreted by the kidneys.

Therapeutic Uses

1. Treatment of **psychomotor seizures** (used alone or with primidone or phenytoin).
2. Treatment of **grand mal seizures** with phenytoin.
3. Adjunctive treatment of **mixed seizures or complex partial seizures**.
4. Relief of pain associated with **trigeminal neuralgia** (tic doloureux).
5. **Experimental uses** include treatment of neurogenic diabetes insipidus, alcohol withdrawal syndrome, bipolar depression and schizophrenia.

Dosage. Carbamazepine is used orally as 200 mg tablets and 100 mg chewable tablets.

Epilepsy: *Adults* - Initially 200 mg bid, increase by 200 mg/day in divided doses till optimal control (maximum 1200 mg/day). *Children* –100 mg bid initially; increase by 100 mg/day till optimal control.

Trigeminal neuralgia: Initially 100 mg bid; increase by 100 mg/12 hours to a maximum of 1200 mg/day till optimal control; maintenance 400-800 mg/day.

Adverse reactions. Common side effects are drowsiness, dizziness, ataxia, nausea and diplopia. Other adverse reactions include: **CNS** - confusion, incoordination, speech disturbances, visual hallucinations, tinnitus, depression, nystagmus; **Dermatologic**- sweating, urticaria, exfoliative dermatitis; **Haematologic** - blood dyscrasias, agranulocytosis, thrombocytopenia; **Genitourinary** albuminuria, glycosuria, urinary retention, impotence; **GI**-abdominal pain, xerostomia, glossitis; **Cardiovascular** - hypotension, syncope, arrhythmias, hypertension, AV block, congestive heart failure; **Others** -abnormal liver function, osteomalasia, jaundice, lenticular opacities, adenopathy. Carbamazepine can result in breakthrough bleeding in women on oral contraceptives.

Benzodiazepines

Clonazepam

Clonazepam, a long-acting benzodiazepine, is used primarily in *absence (petit mal) seizures*, specially for the *akinetic* and *myoclonic* variants. It causes significant CNS depression, and results in **psychological dependence,** and 50 percent of users develop tolerance within 3 to 6 months, requiring dosage adjustment. Withdrawal symptoms appear on discontinuance of therapy. Tolerance limits the usefulness of clonazepam for chronic therapy.

Mode of action. It suppresses the spike-wave discharge of absence seizures, and decreases the frequency, duration, amplitude, and spread of minor motor seizure discharges.

Pharmacokinetics. Onset of action on oral administration is within 30 to 60 minutes; maximum levels occur in 1 to 2 hours; and effects persist for 6 to 12 hours. Half-life of clonazepam varies from 20 to 40 hours. It is metabolized in the liver and excreted in the urine.

Therapeutic Uses

1. Petit mal variant (Lennox-Gestaut syndrome)
2. Myoclonic and akinetic seizures.
3. Simple absence seizures refractory to succinimides (may be used alone or as an adjunct).

Dosage. Clonazepam is administered orally as 0.5, 1.0 or 2.0 mg tablets. In *adults,* initial dose is 0.5 mg tid; increase by 0.5 mg to 1.0 mg every 3 days till optimal control (maximum 20 mg/day). In *children,* initially 0.01 mg/kg to 0.03 mg/kg/day; increase by 0.25 mg to 0.5 mg every 3 days.

Adverse reactions. Common side effects are drowsiness, ataxia and abnormal behaviour. Other adverse reactions include confusion, depression, insomnia, hypotonia, slurred speech, tremor, nystagmus, psychosis, skin rashes, ankle oedema, hirsutism, muscle weakness, blood dyscrasias (rarely), diplopia and lymphadenopathy. Dependence and tolerance can develop on chronic therapy.

Diazepam

Diazepam is a benzodiazepine widely used for *simple anxiety states* **(Chapter 2.4).** It is also useful as an adjunct in the management of *convulsive disorders,* specially *minor motor seizures.* Its main indication is parenterally (IV) for the treatment of **status epilepticus** (see later). It is also used for convulsions accompanying *acute alcohol* *withdrawal.* It facilitates the action of GABA, an inhibitory neurotransmitter in the CNS, although the contribution of this effect to the antiepileptic action of diazepam is unknown. **Oral dosage** for adults ranges from 2 to 10 mg bid to qid, whereas for children the dosage is 1 to 2.5 mg tid or qid. IV doses are 5 to 10 mg in adults, to be repeated as needed at 10 to 15 minute intervals.

Clorazepate

Clorazepate is a benzodiazepine antianxiety agent, also used as an adjunct in the treatment of **partial seizures.** The initial dose is 7.5 mg tid in adults and bid in children from 9 to 12 years of age. For complete information see **Chapter 2.4.**

Valproic Acid Derivatives

Valproic Acid, Valproate Sodium, Divalproex Sodium

Valproic acid, its sodium salt, and divalproex sodium (composed of equal parts of valproic acid and valproate sodium) provide improved seizure control when added to drug regimens of patients with **multiple seizure types,** refractory to other treatments.

Mode of action. Valproic acid induces an **elevation in the functional levels of GABA** in the CNS. This action results from the inhibition of the enzyme gamma-transaminase, which blocks the conversion of GABA to succinic semialdehyde, and more of GABA is available in the CNS. In addition, valproic acid has a *prolactin inhibitory effect,* which may also be related to potentiation of GABA action.

Pharmacokinetics. Valproic acid and valproate sodium are rapidly absorbed orally; divalproex is enteric coated and absorption is delayed by 1 hour, but is uniform and consistent. Peak serum levels occur within 30 to 60 minutes with valproate sodium, and within 1 to 4 hours with other preparations. These drugs are widely distributed and highly (90%) protein bound. Serum half-life ranges from 6 to 16 hours. These drugs are metabolized in the liver, and conjugated metabolites are excreted in the urine.

Therapeutic uses. (*i*) For treatment of *simple and complex absence seizures,* including petit mal seizures (used alone or in combination with other anticonvulsants); (*ii*) used as adjunct in the treatment of *multiple seizure types,* and (*iii*) investigational uses include grand mal seizures, myoclonic seizures, infantile spasms and febrile seizures.

Dosage. Dosages are expressed as valproic acid equivalents. The recommended initial dose is 15 mg/kg/day which may be increased by 5 to 10 mg/kg/day at 1-week intervals till optimal control is obained or side effects occur. The maximum daily dose is 60 mg/kg, and dosages greater than 250 mg/day should be given in divided doses.

Adverse reactions. Common side effects are nausea, vomiting and indigestion. In addition, sedation, abdominal, cramps, and minor elevations of transminases (SGOT, SGPT) and LDH may occur. Lenticular opacities, nystagmus, diplopia, dizziness, alopecia, irregular menses, acute pancreatitis and blood dyscrasias may occur, but cannot be *solely* ascribed to valproic acid derivatives, as these agents are used as adjuncts with other antiepileptics. **Fatal hepatic failure** can occur with valproic acid. Hence, frequent liver function testing is required as a precaution.

Other Unrelated Anticonvulsants

Acetazolamide

Acetazolamide is a carbonic anhydrase inhibitor used as an adjunct to control **petit mal** and other **absence** or **non-localized seizures.** This drug has also been employed as a *mild diuretic* **(Chapter 6.2),** for relief of *migraine,* and for the treatment of **chronic open-angle glaucoma** (reduces formation of aqueous humour).

Acetazolamide is a **carbonic anhydrase inhibitor,** and reduces formation of H^+ and HCO_3 ions, and accumulation of CO_2, which retards abnormal and excessive discharges from CNS neurones. The beneficial effect largely is due to the **mild acidosis** produced by acetazolamide.

The usual starting dose of acetazolamide is 250 mg/day, and the maintenance range is 375 to 1000 mg/day, generally in combination with another antiepileptic. The antiepileptic action of acetazolamide is limited by the **rapid development of tolerance,** and return of seizure activity within a few weeks. **Adverse effects** include paresthesias, polyuria, glycosuria, confusion, myopia, hepatic dysfunction and flaccid paralysis. It is *contraindicated* in patients with **sulphonamide allergy,** since it is a sulphonamide derivative.

Primidone

Primidone is not a true barbiturate, but is structurally related to phenobarbital, and has a similar action profile. Chemically it is 2-deoxyphenobarbital, and is metabolized to phenobarbital and phenylethylmalonamide (PEMA), both active anticonvulsants. Its *mode of action* is similar to phenobarbital. It is used to treat **grand mal seizures** (alone or with other anticonvulsants); **psychomotor seizures;** complex partial motor seizures (Jacksonian); and **benign essential tremor** (investigational use).

It is slowly but well absorbed orally; peak serum levels attained in 3 to 4 hours; has a prolonged action (half-lives of metabolites is 2 to 4 days); and excreted through the kidneys about one-fourth as unchanged drug.

Dosage. Initially, 100-125 mg daily at bedtime for 3 days; gradually increase to 250 mg tid or qid. Common side effects are lethargy, ataxia, vertigo and irritability. Severe skin rashes, lymphadenopathy, rarely megaloblastic anaemia, impotence, visual disturbances, blood dyscrasias and lupus-like reaction can occur.

PROGABIDE

Progabide is an analogue of the amide derivative of GABA, and behaves as a GABA agonist. However, the therapeutic status of the drug remains uncertain. It has displayed anticonvulsant activity in a number of animal models.

PHENACEMIDE

Phenacemide is a structural analogue of hydantoins, and is useful in **severe epileptic states,** specially mixed forms of **psychomotor seizures refractory to other medications.** It is employed as a last resort, because of its extreme toxicity.

The exact mechanism of action is not known. However, it elevates the threshold of *experimental electroshock seizures* in animals.

Phenacemide is available in 500 mg tablets. The recommended dose in adults is 250-500 mg orally tid, initially. The usual maintenance dose is 2 to 3 g a day. Children (5 to 10 years) should receive one-half of the adult dose.

Adverse reactions frequently seen are psychoses, depression, GI disturbances, drowsiness, dizziness, and headache. Other untoward effects include, insomnia paresthesias, fatigue, palpitation, increased serum creatinine, hepatitis (occasionally fatal), blood dyscrasias, and bone marrow depression. It is *contraindicated* in persons with personality disorders, and in pregnant women.

PARALDEHYDE

Paraldehyde is used in **status epilepticus** when other agents have failed to provide relief (see later).

LIDOCAINE

Lidocaine is used as an alternative to general anaesthesia in the treatment of **status epilepticus,** a somewhat paradoxical use. It is infused intravenously as a continuous infusion at a rate of 1 to 3 mg/min, preferably using a continuous injection pump. However, overdosage itself can induce convulsions (see later).

MAGNESIUM SULPHATE

Magnesium, in the form of magnesium sulphate, is an effective anticonvulsant in seizures associated with **toxaemia of pregnancy,** and other conditions with abnormally low plasma magnesium. Other clinical applications are as a cathartic when given orally; topically as an antipruritic; parenterally to control uterine motility; paroxysmal atrial tachycardia; hypertension; and cerebral oedema.

Magnesium controls convulsions possibly by blocking the release of acetylcholine (ACh) from the motor nerve ending. It also has a depressant effect on the CNS. Adult IM doses range from 1 to 5 g of a 25 to 50 percent solution, upto 5 times a day, if necessary. IV injection, 1 to 4 g of a 10 to 20 percent solution may be given at a rate of 1.5 ml/minute. As a guide to dosage, if the *knee jerk* reflex is absent, magnesium should not be administered. **Adverse effects** include sweating, hypotension, sedation, confusion, hypothermia, flaccid paralysis, respiratory depression, and circulatory collapse. The antidote to magnesium sulphate induced respiratory depression is calcium. Thus, an IV calcium preparation should be at hand when magnesium is given.

DRUG THERAPY OF STATUS EPILEPTICUS

Status epilepticus is a medical emergency, resulting from continuous or repetitive grand mal seizures. Serious brain damage is likely to occur in untreated cases, and the degree of potential danger is related to the duration of seizures.

The management of status epilepticus is directed towards securing airway, protection from injury, maintenance of fluid and electrolyte balance and drug therapy. Drug therapy includes the following agents:

1. **Diazepam.** Intravenous diazepam is the drug of choice, and should be administered immediately. The usual adult dose is 10 mg (children over 7 years, 5 mg; infants 0.25 mg/kg body weight). The injection may be repeated after 15 minutes. Continuous IV infusion (1 mg/minute) may be given, if IV bolus injections fail.
2. **Phenobarbital.** In an adult a slow IV injection of upto 250 mg of phenobarbital over a period of 2-3 minutes is given. This dose may be repeated after 30 minutes, if necessary. Higher doses are rarely needed.
3. **Phenytoin.** IV infusion of phenytoin is given not exceeding 50 mg/minute in adults. If an initial dose of 250 mg is not successful, a further 150 mg may be given after 30 minutes.
4. **Chlormethiazole.** An IV infusion of a 0.8 percent solution (total dose 200-1500 ml) is given at a maximum rate of 80 drops/minute. Higher infusion rates may cause hypotension.
5. **Paraldehyde.** It is given in a dose of 0.1 ml/kg body weight by deep IM injection (plastic syringes must not be used).
6. **Lidocaine.** As a last resort, and an alternative to general anaesthesia, lidocaine is sometimes infused IV when all other drugs have failed.

To sum up, diazepam is the drug of choice. If it fails either **paraldehyde** or **chlormethiazole** are given. Barbiturates are best avoided because of the risk of respiratory depression.

Laboratory Screening of Anticonvulsants

Convulsions can be induced in experimental animals (rats and mice) by chemical or electrical stimulation:

1. **Electroshock-induced seizures.** An alternating current is passed through the brain through surface or ear-electrodes. The **minimal current** which produces a convulsion **(threshold current)** can be determined before and after the administration of the test drug to be screened.

A preferred technique is to produce a convulsion of a predictable and set pattern by the application of an alternating current maximal electroshock. Such seizures are designated as **maximal electroshock seizures.** Such convulsions are modified by the hydantoins and the sedatives (extensor component of the seizure is antagonized). Drugs antagonizing the maximal electroshock seizures (extensor component) are very likely to be useful in grand mal seizures.

2. **Chemoshock or pentylenetetrazol seizures.** The convulsions induced by pentylenetetrazol (Cardiazol) are prevented or modified by trimethadione and other agents useful for petit mal epilepsy.

After these preclinical studies in animals, the drugs are subjected to a clinical evaluation for their benefit-risk ratio.

2.6 NARCOTIC ANALGESICS AND ANTAGONISTS

Narcotic analgesics comprise a group of both **naturally occurring** and **synthetic agents** which interact with specific **opioid receptor sites** in the CNS to relieve pain in conscious persons. In contrast, **narcotic antagonists** are those compounds that can occupy the same receptor sites, and antagonize many actions of the narcotic analgesics.

Terminology

Drugs used in the management of severe pain have been designated as **"narcotic analgesics"** or **"potent analgesics"**, to distinguish them from the less potent analgesic drugs like aspirin and paracetamol (non-narcotic analgesics). However, the term "narcotic" is not very appropriate as it is derived from a Greek word *narkotikos* meaning "stuporous" or "unconscious", and these agents produce analgesia without inducing loss of consciousness.The term narcotic in the legal context refers to a substance which produces **dependence.**

Later, the term "opiate" was used to designate drugs derived from opium poppy (morphine and codeine), although it has been loosely applied to morphine derivatives also, thus comprising the **natural** and **semisynthetic** compounds. *Currently,* the term "opioid" is preferred to designate all such substances, *natural, semisynthetic,* or *synthetic* that activate opioid receptors. **Thus, today narcotic analgesics and antagonists are better named as opioid analgesics and antagonists.**

Types of Pain

Pain consists of two components: (*i*) the **perception component;** and (*ii*) the **reaction component.** The perception is presumably the same for everyone, and depends on the intensity of the stimulus; whereas, the reaction is not the same for any two persons. The reaction depends on factors like **past experience, conditioning, memory,** and **judgement.** The **threshold** of reaction to pain varies with different personality types.

Generally, pain is clinically classified into two types: **acute** and **chronic.** Either type may be mild or severe. Acute pain is temporary, instantaneous and eventually subsides by treatment or on its own accord, e.g., renal colic and headache. In contrast, chronic pain is continuous, gradual in onset, and rather refractory to treatment, e.g., pain of rheumatoid arthritis and malignancy. **Psychogenic pain** is said to exist when no anatomic or physiologic reason is available, and relief may be obtained by the use of **placebos** or sedatives.

Neurophysiology of Pain

Peripheral mechanisms: Pain is produced by damage to tissues that leads to the liberation of various chemicals near the nerve endings. The pain receptors are perhaps better called as "nociceptors". There is ample evidence indicating that locally produced chemicals like **bradykinin** and **prostaglandins** are associated with production of pain. Other chemicals like **histamine, acetylcholine, lactic acid, serotonin** and **potassium** are also involved in the initiation of pain impulses.

Two types of fibres in the peripheral sensory nerves, **A-delta** and **C-fibres** are believed to respond to stimulation of pain receptors by generating and transmitting impulses that give rise to pain sensation. The A-delta fibres are large myelinated fibres (3-8 μ), which conduct impulses rapidly (15-20 metres/second), and register discretely localized pain **(epicritic pain).** In contrast the C-fibres are unmyelinated fibres (<1.5 μ), which conduct slowly (1-2 metres/second), and register vaguely localized dull, aching pain **(protopathic pain).**

Axons carrying stimuli from both the periphery and the viscera of the body have their cell stations in the dorsal root ganglia. The A-delta fibres convey pain impulses to the CNS by way of the ipsilateral dorsal columns, whereas the C-fibres relay pain impulses to the CNS by way of the crossed ventrolateral quadrant of the spinal cord, where they ascend as fibres of the spinothalamic tract. These fibres run through the brainstem and reach the posterolateral and posteromedial nuclei of the thalamus. Possibly impulses are integrated by the association nuclei of the thalamus before being relayed. From the thalamic nuclei, fibres project to the hypothalamus, which activates the autonomic response to pain. Some of the fibres transmitting pain terminate in the reticular formation of brainstem, and take part in the initiation of arousal **(Fig. 2.6.1).** The main group of fibres is extended to the **postcentral gyrus,** where the pain sensation is recognized, localized and differentiated.

Visceral pain is primarily conducted by sympathetic nerves, and is dull, aching and vaguely localized. Distension of hollow viscera leads to a sensation of pain due to stimulation of nerve endings located in the muscular wall. Visceral pain impulses enter the CNS via the anterolateral quadrant of the spinal cord. Pain of visceral origin is sometimes felt on certain cutaneous areas of the body surface at some distance from the involved viscera **(referred pain).**

Central neural mechanisms. Of the later theories of pain mechanisms, the current teachings emphasize the **specificity theory,** upon which the description of pain as peripheral, visceral, or referred is based. However, this theory has been challenged by the **gate control theory,** proposed by Melzack and Wall in 1965. This theory differs from the specificity theory in that pain impulses, transmitted from nerve receptors to the brain via the spinal cord, can be modified within the spinal cord, brainstem, and cerebral cortex so that the intensity of pain perceived varies, regardless of the actual intensity of the painful stimuli.

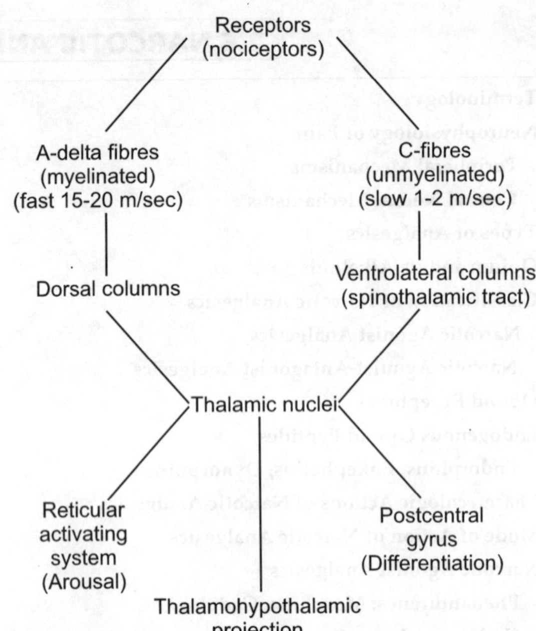

Fig. 2.6.1. The pain pathways (see text).

Although the appreciation of pain is complicated and complex in nature, the "gate control" theory, which essentially is an input control mechanism, has proved useful in explaining some aspects of it. According to this the peripheral sensations are transmitted **via large-diameter** (*L*) fast-conducting nerves, and **via small diameter** (*S*) slower-conducting fibres. The *L* nerve fibres are easily activated by minimal stimulation like touch. Such a stimulation on reaching the spinal cord activates the **first transmission cell** (T_1), and also activates collateral cells possibly in the **substantia gelatinosa** (*SG*). The *SG* cells by a negative feedback system then inhibit T_1 cells and decrease their output reaching the higher centres. If the peripheral stimulus is more intense, not only *L* nerves but also *S* nerves will be activated. The effect of the *S* nerve stimulation on the *SG* cells is to augment rather than diminish T_1 activity and thus increase their output reaching the higher centres **(Fig. 2.6.2).**

Pain has three attributes, namely, **physical, emotional** and **rational.** The physical attribute is subserved by sensory stimuli which ascend in the spinal cord via several pathways, that can be divided into the **oligosynaptic ascending system** (OAS) which ends in the postcentral gyrus and is concerned with the localization of pain, and the **multisynaptic ascending system** (MAS) which joins the limbic system, and is concerned with the emotional attribute of pain. Lastly, the rational attribute of pain is taken care of by the general cortex and depends on memory, judgement and previous experiences of the organism. Pain is considered as an area of intersection of the three attributes mentioned above.

The inhibiting and facilitating mechanisms are to some extent controlled by the higher centres, and emotional factors have considerable effect on the appreciation of pain. Thus, pain can be relieved by:

(*a*) Removal of the peripheral noxious stimulus. This may be done pharmacologically by the use of **non-narcotic analgesics** like aspirin **(Chap. 2.7).**

(*b*) Blockade of transmission in peripheral nerves by local anaesthetics.

(*c*) Modification of the gate mechanism activity. This may be the reason why **vibratory stimulation** and **acupuncture** relieve pain.

(*d*) Interference with the central appreciation of pain, or by inhibiting its emotional attributes, which is how the **narcotic analgesics** like opioids act (see below).

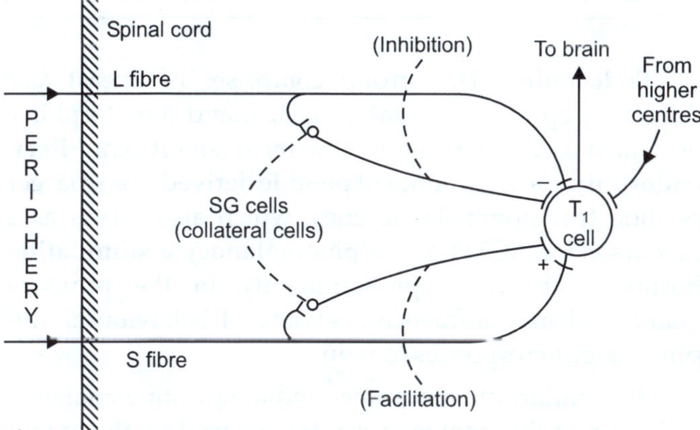

Fig. 2.6.2. Gate control theory of pain (see text).

Types of Analgesics

Analgesia denotes relief of pain, but with simultaneous retention of consciousness. Although the relief of pain is accomplished by the use of corticosteroids in rheumatoid arthritis, nitroglycerin for angina pectoris, and antacids in the treatment of peptic ulcer, these agents are not analgesics.

Analgesic drugs are divided into two main groups:

(*i*) **Narcotic analgesics.** These agents are capable of relieving severe degrees of pain, but are also moderately or strongly addictive. This group includes the opioids, which bind to the opioid receptors.

(*ii*) **Non-narcotic analgesics.** These agents relieve mild to moderate degrees of pain, and are considered non-addictive. This group includes aspirin, and other analgesic-antipyretics, and they have no affinity for the opioid receptors. Their site of action is peripheral **(Chap. 2.7).**

Opium and its Alkaloids

The poppy plant, *Papaver somniferum,* is the source of opium, a substance used since ancient times for relieving pain. Opium was among the earliest drugs discovered by man, and its behavioural effects are described in records dating back to 4000 BC. The poppy plant is found in India, Turkey, China, South-East Asia, Russia, and Mexico, and generally blooms in the month of June.

Opium is obtained by incising the unripe seed capsule of the poppy plant. The milky juice that oozes out is dried in air and forms a brown gummy mass. After further drying, it is powdered. This **powdered opium** contains over 20 alkaloids, but only a few of them have clinical usefulness. Early in the last century, a young German pharmacist, Friedrich Serturner, succeeded in isolating the active ingredient from opium, which he named **morphine,** after Morpheus, the Greek god of sleep and dreams. The application of morphine as an analgesic agent was greatly advanced by Alexander Wood's invention of the hypodermic syringe in 1853. Isolation of morphine, led to the isolation of other crystalline opium alkaloids including codeine. The useful alkaloids of opium are **morphine, papaverine** and **noscapine** (see below).

The alkaloids constitute about 25 percent of the weight of opium, and they have two distinct chemical forms, which differ in their pharmacological properties:

1. **Phenanthrene derivatives.** These are analgesic alkaloids consisting of morphine (10%); codeine (0.5%); and thebaine (0.2%).
2. **Benzylisoquinoline derivatives.** These include papaverine (1.0%) which is a spasmolytic and vasodilator; and *narcotine* or *noscapine* (6.0%) which is an antitussive.

Classification of Narcotic Analgesics

Drugs possessing an opioid-like action fall into two broad categories – the **narcotic agonists,** and the **narcotic agonist-antagonists.**

The narcotic analgesics can be classified as under:

I. Narcotic Agonist Analgesics

A. *Phenanthrenes*

(*i*) Naturally occurring opium alkaloids (*morphine, codeine*)

(*ii*) Semisynthetic derivatives of morphine (*hydromorphone, oxymorphone*)

(*iii*) Semisynthetic derivatives of codeine (*hydrocodone, oxycodone*)

B. *Methadones (methadone, propoxyphene)*

C. *Morphinan (levorphanol)*

D. *Phenylpiperidines (pethidine, fentanyl, alfentanil, sufentanil)*

II. Narcotic Agonist-Antagonist Analgesics

A. *Phenanthrenes (buprenorphine, nalbuphine)*

B. *Morphinan (butorphanol)*

C. *Benzomorphans (phenazocine, pentazocine)*

Table 2.6-1. *The opioid receptors, their endogenous ligands and effects produced on receptor stimulation.*

Receptor	*Endogenous ligand*	*Effects on receptor stimulation*
Mu (μ)	Endorphin	Supraspinal analgesia (μ_1) Dependence (μ_2) Respiratory depression (μ_2) Constipation (μ_2) Miosis (μ_2)
Kappa (κ)	Dynorphin	Spinal analgesia Sedation Miosis
Delta (δ)	Enkephalins	Affective behaviour Respiratory depression
Sigma (σ)	Unknown	Dysphoria Hallucinations

Opioid Receptors

Opioid receptors were first isolated by Pert and Snyder in 1973, and **four** types have been described, **mu** (μ), **kappa** (κ), **delta** (δ), and **sigma** (σ). Recent evidence also suggests subtypes of mu receptors. Sites of high receptor concentration include the *dorsal horn* of the spinal cord, and many subcortical brain areas, such as the *periaqueductal gray matter, hypothalamus, thalamus, locus coeruleus, raphe nuclei, limbic system, substantia gelatinosa,* and *the spinal nucleus of the fifth cranial nerve.* These receptors appear to be the site of action of the endogenous opioids – the *enkephalins, dynorphins,* and *endorphins.* The effects of stimulating the various opioid receptors, and their endogenous ligands are summarized in **Table 2.6-1.**

The narcotic analgesics bind to different receptors to varying degrees, and this relative preference determines their pharmacologic profile. For example most **narcotic agonists** have agonistic activity at μ, κ and possibly also δ receptors, and thereby exert the characteristic narcotic action. The **narcotic agonist-antagonist** drugs appear to preferentially bind to the κ and σ receptors, and may act as **partial antagonists** at the μ sites. This action of the mixed agonist-antagonist drugs may be responsible for their lower abuse potential, reduced euphoric effects, and greater sedative action compared to the narcotic agonists. **Morphine,** the prototype narcotic agonist, is capable of activating both μ_1 and μ_2 receptors.

Endogenous Opioid Peptides

The CNS sites that contain opioid receptors also contain **endogenous** morphine-like peptides that interact with the opioid receptor sites to elicit **physiologic** effects similar to those of exogenous narcotic agonists. Further, electrical stimulation of certain CNS areas evokes potent analgesia that can be attenuated by narcotic antagonist drugs like **naloxone.** This substantiates the presence of endogenous substances that interact with **opioid** receptors. *Three* groups of endogenous opioid peptides have been isolated, and termed **endorphins, enkephalins** and **dynorphins.**

Endorphins. This group comprises of atleast *four* different peptides designated α, β, γ, and δ endorphins, of which *beta-endorphin* is the most significant. **Beta-endorphin** is a 31-amino acid peptide derived from a larger peptide (pro-opiomelanocortin), which also serves as a precursor for ACTH and **alpha-melanocyte stimulating hormone.** It occurs predominently in the pituitary gland, and may influence a variety of behavioural and physiological responses to pain.

Beta-endorphin has potent and long-lasting analgesic activity, and this analgesia can be reversed by the opioid antagonist, **naloxone.**

Enkephalins are pentapeptides, and the two most extensively studied are **methionine-enkephalin** (met-enkephalin) and **leucine-enkephalin** (leu-enkephalin). They are derived from proenkephalin A. The enkephalins are located in nerve endings throughout the CNS, and are particularly abundant in the brainstem, the dorsal horn of the spinal cord, basal ganglia, and portions of the limbic system. Activity of enkephalins is enhanced by the presence of narcotic drugs, and these pentapeptides may be playing a major role in analgesia induced by opioid drugs. Their actions can be blocked or reversed by the narcotic antagonist, naloxone.

Dynorphins are derived from the precursor, prodynorphin. They (Dynorphin *A* and Dynorphin *B*) are larger peptides than enkephalins, but their precise role in pain modulation remains to be established.

Although the **endorphins** and **enkephalins** can mimic the action of opioids in pharmacologic test systems, they are of little clinical value, because they are not absorbed orally and are rapidly degraded by metabolizing enzymes in the brain, blood and other tissues.

Pharmacologic Actions of Narcotic Analgesics

The pharmacologic effects of therapeutic doses of opioids involve many different systems in the body, and are outlined in **Table 2.6-2.**

Table 2.6-2. *Major pharmacologic effects of narcotic analgesics*

Central Nervous System (CNS)
- Analgesia, Sedation, Euphoria, Emesis
- Depressed Cough reflex
- Respiratory depression (depression of medullary respiratory centre)

Cardiovascular System (CVS)
- Orthostatic hypotension (depression of medullary vasomotor centre, and peripheral vasodilation).

Gastrointestinal Tract (GIT)
- Decreased peristalsis and stomach motility
- Delayed gastric emptying
- Constipation

Smooth Muscle
- Increased tone of most nonvascular smooth muscle (e.g., GI, urinary and biliary tracts)

Urinary System
- Urinary tract spasm
- Contraction of urinary sphincter
- Release of antidiuretic hormone (ADH)
- Decreased renal blood flow (?)

Eye
- Miosis

Neuroendocrine
- Release of prolactin and somatotrophin
- Decreased release of luteinizing hormone (LH) and thyrotrophin (TSH)

Most of the actions are dose-dependent, but some effects are seen to a much greater degree with certain drugs, e.g., sedation is much *stronger* with the mixed agonist-antagonists than with the pure agonists. A comparison of their pharmacologic properties is presented in **Table 2.6-3.**

Table 2.6-3. *Comparative pharmacologic properties of narcotic analgesics (opioids)*

Drug	*Equianalgesic Does*	*(mg)**	*Onset of Action (min)***	*Duration of Action (hrs)***	*Analgesic Efficacy*	*Addictive Liability*	*Antitussive Activity*	*Respiratory Depression*	*Sedation*	*Emesis*
	PO	*SC, IM*								
Agonists										
Morphine	60	10	10 – 20	4 – 6	High	High	Strong	Moderate	Moderate	Moderate
Fentanyl	–	0.1-0.2	5 – 15	1 – 2	High	High	–	Weak	–	–
Sufentanil	–	–	2 – 4(IV)	0.5 – 1	High	High	–	–	–	–
Hydromorphone	8	1 – 2	15 – 30	4 – 5	High	High	Strong	Moderate	Weak	Weak
Oxymorphone	6	1 – 1.5	5 – 10	3 – 5	High	High	Weak	Strong	–	Strong
Levorphanol	4	2 – 3	15 – 30	4 – 6	High	High	Moderate	Moderate	Moderate	Weak
Methadone	20	7 – 10	10 – 15	4 – 6	High	High	Moderate	Moderate	Weak	Weak
Oxycodone	30	15	15 – 30	3 – 5	Medium	Medium	Strong	Moderate	Moderate	Moderate
Alfentanil	–	–	2 – 4(IV)	0.5 – 1	High	High	–	–	–	–
Pethidine	300	75 – 100	10 – 20	2 – 4	Medium	High	Weak	Moderate	Weak	–
Codeine	200	120	15 – 30	3 – 5	Low	Medium	Strong	Weak	Weak	Weak
Propoxyphene***	–	–	15 – 30(PO)	4 – 6	Low	Low	–	Weak	Weak	Weak
Agonist-Antagonists										
Buprenorphine	–	0.3	10 – 15	4 – 6	High	Low	–	Moderate	Moderate	Weak
Butorphanol	–	2 – 4	5 – 10	3 – 4	High	Low	–	Weak	Moderate	Weak
Nalbuphine	–	10	10 – 15	3 – 6	High	Low	–	Moderate	Moderate	–
Pentazocine	150	30 – 60	15 – 30	3 – 4	Medium	Medium	–	Moderate	Moderate	Weak

* All doses stated are approximately equal to 10 mg Morphine IM or SC.

** Onset and duration of action is based on SC or IM administration.

*** Propoxyphene is a very weak analgesic, and cannot be compared to other opioids in equianalgesic doses.

Mode of Action of Narcotic Analgesic Central Effects

Analgesia. Narcotic analgesics reduce pain by mimicking the actions of the endogenous opioids **met-enkephalin** and **leu-enkephalin.** In doing so they stimulate the μ, κ, and σ receptors in the CNS. The μ receptors probably mediate morphine-like analgesia and euphoria; κ receptors the analgesia, sedation and miosis produced by agonist-antagonist narcotics; and σ receptors the dysphoria and psychotomimetic effects produced by agonist-antagonist narcotics. **Analgesia** and **mood changes** appear to be interdependent. The euphoria and drowsiness caused by the opioids enhances the ability of the patient to tolerate pain.

Opioids impair the transmission of incoming noxious impulses in the **substantia gelatinosa** of the spinal column, probably by blocking release of **substance *P*,** an excitatory neurotransmitter. In short, the opioids produce analgesia by: reducing the patients **perception** of pain, and **elevation of pain perception threshold; modulation** of pain impulses; and changed **reaction** to pain as a result of sedation, drowsiness and production of sleep.

Sedation. Opioid analgesics in therapeutic doses induce drowsiness, and sleep sometimes ensues, from which the patient can be aroused.

Respiratory depression. Narcotic agonists decrease respiratory rate, minute volume, and tidal exchange by reducing the sensitivity of the brainstem respiratory centre to CO_2. Death from overdose results from respiratory failure.

Emesis. Narcotic analgesics induce nausea and vomiting in therapeutic doses, primarily due to the direct stimulation of the **chemoreceptor trigger zone** (CTZ) in the medulla.

Miosis. Most narcotic analgesics stimulate the autonomic segment of the oculomotor nerve, resulting in miosis. Tolerance does not develop to the miotic effect of opioids.

Cough suppression. All opioids cause a **direct** depression of the medullary cough centre. Codeine and hydrocodone are the most used antitussives. Tolerance and habituation occurs on long-term use.

Peripheral Effects

Constipation. It is a major adverse effect of most narcotic analgesics. It results from: (*i*) a delayed emptying of the stomach; (*ii*) a decrease in peristalsis of the small intestines, together with an increase in the non-propulsive contractions and colonic tone; and (*iii*) an increased tone of the anal sphincter.

Dependence. *Psychological* and *physical* dependence develop during chronic administration, together with an increasing degree of tolerance. **Tolerance** readily develops to the **analgesic, euphoric** and **respiratory depressant** effects, but no tolerance has been reported to the **miotic** and **constipating** effects of narcotics. Tolerance to one narcotic implies tolerance to all narcotics. **Cross-tolerance** does not extend to other CNS depressants, such as alcohol and barbiturates.

Hormonal effects. Release of **prolactin** and possibly **growth hormone** are enhanced by narcotics, whereas, secretion of **luteinizing hormone** (LH) and thyrotrophin (TSH) are inhibited.

The actions, and mechanisms of action of opioids are complex and involve multiple sites. They are summarized below:

1. Opioids **elevate the pain perception threshold,** alter perception of pain, blunt the **anxiety or apprehension** associated with pain, and induce **clouding of mentation** and sleep. Several mechanisms are operative in the above actions, and include; (*i*) **direct activation of opioid receptor** sites in the CNS; (*ii*) **potentiation** of the effects of endogenous opioids; and (*iii*) activation of the descending spinal cord pathways, which **reduces the level of incoming pain impulses** at various segmental levels of the spinal cord.
2. Opioids can **reduce calcium influx** into neuronal cells, thereby impairing the release of neurohormones like **noradrenaline, dopamine, serotonin** and **substance P.**
3. Opioids cause **respiratory depression by reducing the sensitivity of medullary respiratory centre neurones to carbon dioxide,** leading to a dose-dependent respiratory depression.
4. The **chemoreceptor trigger zone** (CTZ) is activated by the opioids causing nausea and vomiting.
5. The responsivity of the peripheral alpha-adrenoceptors is decreased, leading to visceral pooling of blood and **orthostatic hypotension.** Hypotensive effect is also due to depression of the medullary vasomotor centre (VMC), and **histamine** release, causing peripheral vasodilation.
6. Other actions of opioids are a **direct** inhibitory effect on GI motility. In addition there is biliary constriction, increased tone of urinary sphincter, and reduced uterine tone.

Narcotic Agonist Analgesics

Phenanthrenes

Morphine

Morphine isolated by Serturner in 1806 is the prototype narcotic analgesic. The structure of morphine consists of a partially hydrogenated phenanthrene oxide bridge and the ethenamine chain CH_2 CH_2 N (CH_3). It has a **phenolic hydroxyl** group at the 3-position, and an **alcoholic hydroxyl** at the 6-position. Attempts at molecular modification of the morphine structure, made with the intention of reducing the addiction liability and respiratory depressant action, while retaining the analgesic potency, has yielded important information. Masking of the phenolic hydroxyl group, by methylating it to form **codeine,** results in a marked reduction in analgesic potency, respiratory depressant activity, and addiction liability, but also results in an increased excitation of the CNS. In contrast, masking of the alcoholic hydroxyl group to form compounds like **dihydromorphinone** leads to an increase in analgesic and respiratory depressant activities **(Fig. 2.6.3)**

Pharmacological Actions

The central nervous actions can be divided into **suppressant** and **excitatory** actions.

Central nervous system. The most important action of morphine is relief from pain, and it relieves nearly all types of pain, but it is most effective when the pain is prolonged, rather than short-lived. No drug has been developed that is more effective than morphine for the relief of **severe pain.** Morphine *elevates the pain perception threshold,* and modifies the patient's subjective awareness of pain. The anxiety and stress associated with pain are markedly reduced. **Euphoria** may also occur in patients with clinical pain. **Tolerance** and **dependence** develop to the analgesic effect of morphine.

Other **suppressant central effects** produced by morphine include drowsiness, and with larger doses *sleep.* Morphine depresses the sensitivity of the **respiratory centre** to carbon dioxide, but not to hypoxia, thus causing a progressively decreasing respiratory rate and depth of breathing. The **cough centre** is also depressed by morphine.

Central stimulating actions. Morphine causes vomiting in 10-15 percent of patients by stimulation of the **chemoreceptor trigger zone,** and for this reason it may be combined with a phenothiazine like prochlorperazine (12.5 mg) by injection. **Epileptic fits** may be provoked. Morphine causes **pupillary constriction** by stimulating the Edinger-Westphal nucleus in the midbrain. Although this action is of no pharmacological importance, but miosis and "pinpoint pupils" are pathognomic of overdose with opioids. Morphine releases ADH, but suppresses the release of ACTH, FSH, and LH.

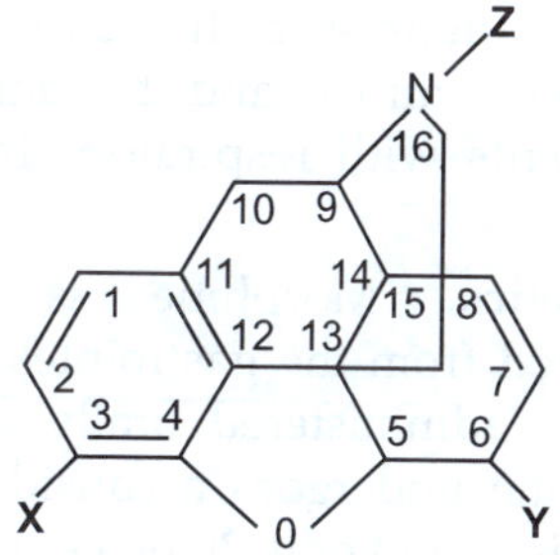

Analgesic	X	Y	Z
Morphine	– OH	– OH	– CH_3
Heroin	–$OCOCH_3$	– $OCOCH_3$	– CH_3
Codeine	–OCH_3	– OH	– CH_3
Dihydromor phinone	–OH	= O	– CH_3
Oxymorphone	–OH	= O	– CH_3
Oxycodone	–OCH_3	= O	– CH_3
Dihydrocode inone	–OCH_3	= O	– CH_3
Nalorphine	–OH	= OH	– CH_2 CH=CH_2
Naloxone	–OH	= O	– CH_2 CH=CH_2
Naltrexone	–OH	= O	– CH_2 CH $(CH_2)_2$

Fig. 2.6.3. Structural formulae of the opioids (see text).

Gastrointestinal and urinary tracts. Morphine increases the muscle tone throughout the gastrointestinal tract, which is combined with decreased peristalsis, leading to constipation. The tone of the anal sphincter is also augmented. The effect on the gut is mediated by the ganglion plexus in the gut wall. Tolerance **does not** develop to the constipating effect of opioids. The increased muscle tone also involves the sphincter of Oddi, and in therapeutic doses morphine causes a variable rise in intrabiliary pressure lasting for 2-3 hours.

In man the effect of morphine on the smooth muscle of the ureters is variable, but there may be some increase in tone.

Cardiovascular system. In therapeutic doses in the supine position, there is no major effect on blood pressure or heart rate, and the vasomotor centre is little affected. Even in toxic doses, despite respiratory depression, the blood pressure is usually maintained till late in the course of intoxication. Morphine causes peripheral arteriolar and venous dilatation, causing venous pooling.

The effects on the myocardium are not significant in normal man, but in some patients morphine may cause bradycardia due to stimulation of the vagal centre in the medulla. Cerebral circulation is not directly affected.

Respiratory system. Morphine depresses the respiratory centre in the brainstem. The voluntary control of breathing is retained in the conscious patient.

The **cough reflex** is **depressed.** It causes constriction of the bronchial smooth muscle, and it is dangerous to use morphine in patients with respiratory insufficiency or bronchial asthma.

Pharmacokinetics. Morphine is slowly and irregularly absorbed from the gastrointestinal tract, and is therefore rarely administered orally for pain relief. Moreover, morphine undergoes a considerable heptatic first-pass metabolism, and only 30 percent of an oral dose reaches systemic circulation. The oral route is useful in the management of cancer pain, as the duration of action is longer than after IM injection. Morphine and its congeners are well absorbed by diffusion from parenteral sites, and can be given by SC, IM or IV injection. After IM injection the peak therapeutic effect is achieved in about 1 hour and it lasts for 3-4 hours.

In therapeutic concentrations about one-third of morphine leaves the blood and accumulates in parenchymatous organs like kidney, liver, lung and spleen. Although the CNS is the primary site of action of morphine, only small amounts pass the blood-brain barrier.

Morphine undergoes metabolism by N-dealkylation, oxidation and conjugation with glucuronide and sulphate. The major route of elimination of metabolites is by glomerular filtration into the urine.

Therapeutic Uses

1. **Pain.** For acute pain following injury, myocardial infraction, or in the immediate postoperative period, the average adult dose is 10 mg SC or IM repeated 4-6 hourly. Morphine may be given intravenously in a dose of 5.0 mg when rapid relief is required.

Morphine or one of its congeners may be used for **relief of pain in terminal illness** due to cancer. The guidelines for the use of analgesics in terminal disease are: (*i*) use a dose large enough to relieve the pain completely; (*ii*) drug dependence is not a problem in the patient with terminal disease; and (*iii*) regular administration is necessary to keep the associated anxiety suppressed. A mixture containing **diamorphine** (Heroin) and **cocaine** may be used in terminal illness, although cocaine probably contributes little. **Morphine, cocaine** and **chlorpromazine** elixir may also be used for relieving pain of terminal illness. Tolerance and physical dependence are inevitable when these drugs are administered regularly.

2. **Preanaesthetic medication.** The preoperative use of opioids for their antianxiety or sedative effects is not preferred now. Anxiolytics such as parenteral diazepam, or hydroxyzine are used for the purpose.
3. **Left ventricular failure.** Morphine is effective in the relief of acute left ventricular failure and dyspnoea (paroxysmal nocturnal dyspnoea) due to associated pulmonary oedema. It allays anxiety, and produces peripheral vascular pooling of blood, which reduces the workload on the heart. The dose is usually 10 mg by injection.
4. **Diarrhoea.** The constipating action of morphine and other opioids make them useful for treating diarrhoea, but now codeine phosphate 30 mg tid is preferred.
5. **Gastrointestinal and urinary tract spasm.** Acute severe pain associated with biliary, renal, or ureteric colic can be relieved by the use of an opioid.
6. **Cough.** The cough reflex is suppressed or abolished by the opioids. For this purpose codeine is prefered.

Adverse Reactions

Despite their effective analgesic action the opioids cause the following adverse reactions that limit their usefulness: *nausea, vomiting, constipation, respiratory depression, histamine release, cardiovascular effects* (hypotension and bradycardia), *increased intracranial pressure, bronchial spasm, spasm of biliary and urinary tracts, urinary retention,* and rarely *hypersensitivity phenomena* (urticaria, rash and anaphylactoid reactions with IV administration). On repeated administration they cause **tolerance** and **dependence.**

Contraindications and precautions. Morphine and related compounds must be used with caution when there is a decreased respiratory reserve like in **emphysema, kyphoscoliosis, severe obesity** and **cor pulmonale.** It is contraindicated in *bronchial asthma,* as it may precipitate an acute attack. It is also contraindicated in patients with **head injuries,** as it tends to further increase intracranial pressure, and mask useful diagnostic and prognostic signs, making management difficult. Patients with **myxoedema** and **Addison's disease** are more sensitive to the depressant effects, whereas those with hyperthyroidism are more tolerant. It must be employed cautiously in patients with severely impaired liver or kidney function. Morphine hypersensitivity is an absolute contraindication. **To sum up,** morphine and other opioids are to be used with caution, or are contraindicated in the following conditions:

(*i*) Head injuries, delirium tremens, increased intracranial pressure;

(*ii*) Severe bronchial asthma, emphysema, and other diseases with a limited pulmonary reserve;

(*iii*) Metabolic disorders like myxoedema, Addison's disease, hepatic cirrhosis, and also renal failure, and

(*iv*) Prostatic hypertrophy, hypovolaemic shock and hypersensitivity.

Preparations and dosage. Morphine is available in the form of *morphine sulphate* and *morphine hydrochloride.* It is usually administered by IM or SC injection in a dose of 10 mg/70 kg body weight (range 5 to 20 mg). It may also be given IV in a dose of 2.5 to 15 mg in 4 to 5 ml of water for injection, administered slowly over 4 to 5 minutes.

Drug interactions. The CNS-depressant effects of opioids may be potentiated or prolonged by concurrent use of other CNS depressants like **barbiturates, alcohol, anaesthetics,** and **phenothiazines.** Respiratory depression may be intensified by the concurrent use of neuromuscular blocking agents like *succinylcholine.*

Acute Opioid Poisoning (Acute Toxicity)

Acute opioid poisoning may result from clinical overdosage, accidental overdosage usually in addicts, or attempts at suicide. There is great individual variation in sensitivity, and the oral toxic dose of morphine is between 100-300 mg, and about 250-500 mg constitutes a lethal dose for the nontolerant person. The addict is capable of taking a dose of morphine that is 10 to 20 times the lethal dose.

Symptoms and signs. The triad of **coma, pinpoint pupils** and **depressed respiration** strongly suggest poisoning. With large overdosage there is profound coma, and the patient cannot be aroused. The respiratory rate is slow (at times 2 to 4/minute), and has alternating periods of apnoea and hyperpnoea **(Cheyne-Stokes breathing),** and cyanosis may be present. The **blood pressure** progressively falls. The **pupils** are symmetrical and pinpoint, but if hypoxia is severe they may be dilated. **Urine formation** is depressed, **body temperature** falls and the skin is cold and clammy, and the skeletal muscles are flaccid. **Pulmonary oedema** may occur following toxic doses of morphine, propoxyphene and methadone.

Treatment. The first step is to establish a patent airway and ventilate the patient. In the relatively rare cases of oral methadone or opium overdosage, it is desirable to administer a *charcoal mixture,* or to wash the stomach (gastric lavage) with solutions of **alkaloidal precipitants** (e.g., tannic acid), or oxidizers (i.e., potassium permanganate 1:5,000 dilution).

Immediate steps should be taken to combat advancing respiratory depression. For this **opioid antagonists** like **naloxone** can produce a dramatic reversal of severe respiratory depression. Naloxone is now the drug of choice as it is a pure antagonist, and it is administered in small doses of 0.4 mg IV, repeated after 2 to 3 minutes. **Pulmonary oedema** may be countered by positive pressure respiration. **Grand mal seizures** are suppressed by treatment with naloxone.

Chronic Toxicity (Opioid addiction). The nature of opioid dependence has been discussed in **Chapter 2.10.**

Codeine

Codeine is the second most important alkaloid of opium poppy. It is widely used as an **analgesic, antidiarrhoeal** and **cough suppressant.** Analgesic potency is considerably lower than morphine. Codeine 120 mg IM is equivalent to 10 mg of parenteral morphine. Codeine is demethylated in the body to morphine and norcodeine. It produces slight sedation, practically no euphoria, and no noticeable respiratory depression in therapeutic doses. **Tolerance** develops far less rapidly than with morphine and dependence occurs rarely. Codeine suppresses cough by direct suppressant effect on the medullary cough centre. **Dosage** of codeine phosphate for **analgesia** in adults ranges from 15 mg to 60 mg qid orally, SC, IM, or IV. For **cough suppression** the dose is 10 mg to 20 mg every 4 to 6 hours to a maximum of 120 mg/24 hours.

Hydromorphone (Dihydromorphinone)

Hydromorphone is a clinically used semisynthetic derivative of morphine. It is 10 times more potent than morphine as an analgesic, and so also its respiratory depressant effect is greater. It produces less sedation, vomiting and nausea. It has a high abuse potential and is a popular "street drug" due to extreme potency and lack of strong hypnotic effect. Oral form is useful in treating **severe chronic pain,** but the drug is relatively short-acting. Suppositories may give a prolonged effect. *Dosage* of hydromorphone hydrochloride is 2 mg to 4 mg orally, SC, IM every 4 to 6 hours.

Oxymorphone

Oxymorphone is 10 times more potent than morphine as an analgesic, with a rapid onset of action. Incidence of euphoria, nausea and vomiting is also greater. It depresses the respiratory centre, and has a high addiction liability. It is used for **preoperative sedation, obstetrical analgesia,** and relief of anxiety in patients with dyspnoea due to pulmonary oedema. **Dosage:** SC, IM–1 mg to 1.5 mg every 4-6 hours; IV–0.5 mg as needed; Rectal–5 mg every 4-6 hours; Analgesia during labour–0.5 mg to 1 mg IM every 4-6 hours.

Heroin (Diacetylmorphine)

Heroin is another semisynthetic derivative of morphine. It is 3 times more potent than morphine as an analgesic. It causes less sedation, less constipation, and less nausea and vomiting compared to morphine. It produces **marked euphoria** and has a very high addiction liability. Hence, it is not available as a drug for routine use. In some institutions it is available for the management of **terminal illness due to cancer.** It is a much abused drug and has a rapid onset of action on IV administration **(Chapter 2.10).**

HYDROCODONE

Hydrocodone is slightly more potent as an analgesic than codeine. In doses of 5 to 10 mg orally it is chiefly employed as an **antitussive** agent.

OXYCODONE

Oxycodone is used for relief of moderate to severe pain, and possesses good **antitussive** action. It is more potent than codeine, and has a greater addiction liability. Oxycodone hydrochloride is usually administered orally in a dose of 5 mg every 6 hours.

METHADONES

METHADONE

Methadone differs structurally from morphine, but has similar actions. Its analgesic action is equal to that of morphine, and it causes respiratory depression and constipation, but it produces less euphoria and drowsiness. It is slower in onset and longer in duration of action.

Methadone may be used to relieve **severe pain** in a dose of 2.5 to 10 mg IM, SC or orally. For **chronic pain** relief it is administered in a dose of 5 mg every 12 hours to 20 mg every 5 hours. Methadone is also used for **detoxification** and maintenance of opioid (morphine or heroin) addicts. It acts in two ways: (*i*) **suppresses the withdrawal syndrome** in patients who are being withdrawn from morphine or heroin; and (*ii*) **maintains patients** who have been withdrawn from narcotics, and are in a stage of minimal craving for the narcotic **(Chap. 2.10).** Dosage is highly individualized depending on the severity of withdrawal symptoms (about 15-40 mg orally used to suppress symptoms, and treatment should not exceed 21 days). Maintenance dose is 20 mg daily.

PROPOXYPHENE

Propoxyphene is a **very weak analgesic,** structurally related to methadone, and has little antitussive activity. Its **addiction liability** equals that of codeine. Propoxyphene (dextropropoxyphene) is superior to codeine as it does not produce constipation, and the incidence of nausea, vomiting, drowsiness and dizziness is lower. It has also been classified as a **non-narcotic analgesic,** but is devoid of antipyretic and anti-inflammatory activity. Propoxyphene is usually administered in fixed-dose combination with aspirin and caffeine, and is usefully employed in the treatment of chronic pain. It may also be used to treat **myalgia, neuralgia, migraine, backache,** and **arthritic pain**. In high doses it produces euphoria and dependence. The oral dose of dextropropoxyphene hydrochloride is 65 to 130 mg every 4 hours.

MORPHINAN

LEVORPHANOL

Levorphanol is a very potent analgesic (5 times more potent than morphine), and 2 mg of levorphanol has a greater sedative effect than 10 mg of morphine administered SC. It is used **preoperatively** to potentiate and prolong general anaesthesia, and to shorten recovery time. The usual dose is 2 to 3 mg orally or SC every 4-6 hours.

PHENYLPIPERIDINES

PETHIDINE (MEPERIDINE)

Pethidine was introduced in 1939 as the first synthetic narcotic analgesic. It is the most frequently prescribed opioid. Pethidine is a moderately potent analgesic (1/10 morphine), with weak antitussive activity. It is less spasmogenic and constipating than most other narcotics. It has a rapid onset and shorter duration of action (2-4 hours) compared to morphine.

Pethidine is used for treating **moderately severe pain,** and the usual dose is 25-100 mg IM, SC and occasionally by slow IV drip. It may also be given orally in a dose of 50-150 mg. It is useful for relief of pain of **coronary occlusion, biliary** or **renal colic.** It is less likely to cause GI spasm, but it does not have an antispasmodic action of its own in therapeutic doses. It is used preoperatively as an **adjunct to anaesthesia,** and for **obstetrical analgesia** (50-100 mg IM or SC, repeated at 1-3 hours intervals).

Adverse effects of pethidine include dizziness, tachycardia, nausea, vomiting, orthostatic hypotension, and excitement. Respiratory depression occurs with higher doses. Its addiction liability is responsible for most iatrogenic (doctor-induced) addictions.

FENTANYL

Fentanyl is a very potent (100 times more potent than morphine) **analgesic** used for short durations (e.g., preoperatively, during surgery or postoperatively to relieve pain and anxiety). It has a rapid onset (10-15 min) and short duration (1-2 hours) of action on IM administration. Respiratory depression outlasts analgesia. **Fentanyl** plus **droperidol** (Innovar) is a combination preparation used to produce analgesia and tranquillization called **neuroleptanalgesia** for short surgical and diagnostic procedures **(Chap. 2.3).**

ALFENTANIL

Alfentanil is a rapid-acting narcotic used intravenously as an **analgesic adjunct** (50 mcg/kg IV) during nitrous oxide/oxygen/barbiturate anaesthesia. It is also used as a **primary induction anaesthetic** (130-245 mcg/kg IV) in general surgery where intubation and mechanical ventilation are required.

SUFENTANIL

Sufentanil is an **anaesthetic agent** which can induce and maintain anaesthesia with 100 percent oxygen in patients undergoing major cardiovascular or neurosurgery. It is also used as an **analgesic adjunct** to maintain **balanced anaesthesia.** Doses above 8 mcg/kg produce sleep. Postoperative mechanical ventilation is necessary due to extended respiratory depression.

Narcotic Agonist-Antagonist Analgesics

Phenanthrenes

Buprenorphine

It is a semisynthetic derivative of thebaine, and has a high affinity for μ receptors, where it acts as a **partial agonist.** It dissociates from the μ receptors slowly, and thus exhibits a long duration of action (upto 6 hours). Its **antagonist** activity is equal to that of naloxone. Buprenorphine is highly lipophilic and is 20 to 30 times more potent than morphine as an analgesic. It may precipitate withdrawal symptoms in narcotic-dependent patients. Buprenorphine has also been abused by the IV route.

Buprenorphine is used in the treatment of **moderate to severe pain.** It has also been used after **myocardial infarction** and in **terminal care.** The usual dose range is 0.3 to 0.6 mg IM, or slow IV every 6 hours, as needed.

Nalbuphine

Nalbuphine is chemically related to oxycodone and naloxone. It possesses both **agonistic** activity at κ and δ receptors, and weak **antagonistic** activity at μ receptors. Analgesia produced is equivalent to morphine, with a somewhat lower abuse potential. The incidence of sedation is high. Duration of **analgesia** ranges from 3-6 hours. The usual dose is 10 mg/70 kg body weight SC, IM, or IV, repeated every 3-6 hours, as necessary. Maximum dose is 160 mg/day.

Morphinan

Butorphanol

Butorphanol is a potent analgesic, about 4 to 7 times more potent than morphine on weight basis. Respiratory depression is more marked than with morphine. It possesses weak narcotic antagonistic activity, and withdrawal symptoms can occur in narcotic dependent patients. The usual dose is 2 mg IM every 3-4 hours, or 1 mg IV every 3-4 hours. It is ineffective by mouth.

Benzomorphans

Phenazocine

Phenazocine is one of the most potent narcotic analgesics on a weight basic. It is about 3 times more potent than morphine, and is useful for the rapid relief of pain. It is claimed that phenazocine does not cause spasm of the sphincter of Oddi, and thus is useful in treating **biliary** and **pancreatic** pain. It is used as an analgesic in **terminal care** of cancer patients in doses of 5 mg (upto 20 mg, if needed) to produce rapid analgesia lasting for 5-6 hours. Phenazocine can also be given by injection in doses of 1-2 mg for **premedication,** for **postoperative pain** and for **obstetrical analgesia.** It produces minimal sedation, and tolerance is rather slow to develop.

Pentazocine

Pentazocine is the N-allyl derivative of phenazocine. It is one-third as potent as morphine parenterally. It possesses some narcotic antagonistic activity also, and therefore can produce withdrawal symptoms in narcotic dependent patients. Pentazocine is of value in the relief of **chronic intractable pain.** Onset of action is in 15-30 minutes on oral, IM or SC use, and the duration of action is 2-3 hours. Pentazocine can cause hallucinations and bizarre thought processes. The usual dose is 50 mg every 3-4 hours orally (maximum dose 600 mg/day); 30 mg every 3-4 hours IM, SC, IV (maximum dose 360 mg/day); 30 mg IM or 20 mg IV every 2-3 hours for **obstetrical analgesia.**

Narcotic Antagonists

In 1951, N-allylnormorphine or **nalorphine** was introduced for the treatment of narcotic poisoning, followed by N-allylnorlevorphanol or **levallorphan** in 1952 as a narcotic antagonist. Both of them have agonist-antagonist activity, and hence no longer used. Considering the **agonist-antagonist ratios** of various opioids and opioid antagonists, morphine is a **pure agonist** and **naloxone** is a **pure antagonist,** as illustrated in **Fig. 2.6.4.**

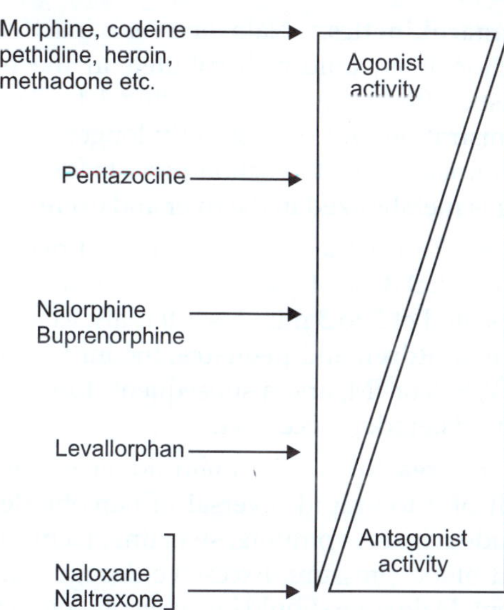

Fig. 2.6.4. The agonist-antagonist ratios of some opioids and opioid antagonists (see text).

Drugs capable of reversing the effects of narcotic agonists are termed *narcotic antagonists* or opioid antagonists. Both the drugs currently in use in this category – **naloxone** and **naltrexone** – are viewed as **"pure" antagonists,** because they possess no intrinsic agonistic activity. The two narcotic antagonists, **naloxone** and **naltrexone,** are the N-allyl and methylcyclopropyl analogues of oxymorphone respectively. Narcotic antagonists competitively block opioid receptors.

In short, **naloxone** is a rapid-acting drug, given parenterally to reverse or prevent the effects of opioids, specially on overdosage. It reverses the **respiratory**

depressant, sedative, hypotensive, analgesic and **psychotomimetic** effects of opioids. In the absence of opioids, naloxone exhibits no pharmacologic activity. **Naltrexone** is an orally effective narcotic antagonist, which attenuates or **blocks subjective effects** of opioids, and **reduces the physical dependence** on these drugs. It is used as an adjunct to maintain an opioid-free state in detoxified former addicts.

NALOXONE

Mode of action. Naloxone exhibits a very high affinity for the μ receptors, and is capable of displacing narcotic drugs from these sites, reversing their effects. Naloxone can also reverse the **dysphoric** and **psychotomimetic** effects of mixed agonist-antagonists like pentazocine. In the absence of narcotics, naloxone exhibits no activity, except mild sedation at very high doses. No tolerance or dependence has been reported.

Therapeutic uses. Naloxone is used for: (*i*) **Reversal of respiratory depression** and other adverse effects induced by overdosage of opioids; (*ii*) Diagnosis of acute opioid overdosage; and (*iii*) **Investigational** uses include reversal of *alcoholic* coma, and improvement of circulation in **refractory shock.**

Pharmacokinetics. Naloxone is inactive orally. On injection it is rapidly distributed in the body, and antagonistic effects are evident within 1 to 2 minutes of IV administration and only slightly longer following SC or IM administration. The action persists for 1 to 4 hours. The drug is metabolized in the liver and excreted in urine.

Dosage. To treat known or suspected overdosage in **adults,** an initial dose of 0.4 mg to 2 mg IV with additional doses repeated at 2 to 3 minutes intervals, as needed upto 3 doses. In **children** and **neonates,** the initial dose is 0.01 mg/kg IV, SC, or IM, and a subsequent dose of 0.01 mg/kg is administered, if necessary.

Adverse reactions. The main adverse reactions are the result of a too-rapid reversal of narcotic depression, and include nausea, vomiting, sweating, tachycardia, and increased blood pressure. Excessive dosage can result in excitement. Naloxone should be given *cautiously* to known or suspected narcotic addicts, as severe withdrawal syndrome may be precipitated.

NALTREXONE

Mode of action. Naltrexone blocks the effects of opioids by a *competitive binding* at opioid receptors. It is a **pure antagonist,** completely devoid of agonistic action at the receptor sites. When given concurrently with opioids, it markedly attenuates the euphoria and other subjective effects, and in a properly motivated individual, provides an adjunctive means for maintaining an opioid-free state. The receptor blocking action persists for at least 24 hours, and may be extended upto 72 hours with increasing dosage.

Therapeutic use. Used as adjunctive therapy in the maintenance of an opioid-free state in detoxified former addicts.

Pharmacokinetics: On oral administration, peak blood levels occur within 1 hour. Naltrexone undergoes extensive first-pass hepatic metabolism, and some of the metabolites also are active antagonists. Effects persist from 24 to 72 hours. Metabolites are excreted by the kidneys.

Dosage. Naltrexone is available as 50 mg tablets. The initial dose is 25 mg and the patient should be observed for 1 hour. If no withdrawal signs occur, an additional 25 mg is given. Thereafter, 50 mg once daily will provide effective blocking action. Dosage schedule is flexible.

Adverse reactions. Major side effects are due to the precipitation of a withdrawal syndrome, and include nervousness, headache, insomnia, cramps, nausea, vomiting, muscle pain and nasal congestion. Naltrexone causes dose-related hepatocellular damage, and should be used with extreme caution in persons with pre-existing liver disease.

ANTITUSSIVES

Most drugs used for the suppression of cough act by **blocking the central component of the cough reflex.** Narcotics are particularly effective in this respect. **Codeine** is the most widely used agent for this purpose, and still is a **standard** for comparison. Other agents are discussed herewith.

DEXTROMETHORPHAN

Dextromethorphan, which is the dextro-isomer of the methyl ether of levorphanol has **antitussive** activity, but no analgesic activity. **It acts centrally to elevate the cough threshold.** The usual adult dose is 15-30 mg every 4 to 6 hours.

LEVOPROPOXYPHENE

Levopropoxyphene has weak antitussive properties, and is devoid of analgesic activity. The average adult dosage of levopropoxyphene napsylate is 50-100 mg every 4 hours.

NOSCAPINE

Noscapine is one of the non-narcotic benzylisoquinoline alkaloids of opium, and has antitussive properties. It has minimal other effects on the CNS in therapeutic doses. Noscapine is the principal antitussive in several proprietary preparations. The usual adult dose is 15-30 mg every 4 to 6 hours.

BENZONATATE

Benzonatate is a non-narcotic antitussive compound, chemically related to the local anaesthetic tetracaine. Its antitussive effect is mediated by an action on both central and peripheral respiratory mucosal stretch receptors. It is less effective than codeine in suppressing cough. The usual adult dose is 100 mg every 4 to 6 hours.

2.7 NON-NARCOTIC ANALGESICS AND ANTIPYRETICS (ANTI-INFLAMMATORY AGENTS, DRUGS FOR GOUT, RHEUMATOID ARTHRITIS, AND MIGRAINE)

Pain has been defined as a characteristic sensation arising from a noxious stimulus, which includes its neurophysiological aspect. Sherrington, in his classic definition has further included the reactive component of pain, i.e., the "psychical adjuvant of an imperative protective reflex". This indicates that pain also has a survival value for the species. There are two main classes of pain: **superficial** (integumental), and **deep.** Superficial pain is usually a quick response of sudden onset, while deep pain is more lingering and aching. Some pain receptors in the body are probably **chemoreceptors,** as a wide variety of compounds, including autacoids like **bradykinin,** and several of the **prostaglandins,** can elicit pain. The main physiological pain receptors, however, are the free nerve endings.

Drugs can alter the pain experience in *three* ways (pain **reception, perception,** and **reaction**). The **first step** that can be interrupted is peripheral **pain reception** at the nerve endings. This modality is susceptible to **non-narcotic analgesics** and **local anaesthetics.** The **second step** which can be modified is **pain perception** at the level of the CNS. Both, **narcotic** and **non-narcotic analgesics** interfere with this level of pain integration. The *third step* which can be influenced is **pain reaction.**

Terminology

The non-narcotic analgesics are a heterogeneous group of drugs which have the properties of being analgesic, antipyretic and anti-inflammatory. These agents have been variously named – **analgesic-antipyretics; aspirin-like drugs;** and **nonsteroidal anti-inflammatory drugs** (NSAIDs). The non-narcotic analgesics have a peripheral site of action, and have no affinity for the opioid receptors. They are considered to be **non-addictive.**

Classification

The non-narcotic analgesics and anti-inflammatory drugs may be classified as under :

1. **Salicylates:** Aspirin, calcium carbaspirin, choline salicylate, diflunisal, magnesium salicylate, methyl salicylate, salicylamide, salicylic acid, salsalate, sodium salicylate, sodium thiosalicylate, sulfasalazine, mesalazine, olsalazine.
2. **Para-aminophenol:** Paracetamol.
3. **Pyrazolones:** Phenylbutazone, oxyphenbutazone, sulfinpyrazone.
4. **Nonsteroidal anti-inflammatory drugs** (NSAIDs).
   (*a*) *Indole derivatives:* Indomethacin, sulindac, tolmetin, etodolac.
   (*b*) *Propionic acid derivatives:* Ibuprofen, fenoprofen, ketoprofen, naproxen, flurbiprofen, oxaprozin.
   (*c*) *Fenamates:* Mefenamic acid.
   (*d*) *Phenylacetic acid derivative:* Diclofenac.
   (*e*) *Oxicams:* Piroxicam.
   (*f*) *Miscellaneous:* Hydroxychloroquine, penicillamine.

5. **Gold compounds:** Auranofin, aurothioglucose, gold sodium thiomalate.
6. **Antigout drugs:** Colchicine, probenecid, sulfinpyrazone, allopurinol.

The non-narcotic analgesics in certain texts have been classified as the **salicylates** (Group 1), and **non-salicylates** (Group 2-6).

SALICYLATES

The salicylates, are derivatives of salicylic acid. Aspirin, a product developed in 1899 by Bayer, is by far the most popular analgesic.

ASPIRIN (ACETYLSALICYLIC ACID)

Hippocrates and other ancient physicians employed plants in the treatment of disease, now known to contain natural salicylates. These include species of willow and poplar, and a species of Gaultheria, from which **oil of wintergreen** (methyl salicylate) is obtained. Actually the word **salicylate** is derived from **Salix,** the Latin name for the willow tree. The **prototype** synthetic salicylate, aspirin, was introduced as a substitute for sodium salicylate.

PHARMACOLOGICAL ACTIONS AND MODE OF ACTION

The salicylates act both **centrally** and **peripherally** to produce their therapeutic and toxic effects. Aspirin exhibits analgesic, antipyretic, and anti-inflammatory activity. The **salicylic acid** portion of the salicylate molecule is the pharmacologically active moiety. It is essential that the hydroxyl group of this molecule remains in the *ortho* position.

Analgesic/anti-inflammatory actions. The salicylates have been found to be most useful for the treatment of headache, rheumatic and muscular pain, arthritic pain and pain arising from integumental structures.

The exact mechanism of analgesic action of the salicylates is not known. The analgesic action is **mainly** a peripheral effect, in the form of blockade of pain impulse generation. They have no effect on the reticular activating system or the limbic system, but may be they exert some action on subcortical sites like the thalamus and hypothalamus.

The peripheral analgesic action of salicylates has been extensively worked upon, and depends essentially on reducing the production of certain **prostaglandins.** The prostaglandins are universally released on tissue damage, and are present in the inflammatory exudate. It is evident that prostaglandins (particularly prostaglandin E_2) plays an important role in several aspects of the inflammatory process. Lately, attention has been focussed on **inhibition of prostaglandin synthesis** as a machanism of analgesic, anti-inflammatory and antipyretic activity. The synthetic pathway of the relevant prostaglandin (PGE_2) is shown in **(Fig. 2.7.1).** The final step in prostaglandin synthesis depends on the activity of the enzyme complex prostaglandin synthetase, and aspirin inhibits its activity. The analgesic anti-inflammatory drugs, including aspirin, are believed to inhibit **cyclo-oxygenase** and thus reduce prostaglandin production. They have an **anti- bradykinin** action, which is reflected as an elevation in pain threshold. Bradykinin is one of the major mediators of the inflammatory response, and is formed through action of activated kallikrein, potentiated by fibrinopeptide B **(Fig. 2.7.2).** The analgesic and anti-inflammatory activity go hand in hand.

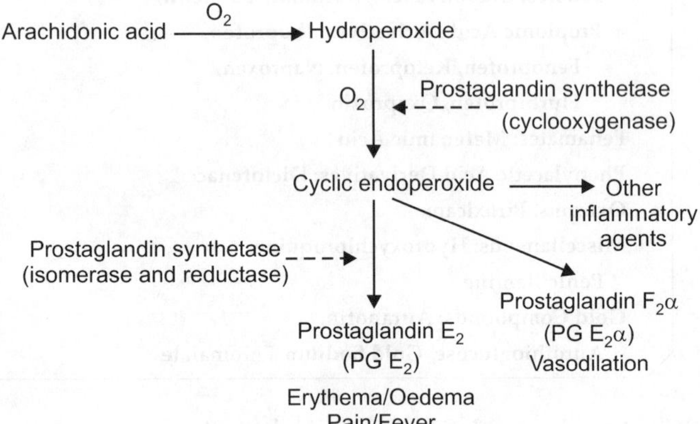

Fig. 2.7.1. The synthetic pathway of Prostaglandin E_2 and Prostaglandin $F_2\alpha$, the mediators of inflammation (simplified).

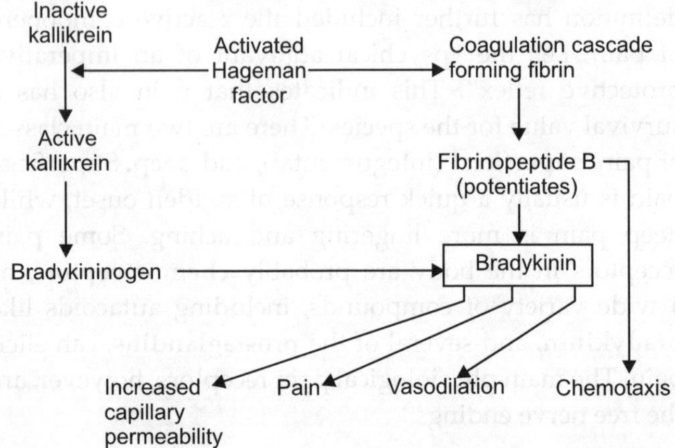

Fig. 2.7.2. Formation and role of bradykinin in inflammation (see text).

Antirheumatic action. In **acute rheumatic fever** the pain and fever are reduced and the joint inflammation settles down. The mechanism of antirheumatic action is unclear. It was suggested that salicylates stimulate the adrenocortical hormones **cortisone** and **hydrocortisone,** which have potent anti-inflammatory activity. However, this theory has lost favour now due to contradictory evidence. The view now held is that the salicylates directly check some steps in the sequence of the inflammatory process, e.g., keeping **bradykinin** and **prostaglandin** from being released to cause vasodilation, increased capillary permeability and pain. The salicylates and other antirheumatic drugs like the corticosteroids, may also prevent the release of **lysosomal enzymes** which destroy the cartilage of rheumatic joints.

Antipyretic action. Body temperature is controlled from a hypothalamic integrating centre (thermostat), which detects changes in the deep body (core) and environmental (cutaneous) thermoceptors and then adjusts the functioning of peripheral effectors. This dynamic equilibrium is maintained through the cutaneous blood vessels, sweat glands and other peripheral structures **(Fig. 2.7.3).**

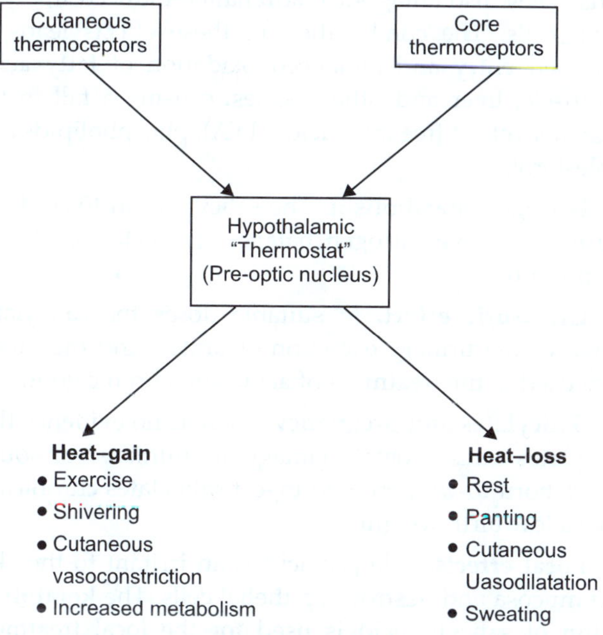

Fig. 2.7.3. Regulation of body temperature.

Fevers caused by bacterial endotoxins or viruses, are caused by **endogenous pyrogens** which act directly upon the thermoregulatory neurones in the hypothalamus to increase the set point temperature. The effectors raise the core temperature so that it is higher than normal. In this febrile process mainly the prostaglandin (PGE_2) is involved.

Salicylates have a marked antipyretic action, and reduce elevated body temperature (normal body temperature is not reduced). This is usually accompanied by profuse sweating, and is believed to be due to inhibition of the synthesis and release of prostaglandin E in the **pre-optic nucleus of the hypothalamus,** which is the site of the temperature regulating area.

Respiration and acid-base balance. The salicylates cause serious acid-base imbalances. They increase respiratory rate and volume by two mechanisms: (*i*) by a **direct** stimulation of the respiratory centre, and (*ii*) by **uncoupling oxidative phosphorylation** causing increased oxygen utilization and production of carbon dioxide. As a secondary effect respiratory alkalosis occurs. In very high doses the respiratory centre is depressed, and salicylates cause central respiratory paralysis.

As mentioned above, initially in therapeutic doses salicylates cause respiratory alkalosis. The kidney compensates by excretion of bicarbonate accompained by an increased excretion of sodium and potassium. As a result plasma bicarbonate falls, and blood pH returns towards normal. This is the stage of **compensated respiratory alkalosis.** Further, in toxic doses the respiratory centre in the medulla is depressed, and there is an enhanced production of CO_2; consequently the plasma PCO_2 increases and the blood pH decreases. Since the plasma bicarbonate is already low, the acid-base status at this stage is essentially an **uncompensated respiratory acidosis.** Superimposed however, is a true metabolic acidosis caused by accumulation of acids as a result of : (*i*) displacement of plasma bicarbonate by salicylic acid derivatives; (*ii*) vasomotor depression by toxic doses impairs renal function leading to accumulation of strong acids of metabolic origin; and (*iii*) organic acids accumulate as a result of salicylate-induced derangement of carbohydrate metabolism, like pyruvic acid, lactic and acetoacetic acids. Such a state further enhances metabolic acidosis **(Fig. 2.7.4).**

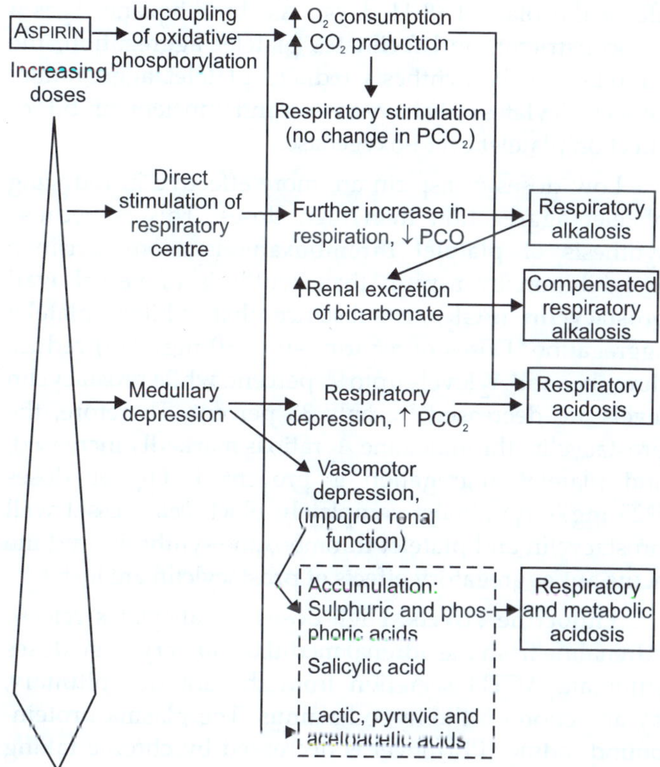

Fig. 2.7.4. Acid-base disturbances caused by increasing doses of aspirin (see text).

The acid-base disturbances also cause alterations of **water** and **electrolyte balance.** In addition water is lost by salicylate-induced sweating, and insensible water loss due to hyperventilation, leading to **dehydration.**

Gastrointestinal effects. The gastric mucosa shows gastritis with superficial gastric ulceration. Solid particles of the drug are particularly damaging and can cause severe gastric bleeding, which is painless, and frequently leads to blood loss in the stool and occasionally to an iron-deficiency anaemia. Bleeding is increased if aspirin is taken with alcohol, and reduced if taken with antacids.

Cardiovascular effects. Therapeutic doses of salicylates have no important direct cardiovascular actions. The peripheral vessels dilate after large doses, due to a direct effect on the smooth muscle. Toxic amounts depress the circulation directly.

Hepatic and renal effects. Salicylates elevate enzyme activities in the plasma which indicate hepatic dysfunction (SGOT, SGPT, alkaline phosphatase), and occasionally hepatomegaly occurs. Aspirin should be avoided in patients with severe hepatic damage, hypoprothrombinaemia, vitamin *K* deficiency or haemophilia, because inhibition of platelet function can lead to bleeding.

Platelet antiaggregatory action. Platelet aggregation is inhibited by aspirin. This difference is probably due to the acetyl group of aspirin, which is capable of **irreversibly inhibiting platelet cyclo-oxygenase and the subsequent synthesis of thromboxane A_2** for the entire life of the platelet (8-11 days). As thromboxane A_2 is a vasoconstrictor, and facilitates platelet aggregation, the inhibition of its synthesis reduces platelet aggregation. Other salicylates only have a weak and transient inhibitory effect on platelet cyclo-oxygenase.

Low doses of aspirin are more effective in reducing platelet aggregation than high doses. This is because synthesis of **platelet thromboxane** is more sensitive to inhibition by aspirin than synthesis of **vessel wall prostacyclin** (PGI_2), a substance that inhibits platelet aggregation. Doses of aspirin (40 to 80 mg/day) reduce thromboxane A_2 levels upto 95 percent, while prostacyclin levels are decreased by only 35 percent. Therefore, the prostacyclin: thromboxane A_2 ratio is markedly increased, and platelet aggregation is prevented. Higher doses (325 mg/day) almost completely block *both* vessel wall prostacyclin and platelet thromboxane synthesis, and the acute antiaggregatory effects of prostacylclin are lost.

Endocrine effects. High doses of salicylates release adrenaline from the adrenal medulla and very large doses stimulate ACTH secretion from the anterior pituitary, by an action on the hypothalamus. The plasma protein-bound iodine (PBI) level is decreased by chronic taking of aspirin. In diabetes mellitus, **aspirin lowers the blood glucose level,** probably by an increased peripheral utilization of glucose.

Metabolic effects. The salicylates affect many metabolic processes, and only a few salient aspects are presented below:

Oxidative phosphorylation. The salicylates uncouple oxidative phosphorylation in a manner similar to 2, 4-dinitrophenol. This effect is evident in man in doses employed for rheumatoid arthritis. As a result of uncoupling, a number of adenosine triphosphate (ATP)-dependent reactions are inhibited.

Carbohydrate metabolism. In large doses the salicylates may cause **hyperglycaemia** and **glycosuria** and deplete liver and muscle glycogen.

Fat metabolism. The salicylates reduce lipogenesis, partly by blocking the incorporation of acetate into fatty acids. They also antagonize adrenaline-induced lipolysis in fat cells. The combination of these effects leads to increased entry and enhanced oxidation of fatty acids in muscle, liver and other itssues, causing a fall in the plasma levels of free fatty acids (FFA), phospholipids and cholesterol.

Nitrogen metabolism. The salicylates in toxic doses cause a negative nitrogen balance, characterized by an aminoaciduria.

Uricosuric effect. In suitable doses the salicylates increases the urinary excretion of urates, and they were once used in the treatment of acute and chronic gout.

Salicylates and pregnancy. There is no evidence that salicylates cause foetal damage in humans, although babies born to women who ingest salicylates chronically have a low birth weight.

Local effects. Salicylic acid is an irritant to the skin and mucosa and destroys epithelial cells. The **keratolytic action** of salicylic acid is used for the local treatment of corns, warts, fungal infections and certain types of eczematous dermatitis. The tissue cells soften, swell and desquamate. **Methyl salicylate** (oil of wintergreen) is irritating both to the skin and mucosa. It is only used externally, in liniments as a **counterirritant.**

PHARMACOKINETICS

Orally ingested salicylates (aspirin and sodium salicylate) are absorbed rapidly, partly from the stomach, but mostly from the upper small intestine. The rate and extent of absorption depends on the disintegration and dissolution rate of the tablets, the pH of the mucosal surface, and gastric emptying time. Appreciable plasma concentrations are reached within 30 minutes, after a single dose, and a peak is reached within 2 hours followed by a gradual decline. The pharmacokinetics of salicylate elimination is complex. The $t_{1/2}$ of the salicylate lengthens as the dose increases. In addition, as the $t_{1/2}$ increases, urinary excretion decreases. Thus, increasing the dose without increasing the interval between doses may result in **accumulation** and **toxicity** of the drug.

After absorption, salicylates are distributed throughout most body tissues and fluids, primarily by pH dependent passive processes. Salicylates cross the blood-brain barrier slowly as a large fraction of the drug is ionized. They are considerably bound (80-85%) to plasma proteins, mainly albumin.

Salicylates are metabolized mainly in the liver by five parallel pathways, two of which are saturable, and are also excreted unchanged by a first-order process **(Fig. 2.7.5).**

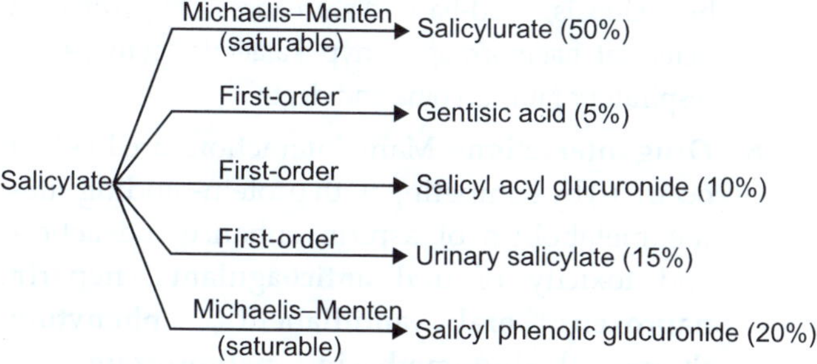

Fig. 2.7.5. The scheme of salicylate metabolism.

Based on the scheme of salicylate metabolism, it has been observed that for doses lower than 4 mg/kg the plasma disappearance of salicylate follows **first-order kinetics,** and the $t_{1/2}$ is 2 to 4 hours, but for higher doses the elimination is overall non-linear and the $t_{1/2}$ may be 15 to 30 hours **(Chap. 1.5).** Salicylate elimination is mainly via the urine, and is influenced by urinary pH, the loss being greater if the urine is alkaline.

Therapeutic Uses

1. **Analgesia.** Aspirin is used for the relief of mild to moderate pain of musculoskeletal origin, e.g., *headache, myalgia, neuralgia, toothache, dysmenorrhoea* and *backache.*
2. **Antipyresis.** Aspirin lowers elevated body tempeature (pyrexia). The antipyretic response is non-specific, and offers only a symptomatic relief. Use of aspirin should be avoided in cases of very high fever (hyperpyrexia), as it may produce

Table 2.7-1. *Preparations and dosage of salicylates*

Drug	*Preparations*	*Dosage Range*	*Comments*
Aspirin	Tablets, Gum Tablets, Enteric-coated tablets, Timed-release tablets, Enteric-coated capsules, Suppositories	*Adults:* Pain, fever - 325 to 650 mg Inflammation 3-7 g/day Transient ischaemic attacks 40-1300 mg/day Prevention of myocardial infarction - 325 mg/day *Children:* Pain, fever - 65 mg/kg/day in divided doses Inflammation 90-130 mg/kg/day in divided doses	Keep aspirin in a cool, dry place; do not use if vinegar-like odour is detected; use suppositories for a vomiting patient
Choline salicylate	Liquid - 870 mg/5 ml	1 teaspoonful every 3 to 4 hours Rheumatoid arthritis - 1 tsp to 2 tsp upto 4 times a day	Liquid preparation giving more rapid absorption and less gastric irritation
Diflunisal	Tablets - 250, 500 mg	Pain - 250-500 mg initially followed by 250 mg every 8 to 12 hours Rheumatoid arthritis/osteoarthritis - 500 mg to 1 g daily in 2 divided doses (maximum 1500 mg/day)	A salicylic acid derivative *not* metabolized to salicylic acid; platelet inhibitory effect is dose related and reversible; at 1 g/day the bleeding time is only slightly increased; anti-inflammatory efficacy is equal to 2-3 g/day of aspirin, with less GI distress; not to be used in children under 12 years of age
Methyl salicylate (oil of wintergreen)	10% to 50% in Ointment or Liniment	Applied topically as a *counterirritant* to relieve muscular and rheumatic pain	Significant absorption can occur through skin and produce untoward effects; very toxic if ingested orally
Salicylic acid	Cream - 2.5, 10% Ointment - 25, 40, 60% Gel - 6, 17% Soap - 3.5% Liquid - 13.6, 17% Plaster - 40%	Applied to the affected area at night, and wash off in the morning	Used topically as a *keratolytic* agent for psoriasis, acne, keratosis, fungal infections, or other conditions requiring removal of dead skin; skin must be hydrated for 5 minutes prior to use, may cause irritation or burning of skin; may be applied as an ether-alcohol or a colloidian solution (Freezone) for removal of corns, warts and calluses; avoid contact with eyes and mucous membranes
Sodium salicylate	Tablets - 325, 650 mg Enteric-coated Tablets - 325, 650 mg Injection - 1g/10ml Injection - 50 mg/ml	325 to 650 mg every 4 to 8 hrs as needed	Irritating to GI mucosa; less effective than an equal dose of aspirin

a shock-like state due to profuse sweating and a sudden fall in body temperature.

3. **Anti-inflammatory activity.** Salicylates may be used for various inflammatory conditions, e.g., *rheumatoid arthritis, osteoarthritis, bursitis,* and *acute rheumatic fever.* Large doses of aspirin (3 g to 7 g/day) are usually necessary, and therapy is palliative.
4. **Prophylaxis** of thromboembolic complications like *venous emboli and cerebral ischaemia* associated with cardiovascular disorders. Aspirin reduces the risk of *transient ischaemic attacks* (TIA) in men, but effectiveness in women is doubtful.
5. Prevention of re-infarction in patients with previous history of **acute myocardial infarction** or **unstable angina.**

Contraindications and Precautions

Salicylates are contraindicated in cases of **salicylate hypersensitivity, haemophilia, bleeding ulcers,** and **other haemorrhagic states.** The **Reye's syndrome,** a rare but life threatening disease, has been linked with the use of aspirin and other salicylates in children under the age of 12 years who have influenza or chickenpox. **Cautious use** is desirable in patients with gastric ulcers, anaemia, impaired hepatic or renal functions, asthma, nasal polyp, and in pregnant or nursing mothers.

Preparations and dosage of salicylates. The various preparations and usual dosage range of salicylates are listed in **Table 2.7-1.**

Adverse Reactions

The most frequent side effects with salicylates are **heartburn, nausea** and **gastric distress.** These can be overcome by taking the drug with food, a full glass of water, an antacid, or in one of the enteric-coated dosage forms **(Table 2.7-1).**

1. **Salicylism.** Large doses of salicylates result in this syndrome, characterized by headache, dizziness, tinnitus, confusion, sweating, deafness, palpitation and hyperventilation.
2. **Haemorrhage.** Major GI bleeding has been estimated to occur in 15 out of 100,000 chronic users of aspirin per year.
3. **Hypersensitivity reactions** range from rash and pruritus to bronchoconstriction, oedema and shock. Fixed drug eruptions and rhinorrhoea may occur.
4. **Reye's syndrome.** Use of salicylates, specially aspirin, in children with influenza or smallpox has been associated with Reye's syndrome, a life-threatening condition marked by initial severe vomiting, lethargy, delirium, coma and death. Mortality rate is about 25 percent, and permanent brain damage is common in survivors. Aspirin and other salicylates are not recommended in children below 12 years with influenza or smallpox.
5. Other adverse reactions include **renal dysfunction,** delirium, hallucinations, **respiratory alkalosis** followed by **acidosis,** acid-base disturbances, hyperthermia, petechial haemorrhages, hypokalaemia, convulsions, respiratory failure, coma and death.
6. **Drug interactions.** Many interactions are likely to occur: (*i*) by competing with protein-binding sites, the metabolites of aspirin enhance the actions and toxicity of **oral anticoagulants, heparin, naproxen, oral antidiabetics, phenytoin, thiopental, indomethacin, methotrexate,** and **valproic acid;** (*ii*) aspirin in small doses can inhibit the uricosuric action of probenecid and sulfinpyrazone; (*iii*) the effects of aspirin are enhanced or prolonged by drugs that acidify the urine, e.g., ascorbic acid, ammonium chloride, and decreased by urinary alkalinizers, e.g., sodium bicarbonate; (*iv*) aspirin may increase the risk of bleeding with oral anticoagulants and antiplatelet aggregatory drugs; (*v*) **phenobarbital** may decrease the efficacy of aspirin by enzyme induction; (*vi*) the antihypertensive action of **beta-blockers** is lessened possibly due to prostaglandin inhibition; (*vii*) the incidence of GI-distress and bleeding is increased by steroids, alcohol, indomethacin, pyrazolones, and other anti-inflammatory drugs; (*viii*) **furosemide** may decrease salicylate excretion, resulting in toxicity at lower doses; (*ix*) salicylates have a hypoglycaemic action and may **potentiate** the effects of insulin and sulphonylureas; (*x*) aspirin may lower the clinical effectiveness of nonsteroidal anti-inflammatory drugs; and (*xi*) antacids and activated charcoal can reduce the oral absorption of aspirin.

Salicylate Poisoning

In adults the intoxication is generally **accidental** or **suicidal.** A single dose of 10-30 g of aspirin or sodium salicylate is the usual lethal dose for adults. The lethal dose of methyl salicylate is much lower, and 4 ml (4.7 g) of it may be fatal in children.

Symptoms and signs. Gastrointestinal symptoms like **epigastric distress, nausea, vomiting, anorexia** and **abdominal pain** are often conspicuous. A more severe intoxication is characterized by CNS abnormalities and skin eruptions. **Restlessness, apprehension, vertigo, tremors, hallucinations, convulsions** and **coma** may occur. Fever is usually prominent, specially in children. Dehydration occurs as a result of *hyperpyrexia.* Disturbances of acid-base balance, and electrolytes of the plasma occur. Haemorrhagic phenomena are evident due to hypoprothrombinaemia. Dangerous hypoglycaemia may occur in children.

Treatment. The patient should be hospitalized, and blood obtained for plasma salicylate determination and electrolyte studies. **Gastric lavage, alkalinization, diuresis** and **intensive supportive measures** are necessary to treat salicylate poisoning. **Activated charcoal** reduces the absorption of salicylate from the gut. Hyperthermia and dehydration need immediate management, for which external sponging with tepid water or alcohol provides quick relief, and adequate amount of intravenous fluids must be given. **Bicarbonate solutions** must be infused intravenously to maintain alkaline diuresis. Glucose is administered intravenously to correct ketosis and hypoglycaemia. If potassium deficiency occurs, the cation K^+ should be added to the intravenous fluids. **Plasma transfusion** may be beneficial. Haemorrhagic phenomena may necessitate **whole-blood transfusion** and vitamin *K* (phytonadione). In very severe intoxication, extrarenal measures like **exchange transfusion, peritoneal dialysis, haemodialysis** and **haemoperfusion** are most effective in removing the salicylate from the system. Thus, treatment of salicylate poisoning is an acute medical emergency.

NON-SALICYLATES

PARA-AMINOPHENOLS

The parent compound of this group of analgesics was **acetanilide,** but it is no longer used because of its excessive toxicity.

PARACETAMOL (ACETAMINOPHEN, N-ACETYL-PARA-AMINOPHENOL)

Paracetamol is the major metabolite of phenacetin and has similar analgesic antipyretic actions, but it does not possess any anti-inflammatory or antirheumatic activity. It has no effect on platelets or blood-clotting mechanisms. Its site of analgesic action is incompletely understood. Paracetamol is a week inhibitor of peripheral prostaglandin synthetase, and is as potent as aspirin in inhibiting the brain prostaglandin synthetase. It is antipyretic presumably due to its effects on brain prostaglandins. Paracetamol is a popular analgesic.

Pharmacokinetics. The absorption rate and relative bioavailability of paracetamol are increased by concomitant administration of metoclopramide, and there is a significant relationship between gastric emptying and absorption. It is bound to plasma proteins (25-50%) to a much lesser degree than the salicylates. It is evenly distributed throughout the body. The major metabolites are sulphate and glucuronide which are excreted in the urine. Paracetamol has a $t_{1/2}$ of about 2 hours.

Therapeutic uses. Paracetamol is a mild analgesic-antipyretic, with little, if any, anti-inflammatory properties. It does not irritate the gastric mucosa, and has therefore been employed as a **substitute for aspirin.** The usual adult dose is 0.5 to 1 g (1-2 tablets) repeated 4-6 hourly to maintain analgesia.

Adverse effects include drug rashes, methaemoglobinaemia, and blood dyscrasias occasionally. As paracetamol has no anti-inflammatory activity, it cannot be used as a substitute for salicylates in the treatment of acute rheumatic fever. On prolonged usage, or overdosage or abuse, **paracetamol liver damage** may occur. Hepatotoxicity is caused by a toxic metabolite of paracetamol, *N*-acetyl-*p*-benzoquinone, which is inactivated by conjugation with **glutathione.** Thus glutathione is ultimately depleted and the toxic metabolite causes necrosis of liver cells. Kidney tubules may also be damaged. **Treatment** consists of administering agents which increase glutathione in liver cells, like **acetylcysteine;** and agents which increase conjugation reactions like **methionine** and **cysteamine.**

ANALGESIC NEPHROPATHY

Phenacetin was introduced in 1887, paracetamol in 1893, and aspirin in 1899. Much later in 1953 postmortem studies revealed that high consumption of non-narcotic analgesics increased the incidence of chronic renal disease manifested as **papillary necrosis, interstitial fibrosis** and **tubular atrophy.** Later, this relationship between analgesic abuse and renal disease was confirmed the world over.

Originally, **phenacetin** was thought to be the causative agent. But more recently nephrotoxicity has also resulted in patients after taking **aspirin** or **paracetamol** for long periods. There is evidence that **analgesic mixutres** are more likely to produce renal damage than single agents.

Analgesic nephropathy occurs most commonly in middle aged individuals who have been heavy consumers of analgesics over several years. They develop a form of **dependence** on the drugs, usually taken for medical reasons, as for the treatment of chronic arthritis. Anaemia due to chronic loss of blood from the gut caused by aspirin may be evident. **Treatment** consists of stoppage of analgesics and symptomatic therapy.

PYRAZOLONES

This group includes **antipyrine, aminopyrine, phenylbutazone, oxyphenbutazone** and **sulphinpyrazone.**

Table 2.7-2. *Pharmacokinetic parameters of nonsteroidal anti-inflammatory drugs (NSAIDs)*

Drug	*Peak Blood Levels (hrs)*	*Plasma Half-life (hrs)*	*Single Dosage Range (mg)*	*Dosage Interval (hrs)*
Indole derivatives				
Indomethacin	1-2	4-6	25-50	6-8
Sulindac	1-2	8-16	150-200	12
Tolmetin	0.5-1	1-3	200-400	4-6
Propionic acid derivatives				
Ibuprofen	1-2	1.5-2.5	400-800	6-8
Fenoprofen	1.5-2	2-3	300-600	6-8
Ketoprofen	0.5-1.5	2-4	25-50	6-8
Naproxen	2-4	12-15	250-375	8-12
Flurbiprofen	0.5-4	3-8	100-150	6-12
Oxaprozin	3-5	40-60	1200	24
Fenamates				
Mefenamic acid	2-4	2-4	250-500	4-6
Phenylacetic acid derivative				
Diclofenac	2-3	1.5-2.5	25-75	6-12
Oxicams				
Piroxicam	3-5	30-75	10-20	24

The earliest members of this group were antipyrine and aminopyrine, but they are not used now because of their potential bone marrow toxicity.

Phenylbutazone

Phenylbutazone (originally used as a solubilizing agent for aminopyrine) was introduced in 1949 for the treatment of rheumatoid arthritis and allied disorders. It has **analgesic-antipyretic** and **anti-inflammatory** properties similar to aspirin, but is much more toxic, and is no longer used.

Phenylbutazone is extensively metabolized in the liver, the most important reactions being glucuronide formation, and hydroxylation to **oxyphenbutazone,** which has similar properties to phenylbutazone (see later).

Oxyphenbutazone

Oxyphenbutazone, the hydroxy analogue of phenylbutazone, is one of the active metabolites of the parent drug. It has the same profile of pharmacological activity. It is claimed to be a *lesser* gastric irritant than phenylbutazone. It is available in 100 mg tablets, and the dosage is 100 to 200 mg bid or tid, when other drugs have failed.

Nonsteroidal Anti-inflammatory Drugs (NSAIDs)

In a search for effective anti-inflammatory drugs with **lesser** toxicity than the older established NSAIDs (salicylates and pyrazolones), several organic acids were shown to have a lower incidence of side effects like tinnitus and GI distress. The NSAIDs belong to various chemical classes, and display significant differences in their pharmacokinetic properties **(Table 2.7-2).**

The relative **nephrotoxicity** among NSAIDs is indomethacin > fenoprofen > ibuprofen = mefenamic acid = naproxen > piroxicam = sulindac = tolmetin.

The NSAIDs possess **analgesic** and **antipyretic** properties, but should not be used for minor headaches or pyrexia in place of aspirin or paracetamol. However, with the exception of **indomethacin** and **meclofenamate,** the NSAIDs may be used for relieveing other types of mild to moderate pain like **dysmenorrhoea, postextraction dental pain, episiotomy pain** and **soft-tissue athletic injuries,** in addition to their use as anti-inflammatory drugs.

Indole Derivatives

Indomethacin

Indomethacin is used in **rheumatoid arthritis** and **ankylosing spondylitis** for its anti-inflammatory and antipyretic effects. Indomethacin inhibits prostaglandin E_2. It inhibits the motility of polymorphonuclear leucocytes, an action similar to that of colchicine, and it uncouples oxidative phosphorylation in cartilaginous and hepatic mitochondria.

Pharmacokinetics. Indomethacin is rapidly and completely absorbed from the gut following oral adminsitration. Peak concentration in plasma is reached within 3 hours in the fasting subject, and somewhat later if the drug is taken after meals. The plasma concentration required for its anti-inflammatory activity is probably less than 1 mcg/ml. It is about 90 percent bound to plasma proteins and also extensively bound to tissues. The concentration in the CSF is low. Indomethacin undergoes extensive hepatic metabolism and both the parent substance and the metabolites take part in an **enterohepatic circulation.** The $t_{1/2}$ is 4 to 6 hours, but is prolonged in biliary obstruction. Indomethacin and its metabolites are excreted in the urine.

Therapeutic uses. Because of a high incidence of serious side effects associated with chronic use, indomethacin must never be used as a routine analgesic-antipyretic. However, it has proved to be useful as an antipyretic in **Hodgkin's disease** when fever is refractory to other agents.

Indomethacin is as effective as oxyphenbutazone, and more effective than aspirin in the treatment of **ankylosing spondylitis, rheumatoid arthritis,** and **acute gout** (though it does not promote uricosuria). As an anti-inflammatory agent indomethacin reduces pain, swelling and tenderness of joints, increasing grip strength, and decreases the duration of morning stiffness. Indomethacin is also used to treat **uveitis** and inflammation following **eye surgery.** It has also been effective in reducing pain and inflammation of **pleurisy, pericarditis** and **pericardial effusion.** It appears to be more effective than aspirin in relieving pain of **dysmenorrhoea.**

Indomethacin is available for oral use in capsules containing 25 or 50 mg of the drug. The initial dose is 25 mg twice daily, and can be increased by 25 mg increments weekly to a total daily dose of 100 to 200 mg.

Toxicity. A high percentage of patients (35 to 50%) receiving indomethacin in therapeutic doses experience adverse effects. The most common adverse effects are headache, light-headedness confusion or hallucinations. Gastric bleeding is not common but can occur. Gastrointestinal complaints consist of anorexia, nausea and abdominal pain. Gastrointestinal ulceration with perforation has been reported. Occult blood loss in stools may lead to anaemia. *Haemopoietic reactions* like *neutropenia, thrombocytopenia,* and rarely *aplastic anaemia* may occur. *Hypersensitivity reactions* have been reported. It is contraindicated in pregnant women, psychiatric disorders, epilepsy, or parkinsonism.

Drug interactions. Antagonism between indomethacin and aspirin regarding the anti-inflammatory activity are possibly of little clinical significance. But the question remains unanswered whether concurrent administration of the two drugs in rheumatoid arthritis is beneficial or not. *Probenecid,* 1 g/day, inhibits the renal tubular secretion of indomethacin. When both are given together, plasma levels of indomethacin are almost doubled. Indomethacin dosage must be reduced when combined with probenecid. Indomethacin does not interfere with the uricosuric effect of probenecid, and it does not modify the effect of **oral anticoagulants.**

Sulindac

It is closely related to indomethacin, and has analgesic-antipyretic and anti-inflammatory activity, which depends on its active sulphide metabolite. Thus sulindac is another example of a **prodrug.** The sulphide metabolite is about 500 times more potent than sulindac as an inhibitor of cyclo-oxygenase.

It is well absorbed when given orally, and is half as potent as indomethacin on a weight basis, but the safety ratio (as determined in animals) is much higher than indomethacin. **Enterohepatic recycling** of sulindac followed by conversion back to the active sulphide metabolite contributes to the maintenance of high plasma levels of the active compound.

Sulindac is used in **rheumatic conditions** of all types and **gout,** in a dosage of 100-200 mg twice daily. It is generally well tolerated, and the main adverse effects are gastrointestinal disturbance, hypersensitivity reactions, and vertigo.

Tolmetin

Chemically tolmetin resembles indomethacin, but its properties are more like the propionic acid derivatives (ibuprofen, neproxen). It is more active than aspirin in its ability to inhibit prostaglandin synthetase. On oral administration it is almost completely absorbed, and peak plasma levels are attained within 1 hour. It is extensively bound (99%) to plasma proteins. Its $t_{1/2}$ in plasma is between 1 and 3 hours.

Therapeutic uses of tolmetin are the same as for other NSAIDs. It is used in the treatment of **rheumatoid arthritis,** specially the juvenile form of the disease; **osteoarthritis** and **rheumatoid arthritis.** *Adverse effects* include headache, tinnitus, vertigo, peptic ulcer and sodium retention. Incidence of gastrointestinal bleeding is lesser than that of aspirin. It is available as 200 mg tablets for oral use, and the recommended dose is 400 mg 3 times daily.

Propionic Acid Derivatives

The members of this group offer significant advantages over aspirin, phenylbutazone, and indomethacin, as they are better tolerated.

Ibuprofen

Like aspirin, ibuprofen has analgesic, anti-inflammatory, and antipyretic actions. It is rapidly absorbed from the gastrointestinal tract, and peak plasma concentrations are reached in 1 to 2 hours. It is rapidly metabolized and eliminated in the urine. The plasma $t_{1/2}$ is about 2 hours. It is extensively (99%) and firmly bound to plasma proteins.

Clinically it is used in the treatment of **rheumatoid arthritis (including Still's disease), osteoarthritis, ankylosing spondylitis, dysmenorrhoea, cervical spondylosis,** and **ophthalmic, dental** and **ENT inflammations.** Ibuprofen is available as 200, 300 and 400 mg tablets, and also as a suspension. The usual adult dose is 400 mg tid or 300 mg qid. Side effects include gastrointestinal disturbances, headache, dizziness and fluid retention.

Fenoprofen. Fenoprofen is chemically and pharmacologically similar to ibuprofen. It is as effective as aspirin for **rheumatoid arthritis,** and as effective as oxyphentutazone for *osteoarthritis*. It is said to be as potent as naproxen, and more potent than ibuprofen and ketoprofen. **Dosage** ranges between 1.2 and 1.8 g per day in three to four divided doses.

Ketoprofen. Peak plasma level of 2 to 5 mcg/ml is reached in 1 hour after a single 50 mg oral dose of ketoprofen. It is virtually completely absorbed from the gut. The recommended daily dose is 100 to 150 mg per day in divided doses.

Naproxen

Like aspirin, it has analgesic-antipyretic and anti-inflammatory actions. It is fully absorbed when adminsistered orally. It is almost completely bound (98 to 99%) to plasma proteins following therapeutic doses. Naproxen crosses the placenta, and appears in the milk of lactating women. It has a long plasma $t_{1/2}$ of 12 to 15 hours. Clinically it is used in the treatment of **rheumatoid arthritis, osteoarthritis,** and **ankylosing spondylitis.** The recommended dosage is 250 mg given twice daily with meals if gastric discomfort is experienced.

Flurbiprofen

Flurbiprofen is a newer propionic acid derivative, and shares the same mechanism of action as other NSAIDs. It is considered to be one of the potent inhibitors of prostaglandin synthesis. **It suppresses both PGE_2 and PGF_2 alpha** through inhibition of the cyclo-oxygenase enzyme. Flurbiprofen also is a potent **inhibitor of leucocyte migration** into inflamed tissues. It **does not inhibit lipoxygenase activity,** except at high concentrations.

Flurbiprofen is well absorbed orally; peak blood levels occur 0.5 to 4.0 hours after administration. The average elimination half-life is 5.7 hours. No accumulation of the drug occurs; upto 98 per cent is excreted within 24 hours after the last dose. It is highly bound (99%) to plasma proteins, and is extensively hydroxylated (50%), and primarily excreted in the urine.

Flurbiprofen is used in the treatment of **rheumatoid arthritis, osteoarthritis** and **ankylosing spondylitis,** and the daily dosage is 200 to 300 mg in 2 to 4 divided doses. **Adverse reactions** include GI disturbances like diarrhoea, dyspepsia and vomiting. GI bleeding and ulceration is rare. Rashes and angioedema may occur.

Oxaprozin

Oxaprozin is a newer propionic acid derivative, and can be effectively administered once daily (half-life 40-60 hrs). It is well absorbed orally, metabolized in the liver, and mainly excreted by the kidney. It is used in doses of 1.2 g daily by mouth in patients of *osteoarthritis* and *rheumatoid arthritis*.

Fenamates

The anthranilic acid derivatives (fenamates) are aspirin-like drugs, but therapeutically they have no clear advantage over other aspirin-like drugs.

Mefenamic Acid

It is another NSAID, and may be useful in the relief of pain in conditions which do not ordinarily require strong analgesics. It is absorbed rather slowly from the gut, reaching peak concentrations in 2-4 hours. It is 98.5 percent bound to plasma proteins. It is used as a mild analgesic, and the usual dose is 500 mg 3 times daily.

Gastrointestinal symptoms are the most common adverse effects. **Diarrhoea** occurs in a large number of patients. Other infrequent side effects include dizziness, rashes, haemolytic anaemia, agranulocytosis, thrombocytopenic purpura, and megaloblastic anaemia. It is contraindicated in gastrointestinal inflammation or ulceration, and impairment of renal function.

Phenylacetic Acid Derivative

Diclofenac

Diclofenac has analgesic, antipyretic, and anti-inflammatory activities. It is an inhibitor of cyclo-oxygenase and its potency is appreciably greater than that of indomethacin, naproxen, and several other NSAIDs. It is completely absorbed on oral administration; peak plasma levels occur in 2 to 3 hours; and the drug undergoes *first-pass* metabolism and only 50 percent is bioavailable. Its average half-life is 2 hours; 65 percent of the dose is eliminated in the urine, while 35 percent is found in bile, largely as conjugates of both the unchanged drug and its metabolites. Diclofenac is 99 percent bound to plasma proteins.

Diclofenac is approved for long-term treatment of **rheumatoid arthritis, osteoarthritis,** and **ankylosing spondylitis.** Also used in short-term treatment of acute musculo-skeletal injury, acute painful shoulder, postoperative pain, and dysmenorrhoea. The usual daily dosage is 100 to 200 mg bid or tid. **Adverse reactions** include GI disturbances and headache, and a reversible elevation of serum transaminases occurs in 15 percent of patients. Skin rashes, allergic reactions, fluid retention and oedema, and impairment of renal function can occur.

Oxicams

Piroxicam

It possesses anti-inflammatory, analgesic and antipyretic activity. It is the NSAID offered for **once-a-day treatment of rheumatoid arthritis** and **osteoarthritis,** and this helps patient compliance. In therapeutic doses, piroxicam equals the efficacy of indomethacin and naproxen for the long-term treatment of rheumatoid arthritis and osteoarthritis.

Piroxicam is an inhibitor of prostaglandin biosynthesis, comparable to indomethacin. It also inhibits activation of neutrophils, which is an additional mode of its anti-inflammatory action. It is well absorbed on oral administration, and peak plasma levels are attained in 3 to 4 hours. The average plasma half-life is 50 hours (range 30-75 hours), and as such piroxicam is likely to accumulate in the body. Steady-state levels are reached in 7 to 12 days. Piroxicam is extensively metabolized to inactive compounds and excreted in urine (two-thirds) and faeces (one-third). Concurrent administration of aspirin causes a 20 percent reduction in plasma levels of piroxicam. **The use of piroxicam (or any other NSAID) in conjunction with aspirin is not recommended,** as such combinations **do not** increase efficacy, but may increase the potential for adverse reactions. Adverse GI reactions are most common, but oedema, dizziness, headache, rash, and haematological changes can occur in 1 to 6 percent of patients. Serious GI toxicity in the form of bleeding, peptic ulceration, and perforation have been reported. Piroxicam is available in 10 and 20 mg capsules. The usual dose is 20 mg daily as a single dose. Maximal therapeutic response should not be expected before 2 weeks.

Miscellaneous Anti-inflammatory Agents

Hydroxychloroquine

Hydroxychloroquine, a 4-aminoquinoline used primarily as an antimalarial, has also been employed in the treatment of **rheumatoid arthritis** and **systemic lupus erythematosus.** Hydroxychloroquine is preferred over chloroquine, as it is slightly less toxic, although not an innocuous drug.

The antiarthritic mechanism of action of the 4-aminoquinolines is not exactly known, but they **stabilize lysosomal membranes, inhibit nucleic acid synthesis, interfere with replication of viruses, and suppress formation of antigens** that cause hypersensitivity reactions.

Initial dosage is 200 mg bid or tid. Several weeks are required for optimal response, when the dosage can be reduced to 200 to 400 mg/day. Untoward ophthalmic reactions involving the cornea, retina, and ciliary body can occur, and periodic ophthalmic examinations are mandatory during prolonged therapy.

Penicillamine

Penicillamine is a **chelating agent** used to remove excess copper in patients with **Wilson's disease** (hepatolenticular degeneration), and to increase cystine excretion in cystinuria. It is also approved for the treatment of severe **forms of rheumatoid arthritis,** but the use is restricted to patients unresponsive to other less toxic anti-inflammatory agents.

The antiarthritic **mode of action** of penicillamine is not precisely known. But it **inhibits lysosomal enzyme release in connective tissue; interferes with DNA synthesis, collagen, and mucopolysaccharides; suppresses T-cell activity, and lowers the titre of IgM rheumatoid factor.**

In *rheumatoid arthritis,* penicillamine is administered initially in a dose of 125 to 250 mg/day orally for 4 weeks. Dosage may be increased at 4 to 12 week intervals. **Adverse reactions** include stomatitis, pruritus, loss of taste, nausea and proteinuria. Leucopenia, thrombocytopenia, bone marrow depression, agranulocytosis, and aplastic anaemia may occur **(Chap. 14).**

Compound Analgesic Preparations

Combinations of analgesic agents, or analgesics with drugs of another class are among the most widely used (or abused) pharmaceutical products. Most of them are formulated on a theoretical basis that they would: (*i*) produce greater analgesic effect (synergism); (*ii*) provide broader therapeutic uses; and (*iii*) cause fewer or less severe adverse effects.

Gold Compounds

Auranofin

Aurothioglucose

Gold Sodium Thiomalate

Aurothioglucose and **gold sodium thiomalate** contain 50 percent gold and are used intramuscularly (IM). In addition, **auranofin** is an orally effective compound containing 29 percent gold. These gold compounds can temporarily *arrest the progression* of bone destruction in the involved joints, but there is no evidence that they can induce remission of *rheumatoid arthritis* (see later).

The antiarthritic mode of action of gold is not completely known. Several actions are thought to contribute to the beneficial effects: (*i*) inhibition of lysosomal activity in macrophages; (*ii*) decreased phagocytic action of macrophages; (*iii*) reduced histamine release from mast cells; and (*iv*) blockade of formation of glucosamine-6-phosphate in connective tissue. The importance of the above actions remains to be determined.

Dosage. The injectable forms (aurothioglucose, gold sodium thiomalate) are available in concentrations of 10 mg/ml, 25 mg/ml and 50 mg/ml. The oral preparation (auranofin) is used as 3 mg capsules.

Aurothioglucose. Weekly IM injections (preferred site is intragluteal); first week, 10 mg; second and third weeks, 25 mg; thereafter, 50 mg/week.

Gold sodium thiomalate. Weekly IM injections; first week, 10 mg, second week, 25 mg; thereafter 25-50 mg/ week until clinical improvement or toxicity occurs.

Table 2.7-3. *Pharmacokinetic parameters of injectable and oral gold preparations*

Drug	*Gold Content*	*Peak Effect (hrs)*	*Protein Binding (%)*	*Serum Half-life (days)*	*Excretion*
Injectable					
Aurothioglucose	50%	4-6	95-100	5-25*	70% urine/ 30% faeces
Gold sodium Thiomalate	50%	2-6	95-100	3-27*	70% urine/ 30% faeces
Oral					
Auranofin	29%	1-2	50-60	20-30	15% urine/ 85% faeces

* Half-life increases after repeated dosage; upto 40 days after 3 to 5 doses, and upto 175 days after 10 doses.

Auranofin. Administered orally 6 mg a day, as a single or 2 divided doses. If response is not adequate after 6 months, increase to 9 mg/day in 3 divided doses.

The pharmacokinetic properties of gold preparations are presented in **Table 2.7-3.** Gold is well distributed in the body, and major sites of localization are bone marrow, liver, skin, and bone. Arthritic joints appears to concentrate more gold than non-involved joints.

Adverse reactions to gold therapy can occur during treatment, or for several months after stoppage of therapy. Most common side effects are dermatitis, stomatitis, pruritus, metallic taste, flushing, sweating, and proteinuria. Diarrhoea occurs in over 50 percent of patients on gold therapy. Other adverse reactions include alopecia, grayish blue skin pigmentation, gingivitis, pharyngitis, vaginitis, blood dyscrasias (rarely), glomerulitis, haematuria, tubular necrosis, nephritis, angioedema and anaphylactic shock. Thus, gold compounds are potentially highly toxic substances.

Antigout Drugs

Gout is a purine metabolism disorder resulting from an excess of uric acid in the blood (hyperuricaemia), due to either its overproduction or faulty elimination. Crystals of **monosodium urate** begin to precipiatate and get deposited in joints, skin, kidney and other tissues. **Gouty arthritis** usually involves a single joint (monoarticular), but may involve many joints (polyarticular) specially in the later course of the disease. Classically the great toe is involved, characterized by pain (podalgia), swelling, tenderness, and other signs of **inflammation.** At the site there is **infiltration of granulocytes that phagocytose the urate crystals.** The granulocytes ultimately breakdown and liberate *lactic acid* and other acidic products, which lower the regional pH, and favour **further precipitation** of urate crystals **(Fig. 2.7.6).** The acute phase of gout is thus a cyclic and self-perpetuating process.

Production of uric acid. Uric acid is formed by the metabolism of nucleoproteins from two sources; the body's own cells and cell-rich food. The nucleic acids from these cells are first converted to the purine bases **hypoxanthine** and **xanthine.** The enzyme, xanthine oxidase, then catalyses the metabolic breakdown of these purines to uric acid **(Fig. 2.7.7).** Thus, uric acid is the end product in the metabolism of the purines **adenine** and **guanine.**

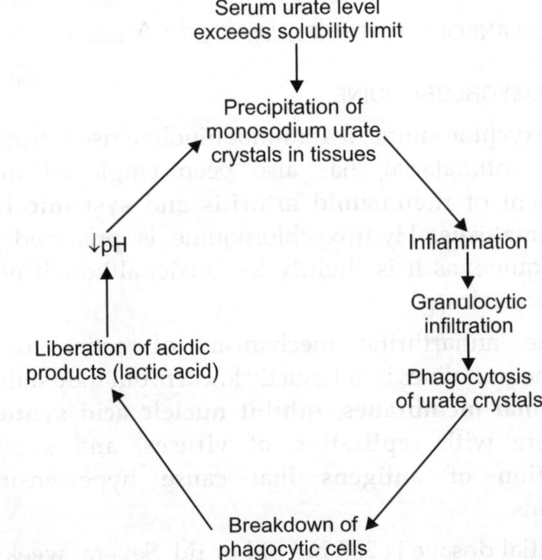

Fig. 2.7.6: The cycle of events occurring during an attack of gout.

Blood ordinarily contains uric acid in a concentration of 3 to 7 mg/dl of serum. The solubility of urates in tissue fluids is limited. When the saturation point is exceeded, microcrystals of **monosodium urate** are precipitated. Urate crystals also trigger the biosynthesis of **bradykinin,** a mediator of inflammation. Thus, gouty inflammation occurs.

Classification

Three types of drugs are employed in the treatment of gout:

1. Drugs used in acute gout to terminate the inflammatory process and prevent its recurrence: **Colchicine, oxyphenbutazone, naproxen, sulindac, indomethacin, corticotrophin, corticosteroids.**

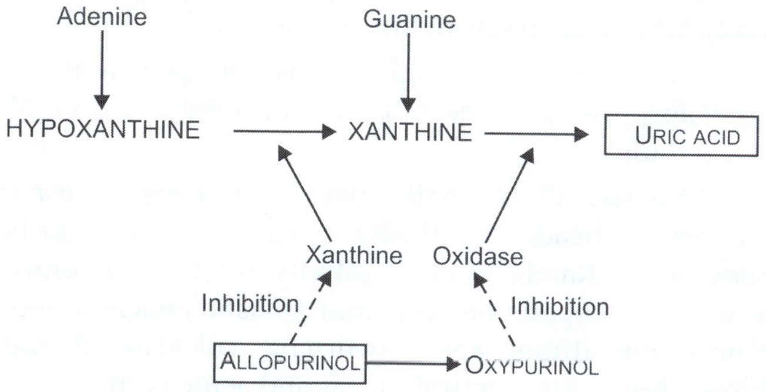

Fig. 2.7.7: Purine metabolism by xanthine oxidase; and its inhibition by allopurinol (see text).

2. Drugs used for long-term control of gout, acting by increasing the excretion of uric acid by the kidneys, i.e., uricosuric agents: **Probenecid, sulphinpyrazine.**
3. Drugs for prevention of urate synthesis in the body: **Allopurinol.**

Acute Gout

The acute attack of gout is due to the precipitation of **monosodium urate** crystals in the joint. These are irritant and an acute inflammatory response occurs which is exceedingly painful. The acute reaction is usually treated by anti-inflammatory analgesics (oxyphenbutazone 200 mg tid; or naproxen 750 mg initially; then 250 mg 8-hourly; or indomethacin 50 mg tid) for a short time. An altenative is **colchicine** which is specific in relieving the symptoms of acute gout, but is probably not as effective as indomethacin, and its use is limited by its toxicity. In resistant cases of acute gout **corticotrophin** (ACTH) is very effective and is given in a dose of 80 units IM, repeated after a day or two, if necessary. The newer agent **sulindac** may also be used to treat acute gout in a dose of 200 mg orally twice daily till relief is obtained.

Colchicine

Colchicine is an alkaloid derived from the corm and seeds of **Colchicum autumnale**, known for centuries for its medicinal qualities. It has no anti-inflammatory or analgesic activity, but is very effective in suppressing inflammation and pain in gouty joints when taken promptly in adequate amounts. It does not enhance renal excretion of uric acid or reduce its concentration in the blood.

Mode of action. The mechanism of action of colchicine in acute gout is incompletely understood. It **inhibits the migration** of granulocytes to inflamed joints, and **phagocytosis is checked.** It checks the leucocytes which get into the joint from releasing lactic acid and lysosomal enzymes (see above), and urate crystal deposition in the joint is reduced. **Bradykinin** biosynthesis also ceases. Thus, it breaks the cycle and reduces inflammation and pain.

Colchicine also is an **antimitotic** agent, arresting cell division in metaphase by blocking spindle formation. Although this phenomenon is not used therapeutically, it is a useful tool in research.

Pharmacokinetics. Colchicine is rapidly absorbed from the gastorintestinal tract. Its plasma $t_{1/2}$ is 30 minutes. It is partly metabolized, and a major portion is excreted via the bile and undergoes **enterohepatic** circulation, which may account for its toxic effects on the gastrointestinal tract. Its half-life is prolonged in renal disease as 20 to 30 percent of the drug is excreted via the urine.

Therapeutic uses. Colchicine is a major drug for reduction of inflammation and relief of pain of **acute gouty arthritis.**

Dosage. For *acute attacks* 0.5 or 0.6 mg is administered orally every hour; or alternatively 1 or 1.2 mg may be given initially followed by 0.5 or 0.6 mg every 2 hourly until pain subsides, or nausea, vomiting and diarrhoea develop. A total dose of 4 to 10 mg may be required.

To avoid gastrointestinal distress, colchicine may be administered intravenously in a dose of 1 or 2 mg initially, followed by 0.5 mg every 3 to 6 hours until a satisfactory response is achieved.

Toxicity. Colchicine causes nausea and vomiting or abdominal pain in about 80 percent of patients. Diarrhoea is considered as the therapeutic end point, and as soon as it occurs, administration should be stopped irrespective of the symptoms. Black tarry stools or light red blood in stools indicates gastsrointestinal bleeding. Antidiarrhoeal agents like **diphenoxylate** (Lomotil) or **paregoric** may be needed to control severe diarrhoea. Gastrointestinal distress is uncommon after IV administration, but extravasation must be avoided as dangerous tissue necrosis may occur. **Bone marrow depression** (agranulocytosis, thrombocytopenia, aplastic anaemia), peripheral neuritis, myopathy, renal damage, hepatocellular failure and alopecia may occur.

Drugs that Precipitate Acute Gout

The following drugs may precipitate an acute attack of gout:

1. **Diuretics.** The *thiazides* by their action on the distal tubule inhibit urate secretion and precipitate gout. Other diuretics like ethacrynic acid, furosemide, and bumetanide also precipitate gout.
2. **Other drugs.** *Pyrazinamide, clofibrate, aspirin* in low doses, and *cytotoxic drugs* used for leukaemia and lymphomas may precipitate gout.

Chronic Gout

Chronic gouty arthritic processes may continue in the absence of acute attacks. Continued deposition of uric acid crystals may destroy cartilage, joints and bone epiphyses.

There are two possible approaches to the long-term control of gout: (*i*) the **uricosuric drugs** *probenecid, sulphinoyrazine*, or *ticrynafen* may be used to increase excretion of uric acid in urine; and (*ii*) the **xanthine oxidase inhibitor** allopurinol may be used to *suppress biosynthesis of uric acid* from purines. The salicylates antagonize the uricosuric drugs, but do not antagonize the action of allopurinol.

Uricosuric Drugs

Probenecid

Probenecid is a sulphonamide derivative, which was developed during World War II in the search for a drug to maintain blood levels of penicillin by interfering with its excretion, because penicillin was then expensive and in short supply. Since 1950, probenecid has been known to be a very **useful uricosuric agent** in gout.

Mode of action. Probenecid acts by inhibiting renal tubular reabsorption of uric acid, thereby greater amounts of uric acid are eliminated in the urine **(Fig. 2.7.8).** The concentration of urates in the plasma falls gradually towards normal; and the size of tophaceous deposits is gradually reduced. Probenecid is **ineffective in acute gout.** Probenecid also blocks the secretion of weak organic acids into the proximal and distal renal tubules. This activity is taken advantage of clinically for **blocking the secretion of penicillins** and **cephalosporins** into the urine. The plasma levels of these antibiotics are maintained at higher levels for a longer duration.

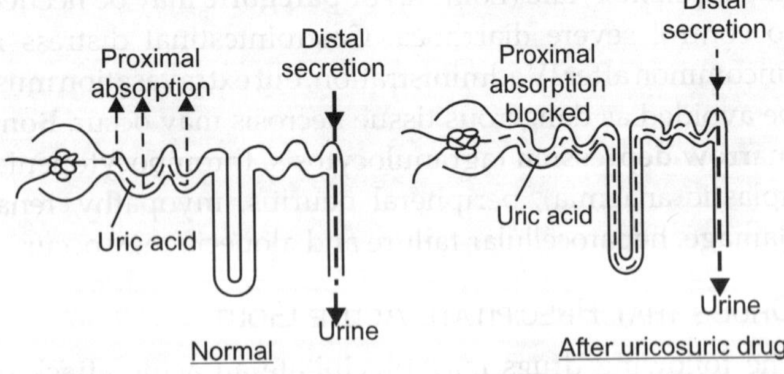

Fig. 2.7.8: Action of uricosuric drugs (probenecid, sulphinpyrazone) on uric acid elimination by the renal tubules (diagrammatic).

Pharmacokinetics. After oral administration, probenecid is rapidly absorbed within an hour, and peak plasma levels are attained in 2 to 4 hours. In the blood 85 to 90 percent of the drug is plasma protein bound; the plasma $t_{1/2}$ is 6 to 12 hours. About 90 to 95 percent of the metabolites are also lost in the urine.

Therapeutic uses. Probenecid is used for the **prophylaxis of gout;** hyperuricaemia; and for the reduction of tubular excretion of penicillins and cephalosporins.

Dosage. For uricosuric therapy, initially 250 mg twice daily orally, is administered preferably after meals, increased after a week to 500 mg twice daily, then upto 2 g daily according to serum uric acid levels.

For maintaining high levels of penicillin and cephalosporin, probenecid is administered in a dose of 1 to 2 g daily.

Toxicity. Occasionally nausea, vomiting, urinary frequency, headache, flushing, dizziness and rashes may occur. Rarely hypersensitivity reactions, nephrotic syndrome, hepatic necrosis and aplastic anaemia occur. **Contraindications** are concurrent salicylate therapy, blood dyscrasias, nephrolithiasis and acute gout.

Probenecid interacts with many drugs. It reduces the renal excretion of nitrofurantoin. It may prolong the half-life of oral hypoglycaemics, and reduction of dosage is required to avoid hypoglycaemia. **Probenecid blocks the renal excretion of indomethacin, sulphipyrazone, dapsone and para-aminosalicylic acid (PAS),** increasing the possibility of adverse reactions. Salicylates inhibit the uricosuric activity of probenecid.

Sulphinpyrazone

Sulphinpyrazone is an analogue of phenylbutazone, but **it lacks the latter's anti-inflammatory, analgesic and sodium retaining** properties. Sulphinpyrazone, like probenecid, markedly inhibits the tubular reabsorption of uric acid from the proximal renal tubules, increasing the urinary excretion of uric acid, and decreasing serum urate levels **(Fig. 2.7.8).** In a dose of 300 to 400 mg, sulphinpyrazone produces uricosuria equivalent to 1.0 to 1.5 g of probenecid.

Sulphinpyrazone also **inhibits platelet adhesiveness and prolongs platelet life.** It is effective in the prevention of thromboembolic diseases like **angina pectoris, transient ischaemic attacks,** and **myocardial infarction** (also see **Chap. 4.5).**

Pharmacokinetics. Sulphinpyrazone is rapidly and completely absorbed on oral administration, and peak blood levels occur in about 1 to 2 hours. It is about 98 percent bound to plasma proteins. Its plasma $t_{1/2}$ is 1 to 3 hours. Most of the drug is excreted unchanged in the urine.

Therapeutic uses. Sulphinpyrazone is used for gout prophylaxis, and in hyperuricaemia.

Dosage. Initially, 100 to 200 mg orally 2 times daily is given with milk or after meals, increasing over 2-3 weeks according to the serum uric acid levels to about 600-800 mg daily in divided doses.

Toxicity. Gastrointestinal disorders, occasionally hypersensitivity reactions, and rarely blood dyscrasias may occur. The frequency of gouty attacks may increase during the first 6-12 months. During these attacks the sulphinpyrazone therapy is to be continued, and the acute attacks may be treated by colchicine or other anti-inflammatory analgesics. Salicylates inhibit the uricosuric action of sulphinpyrazone.

Xanthine Oxidase Inhibitor

Allopurinol

Chemically it is a hypoxanthine analogue. In contrast to the uricosuric agents, allopurinol **inhibits the enzyme xanthine oxidase, reducing the formation of uric acid from xanthine and hypoxanthine.** Thereby xanthine and hypoxanthine are excreted unchanged in the urine. Precipitation of uric acid in joints and elsewhere is minimal, and uric acid is actually mobilized from deposits.

Pharmacokinetics. Allopurinol is rapidly and completely absorbed from the intestine. Its plasma $t_{1/2}$ is about 3 hours. It is largely converted to oxypurinol, which itself is a weak xanthine oxidase inhibitor **(Fig. 2.7.7).**

Therapeutic uses. Allopurinol is used for **gout prophylaxis,** and for **long-term treatment of hyperuricaemia** and its **complications.** Allopurinol alone, or in combination with uricosurics is particularly useful in: (*i*) gout uncontrolled by uricosurics; (*ii*) severe tophaceous gout; (*iii*) urate renal stones; (*iv*) gout with renal failure; (*v*) gouty nephropathy; (*vi*) intolerance to uricosurics; and (*vii*) treatment of leukaemias and lymphomas with cytotoxic drugs.

Dosage. Initially, 100 mg as a single dose is given after meals, gradually increased to 300 my daily, over 1-3 weeks depending on the serum uric acid levels. Usual maintenance dose is 200-600 mg daily. Doses over 300 mg/day should be preferably administered in 2 or 3 divided doses.

Toxicity. Gastrointestinal disorders, drowsiness and hypersensitivity reactions may occur. Rarely vertigo, headache, taste disturbances, hypertension, alopecia, hepatitis and symptomless xanthine deposits in muscles may occur. Rarely it may also cause myelosuppression.

Antirheumatic Drugs

Rheumatic diseases are inflammatory or degenerative disorders that affect mainly the musculoskeletal system,

Table 2.7-4. *Drugs used for rheumatoid arthritis*

Drugs	*Total dose per day (mg)*	*Average Half-life (hrs)*	*Frequency of administration (hrs)*
NSAIDs			
Salicylates			
Aspirin	4000-5000	3-30 (dose dependent)	4-6
Propionic acid derivatives			
Ibuprofen	1200-2400	2	3-6
Naproxen	500-1000	13	8-12
Fenoprofen	1200-3200	3	6-8
Ketoprofen	100-200	3	12
Flurbiprofen	150-200	4	3-4
Indoles			
Indomethacin	50-200	4	3-6
Sulindac	300-400	8	12
Tolmetin	600-1200	1	3-6
Para-aminophenol derivative			
Paracetamol	2000-3000	2	4-6
Fenamates			
Mefenamic acid	1000	3	4-6
Oxicams			
Piroxicam	10-20	45	24
Slow acting antirheumatics (SAARDs)			
Gold	25/week	–	Weekly
Penicillamine	250-750	–	24
Hydorxychloroquine	200	–	24
Immunosuppressives			
Methotrexate	7.5-15/week	–	Weekly
Azathioprine	75-200	–	24
Chlorambucil	4-8	–	24

i.e., the joints, muscles, ligaments, tendons and bursae. The term "rheumatism" is used by the layman to lump together all the different, about 80 chronic and acute disorders, which involve the musculoskeletal system, and include **rheumatoid arthritis, rheumatic fever, osteoarthritis, ankylosing spondylitis, tendinitis, bursitis, fibrositis,** and **myositis.** The primary aim of treatment is reduction of **pain and inflammation, maintenance of joint mobility, and prevention of deformity.** Except for the **gold compounds, chloroquine, penicillamine,** and **immunosuppressants,** which are said to affect the disease process in rheumatoid arthritis and related conditions, the rest of the agents just provide symptomatic relief of pain and inflammation. Penicillamine may retard the radiological progression of the disease.

Classification

The drugs used in the treatment of rheumatic diseases fall into the following categories:

1. **Non-steroidal anti-inflammatory drugs:** Salicylates and non-salicylates.
2. **Gold compounds:** Gold sodium thiomalate.
3. **Chelating agent:** Penicillamine.
4. **Antimalarials:** Chloroquine and hydroxychloroquine.
5. **Adrenocorticosteroids** and ACTH.
6. **Immunosuppressants:** Azathioprine, chlorambucil.

Alternatively, the antirheumatics may be broadly grouped into two: (*i*) the *non-steroidal anti-inflammatory drugs (NSAIDs)*; and (*ii*) the *slow-acting antirheumatic drugs (SAARDs)*. The latter group includes *gold sodium thiomalate, penicillamine, hydroxychloroquine,* the *immunosuppressives* and the *corticosteroids.*

Drug Therapy

Non-steroidal anti-inflammatory drugs (NSAIDs). For full anti-inflammatory effectiveness, aspirin must be taken in much larger amounts than for ordinary analgesia. To avoid gastrointestinal irritation the dose of aspirin (4-5 g/day) should be taken after meals or with milk **(Table 2.7-4).**

The **non-salicylate anti-inflammatory agents** used in the management of rheumatoid arthritis and related disorders include **indomethacin, ibuprofen, fenoprofen, naproxen, sulindac** and **tolmetin.** Their antirheumatic activity probably stems from the resulting reduction of prostaglandins in the arthritic joints. These drugs are detailed in the beginning of this Chapter.

Gold compounds. Chrysotherapy, i.e., treatment with gold salts, sometimes suppresses the rheumatic process in patients. Gold was first used clinically for rheumatoid arthritis in 1927, and by 1934 its use was much popularized.

Gold sodium thiomalate. It is used in severe active or progressive *rheumatoid arthritis, palindromic rheumatism* and *juvenile chronic arthritis.* It is given by IM injection, and usually the treatment is begun with a 10 mg test dose to detect hypersensitive patients. Thereafter, if indicated, doses of 50 mg are given at weekly intervals until response is obtained. Benefit is expected after about 8 doses have been administered. Then the interval between injections is gradually increased to 2 and then to 4 weeks, or even 6 weeks. Treatment is to be continued indefinitely.

Penicillamine. The chelating agent used in the treatment of Wilson's disease, and heavy metal poisoning **(Chap. 14)** is also effective in rheumatoid arthritis. Penicillamine has a similar action to gold. *Comparative studies indicate that penicillamine is as effective as gold or azathioprine.* Because of its potentially hazardous adverse effects, penicillamine is reserved for patients with long-standing disease refractory to standard therapy.

Penicillamine is used for severe active or progressive rheumatoid arthritis, juvenile chronic arthritis, Wilson's disease and cystinuria. An initial dose of 125 to 250 mg orally daily is given, increased after 4 to 6 weeks to 250 to 500 mg daily. Improvement is expected after 6 to 12 weeks of therapy.

Antimalarials. Chloroquine and hydroxychloroquine may be used in **active rheumatoid arthritis, systemic lupus erythematosus,** and **discoid lupus erythematosus.** They have a similar action to gold and are better tolerated than either gold or penicillamine, but their use is limited by their ocular toxicity. However, retinopathy is rare if the dosage mentioned below is not exceeded. Ocular toxicity is reduced if these drugs are not given continuously for periods over 1 year, and the patients are advised to stop treatment for 2 months each year.

Chloroquine is administered initially in a dose of 150-300 mg daily after meals; maintenance 150 mg daily. **Hydroxychloroquine** is given initially in a dose of 400-800 mg daily in divided doses after meals; maintenance 400 mg daily.

Adrenocorticosteroids and ACTH. In 1950 when Hench and his associates administered compound *E* (cortisol) to their patients with rheumatoid arthritis, they observed striking clinical improvement, with disappearance of pain and tenderness of the affected joints. Initially the corticosteroids were hailed as a "cure" for rheumatoid arthritis. In the succeeeding years many patients suffered the adverse effects of corticosteroids, and now they are held in reserve, and used when absolutely necessary to keep the patient from being incapacitated.

Dosage. Patients are started on small doses of prednisone or prednisolone as 5, 7.5 upto 10 mg per day.

This is added to the existing drug regimen of salicylates, non-salicylates, gold salts or antimalarials; and physical measures like heat, hydrotherapy and splints continue. On remission of the active disease process, the steroid dosage is reduced or gradually completely tapered off. Arthritic patients do not respond very well to **alternate day thereapy** (ADT).

Intra-articular steroid therapy. In inflammatory conditions of the joints, particularly in rheumatoid arthritis, corticosteroids are given by **intra-articular injection** to relieve pain, increase mobility, or reduce deformity in one or a few joints. Full aseptic precautions are essential. **Hydrocortisone acetate** 5-50 mg, according to the joint size is injected intra-articularly. Other synthetic analogues like **triamcinolone acetonide** (Kenalog), **triamcinolone hexacetonide** (Lederspan), **dexamethasone sodium phosphate** (Decadron), and **methylprednisolone acetate** may be used intra-articularly for pain relief. Intra-articular steroid injections must be employed sparingly, as aseptic necrosis, particularly of the weight-bearing joints is likely to occur as a result of osteoporosis.

Corticotrophin (ACTH) has also sometimes been employed in rheumatoid arthritis. Its advantages are that it stimulates the production and release of endogenous steroids, and does not suppress adrenal function; and there is less of osteoporosis and muscle weakness. The disadvantage is that ACTH has to be administered IM and has a relatively short half-life (even the repository form).

Immunosuppressants. These agents, when used in rheumatoid arthritis have a similar action to gold, and are useful alternatives in cases that have failed to respond to gold, penicillamine and chloroquine. **Azathioprine** (1.5 to 2.5 mg/kg per day in divided doses), and chlorambucil (5 mg/day) may be used.

The immunosuppressive agents are detailed in **Chapter 10.10.** The use is based on the concept that rheumatoid arthritis is an autoimmune disease, and the immunosuppressants block antibody biosynthesis.

Other measures employed for the management of rheumatoid arthritis include **lymphopheresis, plasmapheresis,** and **total lymphoid irradiation. Sulphasalazine** (salicylazo-sulphapyridine) is a sulphonamide, poorly absorbed from the gut, and primarily used for the treatment of **ulcerative colitis,** has also been used in the treatment of **rheumatoid arthritis** and **ankylosing spondylitis.**

Antimigraine Drugs

Headache is the most common complaint of patients seen by the physician. It may be a serious symptom of intracranial structural changes caused by **brain tumours,** cerebrovascular disorders like **aneurysms** and **angiomas.** Other organic disorders causing headache include **glaucoma, hypertension** and **chronic sinusitis.** The nerve cells of the brain itself are not sensitive to the pain-producing stimuli, but arteries coursing the membranes covering the brain contain pain-sensitive nerve endings. When these **intracranial** arteries are distended pain is perceived. Nerve impulses also arise from **extracranial** structures like skin, blood vessels, and muscles of the scalp and neck, which become a source for pain. In addition, personality factors (psychic causes) may also cause a kind of chronic headache. Thus, headache may be divided into two: (*i*) **tension or muscle contraction headaches;** and (*ii*) **vascular headaches.** The tension headaches are difficult to manage, but respond to non-narcotic analgesics like *aspirin* or *paracetamol.*

Vascular headaches are the result of dilatation of the intracranial and extracranial arteries, and are sometimes classed as **migraine** and **non-migraine** types. Hypertensive vascular headaches with which the patient wakens in the morning are best dealt by controlling blood pressure by antihypertensive agents. Migraine headaches are classified on the basis of differences in the pattern of individual attacks, and they are : (*i*) **classic migraine;** (*ii*) **common migraine;** and (*iii*) **cluster headaches** (a unilateral vascular headache). Chemical substances that are possibly released locally, and play a part in the perpetuation of migraine are, a polypeptide called **neurokinin,** which resembles **bradykinin,** which causes both vasodilatation and stimulation of pain receptors; and **serotonin** which induces certain local tissue changes.

Drug Therapy

Drugs used to treat migraine may be discussed under two heads: (*i*) treatment of acute migraine attack; and (*ii*) prophylaxis of migraine.

Acute migraine attack. Most migraine headaches respond to analgesics like **aspirin** and **paracetamol,** but as peristalsis is reduced during migraine attacks, these drugs may not be effectively absorbed. Soluble preparations are therefore preferable. Other drugs used are **ergotamine tartrate** (Gynergen); **ergotamine tartrate 1 mg, plus caffeine** 100 mg (Cafergot); or **dihydroergotamine mesylate** (DHE-45). These drugs are detailed in **Chapter 3.5.**

Other drugs include **metoclopramide,** or *antihistamine* antiemetics. These drugs relieve the nausea associated with migraine attacks and metoclopramide promotes gastric emptying and peristalsis. A newer drug is **isometheptene mucate** (Midrid), which is as effective as ergotamine, and has much fewer side effects. It is a sympathomimetic, sedative, and an analgesic agent. **Diazepam** or other anxiolytics may be useful adjuncts to counteract muscle spasm and anxiety which is often present in a migraine attack.

Prophylaxis of migraine. The drugs which are helpful in preventing attacks are : (*i*) **Clonidine** in a dose of 50 mcg bid, increased after 2 weeks to 75 mcg bid, if necessary, (*ii*) **Propranolol** 20-40 mg bid or tid for prevention of severe recurrent migraine; (*iii*) **Prochlorperazine** in a dose of 5 mg tid; (*iv*) **Methysergide,** an antiserotonergic drug, in a dose of 1.0 mg at bedtime; (*v*) **Pizotifen,** another antiserotonerigc drug, in a dose of initially 500 mcg daily, increased to 3 mg/day in divided doses, if necessary; and (*vi*) **Cyproheptadine** an older antihistamine-antiserotonergic drug in a dose of 4-20 mg/day in divided doses.

Drugs for Central Pain Syndromes

Central pain syndromes are caused by diseases or injuries affecting portions of the CNS, e.g., **tabes dorsalis, postherpetic neuralgia,** but the aetiology of others, e.g., **trigeminal neuralgia** remains unexplained.

Carbamazepine. It is chemically related to tricyclic antidepressants, but it does not have antidepressive activity. It is primarily employed as an antiepileptic **(Chap. 2.5).** Carbamazepine is the drug of choice for the treatment of **trigeminal** and **glossopharyngeal neuralgia,** and **tabes dorsalis.** It is usually administered in a dose of 200 mg to a maximum of 1.2 g daily.

Phenytoin. It is sometimes used in the treatment of **trigeminal neuralgia,** but is less effective than carbamazepine. Phenytoin is also reported to be effective in several other pain syndromes, e.g., **peripheral neuralgia, phantom limb pain, thalamic pain** and **postherpetic neuralgia.** Phenytoin also is an antiepileptic, and is further detailed in **Chapter 2.5.** For trigeminal neuralgia it is employed in a dose of 300-400 mg daily, and the dose may be increased, if necessary. Recently, **amitriptyline** and **fluphenazine** are under controlled studies for relief of pain of *peripheral diabetic neuropathy.*

In this Chapter mainly the nonsteroidal anti-inflammatory drugs have been discussed. They cause reduction of oedema, erythema, and resulting tissue damage associated with inflammatory conditions, and may also induce analgesia, and antipyresis. This triad of action *anti-inflammatory, analgesic, antipyretic* – is possessed by the classic, and most widely used NSAID, aspirin. Aspirin has been commonly used since the turn of the century, and even today is the drug of first choice for mild pain, fever and arthritis (osteoarthritis and rheumatoid arthritis).

2.8 PSYCHOPHARMACOLOGICAL AGENTS (ANTIPSYCHOTICS, ANTIDEPRESSANTS, ANTIMANICS AND HALLUCINOGENS)

The end of the 19th century saw the influence of Sigmund Freud's psychoanalysis of neurotic disorders, but the treatment of psychotic patients remained crude, and included techniques like isolation, restraint, sleep therapy, hydrotherapy, psychosurgery, insulin shock, and electroconvulsive therapy. Little progress was made until early 1950s, when **clinical psychopharmacology** made major advances with the introduction of **chlorpromazine** and **reserpine.** Today, reserpine is not longer used. However, **chlorpromazine,** and newer antipsychotic drugs are used for treating psychotic patients.

Terminology

In general, drugs primarily used for treating schizophrenia or other psychoses are called **antipsychotics** (neuroleptics, major tranquillizers); those used for treating depressive illness-***antidepressants*** (thymoleptics); those used to control mania – **antimanics;** and those used for treating anxiety neuroses – **antianxiety agents** (anxiolytics, minor tranquillizers). The antianxiety drugs have been discussed in **Chapter 2.4.** Lysergic acid diethylamide (LSD) and drugs with similar activity are called **hallucinogens** (psychotominetics). The hallucinogens are drugs of abuse.

Antipsychotics (Neuroleptics)

The antipsychotic agents are highly effective in excited or **agitated psychotic states,** including acute episodes of **schizophrenia, hypomania** and **delirium.** They have revolutionized the management of schizophrenia. The older term "major tranquillizer" is misleading. The term "antipsychotic" is self-explanatory and most appropriate.

Nature of Psychoses

Psychoses can be divided into two categories: (*i*) **schizoprenic;** and (*ii*) **affective** disorders. The chief characteristic of psychotic individuals is a persistent inability to recognize reality. They have **hallucinations** and **delusions.** Their personality and behaviour become so severely disorganized, that they cannot cope with the environment in which they have to function. For this reason they have to be hospitalized for their own protection, and for the safety of others.

The current understanding of schizophrenia suggests that it has metabolic, genetic and psychosocial components. It is now believed that **noradrenaline,** and **dopamine** in particular are involved in the schizophrenic process, and the imbalance between the two is associated with the disease. Recently a correlation has been demonstrated between the therapeutic potencies of a number of antipsychotic drugs, and their ability to block dopaminergic receptors in *vitro.* These effects are not reversible by levodopa.The antiemetic properties also result from dopaminergic blockade in the chemoreceptor trigger zone. Thus, the therapeutic benefit, and toxicity of the antipsychotics may be partly explained by the dopaminergic blockade they induce.

Classification

Drugs of several different chemical classes have demonstrated an ability to relieve symptoms of schizophenia and other psychoses. They are listed with their pharmacological profile in **Table 2.8-1. Rauwolfia serpentina** the **Indian snakeroot,** is a shrub indigenous to India, and other countries of South-East Asia. For centuries, preparations of this root had been used in Ayurvedic medicine for the treatment of mental diseases, and hypertension. About 20 years later, **reserpine** was isolated as an active ingredient of the plant and used in Western Medicine as an antihypertensive **(Chap. 4.2),** and antipsychotic agent. A high incidence of side effects with reserpine, and the superiority of chlorpromazine as an antipsychotic agent, has led to the removal of reserpine from the list of antipsychotic drugs.

Antipsychotic drugs generally lower the seizure threshold and induce extrapyramidal effects. They do not exhibit an addictive potential or anaesthetic properties. They exert a profound effect on the **autonomic nervous system, hypothalamus, reticular formation** and the **medulla.**

Phenothiazines

Chlorpromazine is the most commonly employed phenothiazine. Prior to the introduction of chlorpromazine, violent patients were physically restrained or heavily sedated. In contrast, the phenothiazines calm the patient without producing clouding of consciousness or incoordination, thus permitting psychotherapy sessions.

Table 2.8-1. *The classification, dosage and pharmacological profile of antipsychotic drugs*

Classification Generic Name	*Total daily dosage (mg; oral)*	*Sedative Effects*	*Extrapyramidal Effects*	*Hypotensive Effects*	*Anticholinergic Effects*
1. **Phenothiazines**					
(a) *Aliphatics*					
Chlorpromazine	50-1500	++++	++	++++	++
Promazine	50-1000	+++	+	+++	++
Triflupromazine	50-200	++++	++	+++	++
(b) *Piperidines*					
Thioridazine	50-800	++++	+	++++	++++
Mesoridazine	50-400	++++	+	++++	+++
Piperacetazine	10-160	+++	+	+++	+++
(c) *Piperazines*					
Prochlorperazine	10-150	++	+++	+	++
Trifluoperazine	5-30	++	+++	+	++
Perphenazine	8-64	++	+++	+	++
2. **Butyrophenones**					
Haloperidol	2-15	+	++++	+	++
3. **Thioxanthines**					
Chlorprothixene	25-600	+++	++	+	+
Thiothixene	5-60	+	+++	+	+
4. Dihydroindolone					
Molindone	10-250	++	+++	++	++
5. Dibenzoxazepine					
Loxapine	20-250	++	+++	++	++
6. Dibenzodiazepine					
Clozapine (atypical antipsychotic; minimal central antidopaminergic activity)					
7. **Diphenylbutylpiperidine**					
Pimozide	1-20	+	++	++	+
8. Bengisoxazole					
Risperidone	4-16	+	+	+	+
9. Thienben					
Zodiazepine					
Olanzepine	5-20	++	+	+	+

+ minimal; ++ mild; +++ moderate; ++++ severe

Pharmacological Actions

Chlorpromazine is a versatile drug in having many actions. It blocks **noradrenaline, dopamine, serotonin, acetylcholine** and **histamine** receptor sites. In addition, it has profound influence on behaviour and on the endocrine glands. Chlorpromazine is not only the prototype neuroleptic drug, it also serves as a standard against which other drugs are compared. Its actions are briefly detailed below:

Behavioural effects. Spontaneous motor activity (SMA) in animals is reduced, and there is sedation. In man, there is drowsiness, and a tendency to fall asleep, but its action is very different from that of the sedative-hypnotics in that `arousal' can be produced by moderate stimulation, and even very large doses do not produce anaesthesia. However, chlorpromazine potentiates the depressant actions of sedative-hypnotics, and anaesthetics. The stimulant effects of amphetamine and related drugs in producing **stereotyped behaviour** are antagonized by chlorpromazine. Under its influence, painful stimuli readily elicit a response, but there is an indifference to pain. The actions of analgesic drugs are potentiated. In savage animals, chlorpromazine has a **`taming'** effect. It prevents **`sham-rage'** induced in cats by stimulating the hypothalamus. Such an activity is thought to be predictive of efficacy in the control of psychotic excitation in man. In man it produces tiredness, sedation, and diminution of emotional responsiveness, with indifference to environmental changes. This is called the **ataractic** state. Thus, it exerts a central antihallucinatory and calming activity. Chlorpromazine disrupts conditioned avoidance reactions in animals which have been trained to act in a specific way to a signal.

Other central effects include: (*i*) inhibition of the **chemoreceptor trigger zone** of the medullary vomiting centre, and thereby exerting an **antiemetic effect;** and (*ii*) inhibition of hypothalamic function; causing loss of temperature control **(hypothermia),** increased prolactin release leading to galactorrhoea, amenorrhoea, delayed menstruation and weight gain. Many of the phenothiazines have powerful extrapyramidal effects.

Chlorpromazine also blocks muscarinic cholinergic receptors, producing *atropine-like effects; blocks histamine* H_1 *receptors;* and *blocks alpha-adrenoceptors.* This latter action plays a part in the production of postural hypotension, which is also due to central impairment of cardiovascular reflexes.

Three classes of phenothiazines are formed according to the substitution in the side chain attached to the nitrogen: (*i*) the **aliphatics** have considerable *alpha-adrenoceptor blocking activity,* and exert greater peripheral effects like hypotension, tachycardia and dry mouth; (*ii*) the **piperidines** are more potent than the aliphatics on a weight-for-weight basis, but sedation is usually prominent, and the extrapyramidal effects are less common than in the other two groups; and (*iii*) the **piperazines** are also more potent antipsychotics than the aliphatics, and produce less sedation. However, extrapyramidal side effects are produced more readily than with the aliphatics **(Table 2.8-1).**

Sites and mode of action. Chlorpromazine and other phenothiazines exert a relatively selective action on those parts of the CNS which are concerned with **alertness** and **performance.** The selectivity, at least in part, is due to their preferential accumulation in the **reticular activating system, limbic system, hypothalamus** and **thalamus.** Very small amounts are found in the cerebral and cerebellar cortices.

It has been suggested that the *tranquillizing action is due to blockade of central adrenergic transmission; antischizophrenic activity is due to blockade of serotoninergic* and *dopaminergic transmission;* and the *antiemetic effect* and *extrapyramidal effects are due to blockade of dopaminergic transmission.*

To sum up, the antipsychotic drugs share two novel pharmacologcial actions: (*i*) their ability to **ameliorate schizophrenia;** and (*ii*) their ability to evoke **extrapyramidal syndromes.** Both of these are mediated through the **postsynaptic dopamine receptor blockade.** The blockade in the **mesolimbic** and **mesocortical dopaminergic systems** is responsible for their antipsychotic activity; and blockade in the **nigroneostriatal** and **tuberoinfundibular dopaminergic system** is responsible for the extrapyramidal and endocrine adverse reactions, respectively. In addition, they also affect the functioning of the three main integrating systems, namely, the *reticular activating system, limbic system,* and *hypothalamus,* whereby the extraneous distracting sensory information and the somatic response to it is reduced.

Animal Tests for Neuroleptic Activity

Some useful pharmacologic tests are: (*i*) Taming of naturally aggressive animals, e.g., the Rhesus monkey; (*ii*) Abolition of sham-rage in operated animals; (*iii*) Suppression of behavioural `arousal' response to noise or electrical stimulation of the reticular formation; (*iv*) Prevention of abnormal behaviour induced by psychotomimetic drugs; (*v*) Suppression of EEG arousal reaction; (*vi*) Suppression of conditioned avoidance response; (*vii*) Reduction of spontaneous motor activity and impairment of muscle coordination; (*viii*) Potentiation of action of depressant drugs like barbiturates;

(*ix*) Antagonism of action of stimulant drugs like amphetamine and apomorphine; and (*x*) Antagonism of experimentally-induced aggression in animals.

Pharmacokinetics

Most studies have been carried out on chlorpromazine. When given orally, it is incompletely absorbed with a bioavailability of about 30 percent. Peak plasma levels are reached in 2-3 hours, but the $t_{1/2}$ varies between 2 and 24 hours in different individuals. The plasma steady-state levels are reached in about 1 week, and range from 10 to 1200 ng/ml in psychotic patients. On intramuscular injection, absorption is irregular possibly due to local precipitation of the drug.

Chlorpromazine has an unstable molecule which rapidly forms an inactive sulphoxide on exposure to light. It has about 168 potential metabolites, out of which 70 have been identified in man. The major routes of metabolism are: **demethylation** producing nor1 and nor2 - chlorpromazine, which are sedative; *oxidation* producing pharmacologically inactive sulphoxides and *N*-oxides; **hydroxylation** producing 3-hydroxy- and 7-hydroxychlorpromazine. Metabolism is primarily by hepatic microsomes, but the brain, kidneys, lungs and the gut also play a part. Levels of 35-350 ng/ml are associated with clinical improvement and severe toxicity is seen above 600 ng/ml. The rate of excretion is slow.

Therapeutic Uses

The phenothiazines have many therapeutic uses, based on their antipsychotic and other pharmacological actions.

1. **Schizophrenia.** They are effective against *acute episodes*, and prevent the general deterioration in *chronic schizophrenia.*
2. **Mania.** The calming and depressant effects are useful in the treatment of all types of mania.
3. **Anxiety neuroses** and **psychosomatic disorders.** Phenothiazines are useful in the treatment of severe anxiety and panic.
4. **Painful terminal illness.** These agents reduce the emotional response to pain, and also potentiate some of the central effects of narcotic analgesics.
5. **Drug-induced psychosis.** Chlorpromazine antagonizes the psychotic effects of intoxication by amphetamines and LSD.
6. **Shock.** The alpha-adrenoceptor blockade induced by the phenothiazines may be of value in the treatment of shock, and also hypertensive reactions.
7. **Nausea and vomiting.** Chlorpromazine exerts its antiemetic action (in nonsedative doses) by depressing the chemoreceptor trigger zone in the medulla. It protects against vomiting produced by apomorphine and ergot alkaloids, but has little action against that produced by cardiac glycosides or copper sulphate. Other phenothiazines used as antiemetics are **prochlorperazine, trifluperazine** and **perphenazine.**
8. **Hiccough** (hiccup) which is intractable to other therapy may be terminated by chlorpromazine.
9. **Withdrawal symptoms** of addictive drugs (opioids) may be partly controlled by chlorpromazine.
10. **Pruritus.** Some of the phenothiazines with antihistaminic activity (promethazine, trimeprazine) are useful antipruritic agents.
11. **Mental retardation.** Antipsychotics may partly alleviate the irritability, disturbed sleep, agitation and hostility associated with mental retardation.
12. **Huntington's disease.** Antipsychotics do not halt the progress of dementia, but they usually control the chorea.

Adverse Reactions

Antipsychotic drugs are remarkably safe with a **wide margin of safety,** and overdoses are seldom fatal in adults.

Disturbances of Central Nervous Function

Drowsiness, lethargy and fatigue. These are the commonest side effects. These effects are more pronounced during initial therapy.

Extrapyramidal effects. Three of the common reactions are: (*i*) **parkinsonism,** marked by coarse tremor and rigidity; (*ii*) **akathesia,** marked by aimless motor restlessness; and (*iii*) **dyskinesia (or dystonia)** characterized by tonic contractions of muscle groups, specially of the face, tongue and neck, and sometimes in the pelvis resulting in adoption of awkward postures. One of the serious but rare reaction to chronic phenothiazine medication is **tardive dyskinesia** (fasciobuccolinguo-masticatory dyskinesia) characterized by uncontrolled, rhythmic, in-and-out ("fly-catching") movements of the tongue, lip smaking and chewing-type movements, and rhythmic shaking and shuffling of the feet. The underlying mechanism is the impairment of dopaminergic transmission in the nigroneostriatal system. These extrapyramidal symptoms are refractory to levodopa, and may be treated with atropine-like antiparkinsonian drugs (benzhexol, benztropine, phenadrine, or procyclidine).

Convulsant action. The phenothiazines may precipitate epileptiform seizures in susceptible individuals.

Endocrine effects. These effects are due to the disruption of the hypothalamic control over the pituitary, leading to a suppression of the secretion of prolactin-inhibitory factor from the hypothalamus, resulting in increased blood prolactin levels. This leads to breast enlargement in men **(gynaecomastia)** and to lactation in women **(galactorrhoea).** There is a suppression of release of pituitary gonadotrophins, causing cessation of ovulation and menstruation (amenorrhoea). Weight gain, oedema and fluid retention can occur. False positive pregnancy tests have been reported.

Disturbances of Autonomic Nervous Function

Postural hypotension with tachycardia is commonly seen, specially during the early stages of treatment.

Anticholinergic effects. These may be manifested as dry mouth, constipation, urinary retention and blurred vision. Atropine-like effect may worsen glaucoma.

Nasal congestion may occur due to alpha-adrenoceptor blockade.

Sexual function. There may be failure of ejaculation, attributable to alpha-adrenoceptor blockade. It is reported that libido is decreased in men and increased in women, probably as a result of complex changes in the secretion pattern of sex hormones (see above).

Temperature control. With higher doses, the temperature regulating mechanism of the thalamus goes out of function; probably due to the blockade of neurotransmitters involved (acetylcholine, noradrenaline, serotonin). This almost leads to a poikolothermic (cold blooded) state, i.e., the body temperature tends to follow the environmental temperature - **hypothermia** is facilitated by peripheral vasodilatation and reduced muscular activity (antishivering effect); and hyperthermia is aided by inhibition of sweating.

Miscellaneous Effects

Allergic reactions in the form of erythema, urticaria, maculopapular rashes have been observed. Photosensitivity resembling sunburn may occur.

Ocular changes. High dose phenothiazine therapy may lead to granular deposits in cornea and lens causing *opacities.* Abnormal conjunctival pigment deposits may occur. Pigmented *retinopathy* is probably the most serious phenothiazine-induced change.

Skin. Purplish pigmentation of the skin occurs on prolonged therapy. This is due to increased melanin deposition as a result of an increased release of melanocyte-stimulating hormone, and also deposition of phenothiazine metabolites forming complexes with melanin.

Hepatotoxicity. Obstructive (cholestatic) jaundice may be produced by chlorpromazine.

Bone marrow toxicity. Agranulocytosis occurs in an approximate frequency of 1 in 250,000 with the aliphatic; 1 in 500,000 with the piperidine; and 1: 400,000 with the piperizine phenothiazines. Agranulocytosis usually occurs during the first 6 to 10 weeks of treatment, manifested as fever, pharyngitis, dysphagia and lymphadenopathy. It is suspected to be a hypersensitivity reaction. *Treatment* consists of immediate stoppage of drug, antibiotic therapy (penicillin), and packed cell transfusion (needed in severe cases). **Eosinophilia, thrombocytopenic or nonthrombocytopenic purpura** and **haemolytic anaemia** occur infrequently.

Teratogenic effects. There is no conclusive evidence that the antipsychotic drugs, can induce foetal malformation. However, as these drugs cross the placental barrier, they should be avoided during the first trimester of pregnancy.

Tolerance and physical dependence. The antipsychotic drugs are not addicting. However, a mild degree of **physical dependence** may occur, manifested as muscular discomfort and insomnia, when the drug is abruptly stopped. **Tolerance** develops to the sedative effects of chlorpromazine and other phenothiazines.

Drug Interactions

Phenothiazines *potentiate* the actions of *analgesics, sedative-hypnotics* and *anaesthetics.* Combination preparations of a phenothiazine with an antidepressant (e.g. perphenazine + amitriptyline) and with stimulants (trifluperazine + tranylcypromine or dextroamphetamine) may sometimes be used for treatment of schizophrenia with depression. The action of muscle relaxants and peripherally acting antihypertensives is also enhanced by phenothiazines. They also potentiate the sedative effects of alcohol, and respiratory depressant action of narcotics. Chlorpromazine is a moderately effective enzyme inducer.

To conclude, the phenothiazines have a wide margin of safety. However, despite their low lethality, they are capable of causing many adverse effects.

Non-Phenothiazine Antipsychotics

These drugs are best employed in the following two situations: (*i*) patients with chronic schizophrenic symptoms which are not completely controlled by the phenothiazines; and (*ii*) patients showing hypersensitivity reactions to the phenothiazines.

Butyrophenones

Haloperidol was the first member of this group to be used clinically. It is an effective alternative drug to the phenothiazines. The main actions of haloperidol are similar to the *piperazine* phenothiazines. Haloperidol possesses alpha-blocking activity, but has weaker autonomic effects than the phenothiazines. **Adverse effects** include sedation, extrapyramidal syndromes, hypotension, depression, leucopenia, agranulocytosis and jaundice.

Droperidol is a butyrophenone with a rapid action of a short duration. It has been used particularly in combination with fentanyl for the production of **neuroleptanalgesia (Chap. 2.3)** It is also effective in relieving attacks of **Meniere's disease.** The usual dose range is 5-20 mg orally.

Thioxanthines

Chlorprothixene was the first member of this group, and an analogue of chlorpromazine. Its pharmacological activity and side effects are similar to the phenothiazines. It is effective both in acute and chronic schizophrenia, and is not superior to the phenothiazines.

Thiothixene is an analogue of thioridazine. It is superior to thioridazine in the treatment of schizophrenic patients. Other newer agents are *clopenthixol* and *flupenthixol.*

Dihydroindolone

Molindone, introduced in 1974, is the only drug in this group which is currently used. It is structurally unrelated to the phenothiazines, thioxanthines or butyrophenones. This drug may be useful in patients refractory to other antipsychotic drugs.

Dibenzoxazepine

Loxapine is the only drug of this group which is currently used clinically. Side effects are similar to those of the phenothiazines, thioxanthines and butyrophenones.

Dibenzodiazepine

Clozapine. It is a unique antipsychotic because with it the incidence of extrapyramidal symptoms is low, and it is devoid of cataleptic activity. In other respects clozapine resembles chlorpromazine.

Diphenylbutylpiperidines

Pimozide, penfluridal, and **fluspirilene** have been developed from the butyrophenones. They are **long-acting neuroleptics,** which are particularly useful in the prevention of psychotic relapse in schizophrenic patients after their discharge from the hospital. These agents are said to be the most selective and potent dopamine antagonists so far discovered. They also have appreciable *alpha-blocking, antiacetylcholine, antihistaminic, antibradykinin* and *antiangiotensin* activity.

Depot Neuroleptics

Fatty acid esters of phenothiazines are being increasingly used for the maintenance therapy in schizophrenics. Single injections may be effective for 2-4 weeks. Acute dystonic reactions may follow initial doses, possibly due to a considerable early release of the drug.

Many depot preparations are available, viz., **fluphenazine decanoate, fluphenazine enanthate, flupenthixol decanoate, perphenazine enanthate** and **flusipirilene.** There is no evidence that the toxic effects are more frequent with these injections as compared to oral therapy. Extrapyramidal effects may be troublesome, and about 30 percent of patients experience them.

Antidepressants

The development of antidepressant drugs, sometimes referred to as "psychic energizers" or "thymoleptics", represents one of the outstanding successes of modern psychopharmacology. The two major categories of antidepressant drugs are: (*i*) the **tricyclic group** of which *imipramine* and *amitriptyline* are the most widely used; and (*ii*) the **monoamine oxidase inhibitors (MAOIs),** of which *tranylcypromaine* and *phenelzine* are the best known. The classic indication for antidepressant medication is endogenous depression; however, these drugs are also helpful in the treatment of agitated depressions and phobic anxiety states.

Classification of Depressions

Depression is an affective disorder which afflicts many individuals. The psychiatric term "affect" refers to the feelings – pleasant and unpleasant – which one experiences. Such feelings may be mild or strong, but all together they regulate the emotional and mental state at any one time.

From the point of view of drug treatment, depression may be classified into: (*i*) reactive depression (exogenous); and (*ii*) endogenous depression.

Reactive depression is characterized by a well-defined precipitating stress, such as the loss of a loved one, adverse effects of drugs or certain disease states. Reactive depression is usually self-limiting and unresponsive to antidepressant drugs. Therapy consists of mainly assurance and support (psychotherapy).

Endogenous depression is characterized by a definite onset of depressive symptoms unrelated to any significant

Table 2.8-2. *Drug therapy of depressive disorders*

Depressive Disorder	*Drug Therapy*
Reactive Depression	
Reaction to emotional stress	Nonspecific treatment, psychotherapy, or treat source if depression is secondary.
Adverse effect of drugs	
Secondary to disease	
Endogenous Depression	
Schizo-affective disorders	Antidepressants + antipsychotics
Manic-depressive disorders	Lithium carbonate

external event. This type of depression is possibly caused by some neurochemical imbalance (see later). The symptoms are usually more severe than those of reactive depression. Endogenous depression often requires life-long therapy. This category also includes **involutional depressions,** which surface at the age of 40 years or above, and depression related to **schizoaffective** or **manic-depressive** disorders. The therapeutic approaches are summarized in **Table 2.8-2.**

Broadly speaking, three main types of therapy are available for the treatment of depression: (*i*) Psychotherapy; (*ii*) **Electroconvulsive therapy (ECT);** and (*iii*) **Pharmacotherapy,** which is our main concern here.

Amine Hypothesis of Depression

As mentioned earlier there are two basic groups of drugs that are used for the treatment of depression: the *tricyclics,* and the *monomine oxidase inhibitors* (MAOIs). The former are more popular, as their side effects are easier to handle.

Many authorities believe that these drugs act by their ability to increase the activity of the *amine transmitters,* such as *noradrenaline* in the brain. The tricyclic antidepressants enhance neurotransmitter activity by *blocking the re-uptake* of amine neurotransmitters released into the synaptic cleft; this re-uptake is necessary for inactivation. This proposed mechanism supports the **"amine hypothesis"** of affective disorders, which attributes depression to a lack of activity of neurotransmitters (mainly noradrenaline and dopamine) in the brain. The MAOIs do this by inhibiting the enzyme monoamine oxidase, and thereby block the inactivation of the pressor amines, and potentiate their action.

Classification of Antidepressants

The antidepressants may be classified as under:

1. Tricyclic antidepressants (Imipramine amitriptyline etc.)
2. Tricylic anxiolytics (Doxepin)
3. Bicyclic antidepressants (Viloxazine)
4. Tetracyclic antidepressants (Maprotiline)
5. Monoamine oxidase inhibitors (MAOIs)
6. Miscellaneous (Nomifensine, trazodone)

Tricyclic Antidepressants

Tricyclic antidepressants are chemically related to the phenothiazine tranquillizers, and like the phenothiazines most of them exert a sedative effect during the first few days of their use. However, after several weeks of treatment, most patients respond quite differently, and sedation is

Table 2.8-3. *Pharmacologic profile of some antidepressants*

Antidepressant Group	*Inhibition of Nor-adrenaline uptake*	*Inhibition of Serotonin uptake*	*Reserpine Antagonism*	*Acetylcholine Antagonism*
Tricyclics				
Impiramine	++	+++	+	++
Amitriptyline	+	+++	+	+++
Nortriptyline	+++	+	+	++
Clomipramine	+	+++	+	++
Desipramine	+++	0	+	+
Protriptyline	+++	++	+	++
Trimipramine	Variable	Variable	+	++
Anxiolytic Tricyclic				
Doxepin	+	+	+	+++
Bicyclic Antidepressant				
Viloxazine	+++	0	+	0
Tetracyclic Antidepressants				
Maprotiline	+++	+	+	+
Mianserin	0	0	0	0
MAOIs	0	0	+	0
Miscellaneous				
Nomifensine	+++	0	+	+

0 denotes none, + slight, ++ moderate, +++ marked activity.

minimal. In general these drugs are most effective for treating **moderate to severe** depressive illness, associated with psychomotor and physiological changes; such as loss of appetite and sleep disturbances. Improvement in sleep is the first benefit of therapy. There may be an interval of 2 or 3 weeks before the antidepressant action is built up, so that electroconvulsive treatment (ECT) may be required in severe depression, where such a delay may be hazardous.

The first tricyclic antidepressant to be developed was **imipramine,** and because of its chemical relationship it was thought to be effective in schizophrenia. But, in fact it turned out to be ineffective in schizophrenia, and showed improvement in patients with depressive illness. The next drug to be introduced was **amitriptyline,** which is chemically related to the thioxanthine neuroleptics. A number of other compounds were subsequently introduced (see later).

Pharmacological Actions

It is generally thought that the tricyclics act by increasing the availability of *noradrenaline* and *serotonin* as central neurotransmitters by blocking their neuronal re-uptake. Actually, the tricyclics block the "amine pump" which is an active transport system for the re-uptake mechanism.

The *second* major pharmacological action of the tricyclics is a variable sedative effect, not too different from that of the phenothiazines. Amitriptyline has a greater sedative property than imipramine.

The *third* pharmacological action of tricyclics is their potent **central** and **peripheral anticholinergic activity.** This action contributes to their side effects. The pharmacological profile of various antidepressants is presented in **Table 2.8-3.**

Pharmacokinetics

The tricyclics being lipid-soluble in their non-ionized form are readily absorbed from the gut, but are subjected to considerable first-pass hepatic metabolism, e.g., nortriptyline is almost completely absorbed, but the bioavailability is only about 65 percent of an oral dose. Tricyclics themselves may delay their own absorption by their anticholinergic effect causing delay in gastric emptying time and intestinal peristalsis.

Protein binding of these drugs is high, just as with the phenothiazines. Thus they can interact with other highly protein bound drugs **(Table 2.8-4).**

The tricyclics are metabolized in a fashion similar to the phenothiazines. As a general rule initial **demethylation** gives monomethyl derivatives that are pharmacologically active. **Ring hydroxylation** abolishes the activity, and **conjugation** occurs before excretion in the urine.

Therapeutic Uses

The following conditions may be treated by using tricyclics alone, or in combination with other drugs.

Depressions. The tricyclics are mainly used in the treatment of *endogenous depression;* however, these may also be useful in the treatment of *agitated depressions* and *phobic anxiety state.*

Enuresis. For this condition imipramine 25-50 mg orally may have a beneficial effect.

Chronic painful states. Many pain clinics use tricyclics for depression associated with chronic vague pain.

The tricyclics are also used in conditions like **school phobia** in children; **hyperactive child syndrome; minimal brain damage;** and **compulsive phobic states.**

Adverse Reactions

Adverse effects of tricyclics may be considered under the following heads:

(*i*) **Autonomic (anticholinergic).** Dry mouth, blurring of vision, and constipation are commonly reported side effects. Hesitancy in micturition and impotence may occur. Aggravation of narrow-angle glaucoma, postural hypotension, retention of urine and paralytic ileus may occur rarely. Postural hypotension is generally attributed to the alpha-blocking activity of tricyclics.

(*ii*) **Central nervous system.** Fine tremor, sedation, insomnia, decreased REM sleep, convulsions, and ataxia may occur. Sometimes confusional states

Table 2.8-4. *Pharmacokinetic characteristics of tricyclic antidepressants*

Drug	*Plasma Half-life (hrs)*	*Therapeutic plasma level (ng/ml)*	*Protein Binding (%)*	*Latency to attain steady-state plasma levels (days)*
Amitriptyline	30-45	100-25	85-95	5-10
Amoxapine	8-12	200-400	85-90	2-8
Desipramine	12-60	150-400	75-90	2-10
Doxepin	8-30	100-250	NA*	2-8
Imipramine	6-20	200-300	80-90	2-5
Maprotiline**	20-30	200-300	NA	5-10
Nortriptyline	20-30	50-150	90-95	4-20
Protriptyline	60-120	100-200	90-95	8-10
Trimipramine	8-30	150-200	NA	2-6

*Data not available; ** Tetracyclic derivative

and extrapyramidal symptoms occur. Rarely mania and schizophrenic excitement may occur.

(*iii*) **Cardiovascular system.** Tachycardia and palpitation are often reported with therapeutic doses. These are due to a combination of factors: an increased sympathetic drive due to inhibition of noradrenaline re-uptake, and an atropine-like suppression of vagal slowing effect on the heart. Overdosage with tricyclics can cause cardiac arrhythmias like atrial fibrillation, ventricular flutter, atrioventricular and intraventricular blocks. Sudden death has been reported in patients taking tricyclics.

(*iv*) **Allergic reactions.** Skin reactions, intrahepatic cholestasis, and agranulocytosis may occur rarely.

(*v*) **Drug interactions.** The tricyclics are likely to interact with the following groups of drugs: (*i*) **Antihypertensives.** The antihypertensive effect of adrenergic neurone blocking agents like guanethidine is blocked; (*ii*) **MAOIs.** There is synergism between the actions of tricyclics and MAOIs, and the combination, under controlled conditions, may be used with advantage to control patients responding poorly to either of the drug-type alone; (*iii*) **Thyroid hormones.** Thyroxine and triiodothyronine have a general stimulant effect, and potentiate the psychotropic effect of tricyclics; and (*iv*) **Sympathomimetics.** The effects of these agents are potentiated by the tricyclics.

Dosage. The dosage guide is presented in **Table 2.8-5.**

Table 2.8-5. *Dosage guide for antidepressant drugs*

Classification, Generic Name	*Total Daily Dosage (mg) (Divided into 2-4 doses)*
Tricyclic Antidepressants	
Doxepin	75-300
Amitriptyline	75-300
Nortriptyline	40-100
Imipramine	75-300
Desipramine	75-300
Protriptyline	30-60
Trimipramine	75-150
MAOI Antidepressants	
Hydrazides	
Phenelzine	15-75
Non-hydrazide	
Tranylcypromine	10-60
Psychomotor Stimulants	
Dextroamphetamine	5-30
Methamphetamine	2.5-20
Methylphenidate	10-40

Anxiolytic Tricyclic Antidepressants

Doxepin. This agent possesses considerable anxiolytic activity, although it is a less potent antidepressant than imipramine or amitriptyline. It is helpful in the treatment of patients of mild depression with anxiety.

Tetracyclic Antidepressants

Maprotiline. Its pharmacological and biochemical properties resemble the tricyclics. It is contraindicated in ischaemic heart disease, as it is cardiotoxic. *Dosage:* 100-150 mg daily in divided doses.

Mianserin. This is a tetracylic compound which increases noradrenaline turnover by an unknown mechanism without affecting the turnover of serotonin or dopamine. One possible mechanism is that mianserin blocks the presynaptic alpha-adrenoceptors modulating synaptic noradrenaline release, resulting in an increased noradrenaline release. *Dosage:* 30-120 mg daily in divided doses.

Miscellaneous Group

Trazodone. Trazodone is chemically unrelated to tricyclics, tetracyclics, or MAOIs. Its efficacy is comparable to that of tricyclics. Trazodone selectively interferes with the uptake of serotonin by nerve endings. It has minimal anticholinergic and cardiotoxic effects, but is a strong sedative. Trazodone is well absorbed orally, and a significant response is seen within 1 week in 50 percent of the patients treated, and within 2 weeks in 75 percent of the patients treated. Its plasma half-life is 4-8 hours. It is used mainly in the treatment of endogenous depression, with or without accompanying anxiety. **Dosage** is initiated at 150 mg/day in divided doses, and may be increased by 50 mg/day increments every 3 to 4 days until optimal control is obtained. **Adverse effects** include drowsiness, fatigue, dry mouth, constipation, and nasal congestion. Hypotension, palpitation, sinus bradycardia, confusion, disorientation, tremors and incoordination have also been reported.

Amoxapine, maprotiline, and trazodone are claimed to have a more rapid onset of action, and a lower incidence of adverse effects. These three second-generation antidepressants require further evaluation.

Monoamine Oxidase Inhibitors (MAOIs)

The development of the MAOIs followed from the observations in 1952, that the antitubercular drug **isoniazid** produced elevation of mood in patients being treated for the disease. In the same year it was discovered that it inhibited MAO. **Iproniazid** (Marsilid), the first MAOI used as an antidepressant, was also originally used in the treatment of tuberculosis. In 1956, Kline and his colleagues introduced it as a treatment for depression.

The **mode of action** of MAOIs, whereby they elevate the mood, is due to the increased availability of monoamine neurotransmitters at synapses in the CNS. The brain levels of *noradrenaline, dopamine* and *serotonin* are increased as a consequence of the inhibition of MAO. The MAOIs produce a feeling of well-being and elation. They also produce an increase in motor activity.

Currently, the most commonly used MAOIs for depression are **phenelzine** and **tranylcypromine (Table 2.8-5).** Favourable results have been observed with tranylcypromine, which is comparable to imipramine in terms of efficacy. All the currently available MAOIs are well absorbed on oral administration. Although they are rapidly metabolized and excreted, their inhibitory effect on the enzyme MAO lasts for as long as several weeks.

Adverse effects. The side effects include effects on the CNS, autonomic effects, hepatic disorders, neurologic disturbances, haematologic abnormalities, and cardiovascular effects. Most often these effects may be minor like dizziness, orthostatic hypotension, oedema, increased intraocular pressure, dry mouth, mydriasis, constipation, difficulty in urination, delayed ejaculation and impotence.

In patients of hypertension, a **hypertensive crisis** may occur on concomitant intake of sympathomimetic amines (including amphetamines, ephedrine, phenylephrine, and phenylpropanolamine), and tyramine or tyramine containing food (aged cheeses, red wines, chicken liver, broad beans, coffee, yoghurt, chocolate and other foods).

Central side effects include agitation, manic excitement and other psychotic reactions. **Hepatotoxicity** manifested as jaundice and other signs of liver damage have been reported particularly with phenelzine.

Psychomotor Stimulants (Psychostimulants)

Some of the sympathomimetic amines like dextroamphetamine and methamphetamine, **(Table 2.8-5)** have been occasionally used in the treatment of depression.

Convulsant Therapy of Depression

Convulsive therapy (shock treatment) was introduced in psychiatry under the mistaken belief that epilepsy prevented schizophrenia.

Electroconvulsive Therapy (ECT). In ECT, a current of 200-150 mA is applied for 0.1-0.6 seconds across the temples. Within a few seconds there is a generalized tonic convulsion; followed by a series of clonic convulsions; and then followed by a period of confusion and amnesia lasting 30-90 minutes before full recovery. In practice light anaesthesia is produced by thiopentone, and a short acting muscle relaxant like **suxamethonium** is administered to the patient before applying the shock.

ECT is of benefit in the treatment of schizophrenia (acute episodes), and in the treatment of endogenous depression with marked suicidal tendencies. A course of 14-20 treatments is usually necessary to prevent relapse in schizophrenia.

The **mode of action** of ECT is not clear. It is suggested that the aberrant neuronal activity which had become 'fixed' in a psychotic is disrupted, and may be normalized.

The ECT carries with it the side effects of a postseizure acute organic mental syndrome with amnesia, confusion and recent memory loss. There is a risk of occasional vertebral or long bone fractures.

Combinations of Antidepressants

A tricyclic-MAOI combination may be used with advantage in relieving certain depressions that are unresponsive to conventional therapy.

Combination of two tricyclic antidepressants is not rational. However, combining *protriptyline* with a sedative tricyclic like *amitriptyline,* might balance the sedative-stimulant effects while summing up the antidepressive action.

Antimanic Drugs

Increase in psychomotor activity, grandiosity and emotional liability characterize the **manic state.** Milder forms of mania are often called **hypomania,** and are less easily recognized as abnormal. Manic attacks may occur in cycles alternating with depression, known as **manic-depressive psychosis.**

With the advent of psychotherapeutic drugs, the management of mania was achieved with antipsychotic drugs like **chlorpromazine** and **haloperidol.** Then **lithium** was introduced as a treatment of mania.

Lithium Carbonate

Lithium is an earth metal with an atomic weight of 7. Lithium carbonate is a simple inorganic salt, and has no known function in normal metabolism. In 1949, Cade in Melbourne discovered that lithium salts had a specific effect in controlling mania, but had no effect in patients with schizophrenia or chronic depression. Lithium counteracts mood changes, without producing sedation, and is considered to be the *only* specific antimanic drug for the prophylaxis and treatment of *manic-depressive disorders.*

Mode of action. Lithium is thought to: (*i*) *accelerate the presynaptic destruction of catecholamines* (an action opposite to that of MAOIs); (*ii*) *inhibit the release of noradrenaline* at the synapse; and (*iii*) *decrease the sensitivity of the postsynaptic receptor.* These actions tend to correct the presumed overactivity of the catecholaminergic systems in mania.

It has also been proposed that lithium interacts with the Ca^{++} and Mg^{++} ions leading to a **stabilization of the neuronal membrane.**

Pharmacokinetics. Lithium is completely absorbed 6-8 hours after oral administration. It is not bound to the plasma proteins, and is well distributed in the body, volume of distribution being 50-90 percent of body weight. Lithium is distributed more evenly in body water than is sodium and potassium. There is possible sequestration in the bone. Plasma $t_{1/2}$ is approximately 7 to 24 hours, and lithium is eliminated almost entirely by the kidneys.

Serum lithium should preferably be between 0.9 to 1.5 mEq/L for therapeutic effect initially, and then maintained within a range of 0.5 to 1.2 mEq/L. It should never be permitted to exceed 2.0 mEq/L, as serious toxicity results.

Therapeutic uses. *Manic-depressive disorder* is the best-established indication for the use of lithium, both for its treatment and prophylaxis. It may sometimes be used for the treatment of selected cases of **endogenous depression, schizoaffective disorder, schizophrenia, alcoholism and uncontrollable aggressive behaviour** in prisoners.

Adverse reactions. Mild to moderate side effects (serum levels 1.5-2.0 mEq/L) include nausea, malaise, diarrhoea, and fine hand tremors. Thirst, polydipsia, fatigue, muscle weakness, slurred speech and nystagmus may occur. Moderate to severe adverse reactions (serum levels 2.0-2.5 mEq/L) include persistent nausea and vomiting, blurred vision, fasciculations, clonic movements of limbs, hyperactive tendon reflexes, hypothyroidism, goitre, choreoathetoid movements, epileptiform convulsions, hypokalaemia, ECG changes, toxic psychosis, acute circulatory failure, stupor and coma. At serum levels above 2.5 mEq/L symptoms rapidly progress to generalized convulsions, oliguria and death. *Thus lithium is a toxic drug, and serum level monitoring is essential for safe therapy.* No specific antidote of lithium is known.

Dosage. Lithium carbonate 0.25-2.0 g orally daily, adjusted by daily blood level tests to achieve a maintenance concentration of 0.5-1.2 mEq/L. Dosage should be individualized on the basis of serum levels and response.

Lithium should not be used in patients with kidney or cardiovascular disease, severe debility, or conditions requiring low sodium diets. Concurrent use of diuretics is contraindicated.

Hallucinogenic Drugs (Psychotomimetics)

Many drugs and chemicals can cause hallucinations, and are known as **hallucinogens.** Other generic names for this class of drugs are: **psychotomimetics, psychodysleptics, psychotogenics, psychedelics, psychotoxics,** and **fantastica.** All these names suggest the capacity of these drugs to produce changes in perception, cause abnormal thinking and behaviour which occurs in natural psychoses.

Classification

The major hallucinogens may be classified according to their chemical structure into five important classes: (*i*) **Indolylalkylamines,** lysergic acid diethylamide (LSD-25), psilocybin and psilocyn (psilocin), bufotenine, harmine and harmaline, N,N-dimethyltryptamine **(DMT);** (*ii*) **Phenylalkylamines,** mescaline, 2-5-dimethoxy-4-methylamphetamine (DOM), trimethoxyamphetamine (TMA); (*iii*) **Arylcycloalkylamines,** phencyclidine; (*iv*) **Tetrahydrocannabinols,** THC and synthetic derivatives; and (*v*) **Glycolate esters,** Ditran (JB-329). In addition to these major classes, many other drugs, including bromides, myristicin and elemicin found in nutmeg, and narcotic antagonists like nalorphine, can produce psychotomimetic effects.

For further consideration these hallucinogens are grouped into four categories; **aminergic, anticholinergic** and **miscellaneous psychotomimetics,** and **cannabis** (marihuana, marijuana).

Aminergic Psychotomimetics

Compounds in this class include LSD and other **tryptamine derivatives** (DMT, bufotenine, psilocybin, psilocyn) and mescaline, and **betaphenylethylamine derivatives** (amphetamine DOM, TMA).

Lysergic Acid Diethylamide (Lysergide, LSD-25, LSD)

LSD was synthesized by Hofmann in 1938 at Sandoz Laboratories in Basel, Switzerland, but it was not until 1943 that he discovered its hallucinogenic properties. Being the twenty-fifth compound prepared in the series it was given the code name LSD-25. Hofmann in the first instance accidentally experienced the hallucinogenic actions of LSD, but later he deliberately took 250 mcg of the material (taking this to be the expected dose to produce minimal effects, but later it turned out to be at least 5 to 10 times the average effective dose of LSD). He also wrote his experiences in his diary about what happened afterwords.

LSD is the most potent hallucinogenic agent presently available, producing clearly demonstrable behavioural effects in adult humans after oral doses of 0.025-0.050 mg (25-50 mcg). Chemically LSD resembles the ergot alkaloid ergonovine.

Pharmacological actions. The ability to alter behaviour is not observed in man only. But LSD interferes with the ability of spiders to spin their webs in an organized manner; it renders cats fearful of mice; and fish maintain a vertical nose-up position and swim backwards after LSD administration. Virtually all actions of LSD are exerted via the CNS.

Physiological effects. Within 20-60 minutes of ingestion of LSD, there is a marked sympathetic stimulation, causing mydriasis, sweating, tachycardia, tremor, gooseflesh, muscular weakness and hyperthermia. Fluctuations in mood, euphoria, dysphoria, hilarity, followed by extreme anxiety, fits of crying and panic are seen.

Psychological effects. The most dramatic effects produced by LSD are those concerned with sensory perception. *Colours,* become more intense and kaleidoscopic. Hallucinations are rare after moderate doses, but illusions, like mistaking a spot on the wall for a face may occur frequently. Enhanced sensitivity to touch, smell and taste have been noted. Significant alterations in the **thought processes** take place. The subject believes he is having a **transcendental** experience. Disorientation of *time* and *space* is common. **Depersonalization** is induced, and there are subjective reports of enhanced creativity while under the influence of LSD. A "bad trip" is horrible, but a "good trip" provides the incentive for continued usage of the drug.

Mode of action. There is a large body of evidence that links LSD action to its effects at the **serotonergic receptor** *sites* in the CNS. Recent evidence shows that LSD binds serotonin in nerve endings and inhibits its breakdown, and holds serotonin in an inactive state. It appears that serotonin is intimately involved in LSD action, but the specific nature of this interaction is ill-understood. Thus, LSD exhibits **anti-serotonin activity.**

Another dimension to LSD action is added by the finding that its chemical analogue *bromolysergide* (bromo-LSD) has only 1 percent of the hallucinogenic activity of LSD, although it is as potent as LSD as an antagonist at peripheral serotonin receptor sites. Bromolysergide antagonizes the hallucinogenic action of LSD.

Adverse reactions. Repeated usage of LSD produces tolerance to the psychic effects of the drug within 4 days, and a similar drug-free period is required for loss of tolerance. Cross tolerance has been demonstrated between LSD and mescaline, psilocybin and psilocyn, but this phenomenon does not occur between LSD and marihuana or amphetamine.

Chronic use of LSD does not produce physical dependence **(Chap. 2.10).** However, in the late 1960s it became evident that *bad trips* could also occur, with an alarming frequency. The adverse reactions include confusion, extreme anxiety, panic and a marked *psychotic state.* During the psychotic state accidental or intentional suicide attempts have been reported. Such bad trips became a scare among the people indulging in this "drug cult". **Flashbacks,** a trip in the absence of the drug have also contributed to general disenchantment with LSD. In addition LSD causes, **chromosomal damage,** probably leading to congenital abnormalities in humans. Thus, because of bad trips, flashbacks and possible chromosomal damage LSD lost prominence on the 'drug scene'.

Morning glory seeds. The seeds of the plant *Ipomoea violacae,* better known to the abuser as *morning glory,* contain the active psychotomimetic principle *lysergic acid amide,* a close relative of LSD but about one-tenth as potent. After chewing several hundred seeds of morning glory, the subject becomes drowsy, with changes in perception, confusion, hallucinations, nausea and vomiting.

Psilocybin and Psilocyn. In 1958, Hofmann (of LSD fame) isolated psilocybin and psilocyn from *Psilocybe mexicana,* the magic mushroom. These substances are equipotent, and have about 1 percent of the potency of LSD. After oral administration of psilocybin, psychic effects are observed within 30-60 minutes and last for about 5 hours.

Mescaline. Chemically, it is 3,4,5-trimethoxyphenyl-ethylamine, and is the oldest known drug, with a primary hallucinogenic activity. It was isolated in 1896 from the Mexican cactus *Lophophora williamsi,* popularly known as the *peyote cactus.* Mescaline is probably the least active of the commonly used psychotomimetic agents, and has about 0.02 percent of the hallucinogenic activity of LSD.

Trimethoxyamphetamine (TMA) is an alpha-methylated analogue of mescaline, and is about 10 times more potent than mescaline.

Amphetamine. This agent also produces a psychosis in which there are visual, auditory, tactile and olfactory hallucinations and excitation.

DOM (2,5-dimethoxy-4-methylamphetamine) is about 100 times more potent than mescaline. It is also known as STP (serenity, tranquillity and peace) to the abuser. It produces euphoric and hallucinogenic effects at doses of 5 mg, and is about 50-100 times more active than mescaline.

MDA (methylene dioxyamphetamine) is twice as active as mescaline. This compound produces psychotomimetic effects, without perceptual distortions, or changes of colour, in sharp contrast to those produced by mescaline.

Anticholinergic Psychotomimetics

The anticholinergic agents (atropine and scopolamine) are capable of producing confusion, delirium, disorientation and hallucinations.

Ditran is a mixture of two esters of substituted glycolate, and is the most studied substance in the series. It is a potent atropine-like drug, and has similar peripheral effects (dry mouth, mydriasis, flushing and tachycardia). Its striking actions on the CNS are: feeling of apprehension, disorientation in time and space, depersonalization, sensory disturbances, and hallucinations (visual, auditory, olfactory). Followed by confusion and a period of amnesia.

Phencyclidine. This agent has anaesthetic activity like *ketamine*, and it was earlier used as an anaesthetic. However, this use was discontinued because of its hallucinogenic activity. It may be noted that ketamine also has mild hallucinogenic activity. The main psychotomimetic effect is distortion of body image, impairment of thought processes, loss of concentration and sense of time.

Miscellaneous Psychotomimetics

Bufotenine (*n,n*-dimethyl-5-hydroxytryptamine) is found in Cohaba Snuff, the skin and parotid gland of the toad (Bufo marinus) and in small quantities in the mushroom *Amanita muscaria*. It causes hallucinations with severe and uncomfortable autonomic effects.

Harmine. It is a Harmala alkaloid obtained from the South American vine *Banisteriopsis caapi*. The Amazon natives use portion of this vine to make snuff and an intoxicating beverage.

Nutmeg. The nutmeg tree, *Myristica fragrans*, is the source for the spices nutmeg and mace. As a flavouring agent nutmeg is popular and pleasant. Nutmeg causes psychotomimetic effects when large amounts are eaten. Its effects include euphoria, visual hallucinations, loss of touch with reality, and distortions of time and space. **Myristicin** is thought to be the active ingredient.

Sodium oxybate. This anaesthetic drug, a portion of which is identical to gamma-hydroxybutyric acid (GHB), a metabolite of GABA and glutamic acid, has been reported to produce hallucinations in some subjects.

Cannabis (Marihuana, Marijuana)

The plant **Cannabis sativa,** the hemp plant, grows freely in Central Asia and the Himalayas. Cannabis, like ethanol has a euphoriant effect. The psychoactive potency of Cannabis depends on the concentration of the naturally occurring substance **delta-9-tetrahydrocannabinol,** which is simply abbreviated as THC. The concentration of THC in Cannabis is influenced by the climate, soil, and method of cultivation of the plant.

Preparations of Cannabis

The resin of the Cannabis plant is the source of the active principle, and the related compounds are known as *cannabinoids.*

In this country there are three main types of preparations of Cannabis: (*i*) **Bhang** is the preparation of dried leaves and flowering shoots of *Cannabis sativa,* male and female plants, cultivated or wild. This is roughly equivalent to marihuana (usually smoked) as it is known in North America; (*ii*) **Ganja** is the dried flowering tops of *Cannabis sativa,* usually the female plants. This product has a higher concentration of THC than bhang. Ganja is usually smoked; and (*iii*) **Charas** is the resinous exudate collected from the flowering tops and leaves of *C. sativa.* This is the most potent form of Cannabis, equivalent to *hashish,* as it is known in the United States. Charas or hashish possesses 5 to 10 times the potency of bhang or marihuana.

Pharmacological Actions

Physiological effects. There is an increase in heart rate, and dilatation of the small conjunctional arteries which gives the "red eye" look to the smoker. Salivation followed by dryness of the mouth occurs. There is an increased frequency of urination.

Behavioural effects. These effects depend on the *set* and *setting*. The term "set" refers to the "internal environment" of the subject and is influenced by his personality, life style previous experience and other drugs. In contrast, "setting" refers to the "external environment", i.e., the company of other drug users, presence of music etc., which to a very great extent influence the behavioural effects.

The subject continues to look normal to an observer. It has a biphasic action, with an initial stimulatory phase followed by sedation. During the **initial phase** the subjects are anxious, restless and experience euphoria, and have enhanced perception of the five senses. In the **sedative phase,** the subject passes into a dream-like state. In high doses, marihuana produces a loss of personal identity, fantasies, sensory and mental illusions, disordered thought process and hallucinations. In "bad trips" panic and psychotic reactions may occur.

Adverse reactions. Cannabis has a very low toxicity. The therapeutic index of THC is 40,000. In contrast, the therapeutic indices for alcohol and secobarbital are 10 each.

Regarding the "abuse potential" of Cannabis, there is little **psychological dependence; tolerance** does develop on continuous use; and there is **no physical dependence,** as evidenced by the absence of the withdrawal symptoms.

The possible *hazards* associated with long-term heavy use of Cannabis are: (*i*) chromosomal damage; (*ii*) interference with the functioning of the immune system;

(*iii*) hormonal changes which may lead to impotence and temporary sterility, and gynaecomastia in males; (*iv*) injury to the bronchial tract and lungs; (*v*) severe personality changes; and (*vi*) irreversible brain damage.

To sum up, **Cannabis sativa,** is the natural source for bhang (marihuana), charas (hashish) and ganja (a preparation of cannabis, usually smoked in India only; it may also be made into a tea). The psychoactive effects are attributed to their delta-9-tetrahydrocannabinol content.

The hallucinogenic drugs are drugs of abuse, and are related to problems of drug dependence, dealt with separately in **Chap 2.10.**

2.9 CENTRAL NERVOUS SYSTEM STIMULANTS

Classification

- **Psychomotor Stimulants**
  - **Methylxanthines**
  - **Amphetamines**
  - **Methylphenidate**
  - **Pemoline**
- **Respiratory Stimulants or Analeptics**
  - **Nikethamide**
  - **Doxapram**
- **Convulsants: Strychnine, Picrotoxin, Pentylenetetrazol**

Stimulation of the central nervous system (CNS) can be produced in man and animals by a large heterogeneous group of **natural** and **synthetic** substances. Only a few of them are used therapeutically.

CLASSIFICATION

CNS stimulants can be grouped on the basis of their dominant site of action:

1. **Cerebral, or Psychomotor stimulants**
   Amphetamines (Chap. 3.4)
   Atropine (Chap. 3.3)
   Cocaine (Chaps. 2.10, 3.8)
   Ephedrine (Chap. 3.4)
   Xanthines (Caffeine)
   Methylphenidate
   Pemoline
2. **Brainstem Stimulants, or analeptics**
   Pentylenetetrazol
   Picrotoxin
   Nikethamide
   Doxapram
3. **Spinal Stimulants, or convulsants**
   Strychnine

A list of therapeutically effective CNS stimulants is as follows:

1. Xanthines (Caffeine)
2. Amphetamines (Dextroamphetamine, Methamphetamine)
3. Methylphenidate
4. Pemoline
5. Respiratory stimulants or analeptics (Doxapram)

PSYCHOMOTOR STIMULANTS

XANTHINES (METHYLXANTHINES)

The xanthines - **Caffeine, theophylline, theobromine** - are closely related plant alkaloids. **Caffeine** is found in coffee bean **(Coffea arabica),** in the leaves of tea **(Thea sinensis),** in the bean of cocoa **(Theobroma cacao),** and in kola nut **(Cola acuminata).** In addition, **theophylline** is found in tea, and **theobromine** in cocoa. These methylxanthines are related to purines and uric acid.

Pharmacological actions. The methylxanthines have qualitative similarity, but quantitative differences in their effects.

Central nervous system. Caffeine, theophylline and theobromine, in order of decreasing potency, stimulate the CNS. Mental activity, performance and association of ideas are facilitated. Fatigue and drowsiness are allayed. Effects on the brainstem and spinal cord are only evident with higher doses.

Under experimental conditions, caffeine produces an increased capacity for sustained intellectual work, shortened reaction time, perfect association of ideas, and better memory. Typists work faster with lesser errors. However, performance in recently acquired delicate motor skills may deteriorate. The above mentioned effects are produced by 85 to 250 mg of caffeine, the amount contained in 1 to 3 cups of coffee **(Table 2.9-1).**

Table 2.9-1 *The caffeine concentrations in commonly consumed beverages*

Beverage	*Caffeine Content (mg)*
Coffee	
Brewed	100-150/cup
Instant	85-100/cup
Decaffeinated	2-4/cup
Tea	65-75/cup
Cocoa	5-40/cup
Cola drinks	3-5/30 ml

Methylxanthines also stimulate the medullary respiratory centres. This action is more prominent in certain pathophysiological states like Cheyne-Stokes breathing.

Cardiovascular system. The methylxanthines stimulate the myocardium; increase coronary blood flow, cardiac output, myocardial work and oxygen consumption. They also stimulate the vasomotor centre. With the exception of cerebral vessels, they relax vascular smooth muscle.

Smooth muscles. The xanthines relax smooth muscles, and their **bronchodilator** activity has been utilized in the treatment of bronchial asthma **(Chap. 13).**

Skeletal muscles. Caffeine increases muscular work capacity in man at doses of about 3.5 mg/kg. It increases twitch tension of indirectly (through nerve) stimulated muscles, possibly by increasing the release of acetylcholine (ACh) at the myoneural junction.

Diuretic action. The methylxanthines, specially **theophylline,** increase urine production, and the pattern of enhanced water excretion is similar to the thiazides **(Chap. 6.2).** Inhibition of renal tubular reabsorption of sodium is the major factor causing diuresis, while the increased glomerular filtration rate is of *minor* importance.

Other actions. Caffeine promotes secretion of hydrochloric acid and pepsin in the stomach. Both *caffeine* and *theophylline* raise plasma renin activity (PRA), and circulating catecholamine levels in man. The basal metabolic rate (BMR) is increased slightly.

Mode of action. There are *three* basic cellular actions of the methylxanthines: (*i*) caffeine augments skeletal muscle twitch response by sensitization of the mechanism for the release of Ca^{++} from sarcoplasmic reticulum; (*ii*) the xanthines increase the accumulation of c-AMP in the cell. They are **competitive inhibitors of phosphodiesterase,** and inhibit the breakdown of c-AMP. This direct action is augmented by the **indirect** adrenergic effects which activate adenylcyclase that catalyses the conversion of ATP to c-AMP. Such an increase in c-AMP in the myocardium produces a positive inotropic effect; and (*iii*) caffeine appears to **competitively block receptors for adenosine,** a naturally occurring substance which depresses neuronal firing in the CNS, thereby permitting these neurones to fire more readily. Caffeine can stimulate all levels of the CNS when used in sufficient amounts.

Pharmacokinetics. The methylxanthines are absorbed on oral, rectal or parenteral administration. Oral absorption of theophylline at times is erratic. Soluble salts of theophylline (choline theophyllinate, theophylline sodium glycinate) are lesser irritants and are better absorbed. Methylxanthines are distributed into all body compartments, and they cross the placental barrier. These drugs are primarily metabolized in the liver, and excreted largely in the urine as metabolites and some unchanged drug.

Therapeutic uses. *Caffeine* is used to allay fatigue and increase sensory awareness; used to treat **mild to moderate respiratory depression** caused by overdosage with CNS depressants like morphine or alcohol (parenteral caffeine sodium benzoate); relief of pain associated with **vascular headaches** or spinal puncture (orally or parenterally usually with ergotamine); and as an adjunct in many over-the-counter (OTC) analgesic remedies for its mood elevating effect. **Aminophylline** is used to treat **bronchial asthma** and **status asthmaticus;** and to relieve acute **left ventricular failure.** Caffeine with ergotamine tartrate is used to treat **migraine.** Aminophylline also has clinically useful diuretic activity **(Chap. 6.2).** Caffeine (IV) has proved beneficial in the treatment of **neonatal apnoea.**

Adverse reactions. On ingestion of 1 g or more of caffeine **insomnia, restlessness, excitement, tachycardia, extrasystoles, quick respiration** and **delirium** have been observed. An anxiety neurosis-like syndrome can occur. Overuse of xanthine beverages leads to chronic poisoning manifested as restlessness, disturbed sleep, tachycardia and premature beats. High tannin content of tea is likely to cause constipation. Some degree of **tolerance** and **psychic dependence** develops to xanthine beverages. Acute lethal dose of caffeine ranges from 5 to 10 g. Treatment is symptomatic and supportive including sedatives and anticonvulsants. **Aminophylline** (IV) should be injected slowly to avoid **palpitation, headache, dizziness, hypotension** and **precordial pain.** Generalized seizures may occur with methylxanthines, and can be controlled by diazepam. **Mutagenic** effects are produced by very high doses of caffeine in both plant and animal cells. Increased caffeine effects can occur in combination with oral contraceptives or cimetidine, because they inhibit caffeine metabolism.

Preparations and Dosage

1. **Aminophylline** (Theophylline ethylenediamine) is the most widely used soluble theophylline salt. It may be administrated orally (100-300 mg); by slow IV injection (250-500 mg); or per rectum (360 mg) in suppositories.
2. **Caffeine citrate.** Orally 100 to 200 mg every 4 hours is the usual dose.
3. **Caffeine sodium benzoate** is employed for stimulation of individuals depressed by alcohol or other CNS depressants. It is given in doses upto 500 mg IM or SC.
4. **Dyphylline** is 7-(2-3-dihydroxypropyl) theophylline. It is not converted to theophylline in the body. It has been extensively used in the treatment of **bronchial asthma** in oral doses of 15 mg/kg, but its efficacy is limited.
5. **Pentoxifylline** is a derivative of theobromine. It is a **haemorheological agent,** a newly introduced class of drugs that lower blood viscosity and improve erythrocyte flexibility and deformability, i.e., the ability of red cells to change their shape in response to mechanical forces and stresses. It has been used in the treatment of **intermittent claudication, cerebral ischaemia, transient ischaemic attacks (TIAs), chronic occlusive arterial disease of the limbs,** and it improves

psychopathological symptoms in patients with cerebrovascular insufficiency. The **mode of action** of pentoxifylline is poorly defined, but there is evidence that tissue perfusion improves. Pentoxifylline is usually administered in a dose of 400 mg 3 times daily with meals. The dose for IV infusion is 100 mg in 250-500 ml of sodium chloride or dextrose injection over 90-180 minutes. **Adverse effects** include angina, dyspnoea, hypotension, dizziness, anxiety and confusion. Rarely cardiac arrhythmias, hepatitis, jaundice and bone marrow suppression may occur.

AMPHETAMINES

AMPHETAMINE, DEXTROAMPHETAMINE, METHAMPHETAMINE

The amphetamines are synthetic sympathomimetic amines causing marked CNS stimulation. On short-term use they increase alertness and concentration, elevate mood, and stimulate motor activity. Amphetamines induce varying degrees of euphoria depending on the dose, and the personality of the user. Peripheral effects include elevation of blood pressure, bronchodilation, contraction of urinary sphincter and mydriasis.

The initial effects of amphetamines are generally pleasant, but **tolerance** soon develops to the mood-elevating action of these compounds. Prolonged use can lead to **irritability, insomnia, dizziness, jitteriness, easy distractibility** and **confusion.** Amphetamine-induced stimulation is followed by intense depression, fatigue and restlessness. To overcome this poststimulatory depression amphetamine is used repetitively, and in emotionally unstable persons **habituation** and **dependence** occurs. Large, repeated doses of amphetamines can lead to a paranoid-like state, hard to differentiate from paranoid schizophrenia. Amphetamines have very few approved clinical uses.

Mode of action. Amphetamines promote the release of catecholamines from presynaptic nerve terminals, and prevent their re-uptake into the neurone. The net effect is **potentiation of endogenous catecholamine (noradrenaline, dopamine) activity.** In addition, these drugs have a direct-activating effect on adrenergic receptor sites (alpha and beta), and interfere with the functioning of monoamine oxidase (MAO), an enzyme responsible for intracellular breakdown of noradrenaline, dopamine, and serotonin. The CNS stimulant effect is exerted on the **cerebral cortex** and the **reticular formation.** The **anorexiant** (appetite suppressant) effect is the result in part of **stimulation of a beta-receptor mediated satiety system in the lateral hypothalamus.** Elevated mood contributes to the anorectic action by lessening the desire to eat. Usefulness of amphetamines in **attention deficit disorders in children** is related to their ability to potentiate catecholamine activity in the CNS, and the increased activity of the recticular activating system.

Pharmacokinetics. Oral absorption of amphetamines is complete, and they are widely distributed in the body. They attain high concentrations in the CNS. Effects are seen within 30-60 minutes, and may persist upto 24-36 hours. Urinary excretion of unchanged drug is pH-dependent, and plasma half-life increases by about 7 hours for every 1 unit increase in pH.

THERAPEUTIC USES

1. As short-term (4-8 weeks) adjunct in the treatment of obesity (potential benefit does not outweigh the risks, i.e., benefit:risk ratio is low, hence its use is hazardous).
2. Treatment of **narcolepsy,** a neurologic disorder characterized by excessive sleepiness, *cataplexy* (sudden loss of muscle tone) and *hypnogogic hallucinations.* "Sleep attacks" may last for several seconds to 30 minutes.
3. Treatment of **attention deficit disorder** (ADD) in children, characterized by increased motor activity, impaired coordination, short attention span, easy distractibility, and learning disability.

PREPARATIONS AND DOSAGE

1. **Amphetamine sulphate.** *Narcolepsy:* 5-60 mg daily in divided doses: *ADD:* 5 mg one to two times daily, increase by 5 mg/week until optimal response.
2. **Dextroamphetamine sulphate**. *Narcolepsy:* 5-60 mg/day in divided doses: *ADD:* 2.5 to 5 mg/day, increase gradually to optimal effect.
3. **Methamphetamine**. *ADD:* 5 mg bid or tid, increase gradually to optimal effect.

Adverse reactions. Side effects with acute amphetamine usage are nervousness, palpitation, tachycardia and insomnia. Other adverse reactions include:

CNS—Dizziness, euphoria or dysphoria, headache, chills, tremors; large doses cause confusion, hallucinations, aggressiveness and psychosis.

Cardiovascular—Hypertension, cardiac arrhythmias, anginal pain.

GIT—Nausea, vomiting, diarrhoea, anorexia, weight loss.

Others—Impotence, urticaria, difficulty in urination; large doses may cause convulsions, syncope and coma.

Amphetamines are frequently abused, and **psychological dependence** occurs. Tolerance to amphetamines is extreme, and daily intake of 1 g to 2 g has been noted. Abrupt withdrawal results in extreme fatigue and depression. Amphetamines are contraindicated in moderate to severe hypertension, arteriosclerosis, hyperthyroidism, glaucoma, and agitated states.

Interactions. Amphetamines reduce the antihypertensive effects of guanthidine, methyldopa, hydralazine and other antihypertensives. Amphetamine effects can be potentiated by cocaine, acetazolamide, propoxyphene, tricyclic antidepressants, and monoamine oxidase inhibitors. Amphetamines delay the effects of phenytoin, ethosuximide and other anticonvulsants. Insulin requirement in diabetes may be altered by amphetamines.

METHYLPHENIDATE

Methylphenidate is a CNS stimulant with a pharmacologic profile similar to that of amphetamine, but with a more marked effect on mental rather than physical or motor activities at usual doses. It shares the same potential for **habituation** and **psychological dependence** as with amphetamines, although its central excitatory effects are less intense.

Mode of action. Its stimulatory effect is exerted at the cortical level. Release of catecholamines from presynaptic nerve terminals may be contributing to the action of the drug.

Pharmacokinetics. The drug is readily absorbed from the GI tract, and distributed throughout the body, including the CNS. The onset of action occurs within 30-60 minutes, and peak blood levels are achieved in 1-3 hours. Effects persist for 6 hours on oral administration. About 80 percent of the dose is metabolized and excreted in urine.

THERAPEUTIC USES

1. Adjunctive therapy of attention deficit disorder (ADD) in children.
2. Narcolepsy.
3. Relief of mild depression and withdrawn senile behaviour.

Dosage. Methylphenidate is used orally in a dosage of 20 to 30 mg daily in 2 or 3 divided doses. The maximal dose is considered to be 60 mg/day.

Adverse reactions. Nervousness and insomnia are the most commonly encountered side effects. Other adverse effects include dizziness, drowsiness, agitation, toxic psychoses, chorea, palpitation, tachycardia, anginal attacks, arrhythmias, skin rashes, exfoliative dermatitis, anorexia, visual disturbances, alopecia, anaemia and leucopenia. Prolonged use in children can suppress growth and exacerbate behavioural disorders.

PEMOLINE

Pemoline is a chemically unique CNS stimulant having minimal sympathomimetic effects. It is otherwise pharmacologically comparable to amphetamine and methylphenidate. It has a lower abuse potential than most other CNS stimulants. The exact mechanism of action is unknown. This drug increases dopaminergic function in the CNS, and exerts a direct action on the cerebral cortex. Its main effects are increased alertness, enhanced motor activity, and mild euphoria.

Pemoline is well absorbed from the GI tract, with peak levels within 2 to 4 hours. The plasma half-life is about 12 hours. It is metabolized in the liver, and excreted in the urine both as unchanged drug (45%), and conjugated metabolites. The drug has a gradual onset of action, and clinical effects may not be evident for 3 to 4 weeks.

Pemoline is used as adjunctive therapy of **attention deficit disorder** in children, and in the treatment of **narcolepsy** and **excessive sleepiness.** The recommended starting dose is 37.5 mg/day as a single morning dose. Increments of 18.75 mg/week may be given till the desired response is obtained. The maximum dose is 112.5 mg/day.

The most frequent **side effects** of pemoline therapy are insomnia, anorexia with weight loss. Other adverse reactions are skin rash, dyskinesias of the tongue, lips, face and extremities, nystagmus, dizziness, depression and hallucinations. Elevated levels of SGOT, SGPT and serum LDH have occurred, but are reversible on drug withdrawal.

RESPIRATORY STIMULANTS OR ANALEPTICS

Respiratory stimulants, or **analeptics,** are believed to act at the level of the brainstem and peripheral carotid chemoreceptors. They may be used primarily as **physiologic antagonists** of respiratory depression due to overdosage of CNS depressants. They have a limited place in the treatment of ventilatory failure in patients with chronic obstructive airway disease. **Their use has largely been replaced by ventilatory support.** The current status of analeptics in therapy is discussed in **Chapter 13.**

NIKETHAMIDE AND DOXAPRAM

Nikethamide and **doxapram** stimulate the entire CNS, although at one time they were considered to be "specific" respiratory stimulants, and thus useful as an antidote in cases of CNS depressant overdose. Clinical use has proved their "nonselective" nature of action with a **narrow margin of safety** between the respiratory stimulant dose and the convulsant dose. Large doses of these drugs can produce tonic-clonic convulsions. **Doxapram** has a greater margin of safety, but is still not safe enough when used in cases of severe CNS depression.

Strychnine, picrotoxin, and **pentylenetetrazol** are strong convulsants, and are **not used therapeutically.** They are used as pharmacological tools in screening procedures for discovering antiepileptic drugs.

2.10 DRUG DEPENDENCE

The use of drugs for "nonmedical" or "recreational" purposes is becoming increasingly common, specially among the younger age groups of society. This spread of "drug abuse" has been a startling phenomenon from 1970 onwards, and in recent years has reached near-epidemic proportions in certain segments of the population. Most of the drugs that are subject to misuse have legitimate uses also, e.g., the **sedatives, narcotics, tranquillizers** and **stimulant** drugs, which form an important part of the physicians' armamentarium for the practice of medicine.

Definitions

Terminology in relation to drug dependence has been under constant debate and revision. Currently accepted definitions according to the WHO Expert Committee on Drug Dependence are as under:

Drug. A drug is a substance (natural or synthetic) which when taken into the living organism, may modify one or more of its functions.

Drug dependence. It is a state, **psychic** and sometimes also **physical,** resulting from the interaction between a living organism and a drug, characterized by behavioural and other responses that always include a **compulsion** to take the drug on a continuous or periodic basis in order to experience its psychic effects. Absence of the drug impairs the ability of the person to function in a socially acceptable manner. Two distinct types of dependence are recognized.

(*i*) **Psychologic (psychic) dependence.** It denotes the *compulsive* need to experience a pleasurable drug reaction, ranging from a mild *desire* for the drug to an **overwhelming** need to have the drug at any cost. Many drugs can lead to a more severe type of dependence, i.e., physical dependence.

(*ii*) **Physical dependence.** It is an altered physiologic state resulting from prolonged use of a drug, and regular usage becomes *necessary* to avoid intense physical disturbances manifested as the **withdrawal** or **abstinence** syndrome. Physical dependence is usually associated with tolerance (see later).

Habituation. It is a pattern of repeated drug usage, although the actual physical need for the drug is **minimal.** There is no desire to increase the dose of the drug taken, and removal of the drug is not accompanied by withdrawal symptoms or by a compulsive need to obtain the drug.

Tolerance. It describes the reduced effect of a drug resulting from repeated exposure to that drug, or to a similar drug. The latter condition is known as **cross-tolerance.** Without tolerance to a drug physical dependence is most unlikely.

Addiction. It is a vague term that refers to compulsive drug usage, the necessity of obtaining the drug at any cost, and the appearance of withdrawal symptoms if the drug is unavailable. Now the term **drug dependence** has replaced the terms addiction and habituation.

Drug misuse. This term refers to the improper use of medicines in a way that can lead to acute and chronic toxicity. This kind of drug-taking is caused by ignorance rather than by any desire to get "high". The unsupervised use of many self-administered non-prescription drugs can lead to various harmful consequences.

Drug abuse. It is the persistent or sporadic excessive drug use inconsistent with, or unrelated to medical practice. Drug abuse goes well beyond mere misuse of drugs.

In short, drug dependence produced by repeated consumption of a **natural** or **synthetic** drug, is characterized by: (*i*) an overpowering desire or need **(compulsion)** to continue taking the drug and to obtain it by any means; (*ii*) a tendency to increase the dose; (*iii*) a **psychic** or **physical** dependence on the effects of the drug; (*iv*) appearance of a characteristic **withdrawal syndrome** on withholding the drug; and (*v*) a general **detrimental effect** on the patient and society.

Drugs of Abuse

The drugs of abuse may be grouped into: (*i*) permissive drugs; (*ii*) prescriptive drugs; and (*iii*) proscriptive drugs.

Permissive drugs. The use of these drugs is generally permitted by the society as almost a norm. For example,

caffeine in tea, coffee and cola beverages; **nicotine** for smoking, chewing and intranasal administration; and **ethyl alcohol** is readily available in a great variety of beverages to adults in unlimited quantities.

Prescriptive drugs. These drugs are used therapeutically for their beneficial effects, and are available on a physicians' prescription. The same drugs can be abused by vulnerable individuals. For example, **barbiturates, nonbarbiturate sedative-hypnotics, anxiolytics,** and **amphetamines.**

Table 2.10-1 *Abuse characteristics of drug groups*

Drug group	*Psychic dependence*	*Physical dependence*	*Tolerance*
CNS depressants	++	+++	++
Amphetamines	+++	+	+++
Cocaine	++	++	+
Narcotic analgesics	+++	+++	+++
Psychotomimetics			
LSD	0	0	++
Phencyclidine	++	+	+
Marihuana	0	+	+

Key: +++ = marked; ++ = moderate; + = slight; 0 = absent.

Proscriptive drugs. This group covers those drugs which have been placed under strict drug control to avoid their illicit or illegal use. Some of the medically used drugs like **opioids, sedatives** and **stimulants,** when used for nonmedical purposes belong to the proscriptive group of drugs. In addition, **marihuana** and other **hallucinogens** like *lysergic acid diethylamide* (LSD) which have no established medical use belong to this group.

Classification

A useful, but incomplete classification of *drugs of abuse,* based on commonality of characteristics is as under:

I. CNS depressants

(*a*) Alcohol

(*b*) Barbiturates

(*c*) Nonbarbiturate sedatives and antianxiety drugs

II. CNS stimulants

(*a*) Amphetamines

(*b*) Anorectics

(*c*) Cocaine

III. Narcotics

(*a*) Heroin

(*b*) Morphine

(*c*) Codeine

IV. Psychotomimetics

(*a*) LSD, DOM, DMT

(*b*) Psilocybin

(*c*) Mescaline

(*d*) Phencyclidine (PCP)

V. Volatile inhalants

Acetone, benzene, trichloroethylene, toluene, paint thinner, amyl nitrite, nail polish remover, and petrol

VI. Marihuana (Cannabis)

VII. Nicotine

The abuse characteristics of the main drug groups are listed in **Table 2.10-1.**

CNS Depressants

Alcohol

Alcohol abuse is a major drug problem in terms of damaged health, accidents, family discord, business interruptions, and socially unacceptable behaviour.

The characteristics of **acute alcohol intoxication** depend on the blood level, ranging from euphoria (50 mg/dl) to impaired motor coordination, concentration and memory (100-150 mg/dl), to profound cardiorespiratory depression and coma (300-400 mg/dl). **Chronic alcohol abuse** is marked by GI disturbances, liver damage, pancreatitis, malnutrition, cardiac impairment, and psychotic disturbances, e.g., Wernicke's encephalopathy and Korsakoff's psychosis **(Chap. 2.2).**

Chronic alcohol ingestion results in development of *tolerance* and ultimately **physical dependence** similar to barbiturates. Withdrawal of alcohol after several weeks of consumption may result in **tremors, anxiety, confusion; GI disturbances, weakness, insomnia** and **delusions.** Abrupt termination after longer periods of alcohol abuse can lead to **delirium tremens** (fever, tachycardia, tremors, profuse sweating, agitation, disorientation, hallucinations and convulsions).

Treatment of acute alcohol withdrawal is largely symptomatic, and involves use of sedatives or anticonvulsants (e.g., diazepam and barbiturates) or both along with supportive therapy. Chronic alcoholism management requires psychiatric counselling, supportive social interaction **(Alcoholics Anonymous),** pharmacotherapy with antianxiety agents, and aversion therapy with agents like disulfiram **(Chap. 2.2).**

Barbiturates

The shorter-acting barbiturates like *amobarbital, pentobarbital, secobarbital* are most sought after agents because they produce *euphoria.*

Symptoms of barbiturate intoxication resemble those of alcohol poisoning, and depend on the blood level, and include **slurred speech, disorientation, impaired motor coordination, poor judgement, confusion** and **emotional instability.** Severe overdosage results in depressed respiration, rapid and weak pulse, cyanosis, mydriasis, coma and respiratory paralysis. Regular barbiturate usage leads to reduced time spent in rapid eye movement (REM) sleep, and resultant behavioural changes.

Withdrawal reactions on abrupt termination of barbiturate use range from **anxiety, confusion, weakness, anorexia, insomnia** due to rebound REM sleep, and **tremors** to **delirium, disorientation, hallucinations and convulsions.**

Management of the withdrawal state is symptomatic. Treatment of chronic barbiturate dependence may be done by **substituting phenobarbital** for the barbiturate being abused at a dose which provides a similar effect, and then gradually reducing the phenobarbital dose over a period of weeks.

Nonbarbiturate Sedatives and Antianxiety Agents

Chronic use of a number of other sedative-hypnotics, and antianxiety drugs can result in **dependence** and an **abstinance syndrome (Chap. 2.4). Methaqualone** has been withdrawn from the market, but remains one of the "street drugs of choice", and is widely abused. It is used orally and produces effects like barbiturates. Prolonged use leads to **dependence.** A combination of the antihistamine diphenhydramine and methaqualone (Mandrax) is more dangerous than methaqualone alone, as the antihistamine can produce ataxia and psychotic behaviour in large doses. **Withdrawal symptoms** include nausea, headache, cramps, insomnia, toxic psychoses and severe convulsions.

The **benzodiazepines** are the most widely used antianxiety drugs, because their margin of safety is greater than other sedative-hypnotics. **Diazepam** is the most frequently prescribed member. Benzodiazepines are not preferred as "street" drugs, but are frequently misused by patients of anxiety neuroses or other psychosomatic disorders.

Prolonged use of benzodiazepines has resulted both in **psychologic** and **physical dependence.** Abrupt discontinuation of usage (60-120 mg/day for 2 months) results in cramps, sweating, agitation, aggressivity, disorientation, confusion, tremors, depression, auditory and visual hallucinations, and paranoia. For further information on benzodiazepines see **Chapter 2.4.**

CNS Stimulants

Amphetamines

The approved clinical uses of the three amphetamines (DL-amphetamine, dextroam-phetamine, methamphetamine) are limited to **attention deficit disorder** (ADD in children, and symptomatic control of **narcolepsy.** They are however, widely abused drugs for their CNS stimulant effects by students, truck drivers, executives, athletes, doctors, nurses and pharmacists. Amphetamine abuse refers to the parenteral or oral administration of large doses to attain intense "rush" or "rapid" high characteristic of these agents. **Methamphetamine** (speed) by IV injection elicits an almost instantaneous euphoria or orgasm-like reaction. **Tolerance** to this effect develops rapidly. The therapeutic doses of amphetamines range from 5-15 mg/day, but "speed freaks" have been known to use upto 5000 mg/day.

Amphetamines induce **physical dependence,** and abrupt withdrawal results in fatigue, muscle pain, lethargy and depression.

Diazepam may be used if sedation is required. Acidification of urine with *ammonium chloride* markedly increases the excretion of amphetamines.

Anorectics

A number of amphetamine-related anorectics (fenfluramine, phenmetrazine, phetermine, phenylpropanolamine) are employed as adjuncts in the short-term treatment of obesity. They are frequently misused chronically as appetite suppressants, and produce symptoms of chronic amphetamine use, like insomnia, elevated blood pressure, tachycardia and anxiety. Like the amphetamines these drugs on chronic usage result in the development of **tolerance** and **physical dependence.**

Cocaine

Cocaine is a natural product extracted from the leaves of **Erythoxylon coca** (coca plant). Its legitimate use in medicine is as a local anaesthetic for the nasal and oral cavity. In high doses cocaine induces **euphoric excitement** and **hallucinations.** This property ranks it highest among the drugs causing **psychic dependence.** No physical dependence develops, and as such there is no typical withdrawal syndrome.

The powdered drug is commonly administered by inhalation or "snorting", and is rapidly absorbed from the nasal mucosa. On IV administration a brief rapturous sensation follows. Owing to the vasoconstrictor action of cocaine, perforated nasal septa are characteristic of chronic snorters. **Crack,** a new hardened form of cocaine, is heated in a glass pipe and smoked; it produces intense euphoria within minutes.

Chronic use of cocaine results in the following systemic effects: (*i*) **Cardiovascular:** arrhythmias, acute myocardial infarction; cerebrovascular accidents; (*ii*) **Respiratory:** pulmonary oedema, rhinitis, rhinorrhoea, perforation of the nasal septum; (*iii*) **Gastrointestinal:** intestinal ischaemia which may cause gangrene, weight loss, nausea; (*iv*) **CNS:** anxiety, irritability, tactile hallucinations (imaginary skin insects or "cocaine bugs", visual disturbances (flashing lights, "snow effect"), paranoia, insomnia; and (*v*) **Genitourinary:** difficulty in maintaining erection, and delay in orgasm in both sexes.

Treatment of abuse is difficult. Regular supportive therapy, along with tranquillizers and antidepressant drugs is employed.

Narcotics

Opioid addiction is one of the oldest afflictions of mankind. The **narcotic analgesics** including **heroin, morphine, codeine** and other *synthetic* and *semisynthetic* derivatives have similar abuse characteristics. **Heroin** is the opioid with the widest illicit use. **Morphine** and **pethidine** are sometimes abused by persons (doctors, nurses and pharmacists) who have ready access to these drugs. Recently, there has been a rise in the abuse of cough remedies containing codeine by youths seeking "kicks". A crude form of heroin called **"brown sugar"** has lately found wide illicit use, and is smoked.

The WHO has listed nearly 100 substances belonging to the **opiate** and **opioid** group. **Opiates** are compounds derived from opium alkaloids containing an oxyphenanthrene ring as their basic structure. **Opioids** are synthetic compounds with opiate-like pharmacological activity, although they lack the oxyphenanthrene ring. The term **"narcotic"** is used most frequently in connection with the opiate family, and applies medically to drugs that produce profound sleep and relief from pain.

The *characteristics of dependence* of the morphine type are: strong **psychic dependence;** and early development of **physical dependence,** which increases in intensity, parallel to the development of **tolerance.**

Heroin or **opium** may be smoked, but most heroin addicts resort to IV injection of heroin and other potent narcotics as it promptly results in a sensation of exquisite pleasure (orgasmic effect, "rush"), and a feeling of extreme contentment. Oral use of narcotics does not produce the "rush", but only leads to relaxation, euphoria, and a feeling of detachment. Heroin is about three times as potent as morphine, and therefore a more acceptable illicit drug. Heroin may also be taken subcutaneously. Other favourite narcotics of abuse are hydromorphone (Diluadid), a potent short-acting opiate used orally or parenterally, and *oxycodone,* available for oral use only.

Abuse syndrome. The effect sought by opiate addicts is a drowsy and relaxed feeling called "getting high". Shortly after a SC injection, the heroin addict "takes off" and drifts into a state between sleep and waking. Restlessness and excitement sometimes occur and the pupils are constricted to a "pinpoint". Secondary effects of opiate addiction include personal neglect, malnutrition, vitamin deficiency, hepatitis, vasculitis, thromboembolic complications, and infections due to unclean hypodermic needles, specially the dreaded acquired immune deficiency syndrome (AIDS). Late effects include pulmonary oedema, cardiorespiratory failure, and coma.

Diagnosis of opiate addiction. The best evidence of narcotic addiction is provided by the injection of a narcotic antagonist like **naloxone, nalorphine** or **levallorphan,** which precipitates a sudden withdrawal syndrome. The inner side of the arms of addicts usually bear needle marks or "tracks" along the course of veins.

Withdrawal syndrome. Dependence on opiates can develop in 10 days to 3 weeks with full therapeutic doses. On sudden withdrawal of opiates the symptoms develop in 12 to 18 hours. There are signs of marked ANS hyperactivity and irritability of CNS, manifested as insomnia, restlessness, gooseflesh, muscle aches, twitching, nausea, vomiting and diarrhoea. Weight loss, hypertension and generalized weakness may occur.

Treatment of abuse. Withdrawal symptoms can be suppressed by substitution of another narcotic for an opiate. Frequently oral **methadone** initially 20 mg once or twice daily is given, then the dose is gradually reduced. The long duration of action of methadone (upto 24 hours) also permits for single daily dosing. Thus temporarily methadone dependence is substituted for a previous opiate (heroin) dependence, and its withdrawal results in a much milder abstinence syndrome, though it is more prolonged.

A newer chemically related compound, levo-alpha-acetylmethadol (LAAM), an even longer acting drug (48-72 hours) is being used now for narcotic addiction. This agent is superior to methadone as it is not to be administered daily.

Naltrexone is a long-acting antagonist which is now available for treatment of narcotic addiction. The effects of heroin can be blocked for upto 3 days, depending on naltrexone dose. The patient must be narcotic-free for the last 7 days, and have normal liver function before receiving naltrexone.

Detoxification programmes work best in conjunction with psychiatric and social counselling, as withdrawal alone is rarely fully successful in overcoming narcotic dependence.

Psychotomimetics

Psychotomimetic drugs, also termed **hallucinogens,** are a group of naturally occurring compounds (like psilocybin, mescaline), and synthetic compounds (like LSD, DOM) capable of producing profound distortion of reality, resulting in confusion, delirium, amnesia, and a loss of sense of direction, time and space. In large doses, delusions and hallucinations occur, judgement is impaired, and frequently depression results.

The term **psychedelic** is also used and means "mind expanding", i.e., these drugs can increase creativity of the mind. Although no single term is adequately descriptive, these drugs are capable of producing changes in (*i*) **perception;** (*ii*) **thought;** (*iii*) **mood;** and (*iv*) **behaviour.** Among the hallucinogens, LSD is the most potent drug and the prototype of the group. The use of these drugs is periodic, rather than continuous, due to the difficulty in obtaining their supply.

The most commonly used hallucinogens are the following:

Lysergic acid diethylamide (LSD). In 1943 Hofmann accidentally discovered the potent psychotomimetic effects of LSD. It is the most potent hallucinogen currently available, and effects usually last for 8-12 hours. It is sold as tablets, thin squares of gelatin ("window panes"), or impregnated paper ("blotter acid"). The average effective oral dose is 25 to 50 mcg.

Mescaline *(Peyote).* Peyote buttons are chewed or swallowed. Mescaline is the active ingredient of the flowering heads of the peyote cactus. Oral doses of 250-500 mg produce LSD-like hallucinations for 6-12 hours, although milder.

DOM. Structural analogue of mescaline, also known as STP, an acronym for "serenity, tranquillity, and peace". DOM (2,5-dimethoxy-4-methylamphetamine) is a potent synthetic, psychotomimetic producing intense, prolonged psychic alterations at a dose of 5 mg, lasting for several days following a single dose.

DMT *(N,N-dimethyltryptamine).* It is a naturally occurring hallucinogen, and must be inhaled or smoked to produce rapid and brief alteration in perception and mood. It is not effective orally.

Psilocybin and psilocin. They are active ingredients of *Psilocybe* mushrooms, chemically related to LSD, although much less potent and shorter acting; usually taken orally.

Phencyclidine *(PCD).* This compound (also known as "peace pill") was developed in 1957 as an adjunct to anaesthesia similar to **ketamine,** to which it is chemically related. However, owing to adverse reactions like disorientation and agitation, and the frequently caused "bad trips" this agent never became popular with drug takers.

Drugs of the LSD-type induce a state of excitation of the CNS, and central autonomic heperactivity manifested by changes in mood (usually euphoria, sometimes depression), anxiety, distortion in sensory perception (chiefly visual), delusions, depersonalization, mydriasis, increased blood pressure and body temperature. An individual's response to these drugs depends not only on his personality, but also upon the **set** and **setting,** i.e., upon the total environment. Some persons experience the opposite type of effects like anxiety, dysphoria, panic, severe depression, and suicidal tendencies, the so-called "bad trips". Recurrences of the various perceptual distortions are experienced, specially with LSD, and can occur upto 5 years after initial usage. These "flashbacks" may be potentially harmful.

Abuse syndrome. Daily use of hallucinogens produces *tolerance,* although it dissipates rapidly and ends after 3 days. *Psychic dependence* to the LSD-type of drugs varies greatly, but is usually not intense. There is no evidence of the development of *physical dependence* or a withdrawal syndrome. The hallucinogens differ in potency, onset of action, and duration of intoxication. LSD is the most potent agent among them.

Treatment of abuse. Rest, reassurance, sympathy and support in a quiet environment are most successful in treating the anxiety and panic reactions. If the "talking down" method fails, benzodiazepines like *diazepam* can be safely used.

Volatile Inhalants

Volatile hydrocarbons such as **acetone, benzene, carbon tetrachloride, trichloroethane, trichloroethylene,** and **toluene** are present in many household products like, **glue, paint, lighter fluid, nail polish remover,** and **varnish thinner.** These volatile liquids are commonly placed on a handkerchief, and inhaled. The initial effects are CNS excitation, sense of exhilaration, dizziness, and occasionally auditory or visual hallucinations. Tinnitus, blurred vision, slurred speech, and a staggering gait may develop. These effects last for 30-60 minutes. Larger amounts can lead to unconsciousness, delirium, stupor, coma, cardiac arrest and death. Lately, **amyl nitrite** inhalation has been abused as a sexual stimulant.

Treatment of acute intoxication resembles that of barbiturate overdosage. Oxygen, respiratory assistance and other supportive measures are required. Sympathomimetic vasopressors should be avoided, due to the likely danger of myocardial sensitization by volatile hydrocarbons, and precipitation of cardiac arrhythmias.

Psychologic dependence can develop, but physical dependence is rare, due to the rather brief duration of action. Chronic misuse of volatile hydrocarbons can result in organ damage, specially of the liver, kidney, heart and CNS. This factor is often overlooked by young users.

Marihuana (Cannabis)

Cannabis, obtained from the leaves and flowering tops of *hemp* plants **(Cannabis sativa, Cannabis indica)** is a very ancient drug. Other names for cannabis and its products are **hashish, charas, bhang, ganja** and **marijuana** or **marihuana.** The dried resinous exudate of the tops is called **hashish** in the United States, and **charas** in India and the Far East. The dried leaves and flowering shoots, containing smaller amounts of the active substance, are called **bhang,** and the resinous mass from the small leaves and inflorescence is called **ganja.** The term **marihuna** or

marijuana refers to any part of plant that induces somatic and psychic changes in man. The biologically active constituents of marihuana are termed **cannabinoids,** and among them more than 60 known compounds are psychoactive. **Delta-9-tetrahydrocannabinol** (THC) is the major psychoactive ingredient. The THC content of marihuana varies widely, depending on the growing climate, and heredity of the individual plant. The usual route of administration is smoking marihuana cigarettes ("reefers"), although it is also chewed, sniffed or swallowed. The average 1 g marihuana cigarette contains less than 1 mg of THC. Marihuana is also nicknamed as "pot", "weed", and "grass". **Hashish oil** is a liquid concentrate extracted from the plant, and by some users has been injected IV, but it is hazardous and the mortality rate is high.

The most commonly reported effects that smokers report within 15 minutes of inhaling an adequate dose is a feeling of floating and drowsiness, and they find it pleasurably relaxing. There is heightened sensitivity to external stimuli. Colour seems brighter and richer. Perception of time and distance is distorted. Psychic symptoms include impaired concentration, expression and recall. Feelings of depersonalization and hallucinations occur. There may be confusion, disorientation and gross memory impairment. Acute psychotic reactions may occur in persons with pre-existing personality problems.

Chronic use of marihuana may result in **psychologic** dependence, but **physical dependence** is rare. Some tolerance occurs with chronic usage, but without physical dependence and withdrawal symptoms. A phenomenon of **"reverse" tolerance** has been reported in some users, whereby smaller amounts of the drug are able to elicit the desired psychic effects with repeated use. This may be in part due to cumulative effects of the drug.

Currently, potential clinical applications of THC are receiving much attention. Two areas of potential therapeutic benefit are for the *control of nausea and vomiting* produced by cytotoxic drugs, and *reduction of intraocular pressure* (IOP) in glaucoma. Other possible uses of THC are its *analgesic, anti-inflammatory, tranquillizing, bronchodilatory,* and *anticonvulsant* actions.

For the management of acute overdosage with marihuana (which is rare), a quiet environment and reassuring attitude are helpful during the acute psychotic phase. Extreme agitation is best controlled by diazepam.

Nicotine

Nicotine is an alkaloid found in tobacco in a concentration between 1 to 2 percent. It is rapidly absorbed by the lungs and causes mild CNS stimulation. Simultaneously there is decreased skeletal muscle tone and reduced appetite. In fresh users occasionally nausea, vomiting, dizziness and irritability occur. **Tolerance** develops to these later effects, but is variable in nature and duration. Withdrawal from nicotine may result in nausea, diarrhoea, increased appetite, headache, drowsiness, insomnia, irritability and poor concentration. For management of the psychic dependence, gradual reduction of nicotine consumption is usually less effective over the long term than abrupt cessation.

Other risks associated with cigarette smoking are lung and **bladder cancer, coronary artery disease, emphysema,** and **other chronic pulmonary disorders.**

Mechanisms of Tolerance and Dependence

There are interactions between man and drug, which are responsible for the development of dependence. **Tolerance** to and **dependence** on drugs are very closely linked. Without tolerance to a drug, physical dependence is most unlikely.

Tolerance. Several mechanisms of tolerance to a drug may be delineated: (*i*) **behavioural tolerance** may be developed as in the case of chronic alcoholics, who even with high plasma levels of ethyl alcohol may appear to be functioning normally; (*ii*) **metabolic tolerance** may occur due to continued exposure to the drug. Enzymes may be induced that enhance the biotransformation of the drug to inactive metabolites. (*iii*) **immune tolerance** may develop through the formation of antibodies to the drug, and (*iv*) **pharmacodynamic tolerance,** i.e., tolerance based on a lessened degree of drug effect due to the operation of homeostatic or compensatory mechanisms elicited by its initial use may develop. This last type of tolerance appears to be conceptually linked with physical dependence (see below).

Dependence. Two types of dependence are recognized: **psychological** and **physical,** although boundaries between the two of them are sometimes difficult to define. **Psychological dependence** is manifested by a strong craving for the drug, but not necessarily with the appearance of physical signs on abrupt withdrawal of the drug. In **physical dependence** psychologic and physical symptoms of withdrawal develop, as exemplified by the well known withdrawal reactions that occur in heavy users of alcohol, barbiturates and opiates. As a rule, psychological dependence is seen in all who develop physical dependence, although the converse is not true.

The social or permissive drugs, caffeine and nicotine, or the abused drugs like marihuana, hallucinogens or amphetamines in small doses produce largely **psychic dependence.** The result of stopping them is the loss of comfort or well being they cause, but physical symptoms are minimal. **Physical dependence** manifests as dangerous physical symptoms, which if uncontrolled may be fatal. Usually first tolerance and then physical dependence develop. The ability of one drug to suppress the manifestations of physical dependence produced by another drug, and to maintain the physically dependent state is referred to as **cross-dependence.** Cross-dependence may be **partial** or **complete** depending more on the pharmacological effect, rather than on chemical similarities. In general any morphine-like opioid shows cross-dependence with other opioids. Partial cross-dependence is seen between alcohol and barbiturates. **Cross-dependence** has important clinical implications, since the withdrawal symptoms produced by drugs with longer half-lives (methadone, phenobarbital, chlordiazepoxide) are usually less severe but more prolonged. This phenomenon is the basis for the substitution treatment of physical dependence by opoids in the form of methadone therapy (see above).

Most theories attempt to explain the phenomenon on the basis of some form of CNS **counteradaptation** to the agonistic actions of the drug. Counteradaptation results in the development of a "latent hyperexcitability" in the nervous system affected by the drugs. On stoppage of the drug this is manifested as a **rebound** or **overshoot** phenomenon. This phenomenon may be precipitated by the displacement of the agonist by the antagonist from the receptor, as is the case with morphine and naloxone.

To sum up, factors associated with the nonmedical use of drugs are many. A large number of personal and environmental factors are involved, and initiate some persons to use the drugs out of the many to whom they are available. The WHO study group on youth and drugs has listed the following motives for the initiation and continuation of drug-taking: (*i*) to **satisfy curiosity** about drug effects; (*ii*) to achieve a **sense of belonging,** to be "accepted" by others; (*iii*) to **express independence** and sometimes hostility; (*iv*) to have **pleasurable, new, thrilling, or dangerous experience;** (*v*) to gain an improved **"understanding" or "creativity";** (*vi*) to foster a **sense of ease or relaxation;** and (*vii*) to **escape** from something real.

2.11 ANTIPARKINSONIAN DRUGS

Parkinson's disease, or **paralysis agitans,** is a chronic progressive disorder of the central nervous system (CNS), which is the result of damage to cells located in the basal ganglia of the brain. The term **parkinsonism** is used to describe the symptom complex which results from either the normal course of the disease, or from administration of drugs like the *phenothiazines, butyrophenones, reserpine, methyldopa, procaine* and *tetrabenazine.* The *three* cardinal manifestations of Parkinson's disease are:

1. **Akinesia (bradykinesia).** This is a lack or difficulty in initiating voluntary muscle movement, and in advanced stages is characterized by "frozen" muscles, resulting in a mask-like facies; impaired postural reflexes; and inability to care for oneself.
2. **Rigidity.** This is usually of the "plastic" or "cogwheel" type, i.e., it gives way in a series of jerks.
3. **Tremor.** Coarse (3-6 cycles/sec), repetitive muscle activity, usually worse when the patient is at rest, is commonly manifested as a "pill-rolling" motion of the hands and "bobbing" of the head.

In addition, the patient may show disturbances in gait, impaired speech, muscle weakness, and autonomic hyperactivity like salivation and seborrhoea. Parkinson's disease affects either sex usually over the age of 50 years, and mild tremor at rest is often the initial sign. As the disease progresses, common functions like walking, eating, and writing become increasingly difficult.

Neurochemical Basis of Parkinsonism

This neurological syndrome is a disorder of the extrapyramidal system which normally governs the quality and smoothness of voluntary muscle movement. The normal function of the extrapyramidal system depends on a **balanced action** of the excitatory and inhibitory components. The excitatory transmitter is **acetylcholine,** while the inhibitory transmitter is **dopamine.** In parkinsonism the inhibitory component is deficient, and the concentration of dopamine in the basal ganglia is low.

The pathological lesion in parkinsonism lies in the **corpus striatum** and **basal ganglia (Fig. 2.11.1).** Gamma-aminobutyric acid (GABA), an inhibitory neurotransmitter also plays an important role in striatal function.

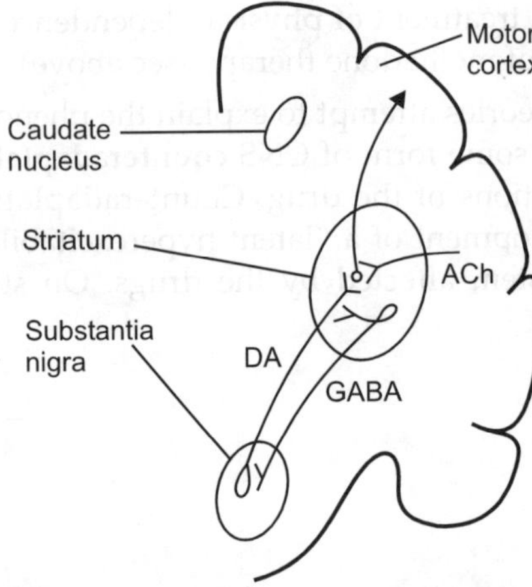

Fig. 2.11.1. Relationship between the dopaminergic (DA), cholinergic (Ach) and GABA-ergic neurones in the basal ganglia. The connection to the caudate nucleus is indirect (see text).

Histochemical studies have shown that these areas are selectively depleted of their **dopamine** content, due to degeneration of dopaminergic neurones having their cell bodies in the **substantia nigra** in the midbrain. Because motor-regulatory areas such as the **corpus striatum** receive their dopamine supply from the substantia nigra, **degeneration of these nigrostriatal neurones decreases the functional amount of dopamine** available to the nuclei of the corpus striatum, i.e., the caudate nucleus, and the putamen. This upsets the normal balance between DA and ACh in these brain regions **(Fig. 2.11.2).** The only true symptom resulting from low striatal dopamine content

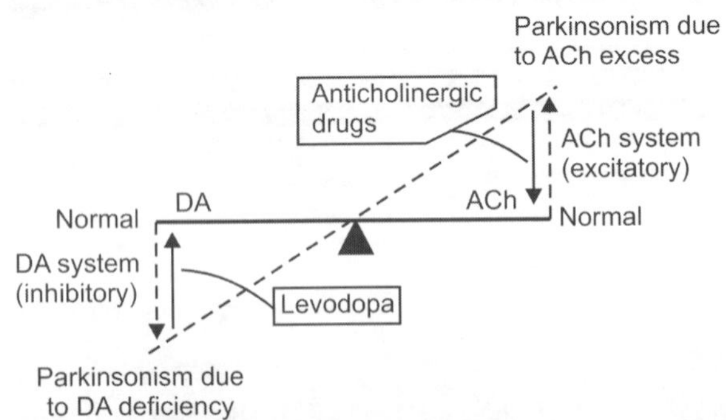

Fig. 2.11.2. Diagrammatic respresentation of the balance between dopamine (DA) and acetylcholine (ACh) acting as antagonistic neurotransmitters in the corpus striatum, and the two major methods of treating parkinsonism (see text).

is **akinesia,** and as such akinesia is the abnormality most benefitted by dopamine-replacement therapy. The rigidity and tremor are less well controlled by supplemental dopamine, and respond better to a combination of DA replacement and antichlolinergic therapy.

To summarize, according to current concepts, dopamine (DA) acts mainly as an inhibitory transmitter, and acetylcholine (ACh) as an excitatory transmitter, within the nigrostriatal pathways of the extrapyramidal motor system. However, a proper balance between the two neurotransmitters is essential for normal function. In view of the selective degeneration of dopamineric neurones, the balance becomes tipped towards cholinergic predominence. Correction of this imbalance is the basis for the drug therapy of parkinsonism.

Antiparkinsonian Drugs

Drug therapy of parkinsonism aims towards augmentation of central dopaminergic function, or reduction of central cholinergic activity. On this basis antiparkinsonian drugs may be classified as :

I. **Dopaminergic agents**
   (*a*) Dopamine precursor (e.g., levodopa)
   (*b*) Dopamine-releasing agent (e.g., amantadine)
   (*c*) Dopamine receptor agonists (e.g., bromocriptine, pergolide)
   (*d*) Inhibition of dopamine inactivation (e.g., selegiline)

II. **Anticholinergic/antihistaminic agents**
   (*a*) Anticholinergics (e.g., benztropine, biperiden, ethopropazine, orphenadrine, procyclidine, trihexyphenidyl)
   (*b*) Antihistaminic (e.g., diphenhydramine)

In addition to drug therapy, which only offers a symptomatic relief, adjunctive therapy for parkinsonism includes **physical therapy** to delay disability, and **emotional support** to lessen feelings of helplessness and inadequacy in the patient.

Some new methods for the treatment of parkinsonism are also under experimentation. Important among them are: (*i*) **implantation of adrenal medullary tissue in the brain** to provide a source of dopamine; and (*ii*) **implantation of foetal nigral tissue in the brain** to replace the deficient dopamine-producing cells of the substantia nigra.

Dopaminergic Agents

Levodopa

Carbidopa/Levodopa

Benserazide/Levodopa

Levodopa (L-DOPA, 1-dihydroxyphenylalanine), the metabolic precursor of dopamine, penetrates the blood-brain barrier, and is converted to dopamine in the brain, thereby replenishing the deficient neurotransmitter. The enzyme **dopa decarboxylase** which converts dopa to dopamine is not only present in the brain, but also in the plasma as well. As such a significant fraction of an oral dose of L-DOPA is converted to DA in the plasma and cannot penetrate the blood-brain barrier. Thus, very large amounts of L-DOPA are required to provide clinically effective levels of dopamine in the brain, and this is associated with many adverse reactions.

For this reason L-DOPA is seldom used alone today. To overcome this problem fixed dose combinations of carbidopa and levodopa (1:4, 1:10) are available. **Carbidopa** is also available alone as 25 mg tablets, which allows the clinician to more carefully titrate the dosage ratio to obtain better symptom control. Carbidopa is a peripheral dopa decarboxylase inhibitor (DCI), which retards the peripheral (extra-cerebral) conversion of L-DOPA to DA **(Fig. 2.11.3).**

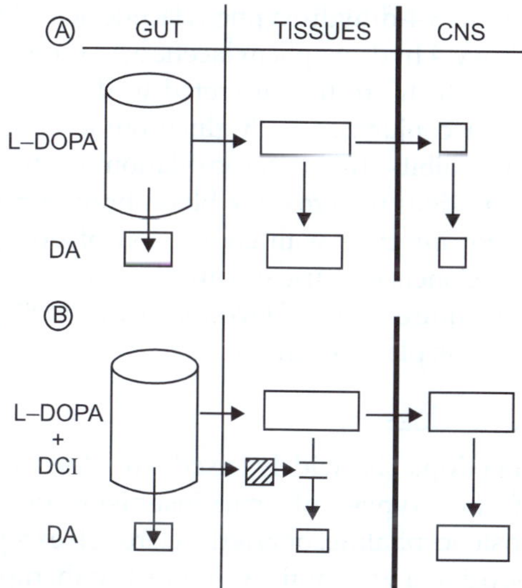

Fig. 2.11.3. Diagrammatic representation of the distribution of levodopa (L-DOPA), and its metabolism when given alone (A), and (B) when combined with a peripheral dopa dicarboxylase inhibitor (DCI). The latter prevents decarboxylation of L-DOPA to dopamine (DA) outside the CNS, whereas decarboxylation occurs normally within the CNS. Hence, more of dopamine reaches the brain, even with smaller doses of L-DOPA (see text).

Carbidopa is a peripheral dopa decarboxylase inhibitor. It competes with the enzyme dopa decarboxylase, thereby retarding the peripheral breakdown of L-DOPA. This allows a greater fraction of the L-DOPA dose to cross the blood-brain barrier, producing higher DA levels in the central motor regulatory areas. Carbidopa itself does not cross the blood-brain barrier, and hence does not interfere with the conversion of L-DOPA to DA in the CNS. Levodopa dosage requirements are reduced by about 75 percent by combination with carbidopa, as the plasma levels and plasma half-life are increased. In addition, as much less DA is formed peripherally, the incidence of systemic side effects is lower, specially nausea, vomiting, and cardiovascular disturbances.

Benserazide is another peripheral dopa decarboxylase inhibitor which is used in combination with levodopa in a ratio of 1 : 4.

Mode of action. Levodopa is a precursor of DA that readily passes the blood-brain barrier, where it is decarboxylated to DA. This increased formation of DA in the motor regulatory areas of the CNS restores depleted DA levels and improves the symptoms of parkinsonism. Levodopa is most effective in relieving **akinesia** and **bradykinesia,** but somewhat less effective in controlling rigidity and tremor. Response to levodopa is greatest at the initiation of therapy, but gradually diminishes over 2 to 5 years.

Pharmacokinetics. Levodopa is well absorbed from the GI tract by an amino acid transport system. Levodopa is rapidly metabolized in the GI tract, and the liver by **dopa decarboxylase.** This enzyme rapidly converts levodopa to DA, and this amine is further metabolized to 3,4-dihydroxyphenylacetic acid (DOPAC) and 3-methoxy-4 hydroxyphenylacetic acid (homovanillic acid, HVA), which are then excreted in the urine either unchanged or conjugated with glucuronide or sulphate. **Carbidopa** inhibits the decarboxylation of peripheral levodopa, but does not cross the blood-brain barrier, and thus does not interfere with conversion of dopa to DA in the CNS. Concurrent use of carbidopa with levodopa reduces the required dose of levodopa by 70 to 80 percent and increases its plasma half-life.

Therapeutic Uses

1. Levodopa is widely used for the treatment of **all types of parkinsonism** (idiopathic, postencephalitic, or arteriosclerotic), except those associated with antipsychotic drug therapy.
2. Relief of pain associated with herpes zoster (investigational use).

Preparations and Dosage. *Levodopa* is available in tablets and capsules (100, 250, 500 mg). Initially 0.5 to 1.0 g daily is given in 2 or more divided doses. Optimal clinical response may not be obtained for upto 6 months. Dosage is highly individualized and must be reassessed frequently.

Carbidopa/Levodopa tablets are available in a fixed ratio of either 10 mg carbidopa/250 mg levodopa, 25 mg carbidopa/100 mg levodopa, or 25 mg carbidopa/250 mg levodopa. Initially 1 tablet (10/100 or 25/100) 3 times a day; increase by 1 tablet daily until 6 tablets per day.

Adverse reactions. Common side effects are nausea, vomiting, anorexia, orthostatic hypotension, salivation, dysphagia, ataxia, headache, confusion, dizziness, weakness, hand tremor, insomnia, anxiety, euphoria, choreiform and other involuntary movements, nightmares, and agitation. Dyskinesias occur on long-term therapy.

Other adverse reactions include: **Gastrointestinal** - diarrhoea, GI bleeding, ulceration; **Cardiovascular** - palpitation, tachycardia, arrhythmias, haemolytic anaemia; *CNS* - bradykinetic episodes ("On-off" phenomenon with sudden loss of symptom control lasting minutes or hours which is apparently due to excessive L-DOPA levels in the body occuring temporarily), muscle twitching, grinding of teeth, paranoid ideation, psychosis, convulsions, and dementia; **Ocular** - blepharospasm, diplopia and blurred vision; and others - urinary retention, bitter taste, sweating, flushing, oedema, alopecia and leukopenia. Levodopa may elevate blood urea nitrogen (BUN), SGOT, SGPT, LDH, bilirubin, alkaline phosphatase and PBI levels.

Contraindications to the use of levodopa include narrow-angle glaucoma, acute psychoses, undiagnosed skin lesions or history of melanoma (as levodopa can activate a malignant melanoma), and concomitant use of monoamine oxidase inhibitors (MAOIs). The drug should be used cautiously in patients with severe cardiovascular, pulmonary, renal, hepatic and endocrinal diseases.

Drug Interactions

1. Effects of L-DOPA are **decreased** by antipsychotics, papaverine, pyridoxine, and benzodiazepines.
2. Effects of L-DOPA may be **potentiated** by propranolol, methyldopa, and anticholinergics.
3. L-DOPA may **enhance** the hypotensive effect of methyldopa, guanethidine, diuretics and other antihypertensive drugs.
4. L-DOPA **enhances** the cardiovascular effects of sympathomimetic drugs: adrenaline, ephedrine, and amphetamines.
5. Concurrent use of L-DOPA and either tricyclic antidepressants or MAOIs can result in tachycardia and hypertension.
6. Diabetic control with oral hypoglycaemic drugs may be adversely affected by L-DOPA.

Amantadine

Amantadine is a synthetic **antiviral** agent, originally used for prophylaxis against the Asian strain of influenza. It also effectively relieves symptoms of parkinsonism, specially **akinesia** and **rigidity.** It may be used as initial therapy of mild Parkinson's disease, but in more advanced stages it has to be combined with levodopa.

The **mode of action** of amantadine is incompletely understood. It causes release of DA from presynaptic nerve endings, and blocks its presynaptic re-uptake. Its effectiveness is greatly reduced in the absence of functional dopaminergic neurones in the corpus striatum. Its antiviral action has been attributed to prevention of the release of viral nucleic acid into host cells **(Chap. 9.9).**

Amantadine is used for the symptomatic treatment of **parkinsonism** in doses of 100 mg once or twice daily (maximum 400 mg/day). It is well absorbed orally; peak plasma levels are reached in 2 to 4 hours; and has a long duration of action (half-life 18-24 hours). It is not metabolized in the body, and is excreted unchanged through the kidneys (excretion is enhanced in an acid urine). Amantadine may be usefully combined with levodopa or with centrally acting anticholinergic drugs.

Side effects seen with amantadine are irritability, anxiety, nausea, dizziness, ataxia, confusion, depression, constipation, urinary retention, oedema, and livedo reticularis (skin mottling). Severe adverse reactions include orthostatic hypotension, fatigue, dyspnoea, congestive heart failure, psychosis, neutropenia and leukopenia.

Bromocriptine

One of the newer drugs approved for the treatment of parkinsonism is the ergoline derivative, **bromocriptine.** It is a dopamine agonist acting directly on the postsynaptic dopamine receptors. It is primarily used orally as adjunctive therapy to provide additional therapeutic control in patients maintained on L-DOPA, who start showing signs of deterioration. Such cases are referred to as "late L-DOPA failures". In such patients there is a return of tremor and rigidity, akinesia and on/off phenomena. Bromocriptine may delay the onset of late L-DOPA failure, and provide symptomatic relief.

Bromocriptine also activates dopamine receptors in the **tuberoinfundibular dopaminergic system** of the pituitary, resulting in the secretion of prolactin inhibitory factor (PIF) from the hypothalamus; secretion of PIF suppresses the release of prolactin from the anterior pituitary **(Chap. 7.1).** Based on this action bromocriptine is used in the treatment of **amenorrhoea, female infertility,** and **galactorrhoea associated with hyperprolactinaemia.** It may also be used for reduction of plasma growth hormone levels in patients of **acromegaly.**

Bromocriptine mesylate is available in 2.5 mg tablets and 5 mg capsules. For Parkinson's disease the dosage varies from 30 to 50 mg/day, depending on the severity of the disease. **Adverse reactions** include nausea, vomiting, dizziness, ankle oedema, skin mottling, skin rashes, muscle cramps and Raynaud's syndrome. **Contraindications** include ischaemic heart disease, peripheral vascular disease, and during pregnancy and lactation.

Pergolide

Pergolide is another ergoline derivative, which is now available for adjunctive treatment with carbidopa/levodopa in the symptomatic management of Parkinson's disease. It is likely that pergolide effectively prevents or delays the "late L-DOPA failures" seen with the use of levodopa alone.

Pergolide mesylate is available as 0.05, 0.25, and 1.0 mg tablets. The recommended starting dose is 0.05 mg/day, and may be gradually increased. The optimal maintenance dose is 3 mg daily in 3 divided doses.

Selegiline

Physiologically, the enzyme MAO-B catalyzes the metabolism of dopamine in the brain. Selegiline (formerly deprenyl) irreversibly inhibits MAO-B enzyme in the nerve endings in the brain, thereby increasing the intraneuronal levels of dopamine. Further, selegiline facilitates dopamine release, and perhaps also interferes with dopamine re-uptake into nerve endings. It does not interfere with the activity of MAO-A, the enzyme found in the liver and intestines. Selegiline has been usefully employed in the adjunctive treatment of Parkinson's disease.

The usual **dosage** is 5 mg twice a day, at breakfast and lunch. **Adverse reactions** include confusion, vivid dreams, headache, anxiety, insomnia, hallucinations, palpitation and urinary retention.

Anticholinergic/Antihistaminic Agents

For more than 100 years, the belladonna alkaloids (atropine and scopolamine) were the primary agents used in the treatment of parkinsonism. These agents, although still occasionally employed, have been largely replaced by a group of synthetic drugs, having a more **selective central anticholinergic activity.**

The centrally acting anticholinergics may be used in all forms of Parkinson's disease, although they are less effective than levodopa. Since the introduction of levodopa, these agents have played a **secondary** role in the management of parkinsonism. They are used in combination with levodopa to obtain a better control on the disease. In addition, these drugs are also widely employed to control the *extrapyramidal manifestations* (akinesia, dystonias, akathesia, tremor) of treatment with antipsychotic agents.

Mode of action. These agents exhibit a postsynaptic blocking effect on central cholinergic excitatory pathways, which in parkinsonism became predominant, specially due to the lack of functional dopamine in the corpus striatum. Central anticholinergics also retard the reuptake of dopamine into the presynaptic nerve endings, thereby blocking its inactivation.

Therapeutic uses. The central anticholinergics are used as *sole* or *adjunctive* agents in the treatment of parkinsonian symptoms, specially rigidity. They are also used for the prevention and relief of **extrapyramidal reactions resulting from antipsychotic drug therapy.** Their usual dosage range is detailed in **Table 2.11-1.**

Table 2.11-1. *The central anticholinergic drugs used for parkinsonism*

Drug	*Dosage Range*	*Comments*
Benztropine	0.5-6 mg	Tropanol derivative used orally and parenterally for parkinsonism and extrapyramidal system reactions induced by antipsychotic drugs; effects may take several days to develop; usually not effective against tremors.
Biperiden	2-20 mg	Most effective against akinesia and rigidity; reduces salivation and seborrhoea; may produce euphoria; IV injection can cause hypotension and incoordination.
Diphenhydramine	75-200 mg	Antihistamine with a strong anticholinergic component; effective in mild parkinsonism and extrapyramidal reactions (dystonias); usually combined with L-DOPA.
Ethopropazine	50-500 mg	A phenothiazine derivative with strong anticholinergic component; controls most symptoms including tremor; *does not* potentiate other CNS depressants; high incidence of side effects and poorly tolerated by older patients; used to treat extrapyramidal reactions, even though itself being a phenothiazine.
Orphenadrine	150-250 mg	Antihistamine with a central muscle relaxant activity; relieves rigidity and controls autonomic manifestations; minimal drowsiness but high incidence of atropine-like side effects.
Procyclidine	10-20 mg	Anticholinergic and smooth muscle antispasmodic; most effective against rigidity; controls excessive salivation; may temporarily worsen tremor as rigidity is relieved; agitation and behavioural changes may occur.
Trihexyphenidyl	4-20 mg	Anticholinergic and antispasmodic; major effect is on rigidity but most symptoms improve; effects may be potentiated by MAOIs.

Adverse reactions. Common side effects are dryness of mouth, blurred vision, dizziness, nausea, nervousness, and urinary hesitancy. Severe adverse effects include confusion, agitation, delirium, hallucinations, depression, memory loss, constipation, paralytic ileus, flushing, tachycardia, palpitation, mild orthostatic hypotension, muscle cramps, mydriasis, diplopia and increased intraocular pressure. **Contraindications** to their use are acute narrow-angle glaucoma, pyloric and duodenal obstruction and prostatic hypertrophy.

Drug interactions. These agents when combined with other drugs having anticholinergic activity (e.g., phenothiazines, tricyclic antidepressants) may result in increased toxicity. They may potentiate the sedative action of other CNS depressants like alcohol, barbiturates and narcotics.

Drug Management of Parkinsonism

Patients with *mild*, early parkinsonism are good candidates for *anticholinergic* drug therapy. Treatment is started with small doses of **diphenhydramine** or **trihexyphenidyl.** Later, the patient may be switched on to a more potent agent like **benztropine.** Patients with more advanced disease may be better controlled when **amantadine** is added to anticholinergic drug therapy. However, this combination increases the risk of drug-induced mental disturbances, specially in the elderly.

The combination of **carbidopa with levodopa** is considered to be the most effective current drug treatment for most *advanced* cases of parkinsonism. If necessary, for more complete control **carbidopa/levodopa** may be combined with **amantadine** and an **anticholinergic** drug. Patients who become less responsive to all these drugs on long-term treatment may improve with the addition of **bromocriptine.** The current status of **selegiline** is under assessment and clinical evaluation.

Other Basal Ganglia Disorders

Huntington's Chorea

Huntington's chorea is an autosomal dominant, inherited disorder of the CNS. Each child of a Huntington's disease-affected parent has a 50 percent chance of inheriting the disorder. This disease is associated with diminished levels of ACh and choline acetylase, due to widespread degenerative changes in the cholinergic interneurones of the corpus striatum. This results in a relative excess of dopamine.

Drug Therapy

It is aimed at either antagonizing brain dopamine activity, or enhancing cholinergic activity.

Antipsychotic drugs. Huntington's disease can be controlled by antipsychotic drugs which antagonize dopamine. There is no specific antipsychotic drug of choice, but drugs with minimal anticholinergic activity are usually chosen.

Tetrabenazine. It is a dopamine-depleting drug used to treat Huntington's disease. Initially it is given in a dose of 25 mg orally 3 times daily, which may be increased to a maximum of 200 mg daily.

Choline and Deanol. These agents enhance cholinergic activity. Deanol is a putative precursor of ACh.

Baclofen. It is an analogue of GABA, and may be useful as this transmitter is possibly deficient in Huntington's disease.

Tardive Dyskinesia

Tardive dyskinesia is a choreiform movement disorder frequently produced by prolonged use of antipsychotic drugs. It often follows abrupt cessation of antipsychotic drug therapy. It is attributed to supersensitivity of the postsynaptic dopamine receptors, rather than to reduction of cholinergic activity as in Huntington's chorea (see above). However, both the defects are the result of an acetylcholine/dopamine imbalance in the brain.

For the treatment of tardive dyskinesia various drugs **like anticholinergic drugs, cholinergic agents, lecithin** and **lithium carbonate** have been employed with limited success.

❑❑❑

3

DRUGS ACTING ON THE PERIPHERAL NERVOUS SYSTEM

3.1 GENERAL CONSIDERATION

The peripheral nervous system is composed of the **afferent** and **efferent** neurones of the autonomic and somatic nervous system. The region of contact between two nerve cells, or between a nerve cell and an effector cell is termed as a **synapse**. The synapse between a motor neurone (autonomic) and an effector cell is known as the **neuroeffector junction** whereas, the synapse between the motor nerve (somatic) and voluntary muscle is known as the **neuromuscular junction**. A comparison of the somatic and autonomic reflex arcs is shown in **Fig. 3.1.1**.

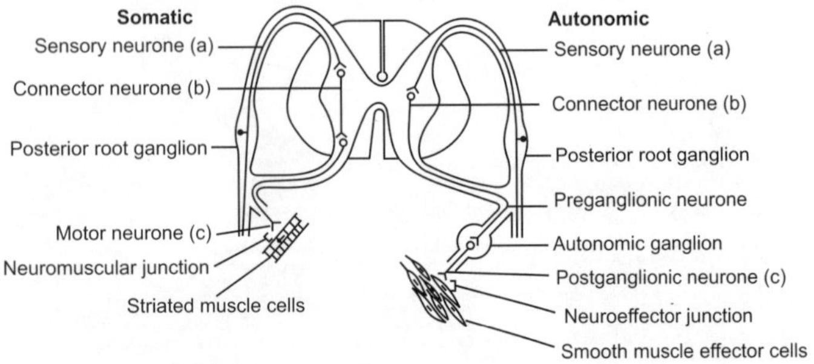

Fig. 3.1.1: Diagrammatic comparison of the somatic and autonomic reflex arcs. Each arc consists of three neuronal components: (a) Sensory neurones (afferent) with cell bodies in the posterior root ganglion, which synapse with the connector neurones (b) in the dorsal horn (somatic) or the lateral horn (autonomic) of the grey matter. The connector neurones in the somatic system remain within the grey matter, and the somatic motor neurone (c) leaves the spinal cord to innervate the striated muscle. In the autonomic system the connector neurones leave the spinal cord as myelinated preganglionic fibres and they synapse in the autonomic ganglia. From the autonomic ganglia the nonmyelinated postganglionic fibres (c) emerge and innervate the effector organs.

The functioning of the autonomic nervous system (ANS) is independent of conscious thought, and the word autonomic is derived from Greek *autos* (self) and *nomos* (governing). The ability of the ANS to maintain constancy of the internal environment in the body is termed as **homeostasis**. By convention the term ANS includes mainly the efferent neurones supplying the viscera, i.e., the preganglionic (connector) and postganglionic (excitor) neurones.

ANATOMY OF THE ANS

The ANS regulates the vital functions in the body including **blood pressure, body temperature, water balance, urination, digestion and many others**.

The ANS comprises of two major subdivisions: **sympathetic** and **parasympathetic**. The main nerve centres for these autonomic reflex arcs are located in the hypothalamus, medulla oblongata and spinal cord. Depending on the anatomical situation of the connector cells and their fibres there is a **cranial** and **sacral outflow** which forms the parasympathetic division, and the **thoracolumbar outflow** which forms the sympathetic division of the ANS. Both these divisions have opposing effects on the innervated viscera, and most of the viscera have a dual nerve supply. However, some of the organs are innervated by one division only (e.g., uterus, adrenal medulla, and most arterioles by sympathetic only; glands of the stomach and pancreas by parasympathetic only). The general arrangement of the ANS is shown in **Fig. 3.1.2.**

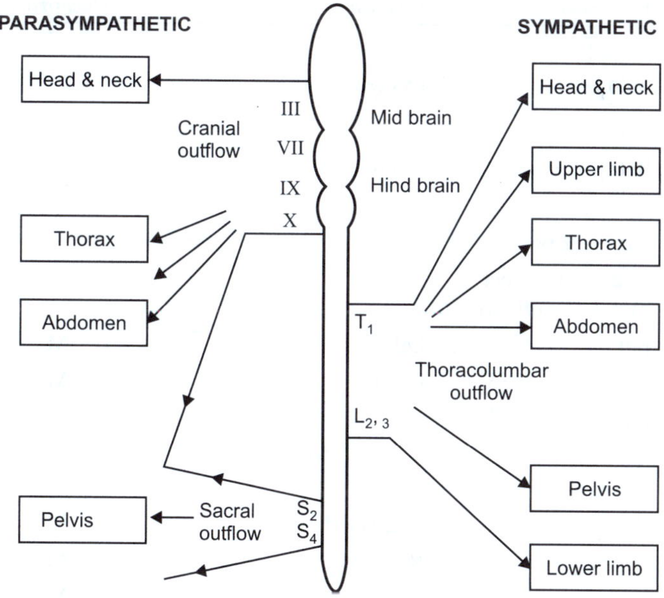

Fig. 3.1.2: The efferent outflow of the autonomic nervous system. The parasympathetic pathways (left) are bilaterally paired. Most of the sympathetic pathways (right) are paired except the prevertebral ganglia (coeliac, superior and inferior mesenteric ganglia).

The visceral afferent or sensory fibres of the ANS reach the cerebrospinal axis via the somatic nerves or various ramifications of the ANS. They carry general visceral sensations and information from the reflexogenic areas of the heart, respiratory and alimentary systems. The integration of autonomic activity occurs at all levels of the cerebrospinal axis. The medulla and pons contain the vital centres for the control of respiratory and cardiovascular systems. **The major site of coordination of autonomic activity is the hypothalamus**. The sympathetic functions are controlled by the posterior, and the parasympathetic by the middle and anterior hypothalamic nuclei. The integration of autonomic with somatic functions occurs in higher centres. The visceral efferent fibres are categorized into two parasympathetic and sympathetic divisions, and consist of two serial neurones, i.e., the **proximal preganglionic** and the **distal postganglionic** neurones with the synapse in the autonomic ganglia.

Parasympathetic Nervous System

The parasympathetic outflow comprises both cranial and sacral components. Cranial outflow is carried in cranial nerves III (oculomotor), VII (facial), IX (glossopharyngeal) and X (vagus). Sacral outflow is carried in the spinal nerves of sacral segments 2, 3 and 4 of the spinal cord. Many parasympathetic ganglia are located close to or are embedded within the wall of the effector organ. Such ganglia are called **terminal ganglia**. In general, the parasympathetic preganglionic neurones are long, while the postganglionic neurones are short. Acetylcholine (ACh) is the chemical transmitter between the postganglionic parasympathetic neurones and the effector cells.

Sympathetic Nervous System

The sympathetic outflow is described as thoracolumbar, since the preganglionic neurones emerge from the CNS in the ventral roots of the spinal nerves of the first thoracic to second or third lumbar segments. The sympathetic preganglionic fibres briefly join the mixed spinal nerve, but soon branch away to form **white communicating rami** (myelinated fibres) which enter the chains of paravertebral ganglia on either side of the vertebral column. The postganglionic fibres are distributed to visceral structures via the **grey communicating rami** (nonmyelinated fibres) and the spinal nerves. In general, the preganglionic sympathetic neurones are short while the postganglionic neurones are long. Noradrenaline (NA) is the chemical transmitter between the postganglionic sympathetic neurones and the effector cells, except to the **sweat glands** which are supplied by sympathetic cholinergic fibres. The **adrenal medullae** are embryologically and functionally equivalent to sympathetic ganglia, and are innervated by preganglionic sympathetic fibres with ACh as the transmitter. Thus, they form an integral part of the sympathetic autonomic division (see later).

Physiological Functions of the ANS

The sympathetic system, working with the adrenal medulla regulates the expenditure of energy, specially in times of **stress**. The parasympathetic system, on the contrary, helps the body to store and save energy. The opposing functions of two divisions of the ANS may be understood by carefully studying the organ responses listed in **Table 3.1-1**.

Table 3.1-1. *Comparison of effector organ responses to sympathetic and parasympathetic nervous stimulation.*

Effector organ	*Sympathetic Stimulation*		*Parasympathetic Stimulation*	
	Response	*Receptor*	*Response*	*Receptor*
Heart				
Rate	Increased	$Beta_1$	Decreased	M*
Contractility	Increased	$Beta_1$	–	–
AV Conduction	Increased	$Beta_1$	Decreased	M
Blood Vessels				
Coronary	Dilated	Alpha & $Beta_2$ (mainly indirect metabolic effects)	–	–
Skeletal muscle	Dilated	$Beta_2$	Dilated	M
Skin and mucosa	Constricted	Alpha	Dilated	M
Cerebral, pulmonary, abdominal viscera	Constricted	Alpha	–	–
Stomach & Intestine				
Motility and tone	Decreased	$Beta_2$	Increased	M
Sphincters	Contracted	Alpha	Relaxed	M
Glandular secretion	Decreased	–	Increased	M
Urinary Bladder				
Detrusor muscle	Relaxed	$Beta_2$	Contracted	M
Trigone and sphincter	Contracted	Alpha	Relaxed	M
Other Smooth Muscles				
Bronchial, ureters, gall bladder, bile duct	Relaxed	$Beta_2$	Contracted	M
Salivary Glands				
Secretion	Stimulated (sparse, thick, mucinous)	Alpha	Stimulated (watery, profuse)	M
Eye				
Iris radial muscle	Contracted (mydriasis)	Alpha	–	–
Iris sphincter muscle	–	–	Contracted (miosis)	M
Ciliary muscle	Relaxed (for far vision)	Beta	Contracted (for near vision)	M
Spleen Capsule	Contracted	Alpha	–	–
Liver	Glycogenolysis: gluconeogenesis	Alpha, $Beta_2$	–	–
Uterus (Pregnant)	Relaxed	$Beta_2$	–	–
Kidney	Renin secretion	$Beta_1$	–	–
Skin				
Sweat glands	Stimulated	M, Alpha	–	–
Pilomotor muscle	Contracted	Alpha	–	–
Pancreas				
Islet cells	Decreased insulin secretion	$Alpha_2$	–	–
Acinar cells	–	–	Increased enzyme secretion	M
Adrenal Medulla	–	–	Secretion of adrenaline and noradrenaline	N**
Fat Cells	Lipolysis	Alpha, $Beta_1$	–	–

*M = Muscarinic; ** = Nicotinic

The **sympathetic** response prepares the body for a "fight or flight" reaction, which occurs when the integrity of the organism is threatened under conditions of stress. The heart rate and the stroke volume is increased, leading to an elevation in the cardiac output. There is generalized venous constriction and contraction of the spleen. The cardiac output is redistributed. The blood supply is shifted from the skin, gastrointestinal tract, kidney and glands to the heart, skeletal muscle, brain and lungs. Pupils and bronchi are dilated. Erector pili and sweat glands are activated. Glycogenolysis occurs. Thus, the body is prepared for the **anti-stress** response.

The **parasympathetic** response on the contrary, is designed to conserve energy. The heart is slowed and the pupils are constricted. The gastrointestinal movements are facilitated so that digestion and assimilation of foodstuffs occurs. Thus, the balance between these two opposing systems is responsible for **homeostasis**. Both divisions of the ANS do not exert equal control over all organs. The *parasympathetic system* has greater influence on the *gastrointestinal* tract function than the sympathetic. Whereas, the *sympathetic system* regulates the activity of the *cardiovascular system* to a greater extent than the parasympathetic system.

Neurohumoral Transmission in the ANS

Convincing evidence for the phenomenon of neurohumoral transmission was provided by simple and direct experiments of the German physiologist **Otto Loewi** in 1921. He cross-perfused two isolated frog hearts, and stimulated the vagus (vago-sympathetic trunk) of one of them, and transferred the perfusate of this heart to the second which was inhibited. Loewi suggested that the inhibition of the second heart was brought about by release of a chemical substance, which he called "**vagusstoff**", which later turned out to be **acetylcholine**. Loewi further observed that the effect of vagusstoff could be blocked by **atropine**. After atropinization the stimulation of the vago-sympathetic trunk no longer caused inhibition, but caused an acceleration of the heart. This excitatory substance he called **acceleransstoff**, and later suggested that this might be **adrenaline**. This classical experimentation led to the concept of neurohumoral transmission of nerve impulses.

There are certain minimum **qualifications** to be possessed by a substance to be labelled as a neurohumoral transmitter (neurotransmitter): (*a*) it should be liberated from the jutional sites during presynaptic nervous activity; (*b*) it should be identified by chemical or biologic methods; (*c*) there should be a similarity in the response to nerve stimulation and local injection of the liberated substance; (*d*) there should be similar modification of responses both to nerve stimulation and local injection of the transmitter substance to drugs and other procedures; (*e*) the enzymes capable of its synthesis must be present in the neurone; and (*f*) the enzymes capable of inactivating the proposed transmitter must be present in the junctional tissue.

Henry Dale in 1933 suggested the terms `cholinergic' to describe nerves releasing acetylcholine, and `adrenergic' for those releasing adrenaline or a closely related substance. The word adrenergic led to some confusion as it was well established that ***noradrenaline*** was the neurotransmitter at the postganglionic sympathetic neuroeffector junction. Hence strictly speaking ***noradrenergic*** is the correct term, although conventionally the term adrenergic is used.

The Neurone

The current concepts of the typical neurone are based on the idealized model illustrated in **Fig. 3.1.3.** The cell body has the general function of maintaining neuronal integrity. The nucleus contains DNA, in which is encoded information for all the enzymes needed for normal cell function. Amongst the enzymes are those needed for the synthesis and degradation of the particular neurotransmitter. The cell bodies possess the appropriate mechanism to take up the specific neurotransmitter precursor from the surroundings, i.e., the cholinergic neurone takes up **choline**; the adrenergic neurone takes up **tyrosine** and the tryptaminergic neurone takes up **tryptophan**.

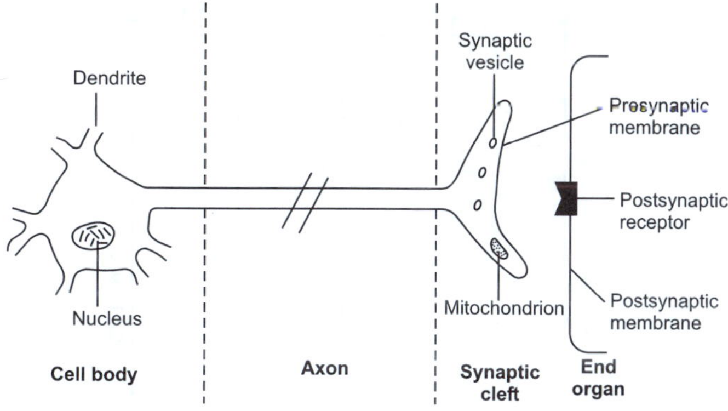

Fig. 3.1.3. Schematic diagram of a typical neurone

The synaptic vesicles are aggregated in neuronal terminations, and store the neurotransmitter. During nervous activity the vesicles migrate towards the neurilemma and release the neurotransmitter into the **synaptic cleft** by a process of **exocytosis**. The released transmitter diffuses across the synaptic cleft which is 200 to 400 Å (Angstrom units) in width. Sometimes the synaptic cleft may be upto 10,000 Å in width. Across this cleft the transmitter combines with the specific receptors on the **postsynaptic membrane** in the end organ and produces the response. There are a number of feedback mechanisms which regulate the synthesis and release of the neurotransmitters from the neurones (see later).

Drugs which activate receptors are termed "agonists" and those which block the effect of **agonists** are termed "**antagonists**".

Cholinergic Transmission

Autonomic and somatic nerves that synthesize, store and release acetylcholine (ACh) are called **cholinergic**. For details of the synthesis, stroage, release and inactivation of ACh see **Chapter 3.2.** ACh molecules are stored in a bound, or inactive form in tiny storage sacs, called **synaptic vesicles.** On the arrival of the action potential at the nerve ending, in the presence of calcium, free ACh molecules are discharged into the synaptic cleft by a process of **exocytosis.** This active ACh combines with the cholinergic receptor, or precisely cholinoceptors on the cell membrane. The permeability of the cell membrane is changed which brings about the response. The cholinergic receptors are of two types-**muscarinic** and **nicotinic (Table 3.1.-2).** The *muscarinic* receptors are responsible for actions resembling ACh that take place at postganglionic parasympathetic neuroeffectors, and the *nicotinic* receptors are responsible for actions resembling ACh that take place at the autonomic ganglia, adrenal medulla, the CNS, and the skeletal neuromuscular junctions of somatic nerves. The muscarinic receptors are subdivided into M_1, and M_2 sites based on the selectivity of various cholinergic agonists and antagonists. There are three main classes of cholinergic nerves.

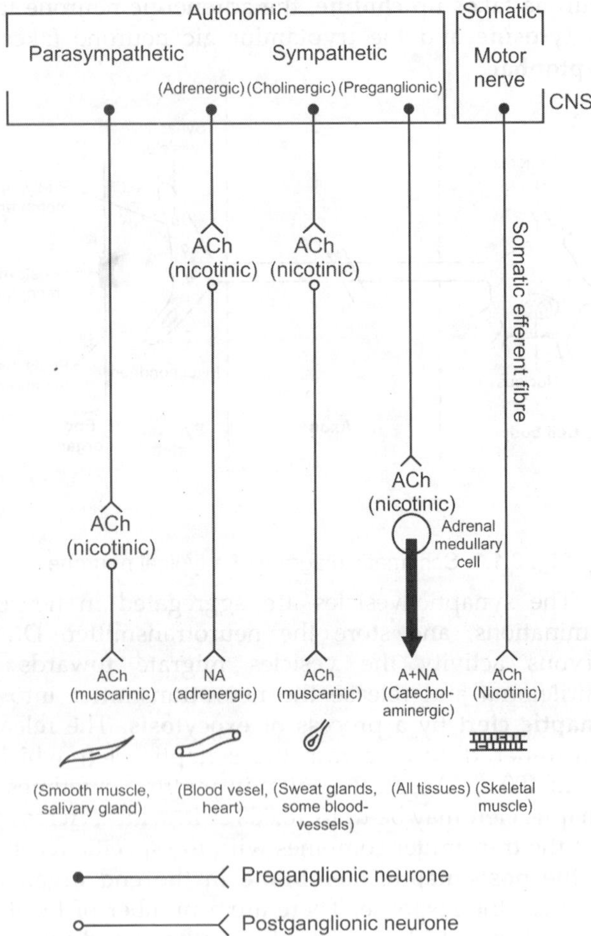

Fig. 3.1.4: Diagram showing the organization of the peripheral nervous system (ANS and somatic nervous system), and the major neurotransmitters released at various sites. ACh, acetylcholine; A, adrenaline; NA, noradrenaline

(*i*) **Postganglionic cholinergic fibres**, which include all the parasympathetic postganglionic fibres, and a few exceptional sympathetic postganglionic fibres to the sweat glands and to some blood vessels.

(*ii*) **Preganglionic cholinergic fibres**, which include all the preganglionic fibres of both the sympathetic and parasympathetic divisions of the ANS, and the cells of the adrenal medulla.

(*iii*) **Somatic motor nerve fibres**, which though not a part of the ANS, also release ACh from their nerve endings at the skeletal neuromuscular junction. The above three types of fibres are diagrammatically shown in **Fig. 3.1.4.**

Table 3.1-2. *Some characteristics of autonomic receptors*

Type	*Location*	*Agonists*	*Antagonists*
Cholinergic			
Muscarinic (M)	Postganglionic parasympathetic fibres (heart, smooth muscle, exocrine glands); brain	Acetylcholine; pilocarpine	Atropine
Nicotinic (N)	Autonomic ganglia; skeletal neuromuscular junction, adrenal medulla	Acetylcholine; nicotine	Trimethaphan (ganglia); d-tubocurarine (neuromuscular junction)
Adrenergic			
$Alpha_1$	Most blood vessels; GI tract; pancreas; eye; skin	Nonadrenaline, adrenaline, phenylephrine	Phentalamine, tolazoline
$Alpha_2$	Presynaptic terminals of adrenergic fibres; platelets; fat cells; vascular smooth muscle	Noradrenaline, adrenaline, clonidine	Imipramine
$Beta_1$	Heart; GI tract; urinary bladder; eye; adipose tissue; presynaptic sympathetic nerve endings	Adrenaline, isoprenaline	Propranolol, metoprolol
$Beta_2$	Bronchioles; uterus; skeletal muscle; blood vessells; liver	Adrenaline, isoprenaline	Propranolol
Dopamine	Renal, visceral and coronary blood vessels; brain; presynaptic nerve terminals	Dopamine	Haloperidol

Table 3.1.3 *Drugs that interfere with specific steps in chemical neurotransmission*

	Transmission step	*Adrenergic neurone*	*Cholinergic neruone*
1.	Biosynthesis of transmitter	Methyldopa	Hemicholinium
2.	Storage of transmitter	Reserpine	None known
3.	Release of transmitter	Guanethidine	Botulinum toxin
4.	Interaction with postsynaptic receptor (depolarization)	Phentolamine (α-receptors) Propranolol (β-receptors)	Atropine (muscarinic receptors) Trimethaphan (nicotinic receptors)
5.	Inactivation of transmitter	Pyrogallol (COMT inhibitor) Pargyline (MAO inhibitor) Tricyclic antidepressants (inhibit neuronal re-uptake)	Pysostigmine (cholinesterase inhibitor)
6.	Recovery of the postsynaptic membrane (repolarization)	Not known	Succinylcholine

Cholinergic transmission is not limited to the ANS and the somatic nerves alone. ACh also functions as a neurotransmitter at certain synapses within the central nervous system (CNS).

Adrenergic Transmission

Sympathetic postganglionic nerve fibres that synthesize, store and release noradrenaline (NA) are called **adrenergic**. For details of the synthesis, storage, release and inactivation of NA see **Chapter 3.4.** NA is stored in a bound, or inactive form, the granules (synaptic vesicles) of adrenergic neurones. On the arrival of the action potential at the nerve ending, free NA is liberated in the synaptic cleft by a process of exocytosis. This free NA then combines with the adrenergic receptors located on the postsynaptic membrane and produce the response. The adrenergic receptors are of two types **alpha** and **beta**. The alpha receptors are mainly excitatory in nature, except in the intestines where their stimulation produces relaxation. The beta receptors are mainly inhibitory, except in the heart where their stimulation produces cardioacceleration and increased myocardial contractility (positive inotropism). Each receptor type is further subdivided to reflect differences in location and function (**Table 3.1-2**). **Alpha$_1$** receptors are found postsynaptically in vascular smooth muscle, GI and urinary sphincter muscles, and in the eye, skin, pancreas, and salivary glands. **Alpha$_2$** receptors occur presynaptically (where they control release of noradrenaline), and in platelets, fat cells, and possibly vascular smooth muscle. **Beta$_1$** receptors occur in the heart and adipose tissue, and may also be found in the CNS, and on presynaptic noradrenergic nerve endings. **Beta$_2$** sites are present in the bronchioles, skeletal muscle vasculature, liver, kidney, and urinary bladder. A fifth type of adrenergic receptor responds selectively to **dopamine**, and is found on visceral and splanchnic blood vessels, in various brain areas, and also possibly on presynaptic sympathetic nerve terminals.

Steps in Neurohumoral Transmisison

Irrespective of the type of neurone, the fundamental steps in chemical transmission are the same. Each of these steps is a potential site for pharmacological intervention. The steps are as under:

1. Biosynthesis of the neurotransmitter.
2. Storage of the neurotransmitter.
3. Release of the neurotransmitter.
4. Interaction with the postsynaptic membrane.
5. Inactivation of the neurotransmitter.
6. Recovery of the postsynaptic membrane (Repolarization).

Drugs that interfere with one or more of the preceding steps in the process of chemical transmission are listed in **Table 3.1-3.**

To summarize, the **parasympathetic** system is mainly concerned with sedentary activities like digestion, emptying of the bowels and urinary bladder. Whereas, the **sympathetic** system is concerned with functions involving increased activity of tissues, e.g., stimulation of the heart during exercise, and stress. Generally the viscera have a nerve supply from each of the two divisions of the ANS, e.g., the heart, pupil and intestines. Certain tissues are innervated predominently by one divison, e.g., most blood vessels have only a sympathetic innervation causing vasoconstriction. The *two* divisions of the ANS balance each other, and are responsible for the maintenance of homeostasis.

3.2 CHOLINERGIC AGENTS (PARASYMPATHOMIMETICS)

The cholinergic drugs are chemicals that act at the same sites as the neurotransmitter acetylcholine (ACh). They are drugs which stimulate the parasympathetic system, and imitate or mimic the actions of acetylcholine. Thus, these drugs are also called **parasympathomimetics** or **cholinomimetics**.

Acetylcholine is of no therapeutic value, because **firstly** it has a widespread action at all cholinergic sites throughout the body, and **secondly** it has a short duration of action as it is very susceptible to hydrolysis by cholinesterase. However, the knowledge of its actions forms the basis for understanding the pharmacology, toxicology and therapeutic usefulness of other muscarinic agents. Hence, it is the **prototype** cholinergic drug.

THE CHOLINERGIC RECEPTORS

The cholinergic receptors are of two types: (*i*) **muscarinic** which are located in tissue innervated by the postganglionic parasympathetic nerves, sweat glands and blood vessels; and (*ii*) **nicotinic** which are located in the autonomic ganglia (both parasympathetic and sympathetic), the neuromuscular junction, the adrenal medulla and in the CNS. ACh is the physiological stimulant of both muscarinic and nicotinic receptors.

The distinction between the two types of receptors has practical importance, because the response of organ systems to other stimulants (agonists) and blockers (antagonists) differs **(Table 3.2-1)**.

The **muscarinic receptor** is located on the outer lipoprotein layer of the postsynaptic membrane, and the ACh molecule combines with it due to a spatial fit and electrostatic attraction. The ACh molecule is presumably composed of *three* parts, each of which plays a role in the drug receptor combination. The quaternized nitrogen atom bearing a strong **positive** charge is the centre of the so called **cationic head** and gives ACh its basic character. The cationic head fits into a depression in the receptor surface, the **anionic site**, which bears a negative electrical charge **(Fig. 3.2.1)**.

The **alkylamine chain** provides a bridge of the correct length between the cationic head and the acetyl group of the ACh molecule. Increase or decrease in the length of the alkylamine chain markedly reduces the muscarinic potency. This chain also aids the combination of the ACh molecule with the receptor by van der Waal's forces or bonds.

Table 3.2-1 *The cholinergic receptors and drug response*

	Muscarinic receptors	*Nicotinic receptors*	
Agonists	Acetylcholine	Acetylcholine	
	Carbachol	Carbachol	
	Muscarine	Nicotine	
	Methacholine		
	Pilocarpine		
Antagonists	Atropine	Hexamethonium	at autonomic ganglia
	Hyoscine	Mecamylamine	
	Homatropine etc.	Pempidine etc.	
		Tubocurarine	at skeletal neuromuscular junction
		Gallamine etc.	

The **acetyl group** forms the third part of the ACh molecule and bears an overall **negative** charge. This group is thought to fit into a depression in the receptor surface bearing a positive charge and called the **esteratic site**. It may be stressed here that this is only a hypothetical picture of the ACh-receptor interaction and some experimental observations remain unexplained.

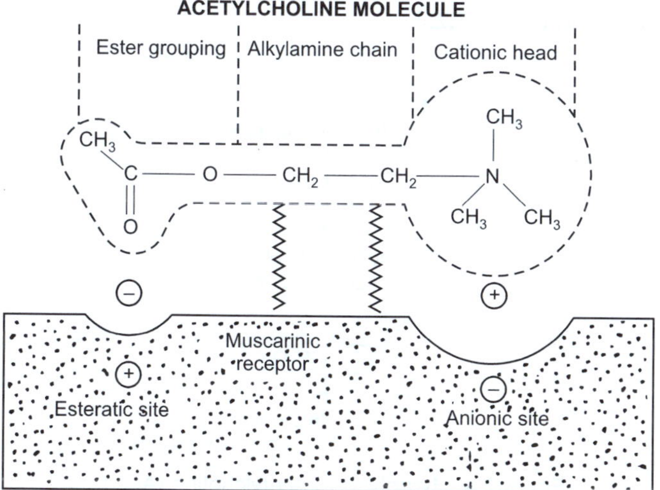

Fig. 3.2.1: Hypothetical illustration of the mechanisms involved in the combination of an acetylcholine molecule with a muscarinic receptor.

The nature of the **nicotinic receptor** is rather unclear. The features which distinguish drug molecules with nicotinic activity from those with muscarinic receptors are insignificant. There is evidence that nicotinic receptors in autonomic ganglia are partly anionic in nature, so that they can enter into salt formation with the cationic head of the ACh molecule and cationic heads of bi-quaternary compounds. A recent concept about the nicotinic receptor in the skeletal muscle pictures it as a **pore** in the end plate membrane. The rim of the pore is composed of **anionic sites** and inside the lumen of the pore are the sites at which the ester groups are bound to **esteratic sites**. It has been suggested that ACh antagonists at nicotinic sites in the skeletal muscle, like d-tubocurarine, have molecules bulky enough to cover the orifice of the pore, and thus prevent the access of acetylcholine to the **anionic** and **esteratic** sites.

Biosynthesis, Storage and Release of Acetylcholine

ACh is the acetic acid ester of choline. It is synthesized within the cholinergic neurones by the transfer of an acetyl group from acetyl-coenzyme A to the organic base choline. A specific enzyme choline acetyltransferase (choline acetylase) is necessary for this reaction. Coenzyme A is widely distributed in the body and choline is an essential dietary constituent, belonging to the B complex group of vitamins. Choline acetyltransferase is synthesized in the cell bodies of the cholinergic neurones. ACh is produced throughout the neurone, and is stored in the **synaptic vesicles** which are mainly accumulated at the nerve ending. Another view is that the synthesis of ACh takes place within the synaptic vesicles. ACh synthesis takes place in *three* steps:

In mitochondria:

Step I Acetate + ATP → Adenylacetate

In axonal cytoplasm:

Step II Adenylacetate + coenzyme A $\xrightarrow{\text{acetylkinase}}$ Acetyl-Coenzyme A (Acetyl-Co A)

Step III Acetyl-CoA + Choline $\xrightarrow{\text{Choline acetylase}}$ ACETYLCHOLINE + CoA

The major source of energy for Step II is adenosine triphosphate (ATP)

Neuronal ACh is mainly stored in the synaptic vesicles, which are 300 to 600 Angstrom units in diameter. In the vesicles it is protected from hydrolysis. On the receipt of a stimulus they combine with the membrane of the nerve ending and discharge their content of ACh into the synaptic cleft by a process of **exocytosis**. Sufficient "quanta" of ACh are released which combine with the specific receptors to produce a response. Under resting conditions insufficient quanta of ACh are released to combine with the postsynaptic receptors and no response is produced. Synthesis of ACh in the neurone is in some way controlled by the passing impulses themselves. It seems that the calcium ions play a major role in the release process of ACh **(Fig. 3.2.2)**. Experimentally it has been found that hemicholinium (HC-3) and triethylcholine (TEC) are two substances which induce a failure of transmission in cholinergic nerves by interfering with ACh synthesis. The ACh released in the synaptic cleft is rapidly hydrolysed by the enzyme acetylcholinesterase (AChE) within a few milliseconds. A part of the choline thus formed is reabsorbed by the presynaptic terminals and later reused in ACh synthesis, and the other part is washed off in the circulation.

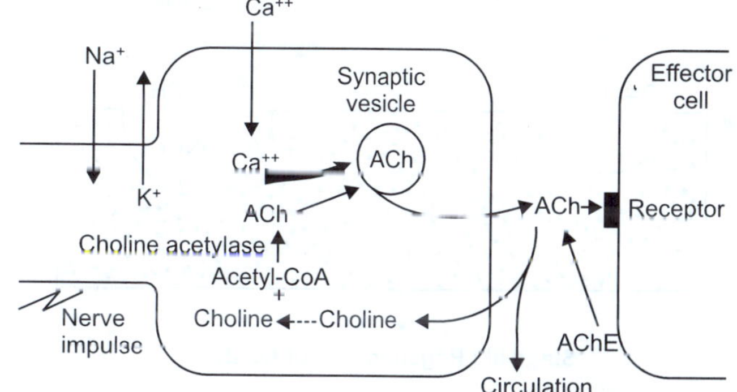

Fig. 3.2.2: Diagrammatic representation of events taking place at a typical cholinergic synapse. The mechanism of release of ACh is uncertain, and possibly requires calcium. On hydrolysis by acetylcholinesterase (AChE) choline is released into circulation and a part of it is taken up by the presynaptic terminals. (see text).

Hydrolysis of Acetylcholine

The members of the family of enzymes responsible for the hydrolysis of ACh and other choline esters are called

cholinesterases. Various types of esterases are found in animal tissue, but only two are discussed here. "True" cholinesterase is the enzyme which hydrolyses ACh liberated at the nerve endings. It is found in the nervous tissues, human placenta and the erythrocytes. It is also called **specific cholinesterase** or **acetylcholinesterase**. AChE has a high affinity for ACh and is mainly responsible for the hydrolysis of endogenously released ACh. "Pseudo" cholinesterase, also known as **nonspecific cholinesterase** is found in the blood serum, intestines, skin and many other tissues. The physiological function of pseudocholinesterase is uncertain.

Acetylcholinesterase is responsible for the *in vivo* hydrolysis of ACh, which is evidenced by the fact that there is a good correlation between the distribution of AChE, ACh and choline acetylase. The hydrolysis of ACh by AChE takes place in **three** stages **(Fig. 3.2.3)**.

In the **first stage** the cationic head of ACh is adsorbed on the anionic site of the AChE molecule and forms a salt. The ester group of ACh is adsorbed on the esteratic site of the AChE molecule. ACh is thus adsorbed on the enzyme to form a substrate enzyme complex. The exact mode of adsorption is uncertain.

Stage I : Adsorption of ACh on AChE (substrate:enzyme complex)
Ester grouping | Alkylamine chain | Cationic head
Esteratic site | ACh E molecule | Anionic site
Stage II : Splitting and choline release
Choline
Stage III : Regeneration of AChE
Acetic acid

Fig. 3.2.3: Hydrolysis of acetylcholine (ACh) by acetylcholinesterase (AChE).

The **second stage** of hydrolysis involves splitting. The substrate enzyme complex reacts to release choline and leaves an acetylated enzyme.

The **third stage** of hydrolysis leads to regeneration of the enzyme. The acetylated enzyme reacts with water to give acetic acid and liberates the enzyme. Thus, the enzyme is regenerated. In a simplified manner it is presented in **Fig. 3.2.4**.

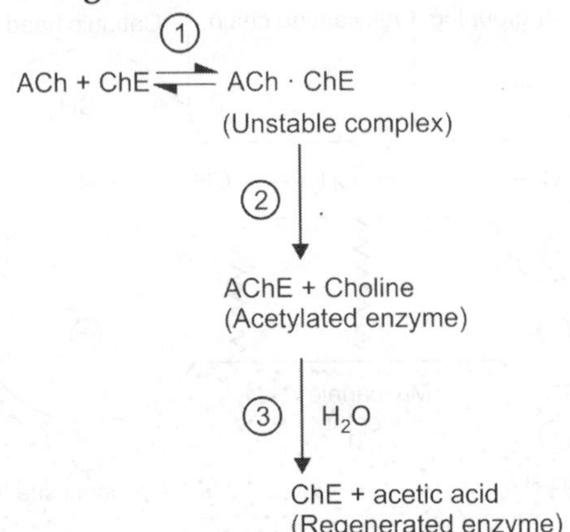

Fig. 3.2.4: Hydrolysis of acetylcholine (ACh)

Basically cholinergic transmission is similar at all sites in the body. It is summarized in **Fig. 3.2.5**.

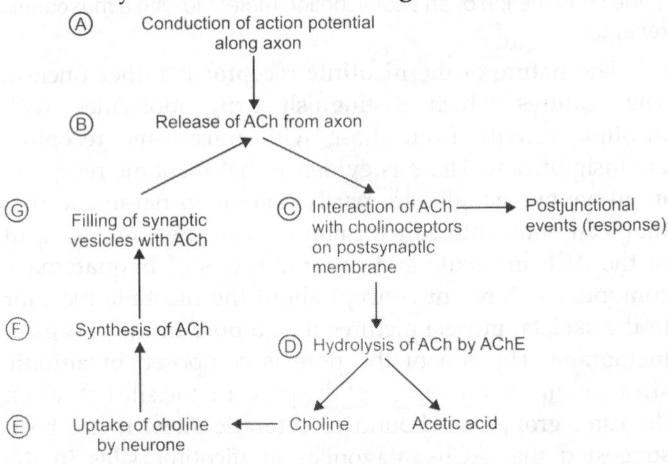

Fig. 3.2.5: Cholinergic neurotransmission in the body.

Classification of Cholinergic Drugs

The cholinergic drugs may be grouped as under:

Direct-acting Cholinergics

Group I. Acetylcholine and related choline esters

(*i*) Acetylcholine
(*ii*) Methacholine
(*iii*) Carbamylcholine
(*iv*) Bethanechol

(These drugs stimulate structures innervated by the preganglionic sympathetic fibres, and the pre- and postganglionic parasympathetic fibres.)

Group II. Cholinomimetic alkaloids

(*i*) Pilocarpine
(*ii*) Muscarine
(*iii*) Arecholine

(These drugs stimulate structures innervated by the postganglionic parasympathetic fibres mainly).

Indirect-acting Cholinergics

Group III. The anticholinesterase agents

(*a*) **Reversible anticholinesterases**

(*i*) Physostigmine
(*ii*) Neostigmine
(*iii*) Pyridostigmine
(*iv*) Ambenonium
(*v*) Edrophonium
(*vi*) Distigmine
(*vii*) Demecarium

(*b*) **Irreversible anticholinesterases** (Organophosphorus compounds)

(*i*) Di-isopropylfluorophosphonate (DFP)
(*ii*) Ecothiopate
(*iii*) Tetraethyl pyrophosphate (TEPP)
(*iv*) Octamethyl pyrophosphoramide (OMPA)
(*v*) Malathion
(*vi*) Parathion

(These compounds inhibit cholinesterase, preserve ACh and indirectly act as cholinergic agents).

CHOLINE ESTERS

Acetylcholine (ACh)

Choline, the parent substance, produces ACh-like effects but the activity is very feeble. Its activity is increased several thousand times by esterification. Choline as such is used in the treatment of hepatic dysfunction as a **lipotropic factor**.

ACh is the acetic acid ester of choline, and is the physiological stimulant of both muscarinic and nicotinic receptors. For this reason ACh administration produces widespread effects on various organs which are of little clinical value. In addition to this lack of specificity, its use as a drug is further limited by its rapid hydrolysis by cholinesterase in the body, and by its total ineffectiveness on oral administration.

Pharmacological Actions

Henry Dale (1914) through his classical experiment demonstrated the **muscarinic** and **nicotinic** actions of ACh on the blood pressure of anaesthetized cat. It is an ingeneous and informative experiment marked by its simplicity **(Fig. 3.2.6)**.

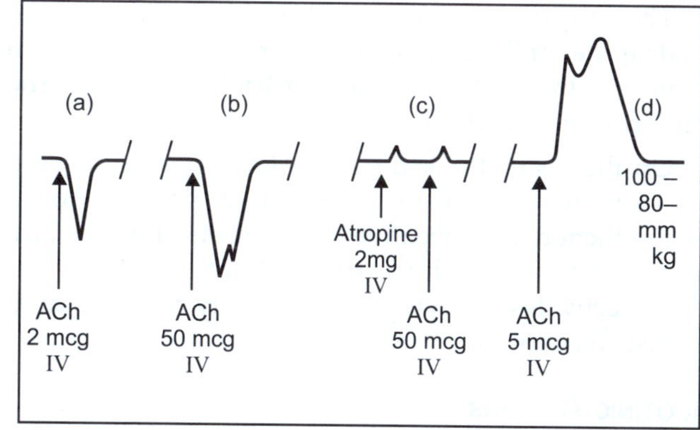

Fig. 3.2.6: Dale's demonstration of the muscarinic and nicotinic actions of ACh on the blood pressure (BP) of anaesthetized cat (diagrammatic). In (*a*) ACh 2 mcg injected intravenously (IV) caused a fall in BP mainly due to peripheral vasodilation; (*b*) ACh 50 mcg IV caused a fall due to slowing of heart plus vasodilatation; (*c*) after atropinization (2 mg IV, interval 20 minutes) ACh 50 mcg IV showed no effect; and (*d*) after atropinization ACh 5 mg caused a rise in BP - *first* due to stimulation of autonomic ganglia, and *second* due to stimulation of the adrenal medulla and discharge of catecholamines, adrenaline and noradrenaline. Panels (*a*) and (*b*) show *muscarinic* and (*d*) shows *nicotinic* actions of ACh following atropinization.

The muscarinic action of ACh is the predominent action on BP, whereas the nicotinic action is unmasked only on **atropinization** of the animal. The nicotinic action (rise in BP) can be further accentuated by injection of **physostigmine** or **neostigmine** into the atropinized animal, followed by ACh administration. This step conserves ACh at cholinergic sites.

Muscarinic Actions

The muscarinic actions of ACh correspond to those produced by the alkaloid, **muscarine**. ACh released from the postganglionic parasympathetic nerves produces most of these effects, and they are exerted on the **cardiovascular system, smooth muscles** and **exocrine glands**. A few sympathetic postganglionic nerves are also cholinergic, and produce muscarinic actions like secretion of sweat, and vasodilatation in skeletal muscle and in some areas of the skin. The muscarinic actions are enumerated below:

1. Slowing of the heart, and arteriolar vasodilatation in slightly higher doses, and a fall in blood pressure.
2. Stimulation of the smooth muscles of the bronchi, the gastrointestinal tract, the gall bladder and bile duct, urinary bladder and ureters.
3. Relaxation of the sphincters in the gastrointestinal, biliary and urinary tracts.
4. Stimulation of the salivary, sweat, nasopharyngeal, and lacrimal glands, and stimulation of the secretory activity of the stomach, intestines and pancreas.
5. Constriction of the pupil (miosis) and accommodation of the lens for near vision.

The muscarinic actions of ACh are blocked or inhibited by **atropine**, and other anticholinergic drugs. They are mimicked by **methacholine**, **carbachol**, **pilocarpine**, **muscarine** and **arecholine**.

On the heart, the actions of ACh resemble those of vagal stimulation, causing bradycardia, prolongation of AV conduction, and negative inotropic effect on the atria and ventricles. The fall in arterial BP produced by ACh reflexly activates the sympathetic activity resulting in an increase in heart rate.

Nicotinic Actions

These are so called because they resemble the pharmacological actions of small quantities of the alkaloid, **nicotine**. They are exerted at the skeletal neuromuscular junction, autonomic ganglia, adrenal medulla and the CNS. The nicotinic actions are enumerated below:

1. Stimulation of the skeletal muscle.
2. Stimulation of sympathetic and parasympathetic ganglia, and stimulation of the adrenal medulla (the arterial BP rises).
3. The actions of ACh in the CNS are described in **Chapter 3.6.** The CNS seems to possess both muscarinic and nicotinic receptors.

The nicotinic actions of ACh are blocked or inhibited by **curare (d-tubocurarine)** at the neuromuscular junction, and by ganglion blocking agents **(pentolinium)** at the autonomic ganglia.

Mechanism of Action

The interaction of ACh with the cholinergic receptor may produce one of the following types of changes in the permeability of the postsynaptic membrane: (*i*) **nonspecific** changes causing an increased permeability to all ions (sodium, potassium and chloride) which result in depolarization or an excitatory postsynaptic potential (EPSP); and (*ii*) **selective permeability** changes to only small ions (potassium and chloride) which produce stabilization or hyperpolarization of the membrane termed as inhibitory postsynaptic potential (IPSP).

In the presence of ACh the membrane becomes more permeable to one or more of the various ions (potassium, sodium and calcium). The pre-existing flux equilibrium is disturbed, and the membrane potential is altered. The direction of change (depolarization or hyperpolarization) depends on the magnitude of the membrane potential and the ratio between the increase in sodium (Na^+) and potassium (K^+) conductance. Under the influence of ACh the membrane permeabilities for K^+ and Na^+ increase unequally. Either the ratio of permeability for K^+ to that of Na^+ is increased, leading to **hyperpolarization**, or the ratio is decreased leading to **depolarization**. In general, hyperpolarization depresses cellular activity, and depolarization increases cellular activity. The result of ACh action is either hyperpolarization (as in myocardial pacemaker cells), or depolarization (as in smooth muscles). Because of such a **dual action** ACh relaxes the smooth muscle in many peripheral blood vessels (hyperpolarization), and stimulates the smooth muscle of the gut (depolarization).

Therapeutic uses. ACh has no safe therapeutic uses as discussed earlier. Lately, a 1 percent solution of **acetylcholine chloride** with 5 percent mannitol (Miochol) has been used for constricting the pupil during corneal grafting operations.

Methacholine (Acetyl Beta-Methylcholine)

Methacholine only differs from ACh in having a methyl group substituted on the beta-carbon atom **(Fig. 3.2.7)**. This chemical change has little effect on its muscarinic activity, but has completely **abolished its nicotinic effects**. In addition, compared to ACh, methacholine is very slowly hydrolysed by acetylcholinesterase, and is virtually resistant to destruction by pseudocholinesterase. **Thus methacholine has a longer duration of action than ACh, and is practically specific for muscarinic receptors.** Methacholine can be administered orally but is poorly and irregularly absorbed.

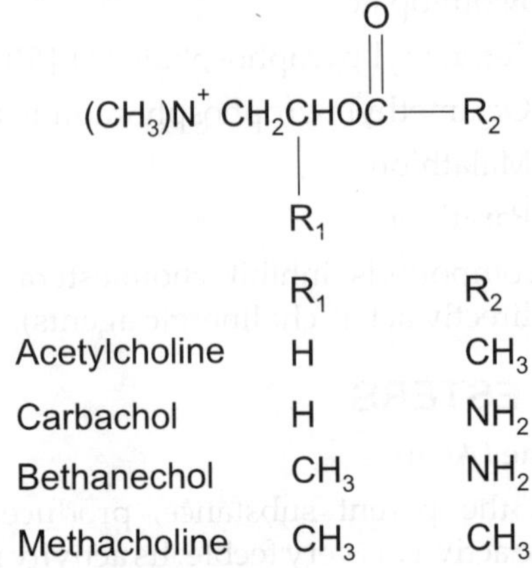

Fig. 3.2.7: Chemical structures of the choline esters

Therapeutic Uses

1. **Paroxysmal atrial tachycardia**. When mechanical measures have failed to stimulate the vagus, methacholine in a dose of 10 to 40 mg subcutaneously may be administered. This use is not without hazards, and the action may be blocked by administration of atropine 0.5 to 1 mg subcutaneously, if need arises.
2. It may be used to treat **glaucoma**, but pilocarpine is a better drug.

Carbamylcholine (Carbachol)

Carbachol is the most potent choline ester. It is derived from ACh by the substitution of an amide group on the acyl carbon atom. Carbachol is not readily hydrolysed by cholinesterase, and has *both* muscarinic and nicotinic actions, but the muscarinic actions predominate **(Table 3.2-2)**.

Table 3.2.-2: *Cholinergic receptor activation profile of choline esters*

Drug	*Muscarinic Receptor Activation*			*Nicotinic Receptor Activation*	*Inactivation by Cholinesterase*
	GI/Urinary	*Cardiovascular*	*Ocular*		
Acetylcholine	++	++	+	++	Yes
Methacholine	++	++	+	None	Slow hydrolysis
Carbamylcholine	+++	+	++	+++	No
Bethanechol	+++	+	++	None	No

Key: Strong +++; Moderate ++; Weak +

Therapeutic uses. Carbachol may be used to treat postoperative **intestinal atony** and **retention of urine**. **Occasionally**, it is used to treat **paroxysmal atrial tachycardia** and **glaucoma**. Carbachol is usually administered subcutaneously in doses of 0.25 to 0.5 mg or orally 1 to 4 mg daily.

Bethanechol (Urecholine)

Bethanechol has structural features common to both methacholine and carbachol, i.e., it contains both the amide group of carbachol and the beta-methyl group of methacholine. It is not hydrolysed by cholinesterase. It is **devoid of nicotinic actions of ACh**, and is principally a muscarinic agent, with a selective action on the gastrointestinal tract and urinary bladder. It is used as a long-acting muscarinic stimulant.

Therapeutic uses. It is used to treat abdominal distention, **paralytic ileus** and for **postoperative urinary retention**. Bethanechol is active by mouth (dose 30-120 mg daily), and by subcutaneous route (dose 2.5 to 30 mg daily). It should never be administered by the IV or IM route, as severe cholinergic overstimulation can occur.

Cholinomimetic Alkaloids

Pilocarpine

Pilocarpine is an alkaloid obtained from the leaflets of **Maranham jaborandi** or **Pilocarpus microphylus**. The hydrochloride salt is hygroscopic and inactivated by light. The nitrate salt is not hygroscopic and is often preferred to the hydrochloride. It stimulates the muscarinic receptors at the postganglionic neuroeffector junction **directly**.

Pilocarpine is a potent stimulant of glandular tissue such as sweat and salivary glands. It has a marked **diaphoretic** effect and produces profuse sweating, as much as 2 to 3 litres in a few hours. It acts as a **sialogogue** and increases salivary secretion to about 350 ml in a few hours.

On the smooth muscles, pilocarpine augments gastrointestinal motility, and increases gastric and pancreatic secretions. Pilocarpine when injected subcutaneously or instilled in the eye causes a constriction of the pupil (miosis) within 10 to 15 minutes, and spasm of accommodation which lasts for 2 to 3 days.

On the cardiovascular system, pilocarpine may induce hypertension and tachycardia due to its nicotinic actions. Atropine blocks the peripheral actions of pilocarpine, and is the best physiologic antidote for pilocarpine intoxication.

Clinically pilocarpine is mainly employed in the treatment of *chronic glaucoma* as a 0.5 to 4 percent solution. It may be used to control **mydriasis** and **cycloplegia** produced by atropine and ganglion blockers. Pilocarpine ocular therapeutic system (Ocusert Pilo) is a continuous-release form of pilocarpine (20 mcg/hour or 40 mcg/hour) placed into the lower conjunctional cul-de-sac. It provides for effective concentrations of pilocarpine in **open-angle glaucoma** for a week.

Muscarine

Muscarine is an alkaloid obtained from the poisonous mushroom **Amanita muscaria**. It is a choline derivative and like ACh stimulates the activity of the effector cells in organs innervated by cholinergic nerves. Unlike ACh it does not stimulate the skeletal muscle and the autonomic ganglia. The cholinergic and toxic actions of muscarine can be effectively blocked by **atropine**. Muscarine has no therapeutic use.

Arecholine

Arecholine is obtained from the betel nut **Areca catechu**. It has a muscarinic and weak nicotinic activity somewhat like pilocarpine. Betel nuts as such, and preparations containing powdered betel nuts are popularly chewed in India to promote salivary secretion and to aid digestion. Arecholine has no therapeutic application in man, but it is used as a laxative and vermifuge for dogs in veterinary medicine.

Side Effects and Contraindications of Muscarinic Agents

The muscarinic agents affect various organ systems. The muscarinic type effects on gastrointestinal tract include belching, epigastric distress, abdominal cramps, tenesmus, diarrhoea, nausea and vomiting. On the cardiovascular system they may cause bradycardia and sometimes reflex cardioacceleration and hypertension.

Involuntary micturation; blurring of vision and miosis; and bronchospasm with increased bronchial secretion and wheezing may occur. There may be profuse sweating, salivation and lacrimation. The exaggerated nicotinic effects are skeletal muscle fasciculations, twitching, cramps, weakness and paralysis of skeletal muscles.

Based on the above adverse effects, muscarinic agents, are **contraindicated** in peptic ulcer, recent myocardial infarction, hyperthyroidism, urinary bladder neck obstruction, bronchial asthma, pulmonary oedema and in cholinergic crisis.

ANTICHOLINESTERASES

Anticholinesterases or **cholinesterase inhibitors** effectively inhibit the enzyme acetylcholinesterase so that it is unable to hydrolyse ACh, and thus they preserve ACh at the nerve ending. Their action is **indirect**. Anticholinesterase agents are classified as **reversible** or **irreversible** inhibitors of acetylcholinesterase (AChE).

Mechanism of Action

The **reversible** inhibitors can interact with AChE in two ways. **Firstly**, a reversible complex between the inhibitor and the enzyme is formed (step I), and steps I and III occur slowly. **Physostigmine** and **neostigmine** are examples of this type, and can delay hydrolysis of ACh from 1 to 8 hours. **Secondly**, a reversible complex between the enzyme and the inhibitor is formed (step I), but steps analogous to steps II and III do not occur, and the duration of action is short. **Edrophonium** is an example of this type. In addition, neostigmine and edrophonium have a direct stimulating action at cholinergic sites.

The **irreversible cholinesterase inhibitors** are mostly organophosphate compounds. They are widely used as ingredients of many insecticides (malathion, parathion) and war gases (sarin, tabun). With the organophosphates steps corresponding to steps I and II occur very rapidly, but step III either does not occur, or occurs extremely slowly with the result that the enzyme AChE is not regenerated. Thus, these drugs produce almost a permanent inactivation of the enzyme AChE, and for this reason their therapeutic usefulness is very limited.

Pharmacological Actions

As mentioned earlier, clinically the reversible cholinesterase inhibitors are used. They induce generalized muscarinic cholinergic responses which include decrease in heart rate; vasodilatation with fall in arterial blood pressure; increase in skin temperature; increased gastrointestinal motility; bronchial constriction; pupillary constriction (miosis); increased secretions of salivary, sweat, gastric and mucosal glands. Local application into the conjunctival sac results in miosis, spasm of the ciliary muscle and accommodation for near vision.

Cholinesterase inhibitors, in low doses have little effect at the skeletal neuromuscular junction. At higher doses muscle fasciculations occur, associated with an increase in the miniature end plate potentials and excitatory postsynaptic potentials, conversion of twitch to tetanus and ultimately a depolarizing block may be seen, as in cases of **myasthenia gravis in cholinergic crisis** (see later).

A variety of effects are produced on the CNS by cholinesterase inhibitors which cross the blood-brain barrier e.g., physostigmine which contains a tertiary nitrogen (neostigmine does not penetrate the blood-brain barrier as it has quaternary nitrogen). The effects on the CNS include stimulation followed by depression, sleep disturbances, tremor and ataxia, hallucinations and dyssynchronization of the electroencephalogram (EEG).

REVERSIBLE ANTICHOLINESTERASES

Physostigmine (Eserine)

Physostigmine salicylate and sulphate are the salts of an alkaloid obtained from the dried ripe seeds of **Physostigma venenosum** which is indigenous to tropical West Africa.

Physostigmine is a tertiary ammonium alkaloid. It is well absorbed from the gastrointestinal tract and enters the CNS. It is equally active against true cholinesterase (AChE) and pseudocholinesterase.

Therapeutic uses and dosage. Physostigmine salicylate is administered orally in doses of 0.5 to 1.0 mg with a maximum recommended dose of 3 mg in 24 hours, or by IM route in a dose of 0.5 mg. Physostigmine sulphate is preferred to salicylate in eye-drop preparations which usually contain 0.25 or 0.5 percent physostigmine sulphate. Physostigmine (0.25–0.5%) and pilocarpine (2–4%) drops are available as a mixture.

The main clinical use of physostigmine in the form of eye-drops is as a miotic to treat **glaucoma**. It is also used to reverse the mydriatic effect of atropine or homatropine, when used for refraction of the eye. Physostigmine drops may be used alternately with homatropine to prevent adhesions between the cornea and the iris after certain surgical ocular procedures. The use of physostigmine is presently confined to the eye conditions. Its main systemic use is in the **treatment of atropine poisoning**. Physostigmine may be used in the early stages of **Alzheimer's disease** to improve memory, although results have been variable.

Neostigmine (Prostigmin)

Neostigmine is a synthetic quaternary ammonium compound with a rapid onset of action, and similar reversible anticholinesterase activity to physostigmine. It differs from physostigmine in that it is a **quaternary nitrogen compound**, and is irregularly absorbed from the gastrointestinal tract, and it does not cross the blood-brain barrier. Neostigmine also has somewhat stronger effects at nicotinic sites, including the skeletal myoneural junction. Because of the presence of quaternary nitrogen it has a **direct** action on both nicotinic and muscarinic receptors, which makes it specially useful for its effect at the neuromuscular junction. Thus at the neuromuscular junction, it produces the contraction of the skeletal muscle by two ways: **firstly**, by a direct action on the skeletal muscle, and **secondly** by inactivation of cholinesterase. Neostigmine has a powerful anticurare action.

Therapeutic uses. Neostigmine is extensively used in the treatment of **myasthenia gravis**. The unwanted autonomic side effects may be abolished by atropine. In myasthenia neostigmine may be given by injection, or more conveniently orally (dose 15 to 30 mg tid or qid daily). It is also used as an **antidote for curare poisoning**.

Dosage. Orally, neostigmine bromide 15 mg thrice daily; neostigmine methylsulphate 0.25 to 1.0 mg SC or IM.

PYRIDOSTIGMINE

Pyridostigmine is chemically and pharmacologically closely related to neostigmine. It is slow in onset, weaker in action (1/2 to 1/4th) than neostigmine, but has a longer duration of action. It offers little advantage over neostigmine in its clinical use. Pyridostigmine is mainly used in the treatment of **myasthenia gravis**. The usual dosage of pyridostigmine bromide is 60 to 240 mg orally, or 1 to 5 mg IM or SC.

AMBENONIUM

Ambenonium is a bis-quaternary reversible anti-cholinesterase agent with about six times greater activity than neostigmine. It facilitates transmission at the neuromuscular junction, and has **anticurare** actions, but in higher doses it blocks the neuromuscular junction. It is usually given orally in a dose of 5 to 25 mg to patients of **myasthenia gravis** who cannot tolerate neostigmine or pyridostigmine.

EDROPHONIUM

Edrophonium is a short-acting cholinesterase inhibitor. It acts only at the anionic site to form a rapidly reversible enzyme-substrate complex, and for this reason is a weak anticholinesterase agent. It also has a direct stimulant action at the motor end plate. Edrophonium has little effect at the postganglionic parasympathetic neuroeffector junction. It is an effective anticurare agent, but its application in patients of myasthenia gravis is limited to its use in the **differential diagnosis** of the disease, and in emergency treatment of a myasthenic crisis.

Edrophonium is an important agent in establishing the **diagnosis** of myasthenia gravis and in differentiating between "myasthenic crisis" and "cholinergic crisis". Both these crises are marked by muscle weakness and sometimes clinical differentiation is not possible, though the line of treatment is grossly different. Myasthenic crisis is due to ACh lack, whereas, cholinergic crisis is due to ACh excess.

The **edrophonium test** has been devised to differentiate between **myasthenic** and **cholinergic crises**. Edrophonium chloride is administered in a dose of 1 to 2 mg IV. If the patients condition improves within 3 minutes the crisis is myasthenic, but if there is no response or exacerbation of symptoms occurs the crisis is cholinergic.

DISTIGMINE

Distigmine has a longer duration of action than neostigmine and its action lasts for 24 hours. It is used to treat **atony** of the bladder and intestines, and may be repeated every second or third day. The usual dose is 5 mg orally or 0.5 mg by IM injection.

DEMECARIUM

This compound consists of two neostigmine molecules joined together. It is more potent than neostigmine and has a very prolonged effect. Its main use is in the management of **glaucoma**. The usual dosage in **glaucoma** is from 2 drops of a 0.25 percent solution instilled twice weekly to 1 to 2 drops twice daily. Demecarium is also used in the management of **accommodative convergent strabisums** (esotropia), affecting children.

IRREVERSIBLE ANTICHOLINESTERASES

As mentioned earlier, organophosphate cholinesterase inhibitors like DFP, phospholine, parathion and malathion are highly toxic compounds as they produce an *irreversible* inhibition of both acetylcholinesterase and pseudocholinesterase. These agents were developed for potential **chemical warfare**, mainly in Germany. Later they were developed as **insecticides** and **pesticides** for use in agriculture. Only the following two agents are used in ophthalmic practice.

DI-ISOPROPYLFLOUROPHOSPHONATE (ISOFLUROPHATE, DFP)

DFP is a clear liquid and forms **unstable** solutions in water. For clinical use it is dissolved in arachis oil. It first inhibits pseudocholinesterase and then acetylcholinesterase, and its duration of action is about 10 days.

DFP is used topically as an instillation of 0.1 percent solution into the conjunctival sac for the treatment of **glaucoma**. It is employed only when other miotics have failed. A 0.02 percent solution is occasionally used in the treatment of **esotropia**.

ECOTHIOPATE (ECHOTHIOPHATE)

Ecothiopate has the advantage over DFP that it forms a *stable* solution in water, and avoids the need for oily drops. When instilled into the eye, escothiopate produces a miotic effect within 45 minutes which may persist for one to four weeks.

Ecothiopate iodide is available as a 0.06, 0.0125 and 0.25 percent aqueous solution. The usual dose in the treatment of **glaucoma** is 1 drop once or twice daily. Ecothiopate 0.25 percent strength may be used for short periods in the treatment of **esotropia**.

In general, the same contraindications apply to the anticholinesterases as to choline esters and cholinomimetic alkaloids. Thus, they may produce bronchoconstriction and precipitate attacks of asthma. They may induce gastric ulceration and other toxic manifestations as enumerated earlier.

Organophosphate Anticholinesterase Poisoning

Most pronounced effects are profuse sweating and salivation; muscular weakness and fasciculations; mental confusion and marked ataxia; severe dehydration; severe nausea, vomiting and intestinal cramps; bronchoconstriction and increased bronchial secretions; respiratory paralysis and death. Delayed neurotoxic effects are seen on chronic poisoning or exposure to organophosphate pesticides. Polyneuritis with flaccid paralysis of the extremities may result.

Treatment of Anticholinesterase Poisoning

1. **Atropine.** The autonomic effects can usually be controlled with atropine as a specific and effective antidote. It is given in a dose of 1 mg IM or subcutaneously, repeated frequently until the muscarinic effects are controlled.

2. **Supportive measures** include artificial respiration and fluid/electrolyte therapy.

3. **Pralidoxime (Pyridine-2-aldoxime methiodide, PAM).** It is an antidote of a different kind and is a **cholinesterase reactivator**. PAM breaks the bonds between the organophosphate poison and the molecular surface of acetylcholinesterase. Thus the enzyme is freed and reactivated to hydrolyse the excess of ACh at the receptor sites. Pralidoxime is effective mainly at the skeletal neuromuscular junction, and to some extent at the muscarinic sites, but is ineffective in the CNS.

In severe poisoning by parathion or similar pesticides, pralidoxime is given in an **initial** dose of 1 to 2 g infused intravenously with 1 to 2 mg of atropine. A **second** similar dose may be administered if muscle weakness continues for 1 hour after the first injection. Additional doses may be given IM or subcutaneously later, if needed, along with atropine.

Pharmacotherapy of Myasthenia Gravis

Myasthenia gravis is a chronic disease characterized by progressive weakness and rapid fatiguability of the skeletal muscles due to impaired neuromuscular transmission. It is suggested that the end plates are morphologically abnormal. They are elongated with widening of the synaptic cleft. The number and size of the synaptic vesicles is normal. The muscles commonly affected are those of the head and neck, and later the disease progresses to permanent muscle paralysis. Dysphagia and dysarthria may be the first symptoms, and this disease is more common in women. Further the cause of myasthenia gravis is almost certainly due to antibodies directed towards the ACh receptors. Such antibodies can be detected in most patients with acute myasthenia, and it is postulated that they interfere with ACh reception at the motor end plate. Recent studies show that this **autoimmune reaction** reduces the number of available ACh receptors on the postsynaptic membrane of the neuromuscular junctions. The drugs employed are:

(*a*) **Reversible anticholinesterases**. The drugs used are neostigmine, pyridostigmine, ambenonium and edrophonium (diagnosis only). Parasympathetic side effects (abdominal pain, diarrhoea, excessive salivation, nausea and sweating) often are an indication for atropine. The usual dosage is as under:

Neostigmine 15–30 mg tid or qid orally

Pyridostigmine 60–120 mg 3 to 4 hourly orally

Ambenonium 5–25 mg tid or qid orally.

(*b*) **Adrenal glucocorticoids**. Oral treatment with prednisone is beneficial in patients with severe myasthenia gravis not controlled by anticholinesterases or thymectomy. Long-term alternate-day treatment with prednisone reportedly produces good results. **Plasmapheresis** may be useful to prepare patients for **thymectomy**.

(c) **Ephedrine sulphate**. This sympathomimetic amine has appreciable anticurare action. In a dose of 12 mg with each dose of neostigmine, it often enhances the action of neostigmine.

Patients with myasthenia gravis are at risk of respiratory insufficiency due to an acute exacerbation of weakness, mainly affecting the bulbar and respiratory muscles. An acute myasthenic crisis can be precipitated by infection, surgery, childbirth, emotional stress and certain drugs which affect neuromuscular transmission **(Table 3.2-3)**.

Table 3.2-3. *Drugs contraindicated, or used with caution in myasthenia gravis.*

Group	*Drug*
Aminoglycoside antibiotics	Streptomycin
	Gentamicin
	Kanamycin
Antiarrhythmic agents	Lignocaine
	Beta-blockers
	Procainamide
	Quinidine
CNS depressants	Chlorpromazine
	Barbiturates
	Morphine

Pharmacotherapy of Glaucoma

The glaucomas constitute a group of ocular diseases in which an elevated intraocular pressure (IOP) damages the optic nerve head, causing visual loss. The pathophysiology of pressure-induced nerve damage is poorly understood; probably ischaemia and direct compression cause the damage. There are **two** types of primary glaucoma: (*i*) **open or wide angle** (chronic, simple); and (*ii*) **narrow angle** (acute, congestive). In addition, there is **secondary** and **congenital** glaucoma. The drugs employed are:

(*a*) **The miotics**. The miotics are cholinergic drugs that stimulate the parasympathetic effector cells directly (parasympathomimetics) or inhibit cholinesterase (anticholinesterases). When applied topically to the eye these drugs cause constriction of the pupil, contraction of the ciliary muscle, and a fall in IOP due to the decreased resistance to the outflow of the aqueous humour.

(*i*) *Parasympathomimetics:* Pilocarpine, Carbachol.

(*ii*) *Short-acting anticholinesterases:* Physostigmine.

(*iii*) *Long-acting anticholinesterases:* Demecarium, DFP, Ecothiopate.

(*b*) **Adrenergic agents**. Dipivalyladrenaline is a new adrenaline analogue. It is a `prodrug' that undergoes biotransformation to become active adrenaline. This drug has better penetrability than adrenaline, and can be used in far smaller amounts without sacrificing its IOP reducing effects. Both local and systemic levels of this agent are lower, and hence fewer side effects. It is possible that dipivalyladrenaline will be used in place of adrenaline in combination with guanethidine for the treatment of glaucoma. Topical adrenaline lowers IOP apparently both by increasing aqueous outflow, and by decreasing aqueous humour formation.

(*c*) **Beta-adrenoceptor blockers.** Timolol is the agent used to lower IOP in patients with primary open-angle glaucoma and secondary glaucomas. The mode of action is unclear, but it possibly decreases the production of aqueous humour.

(*d*) **Carbonic anhydrase inhibitors.** Acetazolamide, dichlorphenamide, ethoxzolamide and methazolamide may be used. These agents are given systemically to reduce IOP.

(*e*) **Osmotic agents.** Hypertonic solutions of glycerine, isosorbide and mannitol are used for the short-term reduction of IOP.

To summarize, ACh is the neurotransmitter released from the postganglionic parasympathetic nerve endings, where it produces its effects by combining with the muscarinic receptors on the postsynaptic membrane. The combination of ACh with muscarinic receptors is the result of a spatial fit and electrostatic attraction.

ACh is not used clinically because of its widespread and transient effects. **Methacholine, carbachol** and **bethanechol** are clinically useful choline esters, and are more stable to hydrolysis by cholinesterases. **Pilocarpine** is a naturally occurring parasympathomimetic drug, with little structural resemblance to ACh. Pilocarpine acts predominantly on the muscarinic receptors.

The anticholinesterases are divided into two groups- **reversible** and **irreversible-** according to the stability of the complex formed with AChE. The reversible inhibitors which include *physostigmine, neostigmine, pyridostigmine, ambenonium* and *demecarium* are clinically used to treat atony of the gut and bladder, and to reduce intraocular pressure in glaucoma. Some members of this group are used to increase skeletal muscle strength in **myasthenia gravis** and to antagonize muscle relaxants of the d-tubocurarine type. The irreversible anticholinesterases are mostly organophosphorus compounds which produce a very stable phosphorylated form of AChE. They are highly toxic and are used as insecticides. Two members of this group, **DFP** and **ecothiopate**, are used in the treatment of **glaucoma**. Poisoning by organophosphorus compounds is treated by repeated administration of **atropine**, and **pralidoxime**. Pralidoxime regenerates the enzyme AChE.

3.3 CHOLINERGIC BLOCKING AGENTS (PARASYMPATHOLYTICS)

The Belladonna Family
- Atropine
- Atropine/Belladonna Poisoning
- Scopolamine (Hyoscine)

Synthetic Antimuscarinics (Atropine Substitutes)
- Atropine-like Mydriatics: Homatropine, Eucatropine, Cyclopentolate, Tropicamide
- Antisecretory-antispasmodics: Methantheline, Propantheline, Oxyphenonium, Homatropine Methyl Bromide
- Antiparkinsonian Drugs: Benzhexol, Procyclidine, Cycrimine, Ethopropazine, Benztropine, Orphenadrin

Cholinergic blocking agents **block** or **interfere** with the actions of acetylcholine (ACh) at the postganglionic parasympathetic nerve endings. These agents have been variously named as **parasympatholytics, spasmolytics** and **anticholinergics**. The most expressive and precise terms are **muscarinic receptor blocking agents** or **antimuscarinics**. Atropine is the classical antagonist which blocks the effects of ACh on the muscarinic cholinergic reeptors. In fact, Henry Dale in 1914 classified those actions of ACh as muscarinic actions which were mimicked by **muscarine** and abolished by **atropine**.

THE BELLADONNA FAMILY

A number of plants in the potato or *Solanaceae* family contain alkaloids of a similar chemical constitution, which dilate the pupil. They are also referred to as **mydriatic alkaloids**. The three noteworthy plants are **Atropa belladonna** (deadly night shade), **Hyoscyamus niger** (black henbane), and **Datura stramonium** (thorn apple or Jimson weed).

ATROPINE

Atropa belladonna is a bushy perennial plant, growing to a height of 1 to 1.5 metres. The principal alkaloids of belladonna are **atropine, hyoscyamine** and **scopolamine** (hyoscine). The most important alkaloid is **atropine**, which probably does not pre-exist in the plant, but is formed from its isomer l-hyoscyamine by racemization during the extraction process. **Atropine is dl-hyoscyamine**, and it may be manufactured synthetically. The l-isomer is more potent both peripherally and centrally compared to the d-form, but the racemic form is preferred as it is more stable chemically.

Mode of action. The antimuscarinic activity of atropine, hyoscine and most synthetic antimuscarinic agents is the consequence of their prolonged occupation of the muscarinic cholinergic receptors, which prevents access of ACh or choline esters to the muscarinic receptor sites. This antagonism is competitive in nature. Thus, antimuscarinic agents are **competitive antagonists** of acetylcholine at muscarinic receptor sites in the smooth muscle, cardiac muscle, exocrine glands and the CNS. Their blocking action is **surmountable** as it can be overcome by increasing the local concentration of ACh or choline esters. The antimuscarinic agents do not react chemically with ACh, nor do they alter the rate of hydrolysis of ACh. The effectiveness of these agents is greater against the muscarinic effects of injected cholinergic drugs (exogenous) than to the stimulation of cholinergic postganglionic nerves (parasympathetic system). The reason for this is possibly anatomic, as the chemical mediator (ACh) during stimulation of the parasympathetic system is released so close to the receptor that the atropine molecule which is bulky, is unable to effectively interpose itself between the agonist (ACh) and the muscarinic receptor. The actions of atropine and hyoscine on the CNS differ, atropine being a stimulant and then a depressant, while hyoscine is a depressant in all doses. The mechanism responsible is unclear.

Atropine bears some distinct chemical similarities to ACh. The most important being that the **critical distance** between the nitrogen (N) and the carbonyl oxygen (-CO-) is 7 Angstroms. This may be responsible for the interaction and competition between ACh (agonist) and atropine (antagonist) for the muscarinic receptor sites. A view is that atropine and related drugs form a three point spatial attachment with the muscarinic receptors.

Atropine is a highly specific antagonist at all muscarinic receptor sites. With the advent of **pirenzepine** (a tricyclic benzodiazepine) at least *three* muscarinic subtypes, M_1, M_2 and M_3 have been demonstrated. They have different affinities for agonists and antagonists, different anatomic distributions, and different relationships to the guanine nucleotide binding system governing adenyl cyclase activity. Pirenzepine has a strong affinity for M_1 sites (corpus striatum, cerebrum, sympathetic ganglia), but a lower affinity for M_2 sites (cardiac muscle), and M_3 sites (smooth muscle and glands). Thus, the more selective drug pirenzepine suppresses both resting and stimulated acid and pepsin secretion, without significant effects on the salivary glands, urinary bladder, or ocular structures, all locations where M_2 and M_3 receptors predominate **(Chap. 12)**. Further, **methoctramine** has selectivity for cardiac muscarinic receptors (M_2), while **hexahydrosiladifenidol** is selective for smooth muscle and glandular receptors (M_3).

PHARMACOLOGICAL ACTIONS OF ATROPINE

Central Nervous System

Atropine stimulates the cerebral cortex and the medulla. The action is dose-dependent. In therapeutic doses (0.5 to 1.0 mg) it has no significant effect. In larger doses (2 to 4 mg) it stimulates the cells of the cerebral cortex, and the effect resembles that of caffeine. A **cerebral toxic syndrome** similar to alcoholic intoxication occurs and the individual is talkative, restive and disorientated. This stimulation is followed by depression, stupor and coma.

Atropine stimulates the respiration in small doses. In a dose of 1 mg it antagonizes morphine-induced respiratory depression. In larger doses it may depress the respiratory centre. Other central anticholinergic effects of atropine and its substitutes are utilized in the treatment of **parkinsonism**, the possible locus of action being the brainstem. Atropine also checks **motion sickness**.

Cardiovascular System

The primary action of atropine is to **alter the heart rate**. In small doses (0.5 to 0.6 mg) it stimulates the vagus centrally, and the pulse rate is slightly slowed. Larger doses (1 to 2 mg) block the cardiac vagus peripherally, and the central action is masked, resulting in an increase in heart rate. The effect of atropine on the heart rate depends on the existing vagal tone. In infancy and old age when the vagal tone is lower, atropine produces a lesser effect on heart rate. Thus atropine is better tolerated by children and old people.

Very few blood vessels receive parasympathetic innervation, although blood vessels of the skeletal muscle receive a cholinergic supply from sympathetic fibres. These fibres are vasodilator and are active mainly during exercise. Atropine produces no significant changes in blood pressure. In very large doses it may produce *postural hypotension due to peripheral vascular pooling*. In large doses atropine causes profound vasodilatation of the superficial skin vessels, specially of the face and neck giving rise to "atropine flush".

Gastrointestinal System

The cholinergic supply is secretomotor to the stomach, and motor to the intestines. Atropine causes a prolonged reduction in the tone and movement of the gut from the stomach to the rectum. It is also capable of blocking the stimulant effect of cholinergic drugs on the gut.

In small doses atropine **diminishes gastric secretion in peptic ulcer**. It has a marked effect on the nervous phase (vagal phase) of gastric secretion, whereas the hormonal phase (gastrin) of gastric secretion is not effectively inhibited. Atropine relaxes the gall bladder and the bile duct.

Other Smooth Muscles

Atropine relaxes the bronchi and bronchioles, resulting in a widening of the airway. The bronchial secretions are dried up and may lead to "mucus plug" formation and obstruction. The tone and contractions of the ureter are decreased. The detrusor muscle of the bladder is relaxed.

Effect on Secretions

Atropine reduces the secretion of glands normally activated by the parasympathetic system. The secretion of mucous glands lining the respiratory tract, mouth, nose, pharynx and bronchi is diminished. Sweating (which involves sympathetic cholinergic nerves) is suppressed and the skin becomes hot and dry, and the body temperature rises, in spite of cutaneous vasodilatation.

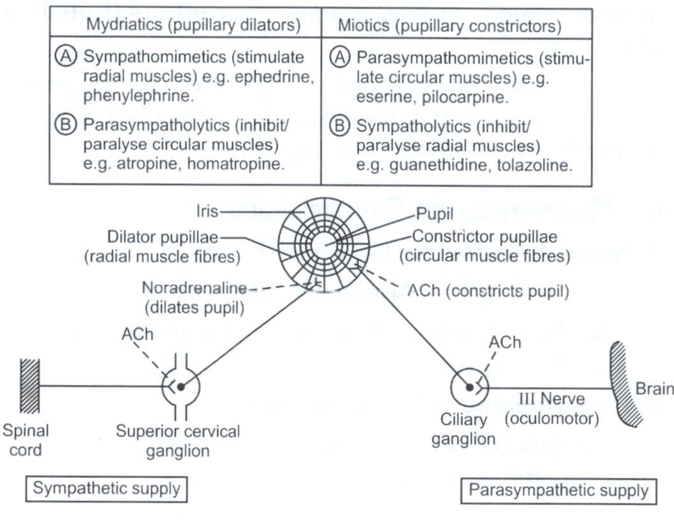

Mydriatics (pupillary dilators)	Miotics (pupillary constrictors)
Ⓐ Sympathomimetics (stimulate radial muscles) e.g. ephedrine, phenylephrine.	Ⓐ Parasympathomimetics (stimulate circular muscles) e.g. eserine, pilocarpine.
Ⓑ Parasympatholytics (inhibit/ paralyse circular muscles) e.g. atropine, homatropine.	Ⓑ Sympatholytics (inhibit/ paralyse radial muscles) e.g. guanethidine, tolazoline.

Fig. 3.3.1: Innervation of the intrinsic muscles of the eye (diagrammatic), and the mode of action of mydriatics and miotics.

Effect on the Eye

The intrinsic muscles of the eye have a dual (parasympathetic and sympathetic) nerve supply **(Fig. 3.3.1)**. The parasympathetic supply is carried via the oculomotor nerve and innervates the **constrictor pupillae**, the stimulation of which causes **miosis**. The sympathetic supply is via the superior cervical ganglion, and innervates the **dilator pupillae**, the stimulation of which causes **mydriasis**. When atropine is administered orally, parenterally or a dilute solution (0.5 to 1.0%) is instilled into the conjunctional sac, a dilatation of the pupil (mydriasis) and paralysis of accommodation (cycloplegia) occurs. The lens becomes less convex, and the eye is **fixed for distant vision**. When a 1 percent solution of atropine sulphate is instilled repeatedly into the conjunctival sac, the pupil begins to dilate in 10 to 20 minutes. Maximum effect is reached in 2 hours and may last for 2 days. The cycloplegic effect of atropine begins within 30 minutes and lasts for 24 to 48 hours.

Atropine produces mydriasis by the relaxation of the constrictor pupillae (circular muscles) of the iris. The dilator pupillae (radial muscles) innervated by adrenergic fibres then acts unopposed and the pupil is dilated. Thus, the dilatation with atropine is a **passive** process. An adrenergic agent like ephedrine can further dilate the pupil by actively contracting the radial muscles. The mydriasis produced by atropine pushes the mass of the iris muscle against the cornea, blocking the cornea-iris angle where the drainage canal of Schelmm lies. This reduces the efficiency of drainage of ciliary fluid, and the intraocular pressure (IOP) has a tendency to rise. The IOP is not much elevated in young adults with normal eyes. However, when the IOP is already raised, and in people aged above 40 years, an attack of glaucoma may be precipitated. Hence, atropine is **contraindicated in glaucoma**.

All classes of autonomic drugs affect the pupillary size by acting on the smooth muscles of the iris directly or indirectly. The following is a partial list:

I. Mydriatics and Cycloplegics

A. Sympathomimetics (mydriasis)

(*i*) *Direct acting*: Adrenaline, Phenylephrine.

(*ii*) *Indirect acting*: Hydroxyamphetamine, Cocaine, Ephedrine.

B. Parasympatholytics (cycloplegia)

Atropine, Homatropine, Cyclopentolate, Tropicamide, Oxyphenonium, Scopalamine.

II. Myotics Causing Accommodation Spasm

A. Parasympathomimetics

(*i*) *Direct acting*: Acetylcholine, Methacholine, Carbachol, Pilocarpine.

(*ii*) *Indirect acting*

(*a*) *Reversible:* Eserine, Edrophonium.

(*b*) *Irreversible:* Isoflurophate, Ecothiopate, Demecarium.

B. Sympatholytics

Guanethidine, Dibenamine, Dihydroergocornine, Tolazoline.

Other Actions

Atropine in large doses exerts a weak **local anaesthetic action**, possibly due to its chemical similarity to cocaine. It also exerts a **weak antihistaminic** activity. Large doses of atropine may increase the body temperature as a result of diminished sweat secretion (anhidrotic action), and a reduced heat loss.

The pharmacologic actions of anticholinergics are summarized in **(Table 3.3-1)**.

Pharmacokinetics

Atropine is readily and completely absorbed from the intestines within 2 hours of ingestion. In the blood it is appreciably bound to the plasma proteins and elimination by the kidney is almost complete (85 to 90%) within 24 hours. It is absorbed to a limited extent from the eye or through the intact skin. About 50 percent absorbed atropine is excreted unchanged in the urine. This is a faithful criterion for the detection of atropine in cases of belladonna/atropine poisoning. A drop of the suspected urine, when instilled into the conjunctival sac of a cat, produces mydriasis. Rabbits are inherently resistant to large quantities of belladonna, and do not suffer the ill effects. Metabolism of atropine in the body is incompletely understood. It is mainly inactivated in the liver to **tropic acid esters** or **tropine**. Atropine is possibly hydrolysed in the liver by **atropine esterase**.

Therapeutic Uses

The therapeutic uses are listed below:

1. CNS disorders. Scopolamine and antihistamines are effective in the treatment of nausea and vomiting of **motion sickness**. They are more effective as preventive agents. Anticholinergics are used to reduce tremor and rigidity of **Parkinson's disease** (paralysis agitans).

2. As antispasmodics. They relax the spasm of smooth muscles (colic) of the **intestinal, urinary** and **biliary** tracts. Atropine is used as a **bronchodilator** in cases of bronchial

Table 3.3-1. *The pharmacologic effects of anticholinergics in man*

Tissue/System	*Pharmacologic effects*
Central nervous system	Decreased concentration and memory; sedation; drowsiness; excitation; ataxia; asynergia; decrease in alpha EEG and increase in low voltage slow waves (drowsy State); hallucinations; coma.
Cardiovascular system	Bradycardia at low doses (CNS effect), and tachycardia at higher doses (peripheral effect); increased cardiac output in recumbent patients.
Gastrointestinal system	Decreased salivation; reduced tone and motility of the gut; decrease in vagus-stimulated gastric, pancreatic, intestinal and biliary secretions.
Respiratory system	Bronchial dilatation and decreased secretions.
Urinary Tract	Relaxation of detrusor muscle and contraction of the sphincter leading to urinary retention; relaxation of ureter.
Eye	Cycloplegia (relaxation of ciliary muscle); mydriasis (relaxation of sphincter pupillae); increased intraocular pressure (IOP) due to increase in aqueous outflow resistance; increased IOP in case of glaucoma.
Skin	Flushing; inhibition of sweating (hyperpyrexia may result).

asthma. **Ipratropium** is a synthetic anticholinergic with a bronchoselective action, producing bronchodilatation **(Chap. 13)**.

3. As antisecretory agents. They are used to reduce gastric secretion in cases of **peptic ulcer** and to reduce sweating in cases of tuberculosis with profuse night sweats.

4. As preanaesthetic medication. Atropine is used to reduce salivary and bronchial secretions. It is usually combined with morphine as a preanaesthetic medicament to antagonize the central depressant action of morphine on respiration.

5. Ophthalmic uses. Atropine is used (with precautions already mentioned) to produce **mydriasis** and **cycloplegia** for the measurement of refractive errors, and other diagnostic procedures. Atropine is instilled into the conjunctival sac in cases of **corneal ulcers** for its local anaesthetic activity. **Homatropine** is better (see later). Mydriasis alone or alternate with miosis is used to keep the lens from adhering to the iris. Also used to relax ocular muscles and reduce irritation in **iridocyclitis** and **choroiditis**.

6. As a cardiac stimulant in cases of **vasovagal syncope** and bradycardia. Atropine is also used to treat **heart block** due to digitalis toxicity. Attropine is useful in preventing the cardiovascular effects of anticholinesterases when used in the treatment of myasthenia gravis.

7. As an antidote in anticholinesterase poisoning, and poisoning by other cholinergic drugs.

8. May be tried in cases of **urinary incontinence** (enuresis).

Dose: Atropine sulphate (oral, subcutaneous) 0.5 to 1.0 mg. For instillation into the eye a 1-2 percent solution is used.

Contraindications

Atropine is contraindicated in patients with **narrow-angle glaucoma** and caution is required in all patients above 40 years of age (homatropine preferred) because of their increased susceptibility to attacks of acute glaucoma. It is contraindicated in patients with **prostatic hypertrophy**. Synthetic atropine-like drugs with a ganglion blocking component may produce impotence in young males. Atropine has to be administered with caution in patients of angina or congestive heart failure. In case of partial pyloric obstruction atropine may cause a complete obstruction due to the peripheral vagal block and an unopposed sympathetic activity.

Adverse Reactions

The usual side effects are:

1. Dryness of the mouth and throat (xerostomia) due to reduced salivation, leading to dysphagia. Dryness of the respiratory tract may harden the bronchial secretions and mucus plugs may be formed.

2. The skin is dry, hot and red, specially in the region of the face and neck (atropine flush).

3. The body temperature may be raised due to abolition of sweating, and reduced heat loss, specially in children and infants who may suffer **hyperpyrexia**.

4. Blurred vision due to paralysis of accommodation. Photophobia may result due to widely dilated pupils. Due to reduced drainage of the anterior chamber the intraocular pressure may rise leading to **glaucoma**.

5. Urinary retention may occur due to loss of bladder tone specially in the elderly males with an enlarged prostate.

6. Palpitation and tachycardia may occur due to peripheral blockade of cardiac vagus. Atropine may cause coronary insufficiency, angina and cardiac decompensation in patients with heart disease.

7. Constipation occurs due to the reduced tone and motility of the gastrointestinal musculature.

Atropine/Belladonna Poisoning

Acute poisoning by belladonna alkaloids may result accidentally or from dosage errors. Atropine has a wide margin of safety and persons even after having ingested 1 g have survived. The symptoms of intoxication are: severe dryness of the mouth and throat, wide pupillary dilatation, dsyphagia and thirst, tachycardia, redness of the skin specially in the blush area, muscle incoordination, rise in body temperature, delirium, hallucinations, mania, apathy, stertorous breathing, stupor, coma and finally respiratory collapse.

Treatment of Poisoning

1. The rational antidote of choice is **physostigmine salicylate.** A slow IV injection of 1-4 mg of physostigmine readily controls the delirium and coma. If coma persists it may be repeated within 1 to 2 hours.
2. Hyperpyrexia and delirium may be treated by an ice cap, and cold sponging.
3. Respiratory stimulants like **caffeine with sodium benzoate** or **oxygen-carbon dioxide mixtures** may be used.
4. Artificial respiration is instituted, if necessary.
5. **Diazepam** may be used if mental symptoms are disturbing.
6. Other usual supportive measures are to be instituted.

Scopolamine

Atropine and scopolamine have almost similar anticholinergic activity, except that scopolamine is a more powerful mydriatic and cyclopegic, a more potent anhidrotic, and is less active on the cardiac vagus.

The main difference in the action of atropine and scopolamine is on the CNS. Atropine in therapeutic doses has little effect on the CNS, but in higher doses it produces a mild stimulation. With still higher doses atropine is a strong stimulant of the CNS producing irritability, restlessness, disorientation, hallucinations and delirium. This stimulation may be followed by depression. Scopolamine on the contrary, is a **primary depressant** of the CNS, and in therapeutic doses causes drowsiness, amnesia, euphoria, fatigue and sleep. **Physostigmine** is highly effective in reversing these central effects.

Therapeutic uses. Scopolamine is mainly used for its *sedative* effect on the cerebrum.

1. Scopolamine is used with Morphine in obstetrics to produce amnesia or **"twilight sleep"**. The drug combination produces a blurred consciousness, in which the pain is dulled. The memory of the patient about pain is impaired. For producing amnesia morphine 15 mg and scopolamine 0.5 mg is injected subcutaneously.

2. Scopolamine may be used for preanaesthetic medication to reduce salivary and bronchial secretions. The sedative effect soothes the patient before operation.

3. Scopolamine may be used to sedate patients with **delirium tremens** and **acute maniacal states.**

4. Used in some cases of **motion sickness.**

5. May be used in cases of **Parkinson's disease**.

Dose: Scopolamine hydrobromide 0.3 to 0.6 mg orally or subcutaneously. **Transdermal hyoscine** is also available for prevention of motion sickness.

SYNTHETIC ANTIMUSCARINICS (ATROPINE SUBSTITUTES)

Numerous synthetic compounds, as well as derivatives of the natural alkaloids have been prepared to: (*i*) obtain a greater **selectivity** of action than atropine, and (*ii*) to lessen the side effects produced. To a certain extent these aims have been achieved. These agents are mainly employed for their **mydriatic**, or **antispasmodic**, or **antiparkinsonian activity**. These atropine-like drugs may be classified into the following three groups:

Group I. Antropine-like Mydriatics

Homotropine hydrobromide
Eucatropine hydrochloride
Cyclopentolate hydrochloride
Tropicamide

Group II. Antisecretory Antispasmodics (Peptic ulcer)

Methantheline bromide
Propantheline bromide
Oxyphenonium bromide
Homatropine methylbromide
Hyoscine methobromide
Hyoscine-N-butylbromide
Tricyclamol
Atropine methonitrate
Dicyclomine

Group III. Antiparkinsonian Drugs

Benzhexol
Procyclidine
Cycrimine
Ethopropazine
Benztropine
Orphenadrin

The above is a partial list of compounds in the various groups.

The synthetic antimuscarinic agents belonging to **Group I** are applied topically by instillation into the conjunctival sac to produce **mydriasis** and **cycloplegia** of various durations, as shown in **Table 3.3-2.** Clinically muscarinic agents like physostigmine or pilocarpine are frequently employed topically to terminate the mydriatic and cycloplegic effects of antimuscarinic agents more rapidly.

Compounds belonging to **Group II** i.e., antisecretory-antispasmodic agents are as a class employed in the treatment of **peptic ulcer, functional indigestion, gastritis,**

Table 3.3-2 *Antimuscarinic agents commonly employed to produce mydriasis and cycloplegia*

Drug	*Concentration used (%)*	*Duration of action*	*Cycloplegia*
Atropine sulphate*	1–4	6–12 days	+++
Homatropine hydrobromide	2	12–48 hrs	+
Eucatropine hydrochloride**	5–10	2–4 hrs	–
Cyclopentolate hydrochloride	1–2	12–24 hrs	++
Tropicamide	0.5–1	1–2 hrs	++

* Atropine is a naturally occurring alkaloid listed here for comparison (synthetic atropine available).

** Note that eucatropine does not produce cycloplegia; useful for ophthalmoscopy.

dumping syndrome and **irritable colon syndrome**. They are quaternary nitrogen containing compounds, and in general quaternization results in an enhanced antimuscarinic activity on the intestines (antispasmodic action). They do not readily penetrate the CNS, hence they have little or no central action, and the side effects are fewer **(Chap. 12)**.

Compounds included in **Group III** are mainly employed for their ***antiparkinsonian activity***. Parkinsonism is the result of lesions of the basal ganglia, the substantia nigra, their interconnecting fibres and their extrapyramidal pathways. It is characterized by **tremors, rigidity** and **akinesia**.

To summarize, atropine is a typical **competitive antagonist** for the muscarinic effects of ACh in the body. Atropine and scopolamine are more effective in abolishing the effects of exogenously administered cholinergic agents, than against ACh released by parasympathetic stimulation at the nerve endings.

Several synthetic compounds with atropine-like action have been prepared with the aim of producing drugs with a **selective** and **shorter** duration of action. They have been variously employed for producing **mydriasis**, and for the management of **peptic ulcer** and **parkinsonism**.

3.4 ADRENOCEPTOR STIMULANTS (SYMPATHOMIMETICS)

Sympathomimetic (adrenomimetic) drugs, as the name suggests, mimic the effects of sympathetic nervous stimulation of organs and structures that contain the adrenergic receptors. The adrenergic receptors (adrenoceptors) are subdivided into **two** main categories: alpha- and beta-type (see later). In general, the term sympathomimetic amines includes all drugs that are chemically related to noradrenaline, and act on the effector organs innervated by the sympathetic nervous system.

Numerous sympathomimetic amines have been synthesized, and many are used clinically. However, the prototype **adrenaline**, and five other drugs– **noradrenaline**, **isoprenaline**, **dopamine**, **amphetamine** and **ephedrine** will be discussed in detail.

THE ADRENOCEPTORS

Barger and Dale in 1910 were the first to systematically examine the effects of a series of compounds with actions resembling those of **adrenaline**, and it is they who suggested the term "sympathomimetic" to describe these actions. Ahlquist in 1948 emphasized the qualitative differences between sympathomimetics, and generated the idea that there were *two* different types of adrenoceptors possessing different structural requirements for their activation. He suggested that the effects of adrenaline at peripheral sympathetic sites could be divided into two groups, which depended on two types of postsynaptic receptors: **alpha-** and **beta-type**. These were originally called **excitatory** and **inhibitory** receptors respectively, but there are certain important exceptions to this rule. Stimulation of alpha-receptors produces excitation in most adrenergically innervated organs and tissues, except in the gastrointestinal tract. In contrast, stimulation of beta-receptors produces inhibition in most adrenergically innervated organs and tissues, except in the heart.

The above is an oversimplification, because the two basic types of adrenoceptors have been further subdivided. There are two distinct types of alpha receptors (alpha$_1$, alpha$_2$), and two types of beta receptors (beta$_1$, beta$_2$). The difference is based primarily on their location. Thus, **alpha$_1$** receptors are found **postsynaptically** on vascular smooth muscle, gastrointestinal and urinary sphincters, eye, pancreas, spleen, and certain glands. **Alpha$_2$** receptors are located **presynaptically** where they control the release of noradrenaline by a **negative feedback** mechanism. Other sites where alpha$_2$ receptors are found include platelets, fat cells, and certain vascular smooth muscle cells. Beta$_1$ receptors are located primarily in the heart and adipose tissue, while beta$_2$ receptors are located in the bronchial, gastrointestinal, uterine and urinary smooth muscle, skeletal muscle, blood vessels, and in the liver and kidney. The sensitivity of adrenoceptor *subtypes* to catecholamines has the following *rank order* of potencies:

Alpha$_1$

adrenaline ≥ noradrenaline > isoprenaline

Alpha$_2$

adrenaline = noradrenaline (isoprenaline is ineffective)

Beta$_1$

isoprenaline > adrenaline = noradrenaline

Beta$_2$

isoprenaline ≥ adrenaline > noradrenaline

Thus, **adrenaline** has a mixed action; **noradrenaline** is a predominent alpha-agonist; and **isoprenaline** is a beta-agonist. The adrenergic responses elicited by the stimulation of the predominent adrenoceptor type in the body are listed in **Table 3.4-1**.

Table 3.4-1 *Classification of adrenoceptors, their distribution, and effects produced*

Organ/tissue function	*Predominent adrenoceptor type*	*Adrenergic response*
*Heart**		
Rate (Chronotropic effect)	β_1	Increased
Contractility (inotropic effect)	β_1	Increased
Conduction velocity (dromotropic effect)	β_1	Increased

Table 3.4-1 Contd...

Organ/tissue function	*Predominent adrenoceptor type*	*Adrenergic response*
Excitability (bathmotropic effect)	β_1	Increased
Eye		
Pupillary size	α_1	Conraction of radial muscles of iris (mydriasis)
Accommodation	–	No innervation
Bronchial muscle	β_2	Relaxation
*Blood vessels (arteries and arterioles)***		
Cutaneous	α_1	Constriction
Visceral	α_1	Constriction
Pulmonary	α_1	Constriction
Skeletal muscle	α_1, β_2	Constriction, dilatation
Coronary	α_2, β_2	Constriction, dilatation
Cerebral	α_1	Constriction
Veins	α_1	Constriction
Gastrointestinal tract (tone, motility and secretions)	α_2, β_2	Decreased
Sphincters	α	Contraction
Splenic capsule	α_1	Contraction
Urinary bladder		
Detrusor muscle	β	Relaxation
Sphincter muscle	α_1	Contraction
Uterus	α_1, β_2	Contraction, relaxation
Glycogenolysis		
Skeletal muscle	β	Increased
Liver	α_1, β_2	Increased
Lipolysis	β_1	Increased
Renin secretion	β_1,	Increased
Insulin secretion	α_2	Decreased

* There are some β_2 receptors in the heart also. The ratio of $\beta_1 : \beta_2$ in the human heart is about 3:2 in the atria, and 4 : 1 in the ventricles.

** There are some α_2 receptors in some vascular smooth muscles.

In addition to adrenergic alpha and beta receptors, there are specific **dopaminergic receptors** located on the renal and visceral blood vessels. Their activation by *dopamine* results in vasodilation, and reduced vascular resistance in the renal and mesenteric circulation. This selective effect is present only with small doses of exogenously administered dopamine. At higher dose levels, dopamine activates cardiac beta$_1$ sites, and systemic alpha$_1$ sites, producing typical catecholamine effects (see later). **Isoprenaline** is an example of a mixed beta$_1$/beta$_2$ adrenoceptor agonist, whereas **salbutamol** and **terbutaline** act selectively on beta$_2$ adrenoceptors. Examples of compounds which selectively activate (agonists) or block (antagonists) the adrenoceptors are given in **Table 3.4-2.**

Table 3.4-2. *The selective agonists of alpha, beta$_1$ – and beta$_2$ -adrenoceptors. The last column on the right lists beta drenoceptor blockers having a non-selective (beta$_1$ and beta$_2$) beta-blocking activity*

Receptor type	*Selective activation (agonist)*	*Selective blockade* (antagonist)*	*Non-selective blockade (antagonist)*
Alpha	Noradrenaline	Phenoxybenzamine	
	Phenylephrine	Phentolamine	
	Methoxamine	Thymoxamine	
		Indoramin, Tolazoline	

Table 3.4-2 Contd...

Receptor type	*Selective activation (agonist)*	*Selective blockade* (antagonist)*	*Non-selective blockade (antagonist)*
Beta			
Beta$_1$	Dobutamine	Acebutolol Atenolol Metoprolol	
			Propranolol Sotalol
Beta$_2$	Orciprenaline		
	Isoetharine		Timolol
	Salbutamol, Terbutaline		Alprenolol, Oxprenolol

* Selective beta$_2$-adrenoceptor blockers are not available.

Regarding the nature of adrenoceptors little is known. Belleau in 1963 proposed that the receptor for catecholamines (noradrenaline, adrenaline, isoprenaline) is a single structure with both alpha- and beta-sites **(Fig. 3.4.1)**. At physiological pH the catecholamines exist in an ionic form with a *positively* charged nitrogen atom. According to Belleau the combination of catechol hydroxyl groups to the beta-site of the receptor through formation of a metal ion complex is responsible for beta effects (inhibitory responses). Combination of the positively charged nitrogen atom of the catecholamine with a negatively charged group, possibly phosphate, on the alpha site by ion-pairing is responsible for alpha-effects (excitatory responses). Substitution on the nitrogen atom with bulky groups such as isopropyl (e.g. isoprenaline) interferes with attachment to the alpha site and therefore favours beta effects through combination of the catechol hydroxyl groups to beta-sites. When both sites are occupied the alpha effects are produced while combination through the catechol hydroxyl groups alone produces beta effects. In accordance with the Belleau's concept it has been suggested that alpha- and beta-adrenoceptors are different allosteric forms of the same basic structure.

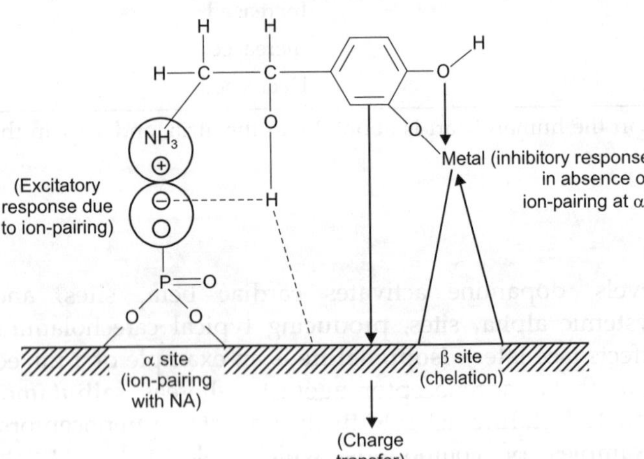

Fig. 3.4.1: Interaction of noradrenaline with alpha and beta sites of the adrenergic receptors (Belleau's concept of a single adrenoceptor mediating both apha and beta effects). Ion-pairing at the alpha-site between positively charged nitrogen atom of the NA molecule and a negatively charged phosphate group on the receptor produce alpha effects (excitatory), whereas, beta-effects (inhibitory) are produced by the combination of the catechol hyroxyl groups of the NA molecule with the beta-site of the receptor through a metal ion chelate, in the absence of ionic bond at the alpha site (see text).

It has been suggested that beta-adrenoceptors are possibly localized on the enzyme adenylcyclase of the effector cell wall. Activation of adenylcyclase catalyses the conversion of ATP to cyclic-AMP, and the beta effects are mediated by this formation of cyclic-AMP in the effector cells.

Biosynthesis, Storage and Release of Catecholamines

To revise, noradrenergic neurones include most *postganglionic sympathetic* neurones (except those supplying the eccrine sweat glands; and those providing the vasodilator supply to the arterioles of skeletal muscle which are cholinergic), and some neurones lying entirely within the CNS.

In 1939 Blaschko proposed a series of steps for the synthesis of noradrenaline and adrenaline in the body from **phenylalanine**. Later light and electron microscopy and various experimental studies verified these steps of synthesis occurring in the noradrenergic and chromaffin cells of the adrenal medulla.

The synthesis of NA is the first step in the process of noradrenergic transmission. Starting material is dietary L-phenylalanine, which is actively absorbed from the gut and oxidized by hepatic **phenylalanine hydroxylase** to form L-tyrosine. This L-tyrosine circulates in the blood stream and is actively transported into the cytoplasm of the noradrenergic neurones. Within the neuronal cytoplasm, L-tyrosine is hydroxylated to form L-dihydroxy phenylalanine (L-DOPA). This reaction is catalysed by cytoplasmic **tyrosine hydroxylase** and is the "rate-limiting step" in the biosynthesis of NA i.e., the activity of tyrosine hydroxylase is governed by the cytoplasmic concentration of NA, and high NA concentration inhibits the conversion of L-tyrosine to L-DOPA. This is an example of **feedback inhibition (Figs. 3.4.2 and 3.4.3).** Further **L-dopa decarboxylase** is the enzyme which converts L-DOPA to **dopamine** within the neuronal cytoplasm. Dopamine is actively transported into the storage vesicles, and here it is oxidized by **dopamine-beta-hydroxylase** to form NA. This endogenous NA is stored in the synaptic vesicles as a complex with ATP and a soluble protein called **chromogranin.**

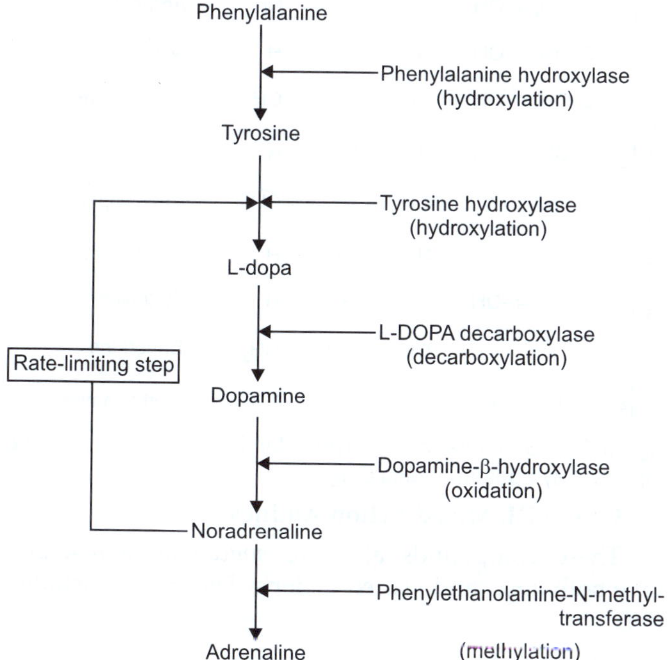

Fig. 3.4.2. Biosynthesis of catecholamines. Phenylalamine is converted in the circulation (extraneuronally) into tyrosine. Tyrosine is taken up from the blood stream by noradrenergic neurones and chromaffin cells of the adrenal medulla. In the cytoplasm of the neurones tyrosine is converted to L-DOPA, and L-DOPA to dopamine. Dopamine is taken up into the noradrenaline storage vesicles and converted to noradrenaline. The conversion of noradrenaline to adrenaline does not occur in the noradrenergic neurones, but takes place in the chromaffin cells of the adrenal medulla which store adrenaline (see text).

Regarding the release of stored NA (bound NA) two physiological mechanisms operate: (*i*) when an action potential reaches the nerve terminal, the membrane permeability is altered. Na^+, Cl^- and Ca^{++} enter the cell and K^+ leaves the cell. This influx of Ca^{++} triggers many synaptic vesicles to release NA, ATP, chromogranin and dopamine-beta-hydroxylase into the synaptic cleft by a process of **exocytosis.** The empty vesicles are retained within the nerve terminal and are refilled with NA; and (*ii*) some storage vesicles randomly migrate to the terminal and release their contents into the **synaptic cleft**, which is designated as NA leak. Some free NA also leaks from the storage vesicles into the neuronal cytoplasm **(Fig. 3.4.3).** The free NA released into the synaptic cleft is active, and attaches itself to the adrenoceptors to produce the response. Part of it is washed off in circulation and metabolized by **catechol-O-methyl transferase** (COMT), and a major part of released NA is re-incorporated (re-uptaken) into the neurone. This sequence of events is shown in **Fig. 3.4.3.**

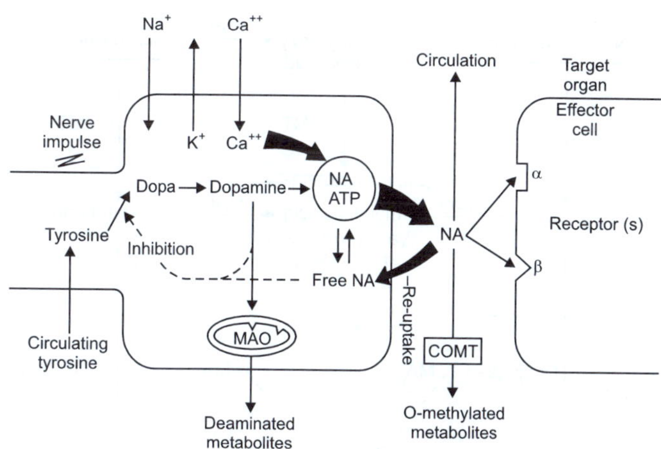

Fig. 3.4.3. A diagrammatic representation of the noradrenergic nerve terminal. The level of free NA in the intraneuronal cytoplasm regulates the rate of synthesis of NA by a negative feedback mechanism (dotted line). Free NA released into the synaptic cleft is partly metabolized by COMT, and partly lost in circulation. A major part is re-uptaken into the neurone, and a small amount produces the biological response by attaching itself to the adrenoceptors on the surface of the effector cells of the target organ (see text).

FATE OF CATECHOLAMINES

The two major enzyme systems involved in the metabolism of catecholamines are **monoamine oxidase (MAO)** and **catechol-O-methyl-transferase** (COMT). A major mode of termination of the action of noradrenaline is by re-uptake (80-90 percent) into the adrenergic neurone **(Uptake 1)** to be re-used as transmitter. Uptake 1 is energy-dependent membrane transport system which is able to transport NA and some structurally related substances into the neurone. The remainder is metabolized by MAO (oxidative deamination), and COMT (O-methylation). The end products, **vanillylmandelic acid** (VMA) and **metanephrines** are excreted in the urine. In addition to the specific neuronal uptake (Uptake 1) mechanism for noradrenaline and related substances, there is an extraneuronal uptake (Uptake 2) mechanism. Uptake 2 operates only when high concentrations of catecholamines are circulating in the blood stream. After transport by Uptake 2, the catecholamines are not stored but are rapidly metabolized intracellularly by both COMT and MAO.

MAO and COMT are widely distributed in the body, but only MAO is present in the adrenergic neurone, located in the mitochondria. It is likely that MAO mainly regulates the amount of NA stored intraneuronally, while COMT is mainly responsible for the inactivation of circulating catecholamines by methylation. The steps in the metabolic fate of noradrenaline and adrenaline are shown in **Fig. 3.4.4.**

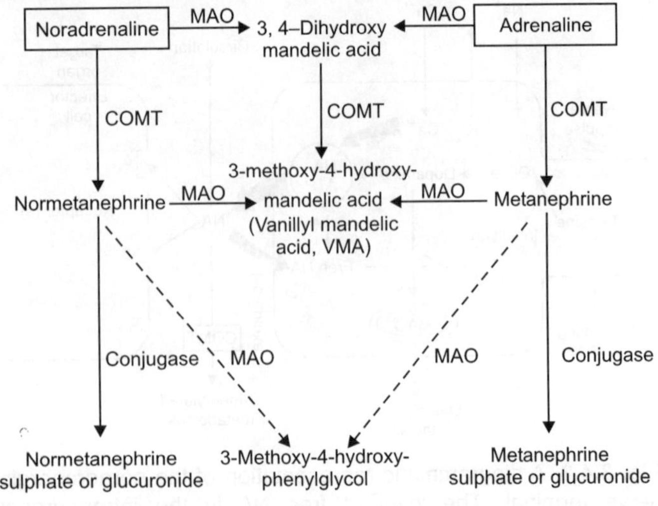

Fig. 3.4.4. The metabolic pathways of catecholamines. Both noradrenaline and adrenaline may be initially oxidized by MAO to 3, 4-dihydroxymandelic acid. Alternatively they can be methylated by COMT to normetanephrine and metanephrine respectively. These three products (3, 4-dihydroxymandelic acid, normetanephrine and metanephrine) are then metabolized to form the major excretory product 3-methoxy-4-hydroxymandelic acid or venillyl-mandelic acid (VMA). Small quantities of normetanephrine and metanephrine are conjugated to form corresponding sulphates or glucuronides. Small portions of normetanephrine and metanephrine form 3-methoxy-4-hydroxy phenylglycol (dashed arrows). VMA is the major metabolite of catecholamines excreted in the urine.

CLASSIFICATION OF SYMPATHOMIMETIC AMINES

Sympathomimetic amines can be classified into *three* groups on the basis of their mechanism of action:

Group I. Directly-acting Amines

These agents interact with the receptor sites on the effector cell membrane. Chemically most of them are amine derivatives of catechol i.e., *catecholamines*. The agents included are:

(*i*) Adrenaline
(*ii*) Noradrenaline
(*iii*) Isoprenaline
(*iv*) Dopamine
(*v*) Dobutamine

Note: Phenylephrine is a directly-acting amine which is not a catecholamine.

Group II. Indirectly-acting Amines

Most of these compounds are noncatecholamines, and act by being taken up by the adrenergic nerve endings and releasing noradrenaline into the synaptic cleft. The agents are:

(*i*) Amphetamine
(*ii*) Tyramine

Group	Ring (positions 1–6)	β-CH	α-CH	NH	Compound
		H	H	H	Phenylethylamine
Catecholamines	3–OH, 4–OH	OH	H	CH_3	Adrenaline
Catecholamines	3–OH, 4–OH	OH	H	H	Noradrenaline
Catecholamines	3–OH, 4–OH	OH	H	$CH(CH_3)_2$	Isoprenaline
Catecholamines	3–OH, 4–OH	H	H	H	Dopamine
Non-Catecholamines	3–OH,	OH	H	CH_3	Phenylephrine
Non-Catecholamines		H	CH_3	H	Amphetamine
Non-Catecholamines	4–OH	H	H	H	Tyramine
Non-Catecholamines		OH	CH_3	CH_3	Ephedrine
Non-Catecholamines	2–OCH_3, 5–OCH_3	OH	CH_3	H	Methoxamine

Fig. 3.4.5: Structure of phenylethylamine, and some of the important sympathomimetic drugs.

Group III. Mixed Action Amines

These compounds also are *noncatecholamines*, and have both *direct* and *indirect* actions. The agents included are:

(*i*) Ephedrine
(*ii*) Metaraminol
(*iii*) Methoxamine

Chemically speaking, the sympathomimetic amines can be classified under two heads: (*i*) **Catecholamines** (Group I), and (*ii*) **Noncatecholamines** (Groups II and III).

STRUCTURE-ACTIVITY RELATIONSHIP OF SYMPATHOMIMETICS

The parent substance of many sympathomimetics is **phenylethylamine (Fig. 3.4.5)**. This compound itself is a weak sympathomimetic agent with predominantly indirect effects. The activity may be increased or modified by substitution of groups on the aromatic ring, on the aliphatic side chain or on the amine group.

The pharmacology of the compounds included in **Fig. 3.4.5** is discussed in this Chapter. It may be appreciated as to how the activity profile is changed as a result of alteration in the chemical structure.

CATECHOLAMINES

Adrenaline (Epinephrine)

The naturally occurring l-isomer of adrenaline, is about 50 times more active pharmacologically than the d-isomer. Adrenaline is found in nervous tissue, adrenal medulla and in the chromaffin cells scattered throughout the body. Activation of the adrenal medulla leads to release of varying proportions of adrenaline and noradrenaline.

The clinically used form of adrenaline is its l-isomer. The presence of the methyl substituent on the amine group of the molecule confers marked beta-adrenoceptor stimulant potency to adrenaline, while its alpha-potency is almost equivalent to noradrenaline. Thus, adrenaline is a *prototype* sympathomimetic agent, and exerts both alpha- and beta-effects, on which its clinical uses are based.

PHARMACOLOGICAL ACTIONS

Cardiovascular System

Blood pressure. A characteristic series of changes in arterial blood pressure occurs when adrenaline is administered intravenously into a suitably anaesthetized experimental animal. In an adequate dose there is a prompt and sharp rise in blood pressure, followed by a moderate fall below the previous level before normal levels are resumed, i.e., the action is **biphasic**, and lasts for about 2 to 4 minutes. Henry Dale in 1906 demonstrated in the anaesthetized cat that ergotoxine (an alpha-blocker) converted the usual predominantly pressor response of adrenaline to a depressor response, and labelled it as the **"adrenaline vasomotor reversal"** phenomenon **(Chap. 3.5)**.

Regarding the **mode of action**, adrenaline possesses both alpha- and beta-stimulating properties. In small doses it causes a predominantly beta-effect, as beta-receptors are more sensitive than alpha-receptors. The effect of higher doses depends upon the relative importance of alpha- and beta- responses in any particular organ. Considering the effect of adrenaline on blood pressure in an anaesthetized animal there is an increase in both **systolic** and **diastolic** arterial pressures. The causes are **cardiac** and **vascular**. The cardiac output is increased due to an increased heart rate and stroke volume, both of which are beta-effects. In addition, adrenaline causes direct myocardial stimulation. The total peripheral resistance is increased, as adrenaline constricts resistance and capacitance vessels in the skin, mucosa, splanchnic organs and kidney, because the alpha-effects predominate over the beta-effects in these regions. These factors are responsible for the **hypertensive phase** of action. At the peak of the pressor response there is a bradycardia, due to **compensatory vagal activity** evoked by the carotid and aortic sinus reflexes. As the extracellular concentration of adrenaline falls, the beta-effects predominate. The decrease in peripheral resistance outweights the cardiac excitatory effects of adrenaline, and the arterial pressure, particularly the diastolic pressure falls. Soon afterwards the blood pressure returns to normal. Little or no tolerance is developed to the pressor action of adrenaline.

Vascular effects. Adrenaline has a differential effect on various vascular beds. It constricts the blood vessels of the skin, mucosa and kidney, whereas the vessels supplying skeletal muscles are dilated (beta$_2$ effect). The coronary vessels are dilated and the flow is enhanced. Adrenaline constricts the veins, decreases venous volume and increases venous return resulting in an increased cardiac output. The data described so far are based on **animal studies**.

The cardiovascular effects produced in **man** by an intravenous infusion of adrenaline are shown in **Fig. 3.4.6.** The systolic blood pressure is raised, while the diastolic pressure is lowered and the mean blood pressure registers little change. Heart rate is increased and the **overall peripheral resistance is reduced**. The increase in systolic pressure is entirely due to the increased cardiac output, resulting from beta$_1$ adrenoceptor stimulation, which in turn increases both cardiac contractility and rate. Adrenaline causes a **mixture of vasoconstriction and vasodilatation** in different vascular beds depending on the relative proportion of alpha- and beta-receptors present. **But the overall effect is a reduction in peripheral resistance which leads to a drop in diastolic pressure. The cardiac output is also elevated by adrenaline, because it causes venoconstriction and increases the venous return to the heart.** The differences in the cardiovascular effects of adrenaline and noradrenaline are explainable in terms of the added beta-effects of adrenaline. Adrenaline, like noradrenaline, causes an increase in the coronary flow. But the marked cardiac stimulant actions of **adrenaline greatly increase the myocardial oxygen demand**, which the increased blood flow is unable to satisfy. Thus, adrenaline is **absolutely contraindicated** in cases of coronary insufficiency.

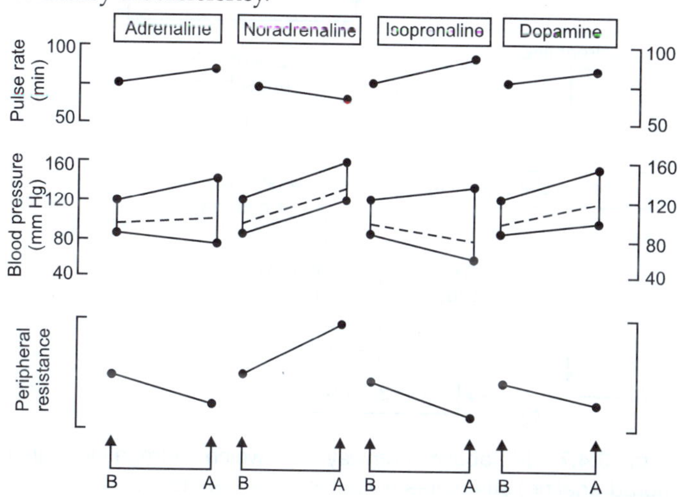

Fig. 3.4.6: Comparison of the circulatory effects of adrenaline, noradrenaline, isoprenaline and dopamine (diagrammatic). The middle panel depicts the drug effect on arterial blood pressure as: upperline for systolic, lower line for diastolic, and dashed line for mean (diastolic + 1/3 pulse pressure) blood pressure B = before drug; A = after drug.

Respiratory System

Adrenaline has a brief stimulant effect on the respiratory centre, but it is of no therapeutic value. The bronchial muscle is relaxed (beta effect), and the microcirculation in the bronchial mucosa is constricted (alpha effect), whereby mucosal oedema tends to diminish. These changes (bronchodilatation and mucosal vasoconstriction) lead to a decreased bronchial resistance. Adrenaline given intravenously to animals or man, may cause a brief period of apnoea (adrenaline apnoea) before ventilatory stimulation.

Metabolic Effects

The metabolic actions of adrenaline lead to: (*i*) a marked **increase in oxygen consumption** by tissues; (*ii*) an **increased glycogenolysis** in liver; (*iii*) **decreased glucose utilization** by tissues; (*iv*) **release of lactic acid** from muscle; and (*v*) an **elevation of free fatty acid (FFA)** levels in blood. These actions are largely caused by the promotion of the formation of 3, 5- adenosine monophosphate (c-AMP), which is the energy controlling reaction in effector cells.

Adrenaline increases blood glucose levels by promoting the formation of c-AMP from ATP by activation of the enzyme adenylcyclase. Cyclic-AMP in turn stimulates phosphorylase enzyme which catalyses the breakdown of glycogen in liver and muscle first to glucose-1-phosphate and later to glucose in liver cells and lactic acid in muscle cells **(Fig. 3.4.7)**. It may be mentioned here that adrenaline has a glucagon-like effect.

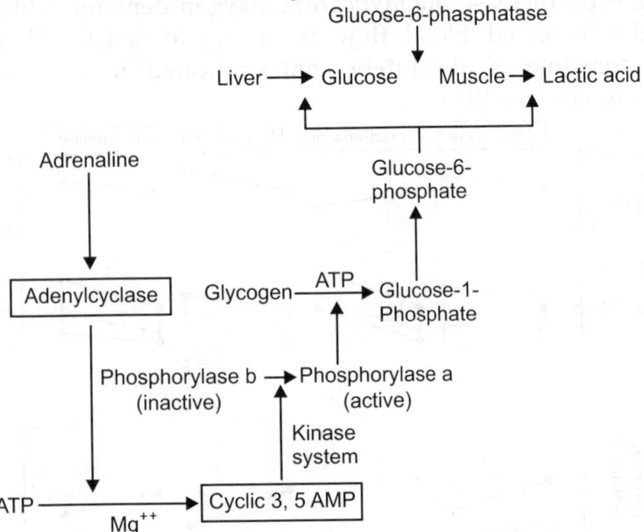

Fig. 3.4.7: Metabolic pathway by which adrenaline (also noradrenaline) stimulates glycogenolysis (see text).

The glycogenolytic action of adrenaline exerted on the liver and skeletal muscle leads to *hyperglycaemia*. This action is thought to be mediated via the beta adrenoceptors.

Adrenaline raises the plasma FFA levels by activating a lipase which promotes the breakdown of triglycerides. This **lipolytic action** is also medicated via c-AMP and $beta_1$-adrenoceptors. Adrenaline also produces a transient rise in plasma potassium level mainly due to release of potassium from the liver. Adrenaline increases total leucocytic count, but causes *eosinopenia*.

Adrenaline in conventional doses causes an overall stimulation of metabolism in man. The oxygen consumption is raised by 20 to 30 percent. This increase in basal metabolic rate has a calorigenic effect and the body temperature rises.

Eyes. On intravenous administration adrenaline contracts the radial muscles of the iris inducing active mydriasis (alpha-effect), but no cycloplegia. It has little mydriatic effect on the pupil when applied locally. Adrenaline lowers intraocular pressure in normal subjects and in glaucoma.

Skeletal muscle. Adrenaline does not directly stimulate the skeletal muscle, but it facilitates neuromuscular transmission by a presynaptic alpha-receptor action which increases the amount of acetylcholine liberated at the myoneural junction. It improves blood flow to the skeletal muscle, and due to this under conditions of stress it has an *antifatigue action*.

Gastrointestinal tract. The tone, frequency and amplitude of peristalsis are reduced (alpha and beta-effects). The sphincters are constricted (alpha-effect).

Glandular secretions. In most glands secretion is inhibited partly due to reduced bood flow caused by vasoconstriction. The salivary secretion becomes thick and mucoid. Sweating and pilomotor activity are not produced by systemic administration of adrenaline, but occur locally on intradermal injection of very dilute solutions. Adrenaline-induced sweating provides indirect evidence for an adrenergic sweating mechanism in man. Intravenous injection of adrenaline does not produce generalized sweating, as the nerves supplying the sweat glands are cholinergic.

Urogenital tract. The detrusor muscle of the bladder is relaxed (beta effect). The trigone and the sphincters are constricted (alpha effect). On the **uterus** the effect varies with the dose, species, pregnancy and the stage of the oestrous cycle. The human gravid uterus contracts, but in late pregnancy and parturition the uterine tone is decreased. The uterine relaxant action of **relaxin** is possibly due to a release of catecholamines.

Central nervous system. In therapeutic doses adrenaline does not stimulate the CNS. In certain individuals it may induce a feeling of anxiety, apprehension and restlessness, and sometimes tremors and weakness. In patients of Parkinson's disease adrenaline increases tremors and rigidity.

Absorption, Fate and Excretion

Adrenaline is poorly absorbed and rapidly destroyed in the gastrointestinal tract. Hence it has to be given parenterally by the intramuscular or subcutaneous route, or by inhalation. Absorption from the subcutaneous site may be hastened by massage. Injection of adrenaline suspension in oil delays the absorption and prolongs the duration of action. The fate and excretion of adrenaline has been described earlier in this Chapter.

Therapeutic Uses

Clinical uses are based mainly on the actions of this drug on the bronchial muscle, heart and blood vessels.

1. Bronchial asthma. Adrenaline may be used in the treatment of acute and moderately severe attacks of bronchial asthma. It induces a fairly prompt bronchodilation, shrinkage of muscosa and inhibits mucoid secretion. It is given in a dose of 0.2 to 0.5 ml of 1 in 1000 solution. Lately, it has been superseded by the selective $beta_2$-stimulant drugs. Adrenaline may be used in the emergency treatment of *epiglottiditis* and *croup*.

2. Hypersensitivity reactions. In allergic emergencies the first drug to use is adrenaline. It is a potent antiallergic agent and produces prompt relief in life-threatening allergic reactions like serum sickness, angioneurotic oedema, hay fever and anaphylactic shock. It may be administered in a dose of 0.5 to 1.0 ml of adrenaline (1 in 1000) subcutaneously or intramuscularly. In extreme emergency upto 0.25 ml (1 in 1000), well diluted, may be given very slowly intravenously, but is hazardous.

3. Heart block and cardiac arrest. For the treatment of heart block with syncope (Stokes-Adams attacks) 0.3 to 0.6 ml of adrenaline (1 in 1000) may be given subcutaneously. For the treatment of cardiac arrest about 0.3 to 0.5 ml of adrenaline (1 in 1000) may be injected directly into the right atrium. Cardiac massage and other supportive measures may prove useful.

4. Control of bleeding. Adrenaline is frequently used as a topical haemostatic agent to produce vasoconstriction, which stops epistaxis (nose bleed) and bleeding from the gums. Adrenaline soaked packs are applied locally, or it may be sprayed over the bleeding region.

5. Adrenaline is frequently **added to local anaesthetics like lignocaine** to limit the absorption from the site of infiltration, and prolong the duration of action. It also lessens the toxicity.

6. **Adrenaline** solutions may be instilled into the eye to treat conjunctival congestion, to control haemorrhages and to reduce intraocular pressure in simple open-angle glaucoma.

Contraindications

Adrenaline is contraindicated in thyrotoxicosis and cardiovascular disease like hypertension, arteriosclerosis, and coronary insufficiency. It should not be given while using volatile halogenated hydrocarbon general anaesthetics like *halothane*. It is contraindicated in spinal anaesthesia as it may damage the cord. It should be given cautiously in diabetic patients as its hyperglycaemic effect may need increased insulin or oral hypoglycaemic dosage.

Adverse Reactions

The most common ill effects of adrenaline are anxiety, fear, pallor, tachycardia, palpitation, tremors, restlessness and throbbing headache. Extreme hypertension may occur and precipitate cerebral haemorrhage, and there may be convulsive episodes. Cardiac arrhythmias and fatal ventricular fibrillation may develop. Anginal pain can be readily precipitated by adrenaline in patients of angina pectoris. Cyclopropane or halogenated hydrocarbon anaesthetics accentuate the cardiotoxicity of adrenaline.

Dosage. *Adrenaline hydrochloride* in a 1:1000 aqueous solution is available for subcutaneous or intramuscular injection. The usual adult dose ranges between 0.1 to 0.5 ml subcutaneously. The intravenous route is rarely used.

Adrenaline hydrochloride 1 percent aqueous solution is used intranasally; a 1 to 2 percent solution is instilled into the conjunctival sac for local vasoconstriction. A 1:500 suspension of adrenaline in peanut oil given in a dose of 0.2 to 1.5 ml intramuscularly produces a longer lasting bronchodilator effect.

NORADRENALINE (NOREPINEPHRINE, LEVARTERENOL)

The prefix *Nor* is derived from the German N (itrogen) O (hne) R (adikal)-nitrogen without radical. Noradrenaline chemically differs from adrenaline in that the nitrogen is without the methyl substitution **(Fig. 3.4.5)**. The l-isomer of noradrenaline (l-noradrenaline) is the neurotransmitter released from the postganglionic sympathetic nerve endings. Clinically the l-noradrenaline is used.

Pharmacological Actions

Noradrenaline predominantly acts on the alpha adrenoceptors, *i.e., it is an alpha agonist*, and it has only minimal effects on cardiac beta receptors. Its pharmacological actions are compared with adrenaline and isoprenaline in **Table 3.4.-3**.

Cardiovascular System

The basis for the clinical use of noradrenaline is its ability to raise systemic arterial blood pressure by causing vasoconstriction as a result of its alpha-agonistic activity. Noradrenaline raises both *systolic* and *diastolic* blood pressures; mainly due to an increase in the total peripheral resistance **(Fig. 3.4.6, Table 3.4.-3)**. The cardiac output is either unchanged or slightly affected. Clinically noradrenaline produces a bradycardia as a result of activation of the aortic and carotid baroreceptors, leading to an increased reflex vagal activity. The increased reflex cardioinhibition also antagonizes the weak beta-stimulating effect of noradrenaline on the heart. Cardiac oxygen consumption is increased by noradrenaline as it increases the cardiac work, but to a lesser extent compared to adrenaline. The coronary arteries are dilated and the coronary flow is increased by noradrenaline. The coronary flow mainly increases due to a **raised mean arterial pressure**, and possibly also due to the production of adenosine, which is a vasodilator metabolite of myocardial metabolism. Noradrenaline also possesses a **positive inotropic effect** on the heart.

The other sympathomimetic actions of noradrenaline (hyperglycaemia, bronchodilatation, CNS stimulation etc.) in therapeutic doses are minimal and clinically unimportant.

Noradrenaline is ineffective by mouth due to its rapid destruction by MAO and COMT in the gut wall and the liver. Its pressor effect is rapid in onset but brief, and therefore it has to be given as an intravenous infusion.

Therapeutic Uses

Noradrenaline is used as a vasopressor agent in the treatment of **hypotensive states** like **surgical shock** or **myocardial infarction** (cardiogenic shock), where there is peripheral vascular pooling of blood. Noradrenaline may also be used to combat hypotension caused by overdosage of hypotensive drugs or removal of a pheochromocytoma.

Adverse Reactions and Contraindications

Whenever noradrenaline is indicated, it is administered by slow intravenous infusion, at a rate (10 to 13 drops per minute of a solution containing 4 mcg/ml of noradrenaline bitartrate) which stabilizes the blood pressure at the desired level. Long-term infusions lead to loss of responsiveness, which necessitates the increase in dosage. Infusions should be discontinued gradually, otherwise a profound fall in blood pressure may occur. The reason for this fall is possibly related to the **desensitization** of the vascular alpha-adrenoceptors and to a reflex reduction in sympathetic nerve traffic due to a **partial ganglionic blockade** caused by noradrenaline. Other complications include, severe tissue necrosis around the infusion site, and the pressor effect may be profoundly increased in patients who are concurrently receiving drugs like **tricyclic antidepressants** or **adrenergic neurone blocking agents**, which inhibit the neuronal amine uptake mechanism (Uptake 1). Cyclopropane or halothane anaesthesia are **contraindications** to the use of noradrenaline. Rapid administration may cause dangerous cardiac arrhythmias. Extreme caution is to be observed in patients of hypertension and cardiovascular diseases.

Dosage. *Noradrenaline bitartrate* (Levarterenol bitartrate) is the salt used, and 2 mcg of noradrenaline bitartrate are approximately equivalent to 1 mcg of noradrenaline base.

Noradrenaline bitartrate injection is usually available in 2 ml ampoules containing 1 mg/ml noradrenaline base (1 in 1000 solution of noradrenaline base). It should not be used if the solution is brown in colour or contains a precipitate. This solution is too strong for direct injection, but is used to prepare dilute solutions for intravenous infusion immediately before use. The solution is diluted to contain 4 mcg/ml of noradrenaline base which is obtained by diluting 4 ml of official injection (2 ampoules) in 1000 ml of 5 percent dextrose injection, which may contain variable amounts of sodium chloride. The rate of infusion (0.5 to 1.0 ml/min) is adjusted to maintain the desired level of blood pressure. Ascorbic acid (0.5 g/litre) is added to prevent degradation of noradrenaline in the infusion system. Blood pressure is taken every 2 to 5 minutes till it is stabilized.

Isoprenaline (Isoproterenol, Isopropyl-noradrenaline)

Isoprenaline is a synthetic catecholamine derived from noradrenaline by substitution of an isopropyl group on the nitrogen atom of the aliphatic side-chain **(Fig. 3.4.5)**. The commercially available form is the racemic form. Amongst the beta-active sympathomimetics, isoprenaline is the most active agent, and acts almost exclusively on the beta adrenoceptors.

Pharmacological Actions

The pharmacological actions of isoprenaline are due to its powerful beta-stimulant activity, and it has almost no action on alpha receptors.

Cardiovascular System

As a result of stimulation of the cardiac beta-adrenoceptors isoprenaline exerts a **positive inotropic** and **chronotropic** effect on the heart, causing an increase in the cardiac output. It lowers peripheral vascular resistance, mainly in the skeletal muscle and also in the renal and mesenteric vessels. Isoprenaline in usual doses in man increases the cardiac output usually sufficiently to raise the systolic blood pressure, but there is a fall in the diastolic pressure, and the pulse pressure increases. As a result the mean pressure is slightly reduced **(Fig. 3.4.6; Table 3.4-3).**

Table 3.4-3 *Comparison of the effects of adrenaline, noradrenaline and isoprenaline in man*

*Effect on**	*Adrenaline (alpha + beta)*	*Noradrenaline (alpha)*	*Isoprenaline (beta)*
Heart			
(a) Heart rate	Increased (direct action)	Slowed (reflexly via vagus)	Increased
(b) Force of contraction	Increased (direct action)	Little effect	Increased (direct action)
(c) Cardiac output	Increased	No change or reduced	Increased
(d) Excitability & conductivity	Much increased	Increased	Much increased
(e) Coronary blood flow	Increased	Increased	Increased
Arterial blood pressure			
(a) Systolic	Rise	Rise	Little change or fall
(b) Mean	Slight rise	Marked rise	Fall
(c) Diastolic	Fall	Rise	Fall

Table 3.4-3 Contd...

*Effect on**	*Adrenaline (alpha + beta)*	*Noradrenaline (alpha)*	*Isoprenaline (beta)*
Vascular beds			
(a) Skeletal muscle	Dilated	Constricted	Dilated
(b) Skin & viscera	Constricted	Constricted	Dilated
(c) Brain	Dilated	No change or constricted	Dilated
(d) Heart	Dilated	Usually dilated	Dilated
(e) Kidney	Constricted	Constricted	No change
Total peripheral resistance	Decreased	Increased	Decreased
Metabolic effects			
(a) Oxygen consumption	Increased	Little effect	Increased
(b) Blood glucose	Increased	Little effect	Increased
Smooth muscle			
(a) Bronchi	Relaxed	Little effect	Relaxed
(b) Intestines	Relaxed	Relaxed	Relaxed
(c) Urinary bladder	Relaxed	Relaxed	Relaxed
(d) Sphincters	Constricted	Constricted	Constricted
(e) Gravid uterus	Usually inhibited	Stimulated	Inhibited
Central nervous system	Stimulation	Little effect	Stimulation
Capillary permeability	Reduced	Little effect	

* The responses to these catecholamines are much influenced by the dose and the ratio of alpha and beta-receptors in the tissues.

Renal blood flow is normally decreased in normotensive patients, but is appreciably increased in cases of septicaemic or cardiogenic shock.

Bronchial Muscles

Isoprenaline relaxes all smooth muscles in the body, specially when the tone is high. This **spasmolytic action** is most marked on the **bronchial** and **gastrointestinal** musculature. It prevents or relieves bronchoconstriction in cases of bronchial asthma, but tolerance can develop with overuse of the drug. Isoprenaline also decreases the tone and motility of the intestines and inhibits uterine motility.

Other Actions

Isoprenaline, like adrenaline induces **hyperglycaemia**, though lesser than adrenaline. However, it is as effective as adrenaline in raising plasma free fatty acid levels. The **calorigenic action** is similar to that of adrenaline.

Isoprenaline is erratically absorbed when given orally, but absorption is more regular and complete when the tablets are allowed to slowly dissolve under the tongue (*sublingual administration*). It is readily absorbed when given parenterally or as an *aerosol*. Its metabolism in the body is the same as that for adrenaline.

Therapeutic Uses

1. **Bronchial asthma.** In the treatment of a moderate to severe attack of bronchial asthma, isoprenaline may be administered as a sublingual tablet or by oral inhalation.

2. **Heart block.** As isoprenaline is a potent cardiac stimulant, it is useful for the immediate treatment of heart block. In cases of Stokes-Adams syndrome, the heart rate is increased and the syncopal seizures are reduced. Later, preferably a cardiac pacemaker should be implanted.

3. Isoprenaline may be employed in **cardiogenic shock** after myocardial infraction and in septicaemic shock (see Chap. 4.6). For treating shock 5 ml of a 1:5000 solution may be diluted with 500 ml of 5 percent dextrose and infused intravenously at carefully adjusted flow rates.

Adverse Reactions and Contraindications

Isoprenaline may cause palpitation, tachycardia, headache and flushing of the skin. Serious arrhythmias, anginal pain, tremors, dizziness and sweating occasionally occur. Isoprenaline is contraindicated in patients of cardiac arrhythmias, coronary insufficiency, hyperthyroidism and diabetes mellitus.

Dosage. *Isoprenaline hydrochloride* inhalation solutions are available in strengths of 1:100, 1:200 and 1:400 solution of isoprenaline base. Sublingual tablets of 10 and 15 mg, and sustained release tablets of 30 mg are available.

Dopamine

Dopamine is the naturally occurring catecholamine, which is the immediate precursor of noradrenaline in the body. Additionally it has a neurotransmitter function in the CNS **(Chap. 2.1)**, and possibly also in some peripheral tissues. Alteration in the dopaminergic neuronal mechanism in the substantia nigra is linked with parkinsonism **(Chap. 2.11)**. Although dopamine has specific **dopaminergic** receptors in the CNS, injected dopamine has no central effects as it does not cross the blood-brain barrier. The metabolism of dopamine is shown in **Fig. 3.4.8.** The enzymes MAO and COMT also metabolize dopamine. The end products are different than those of adrenaline and noradrenaline. They are excreted in the urine.

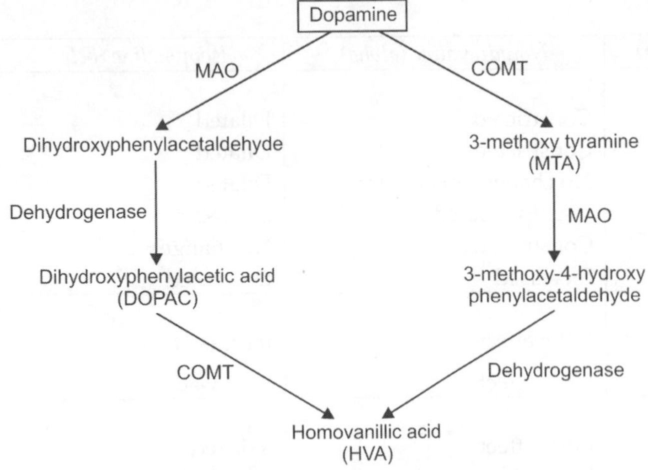

Fig. 3.4.8: Metabolism of dopamine

Dopamine hydrochloride has recently been used in the treatment of **shock syndromes associated with reduced cardiac output and blood pressure (Chap. 4.6).** Dopamine stimulates the beta and alpha adrenoceptors, but certain vasodilator effects, particularly in the renal and mesenteric vasculature appear to be mediated by specific "dopaminergic receptors", which are distinctly different from alpha- and beta-receptors. Small doses of dopamine dilate renal and mesenteric vascular beds by acting on these receptors. This effect is blocked by **haloperidol**, and is not blocked by alpha- or beta-blocking agents.

Pharmacological Actions

Dopamine exerts alpha-adrenergic vasoconstrictor activity in both arterial and venous beds. With higher doses the peripheral vasoconstrictor effect predominates over the vasodilating action. Through beta-adrenoceptor stimulation dopamine augments myocardial contractility, and in addition it exerts an indirect positive inotropic action through the release of noradrenaline. Dopamine also exerts a mixed (direct and indirect) positive chronotropic action. Thus, dopamine is a catecholamine which is unique in having a mixed action.

The haemodynamic response in man to an infusion of dopamine is that the cardiac output is increased, peripheral resistance is decreased, and there is little change in the mean arterial pressure and the heart rate **(Fig. 3.4.6)**. Compared to other sympathomimetic amines, dopamine causes a lesser increase in myocardial oxygen consumption, and the incidence of cardiac arrhythmias is lower.

Therapeutic Uses

Dopamine is recommended for the treatment of shock resulting from **trauma, surgery** and **myocardial infarction**. Also used in the treatment of **congestive heart failure, renal and liver failure.**

Adverse Reactions and Contraindications

Toxic effect include nausea, vomiting, tachycardia and ectopic beats. Precordial pain and occasionally hypertension may develop. Dopamine is contraindicated in patients of *tachyarrhythmias* and *pheochromocytoma*. **Before administering dopamine to patients in shock, hypovolaemia, if present, must be corrected.**

Dosage and Administration. *Dopamine hydrochloride* (Intropin) is available as a sterile solution containing 40 mg/ml of the drug in 5 ml ampules. The contents of the ampule are diluted in 250 or 500 ml of 0.9% sodium chloride, or 5% dextrose solution, to give a final concentration of 800 or 400 mcg/ml. This is given as a drip infusion at a rate between 5 to 20 mcg/kg body weight. The blood pressure, heart rate and urine flow must be continuously monitored to adjust the dose.

Dobutamine

Dobutamine is a synthetic catecholamine, an analogue of dopamine with a large substituent on the amine nitrogen.

Pharmacological Actions

Dobutamine acts directly on beta$_1$-adrenoceptors in the heart. It has little or no action at beta$_2$- or alpha-receptors. It does not cause release of noradrenaline. It increases the contractile force of the heart raising the stroke volume and cardiac output. These actions are produced without marked increase in heart rate. Compared to dopamine, dobutamine increases the oxygen demand of the heart to a lesser extent. Like dopamine, it produces vasodilation of the renal and mesenteric vessels. Systemic vascular resistance is decreased, however, the systolic blood pressure remains unchanged or is slightly increased. Dobutamine has a very short duration of action (plasma $t_{1/2}$ is 2 minutes), as it is rapidly metabolized and excreted.

Therapeutic Uses

Dobutamine (Dobutrex) is used in the short-term management of **acute cardiac decompensation** due to depressed contractility resulting from organic heart disease on cardiac surgery. Dobutamine is more useful than dopamine in the treatment of *cardiogenic shock*.

Adverse Reactions and Contraindications

Premature ventricular beats occur in about 5 percent of patients. Less frequently headache, palpitation, nausea, anginal pain and dyspnoea may occur. Very large doses may dangerously raise blood pressure and heart rate. **Contraindications** include idiopathic hypertrophic subaortic stenosis, pre-existing hypertension, cardiac valvular disease, and cardiac carrhythmias.

Dosage and Administration

Dobutamine is available as a powder for injection (250 mg/vial). It is administered by IV infusion, diluted in

5 percent dextrose injection. The usual dosage range is 2.5 to 10 mcg/kg/min of either 250, 500 or 1000 mcg/ml solution. Doses upto 40 mcg/kg/min have been used occasionally.

Terbutaline and Albuterol

Terbutaline and albuterol are beta-adrenoceptor agonists with a relative **selectively** for beta$_2$-adrenoceptors. Both have a longer duration of action than isoprenaline as they are not metabolized by COMT. Like isoprenaline they also are not transported into the adrenergic neurones, and are not metabolized by MAO. Because of their selectivity for beta$_2$-adrenoceptors, they produce less cardiac stimulation than isoprenaline, but are not completely without action on the heart.

Terbutaline and **albuterol** are used to treat **bronchial asthma** and **emphysema (Chap. 13)**. Side effects include tremor, nervousness, tachycardia, palpitation and sweating.

NONCATECHOLAMINES

A large number of sympathomimetics lack the catechol nucleus, and are used clinically. Their effects depend partly upon **release** of stored noradrenaline from the noradrenergic nerve terminals, and partly upon a direct action on the effector cells. The ratio of the direct to indirect action varies in these compounds. The indirectly acting compounds (amphetamine, tyramine) predominantly act by releasing noradrenaline, which in turn stimulates the adrenoceptors, whereas ephedrine, metaraminol and methoxamine have a mixed action. **Amphetamine** and **ephedrine** are prototypes and would be discussed in further detail.

In contrast to catecholamines, most of the noncatecholamines are effective orally and have a much longer duration of action. The noncatecholamines are found in high concentrations in the brain and cerebrospinal fluid, which explains their powerful CNS activity. Both amphetamine and ephedrine are resistant to the action of MAO. In fact, it has been suggested that MAO inhibition is responsible for their CNS stimulant action.

Repeated injections of ephedrine, close to each other, ultimately fail to elicit the hypertensive response in animals by the third or fourth injection. As ephedrine depends on the noradrenaline available in the neurone for this effect, it leads to transmitter (NA) depletion, and the synthesis fails to keep pace with the release. This acute phenomenon in which the biologic responses to repeated doses become progressively smaller is known as **tachyphylaxis**, or **acute tolerance.**

Amphetamine

Amphetamine has powerful CNS stimulant activity, in addition to peripheral actions on the alpha- and beta-adrenoceptors. The name amphetamine (Benzedrine) refers to the racemic form of the drug, and dextroamphetamine (Dexedrine) to the d-isomer. Both are synthetic in origin. In therapeutic doses the CNS actions overshadow the peripheral actions.

Pharmacological Actions

Cardiovascular System

Amphetamine given orally raises both systolic and diastolic blood pressures. The pulse pressure is usually increased as it has an effect on both alpha- and beta-receptors. The heart rate is reflexly slowed. The l-isomer is slightly more active than the d-isomer on the cardiovascular system.

Central Nervous System

Amphetamines have a powerful psychostimulant action on the CNS. **Dextroamphetamine** is most active in this respect, and is 3 to 4 times as potent as the l-isomer. Amphetamine stimulates the respiratory centre, increases motor activity, and induces sleeplessness. These effects are due to **cortical stimulation** and possibly **stimulation of the reticular activating system**. Amphetamine counteracts the undesirable effects of CNS depressants.

The psychic effects in man depend on the dose, the mental state and personality of the individual. The effects of an oral dose (10 to 30 mg) of amphetamine are: alertness, wakefulness, decreased fatigue, elevation of mood, increased initiative, confidence and ability to concentrate. This is often associated with elation, euphoria, increased motor and speech activity. Performance of simple mental tasks may be improved. The effect on memory is undecided. Physical performance is improved. Prolonged use leads to mental depression and fatigue. Amphetamine has a mild analgesic effect in man and animals.

Amphetamine leads to a suppression of appetite i.e., it has an **anorexigenic** or **anorexiant** effect. It has been considered useful as an adjunct in the treatment of **obesity**. Weight loss is mainly due to a reduced food intake. The site of anorexiant action is the feeding centre in the lateral hypothalamus, whereby the hunger drive is diminished. Unfortunately tolerance and addiction develop, which are a serious hazard to its use. Some other amphetamine-like appetite suppressants may be safer (see later). The *mode of action* on the CNS is illunderstood. Possibly it is a combination of MAO inhibition, **direct** action on the CNS cells, and **indirect** action via the release of noradrenaline in the cerebrospinal axis.

Therapeutic Uses

It is employed in the treatment of: narcolepsy, hyperkinetic behaviour disorders in children, **depressive states, enuresis, epilepsy, motion sickness, postencephalitic parkinsonism, orthostatic hypotension** and **obesity**. It is also employed as an analeptic in the management of poisoning by barbiturates and other CNS depressant drugs.

Table 3.4-4 *Some commonly employed sympathomimetics*

	Generic name	*Dosage*
A.	**Adrenergic Nasal Decongestant Drugs**	
1.	Ephedrine sulphate/HCl	0.5-3% topically
2.	Cyclopentamine HCl	0.5-1% topically
3.	Mephentermine sulphate	0.5% topically
4.	Naphazoline HCl	0.5% topically
5.	Oxymetazoline HCl	0.5% topically
6.	Phenylephrine HCl	0.125-0.5% topically
7.	Phenylpropanolamine HCl	25-50 mg orally
8.	Propylhexedrine HCl	Topically by inhaler
9.	Tetrahydrozoline HCl	0.05-0.1% topically
10.	Tuaminoheptane sulphate	1-2% by inhaler
11.	Xylometazoline HCl	0.05-0.1% topically
12.	Pseudoephedrine HCl	30-60 mg orally
B.	**Adrenergic Bronchodilator Drugs**	
1.	Epinephrine bitartrate	0.3 mg per inhalation
2.	Adrenaline	0.2-0.5 mg IM, SC or by inhalation
3.	Ephedrine sulphate	15-50 mg orally
4.	Isoprenaline HCl	10-15 mg sublingually
5.	Isoprenaline sulphate	3 mg orally or 0.125 mg per inhalation
6.	Orciprenaline sulphate	0.65 mg per inhalation or 20 mg orally
7.	Methoxyphenamine HCl	50-100 mg orally
8.	Pseudoephedrine HCl	30-60 mg orally
9.	Terbutaline sulphate	5 mg orally or 0.25 mg SC
10.	Salbutamol Sulphate	2-4 mg orally or 100-200 mcg per inhalation
11.	Isoetharine HCl	30-40 mg orally or 350 mcg per inhalation
12.	Rimiterol hydrobromide	200 mcg per inhalation
C.	**Adrenergic Drugs in Shock and Acute Hypotension**	
I.	**Catecholamines**	
1.	Noradrenaline bitartrate (Levarterenol)	IV infusion containing 4 mcg/ml base
2.	Isoprenaline HCl	Dilute a 1:5000 solution to 1:500,000 infuse IV
3.	Dopamine HCl	Initiate IV infusion at 2-5 mcg/kg/min and increase upto 20-50 mcg/kg/min
4.	Dobutamine HCl	Initiate IV infusion at 2.5-10 mcg/kg/min and increase upto 40 mcg/kg/min
II.	**Noncatecholamines**	
1.	Ephedrine sulphate	20 mg IV or 15-50 mg IM or SC
2.	Metaraminol bitartrate	2-10 mg IM or SC; IV bolus or infusion may be given
3.	Methoxamine HCl	3-5 mg IV slowly or 10-15 mg IM
4.	Phenylephrine HCl	2-5 mg IM or SC; 0.1-0.5 mg IV or a 1:50,000 solution by IV infusion
D.	**Adrenergic Anorexiants (Appetite suppressants)**	
I.	**Amphetamines**	
1.	Amphetamine sulphate	5-10 mg tid
2.	Dextroamphetamine sulphate	5-10 mg tid
3.	Methamphetamine HCl	2.5-5 mg tid
II.	**Amphetamine-like Drugs**	
1.	Benzphetamine HCl	25-50 mg bid or tid
2.	Clortermine HCl	50 mg once daily
3.	Diethylpropion HCl	25 mg tid
4.	Fenfluramine HCl	20 mg tid
5.	Phenmetrazine HCl	25 mg bid or tid
6.	Phentermine HCl	8 mg tid
E.	**Adrenergic Vasodilator Drugs**	
1.	Isoxsuprine HCl	5-10 mg orally
2.	Nylidrin HCl	6 mg orally

Adverse Reactions and Precautions

Amphetamine may induce dryness of mouth, difficulty in micturition, agitation, restlessness, insomnia and anorexia. With higher doses there may be hypertension, tachycardia, anginal pain and cardiac arrhythmias. With large doses psychotic reactions, disorientation, aggressive behaviour, hallucinations and convulsions occur. On prolonged use **tolerance** and **dependence** (addiction) on amphetamine develop.

Dosage. *Amphetamine sulphate, amphetamine phosphate and dextroamphetamine sulphate* are available usually in 5 or 10 mg tablet forms. The usual initial oral dose is 2.5 to 5.0 mg.

The other two amphetamines used clinically are *methamphetamine hydrochloride* and *hydroxyamphetamine hydrobromide*. The former is mainly employed for its CNS effects, and the latter for its peripheral effects in hypotensive states.

Ephedrine

In olden days ephedrine was isolated from plants like **Ephedra equisetina** or **E. sinica**. It is now obtained entirely by chemical synthesis. It is a noncatecholamine and a number of isomeric forms of varying potency are known. Its central actions are less pronounced than those of the amphetamines. Ephedrine partly owes its peripheral action to release of noradrenaline from neuronal storage sites, and has direct action also on the adrenoceptors, i.e., it has a mixed action. Ephedrine stimulates both alpha- and beta-receptors. An injection of ephedrine causes a prolonged pressor effect in experimental animals (dogs, cats), which diminishes if the same dose is repeated at close intervals (tachyphylaxis). It is a stable compound and is a competitive inhibitor of the enzyme MAO.

Pharmacological Actions

Cardiovascular system. Ephedrine differs from adrenaline in that it is active orally, has a much longer duration of action, and has more pronounced central actions. The drug increases both the systolic and diastolic blood pressures in man, and the pulse pressure increases. It raises the cardiac output, but the heart rate is not appreciably altered in therapeutic doses. The pressor response of ephedrine can be blocked by alpha blockers, but the reversal is slight.

Smooth muscles. The *bronchodilator* effect of ephedrine is weaker, slower in onset, but more persistent than that of adrenaline. Consequently, ephedrine is of value only in the prevention of acute attacks of bronchial asthma for which continued medication is required. Ephedrine instilled into the conjunctival sac dilates the pupil, but the accommodation is unaffected, *i.e.*, there is a mydriasis without cycloplegia. The intraocular pressure remains unchanged.

Central nervous system. The central stimulant effects of ephedrine are similar to those of amphetamine, but are less marked. It is a weak analeptic.

Therapeutic uses. Ephedrine is used in mild or moderate cases of **bronchial asthma**. Its use is limited by its slow onset of action, modest potency, tachyphylaxis and CNS stimulant action. The advantage is its long duration of action. It may be used as a **nasal decongestant** and a **mydriatic**. Other uses include **Stokes-Adams syndrome, hypotension during spinal anaesthesia**, and **narcolepsy**.

Adverse Reactions and Precautions

The adverse cardiovascular effects are similar to those of adrenaline. In therapeutic doses ephedrine stimulates the CNS, manifested as insomnia, restlessness, tremors, anxiety and agitation. It does not cause addiction. It may cause urinary retention in the elderly men and glycogenolysis in diabetics. **Tolerance** develops after several weeks of continued use, but disappears on discontinuing the therapy for 3 or 4 days. Precautions in the use of ephedrine are the same as for adrenaline and the amphetamines.

Dosage. *Ephedrine sulphate* and *ephedrine hydrochloride* are preparations of the l-isomer, and are available as nose drops, sprays or tablets. The oral dose varies from 15 to 50 mg. In **hypotensive states** ephedrine sulphate 15 to 50 mg may be given subcutaneously.

Other Sympathomimetic Amines

A large number of sympathomimetic amines, some of them not included in the text so far, are usefully employed clinically. They are listed in **Table 3.4-4**, together with the *prototype* agents.

The above is a partial list of sympathomimetic agents which are clinically extremely useful. It is noteworthy that the adrenergic drugs have a wide variety of uses in medicine.

3.5 ADRENOCEPTOR BLOCKING AGENTS (SYMPATHOLYTICS)

Adrenoceptor blocking drugs **inhibit** or **prevent** the response of effector cells to both sympathetic nerve activity, or sympathomimetic amines by their blocking action on the adrenoceptors. Circulating adrenaline and noradrenaline are antagonized more readily than the effects of sympathetic nerve stimulation. Their primary site of action is distal to the synaptic cleft, i.e., on the **postsynaptic membrane**. These agents must be **differentiated from the adrenergic neurone blocking agents**, like **guanethidine**, with an action proximal to the synaptic cleft. The adrenergic neurone blockers are used as antihypertensives **(Chap. 4.2)**.

ADRENOCEPTORS

Noradrenaline is the neurotransmitter released at the noradrenergic nerve terminals. On the basis of **selectivity** of action among **agonists** and **antagonists**, two types of adrenoceptors were recognized, and designated as α (alpha) and β (beta) adrenoceptors **(Chap. 3.4).** Subsequently they were further classified into α_1 and α_2, and β_1 and , β_2 receptor sybtypes.

The α_1 adrenoceptors are located at **postsynaptic** sites on tissues innervated by adrenergic neurones. The α_2 adrenoceptors have **presynaptic** location, and are involved in the **feedback inhibition** of noradrenaline release from nerve terminals. The β_1 adrenoceptors are found chiefly in the **heart**, and **adipose tissue** while β_2 adrenoceptors are located in a number of sites including bronchial muscle and skeletal muscle blood vessels.

Presynaptic receptors. There is evidence that a second population of receptors also plays a role in neurotransmission. These are called **presynaptic** or **prejunctional receptors**. They are located on the presynaptic nerve endings. Their function is to control the amount of neurotransmitter released per nerve impulse.

The presynaptic α-adrenoceptors on noradrenergic neurones are of the α_2 subtype; and **presynaptic β** adrenoceptors are of the β_2 subtype. **The physiological and pharmacological imoportance of the presynaptic β_2-receptors, however, is less certain than it is for presynaptic α_2 receptors.**

The presynaptic beta-receptors have a **low threshold** for stimulation, and cause a **facilitation** of noradrenaline release (positive feedback) from the adrenergic neurone, while the presynaptic alpha-receptors have a **higher threshold** and inhibit the release of noradrenaline **(negative feedback) (Fig. 3.5.1)**. This may be a regulatory mechanism for first amplifying, i.e., **"turning on"**, and later terminating, i.e., **"turning off"** the action of noradrenaline. Therefore, presynaptic alpha-blockade facilitates noradrenaline release, and presynaptic beta-blockade inhibits transmitter release **(Table 3.5-1)**.

Table 3.5-1 *Control of the release of noradrenaline from the sympathetic nerve ending*

Activity/drug	*Mode of action*	*Noradrenaline release*
Sympathetic nerve activity	Promotes exocytosis of storage vesicles	↑
Alpha-agonist	Activates inhibitory presynaptic alpha-receptors	↓
Alpha-blocker	Inhibits inhibitory presynaptic alpha-receptors	↑
Beta-agonist	Activates stimulatory presynaptic beta-receptors	↑
Beta-blocker	Inhibits stimulatory presynaptic beta-receptors	↓

↑ = increased ↓ = decreased

Alpha Adrenoceptor Blocking Agents

The main action of alpha adrenoceptor blocking agents (alpha blockers) is to produce **peripheral vasodilatation.** The hypertensive response of adrenaline in an experimental animal (dog, cat), is changed to a mainly hypotensive response after alpha blockade **(adrenaline reversal)**. It is because the beta dilator effects on the blood vessels overshadow the beta stimulant actions on the heart **(Chap. 3.4)**.

Pre-synaptic membrane | Post-synaptic membrane
NA ATP; β+; > NA >; α or β adrenoceptor; α−
Sympathetic nerve ending | Effector cell

Fig. 3.5.1: Diagrammatic representation of the pre- and post-synaptic adrenoceptors (see text). NA = noradrenaline; ATP = adenosine triphosphate; + = positive feedback; - = negative feedback.

Classification of Alpha-Blockers

1. **Haloalkylamine.** Dibenamine, Phenoxybenzamine
2. **Imidazolines.** Tolazoline, Phentolamine.
3. **Dibenzazepines.** Azapetine.
4. **Ergot alkaloids.** Ergotamine & dihydroergotamine, Ergotoxine and dihydroergotoxine, Ergometrine (mainly oxytoxic action).
5. **Other compounds.** Thymoxamine, Prazosin, Chlorpromazine, Yohimbine.

Mode of Action

Based on the mode and duration of action the alpha-adrenoceptor blockers are grouped into:

1. **Competitive, Short-acting antagonists.** The ergot alkaloids, tolazoline phentolamine and azapetine belong to this group. These agents selectively block the alpha-adrenoceptors by competition with alpha-agonists like noradrenaline for the receptor sites. The degree of blockade obtained is dependant on the relative concentrations of the agonist and antagonist, i.e., they produce and **equilibrium type** of blockade, which is **competitive** and **surmountable**. Their duration of action is short. These agents are also called **reversible** alpha-blockers.
2. **Noncompetitive, Long-acting antagonists.** Phenoxybenzamine belongs to this group, and produces a **non-competitive** antagonism which cannot be overcome by increasing the concentration of the alpha-agonist noradrenaline, i.e., they produce a **non-equilibrium blockade**. These agents are related to the nitrogen mustards, and they alter the alpha-adrenoceptors chemically be alkylation (cyclization reaction). In the initial stages the blockade is competitive, but when fully developed it becomes non-competitive. Thus, phenoxybenzamine produces an **insurmountable**, non-equilibrium (non-competitive) blockade of the alpha-adrenoceptors, which is long lasting. They are also called **irreversible** alpha-blockers.

Adrenaline Reversal Phenomenon

Originally Dale in 1906 demonstrated this phenomenon known as **vasomotor reversal** by using the extract of ergot (ergotoxine) in the anaesthetized cat, which changed the usual pressor response of intravenously administered adrenaline to a depressor response on blood pressure. Later, the classification of adrenoceptors into alpha- and beta-types by Ahlquist in 1948, satisfactorily explained this "**adrenaline reversal**" phenomenon. In fact the ergot alkaloids block the alpha-adrenoceptors only, which are responsible for peripheral vasoconstriction. The beta-receptors are not blocked even after ergot pre-treatment, and respond to adrenaline, causing a fall in the blood pressure. Any one of the other alpha-blockers like **phentolamine, dibenamine, tolazoline** or **chlorpromazine** may be used to demonstrate this adrenaline reversal phenomenon **(Fig. 3.5.2)**. The experimental animal may be the cat or the dog.

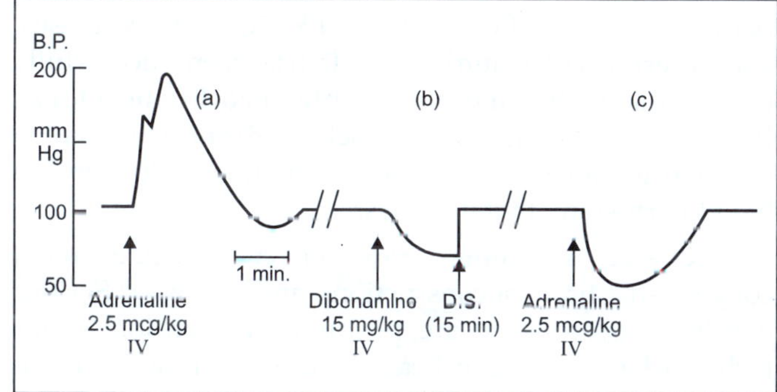

Fig. 3.5.2: The "adrenaline reversal" phenomenon demonstrated on the blood pressure (BP) of anaesthetized cat (diagrammatic kymographic record). (*a*) the biphasic (hypertension followed by hypotension) response of adrenaline; (*b*) dibenamine slightly lowers blood pressure; and (*c*) now adrenaline causes a hypotensive response. The predominantly pressor response is converted to a depressor response by dibenamine due to selective blockade of the vasoconstrictor (alpha-receptor) action of adrenaline, which allows for the vasodilator (beta-receptor) action D.S = Drum stopped.

HALOALKYLAMINES

DIBENAMINE

It is structurally related to nitrogen mustards, and is a **long-acting** alpha-blocker as it combines firmly with the alpha-adrenoceptors. Clinically it has been replaced by its close relative phenoxybenzamine.

PHENOXYBENZAMINE

Phenoxybenzamine is the only haloalkylamine in clinical use at present. It is a potent alpha-adrenoceptor blocker. Phenoxybenzamine has a number of other actions like antagonism of acetylcholine, histamine and 5-hydroxytryptamine. However, it appears that the vasodilator actions of the drug in man are essentially due to alpha-blockade.

The slow onset of action of phenoxybenzamine is due to the formation of an intermediate compound, an **ethylene imminium ion** which firmly attaches itself to a negatively charged site on the alpha-receptor. In the early stages the alpha-blockade induced by phenoxybenzamine is **competitive** in nature, but once the blockade is fully developed, it becomes **non-competitive** (non-equilibrium blockade) in nature.

Phenoxybenzamine effectively prevents the responses mediated by the alpha-receptors. In normotensive patients it produces variable effects on resting arterial blood pressure. The diastolic blood pressure tends to fall. It interferes with the reflex adjustment of blood pressure and produces **postural hypotension**. Phenoxybenzamine increases the cardiac output and decreases the total peripheral resistance, which leads to a better tissue perfusion **(Chap. 4.6)**. Phenoxybenzamine stimulates the CNS.

Therapeutic uses. Phenoxybenzamine is used to treat peripheral vasospatic conditions like **Raynaud's disease** and **intermittent claudication**. It has been successfully used in the treatment of **inoperable pheochromocytoma**. It is used in the treatment of **shock syndromes** marked by hypotension and extreme vasoconstriction, as it increases blood perfusion of vital tissues.

Adverse reactions. Side effects include nasal congestion, bronchoconstriction and miosis. Serious effects of overdosage are postural hypotension, reflex tachycardia, congestive heart failure, cerebral stroke or kidney failure.

Dosage. *Phenoxybenzamine hydrochloride* (Dibenzyline) is started at a dose level of 10 mg daily orally. The optimal daily dose is adjusted usually between 20 and 60 mg.

IMIDAZOLINES

TOLAZOLINE

Tolazoline is a weak alpha-blocker, and causes peripheral vasodilatation mainly by its direct relaxant effect on the vascular smooth muscle. In addition, the drug has a direct cardiac stimulant action, and often causes tachycardia. It causes a weak **competitive blockade** of alpha-receptors. In man, tolazoline decreases peripheral resistance, increases venous capacity, with little change in the arterial pressure as the cardiac output is increased.

Tolazoline is used to increase blood flow in peripheral vasospastic conditions like **Raynaud's syndrome, chilblains, causalgia, frostbite, acrocyanosis** and **intermittent claudication**. It has also been used to increase blood flow through recently grafted tissues after plastic surgery.

Adverse effects include pilomotor stimulation (goose flesh), tachycardia, increased gastrointestinal motility, and hyperchlorhydria as it is chemically related to histamine.

Dosage. *Tolazoline hydrochloride* 25 to 50 mg three times a day. An injection solution (25 mg/ml) is also available.

PHENTOLAMINE

Phentolamine is a more potent alpha-blocker compared to tolazoline. This alpha-blocker is almost exclusively used for the **diagnosis of pheochromocytoma**, and for the prevention of hypertension during operative removal of this adrenal medullary tumour. Another important use of phentolamine is as an **antidote** to the pressor effects of overdosage of alpha-adrenoceptor agonists.

DIAGNOSTIC TESTS FOR PHEOCHROMOCYTOMA

1. **Phentolamine test.** It is done when hypertension is sustained. Phentolamine 5 mg is given intravenously, and if the high arterial pressure is due to excess of circulating catecholamines, there is a fall of arterial pressure within 2 minutes by at least 35 mm Hg systolic and 25 mmHg diastolic in most patients suffering from pheochromocytoma. This fall is not observed in patients suffering from other types of hypertension.
2. **Histamine test.** This is a **provocative** test done if hypertension is **intermittent.** An equivalent of 0.05 mg histamine base is given intravenously. This directly stimulates the tumour, and the blood pressure shoots up, often preceded by a fall. **It precipitates almost a typical hypertensive paroxysm**. Phentolamine should be available at hand to terminate this, if needed. In normal individuals the rise in blood pressure does not exceed 10 mm Hg systolic.

Adverse reactions to phentolamine include orthostatic hypotension, tachycardia and nasal stuffiness. It is contraindicated in patients of coronary artery disease and angina pectoris.

Dosage. Phentolamine hydrochloride 50 mg four to six times a day orally prior to surgery on patients of pheochromocytoma. *Phentolamine mesylate* is injectable intravenously and 5 mg ampules are available. Dosage as above.

DIBENZAZEPINES

AZAPETINE

Azapetine closely resembles tolazoline in possessing both alpha-blocking and direct vasodilating action. Its actions are less pronounced than those of tolazoline. Its clinical uses are the same as for tolazoline. ***Azapetine phosphate*** is used in a dose of 25 mg three times a day orally.

ERGOT ALKALOIDS

Ergot is a parasitic fungus **(Claviceps purpurea)** which grows on rye and certain other grains. It contains twelve alkaloids (six isomeric pairs) of complex chemical structure, and each is derived from lysergic and isolysergic acids **(Table 3.5-2)**. The naturally occurring l-forms are much more active than the d-forms, and they are readily interconvertible. Two major actions of ergot alkaloids are: (*i*) **to stimulate smooth muscles**, and (*ii*) **to block alpha-adrenoceptors**.

Table 3.5-2 *The natural alkaloids of ergot and their dextro-isomers*

Group	*Natural alkaloid*	*Dextrorotatory isomer*
1. Ergotamine group	Ergotamine Ergosine	Ergotaminine Ergosinine
2. Ergotoxine group	Ergocristine Ergocryptine Ergocornine	Ergocristinine Ergocryptinine Ergocorninine
3. Ergobasine group	Ergonovine (ergometrine)	Ergonovinine (ergometrinine)

DRUGS USED IN MIGRAINE

Ergotamine is an important alkaloid and possesses both **vasoconstrictor** and **alpha-blocking** activity. Dihydrogenation of ergotamine (Dihydroergotamine) increases the alpha-blocking potency and reduces the smooth muscle stimulant activity. Both, ergotamine and dihydroergotamine are used to treat migraine.

The ergot alkaloids: (ergotamine and dihydroergotamine) are effective due to their action on the vascular smooth muscle, and should be preferably given during the prodromal period (vasoconstriction phase). They are much less effective in aborting an attack of migraine when headache has set in.

Ergotamine tartrate for the prevention of migraine may be given orally as 2 or 3 tablets (1 mg/tablet), repeated for 2 to 3 doses. It may be injected in a dose of 0.25 mg SC. If headache has already started 0.5 mg IM may be administered. Combination of ergotamine tartrate 1 mg and caffeine 100 mg (Cafergot) in tablet form is available for use, and 2 tablets may be administered at onset of attack. Dihydroergotamine (DHE) is generally less effective than ergotamine, but is preferred by some patients. In addition, dihydroergotamine has been tried in *herpes zoster, herpes cornea* and *symptomatic relief in mumps.*

Methysergide, a congener of ergonovine, and a potent serotonin antagonist is used in the **prevention of migraine** and **vascular headaches**. Adverse effects like angina, peripheral vascular insufficiency and retroperitoneal fibrosis limit its use.

In addition *sedatives, antiemetics* (prochlorperazine), *clonidine* and *propranolol* have been employed in the management of migraine **(Chap. 2.7).**

OTHER ERGOT ALKALOIDS

Ergometrine has weak alpha-blocking activity, but is a powerful stimulant of the uterus (oxytocic action), and is mainly used in obstetrics to reduce **post-partum haemorrhage (Chap. 6.3)**.

Ergotoxine is a mixture of three different alkaloids *ergocornine, ergocristine* and *ergocryptine.* It has alpha-blocking activity, and in addition stimulates the vascular smooth muscle, and the uterus. The dihydrogenated derivatives of this mixture (dihydroergotoxine) have increased alpha blocking potency, and very little smooth muscle stimulant activity.

Dihydroergotoxine is a mixture containing equal parts of methane sulphonate salts of **dihydroergocorine, dihydroergocristine** and **dihydroergocryptine** (Hydergine). It has been used to cause peripheral vasodilatation in vasospastic disorders like **Raynaud's syndrome**. In recent years it has been used to **improve the mental status of elderly patients** with signs of inadequate cerebral blood flow. However, little supporting evidence is available. Dihydroergotoxine is poorly absorbed from the gut, but may be administered sublingually in doses upto 4.5 mg per day in tablet form containing a total of 1.5 mg of the alkaloids in equal proportions. It may be injected IM or intra-arterially in doses of 150 to 600 mcg to relieve vasospasm.

BROMOCRIPTINE

Bromocriptine (2-bromo-alpha-ergocryptine) is a new compound related to the ergot alkaloid ergocryptine. It interestingly suppresses prolactin secretion by a direct action on the anterior pituitary, possibly by a **specific dopamine receptor agonistic action**. It functions as an analogue of the prolactin-release-inhibiting factor (PIF) of the hypothalamus **(Chap. 7.1)**.

Bromocriptine has been employed in the treatment of **hypogonadism** in both men and women. It has been shown to restore fertility in women with or without **hyperprolactinaemia**. It is also used for the **suppression of puerperal lactation**. Bromocriptine is being tried in the treatment of **parkinsonism, acromegaly** and has been recommended for **migraine**.

Side effects on the initiation of therapy include nausea, vomiting, postural hypotension and micturition syncope. On prolonged therapy mild constipation, muzziness, nasal congestion, night cramps in legs and dystonic reaction in parkinsonism may occur. Cardiac arrhythmias have been reported with high doses.

Dosage. *Bromocriptine mesylate* for suppression of lactation is given orally in a dose equivalent to 2.5 mg bromocriptine base daily for 2 to 3 days, and later 2.5 mg twice daily for 14 days. Each tablet contains equivalent of 2.5 mg of bromocriptine. It should be taken with food to minimize side effects. Special dosage schedules are employed in the treatment of **hypogonadism** and **galactorrhoea** syndromes.

OTHER COMPOUNDS

THYMOXAMINE

Thymoxamine is a **competitive** alpha-adrenoceptor antagonist. It has weak antihistaminic properties. It is used for the treatment of peripheral vasospastic disorders like **acrocyanosis** and **Raynaud's syndrome**. The usual oral dose is the equivalent of 40 mg of thymoxamine base four times a day. It can be given intravenously in a dose of 100 mcg/kg body weight four times a day. Overdosage may cause palpitation, hypotension, headache and flushing of the face.

PRAZOSIN

Prazosin is of value in the treatment of hypertension **(Chap. 4.2)**, and congestive heart failure **(Chap. 4.3)**. It has potent alpha$_1$-adrenoceptor blocking activity. The haemodynamic effects of prazosin in man differ from those of phenoxybenzamine. It produces much less postural hypotension and almost no tachycardia.

CHLORPROMAZINE

Chlorpromazine amongst its many actions **(Chap. 2.10)** possesses alpha-adrenoceptor blocking activity. However, it is not used clinically as an alpha-blocker.

YOHIMBINE

Yohimbine is a plant alkaloid (an indolealkylamine) related to reserpine. It produces a short-acting competitive blockade of alpha-receptors, and also blocks the 5-hydro- xytryptamine receptors. In addition, it is a strong stimulant of the brain, and is reputed to possess **aphrodisiac** properties, which presumably are attributable to stimulation of the CNS and/or to vasodilatation in the genitalia. However, convincing evidence for its aphrodisiac action is lacking.

BETA-ADRENOCEPTOR BLOCKING AGENTS

All beta-adrenoceptor blocking agents (beta-blockers) are synthetic compounds and competitively inhibit the actions of adrenergic agonists on beta-receptors. The first beta- blocker **dichloroisoprenaline** (DCl) was introduced by Powell and Slater in 1958. As DCI was a partial beta-agonist, and exhibited beta-receptor stimulation before blockade, it was not clinically useful. Almost all the later beta-blockers, have the isoprenaline side-chain as a part of the molecule. In 1962 **pronethalol** was synthesized as a fairly pure beta-blocker, but subsequently it was found to produce *tumours of the thymus in mice*, and its use was discontinued. In 1965 Black, Duncan and Shanks introduced **propranolol** as a non-carcinogenic beta-blocker, more potent than pronethalol, and virtually devoid of intrinsic sympathomimetic activity (ISA) or beta-agonistic activity. Numerous beta-blockers have been synthesized later, and differ from propranolol in their relative effects on the cardiac and bronchial beta-receptors, ISA, lipid solubility and direct membrane stabilizing or local anaesthetic activity **(Table 3.5-3)**.

Table 3.5-3. *Actions of beta-adrenoceptor blocking agents*

Generic name	*Beta-blockade potency ratio* **(propranolol =1)**	*Bronchoconstrictor action*	*Cardio-selectivity*	*Membrane stabilizing activity (MSA)*	*Partial agonistic activity (ISA)*	*Plasma $t_{1/2}$ (hrs)*
Propranolol	1	+++	0	+	0	3-5
Sotalol	0.3	+	0	0	0	6-8
Alprenolol	0.3	+	0	+	++	2-4
Oxprenolol	0.5-1	+	0	+	++	3-5
Pindolol	6	++	0	±	+++	2-5
Timolol	6	+	0	0	±	4-6
Nadolol	2-9	+	0	0	0	16-20
Atenolol	1	0	+	0	0	6-7
Metoprolol	1	0	+	±	0	2-4
Acebutolol	0.3	0	+	+	+	7-12

+ = present; 0 = absent; ± = negligible

Classification

The clinical actions of beta-blockers seem to be a property of their beta-receptor inhibitory activity. In addition, the presence or absence of **cardioselectivity, membrane stabilizing (or quinidine-like, or local anaesthetic) activity (MSA)**, and **intrinsic sympathomimetic activity** (ISA) have been used as the basis for their classification. Accordingly they are divided into **non-cardioselective** (Division I), and **cardioselective** (Division II) agents. Later, another group (Division III) was formed comprising beta-blockers which also have alpha-adrenoceptor blocking activity. Thus structured is the following classification:

Division I (Non-cardioselective)

Group I: agents with both MSA and ISA, e.g., *alprenolol* and *oxprenolol*.

Group II: agents with MSA, but no ISA, e.g., *propranolol*.

Group III: agents without MSA, but with ISA, e.g., *pindolol*.

Group IV: agents without both MSA and ISA, e.g., *sotalol and timolol*.

Division II (Cardioselective)

Group I: agents with both MSA and ISA e.g., *acebutolol*.

Group II: agents with MSA, but no ISA, agents not available.

Group III: agents without both MSA and ISA, e.g., *atenolol* and *metoprolol*.

Division III (Beta plus Alpha Blockade)

Labetalol

The above classification was devised by J.D. Fitzgerald in 1972. Later, a much simpler working classification has been developed (also including some newer agents) as under:

I. **Non-selective beta-blockers:** Propranolol, nadolol, pindolol, oxprenolol, sotalol, timolol, alprenolol, penbutolol.

II. **Cardioselective beta-blockers:** Metoprolol, atenolol, acebutolol, bevantolol, pafenolol, betaxolol, tolamolol, celiprolol.

III. **Beta-plus alpha-blockers:** Labetalolol, celiprolol.

IV. **Agents with direct vasodilator effect:** Bucindolol, prizidolol.

Mode of Action

Beta-adrenoceptors are located predominantly in the heart (beta$_1$), in the arteries and arterioles of skeletal muscle (beta$_2$), and in the bronchi (beta$_2$), where their stimulation induces cardiac excitation, peripheral vasodilation, and bronchial relaxation respectively. Beta-blockers combine **reversibly** with these receptors to block the responses to sympathetic nerve stimulation or circulating catecholamines. Blockade of cardiac (beta$_1$) receptors **reduces heart rate, myocardial contractility** and **cardiac output**. **The atrioventricular conduction time** is slowed, and the **automaticity** is suppressed. Consequent upon this the blood pressure falls. Studies show that the cardiac output falls by 15-20 percent. It is believed that partly propranolol exerts its antihypertensive effect by **inhibiting the secretion of renin from the juxtaglomerular apparatus** of the kidney by inducing beta-receptor blockade. The peripheral beta$_2$-blockade allows alpha-adrenergic mediated vasoconstriction to be unopposed, and the **peripheral vascular resistance** increases initially. Within weeks the peripheral resistance returns to normal or rather below normal. A number of suggestions have been made to explain their hypotensive effect, including an effect on the CNS leading to a **decreased outflow of sympathetic impulses, an adrenergic neurone blocking effect**, an **anti-renin effect**, and the **resetting of the baroreceptors**.

Blockade of noncardiac (beta$_2$) receptors increases airway resistance, inhibits catecholamine-induced glycogenolysis and lipolysis, and inhibits the vasodilating effect of catecholamines on peripheral circulation. These noncardiac actions are responsible for some of the adverse effects of beta-blockers, like bronchospasm, hypoglycaemia, interactions with sympathomimetic amines, and aggravation of peripheral vascular insufficiency.

Beta-blockers differ in their relative affinity for beta$_1$- and beta$_2$-receptors. The **non-selective agents** (propranolol, nadolol, timolol, pindolol, alprenolol, oxprenolol, sotalol) block beta-receptors at all sites. Whereas, the **cardioselective** agents (metoprolol, atenolol, acebutolol, beventolol, tolamolol) have greater affinity for the beta$_1$-receptors, and may be safer in asthmatics, in patients prone to hypoglycaemia, and patients with peripheral vascular disease.

Pharmacokinetics

Hydrophilic beta-blockers (atenolol, nadolol, sotalol) are not as readily absorbed from the gut as lipophilic agents (propranolol, metoprolol, oxprenolol). Hydrophilic agents are not extensively metabolized, and have relatively longer plasma half-lives. Hydrophilic beta-blockers do not cross the blood-brain barrier as readily as lipophilic agents, and are thought to be less likely to be produce CNS side effect.

Propranolol is almost completely absorbed from the gut, but much of the administered drug is metabolized by the liver during its **first-pass** through the portal circulation, and only one-third reaches the systemic circulation. Propranolol is bound to plasma proteins to an extent of 90 to 95 percent. Propranolol is almost completely metabolized before excretion in urine. One of the products of hepatic metabolism is **4-hydroxypropranolol**, which exhibits beta-blocking activity comparable to the parent compound. Other products of metabolism lost in urine are **napthoxylactic acid, isopropylamine** and **propranolol glycol**. A large fraction of the metabolites of propranolol is of glucuronide conjugates. The half-life of propranolol is 3 to 5 hours, but the therapeutic effect lasts longer.

Therapeutic Uses

Beta-blockers have many therapeutic uses. The principles of therapy are detailed below:

1. **Hypertension.** Propranolol is useful in the treatment of all degrees of hypertension. When used alone, the antihypertensive effect of propranolol is equivalent to that of a thiazide diuretic.
2. **Angina pectoris**. Propranolol or nadolol may be used for the long-term management of patients with angina pectoris.
3. **Cardiac arrhythmias.** Beneficial effects have been observed in patients of *supraventricular arrhythmias; tachyarrhythmias due to thyrotoxicosis: persistent atrial extrasystoles* refractory to conventional treatment, *atrial flutter* and *fibrillation* when ventricular rate cannot be controlled by digitalis alone, or digitalis is contraindicated; *ventricular tachycardias; persistent premature ventricular extrasystoles; tachyarrhythmias of digitalis intoxication; and resistant tachyarrhythmias due to excessive catecholamine action during anaesthesia.*
4. **Myocardial infarction.** Propranolol and timolol are indicated in clinically stable patients who have survived the acute phase of MI to reduce cardiovascular mortality and risk of reinfarction.
5. **Pheochromocytoma.** After primary treatment with an alpha-blocker, propranolol may be useful as adjunctive therapy if the control of tachycardia becomes necessary before or during surgery.
6. **Idiopathic hypertrophic subaortic stenosis.** Propranolol relieves angina, dyspnoea, palpitation and syncope in patients with hypertrophic cardiomyopathy.
7. **Migraine.** Propranolol is used for the **prophylaxis** of migraine headache, specially in patients who cannot take ergot preparations due to associated disease like hypertension, cerebrovascular disease, angina pectoris, severe peripheral vascular disease or thyrotoxicosis.
8. **Hyperthyroidism.** Propranolol rapidly controls tachycardia, tremors and anxiety in patients of **thyrotoxicosis**. It is useful as an adjunct to other appropriate therapy for *thyrotoxic crisis* and *neonatal thyrotoxicosis*. It has been suggested that propranolol reduces the peripheral conversion of thyroxine (T_4) to tri-iodothyronine (T_3).
9. **Parkinson's disease and essential tremor.** Propranolol combined with levodopa may benefit a patient of Parkinson's disease. Beta-blockers also diminish essential tremor which primarily involves the upper extremites.
10. **Glaucoma.** Beta-blockers lower intraocular hypertension by decreasing the production of aqueous humour. The topical route is preferred because of a lower incidence of systemic side effects. **Timolol** is the best topical ophthalmic preparation available. In patients with **open-angle glaucoma**, timolol appears to be as effective as pilocarpine or adrenaline. Topically one drop of a 0.25 percent solution is instilled into the conjunctival sac twice daily. Lately, a number of cases of sexual dysfunction with use of timolol eye drops have been reported, labelled as "eye drop impotence".
11. **Anxiety.** Propranolol and other beta-blockers suppress objective signs of anxiety like diarrhoea, palpitation, tachycardia and tremor. The antianxiety action of beta-blockers is more peripheral than central. There is increasing interest in the use of beta-blockers for acute situational anxiety of the anticipatory type, e.g., public speaking, stage fright and competitive activities. The lay press popularizes these drugs by using the term "confidence drugs".
12. **Propranolol** has also been evaluated for use in conditions like, schizophrenia, tardive dyskinesia, and acute panic symptoms.

Contraindications

Beta-blockers are contraindicated in sinus bradycardia; greater than first degree heart block; congestive heart failure; cardiogenic shock; overt cardiac failure; and hypersensitivity to beta-blockers. Propranolol, nadolol, timolol and pindolol are contraindicated in patients with bronchial asthma, or severe chronic obstructive pulmonary disease. Beta-blockers are contraindicated in the management of myocardial infarction patients with a heart rate below 45 beats/min; heart block greater than first degree (PR interval more than 0.24 sec); systolic blood pressure less than 100 mmHg; or moderate to severe heart failure.

Adverse Reactions and Precautions

Gastrointestinal: Vomiting, diarrhoea and flatulence.

Cardiovascular: Marked **bradycardia** and **hypotension**, specially on intravenous administration. IV or IM atropine can control excessive bradycardia if severe myocardial depression occurs.

Propranolol may precipitate **heart failure** in patients with inadequate cardiac reserve. It should be given with great caution to patients with frank or borderline congestive heart failure (CHF) who mainly depend upon the sympathetic drive to remain compensated.

Abrupt withdrawal of large doses of propranolol is occasionally followed by recurrence of **unstable angina, ventricular tachycardia, myocardial infarction and sudden death**. This is due to hypersensitivity of beta-receptors to catecholamines developed over time. Dosage should be gradually reduced over a 1 to 2 week period.

Propranolol may cause cold extremities and precipitate or aggravate **Raynaud's phenomenon** or **intermittent claudication**.

Paradoxical hypertension may occur occasionally when propranolol is administered in patients with pheochromocytoma without prior alpha-blockade.

Respiratory. Propranolol induces **bronchoconstriction** and may provoke *asthmatic attacks*.

Metabolic. Propranolol impairs the sympathetically medicated **rebound response to hypoglycaemia**, and may mask some hypoglycaemic symptoms like tachycardia in patients on insulin therapy.

Neurologic. Fatigue and lethargy are common central side effects. **Vivid dream** or **nightmares**, with or without insomnia occur frequently. **Depression and memory loss** are not uncommon. **Hallucinations, delirium, psychotic reactions** and **paresthesias** have also been reported.

Pregnancy and lactation. Propranolol crosses the placenta and may cause bradycardia, hypotension and hypoglycaemia in neonates born to mothers on propranolol therapy. It is also excreted in breast milk.

Miscellaneous. Propranolol may cause sexual dysfunction (impotence or decreased libido) fever, rash, myopathy, cheilostomatitis, alopecia and Peyronie's disease. **Thrombocytopenia** and **agranulocytosis** may occur rarely. Propranolol masks the signs and symptoms of hyperthyroidism. Indomethacin antagonizes the antihypertensive action of propranolol, and *cimetidine increases its bioavailability by inhibiting the hepatic enzymes responsible for first-pass metabolism of propranolol.*

Drug Interactions

Catecholamine depleting drugs like reserpine have an additive effect with beta-blockers. Beta-blockers further add to the antihypertensive effect of **captopril**, but the overall response is less than additive. The bronchodilating and cardiostimulating actions of **sympathomimetics** are antagonized. Concomitant use of **verapamil** and beta-blockers asks for caution; specially in patients with left ventricular dysfunction or conduction abnormalities, since both drugs may depress myocardial contractility and AV conduction. Concomitant use of **nifedipine** and beta-blockers is usually well tolerated, although there is an increased likelihood of CHF, severe hypotension, or exacerbation of angina. Increased beta-blockade may occur during concomitant administration with *chlorpromazine, cimetidine, oral contraceptives, furosemide* and *hydralazine*. *Smoking* reduces the serum levels of propranolol by increasing its clearance from the body. The effects of beta-blockers can be reversed by *isoprenaline, noradrenaline, dopamine* or *dobutamine*. In refractory beta-blocker induced cardiac failure **glucagon** may be useful. Insulin hypoglycaemia is prolonged by beta-blockers.

Individual Beta-Blockers

1. **Propranolol.** It is the most commonly used non-selective beta-blocker. It is completely absorbed from the gut. One-third reaches systemic circulation. The degree of first-pass hepatic extraction is less as the dose increases suggesting that a saturable reduction is involved. Ingestion with food enhances absorption, reduces first-pass metabolism and increases its bioavailability. Propranolol is usually given in doses of 40 mg bid upto 480 mg/day. It may be given IV in a dose of 1 to 3 mg slowly and repeated after 2-3 minutes, if necessary.
2. **Nadolol.** It is long-acting (half-life 16-20 hrs) non-selective beta-blocker. Its antianginal effect is comparable to that of propranolol. It does not cross the blood-brain barrier. It is given in a dose of 80-320 mg once a day.
3. **Timolol.** It is useful for chronic wide-angle glaucoma and aphakic glaucoma. It can be used as an antihypertensive agent in a dose of 10-40 mg/day in 2 divided doses. Timolol may also reduce mortality and the reinfarction rate when given as a long-term therapy after acute myocardial infarction. Timolol is known to cause gastrointestinal and CNS disturbances, rash, sexual dysfunction, alopecia and Peyronie's disease.
4. **Oxprenolol.** It resembles propranolol in its action, but is specially useful in elderly patients with a hyperkinetic heart, and during pregnancy. It has mild ISA.
5. **Pindolol.** It is a non-selective beta-blocker with marked ISA. It lacks MSA in usual doses. It is given in a dose of 5 mg tid upto 60 mg/day.
6. **Metoprolol.** It is selective $beta_1$-receptor blocker devoid of ISA. It reduces plasma renin activity in hypertensives. Because of its relative *cardioselectivity*, metoprolol may be preferred to a nonselective agent in asthmatics, patients prone to develop hypoglycaemia, and in those with peripheral vasospatic diseases. It is given in a dose of 50-200 mg twice daily.
7. **Atenolol.** The antianginal effect of this long-acting (elimination half-life 6 hrs) beta-blocker appears to be comparable to that of propranolol. It is a selective $beta_1$-antagonist with insignificant ISA. It may be preferred to non-selective agents in asthmatics, patients prone to develop hypoglycaemia and patients with peripheral

vascular disease. It is given in a dose of 50-200 mg once daily.

8. **Labetalol.** This agent combines both selective, post-synaptic alpha$_1$-adrenergic blocking, and non-selective beta-adrenergic blocking activity. The ratios of alpha to beta-blockade are approximately 1:3 and 1:7 following oral and IV administration respectively. Both alpha- and beta-blocking actions of labetalol contribute to a decrease in blood pressure in hypertensives. Due to alpha-blocking activity, the standing blood pressure is lowered more than the supine, and postural hypotension can occur. Labetalol is effective in patients with **mild to moderate hypertension**. It may also be administered IV to treat hypertensive emergencies. **Side effects** include orthostatic hypotension, sexual dysfunction, depression, nightmare and oedema. Systemic lupus syndrome has been reported rarely. It is given in a dose of 100 mg bid to patients of mild hypertension. Patients of severe hypertension may require 1.6 to 2.4 g daily in 2 or 3 divided doses. In *hypertensive emergencies* initially 20 mg is given IV slowly over a 2 minute period. The supine blood pressure should be measured.

To **summarize**, the oldest group of alpha-blocking drugs was the ergot alkaloids. Other **competitive antagonists** in clinical use are **tolazoline, phentolamine** and **thymoxamine**. **Phenoxybenzamine** is an alpha-blocker which produces a persistent non-competitive antagonistic effect. The main clinical use of alpha-blockers is in the treatment of vasospastic conditions like **Raynaud's syndrome**, in the diagnosis and treatment of **pheochromocytoma** and to antagonize vasoconstrictor effects of overdosage with sympathomimetic drugs. With the exception of **prazosin**, the alpha-blockers are ineffective in the treatment of essential hypertension.

Cardioselective agents like *atenolol*, *metoprolol* and *acebutolol* are available for clinical use. Labetalol is an agent possessing both alpha- and beta-blocking activity, and may be of advantage for the treatment of *essential hypertension*.

Propranolol till date is the most extensively used beta-blocker. Propranolol is used clinically in a large number of conditions including **angina pectoris, essential hypertension, cardiac arrhythmias, thyrotoxicosis** and **anxiety**. Lately, it is being tried as an **antipsychotic** agent.

3.6 GANGLION BLOCKING AGENTS

Drugs which inhibit or block the nerve impulse transmission across the synapses in autonomic ganglia are known as **ganglion blocking agents.** These agents block transmission across both **sympathetic** and **parasympathetic ganglia**, i.e, they are non-selective in their action, although some specificity has been attained with the newer agents. Transmission across the ganglia is **cholinergic** in nature, and the **nicotinic receptors** are involved.

The ganglion blocking agents were used mainly for their blocking effects on the sympathetic ganglia in the treatment of severe hypertension to produce a **medical sympathectomy**. However, now these agents have been largely replaced by the **adrenergic neurone blocking drugs (Chap. 4.2)**.

Ganglionic Transmission

The cholinergic receptors at the autonomic ganglia (skeletal muscle and adrenal medulla) were originally designated as "nicotinic" since nicotine could mimic the actions of acetylcholine (ACh) at these sites. The normal sequence of events during ganglionic transmission is: (*i*) arrival of an optimal number of action potentials at the preganglionic nerve terminals; (*ii*) release of ACh into the synaptic cleft by exocytosis; (*iii*) interaction of ACh with the nicotinic cholinoceptors located on the postsynaptic membrane; (*iv*) development of the excitatory postsynaptic potential (EPSP), which when crosses the threshold of excitability, an action potential is triggered and moves down the postganglionic axon; (*v*) dissociation of ACh: Cholinoceptor complex; (*vi*) hydrolysis of ACh; (*vii*) transport of choline back into the preganglionic nerve terminal; (*viii*) resynthesis of ACh; and (*ix*) storage of ACh in vesicles.

Mode of Action

Simply speaking, suppression or blockade of ganglionic transmission by drugs may be induced: (*i*) by the occupation of nicotinic cholinoceptors on the postsynaptic membrane which does not permit the released ACh to occupy these receptors and cause a depolarization, i.e., such drugs act by **competition** with ACh and are called **non-depolarizing ganglion blockers**; and (*ii*) by causing persistent depolarization of the postsynaptic membrane and thereby rendering it inexcitable. Such drugs are called **depolarizing ganglion blockers**, and they cause an initial facilitation of ganglionic transmission followed by paralysis.

Classification

On the basis of their mode of action the ganglion blocking agents can be classified as under:

I. Non-depolarizing blocking agents. They act by simple competition with acetylcholine, and stabilize the postsynaptic membrane.

(*i*) Pentolinium
(*ii*) Trimetaphan
(*iii*) Mecamylamine
(*iv*) Pempidine

II. Persistent depolarizing blocking agents. They cause prolonged depolarization of the postsynaptic membrane, and render it inexcitable (also called autonomic ganglion stimulants).

(*i*) Nicotine

Non-depolarizing Blocking Agents

The autonomic ganglion blockers today, as mentioned earlier, are of historical interest and have a small but not insignificant place in therapeutics.

All ganglion blocking agents essentially produce the same qualitative effects, since they block both sympathetic and parasympathetic ganglia **(Table 3.6-1).**

Table 3.6-1. *Some important effects of ganglionic blockade induced by a competitive antagonist like pentolinium, exerted on various body organs/tissues*

Organ/Tissue	*Sympathetic ganglionic blockade*	*Parasymapthetic ganglionic blockade*
Eye		
Ciliary muscle	—	Relaxed
Pupil	—	Dilatced

Table 3.6-1. Contd...

Organ/Tissue	*Sympathetic ganglionic blockade*	*Parasymapthetic ganglionic blockade*
Nictitating membrane	Relaxed	—
Lacrimal glands	—	Reduced secretion
Heart		
SA Node	—	Tachycardia
Gastrointestinal tract		
Propulsive muscle	—	Reduced motility and constipation
Salivary, gastric and pancreatic exocrinic glands	—	Reduced secrcetion
Urogenital system		
Urinary bladder	—	Retention of urine
Seminal vesicles and vas deferens	Failure of ejaculation	—
Blood vessles of the erectile tissue of external genitalia	—	Impotence
All blood vessels		
Skin	Dilated, postural hypotension	—
Pilomotor muscles	Relaxed	—
Eccrine sweat glands	Reduced secretion	—

PENTOLINIUM TARTRATE

Pentolinium is a bisquaternary compound, and resembles hexamethonium in most respects. It is about *five times* as potent as hexamethonium in lowering blood pressure. It is alleged that it has **some selectivity for the sympathetic ganglia**. Pentolinium is slightly better absorbed orally, but produces the same adverse effects, and tolerance develops on continued use.

Pentolinium is occasionally used to treat **severe hypertension** when other drugs have failed. The usual starting dose is 10 to 20 mg orally or 1 to 2.5 mg SC. The doses may be increased upto 900 mg per day orally or 20 mg per day SC.

Contraindications to the use of pentolinium are pyloric stenosis, marked arteriosclerotic cerebral or coronary vascular disease, impaired renal function and recent myocardial infarction.

TRIMETAPHAN CAMSYLATE

Trimetaphan is a very short-acting ganglion blocker. It is used to produce "**controlled hypotension**" during surgical procedures, specially in vascular and neurosurgery to provide a "**bloodless field**" for the operation. Bleeding is much reduced due to the low arterial pressure.

Trimetaphan is administered in a dose of 50 mg to 1 g as an intravenous infusion (1 mg/ml). The infusion may continue upto 2 hours, and on stoppage the blood pressure returns to normal in about 5 minutes.

MECAMYLAMINE HYDROCHLORIDE

Mecamylamine was the first **non-quaternary** ganglion blocker to be used clinically in the treatment of **moderate to severe hypertension (Chap. 4.2)**. It is a secondary amine and is well absorbed by mouth. The onset of hypotensive action is smooth, lasting for 6 to 12 hours. It has lesser visceral anticholinergic activity compared to pentolinium. **Tolerance** to the drug develops on prolonged use.

The **adrenergic neurone blockers** have superseded mecamylamine in the treatment of hypertension. But mecamylamine is sometimes used to control **severe hypertension** in patients refractory to other antihypertensives. The initial oral dose is 2.5 mg twice daily, and may be increased upto 60 mg daily, if necessary.

PEMPIDINE TARTRATE

Pempidine is a tertiary amine. It is well absorbed on oral administration, and does not pass into the brain as readily as mecamylamine. It is less likely to cause central side effects. Tolerance on prolonged use develops rerely. Side effects are the same as for other ganglion blockers, but milder.

Pempidine is sometimes used for **severe hypertension**. The initial does is 2.5 mg orally every 6 hours increasing upto a maximum of 80 mg per day. Larger doses may cause curare-like effects on the skeletal muscle, and CNS stimulation.

PERSISTENT DEPOLARIZING BLOCKING AGENTS

AUTONOMIC GANGLION STIMULANTS

NICOTINE

Nicotine is the colourless, volatile and highly toxic **liquid alkaloid** obtained from the leaves of the tobacco plant, **Nicotiana tabacum**, and acquires a brown colour on standing. It is a strongly basic substance, readily miscible with water. It has no therapeutic use, but is of considerable interest because of its wide use in **tobacco smoking** and **chewing,** and as an **experimental tool** in pharmacology.

Mode of Action

Nicotine is a persistent depolarizing ganglion blocker, as initially it behaves like a **partial agonist** at the ganglia producing depolarization, and later due to **prolonged depolarization** it blocks the ganglia. Thus, it has a "dual action". Nicotine first stimulates and then depresses the autonomic ganglia, adrenal medulla, neuromuscular junction, and the central nervous system.

Pharmacological Actions

Central nervous system. Small doses of nicotine have a stimulating effect on the CNS, and larger doses depress it. The **conditioned reflexes** are first inhibited and later completely lost. In man cigarette smoking leads to an increased dominant alpha rhythm in the electroencephalogram (EEG), which appears to be the result of psychophysiologic changes in the CNS. **Tremors** are a characteristic effect in man, which are due to both central and direct stimulation of the skeletal muscle. Nicotine first stimulates and then depresses the following centres: (*i*) the vagal centre; (*ii*) the respiratory centre; (*iii*) the vomiting centre; (*iv*) the supraoptic nucleus of the hypothalamus causing an increased formation and output of the antidiuretic hormone (this is the reason for the antidiuresis observed after cigarette smoking); and (*v*) the vasomotor centre. In animals, tremors may be followed by convulsions, possibly due to the stimulation of the upper levels of the CNS.

Cardiovascular system. In animals the observed **rise in blood pressure** is the combined result of stimulation of the medullary vasoconstrictor centres and the ganglia of the vasoconstrictor nerves, combined with the release of adrenaline and noradrenaline from the adrenal medulla. Later with higher doses the blood pressure **falls** due to ganglion blockade and loss of vascular tone. Nicotine releases **oxytocin** from the posterior pituitary which may be responsible for constriction of the coronary arteries in smokers.

Administration of 2 mg of nicotine by injection or through cigarette smoking in man results in a **tachycardia, increased blood pressure, stroke volume,** and **cardiac output**. These effects are mainly due to release of catecholamines from the adrenal medulla. The electrocardiogram (ECG) may show a **depression or inversion of the T wave**, which is due to the increase in heart rate and not myocardial ischaemia as commonly believed.

Smooth muscles. On the gastrointestinal tract nicotine induces *powerful contractions of the stomach, which extend to the intestinal tract exhibiting a marked increase in the tone and peristalsis*. Sometimes repeated evacuations of the bowel occur. Larger quantities of nicotine may lead to a tetanic contraction of the entire intestine. This is followed by a reduction in tone and peristalsis. The detrusor muscle of the urinary bladder contracts and causes expulsion of urine. Nicotine contracts the uterus. The glandular secretions are first increased, but later diminished.

Metabolism. Nicotine increases the free fatty acid (FFA) levels in the plasma, and it inhibits the anticoagulant effect of heparin. It stimulates anaerobic glycolysis in brain tissue. It stimulates the hypothalamo-hypophysial system, releasing vasopression which explains its **antidiuretic action.**

Fate of Nicotine

Nicotine ingested or inhaled by man from tobacco smoke is partially degraded in the body, mainly in the liver. The remainder is excreted in the urine unchanged.

Tolerance to Nicotine

Tolerance to nicotine develops fairly rapidly. The excitation, salivation, nausea and the burning sensation of the buccal mucosa in the uninitiated individual (non-smoker) diminish on repeated use of tobacco. *Non-smokers are nauseated by 1 to 2 mg of nicotine administered orally, whereas, smokers may tolerate upto 8 mg of the alkaloid.* Smokers usually absorb about 0.3 to 0.6 mg of nicotine per cigarette, although the amount may range between 2.5 to 3.5 mg depending on the number of puffs inhaled per cigarette.

Nicotine and Tobacco Smoking

Tobacco through the ages has been **snuffed**, **chewed**, and **placed under the lips**, but the most popular route of intake is by smoking. The pleasurable qualities of tobacco consumption are usually ascribed to the soothing and satisfying effect exerted by nicotine on the CNS. This leads to the tobacco habit. **Physical dependence does not develop**. The nicotine content of tobacco varies from 0.5 to 8.0 percent. The nicotine content of the so called "denicotinized" cigarettes is about 1 percent. About 90 percent nicotine is absorbed from the smoke inhaled into the lungs, whereas only 10 to 25 percent is absorbed if the smoke is merely taken in the mouth and expelled. In addition to nicotine, numerous other compounds have also been isolated from tobacco smoke. Some of these are **polycyclic hydrocarbons** known as "**tars**", and are responsible for the greater incidence of **lung cancer** among smokers. Efforts are being made to discourage the use of tobacco and to eliminate the carcinogenic agents assumed to be responsible for the bad effects of smoking.

In addition to **lung cancer, respiratory, cardiovascular** and **gastrointestinal** diseases have been related to cigarette smoking. The higher mortality rate among smokers has been correlated with the number of cigarettes smoked daily, the age at which smoking was started, and whether or not the smoke was inhaled.

The use of tobacco may lead to **palpitation, extrasystoles** and **paroxysmal auricular tachycardia.** It induces peripheral vasoconstriction evidenced by an **increase in the systolic** *and* **diastolic blood pressures**, decline in skin temperature and volume of the extremites, and narrowing of the retinal arterioles. Hypersensitivity to tobacco smoke possibly is responsible for **necrotizing angiitis. Emphysema and bronchitis** are six times more prevalent in smokers than in non-smokers. There is a demonstrable reduction in pulmonary function. Anginal attacks may be provoked by tobacco. Statistical studies indicate that the incidence of heart disease, chronic bronchitis, emphysema, carcinomas of the lung, mouth and throat, and atherosclerotic occulsive vascular disease is greater in smokers. Abuse of tobacco may result in dimness of vision, imperfect accommodation, degenerative changes in the ganglion cells of the macular region of the retina, and complete blindness in one or both eyes (**tobacco amblyopia**).

Cigarette smoking is contraindicated in: hypertension, angina pectoris, postcoronary conditions, Raynaud's disease, Buerger's disease, intermittent claudication and other vasospastic conditions, atheroslerosis, peptic ulcer, bronchial coughs, emphysema and lung cancer.

3.7 SKELETAL MUSCLE RELAXANTS

There are *three* distinct varieties of clinically useful skeletal muscle relaxants: (*i*) those that act peripherally at the neuromuscular junction termed as **neuromuscular blocking agents** (*ii*) those that act in the brain and spinal cord termed as **centrally acting muscle relaxants**; and (*iii*) the **directly acting muscle relaxant** dantrolene sodium.

The neuromuscular blocking agents interfere with transmission of nerve impulses from the somatic motor nerve endings to the skeletal muscle fibres which they innervate.

Historically **curare** was used by South American Indians as **arrow poison**. The paralysing effect of curare on skeletal muscle insured capture of the animal hunted, even if it was not killed outright by the arrow itself. **Claude Bernard** in 1856 carried out his classical experiment, in which he applied curare to a nerve-muscle preparation of the frog, and found that although the muscle did not contract following nerve stimulation, it continued to respond to direct electrical stimulation. He concluded that curare induces a blockade at the neuromuscular junction. The chemicals possessing this quality are designated as **curariform agents**, and their site of action is the **motor end plate.**

Neuromuscular Transmission

A **motor nerve unit** consists of an anterior horn cell, its processes (lower motor neurone) and the skeletal muscle fibres it supplies. Transmission of impulses at the neuromuscular junction (neuromuscular synapse) is mediated by the neurotransmitter **acetylcholine** (ACh), which is released from the nerve terminals where it is stored in the presynaptic vesicles **(Fig. 3.7.1).** The molecules of ACh then diffuse across the synaptic cleft and combine with the **nicotinic cholinergic receptors** on the **postjunctional membrane** (postsynaptic membrane) of the motor end-plates. This in turn makes the membrane more permeable to sodium (Na^+ influx), and potassium (K^+ efflux) ions, with local depolarization of the end-plates to give the end-plate potential (epp), which excites the muscle fibres of the motor units causing a contraction (propagated muscle potential). The enzyme acetylcholinesterase (AChE), in the synaptic cleft inactivates ACh, repolarization of the membrane occurs, the muscle fibre is relaxed, and is ready for stimulation afresh.

The sequence of events during neuromuscular transmission may be **summarized** as under:

1. Arrival of nerve action potential in the nerve terminal.
2. Release of ACh into the synaptic cleft (width 20 nm) from the synaptic vesicles by *exocytosis*.
3. Diffusion of ACh across the synaptic cleft and its association with the nicotinic cholinoceptors.
4. Depolarization of the motor end-plate to give the end-plate potential (epp).
5. The epp crosses the **threshold potential** and the **action potential** is triggered to the muscle cell (propagated muscle potential).
6. Ca^{++} release from intracellular sites causes shortening of myofibrils and development of muscle tension.
7. Dissociation of ACh: receptor complex, followed by hydrolysis of ACh by AChE.
8. Transport of choline back into the nerve terminal.
9. Resynthesis of ACh.
10. Storage of ACh in synaptic vesicles.

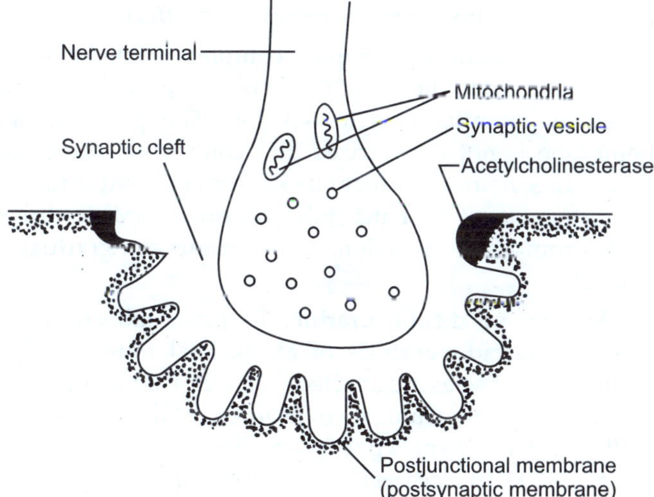

Fig. 3.7.1: The skeletal neuromuscular junction (diagrammatic).

Under normal conditions a single nerve action potential releases sufficient ACh to depolarize the end-plate to threshold potential, and only one muslce action potential is generated, as ACh is hydrolysed within the refractory period of the muscle.

Classification of Neuromuscular Blocking Agents

Based on their *mode of action* the neuromuscular blocking agents can be classified into two groups:

1. **Nondepolarizing Blockers.** These agents competitively block the receptor sites, and ACh fails to reach the nicotinic cholinoceptor. The postsynaptic membrane is maintained in a **hyperpolarized** state, and no stimulation or depolarization occurs. *Examples* include **d-tubocurarine,** its semisynthetic derivative **dimethyltubocurarine**, and synthetic agents **gallamine, pancuronium, atracurium, vecuronium**.

2. **Depolarizing Blockers.** These agents *depolarize* the postsynaptic membrane, and maintain it in a refractory state. Unlike curare there are initial muscle contractions referred to as fasciculations. *Examples* include **succinylcholine** and **decamethonium** (rarely used).

Nondepolarizing Blockers

d-Tubocurarine Chloride

King in 1935 isolated the pure crystalline material d-tubocurarine from *Chondrodendron tomentosum.* Synthetic tubocurarine is also available. Currently the term "curare" is used to denote d-tubocurarine.

Mode of action. When d-tubocurarine is injected intravenously, it is distributed throughout the extracellular body fluid, but does not cross the blood-brain barrier. A small part combines locally and **reversibly** with the **nicotinic cholinoceptors** on the surface of the skeletal muscle fibres in the region of the end-plate. A large portion of the drug combines with "acceptors" or "sites of loss" throughout the body producing no direct effects.

The **tubocurarine receptor complex** formed, keeps ACh away from the nicotinic cholinoceptors, and the end-plate potential fails to develop. The postsynaptic membrane is not depolarized and contraction does not occur. Thus, neuromuscular blockade is achieved through *competitive inhibition*. Later, tubocurarine *dissociates* from the neuromuscular junction, and transmission gradually recovers.

Actions of d-tubocurarine. In man, tubocurarine, causes a **flaccid paralysis** of all skeletal muscles. The extraocular muscles are affected *first*, followed by those of the face, limbs and trunk, then the intercostal muscles, and *finally* the diaphragm is paralysed. The *use of tubocurarine, therefore, almost always requires some ventilatory assistance.*

Therapeutic uses. Tubocurarine is used with **general anaesthesia** to produce muscle relaxation during surgical procedures of moderate or long duration; to reduce the severity of muscle spasm in severe **tetanus**; to facilitate **controlled ventilation**; and occasionally in the **diagnosis of myasthenia gravis.**

Toxicity. In doses commonly employed during anaesthesia, tubocurarine produce few side effects. A **fall in blood pressure** with a slight increase in heart rate may occur. Rarely it may induce **bronchospasm** due to histamine release. Overdosage causes **respiratory failure** by paralysing, the intercostal muscles and the diaphragm. Occasionally **postoperative apnoea** resistant to neostigmine may occur.

Dose: Average dose is 6 to 9 mg intravenously.

Dimethyltubocurarine Iodide

This is a **semisynthetic** derivative of tubocurarine, and is about **twice as potent** as tubocurarine, but has a **shorter duration of action**. It should not be used in patients sensitive to iodides. Dimethyltubocurarine produces a nondepolarizing neuromuscular blockade like tubocurarine. Its average dose is 2 mg intravenously.

Gallamine Triethiodide

Gallamine is a **synthetic** agent. Its mode of action is similar to tubocurarine, except that there is a **parasympatholytic action** at vagal sites, which may cause **sinus tachycardia**, occasionally **hypertension** and an **increased cardiac output**. Gallamine has a shorter duration of action, and lesser potency than tubocurarine. Patients sensitive to iodine may suffer hypersensitivity reactions. Its average dose is 80 mg intravenously.

Pancuronium Bromide

Pancuronium is approximately 5 **times as potent** as tubocurarine, the basic mechanism of neuromuscular blockade is the same. With pancuronium the histamine release seen with tubocurarine is largely absent, without the consequent symptoms of bronchoconstriction and hypotension. This agent occasionally produces *ventricular extrasystoles.* The average dose is 4 to 6 mg intravenously.

Atracurium

Atracurium is a nondepolarizing skeletal muscle relaxant, which functions as a **competitive antagonist** with ACh at the cholinergic receptor sites on the motor end-plate. Histamine release is minimal, and significant haemodynamic changes seldom occur.

Atracurium is used as an **adjunct** to general anaesthesia as a muscle relaxant during **surgery** or **mechanical intubation**. An initial dose of 0.4 mg/kg produces neuromuscular blockade within 2 to 5 minutes. Recovery begins 20-30 minutes after injection, and is complete by 60-75 minutes. **Adverse reactions** include skin rash, dyspnoea, bronchospasm, laryngospasm, hypotension, and prolonged muscle relaxation.

Vecuronium

Vecuronium is another nondepolarizing neuromuscular blocker. It is used as an adjunct to general anaesthesia during **surgery** or **mechanical intubation**. An initial dose of 0.08 to 0.1 mg/kg given as an IV bolus produces neuromuscular blockade within 3 to 5 minutes. Recovery is almost complete within 45 to 60 minutes. **Adverse reactions** include excessive muscle weakness, decreased respiratory reserve and apnoea. *Caution* must be observed in patients of myasthenia gravis.

Antagonists of Nondepolarizing Blockers

The **anticholinesterases** are useful in combating the toxic effects of nondepolarizing blockers by prolonging the life of liberated ACh at the neuromuscular junction. They exert a **decurarizing effect** mainly by inhibiting the enzyme acetylcholinesterase at the motor end-plate. The compounds which may be used (SC or IM or IV) are **neostigmine methylsulphate** 1 to 3 mg or pyridostigmine 5 to 15 mg, with atropine 1 mg to antagonize the muscarinic actions. **Edrophonium** or **ambenonium** may also be used with advantage. **Artificial respiration**, preferably with oxygen under pressure, should be carried out until it is safe to discontinue it. The nondepolarizers (curariform drugs) should not be used in myasthenia gravis.

Depolarizing Blockers

These drugs cause a persistent depolarization of the neuromuscular junction, i.e., they have the same effect as the natural neurotransmitter ACh but of a longer duration.

Mode of action. Succinylcholine acts by depolarizing the postsynaptic membrane in a manner similar to the neurotransmitter ACh. This action produces **muscle fasciculations**. After the initial muscle stimulation, continued occupation of the nicotinic cholinoceptor results in **persistent depolarization** (Phase I), and paralysis ensues. **This type of neuromuscular block is not antagonized by anticholinesterases**. On the contrary the anticholinesterases prolong the Phase I block produced by succinylcholine. This Phase I block declines in spite of the presence of the depolarizer, and the recovery of transmission marks the end of Phase I block. Later, due to a decreased receptor sensitivity, as a result of a single large dose or prolonged infusion these drugs cause a **desensitization block**, which results in a slowly increasing muscle paralysis (Phase II). Phase II block is also known as the *dual, biphasic* or *antidepolarizing block. It differs markedly from phase I block as it is slow in onset, and is similar to that produced by nondepolarizers like tubocurarine, since it is antagonized by the anticholinesterases*. This dual block is a characteristic feature of the action of depolarizers on all voluntary muscles. With succinylcholine Phase II block occurs very readily in patients with **atypical** or **reduced cholinesterase**. The safest treatment for a prolonged Phase II block is **maintenance of controlled ventilation** until the block reverses spontaneously. **Succinylcholine has the shortest duration of action.**

Succinylcholine Chloride

Succinylcholine (suxamethonium) is the dicholine ester of succinic acid. It resembles decamethonium in being a long, slender, flexible bis-quaternary positively charged molecule, and is equivalent to **two ACh molecules joined back to back**. In contrast to the bulky molecules (pachycurares) of tubocurarine and gallamine, the two depolarizers succinylcholine and decamethonium have thin long molecules (leptocurares).

Succinylcholine has a rapid onset (1 minute) and short duration of action (5 minutes), because it is rapidly hydrolysed by the plasma cholinesterase (pseudocholinesterase). Prolonged paralysis **(succinylcholine apnoea)** does not occur unless the plasma cholinesterase level is low or the individual has an atypical plasma cholinesterase **(Chap. 1.4)**. The drug is first hydrolysed by pseudocholinesterase into pharmacologically inactive **succinylmonocholine** and **choline**. Later succinylmonocholine is further hydrolysed into succinic acid and *choline*.

Therapeutic uses. Succinylcholine is used primarily as an ultrashort-acting muscle relaxant. It is used for brief procedures like **endotracheal intubation**, relief of **laryngospasm**, endoscopy, **orthopaedic manipulations** and **electroconvulsive therapy**.

Toxicity. The initial stimulation of muscle fibres leads to **muscle fasciculations**, which may cause considerable **soreness of the muscles**. Severe **ventricular arrhythmias** and **cardiac arrest** have followed succinylcholine administration to patients with severe burns, massive trauma, brain or spinal cord injuries, or tetanus. Succinylcholine may precipitate **malignant hyperthermia** in genetically predisposed patients, particularly when employed with inhalation anaesthetics like **halothane**, **cyclopropane** and **diethyl ether**.

Dose. Average initial dose is 30 mg intravenously. For continuous infusion the average rate is 2.5 mg/minute.

Plasma Cholinesterase Inhibitor

Hexafluorenium Bromide

Hexafluorenium inhibits the enzyme cholinesterase in the plasma, but apparently not at the neuromuscular junction. It also has some nondepolarizing activity (tubocurarine-like) at the postjunctional membrane. In man, **hexafluornium potentiates the muscle relaxant effects of succinylcholine**. Facilities for artificial respiration should always be at hand while using these agents. Hexafluorenium has been employed in a dose of 0.4 mg/kg intravenously to prolong the relaxant effects of succinylcholine.

Antagonists of Depolarizing Blockers

There are no clinically effective antagonists for the depolarizers. The anticholinesterases do not effectively antagonize the effect of depolarizers, but on the contrary are harmful. The safest treatment as mentioned earlier is **controlled ventilation** until the block reverses spontaneously.

Clinical Pharmacology of Neuromuscular Blockers

The neuromuscular blocking agents are used chiefly by anaesthesiologists to relax skeletal muscle in preference to deepening the level of general anaesthesia. Without good muscular relaxation, it is virtually impossible for the surgeon to gain access to the abdominal cavity.

Relaxants also facilitate **endotracheal intubation** and **reduction of dislocations** and **fractures**.

In **ophthalmic surgery** the nondepolarizers are the agents of choice when it is necessary to mobilize the eyeball.

In **thoracic surgery** muscle relaxants are used to relax the chest wall and paralyse the diaphragm to reduce the movement of the mediastinum. Relaxants are also used in **electroconvulsive therapy** to protect the patient from his own violet muscular contraction, which may otherwise lead to vertebral fractures or dislocations.

Selection of a Neuromuscular Relaxant

The choice of a muscle relaxant and its dosage is made mainly, but not exclusively on the basis of the needed duration of relaxation. The site of operation, the general anaesthetic used, patient's sensitivity, and other associated pathologic conditions must also be considered.

In general, a single dose of **succinylcholine** is the most suitable agent for procedures not exceeding 3 minutes, such as endotracheal intubation, reduction of dislocations and fractures, and electroconvulsive shock therapy. For procedures not exceeding 15 to 20 minutes, a single dose of **d-tubocurarine** or **gallamine** is used. For prolonged procedures relaxation may be induced by d-tubocurarine or gallamine, and maintained by small repeat doses of these agents.

Drug Interactions

Some clinically relevant interactions with neuromuscular blocking agents are summarized in **Table 3.7-1**.

Fatal ventilatory depression has been reported in anaesthetized patients following the peritoneal or immediate postoperative administration of antibiotics like **gentamicin, neomycin, streptomycin** and **polymyxin** B, which themselves have neuromuscular blocking activity.

Centrally Acting Muscle Relaxants

In addition to the neuromuscular blocking agents, certain other drugs can cause muscle relaxation by acting on the **internuncial spinal neurones** to depress polysynaptic pathways **(Fig. 3.7.2)**. These centrally acting muscle relaxants also act on higher centres, and are commonly employed as **antianxiety** agents.

Injuries or poisons that interfere with the normal flow of nerve inpulse between the brain and spinal cord and the skeletal muscles produce various signs and symptoms of abnormal muscle function. This may range from temporary minor **muscle spasm** following excessive activity, to permanent **muscle spasticity**. Muscle spasm often results from injury to peripheral musculoskeletal system structures, like overstretching a muscle, wrenching a joint, or tearing of tendons or ligaments, leading to involuntary muscle contraction, usually associated with pain. These are the results of excessive reflex action at the spinal level. **Muscle spasticity** is the result of damage to the neurones in the CNS rather than in the peripheral structures. The resulting hypertonicity is permanent rather than temporary, and can lead to crippling **contractures**. Spasticity results from either an increase in excitatory (facilitatory) influences or a decrease in inhibitory impulses. Such a situation may result in loss of coordinated activity and even in **spastic paralysis**.

Table 3.7-1. *Some relevant drug interactions*

Interacting agent	*Non-depolarizing blocker (d-Tubocurarine)*	*Depolarizing blocker (Succinylcholine)*
General *anaesthetics*-ether halothane, cyclopropane, methoxyflurane,	+	0
Aminoglycoside antibiotics - streptomycin, neomycin, gentamicin, colistin,	+	0
Quinine, quinidine, magnesium sulphate	+	0
Anticholinesterases- neostigmine	—	0
Hypothermia	—	+

\+ Increased neuromuscular blockade
— Decreased neuromuscular blockade
0 No pronounced effect on neuromuscular blockade

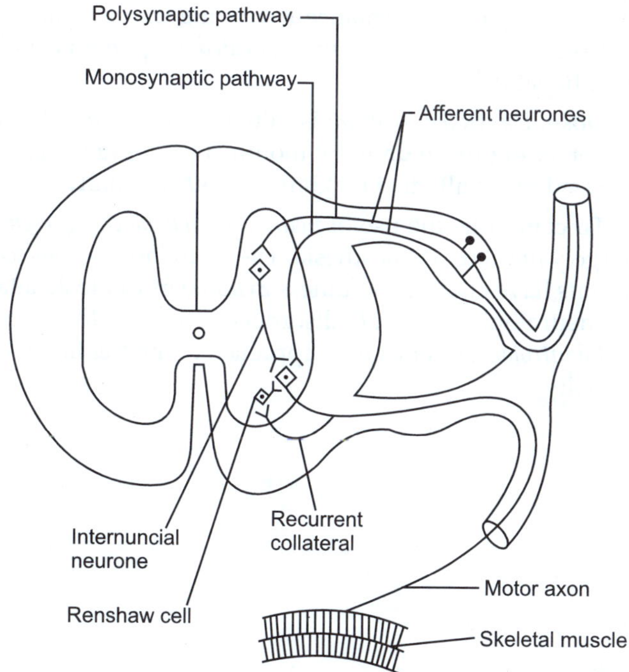

Fig. 3.7.2: Cross section of the spinal cord showing the internuncial spinal neurone, polysynaptic and monosynaptic pathways innervating the skeletal muscle.

Drugs for Relaxing Muscle Spasm and Spasticity

Several different kinds of centrally and peripherally acting drugs can relax skeletal muscle spasms and spasticity, e.g., **neuromuscular blockers**; **local anaesthetics** injected at specific spots in the skeletal muscle; **spinal anaesthesia** can block conduction of all motor impulses; **general anaesthetics** and barbiturates also can bring about muscle relaxation.

Selective Antispasmodics. These agents differ from the above in that they have a greater selectivity for motor neuronal pathways. Although the exact mechanism of action of these **neurospasmolytic** or **lissive** drugs is uncertain, their site of action is thought to be at the spinal and supraspinal **interneurones** that are involved in the hyperactive polysynaptic reflex activity. **Thus these centrally acting antispasmodics depress the overactivity of these internuncial neurones, which is responsible for hypertonicity, spasm and spasticity**.

Therapeutic Uses

The dosage and therapeutic uses of some commonly employed centrally acting muscle relaxants are summarized in **Table 3.7-2**.

Thus, the available neurospasmolytic agents are used in two clinical conditions: (*i*) **Musculoskeletal disorders**, e.g., muscle strains and sprains, whiplash injuries of the cervical spine processes, cervical root syndromes, herniated disc syndromes, low backache syndromes, dislocations and fractures, arthritis, fibrositis, bursitis and neuritis; and (*ii*) **Neurological disorders**, e.g., cerebral palsy, multiple sclerosis, poliomyelitis, hemiplegia, quadriplegia, Parkinson's disease, and strychnine poisoning.

Directly Acting Muscle Relaxant

Dantrolene Sodium

Dantrolene is a new hydantoin derivative that acts **directly** on the contractile mechanism of the voluntary muscle. It has no effect on nerve conduction or neuromuscular transmission, i.e., its site of action is beyond the neuromuscular junction. It probably acts by interfering *with the release of calcium*. It has the advantage of being orally active and has a long duration of action.

Table 3.7-2. *Some commonly used centrally acting muscle relaxants*

Compound	*Usual single oral dose (mg)*	*Therapeutic use*
Diazepam	2-10	For control of seizures and skeletal muscle spasm and spasticity; stiffman syndrome; cerebral palsy and athetosis, and for facilitating orthopaedic manipulations; convulsions in status epilepticus and tetanus.
Methocarbamol	500-2000	For spasm and pain with muscle strains, and inflammatory musculoskeletal conditions like arthritis, bursitis, fibrositis and myositis.
Carisoprodol	250-350	In addition to central antispasmodic activity, it is claimed to have analgesic activity.
Chlordiazepoxide	25-50	For active delirium tremens of alcohol withdrawal states.
Chlormezanone	100-200	Antianxiexty with mild central antispasmodic activity.
Chlorzoxazone	250-750	Available in combination with analgesics.
Baclofen	5-20	Used for spasticity in multiple sclerosis and in spinal cord injuries.
Cyclobenaprine	10	Used for acute traumatic and inflammatory muscle spasm for not more than 2 to 3 weeks.

The effect starts in 1 to 2 hours and continues for several hours. Dantrolene facilitates the effects of GABA, which results in reduced *efferent* spinal motor neurone activity, and *depressed* brainstem reticular function.

Therapeutic uses. Dantrolene has been used in patients with strokes, multiple sclerosis, cerebral plasy, spinal cord injury, postencephalitic athetosis and dystonia, and preoperative prophylaxis of malignant hyperthermia in high-risk patients.

Toxicity. The common adverse effects are weakness and diarrhoea. Hepatic dysfunction, and phototoxicity may also occur. Rarely insomnia, nervousness, skin rashes, visual disturbances and psychotic reactions may occur. It may also impair performance in driving motor vehicles. Dantrolene is *absolutely contraindicated* in patients with active hepatic disease.

Dose. *Dantrolene sodium* is initially administered in a dose of 25 mg twice daily by mouth. The dosage may be increased gradually to a maximum of 400 mg daily.

To conclude, the use of *neuromuscular blocking agents* is largely limited to anaesthesia. The *centrally acting muscle relaxants* have clinical usefulness in some musculoskeletal and neurological spastic disorders. The *directly acting agent dantrolene*, offers a new approach to the treatment of spasticity.

3.8 LOCAL ANAESTHETICS

Local anaesthetics are drugs that cause a loss of sensation in a limited area of the body. Unlike general anaesthetics, these drugs do not cause unconsciousness. The effects of local anaesthetics are not necessarily limited to the sensory fibres alone. When they come in direct contract with other parts of mixed spinal nerves, they interfere with skeletal muscle and smooth muscle activity in the regions supplied by the nerves blocked.

Local anaesthetics may be defined as drugs which reversibly block nerve conduction beyond the point of application, when applied locally in an appropriate concentration. Thus, local anaesthesia is a drug-induced *reversible* blockade of nerve impulses in a restricted region of the body (regional anaesthesia). Local anaesthesia of the skin can be produced by the rapid evaporation of a volatile liquid e.g., *ethyl chloride.*

Historically, in 1884 Carl Koller studied **cocaine** (derived from the leaves of **Erythroxylon coca**) with Sigmund Freud, and introduced the drug as a topical anaesthetic in ophthalmology. Later, Einhorn in 1904 introduced **procaine** as the first safe local anaesthetic for injection. Procaine remained the most widely used local anaesthetic till the introduction of **lidocaine** (Xylocaine), which is considered to be the agent of choice for infiltration anaesthesia. Lidocaine in addition to being an important local anaesthetic, is an important antiarrhythmic agent **(Chap. 4.4).**

Classification

The local anaesthetics may be classified according to their **chemical structure** or their **clinical usage**.

Based on their chemical structure, local anaesthetics are either *esters* or *amides*, and agents of clinical utility in general, possess the following chemical arrangement:

Aromatic portion - Intermediate chain - Amine portion. The aromatic portion confers **lipophilic** properties to the molecule, whereas the amine portion is **hydrophilic**. The currently used agents may be devided into *three* classes:

1. **Esters of Benzoic or Aminobenzoic Acid**
   Benoxinate
   Butamben
   Chloroprocaine
   Cocaine
   Cyclomethicaine
   Dyclonine
   Ethyl aminobenzoate
   Procaine
   Proparacaine
   Tetracaine
2. **Amides**
   Bupivacaine
   Dibucaine
   Etidocaine
   Lidocaine
   Mepivacaine
   Prilocaine
3. **Ether**
   Pramoxine

According to their *clinical usage*, the local anaesthetics are classified into the following types:

1. **Topical anaesthetics:** *benzocaine, butacaine, butyl aminobenzoate, cocaine, benoxinate.* Others are dibucaine, hexylcaine, lidocaine, tetracaine, and also benzyl alcohol and ethyl chloride.

2. **Infiltration and block anaesthetics:** *procaine, chloroprocaine, hexylcaine, lidocaine.* Others are bupivacaine, mepivacaine, piperocaine, prilocaine and tetracaine. In *dentistry* butethamine, metabutethamine and isobucaine may be used.

3. **Spinal anaesthetics:** *tetracaine.* Others are procaine, dibucaine, lidocaine, mepivacaine, and piperocaine.

4. **Epidural and caudal anaesthetics:** *lidocaine, prilocaine,* and *mepivacaine.* Others are procaine, piperocaine, and tetracaine.

Clinical Uses and Techniques of Administration

The technique by which regional anaesthesia is to be produced influences the choice of the local anaesthetic agent, and some guidelines are summarized below:

1. **Topical anaesthesia.** In this the local anaesthetic is applied in the form of a solution, ointment, cream or powder directly to the site which is to be anaesthetized. Topical anaesthesia is restricted to mucous surfaces, damaged skin surfaces, wounds or burns **(Fig. 3.8.1).** They are ineffective in penetrating the keratinized surface of the intact skin. The *corneal surface, mucosa of the mouth,*

nose, pharynx, larynx, trachea and *the urethra* are easily anaesthetized.

2. **Infiltration and block anaesthesia.** Infiltration anaesthesia is produced by injecting the agent throughout the area to be rendered insensitive **(Fig. 3.8.1)**. The object is to ensure that the finer nerve endings in the region are anaesthetized.

Two types of block anaesthesia are usually applied:

(*i*) **Field block**, in which the anaesthetic agent is not injected in the area to be dissected, but into the surrounding area. Field blocks are applied to the **scalp** and **anterior abdominal wall** where the nerves travel superficially to supply the area; and (*ii*) **Nerve block**, in which the local anaesthetic is deposited close to the mixed nerve, e.g., radial, ulnar, palatine, pudendal or a cord of the brachial plexus, and many others. The block is usually described by adding the name of the anaesthetized nerve, e.g., radial nerve block, ulnar nerve block and so on.

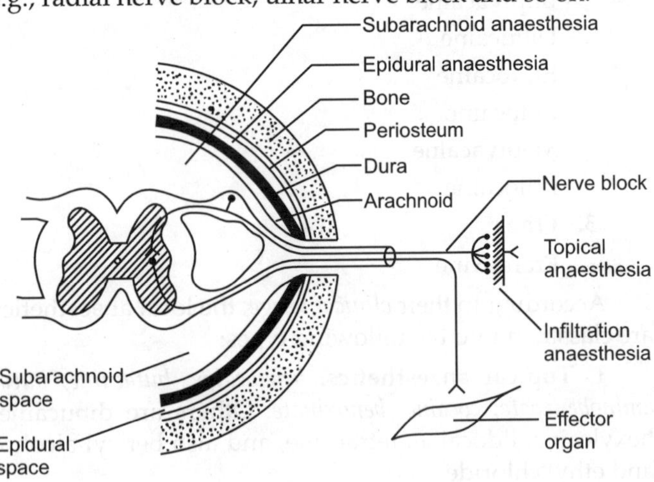

Fig. 3.8.1: Sites of application of local anaesthetics.

3. **Spinal anaesthesia.** In spinal anaesthesia (also called subarachnoid or intrathecal anaesthesia or block) the solution is injected into the **subarachnoid space**, so that it reaches the roots of the spinal nerves and dorsal root ganglia **(Fig. 3.8.1)**. The site of injection is chosen to block the roots of those nerves which supply the site of operation. Solutions which possess the same specific gravity (SG) as the cerebrospinal fluid (1.003 to 1.009) act primarily at the site of injection (isobaric), but solutions which are heavier (SG>1.009; hyperbaric) or lighter (SG<1.003; *hypobaric*) may be used if it is desired that the anaesthetic solution moves down or up the subarachnoid space respectively. Spinal anaesthesia by **tetracaine** which is the most commonly used agent lasts for 1 to 2 hours. **Procaine** is a shorter acting agent.

A variation of spinal anaesthesia is the **saddle block.** With the patient in the sitting position, a **hyperbaric** solution is injected, which settles down to the lowest portion of the dural sac, and anaesthetizes the nerve roots supplying the saddle areas. Saddle block is used in obstetrics and for surgery of the vaginal and perineal regions.

4. **Epidural and caudal anaesthesia.** The point of the needle rests in the epidural space **(Fig. 3.8.1)**, which is not fluid filled and extends from the foramen magnum to the sacral hiatus. The concentration and total dose of the local anaesthetic is large, and care must be taken to prevent its subarachnoid injection. Epidural anaesthesia has proved to be useful for operative procedures on the upper and lower abdomen and the pelvis. It is employed prior to *total hysterectomies* and *caesarean section* deliveries.

Caudal anaesthesia is a simple variation of epidural anaesthesia in which the needle enters the epidural space through the sacral hiatus below the termination of the dural sac. Anaesthesia of the most caudal segments only can be achieved, making the method suitable for obstetric analgesia.

ABSORPTION AND METABOLISM

The rate of absorption from the sites of injection depends upon the **vascularity** and blood flow of the region. It occurs just like any other material injected intramuscularly or subcutaneously.

Metabolism of the local anaesthetics does not take place at the site of application but in the plasma or liver. Esters like procaine are hydrolysed by plasma pseudocholinesterase. Amides like lidocaine are hydrolysed more slowly in the liver. Reducing blood flow to the site of injection by the addition of a vasoconstrictor (adrenaline) to the local anaesthetic solution slows down the absorption, prolongs the duration of action, and reduces systemic toxicity.

MODE OF ACTION

The local anaesthetics in current use consist of an aromatic **lipophilic** group, connected by an intermediate carbon chain to the **hydrophilic** amino group. The linkage between the intermediate group and the aromatic group may be an amide (lignocaine) or an ester (procaine).

The local anaesthetics are weak bases (pKa = 8 to 9) because of the amine group, due to which they combine with an acid to form salts, e.g., **lignocaine hydrochloride**. The salt can exist both in the form of uncharged molecules (B) and as positively charged cations (BH^+). The proportion of each depends on the pH and the pKa:

$$BH^+ \rightleftharpoons B + H^+$$

$$pH = pKa + \log \frac{[B]}{[BH^+]}$$

In acid conditions more cation will be present than free base, whereas in alkaline conditions more free base will be present. The active form of the molecule is the **cation**, which at pH 7.4 forms about 90 percent of the drug in solution. However, it is the **unionized form** of the drug which is important for optimal penetration of the nerve sheath to reach its actual site of action. Thus both the **charged** and the **uncharged** forms are involved in the process of conduction block.

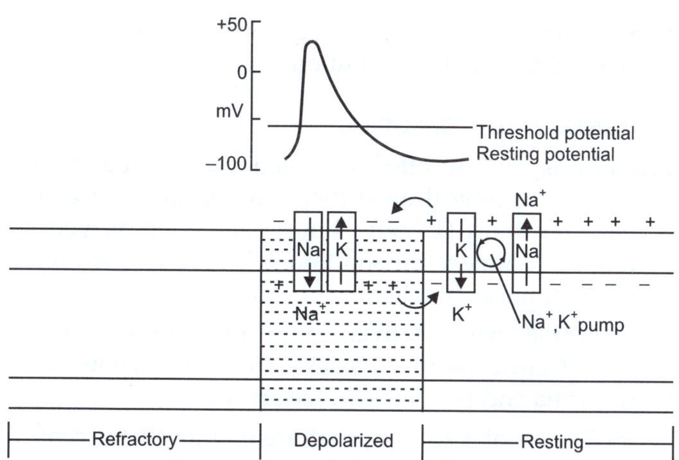

Fig. 3.8.2: The conduction of nerve impulse (left to right). The dotted segment shows the depolarization and repolarization phase, with the action potential curve on top. The segment of the nerve on the left of this dotted area is refractory to stimulation, and segment on the right is in the resting phase awaiting depolarization. The impulse thus can move only in one direction (see text).

During nerve inactivity, a resting potential of 50-70 mV exists across the nerve cell membrane, the inside of the nerve being negative **(Fig. 3.8.2)**. When excitation occurs, there is at first a relatively **slow phase of depolarization** during which the electrical potential within the nerve cell becomes progressively less negative. When a critical potential difference is reached (the firing level), there is a **rapid phase of depolarization** which reverses the electrical potential of 40 mV. The process of repolarization starts and the resting potential is re-established.

The local anaesthetics block transmission through all nerve fibres, namely sensory, motor or autonomic, i.e., they are relatively **nonspecific** in their action. About their site of action the current view is that the cationic form attaches itself to the internal axoplasmic membrane, probably a **phospholipid receptor**, whereby sodium influx is mainly decreased. The rate of increase and amplitude of the local action potential are depressed, and are insufficient for a propagated action potential. **Thus, the local anaesthetics have a stabilizing (nondepolarizing) effect on the nerve membrane, and the nerve impulse transmission is blocked**. According to the diameter, myelination and conduction velocities, the nerve fibres are classified into three types: A, B, and C fibres **(Table 3.8-1)**.

Blockade of A fibres results in **skeletal muscle relaxation, loss of thermal** and **tactile sensation** and **loss of sharp pain sensations**. Blockade of B fibres results in **autonomic paralysis**, and blockade of C fibres results in **autonomic paralysis, loss of sensation of itch, dull pain and temperature**. Clinically the order of loss of function is: **pain, temperature, touch, proprioception** and **skeletal muscle tone**.

To summarize, the principal site of action of the local anaesthetics is the outer part of the cell membrane (outer protein monolayer, and the phospholipid monolayer lying below it). The **sequence of events** of a local anaesthetic block are: displacement of calcium ions from the nerve receptor binding of local anaesthetic to the receptor site → blockade of sodium channel → decrease in sodium conductance → depression of rate of electrical depolarization → failure to achieve threshold potential level → lack of development of propagated action potential → conduction blockade.

Pharmacological Actions

Local anaesthetics largely exert their effect on a restricted area, as they cause blockade of nerve conduction at the site of application. In addition, they are also absorbed in appreciable amounts from the site of injection and exert effects on the CNS, and the cardiovascular system, particularly when high doses have been employed.

Central Nervous System

All local anaesthetics, under certain conditions have CNS stimulating effects like the convulsant stimulants **(Chap. 2.9)**. High doses may cause convulsions and respiratory depression. Very large doses depress both inhibitory and facilitatory neurones, leading to depression. Cocaine used by injection, ingestion or snuff produces long-lasting CNS stimulation comparable to amphetamine. It produces euphoria, and for this reason is an abused drug causing dependence **(Chap. 2.10)**.

Cardiovascular System

During the phase of CNS stimulation the blood pressure may be elevated. But later during the phase of CNS depression profound and dangerous hypotension may occur. They have a **direct depressant action** on the heart and also cause a **direct peripheral vasodilatation**. Vasoconstrictors, particularly adrenaline is commonly

Table 3.8-1 *The types of nerve fibres*

Type of fibre	*Function*	*Fibre diameter (μ m)*	*Conduction velocity (m/sec)*	*Myelination*
A	Somatic motor and sensory fibres	1-20	12-120	Yes
B	Preganglionic autonomic fibres	1-3	3-15	Minimal
C	Postaganglionic sympathetic and somatic sensory fibres	0.3-13	0.5-2	No

added to local anaesthetic solutions in a dose of 2 to 10 mcg/ml (1:500,000 to 1:100,000), to prolong the duration of action and to reduce systemic absorption and reactions.

Local anaesthetics have a **quinidine-like action** on the heart, and lidocaine is used in the treatment of **cardiac arrhythmias (Chap. 4.4)**.

Miscellaneous Actions

Procaine and related drugs are weak **antihistamines** and even weaker **parasympatholytics**. They have a **curare-like** effect on neuromuscular transmission. They also **depress ganglionic transmission**.

Toxicity of Local Anaesthetics

Transient or persistent CNS stimulation followed by CNS and cardiovascular depression may occur. Very profound CNS stimulation may lead to convulsions, which may be treated with **diazepam** and **barbiturates** intravenously. Rarely systemic allergic reactions may occur, and **topical sensitization** may lead to dermatitis on the fingers of dentists who repeatedly come in contact with the drug.

The sequelae of spinal anaesthesia are **hypotension** due to blockade of sympathetic vasoconstrictor fibres. Trauma of lumbar puncture may cause a **transient headache**. Spinal cord or nerve root damage may also occur.

Common Local Anaesthetic Agents

Some of the more common agents are detailed below:

Cocaine Hydrochloride

This alkaloid obtained from the coca shrub was the first clinically important local anaesthetic. The use of cocaine is restricted to **topical anaesthesia** of the eye, nose and throat, and in bronchoscopy. Because of its amphetamine-like stimulation of the CNS, it has been a popular drug of abuse **(Chp. 2.10)**.

Adverse effects are mydriasis, dryness and damage to the cornea. On systemic absorption it can lead to hypertension, tachycardia, tremors and convulsive seizures. It causes **psychological** and possibly **physical dependence** on repeated use. For topical application it is used as a 5 to 10 percent solution.

Procaine Hydrochloride

Procaine is rapidly effective when injected, but is not effective as a topical anaesthetic. Its duration of action is relatively short (1 hour), but it can be lengthened by adding adrenaline to the solution. It is used for peripheral and central **nerve blocks**.

Procaine has relatively low local and systemic toxicity. Cardiovascular toxicity includes hypotension, bradycardia and possible cardiac arrest.

Solutions of 1 to 2 percent are employed for central block procedures. The total dose for spinal anaesthesia is 50 to 200 mg intrathecally. One to 2 percent solutions are used for infiltration purposes, and the maximum dosage is 10 mg/kg.

Lidocaine Hydrochloride

This amide is one of the most widely used local anaesthetics for **infiltration, regional, nerve block, epidural and subarachnoid anaesthesia**. It also is commonly used for topical anaesthesia. Compared to procaine the action is more prompt, intense and of a longer duration **(Table 3.8-2)**. It is also employed to control ventricular arrhythmias.

Adverse reactions include stimulation or depression of the CNS. There may be a bradycardia and hypotension. Allergic reactions may occur.

Usually a 1 to 2 percent solution is employed for nerve blocks. For **spinal anaesthesia** a 5 percent hyperbaric solution is used. It may be applied topically as a 2 percent ointment. Also available as suppositories (100 mg) for use prior to proctoscopic and sigmoidoscopic examination.

Tetracaine Hydrochloride

Tetracaine is the most widely used subarachnoid (spinal) anaesthetic. It is not recommended for infiltration or peripheral nerve blocks. Tetracaine is possibly 10 times more potent and toxic than procaine when injected. The onset of action is slow (5-10 minutes), but the duration of action is 2 hours **(Table 3.8-2)**.

Table 3.8-2 *Comparison of some commonly used local anaesthetics*

Drug	*pKa*	*Concentration (%)*	*Latency (min)*	*Duration (hours)*	*Uses*	*Comments*
Procaine	8.9	1-2	2-5	1	Infiltration, nerve block and spinal anaesthesia; also for analgesia	Replaced by lidocaine
Lidocaine	7.9	0.5-2.0	1	4-5	Topical, infiltration, nerve block and spinal anaesthesia	About equal toxicity to procaine
Tetracaine	8.2	0.25	5-10	3	Topical, infiltration, nerve block and spinal anaesthesia	Ten times potency and toxicity of procaine

Table 3.8-2 Contd...

Drug	*pKa*	*Concentration (%)*	*Latency (min)*	*Duration (hours)*	*Uses*	*Comments*
Dibucaine	8.8	0.1-0.5	10	3-4	Infitration, surface or spinal anaesthesia	Fifteen times potency and toxicity of procaine
Mepivacine	7.6	1-2	3-5	2-3	Infiltration, nerve block and epidural anaesthesia	Similar to lidocaine with slightly faster onset and longer duration
Bupivacaine	8.1	0.25	12-15	10-12	Infiltration, nerve block and epidural anaesthesia to relieve pain during labour	Potency 4 times greater than mepivacine
Prilocaine	7.9	0.5-4.0	1-2	2-3	Infiltration, spinal anaesthesia	Overdosage may cause methaemoglobinaemia

The chief adverse effect in spinal anaesthesia is hypotension. As a general guide, the maximal single dose is 50 mg topically and 1.5 mg/kg of body weight by injection.

Dibucaine Hydrochloride

Dibucaine is one of the **most potent** and **most toxic** of the long-acting anaesthetics. It is 15 to 20 times more potent, and 15 times more toxic than procaine when injected. The onset of action is slow (upto 15 minutes), and the duration of spinal anaesthesia is 3 to 4 hours, and can be prolonged upto 6 hours by the addition of *adrenaline*.

Mepivacaine Hydrochloride

This agent is chemically and pharmacologically related to lidocaine, and is indicated for **infiltration, nerve block** and **epidural anaesthesia (Table 3.8-2)**. It is not effective topically except in very high doses. The maximal single dose is 7 mg/kg of body weight or 400 mg total, whichever is less.

Bupivacaine Hydrochloride

This agent is chemically related to mepivacine, and is used for **infiltration, nerve block** and **epidural** anaesthesia. It is particularly useful when administered by continuous epidural technique to **relieve pain of labour**. The maximal single dose should not exceed 200 mg without adrenaline, and 250 mg with adrenaline.

Prilocaine Hydrochloride

The agent is at least as effective as lidocaine in concentration, latency and duration of action. A disadvantage is that it causes methaemoglobinaemia. It should not be used in patients of anaemia, or in obstetric anaesthesia where placental transfer may cause foetal methaemoglobinaemia.

Pramoxine

Pramoxine (1 percent) is available as a cream, lotion, suppositories, foam and rectal ointment, and is to be applied topically or rectally 2 or 3 times daily, as needed. Anorectal preparations (ointments, foams, suppositories) are used mainly to relieve pain and itching of **haemorrhoids**. It is also used to facilitate **endotracheal, intragastric**, and **rectal intubation** procedures.

Clinical Properties of Local Anaesthetics

The **latency** of a local anaesthetic is defined as the time required for the onset of analgesia/anaesthesia after its administration. They fall into the following categories:

Fast acting: lidocaine, mepivacaine, prilocaine.

Intermediate acting: procaine, bupivacaine.

Slow acting: tetracaine, dibucaine.

Another factor to be considered while choosing a local anaesthetic agent is its **duration of anaesthetic action**, for which they are categorized as under:

Short duration (about 1 hour): procaine, chloroprocaine.

Intermediate duration (1-2 hr): lidocaine.

Long duration (2-3 hrs): prilocaine, mepivacaine.

Very long duration (over 3 hrs): tetracaine, dibucaine, bupivacaine.

Great *caution* should be observed while administering local anaesthetics, as their improper use can be dangerous. Some recommended steps are: (*i*) the lowest concentration and amount of the solution should be used to produce the desired degree of blockade; (*ii*) the total amount of the agent by weight must be recorded each time it is injected; (*iii*) these agents should not be applied to traumatized mucous membranes or areas of infection; (*iv*) injections should be made slowly and cautiously, taking care not to inject in a blood vessel; (*v*) adrenaline may be added to delay systemic absorption and prolong the duration of anaesthesia; (*vi*) patients should be placed in a proper position before spinal anaesthesia is given, and the patient should be lying flat or with head down (Trendelenberg position) after spinal anaesthesia; and (*vii*) oxygen, rapid-acting barbiturates and vasopressor drugs with apparatus for resuscitation should be available at hand, if needed.

❑❑❑

DRUGS ACTING ON THE CARDIOVASCULAR SYSTEM

4.1 GENERAL CONSIDERATION

The human heart is a four-chambered muscular organ, which by means of its rhythmic contractions pumps blood through two circuits—a shorter **pulmonary** circulation, and a longer **systemic** circulation. A unidirectional flow of blood is ensured by valves within the heart and in some of the veins. The blood outputs of the right and left sides of the heart are equal, and this is essential for the maintenance of optimal pressures and volumes throughout the circulatory system. Each circulation circuit consists of **arteries, capillaries**, and **veins** which carry the blood back to the heart. This capillary network serves the prime functions of the circulatory system, which are to carry: (*i*) oxygen from the lungs and nutrients from the gut to the tissues; (*ii*) excretory products from the tissues to the lungs and kidneys; (*iii*) hormones from the endocrine glands to their target tissues; and (*iv*) heat between the body core and body surface. The cardiac muscle fibres are **partially striated** and form two intertwining networks or **syncytia.** This interlacing accounts for the first both atria, and then both ventricles contract synchronously when excited by the same rapidly moving stimulus. Complete simultaneous contraction is necessary for the heart to function as an efficient pump.

The Conducting System

The special system for initiating and conducting the impulses which control cardiac rhythm is made up of: (*i*) the **sinoatrial**, or SA node, which sends impulses over certain atrial pathways (internodal tracts) to (*ii*) the **atrioventricular**, or AV node, from which they are passed onto (*iii*) the AV bundle or **bundle of His.** This divides into (*iv*) **two bundle branches,** the right and left, which break up into a network of fine fibres, the **Purkinje fibres,** which make contact with the muscle fibres of the ventricles. This conduction system is responsible for the normal heart beat rhythm.

Blood Supply to the Heart

The heart is supplied by two **coronary arteries,** which are the first branches of the aorta and arise just above the aortic valves. The myocardium is richly supplied by blood, with a 1:1 ratio between muscle cells and capillaries. Coronary venous blood is collected into the **coronary sinus,** which opens into the right atrium. The coronary arteries supply the heart with about 4 to 5 percent of the total cardiac output. During strenuous activity, this coronary flow may increase as much as 4 to 6 times. Oxygen lack of the myocardium results in **angina.**

Nerve Supply to the Heart

The heart receives fibres from both the **parasympathetic** and **sympathetic** divisions of the autonomic nervous system. The parasympathetic fibres are carried in the **vagus** nerves and mainly supply the atria, the SA node, and the AV node. The sympathetic fibres are carried in several nerves which have their axons located in the **upper thoracic** and **inferior cervical ganglia,** and these sympathetic fibres supply all parts of the heart. Because of this arrangement, the **vagus mainly affects heart rate and conduction, whereas the sympathetic nerves**

influence force of contraction together with the rate and conduction.

AUTOMATICITY

The heart exhibits an **intrinsic rhythmicity**, which is independent of external nervous or hormonal activity. The beat is initiated by spontaneous generation of action potentials by specialized cells in the SA node, or the **pacemaker.** The pacemaker cells exhibit a **spontaneous depolarization**, because their membrane is specially permeable to Na^+ ions. These Na^+ ions move continuously into the cells during the resting phase between two impulses (phase 4). As a result of this steady leak the **resting membrane potential** (– 90 mV), moves towards the trigger point—the **threshold potential** (– 55 mV). When this point is reached, sodium ions rush into the interior of the cells at a very rapid rate, and cause a **rapid depolarization** of the cardiac cell membrance to develop the action potential (phase O). The action potentials are conducted across the atria via the internodal tracts to the AV node. The conduction at the AV node is slower to provide time for the atria to empty into the ventricles, before the ventricles contracts **(Fig. 4.1.1).**

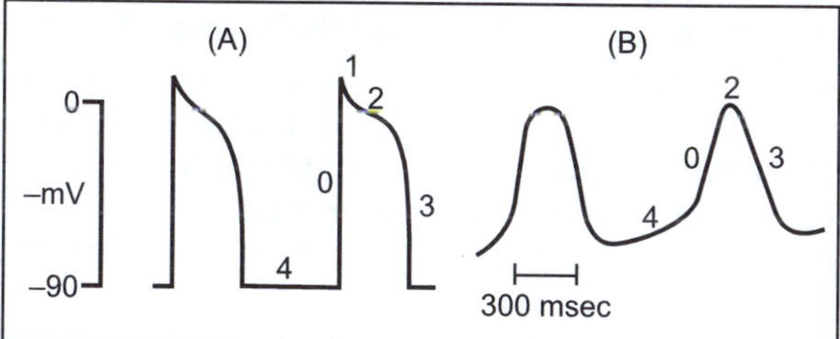

Fig. 4.1.1: Action potentials from (A) a ventricular myocardial cell, and (B) from a pacemaker cell (automatic cell).

Ordinary cardiac muscle cells (non-automatic cells) *do not* possess this property of spontaneous depolarization, instead they are excited to depolarize when they catch the propagated action potentials from the nodal or pacemaker cells, or other cells of this specialized conduction system. Rapid depolarization (phase O) is followed by repolarization of the membrane to the resting level of almost – 90 mV (phases 1 to 3).

There is another variety of automatic cells known as the "**latent pacemakers**", located in the AV node and Purkinje system. The rate of phase 4 spontaneous depolarization of latent pacemaker cells is much **slower** than the pacemaker cells. Normally these cells catch the propagated impulse from other cells before they reach their threshold potential, and thus their spontaneous activity remains latent. However, if their rate of phase 4 depolarization is increased, or the SA nodal cells are damaged, they may take up cardiac pacemaker function.

CONDUCTIVITY

Under normal conditions the cells of the SA node depolarize at a much faster rate than any of the other automatic cells. The SA node, or **pacemaker**, triggers the passive firing of the rest of the conducting system by means of its excitatory action potentials.

The speed at which the impulses are propagated through the conducting system and the myocardium, i.e., **conduction velocity** is slowest in the AV node and fastest in the Purkinje system fibres. The delay in conduction at the AV node is responsible for the fact that the atria contract a fraction of a second before the ventricles, which allows for the ventricles to fill fully before contracting **(Fig. 4.1.2).** The impulse spreads almost instantananeously through the ventricular muscle via the Purkinje fibres, which is responsible for the powerful and efficient pumping function of the heart.

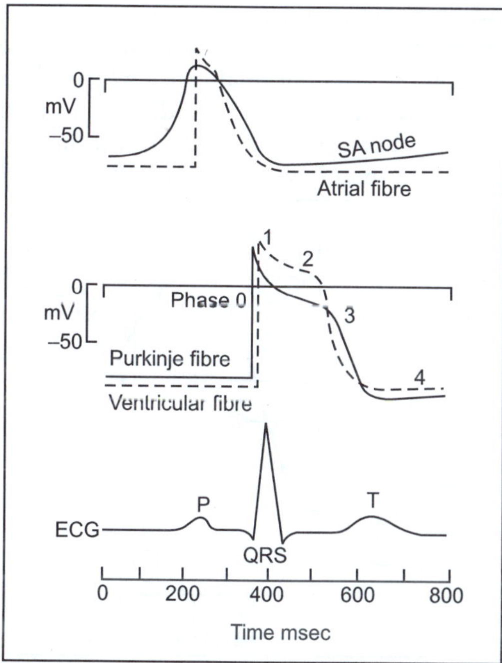

Fig. 4.1.2: Tracing of the typical transmembrane potential recording from the SA node, atrial fibre, Purkinje fibre and venticular fibre. The SA nodal fibre has a slow action potential upstroke, low overshoot and rapid diastolic depolarization (pacemaker), whereas the atrial action potential has a faster upstroke and flat diastolic potential (non-automatic). The Purkinje fibre shows slower diastolic depolarization (latent pacemaker), and the ventricular fibre has a stable diastolic potential (non-automatic), and relatively shorter action potential duration. The ECG shows the gap between atrial and ventricular activity, i.e. the P-R interval with the AV conduction delay. The Q-T interval represents the ventricular action potential duration.

The **conduction velocity** is a function of the amplitude of the action potential (*dv*) and its rate of rise (*dt*), expressed as *dv*/*dt* of phase O, or **membrane responsiveness.** Both *dv* and *dt* are related to the membrane potential present at the onset of the action potential. A smaller (less negative) membrane potential results in a decrease in the amplitude of the action potential, a decrease in the slope of phase O, and a decreased conduction velocity. **A decrease in intraventricular conduction is manifested in the ECG as a widening of the QRS complex, and a decrease in AV conduction is indicated by a prolonged P-R interval.**

Refractory Period

The inability of the myocardium to be re-excited immediately after an action potential is called **refractoriness**, and the period during which the excitability is reduced is called the **refractory period.** For a time after an impulse has stimulated a myocardial cell, and the membrane potential is less negative than – 45 to – 50 mV, it is generally unresponsive to even strong stimuli. Referring to myocardial excitability, the term absolute refractory period has gone out of use and the choice term is **effective refractory period** (ERP). Recent studies have shown that electrical stimuli delivered later during the ERP, if they are strong enough, elicit a local response leading to a transient depolarization which is not propagated. Such responses are important in the genesis of some conduction abnormalities, e.g., the phenomenon of **concealed conduction.** The ERP lasts from the onset of depolarization until the myocardium has partly repolarized to a membrane potential of about – 50 mV.

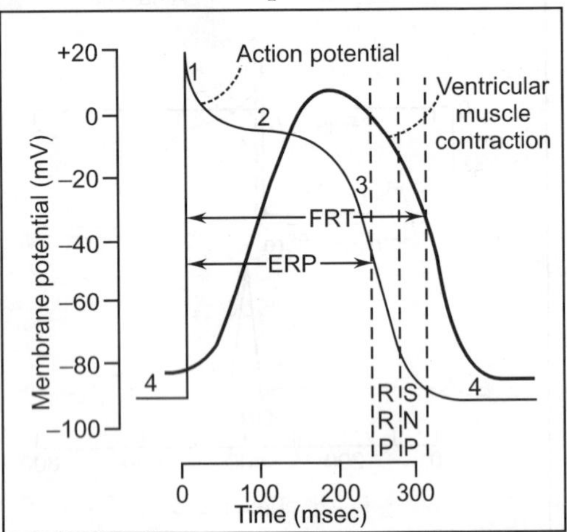

Fig. 4.1.3: Relationship between the ventricular cell action potential (phase 0, 1, 2, 3, 4) and the cardiac muscle contraction. ERP = effective refractory period; RRP = relatively refractory period; SNP = supernormal period; FRT = full recovery time (FRT).

The ERP outlasts the peak of the tension curve **(Fig. 4.1.3).** There is a considerable overlap of the action potential record with that of isometric tension, although the peak tension has passed by the time that the membrane has repolarized to – 50 mV. The ERP is followed by the **relative refractory period** (RRP), in which only an abnormally strong stimulus can initiate a propagated muscle potential. The RRP is followed by the **supernormal period** (SNP), in which even stimuli slightly smaller than the threshold stimuli elicit a propagated response. The interval between depolarization and complete recovery to normal resting excitability is the **full recovery time** (FRT). Thus, the FRT is the sum of the ERP, RRP and SNP. At the end of the FRT the myocardial cell responds with a normal threshold resulting in a normal action potential.

The mechanical muscle contraction soon begins after the action potential reaches its peak towards the end of phase 2 (plateau phase). The contraction phase of the cardiac muscle occurs within the ERP. Thus, the heart, unlike the skeletal muscle, *cannot be tetanized.*

Regulation of Heart Rate

Under resting conditions, the normal heart rate of an adult man is about 70 beats per minute. In well trained athletes the heart rate is about 50 beats per minute, which indicates a higher efficiency of the heart to function as a pump. Streneous exercise, fever and emotional stress increase the heart rate. Basically the heart rate is maintained by means of nervous control mechanisms, which can quicken or slow down the heart rate according to the needs of body tissues.

Electrophysiologically, the rate of firing of the sinus node can be **increased** in three ways: (*i*) if the rate of phase 4 spontaneous depolarization is increased, i.e., its slope is increased, the heart rate is increased as the threshold potential will be reached earlier; (*ii*) if the threshold potential becomes more negative,with the other factors constant, phase 4 depolarization will trigger off an action potential earlier; and (*iii*) if the resting membrane potential at the start of phase 4 becomes less negative, it will be closer to the firing threshold, and the heart will accelerate **(Fig. 4.1.4).** The reverse of these changes can cause cardiac slowing. Many drugs and conditions affect the diastolic depolarization in phase 4, and lead to either an increase or decrease in the heart rate **(Table 4.1-1).**

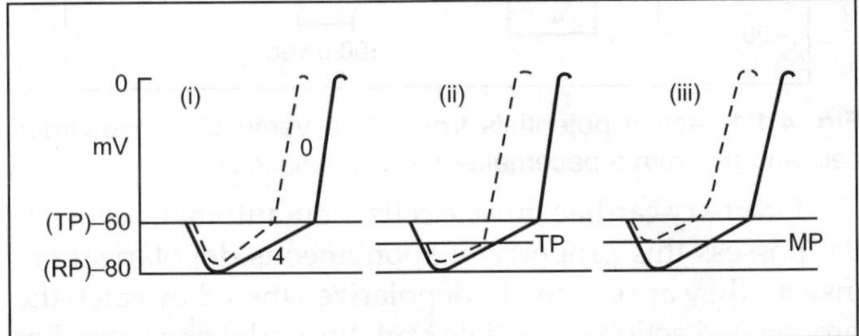

Fig. 4.1.4: Three conditions which increase the discharge rate of nodal cells accelerating the heart: (*i*) increased slope of phase 4 depolarization; (*ii*) the threshold potential becomes more negative; and (*iii*) the membrane potential becomes less negative. The potentials with increased rate (dashed line) are compared with the control rate (solid line). TP = threshold potential; RP = resting potential.

If the normal pacemaker is suppressed, or if latent pacemakers are stimulated, then the normal pacemaker no longer discharges at the fastest rate, and an **ectopic** focus takes over as the dominant pacemaker. **Myocardial ischaemia** and **stretch, catecholamines** or **acidosis may cause arrhythmias** by increasing the discharge rate of latent pacemakers. Enhanced vagal activity can decrease the discharge rate of the SA node, and ectopic foci dominate the cardiac rhythm. Thus, cardiac arrhythmias arise as a result of abnormalities in either or both of the fundamental electrophysiological properties of the heart, i.e., **automaticity** and **conductivity.**

Table 4.1-1. *List of drugs or conditions affecting diastolic depolarization*

Favouring rapid diastolic depolarization	*Fabouring slow diastolic depolarization*
Digitalis	Quinidine
Catecholamines	Procainamide
Atropine	Acetylcholine
Hypokalaemia	Hyperkalaemia
Marked hypocalcaemia	Lidocaine
Ischaemia and damage	Phenytoin
Respiratory acidosis	Propranolol

The Electrocardiogram (ECG)

The electrocardiograph records the patterns of electrical activity generated in the heart and spread to the surface of the body, where they are picked up by recording electrodes. These patterns of electrical activity are shown by the electrocardiogram (ECG) recorded on a moving strip (25 mm/sec) of calibrated paper. Electrocardiography is an important **diagnostic** and **prognostic** tool for the detection and management of cardiac arrhythmias. Electrophysiologically, the ECG is a record of depolarization and repolarization waves that sweep over the atria and ventricles.

In the normal ECG three main components are seen. The P wave corresponds to atrial depolarization, the QRS complex indicates ventricular depolarization, and the T wave records ventricular repolarization. A small U wave of uncertain origin follows the T wave in some leads. By convention any positive (upward) deflection of the QRS complex is the R wave. A negative deflection that precedes the R wave is a Q wave, and negative deflection which follows the R is an S wave **(Fig. 4.1.5).**

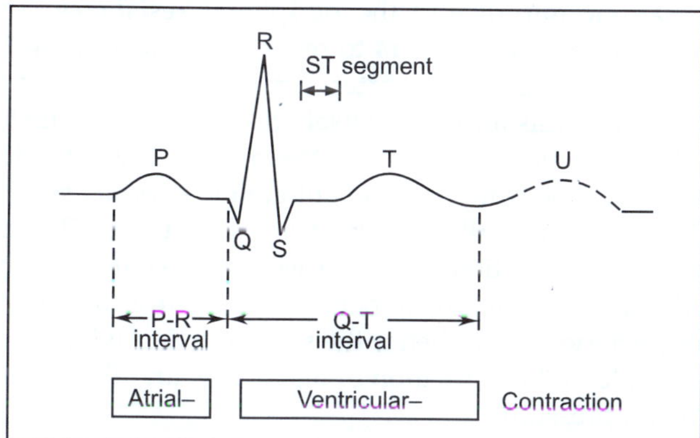

Fig. 4.1.5: The normal electrocardiogram, its waves,complexes and intervals. The boxes at the bottom roughly indicate the timing of the atrial and ventricular muscle contraction.

The following values for various waves and intervals for average adults are of clinical importance:

P Wave	0.07-0.14 second
P-R interval	0.10-0.21 second
QRS complex	0.06-0.10 second
Q-T interval	0.28-0.44 second

In cardiac arrhythmias these normal values are altered, with the result that the heart becomes a less efficient or even an inefficient pump.

Cardiac Output

The volume of blood pumped by the heart per minute is termed as the **cardiac output.** It depends upon the amount of blood expelled by each contraction or stroke of the left ventricle (stroke volume) and the heart rate.

Cardiac ouput (ml/min) = Stroke volume (ml/contraction) × Heart rate (beats/min)

The normal cardiac output in man is 5.5 litres of blood per minute. Trained athletes can raise their cardiac output to 6 times above the resting level during exercise. The factors which regulate the cardiac output are summarized in **Fig. 4.1.6.**

In **congestive heart failure** (CHF) the heart beats rapidly and weakly. This rapid rate prevents adequate diastolic filling, and the weak contraction incompletely expels the blood, and thereby the cardiac output and efficiency falls.

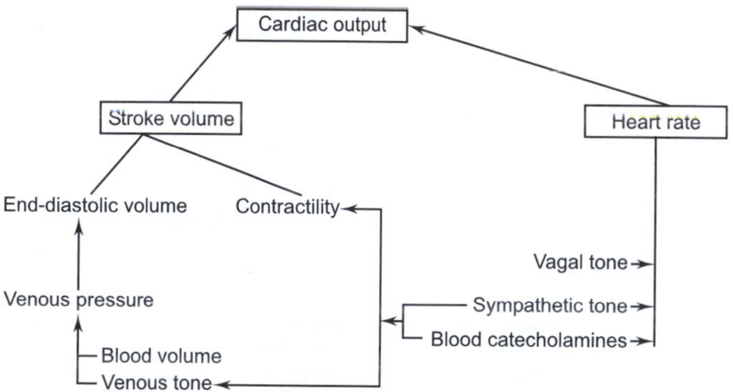

Fig. 4.1.6: Factors that regulate cardiac output.

Myocardial Mechanics

The left ventricular performance is dependent on mainly five variables: **preload, contractility, afterload, heart rate,** and **synergy** of contraction. The "**preload**", or the end diastolic fibre length of the left ventricular muscle refers to the filling volume of the left ventricle. To the extent that the left venticular end-diastolic pressure reflects its end-diastolic fibre length and volume, this end-diastolic pressure is considered as preload. The "**afterload**" is the impedance or resistance to the ejection of blood offered by the vascular system during the course of the ventricular systole. An **elevated mean arterial pressure** and **peripheral vascular resistance** represent an increased afterload and require the heart to work harder in pushing a given volume of blood through the vessels. Myocardial "**contractility**" is an intrinsic ability of the heart muscle to contract more or less vigorously for a given end-diastolic volume and afterload. A positive inotropic agent increases myocardial contractility. Regarding the "**heart rate**" it has been worked out that only at a particular rate the cardiac output is maximum, i.e., above this critical value the cardiac output does not proportionately increase with the heart rate. Tachycardia wastes oxygen and nutrients available to the myocardium. The "**synergy of contraction**" means the synchronization of ventricular motion during systole to eject a maximum stroke volume. **Asynergy** may occur due to a hypodynamic infarcted area of the myocardium. Haemodynamically, asynergy decreases cardiac output since the malfunctioning myocardium fails to contribute optimally towards a co-ordinated maximal ejection of blood during systole.

The relationship between stroke volume, and preload (left ventricular output versus input) is given by the length-tension curve called the **Starling's curve (Fig. 4.1.7).** Each curve describes the variation in the stroke volume (ordinate) with increasing levels of preload (abscissa).

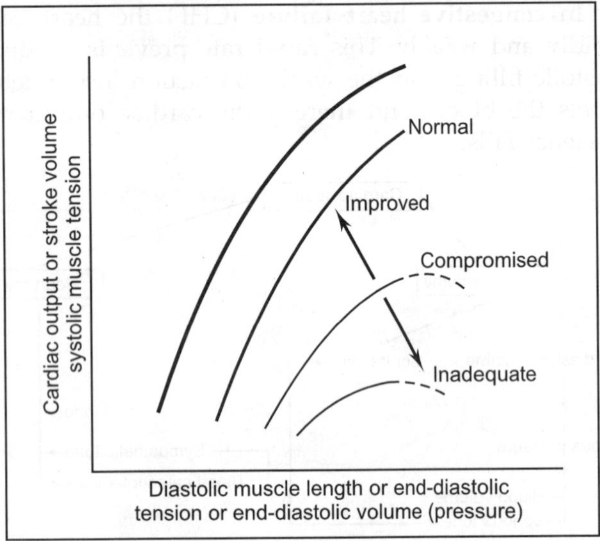

Fig. 4.1.7: The Starling's curves (length-tension curves) in which Stroke Volume is plotted against diastolic filling volume. Movement of the curve upwards indicates improvement in cardiac function, and *vice versa*.

When the contractility is depressed and the output is low, as in congestive heart failure, the myocardial performance is described by a **new length-tension curve,** which lies below the normal curve. On the lower curve, cardiac output is less per given value of preload. On the other hand, augmented contractility secondary to isoprenaline shifts the curve upward, i.e., the cardiac output is increased per given value of preload. This mode of myocardial mechanics operates within **physiological limits.**

Blood Pressure

Circulation of blood across the body tissues occurs via the arteries and veins, because of gradients or differences in blood pressure as it passes along the blood vessels. The mean blood pressure in the aorta is 100 mm Hg; it falls to 60 mm Hg in the arterioles; and to 30 mm Hg in the capillaries. As the blood enters the veins it has a pressure of 10 mm Hg, and in the right atrium it exerts essentially no pressure.

The **arterial blood pressure** fluctuates with each contraction of the heart. The maximum arterial pressure resulting from ventricular contraction or systole, is termed as **systolic blood pressure.** During the relaxation or diastolic phase of the cardiac cycle, the pressure falls, and a steep fall is avoided by the elastic recoil of the arteries. This lower blood pressure is called the **diastolic blood pressure.** The pulse pressure is the difference between the systolic and diastolic blood pressures. The **mean blood pressure** is **not** the arithmetic mean of the systolic and diastolic blood pressures. The value of mean blood pressure is given by the formula.

$$\text{Mean blood pressure} = \text{diastolic pressure} + \frac{\text{pulse pressure}}{3}$$

The average normal blood pressure in an adult man is about 120/80 mm Hg (systolic/diastolic). If on repeated estimations (when the person is at rest), the blood pressure exceeds 140/90 mm Hg, the individual in all likelihood has *hypertension*.

The arterial blood pressure is directly influenced by the **cardiac output** and the **peripheral resistance.** The peripheral resistance refers to resistance which the walls of blood vessels (mainly arterioles) exert on the flow of blood. This resistance is inversely related to the diameter of the arterioles, i.e., smaller the diameter, greater the resistance. The symphathetic autonomic nervous system (ANS) innervates all blood vessels except the capillaries. Under the direction of the **vasomotor centre** in the medulla, the sympathetic nerves can modify the calibre of the arterioles, and hence the sympathetic ANS plays a major role in the regulation of blood flow and the control of blood pressure.

4.2 ANTIHYPERTENSIVE DRUGS

The term "hypertension" literally means an abnormally raised arterial blood pressure. There are many conditions which elevate arterial pressure, including **primary renal disease, pheochromocytoma, hyperthyroidism, hyperaldosteronism** and **coarctation of aorta**, leading to **secondary** hypertension. In about 80 to 85 percent of patients of hypertension, no specific cause is evident, and such a condition is labelled as **primary** or **essential** hypertension. In these patients although the cause is not completely understood; heredity, emotional factors, and various physiological parameters play a major role in raising blood pressure (BP). If this condition is not treated, complication like **left heart failure, congestive heart failure, cerebrovascular disease, kidney damage and atherosclerosis** may develop.

Without entering the debate about normal blood pressure, it is agreed, that if the values of systolic/diastolic BP on repeated determinations exceed 140/90 mm Hg, it is likely that the person is suffering from hypertension.

Regulation of Blood Pressure

In order to understand how antihypertensive drugs act, it would be useful to review the factors which regulate blood pressure **(Fig. 4.2.1).**

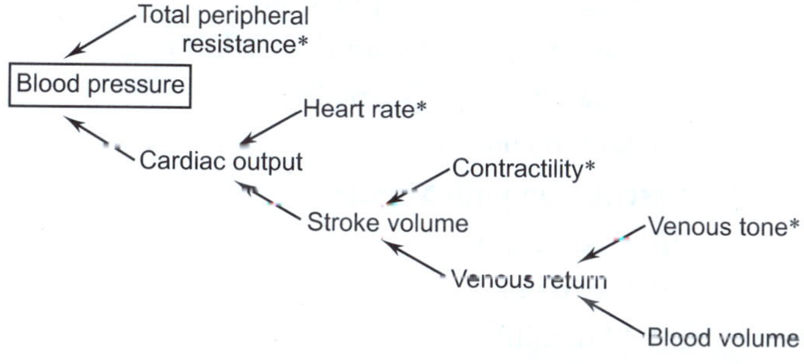

Fig. 4.2.1: Scheme for physiological maintenance of blood pressure (see text).

Thus, we see that many important regulatory factors work in a complex interrelated manner to control BP, and essential hypertension is a **"disease of regulation"**. The *four* factors, namely **total peripheral resistance (TPR), heart rate, myocardial contractility** and **venous return** are directly under the control of the sympathetic nervous system, which is supposed to be defective in a hypertensive patient. There is strong evidence that in the hypertensive patient, the **Renin: Angiotensin:Aldosterone system** is also faulty. Currently, pharmacotherapy aims at: (*i*) decreasing sympathetic influences on vessels; (*ii*) inducing loss of salt; and (*iii*) a combination of the above two factors.

The Renin: Angiotensin: Aldosterone System

The demonstration that renal ischaemia leads to hypertension led to the discovery of a kidney enzyme, **renin,** which is derived from the granules of the juxtaglomerular apparatus. On renal ischaemia renin is released which acts on a substrate in the blood, called **angiotensinogen,** an alpha 2-globulin, which is converted into **angiotensin I**, a decapeptide. This is converted into **angiotensin II** or **angiotensin,** an octapèptide, by the converting enzymes located in the lungs. Angiotensin stimulates the adrenal cortex to release **aldosterone.** Angiotensin is rapidly destroyed in man (Plasma $t_{1/2}$ = 1 to 2 minutes) by the angiotensinases to give inactive peptide fragments **(Fig. 4.2.2).** Lately, it has been shown that a part of angiotensin I and angiotensin II is converted to **angiotensin III.**Generally, angiotension III is less potent than angiotension II.

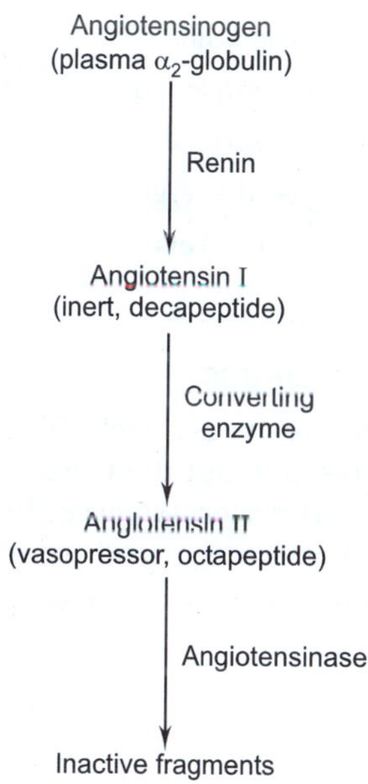

Fig. 4.2.2: The renin: angiotensin: aldosterone system.

Angiotensin is a **very potent vasopressor** agent, and in equimolar doses is 40 times more potent than noradrenaline. It causes strong arteriolar constriction and a rise in both **diastolic** and **systolic** blood pressure **(Fig. 4.2.3).**

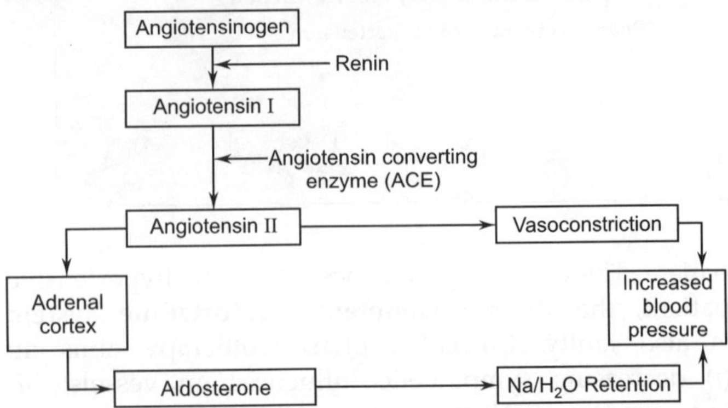

Fig. 4.2.3: The renin: angiotensin: aldosterone system and blood pressure.

The **renin: angiotensin: aldosterone system** is important in the maintenance of cardiovascular homeostasis and the control of electrolyte balance. It also has a modulatory effect on sympathetic nerve activity. A high renin and angiotensin concentration is a common finding in **malignant hypertension**.

With reference to plasma renin activity, about 15 percent of essential hypertensives have high renin activity, 55 percent have normal activity, and 30 percent have low renin activity. Many antihypertensive drugs alter renin activity **(Table 4.2-1).**

Table 4.2-1. *Effect of antihypertensive drugs on plasma renin activity*

Renin elevation	*Renin depression*	*No change*
Thiazide diuretics	Beta-blockers	Prazosin
Loop diuretics	Clonidine	
Spironolactone	Methyldopa	
Triamterene	Reserpine	
Hydralazine	Andrenergic neurone blockers	
Diazoxide		
Minoxidil		

ANTIHYPERTENSIVE DRUGS

Most antihypertensive drugs can effectively reduce mildly elevated blood pressure, but their use is associated with many side effects. Hypertension according to the level of blood pressure may be categorized as under:

Pressure (mm Hg)	**Category**
Diastolic	
Less than 85	Normal
85-90	High Normal
91-105	Mild
106-115	Moderate
Greater than 115	Severe
Systolic *(with diastolic less than 90)*	
Less than 140	Normal
140-160	Borderline systolic
Greater than 160	Isolated systolic

The diastolic reading is usually taken as the **primary** determinant of the degree of hypertension, while the systolic pressure is often utilized to further delineate the category of hypertension. **Borderline hypertension** can be controlled by **weight reduction, salt restriction, cessation of smoking,** and **change in life style.** But drug therapy must be seriously considered in the *high-risk* group, with evidence of end-organ damage or a strong family history of cardiovascular disease. Currently **isolated systolic hypertension** is also recognized as a disease entity, and drug therapy must be seriously considered.

SITES OF ACTION

Many antihypertensive drugs have more than one site or mode of action, but they can be conveniently grouped according to their principal site of action **(Table 4.2-2).**

Table 4.2-2: *The principal sites of action of antihypertensive drugs.*

I. **CNS: Hypothalamus, Medulla**
   (*i*) Clonidine, Guanabenz, Guanfacine
   (*ii*) Methyldopa
   (*iii*) Beta-blockers (propranolol)

II. **Sympathetic Ganglia**
   (*i*) Ganglion blockers (Trimethaphan)

III. **Adrenergic Nerve Endings**
   (*i*) Alpha-blockers (phentolamine, prazosin)
   (*ii*) Beta-blockers (propranolol)
   (*iii*) Alpha + beta blocker (Labetalol)
   (*iv*) Guanethidine, Guanadrel
   (*v*) Metyrosine

IV. **Vascular Smooth Muscle**
   (*i*) Hydralazine
   (*ii*) Diazoxide
   (iii) Minoxidil
   (*iv*) Nitroprusside
   (*v*) Diuretics (hydrochlorothiazide)
   (*vi*) Calcium channel blockers (verapamil)

V. **Kidney**
   (*i*) Diuretics (thiazides, loop diuretics)

VI. **Renin : angiotensin : aldosterone system**
   (*i*) Captopril, Enalapril, Lisinopril

CLASSIFICATION

Drugs influence arterial blood pressure at **four** effector sites–**arterioles** (resistance vessels); **veins** (capacitance vessels); **heart;** and the **kidneys—**by several different mechanisms. They can be classified according to their site or *mode* of action as follows:

I. **Diurectics**

(*i*) *Thiazides* and related agents (hydrochlorothiazide, chlorthalidone etc.)

(*ii*) *Loop diuretics* (frusemide, bumetanide, ethacrynic acid)

(*iii*) *Postassium-sparing diuretics* (spironolactone, triamterene, amiloride)

II. **Sympatholytic Drugs**

(*i*) *Centrally acting agents* (methyldopa, clonidine, guanabenz, guanfacine).

(*ii*) *Ganglion blocking agents* (trimethaphan).

(*iii*) *Adrenergic neurone blocking agents* (guanethidine, guanadrel).

(*iv*) *Beta-adrenoceptor blockers* (propranolol, metoprolol, atenolol etc.)

(*v*) *Alpha-adrenoceptor blockers* (prazosin, terazosin, doxazosin, phenoxybenzamine).

(*vi*) *Alpha*+beta blockers (labetalol, carvedilol)

III. **Vasodilators**

(*i*) *Arterial* (hydralazine, minoxidil, diazoxide)

(*ii*) *Arterial* and *venous* (nitroprusside)

IV. **Calcium Channel Blockers**

Verapamil, diltiazem, nifedipine, nicardipine, nitrendipine, nimodipine, felodipine, amlodipine

V. **Angiotensin Converting Enzyme Inhibitors**

Captopril, enalparil, lisinopril

Alternatively, antihypertensive drugs may be grouped according to the **stepped-care approach** of treating hypertension, as advocated by the Joint National Committee on Detection, Evaluation and Treatment of High Blood Pressure, USA. This approach consists of **sequential** prescribing steps, beginning with a **single** agent in increasing dosage, then adding or substituting other agents in gradually increasing doses until the therapeutic goal is attained, or side effects become intolerable, or maximum dosage is reached. **The stepped-care approach** is outlined below:

Step 1 (Mild Hypertension)

Diuretics

Thiazides

Loop diuretics

Potassium-sparing diuretics

Beta-blockers

Step 2 (Mild to Moderate Hypertension)

Beta-blockers

Labetalol

Clonidine, guanabenz, guanfacine

Methyldopa

Prazosin, terazosin

Calcium channel blockers (verapamil)

Captopril, enalapril, lisinopril

Step 3 (Moderate Hypertension)

Captopril, enalapril, lisinopril

Hydralazine

Step 4 (Severe Hypertension)

Guanethidine, guanadrel

Minoxidil

Hypertensive Emergencies

Diazoxide

Nitroprusside

Trimethaphan

I. Diuretics

Diuretics are still used as initial drugs of choice for mild hypertension in the majority of cases. They can be used alone, or in combination with other classes of antihypertensive drugs. Diuretics of established value in the treatment of hypertension are the **thiazides**, the **loop** or **high-sealing** diuretics, and the **potassium-sparing** diuretics **(Chap. 6.2).**

THIAZIDE DIURETICS

Chlorothiazide was the first potent orally effective diuretic. It was soon observed that it lowered blood pressure (BP) in hypertensive patients. This was possibly due to blockade of Na^+ and Cl^- reabsorption from the renal tubules, leading to sodium and water loss from the body. Side by side K^+ was also lost in urine causing hypokalaemia. The hydrogenated compounds have a more favourable Na^+/K^+ excretion ratio. A few thiazides are lsited in **Table 4.2-3.**

Mode of action. The thiazides initially induce a Na^+ and water loss, leading to a fall in plasma volume and extracellular fluid (ECF), which in turn **lowers** the cardiac output and BP. On prolonged thiazide treatment the plasma volume and ECF return to normal, but their hypotensive effect continues. This is probably due to the **reduced sensitivity** of the vascular bed to circulating **catecholamines** (CA) and **angiotensin.** This, in addition to reduced arteriolar oedema, decreases the TPR and lowers arterial BP.

The main advantages of the thiazides are, that tolerance to the antihypertensive effect does not develop, side effects are mild, and they potentiate the effect of other unrelated antihypertensive drugs, and lower BP in both supine and standing positions.

Table 4.2-3: *The dosage, duration of action and electrolyte excretion pattern of some thiazides*

Thiazide	*Dose (mg)*	*Duration of action (hrs)*	*Electrolyte excretion (mEq/24 hrs)* Sodium excretion	Na^+/K^+ ratio
Chlorothiazide	1000	6-12	44	2.5
Hydrochlorothiazide	25	6-12	90	2.9
Hydroflumethiazide	25	6-12	85	3.4
Bendroflumethiazide	2.5	24	110	8.1
Polythiazide	4	36	136	8.4
Chlorthalidone*	25	72	112	18.2

*pthalimidine derivative

Adverse reactions. Certain degree of hypokalaemia can occur, which can be avoided by combining K^+ sparing diuretics like **spironolactone** or **triamterene.** Other side effects are, hyperglycaemia and hyperuricaemia. Rarely pancreatitis, photosensitivity, cholestatic jaundice, bone marrow depression and postural hypotension may occur. The thiazides are **contraindicated** in cases of renal insufficiency and hepatic cirrhosis.

Dose. Hydrochlorothiazide 25-50 mg bid orally.

Loop Diuretics

The drugs in this class are **frusemide, bumetanide,** and the less used **ethacrynic acid.** They can be used in a manner similar to the thiazides. Loop diuretics inhibit active tubular reabsorption or Na^+ and Cl^- in the thick ascending loop of Henle, and segments of the proximal and distal tubules. Thus they have a strong **natriuretic** activity. Magnesium and calcium excretion is increased secondarily, and their chronic use can result in **hypomagnesemia** and **hypocalcaemia.** Loop diuretics can cause **dangerous hypokalaemia.** In the adjunctive treatment of hypertension usually **frusemide** is used in a dose of 40 mg twice daily, adjusted according to response. Usual maintenance dose is 40 to 80 mg/day in a single or two divided doses.

Potassium-sparing Diuretics

Spironolactone, triamterene and **amiloride** produce modest diuresis in comparison to the thiazides and loop diuretics. The important feature is that the loss of Na^+ is not accompanied by loss of K^+, and they exert a potassium-sparing effect. Potassium-sparing diuretics are usually employed in conjunction with other potent diuretics to minimize K^+ loss.

II. Sympatholytic Drugs

Centrally Acting Agents

Methyldopa

Methyldopa is a structural analogue of dihydroxyphenylalamine (dopa), and differs from it only by the presence of a methyl group on the α-carbon of the side chain. It is preferred for patients with **chronic renal disease,** and in **hypertensive emergencies.**

Mode of action. Methyldopa is a substrate for dopa decarboxylase, and in the neurone is converted to **alpha-methylnoradrenaline,** which acts as a **false transmitter,** and in due course of time leads to noradrenaline (NA) depletion. But subsequently it was found that alpha-methylnoradrenaline is equipotent to noradrenaline as a vasopressor, and the **false transmitter hypothesis** was dropped.

Currently it is held that methyldopa rapidly enters the brain where it accumulates in the adrenergic neurones. In the central neurones it is converted to **alpha-methylnoradrenaline** by the enzyme dopa decarboxylase. Alpha-methylnoradrenaline is a potent **alpha$_2$-receptor agonist** located presynaptically. This leads to a **decreased sympathetic outflow** from the brain, which in turn causes peripheral vasodialation and reduction of TPR. Thus, like **clonidine, guanfacine** and **guanabenz,** alpha-methylnoradrenaline also decreases brainstem sympathetic outflow resulting in reduced TPR. Standing BP, and to a lesser extent supine BP are reduced, but orthostatic effects are infrequent.

Adverse reactions. Marked drowsiness, depression, nightmares, fluid retention, enlargement of breast, drug fever, hepatic dysfunction and haemolytic anaemia may occur. The haemolytic anaemia which may be acute produces a positive direct Coomb's test in upto 20 percent of patients treated with methyldopa. Postural hypotension can occur. In some individuals it can lead to an influenza-like reaction, which may be due to drug sensitization.

Dose. Methyldopa initially 250 mg bid or tid, can be increased upto 500 mg qid.

Clonidine

Guanabenz

Guanfacine

Clonidine is effective orally, and is used primarily in the treatment of moderate hypertension. It is an **imidazoline** derivative, structurally related to the alpha-blockers **phentolamine** and **tolazoline. Clonidine, however, is not an alpha-blocker, but is an alpha$_2$-adrenoceptor agonist.** It activates central alpha$_2$-receptors, thereby reducing sympathetic outflow to the periphery.

Guanabenz and **guanfacine** have considerable structural similarity to clonidine. They exhibit a central α_2-agonistic acitivity similar to that of clonidine.

Clonidine on IV injection may produce a transient pressor response, apparently due to stimulation of peripheral vascular alpha-receptors. This pressor response does not occur after oral administration, because the centrally mediated depressor action overrides it.

Mode of action. Clonidine, guanabenz and guanfacine are central **alpha$_2$-adrenoceptor agonists,** and inhibit the **outflow of sympathetic vasoconstrictor and cardioaccelerator** impulses from the brainstem. BP is reduced equally in the supine and standing position, thus orthostatic effects are infrequent. Heart rate is slowed, but renal blood flow remains unchanged. There is a small reduction in TPR. A *paradoxical* rise in blood pressure may occur in some patients on these drugs, because of a peripheral alpha-receptor stimulation leading to vasoconstriction. The main difference between clonidine and methyldopa is that clonidine acts directly on alpha$_2$-receptors, whereas alpha-methyldopa first must be converted to alpha-methylnoradrenaline which then acts on alpha$_2$-receptors.

Therapeutic uses. Clonidine, guanabenz and guanfacine are used in the treatment of **mild to moderate hypertension,** either alone, or in combination with a diuretic or other antihypertensives. The investigational uses for clonidine include prophylaxis of **migraine, menopausal flushing,** and symptomatic management of **opiate detoxification.**

Adverse reactions. Dry mouth and drowsiness are the most frequent side effects with these agents. Other adverse reactions observed with *clonidine, guanabenz* and guanfacine are; **GI**—anorexia, nausea, vomiting, parotid pain, liver dysfunction; **CNS**—insomnia, nervousness, anxiety, depression, vivid dreams or nightmares; **Cardiovascular**—Raynaud's phenomenon, flushing, congestive heart failure; **Others**—weight gain, hyperglycaemia, gynaecomastia, impotence, muscle aches.

A potentially dangerous effect is **rebound hypertension,** which follows abrupt withdrawl of clonidine therapy.

Dose. Clonidine HCl is available as 0.1 and 0.2 mg tablets. The usual oral dose initially is 0.1 mg bid. If necessary it may be increased to 0.6 mg tid or qid. **Clonidine transdermal patch** is available in three strengths which deliver 0.1 mg, 0.2 mg and 0.3 mg per day. The patch is applied to the skin at 7-day intervals.

Guanabenz is available as 4 mg and 8 mg tablets. The usual starting dose is 4 mg bid. It can be gradually increased over several weeks upto 32 mg/day in divided doses.

Guanfacine is available as 1 mg tablets. The initial dose is 1 mg at bedtime with a thiazide diuretic, and may be increased upto 3 mg/day, if necessary.

Ganglion Blocking Agents

Ganglion blocking agents like **pentolinium, mecamylamine** and **pempidine** have been employed in the past for the management of moderage-to-severe hypertension. They act by **competitive antagonism** with acetylcholine at the cholinergic synapses of the autonomic ganglia. Some may believe that they still have a place in the emergency management of **malignant hypertension,** but they probably should best be regarded as obsolete hypotensive drugs, and they have given way to the **adrenergic neurone blockers.**

Trimethaphan

Trimethaphan is a short-acting ganglion blocking agent **(Chap 3.6).** The blocking action is exerted at the postsynaptic cholinergic receptor in autonomic ganglia. This **competitve antagonism** is short-lived.

Trimethaphan is used to produce **controlled hypotension** during surgery to reduce bleeding. It is also used to control **hypertensive emergencies,** and for the treatment of **pulmonary oedema secondary to pulmonary hypertension.**

Trimethaphan is available as an injection solution (50 mg/ ml) and is administeted by IV infusion. A 1 mg/ ml infusion solution is prepared by diluting 10 ml (500 mg) to 500 ml of 5 percent dextrose injection. The IV drip is started at a rate of 3-4 ml/minute, then adjusted to maintain the desired degree of hypotension.

Adrenergic Neurone Blocking Agents

Guanethidine. Guanethidine is a potent drug for the relief of **severe** hypertension, and has relatively lower incidence of side effects. It depletes the sympathetic nerve endings of their NA content like reserpine, but does not remove serotonin from the body stores (platelets, brain etc.). It does not cross the blood-brain barrier, and lacks the sedative effect of reserpine. It is fairly well absorbed orally, begins its hypotensive effect after 36 to 48 hours, and with continued medication reaches its maximal effect in 72 hours.

Mode of action. Guanethidine is taken up into the adrenergic neurone by the NA transport mechanism. Later (*i*) it releases the NA from tissue stores, which may be termed as a tyramine-like effect; (*ii*) it has an adrenergic neuronal blocking action referred to as a **bretylium-like** effect; (*iii*) it depletes the NA stores exhibiting a **reserpine-like** effect; and (*iv*) finally it blocks the membrane amine-pump, impairing the re-uptake of NA.

The hypotensive effect of guanethidine is mainly due to a fall in the cardiac output. The TPR almost remains unchanged. It can cause severe postural hypotension, possibly due to a greater effect on capacitance vessels than on resistance vessels. Guanethidine sensitizes the adrenergic receptor and thus is **absolutely contraindicated in pheochromocytoma.**

Adverse reactions. Diarrhoea, nasal congestion, postural hypotension and parotid pain occur. In the male it may prevent ejaculation, without affecting erection. Due to sympathetic inhibition and hot environment the BP is likely to markedly fall usually after exercise in the standing position and a heavy meal.

Dose. 10 mg per day initially. Can be increased by 10 mg increments every 7 days. Maintenance dose 25-300 mg daily. Parenteral use is best avoided.

GUANADREL

Guandrel possesses guanethidine-like pharmacologic and toxicologic properties. It is effective in the treatment of **severe** hypertension, but it may also be employed in the treatment of **mild to moderate** hypertension in patients who have not responded to step-2 drugs.

Guanadrel is available as 10 and 25 mg tablets. The initial dose is 10 mg/day, increase gradually until optimal effect is obtained. Usual dosage range is 20 to 75 mg in two divided doses.

BETA-ADRENOCEPTOR BLOCKERS

Propranolol

All beta-blockers share the common property of being **competitive inhibitors** of catecholamines. But they differ in their possession or otherwise of cardioselectivity, local anaesthetic activity and intrinsic sympathomimetic activity **(Chap 3.4).** They have a hypotensive effect. There is no postural or exercise hypotension.

Mode of action. The exact mode of hypotensive action is illunderstood. The suggestions include, an effect on the CNS, an **adrenergic neurone blocking effect, an antirenin** effect and the **resetting of the baroreceptors.** The cardiac output falls, and on prolonged use an intial rise in TPR is followed by a fall. Propranolol has appreciable antirenin activity and its response is good in moderate hypertensive with normal or high PRA, whereas, it is poor if the PRA is low. Propranolol has been lately employed in the management of **malignant hypertensive emergencies.**

Side effects. Depression, lethargy, impotence, headache and vertigo have been observed. Propranolol increases airway resistance and may precipitate bronchial asthma (contraindicated in bronchial asthma). Left ventricular insufficiency, congestive heart failure, hypotension, hypoglycaemia, cardiomyopathy and thrombocytopenic purpura may occur.

Dose. Propranolol 10 mg tid or qid orally. Can be raised upto 0.5 g daily in divided doses.

Beta-blockers like **acebutolol, atenolol** and **metoprolol** are **relatively cardioselective** in blocking beta$_1$-receptors in therapeutic doses. This selectivity is of little advantage in the treatment of hypertension. Although diuretics are still recognized as initial drugs of choice for the treatment of mild hypertension, but on revaluation some authorities feel that **beta-blockers** are better as initial drugs for mild hypertension.

ALPHA-ADRENOCEPTOR BLOCKERS

Prazosin

Prazosin acts by a competitive postsynaptic alpha$_1$-adrenoceptor blockade. It does not block the presynaptic inhibitory effects, which allow reflex action to overcome the postural hypotension usual with alpha-blockade. There is little reflex tachycardia or renin release, and side effects are generally minor. Prazosin produces a balanced reduction in the preload and afterload on the heart. It dilates both resistance (arterioles) and capacitance (veins) vessels. Because of the above activity profile it is usefully employed in the management of essential hypertension and chronic **congestive heart failure.**

Adverse reactions. Although prazosin is fairly well tolerated, severe postural hypotension can occur. Paroxysmal tachycardia and vivid dreams can also occur. Sexual dysfunction is rare.

Dose. 2 mg tid for 4 to 6 weeks. Later, graded increments, but total daily dose not to exceed 20 mg.

PHENOXYBENZAMINE

Phenoxybenzamine is an orally effective, long-acting non-selective (alpha$_1$ and alpha$_2$) alpha-adrenoceptor blocking agent **(Chap. 3.5).** It is used for the control of **episodes of hypertension associated with pheochromocytoma.** It literally produces a "chemical sympathectomy". The initial dose is 10 mg/day, increased by 10 mg every 4 days till the desired response is attained. The usual dosage range is 20-60 mg/day. **Adverse reactions** like orthostatic hypotension, nasal congestion, miosis, tachycardia and impaired ejaculation can occur.

ALPHA+BETA-ADRENOCEPTOR BLOCKER

Labetalol

Labetalol has an alpha$_1$ blocking action, with a non-specific beta$_1$ and beta$_2$-adrenoceptor blocking action. On oral administration the ratio of alpha to beta blockade is about 1:3. It lowers BP primarily by blocking alpha-receptors in the peripheral arterioles, reducing the TPR. At the same time it blocks beta-receptors (cardiac beta$_1$), and prevents reflex sympathetic cardiac compensation induced by peripheral vasodialation. Labetalol lower both systolic and diastolic pressures, without postural or exercise-induced hypotension.

Side effects. Nasal stuffiness, vivid dreams and epigastric pain may occur. This drug should not be used in bronchial asthma.

Dose. Labetalol 100 mg tid orally, increasing upto 200 mg tid or qid after 1 or 2 weeks.

VASODILATORS

Hydralazine

Hydralazine (1-hydrazinopthalazine hydrochloride) is a potent direct relaxant of vascular smooth muscle, but often produces considerable reflex cardiac stimulation. This drug reduces both systolic and diastolic BP. It increases renal blood flow, and is useful in hypertension with renal dysfunction. It is employed in cases of **mild to moderate hypertension**, and **toxaemia of pregnancy.**

Mode of action. Hydralazine directly dilates the arteriole, reducing the TPR. It seems to exert a more favourable effect on the diastolic BP than on the systolic BP, as it affects the **precapillary resistance vessels** much more than the postcapillary capacitance vessels. Hydralazine reflexly stimulates the heart, causing **tachycardia, increased cardiac output** and **renal blood flow.**

Adverse reactions. Headache, palpitation (addition of a beta-blocker can prevent palpitation and enhance the hypotensive effect), nasal congestion, peripheral neuropathy and bone marrow suppression can occur. On chronic administration a **disseminated lupus erythematosus-like syndrome** can occur.

Dose. Hydralazine 20 mg tid, raising to 50-75 mg orally. In *malignant hypertension* upto 20 mg may be given slowly intravenously till the pressure is controlled.

MINOXIDIL

Minoxidil dilates arteriolar resistance vessels with minimal effects on venous capacitance vessels. **It reduces calcium uptake** through the cell membrane, thereby reducing arteriolar tone and lowering peripheral vascular resistance. Orthostatic effects are rare, and renal blood flow is maintained. Reflex tachycardia, increased renin secretion, and salt and water retention occur. Blood pressure is substantially reduced, and this drug is **reserved** for severe hypertension not controlled by other antihypertensives.

Minoxidil is used to treat **severe hypertension**, usually given with a diuretic and beta-blocker to minimize fluid retention and reflex tachycardia respectively. It is also used to treat **alopecia areata** and **androgenic alopecia** (male pattern baldness), as a topical lotion or ointment. This use is based on its ability to cause hypertrichosis.

Adverse reactions. The most commonly seen side effect is hypertrichosis (elongation and thickening of fine body hair). This begins in the facial region and later spreads to the back, arms, legs and scalp. It develops within 3 to 6 weeks, and occurs in upto 80 percent of patients. No endocrine abnormality is associated with this condition. Other side effects include **tachycardia, breast tenderness, skin rash, oedema,** and **headache.** Sometimes **pericardial effusion** occurs in patients with a renal insufficiency. **Anginal symptoms, syncope** and **myocardial infarction** can occur due to a rapid decline in blood pressure.

Dose. Minoxidil is available as 2.5 and 10 mg tablets. Initially 5 mg/day as a single dose; increase step-wise upto 40 mg/day in divided doses (maximum is 100 mg/day).

DIAZOXIDE

It is a non-diuretic thiazide. On prolonged use it leads to diabetes mellitus, although not permanent in nature. Hence, it is not used as a routine hypotensive. It is employed exclusively for **emergency reduction of BP** as a short-term therapy, not exceeding 2 to 3 days. The response sets in within 2 minutes of intravenous administration, lasting for 2-5 hours.

Mode of action. It acts directly on the arterioles, lowering the TPR. The heart rate and cardiac output is increased. the fall in BP ordinarily does not reduce renal blood flow or glomerular filtration rate. There is no postural hypotension indicating that the sympathetic system is not involved. **Its major action is on the precapillary resistance vessels and not on the postcapillary capacitance vessels.** The diabetogenic action is due to direct suppression of pancreatic beta-cell activity, inhibiting the release of insulin.

Adverse reactions. Salt and water retention, hypogammaglobulinaemia, hypotension, dizziness, hyperglycaemia and transient diabetes mellitus may occur.

Dose. Diazoxide 300 mg by rapid intravenous injection over 30 seconds with the patient in the supine position.

SODIUM NITROPRUSSIDE

Sodium nitroprusside is a short-term hypotensive agent. It reduces TPR by a direct action on blood vessels and may be used in the treatment of **hypertensive crisis.** It may also be used for **controlled hypotension** during general anaesthesia. Its effects appear within a few seconds of intravenous infusion. It relaxes both the arteriolar and venous smooth muscles.

Side effects. It may produce anorexia, nausea, vomiting, abdominal pain, apprehension, dizziness, disorientation, palpitation, retrosternal pain and muscle weakness. **Methamoglobinaemia** and **hypothyroidism** may occur rarely.

Dose. Stock solution is prepared by dissolving 60 mg in 25 ml of isotonic saline. This 25 ml of the stock solution is added to 1000 ml of isotonic saline or 5 percent glucose solution. The influsion is started at a rate of 5 to 10 drops per minute, the BP being checked every 10 minutes or less.

CALCIUM CHANNEL BLOCKERS

Verapamil

Verapamil is a calcium channel blocker used in the chronic management of **angina pectoris (Chap. 4.5)**; and in the control of **supraventricular arrhythmias (Chap. 4.4).** Verapamil is also useful in the control of **mild to moderate hypertension.** Verapamil relaxes vascular smooth muscle, thereby decreases peripheral vascular resistance. For complete information refer to **Chap. 4.5.**

Adverse reactions. Constipation occurs frequently, and other side effects include dizziness, nausea and oedema. Due to its **negative inotropic effect,** and **slowing of A-V conduction, it is contraindicated in left ventricular dysfunction, cardiogenic shock, sick sinus syndrome, and II and III degree A-V block.**

Dose. Verapamil is available as 40 and 80 mg tablets, and also as 240 mg **sustained release tablets,** which are administrated once daily. Recommended dosage is 240 mg once daily, or twice daily to adequately control hypertension.

Nifedipine 10 to 20 mg sublingually or orally has been recommended in **hypertensive emergencies,** when close monitoring is not possible. The hypotensive effect is seen within 10 minutes, with a maximal effect in 30-40 minutes.

ANGIOTENSIN CONVERTING ENZYME INHIBITORS

Captopril
Enalapril
Lisinopril

Angiotensin converting enzyme inhibitors are orally effective antihypertensives, used either alone or in combination with other antihypertensive agents for treating **mild to moderate hypertension.**

Mode of action. These drugs inhibit the angiotensin converting enzyme (ACE), which hydrolyses the inactive angiotensin I to the active angiotensin II **(Fig. 4.2.2).** Thus, inhibition of ACE reduces the formation of angiotensin II, and decreases the angiotensin-mediated secretion of aldosterone from the adrenal cortex **(Fig. 4.2.3).** As a result preipheral vascular resistance is lowered, and salt and water retention is reduced. Plasma renin activity increases due to loss of negative feedback, and serum potassium may rise due to less of aldosterone. Both *supine* and *standing* BP are lowered to the same extent. Orthostatic hypotension is rare, and reflex tachycardia seldom occurs.

Inhibition of the converting enzyme by these drugs also **decreases the inactivation of bradykinin,** a potent endogenous vasodilator, and this adds to the BP lowering effect. Increased levels of bradykinin also leads to an increased synthesis of prostaglandin E, which also causes peripheral vasodilation. In patients of congestive heart failure the ACE inhibitors decrease peripheral vascular resistance (afterload), and pulmonary capillary wedge pressure causing an increase in cardiac output.

Adverse reactions. The most common side effects with *captopril* are loss of taste sensation, rash and pruritus. Common side effects with *enalapril* are headache, dizziness and fatigue; with *lisinopril* are GI upset, *lightheadedness*, and *fatigue*.

Other adverse reactions noted occasionally with all the three drugs include: *CNS*—insomnia, paresthesias; *GI*—nausea, vomiting, diarrhoea, altered taste sensation (dysgeusia); *CVS*—chest pain, palpitation, hypotension; *Others*—cough, rash, angioedema, bone marrow depression, impotence, muscle cramps, and broncospasm.

Therapeutic uses. The ACE inhibitors can be used to treat **all degrees of hypertension** either alone or in combination with other antihypertensives. They are specially useful in cases where other Step 1 and Step 2 drugs have failed. These agents are also used as adjuncts in the treatment of **refractory congestive heart failure** with digoxin and a diuretic.

Dose. *Captopril.* The initial dosage for mild to moderate hypertension is 12.5 to 25 mg bid or tid. May be increased gradually up 50 mg bid or tid to obtain adequate control.

Enalapril. The initial dose is 5 mg once daily. The usual dose range is 10 to 40 mg once or twice daily.

Lisinopril. Initially, 10-20 mg once daily. Usual dosage range is 20-40 mg daily.

MISCELLANEOUS ANTIHYPERTENSIVE AGENTS

Phentolamine

Phentolamine is a nonselective alpha-adrenoceptor blocker, used by injection to control hypertensive episodes that occur in patients with **phenochromocytoma** during surgery for removal of the tumour. Phentolamine may also be employed: (*i*) to prevent dermal necrosis and sloughing upon extravasation during IV infusion of noradrenaline, dopamine and adrenaline solutions; (*ii*) for treatment of **rebound hypertension** during withdrawal of antihypertensive therapy; and (*iii*) for **diagnosis of pheochromocytoma (Chap. 3.5).** The usual dosage for reducing BP is 5 mg 1M or 1V.

INDORAMIN

Indoramin is a selective α_1-adrenoceptor blocker that can be used in the treatment of all grades of hypertension. It is also a competitive antagonist of histamine H_1 and 5-HT receptors. **Side effects** include sedation, dry mouth, and failure of ejaculation.

MECAMYLAMINE

Mecamylamine is a **potent, orally effective ganglion blocker** which exhibits a considerable **orthostatic hypotensive effect (Chap. 3.6).** Due to its many side effects, it is used only for control of **severe hypertension** in patients not responding to other antihypertensive drug combinations. The initial dose is 2.5 mg bid, which may be adjusted in increments of 2.5 mg at 2-day intervals. The average dose is 25 mg/day in 2 or 4 divided doses.

METYROSINE

Metyrosine, or alpha-methyltyrosine, is a **competitive inhibitor** of the enzyme tyrosine hydroxylase which catalyzes the conversion of tyrosine to dopa **(Chap. 3.4)**. Because this is a **rate-limiting step**, inhibition of tyrosine hydroxylase results in decreased levels of noradrenaline and adrenaline in the CNS and periphery.

Metyrosine is used in the management of patients of **pheochromocytoma** for preoperative preparation, or for control of BP rise when surgery is contraindicated. Initial dosage is 250 mg orally qid. Optimally effective doses are between 2-3 g/day.

Adverse reactions. Common side effects are sedation, diarrhoea, drooling, mild tremor, and speech difficulty. Infrequent reactions include confusion, depression, hallucinations, impotence, ejaculation disturbances, galactorrhoea, crystalluria and hypersensitivity reactions. A sufficient daily intake of water to achieve a urinary output of 2000 ml/day must be maintained to avoid crystalluria.

INDAPAMIDE

Indapamide [1-4-chloro-3-sulfamyl-benzamido)-2-methyl indoline] decreases peripheral resistance in hypertensive subjects, and reduces vascular reactivity to pressor agents like adrenaline, noradrenaline and angiotensin. It inhibits enhanced ionic migration across the membrane of the vascular smooth muscle cell, particularly produced by pressor agents. It is effective in a single daily dose of 2.5 mg in **mild to moderate hypertension**. As indapamide is an indoline thiazide derivative, in large doses it exerts diuretic activity. **Side effects** like epigastric pain and nausea have been reported. Based on current evidence regarding efficacy of indapamide in a single dose without serious side effects, makes it worthy of trial in the treatment of hypertension. It is **contraindicated** in severe hepatic and renal insufficiency. Its administration during pregnancy is inadvisable. It is also not advisable to combine indapamide with the thiazides.

PHARMACOTHERAPY OF HYPERTENSION

Antihypertensive thereapy has to be tailored to the needs of the individual patient, and a balance struck between the beneficial effects and side effects. The ultimate goal of therapy is to reduce BP to normotensive levels. However, this is not always possible if there is prior evidence of appreciable vascular deterioration or renal damage. In the latter case BP reduction should be induced slowly and cautiously to avoid vascular insufficiency or uraemia. Hence, the BP is reduced to the point of renal and cardivascular system tolerance. Periodic blood urea nitrogen (BUN) estimations are a practical guide to thereapy. The moment there is a tendency of the BUN to rise, thereapy should be titrated afresh.

Based on the study of a large number of hypertensive patients, the WHO has classified hypertension into three stages:

Stage I: *Latent hypertension* (uncomplicated, often labile elevation of BP, usually in *younger* subjects).

Stage II: *Established hypertension* (stable elevation of BP with cardiac hypertrophy, *in middle aged* subjects).

Stage III *Advanced hypertension* (signs of organic damage caused by elevation of BP, coronary sclerosis, renal and myocardial insufficiency, usually in the *elderly*).

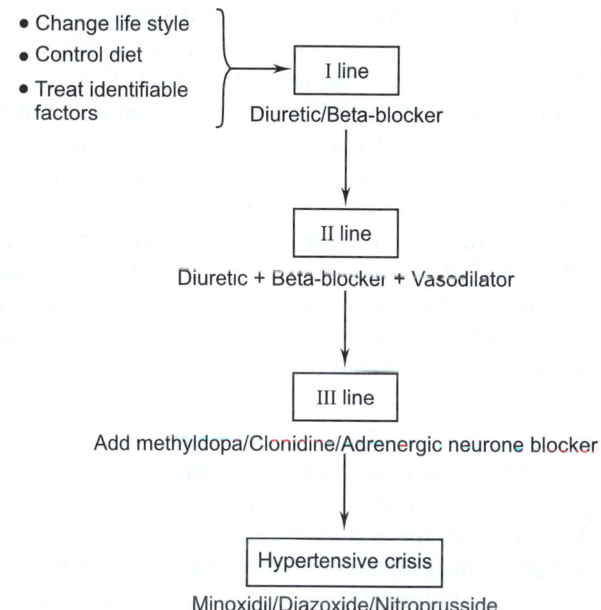

Fig. 4.2.4: Drug management plan for a hypertensive patient.

From the clinical standpoint antihypertensive drugs may be grouped into:

(*i*) **First-line drugs** (thiazides, loop diuretics, potassium-sparing diuretics);

(*ii*) **Second-line drugs** (methyldopa, beta-blockers, clonidine, hydralazine, prazosin, minoxidil, indapamide); and

(*iii*) **Third-line drugs** (adrenergic neurone blockers, ganglion blockers). For the management of hypertensive emergencies the drugs available are *minoxidil, diazoxide* and *nitroprusside*. A suitable drug management plan is summarized in **Fig. 4.2.4.**

Thus, with a proper application of currently available drugs the life of the hypertensive patient can be made much more useful, comfortable and safe.

4.3 CARDIAC GLYCOSIDES

The term "Cardiac Glycosides" is used to describe a group of compounds of common basic chemical structure, which increase the work performance of the heart. They have a cardiotonic action, and this is most marked on the "failing heart". They are used clinically in the management of congestive heart failure, and to control certain cardiac arrhythmias. The best known members of this group are derived from plants of the genus Digitalis. Thus, the terms **digitalis** or **digitalis glycosides** or **cardiac glycosides** are commonly used interchangeably, including a large number of naturally occurring and semisynthetic steroid glycosides, all of which have the same beneficial and toxic effects on the heart.

Historically, the English physician and botanist, **William Withering** (1741-1799) brought this old vegetable drug into modern medicine. In 1775 he singled out the **foxglove plant** as the active ingredient out of a secret folk remedy containing 20 or more herbs, effective for treating "dropsy", the old term for oedema. Over the next decade, Withering administered this drug to his "sick poor" patients, and carefully observed its therapeutic and toxic effects. In 1785 he published his findings in the medical classic, *An Account of the Foxglove and some of its Medical Uses: with practical remarks on dropsy and other diseases*. At that time Withering attributed the beneficial effect to the diuretic action of digitalis in dropsy. However, by 1800, the primary site of action was correctly identified as the heart. The main use of cardiac glycosides is in the management of heart failure. The characteristics of this disease state may be considered under two heads: **congestive heart failure** and **acute pulmonary oedema**.

Congestive Heart Failure (CHF)

Congestive heart failure is a gradually developing inability of the heart to pump sufficient blood to satisfy the needs of the body, i.e., it fails to function as an efficient pump. There is a depression of the **Starling's curve** relating cardiac performance to the ventricular filling pressure. The fundamental cause is unknown, but the biochemical defect is an ineffective conversion of chemical energy (adenosine triphosphate and creatine phosphate) to mechanical work.

In the early stages of heart failure, the compensatory mechanisms are activated to maintain cardiac ouput. These mechanisms are normally reserved for times of cardiovascular stress and exercise. During heart failure these mechanisms are required even during rest, and the cardiac reserve and exercise tolerance is diminished. Ultimately, in advanced congestive heart failure, the heart has no functional reserve, and the heart becomes **decompensated** and **dilated**.

One of the compensatory mechanisms is the **Frank-Starling mechanism**. In early heart failure the kidney retains sodium and water, with an associated increase in blood volume, which increases the venous return. The increased venous return lengthens the myocardial fibre during diastole and the stroke volume is increased (Starling's law). Such a sequence operates within certain limits and ultimately decompensation occurs. In addition, a decreased cardiac output activates both the baroreceptor reflex (increased sympathetic activity produces tachycardia and vosoconstriction), and the **renin-angiotension-aldosterone system** (NaCl and water retention with K^+ and H^+ ion loss, which is the effect of **secondary hyperaldosteronism** on the distal tubule). **Ultimately these mechanisms fail, the heart is decompensated, and congestive heart failure occurs.**

Acute Pulmonary Oedema

Acute pulmonary oedema usually occurs in the presence of underlying cardiovascular disease *like acute myocardial infarction, cardiac arrhythmias, malignant hypertension, aortic valvular diseases, pulmonary embolism or acute fluid or salt overload.* It is precipitated by an acute decrease in left ventricular output. This results in an increase in the pulmonary capillary hydrostatic pressure above a critical level (25 to 40 mm Hg). Fluid escapes from the capillaries and collects in the interstitial spaces and alveoli. The gas exchange in the lungs suffers, leading to marked breathlessness (orthopnoea).

Aims of Therapy

General measures while treating heart failure, include the treatment of precipitating factors like infection, cardiac arrhythmias, anaemia, hypertension, thyrotoxicosis and fever. In addition there are **three** main aims of therapy:

(*i*) **To reduce cardiac work:** The measures include rest from physical activity; if obese, restrict calorie intake; and restrict salt intake. In addition, attempts are made to decrease ventricular end-diastolic pressure.

(*ii*) **To decrease pulmonary congestion and peripheral oedema:** For urgent reduction in pulmonary congestion, the patient should be propped up in bed; administered 60 percent oxygen (6 litres/minute); given **IV aminophylline** for its bronchodilator, vasodilator and postive inotropic effect; given a **loop diuretic** like frusemide for its potent and prompt action.

(*iii*) **To increase cardiac output:** The cardiac glycosides are employed to improve the efficiency of the failing heart. **Digoxin** is the prototype.

CARDIAC GLYCOSIDES

Source and Chemistry

Official digitials is the dried leaf of the **purple foxglove plant** or **Digitalis purpurea**. Other plant sources of cardiac glycosides are the *white foxglove* or **Digitalis lanata**, **Strophanthus gratus**, **Strophanthus kombe** and **Urginea maritima or indica** (squill).

Each of the cardioactive glycosides contains: (*i*) a steroid nucleus; (*ii*) a lactone ring at C17, which is essential for cardioactivity; and (*iii*) a sequence of sugars at C3 hydroxyl group. The steroid-lactone system freed of the sugars by hydrolysis, with a free hydroxyl group at C3 is called an aglycone or *genin* **(Fig. 4.3.1.)**.

The basic pharmacologic properties of all aglycones are similar. The attached sugars are important in determining the potency, solubility, absorbability, onset and duration of action, and plasma/tissue protein binding properties of the glycoside.

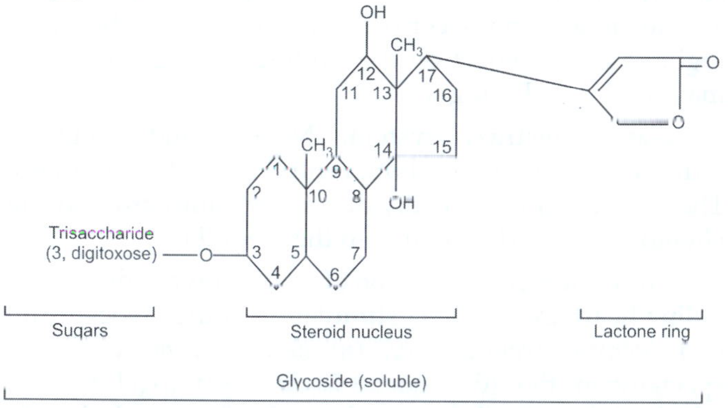

OH
CH_3
12 17
11 13 16
CH_3 14 15
1 9
2 10 8 OH
Trisaccharide (3, digitoxose) —O— 3 5 7
4 6
O
O
Sugars
Steroid nucleus
Lactone ring
Glycoside (soluble)

Fig. 4.31: Structural fromula of digoxin (12 hydroxydigitoxin). The glycoside consists of the basic steroid nucleus, sugar moiety and lactone ring. Removal of sugars by hydrolysis gives the aglycone, digoxigenin. Deletion of hydroxyl (OH) group at C12 in the steroid nucleus changes the compound to digitoxin, a nonpolar compound.

Each glycoside represents the combination of an **aglycone** with **one to four molecules of sugar**. The pharmacological property resides in the aglycone. The aglycones can be released from the cardiac glycosides by hydrolysis.

Pharmacological Actions

The primary action may be divided into three components: (i) **a positive inotropic effect** on the heart; (*ii*) **partial blockade of AV conduction**; and (*iii*) **reduction in the heart rate**. These glycosides cause these effects by their **direct** and **indirect** actions on the cardiac cells.

Effect on myocardial contraction. Digitalis by its direct action increases the contractility of the myocardium (**positive inotropic effect**), and as a result the cardiac output in the failing heart is increased. It causes the heart to contract more forcefully and completely with greater efficiency, without a proportionate extra consumption of nutrients or oxygen. In patients of congestive heart failure the stroke volume is increased; there is more complete filling of the ventricles in diastole; and as the initial diastolic length of the myocardial fibre is greater, there is an increased force of contraction (Starling's law). As the systolic emptying is more complete, the diastolic size of the heart is decreased.

Effect on other myocardial properties. The effects of digitalis on myocardial **automaticity** and **excitability** depend on the dose, and the different parts of the heart react differently. The glycosides exert direct actions on the mycardial cells, and in addition, they increase parasympathetic (vagal) and also sympathetic tone.

(*i*) **Decreased SA nodal rate:** The spontaneous discharge rate of the SA node is decreased (pulse rate slowed) by a direct and indirect action of the glycosides, which is dose dependent. With smaller doses, the effect is mostly due to vagal stimulation (indirect), and is reversed by atropine. With larger doses of digitalis, the decrease in SA discharge rate is a direct effect, and is not blocked by atropine.

In the average patient, the vagal effects (indirect) are dominant. The refractory period is shortened and conduction velocity is increased **(Table 4.3-1)**. Automaticity is increased more in the atria compared to the ventricles.

Table 4.3-1 *The effects of digitalis on the heart*

Parameter	*Indirect effect (via vagus)*	*Direct effect*
SA nodal rate	Decreased	Decreased*
Atrium		
Conduction velocity	Increased	Slowed*
Refractory period	Shortened	Lengthened*
Automaticity	Increased	Increased*
AV conduction system		
Conduction velocity	Slowed	Slowed
Refractory period	Shortened	Lengthened

Table 4.3-1 Contd...

Parameter	*Indirect effect (via vagus)*	*Direct effect*
Ventricle		
Conduction velocity	—	Slightly slowed*
Refractory period	—	Shortened
Automaticity	—	Increased*
Contractility	—	Increased

* The predominant effects with toxic doses.

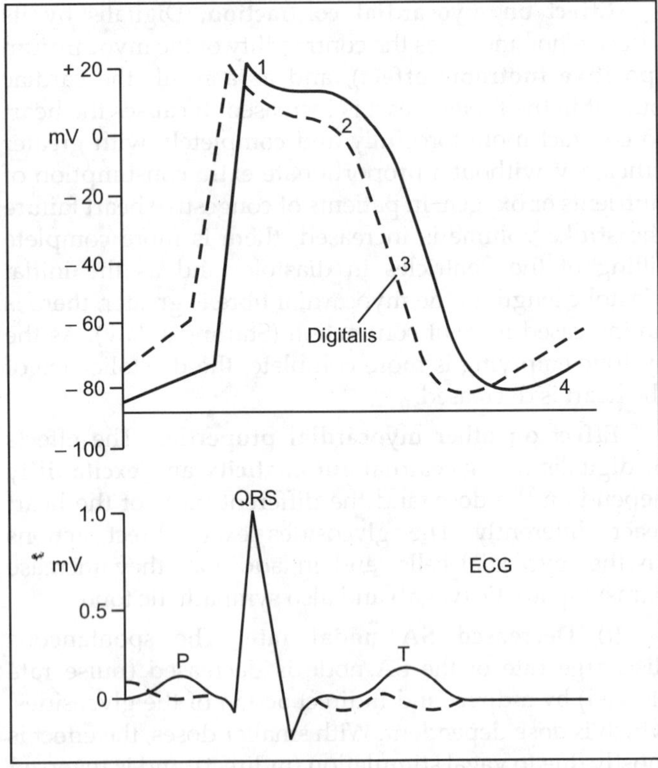

Fig. 4.3.2 Efffects of digitalis on the transmenbrane action potential, and the ECG. The action of digitalis is shown by dashed lines, while solid lines represent normal records (see text).

(*ii*) **Slowed AV conduction:** Digitalis slows conduction through the specialized tissue connecting the atria and the interventricular septum through the AV node and the bundle of His. *The effective refractory period of the AV node is prolonged, and the rate of conduction in the atrioventricular bundle is reduced.* This is the result of an additive effect of both the direct and indirect (vagal) actions of the drug. In toxic doses digitalis glycosides increase the automaticity of all the areas of the heart except the SA node.

(*iii*) **Increased ventricular contractility:** Digitalis exerts a definite direct effect. The **refractory period is shortened**, and the Purkinje cells show enhanced automaticity.

Effect on the membrane potential and the ECG. The effect of digitalis on the membrane potential of Purkinje fibres is a progressive decrease in the duration of the action potential due to a faster repolarization (refractory period shortened). Digitalis increases automaticity at pacemaker and ectopic pacemaker sites by increasing the rate of spontaneous diastolic depolarization **(Fig. 4.3.2)**. The resting potential and the amplitude of action potential also decrease.

The characteristic effects of digitalis on the ECG are: there is a *sagging of the ST-segment* below the isoelectric line; the T-wave becomes smaller, disappeas or may be inverted; the *P-R interval is prolonged* (delayed atrioventricular conduction); and the *Q-T interval is shortened* (shorter ventricular systole; shortening of the plateau phase 2 of the action potential). Such changes are more manifest in the failing heart.

The ECG also reflects the toxicity of higher doses of digitalis. In *mild* toxicity bradycardia and ventricular ecotpic beats appear. In *moderate* or *severe toxicity* ***ventricular premature beats, begeminy, paroxysmal atrial tachycardia with block, AV dissociation, nodal tachycardia, atrial fibrillation, ventricular tachycardia, SA or AV blocks may occur***. In extreme toxicity high degree of **conduction blocks** and ***ventricular fibrillation*** occur.

Effects secondary to relief of CHF. When congestive heart failure is relieved certain secondary changes follow due to improvement in circulatory haemodynamics: (*i*) **diuresis** occurs due to the improved renal circulation, (*ii*) the **blood pressure returns towards normal**, i.e., it *establishes an equilibrium* between the vasomotor centre and the cardiovascular system; (*iii*) the **tachycardia accompanying CHF declines**, mainly due to the fall in pressures in the right heart; (*iv*) the ***venous pressure is reduced*** due to removal of the excess extracellular fluid and improved cardiac function; and (*v*) the **heart size decreases.**

Effects on Other Systems

Blood and vascular system. Digitalis has a direct constrictor action on the vascular smooth muscle. It also leads to venous constriction. In thereapeutic doses digitalis has no effect on the clotting time. Larger doses may diminish clotting time.

Gastrointestinal system. Nausea and vomiting induced by digitalis are both central and reflex in origin. The emetic action is mainly due to the **stimulation of the chemoreceptor trigger zone** in the medulla.

To summarize, the action of cardiac glycosides on the failing heart are: (*i*) direct stimulation of the myocardium and *increased contractility*; (*ii*) *depression of conduction* specially in the AV node; (*iii*) *increased vagal activity*, which decreases the auricular refractory period with conversion of flutter to fibrillation; and (*iv*) *the increased cardiac excitability* makes the heart more vulnerable to arrhythmias.

Pharmacokinetics

The clinically used preparations are: (*i*) *Digoxin* obtained from *D. lanata*, active orally and parenterally; (*ii*)

Table 4.3-2 *Comparison of the pharmacokinetics of digoxin and digitoxin*

Parameter	*Digoxin*	*Digitoxin*
Lipid solubility	Less	Greater
Intestinal absorption	40-80%	80-100%
Single dose	0.25 mg	0.10 mg
Plasma albumin binding	20-30%	More than 90%
Biotransformation	Limited	Hydroxylated in the liver
Kidney excretion	Glomerular filtration and tubular secretion	Filtration of unbound digitoxin, and passive tubular reabsorption
Drug in urine	90% as uncharged	10% as unchanged digitoxin
Half life ($t_{1/2}$)	digoxin 1-2 days	5-9 days

Digitoxin from *D. purpurea* active orally and parenterally; (*iii*) *Lanatoside* C (Cedilanid) is a precursor of digoxin, obtained from *D. lanata, active* orally only; (*iv*) *Deslanoside* (Cedilanid-D) is the deacetyl derivative of Lanatoside C, quick acting IV glycoside; and (*v*) *Ouabain* (Strophanthin-G) obtained from *S. gratus*, quickest acting IV glycoside.

Digoxin and **digitoxin** are the two preparations, generally satisfactory for all purposes. The pharmacokinetics of digoxin and digitoxin is detailed in **Table 4.3-2.**

Both are rapidly absorbed when taken orally. Thus, except in emergency situations, these drugs do not have to be given by injection. Plasma concentration of these glycosides is measured by radioimmunoassay. Because of long half-lives, daily administration of these drugs (digoxin and digitoxin) is likely to lead to accumulation in the body, inducing a **cumulative toxicity**. The comparison of the characteristics of digoxin and digitoxin with other clinically used cardiac glycosides is provided in **Table 4.3-3**. In general, as the cardiac glycosides have long half-lives, the possibility of accumulation in the body is high.

Mode of Action

The digitalis glycosides *inhibit the Mg-dependent Na^+/K^+ ATPase enzyme activity*. This enzyme is located within the cardiac cell membrane and regulates the intracellular Na^+ and K^+ ion concentrations. *The inhibition of Na^+-K^+ activated ATPase reduces the energy available to the sodium pump, with the result that intracellular Na^+ concentration increases, and K^+ is lost from the cells*. Potassium loss effectively lowers the membrane potential with two consequences: (*i*) in certain cells the potential generation and propagation is inhibited resulting in a transmission block. Specially in the AV node this feature is useful in atrial fibrillation; and (*ii*) in other cells specially in the bundle of His, the automaticity is increased and ventricular arrhythmias are produced. The mechanism is possibly responsible for the toxic manifestations of digitalis.

The evidence for the **inhibition of Na^+/K^+ ATPase enzyme** by cardiac glycosides is so strong that it has been postulated that this enzyme acts as a **receptor** for digitalis. Although not firmly established, the intracellular rise in Na^+ concentration allows more calcium (Ca^{++}) to enter the cell with each action potential. More of Ca^{++} available to the myofilaments is responsible for a more powerful muscle contraction.

Table 4.3-3 *Pharmacokinetic properties of common cardiac glycosides*

Glycoside	*Source*	*Route of administration*	*Gastro intestinal absorption*	*Latency*	*Time of maximum effect*	*Half-life ($t_{1/2}$)*	*Duration of action (days)*
Digoxin	*D. lanata*	Oral	40-80%	1½-4 hr	6-8 hr	1-2 days	2-6
Digoxin	*D. lanata*	IV	—	10-30 min	1½-5 hr	1-2 days	2-6
Digitoxin	*D. purpurea*	Oral	80-100%	2-6 hr	4-12 hr	5-9 days	14-21
Digitoxin	*D. purpurea*	IV	—	½-2 hr	8 hr	5-9 days	14-21
Lanatoside C (Cedilanid)	*D. lanata*	Oral	77%	3-4 hr	8 hr	2-3 days	3-6
Deslanoside (Cedilanid-D)	*D. lanata*	IV	—	10-30 min	1-2 hr	1-2 days	3-6
Ouabain (Strophanthin-G)	*S. gratus*	IV	—	5-10 min	½-2 hr	21 hr	2-4

Digitalis enhances excitation, contraction, and coupling by which chemical energy is converted to mechanical work on the depolarization of the membrane. Digitalis probably does not have a direct effect of Ca^{++} influx across the membrane, or does not release Ca^{++} from the sarcoplasmic reticulum.

When the Ca^{++} ion concentration is increased due to an influx from the sarcoplasmic retriculum during an action potential, the myofilaments shorten and contraction occurs. The calcium pump which lowers Ca^{++} ion concentration around the myofilament requires energy which is derived from the hydrolysis of ATP. As digitalis inhibits the enzyme Na^+/K^+ ATPase, it blocks the rapid dissipation of ATP, and less of energy is available for the calcium pump, with the result that there is an increased concentration of Ca^{++} around the myofilament. The free Ca^{++} ion binds to **troponin**, which releases the inhibition by the troponin tropomyosin complex on the interaction of **actin** and **myosin** leading to contraction.

Therapeutic Uses

1. **Heart failure (left sided, right sided, or combined) with sinus rhythm or atrial fibrillation.** Clinical improvement can almost always be expected. In adequately digitalized patients, the heart rate decreases, engorged tender liver and veins regress, venous pressure and circulation time return towards normal, the cardiac size is decreased, pulmonary congestion subsides and oedema fluid is lost.

2. **Atrial fibrillation.** In atrial fibrillation the SA nodal activity is defective. The AV node is bombarded irregularly (upto 500 times/min) by impulses originating from abnormal or ectopic foci in the atria. The ventricular rate may go upto 180 beats/min, and the pulse is irregular in rhythm and force. Digitalis **prolongs the refractory period of the AV node** and the conduction system, with the result that fewer impulses from the atria reach the ventricles. The ventricular rate is reduced.

3. **Atrial flutter.** In this condition also the patient is mainly benefited by the *vagal* and *direct* effect of digitalis on the conduction tissue. The heart block usually present in this condition is increased, and then maintained by digitalis.

4. **Paroxysmal atrial tachycardia (PAT).** The patient benefits by vagal effects on the SA node, and on the conduction tissue.

5. **Prevention of paroxysmal atrial arrhythmias.** Digitalis may be used when quinidine has failed or cannot be tolerated.

Contraindications and Precautions

In the presence of heart failure, digitalis is the drug to be employed. However, there are certain relative contraindications, rather than *absolute,* and certain precautions have to be observed with digitalis use.

1. **Recent myocardial infarction.** After myocardial infarction the heart is more prone to arrhythmias.

2. **Ventricular tachycardia.** Digitalis may have to be used in the treatment of failure associated with persistent ventricular tachycardia.

3. **Partial heart block**. Digitalis may convert a partial to a complete heart block.

4. **Acute myocardial insufficiency.** Patients of infectious myocarditis or shock following myocardial infarction usually do not benefit by digitalis.

5. **Previous digitalis therapy.** Caution should be observed in digitalizing patients who have been on digitalis therapy earlier.

6. **Calcium administration.** Calcium and digitalis administered together increase the toxic effects of digitalis.

7. **Potassium depletion.** Potassium depletion due to diurectics precipitates digitalis toxicity.

Toxicity

The cardiac glycosides have a very **low therapeutic index** (between 2 and 3). Hypersensitivity reactions like urticaria and thrombocytopenia are rare. Gynaecomastia may occur rarely.

1. **Gastrointestinal effects.** Anorexia, nausea and vomiting are usually the early signs.

2. **Neurological effects.** Headache, fatigue, insomnia and mental symptoms like confusion, delirium, psychosis, and convulsions may occur.

3. **Visual disturbances.** Yellow or green vision, white halos around objects, snow-covered appearance of objects is reported by patients.

4. **Cardiac arrhythmias.** The most common being ventricular ecotopic beats, which may progress to "coupling" with a normally generated contraction (bigeminy). Atrioventricular blocks (partial or complete) may occur.

Treatment of Digitalis Toxicity

1. **Withdrawal of the drug or reduction in the dose.**

2. **Administration of potassium.** Hypokalaemia, particularly following diuretic thereapy precipitates digitalis toxicity. To correct hypokalaemia, potassium chloride about 2 g every 4 hourly to a total of 4 to 6 g daily may be given.

3. Elevated serum calcium levels, if detected, may be reduced by chelating agents like **disodium versenate**. However, this measure has not been found to be very effective.

4. **Antiarrhythmic drugs.** *Phenytoin* and *lignocaine* are the preferred agents.

5. **Digoxin Immune Fab-Ovine** (Digibind) contains antigen binding fragments derived from antidigoxin antibodies produced in immunized sheep. Digoxin

Table 4.3-4 *Preparations and dosage of cardiac glycosides*

Glycoside	*Dose*		*Preparations available*
	Digitalizing	*Maintenance (oral)*	
Oral preparations			
Digoxin	1-1.5 mg	0.25-0.75 mg	Tablets 0.25 and 0.5 mg
Digitoxin	1.2-1.5 mg	0.1-0.2 mg	Tablets 0.05, 0.1, 0.15 and 0.2 mg
Lanatoside C (Cedilanid)	6.0 mg	1.0 mg	Tablets 0.5 mg
Parenteral preparations			
Digoxin	0.5-1.0 mg IV	0.25-0.75 mg	Injection IV 0.5 mg/2 ml ampoule
Digitoxin	1.2 mg IV	0.1-0.2 mg	Injection IV 0.2 mg/ml, 1 ml and 2 ml ampoules
Deslanoside (Cedilanid-D)	1.2-1.8 mg (6-8 ml) IV	—	Injection IV 0.2 mg/ml, 2 ml and 4 ml ampoules
Ouabain (Strophanthin-G)	0.5 mg IV	—	Injection IV 0.5 mg in 2 ml ampoules

immune Fab is used to treat life-threatening digoxin or digitoxin toxicity. The preparation contains 40 mg/vial of lyophilized powder for reconstitution, which can bind about 0.6 mg of digoxin or digitoxin.

Preparations, Dosage and Digitalization

Digitalis has to be present in the body in a certain "saturating" amount before any effect on congestive heart failure is seen. **The initial saturating process by larger doses of digitalis is designated as "digitalization".** After adequate digitalization the "maintenance dose" of the glycoside is administered daily, and the attempt is to maintain the patient in a "compensated" state with optimal cardiac efficiency. The size of the *digitalizing dose* and the *maintenance dose* must be determined for each patient. The available preparations and dosages are detailed in **Table 4.3-4**.

Methods of Digitalization

The doses have to be individualized. The methods of digitalization may be considered under two main heads: (*i*) untreated cases, and (*ii*) partially treated cases.

Untreated cases.

1. **Slow digitalization (5-7 days).** When there is no emergency, it is desirable to digitalize the patient slowly over the course of one week. Any of the oral digitalis perparations can be given 2 or 3 times daily, administering the digitalizing dose over a period of 5-7 days.

2. **Rapid oral digitalization (within 24 hours).** Multiple oral doses are usually adequte for initial digitalization, administered over a period of 24 hours. Close observation is essential.

3. **Rapid parenteral digitalization.** This method is reserved for emergency digitalization of patients of **acute pulmonary oedema, severe heart failure or treatment of atrial arrhythmias** when immediate control of the ventricular rate is required. As a general rule one-half of the digitalizing dose is immediately administered IV slowly, and then increments of one-fourth of the initial dose are given at intervals of 2 to 4 hours until the desired effect occurs or toxicity appears. Frequent ECG monitoring is advisable.

Partially treated cases. If digitalis has been taken by the patient within the previous 2 weeks, give one-fourth of the estimated digitalizing dose, and then give additional digitalis cautiously.

Maintenance doses. The oral route is preferred for maintaining digitalization.

Drug Interactions

Digitalis itself is a dangerous drug with a low therapeutic index. During its use it is likely to interact with certain drugs partially listed in **Table 4.3-5.**

Table 4.3-5. *Drug interactions with digitalis*

Drug (a)	*Drug (b)*	*Effect of (b) on (a)*
Digitalis	Thiazide diuretics	Toxicity increased
	Steroids	Toxicity increased
	Quinidine	Toxicity increased
	Calcium	Toxicity increased
	Sympathomimetic amines	Arrhythmias increased
	Propranolol	Arrhythmias decreased
	Potassium	Toxicity increased
	Antacids, oral	Digoxin absorption decreased

To summarize, the drug treatment of congestive heart failure consists of administration of **cardiac glycosides, diuretics** and **potassium supplementation** with other measures like dietary salt-restriction and rest. The treatment of **acute pulmonary oedema** is a medical emergency. In this condition initially measures should be taken to decrease central blood volume like making the patient sit with legs hanging, limb tourniquets and phlebotomy. **Aminophylline** may be administered intravenously, the benefit is due to **(*i*) a positive inotropic effect; (*ii*) reduction in peripheral vascular resistance, venous pooling and reduction in cardiac work; (*iii*) bronchodilatation, relieving bronchospasm due to acute pulmonary congestion; and (*iv*) diuresis. Oxygen inhalations** for hypoxaemic patients, and **intermittent positive pressure breathing** is beneficial. **Loop diuretics** are administered to relieve pulmonary congestion. **Rapid intravenous digitalization** of the patient is carried out cautiously.

Intractable Heart Failure

The `ideal' drug for management of CHF should: (*i*) increase ventricular performance; (*ii*) decrease filling pressure; and (*iii*) increase cardiac output by decreasing afterload. Cardiac glycosides accomplish the first two objectives, but not the last one.

Vasodilators and **positive inotropic agents** are used as alternative or additional drugs in the treatment of CHF.

Vasodilators

Vasodilators used in CHF can be categorized as under:

1. ← **Arteriodilators:** ← Hydralazine, ← minoxidil, phentolamine, nifedipine, diltiazem.

2. **Venodilators:** Isosorbide, nitroglycerin.

3. ← **Combined** ← **arterio-venodilators:** ← Captopril, enalapril, nitroprusside, prazosin.

A reduced left ventricular output is benefited most by an **arteriodilator,** which lower resistance to ventricular ejection, i.e., afterload. Heart failure associated with high ventricular filling pressure, and symtoms of pulmonary congestion is benefited by **venodilators** like nitrates which lower the filling pressure by decreasing venous return as a result of increased venous capacitance, i.e., preload. Many forms of CHF are characterized by both - an increased ventricular filling and reduced cardiac output. Such patients benefit most by the **combined arterio-venodilators,** like **captopril** and **prazosin**.

Positive Inotropic Agents

Amrinone and Milrinone

Amrinone (Inocor) is the first of a new class of positive inotropic agents that are structurally and mechanistically unlike the cardiac glycosides. It is a potent inotropic-vasodilator. **Amrinone** and **milrinone**, its close structural analogue, are phosphodiesterase inhibitors, an action which results in increased intracellular concentrations of cyclic adenosine monophosphate (cAMP), which facilitates the contractions of the myocardial muscle. These agents have been classified as **non-glycoside, non-catecholamine positive inotropic drugs**. Amrinone is a vascular smooth muscle relaxant, thereby **reduces both preload and afterload**. There is little change in heart rate or arterial blood pressure. **Amrinone is used in the short-term management of CHF in patients who have not responded adequately to digitalis glycosides, diuretics and vasodilators**. Currently it is adailable for IV administration only as 20 ml ampoules containing 5 mg/ml as the lactate salt. The initial dose is 0.75 mg/kg by IV bolus over 2 to 3 minutes, followed by a maintenance infusion of 5 mcg/kg/min to 10 mcg/kg/min to a total daily dose of 10 mg/kg (including bolus). The most important **adverse reactions** are cardiac arrhythmias (3%), and thrombocytopenia (2.5%). Other effects include anorexia, abdominal pain, hepatotoxicity, hypotension, and hypersensitivity reactions. Amrinone produces fever, and nephrogenic diabetes insipidus. **Milrinone** is claimed to be 10 to 20 times more potent than amrinone, and free from some of its adverse effects.

Glucagon, a polypeptide hormone produced by the alpha cells of the islets of Langerhans has a potent positive inotropic activity in addition to its hyperglycaemic action **(Chap. 7.4)**. The use of glucagon in refractory CHF is under scrutiny.

Dopamine and **dobutamine,** both potent inotropic agents, have also been used for the **short-term management of intractable CHF**. Both these drugs stimulate beta$_1$ receptors in the heart, and increase the cardiac output. Dopamine produces renal vasodilation, increases renal blood flow, glomerular filtration rate, and sodium excretion. In contrast, doubutamine does not produce any renal effects.

It has been found that often a combination of **dopamine and phentolamine, noradrenaline and phentolamine, or dopamine and noradrenaline** has resulted in clinial improvement in intractable CHF, whereas alone they have failed.

4.4 ANTIARRHYTHMIC DRUGS

Cardiac arrhythmias are defined as disorders of **rate**, **rhythm**, **origin** or **conduction** of impulse within the heart. Successful drug therapy of arrhythmias is dependent on certain basic principles: (*i*) the presence of arrhythmia and its type must be correctly identified; (*ii*) the factors involved in the genesis of the arrhythmia must be evaluated; and (*iii*) the use of a particular antiarrhythmic drug must be justified on the basis of its mechanism of action.

The Genesis of Arrhythmias

Cardiac rhythm disturbances are the result of altered impulse generation (automaticity), altered impulse propagation (conductivity), or both factors acting together. The physiological regulation of automaticity and conduction is detailed in **Chapter 4.1.**

Automaticity Defect (Ectopic Impulse Generation)

Normally the sinoatrial (SA) node, the pacemaker, has the highest degree of automaticity, and is responsible for normal sinus rhythm. This spontaneous electrical activity of the SA node is independent of the CNS control, but is affected both by sympathetic (accelerator) and parasympathetic (slowing) activity of the ANS. Under certain circumstances, due to drugs or pathological changes, when the SA node is suppressed as in some bradyarrhythmias, other specialized conduction tissue with automatic properties takes up the role of the pacemaker. Thus, specialized atrial fibres, atrioventricular nodal tissue, the bundle of His, or the Purkinje fibres develop an enhanced automaticity when the SA pacemaker fails. Such a site is known as an **ectopic focus**, and the cells exhibit an increased tendency to depolarize during diastole. Arrhythmias due to increased automaticity in subsidiary or **latent pacemakers** result from myocardial ischaemia or damage, hypopotassaemia or digitalis intoxication. Circulating catecholamines also increase automaticity and induce arrhythmias.

Common arrhythmias due to ectopic automaticity include **premature ventricular beats**, **ventricular tachycardias**, and **ventricular escape rhythms**.

Conductivity Defect (Altered Impulse Propagation)

Some arrhythmias may be attributed to a defective transmission of the cardiac action potential. In myocardial ischaemic or hypoxic states any region of the heart may transmit impulses slowly or act as a conduction block. Simple slowing in the rate of ventricular contraction follows **AV blockade** or **bundle branch block**. Single re-entry impulses produce **ventricular premature beats**. A continuing self-sustaining re-entrant loop (circus movement) would lead to a **ventricular tachycardia. (Fig. 4.4.1, C)**.

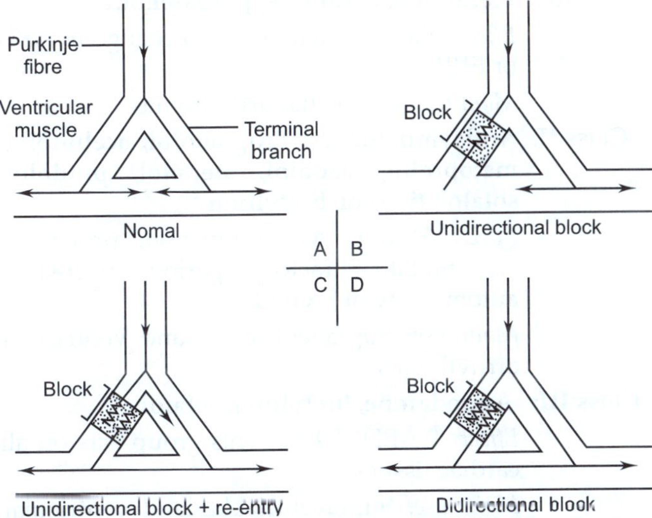

Fig. 4.4.1: The mechanism of a re-entry type of cardiac arrhythmia. A: Normal impulse conduction from terminal branches of Purkinje fibres to ventricular muscle; B: Unidirectional block caused by disease or drug toxicity; C: Unidirectional block of the impulse in left branch and re-entry of the impulse from the right branch into the left branch (retrograde transmission) causing arrhythmia by re-excitation; D: Bidirectional conduction block in left branch due to severe depression caused by drugs like quinidine and procainamide (see text).

Effects of Potassium

The level of extracellular potassium is of critical importance and regulates both automaticity and conductivity. Ectopic automaticity is suppressed by adequate or elevated levels of extracellular K^+, because it reduces the slope of phase 4 (diastolic depolarization) in the Purkinje fibres. Normal cardiac rhythm is the result of minimal automaticity (outside the SA node) and optimal conductivity. Increasing extracellular K^+ may reduce ectopic automaticity but it impairs conduction.

Classification of Antiarrhythmics

Five antiarrhythmic drugs have been commonly employed in the management of arrhythmias, namely **quinidine**, **procainamide**, **propranolol**, **lidocaine**, and to a lesser extent **phenytoin**.

Based on their **primary mode of action** and **electrophysiology** Vaughan Williams (1983) classification divides these drugs into four classes (I-IV) as follows:

Class I: This class is subdivided into *three* subclasses:

IA: Quinidine, procainamide, disopyramide.
Effect: Na^+ channel block, ↑ APD*, ↑ ERP**. These drugs inhibit pacemaker depolarization.

IB: Lignocaine, phenytoin, tocainide, mexiletine.
Effect: Na^+ channel block, ↓ APD, ↑ ERP. These drugs do not inhibit pacemaker depolarization, but inhibit the inward sodium current associated with ectopic beats of ventricular arrhythmias.

IC: Flecainide, encainide, propafenone.
Effect: Na^+ channel block, no change in APD or ERP.
Main use: Ventricular arrhythmias.

Class II: Antisympathetics: Propranolol, acebutolol, metoprolol, nadolol, atenolol, pindolol, sotalol, timolol, bretylium.
Effect: Slowed AV conduction, prolonged AV nodal refractory period, decreased automaticity of SA node.
Main use: Supraventricular and ventricular arrhythmias.

Class III: Amiodarone, bretylium, sotalol.
Effect: ↑ APD, ↑ ERP. This group acts on all cardiac tissues.
Main use: Supraventricular and ventricular arrhythmias.

Class IV: Calcium channel blockers: Verapamil, diltiazam.
Effect: Prolonged AV nodal refractory period, decreased sinus node automaticity.
Main use: Supraventricular arrhythmias.

* APD = Action Potential Duration;
** ERP = Effective Refractory Period.

The above enumerated drugs are used to treat **tachyarrhythmias**. Agents used to treat **bradyarrhythmias** are: (*i*) **Sympathetic agonist:** Isoprenaline; and (*ii*) **Parasympathetic antagonist:** Atropine.

Individual Drugs

Class IA

Quinidine

Quinidine is the dextro-rotatory isomer of quinine, obtained from the bark of the cinchona tree. Quinidine has greater effects on the heart compared to quinine.

Pharmacological actions. Quinidine has mainly direct actions on the cardiac cell membrane, which alter the **automaticity, excitability, conduction velocity** and **effective refractory period**. In addition, quinidine has indirect atropine-like (anticholinergic) effects. Quinidine depresses automaticity in cardiac pacemaker cells, and also in ectopic foci by raising the threshold to electrical stimuli. Quinidine reduces myocardial excitability and conduction velocity while it **lengthens the effective refractory period** in relation to the duration of the action potential passing through Purkinje fibres and ventricular musculature. Because of these actions it is effective in treating arrhythmias due to re-entry phenomena. In such cases, quinidine can abolish re-entry type of arrhythmias by **converting a unidirectional block to a bidirectional block (Fig. 4.4.1)**. Quinidine decreases the conduction velocity and shifts the threshold potential towards zero (less negative), and a greater stimulus is required to initiate an action potential.

The **negative inotropic** effect of quinidine on ventricular muscle has been observed both in experimental animals and in humans. It produces a fall in blood pressure, with a reduction in cardiac output and elevation of the left ventricular end diastolic pressure (LVEDP). A comparison between the effects of digitalis and quinidine is presented in **Table 4.4-1**.

Table 4.4-1. *Comparison of digitalis and quinidine activity on the heart*

Property	*Digitalis*	*Quinidine*
Contractility	Increased specially in failing heart	No effect or depressed
Excitability	Increased	Depressed
Conduction	Slowed, more so in the AV nodal area	Slowed
Spontaneous pacemaker activity	Slowed	Slowed
Refractory period	Shortended, except in AV nodal area	Lengthened, in all areas
Vagal tone	Increased	Decreased
Potassium efflux	Increased	Decreased
Response to adrenaline and noradrenaline	Increased	Decreased

Mode of action. Quinidine reduces the slope of phase 4 depolarization in pacemaker cells. This is probably due to a reduction of diastolic sodium influx. Thus it abolishes ectopic pacemakers activity. Quinidine also reduces the transfer of sodium across the cell membrane during phase O of the action potential. As a result the **conduction velocity is decreased and the refractory period is prolonged**. Due to the decreased sodium influx there is decreased efflux of potassium, which has a specific **membrane stabilizing effect** on the cardiac cell. The reduction in potassium efflux may be responsible for the increase in the duration of the action potential observed with quinidine.

Pharmacokinetics. Orally administered quinidine is readily absorbed into the blood where about 80 percent is bound to plasma proteins. Peak plasma concentrations are reached in 2 to 4 hours. The therapeutic serum level of quinidine is 3 to 6 mcg/ml, and toxicity is manifested with levels in excess of 8 mcg/ml. It is largely hydroxylated in the liver and excreted through the kidneys. The half-life of the parent compound is between 5 to 7 hours.

Toxicity. Quinidine is a dangerous drug. The common toxic manifestations are diarrhoea, nausea and vomiting. **Cinchonism** may occur in a dose-related manner, and consists of tinnitus, headache and blurring of vision. An idiosyncratic response to quinidine may occur, and even very small doses may cause vertigo, tinnitus, visual disturbances, angioneurotic oedema or skin rashes. **Hypersensitivity** to quinidine occurs rarely, marked by hypotension and cardiovascular collapse. A **test dose** may be administered before starting quinidine therapy to detect hypersensitivity. Haematologic abnormalities like thrombocytopenic purpura may occur.

Serious cardiotoxicity may occur. Atrioventricular and intraventricular blocks, ventricular tachyarrhythmias, and myocardial depression with or without hypotension may occur. **Pacemaking** may be needed in patients with advanced AV block.

Therapeutic uses. The major clinical uses of quinidine are in the treatment of **atrial fibrillation, atrial flutter and paroxysmal supraventricular tachycardia**

Preparations and Dosage

1. **Quinidine sulphate:** 200 to 300 mg orally 3 to 4 times daily.

2. **Quinidine gluconate:** 200 to 300 mg orally; 600 mg IM followed by 400 mg repeated every 2 hourly; 300 to 750 mg IV well diluted, administered slowly.

3. **Quinidine hydrochloride:** 200 mg IV or IM injected slowly. Parenteral use of quinidine is dangerous.

Procainamide Hydrochloride

Procainamide differs from the local anaesthetic procaine simply in the replacement of the ester linkage in the molecule by an amide linkage.

Pharmacological actions. The electrophysiologic properties and antiarrhythmic actions of procainamide are similar to those of quinidine, **except** that procainamide has a definite direct depressant effect on the SA node, and could lead to sinus bradycardia. However, this negative chronotropic action of procainamide is countered by its own vagolytic effect. **Like quinidine, procainamide diminishes excitability, decreases conduction velocity, and prolongs the effective refractory period to a greater extent in the atria compared to the ventricles.**

Pharmacokinetics. Procainamide is well absorbed from the gastrointestinal tract, peak concentrations are reached in 1 to 2 hours, and only 15 percent is bound to plasma proteins. Normally between 45 and 60 percent is excreted unchanged via the kidney, but this may be reduced in patients with diminished glomerular filtration rate. The remainder is metabolized in the liver mainly by N-acetylation to form N-acetyl procainamide (NAPA), which itself has antiarrhythmic activity. The half-life is usually between 2 and 4 hours.

Toxicity. In atrial fibrillation or flutter the ventricular rate may suddenly increase when the atrial rate is slowed by procainamide. Procainamide should not be administered when complete AV block is present, and extreme caution should be observed in the presence of partial block. Procainamide may cause anorexia, nausea and vomiting. Its clinical use is limited as it produces a reversible lupus erythematosus-like syndrome in about 30 percent of patients on prolonged maintenance therapy. Flushing of the face and hypotension may occur on rapid IV injection. Hypersensitivity reactions and bone marrow depression (agranulocytosis) may occur. Rarely mental disturbances like depression, hallucinations and psychosis have been noted.

Therapeutic uses. The usefulness of procainamide parallels that of quinidine. It is primarily used to suppress ventricular ectopy in cases of ventricular arrhythmias, except those resulting from digitalis toxicity.

Procainamide is quite effective in suppressing atrial and nodal arrhythmias, but quinidine is the preferred drug. Procainamide administered intravenously is safer than quinidine. Intravenous procainamide administration must always be accompanied by careful minute-to-minute monitoring of blood pressure and the ECG.

Preparation and Dosage

Procainamide hydrochloride. Initially 1 to 1.25 g orally followed by 250 to 750 mg every 4 to 6 hourly depending upon the disorder; IM 0.5 to 1g; IV 50-100 mg every 3 to 5 hours upto 1000 mg under ECG monitoring.

Disopyramide Phosphate

Disopyramide is a newer antiarrhythmic agent, with actions similar to those of quinidine and procainamide. **It depresses automaticity, diminishes conduction velocity and increases the effective refractory period of cardiac cells.** Like quinidine it has both direct and anticholinergic effects on atrioventricular conduction. Disopyramide has been successfully used to prevent **ventricular extrasystoles** and **ventricular tachycardia**, and is effective in suppressing artial tachyarrhythmias.

Disopyramide is well absorbed on oral administration. Peak plasma levels are attained within 2 hours. Therapeutic plasma levels range between 2 and 4 mcg/ml. The plasma half-life is 6 ot 8 hours. About 80 percent of the oral dose is excreted unchanged in the urine, and the rest is metabolized by N-dealkylation in the liver.

The common **adverse effects** are related to its anticholinergic activity, which include dryness of mouth, blurred vision, constipation and urinary retention. Rarely, it may precipitate acute angle-closure glaucoma. The toxic effects on the cardiovascular system are like quinidine. Severe hypotension may occur. It may precipitate or worsen heart block, and it should not be used in second or third degree heart block unless a ventricular pacemaker is already provided. Disopyramide is usually administered orally as 400-800 mg/day in 4 divided doses following an initial loading dose of 300 mg.

Class IB

Lidocaine Hydrochloride

Lidocaine (lignocaine) is a local anaesthetic, useful in the treatment of ventricular tachycardia and abormalities of rhythm occurring after myocardial infarction. Lidocaine differs from quinidine and procainamide in its mode of action, as it **decreases the duration of the action potential. It enhances conduction velocity and increases membrane responsiveness**. Lidocaine is now the drug of choice in managing acute **ventricular arrhythmias** when a rapid onset of antiarrhythmic action is required. It is effective only when administered intravenously.

Electrophysiologically, lidocaine increases both the rate of rise and rate of fall of the action potential of Purkinje fibres. The action potential duration is thereby shortened. **Effective refractory period is reduced and conduction velocity is increased** in these fibres. As a result of the improved conduction, normal transmission is restored in areas of unidirectional block. Re-entry type arrhythmias are thus suppressed.

Lidocaine has little effect on myocardial contractility or peripheral vasculature. It has no vagolytic property. It has little effect on automaticity. On the ECG lidocaine has little effect on the duration of the QRS, indicating that it has little effect on impulse conduction. But it shortens the Q-T interval of normal and ectopic impulses, indicating the shortening of the duration of the action potential.

Pharmacokinetics. Lidocaine is almost always given intravenoulsy. It is metabolized in the liver, with less than 10 percent of the dose excreted unchanged in the urine. The plasma half-life of a single injection is very short (15 minutes). Therefore, it has to be initially given as a "bolus" injection, followed by continuous intravenous infusion. IM administration of lidocaine is used in emergency situations only when facilities for IV administration are not available.

Toxicity. Lidocaine is a relatively safe drug, but bradycardia and hypotension can occur. Toxicity is usually expressed on the central nervous system, leading to drowsiness, parasthesias, disorientation, convulsions, behavioural disturbances and increased irritability. It can lead to heart block or cardiac standstill in patients with pre-existing bundle branch disease.

Therapeutic uses. Lidocaine is of particular use in the emergency treatment of **ventricular tachyarrhythmias following myocardial infarction**. It must be stressed that lidocaine has no place in the treatment of supraventricular tachyarrhythmias. It may also be used for treating **digitalis-induced arrhythmias**.

Dosage. Lidocaine hydrochloride 50-100 mg is administered intravenously as a loading dose, followed by an IV infusion of 1-4 mg/minute.

Phenytoin Sodium

Phenytoin (diphenylhydantoin) is a reliable antiepileptic drug **(see Chap. 2.7)**. The main clinical use of phenytoin is confined to digitalis-induced arrhythmias.

The major cardiac actions of phenytoin resemble those of lidocaine **(Table 4.4-2)**. It acts on the cell membrane of the myocardial fibres to enhance sodium influx during depolarization, and potassium efflux during the repolarization phase. It neither depresses the excitability, nor prolongs the refractory period of atrial or ventricular muscle. Phenytoin toxicity is uncommon when used in small incremental doses.

Table 4.4-2 *The pharmacokinetic and electrophysiological properties of antiarrhythmic drugs*

Class/Drug	*Pharmacokinetics*				*Electrophysiology*							
	Onset (min)	*Duration (hrs)*	*Phasma $t_{1/2}$ (hrs)*	*Protein Binding (%)*	*Automaticity*		*Conduction Velocity*		*Refractory Period*			*Heart Rate*
					SA Node	*Ectopic pace makers*	*AV Node*	*Pur-kinje Fibres*	*AV Node*	*Pur-kinje Fibres*	*Ven-tricle*	
Class IA												
Quinidine	30	6 – 10	6 – 7	70 – 90	↑↓	↓	↑↓	↓	↑	↑	↑	↑↓
Procainamide	30	3 – 5	3 – 5	15 – 25	↑↓	↓	↑↓	↓	↑	↑	↑	↑↓
Disopyramide	30	5 – 7	4 – 8	30 – 60	↑↓	↓	↑	↓	↑	↑	↑	↑↓
Class IB												
Lignocaine	1 – 3*	0.2	1 – 2	40 – 80	0	↓	↑	↑	↑↓	↑↓	↑↓	0
Phenytoin	30 – 60	24	24 – 36	90 – 95	↑↓	↓	↑	↑	↑↓	↑↓	↑↓	↑↓
Tocainide	30 – 60	4 – 8	10 – 15	10 – 20	↑↓	↓	0	0	↓	↑↓	↓	0
Mexiletine	30 – 60	4 – 8	10 –12	50 – 60					↑↓	↑	↑	
Class IC												
Flecainide	30 – 60	8 – 12	12 – 24	40 – 50			↓	↓	0	↑	↑	0
Encainide	30 – 60	8 – 12	1 – 2	75 – 85			↓	↓	↑	↑		
Class II												
Propranolol	30	3 – 6	2 – 4	90 – 95	↓	↓	↓	↓	↑	0	0	↓
Acebutolol	30	12 – 16	3 – 4	25 – 30	↓	↓	↓	↓	↑	0	0	↓
Class III												
Amiodarone	**	**	1 – 4 days	95					↑	↑	↑	
Bretylium	1 – 3*	6 – 8	6 – 10	10	↑	↑	0	↑	↑↓	↑	↑	0
Class IV												
Verapamil	30	6 – 8	4 – 8	90	↓	↓	↓	0	↑	0	0	↓

key ↑ = increase; ↓ = decrease; 0 = insignificant effect; ↑↓ = variable effect
* = Onset after IV administration.
** = Onset takes weeks, and effects persist from weeks to months on discontinuation of drug.

Therapeutic uses. Phenytoin has been employed successfully in the treatment of **arrhythmias associated with digitalis intoxication**. In fact, phenytoin can often counteract a partial AV block while terminating the rapid irregular cardiac rhythms of digitalis intoxication or ventricular tachyarrhythmias. For dosage schedule see **Table 4.4-3**.

Table 4.4-3 *The therapeutic plasma levels, therapeutic uses, and toxicity of commonly used antiarrhythmic drugs*

Generic name	*Dosage*	*Therapeutic plasma levels (mcg/ml)*	*Therapeutic uses*	*Toxicity*
Quinidine sulphate	Orally 200-300 mg 3 or 4 time daily	36	Prevention and suppression of premature atrial and ventricular contraction (PACs, PVCs): paroxysmal atrial tachycardia (PAT); atrial fibrillation and flutter; paroxysmal ventricular tachycardia without complete heart block	Hypotension, cinchonism, vomiting, diarrhoea, drug rash, haemolytic anaemia, thrombocytopenia, asystole, heart block, and intra-ventricular block ventricular arrhythmias

Table 4.4-3 Contd...

Generic name	*Dosage*	*Therapeutic plasma levels (mcg/ml)*	*Therapeutic uses*	*Toxicity*
Procainamide HCl	IV: 50-100 mg, every 3-5 hrs, upto 1g. Oral: 3-6 g/day in 6 divided doses	4-8	Prevention and suppression of premature ventricular contractions and ventricular tachycardia: recurrent ventricular arrhythmias following myocardial infarction	Hypotension respiratory arrest, heart block, AV or intraventricular block, venticular fibrillation, asystole, lupus-like phenomena
Disopyramide phosphate	Oral: 400-800 mg daily in four divided doses following an initial dose of 300 mg	2-4	Prevention and suppression of premature ventricular* contractions (PVCs): ventricular tachycardia; atrial tachycardia	Anticholinergic effects like dryness of mouth, congestive heart failure
Lidocaine HCl	IV: single IV bolus dose of 50-100 mg, followed by continuous IV injection 1-4 mg per min	1.4-6.0	Prevention and suppression of PVCs; ventricular tachycardia in patients following acute myocardial infarction and in cases of digitalis intoxication	Hypotension, respiratory arrest, seizures, heart block specially in patients with pre-existing conduction defect
Penytoin sodium	IV: 5-10 mg/kg by slow IV injection Oral: 100-400 mg orally in divided doses	10-18	Prevention and suppression of atrial and ventricular tachycardia, specially in digitalis intoxication	Gingival hyperplasia, drowsiness, drug interactions with Warfarin and Phenylbutazone
Propranolol HCl	Oral: 10-30 mg 3 or 4 times daily. IV: 1-3 mg at a rate of not more than 1 mg/min with ECG monitoring	Variable	Supraventricular and ventricular arrhythmias specially those induced by catecholamines pheocromocytoma, during general anaesthesia, thyrotoxicoses; digitalis arrhythmias; Wolff-Parkinson-White syndrome	Hypotension, heart block, cardiac failure, bronchospasm, alopecia, altered carbohydrate metabolism
Bretylium tosylate	IV or IM 5-10 mg/kg body weight		Treatment of life threatening ventricular tachycardia or ventricular fibrillation	Severe hypotension

Tocainide

Tocainide, a close structural analogue of *lidocaine*, is resistant to gastric acid and little affected by first-pass hepatic metabolism. Its mode of action is similar to that of lidocaine. It is used for the treatment of ventricular arrhythmias, like **premature ventricular contractions, ventricular tachycardia, and unifocal or multifocal couplets**.

Tocainide is available as tablets (400, 600 mg). The initial dose is 400 mg every 8 hours, and the maintenance dose is 1200 to 1800 mg/day in 2 or 3 divided doses. The maximum dose is 2400 mg/day. **Adverse reactions** include dizziness, nausea, tremor, nervousness, tinnitus, nystagmus, disorientation, hallucinations, bradycardia, hypotension, CHF, AV or bundle branch blocks, lupus-like syndrome, pulmonary fibrosis and pneumonia.

Mexiletine

Mexiletine is an orally effective antiarrhythmic, and is similar to **lidocaine** and **tocainide** in its actions. It reduces the rate of rise of phase O of the action potential, decreases the effective refractory period in Purkinje fibres, and shortens the action potential duration (APD). It has minimal effects on impulse generation and propagation, cardiac output and contractility, pulse rate, blood pressure, and peripheral vascular resistance. Mexiletine, like tocainide, is used for treating various ventricular arrhythmias.

Mexiletine is available as capsules (150, 200, 250 mg). The initial dose is 200 mg every 8 hours, with gradual adjustments in 50-100 mg increments as needed. **Adverse reactions** include GI distress, tremor, incoordination, peptic ulcer, altered taste, oral ulceration, confusion, short-term memory loss, psychosis, bradycardia, hypotension, atrial arrhythmias, rash, arthralgia, lupus-like syndrome and blood dyscrasias.

Class IC

Flecainide

Flecainide is an orally effective antiarrhythmic that possesses **membrane stabilizing activity**, and has local anaesthetic properties. It decreases conduction in all parts of the heart, with greatest effect on the His-Purkinje system. Ventricular refractory period is prolonged. It suppresses single and multiple premature ventricular contractions, and decreases recurrence of ventricular tachycardia. Flecainide is mainly used in the treatment of **life-threatening ventricular arrhythmias.**

Flecainide is available as 100 mg tablets. For ventricular tachycardia initially 100 mg every 12 hours is given. Increased in 50 mg increments twice daily every 4 days until optimal effect. Maximum dose is 400 mg/day. **Adverse reactions** include dizziness, visual disturbances, dyspnoea, sinus bradycardia, second and third degree heart block, hypotension, anxiety, convulsions, morbid dreams, blurred vision, diplopia, nystagmus, decreased libido and impotence.

Encainide

Encainide blocks the sodium channel of the Purkinje fibres and the myocardium, and slows phase O depolarization in a dose-dependent manner. It **increases the ratio of the effective refractory period to the action potential duration**. It decreases intracardiac conduction in all parts of the heart. Peripheral circulation is largely unaffected. Encainide is used for life-threatening arrhythmias like **sustained ventricular tachycardia**.

Encainide is used as 25, 35 or 50 mg capsules. The initial dose is 25 mg every 8 hours. The maximum recommended dose for life-threatening arrhythmias is 75 mg four times a day. **Adverse reactions** include initiation or worsening of ventricular arrhythmias, palpitation, tachycardia, CHF, tremor, tinnitus, altered taste, bradycardia and asystole.

Propafenone

Propafenone possesses class IC properties, together with class II properties like beta-blockers. It also **slows down inward calcium current**. Propafenone is used for the suppression of **ventricular tachycardia and ectopic ventricular rhythms.**

Class II

Propranolol

Acebutolol

Almost all beta-blockers have significant antiarrhythmic activity. Amongest them, **propranolol** and **acebutolol** are the agents which have been used to treat a variety of arrhythmias, specially **exercise-induced arrhythmias**, or those associated with **excessive sympathetic stimulation** or **circulating catecholamine levels**. The beta-blockers are used in many disease states **(Chap. 3.5)**, but the following discussion is limited to their use in treating arrhythmias.

The beta-blockers **competitively** antagonize the action of adrenergic agents, specifically on the heart (beta$_1$-receptors). As a result the sinus rate is slowed, **AV conduction is depressed, contractility is reduced, and the automaticity of the SA node and ectopic pacemakers is decreased. AV nodal refractory period is lengthened and re-entry excitation is reduced**. In short, the antiarrhythmic activity is attributed to two action; (*i*) blockade of cardiac beta-adrenoceptors; and (*ii*) membrane stabilizing activity, also labelled as quinidine-like activity. The direct effects of propranolol resemble those of quinidine and procainamide (class IA drugs). The electrophysiological actions of beta-blockers are summarized in **Table 4.4-4**.

Propranolol is used for the following arrhythmias: exercise-induced ventricular tachycardia; supraventricular tachyarrhythmias (atrial fibrillation, atrial flutter, paroxysmal atrial tachycardia); tachyarrhythmias of digitalis intoxication; tachycardias due to thyrotoxicosis or excessive catecholamine activity during anaesthesia; and persisent premature ventricular extrasystoles. The usual oral dose is 10-30 mg 3 or 4 times daily. IV propranolol is reserved for life-threatening arrhythmias in a dose of 1-3 mg at a rate of 1 mg/minute.

Table 4.4-4 *The pharmacological and electrophysiological actions of beta-blockers*

Drug	*Beta-blocking potency (Propranolol = 1)*	*Cardioselectivity*	*Partial agonist activity*	*Membrane stabilizing activity*	*Electrophysiological actions**
Propranolol	1	—	—	++	Acute increase in VRP and V-APD in animals: A-APD and V-APD in animals.
Acebutolol	0.3	+	+	+	Acute increase in VRP and V-APD
Metoprolol	1	+	—	—	Acute, slight increase in ARP in humans; chronic increase in VRP and V-APD in humans; chronic increase in A-APD and V-APD in animals.
Atenolol	1	+	—	—	Acute increase in VRP and APD in animals; acute increase in ARP in humans.
Sotalol	0.3	—	—	—	Acute and chronic increase in ARP, VRP, A-APD and V-APD in animals and humans.
Timolol	6	—	—	—	Acute increase in VRP in animals.
Pindolol	6	—	+++	+	Acute increase in ARP in humans.
Nadolol	2-6	—	—	—	Acute increase in V-APD in animals.

* ARP = Atrial refractory period; A-APD = atrial action potential duration;
VRP = ventricular refractory period; V-APD = ventricular action potential duration
\+ = increased; — = decreased.

Acebutolol is currently indicated for management of ventricular premature beats. The initial dose is 200 mg twice a day. Dosage range is 600-12000 mg a day.

Adverse reactions are detailed in **Chapter 3.5.** IV propranolol may cause significant hypotension or even left ventricular failure. In addition AV block, severe bradycardia and asystole may occur.

CLASS III

AMIODARONE

Amiodarone is an orally effective agent reserved for life threatening ventricular arrhythmias, refractory to other agents. This drug is **highly toxic**. It prolongs myocardial cell action potential duration (APD) and refractory period. It possesses both **alpha-** and **beta-blocking actions**. The peripheral vascular resistance is reduced. Automaticity is decreased causing marked bradycardia and sinus arrest. ECG changes include increased PR and QT intervals, appearance of U waves, and altered T wave contour.

Amiodarone is used to treat life-threatening recurrent ventricular arrhythmias like **ventricular fibrillation** and haemodynamically unstable ventricular tachycardia. It is used as 200 mg tablets. Loading doses of 800-1600 mg/day in divided doses are required for 1-3 weeks, followed by a maintenance dose of 600-800 mg/day in divided doses for one month, then 400 mg/day as a single dose or in 2 divided doses. **Adverse reactions** include corneal microdeposits, peripheral neuropathy, pulmonary fibrosis, insomnia, decreased libido, bradycardia, CHF, hypotension and conduction abnormalities.

BRETYLIUM

Bretylium, an adrenergic neurone blocker, was originally introduced as an antihypertensive, but later was found to have antiarrhythmic activity. Currently it is used exclusively as an **alternative drug** for the emergency control of serious ventricular arrhythmias. It prolongs the effective refractory period and action potential duration of Purkinje fibres and ventricular muscle cells. **The ventricular fibrillation threshold is increased**.

Bretylium is used to control **life-threatening ventricular arrhythmias** that have not responded to first-line drugs like lidocaine and procainamide. It is usually administered IV in a dose of 5 mg/kg by rapid injection, and may be repeated in dose of 10 mg/kg every 15-30 minutes to a total dose of 30 mg/kg. **Adverse reactions** include orthostatic hypotension, dizziness, bradycardia, substernal pain, and transient tachycardia on initiation of therapy.

CLASS IV

VERAPAMIL

Verapamil inhibits the influx of calcium through the cardiac cell membrane into the cardiac cell. Verapamil only minimally affects the rapid sodium current. Verapamil decreases phase 4 depolarization by inhibiting slow calcium dependent ionic channels in the sarcolemma. **It slows AV conduction and increases the P-R interval. It also produces peripheral vasodilatation**. Verapamil has been therapeutically used in **atrial flutter** and **fibrillation with rapid ventricular rate, supraventricular tachyarrhythmias** (paroxysmal atrial tachycardia and WPW syndrome). Verapamil is effective orally in the prophylaxis of angina pectoris **(Chap. 4.5)**. It should be used with caution in patients with AV conduction defects or cardiac failure. **Side effects** include hypotension, and it should not be administered simultaneously with beta-blockers. Verapamil has a half-life of 2-4 hours and undergoes first-pass metabolism in the liver on oral administration. Verapamil may be given orally in a dose of 80 mg three or four times daily, or in severe cases intravenously 5-10 mg slowly. Verapamil 1 mg/min upto 10 mg intravenously is the drug of choice for an attack of atrial tachycardia.

DIGITALIS

The digitalis glycosides have complex **direct** and **indirect** effects on the heart **(Chap. 4.3)**. The factors responsible for the antiarrhythmic activity of digitalis are: (*i*) lengthening of AV nodal conduction time and refractory period due to its vagotonic and direct effects; (*ii*) shortening of the atrial refractory period due to vagal stimulation; (*iii*) shortening of the ventricular muscle refractory period by a direct action; and (*iv*) enhancement of myocardial contractility. A comparison with quinidine action is shown in **Table 4.4-1.** The above enumerated actions of digitalis collectively account for its antiarrhythmic activity.

In atrial flutter or fibrillation, digitalis is effectively used to slow the ventricular rates. It may be used to terminate **supraventricular tachycardia** and **sinus tachycardia**.

Table 4.4-5 *Choice of antiarrhythmic drugs*

Arrhythmia	*Rate/min*	*Acute treatment of choice*	*Second choice*
Atrial arrhythmias			
Atrial fibrillation	vent. = 70-200	Digitalis to control ventricular rate	DC shock for conversion after starting quinidine or procainamide
Atrial flutter	Atrial = 300; vent. 75, 100, 150,	Digitalis or DC shock	Same as for atrial fibrillation
Paroxysmal atrial tachycardia	130-240	Vagotonic manoeuvres	Verapamil (propranolol, DC shock)*
Ventricular arrhythmisas			
Ventricular premature beats	—	Lidocaine	Procainamide (quinidine, phenytoin, propranolol)
Ventricular tachycardia	80-180	DC shock, if available	Lidocaine (procainamide, phenytoin)
Ventricular fibrillation	—	DC shock, if available	Cardiopulmonary resuscitation; Lidocaine (procainamide, phenytoin)
Digitalis-induced tachyarrhythmias	—	Potassium chloride	Lidocaine or phenytion (propranolol, procainamide)

* Drugs/ manoeuvres within perentheses may be employed if the other drugs fail.

Drugs for Bradyarrhythmias

Isoprenaline Hydrochloride

Isoprenaline (isoprotetrenol, isopropylnoradrenaline) stimulates the beta-adrenoceptors in the heart, blood vessels, and bronchioles. It has a non-selective action and acts as an agonist for both $beta_1$ (heart) and $beta_2$ (blood vessels, bronchioles) adrenoceptors **(see Chap. 3.4).**

Isoprenaline increases heart rate and myocardial contractility, enhances automaticity and increases the conduction velocity by stimulating the cardiac $beta_1$-receptors. It is used in patients with **second- or third-degree AV block**, where it can effectively maintain the heart rate and cardiac output prior to insertion of a pacemaker. It is useful in emergency treatment of **Stokes-Adams seizures**, and for **severe propranolol-induced myocardial depression**. For these conditions isoprenaline 1 to 2 mg diluted in 500 ml of 5 percent dextrose injection in water, is infused slowly at the rate of 0.5 to 2 ml/minute with continuous ECG monitoring.

Atropine Sulphate

Atropine is a cholinergic blocking agent, and it blocks the myocardial cholinergic (muscarinic type) receptors **(see Chap 3.3)**. Atropine increases the heart rate and AV conduction velocity by blocking the parasympathetic neurotransmitter acetylcholine. It is used to treat certain **reversible bradyarrhythmias** which accompany acute myocardial infraction like sinus bradycardia. Atropine may be used in cases of **sinoatrial arrest, vasovagal syndrome and in Wenckebach Type 1 second-degree AV block.** For these conditions initially 0.4 to 1 mg of atropine is given intravenously and repeated every 1 to 2 hours.

Therapeutic doses may cause dryness of the mouth, cycloplegia, and intravenous atropine may induce acute closed-angle glaucoma in predisposed patients. Large doses may cause urinary retention, hyperpyrexia, confusion and hallucinations.

Choice of Antiarrhythmic Drugs

The electrocardiogram (ECG) is an important tool for diagnosing arrhythmias and monitoring the effect of therapy. Firstly, an accurate diagnosis of the arrhythmia is essential for rational, safe and effective drug therapy.

The order of drugs mentioned in **Table 4.4-5** is just for a broad guideline. The objectives of drug therapy in the management of atrial tachyarrhythmias are that: (*i*) drugs are mainly used to **protect the ventricles from excessive supraventricular impulses**; and (*ii*) drugs may also **prevent the recurrence of atrial arrhythmias** when used as maintenance therapy following DC cardioversion to restore normal sinus rhythm. The objective in the case of ventricular tachyarrhythmias is that **drugs used should restore normal rhythm by abolishing premature ventricular contractions (PVCs)** and prevent their extension to more serious arrhythmias.

Combinations of Drugs

In the treatment of cardiac arrhythmias, drug combinations should only be used when absolutely necessary. In general the combination of two drugs, with the same type of actions (quinidine and procainamide) probably has no added advantage. However, certain combinations are rational and useful if cautiously employed.

4.5 ANTIANGINAL DRUGS

Angina pectoris manifests itself in the form of a dramatic and terrorizing retrosternal pain, often of a "crushing" nature. This ischaemic pain may last for several seconds and terminate on rest (angina of effort). At a cellular level it is the result of deficient myocardial perfusion, inadequate to meet the metabolically generated oxygen need of the myocardium.

Angina pectoris is the most frequent symptom of **ischaemic heart disease**, and results from a temporary relative imbalance of oxygen supply and demand in the myocardium. The characteristic central chest pain is due to the metabolites produced by the ischaemic myocardium. The major determinants of myocardial oxygen consumption are: (*i*) the **left ventricular systolic wall tension**, which is related to the systolic intraventricular pressure and left ventricular size; (*ii*) **time spent in systole**, determined by the heart rate and ejection time; and (*iii*) the **inotropic state of the myocardium** which determines the rate of rise of ventricular pressure, and is increased by sympathetic stimulation. Normally coronary flow can increase **five-fold** to meet the oxygen demand, but in angina this capacity is limited. The antianginal drugs act by altering one or more of the above mentioned three factors.

Types of Angina Pectoris

Three types of angina can be described based on the *aetiology* of the myocardial ischaemia and severity of symptoms:

1. **Classic, stable angina.** Occurs on a disproportionate increase in myocardial oxygen demand due to excercise, emotional stress or physical exertion. It is termed as "exertional angina" or "angina of effort". The attacks are transient and cease when the person rests.

2. **Classic, unstable angina.** Chest pain occurs even at rest, ischaemia is severe, and coronary flow is significantly impaired. The person is at high risk of myocardial infarction.

3. **Vasospastic (Prinzmetal's variant) angina.** Myocardial ischaemia is the result of coronary vasospasm, pain is prolonged, and may develop during activity or rest. It can lead to sudden death due to arrhythmias or infarction.

The most attractive goal of therapy is, **to dilate the narrowed coronary vessels** to permit an adequate perfusion of the working myocardium. A second more realistic goal may be, **to cause a reduction of cardiac work** to within appropriate limits.

When a branch of the coronary artery is occluded, the myocardium supplied by it dies, and this is known as **myocardial infarction**.

Classification

Drugs used in the treatment of angina pectoris are:

I. Nitrates and Nitrites

(*a*) **Relief of anginal pain.** (Rapid onset and short-acting agents)

Nitroglycerin (glyceryl trinitrate)

Amyl nitrite

(*b*) **Prevention of anginal attacks** (Slow onset and long acting agents)

Pentaerythrityl tetranitrate

Erythrityl tetranitrate

Mannitol hexanitrate

Isosorbide dinitrate

Isosorbide mononitrate

(*c*) **Treatment of cyanide poisoning**

Sodium nitrite

II. Agents for Prevention of Anginal Attacks

(*a*) **Beta-blockers**

Propranolol

Nadolol

Atenolol

Metoprolol

(*b*) **Calcium channel blockers**

Verapamil

Nifedipine

Diltiazem

(*c*) **Antiplatelet agents**

Dipyridamole

Aspirin

III. Other Measures

(*a*) **Antianxiety drugs**, e.g., Diazepam

Nitrates and Nitrites

Nitroglycerin and *amyl nitrite* were the first members of this group to be used as coronary vasodilators more than 100 years ago.

Pharmacology and Mode of Action

The basic action of the nitrites is a **direct relaxation of the smooth muscles**. All types of blood vessels are dilated, and the coronary arteries share this generalized vasodilatation.

The duration of the cardiac systole is shortened (coronary blood flow occurs chiefly during diastole), and the cardiac size is decreased (due to a lowered diastolic filling pressure that results from venous pooling). Though there is a moderate reflex tachycardia, **the end result is reduced cardiac work**. This is also a major mechanism of relief of angina pectoris.

Nitroglycerin-type compounds appear to have a selective action on the **venous capacitance vessels**, although they also exert some influence (pressure reduction) on the arterial side. This combined effect elicits reductions in both **preload** (venous filling pressure) and **afterload** (arterial impedance), which greatly reduce the high ventricular wall stress on the damaged heart. The decrease in venous return leads to **reductions in left ventricular end-diastolic pressure (LVEDP) and volume, ventricular size, and wall tension**, resulting in an overall increase in ventricular efficiency and reduced oxygen requirements. **These mechanically induced changes are accompanied by increased exercise tolerance, and reversal of electrocardiographic (ECG) manifestations of coronary insufficiency**.

There is evidence that nitroglycerin may cause a **beneficial redistribution of coronary blood flow**. Under normal conditions the ratio of endocardial to epicardial blood flow is fairly even. However, in acute myocardial ischaemia there is a disproportional decrease in endocardial blood flow. **Nitroglycerin has been shown to increase preferentially endocardial blood flow, both in the normal and acutely ischaemic myocardium, without increasing the total coronary blood flow**.

These agents also relax the musculature of the bronchi, the gall bladder and the biliary tract, ureter, uterus, the stomach and the intestines. The mechanism involved is illunderstood. A possibility is that the nitrates and nitrites inhibit ATPase activity, preventing the utilization of ATP, and thus, the interference in energy utilization is responsible for dilatation.

Lately, the organic nitrates are thought to involve the **nitrate receptors** in the vascular smooth muscle. The nitrate receptor has sulfhydryl groups which reduce nitrate to inorganic nitrite and nitric oxide. The formation of **nitrosothiol** stimulates **guanylate cyclase** leading to increased intracellular cyclic guanosine monophosphate (GMP) formation. This increased GMP formation leads to vascular smooth muscle relaxation, possibly by an inhibition of calcium entry, or an increase in calcium efflux from the smooth muscle.

Adverse Reactions

1. The chief disturbances occur due to sudden **hypotension**. Light headedness, dizziness, flushing of the face, throbbing headache, tachycardia, thready pulse and fainting and a complete **nitrite syncope** might occur.

2. **Tolerance** is developed rapidly.

3. **Methaemoglobinaemia.** The nitrite ion readily oxidizes haemoglobin to methaemoglobin. Amyl nitrite has greater effect than other organic nitrites. Whenever 10 percent of the haemoglobin is oxidized to methaemoglobin, the skin appears to be "cyanotic". *Nitrite-induced methamoglobinaemia has a unique application in the treatment of cyanide poisoning.*

Therapeutic Uses

1. In **angina pectoris** to relieve or prevent anginal pain.
2. In **refractory biliary colic**, and **bronchial asthma** as antispasmodics.
3. In abdominal cramps of **lead colic**.
4. In **trigeminal neuralgia** amyl nitrite inhalations may reduce the intensity and duration of pain.
5. In **Raynaud's disease** and **trophic ulcers** topical application of nitroglycerin may provide useful local vasodilatation.
6. In **cyanide poisoning**.

Treatment of Cyanide Poisoning

The lethal action of cyanide is due to its inactivating the enzyme cytochrome oxidase. In the presence of methaemoglobin the cyanide dissociates from the enzyme, and combines instead with methaemoglobin. The **cyanmethaemoglobin** so formed will itself dissociate by recombination of cyanide with cytochrome oxidase, which can be prevented by thiosulphate administration. Thiosulphate reacts with cyanide to produce stable thiocynate. **Sodium nitrite** is usually employed in these cases to induce methaemoglobinaemia. A suggested regimen is as under:

1. **Sodium nitrite** 0.3 to 0.5 g, dissolved in 10 to 15 ml of water is injected intravenously over 3 to 4 minutes. If there is a delay in preparation and injection of solution, amyl nitrite inhalations may be given every 2 minutes for 30 seconds.

2. **Sodium thisulphate** 12.5 g in 50 ml of water, given intravenously over 10 minutes.

3. **Oxygen inhalation** or even a **blood transfusion** may have to be given if severe methaemoglobinaemia, leading to profound hypoxaemia has occurred.

Specific Agents

Glyceryl trinitrate (Nitroglycerin). It is a standard agent for the relief of acute angina pectoris. It is administered in doses of 0.3 to 0.6 mg sublingually. The onset of action is within 2 to 5 minutes, and the duration of action is about 30 minutes. Not more than 2 tablets should be taken at a time. It is advisable to direct the patient to expel the undissolved tablet from the mouth as soon as relief is obtained.

Currently nitroglycerin is available in many dosage forms:

(*i*) **Nitroglycerin sublingual tablets** (0.15, 0.3, 0.4, 0.6 mg) -dose 0.3-0.6 mg under the tongue; (*ii*) **Nitroglycerin translingual oral spray** (0.4 mg/metered dose) - one to two sprays onto oral mucosa; (*iii*) **Nitroglycerin transmucosal** (controlled release buccal tablets 1, 2, 3 mg) - dose 1 tablet placed in buccal pouch; (*iv*) **Nitroglycerin injection** (0.5, 0.8, 5.0, 10 mg/ml) - dose 5 mcg/min IV infusion, increase upto 20 mcg/min; (*v*) **Nitroglycerin topical ointment** (2%) - dose half-inch strip of ointment applied by spreading over 6 × 6 inch area of the skin, do not rub in, increase by half-inch increments; and (*vi*) **Nitroglycerin transdermal systems** (Transderm-Nitro - 2.5, 5, 10, 15 mg/24 hours) - apply one patch to a non-hairy skin area once in 24 hours.

Amyl nitrite. It is a volatile liquid available in small breakable ampoules (pearls) containing 0.3 ml of the drug. The pearl is cracked between the folds of a handkerchief and the vapours inhaled. Its major **disadvantages** are, the inconvenient mode of administration, strong odour, and a tendency to produce nitrite headache. It is now rarely used in the treatment of angina pectroris. As indicated earlier amyl nitrite **may be used to induce methaemoglobinaemia in cyanide poisoning**, and also to reduce the severity of attacks of trigeminal neuralgia.

Long-acting Nitrates

Pentaerythrityl tetranitrate in a dose of 20-60 mg tid has been claimed to reduce the severity and frequency of anginal attacks in about one-third of patients. On the contrary, in some well controlled studies it is no better than a placebo. Thus, the use of these agents continues to be controversial, however, a trial is always indicated in angina patients.

Isosorbide dinitrate is given as a 5 mg sublingual tablet and is effective within 5 minutes. Since this nitrate has a half-life of about 40 minutes it is effective for upto 2 hours. It is used for prophylaxis or treatment of anginal attacks. **Isosorbide-5-mononitrate** is used for the prophylaxis of angina pectoris.

Beta-Adrenoceptor Blockers

The beta-blockers are discussed in detail in **Chapter 3.5.** The agents approved for treatment of angina pectoris include **propranolol, nadolol, atenolol** and **metoprolal**. These agents are particularly suited in patients who get frequent or severe attacks of angina at rest, because they can markedly *reduce myocardial oxygen demand*. The *haemodynamic effects* responsible for the beneficial effects of beta-blockers are a **decreased heart rate, blood pressure,** and **myocardial contractility**, all of which **reduce cardiac workload (Table 4.5-1)**. Propranolol blocks the oxygen wasting effects of catecholamines.

The beta-blockers may slightly increase the end-diastolic pressure due to bradycardia, but this can be avoided by simultaneous use of a nitrate. In addition, the reflex tachycardia induced by nitrates is attenuated by beta-blockers. **Thus, a combined nitrate-beta-blocker therapy is frequently more advantageous, exerting a synergistic effect.**

Propranolol. It is a **nonselective** beta-blocker used for moderate to severe angina. Propranolol is administered orally in combination with nitrates as needed. The initial dose is 10-20 mg tid or qid; dosage may be increased to optimal levels which may range from 80 to 160 mg/day. Sustained-release capsules (60, 80, 120, 160 mg) may be given once daily when the patients have been stabilized on the drug.

Nadolol. The actions of nadolol are similar to propranolol in reducing myocardial oxygen consumption. Nadolol has a long half-life (18-24 hours), and may be used

Table 4.5-1 *The effects of nitrates, beta-blockers and calcium channel blockers on the determinants of myocardial oxygen supply and demand*

Determinant	*Nitrates*	*Beta-blockers*	*Calcium channel blockers*
Wall tension	↓	±	↓
Ventricular volume	↓	↑	±
Ventricular pressure	↓	↓	↓
Heart size	↓	↑	±
Heart rate	↑ (reflex)	↓	±
Contractility	↑(reflex)	↓	±
Endocardial/epicardial blood flow ratio	↑	↑	↑
Collateral blood flow	↑	→	↑

key: ↑ = increase; ↓ = decrease; → = no change; ± = variable effect as a once-a-day dosing schedule. Initial dosage is 40 mg, which may be increased by 40-80 mg increments every 3 to 7 days. The usual maintenance dose ranges from 80 to 240 mg a day.

Atenolol. Atenolol is a long-acting ($t_{1/2}$ 6-9 hours) cardioselective beta-blocker with actions similar to those of propranolol. The usual dose is 50 mg once daily.

Metoprolol. The usual dose is 100-450 mg daily. It has to be adjusted to individual needs.

Calcium Channel Blockers

Calcium channel blockers are a heterogeneous group of drugs that **reduce intracellular calcium transfer,** thereby limiting calcium-triggered ATP release and thus reducing contractility of the muscle cell. The three clinically important agents are **verapamil, diltiazem** and **nifedipine**. Alternative names like calcium antagonists, calcium blockers, calcium slow-channel blockers and inhibitors of the slow calcium current stress the point that this group of agents inhibits the slow calcium channel. They act specially on those tissues in which the slow calcium channel opens without being triggered by the fast sodium channel, e.g., the **nodal tissue** in the heart and the **arterial smooth muscle.**Different calcium antagonists act differently, with **verapamil** and **diltiazem** being most effective on nodal tissue, **nifedipine** on peripheral arteries, and all three agents being **equally effective on coronary arteries**. These three sites of action account for most of the clinical applications of calcium antagonists, namely **angina pectoris** (classical and variant), **supraventricular arrhythmias**, **hypertension** and **peripheral vascular disease**. Verapamil and diltiazem relieve supraventricular tachycardia by inhibition of the AV node; nifedipine is most effective in hypertension. All three benefit angina of effort, acting through a mixture of mechanisms: (*i*) all may increase coronary blood flow; (*ii*) **diltiazem** has negative chronotropic effect and mildly reduces afterload; (*iii*) **verapamil** has a mild negative inotropic effect and decreases afterload; and (*iv*) the major effect of **nifedipine** is to reduce afterload.

Calcium antagonists, like beta-blockers have **antianginal**, **antihypertensive** and **antiarrhythmic** properties. An important difference is in the vascular smooth muscle, where calcium antagonists dilate and beta-blockers constrict the vessels. Further, calcium antagonists do not induce bronchospasm, whereas the beta-blockers precipitate bronchospasm.

Pharmacology and Mode of Action

When a cardiac cell potential reaches its threshold, the membrane permeability for sodium increases rapidly and markedly. This so called **fast channel** is responsible for the influx of sodium, and is blocked by **tetrodotoxin.** The time required for the second inward current to reach its maximum is longer. This current is caused mainly by the movement of calcium ions into the cell through a **membrane pore**. This second channel is known as the **slow channel**. The movement of calcium through this slow channel is inhibited by manganese (Mn^{++}) but not by tetrodotoxin. This movement is blocked by verapamil, and thereby the plateau phase of the cardiac action potential is altered.

It should be appreciated that calcium antagonists, unlike beta-blockers, are structurally heterogeneous compounds, with somewhat different properties **(Table 4.5-2)**. **Verapamil** is a papaverine derivative: **nifedipine** is a dihydropyridine derivative; and **diltiazem** is a benzothiazepine derivative. Despite marked structural differences, they all **block the slow channel selectively** in the heart muscle and smooth muscle, with varying potencies.

Table 4.5-2 *The electrophysiological, haemodynamic and pharmacokinetic properties of conventional calcium channel blockers*

Effects and properties	*Verapamil*	*Nifedipine*	*Diltiazem*
ELECTROPHYSIOLOGY			
Heart rate			
Isolated atria	↓+++	↓+++	↓+++
Intact organism	↓↑	↑→	↑→
AV conduction			
Isolated heart	↓+++	↓++++	↓+++
Intact organism	↓++++	0 to ↑	↓+++
Electorcardiogram			
RR interval	↑↓	↓	↑↓
QRS complex	0	0	0
PR interval	↑	0	↑
A-H	↑	0	↑
H-V	0	0	0
Atrial ERP	0	0	0

Table 4.5-2 Contd...

Effects and properties	*Verapamil*	*Nifedipine*	*Diltiazem*
AV node ERP	↑↑	±	↑
AV node FRP	↑↑	±	↑
Ventricular ERP	0	0	0
His-Purkinje ERP	0	0	0
Ventricular automaticity	0	0	0
HAEMODYNAMICS			
Myocardial contractility	↓↓	↓	↓
Cardiac Output	↑↓	↑	0↑
Peripheral vascular resistance	↓↓	↓↓↓	↓
Afterload	↓↓	↓↓↓	↓
Preload	→	→	→
PHARMACOKINETICS			
Absorption from gut (%)	90	90	80-90
Absolute bioavailability (%)	10-35	45-70	40-67
Onset of action—Oral (min)	30	20	30
Time of peak plasma level (hrs)	1-2	0.5	2-3
Plasma protein binding (%)	83-92	92-98	70-85
Therapeutic serum level (mcg/ml)	0.08-0.3	0.025-0.1	0.04-0.2
Excreted unchanged in urine (%)	3-4	1-2	2-4
Half-life (hrs)	3-7	2-5	4-9

Abbreviations: ↓ = decrease; ↑ = increase; ↑↓ = variable effect; → = unchanged; ± = variable change;
0 = no change.
+ → ++++ = gradation of change from small to marked.
ERP = effective refractory period.
FRP = functional refractory period.
A-H = atrial-His Bundle conduction time.
H-V = His-ventricular conduction time.

Electrophysiology. *Verapamil* and *diltiazem* decrease SA and AV conduction and prolong the AV node effective and functional refractory periods. Some clinical studies have demonstrated a reduction in AV node ERP and FRP with nifedipine.

Verapamil slows AV conduction and prolongs the ERP within the AV node, and thus reduces elevated ventricular rate in **supraventricular tachycardia** due to atrial flutter or fibrillation. By interrupting re-entry at the AV node, verapamil can restore normal sinus rhythm in patients with paroxysmal supraventricular tachycardias (PSVT), including **Wolff-Parkinson-White (WPW) syndrome**. Verapamil can induce AV blocks, though rarely.

Haemodynamics. Calcium antagonists dilate the coronary arteries and arterioles, both in the normal and ischaemic regions of the myocardium, and inhibit coronary artery spasm. This increases myocardial oxygen delivery in patients with vasospastic (Prinzmetal's or variant) angina. All three of the conventional calcium channel blockers decrease coronary vascular resistance and increase coronary blood flow. Nifedipine is a more potent vasodilator than verapamil.

Calcium antagonists reduce arterial blood pressure at rest and at a given level of exercise by dilating peripheral arterioles and thereby reducing total peripheral resistance (afterload) against which the heart works. Such an unloading of the heart reduces myocardial energy consumption and oxygen demand. This probably accounts for their effectiveness in *chronic stable angina*.

The haemodynamic effects of these agents (verapamil, nifedipine, diltiazem) vary depending on the route of administration and the left ventricular function. **Nifedipine** given intravenously increases forearm blood flow with little effect on venous pooling, which indicates a selective dilation of arterial resistance vessels. The heart rate and cardiac output are slightly increased. Recent studies show that sublingual nifedipine produces a more marked improvement in cardiac performance.

Verapamil is a less potent vasodilator *in vitro* than nifedipine. However, the cardiac actions of verapamil are more marked than those of nifedipine. With doses of verapamil which produce peripheral arterial vasodilation, there are more direct negative chronotropic (rate), dromotropic (conductivity), and inotropic (contractility) effects than with nifedipine. Oral administration of verapamil induces a reduction of peripheral resistance and BP with no change in heart rate.

Diltiazem given IV results initially in a reflex increase in heart rate and cardiac output. Heart rate falls below initial levels due to the direct negative chronotropic effect of the drug. Oral administration of diltiazem produces a sustained fall in both heart rate and mean arterial blood pressure.

Pharmacokinetics. Although calcium antagonists are well absorbed (80 to 90%) from the gut, they are subject to extensive **first-pass metabolism**, resulting in a considerably less absolute bioavailability.

Therapeutic Uses

1. **Angina pectoris due to coronary spasm (nifedipine, verapamil, diltiazem).** They are useful in the treatment of spontaneous coronary artery spasm presenting as Prinzmetal's variant angina.

2. **Exertional angina pectoris (nifedipine, verapamil, diltiazem).** Classical chronic stable angina or angina of effort responds to calcium antagonist therapy, specially in patients who cannot tolerate beta-blocker therapy or nitrates, or who remain symptomatic despite adequate doses of these agents. Beneficial effects have been seen after long-term oral administration of any of the three agents. The **double product**, which is calculated as heart rate x systolic blood pressure, is an indirect index of myocardial oxygen demand. **The value of the double product oxygen demand is reduced by these agents.** The beneficial effect in exertional angina is due to the reduced oxygen demand of the myocardium.

3. **Unstable angina (oral verapamil).** This condition is also named as **preinfarction angina** or **crescendo angina**. There is severe reduction of coronary flow, and vasospasm is likely to occur in some patients. Calcium antagonists have been found to be particularly effective if the underlying mechanism is vasospasm with ST segment elevation.

4. **Supraventricular tachyarrhythmias (IV verapamil).** Verapamil 5 to 10 mg (0.075-0.015 mg/kg) IV is given over 2 minutes. The repeat dose is 1 mg after 30 minutes of the initial dose, if response is not adequate.

5. **Hypertensive emergencies.** Nifedipine 10 to 20 mg orally or sublingually has been used to lower blood pressure in hypertensive emergencies.

6. **Miscellaneous uses.** Nifedipine has been found to be useful in the treatment of **Raynaud's phenomenon**. Preliminary studies suggest that nifedipine may also be useful in the treatment of **primary pulmonary hypertension** and **asthma**. Verapamil 80 to 160 mg tid has been used for **paroxysmal supraventricular tachycardia** (PSVT). It has also been used for the prophylaxis of **migraine headaches**. A new use for calcium antagonists has been for myocardial preservation. Calcium antagonists (nifedipine 20 to 40 mg orally) may be used to treat primary dysmenorrhoea and other conditions in which inhibiton of uterine activity is desirable. On an investigational basis calcium antagonists are also being tried for the **prevention of exercise-induced asthma**. The uses of calcium antagonists in cardiovascular diseases are summarized in **Table 4.5-3**.

Contraindications and Precautions

Verapamil and diltiazem are contraindicated in **sick sinus syndrome** except in the presence of a functioning ventricular pacemaker. Other contraindications are **second or third degree AV blocks** and **hypotension**. IV verapamil and IV beta-blockers must not be injected concomitantly, since both depress the myocardial contractility and AV conduction. Hypersensitivity to nifedipine has been reported.

Adverse Reactions

Verapamil is the best tolerated calcium antagonist. **Constipation** is the most common side effect. Headache,

Table 4.5-3 *Calcium antagonist and cardiovascular disorders*

Drug	*Indications*	*Dosage*
Verapamil	1. Supraventricular tachycardia (SCT) - narrow QRS complexes	1. IV bolus 5-0 mg, repeated after 10 minutes, then 0.005 mg/kg/min, if needed. 2. IV infusion 1 mg/min to a total of 10 mg. 3. If myocardial disease, work up from 0.0001 mg/kg/ min., titrating against heart rate.
	2. Atrial flutter/fibrillation (to control ventricular rate)	IV infusion, if needed (3 above); or 80-120 mg tid increasing to 80-120 mg qid
	3. Prophylaxis of SVT, angina of effort, angina at rest, and hypertrophic cardiomyopathy	Orall 80-120 mg Orally 8-120 mg tid increasing to 80-120 qid.
Nifedipine	1. Angina of effort, angina at rest and Prinzmetal's angina	Orally 30-80 mg/day in 3 or 4 divided doses.
	2. Hypertension, acute left-venticular failure (pulmonary oedema)	Orally, 10 mg 2 to 4 times daily; 10 mg sublingually 6 hourly.
Diltiazem	1. Supraventricular tachycardia (SVT)	IV 0.15-0.25 mg/kg giver over 2 minutes.
	2. Atrial flutter/ fibrillation	IV 0.15-0.25 mg/kg given over 2 minutes.
	3. Prophylaxis of SVT, angina of effort and at rest Prinzmetal's angina	Oral 30-90 mg tid increasing to qid.
	4. Hypertrophic cardiomyopathy	Indication/dosage yet to be established.

vertigo, weakness, nervousness, pruritus, flushing and gastric disturbances may occur. **Orthostatic hypotension, AV block, AV dissociation, pedal oedema, pulmonary oedema** and **congestive heart failure** have been reported occasionally. Perceptual disorders (feeling of coldness and numbness), **hyperprolactinaemia**, and **galactorrhoea** also have been reported.

Nifedipine may cause headache, tachycardia, dizziness, fatigue, nausea, oedema, flushing, orthostatic hypotension, tinnitus, leg cramps and skin reactions. It occasionally worsens anginal symptoms and precipitates CHF or cerebral ischaemia. Severe hypotension, heart failure and myocardial infarction have occurred in patients receiving nifedipine. Occasionally glucose intolerance occurs. Hepatitis occurs rarely.

Diltiazem may cause bradycardia, dizziness, headache, flushing and dryness of mouth. Hypersensitivity reactions have been reported. CHF, AV conduction defects and sinus arrest occur rarely.

Felodipine. This is a newer calcium antagonist, and a dihydropyridine derivative. Felodipine has a more selective effect on smooth muscle cells of resistant vessels than nifedipine and verapamil. It interferes with the utilization of intracellular calcium, and causes a fall in total peripheral resistance with a fall in diastolic blood pressure; the systolic blood pressure remaining unchanged. This results in a reflex increase in sympathetic tone and heart rate. This drug also has a marked **diuretic effect** secondary to increased **natriuresis**.

Haemorheology, i.e., the study of the flow properties of blood and its interaction with the vascular system, has received professional attention lately. **Felodipine** enhances red cell deformability or flexibility, i.e., the ability of the red blood cells to change their shape in response to mechanical force or stresses is increased. In short, this intrinsic flexibility of the red blood cells is governed by three factors: (*i*) the rheological characteristics of the fluid inside the cell; (*ii*) properties of the membrane surrounding the cell; and (*iii*) the excess membrane surface area over and above that is needed to encase the cell volume. **Felodipine is an inhibitor of calmodulin**, an intracellular protein which enhances the activity of calcium-dependent ATPase. Thus it inhibits ATP breakdown and reduces intracellular calcium. The former action promotes removal of cations, and the later action prevents formation of rigid crossbridges between **spectrin molecules** lining the cell membrane. Both actions result in enhanced red blood cell membrane flexibility and lowered blood viscosity.

Therapeutic uses. Felodipine lowers blood pressure without any change in renin levels. Hence its **role in renin-independent hypertension**. In hypertensive emergencies it is given in a dose of 0.01 to 0.04 mg/kg IV, over 20 to 120 minutes. The vasodilatory effect is without negative inotropic effect on the heart. The usual dose in **hypertensives** is 10 mg orally bid. Felodipine is also under trial in cases of **congestive heart failure** and **cardiac arrhythmias**. As felodipine increases red cell deformability and promotes better flow; reduces whole blood viscosity and reduces total peripheral resistance, these factors may contribute towards control of hypertension. The use of felodipine in conditions with **reduced tissue perfusion, impaired microcirculation** and both **intra** and **extravascular haemolysis** is under evaluation.

Short-term **side effects** include headache, diarrhoea and flushing in some patients. Long-term use may lead to ankle oedema, but without weight gain, as felodpine has a potent diuretic effect. Its use appears to be safe in renal insufficiency.

Lidoflazine. It is a piperazine derivative that interferes with calcium transport, and also potentiates the vasodilator effect of endogenous adenosine. *Strictly speaking, it is not a selective calcium channel blocker, as it also blocks the fast sodium current in relatively low concentrations.* Lidoflazine slows heart rate and AV conduction velocity; dilates the coronary and peripheral arteries, and reduces venous tone.

Drug Interactions

Concomitant use of *calcium antagonists* and *beta-blockers* is risky, as the cardiac function can be adversely affected because of the combined depressant effects on the myocardial contractility and AV conduction. Elevated **digoxin** levels have been reported with concurrent administration of nifedipine. Verapamil administered with antihypertensive agents may have an additive effect in lowering blood pressure. Verapamil is highly bound to plasma proteins, and should be administered with caution in patients receiving other highly protein-bound drugs like **warfarin** and **oral hypoglycaemic agents**. The therapeutic effectiveness of verapamil may be decreased by administration of **calcium** and **vitamin D**. Calcium has been used to treat verapamil toxicity.

To conclude, the **beta-blockers** and **calcium angatonists** have a somewhat similar spectrum of therapeutic usefulness. Individual calcium channel blockers significantly differ among each other regarding their pharmacologic, electrophysiologic, haemodynamic and pharmacokinetic properties. These considerations govern the choice of a particular calcium antagonist for a specific clinical disorder.

Antiplatelet Agents

Dipyridamole

Dipyridamole is a potent non-nitrate coronary vasodilator used in the long-term prophylactic therapy of angina pectoris. It acts on the small resistance vessels of the coronary bed to increase coronary blood flow. Dipyridamole

inhibits adenosine deaminase, thereby increasing the levels of adenosine and other vasodilatory nucleotides. It also **blocks the action of phosphodiesterase**, resulting in an increased level of cyclic-AMP, causing coronary vasodilation. Increased cyclic-AMP also **reduces platelet aggregation**. For antiplatelet drugs see **Chapter 5.3.**

Therapeutic uses. Dipyridamole either alone or in combination with aspirin has been used to prevent **transient ischaemic attacks** and protect against further *thromboembolic complications.*

Dipyridamole is administered orally as tablets (25, 50, 75 mg). The usual dose is 25-50 mg bid or tid orally. It is a well tolerated drug and side effects are rare. GI distress, headache, flushing, dizziness and skin rash may occur.

Myocardial Oxygen Metabolism

Imbalance between myocardial oxygen need and supply lead to either **reversible** or **irreversible changes**. If the myocardial ischaemia is slight and limited, the biochemical and cellular changes are reversible. But if there is complete occlusion of a branch of a coronary artery with almost no blood supply to a part of the myocardium, there is a severe imbalance between the myocardial oxygen need and supply. This eventually leads to **myocardial infarction**, and a poor left ventricular function, depending on the extent of the myocardium that has lost its contractility. The sequence of events is summarized in **Fig. 4.5.1.**

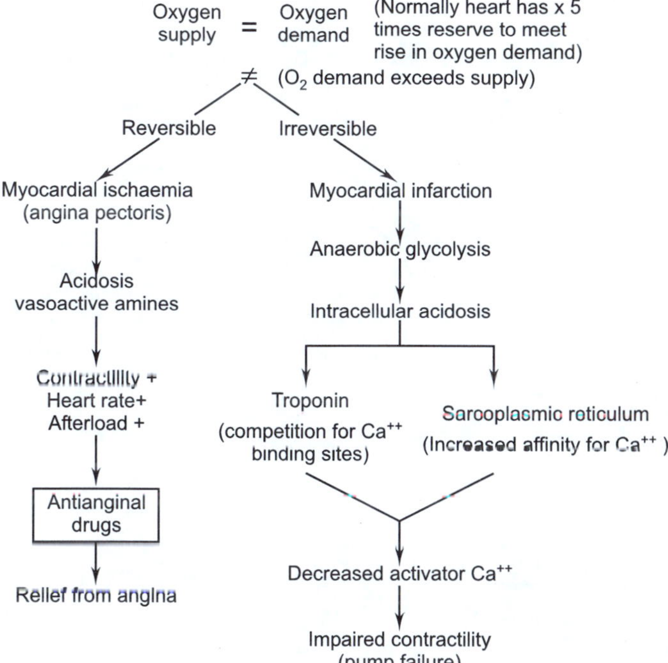

Fig. 4.5.1: The balance between myocardial oxygen supply and demand. Their imbalance causes reversible or irreversible myocellular changes leading to clinical consequences of impaired contractility (see text).

Drug Management of Angina Pectoris

1. Treat the cause, if possible, e.g., anaemia, syphilis.
2. Arrangement of life so as to reduce the number of attacks as far as possible. Weight reduction is helpful.
3. **Nitroglycerin** to be taken before exercise that is expected to induce angina. It is also used to relieve the attack.
4. **Beta-adrenoceptor blockade.** Propranolol is given continuously, and the dosage is adjusted.
5. The **long-acting organic nitrates** may be used for prophylaxis.
6. **Sedation** may help if anxiety is a factor.
7. Smoking should be discouraged.
8. In severe cases **anticoagulant therapy** should be considered.
9. Control of plasma lipids is likely to be helpful.
10. Severe angina, unresponsive to drug treatment is an indication for **surgical bypass grafting** of the affected coronary arteries.

Drug Treatment of Acute Myocardial Infarction

The drug treatment of acute myocardial infarction (MI) is aimed to treat the following major associated abnormalities:

(*i*) **Pain:** Morphine, Pethidine.

(*ii*) **Arrhythmias:** Lignocaine, glucose-insulin-potassium infusion.

(*iii*) **Pump failure:** Digitalis, glucagon.

(*iv*) **Cardiogenic shock:** Mephentermine, dopamine.

The use of drugs for the prophylaxis of arrhythmias in the absence of any rhythm abnormality is controversial. **Lignocaine**, **quinidine**, and **procainamide** have been tried. Treated patients have fewer arrhythmias, but paradoxically there seems to be no improvement in the overall survival. The **anticoagulants** may be used for one month for the prevention of recurrence of myocardial infarction in an uncomplicated case of acute MI. Otherwise, the use of anticoagulants is reserved for patients of MI with complications.

The most important factor to be managed is the extreme apprehension and pain in the patient. To allay anxiety **diazepam** produces adequate sedation, reduces the secretion of catecholamines, and often decreases the need for analgesics. **Intravenous morphine** or **pethidine** are the drugs of choice for analgesia, with 10 mg of morphine being equivalent to 75 mg of pethidine.

Lately for the prevention of arrhythmias, and for limiting the infarct size, **glucose insulin potassium**

infusion (potassium chloride 40 mEq and regular insulin 20 units in 1000 ml of 10% glucose) has been tried, in the hope of increasing the diastolic polarization of the infarcted area by forcing the potassium ions into the fibre. Its usefulness for restricting the myocardial infarction size is yet to be fully evaluated. For the secondary prevention of reinfarction, drugs like **aspirin**, **sulphinpyrazone** and **beta-adrenoceptor blockers** have been employed. **Low-dose heparin therapy** has been shown to reduce the incidence of deep vein thromboses and consequent pulmonary embolism in patients of myocardial infarction. **Oxygen** is given to most patients with complicated MI, and in many units it is given for the first few hours after infarction routinely.

To conclude, drugs employed in the treatment of angina pectoris exert one or more of the following effects: increase in coronary blood flow; decrease in cardiac work; and improvement in myocardial efficiency. The last mentioned factor means an increase in work proportionate to the oxygen needed by the heart.

4.6 DRUG THERAPY OF SHOCK

Shock is a state of acute circulatory failure in which the cardiac output is inadequate to provide normal tissue perfusion. It is an all-inclusive term for inadequate tissue perfusion, produced by a number of diseases, and the symptoms are particularly related to the hypoperfusion of the vital organs like the **brain, heart, kidneys, liver** and **lungs**. The consequences of inadequate tissue perfusion are, **firstly**, stagnation of blood in the capillaries, and **secondly**, tissue hypoxia with metabolic acidosis as a result of accumulation of lactic acid. If hypoxic cellular damage is not promptly reversed by restoring normal blood flow to the vital organs, the state of shock may become **irreversible** and refractory to treatment. **It must be remembered that shock represents a failure of blood flow rather than a fall of blood pressure**.

The diagnosis of shock should not be based on the level of arterial blood pressure, but must take into consideration the signs and symptoms of **inadequate perfusion of vital organs**, like the brain, kidney and myocardium, manifested as a **clouded sensorium, oliguria**, and **cardiac arrhythmias** respectively.

In the great majority of shock patients, there is a fluid deficit. Treatment is first of all directed towards replacement therapy with **plasma, blood substitutes**, or **whole blood** depending on individual needs **(Chap. 5.5)**. The monitoring of such therapy is often done **via central venous pressure** (CVP). The clinical CVP monitoring usually refers to central vena caval or right atrial pressure, and therefore is a general index of right ventricular filling pressure, and right ventricular end-diastolic pressure.

The Peripheral Circulation

The total blood volume is about 5 litres, and this amount is pumped by the heart once each minute. The stroke volume is about 70 ml per beat, ejected about 72 times each minute. Only about 15 percent of the blood volume lies in the arterial bed, and variations in arterial calibre have little effect on vascular capacity. The arterioles are extremely muscular and the tone of the arterioles regulates the blood flow through the organs and tissues. As the greatest fall in mean blood pressure (from 100 to 32 mm Hg) occurs in this region, the arterioles are called **resistance vessels**. Normally they are widely open to permit free perfusion of tissues. **(Fig. 4.6.1)**. Sympathetic autonomic stimulation constricts the arterioles, diminishing tissue perfusion.

Only 5 percent of circulating blood volume is contained in the capillary bed, and normally the capillaries do not influence the vascular capacity greatly. The **pre-capillary sphincter** relaxes as the oxygen tension in tissues falls. Mast cells around the capillaries secrete histamine on anoxia and the pre-capillary sphincter opens. As a result of metabolic acidosis (elevated lactate, pyruvate and ketones) the pre-capillary sphincter relaxes and the blood flow increases. Thus, the pre-capillary sphincter is mainly under **local metabolic control.**

Most of the circulating blood volume (over 70%) lies on the venous side, in the venules. Hence, the venous system is called the **capacitance system**. The veins are less muscular, with a large diameter and offer a low resistance, whereby the blood pressure falls to about 7 mg Hg. The veins and the **post-capillary sphincter** are under sympathetic autonomic control, and failure of venous tone would lead to pooling of blood in the venules and capillaries, resulting in a fall in cardiac output. Such a condition is labelled as **peripheral circulatory failure**.

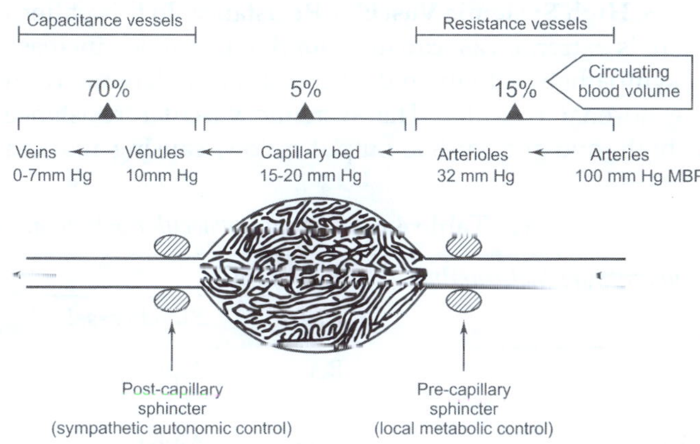

Fig. 4.6.1: Diagrammatic representation of the normal peripheral capillary circulation system. MBP = mean Blood Pressure.

The sympathetic autonomic nervous system (ANS) mainly regulates **blood pressure; distribution of blood; capacity of the venous system; the force and rate of cardiac contraction**. In the earlier stages these haemodynamic abnormalities can be reversed by using drugs which reduce the blood supply to the viscera and preserve or augment the blood supply to the brain, kidney and heart. This stage of shock is labelled as **reversible shock**. In reversible shock there is tissue hypoxia and metabolic acidosis which impairs capillary perfusion. Attempts must be made to reverse this condition soon or it would progress into **irreversible shock**.

Various anoxic tissues release *proteolytic enzymes, bradykinin, histamine* and *5-hydroxytryptamine*. Due to tissue acidosis and anoxia the pre-capillary sphincter widely opens and the post-capillary sphincter calibre remains the same as it is more resistant to anoxia. Thus, the pressure within the capillaries is raised. Plasma is lost by exudation and the circulating blood volume is further reduced. **Thrombosis** occurs due to increased viscosity of blood. Tissue oxygenation further suffers. **Such a state occurs in irreversible shock and it is refractory to drug treatment**.

Haemodynamic Patterns in Shock

In patients of *shock three* haemodynamic patterns have been described:

1. **Inadequate Venous Return.** This pattern is the result of trauma, bleeding, peritonitis or burns. The cardiac output is lowered. For the management, first proper replacement of fluids is necessary **(Chap. 6.1)**.

2. **Low Systemic Vascular Resistance.** This pattern of shock is characterized by low arterial blood pressure, slightly low or normal cardiac output and abnormally low systemic vascular resistance. About 75 percent of patients of **septic shock** and 50 percent of patients in shock **following myocardial infarction** belong to this category. In shock of head **injury** and **chemical toxicity** also the peripheral resistance is low.

3. **High Systemic Vascular Resistance.** In this pattern there is **extreme vasoconstriction** due to a reflex increase in sympathetic activity, and release of catecholamines from the adrenal medulla. The systemic vascular resistance is high, and the cardiac output is low, causing marked tissue hypoperfusion. About 50 percent of patients in **shock following myocardial infarction**, and 25 percent of patients of **septic shock** belong to this category. Shock following **cardiac surgery** also belongs to this category.

Drug Therapy of Shock

The treatment of shock may be divided into **primary therapy** for the presumed cause of the syndrome (haemorrhage, infection, myocardial infarction, anaphylaxis), and **secondary therapy** for the correction of the associated haemodynamic disturbance. The following drugs are employed for their haemodynamic effects:

1. Sympathomimetic amines.
2. Alpha-adrenoceptor blocking agents.
3. Corticosteroids.
4. Oxygen.
5. Cardiac glycosides.
6. Glucagon.
7. Dextrans.

Sympathomimetic Amines

The sympathomimetic amines exert their cardiovascular effects by acting on the beta$_1$-adrenoceptors in the heart, alpha and beta$_2$- adrenoceptors in the blood vessels, and dopamine receptors in the renal, mesenteric, coronary and cerebral vascular beds **(Chap. 3.4)**. When shock is due to inadequate circulating blood volume, blood or plasma volume expanders should be administered first, and later if need be, the sympathomimetics may be used to improve tissue perfusion.

The sympathomimetic amines used in the treatment of shock are **noradrenaline, adrenaline, dopamine**, and the synthetic compounds **isoprenaline, metaraminol** and **dobutamine**. Some sympathomimetic amines are preferably used as pressor agents during anaesthesia which include **mephentermine, methoxamine** and **phenylephrine (Table 4.6-1)**.

Table 4.6-1 *The cardiovascular action and the receptor profile of sympathomimetic amines*

Sympathomimetic amine	*Receptors*		*Haemodynamic action*
	Heart	*Blood vessel*	
Noradrenaline	Beta	Alpha	C.O. ↑ or ↓ ; TPR ↑; Blood flow ↑ in cerebral and coronary beds, ↓ in all others
Adrenaline	Beta	Alpha Beta	C.O↑; TPR ↓ in small doses; Blood flow ↑ skeletal muscles and mesentery; ↓ skin and kidneys
Dopamine	Beta	Dopaminergic Alpha	C.O ↑; TPR↓ in small doses; ↑ in large doses; ↑ blood flow to kidneys and mesentery
Isoprenaline	Beta	Beta	C.O. ↑; TPR ↓; Blood flow ↑ skeletal muscle and mesentery; kidney no effect or ↓
Metaraminol	Beta	Alpha	Acts indirectly; actions like noradrenaline, with longer duration

Table 4.6-1 Contd...

Sympathomimetic amine	*Receptors*		*Haemodynamic action*
	Heart	*Blood vessel*	
Dobutamine	Beta	Beta Alpha	C.O. ↑;TPR↓; Circulatory effects similar to isoprenaline qualitatively
Mephentermine	Beta	Alpha Nonspecific vasodilation	C.O. ↑ or ↓; TPR ↑ or ↓ depending on dose and existing vascular tone
Methoxamine	—	Alpha	C.O.↓; TPR↑
Phenylephrine	—	Alpha	C.O↓; TPR ↑; ↓ blood flow through skin and kidneys

C.O. = Cardiac output; TRP = Total peripheral resistance; ↑ = Increased; ↓ = Decreased.

Noradrenaline raises the perfusion pressure and the cardiac output in patients of shock with very low peripheral vascular resistance. Thus, it is indicated in the patient with low peripheral resistance shock. **In the shock syndrome with high peripheral resistance and low or normal blood pressure, noradrenaline induces further vasoconstriction and is rarely helpful or rather it is harmful.**

Adrenaline although increases the cardiac output and lowers the TRP, the renal blood flow is not increased. On the contrary it is lowered. The use of adrenaline is restricted to **anaphylactic shock**.

Dopamine is a biochemical precursor of noradrenaline and adrenaline, but it exerts haemodynamic effects which are qualitatively different from noradrenaline, adrenaline and other sympathomimetic amines. **Dopamine increases renal and mesenteric blood flow, possibly by acting on the dopamine receptors**. It stimulates the heart through the beta-receptors. Dopamine increases cardiac output and renal blood flow. The TPR remains unchanged. It is possibly most useful in treating oliguric patients with low or normal peripheral vascular resistance. *In the vasoconstricted patient it can be usefully combined with an alpha-blocking agent*. Dopamine has been usefully employed in the management of **cardiogenic**, **septic** and **traumatic shock**.

Isoprenaline has a beta-adrenergic action both on the heart and periphery. Unlike adrenaline it does not cause renal vasoconstriction. It is helpful in patients of shock with high peripheral vascular resistance. **Metaraminol** has haemodynamic actions like noradrenaline, but the duration of action is longer.

Dobutamine is a newer synthetic catecholamine, and acts primarily on the beta$_1$-receptor, with less pronounced actions on beta$_2$- and alpha-receptors. Because dobutamine acts mainly on cardiac beta$_1$-receptors, rather than on the alpha and beta$_2$-receptors of blood vessels, it has relatively fewer vascular effects. Dobutamine has been used for short-term therapy to increase cardiac output in patients with severe congestive heart failure, and in patients following cardiac surgery. It causes lesser tachycardia and fewer arrhythmias than isoprenaline **(Table 4.6-2)**.

Adverse Reactions

Therapeutic doses of sympathomimetic amines may cause *restlessness, headache, pallor, dizziness, precordial pain* and *palpitation*. Overdosage can induce *convulsions, cerebral haemorrhage* and *tachyarrhythmias* leading to *fatal ventricular arrhythmias*.

Alpha-Adrenoceptor Blocking Agents

Alpha-adrenoceptor blocking agents are used to reduce the intense vasoconstriction produced by reflex release of noradrenaline from the adrenergic nerves, and catecholamines from the adrenal medulla as a result of shock. The **advantages** are that: (*i*) the harmful effect of vasoconstriction on microcirculation in tissues is avoided; (*ii*) they permit rapid administration of intravenous fluid without increasing central venous pressure; and (*iii*) the occult plasma volume deficit is unmasked. **Alpha-blocker therapy must follow adequate replacement of fluid volume. Phenoxybenzamine** is the agent usually employed, and has been found to be life-saving in cases of

Table 4.6-2 *The catecholamines commonly used in shock and their effective dosage range*

Catecholamine	*Beta$_1$ receptors*	*Beta$_2$ receptors*	*Alpha receptors*	*Dopamine receptors*	*Dosage range (IV)*
Noradrenaline	++	0	++	0	6-12 mcg (base)/min
Adrenaline	++	++	+→++	0	0.5 mg IV Inj.
Dopamine	++	0	+→++	++	2-5 mcg/kg/min
Isoprenaline	++	++	0	0	0.1-1.5 mcg/kg/min
Dobutamine	++	+	+	0	2.5-10 mcg/kg/min

+ = Stimulation; 0 = no action.

traumatic or **surgical shock**. Alpha-blockers have also been recommended for use with dopamine or noradrenaline, in order to block vasoconstriction produced by these agents, without affecting their cardiac stimulant effects. Phenoxybenzamine produces a dramatic redistribution of plasma volume and blood flow, for which it has to be administered cautiously in a dose of 1 mg/kg body weight IV slowly well diluted in a volume of 500 ml 5 percent glucose.

Corticosteroids

Some authorities consider that massive doses of corticosteroids are useful in shock as they cause **vasodilatation** and a **positive intropic effect**, thereby improving tissue perfusion. In cases of septic shock, they may decrease the sensitivity to endotoxin, but their use is questionable as this would enhance the susceptibility to infection and increase the likelihood of bacteraemia. The high-dose steroid therapy used in shock may possibly be helpful by causing: (*i*) **a positive inotropic effect**; (*ii*) **decreased peripheral resistance**; (*iii*) **stabilization of lysozomes**; (*iv*) preservation of integrity of small vessels, preventing leakage from microcirculation; and (*v*) **reduction in platelet adhesiveness**.

Large doses of corticosteroids have been found to reduce the formation and liberation of cardiodepressant substances released from tissues by virtue of their stabilizing the lysosomal membrane. This lysosomal membrane stabilization may also account for their other cellular effects to save cells from hypoxic damage. Corticosteroids have to be tried then massive doses (methyl prednisolone, 30 mg/kg IV) may be administered. All precautions involved with corticosteriod therapy **(Chap. 7.5)** must be observed.

Oxygen

Oxygen increases the cardiac output, and tissue oxygenation can be significantly improved. Oxygen is necessary in patients who have arterial hypoxaemia, which usually occurs in **cardiogenic shock**. If arterial PO_2 is below 60 mm Hg or if dyspnoea or cyanosis is present, oxygen administration is required. **Positive pressure ventilation** may be required to maintain adequate oxygen exchange.

Cardiac Glycosides

Cardiac glycosides improve myocardial contractility, raise the cardiac output and improve tissue perfusion, specially in cases of congestive heart failure **(Chap. 4.3)**.

Glucagon

Glucagon increases myocardial contractility and raises the cardiac output. These actions resemble those of sympathomimetic amines but cannot be blocked by beta-blockers. Hence glucagon acts by a different mechanism of action **(Chap. 4.3)**. Glucagon definitely improves the haemodynamic status of patients in **acute heart failure following cardiac surgery**, and in **shock following myocardial infarction**. Glucagon 1-2 mg is administered intravenously in these conditions.

Dextrans

Dextrans are effective plasma volume expanders **(Chap. 5.5)** used in the emergency treatment of hypovolaemic shock, but they do not replace blood (or its derivatives) in the treatment of haemorrhagic shock. **High-molecular-weight dextran** (Mol. Wt. 110,000) is used for this purpose, and it remains in the blood for a longer period of time maintaining its oncotic pressure.

Low-molecular-weight dextran (Mol. Wt. 40,000), also known as Dextran 40, is available as a 10 percent solution in either isotonic saline or 5 percent dextrose in water for intravenous use. It has a powerful though temporary oncotic effect on blood, and withdraws fluid into the vascular space, improving blood flow. **It reduces the viscosity of blood** by inducing a negative charge on the erythrocytes causing them to repel each other, thereby it **improves the microcirculation**. Thus dextran 40 may be employed in cases of shock to improve tissue perfusion. Prolongation of bleeding time and anaphylactoid reactions may occur.

A number of other agents like: (*i*) **vasodilator drugs** (diazoxide, nitroprusside, hydralazine) may be used in patients with severe `pump failure' following acute myocardial infarction; (*ii*) **diuretics** may be cautiously employed; (*iii*) **alkalizing agents** may be used to treat metabolic acidosis; and (*iv*) **heparin** may be used to avoid **disseminated intravascular coagulation** in patients of shock syndromes.

Clinical Applications

Shock is generally classified according to its aetiology and there are **four** main types: (*i*) **Hypovolaemic**; (*ii*) **Cardiogenic**; (*iii*) **Septic**; and (*iv*) **Anaphylactic shock.**

Hypovolaemic Shock

The major haemodynamic abnormality is decreased venous return, and a low cardiac output. Therapy consists of **appropriate fluid replacement using saline, plasma or blood, and correction of acidosis**.

Cardiogenic Shock

The most common cause of cardiogenic shock is acute myocardial infarction (AMI). There is a failure of the heart as a pump, i.e., ''pump failure'' **(Fig. 4.6.2)**. The haemodynamic pattern is not always predictable, but usually the **cardiac output is reduced and the peripheral resistance is either normal or increased**.

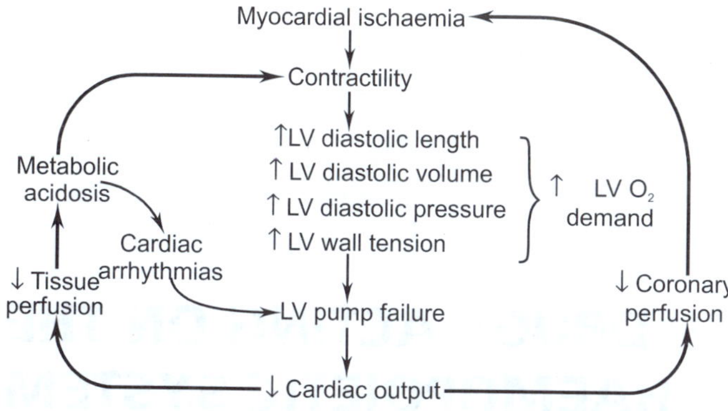

Fi.g 4.6.2: The vicious cycle of cardiogenic shock. LV = left ventricular; O_2 = oxygen.

Therapy consists of relief of pain and anxiety which reduces reflex vasoconstriction. **Oxygen** administration antagonizes tissue hypoxia and acidosis. In uncomplicated AMI the use of **cardiac glycosides** (digoxin) with caution is rational. **Phenoxybenzamine** may be employed in selected cases. **Vasodilator drugs** (sodium nitroprusside) may be useful in selected patients with severe pump failure.

Septic Shock

Shock may occur during the course of gram-negative, or less commonly gram-positive bacterial infection. In the earlier stages the peripheral vascular resistance is low designated as "warm shock". Bacterial shock requires immediate **intensive antibiotic therapy**, and adequate circulating volume should be maintained. **Sympathomimetic amines** should be used with **fluid replacement** and controlled by monitoring the central venous pressure. **Isoprenaline** administration improves tissue perfusion. **Dopamine** is preferred. **Corticosteroids** have been advocated to suppress the systemic reactions to endotoxins.

Anaphylactic Shock

Hypersensitivity reactions may be **immediate** due to circulating antibody, or **delayed** due to cell bound antibody. In anaphylactic reactions there is extreme vasodilatation and increased capillary permeability. Thus, a large volume of blood is trapped in venous pools, and the circulating volume is further reduced due to exudation and angioneurotic oedema. *Treatment consists of:* (*i*) prompt administration of **adrenaline** to act as a vasoconstrictor and for relaxing the smooth muscle. A dose of 0.5 ml of a 1:1000 solution is given intramuscularly or 0.1 ml of 1: 1000 solution diluted in 10 ml of saline is injected intravenously; (*ii*) **Antihistamines** like diphenhydramine are administered; (*iii*) **Corticosteroids** are administered for their anti-inflammatory and antiallergic actions; and (*iv*) treat hypoxia by oxygen inhalations and **positive pressure respiration**, if required. Simultaneously the fluid and electrolyte balance should be taken care of.

Neurogenic shock may occur as a result of spinal anaesthesia; or an autonomic imbalance, as the ANS is responsible for maintaining physiological arteriolar resistance, venous return and cardiac output. A shock syndrome may also occur due to endocrine failure specially due to cortisol deficiency. The treatment of **endocrine shock** is that of the primary disease.

To Summarize, the two basic aims in the therapy of shock are: (i) to eliminate the initiating cause (primary therapy); and (ii) to correct the haemodynamic derangement (secondary therapy), allowing time for specific therapy to be effective or physiologic improvement to take place.

To correct the haemodynamic derangement it is first necessary to assure adequate fluid replacement and venous return regardless of the cause. After this measure categorize the shocks as either (*i*) **low systemic vascular resistance shock**, where the BP is inadequate to perfuse vital organs; or (*ii*) **high systemic vascular resistance shock**, with sufficient central arterial pressure, but blood flow to viscera is drastically reduced due to vasoconstriction. The patient may pass from one category to the other, and therapy has to be accordingly altered.

For **low systemic vascular resistance shock** (vasodilated patient) drugs having a **positive inotropic effect** and vasoconstricting action are indicated, e.g., **noradrenaline** or **metaraminol**.

For **high systemic vascular resistance shock** (vasoconstricted patient) drugs having a **positive inotropic effect** and **vasodilating action are indicated**. In addition they should increase blood flow to the kidneys, brain and mesentery. **Isoprenaline** may be administered, but if BP falls excessively discontinue the drug. Combinations of **noradrenaline** and **phentolamine**, or **dopamine** with **isoprenaline** or **phenoxybenzamine** may be effective in the vasoconstricted patient.

Glucagon is reported to be effective in patients of shock following cardiac surgery or beta-blocker overdosage.

❑❑❑

5 DRUGS ACTING ON THE HAEMOPOIETIC SYSTEM

5.1 HAEMATINICS

Haematinics are agents used for the prevention and treatment of anaemias. In anaemia there is some deficiency in the **quality** or in the **quantity** of blood, the common factor being a diminished oxygen-carrying capacity of the blood, leading to diminished tissue oxygenation. The haemoglobin in the erythrocyte is mainly responsible for delivering oxygen to the tissues. **Anaemias** can be divided into: (a) **microcytic hypochromic** (iron-deficiency anaemia); (b) **megaloblastic or macrocytic hyperchromic** (megaloblastic anaemia); (c) **aplastic**; and (d) **haemolytic** anaemias.

SYNTHESIS OF HAEMOGLOBIN

Haemoglobin is formed in the red bone marrow. The total available tissue in the body for haemopoiesis is 1400 g, and this is capable of manufacturing several times its own weight of erythrocytes every 2-3 weeks. The life span of erythrocytes is about 120 days. Interestingly, about 10^{12} erythrocytes are produced daily, and during a human life span about 1 ton of erythrocytes are released into the blood stream.

Haemoglobin is a conjugated protein, consisting of an iron-containing pigment combined with a proetin (histone), known as **globin**. The iron-containing portion is a porphyrin consisting of 4 pyrrole rings. Haemoglobin is a **metalloporphyrin**, and the metallic atom is iron in the ferrous state (Fe^{++}). This porphyrin is designated as **haem**. Haem synthesis occurs in the immature erythrocyte itself. **Folic acid** and **vitamin** B_{12} are capable of increasing the rate of haem synthesis in the red cells, reflected by an increased iron uptake. Haem is also a constitutent of the cytochrome system involved in oxygen exchange.

The essential raw material to be provided to the red bone marrow for haemoglobin synthesis is: (*i*) **iron**; (*ii*) **pyrrole groups** for porphyrin synthesis; and (*iii*) **amino acids** for globin synthesis. In addition, an adequate diet, providing traces of copper, manganese, cobalt salts, pyridoxine, riboflavin and protein, collectively play an important role in normal erythropoiesis. Most anaemias are due to the deficiency of one or more of the following:

Iron
Folic acid (Pteroylglutamic acid)
Vitamin B_{12} (Cyanocobalamin)

IRON

The human body contains about 3.5 g of iron of which about 2/3 is contained in the blood, and the remainder is stored (as **ferritin** and **haemosiderin**) in the bone marrow, spleen and muscles. Most of the iron released on the destruction of 3 × 10^6 red cells/second is re-utilized for haemoglobin formation. The diet contains about 10-15 mg iron per day. A normal man absorbs upto 10 per cent of iron, whereas, an anaemic man absorbs about 30 percent of dietary iron. Iron is lost from the body mainly by desquamation of the gut and dermis. The iron requirement ranges between 0.5-

1.0 mg daily for adult males and postmenopausal women. During pregnancy and lactation there is an increase in the iron requirement to 2.5-3.0 mg daily.

Iron Absorption, Distribution and Excretion (Ferrokinetics)

Iron is widely distributed in foodstuffs, including **meat, leafy vegetables, pulses, wheat, oat meal, eggs and chocolate**. Milk and its products are a poor source.

Iron absorption mainly takes place in the duodenum and proximal jejunum involving an active transport mechanism, depending on the physiological needs of the body. On administration of large doses, iron is absorbed by diffusion across the mucosal barrier. Iron in foodstuffs is mostly in the ferric form, but gastric acid reduces it to the ferrous state which is more readily absorbed. *In view of this reasonably, achlorhydria, impairs iron absorption; whereas, a reducing agent like ascorbic acid (in high doses of 200 mg, 8-hourly) favours iron absorption.* The ferrous iron passes through the mucosal cell directly into the blood stream, where it is bound to *transferrin* and carried to the storage sites **(Fig. 5.1.1)**.

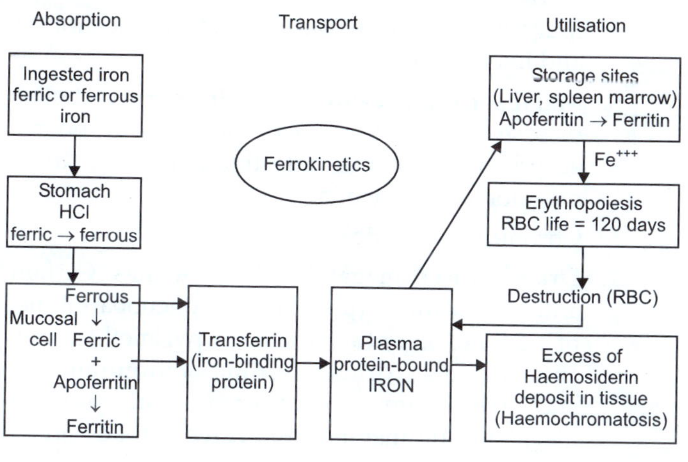

Fig. 5.1: The metabolism of iron (see text).

In the mucosal cell the excess of ferrous iron is re-oxidized to the ferric state (ferric hydroxide phosphate complex), which is insoluble and combines with the protein **apoferritin** to form a complex called **ferritin**. Ferritin is a storage form of iron. When apoferritin is saturated with iron the mucosal cell cannot further assimilate iron and a **mucosal barrier** is established. Quite a few of these mucosal cells are desquamated and lost into the lumen of the gut. Thus the body exerts a control over iron absorption through this mucosal barrier, also called the **ferritin curtain**.

Ferritin releases iron (Fe^{+++}) into the circulating blood which is bound to a glycoprotein beta$_1$ globulin known as **transferrin**. In this form it is carried to the storage depots (liver, spleen, bone marrow), and stored as ferritin, from where it is utilized for erythropoiesis. This is exchangeable iron. In contrast, iron which is utilized in the cytochrome system is not exchangeable.

Excessive quantities of iron are mainly excreted through desquamation of ferritin bearing cells in the gut and skin. It is also excreted in bile, urine, hair, nails and sweat in traces.

Interaction with food and drugs. A diet rich is phytate and milk tends to decrease iron absorption. **Antacids** impair absorption due to their alkalinizing effect on the gut contents. Oral **tetracycline** and iron bind together, and the absorption of both the drugs is impaired.

Therapeutic Uses

The chief indication of iron therapy is **iron-deficiency anaemia**, which is the result of severe or chronic haemorrhage, malabsorption syndromes, simple achlorhydria, malignancy, infection, nutritional deficiency, pregnancy, lactation, or parasitic infestations (specially ankylostomiasis).

Iron Therapy

It has been estimated that 25 mg of iron is required daily by the bone marrow in cases of iron-deficiency anaemia to raise the haemoglobin by 1 percent per day. With oral therapy it is assumed that about 30 percent of iron will be absorbed, and about 180 mg of elemental iron is administered daily.

Oral Iron Preparations. The old preparation ferrous sulphate is as effective as any of the later and more expensive preparations. The following preparations and dosages are employed:

Ferrous sulphate, hydrated*	0.3 g tid
Ferrous sulphate, exsiccated	0.2 g tid
Ferric ammonium citrate	1.0 g tid
Reduced iron	0.5 g tid
Ferrous gluconate*	0.6 g tid
Ferrous fumarate*	0.2 g tid
Ferrocholinate	0.5 g tid

(*most commonly used)

The slow release and chelated forms of iron are also available, and they cause less of gastrointestinal upsets, and are better tolerated by children

Parenteral Iron Preparations. Usually oral iron therapy is adequate to treat the anaemia. Parenteral therapy is only required when there is: (*i*) intolerance to oral therapy; (*ii*) improper iron absorption from the intestines; (*iii*) malabsorption syndromes; (*iv*) inadequate response; or (*v*) severe iron-deficiency anaemia. The total dose to be administered parenterally should be carefully calculated (based on the haemoglobin level) before therapy is started by the following formula:

Total dose (mg) = 4.4 × Body Wt. in kg × Haemoglobin deficit in g/100 ml blood.

Intramuscular Preparations

Iron Dextran Injection (Imferon). Contains elemental iron 50 mg/ml. The dose is 1-4 ml daily by deep intramuscular injection.

Iron Sorbitex Injection (Jectofer), ferrous gluconate, iron adenylate and iron polyisomaltose have no advantage over iron dextran complex.

Intravenous Preparation

Iron Dextran Injection. It is the same as the intramuscular preparation of iron dextran complex, except that it is without preservatives. The initial dose should be limited to 25 mg, and daily increments upto 100 mg per day may be given slowly intravenously.

Toxicity of Iron

Therapeutic doses given orally, may cause *nausea, abdominal discomfort*, and either *constipation or diarrhoea.* High oral doses can cause *serious gastrointestinal irritation,* and *necrosis of the mucous membrane, and shock leading to **acute iron poisoning***. The symptoms include pallor, cyanosis, lassitude, drowsiness, haematemesis, and cardiovascular collapse.

Treatment of acute iron poisoning is: (*i*) administration of raw eggs and milk to help in binding iron in the gut; (*ii*) **Desferrioxamine** (Desferal) 1-2 g IM every 12-hourly. It is an iron chelating agent, and forms a non-toxic complex which is excreted in the urine, and (*iii*) **Calcium disodium edathamil** (Calcium Disodium Versenate) may be used, if desferrioxamine is not available.

On prolonged parenteral iron overdosage, the body is unable to excrete the excess of iron and it accumulates in the body, leading to **haemochromatosis**, i.e., deposition of haemosiderin in the parenchyma of the liver, and other organs. To treat **chronic iron overload** desferrioxamine may be administered by injection daily to remove the excess iron (20 mg iron/day) from the body. **Venesection** of 500 ml may be tried in the absence of anaemia, as it would remove about 200 mg of iron from the body, and may be repeated weekly.

Desferrioxamine mesylate (*deferoxamine mesylate*). It is obtained from *Strepromyces pilosus*, and is a specific iron-chelating agent. It forms a non-toxic ferrioxamine complex with ferric iron, and is excreted in the urine. Children suffering from **thalassaemia** are dependent on regular blood transfusions, which leads to a gradual deposition of iron in the organs and tissues. The build-up of tissue-iron can be prevented by desferrioxamine **(Chap. 14)**.

Folic Acid

Folic acid (pteroylglutamic acid) is a member of the B complex group of vitamins. It is present in yeast, green vegetables and liver, and is capable of curing megaloblastic anaemias. The daily requirement is 50-100 mcg, and rises to about 200 mcg in pregnancy. Folic acid deficiency leads to **macrocytic hyperchromic anaemias**.

Mode of action. Folic acid itself is inactive. In the body it is converted to **folinic acid**, which is its active form. Folinic acid (citrovorum factor, leucovorin) is 5-formyl tetrahydrofolic acid. Ascorbic acid protects active tetrahydrofolic acid from oxidation. Folinic acid further participates in the production of purines and pyrimidines leading to the synthesis of deoxyribonucleic acid (DNA), and thus regulates cell division. The bone marrow changes from a **normoblastic** to a **megaloblastic** appearance in folic acid deficiency. Folic acid deficiency directly leads to megaloblastic anaemia, which is different from the megaloblastic anaemia (pernicious anaemia) of vitamin B_{12} deficiency. In simple terms folic acid utilizes vitamin B_{12} in its metabolic pathway, and can only correct the haematolgical disorder in pernicious anaemia, whereas, the neurological damage continues, or may even be aggravated.

Therapeutic Uses

Folic acid is used in the prevention and cure of *megaloblastic anaemias due to folate deficiency*, enumerated below:

1. Nutritional megaloblastic anaemia.
2. Megaloblastic anaemia of pregnancy.
3. Megaloblastic anaemia in infancy and childhood.
4. Megaloblastic anaemia associated with alcoholism and liver disease.
5. **Malabsorption syndromes.** In sprue, coeliac disease and steatorrhoea folic acid is poorly absorbed from the intestines, leading to a magaloblastic anaemia.
6. Chronic haemolytic states.
7. **Drug-induced magaloblastic anaemias.** Certain anticonvulsants (phenytoin, phenobarbitone, primidone); antimalarials (pyrimethamine); antibacterials (trimethoprim, nitrofurantoin); and the diuretic triamterene can produce megaloblastic anemias responsive to folic acid.
8. Magaloblastic anaemia of malignant disease.
9. **Aplastic or hypoplastic anaemias.** There is a likelihood of improvement in bone marrow function, specially when high doses are given, combined with vitamin B_{12} (cyanocobalamin 1000 mcg + folic acid 15 mg IM daily for a month).
10. Some cases of agranulocytosis.

Based on unsound reasons, folic acid is also included in "shotgun" antianaemic preparations, which are a mixture of liver and stomach extracts, folic acid, iron, copper, cobalt, vitamin B_{12} and other vitamins.

Dose. Synthetic folic acid 10-30 mg orally daily is usually given. The sodium salt is available for injection. The dose for prophylaxis is 50-100 mcg/day.

Toxicity. Folic acid is non-toxic in man. It should never be used as a sole drug in the treatment of pernicious (Addisonian) anaemia. Allergic reactions may occur rarely.

VITAMIN B_{12} (CYANOCOBALAMIN)

There is a big family of cobalamins (natural and semisynthetic) available today, which include cyanocobalamin (vitamin B_{12}) and hydroxycobalamin (vitamin B_{12a}). Vitamin B_{12} is mainly employed in the treatment of pernicious anaemia (Addisonian anaemia).

Sources. In man it is synthesized by the bacteria in the colon, but it cannot be absorbed, and leaves the body via the faeces. Thus man depends on the dietary intake of vitamin B_{12}. The cobalamins in food are bound to protein, and this bond must be split by proteolysis before absorption. Rich sources of cyanocobalamin are **organ meats, lamb and beef liver, kidney and heart**. Egg yolk, fish and some cheeses also have a moderate amount of vitamin B_{12}. The daily dietary requirement ranges from 0.6 to 1.2 mcg. The total vitamin B_{12} store in the human adults in about 5 mg, mostly in the liver.

Pernicious anaemia. This is a vitamin B_{12} deficiency disease, due to the lack of a specific substance secreted by the normal gastric mucosa. This substance is a glycoprotein called the "**intrinsic factor**" of Castle. This intrinsic factor is essential for the intestinal absorption of the dietary "**extrinsic factor**", which is vitamin B_{12} itself. A very small amount (less than 1 mcg daily) is the daily requirement of vitamin B_{12}. The symptoms of vitamin B_{12} deficiency are due to ineffective haemopoiesis (**maturation arrest at the megaloblastic stage**); inadequate epithelial cells of the gut (**histamine-fast achlorhydria and achylia gastrica**); inadequate myelin synthesis (**subacute combined degeneration of the dorsal columns of the spinal cord**); and general debility.

Mode of action. The relationship of vitamin B_{12} and folic acid to haemopoiesis is not fully undertood. They play an important role in the biochemical processes of **methylation** and **transmethylation**, leading to synthesis of nucleic acids. A deficiency of vitamin B_{12} interferes with normal folate metabolism, and induces a functional folate deficiency, although folate intake in diet may be adequate. Clinically folic acid or vitamin B_{12} alone can cure sprue and allied disorders, but both are required together to relieve pernicious anaemia. Vitamin B_{12} favours laying of myelin sheath in the CNS and protects against subacute combined degeneration of the cord. **Thus vitamin B_{12} relieves both neurological and haematological disturbances in pernicious anaemia.**

On administration of vitamin B_{12} in cases of pernicious anaemia there is a prompt increase in the number of circulating reticulocytes. *The bone marrow changes its appearance from megaloblastic to normoblastic, indicating that haemopoiesis is being normalized.*

Pharmacokinetics. The absorption of vitamin B_{12} from the gut is irregular and unreliable, as there is a deficiency of the stomach intrinsic factor, or further there may be an associated intestinal malabsorption syndrome. Intestinal absorption can be improved by adminsitering vitamin B_{12} with stomach intrinsic factor preparations.

Cyanocobalamin is bound to the plasma proteins, and is stored in the liver. When given in doses of 100 mcg or higher, more than half of it is excreted in the urine within 48 hours.

THERAPEUTIC USES

Vitamin B_{12} is used for the prevention and treatment of its deficiency states, commonly presenting as megaloblastic anaemias.

1. **Pernicious (Addisonian) anaemia.** The prognosis in uncomplicated cases, properly treated with vitamin B_{12} is fairly good. The treatment has to be continued throughout life.
2. **Malabsorption syndromes.** In coeliac disease, sprue and idiopathic steatorrhoea there is a vitamin B_{12} and folic acid deficiency, with megaloblastic anaemia in later stages.
3. **Neurological conditions.** Vitamin B_{12} has been employed empirically in high doses of 1 mg or more daily in cases of **trigeminal neuralgia, toxic/ diabetic/ alcoholic neuritis**, and **other nutritional neuropathies**. Hydroxycobalamin is worth a trial in **tabacco amblyopia**. Massive doses of vitamin B_{12} have been used in **neuroblastoma** in children.
4. **Psychiatric disorders.** Disorders met with during old age may favourably respond to vitamin B_{12} therapy.

Preparations and dosage.

Hydroxycobalamin. In cases of uncomplicated pernicious anaemia, and other cobalamin deficiency anaemias, it is given in a dose of 100 mcg IM every 3 days for 7 to 10 doses. The maintenance dose is 1000 mcg every 2 to 4 months, given lifelong.

TOXICITY

The cobalamins are usually well tolerated. Rarely allergic reactions may occur. Their use as `tonics' must be avoided.

ERYTHROPOIETIN

Erythropoietin is a **glycoprotein** produced by the peritubular cells in the proximal tubule of the kidney. In the bone marrow erythropoietin is produced by the macrophages, and functions as a growth factor inducing the differentiation of stem cells into erythrocytes. *It stimulates proliferation, maturation, and haemoglobin* *formation in the erythrocytes.* It also stimulates the early release of reticulocytes from the bone marrow into circulation. **Thus it is the primary hormone involved in the regulation of erythropoiesis in man**. Its levels are regulated by haemoglobin concentration, arterial oxygen saturation, or both.

Therapeutic uses. Erythropoietin is very effective in the treatment of **anaemia of chronic renal failure**. It is also effective in the treatment of anaemia associated with **acquired immunodeficiency syndrome** (AIDS), specially in patients on zidovudine (AZT) therapy; and anaemia associated with **cancer chemotherapy**.

Dosage. Recombinant human erythropoietin is available as **epoetin alfa** (Epogen, Eprex) in buffered saline containing human alubmin in single dose vials of 2000, 4000, or 10,000 units for IV or SC injection. The recommended initial dose is 50-100 units/kg three times a week in patients with chronic renal failure. The dosage can be increased by increments of 25 units/kg at monthly intervals.

To conclude, iron therapy is employed for iron-deficiency anaemias. **Folic acid** and/or **Cobalamins** are employed for treating megaloblastic anaemias. Folic acid should never be used as a sole agent in cases of pernicious anaemia. **Shotgun therapy** with antianaemic preparations must be avoided. **Erythropoietin** is used in the treatment of anaemia of chronic renal failure, AIDS, and anaemia following cancer chemotherapy.

5.2 ANTICOAGULANTS AND HAEMOSTATIC AGENTS

In man coagulation and fibrinolysis are in state of dynamic equilibrium. In both systems an inactive precursor is converted into the active substance, inhibitors being present to prevent excessive activity **(Fig. 5.2.1)**.

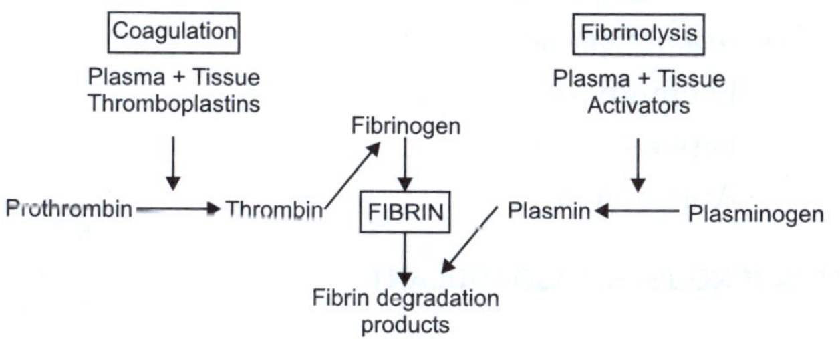

Fig. 5.2.1: The dynamic equilibrium of coagulation and fibrinolysis.

The end result of this dual process is that **thrombin** and **plasmin** are simultaneously active at the site of fibrin formation. The fibrin degradation products themselves have important actions in haemostasis with platelet function, and also have direct anticoagulant effect.

Anticoagulants act on various factors and stages involved in blood coagulation. They are employed in the prevention and treatment of **deep venous thrombosis, myocardial infarction, pulmonary embolism**, and **other thromboembolic disorders**.

Mechanism of Haemostasis

Whenever there is an injury to the blood vessel wall, a **primary mechanism** operates to form a **platelet plug**, followed by the **secondary mechanism** of haemostasis or **blood coagulation** which operates to form the **fibrin clot**.

In the primary mechanism, the platelets interact with the subendothelial structures, mainly collagen, and adhere to the injured site. Subsequently, the platelets undergo morphologic changes, and via a series of biochemical reactions, they release adenine nucleotides, mainly **adenosine diphosphate** (ADP). The released ADP interacts with specific receptors on the platelet membrane, leading to further release of ADP, and initiating **aggregation** of platelets (platelet-platelet reaction). This series of reactions ends in the final reaction, which involves the release of alpha granules and lysosomal enzymes, and finally an amorphous "**platelet mass**" or **platelet plug** is formed **(Fig. 5.2.2)**.

Mechanism of Blood Coagulation

Blood coagulation is the secondary mechanism of haemostasis. Currently this is based on the **Macfarlane's Cascade theory**. The various blood coagulation factors are listed below :

Factor I	Fibrinogen
Factor II	Prothrombin
Factor III	Tissue thromboplastin
Factor IV	Calcium
Factor V	Proaccelerin
Factor VI	(not an independent factor)
Factor VII	Proconvertin
Factor VIII	Antihaemophilic globulin (AHG-A)
Factor IX	Christmas factor (AHG-B)
Factor X	Stuart-Prower factor
Factor XI	Plasma thromboplastin antecedent (AHG-C)
Factor XII	Hageman factor
Factor XIII	Fibrin stabilizing factor

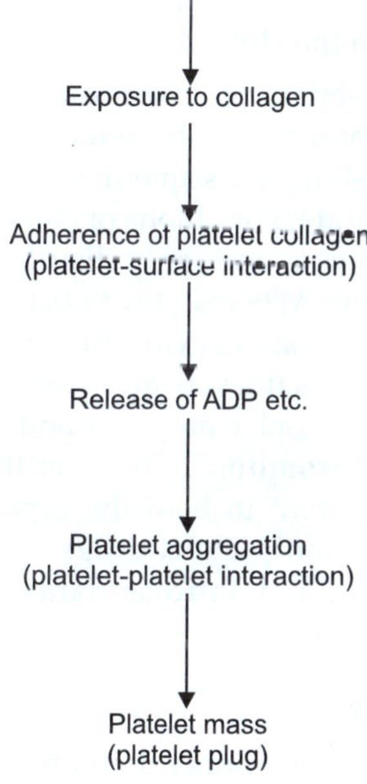

Fig. 5.2.2: The primary mechanism of haemostasis.

The cascade theory consists of : (*i*) the "**intrinsic system**", in which each stage accelerates the next one, and the activated factor is quickly destroyed by an inhibitor. This process is started *in vitro* by contact of factor XII (Hageman factor) with glass, and *in vivo* with collagen of damaged vessels, and (*ii*) the "**extrinsic system**", where coagulation is activated by tissue fluid, outside the blood vessels. The final steps of the two systems are the same, i.e., from the stage where factor X (Stuart-Prower factor) is activated to Xa, as shown in **Fig. 5.2.3.** However, the initiation of this step in the extrinsic system is not by factor VIIIa, but by factor VII (Proconvertin).

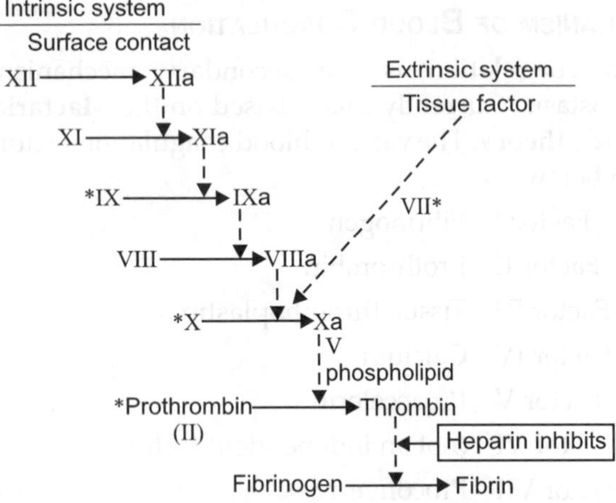

Fig. 5.2.3: Mechanism of blood coagulation. The cascade' system (simplified)' showing the sites of action of major anticoagulant drugs a = activated; * = reduction of synthesis by coumarins and indanediones (oral anticoagulants).

To simplify, the **intrinsic system** requires all factors in blood and damaged platelets to form **thromboplastin**, and simultaneously the **extrinsic system** utilizes tissue factor, factor V, and factor VII to generate **thromboplastin**. Further, thromboplastin and calcium convert prothrombin to thrombin, and thrombin converts fibrinogen to fibrin. Finally the fibrin mesh entraps the erythrocytes and leucocytes to form the **clot**.

The above series of haemostatic mechanisms—platelet plug formation, clot formation and stabilization, and fibrinolysis—follow a sequential order. The thrombi formed in veins, under conditions of **slow-flowing blood**, have cellular elements uniformly distributed all over the gel or fibrin network. Whereas, thrombi formed in arteries, under conditions of **fast-flowing blood**, the distribution of cellular elements is uneven, and there is a platelet-rich zone next to the vessel wall, surrounded by the fibrin gel, i.e., "**white thrombus**". Thus, as the predominant mechanism is different in both the types of thrombi, it is advisable to use **antiplatelet drugs** in the treatment of arterial thrombosis, and **anticoagulants** in the treatment of venous thrombosis.

ANTICOAGULANTS

The anticoagulants commonly used are: (*i*) **Direct acting, like heparin**, which is given parenterally, is quick-acting and effective *in vitro* and *in vivo;* and (*ii*) **Indirect acting,** like warfarin and phenindione, which are given orally, take 36 to 48 hours to act, and are effective only *in vivo.*

CLASSIFICATION OF ANTICOAGULANTS

1. **Intravenous Anticoagulants (Directly acting)**
   Heparin
2. **Oral Anticoagulants (Indirectly acting)**

(*i*) *Coumarin derivatives*
- Warfarin
- Bishydroxycoumarin
- Ethyl biscoumacetate
- Phenoprocoumon
- Acenocoumarin
- Cyclocoumarol

(ii) *Indanedione derivatives*
- Phenindione
- Diphenadione
- Anisindione

INTRAVENOUS ANTICOAGULANT

HEPARIN

Heparin is a mucopolysaccharide with a molecular weight of 20,000. Interestingly, it was discovered in 1916 by a medical student, who was studying the clotting activity of phosphatides, and found that a preparation from the liver prolonged the clotting time. It was thought to be predominantly localized in the liver, hence the name **heparin**. As known today, heparin largely occurs in the *mast cells* around the blood vessels, and many organs are rich in their heparin content. Commercially heparin is prepared from ox lung and standardized on animal blood.

Mode of action. Heparin inhibits clotting both *in vivo* and *in vitro*. In solution it carries a strong **electonegative charge** which is responsible for its interaction with basic proteins needed for clotting. Heparin itself is not an anticoagulant, as it is unable to inhibit the clotting of purified fibrinogen by thrombin. Heparin with a **co-factor** in plasma, probably an alpha-globulin, forms a complex which has a powerful **antithrombin activity.** This chiefly accounts for its anticoagulant activity, **prolonging the clotting time of blood**. In addition, heparin inhibits the conversion of prothrombin to thrombin, and has an **antithromboplastin effect**. Both of these effects are a possible sequence of its primary antithrombin action. To a lesser extent heparin **interferes with aggregation of platelets** induced by thrombin.

Heparin reduces lipaemia following a fatty meal by causing a redistribution of plasma lipoprotein fractions. It releases the enzyme lipoprotein lipase which hydrolyses triglycerides to free fatty acids, which enter the tissues. The **lipaemia-clearing effect** occurs at a much smaller dose campared to the anticoagulant dose of heparin.

Dose. Heparin is ineffective orally. To obtain an anticoagulant effect it has to be injected intravenously or subcutaneously. It is usually given in a dose of 10,000 to 12,500 I.U. (100 mg = 10,000 I.U). The maximum effect is immediate and rapidly wears off. The plasma $t_{1/2}$ is 50 minutes (low dose) and 120 minutes (high dose). The injections should be repeated every 4 to 6 hours. Heparin may be administered subcutaneously in a dose of 5,000 units, every 8 to 12 hourly for the prevention of deep vein thrombosis. *However, it may lead to painful haematomas.* If long-term anticoagulant therapy is intended, then one of the oral anticoagulants should be started at the same time as heparin, so that the oral anticoagulant takes over when heparin is stopped.

Control of therapy. The **clotting time** should be maintained above 15 minutes (normal 5 to 7 minutes), i.e., about twice the normal. It should be measured before start of heparin therapy, and later once daily before an injection is due.

Adverse effects. Haemorrhagic tendency may develop due to prolonged clotting time of blood. Some believe that heparin can lead to cerebral haemorrhage in susceptible patients. Long-term heparin treatment may cause osteoporosis. Transient alopecia and diarrhoea may occur. Hypersensitivity reactions have been recorded.

Heparin Antagonists

Heparin overdosage lasts for a short time, as it is metabolized in a few hours. However, heparin antagonists have an important role to play, as they are used during the **extracorporeal bypass procedure**, so that the blood returns to the body with normal coagulability.

Protamine sulphate, a protein obtained from fish sperm, is strongly basic and nullifies the anticoagulant action of heparin, which is acidic. It is given intravenously and neutralizes and equal weight of heparin. But if heparin is given more than 30 minutes earlier, the dose must be halved or further reduced. Protamine overdosage must be avoided as it has an anticoagulant effect of its own.

Oral Anticoagulants

The **coumarins** and **indanediones** are derivatives of 4 hydroxycoumarin and indane-1, 3-dione respectively. They are active orally, and only *in vivo*.

Mode of action. The coumarins and indanediones act by reducing the synthesis of prothrombin (factor II), factors VII, IX and X **(Fig. 5.2.3)**. The normal synthesis of these four factors requires vitamin K. Thus, oral anticoagulants inhibit the activity of vitamin K. In usual practice a loading (induction) dose of the drug is given, followed by the smaller maintenance dose, which is sufficient to obtain the desired control. The anticoagulant effect on an average takes 36-48 hours to build up. Thus usually heparin is employed in the initial stage of therapy to provide an adequate cover immediately to avoid progressive thrombosis.

Pharmacokinetics. A large number of compounds are available but they differ mainly in their speed of onset of action, and the duration of action **(Table 5.2-1)**. These agents are well absorbed on oral administration, and peak levels occur in 2-3 hours. In the blood they are largely bound to plasma protein, and are concentrated in the liver, which is their main site of action. The half-life of **phenindione** is 5-10 hours, and for **warfarin** may vary from 15 to 70 hours. The coumarins and indanediones cross the placenta and predispose to foetal and neonatal bleeding.

Table 5.2-1. *Oral anticoagulants, their dosage and therapeutic profile.*

DRUG	*DOSE**		*Anticoagulant effect*			*Therapeutic profile*
	Initial (mg/ day)	*Maintenance (mg/ day)*	*Onset (hrs)*	*Peak (hrs)*	*Duration (days)*	
Coumarins						
Warfarin sodium**	30-50	2.5-25	2-12	36-48	4-5	Intermediate
Bishydroxy coumarin	200-300	25-150	12-24	36-72	4-14	Long
Ethylbiscoum- acetate	1800-2400	150-900	8-12	18-36	2-3	Short
Phenprocoumon	18-30	0.75-6.0	12-24	48-72	7-14	Long
Acenocoumarin	16-28	2-12	12-24	36-48	1-2	Short
Cyclocumarol	50-150	10-50	2-12	36-60	6-8	Intermediate
Indanediones						
Phenindione	200-300	25-200	8-12	24-28	1-4	Short
Diphenadione	30-45	3-5	8-12	24-48	15-20	Long
Anisindione	200-300	75-100	8-12	24-36	1-3	Short

* Because of long $t_{1/2}$ and indirect mode of action, if dosage is to be changed, it should be every 5-7 days, when a steady-state is attained.

** Warfarin sodium can be used in a dose of 50 mg IV or IM.

Control of therapy. Quick's one-stage "prothrombin time" or *Quick time* is determined to regulate the dose. A satisfactory control is obtained with the patient's prothrombin time maintained 2 to 3 times normal (normal about 12 seconds).

Adverse effects. Bleeding may occur due to an overdose, specially in the renal and alimentary tracts. **Subdural** and **intracerebral haematomas** may occur. Patients with liver disease or vitamin K deficiency are specially prone to these complications. Other adverse reactions include, *skin rashes, blood dyscrasias, jaundice and vomiting*. Phenindione has caused serious side effects like agranulocytosis and liver damage.

Vitamin K as Antidote

Vitamin K_1 (water soluble) may be administered in a dose of 100-200 mg IV. Alternatively *vitamin K_1 oxide* and *phytonadione* may be administered orally. On IV administration the prothrombin time returns to normal in 3 to 5 hours, and on oral administration within 12 hours. Vitamin K preparations do not antagonize heparin effect. In a serious emergency fresh *whole blood transfusion* may be given to counter the action of oral anticoagulants.

Therapeutic Uses of Anticoagulants

1. **Venous thromboembolism.** The anticoagulants are useful both in the treatment and prophylaxis.
2. **Arterial thrombosis.** Anticoagulants may prevent the extension of the clot, and hasten recanalization. Heparin is the drug of choice in arterial embolism.
3. **Deep venous thrombosis and pulmonary embolism.** This can be prevented by anticoagulants. At least 6 weeks of anticoagulant therapy is advocated.
4. **Acute myocardial infarction.** Anticoagulant therapy may be of benefit, if started within 3 days of the episode, to prevent venous thrombosis due to immobility and sluggish venous circulation in serious patients due to shock and heart failure.
5. **Atrial fibrillation.** Patients who have suffered pulmonary or systemic embolism may benefit from long-term anticoagulant therapy.
6. **Acute coronary insufficiency and angina pectoris.** These patients may benefit, but routine use is not advocated.
7. **Cerebrovascular disease.** There is inconclusive evidence whether the anticoagulants are useful in transient ischaemic attacks (TIA), or not. If therapy is started it should be continued for at least 1 year.
8. **Retinal vein or artery thrombosis.** Anticoagulant therapy is useful.
9. **Vascular surgery.** Anticoagulants may be useful both during and after surgery. Heparin is the drug of choice, as its action can be speedily abolished, if required.

Contraindications

In disorders with a bleeding tendency, like **haemorrhoids, ulcerative colitis, hepatic disease** and **blood disease** the anticoagulants are contraindicated. **Hypertension** increases the risk of cerebral haemorrhage. Severe haematuria may occur if the kidneys are previously damaged.

Drug Interactions

As the oral anticoagulants are bound to plasma proteins, any other drug with a higher affinity for proteins would displace them, leading to an increased sensitivity and toxicity, even when the dose of the anticoagulant given is well within the therapeutic limits. Some drugs likely to interact are listed below:

Drugs enhancing anticoagulation: (*i*) **Displacement of the anticoagulant from plasma albumin**: Phenylbutazone, mefenamic acid, sulphonamides, clofibrate, ethacrynic acid, nalidixic acid; (*ii*) **Inhibition of microsomal enzymes:** Disulfiram, methylphenidate, chloramphenical, clofibrate; (*iii*) **Reduction in availability of vitamin K**: Tetracyclines, D-thyroxine, clofibrate, anabolic steroids; (*iv*) **Depression of the formation of factors II, VII, IX and X in the liver:** Quinine, quinidine, D-thyroxine, salicylates, acetaminophen; (*v*) **Reduction in vitamin K absorption:** Liquid paraffin; and (*vi*) **Increase in the clotting factor catabolism:** Anabolic steroids, D-thyroxine.

Drugs diminishing anticoagulation: (*i*) **Induction of hepatic microsomal enzymes:** Barbiturates, phenytoin, griseofulvin, mercaptopurine, rifampicin, meprobamate; (*ii*) **Stimulation of synthesis of clotting factors:** Vitamin K; and (*iii*) **Genetic variation.**

To conclude, the intravenous and oral anticoagulants are useful agents for the prevention, and management of thromboembolism. For a short-term and immediate anticoagulant effect, **heparin** is useful, whereas, for prolonged therapy one of the **coumarins** may be employed. The **indanediones** are more likely to cause allergic reactions.

Haemostatic Agents

Haemostatics are agents used to arrest bleeding, or to control oozing from minute blood vessels, by the formation of an **artificial clot**, or by providing a matrix which facilitates clotting. They are ineffective in combating bleeding from large arteries and veins. They have to be applied directly on the denuded or bleeding surface. Since they are ultimately absorbed from the site of application, they are known as **absorbable haemostatics**.

Absorbable Haemostatics

1. **Gelatin sponge**. It is used to control capillary bleeding. It is a surgical sponge which is left in place after the closure of the operative wound, moistened with thrombin or thromboplastin solution. It is completely absorbed in 4 to 6 weeks.
2. **Oxidized Cellulose**. It is surgical gauze or cotton specially treated to promote clotting by a reaction between haemoglobin and cellulosic acid. It is not well absorbed, and is suitable for surface haemostasis only.
3. **Human Fibrinogen.** it is used for restoring normal plasma fibrinogen levels in bleeding complications caused by **acute afibrinogenaemia**. Fibrinogen with thrombin solution can be used locally to induce clotting.
4. **Fibrin Foam.** It is used as a mechanical agent to promote blood clotting. It is applied directly to the bleeding area, and may be combined with thrombin. It is absorbed in the body.
5. **Russel's Viper venom**. It has a strong thromboplastin activity, and may be used in cases of **haemophilia**. It is applied locally.
6. **Thrombin.** It is obtained from bovine plasma, and should be only used topically. It can be used in the form of a solution or powder with **gelatin sponge**, or **fibrin foam**. It is non-antigenic when employed topically. Thrombin may be used in **haemophilia**, and together with fibrin in **neurosurgery**.
7. **Adrenaline.** It is useful in *epistaxis*. It stops bleeding by causing local vasoconstriction when the bleeding nostril is packed with gauze soaked in adrenaline solution.

Systemic Haemostatics

Systemic agents for checking bleeding are less well established. The antifibrinolysins (**aminocaproic** and **tranexamic acid**, (see **Chapter 5.3**), **ethamsylate** and **naftazone** have been claimed to reduce capillary bleeding when given systemically.

5.3 FIBRINOLYTIC AGENTS AND ANTIPLATELET DRUGS

The blood has an inborn capacity of dissolving intravascular clots by means of its *fibrinolytic system*. Fibrin deposited on the vascular endothelium in the process of injury-repair in small vessels is cleared by fibrinolysis. Agents which promote fibrinolysis are designated as **fibrinolytics ag2ents** or **thrombolytics agents**.

Fibrinolytic Drugs

The fibrinolytic system works through *fibrinolysin* (also called plasmin), which is a proteolytic enzyme with a marked affinity for fibrinogen or fibrin, and several other clotting factors. The working sequence of this system is detailed in **Fig. 5.3.1.**

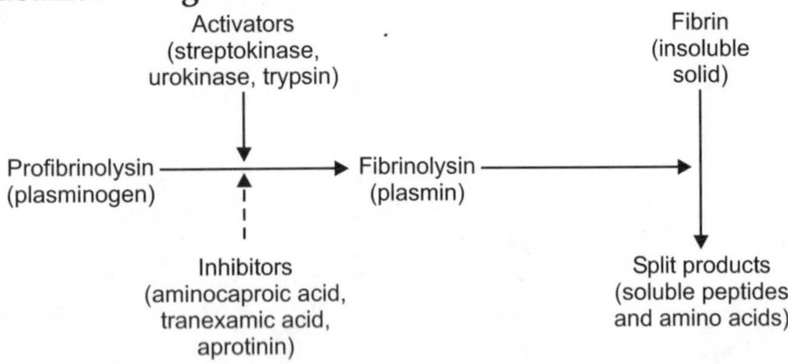

Fig. 5.3.1: Fibrinolytic system, its activators and inhibitors.

The drugs acting on the fibrinolytic system can be divided into: **plasminogen activators**, and **plasminogen inhibitors**. Plasminogen itself is a β-globulin (Mol Wt about 90,000), and plasmin is a trypsin-like endopeptidase.

PLASMINOGEN ACTIVATORS

Streptokinase

Streptokinase is derived from β-haemolytic streptococci, and it acts as a plasminogen activator, leading to fibrinolysis. It can be used in **deep vein thrombosis**, **pulmonary embolism**, or **central retinal vein thrombosis**. Partial or complete thrombolysis is expected in upto 3-day old thrombin. It has been used in **myocardial infarction** with success.

It is given slowly by intravenous infusion upto a loading dose of 500,000 units by an infusion pump over 30 minutes. The patient is protected by hydrocortisone 100 mg IV to avoid possible reactions. This is followed by an infusion of 100,000 units hourly. In deep vein thrombosis this may be continued for 5 days. To control therapy the thrombin time is maintained 2 to 4 times normal.

Urokinase

Urokinase is a plasminogen activator, related to streptokinase, physiologically occurring in human urine. It is extremely expensive. Urokinase can be used in patients allergic to streptokinase.

Human Fibrinolysin

Human fibrinolysin is the proUct of the action of streptokinase on human plasminogen. It has been tried in thromboembolic disease, other than those involving the cerebral or coronary vessels.

PLASMINOGEN INHIBITORS

(Antifibrinolytic Drugs)

Aminocaproic Acid

Aminocaproic acid inhibits **competitively** the activation of plasminogen to plasmin. It is a specific **antidote** for an overdose of a fibrinolytic agent. Local fibrinolysis can also be inhibited, and it is used sometimes to control **haemophilia**. It has also been used in the treatment of haemorrhage due to **severe trauma, major surgery, in obstetric complications, leukaemias, and hepatic cirrhosis**.

The usual dose is 5 g initially (orally or IV), followed by 1.25 g per hour till bleeding stops. The dosage should not exceed 30 g in 24 hours. Rapid IV administration may lead to *bradycardia, hypotension* and *arrhythmias*. Aminocaproic acid may promote d*isseminated intravascular clotting*, due to its antifibrinolytic activity.

Tranexamic Acid

Tranexamic acid acts like aminocaproic acid, and has similar indications. Like aminocaproic acid it may also enhance the tendency towards intravascular coagulation. It is administered IV (divided daily doses of 1.5-3.0 g), or orally (divided daily doses of 1.0 or 1.5 g), and is available as 500 mg tablets or injection (100, 250 mg).

Role of Platelets in Thrombosis

When there is vascular endothelial damage the platelets adhere to the subendothelial basement membrane and collagen. On exposure to collagen they release adenosine diphospate (ADP) from their granules, together with some unstable derivatives of arachidonic acid metabolim, i.e., prostaglandins G_2 and H_2 (PGG_2 and PGH_2), and thromboxane A_2. These released substances lead to platelet aggregation over the area of vessel injury **(Fig. 5.3.2)**.

The **antiplatelet drugs**, also known as **platelet aggregation inhibitors**, possess diverse structures and actions. They are grouped together because all of them inhibit some aspect of platelet function, which may be of potential value for the prevention and treatment of thrombosis, occurring in disorders like **myocardial infarction** and **cerebrovascular stroke**, and **transient cerebral ischaemic attacks**.

Basis of Antiplatelet Drug Therapy

Out of the many approaches to thrombosis prevention, *two* are most noteworthy:

(*i*) **Inhibition of cyclo-oxygenase in platelets:** If there are drugs which inhibit the formation of thromboxane A_2 by inhibiting cyclo-oxygenase (prostaglandin synthetase) which converts arachidonic acid to cyclic endoperoxides (PGG_2* and PGH_2), and further to thromboxane A_2 during the platelet release reaction, it is likely that thrombosis in arteries or veins may be inhibited. **Aspirin, sulphinpyrazone**, and **indomethacin** may be included under this head **(Fig. 5.3.2)**.

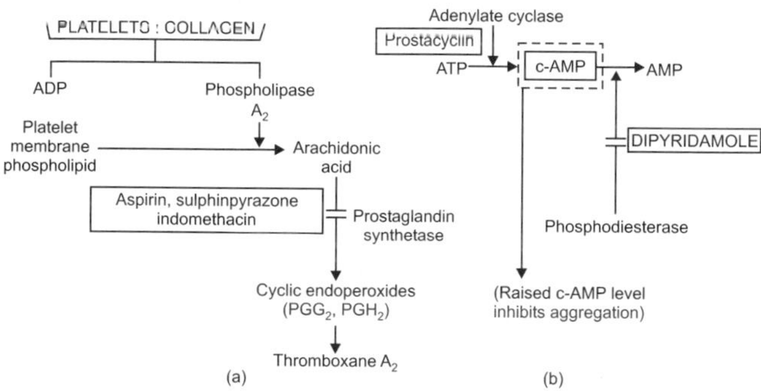

Fig. 5.3.2: Mode of action of antiplatelet drugs: (a) Aspirin inactivates cyclo-oxygenase irreversibly, while sulphinpyrazone, and indomethacin inactivate it reversibly; (b) Dipyridamole elevates c-AMP by inhibiting phosphodiesterase, while prostacyclin raises c-AMP by stimulating adenylate cyclase.

(*ii*) **Elevation of cyclic adenosine 3′5′-monophosphate levels in platelets:** Increased platelet c-AMP levels may impair platelet aggregation by chelating ionized calcium, and inhibiting phospholipase A_2. **Dipyridamole** inhibits platelet phosphodiesterase, therapy raising c-AMP levels. **Prostacyclin increases** c-AMP levels by stimulating adenylate cyclase (**Fig. 5.3.2**).

Individual Drugs

Out of the many drugs which affect platelet function, only **aspirin, dipyridamole**, and **sulphinpyrazone**, have been extensively evaluated clinically, and would be dealt in further detail.

Aspirin

Aspirin inhibits the release of ADP, cationic proteins, PGE_2, PGF_2 alpha, and phospholipase from the granules of the platelets. In addition, aspirin irreversibly inactivates the enzyme cyclo-oxygenase, and thus interferes with the production of cyclic endoperoxides, and diminishes the formation of thromboxane A_2, thereby inhibiting platelet aggregation.

Clinically, aspirin has proved effective in doses of 300 to 1500 mg daily. Higher doses should not be given as they nullify the beneficial effect by blocking prostacyclin formation in the vessel wall. Prostacyclin **(Fig. 5.3.2)** is an agent which elevates platelet-c-AMP and on its own antagonizes platelet aggregation.

Dipyridamole

Dipyridamole elevates endogenous c-AMP levels by inhibiting phosphodiesterase, and inhibits platelet aggregation **(Fig. 5.3.2b)**. **Thus, it has a synergistic action when used in combination with aspirin**. The suggested dosage schedule for combination therapy is, **dipyridamole** 100 mg daily, plus **aspirin** 1 g daily in divided doses orally. The precaution is that very high doses of aspirin antagonize dipyridamole effect. Alternatively, dipyridamole 100 mg qid may be administered alone.

Sulphinpyrazone

Sulphinpyrazone essentially is a uricosuric agent, related to phenylbutazone. It inhibits platelet aggregation by reversibly inactivating cyclo-oxygenase, and thereby leading to the inhibition of prostaglandin and thromboxane A_2 synthesis in the platelets. This drug has been tried in a North American trial, in cases who suffered myocardial infarction, and was administered from the 25th postinfarction day onwards. It was concluded from this study that the annual death rate was significantly reduced. The usual dose employed is 600-800 mg daily.

Therapeutic Uses

The antiplatelet drugs have been variously employed, singly or in combination, for the undermentioned conditions:

(*i*) Prevention of myocardial infarction, and re-infarction after the initial episode.

(*ii*) Myocardial ischaemia and angina pectoris.

(*iii*) Transient cerebral ischaemia and stroke.

(*iv*) Postoperative venous thrombosis.

(*v*) Haemodialysis, arteriovenous shunts, prosthetic heart valves, and arterial surgery.

(vi) Microvascular disorders.

(vii) Organ transplant rejection reactions.

Adverse Effects. Bleeding complications might develop, but are mild and manageable. Other side effects are related to the individual drugs. Interactions of antiplatelet drugs with hypolipidaemic drugs and anticoagulants must be kept in mind.

To conclude, the clinical status and therapeutic regimens of antiplatelet drugs are under evaluation and standardization. There are several other drugs, including *indomethacin, verapamil, prostaglandin* E_1 and *cyproheptadine* which have the capacity of inhibiting platelet aggregation. *Clofibrate* and *hydroxychloroquine* also alter platelet function. The drugs available for the management of thromboembolic disorders may be usefully employed according to the flow chart **(Fig. 5.3.3)**.

Antiplatelet drugs should be employed mainly before the formation of the **white thrombus** to inhibit platelet aggregation. The **anticoagulants** prevent the deposition of fibrin in the thrombus and retard thrombus growth. **The fibrinolytic drugs** attempt to remove deposited fibrin from the **red thrombus,** leading to thrombolysis.

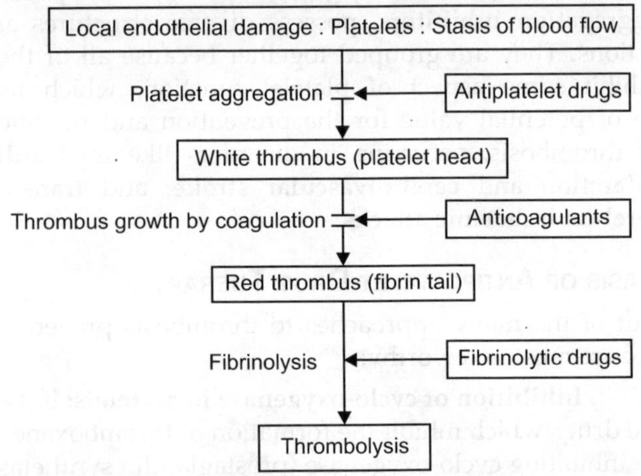

Fig. 5.3.3: Points of therapeutic application of antiplatelet, anticoagulant, and fibrinolytic drugs in various phases of thrombus formation.

5.4 HYPOLIPIDAEMIC AGENTS

Cholesterol is a lipid. It is synthesized from acetate in many tissues of the body. The basic scheme for its synthesis is Acetate → Mevalonate → Squalene → Lanosterol → Cholesterol. It is highly fat soluble with a limited water solubility, and it localizes itself in the lipid regions of cell membranes. The cholesterol molecule is of major importance in maintaining the structural integrity of the plasma membrane of cells. If cholesterol metabolism is defective, the cell membrane ceases to function properly, and ruptures more easily. The **steroid hormones** constitute a large group of hormones synthesized by the adrenal cortex and the gonads, and all of them are derived from a common sterol precursor, i.e. cholesterol. It is converted to **pregnenolone**, which provides the steroid nucleus.

Lipids exist in the blood mainly as **cholesterol** and **triglycerides**. In addition, there are smaller amounts of phospholipids, fatty acids and fatty acid esters. Free fatty acids (FFA) are bound to plasma albumin, while other lipids form complexes with proteins (albumin, globulins). These lipoproteins differ in **density, composition** and **size**, and are separable by **electrophoresis**. Based on their electrophoretic-density patterns they mainly are: (*i*) **chylomicrons**; (*ii*) **very low-density lipoproteins, Pre-β-lipoproteins** (VLDL); (*iii*) **low-density lipoproteins, β-lipoproteins** (LDL); and (*iv*) **high-density lipoproteins,** α-lipoproteins (HDL). The particle size of these four principal lipoproteins decreases from chylomicrons (800-2000 Å) to HDL (70-100 Å).

Classification of Hyperlipidaemias

The World Health Organization (WHO) has proposed an International classification based mainly on that suggested by Fredrickson, which recognizes five different lipoprotein patterns, designated types I through V **(Table 5.4-1)**. The WHO types II and IV cover most of the clinical disorders; types III and V are uncommon; and type I is rare.

Table 5.4-1. *Classification and treatment of primary hyperlipidaemias*

Type	*Classification*	*Lipoprotein increased*	*Main plasma lipids increased*	*Treatment*		*Relationship to Coronary Heart disease (CHD)*
				Drugs	*Diet*	
I	Familial (exogenous) hypertriglyceridaemia (lipoprotein lipase deficiency)	Chylomicrons	Triglyceride	None effective	Low fat, no alcohol, no restrictions on proteins, carbohydrates or cholesterol	None
IIa	Familial hypercholesterolaemia (LDL receptor defect)	LDL	Cholesterol	Cholestyramine Colestipol, Probucol, Lovastatin Dextrothyroxine	Low cholesterol, low saturated fats, increased intake of polyunsaturated fats	Positive
IIb	Familial multiple-type hyperlipoproteinaemia	LDL+VLDL	Cholesterol and triglyceride	Same as IIa and nicotinic acid	Same as IIa	Positive
III	Familial dysbetalipoproteinaemia	β-VLDL (LDL)	Cholesterol and triglyceride	Clofibrate Dextrothyroxine Nicotinic acid	Weight reduction, low cholesterol, low saturated fats, high protein	Positive
IV	Familial (endogenous) hypertriglyceridaemia	VLDL	Triglyceride	Clofibrate Gemfibrozil Nicotinic acid	Weight reduction, low carbohydrate, low cholesterol, low alcohol, maintain protein intake	Questionable

Table 5.4-1. Contd...

Type	*Classification*	*Lipoprotein increased*	*Main plasma lipids increased*	*Treatment*		*Relationship to Coronary Heart disease (CHD)*
				Drugs	*Diet*	
V	Mixed hypertriglyceridaemia	VLDL and chylomicrons	Triglyceride	Clofibrate Gemfibrozil Nicotinic acid	Low fat, high protein, low carbohydrate, no alcohol	Questionable

Lately a receptor-mediated control of cholesterol metabolism has been generated. Certain mammalian cells (fibroblasts) have a **low-density lipoprotein (LDL) receptor** that binds cholesterol-carrying lipoprotein of plasma, and regulates the transfer of cholesterol into the cell. In **familial hypercholesterolaemia** the LDL receptor is defective.

Atherosclerosis is essentially a metabolic disorder characterized by faulty transport, distribution and deposition of lipids. It is influenced by multiple factors. Above all the concept that atherosclerosis is necessarily associated with hypercholesterolaemia, and subsequent formation of **atheromatous plaques** in the intimal walls of the arteries is mostly accepted. This disease mainly affects the large and medium sized arteries, namely, the **cerebral, coronary, vertebral** and **renal** arteries. It also involves the aorta and the arteries of the legs. The important clinical complications are **coronary heart disease, cerebrovascular disease** and **peripheral vascular disease**, which are a major cause of death.

The normal plasma cholesterol and triglyceride levels vary from country to country. Many authorities agree that any person whose plasma cholesterol level is higher than 200 mg/dl, and whose plasma triglyceride level exceeds 150 mg/dl has sufficient hyperlipaemia to require attention. About one-fourth of all adults have elevated levels of one or more plasma lipids or lipoproteins, due to improper diet, excessive alcohol intake, hypothyroidism, diabetes mellitus or an inherited trait.

Hypolipidaemic Drugs

The role of **hyperlipoproteinaemia** as a risk factor in **coronary heart disease** and **cerebrovascular disease** is fairly well established. The available drugs are:

1. **Predominantly effective in hypertriglyceridaemias**:

   Clofibrate

   Gemfibrozil

   Fenofibrate

   Nicotinic acid

2. **Predominantly effective in hypercholesterolaemia:**

   Cholestyramine

   Colestipol.

   Dextrothyroxine

   Probucol

   Lovastatin, Simvastatin, Atorvastatin etc.

   Safflower oil

Clofibrate

Clofibrate is used in patients with hypertriglyceridaemia or hypercholesterolaemia to reduce the respective blood levels. It has shown favourable results in the long-term treatment of hyperlipidaemias. Clofibrate can cause serious toxicity. Hence, it should be reserved for patients who fail to respond to diet control, weight reduction, and less toxic drugs.

Mode of action. Clofibrate probably inhibits hepatic cholesterol synthesis, and decreases the rate of lipoprotein release from the liver. It inhibits cholesterol synthesis at a point between the acetate pool and mevalonic acid, i.e. it acts at a pre-squalene stage. Clofibrate accelerates the conversion of VLDL to LDL. It lowers VLDL and plasma triglycerides, but has little effect on LDL and cholesterol.

Side effects. Nausea, gastrointestinal upset, drowsiness, headache, and dizziness may occur. Weight gain, pruritus, skin rashes, alopecia, leucopenia, and agranulocytosis have been reported. A rise in transaminases may occur. Hypoglycaemia can occur in some patients, and precaution should be observed in diabetics. Clofibrate increases the sensitivity to coumarin anticoagulants.

Therapeutic uses. Clofibrate is useful in hyperlipidaemia types III, IV and V, but is less effective in type II.

Contraindications. Clofibrate should not be administered in patients with renal or liver disease, and to pregnant and lactating mothers.

Dose. Upto 2 g daily in 4 divided doses, depending on the patient's response.

Gemfibrozil

Gemfibrozil is a structural analogue of clofibrate and shares many of its pharmacologic and toxicologic properties. It lowers elevated serum triglycerides, mainly the VLDL fraction, and to a lesser extent the LDL fraction. It may also increase the HDL fraction, and the ratio of HDL cholesterol to total cholesterol. This action is considered to be beneficial in atherosclerosis.

Gemfibrozil is used in the treatment of **types IV and V hyperlipoproteinaemia** in patients with high serum triglyceride, and a definite risk of pancreatitis. The **adverse effects** include GI distress, skin rash, musculoskeletal pain, blurred vision, anaemia and leucopenia. It may enhance the effect of oral anticoagulants. It is administered as 300 mg capsules and the *recommended dosage* is 1200 mg a day in 2 divided doses, 30 minutes before meals.

Fenofibrate

Clofibrate, gemfibrozil and fenofibrate are collectively known as **fibric acids**. Fenofibrate is a relatively newer agent. It has the same indications as gemfibrozil. The *usual dosage* is 100 mg orally after each meal.

Nicotinic Acid

Nicotinic acid when administered in large doses of 1.5 to 8 g daily, lowers plasma triglyceride and cholesterol levels. Probably it acts by inhibiting the release of free fatty acids from adipose tissue, and inhibits cholesterol synthesis in the liver. It has been found effective in hyperlipidaemia types II, III, IV and V. The **side effects** include, flushing of the face, dizziness, pruritus, gastrointestinal upset and liver dysfunction, which occur at a fairly high frequency. Thus, the usefulness of nicotinic acid as a hypolipidaemic agent is limited.

Cholestyramine

Colestipol

Cholestyramine is the chloride salt of a quaternary ammonium **anion-exchange resin**, which in the intestinal lumen binds bile acids, exchanged for chloride. This insoluble resin-complex is not absorbed, and thus it promotes the faecal excretion of bile acids which would have been otherwise largely reabsorbed from the intestines. Such a mechanism may lower serum cholesterol.

Cholestyramine may be used in doses of 4 g thrice daily in hyperlipidaemia type II. However, it is mainly used for the relief of pruritus due to biliary tract obstruction. Being an anion-exchange resin, it may interfere with the gastrointestinal absorption of many drugs and fat soluble vitamins. Common **side effects** include constipation, diarrhoea, heart-burn or nausea. There may be steatorrhoea, impaired calcium absorption and osteoporosis.Lately, the anion-exchange resin **colestipol** has been introduced, which is similar in action to cholestyramine. It is given orally in a dose of 12-25 g/day in 3 or 4 divided doses.

Dextrothyroxine

The dextro-isomer of thyroxine increases the rate of oxidation or hydroxylation of cholesterol to bile acids in the liver, and promotes the biliary excretion of cholesterol. This lowers the blood cholesterol level. Dextrothyroxine may be effective in hyperlipidaemia types II and III, but the **side effects** due to general metabolic stimulation including angina pectoris and arrhythmias, seriously limit its use.

Probucol

Probucol decreases elevated serum cholesterol levels by reducing low-density lipoproteins (LDL) concentrations, but does not reduce serum triglyceride levels appreciably. Like cholestyramine this drug appears to be most effective in type IIa hyperlipoproteinaemia. **Adverse reactions** include gastrointestinal disturbances, headache, paraesthesias, and eosinophilia. The *usual dose* is 500 mg with the morning and evening meal.

Lovastatin

Lovastatin is isolated from a strain of *Aspergillus terreus*. Compared to many other hypolipidaemic drugs it is well tolerated in majority of patients.

Lovastatin is an inactive lactone. In the body it is hydrolyzed to a beta-hydroxy acid form, which is a **potent inhibitor of HMG-CoA reductase**, an enzyme that catalyzes the conversion of HMG-CoA to mevalonate, a **rate-limiting step** in the biosynthesis of cholesterol. Both normal and elevated LDL cholesterol levels are lowered. Lovastatin reduces the concentration of circulating LDL particles, increases HDL cholesterol levels, and reduces VLDL cholesterol and plasma triglycerides. It is mainly used in the treatment of **familial hypercholesterolaemia (types IIa and IIb)** The recommended starting dose is 20 mg (20 mg tablets) once a day with the evening meal. The dosage range is 20-80 mg/day in single or divided doses. **Side effects** include headache, GI distress, myalgia, increased serum transaminases, blurred vision, and peripheral neuropathy.

Other HMG-CoA reductase inhibitors, namely **simvastatin, atorvastatin, fluvastatin**, and **pravastatin** have actions and uses similar to **lovastatin**.

Safflower Oil

This fixed oil is extracted from the seeds of safflower, *Carthamus tinctotius*. It contains 74.5 percent of linoleic acid (unsaturated fatty acid), and only 6.6 percent of mixed saturated fatty acids. Safflower oil reduces serum cholesterol when used instead of saturated fats (animal fats). The exact mechanism of action is illunderstood. Safflower oil is available as a 65 percent emulsion of the oil, and may be used as a cooking medium. The suggested dose is 75 ml of the emulsion, which provides 450 calories, and the expected weight gain has to be checked by adjusting the diet accordingly.

Other agents like **β-sitosterol, oestrogens, neomycin,** and **aminosalicylic acid** also possess hypolipidaemic action, but are not used therapeutically.

To conclude, a reasonably effective control of hyperlipidaemia is possible with the judicious employment of drug therapy and dietary restriction. The presently available drugs act by: (*i*) interference in the absorption of bile acids from the gut, e.g., **cholestyramine**; (*ii*) reduction in the release of lipoproteins from the liver, e.g., **clofibrate**; (*iii*) inhibition of the synthesis of cholesterol, e.g., **clofibrate** and **nicotinic acid**; (*iv*) blockade of the release of triglycerides as free fatty acids from adipose tissue, e.g., **nicotinic acid**; and (*v*) increased catabolism and biliary excretion of cholesterol, e.g. **dextrothyroxine**.

5.5 BLOOD AND PLASMA VOLUME EXPANDERS

Anaemias caused by hypoplasia or aplasia of the bone marrow can only be managed by blood transfusions. Similarly, in the management of haemorrhagic shock whole blood transfusion has no better substitute.

A search for suitable plasma substitutes has been rewarding. The plasma substitute must have the qualities of plasma itself, i.e., (*i*) its osmotic pressure should match with that of blood, so that it remains in circulation for a reasonably long time; (*ii*) it should be metabolized and excreted without toxic effects; (*iii*) it should be non-antigenic; and (*iv*) it should be compatible with the elements of blood.

Plasma volume expanders are agents which may overcome the imbalance in conditions of shock, and tide over the critical period until the ideal material is available, or the patient recuperates to restore his own blood volume. The agents available are: (*i*) *Blood and its elements*; and (*ii*) *Macromolecular colloidal solutions*.

BLOOD AND ITS ELEMENTS

Citrated Whole Human Blood

Human blood is collected from healthy donors under aseptic conditions. It is **mandatory** to ensure that the donors are free from AIDS (Acquired immuno-deficiency syndrome) infection, or viral hepatitis B infection, as blood transfusion is a mode of transmission of these ghastly viral diseases. Due care is taken to reduce haemolysis during storage. The usual anticoagulant used for preservation is acid citrate dextrose (ACD) solution. Whole human blood is stored soon after collection and mixing with anticoagulant, in sterile containers at a temperature of 4° and 6°C. Material with signs of haemolysis should not be used.

Whole human blood is used to replace blood volume and elevate oxygen-carrying capacity following blood loss due to surgery or severe haemorrhage. The haemoglobin concentration of blood is raised by about 1 g/100 ml by transfusion of 540 ml of whole blood. **Due precautions should be taken to properly match the blood to avoid dangerous blood transfusion reactions**. Transfusion of massive quantities may overload the circulation and lead to pulmonary oedema.

Packed Red Cells

Packed red cells are used in severe forms of anaemia which do not usually require a simultaneous restoration of blood volume. It also reduces the danger of circulatory overload and pulmonary oedema. **Packed red cells** are separated from citrated whole blood and cannot be safely stored for longer than 24 hours at a temperature of 10°C.

Dried Human Plasma

This is prepared by drying a sterile pool of supernatant fluid from quantities of whole blood. It is stored below 25°C in an atmosphere of nitrogen in sterile containers, protected from light. **Dried human plasma** is completely soluble in water for injection, and should be used immediately after reconstitution. There is a danger of transmitting viral hepatitis type B, which must be kept in mind.

Human Serum Albumin

Human serum albumin is a sterile solution of the serum albumin fraction of blood from healthy donors. It is used in the management of *shock, hypoproteinaemia and oedema of nephrosis*. **Human albumin** (5 and 20%) is available as a sterile, pyrogen-free solution for IV use. *Dried human albumin fraction* is also available.

MACROMOLECULAR COLLOIDAL SOLUTIONS

Gelatin Solution

This is a special solution (5 or 6%) obtained from collagen of bones and skin. It has been used as a plasma expander in the management of **shock, haemorrhage** and **burns**. The osmotic action lasts for about 25 hours after one injection. The disadvantages are that its fate in the body is illunderstood, and it is known to interfere with blood typing, and gelatin preparations solidify at room temperature.

Polygeline

Polygeline is a polymer from degraded gelatin, and is available as a sterile pyrogen-free solution for IV use. It can replace upto 70-80 percent of circulating plasma. It can be used in all forms of **oligaemic shock, burns and endotoxic shock**. It has also been employed for **preoperative haemodilution**, and **perfusion of isolated organs**. The dose depends on the amount of intravascular fluid lost, and is approximately equal to the calculated volume deficit. Hypersensitivity reactions can occur.

Dextran 70 and Dextran 110

The dextran used clinically is a complex polysaccaride obtained by the action of *Leuconostoc mesentroides* on sucrose. The average molecular weights are 70,000 for dextran 70, and 110,000 for dextran 110. The usual dose is about 50 ml of a 6 percent solution infused intravenously at a rate of 20-40 ml/minute. Dextran solutions may cause allergic reactions. **Dextrans 70 and 110 are mainly used to restore and maintain the blood volume**. Their advantages over whole blood are their wide availability, lack of incompatibility problems, and their use has no danger of transmitting viral hepatitis or AIDS.

Dextran 40

This preparation is popularly designated as low molecular weight dextran (Mol. Wt. 40,000). It is available as a 10 percent solution in dextrose or sodium chloride injection. It is known that dextrans disrupt aggregation of red cells, and have a "**desludging action**" in the blood vessels. For this reason dextran 40 has been primarily used for the **prevention** and **therapy of venous thrombosis.** There are claims that dextran 40 also improves capillary microcirculation by its *desludging* action.

Hetastarch

Hetastarch is a synthetic polymer prepared from amylopectin. Its actions are similar to dextran, and can be used for blood volume expansion. Hetastarch is available as 6 percent solution in sodium chloride 0.9 percent injection. The usual dose is 500-1000 ml, upto a maximum of 1500 ml daily.

To conclude, agents are available to make up for the lost blood volume, and for maintaining optimal fluidity and osmotic pressure of blood. Judiciously employed they can be life-saving in many critical cases of shock due to haemorrhage and burns.

❑❑❑

6

DRUGS ACTING ON THE GENITO-URINARY SYSTEM

6.1 FLUID AND ELECTROLYTE BALANCE

Next to oxygen, water is most important to life. The volume and composition of the body fluids varies within a narrow range from day to day, there being a state of balance between the intake and elimination from the body. This balance between the **intput** and **output** is a general concept applicable to **water, sodium, potassium, calcium** and **nitrogenous material**, and also **anions like chloride** and **bicarbonate**, which in turn are responsible for the acid-base balance. Such a balance between **water, electrolytes** and **acid-base content** of the body is extremely important for **homeostasis (Fig. 6.1.1)**.

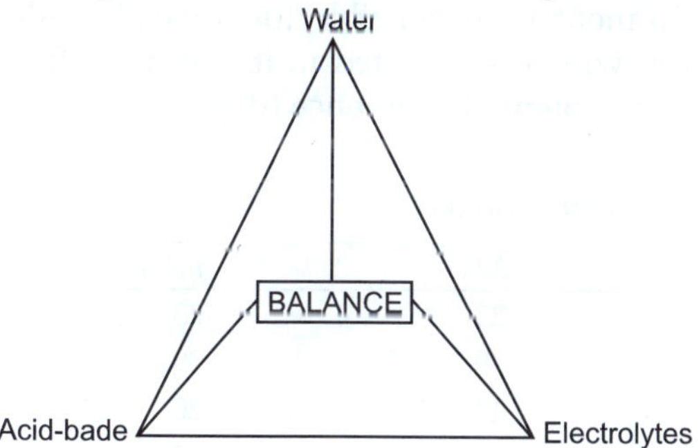

Fig. 6.1.1: The triangle of homeostasis.

Disturbances in fluid and electrolyte metabolism involve *four* major properties of the body fluids, namely, **volume, osmolality, hydrogen ion concentration** (pH), and *specific* **ion concentrations**. The kidney is the major regulator of the salts and water content of the body.

WATER BALANCE

The prime importance of water is evident by the fact that 45-65 percent of body weight in man is water, i.e., about 42 litres is the total body water (TBW). Various tissues have different water contents, the **brain** has 82 percent, the **bone** has 20 percent, and **adipose tissue** has 10 percent by weight. The total volume of water is divided into *two* major compartments – **the extracellular fluid** (ECF) compartment, and **the intracellular fluid** (ICF) compartment. The body water distribution is detailed in **Table 6.1-1.**

Table 6.1-1. *The distribution of body water in an adult male*

	Adult (weight 70 kg)		
	Litres		*Percentage of body weight*
Total extracellular fluid (ECF)	14		20
Intravascular fluid (Plasma)		3	
Extravascular fluid		11	
Total intracellular fluid (ICF)	28		40
Total body water (TBW)	42		60

The concept of the extracellular fluid and intracellular fluid compartments is not adequate. A better description is that the ECF is likened to the **continuous phase** of an emulsion, and the ICF to the **dispersed phase.** The ECF is an all-pervading fluid surrounding the cells. Its composition is kept constant within narrow limits, as regards its osmolality, chemical and ionic composition, and pH. The ECF thus plays the major role in the **homeostasis** as conceived by Claude Bernard. In such a system, extremes of diet, overhydration or underhydration have minimal effects on the composition of the ECF, and the cells are protected from changes in the external environment.

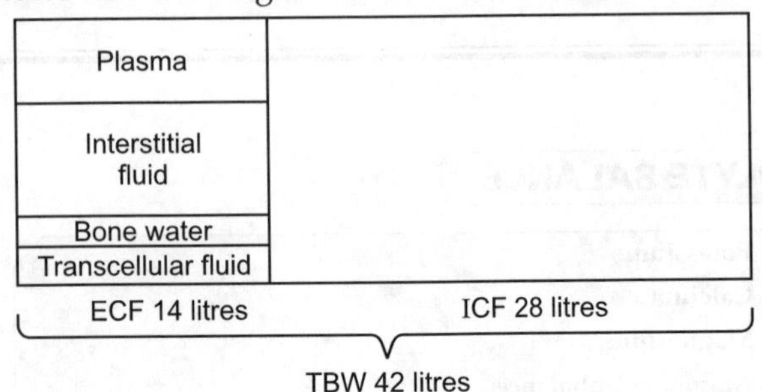

Fig. 6.1.2: Relative sizes of the intracellular and extracellular fluid compartments, with sub-divisions of the ECF.

The ECF is divided into *four* compartments: (*i*) **intravascular fluid compartment** (plasma); (*ii*) **extravascular fluid compartment** (interstitial fluid, lymph; (*iii*) **inaccessible bone water** (water trapped in the deep layers of the bone, not readily exchangeable); and (*iv*) **transcellular fluid** (secretions of glandular tissue, gastrointestinal fluid, renal tract, respiratory tract, aqueous humour, and the cerebrospinal fluid). The relative sizes of the various compartments are illustrated in **Fig. 6.1.2.** Almost all cell membranes are freely permeable to water, except the **sweat glands** and the **distal nephron**. Hence, as a consequence of free diffusion of water, the extracellular and intracellular fluids have equal osmolality.

A disturbance in the hydrostatic:oncotic pressure equilibrium would lead to oedema, and its drug management is dealt in Chapter 6.2.

ELECTROLYTE BALANCE

Electrolytes are inorganic salts present in solution as charged ions (cation$^+$, positive; anion$^-$, negative). The cations and their movement across the cell membrane play an important role in the function of cells and the action of drugs. They also maintain the osmotic pressure, which in turn maintains the volume of the solvent water. The balance of electrolytes across the cell membranes determines the size of the two body fluid compartments. An **isotonic solution** is one which exerts a physiological osmotic pressure, and causes no passage of water across the cell membrane. .

All the electrolytes in the body are present as ions. Prior to the introduction of SI units (see Appendix I) these were recorded in equivalent weights, i.e., the molecular weight of the ion in mg, and the sum of its constitutent atomic weights divided by the valency. **A convenient notation was the milliequivalent (mEq). Now the unit of quantity of SI notation is one mole, i.e., the molecular weight in grams. A molar solution (M) contains a mole/litre.** For a monovalent substance (Na^+, K^+, Cl^-) **normality**, i.e., the concentration in mEq/l equals the molarity, whereas for divalent substances (Ca^{++}, SO_4^{++}) normality will be half molarity **Table 6.1-2.**

Molarity is applicable to any soluble substance the molecular weight of which is known. Thus it is possible to compare **equimolar** amounts of two drugs, and to make a statement about their **potency**. If the drug has a carrier portion (e.g., noradrenaline acid tartrate) the activity is described in terms of the active part only, i.e., noradrenaline base in this case.

The cell membrane separates two fluids of different compositions but equal osmolarity. The ECF has most of the cationic sodium and the accompanying anions are Cl^- and HCO_3^-. Whereas, in the ICF the cations are K^+ and Mg^{++} accompanied by a large variety of anions like **phosphate, sulphate, citrate,** Cl^-, HCO_3^-. The **sodium pump,** which is an active chemical pump in the cell membrane, continuously extrudes Na^+ from the cell, and K^+ is transported inwards. The movement of ions in some cases is linked, e.g., efflux of Na^+ is linked with that of Ca^{++}, and influx of Na^+ occurs with efflux of K^+. Such an arrangement is responsible for a steady-state in the resting cell which is reflected in its resting intracellular-extracellular potential difference (degree of polarization).

Table 6.1-2. *Molar and mEq weights of common cations and anions*

		Valency	*M*	*mEq*
Cation	Sodium (Na^+)	1	23	23
	Potassium (K^+)	1	39	39
	Calcium (Ca^{++})	2	40	20
Anion	Chloride (Cl^-)	1	35.5	35.5
	Bicarbonate (HCO_3^-)	1	61	61
	Sulphate (SO_4^{--})	2	96	48

Table 6.1-3: *Comparison of the composition of the extracellular fluid (plasma) and intracellular fluid (muscle-cell fluid).*

Extracellular fluid (mEq/l)				*Intracellular fluid (mEq/l)*			
Cations		*Anions*		*Cations*		*Anions*	
Sodium	135-145	Chloride	98-106	Sodium	10	Bicarbonate	10
Potassium	3.5-5.0	Bicarbonate	24-28	Potassium	150	Phosphate	150
Calcium	4.5-5.3	Phosphate	2-5	Magnesium	40	Protein	40
Magnesium	1.5-2.0	Organic anions	3-6				
		Protein	15-20				

The resting state may be abruptly disturbed by a stimulus or a drug, which is then responsible for the transmembrane movement of ions and electrical potential changes.

Solutions: Definitions and Terms

Solution. A physically homogeneous liquid mixture of two or more substances.

Isotonic solutions. Solutions exerting equal osmotic pressures whatever their composition (Synonym: isosmotic solutions.)

Buffer solution. Aqueous solution able to resist changes of pH upon addition of an acid or base.

Normal (N) solution. One gram equivalent weight (GEW) of the solute per litre of solution.

Mole (abbr. Mol.) Gram molecular weight; a weight of a substance in grams equal numerically to its molecular weight.

Molar solution. One mole of solute per litre of solution (1 mol/1).

Molal solution. One mole of solute per kg of solvent (1 mol/kg).

Molarity. The concentration of a solution expressed in moles per litre of solution.

Molality. The concentration of a solution expressed in moles per kilogram of pure solvent.

Osmole solution. Molarity x number of particles per molecule.

Osmolar solution. One osmole per litre of solution.

Example: Normal, and Physiologic (isotonic) saline.

One Normal solution of NaCl

Gram equivalent weight of NaCl = 58.5 g

∴ 1N solution of NaCl = 58.5 g/l, or

= 5.85 g/100 ml, or 5.85% solution.

Physiologic saline = 0.9% NaCl (isotonic to body fluid) 0.9 g/100 ml.

The 0.9 percent saline solution is isotonic to body fluid, and is usually termed "**normal saline**", but it is not of the same strength as a normal solution of NaCl.

Composition of Body Fluids

There are marked differences in the composition of the *extracellular* and *intracellular* fluid. More information is available about the extracellular fluid, and electrolyte concentrations in plasma are an index for the entire compartment. Whereas, intracellular fluids of various tissues differ from each other, and information is limited. The muscle tissue constitutes the largest segment of intracellular fluid and the composition of the muscle-cell fluid is known **(Table 6.1-3)**.

Sodium is the major cation in the extracellular fluid, with **chloride** and **bicarbonate** as the major anions in ECF. In contrast, the major cations in the intracellular fluid are **potassium** and **magnesium**, with very little sodium, and the main anions are **phosphate** and **protein** with **very little bicarbonate**.

Abnormal States of Hydration

Physiological or normal hydration of the body is maintained by a balance between the water **intake** and the **output** in a healthy individual (**Table 6.1-4**).

Table 6.1-4. *Average daily water intake and output in a healthy adult*

Intake	*ml*	*Output*	*ml*
Water drunk	1500	Urine output	1600
Water in food	750	Faecal water	50
Water from metabolism of food	250	Water lost in expired air:	850
		Insensible and sensible perspiration	
	———		———
Total	2500		2500

A dynamic interrelationship exists between the extracellular cation sodium and fluid volume. Hence they are considered together. An abnormal state of hydration may be characterized by:

(i) **Isotonic loss of sodium and water** (volume depletion) may be caused by *vomiting, diarrhoea,* or *haemorrhage*. For this sodium chloride injection 0.9 percent, or balanced isotonic electrolyte solutions may be used to restore the extracellular fluid volume.

(ii) **Loss of water in excess of sodium** (hypernatraemia) may result from reduced intake or **unusual water losses**. There is a decrease in the volume of both ECF and ICF with an increased concentration of solutes in both the fluid compartments. There is a marked increase in the concentration of sodium in ECF and hyperosmolality results. There may be a reduced water intake due to the patient being comatosed. **Fever** or **hot environment** increase water loss from the lungs and skin. The kidneys may fail to conserve water due to ADH deficiency (**diabetes insipidus**). Increased water loss may be due to osmotic diuresis in **diabetes mellitus**. All such situations would lead to dehydration. To treat dehydration water must be provided initially without electrolyte, and 5 *percent dextrose injection* is recommended. If more fluid is needed after plasma has reached normal tonicity, *0.9 percent sodium chloride injection* may be infused. Electrolyte levels should be monitored closely.

(iii) **Loss of sodium in excess of water** (hyponatraemia) occurs when the kidneys are unable to conserve sodium adequately in conditions like **adrenocortical insufficiency, vigorous diuretic therapy, water retention as a result of abnormal ADH secretion, or excessive sweating when fluid is replaced by water without adequate salt**. To manage low serum sodium concentrations, when the renal function is normal, 0.9 percent sodium chloride injection is given. In severe hyponatraemia 3 percent to 5 percent sodium chloride injection may be given cautiously. Hyponatraemia due to adrenocortical insufficiency should be treated with hormone replacement therapy **(see Chap. 7.5)**.

(iv) **Volume excess** (oedema) is manifested as an excess of fluid in the interstitial space with salt retention. This is observed in patients with **congestive heart failure, nephrotic syndrome,** or **cirrhosis with ascites.** The **diuretics** are employed in the management of these conditions together with dietary salt restriction **(see Chap. 6.2)**.

ACID-BASE BALANCE

In the ECF the pH is normally maintained with remarkable constancy, at about 7.4 in arterial blood, and about 7.35 in venous blood and interstitial fluid. The pH of the ICF has not been measured directly, but from indirect evidence ranges from 4.5 to 8.0 in different cells, with an average of about 7.0 units. A small variation in the pH units can have lethal effects: pH of the ECF below 7.0 or above 7.8 are incompatible with life. In general, pH values of arterial blood below 7.4 are classified as **acidosis**, and a pH value above 7.4 is classified as **alkalosis (Fig. 6.1.3)**.

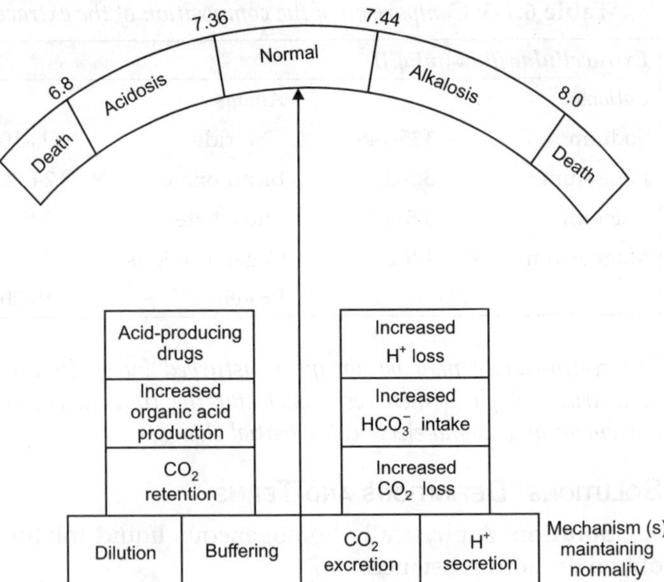

Fig. 6.1.3: The factors affecting body fluid pH, and the mechanisms which operate to control the pH.

Three main mechanisms operate to control the pH in the body fluids:

1. Action of chemical buffer systems.
2. Respiration which removes carbon dioxide.
3. Renal excretion of acid and base.

The **buffer systems** of the body are so efficient that they can neutralize 1 litre of 1 N hydrochloric acid infused into the blood stream, without letting the blood pH to fall below the critical value of 7.0. The buffer systems consist of a weak acid and its sodium or potassium salt. The **three** most important buffer systems of the body are:

(*i*) $$\frac{\text{Carbonic acid } (H_2CO_3)}{\text{Sodium bicarbonate } (NaHCO_3)}$$

(*ii*) $$\frac{\text{Sodium dihydrogen phosphate } (NaH_2PO_4)}{\text{Disodium hydrogen phosphate } (Na_2HPO_4)}$$

(*iii*) Protein buffer systems.

A buffer system can be effective in keeping the pH of the medium unchanged only as long as both the components of the buffer system are available.

To summarise, an excess of CO_2 produces acidosis which stimulates the respiratory centre to eliminate the CO_2 in the expired air, correcting the acidosis. Wheareas, in alkalosis the CO_2 level of ECF is reduced, the respiratory centre is depressed causing temporary apnoea which restores the body fluid pH to normal. The kidneys regulate the pH of body fluids by: (*i*) excreting NaH_2PO_4 in acidosis, or Na_2HPO_4 in alkalosis; (*ii*) reabsorbing bicarbonate ($NaHCO_3$) in acidosis; and (*iii*) producing ammonia from glutamine breakdown, and excreting it as ammonium (NH_4^+) salts in acidosis.

Alkalosis and acidosis are disturbances of the acid-base balance. The induced disturbance may be compensated or uncompensated **(Table 6.1-5)**.

Table 6.1-5. *The acid-base disturbances*

Acid-base disturbance	*Bicarbonate content (plasma)*	*pH*
Compensated alkalosis	Increased	Unchanged
Uncompensated alkalosis	Increased	Rises
Compensated acidosis	Decreased	Unchanged
Uncompensated acidosis	Depleted	Falls

Acid-Base Disturbances

In simple terms, **acidosis** denotes a decrease in pH (rise in H^+), and alkalosis denotes an **increase** in pH (fall in H^+) of the extracellular fluid. These changes are the result of **respiratory** or **metabolic** abnormalities.

Respiratory Acidosis

Respiratory acidosis is due to ventilatory abnormalities which impair the gaseous exchange, e.g., poor ventilation during anaesthesia, pneumonia, pulmonary oedema, suppression of the respiratory centre, emphysema, myasthenia gravis, poliomyelitis, asthma and respiratory muscle weakness. It is characterized by retention of CO_2 and an elevation of PCO_2 in the alveoli and arterial blood (hypercapnia). The compensatory reabsorption of HCO_3^- by the kidneys operates to buffer and reduce the H^+ concentration, but this protection develops very slowly, and immediate treatment is required.

Treatment. Measures should be taken to improve ventilation by mechanical means, bronchodilators and correction of heart failure. The PCO_2, PO_2 and pH of arterial blood should be monitored.

Respiratory Alkalosis

Respiratory alkalosis results from hyperventilation during anaesthesia, or due to incorrect use of mechanical respirators, or psychogenic hyperventilation. It is characterized by a lowered PCO_2 and an elevated pH of the extracellular fluid to more than 7.45.

Treatment. Psychogenic hyperventilation may be controlled by antianxiety drugs or psychotherapy. Tetany may be relieved by rebreathing exhaled air which increases the PCO_2 and lowers blood pH. The use of mechanical respirators should be based on the PCO_2 and pH values of arterial blood.

Metabolic Acidosis

Metabolic acidosis is accompanied by dehydration, and is caused by excess production of lactic acid; or starvation and uncontrolled diabetes mellitus (ketoacidosis); inability of the kidney to acidify the urine (renal tubular acidosis); chronic renal failure; intestinal loss of base in diarrhoea; or certain drugs and toxins like paraldehyde, salicylates, methanol or ethylene glycol. As a result there is a cation loss (Na^+, K^+, Ca^{++}) and organic anion retention occurs in starvation and diabetes mellitus. Respiratory compensation occurs for metabolic acidosis by hyperventilation and reduction of PCO_2, and in turn reduction in H_2CO_3 in extracellular fluid.

Treatment. Attempts are made to correct the metabolic defect (insulin for control of diabetes), water is replenished and deficit of Na^+, K^+, HCO_3^- and other electrolytes is made up. If plasma HCO_3^- levels fall below 16 mEq/l or blood pH below 7.25, then preferably sodium bicarbonate solution is given.

Metabolic Alkalosis

Metabolic alkalosis with dehydration is caused by excessive loss of hydrochloric acid due to vomiting, or from excessive sodium bicarbonate ingestion. Potassium deficit occurs due to increased urinary excretion of H^+ ions, which results in retention of HCO_3^-. Respiratory compensation by hypoventilation elevates PCO_2 and increases the H_2CO_3 fraction of the bicarbonate buffer system.

Treatment. Administration of **potassium chloride** and/or **sodium chloride** is essential in all types of metabolic alkalosis as bicarbonate levels cannot be effectively reduced unless chloride is made available for reabsorption with sodium in the renal tubules.

Potassium

Potassium is the major intracellular cation. It is also found in low but critical concentration in the extracellular fluid. Its concentration varies from 3.4 to 5.6 mEq/litre in health, and it is emphasized that plasma levels do not correctly reflect the total intracellular K^+ content. Potassium plays an important role in muscle contraction, enzyme action, nerve conduction, and cell membrane function. The myocardial excitability, conduction, and rhythm are markedly affected by the concentration of K^+ in ECF. Excretion of potassium ingested in daily diet is mainly through the kidney.

Hypokalaemia

Diuretic therapy is the most common cause of hypokalaemia. It is also found in patients suffering from **hyperaldosteronism, nephrotic syndrome, renal tubular acidosis, Cushing's syndrome, hypoproteinaemia** of any cause, K^+ wasting renal disorders and **uraemia**. Hypokalaemia manifests as a depression of the ST segment and a lowering of the T-wave in the electrocardiogram (ECG), and a prominent U wave which may be biphasic

(Fig. 6.1.4). Atrioventricular block and cardiac arrest occurs in severe cases.

Treatment. Oral or parenteral replacement therapy is indicated. Potassium chloride solution is preferred to other salts of potassium, because, if there is associated alkalosis, the Cl^- ion is needed for hypochloraemic alkalosis. Potassium chloride in a total dose of 1 to 3 mEq/kg/24 hours may be given parenterally in glucose or saline solution at a rate which does not cause hyperkalaemia.

HYPERKALAEMIA

Hyperkalaemia is usually the result of ***inefficient potassium excretion by the kidneys due to impaired renal function, or due to large amounts of K^+ ingested in diet, or as a result of overenthusiastic use of potassium sparing diuretics, or fast intravenous infusions of potassium containing solutions.*** The extracellular concentration of K^+ increases, and the ECG manifests an absence of P-wave, an impaired conduction by peaked and tall T-waves, atrial arrest, widening of the QRS, biphasic QRS-T complexes, ventricular fibrillation and cardiac arrest **(Fig. 6.1.4).**

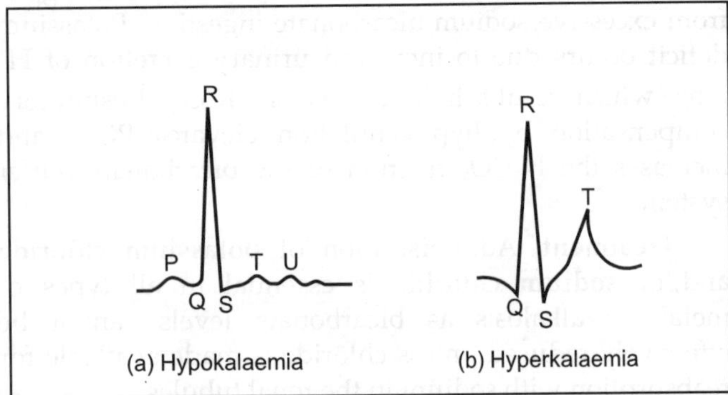

Fig. 6.1.4: The electrocardiogram in potassium imbalance.

Treatment. Treatment consists of immediately withholding K^+ and administering cation exchange resins by mouth (40-80 g/day) in divided doses. **Insulin** may be employed to deposit K^+ with glycogen intracellularly in the liver and muscle. Calcium may be administered intravenously as an antagonist ion. **Sodium bicarbonate** administration may be done in severe cases to increase the blood pH and cause a shift of K^+ into the cells. **Haemodialysis** or **peritoneal dialysis** may be employed in cases of chronic renal insufficiency.

CALCIUM

Calcium levels in the blood range between 10 to 10.5 mg/dl. In the blood it exists in two forms, half of it bound to protein as **non-diffusible** calcium, and the other half as **diffusible** calcium in chemically complexed and ionized form. The serum calcium level is largely controlled by opposing effects of two polypeptide hormones—**parathormone** and **calcitonin**–both exerting their major effect on bone which is the calcium depot.

MAGNESIUM

Magnesium is an important activator ion participating in many enzyme actions, including those requiring ATP or other nucleotides as co-enzymes. About 50 percent of total body Mg^{++} exists in an insoluble state in the bone. Only 5 percent is present as extracellular cation, and the remaining 45 percent is contained in cells as an intracellular cation. The normal plasma level is 1.5-2.5 mEq/litre, out of which one-third is bound to protein and two-thirds is in a free state. Excretion of Mg^{++} is via the kidney, although there is no evidence of an active tubular secretion.

HYPOMAGNESAEMIA

Magnesium deficiency is encountered in *chronic alcoholism with delirium tremens, starvation, diarrhoea, malabsorption, vigorous diuresis, hypoparathyroidism and renal tubular damage.* It is manifested as CNS hyperirritability.

Treatment. Parenteral fluids may be administered containing magnesium as chloride or sulphate in a dose of 10-40 mEq/day in the severe phase, maintained by 10 mEq/day later. Magnesium sulphate 4-8 g may be given IM daily in four divided doses.

HYPERMAGNESAEMIA

Magnesium excess results from **renal insufficiency**, and the inability of the kidney to excrete magnesium. The ECG shows prolonged P-R interval, broad QRS complexes and elevated T-waves.

Treatment. Calcium salts counteract the respiratory effects. **Haemodialysis** or **peritoneal dialysis** is indicated in severe hypermagnesaemia with coexisting renal insufficiency.

AMMONIA IMBALANCE

In cases of advanced and complicated cirrhosis the blood ammonia level is elevated, leading to a *portal systemic encephalopathy*, which is a metabolic disorder of the central nervous system. The blood ammonia levels may be reduced by the use of **laxatives**. Formation of ammonia is decreased by restricting dietary protein and preventing gastrointestinal bleeding. **Neomycin** and/or **lactulose** (a synthetic disaccharide) may be employed to decrease ammonia production and/or enhance its excretion. Neomycin possibly acts by destroying some of the intestinal bacteria that produce ammonia.

PERITONEAL DIALYSIS SOLUTIONS

These special solutions are used to remove urea, creatinine, uric acid, serum electrolytes, and excess of body fluids and toxins from the body. They are indicated in *acute* and *chronic renal failure, intractable oedema, hyperkalaemia, hypercalcaemia, and poisoning with dialysable agents.* Peritoneal dialysis is a specialized technique, and both overhydration and hypovolaemia should be avoided. Protein loss may occur during prolonged dialysis, and plasma proteins should be measured to avoid hypoproteinaemia. Fluid and electrolytes must be monitored simultaneously and requirements maintained accordingly. Some commonly used intravenous solutions are detailed in **Table 6.1-6**.

Table 6.1-6. *Some commonly used intravenous solutions*

Solution	*Electrolytes (mEq/litre)*						
	Na^+	K^+	Ca^{++}	Mg^{++}	Cl^-	HCO_4^-	HCO_3^-/precursor
Sodium chloride* 0.9%	154				154		
Sodium lactate (M/6) 1.72%	167						Lactate 167
Sodium bicarbonate 5%	595						595
Sodium chloride 0.9% + Dextrose 5%	154				154		
Potassium chloride 0.7% + Dextrose 5%		10			10		
Ringer's solution	147	4	5		156		
Lactated Ringer's solution (Hartmann's solution)	130	4	3		109		Lactate 28
Acetated Ringer's solution	130	4	3		109		Acetate 28

* also known as `normal saline'

6.2 DIURETICS

Diuretics are commonly defined as drugs that increase the amount of urine produced by the kidneys. **A precise definition is that diuretics are agents which augment the renal excretion of sodium and either chloride or bicarbonate primarily, and water excretion secondarily.** The term "saluretic" is sometimes used to describe a drug that increases the renal excretion of sodium and chloride ions.

Clinically diuretics are the mainstay of treatment of **hypertension** and oedematous states like **congestive heart failure, cirrhosis with ascites, nephrotic oedema,** and **oedema of pregnancy**. The pathophysiologic processes involved in the development of oedema include: an increased venous pressure; an increased capillary permeability; obstruction of the lymphatic channels; hypoproteinaemia with a resultant fall in the colloid osmotic pressure of blood; and aldosterone excess. These factors usually operate in combination. Physiologically fluid exchange is controlled by the balance between the blood colloid osmotic (oncotic) pressure, and the hydrostatic pressure along the capillary system **(Fig. 6.2.1). But due to an abnormal pressure relationship more of fluid leaves the capillary system at the arterial end, and less of it returns at the venous end resulting in oedema.**

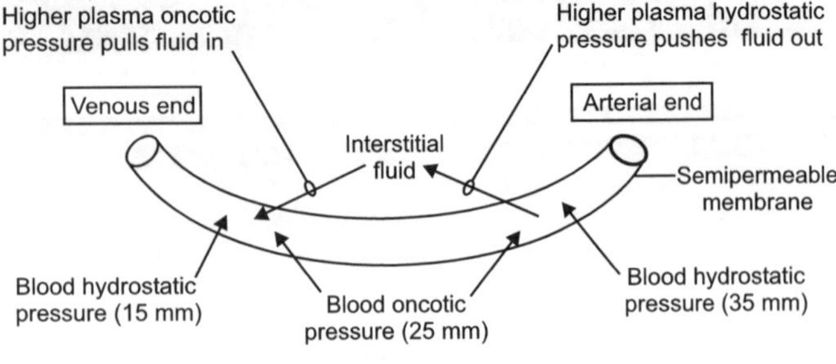

Fig. 6.2.1: The normal capillary system of fluid exchange.

RENEAL REGULATION OF WATER AND ELECTROLYTE BALANCE

The kidney is primarily a regulatory organ. The major functions of the kidney are:

1. Excretion of nitrogenous waste products of protein metabolism,
2. Maintenance of acid-base equilibrium, and
3. Maintenance of sodium, potassium, chloride, and bicarbonate ions in a proper balance within the two fluid compartments.

The functional unit of the kidney is the **nephron**, and the above three functions are carried out by the complex process of urine formation, which consists of the production of an **ultrafiltrate of plasma** in the glomeruli, reabsorption and secretion of electrolytes and other solutes in the tubules, and a passive diffusion of water and solutes according to the concentration gradients caused by the active transfer of sodium and chloride ions across the tubules.

Under normal conditions, the glomerular filtration rate is about 120 ml per minute, which works out to more than 150 litres per 24 hours. Out of this protein-free filtrate 99 percent is reabsorbed, and the urine volume each day is about 1.5 litres. This one hundred fold reduction in volume of the glomerular filtrate is by an **active reabsorption of sodium and chloride**, accompanied by the passive reabsorption of water along the course of the tubule. There are **four** major sites of sodium reabsorption, and water and electrolyte transport along the nephron: (A) proximal convoluted tubule or **isosmotic site;** (B) the thick ascending limb of the loop of Henle, which constitutes the **counter-current multiplier system**, and with the collecting duct is known as the **concentration site;** (C) the cortical distal **dilution site**; and (D) the distal convoluted tubule where **sodium** and **bicarbonate** ions are *reabsorbed*, while **potassium** and **hydrogen** ions are *secreted* to regulate the potassium and acid-base balance of the body **(Fig. 6.2.2)**, and **(Fig. 6.2.3)**.

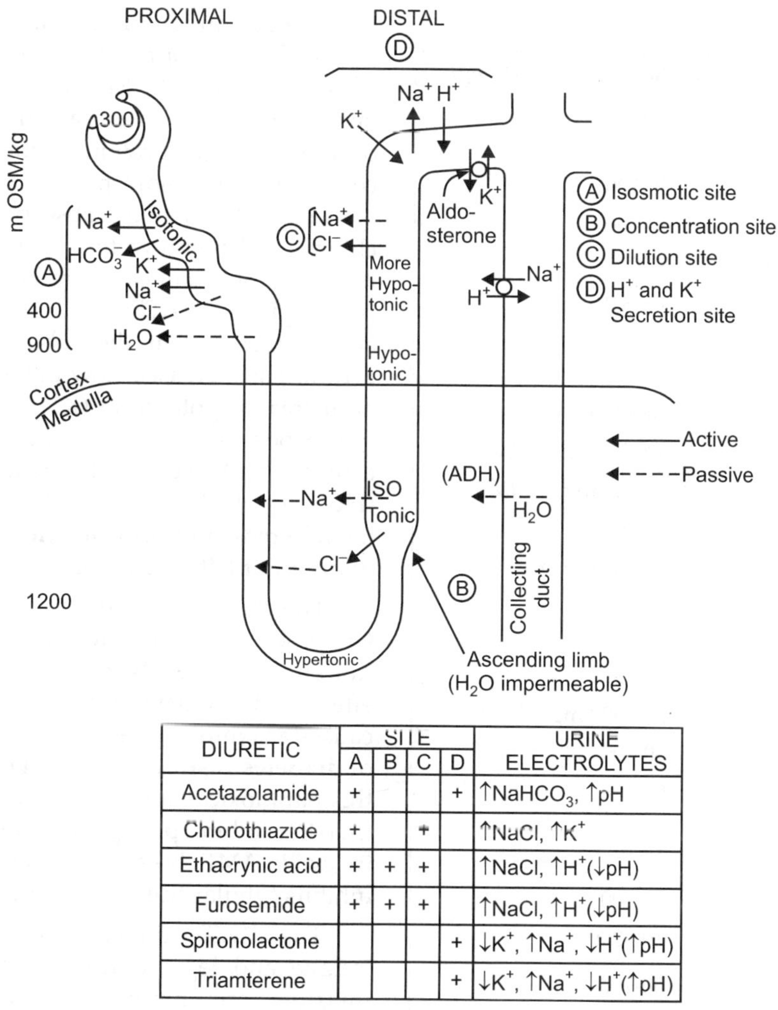

DIURETIC	SITE A	SITE B	SITE C	SITE D	URINE ELECTROLYTES
Acetazolamide	+			+	↑$NaHCO_3$, ↑pH
Chlorothiazide	+		+		↑NaCl, ↑K^+
Ethacrynic acid	+	+	+		↑NaCl, ↑H^+(↓pH)
Furosemide	+	+	+		↑NaCl, ↑H^+(↓pH)
Spironolactone				+	↓K^+, ↑Na^+, ↓H^+(↑pH)
Triamterene				+	↓K^+, ↑Na^+, ↓H^+(↑pH)

Fig. 6.2.2: The four major sites of sodium reabsorption and electrolyte and water transport in the nephron. The major sites of action of diuretics are tabulated (see text).

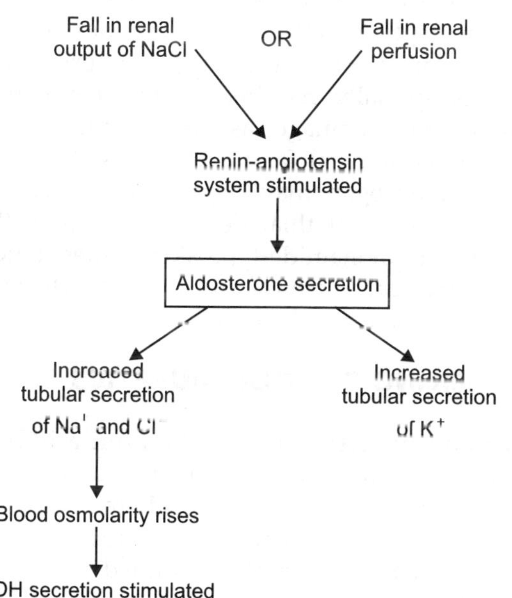

Fig. 6.2.3: Role of the renin-angiotensin-aldosterone system, and the antidiuretic hormone (ADH) in the maintenance of the fluid and electrolyte balance (homeostasis).

CLASSIFICATION OF DIURETICS

Although these drugs vary in their chemical structure and mechanisms of action, almost all of them **interfere with the tubular reabsorption of sodium**. A convenient classification of diuretics is presented in **Table 6.2-1.**

Table 6.2-1. *The diuretic agents*

Class and Generic name	*Total daily dose (mg)*
I. BENZOTHIADIAZIDES AND RELATED COMPOUNDS	
The thiazides	
Chlorothiazide	250-1000*
Hydrochlorothiazide	25-100
Bendroflumethiazide	5-20
Benzthiazide	25-100
Cyclothiazide	1-2
Hydroflumethiazide	25-100
Methyclothiazide	2.5-10
Polythiazide	1-4

Table 6.2-1. Contd...

Class and Generic name		Total daily dose (mg)
	Trichlormethiazide	2-4
	Related Compounds	
	Chlorthalidone	50-100
	Quinethazone	50-100
	Metolazone	5-20
	Indapamide	2.5-5.0
II.	HIGH-CEILING OR LOOP DIURETICS	20-28
	Furosemide	20-40 mg 0.5-2.0 mg/kg IV
	Bumetanide	0.1-1.0 mg/kg IV
	Ethacrynic acid	25-50 50-100 mg IV
III.	CARBONIC ANHYDRASE INHIBITORS	
	Acetazolamide	250-500
	Acetazolamide sodium	250-500 mg IV
	Dichlorphenamide	50-200
	Methazolamide	50-100
IV.	POTASSIUM-SPARING DIURETICS	
	Spironolactone	25-100
	Triamterene	100-200
	Amiloride	50-100
V.	OSMOTIC DIURETICS	
	Mannitol	50-100 g IV in 15-20% solution
	Urea, sterile	40-120 g IV in 4% or 30% solution
	Glycerin	1-1.5 g/kg
	Isosorbide	1-3 g/kg
VI.	METHYLXANTHINES	
	Aminophylline	250-500 mg, IV slowy

* Daily dosage in mg orally, unless otherwise mentioned.

INDIVIDUAL AGENTS

BENZOTHIADIAZIDES (THIAZIDES)

The prototype agent, **chlorothiazide**, was introduced in 1958, and became widely used as an orally effective agent. The thiazides are related chemically to the **sulphonamides**, but have no antibacterial activity. Most of these diuretics are derived from benzothiadiazine and thus known as 'thiazides'. The other four sulphonamide diuretics, **chlorthalidone, quinethazone, metolazone** and **indapamide** differ in their chemical structure from the thiazides, but act exactly like the thiazides and have a relatively longer duration of action.

Site and mode of action. The main action is exerted on the *first part of the distal tubule*, and possibly also on the proximal tubule. Members of this group very in their onset and duration of action. The duration depends on the degree of protein-binding, and the longer acting compounds are more portein bound. Their main action is to block the active reabsorption of sodium (Na^+) and chloride (Cl^-) with water in the distal tubule, possibly by inhibition of glycolysis, as inhibition of Na^+/K^+ adensoine triphosphatase (ATPase), limits the energy supply for active transport in the tubule. They have a **saluretic action**. The increased flow in the distal tubule also causes an increased potassium (K^+) loss. Some members of this group possess significant carbonic anhydrase inhibiting activity, and reduce the reabsorption of bicarbonate (HCO_3^-), which is lost in the urine. Other renal effects include **reduction in uric acid secretion** and a **decreased glomerular filtration rate**.

The thiazides have an **antihypertensive action (see Chap. 4.2)**. It is of interest here to note that the non-diuretic thiazide, **diazoxide**, has a potent hypotensive effect without having any renal action. Chlorothiazide causes a significant reduction in urine volume in patients of **diabetes insipidus (see Chap. 7.1).** The mechanism of this paradoxical antidiuretic effect is not understood. The thiazides inhibit phosphodiesterase, the enzyme involved in cyclic-AMP breakdown, and the conserved c-AMP inhibits tubular fluid reabsorption.

Toxicity. The thiazides may cause dizziness, weakness, fatigue and leg cramps. But the major side effects of thiazides are: **hypopotassaemia, hyperuricaemia** and **aggravation of diabetes mellitus.** Hypopotassaemia may require supplemental administration of potassium chloride. *Hyperuricaemia*, which is due to the decreased secretion of uric acid by the tubular cells, may precipitate **gout** in susceptible patients. The thiazides and uric acid probably share a common tubular secretory mechanism. *Caution* is specially required in patients with severe hepatic or renal damage, as the thiazides may induce hepatic coma or renal failure. A reversible elevation of blood urea nitrogen may occur. **Hypercalcaemia** is a rare complication of thiazide therapy. Rarely thiazides may cause sulphonamide-type **skin rashes, leucopenia, thrombocytopenic purpura,** and **agranulocytosis.** Overall the thiazides have a wide margin of safety.

HIGH-CEILING OR LOOP DIURETICS

Furosemide, bumetanide and **ethacrynic acid** have been labelled as "high-ceiling" or "loop diuretics", because they inhibit the **sodium** and **chloride** reabsorption in the thick segment of the ascending limb of the loop of Henle as well as in the proximal convoluted tubule, and the distal diluting site **(Fig. 6.2.1)**. Thus they are very **potent** diuretics, and induce a dramatic and copious flow of urine rich in sodium chloride.

Site and mode of action. Their major action is to reduce active Cl^- reabsorption in the ascending limb of the loop of Henle. In addition, there are minor actions on Na^+ reabsorption in the proximal tubule, and the distal tubule. There is an increased urine volume with loss of Na^+, K^+ and Cl^-. The Cl^- loss induces **hypochloraemic alkalosis** and K^+ loss may provoke digoxin intoxication. Uric acid secretion is reduced and this may induce gout in susceptible individuals. *Unlike most other diuretics, the loop diuretics continue to be effective even in the presence of electrolyte and acid-base imbalance, and nitrogen retention.*

Like the thiazides these agents are absorbed on oral administration, are protein bound in the plasma, enter the kidney partly by glomerular filtration and partly by secretion in the proximal tubule. The diuretic action is rapid in onset, short in duration, and more marked than other diuretics.

Furosemide and **bumetanide** are sulphonamide compounds. Both of them as well as **ethacrynic acid**, contain a free carboxyl group, which helps them to be transported into a longer segment of the tubule than the thiazides. *Hence, the loop diuretics inhibit sodium and chloride reabsorption over a longer length of the nephron producing more diuresis than the thiazides.*

Toxicity. Because of high potency, therapy with loop diuretics must be instituted cautiously to avoid excessive diuresis. A rapid reduction in extracellular fluid volume can result in a cardiovascular collapse, with associated hypokalaemia, and **hypochloraemic alkalosis**. Thus, during therapy, serum electrolytes should be monitored closely and prophylatic measures taken to prevent severe **hypokalaemia**. A **potassium-sparing diuretic** or **potassium supplements** are indicated in digitalized or cirrhotic patients. Furosemide and ethacrynic acid may cause **azotaemia, hyperuricaemia**, and **hyperglycaemia**. Acute pancreatitis, allergic interstitial nephritis, severe gastrointestinal disturbances, **agranulocytosis** and **thrombocytopenia** have been reported. Dose-related **reversible ototoxic effects** like tinnitus, hearing impairment, and rarely deafness can occur.

The use of loop diuretics should be reserved for patients refractory to thiazides, or when an immediate diuresis is indicated to control the fluid overload, or the glomerular filtration rate is markedly reduced.

CARBONIC ANHYDRASE INHIBITORS

Acetazolamide is a sulphonamide and is the *prototype* carbonic anhydrase inhibitor. Carbonic anhydrase inhibitors have a limited use as diuretics.

Site and mode of action. Carbonic anhydrase influences the tubular reabsorption of sodium at two sites: in the **proximal tubule** where bicarbonate absorption occurs; and in the **distal tubule** where sodium is exchanged for potassium or hydrogen ion and bicarbonate is formed as the accompanying anion.

The hydration of carbon dioxide takes place under the influence of carbonic anhydrase to form carbonic acid which dissociates to give hydrogen and bicarbonate ions:

$$CO_2 + H_2 \underset{\text{anhydrase}}{\overset{\text{carbonic}}{\rightleftharpoons}} H_2CO_3 \rightleftharpoons H^+ + HCO_3^-$$

In relation to the tubular cells, carbonic anhydrase helps to produce the hydrogen ions, which are secreted into the tubules in exchange for sodium ions. The *sodium-hydrogen ion exchange* takes place almost all along the length of the renal tubule, and normally is responsible for the formation of acid urine, while conserving the stores of bicarbonate along with sodium.

Acetazolamide competitively inhibits the enzyme carbonic anhydrase, and interferes with the ability of the renal tubular cells to produce and secrete hydrogen ions. As a result fewer hydrogen ions are available for exchange with filtered sodium. The sodium is eliminated along with bicarbonate ions and the water in which they are dissolved. **The urine become alkaline**. Ultimately, these agents lead to a build up of acidity in the interstitial fluid and **metabolic acidosis** results which initiates compensatory mechanisms. The moment there are enough of H^+ ions for exchange with Na^+ ions in the tubules, diuresis ends. Thus, the diuretic effect of acetazolamide is self-limiting.

These agents also decrease the activity of carbonic anhydrase at other sites in the body like the CNS, the eye, the lungs and the gastrointestinal tract.

Therapeutic uses. The carbonic anhydrase inhibitors are rarely used as primary diuretics, because their action is weak and self-limiting. Their combination with thiazides has a **synergistic** effect. Acetazolamide may be used to alkalinize the urine in conditions like *salicylate poisoning*.

Acetazolamide or dichlorphenamide is used as an adjunct to miotic drugs in the treatment of **acute open angle glaucoma**. It reduces the secretion of aqueous humour, and the intraocular pressure falls. Acetazolamide may be used as an adjunct to antiepileptic drugs in the management of **petit mal epilepsy**. Acetazolamide has been used with benefit in cases of **premenstrual tension, migraine** and **acne vulgaris**. It possibly acts by antagonizing the tendency towards sodium retention. Acetazolamide may provide relief in cases of **acute mountain sickness**. Dichlorphenamide may be used in cases of *chronic bronchitis with emphysema* who suffer from effect of CO_2 retention.

Toxicity. Parasthesias and drowsiness are common with large doses. **Hepatic coma** or **pre-coma** may be precipitated in cases of hepatic cirrhosis due to systemic accumulation of ammonia and hypopotassaemia. **Renal calculus formation** and ureteric colic may occur due to the alkaline urine leading to precipitation of calcium phosphate crystals. Acetazolamide depresses the uptake of iodide by the thyroid gland, this may have a **goitrogenic effect**. **Hypersensitivity reactions, agranulocytosis** and **other blood dyscrasias** may occur.

POTASSIUM-SPARING DIURETICS

The potassium-sparing diuretics, **spironolactone, triamterene** and **amiloride**, interfere with sodium reabsorption at the distal exchange sites, and promote sodium excretion while **potassium is conserved**. Their major use is in conjunction with the thiazides or loop diuretics. Such a combined therapy reduces potassium loss, minimizes alkalosis, and is sometimes effective in refractory oedema. Since hypokalaemia predisposes to digitalis toxicity, such a combined therapy is useful in digitalized patients.

SPIRONOLACTONE

Spironolactone is an **aldosterone antagonist**. Aldosterone is an adrenal mineralocorticoid responsible for the maintenance of electrolyte balance in the body **(see Chap. 7.5)**. It stimulates the sodium pump at the distal tubular ion exchange site inducing **sodium reabsorption**, and **potassium loss**. Spironolactone antagonizes this tubular effect of aldosterone, leading to **sodium and water loss in the urine, and potassium is conserved**.

Site and mode of action. Spirolactones are synthetic steroidal lactones which **competitively antagonize** the effect of aldosterone and deoxycorticosterone on tissues, and particularly at distal tubular ion exchange sites. One of these compounds, **spironolactone**, produces a considerable loss of Na^+ and water, and diminishes loss of K^+ and H^+. Thus, the ionic effects of aldosterone are antagonized.

Therapeutic uses. Spironolactone is generally used in combination with other diuretics, and has been specially useful in cases of **congestive heart failure, hepatic cirrhosis** and **nephrotic syndrome**. It may be given a trial in refractory oedematous states.

Toxicity. Spironolactone may induce **hyperkalaemia**, specially if diuretic therapy is accompanied by high potassium intake, particularly in patients with renal insufficiency. Minor side effects like drowsiness and rashes may occur. It may cause **gynaecomastia, androgen-like side effects**, and **gastrointestinal upset**. **Menstrual disturbances** may occur in women.

TRIAMTERENE

Triamterene is a nonsteroidal compound, which produces a spironolactone-like effect by acting on the distal tubule to increase Na^+, Cl^- and HCO_3^- loss and conserve K^+. **But it is not an aldosterone antagonist**. Presumably triamterene acts directly on the renal tubule, independently of aldosterone. Triamterene is usually employed in combination with a thiazide or loop diuretic in the management of oedema associated with **congestive heart failure, cirrhosis** or **nephrotic syndrome**. Like spironolactone, triamterene may cause **hyperkalaemia**. It may also increase blood urea nitrogen and serum uric acid levels.

AMILORIDE

Amiloride is an organic base and has renal actions like triamterene. Its mode of action is incompletely understood. It has no aldosterone antagonistic activity. Triamterene and amiloride are equally effective in inhibiting the distal tubular sodium-potassium exchange mechanism.

OSMOTIC DIURETICS

Mannitol, urea, glycerol and **isosorbide** are four osmotic diuretics, which are freely filtered through the glomerulus and are insignificantly reabsorbed from the tubules. They mainly induce diuresis by inhibiting sodium and water reabsorption in the proximal tubules and the Henle's loop.

Site and mode of action. Under normal conditions Na^+ and Cl^- are reabsorbed in the proximal tubule, and since the tubule is permeable to water, there is a passive back diffusion of water. Such a process keeps the tubular fluid isosmotic. This continues till the major fraction of the glomerular filtrate is reabsorbed. In the presence of a non-reabsorbable solute like mannitol and urea, the overall osmotic relationship within the proximal tubule remains almost unaltered and the tubular fluid is isosmotic with plasma. Thus, **back diffusion of water does not take place** and **less of sodium is reabsorbed**. Such a mechanism also applies to the loop of Henle. Osmotic diuretics by this mechanism are able to maintain urine volume even when the glomerular filtration rate is reduced.

MANNITOL

This osmotic diuretic is administered intravenously, and is useful for the **prophylaxis of acute renal failure**. It is also used to **reduce intraocular pressure and vitreous volume prior to ocular surgery; to reduce intracranial pressure in patients of cerebral oedema**; and to promote **excretion of toxic substances**. Headache, nausea, chills, lethargy and confusion may occur. There may be a feeling of constriction or pain in the chest. On rapid administration it may pass into the extracellular space and lead to an expansion of extracellular fluid volume. **Congestive heart failure and pulmonary oedema may occur**. Thus, in an oliguric patient it is important to predict the response to mannitol. For this a **test dose** of 12.5 g of mannitol is given intravenously over a period of 3 to 5 minutes. Unless urine output increases within the next 3 hours to 40-60 ml/hour, the condition is probably unresponsive to mannitol. Further mannitol administration should only be done if the patient shows an adequate diuretic response to the test dose.

UREA

Urea also is administered intravenously, and tends to draw fluid from the extracellular space into the blood. Urea is useful for **reducing a raised cerebrospinal fluid pressure during neurosurgical operations and cerebral oedema following head injury**. Intraocular pressure may also be reduced by its use. Use of urea is contraindicated in patients with impaired hepatic, cardiac or renal function. Disorientation, confusion, headache, nausea and vomiting may occasionally occur.

GLYCEROL

Glycerol is of particular use prior to ophthalmological procedures to **reduce intraocular pressure**. As it is metabolized in the body, it produces poor diuresis. It is given orally in a dose of 1 to 1.5 g/kg usually as a 50 percent solution. The intraocular pressure falls within an hour and the effect continues till 5 hours.

ISOSORBIDE

Isosorbide is available as an oral solution (45%) for reduction of intraocular pressure prior to, or following eye surgery for glaucoma or cataract, or to check an acute attack of glaucoma. This drug should not be confused with isosorbide dinitrate, which is an antianginal drug.

METHYLXANTHINES

The xanthines (theophylline, theobromine, caffeine) have a weak diuretic activity. **Aminophylline** (theophylline ethylenediamine) is the most used member. The diuresis is partly a result of cardiac stimulation, better renal haemodynamics, and an increased glomerular filtration rate (GFR). In addition, there is a direct action on the tubule and **sodium reabsorption is inhibited together with an increased Cl^- and water loss**. They are rarely used as primary diuretics. **Aminophylline** is used in the management of **acute pulmonary oedema**, but its efficacy stems from its cardiac and bronchial action rather than its diuretic action.

THERAPEUTIC USES OF DIURETICS

For the management of oedematous states three approaches are available: (*i*) **treat the primary cause**, (*ii*) **suppress renal tubular reabsorption of salt and water** by the administration of diuretics; and (*iii*) **reduce the intake of sodium salts** which is achieved by **a low-salt diet.**

1. **Congestive Heart Failure (CHF).** Digitalis is used in adequate doses to increase the cardiac output, and improve renal haemodynamics, which results in diuresis. Dietary sodium intake is restricted. The choice of the diuretic would depend on the severity of the disorder. In an emergency like acute pulmonary oedema, intravenous **furosemide** or **sodium ethacrynate** may be given. Potassium-sparing diuretics like *spironolactone* or *triamterene* may be added to thiazide therapy.

2. **Essential hypertension.** The thiazides usually serve as primary antihypertensive agents.

3. **Hepatic cirrhosis with ascites.** Potassium-sparing diuretics like **spironolactone** may be employed. If spironolactone alone fails, then a thiazide diuretic can be added cautiously. **Furosemide** or **ethacrynic acid** may have to be used if the oedema is refractory, together with spironolactone to lessen potassium loss.

4. **Nephrotic syndrome.** Dietary sodium restriction may be combined with a **thiazide** diuretic, adding **spironolactone** to control secondary hyperaldosteronism.

5. **Chronic renal failure.** A loop diuretic like **furosemide** may be useful in controlling both oedema and hypertension.

6. **Acute oliguric renal failure. Mannitol** may be employed diagnostically, prophylactically and therapeutically. This osmotic diuretic keeps enough fluid in the nephrons to avoid further damage.

7. **Acute glomerular nephritis.** The hypervolaemia and oedema associated with acute glomerular nephritis is now sometimes treated successfully with **furosemide**.

8. **Cerebral oedema.** Oral **glycerol** may be given a trial. Intravenous *mannitol* is usually preferred as a short-term therapy.

9. **Glaucoma.** The *carbonic anhydrase inhibitors* (acetazolamide) may be used in the long-term treatment of primary open-angle glaucoma.

10. **Intraocular surgery.** The osmotic diuretics (glycerol, mannitol) are used to reduce intraocular pressure and vitreous volume prior to iridectomy, and other ocular surgical procedures.

11. **Diabetes insipidus.** The **thiazides** exhibit **paradoxical antidiuretic action** in patients with diabetes insipidus.

USE OF DIURETICS IN NONOEDEMATOUS DISORDERS

The conditions in which they may be of benefit are:

1. **Renal tubular acidosis.** The thiazides may cause the blood pH, serum bicarbonate and chloride levels to return to normal in the proximal form of this disease, in which there is a deficient bicarbonate reabsorption.

2. **Hypercalciuria, hypercalcaemia and renal calculi.** *Furosemide* increases urinary excretion of calcium, and may be used to treat acute hypercalcaemia.

3. **Salicylate and barbiturate poisoning.** Alkalinization of the urine, achieved by **acetazolamide** administration is used to increase the urinary clearance of salicylates and barbiturates.

4. **Hyperuricaemia.** In patients of lymphomas or leukaemias during cytotoxic drug therapy the serum uric acid levels rise due to rapid metabolism of nucleoproteins, and may lead to acute renal shutdown. Alkalinization of urine increases the solubility of uric acid. **Acetazolamide** and **osmotics diuresis** may help in alkalinization of urine and flushing of the kidneys.

5. **Cystinuria.** The proximal tubular transport of dibasic amino acids like cystine, lysine, arginine or

ornithine may be defective in certain genetic disorders. Cystine is poorly soluble in acid pH of the urine, and may precipitate in the urinary tract to form stones. Alkalinization of the urine with **acetazolamide** and large fluid intake helps in preventing stone formation.

COMPLICATIONS OF DIURETIC THERAPY

The aim of diuretic therapy is to mobilize oedema fluid from the extracellular space so that the extracellular fluid is restored to normal.

1. **Metabolic acidosis.** Acetazolamide, and other acidifying salts lead to a metabolic acidosis due to accumulation of Cl^- ions, in relative excess to HCO_3^-, which is lost in the urine. Retention of H^+ ions also occurs as a result of the **decreased alkali reserve**.

2. **Alkalosis.** The thiazides, and loop diuretics cause excessive Cl^- ion loss with retention of bicarbonate. It may be managed by providing Cl^- ions by administration of *ammonium chloride* and other acidifying salts.

3. **Hypokalaemia.** Loop diuretics, thiazides, or carbonic anhydrase inhibitors cause an excessive loss of K^+ *via* the urine.

4. **Hyperkalaemia.** High levels of plasma K^+ can be the result of hypovolaemia, or administration of K^+-sparing diuretics, or due to a reduced distal excretion of K^+ ions.

5. **Dilutional hyponatraemia.** In this there is a decreased extracellular Na^+ in proportion to water content. The **loop diuretics** or **thiazides** may cause such a situation.

6. **True hyponatraemia.** In this condition there is an actual depletion of the body's salt reserve, and the Na^+ ion levels in the plasma are low. The **loop diuretics** or **thiazides** may cause an excessive salt loss (low-salt syndrome).

PRECAUTIONS AND CONTRAINDICATIONS

In general, following are the *relative contraindications* to diuretic therapy:

1. In advanced **liver cirrhosis** diuretics induce electrolyte imbalances leading to encephalopathy and hepatic coma which may be fatal.

2. In patients on **digitalis therapy** the diuretic-induced hypokalaemia can cause fatal arrhythmias.

3. **Diabetic patients** may develop hyperglycaemia specially with the thiazides.

4. In patients of **gout,** hyperuricaemia may occur and an acute attack may be precipitated, specially with the thiazides.

5. The antihypertensive drug schedules must be revised, if a diuretic is combined freshly, as the patient may have episodes of postural hypotension.

6. Patients on **lithium therapy** should not be administered diuretics as far as possible, as they decrease the renal excretion of lithium leading to lithium intoxication.

Absolute contraindications for the use of diuretics are **severe kidney damage, extreme oliguria or anuria, severe electrolyte and acid-base imbalances, hypersensitivity reactions, and bone-marrow suppression.**

REFRACTORY OEDEMA

Diuretics are likely to lose their efficacy due to factors like: **hyponatraemia; reduction in glomerular filtration rate; hypochloraemic alkalosis; and other electrolyte and acid-base imbalances.** When a patient develops refractoriness to a particular diuretic regimen, the entire regimen should be reassessed. Patients refractory to the **thiazides** may respond to the **loop diuretics** satisfactorily. **Corticosteroids** are sometimes helpful in refractory oedema of cirrhosis liver with ascites. *Combination of thiazides/loop diuretics with* K^+*-sparing diuretics like spironolactone or triamterene avoids serious hypokalaemia.* Thus, with such steps a satisfactory response may be achieved in a diuretic refractory patient.

6.3 DRUGS ACTING ON THE UTERUS

Uterine Stimulants
- Indirect Oxytocics: Purgatives
- Direct Oxytocics: Oxytocin, Ergometrine, Prostaglandins

Urerine Relaxants (Tocolytics)
- Ethyl Alcohol
- Isoxsuprine
- Ritodrine
- Magnesium Sulphate

Dysmenorrhoea

The uterine smooth muscle (myometrium) has its own *inherent rhythm* of contraction and relaxation independent of its nerve supply. In the non-gravid uterus, during the menstrual cycle, the rhythm is influenced by **two** hormones: (*i*) **oestrogens**, in the first half of the cycle induce contractions of low amplitude and high frequency; and (*ii*) **progesterone**, in the second half of the cycle induces contractions of greater amplitude and lower frequency. At the onset of menstruation the contractions become stronger, and sometimes cause pain and discomfort (**dysmenorrhoea**). This may be due to prostaglandins.

The physiologic and pharmacologic factors favouring uterine *contraction* include *oestrogens, oxytocin, prostaglandins*, and *stretching of the muscle*. Whereas, the factors favouring *relaxation* include *progesterone* and *beta-adrenoceptor stimulants*. The progesterone production increases through the course of a pregnancy, and is responsible for maintaining the uterus in a non-excitable state. The increasing oestrogen production during pregnancy is partly responsible for the **increased sensitivity to oxytocin**, as oestrogen increases both the binding sites and the affinity of the uterine **oxytocin receptors**. The local hormones, **prostaglandins**, also play a complex and important role in the timing mechanism of labour.

During pregnancy the capacity of the uterus increases, and this enlargement involves both stretching and hypertrophy of the existing muscle fibres. The uterine contractions continue, but they are irregular and painless. As pregnancy advances these contractions become stronger and more regular till **during labour they are painful, rhythmic and regular, with periods of relaxation in between**. The intensity, duration, and frequency reaches its maximum during the **second** and the **third stage** of labour. After a short interval of rest the contractions return and lead to the **separation and expulsion of the placenta**, and then the **involution of uterus** takes place, and the uterus returns to almost its non-gravid shape and size within a period of six weeks.

The drugs acting on the uterus can be classed into two groups:

1. Uterine stimulants (Oxytocics or Ecbolics)
2. Uterine relaxants (Tocolytics)

UTERINE STIMULANTS

Oxytocics or **ecbolics** are drugs which stimulate uterine contractions indirectly or directly, and help in the expulsion of its contents.

(*i*) **Indirect Oxytocics:** These drugs induce pelvic congestion and stimulate uterine activity, e.g., *purgatives*.

(*ii*) **Direct Oxytocics:** *Oxytocin, ergometrine* and *prostaglandins*.

OXYTOCIN

Oxytocin is a *polypeptide hormone* obtained from the posterior pituitary gland. It is a neurosecretory product mainly synthesized in the cell bodies of the **paraventricular nucleus of the hypothalamus**. The actions of oxytocin are detailed in **Chapter 7.1**. *The sensitivity of the uterus to oxytocin increases with advancing pregnancy.* Oestrogens intensify and progesterone diminishes the uterine effect of oxytocin. The action of oxytocin is also influenced by cations like **calcium, magnesium** and **potassium.**

The physiological function of oxytocin is to help labour at term. Oxytocin concentration is highest in the second stage of labour. It causes **fundal contraction** and **dilatation of the cervix**. The intrauterine pressure in between contractions remains almost normal. Oxytocin is also released in response to **suckling** by the baby, and helps in **expression of milk**, and also in the **involution of the uterus** during the postnatal period. Oxytocin has very little pressor or antidiuretic action.

Oxytocin causes a *direct* stimulation of the uterine muscle, which involves changes in membrane permeability to sodium, and changes in the membrane potential favouring formation of contractile **actomyosin**.

THERAPEUTIC USES

1. **Induction of labour.** For induction 2 to 5 units of oxytocin in 1000 ml of 5 percent dextrose injection may be given by slow IV drip. If there is no evidence of tetanic contractions of the uterus, the drip may be continued safely till the expulsion of the placenta.
2. **Hypotonic uterine inertia.** To manage uterine inertia 1 to 5 units of oxytocin may be administered by a similar regimen as above, until the inertia is overcome.
3. **Retained placenta and postpartum haemorrhage.** Oxytocin 2 to 5 units may be given subcutaneously, IM, or in the form of a drip. It may also be used in combination with **ergometrine** (Syntometrine

contains oxytocin 5 units with ergometrine 0.5 mg in 1 ml, to be given IM in the third stage of labour).

4. **Oxytocin challenge test.** This is one of the tests to determine foetal well-being in high-risk obsterical patients (pre-eclampsia, prolonged pregnancy, diabetes mellitus). It is performed at intervals during late pregnacy **to determine the oxytocin sensitivity of the uterus**. For this 0.01 units of oxytocin are given IV every minute to a maximum of 10 doses. A strong contraction with 0.03 units or less indicates positive sensitivity.
5. **Engorged breasts.** For let-down of milk from engorged breasts 5 units oxytocin may be given IM before expression of breast milk manually or by a breast pump.
6. **Incomplete abortion.** Oxytocin may be occasionally employed to expel the dead foetus from the uterus in early pregnancy.

The *preparations, toxicity,* and *contraindications* to the use of oxytocin are detailed in **Chapter 7.1.** Oxytocin is not administered to women with a previous history of uterine surgery, or cesarean section, or when the uterus is overdistended, as rupture of the uterus can occur. Oxytocin should only be administered by a well trained staff.

ERGOMETRINE

Ergot is the product of a fungus *Claviceps purpurea* which grows on rye and other grains. It is a source for many alkaloids, each of which has laevo- and dextro-isomers. The laevo-isomers are active. The major alkaloids of ergot are: **ergotoxine, ergotamine** and **ergometrine**. Out of these, **ergometrine is the only alkaloid used as an oxytocic**, as it has greater selectivity for the uterus compared to the others. Ergometrine, and its semisynthetic derivative **methylergometrine** are extensively used as oxytocics.

Ergometrine acts *directly* on the uterine smooth muscle, and increases the frequency and duration of uterine contractions. **These contractions are superimposed on a tonic contraction with no relaxation in between.** This is in contrast to the action of oxytocin, which produces a contraction of the uterus with complete relaxation in between. Ergometrine increases the basal level of uterine tone, and clamps the open arterioles, which checks postpartum bleeding.

THERAPEUTIC USES

1. **To prevent and control postpartum haemorrhage.** These alkaloids (ergometrine, methylergometrine) are usually administered towards the end of labour, to promote a firm contraction of the uterus, which closes the bleeding uterine sinuses.
2. Ergometrine is sometimes administered during puerperium to promote recovery of uterine tone, and **involution of the uterus.**
3. **Incomplete abortion.** Oxytocin is considered superior for initiation of contractions, but ergometrine may be more effective for reducing the bleeding which follows the expulsion of the dead foetus and membranes.

Contraindications. The use of ergot alkaloids in *preeclampsia, hypertension, coronary artery disease* and *thrombophlebitis* is contraindicated.

Toxicity. Side effects are uncommon with ergometrine and methylergometrine. Cramp-like pains may occur. Overdoses are likely to cause *peripheral gangrene.*

Preparations and Dosage

1. *Ergometrine maleate*: Injection 0.25 mg/ml IM or IV. Maximum dose 1 mg. Orally 0.5 mg tablets three times a day.
2. *Methylergometrine maleate (Methergin)*: Injection 0.2 mg/ml IM or IV. Orally 0.25 to 0.5 mg two or three times daily.
3. *Oxytocin and ergometrine injection (Syntometrine).* Available as synthetic oxytocin 5 units and ergometrine 0.5 mg in 1 ml. Usually given IM in the *third stage* of labour. The advantage of this combination is that oxytocin provides prompt effect and ergometrine provides a sustained action.

PROSTAGLANDINS

The prostaglandins are **long-chain fatty acids**, and derive their name from their high concentration in seminal fluid. They are found almost in all tissues, and those used as drugs are prepared synthetically.

Two prostaglandins, **dinoprost tromethamine** (PGF_2 alpha) and **dinoprostone** (PGE_2) possess oxytocic activity. PGF_2 alpha is found in aminotic fluid, blood and decidua during labour. It is believed that PGF_2 alpha functions as a physiological oxytocic which initiates and maintains uterine contractions during labour, and also is responsible for the **induction of menstruation** in the non-gravid state of the uterus.

Mode of action. There is evidence that PGF_2 alpha causes an increase in the free calcium (Ca^{++}) level in the myofibril by two processes:

(*i*) It increases the Ca^{++} influx across the myometrial cell membrane, and (*ii*) it blocks the binding of Ca^{++} to the cytoplasmic membrane protein by inhibiting adenylcyclase. This in turn leads to decreased phosphorylation. As a consequence, there is an **increase in the free Ca^{++} levels intracellularly, triggering contraction of the myofibril.** The increased contractility of the uterus is similar to the spontaneous contractions seen during labour in the term uterus.

Therapeutic uses. Both, *dinoprost tromethamine* (PGF_2 alpha) and *dinoprostone* (PGE_2), can be employed for induction of therapeutic or elective abortion; and induction of labour.

1. **Therapeutic or elective abortion:** They may be administered in the form of vaginal suppositories (PGF_2 alpha, 50 mg/2 hourly; PGE_2, 20 mg/2 hourly). They are successful in terminating pregnancy in 85 to 90 percent of cases within 30 hours. In the remaining cases evacuation may be completed by other means like **suction curettage** or **hypertonic saline** administration. The prostaglandins can also be administered by the extra-amniotic or intra-amniotic route.

Lately, **hypertonic urea solution** is being used as an alternative to hypertonic saline, dinoprost and dinoprostone to induce second-trimester abortions.

2. **Induction of labour:** These agents (PGF_2 alpha, 1.25 mcg/minute; PGE_2, 0.5 mcg/minute) may be administered as an IV drip. The advantages of prostaglandins over oxytocin are that: (*i*) the prostaglandins (PGs) are more effective when premature delivery is desired and the cervix is incompletely dilated; (*ii*) the PGs do not cause water intoxication; and (*iii*) the PGs can be safely used in pre-eclampsia, cardiac and renal diseases. The oral and extra-amniotic routes of administration can also be tried.

Toxicity. The side effects are mainly gastrointestinal like *nausea, vomiting* and *diarrhoea*. They may cause *tetanic contraction of the uterus*. Caution is to be exercised in patients of asthma, epilepsy, hypertension and glaucoma.

UTERINE RELAXANTS (TOCOLYTIC AGENTS)

Drugs capable of reducing uterine hypermotility would be useful for preventing premature labour, which is the commonest single cause for increased perinatal mortality and morbidity. Other uses would be for relaxing tetanic uterine contractions during abnormal labour, and for relief of cramp-like pains of dysmenorrhoea. The term "tocolysis" was first used in 1966, derived from the Greek, *tocos* = birth, and *lysis* = dissolution. Thus *tocolytic agents* include all drugs inhibiting labour.

Ethyl Alcohol

Ethyl alcohol is sometimes administered intravenously for its sedative and analgesic effect, and has been found to **reduce uterine contractions during premature labour**. The mode of action is possibly by: (*i*) inhibition of the release of vasopressin and oxytocin from the posterior pituitary; (*ii*) adrenaline release through sympathetic activation, and (*iii*) inhibition of prostaglandin synthesis. Thus, an intravenous ethyl alcohol infusion may slow down labour. For this 50 ml of 95 percent ethyl alcohol is mixed with 450 ml of 5 percent dextrose in distilled water to give a 9.5 percent alcohol solution. The loading dose is 15 ml/kg of body weight of 9.5 percent alcohol given over 2 hours. Followed by a maintenance dose of 1.5 ml/kg of body weight. The disadvantage of this regimen is that the patient sometimes feels intoxicated.

Beta-adrenoceptor Stimulants (Beta-agonists)

Isoxsuprine Hydrochloride

Isoxsuprine is a smooth muscle relaxant. It acts by stimulating the beta-adrenoceptors. It relaxes the uterine muscle and also improves cerebral and peripheral blood circulation. Diminished uterine contractility can be maintained for long periods provided the cardiovascular system tolerates the amount infused. Uterine blood flow also increases.

Isoxsuprine is used to inhibit **premature labour**, and to manage **tetanic uterine contractions**, and **toxaemia** of pregnancy. It can be administered orally, intramuscularly, or as an IV drip depending on the need, cardiovascular tolerance, and the response of the patient. Initial dose is 80 mg in 250 ml of 5 percent dextrose IV, followed by 0.1 to 0.2 mg/min, until uterine relaxation is obtained.

Ritodrine Hydrochloride

Ritodrine is a more specific $beta_2$-adrenoceptor stimulant (causing uterine and bronchial relaxation), and produces fewer cardiovascular reactions. It relaxes the uterus and delays the onset of labour. It is administered as an IV drip at a rate of 50 mcg/minute, gradually increased by 50 mcg/minute every 10 minutes (not to exceed 400 mcg/min), until adequate relaxation is obtained, Ritodrine can also be administered intramuscularly or orally. **Side effects** include tachycardia and hypotension.

Other beta-agonist like **fenoterol, terbutaline** and **salbutamol** have also been tried for inhibiting uterine activity.

Magnesium Sulphate

High concentrations of magnesium depress uterine activity. Magnesium sulphate is used as an *intravenous infusion* in the management of pre-eclampsia to prevent convulsions and to inhibit uterine contractions.

Various other drugs like *progesterone*, *pethidine* and *promethazine* have been used to inhibit uterine motility with limited success. As a last resort, **inhalation anaesthetics like halothane** can be used to suppress uterine contractions, although they predispose the patient to postpartum haemorrhage (PPH).

DYSMENORRHOEA

In dysmenorrhoea there are cramp-like painful contractions of the uterus, more so at the onset of menstruation. Currently, it is thought that the **prostaglandins** are involved in this disorder, and substances which inhibit the synthesis of PGs like **aspirin** and **indomethacin** may be of some use.

Belladonna alkaloids (atropine and other cholinergic blocking agents) in combination with aspirin and codeine have been tried to treat severe dysmenorrhoea. However, this disorder is not helped much by drugs. Lately, the calcium antagonist, **nifedipine**, has been tried for **dysmenorrhoea** and management of preterm labour.

❑❑❑

DRUGS ACTING ON THE ENDOCRINE SYSTEM

7.1 HYPOTHALAMIC AND PITUITARY HORMONES

Cells are essentially chemical machines, and respond to chemical signals. Messages are carried by two well defined systems: (*i*) the **hormonal system** in which the chemical messengers (hormones) are produced by special glands, released into the blood stream, and **slowly** act upon the target cells in the body; and (*ii*) the **nervous system** in which messages travel across the body in milliseconds. Nervous communication is rapid and more specific than hormonal communication.

Hormones are chemical substances produced endogenously by endocrine glands, and certain nerve cells. They are carried by the blood throughout the body, but influence the activity of specific **target** tissues and organs, the cells of which lodge special receptors capable of binding the hormones. The term "endocrine" refers to the system of glands or tissues that synthesize the hormones and secrete them directly into the circulatory system.

The endocrine system is more precisely a **neuroendocrine** system, as it not only includes the glands, but also sites in the **central nervous system** with which this system interacts. The coordinated activity of these two major systems is responsible for the stability of the internal environment (homeostasis) in the body.

The **pituitary gland** is placed at the base of the brain, and is connected to the hypothalamus by the pituitary stalk containing nerve fibres and blood vessels. It consists of an **anterior lobe** (adenohypophysis), and a **posterior lobe** (neurohypophysis). The posterior lobe produces **oxytocin** and the **antidiuretic hormone** (ADH), which have effects on the uterus and the renal tubules respectively **(Fig. 7.1.1).**

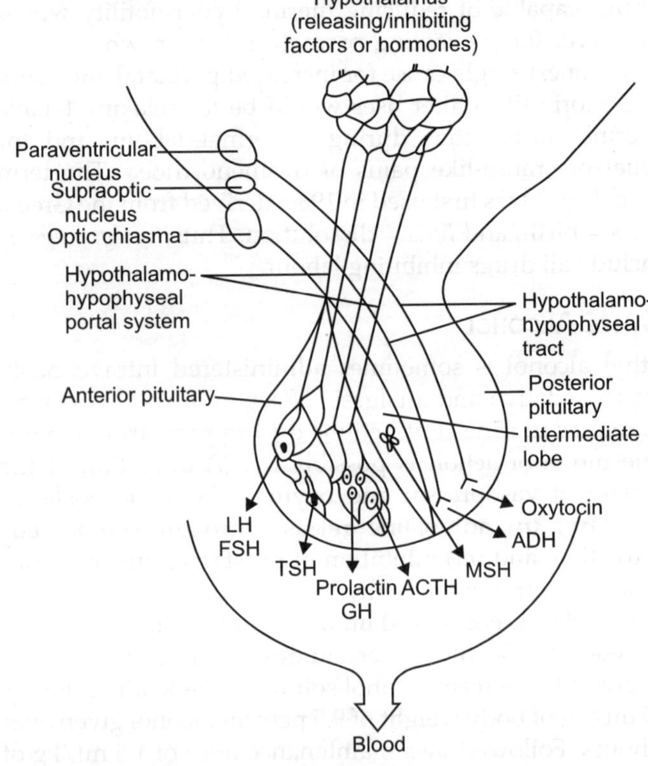

Fig. 7.1.1: The hypothalamo-pituitary axis.

Table 7.1.-1. *The hypothalamic hormones and their specific trophic hormones in the anterior pituitary gland*

Hypothalamus (hormone or factor)	*Anterior Pituitary Gland (trophic hormone)*
RELEASING HORMONES	
Thyrotrophin-releasing hormone (TRH)	Thyrotrophic hormone (TSH)
Corticotrophin-releasing hormone (CRH, CRF)	Adrenocorticotrophic hormone (ACTH)
Follicle stimulating-releasing hormone (FSH-RH, FRH)*	Follicle stimulating hormone (FSH)
Luteinizing hormone-releasing hormone (LH-RH, LRH)*	Luteinizing hormone (LH)
Prolactin-releasing hormone (PRH, PRF)	Prolactin (PL)
Somatotrophin-releasing hormone (SRH, GH-RH, GRF)	Somatotrophin (STH)
Melanocyte stimulating-releasing hormone (MRF, MSH-RH, MRH)	Melanocyte stimulating hormone (MSH)
INHIBITING HORMONES	
Prolactin inhibiting hormone (PIH, PIF)	Prolactin (PL)
Somatostatin (SIH, SIF, GH-RIH)	Somatotrophin (STH)
Melanocyte stimulating-inhibiting hormone (MSH-IH, MIF)	Melanocyte stimulating hormone (MSH)

* A single substance released from the hypothalamus appears to promote release of both FSH and LH, sometimes designated as gonadotrophin releasing hormone (GRH) which is a decapeptide.

The **anterior lobe** comprises of six or seven different types of non-innervated secretory cells which synthesize, store and secrete **trophic hormones** regulating other endocrine glands. The hormones of the anterior pituitary are: the **thyroid stimulating hormone** (thyrotrophin, TSH), **adrenocorticotrophic hormone** (corticotrophin, ACTH), **follicle stimulating hormone** (FSH), **luteinizing hormone** (LH), **prolactin** (PL), **growth hormone** (somatotrophin, STH, GH), and **melanocyte stimulating hormone** (MSH).

REGULATION OF ANTERIOR PITUITARY SECRETION

The anterior pituitary gland has been traditionally termed as the master of the endocrine system. However, more recently this regulatory role has been attributed to the hypothalamus. Thus, the secretion of the trophic hormones from the anterior pituitary gland is controlled in two ways: (*i*) by the **hypothalamus**: and (*ii*) by **feedback** of hormones from the endocrine target glands **(Fig. 7.1.2)**.

Hypothalamic Control

The secretion of hormones from the anterior pituitary is controlled by the hypothalamo-pituitary neurohormones. They are also called **hypothalamic releasing** or **release inhibiting hormones**. These neurohormones are synthesized in the hypothalamic neurones (median eminence), and released into the blood capillaries which unite to form the sole blood supply (a portal system) to the anterior pituitary gland. The **median eminence** is now established to perform a neuroendocrine function. It produces the hypothalamic hormones which control the release of trophic hormones from the anteriory pituitary gland **(Table 7.1-1)**. Three **inhibiting hypothalamic hormones** have also been demonstrated which inhibit the release of **prolactin, somatotrophin**, and **melanocyte stimulating hormone**.

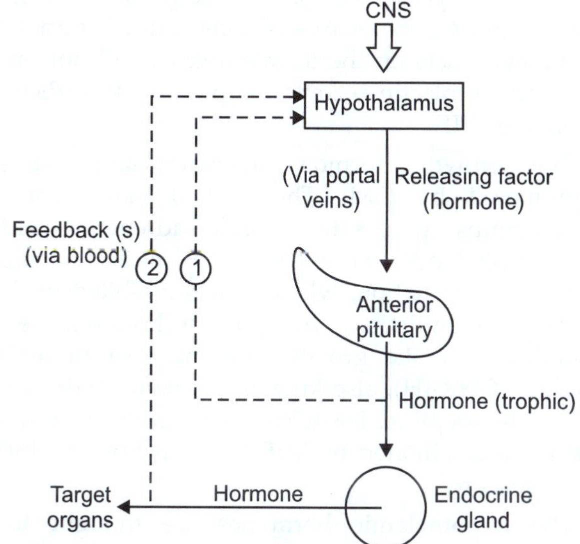

Fig. 7.1.2: The negative feedback control of the anterior pituitary secretion. Environmental or endogenous stimuli act upon the hypothalamus, which secretes specific releasing factors conveyed to the anterior pituitary. As a result specific trophic hormones are released–higher the blood level of the trophic hormone, less of it is released (feedback 1). The trophic hormone induces its target endocrine gland to secrete specific hormone(s). The raised blood level of this specific hormone also suppresses the trophic hormone release through the hypothalamus (feedback 2). Thus, there are short-and long-loop controls operating on the anterior pituitary.

Feedback Control

The trophic hormone-producing and secreting activity of the anterior pituitary is also influenced by the hormones of the respective target glands, i.e., by a **feedback** from the glands which it influences. Thus, when the plasma levels of hormones of the **adrenals, thyroid** and **gonads** fall, the hypothalamus is stimulated to secrete the appropriate releasing hormones, which in turn step up the production of **corticotrophin, thyrotrophin** and the **gonadotrophins**. On the contrary, when the blood levels of the target gland hormones are high, the release of the hypothalamic releasing hormones is inhibited. Thus, such a **negative feedback mechanism** is responsible for the maintenance of normal target gland hormonal blood levels **(Fig. 7.1.2)**.

HYPOTHALAMIC HORMONES

TRH is a **tripeptide**, and it promotes the secretion of TSH from the anterior pituitary. It is not very specific as it can also release prolactin. The neurohormone CRF controls ACTH secretion, and its nature is yet to be fully identified **(Table 7.1-1)**. Dextroamphetamine promotes the release of CRF, and the alpha-adrenoceptor blockers reduce the secretion.

The mechanism of the differential release of FSH and LH is poorly understood. **Dopamine** is a stimulatory, and **serotonin** is an inhibitory neurotransmitter in the release of the gonadotrophin releasing hormone. Prolactin (lactogenic hormone) is the pituitary hormone which stimulates the ovaries of some animal species, but in humans it acts on the female breasts and not on the sex glands. Prolactin secretion is promoted by PRF and inhibited by PIF.

The growth hormone (somatotrophin) release is promoted by GRF. The GRF release from the hypothalamus appears to be under adrenergic control. Dextroamphetamine stimulates GRF release by alpha-adrenergic stimulation, whereas it is inhibited by beta-adrenergic stimulation. The growth hormone release is inhibited by the growth-hormone-release-inhibiting hormone (GHR-IH), also known as **somatostatin**, which is a tetradecapeptide. The release of the MSH is promoted by MRF and inhibited by MIF. The function of MSH in man is obscure.

The hypothalamic hormones are thought to be liberated as a result of aminergic neuronal activity – **dopamine, noradrenaline** and **serotonin**.

ANTERIOR PITUITARY HORMONES

Thyroid Stimulating Hormone (TSH, Thyrotrophic Hormone, Thyrotrophin)

The TSH controls the activity of the thyroid gland by regulating the uptake of iodide by the gland. It also affects the enzymes involved in the various stages of synthesis and release of the thyroid hormones **(Chap. 7.2)**. The hormones of the thyroid gland (thyroxine, triiodothyronine) exert a **negative feedback** effect, which controls the secretion of TRH by the hypothalamus, and TSH by the anterior pituitary. TSH is a glycorprotein with a molecular weight of 25,000 and its blood level can be assessed by **radioimmunoassay**. Commercially TSH is obtained from bovine anterior pituitary glands, and allergic reactions are likely. Administration of antithyroid drugs like carbimazole suppress thyroxine production and stimulate the release of TSH. This results in **colloid hypertrophy** (goitre). Lack of iodides in diet has a similar effect.

The main use of TSH (Thytropar) is as a **diagnostic agent** to differentiate between **primary hypothyroidism** and **secondary hypothyroidism** due to pituitary failure. On TSH administration there is no increase in the thyroid uptake of I^{131} in cases of primary hypothyroidism, whereas, the uptake greatly increases in cases of secondary hypothyroidism.

Adrenocorticotrophic Hormone (ACTH, Corticotrophin)

The ACTH is a single chain polypeptide containing 39 amino acids, produced by the anterior pituitary, and is released into the systemic circulation in response to the neurohormone, **corticotrophin releasing hormone** (CRH). The ACTH stimulates the adrenal cortex to increase the production of glucocorticoids mainly, and sex hormones to some extent **(Chap. 7.5)**. These adrenocortical steroids released into the blood control the secretion of CRH from the hypothalamus and ACTH from the anterior pituitary by a **negative feedback** mechanism.

Actions. The site of action of ACTH is the **zona fasciculata** and **zona reticularis** of the adrenal cortex, of which it causes a hyperaemia and hypertrophy. The production of aldosterone from *zona glomerulosa is independent* of ACTH action. Thus, ACTH stimulates the synthesis and secretion of the glucocorticoids cortisol and corticosterone mainly, and to some extent the secretion of androgens like dehydroepiandrosterone. The cholesterol and vitamin C levels of the adrenal cortex fall sharply. The *actions of* ACTH are largely due to the released adrenal glucocorticoids, and include reduced excretion of sodium and oedema; increased urinary excretion of uric acid, 17-hydroxycorticosteroids, 17-ketosteroids and potassium; hyperglycaemia and glycosuria; eosinopenia, lymphopenia and polymorphonuclearcytosis. In addition ACTH has an **anti-inflammatory** and **antiallergic** action.

Mode of action. ACTH first binds to specific **receptors** on the membrane of the adrenocortical target cells. This hormone–receptor complex activates the membrane enzyme, adenylate cyclase. This, in turn, promotes the formation of the intracellular cyclic nucleotide, cyclic adenosine 3′,5′, monophosphate (c-AMP). This second messenger (ACTH is the first chemical messenger in this case) then stimulates the enzymatic reactions that **catalyse the steps in the biosynthesis of both adrenocortical protein and adrenocortical steroid hormones**.

Cyclic-AMP also probably activates adrenal phosphorylase activity, which promotes the conversion of glycogen through glucose-6-phosphate to triphosphopyridine nucleotide (TPN). Then TPN provides the energy for adrenal steroidogenesis.

Therapeutic uses. Amongst the anterior pituitary hormones, ACTH is the most extensively employed, both *diagnostically* and *therapeutically*.

1. Used **diagnostically** to determine whether adrenal insufficiency is due to pituitary or adrenal failure.

2. Used intermittently to avoid adrenocortical insufficiency and atrophy as a result of long-term administration of adrenocorticosteroids.

3. Used **therapeutically** to treat nonendocrine disorders like **status asthamaticus, anaphylactic shock, rheumatic** and **collagen disease**.

4. ACTH is claimed to have special advantages over adrenocorticoids in the therapy of **multiple sclerosis, ulcerative colitis, infantile convulsions** and **severe myasthenia gravis**.

Contraindications. The problems with therapeutic use of ACTH are that: (*i*) it has to be administered parenterally to avoid proteolytic destruction; (*ii*) it usually offers a temporary remission; (*iii*) its efficacy depends on an optimally active adrenal cortex; and (*iv*) hypersensitivity reactions may occur though rarely. **Tetracosactrin**, the synthetic ACTH, produces the least of allergic complications.

Contraindications are the same as those for adrenocorticosteroids, including *tuberculosis, azotemic nephritis, acute psychosis, active peptic ulcer, congestive heart failure and diabetes mellitus.*

Toxicity. Long-term administration of ACTH induces disturbances of the endocrine system, including suppression of ACTH production; **exacerbation of diabetes mellitus; hypertrophy of the adrenal medulla; oedema; hypertension; and difficulty in withdrawing the drug**. In addition, there may be **rounding of facial contour** (Cushingoid appearance), **mild hirsutism, acne, menstrual irregularities** and **hypopotassaemic alkalosis (Chap. 7.5)**. Hypersensitivity reactions may occur.

Preparations

Short-acting Preparation

Corticotrophin Injection (ACTH *Inj., Acthar*). A sterile solution in water should be prepared immediately before use. Usual dose is 25–40 units IM, or SC 6 hourly. Or 10–25 units diluted in 500 ml of 5 percent glucose given by slow IV infusion over 8 to 24 hours.

Long-acting Preparation

Corticotrophin Gelatin Injection (ACTH Gel *Inj., Acthar Gel*). Usual dose 25–40 units IM or SC every 24–72 hours.

Corticotrophin Zinc Injection (ACTH *Zinc Inj.*). Dose 20-60 units IM or SC every 24–72 hours.

Synthetic Corticotrophin Preparations

Tetracosactrin (*Synacthen, Cortrosyn*): Dose 0.25–0.75 mg IM or IV. Depot preparations are also available in a zinc phosphate complex for prolonged action.

Gonadotrophins

A gonadotrophin is a substance which promotes the growth and development of the gonads. The anterior pituitary stimulates the ovary by means of two gonadotrophins: **follicle stimulating hormone** (FSH) is responsible for the development of the ovarian follicle; and **luteinizing hormone** (LH) is the stimulus to ovulation, and later it maintains the corpus luteum. Both FSH and LH are glycoproteins (Mol. Wt. 25,000–70,000), and their cyclic activity regulates the menstrual cycle **(Chap. 7.6).**

Human menopausal gonadotrophin (HMG) is prepared from the urine of postmenopausal women. HMG is a mixture of gonadotrophins, and mainly acts like FSH. It is used to induce ovulation in infertile women having anovalar ovaries.

The placenta and the endometrium produce **homologous chorionic gonadotrophin** (HCG), which is extracted from the urine of pregnant women, partially purified, and is available for therapeutic use as an injection. HCG acts like LH.

In **males** the FSH stimulats **spermatogenesis**, and the LH is identical with the interstitial cell stimulating hormone (ICSH) which stimulates the testicular Leydig cells to produce testosterone (**Chap. 7.7**).

A third pituitary hormone **prolactin** (PL), which stimulates the ovaries of some animal species, **acts in humans on the female breast only** and not on the gonads.

Classification of Gonadotrophic Activity

Gonadotrophins can be subdivided and characterized by the actions they produce **(Table 7.1-2)**. HMG and *pregnant mare's serum gonadotrophin* (PMSG) have mainly FSH-like actions, and HCG has mainly LH-like actions.

Table 7.1-2. *Classification of gonadotrophic activity*

FSH-like activity (HMG & PMSG)	*LH-like activity (HCG)*
In the female	
Oocyte growth	Maturation of the ovum
Follicular growth	Ovulation and structural integrity of corpus luteum
17-β-oestradiol secretion	17-β oestradiol and progesterone secretion
In the male	
Spermatogenesis	Testosterone secretion

Gonadotrophins in the Female

Both FSH and LH act in harmony and follow a cyclic pattern in the female, characterized by the human menstrual cycle (28 days). At birth each human ovary has about 200,000 *oocytes*, each enclosed in follicular cells to form the primordial follicles. At puberty a preset "biological clock" in the brain makes the hypothalamus increase its secretion of a neurohormone, (gonadotrophin releasing hormone, GRH), which stimulates certain pituitary cells to secrete the **follicle stimulating hormone** (FSH).

Actions of FSH on the ovary. After puberty, FSH continues to affect ovarian function cyclically throughout the reproductive years of the women. Early in each cycle FSH stimulates the growth of several primordial follicles. Later, FSH (with a low concentration of LH during the follicular phase of menstrual cycle) promotes the growth of a few oocytes, and promotes 17-β-oestradiol (oestrogen) secretion by the thecal cells of these follicles. This oestrogen is responsible for the gradual thickening of the endometrium known as the **proliferative phase** of the ovulatory cycle **(Chap. 7.6)**.

Actions of LH on the ovary. The midcycle LH surge is preceded by high levels of plasma oestradiol occurring upto 24 hours previously. The LH induces final maturation of usually one occyte, and completes the first **meiotic division**. Ovulation and conversion of the follicle to a corpus luteum occurs about 10 hours later. This corpus luteum secretes both 17-β-oestradiol and progesterone under LH effect.

If the ovum is **not fertilized**, the corpus luteum regresses due to lack of gonadotrophins, and the ovarian steroid secretion declines. This withdrawal of ovarian sex steroids produces loss of the endometrium and **menstruation** occurs.

If the ovum is **fertilized**, the blastocyst implants into the endometrium about 7 days after ovulation. The trophoblast soon starts secreting HCG (human chorionic gonadotrophin) which maintains the steroidogenesis by the corpus luteum. HCG is **non-pituitary gonadotrophin** which appears in the woman's urine within a week after pregnancy–a fact that is the basis for several **pregnancy tests**.

Gonadotrophins in the Male

In the male spermatogenesis is mainly controlled by FSH and steroidogenesis by LH, named as the **interstitial-cell-stimulating hormone** (ICSH). The sites of sperm production are the seminiferous tubules, and the testicular interstitial cells of Leydig are the major site for testosterone synthesis and secretion.

Before puberty the seminiferous tubules are lined by diploid **spermatogonia**. The FSH **stimulates** the growth of the seminiferous tubules and induces the Sertoli cells to secrete an androgen-binding protein which maintains a high concentration of testosterone in the lumen of the tubule. FSH stimulates cell division and the number of spermatogonia and spermatocytes is increased. The ICSH promotes the synthesis and secretion of testosterone by the Leydig cells. FSH and testosterone are responsible for **meiosis**. Later through a series of steps the spermatozoa are formed and pass to the **epididymis** where final maturation takes place. The duration of spermatogenesis and sperm transport into the ejaculate in man ranges between 12 to 15 weeks. **Gametogenesis in the male is a continuous process in contrast to a cyclic process in the female.**

Therapeutic Uses of Gonadotrophins

1. **Female infertility.** Replacement therapy with HMG (FSH-like activity), followed by HCG (LH-like activity) may lead to ovulation and pregnancy, if the ovaries are responsive.

2. **Male infertility.** Exogenous gonadotrophins are of little value in the treatment of male infertility. **For cryptorchidism** (undescended testes) HCG is the preferred treatment, as it apparently acts like ICSH, and produces testosterone which brings about the descent of the testes.

3. HCG has been tried in cases of **metropathia haemorrhagica, habitual abortion**, and **secondary amenorrhoea**.

Toxicity. Serious side effects of gonadotrophin therapy may occur in women, such as the **hyperstimulation syndrome**. This occurs after ovulation due to an exaggerated oestrogen response, characterized by abdominal pain, nausea, distention, ovarian enlargement, ascities, hydrothorax and paralytic ileus. Additional complications can be a febrile response, multiple pregnancy, ovarian rupture with haemoperitoneum.

Preparations and Dosage

1. **Human menopausal gonadotrophin injection** (*Pregonal*). HMG is extracted from the urine of postmenopausal women, and used for its FSH activity. A sterile solution is prepared immediately before use containing 75 IU FSH and 75 IU LH in 1 ml of normal saline. One injection of HMG is given IM daily for 9 to 12 days, and is followed one day after the last injection by an injection of HCG, which has a luteinizing action leading to ovulation and secretion of progesterone from the corpus luteum.

2. **Human chorionic gonadotrophin injection** (Pregnyl). HCG is extracted from the urine of pregnant women, and used for its LH activity. The powder contains not less than 1500 IU LH per mg. The solution is prepared freshly and injected in a dose of 500 to 5000 IU IM according to the indication and regimen chosen.

3. **Serum gonadotrophin injection** (*Gestyl*). PMSG is extracted from the serum of pregnant mares, and used for its FSH activity. The powder contains not less than 100 IU per mg. It has the same use as HMG.

Prolactin

Prolactin is a trophic hormone from the anterior pituitary which in humans acts mainly on the mammary glands.

It has a molecular weight of about 25,000, and has some chemical similarities with the growth hormone (GH).

Prolactin acts upon the oestrogen and progesterone primed mammary gland and initiates milk production (lactogenic action). Oxytocin from the posterior pituitary is responsible for the "let down" or the flow of milk. Prolactin is not ordinarily produced by nonpregnant women because the hypothalamus secretes a prolactin release-inhibiting hormone (PIH). During pregnancy there is a reduction in this hypothalamic inhibition, and prolactin reaches peak plasma levels at the time of the baby's birth. The infant's suckling of the mother's breast stimulates further secretion of prolactin and oxytocin from the posterior pituitary, and the latter is responsible for the "let down" of milk. It has no known physiological role in males. In humans prolactin has no established therapeutic or diagnostic use.

The release of prolactin is **stimulated** by methyldopa, phenothiazines, haloperidol and reserpine possibly by inhibiting the release of PIH from the hypothalamus. These agents sometimes may even cause milk secretion (galactorrhoea) in nonpregnant and nonlactating women. On the other hand prolactin release may be **inhibited** by dopaminergic agents like bromocriptine.

The semisynthetic ergot alkaloid **bromocriptine** (2-bromo-alpha-ergocryptine) has a specific dopamine receptor–agonist action. It lowers prolactin release by activating dopamine receptors on the pituitary cells, and functions as an analogue of the prolactin-release inhibiting hormone (PIH). Bromocriptine is being used for **galactorrhoea, suppression of puerperal lactation, hyperprolactinaemia, hypogonadism** and **restoring fertility in women**. It is also being tried in cases of **acromegaly** and **parkinsonism**.

Human Growth Hormone (Somatotrophin, STH, GH, HGH)

The *growth hormone* from the anterior pituitary promotes the growth of all body tissues. Its secretion is regulated by two hypothalamic hormones: somatotrophin releasing hormone (SRH), and somatotrophin inhibiting hormone (SIH, somatostatin).

The deficiency of STH leads to **hypopituitary dwarfism**. On the other hand hyperfunction leads to **acromegaly, gigantism** and other forms of **hyperpituitarism**, which is treated by irradiation or surgical excision of the pituitary gland tumours.

The STH stimulates cartilage growth (chondrogenesis) and therefore promotes the growth of the skeletal system. Possibly STH acts indirectly in promoting growth through **somatomedin**, which is formed in the liver and kidney. It exerts many metabolic effects. It has a **protein anabolic action**. It interferes with the metabolism of intracellular glucose and has a **diabetogenic action**, i.e., an anti-insulin action. Many drugs can influence the plasma levels of STH, namely oestrogens, insulin, vasopressin, noradrenaline, dopamine and beta-adrenoceptor blockers raise STH levels; while glucocorticoids, chlorpromazine and alpha-adrenoceptor blockers lower STH levels.

Human growth hormone is a polypeptide (Mol. Wt. 21,500) containing 188 amino acids. The growth hormone is species specific, and only that of human origin is active in man. It can be measured by radioimmunoassay and has been used in the diagnosis of gigantism, acromegaly, hypopituitarism and growth retardation syndromes.

Therapeutic uses. Human growth hormone (HGH) is used in the management of growth disorders, particularly *dwarfism*. HGH therapy may be useful in certain phases of *renal failure, bone marrow hypoplasia, juvenile spontaneous hypoglycaemia*, and *to antagonize catabolism in response to burns or severe trauma*, as the anabolic action of HGH may be helpful.

Somatostatin is being tried in the treatment of *diabetes mellitus*, and its use in conditions marked with excessive growth is under evaluation.

Toxicity. HGH can precipitate diabetes and severe ketoacidosis develops in diabetic patients even after a single dose. Antibodies to HGH may develop in some patients.

Posterior Pituitary Hormones

The posterior pituitary (neurohypophysis) stores and secretes two neurosecretions made by certain nerve cells of the hypothalamus: the **antidiuretic hormone** (ADH or vasopressin) and **oxytocin**. ADH is synthesized in the cell bodies of the **supraoptic** and **paraventricular nuclei** of the hypothalamus. Oxytocin is mainly synthesized in the cell bodies of the **paraventricular nucleus**. These hormones are carried to the posterior pituitary by axoplasmic flow *via* the **neurohypophyseal tract**, complexed with a protein named **neurophysin**, and stored in the nerve terminals.

Antidiuretic Hormone (ADH, vasopressin)

The ADH is a polypeptide containing 8 amino acids. In mammals arginine vasopressin is more prevalent than lysine vasopressin. ADH modulates the tubular reabsorption of water. It is secreted from the nerve terminals in response to a decrease in plasma volume, increased osmolarity of blood, stress, coitus, and drugs like nicotine, barbiturates and morphine. The **osmoreceptors** in the hypothalamic nuclei, which are sensitive to the osmolarity of blood, regulate the release of ADH into the blood. When osmolarity is increased (dehydration), ADH secretion is increased, and conversely reduction in osmolarity (overhydration) inhibits the release of ADH. There is evidence that certain "**volume receptors**" exist in the left atrium and pulmonary veins, which influence the activity of the hypothalamo-neurohypophyseal system and maintain the osmotic pressure of blood and body fluids within a narrow homeostatic limit. **Alcohol inhibits the release of ADH.**

The deficiency of ADH is the cause of diabetes insipidus, also designated as neurohypophyseal or neurogenic or **central diabetes insipidus** (ADH-responsive). This is the uncommon variety of the disease. In contrast, **nephrogenic diabetes insipidus** (ADH-resistant) is a rare hereditary disorder, mostly affecting males, and the epithelium of the collecting ducts does not respond to ADH, although the hormone is present in normal amounts. About 25 percent of cases are *idiopathic*.

ADH or **vasopressin** preparations have a brief half-life in blood (in humans less than 30 minutes). It is rapidly metabolized in the liver and the kidney.

Mode of action. The ADH *via* the blood reaches the kidney and attaches itself to the membrane of the distal and collecting tubules. ADH activates the adenylcyclase system and thus involves c-AMP which is known to enhance the permeability of the collecting tubule. In addition, ADH also probably releases hyaluronidase which partially digests the intercellular cementing substance in the collecting duct system leading to an increased water permeability. Thus, both the mechanisms reduce free water clearance *via* the renal tubules. The urine volume decreases and the solute concentration in urine rises.

The oral hypoglycaemic sulphonylurea, **chlorpropamide**, has an antidiuretic action in patients with **central diabetes insipidus**. It probably acts by sensitizing the renal tubule to ADH action.

The **thiazide diuretics** are effective in **nephrogenic diabetes insipidus**, which is ADH or chlorpropamide resistant. The mechanism of this antidiuretic action is unclear. The thiazides may also be used in the central form of the disease, and may even be combined with chlorpropamide with advantage.

Therapeutic Uses

1. **Diabetes insipidus.** ADH or vasopressin is used as a diagnostic agent and for the maintenance therapy of diabetes insipidus. The posterior pituitary extract contains both *vasopressin* and *oxytocin*, and the latter produces some side effects. So the purified forms of ADH, namely **vasopressin tannate**, **lysine vasopressin** or **arginine vasopressin** should be employed.

2. Vasopressin has a **spasmogenic** action, and may be used in the management of **postoperative abdominal distension** and **paralytic ileus**. May be employed as an emergency measure to control bleeding from **oesophageal varices** and massive haemorrhage in the upper gastrointestinal tract. Vasopressin injection can also be infused intravenously to control continued gastrointestinal bleeding in cases of **bleeding peptic ulcers** and **cirrhotic patients**.

Toxicity. The antidiuretic effect of vasopressin may lead to **water retention** and **hyponatraemia (water intoxication)**. Large doses of vasopressin may give rise to pallor, nausea, cramps and desire to defecate. In women it may cause **uterine cramps of a menstrual character, and menorrhagia**. Vasopressin causes coronary constriction, may precipitate **angina pectoris, precipitate cardiac arrhythmias** and **myocardial infarction. Hence it is contraindicated in coronary artery disease**. Allergic reactions may occur.

PREPARATIONS

1. **Posterior pituitary powder.** It is extracted from posterior pituitary of cattle and swine. The dose is 5 to 40 mg administered topically (intranasal) as a snuff. The dosage has to be individualized.

2. **Posterior pituitary injection** (*Pituitrin*). This preparation is *obsolete*.

3. **Vasopressin Injection** (*Pitressin*). Dose 5 to 10 units SC or IM three or four times daily. Duration of action is 4 to 6 hours.

4. **Vasopressin tannate injection** (*Pitressin tannate in oil*). It is a long-acting preparation. Dose: 2.5 to 5 units every 1 to 3 days.

5. **Lysine vasopressin** (*Lypressin, Diapid*). It is synthetic, and differs from human ADH in that arginine is substituted by lysine in the molecule. Administered intranasally as a spray and each spray contains 2 units of activity. The dose has to be titrated according to the need.

6. **Desamino Arginine Vasopressin** (*Desmopressin, DDAVP*). It is a synthetic analogue of natural ADH. The usual dose is 2.5 to 15 mcg intranasally twice daily.

OXYTOCIN

Oxytocin is a polypeptide containing 8 amino acids, and differs slightly from vasopressin in its structure. This similarity is responsible for the overlapping of their biological activities when used in supraphysiologic doses.

Actions: The physiologic role of oxytocin is to stimulate the contractions of the uterine smooth muscle and the mammary gland. The **ductile system** of the mammary gland contracts to squeeze the milk from the alveoli of the lactating breast into the sinusoids. Many hormones, namely oestrogen, progesterone and prolactin are responsible for the production of milk by the mammary gland, but **milk ejection requires oxytocin**. It contracts the myoepithelium of the mammary glands and forces the milk into the large ducts. Oxytocin contracts the smooth muscle of the nipple and causes a flow of milk (let down). Oxytocin does not have any galactopoietic properties. Suckling by the infant releases oxytocin which is responsible for **milk ejection**, and in addition **facilitates the contraction of the uterus, prevents postpartum haemorrhage** and **hastens restoration of the uterus to its pregravid state**. The increasing sensitization of the uterus to oxytocin effect with advancing pregnancy is dependent on the relative levels of oestrogen and progesterone. **The sensitivity is increased by oestrogens and decreased by progesterone.** When oxytocin is given by a slow IV infusion it produces a rapid increase in the tone and motility of the human uterus at term. The non-pregnant uterus is not as sensitive to oxytocin as the pregnant uterus. Oxytocin is ineffective orally as it is degraded by proteolytic enzymes. Regarding the mode of action, oxytocin causes a release of c-AMP, but whether this plays a role in its action is not established.

Therapeutic Uses

1. **Induction of labour at term.** It may be given by injection or infusion at the beginning of the *third stage* of labour.

2. Oxytocin may be used to **promote milk ejection** in lactating mothers where milk let-down is poor.

3. As a adjunct in controlling postpartum haemorrhage.

4. Management of **uterine inertia** and **missed abortion**.

5. To cause **uterine contraction after cesarean section**.

Contraindications to the use of oxytocin for induction of labour are: major *cephalopelvic disproportion; during first* and *second stage of labour; foetal distress; malpresentation; breech presentation; uterine scar from previous cesarean section; central placenta praevia; hysterotomy* and *unengaged head*.

Toxicity. Excessive amounts of oxytocin may lead to a tetanic spasm of the uterus, foetal distress and even **rupture of the uterus and cervix**. It may produce hypotension and tachycardia. Anaphylactoid and *allergic reactions* may occur in the mother. The *foetus may suffer cardiac arrhythmias*.

Preparations And Dosage

All commercial preparations now available are *synthetic*.

1. **Oxytocin injection** (*Pitocin, Syntocinon*). It contains 10 units (10,000 milliunits) per ml. It is the drug of choice for induction of labour. A suitable concentration is 10 milliunits per ml (10 units added to 1 litre of 5% dextrose). The infusion rate is 0.5 ml (5 milliunits) per minute. For control of postpartum haemorrhage 2–5 units are given SC, IM or by slow IV injection. Oxytocin is available as a nasal spray containing 40 units per ml.

2. **Oxytocin citrate** (*Pitocin citrate*). Available as buccal tablets, each containing 200 units.

The posterior pituitary elaborates two important hormones—oxytocin and vasopressin. Both of them are octapeptides and have marked chemical similarity (oxytocin contains leucine and isoleucine instead of phenylalanine and arginine; the other six amino acids are common). However, they have certain marked differences in their action. **Oxytocin differs from vasopressin in the following aspects**:

1. It has no effect on water diuresis.

2. It is a strong stimulant of the gravid uterus at term and postpartum.

3. It produces milk let-down during the postpartum period.

4. It has little effect on the smooth muscles of the intestines and coronary arteries.

5. It does not produce vasoconstriction, and may even lead to peripheral vasodilatation and fall of blood pressure.

Clinically oxytocin is the drug of choice for the **induction of labour at term**, and vasopressin is the drug of choice for the management of **central diabetes insipidus**.

7.2 THYROID HORMONES AND ANTITHYROID DRUGS

The main function of the thyroid gland is to synthesize, store and secrete **thyroxine** (T_4) and **triiodothyronine** (T_3), under the control of **thyrotrophic hormone** (TSH) from the anterior pituitary. These hormones are essential for normal energy metabolism, body growth and mental development. It also secretes the hypocalcaemic hormone **calcitonin (Chap. 7.3)**.

THYROID HORMONES

BIOSYNTHESIS, RELEASE AND TRANSPORT

The following steps are involved:

1. **Uptake of iodide** (iodide trapping).
2. **Oxidation of iodide** to free iodine and **iodination of tyrosine.**
3. Formation of thyroxine and triodothyronine by **coupling of iodotyrosines.**
4. **Proteolysis of thyroglobulin** and release of thyroxine and triodothyronine into the blood.

The biosynthesis of thyroid hormones is carried out in the thyroid follicular cells by an iodination and a condensation reaction involving tyrosine. The dietary iodide (I^-) is readily absorbed from the upper gastrointestinal tract, and actively concentrated by the "iodide pump" into the follicular cells. The activity of the iodide pump is controlled by TSH. Inside the cell, iodide is oxidized to the more reactive elemental iodine (I_2) by a peroxidase enzyme. This iodine then is incorporated into tyrosine amino acid groups (tyrosyl groups). This leads to the formation of **monoidotyrosine** (MIT) and **diiodotyrosine** (DIT). Further, it is generally agreed that the synthesis of triiodothyronine (T_3) is by a coupling reaction between a molecule of MIT and a molecule of DIT. **Thyroxine** or **tetraiodothyronine** (T_4) is formed by the condensation of two molecules of DIT. The **thyroglobulin** with T_3 and T_4 attached to it by peptide linkage, is present in high concentrations within the colloid substance of the follicular cells. Thus thyroglobulin stores T_3 and T_4 in the gland. The release of T_3 and T_4 from thyroglobulin is by a process of proteolysis, which is under the control of TSH. These two hormones are released into the blood by diffusion **(Fig. 7.2.1)**.

In the blood the two hormones (thyroxine 80%; triiodothyronine 20%) are transported mostly bound to plasma proteins. T_4 is mainly bound to thyroxine-binding globulin (TBG), and T_3 is mainly bound to thyroxine-blinding prealbumin (TBPA). These proteins carry the two hormones to the body cells, where they deliver them in their free forms. **It is generally agreed that in the body cells thyroxine is converted (deiodinated) to triiodothyronine, which is the active form of the hormone.**

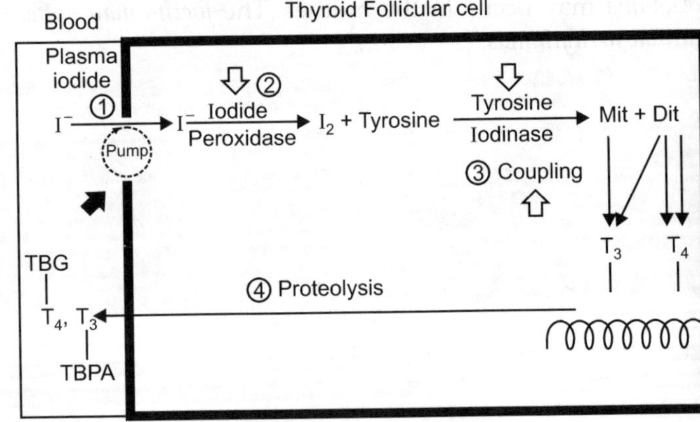

Fig. 7.2.1: Biosynthesis, release and transport of thyroxine and triiodothyronine. Steps: (1) Iodide trapping; (2) Oxidation of iodide; (3) coupling of iodotyrosines; (4) proteolysis of throglobulin (Abbreviations: MIT = monoiodotyrosine; DIT = diiodotyrosine; T_3 = triiodothyronine; T_4 = thyroxine; TBG = thyroxine-binding globulin; TBPA = thyroxine-binding prealbumin).

Sites of action of antithyroid drugs:

⇧ T_4 synthesis inhbitors (Propylthiouracil, Methimazole).

⬆ ionic/pump inhibitors (Thiocynates, Perchlorates).

Metabolism and Excretion

Only the free forms of the hormones (T_4 0.05% and T_3 0.5%) are active; with their half-lives as 7 and 2 days respectively. Many tissues can metabolize T_4 and T_3, however the important organs are the liver and the kidney. The products of catabolism include **tetraiodothyroacetic acid** (TETRAC) and **triiodothyroacetic acid** (TRIAC). These products are conjugated with glucuronides, and deiodinated. The iodine so liberated is retained and reused in the body. The conjugates are excreted via the bile in the stools. In man about 20 to 40 percent of thyroxine is excreted in faeces.

Control of Release

The plasma levels of thyrotrophin (TSH) control the rates of synthesis and release of T_4 and T_3. The plasma concentrations of the active (free) hormones in turn control the rate of TSH secretion from the anterior pituitary–increase in active T_3 and T_4 inhibits, and decrease stimulates the release of TSH **(Fig. 7.2.2)**. This **negative feedback mechanism** ensures physiological hormone levels within a narrow limit. The release of TSH is under the control of the hypothalamic **thyrotrophin releasing hormone** (TRH). There is evidence that the negative feedback by T_4 and T_3 occurs at two levels: the anterior pituitary, and the hypothalamus. **TSH stimulates the iodide pump and thyroglobulin synthesis, and increases the rate of proteolysis of thyroglobulin**. Circulating iodide levels also inversely regulate the release of TSH. Prolonged TSH stimulation to the thyroid leads to an increased vascularity and hypertrophy of the gland (goitre). In Graves' disease (toxic goitre) it has been suggested that a **long-acting thyroid stimulator** (LATS) is present in the body. LATS is a gamma globulin and its mode of action is not understood. It is unrelated to thyrotrophin.

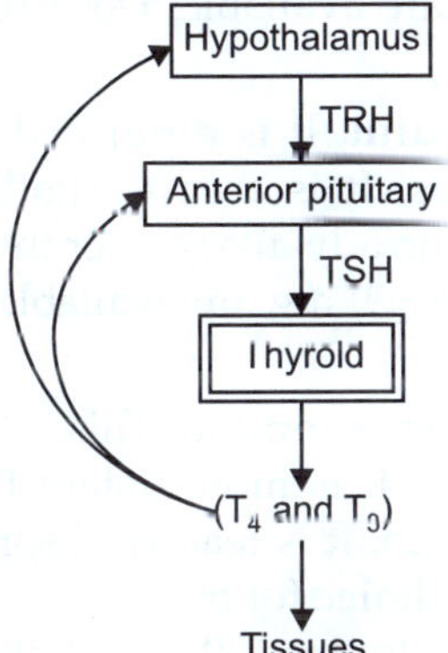

Fig. 7.2.2.: Control of the thyroid hormone production.

TRH = thyrotrophin-releasing hormone;

TSH = thyroid stimulating hormone;

T_4 = thyroxine;

T_3 = triiodothyronine.

Actions

Both thyroxine and triiodothyronine produce a **calorigenic action**, and raise the basal metabolic rate (BMR). This is manifested by an increase in oxygen consumption by the tissue, excessive protein breakdown, and loss of body weight. Thyroid secretions are increased in cold environment.

Thyroid hormones have a profound influence on carbohydrate metabolism. **They enhance the glycogenolytic action of adrenaline, possibly by increasing the sensitivity of the adenyl cyclase-cyclic AMP system**. They potentiate the effects of insulin by promoting insulin-induced glycogen synthesis, and an increased glucose uptake in muscle and adipose tissue. They also directly stimulate the rate of intestinal glucose absorption.

Thyroid hormones stimulate the synthesis and mobilization of lipids in the body on one hand. However, on the other hand the degradation of lipids is increased to a much greater extent, leading to a fall in the circulating plasma lipids (triglycerides, cholesterol, phospholipids).

Thyroid hormones have a variety of effects on the cardiovascular system. **They synergize the effect of catecholamines by increasing the sensitivity of the beta-receptors**. The pulse rate, pulse pressure and the cardiac output are increased. The thyroid hormones also have a **diuretic effect**.

Thyroid hormones are **essential for the normal development of the central nervous system**. In hypothyroidism there may be poor mentation, memory and initiative. They regulate haemopoiesis. A deficiency may cause anaemia due to suppression of bone marrow function. They mobilize calcium from the bone, and simultaneously facilitate calcium clearance through the kidneys. Hence in contrast to parathormone, there is no hypercalcaemia.

The actions of thyroid hormones may be **summarized** as under:

(*i*) Increased calorigenesis, and raised BMR.

(*ii*) Increased carbohydrate and protein metabolism.

(*iii*) Increased cholesterol turnover (hypolipidaemic effect).

(*iv*) Increased heart rate, contractility and cardiac output.

(*v*) Increased calcium mobilization from bone.

(*vi*) Synergism with the action of catecholamines on the cardiovascular system, and carbohydrate metabolism.

(*vii*) Regulation of water and electrolyte balance.

(*viii*) Normal development of the nervous system.

(*ix*) Essential for normal body growth, development and reproduction.

Mode of Action

High-affinity binding sites (receptors) for T_3 and T_4 in the **nucleus, mitochondria,** and **plasma membrane** of cells, suggest multiple sites of action. The affinity of these receptors for T_4 is about 10 times lower than that for T_3. Thyroid hormones bind to receptors on cell surfaces increasing the uptake of glucose and amino acids. They also enter the cells to interact with receptors on mitochondria and chromatin material, resulting in **increased synthesis of RNA,** leading to accelerated protein synthesis, and enhanced enzymatic and cellular activity. Thyroid hormones stimulate Na^+, K^+ -ATPase directly, and thereby increase ATP turnover and oxygen consumption. This is responsible for the **calorigenic action** of thyroid hormones.

Thyroid Function Tests

(*i*) **Protein-bound iodine.** It is a measure of organically bound iodine in blood (normal 4–8 mcg/dl; myxoedema 2 mcg/dl; thyrotoxicosis 10–12 mcg/dl).

(*ii*) **Serum T_4.** It is measured by **radioimmunoassay** (normal 5–12 mcg/dl). Serum T3 assays can also be done (normal 80-180 ng/dl).

(*iii*) **Serum TBG.** It is measured by radioimmunoassay or immunoelectrophoresis, and the ratio of T4 to TBG is used as an index of free hormone activity.

(*iv*) **Free thyroxine index and effective thyroxine ratio.** These are calculated from the serum T_4 and serum TBG levels. There is a good correlation between these values and free T_4 levels.

(*v*) **Scintillography.** The radioiodine uptake by the gland is recorded photographically and scanned.

(*vi*) **T_3 Suppression test.** It is based on the premise that whereas normally the drive to thyroid function is exclusively from TSH, in Graves' disease (hyperthyroidism) the drive is from another substance, probably **long-acting thyroid stimulator** (LATS). In the standard test, the pretreatment radioactive iodine uptake (RAIU) is determined. Then triiodothyronine (as Cytomel) 25 mcg tid, is given for 7 to 10 days. On the last day a repeat RAIU is performed. In a normal person the RAIU will be suppressed by 50 percent or less of the original value. **Whereas in Graves' disease there is no suppression as the thyroid is functioning autonomously**.

The determination of **basal metabolic rate** (BMR) and the **serum cholesterol** estimation are poor indicators of thyroid function.

Therapeutic Uses

1. **Thyroid deficiency states.** Thyroid hormones are mainly used in the treatment of **myxoedema** in adults, and **cretinism** and **juvenile myxoedema** in children.
2. **Hypothyroidism secondary to anterior pituitary destruction (Simmonds' disease).** Used in conjunction with corticosteroids, because thyroid hormones increase the degradation of adrenocorticosteroids, and may precipitate acute adrenal insufficiency.
3. **Chronic thyroiditis (Hashimoto's disease), nontoxic and nodular goitre.**
4. **Hyperlipidaemia** associated with hypothyroidism.
5. Thyroid hormones may be given a trial in various other disorders including **delayed union of fractures, hypogonadia, menopausal arthralgia, infertility, menstrual disorders, nephrotic syndrome, refractory chronic constipation,** and **refractory eczema.**

Toxicity

The toxicity of thyroid preparations resembles the manifestations of hyperthyroidism, like *hyperirritability, insomnia, nervousness, tachycardia, palpitation, arrhythmias, angina pectoris, polyphagia* and *emaciation*. They may also lead to hypertension and gastrointestinal disturbances. Thyroidal preparations must be used with caution in patients with hypertension and coronary artery disease.

Preparations

The following preparations are available commercially:

(*i*) **Thyroid USP.** It is a dried thyroid extract obtained from defatted thyroid glands of cows and pigs. It is standardized by chemical means, and should contain 0.17 percent to 0.23 percent of iodine by weight in organic combination with thyroid tissue. Various tablet strengths from 15 to 30 mg are available. Dose 30 to 250 mg daily orally.

(*ii*) **Thyroglobulin**. It is a purified extract of frozen hog thyroid glands. It is assayed both chemically and biologically. It has no advantage over thyroid USP. Tablets ranging from 15 to 300 mg are available. Average dose is 150 mg.

(*iii*) **Levothyroxine sodium**. This is the sodium salt of synthetic thyroxine. It is more potent than both thyroid USP or thyroglobulin. It is readily absorbed from the gut and is the **drug of choice** for management of hypothyroid disorders. Average dose is 150 mcg daily. Range 50 to 300 mcg daily.

(*iv*) **Liothyronine sodium**. It is the sodium salt of synthetic triiodothyronine (T_3). It has a rapid onset of action, and a short duration of action. It is an expensive preparation and not suitable for routine use. However, it is the drug of choice in an emergency situation like myxoedema coma. *Dose.* 5 to 100 mcg daily orally. Injectable preparation for intravenous use is also available (20 mcg ampoules).

(*v*) **Liotrix.** It is a 4 : 1 mixture of the synthetic sodium salt of T_4 and T_3 (levothyroxine sodium and liothyronine sodium). It is orally effective. However, it offers no advantage over thyroid USP or thyroglobulin.

On a quantitative clinical response basis thyroid USP 60 mg = Thyroglobulin 60 mg = Levothyroxine 0.1 mg = Liothyronine 25 mcg = Liotrix (levothyroxine 0.05 mg + liothyronine 0.0125 mg).

Thyrotrophin (TSH) and Thyrotrophin-releasing Hormone (TRH)

Thyrotrophin or TSH is an anterior pituitary hormone that stimulates production of thyroid hormones. It is used in tests of thyroid function. **Thyrotrophin-releasing hormone** or TRH is a hypothalamic hormone. TRH may be useful as a diagnostic agent to assess the pituitary reserve, and to *differentiate between hypothalamic hypothyroidism* and *pituitary hypothyroidism*.

Iodine and Thyroid Function

A minute amount of iodine intake (100 mcg daily) is necessary for the normal synthesis of the thyroid hormones. Except in "goitre belts" (geographical regions in which iodine-deficiency goitre is prevalent due to the washing out of iodides from the soil) man receives a sufficient supply of iodine from **vegetables** and **animal muscle meat**. Specially **sea fish** is a rich source of iodine. If there is a lack of ingested iodine, normal amounts of thyroid hormones cannot be formed, and this leads to the release of excess of thyrotrophin (TSH), which in its turn induces a thyroid follicular proliferation and thyroid hypertrophy. This cycle of events was based on extensive work done by Marine. A prolonged repetition of this **Marine cycle** would lead to large goitres in the people living along the goitre belts. In the early stages of this disease simple iodine therapy may be helpful, but in later stages a short-course of *thyroid* USP or *thyroglobulin* has to be administered in 60 mg daily doses to reduce the size of the gland. Later, iodine intake in diet should be maintained to avoid chronic iodine lack.

Prophylaxis of Iodine-deficiency Goitre

An average iodine intake of 0.2 to 1.0 mg per day substantially reduces the incidence of goitre in goitre belts. Iodine intake may be increased by the administration of:

(*i*) **Lugol's iodine:** It contains 5 percent iodine and 10 percent potassium iodide in water. Lugol's iodine (0.2 to 0.5 ml orally daily) is administered.

(*ii*) **Iodized table salt** may be used in goitre regions.

Toxicity of Iodine

Severe **hypersensitivity reactions** like angioedema, swelling of the larynx and multiple cutaneous haemorrhages may occur. On continued administration chronic iodine poisoning or "iodism" may set in. It is marked by irritative phenomena of the mucous membranes and skin like **coryza, conjunctivitis, laryngitis, bronchitis, urticaria** and **vesication**. There may be symptoms of *gastric irritation* and *diarrhoea. Brassy taste, anorexia* and *fever* may occur. On prolonged iodine administration latent inflammatory processes like chronic fibrocaseous tuberculosis and gummatous lesions may flare up.

Antithyroid Drugs

In **hyperthyroidism** there is an excessive secretion and hyperactivity of the thyroid hormones. It occurs in two major forms: (*i*) **Diffuse toxic goitre** (Graves' disease, Exophthalmic goitre) characterized by thyrotoxicosis and ophthalmopathy; and (*ii*) **Toxic nodular goitre** (Pulmmer's disease) which occurs in older patients of non-toxic goitre, and in these ophthalmopathy is not marked. The manifestations of hyperthyroid states are due to a generalized increase in the basal metabolic rate, neuromuscular activity and activity of the sympathetic nervous system. Thus, there are symptoms of **fatigue, irritability, agitation, hyperkinetic behaviour, voracious appetite, loss of weight, excessive sweating, tremors, tachycardia, palpitation** and **hypertension**. There may be **exophthalmos** and thyroid enlargement. Existing angina pectoris may be exacerbated.

Classification

The following classification of antithyroid drugs is based on their *mode of action*:

1. **Inhibitors of thyroxine synthesis**
   Propylthiouracil
   Methylthiouracil
   Methimazole
   Carbimazole
2. **Drugs that destroy thyroid tissue**
   Radioactive iodine (I^{131})
3. **Antiadrenergic drugs**
   Propranolol
   Guanethidine
4. **Drugs with uncertain mode of action**
   Potassium iodide
   Sodium iodide
   Lugol's iodine (Strong Iodine Solution)

Inhibitors of Thyroxine Synthesis

Thioamides

Propylthiouracil, a thioamide, is the prototype in the group, and has completely replaced the parent compound thiouracil. It **inhibits the synthesis of the thyroid hormones** in usual doses, but does not inactivate or interfere with the action of the already formed and stored thyroxine in the gland. Thus its effect does not appear till the already available hormone supply is exhausted. This *time lag* in its antithyroid effect may range from several days to weeks. By the use of these antithyroid drugs when thyroxine synthesis is diminished, the secretion of TSH is increased. This leads to thyroid hyperplasia and increased vascularity, manifested as an **enlargement of the gland**. For this reason they are also labelled as **goitrogens**. **Methylthiouracil** is equal in potency to propylthiouracil, but is less desirable as allergic manifestations are more frequently observed with its use. **Methimazole**, which is also chemically related to propylthiouracil has similar actions and uses. It is about 10 times more potent than propylthiouracil, but has no distinct advantage over it. **Carbimazole** is as effective as propylthiouracil.

Mode of Action

These antithyroid drugs (thioamides) inhibit the formation of thyroxine mainly by interfering with: (*i*) the **iodination** of tyrosine; and (*ii*) the **coupling** and **condensation** of the iodotyrosines. They may also block the oxidation of iodides. They inhibit the cytochrome/cytochrome oxidase and peroxidase enzyme systems.

Therapeutic Uses

1. **Hyperthyroidism** (Graves' disease). Relief is marked by a fall in BMR, increase in body weight, and reversion of arrhythmias if present. There is little effect on associated exophthalmos in Graves' disease.

2. Preparation of the thyrotoxic patient for surgical treatment.

Contraindications

As the thioamides cross the placenta, they can cause **foetal goitre**. Their use should be minimized in pregnancy. They should not be used in lactating mothers as they are concentrated in milk.

Toxicity

They have a **goitrogenic action** as already mentioned. Allergic reactions (urticaria, purpuric rashes) may occur. A **hypothyroid state** may be induced. Severe **leucopenia** and **agranulocytosis** have been reported. The incidence of agranulocytosis with propylthiouracil and **methimazole** is 0.44 percent and 0.12 percent of cases respectively. **Drug fever, hepatitis** and **nephritis** may occur rarely. Carbimazole is claimed to produce fewer adverse effects than methiamazole.

Dosage and Preparations

Depending on the severity of thyrotoxicosis the following working oral dosage schedules are suggested:

Propylthiouracil 75–100 mg every 8 hourly.
Methylthiouracil 50 mg every 6 hourly.
Methimazole 5–10 mg every 8 hourly.
Carbimazole 5–10 mg every 8 hourly.

Many *sulphonamides* and related compounds possess antithyroid activity.

Drugs that Destroy Thyroid Tissue

Radioactive Iodine (I^{131})

Several radioactive isotopes of iodine are available, but radioiodine I^{131} is most used. It has a half-life of 8.04 days, and emits **beta** and **gamma** radiations. I^{131} accumulates in the thyroid gland as does nonradioactive iodine. The destructive action of I^{131} on the thyroid gland is induced by beta radiations. The gamma radiations are only useful for estimating the quantity of radioactive material in the gland by placing the counting equipment in front of the neck. Thus, on I^{131} administration there is thyroid tissue damage as a result of beta radiation, followed by fibrosis. The objective of therapy is to leave the patient with enough thyroid tissue to provide a normal metabolic rate.

Mode of Action

The biological activity of I^{131} is attributed to **ionizing beta radiations**, which destroy the functional and regenerative capacity of the thyroid cells within few weeks of administration. **The follicular cells are necrosed, the colloid disappears, followed by fibrosis.**

Therapeutic Uses

1. Selected cases of **hyperthyroidism**. The treatment is effective and recurrence rate after successful I^{131} therapy is very low.
2. **Thyroid carcinoma**. Mainly follicular carcinomas continue to accumulate iodine, and therapy with large doses may prolong life specially in younger patients. Also given in *thyroid carcinomas with multiple metastases*.
3. **Diagnostic uses.** Radioiodine uptake studies are useful in the diagnosis of thyroid disorder. It may also be used for **localization of metastatic deposits** of thyroid cancer in the lungs and bones.
4. Occasionally I^{131} has been employed in the treatment of **intractable angina pectoris**.

The following are guidelines for selection of patients of thyrotoxicosis for radioiodine therapy: (*i*) **uncomplicated hyperthyroidism** over the age of 40 years; (*ii*) **recurrent or persistent hyperthyroidism** after subtotal thyroidectomy; (*iii*) **failure of response to antithyroid drugs**; (*iv*) presence of **severe exophthalmos**; and (*v*) **refusal to surgery**. In 76 percent of properly selected cases remission occurs with 1 to 2 doses of I^{131}.

CONTRAINDICATIONS

I^{131} is contraindicated during **pregnancy** and **lactation**, in **large toxic nodular goitres**, and in **severe thyrotoxic cardiovascular disease**.

TOXICITY

There may be *mild pain and tenderness in the thyroid area, acute swelling of the thyroid gland, radiation thyroiditis, exacerbation of the thyrotoxicosis*, and *bone marrow depression*. Overdosing may lead to *hypothyroidism*. Late adverse reactions occurring after years of treatment are *thyroid carcinoma, leukaemias* and *chromosomal abnormalities*.

PREPARATION AND DOSAGE

Sodium Iodide I^{131} (Iodotope) is available as a solution or in capsules containing I^{131}, suitable for *oral* or *intravenous* administration.

The dose is calculated on the *percentage of radioiodine uptake* by the thyroid, *estimated thyroid weight*, and a *desired radiation of 80 microcuries per gram of thyroid tissue for the first 50 g, and 40 microcuries of radiation per gram for the additional thyroid tissue*. The usual total dose works out to 4,000 to 10,000 microcuries or 4 to 10 millicuries (1000 microcuries = 1 millicurie). The total calculated dose may be administered orally as a single dose, or *equally divided into two or more doses given at 6 to 8* week intervals.

ANTIADRENERGIC DRUGS

Propranolol, the beta-blocker, and *guanethidine*, the adrenergic neurone blocking agent, may be used as adjuncts to antithyroid therapy to control the adrenergic mediated symptoms of thyrotoxicosis, like **tachycardia, palpitation** and **hypertension**. They have no effect on the underlying cause of the disease. Propranolol appears to be superior to guanethidine in this respect and also in addition relieves anxiety and tension. Propranolol has found a special use in the management of thyroid crisis. Propranolol reduces the peripheral conversion of T_4 to T_3.

DRUGS WITH UNCERTAIN MODE OF ACTION

Iodide

As mentioned earlier it is used in the treatment of **iodine-deficiency goitre, and this prevents endemic goitre and cretinism**. Paradoxically, if iodide is administered to hyperthyroid patients, there is a reduction in the vascularity and swelling of the gland. The gland shrinks and the symptoms improve. This response reaches its maximum in 10 to 15 days, but on prolonged iodide therapy hyperthyroidism reappears perhaps in a more severe form and **thyroid crisis** may be precipitated. Thus, after sometime the thyroid gland "escapes" the inhibitory effect of iodine and a large amount of thyroid hormone is released in the blood which may be dangerous.

MODE OF ACTION

High iodide content in blood inhibits thyroid hormone release. It antagonizes the ability of both TSH and c-AMP to stimulate the proteolysis and hormone release. Ultimately the thyroid escapes this action and a thyroid crisis may occur. This is designated as the "**escape phenomenon**".

THERAPEUTIC USES

To prepare hyperthyroid patients for surgery potassium iodide 60 mg thrice daily is given for 14 days before operation. This therapy is combined with the administration of *carbimazole* or *propylthiouracil* to suppress hormone synthesis and thus to avoid a thyrotoxic crisis.

DRUG THERAPY OF THYROTOXIC CRISIS

Thyrotoxic crisis (thyroid storm) is an exacerbation in the intensity of the features of thyrotoxicosis. It is usually precipitated by surgery, and is most likely to occur in patients who have been inadequately prepared pre-operativity. This crisis *has become uncommon with the growing use of beta-adrenoceptor blockers in the pre-operative treatment of thyrotoxic patients*. *Plasmapheresis* is an adjunct of therapy of thyroid crisis. The guidelines for drug therapy are:

1. **Correction of symphathetic overactivity**
   (*i*) *Propranolol* 40 mg 6-hourly orally, 2 mg IV 6-hourly.
2. **Correction of relative adrenal insufficiency by administering hydrocortisone** 200 mg IV.
3. **Blockade of further thyroid hormone synthesis and release**
   (*i*) *Sodium iodide* 1–2 g by slow IV infusion.
   (*ii*) *Oral antithyroid drugs*. Neomercazole 100 mg stat, and maintenance dose of 15 mg tid for 72 hours.
4. Heart failure may require **digitalization** and **diuretics**.
5. **General measures.** Tepid sponging of the patient for hyperpyrexia, oxygen inhalations; IV glucose infusion for severe dehydration.

To conclude, the mainstay for the pharmacotherapeutic management of hyperthyroidism is on the inhibitors of thyroxine synthesis (propylthiouracil, carbimazole, methimazole) and radioactive iodine. The antiadrenergic agents (propranolol, guanethidine) are used as adjuncts to allay the sympathetic mediated symptoms of thyrotoxicosis. Potassium iodide only controls thyrotoxic symptoms temporarily.

7.3 PARATHYROID HORMONE, CALCITONIN, VITAMIN D AND CALCIUM METABOLISM

Parathormone (PTH)
- **Control of Release**
- **Actions**
- **Mode of Action**
- **Therapeutic Uses**
- **Dose**
- **Toxicity**

Calcitonin (Thyrocalcitonin)
- **Mode of Action**
- **Therapeutic Uses**
- **Dose**
- **Toxicity**

Vitamin D
Etidronate
Calcium Homeostasis
Hypoparathyroidism
Hyperparathyroidism

The total calcium in the body is between 1000 and 1200 g, and 99 percent of it is in the bony skeleton. The normal calcium level in blood is 10 to 10.5 mg/dl. In the blood it exists in two forms: (*i*) **non-diffusible** calcium (50%), which is protein bound; and (*ii*) **diffusible** calcium (50%), a part of which is complexed with phosphate and carbonate (1 mg/dl) and another part is ionized Ca^{++} (3-4 mg/dl).

The main functions of calcium in the body are: (a) ossification of bone and formation of teeth; (b) maintenance of the integrity of the intercellular cement material; (c) selective cell permeability—calcium appears to be involved in the selective absorption of sugars from the intestinal tract; (d) control of excitability of nerve tissue—lack of blood calcium leads to increased excitability of the central nervous system; (e) maintenance of rhythm, tonicity and contractility of the heart; and (f) control of contraction of the skeletal and smooth muscles.

Calcium metabolism in the body is mainly governed by two hormones, **parathormone** from the parathyroids, and **calcitonin** from the parafollicular cells of the thyroid gland. In addition, **vitamin D** and its metabolites regulate plasma calcium levels.

PARATHOROME

The parathyroid hormone, parathormone (PTH) is a large polypeptide (Mol. wt. 9,500) containing 84 amino acids. It is obtained from bovine parathyroid extract. Parathormone is synthesized initially as a component of **pro-parathormone** (Mol. wt. about 12,000), which is present in the gland only in small amounts. A cleavage of this precursor molecule (pro-parathormone) probably occurs just prior to the release of parathormone from the gland. The chief physiologic role of PTH is the maintenance of **calcium homeostasis,** which is an essential requirement for normal body function. Removal of the parathyroid gland results in a progressive hypocalcaemia, tetany, convulsions and death.

CONTROL OF RELEASE

Pararthormone release is regulated by the Ca^{++} ion concentration in the blood. Release of PTH is stimulated by a fall, and inhibited by a rise in the ionized Ca^{++} levels of plasma. Thus, there is an **inverse correlation** between plasma calcium concentration and parathormone concentrations. The **magnesium** ion also appears to be necessary for this negative feedback control. No effective control by the nervous system or the anterior pituitary has been demonstrated.

ACTIONS

The major effects are exerted on the Ca^{++} transport in the (*i*) bone, (*ii*) kidneys, and (*iii*) intestines.

(*i*) **Bone.** PTH leads to **resorption** of the bone, releasing calcium into the blood. By stimulation of adenyl cyclase activity in the bone, PTH promotes osteoclastic activity, and transiently depresses osteoblastic activity. These factors result in an increased absorption of bone matrix and release of calcium from bone, and the plasma calcium ion concentration is raised.

(*ii*) **Kidneys.** PTH inhibits the renal tubular reabsorption of phosphate, possibly due to the activation of renal adenyl cyclase. This results in an increased phosphate clearance and a **phosphaturia.** In addition, PTH decreases calcium clearance. This explains the low incidence of hypercalciuria in hyperparathyroidism.

(*iii*) **Intestines.** PTH has no direct effect on the intestinal calcium transport. It is suggested that in the presence of vitamin D it promotes the absorption of calcium from the intestines.

MODE OF ACTION

The precise mechanism of PTH action is incompletely understood. Parathormone stimulates adenyl cyclase activity in the bone and kidney cells, leading to an increase in cyclic-AMP formation, which is believed to be an important factor involved in the regulation of the intracellular calcium ion concentration.

THERAPEUTIC USES

Parathyroid injection is only used for the early control of tetany due to **hypoparathyroidism**. Once the tetany has been controlled the treatment is mainly dietetic and administration of vitamin D. PTH has also been used for the diagnosis of **pseudohypoparathyroidism**.

DOSE

Parathyroid injection. 20 to 40 USP units twice daily subcutaneously or intramuscularly, but in emergencies it may be given intravenously. Dose ranges from 40 to 300 units daily.

TOXICITY

Overdosage with PTH causes **hypercalcaemia**, manifested as weakness, vomiting, diarrhoea and lack of muscle tone. **Hypersensitivity reactions** may occur. Prolonged use of PTH can lead to **demineralization of bone**, and **metastatic calcification** in the kidneys (nephrocalcinosis, urolithasis) and in other organs and tissues. The development of antibodies may cause intolerance and resistance.

CALCITONIN (THYROCALCITONIN)

Calcitonin is a small polypeptide (Mol. wt. about 3600), with 32 amino acids, synthesized and secreted by the parafollicular cells (C cells) of the thyroid gland. The main action of calcitonin is to produce **hypocalcaemia** by inhibiting bone resorption, and by promoting the urinary excretion of calcium and phosphate. It has no action on the calcium transport in the intestines. Calcitonin release is regulated by the ionized calcium concentration of blood perfusing the thyroid gland. Hypercalcaemia promotes the release of calcitonin, and *vice versa*. **Glucagon** and **magnesium** also stimulate the release of calcitonin. The calcitonin products available for use are synthetic compounds that resemble the polypeptide hormones **salmon calcitonin** and **human calcitonin**. Salmon calcitonin is considerably more potent in humans than is human calcitonin.

MODE OF ACTION

Calcitonin produces hypocalcaemia possibly by decreasing osteoclastic activity and increasing osteoblastic activity in the bone. Thus it inhibits bone resorption and antagonizes the action of PTH.

THERAPEUTIC USES

The use of calcitonin in **hypercalcaemic states** is limited, due to its short duration of action, and rapid development of resistance as a result of a compensatory increase in the secretion of PTH. **Salmon calcitonin** has a longer half-life and has been used with some success in **Paget's disease** (osteitis deformans) and in **osteoporosis**.

Dose. *Salmon calcitonin* 40 to 160 units daily by subcutaneous, intramuscular, or intravenous injection. *Human calcitonin* is initially given in a dose of 0.5 mg/day, and the dose is adjusted on clinical response.

TOXICITY

Inflammatory reactions may be caused at the site of injection. It may produce mild hypocalcaemia, but does not produce tetany. Circulating antibodies form to salmon caliitonin, and its efficacy declines with continued use.

VITAMIN D

Vitamin D designates a group of related sterols active against rickets **(Chap. 8)**. The effects of vitamin D (cholecalciferol) are mainly due to its more potent hydroxylated metabolites formed in the liver and kidneys. **Dihydrotachysterol** (AT_{10}) is a synthetic compound chemically related to calciferol. Its ability to raise calcium concentration in blood is equal to that of calciferol, but it is much less potent as an antirachitic agent. *Dihydrotachysterol is used to correct hypocalcaemia of hypoparathyroidism and to treat acute, chronic and latent forms of parathyroid tetany*. It has also been employed in cases of vitamin *D-resistant rickets* and *osteomalasia*.

MODE OF ACTION

Vitamin D, and its more active hydroxylated metabolites participate in the regulation of plasma calcium ion concentration by acting on the bone, *kidneys* and the *intestines*.

In the *bone* vitamin D maintains the stores of calcium in the mitochondria, and thus is essential for the PTH-induced bone resorption. In the **kidneys** the vitamin D metabolites increase calcium reabsorption from the proximal tubules. In the **intestines** the vitamin D metabolites promote the absorption of calcium. The PTH action on intestinal calcium transport is indirect, and is dependent on the presence of vitamin D in the gut.

TOXICITY

Hypervitaminosis D is likely to occur if the individual with normal vitamin D sensitivity receives a dose of 150,000 units or more daily for a prolonged period. It is characterized by **generalized decalcification of bones, hypercalcaemia, hyperphosphataemia, hypercalciuria** and **metastatic calcification**.

ETIDRONATE

Etidronate is a nonhormonal substance that reduces the rate of bone turnover. It is related to pyrophosphate, which has a role in bone mineralization. It *adsorbs* onto the surface of *hydroxyapatite crystals*, disrupting the formation, growth, and dissolution of these crystals. The accelerated bone turnover in Paget's disease in slowed down, and bone pain and incidence of factures is reduced.

Etidronate is used in the treatment of moderate to severe **Paget's disease, hypercalcaemia of malignancy,** and for reduction of **heterotrophic bone ossification** due to spinal cord injury or total hip replacement. Its advantages over calcitonin are its lack of antigenicity, lower cost, and oral effectiveness. The *usual dose* is 5 to 10 mg/kg/day for upto 6 months. Retreatment is needed on reactivation of the disease.

Calcium Homeostasis

By means of PTH from the parathyroids, calcitonin from the parafollicular cells of the thyroid, and vitamin D metabolites, the plasma calcium ion concentrations are regulated within the physiological limits. **PTH** raises blood calcium level by increasing bone resorption, increasing calcium reabsorption from the kidneys, and by stimulating the renal conversion of vitamin D to its metabolites. **Calcitonin** lowers blood calcium levels by antagonizing the action of PTH. It inhibits bone resorption. The physiological role of calcitonin in man is debtable. The **vitamin D metabolites** raise plasma calcium concentrations by promoting intestinal calcium absorption, and renal calcium reabsorption. In addition, vitamin D is also essential for the action of PTH on bone. Thus, the action and interaction of the above three agents is responsible for the maintenance of an equilibrium between the plasma calcium ion and the bound/stored calcium ion concentrations.

Hypoparathyroidism

Hypofunction of the parathyroid gland may be due to an accidental extirpation of the gland during thyroid surgery, or due to an interruption of its vascular supply, or due to idiopathic hypoparathyroidism. The *symptoms* are mainly due to hypocalcaemia, and there are fine fibrillary twitchings of the skeletal muscles which may become coarse. The syndrome thus induced is known clinically as **tetany**.

Treatment

The following measures may be employed:

(*i*) **Calcium gluconate.** In acute hypocalcaemia 10 to 30 ml of 10 percent calcium gluconate in 500 to 1000 ml of isotonic saline is administered intravenously. Usually 1 g is administered, and therapy is monitored by determination of plasma calcium levels and the electrocardiogram (ECG).

(*ii*) **Parathyroid injection.** In acute phases 100-200 units IV slowly, followed by 25 to 50 units IM 6 to 12 hourly is administered till the crisis is over. Administration must be stopped within a week.

(*iii*) **Vitamin D**

(a) *Vitamin D_2 (Calciferol or Ergocalciferol) oily Injection. Initially* 400,000 IU IM daily, and a maintenance dose of 100,000 IU IM daily is given.

(b) *Dihydrotachysterol (AT_{10}).* Initially 0.8 to 2.4 mg once daily orally, and for maintenance 200 mcg weekly to 1 mg daily orally, is administered.

(*iv*) *A calcium rich and phosphate poor diet.*

An average case of hypoparathyroidism can be well maintained on vitamin D, high calcium and low phosphate diet. Parathyroid injection is seldom required. Acute phases are managed by IV calcium gluconate administration.

Hyperparathyroidism

Hyperfunction of the parathyroid gland may be due to a diffuse hyperplasia of the glands, adenomas, carcinoma and aberrant production of PTH. *Symptoms* include polyurea, polydipsia, disordered cardiac rhythm, renal calculi and subperiosteal bone resorption, with hypercalcaemia and hypercalciuria.

Treatment

(*i*) **Surgical removal** of the diseased gland.

(*ii*) **Intravenous saline infusion** to correct dehydration.

(*iii*) Intravenous infusion of 0.1 **M solution of dibasic sodium phosphate** to promote calcium excretion.

(*iv*) **Isotonic sodium sulphate and sodium chloride** administered intravenously to induce calciuresis.

(*v*) **Disodium edetate (EDTA).** It chelates calcium, but is too toxic for routine use. In an emergency 50 mg/kg in 500 ml saline may be given intravenously.

(*vi*) **Mithramycin.** It is a cytotoxic agent and reduces serum calcium levels. In an emergency 25 mcg/kg/day may be given IV for 3 to 4 days.

(*vii*) **Calcitonin** 5 to 25 mcg/kg may be of therapeutic value, but experience with this agent is limited.

(*viii*) **Glucocorticosteroids** may be tried. They are claimed to be effective in hypercalcaemia of vitamin D therapy, sarcoidosis and malignancy.

(*ix*) **Haemodialysis** may be of value when all other measures have failed.

Mainly the treatment is operative. *Hypercalcaemic crisis* may be controlled by drugs preoperatively to make safe surgery possible.

7.4 INSULIN AND ORAL HYPOGLYCAEMIC AGENTS

The external secretion of the pancreas is digestive in function, and the endocrine functions are performed by the **islets of Langerhans**. They are small, highly vascularized masses of cells scattered throughout the pancreas, forming only 1 to 3 percent of the entire organ.

The islets of Langerhans contain *four* types of secretory cells:

(*i*) Alpha (A) Cells, secrete *glucagon;*

(*ii*) Beta (B) Cells, secrete *insulin;*

(*iii*) Delta (D) Cells, secrete *somatostatin;* and

(*iv*) PP (F) cells, secrete *pancreatic polypeptide.*

The insulin-secreting beta-cells are the most numerous (upto 70-80% of islet cells). The alpha-cells comprise about 20 percent of islet cells. Whereas, the D-cells and F-cells account for 4 percent, and less than 2 percent of islet cells respectively. The physiologic role of **glucagon** and **insulin** in the regulation of intermediary metabolism is well established, but the exact physiologic role of pancreatic somatostatin remains unclear. The pancreatic polypeptide is believed to assist in digestion in a yet undefined manner.

Diabetes mellitus (DM) is a chronic metabolic disorder, resulting from insulin deficiency, characterized by hyperglycaemia, altered metabolism of carbohydrates, protein and lipids, and an increased risk of vascular complications. The insulin deficiency may be **absolute** or **relative**, and the metabolic abnormalities lead to the classic symptoms of **polyuria** (frequent urination), **polydipsia** (excessive thirst), **polyphagia** (excessive hunger), and fatigue. Long-term complications of DM include gangrene, proliferative retinopathy, myocardial infarction, polyneuropathy, and uraemia. The disordered microcirculation (microangiopathy) underlies the majority of these complications.

Predisposition to DM is **inherited**, although the genetic factors are complex. There are two recognized types of DM:

(*i*) **Insulin Dependent** (Type I or juvenile onset; IDDM), and (*ii*) **Noninsulin Dependent** (Type II or maturity onset; NIDDM). Type I or IDDM usually occurs in nonobese persons before the age of 20 years. Circulating insulin is virtually absent, and beta-cells fail to respond to normal stimuli. **It is an autoimmune disease of beta-cells**. The Type II or NIDDM usually occurs after the age of 40 years, and obesity is a major risk factor. The beta-cell mass is moderately reduced, and autoimmunity is not demonstrable. **Gestational diabetes** refers to the onset of glucose intolerance in women during pregnancy. It excludes women who were diabetic before pregnancy. If the woman remains diabetic after pregnancy, she must be reclassified as Type I or Type II diabetic.

In short, all forms of DM are due to either a decrease in circulating free insulin (insulin deficiency), or a decrease in the response of peripheral tissues to insulin (insulin resistance).

INSULIN

Insulin was first isolated in 1921 by **Banting and Best**, and used in the treatment of diabetes mellitus in 1922. It was completely synthesized in 1966.

Insulin is a polypeptide with a molecular weight of about 6,000. It is composed of an **A-chain** (acidic) made up of 21 amino acids, and **B-chain** (basic) of 30 amino acids, linked by **two disulphide (-S-S-) bridges**. The immediate precursor of insulin within the pancreatic beta-cell is **proinsulin** in which the A and the B chains are joined by the "connecting" peptide (C-peptide) composed in man of 31 amino acids. Proinsulin has a molecular weight of about 9,000. Insulin has been completely synthesized, however the present supplies are obtained mainly from the pancreas of cattle (**bovine**). Insulins derived from different animal sources show differences in their amino acid sequences, but are active in almost all species with a biological activity of approximately 25 units per mg. The pig (**porcine**) insulin closely resembles human insulin, which may account for its low antigenicity. The "active centre" of insulin has not been recognized, however, the disulphide bridges are essential for its biological activity.

Insulin is soluble in water, but undergoes molecular aggregation at extremes of pH (3.2 and 10). Such aggregations are also encouraged by the presence of Zinc (Zn) which brings about crystallization of insulin. Insulin, with an isoelectric point of 5.3, is relatively insoluble between pH 4 and 7. It can combine with proteins like **globin** and **protamine**, whereby its activity is retained and the duration of action is prolonged. Recently **human insulin** has been successfully produced through E. coli by recombinant DNA technique, or by chemical modification of pork insulin to replace the lone amino acid that is different from human insulin.

Biosynthesis, Storage and Release

The islet tissue constitutes about 1 percent by weight of the pancreas, and there are about 2,000,000 islets in the human pancreas, mostly concentrated in the tail. The **beta-cells** synthesize, store and release insulin. Electron microscopic studies indicate that insulin is present in beta-cells in particulate form (granules), and the insulin content runs parallel to the granulation of beta-cells. Storage is facilitated by zinc which renders insulin less soluble. **The normal pancreas contains about 200 units of insulin, and man secretes about 50 units daily, most of which is metabolized in the liver.**

Proinsulin is a transient intermediary in the synthesis of insulin, and is not the storage form of insulin. **Proinsulin** is derived from a larger precursor, **pre-proinsulin**. Conversion of proinsulin to insulin takes place in the beta-cells by a proteolytic **removal** of the **C-peptide** and four basic amino acids. Thus, plasma has **proinsulin, insulin** and **C-peptide** circulating in it, and normally proinsulin forms 30 percent of the total plasma insulin. Plasma **proinsulin:insulin ratio** is a useful index of islet function–this ratio is high in juvenile diabetes; *normal* in maturity-onset diabetes; and very high in insulinomas (8 : 2). Biologically proinsulin is 1/10th to 1/8th as active as insulin, while the separate A and B chains are inactive. The function of the C-peptide is unclear.

The release of insulin from the beta-cells involves a complex interplay between food products, hormones, gastrointestinal hormones, and the neural stimuli from the autonomic nervous system, and the central nervous system **(Table 7.4-1)**.

Table 7.4-1 *Factors affecting insulin release*

Stimulation of release	*Inhibition of release*
Glucose	Catecholamines
Glucagon	Exogenous insulin
Sulphonylureas	Starvation
Cyclic-AMP	Diazoxide
Leucine and certain other amino acids	Phenytoin
ACTH and corticosteroids	Potassium deficiency
Secretin and Pancreozymin	Vagotomy
Vagal stimulation	

The most important factor controlling insulin secretion is glucose. An increase in blood glucose level promotes both synthesis and secretion of insulin from the beta-cells. The beta-cells have an adenyl cyclase system, which is stimulated by **glucose** or **beta-adrenergic stimulation** (on the contrary alpha-adrenergic stimulation inhibits insulin secretion). The secretion of insulin is independent of a hypothalmo-pituitary axis (HPA).

Transport, Metabolism and Excretion

Orally administered insulin is rapidly proteolysed in the gut, hence oral administration is ineffective. It has to be given parenterally, usually by subcutaneous injection. The rate of absorption from the site of injection varies with the type of insulin used. Insulin circulates in plasma essentially in a **free** state, and only a negligible fraction is bound to the plasma globulins. Insulin disappears rapidly from the plasma, and is taken up by the liver and kidney, where it is mainly degraded. The disulphide bridges are split in the liver by the enzyme **glutathione insulin transhydrogenase** (insulinase) which breaks the insulin molecule into its A and B chains. A small amount of insulin is also bound and inactivated by the muscle and fat tissue. Elimination is primarily by metabolism, and no free insulin is excreted in the urine and faeces. The plasma half-life of intravenously injected insulin is less than 9 minutes in man. The plasma half-life of crystalline insulin injected subcutaneously is 40 minutes.

Actions

In DM there are disturbances in the metabolism of carbohydrate, fat, protein, electrolytes and water. Considering them in order:

(a) **Carbohydrate Metabolism**

Insulin deficiency produces two fundamental defects: (*i*) reduced entry of glucose into cells; and (*ii*) increased release of glucose from the liver into circulation. Both of these raise the blood glucose level **(hyperglycaemia)**, and lead to the excretion of glucose in urine (**glycosuria**). In addition, in insulin deficiency there is an abnormally high rate of conversion of protein to glucose (**gluconeogenesis**). Insulin replacement facilitates entry of glucose and other sugars into the cell. After entry into the cell it facilitates the phosphorylation of glucose, and promotes glycogen synthesis. Further, insulin inhibits glycogenolysis and gluconeogenesis. *Thus, by promotion of glycogenesis and inhibition of glycogenolysis and gluconeogenesis, the utilization of glucose is increased*. This leads to a fall in the glucose content of the blood and tissues.

(b) **Fat Metabolism**

Insulin deficiency leads to a mobilization of fat from adipose tissue into the blood stream (lipaemia). The blood concentrations of triglyceride and FFA rise. In the absence of normal carbohydrate metabolism the liver cells can only partially oxidize fatty acids. The greater availability of FFA to the liver leads to an increased production of **acetoacetic** and **β-hydroxybutyric acids** (ketone bodies). These ketone bodies enter the blood and produce a **metabolic ketoacidosis**. In diabetes the blood cholesterol level also rises.

(c) **Protein Metabolism**

Insulin deficiency and a disordered glucose utilization impair protein synthesis, and promote protein breakdown specially in the muscle. Increased protein catabolism leads to wasting. This protein depletion together with glucose-rich tissues and body fluids predispose the individual to infection.

Insulin replacement has an **anabolic** effect. It accelerates the transfer of amino acids into cells, and promotes their incorporation into protein. Insulin also promotes the action of the growth hormone on protein synthesis.

(d) **Electrolytes**

Due to an increased protein breakdown, glycogenolysis, and tissue hypoxia, intracellular potassium (K^+) escapes into the extracellular fluid and is lost in the urine. Insulin facilitates entry of potassium into the cells, and its involvement in glycogenesis.

(e) **Water**

As an osmotic consequence of glycosuria, there is an extra loss of water from the body (polyuria). This leads to dehydration and polydypsia. Insulin replacement due to its overall effect on various metabolisms specially the carbohydrate metabolism, antagonizes this excess of body water loss.

The main actions of insulin may be summarized as:

Membrane effects

1. Glucose transport increased.
2. Amino acid transport increased.
3. Fatty acid transport increased.
4. Cellular uptake of K^+ and Mg^{++} increased.

Intracellular effects

1. Increased RNA and DNA synthesis.
2. Increased protein synthesis.
3. Stimulation of glycogen synthetase.
4. Stimulation of glycokinase.
5. Inhibition of glucose-6-phosphatase.
6. Increased lipogenesis.
7. Decreased lipolysis.
8. Inhibition of cyclic-AMP synthesis.
9. Increased Mg^{++} activated Na^+, K^+ ATPase activity.

The overall effect of insulin on carbohydrate metabolism is expressed as a fall in blood glucose, while inhibition of fat breakdown in adipose tissue produces a fall in plasma free fatty acids. Simultaneously the utilization of fat is reduced and the incorporation of amino acids into muscle protein is facilitated. These actions are illustrated in **Fig. 7.4.1.**

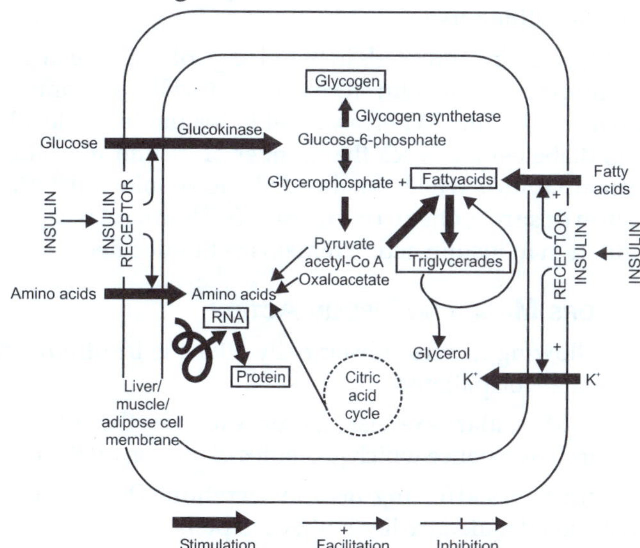

Fig. 7.4.1: *Actions of insulin.* Insulin acts primarily as an anabolic hormone. It stimulates the formation of glycogen, ribonucleic acid (RNA), protein, fatty acids and triglycerides from their precursors.

Mode of Action

The major effects of insulin on glucose, fatty acid, and amino acid metabolism, and on ion flux are initiated by the attachment of the insulin molecule to a **specific insulin receptor** on the cell surface. This hormone–receptor interaction is **reversible**, and the insulin molecule is not chemically altered during this contact. The hormone-receptor complex is then internalized by an endocytotic mechanism, with insulin molecule eventually being metabolized, and the insulin receptor is recycled to the membrane for use again.

Insulin lowers the c-AMP content in some tissues, perhaps by **inhibiting** the adenyl cyclase system. This lowering is more marked when c-AMP synthesis is first stimulated by hormones like **glucagon** and **catecholamines**. Thus, insulin and glucagon are mutally antagonistic to each other in function. Basal levels of c-AMP are not much affected by insulin, and this is an argument against its direct relationship with c-AMP metabolism. Further, it has been postulated that insulin **stimulates cyclic nucleotide phosphodiesterase** (the enzyme which destroys c-AMP) activity, thereby lowering c-AMP content of cells. Because of less of c-AMP in the cell less of glycogen breakdown (glycogenolysis) occurs, and in addition glycogen synthesis is facilitated due to **activation of glycogen synthetase** by insulin. Such a state leads to an increase in the glycogen content of the cells specially in the liver and skeletal muscle. Insulin facilitates **potassium** transport into the cell, and potassium is important in the regulation of the membrane potential and enzyme activity. Insulin also promotes intracellular magnesium accumulation. It is proposed that **magnesium** is responsible for the activation of many critical intracellular enzymes. Many facets of insulin action are illunderstood.

Elevated insulin levels in blood (e.g., obesity) decrease the number of insulin receptors on cell membranes (**downregulation**). Whereas, a fall in insulin blood levels (e.g., diabetes) increases the number of insulin receptors (**upregulation**), which in the diabetic would **shift the insulin dose response curve to the left**. The role of receptor regulation in insulin action remains yet undecided.

Factors Modifying Insulin Action

The following factors substantially alter the insulin need in the diabetic patient:

(*i*) **Muscular exercise.** After exercise the plasma contains a substance which promotes oxidation of glucose.

(*ii*) **Factors affecting insulin secretion.** These factors have been detailed earlier in this Chapter.

(*iii*) **Insulin antibodies.** On repeated injections of insulin specific insulin antibodies develop in the plasma. These antibodies bind insulin and it loses its physiological activity. *Insulin resistance* is arbitrarily defined as a state when the daily insulin requirement of the individual exceeds 200 units.

(*iv*) **Insulin antagonists.** In addition to insulin antibodies certain other factors interfere with insulin action, e.g., *growth hormone, glucocorticoids, glucagon, and other unidentified materials.*

(*v*) **Diet.** The diet has to be specially adapted to meet the metabolic needs.

Preparations

Commercial insulin is a mixture of the hormone extracted from the pancreas of cattle (bovine) and pigs (porcine). The potency of insulin is assayed by comparing the new sample with an **International Standard** for its hypoglycaemic effect, measured in groups of mice, the endpoint being hypoglycaemic coma. The potency is described in **units**. Preparations are adjusted to contain 40, 80, 100 or 500 units/ml. Various insulin preparations differ mainly in the **rate of absorption** from the site of subcutaneous injection. Regular insulin (Crystalline Insulin) is modified to form suspensions by two procedures: (*i*) basic **protamine** is added to raise the isoelectric point of acidic insulin; and (*ii*) high concentrations of **zinc** and **acetate buffer** make it possible to prepare suspensions having varying particle size. On these factors the onset and duration of action of the preparation would depend. The available preparations of insulin are detailed in **Table 7.4-2.**

All insulin preparations are usually given **subcutaneously**. Only Insulin Injection or Regular Insulin can be given **intravenously**. The insulins are marketed in 10 ml vials.

The duration of action of short-acting insulins is so short that many injections would be required daily for adequate control. On the other hand long-acting insulins start acting too late to cover the first meal (breakfast) of the day. Hence, appropriate mixtures of the two are used in

Table 7.4-2. *The characteristics of insulin preparations*

Type	*Preparation*	*pH and appearance*	*Hours after subcutaneous injection*			*Can be safely mixed with*	*Time of injection*	*Time of hypoglycaemic risk*
			Onset of action	*Maximal action*	*Duration of action*			
Fast-acting	Insulin Injection(regular, crystalline insulin)	3.2 clear	1	2-3	5-7	All preparations	Before breakfast	Late morning
	Prompt Insulin Zinc Suspension (SEMILENTE)	7.2 cloudy	1	4-6	12-16	LENTE preparations	Before breakfast	Late morning to mid-afternoon
Intermediate acting	Isophane Insulin Suspension (NPH Insulin)	7.2	2	8-12	18-24	Insulin injection	Before breakfast	Late afternoon to bedtime
	Insulin Zinc 7.2 Suspension (LENTE)	2-4	8-12	18-24		Insulin injection, SEMILENTE	Before breakfast	Late afternoon to bedtime
	Globin Zinc Insulin Injection (Globin Insulin)	3.4 clear	1-2	6-10	12-18	–	Before breakfast	Early morning
Long-acting	Protamine Zinc Insulin Suspension (PZI)	7.2 cloudy	4-6	16-18	24-36	Insulin injection	At breakfast	During the night until breakfast time
	Extended Zinc Insulin Suspension (ULTRALENTE)	7.2 cloudy	4-6	16-18	24-36	Insulin injection SEMILENTE	At breakfast	During the night until breakfast time

practice **Crystalline insulin** (regular insulin) is commonly injected ½ hour before a meal, and the **intermediate-acting preparations** are injected once a day before breakfast.

Newer Insulins

1. **Actrapid** (*Nusol*). It is a clear neutral solution of recrystallized porcine insulin. It acts faster than regular insulin, and has a greater hypoglycaemic action than bovine insulin in patients who have been receiving the latter over long periods.

2. **Rapitard** (*Biphasic Insulin*). It is a cloudy mixture of actrapid (1 part) and insoluble crystals of bovine insulin (3 parts) buffered to pH 7. Its action is similar to Lente insulin, except that the onset of action is quicker and the blood sugar control is smoother.

In some diabetics antibody production and insulin allergy are a problem. Various purification techniques have been perfected to remove allergenic contaminants (e.g., proinsulin), and a new class of purified single-peak insulins are now available. These products are labelled as "**purified insulins**" or "**monocomponent insulins**", and contain less than 10 ppm (parts per million) of proinsulin, and they elicit fewer allergic reactions compared to conventional insulins.

3. **Monotard**. It is **monocomponent insulin zinc suspension** containing highly purified porcine insulin, and is claimed to be devoid of antigenic property.

4. **Human insulins**. Human insulins are highly purified insulins prepared by recombinant DNA technique, or semisynthetically using porcine insulin as starting material, followed by chemical modification of the **threonine** and **alanine** residues. The rDNA human insulin is synthesized in **Escherichia coli**, and is available as: Fast-acting Neutral Regular Human Insulin (Humulin R); and Intermediate-acting NPH human insulin, isophane-type (Humulin N). *Insulatard NPH Human* is a suspension of isophane and purified human (semisynthetic) insulin (100 units/ml). *Velosulin Human* is a semisynthetic purified human insulin (100 units/ml).

Human insulins are as safe and as effective as conventional insulins, and are much less immunogenic than beef or pork insulins, because they do not contain proinsulin or any other animal derived contaminants.

Insulin pumps. There are two types of pump systems: the open-loop and the closed-loop. The **open-loop** uses a microcomputer to regulate the flow of insulin from the syringe to the needle inserted subcutaneously into the diabetic patient. The **closed-loop** automatically reads blood glucose levels and adjusts the rate of insulin delivery. Both pumps deliver insulin subcutaneously. Lately the FDA (Food and Drug Administration, USA) has approved a **transdermal insulin patch** for use in diabetics. The very new approach for *oral administration of insulin* involves coating insulin molecules with *polymers crosslinked with azoaromatic groups* so as to protect the hormone from digestion in the stomach and small intestines.

Adverse Reactions and Precautions

1. **Hypoglycaemia.** This is an extension of insulin action. It may occur due to insulin overdosage, failure to eat, unaccustomed physical exercise, or ingestion of alcohol.

2. **Insulin allergy.** It occurs infrequently. Manifestations may range from local itching to lymphadenopathy. Protein containing insulins are more likely to produce allergy than Lente insulins.

3. **Insulin lipoatrophy.** Atrophy of subcutaneous fat occurs at the sites of frequent insulin injections. The absorption of insulin from these sites becomes erratic. It can best be avoided by frequently changing the site of injection.

4. **Insulin presbiopia.** When a diabetic is rapidly controlled with insulin he may develop a difficulty or loss of accommodation. This disorder gradually settles down.

5. **Insulin neuropathy.** Rapid control of diabetes with insulin may precipitate or worsen pre-existing neuropathy. The mechanism involved is unclear.

6. **Insulin resistance.** On prolonged insulin administration the daily requirement gradually rises due to the formation of **insulin antibodies**. Insulin resistance can be managed by administering **glucocorticoids** (prednisone); or change over from bovine to porcine insulin. Infection if present should be treated vigorously.

7. **Obesity.** Insulin therapy without dietary restriction may lead to obesity.

Every diabetic should carry an *identification card* containing related medical information which may be useful in managing an emergency.

Therapeutic Uses

1. **Diabetes mellitus.**

2. **Schizophrenia.** Insulin shock (coma) therapy is a useful therapeutic measure. The coma is allowed to last for 20–30 minutes, and then terminated by administering *glucose* by a stomach tube or intravenously. Glucagon can also be used to terminate coma.

3. **Myocardial infarction.** Insulin, glucose and potassium chloride have been used with benefit for myocardial salvage.

4. **Anorexia nervosa.** Insulin improves the appetite and there is a simultaneous gain in body weight.

5. **Burns.** Insulin with glucose administration reduces the nitrogen and potassium losses in severely burnt patients.

PHARMACOTHERAPY OF DIABETES MELLITUS

Diabetes mellitus is a condition of impaired carbohydrate metabolism due to a **relative** or **absolute deficiency** of insulin. DM clinically is of two types:

(*i*) **Maturity-onset diabetes (noninsulin dependent, ketoacidosis-resistant)**. These patients have functional beta-cells evidenced by the presence of both IRI and C-peptide in plasma. There is some defect in the glucoreceptor of the beta-cell membrane, which accounts for the delay in the secretion of insulin. This is the *milder* form of the disease.

(*ii*) **Juvenile-onset diabetes (insulin dependent, ketoacidosis prone)**. The onset is prior to the age of 20 years, and the patient is dependent on exogenous insulin to prevent ketoacidosis, due to an almost complete absence of circulating IRI. The function of the beta-cells is almost totally lost. This is the *severe* form of the disease.

Indications for Insulin Therapy

All diabetics do not require insulin. Some patients of the maturity-onset type of the disease can be controlled on diet and exercise alone. However, the following categories of diabetics necessarily require insulin administrations:

(*i*) Juvenile diabetics, specially of more than 2 years duration.

(*ii*) Older diabetics with maturity-onset diabetes.

(*iii*) All diabetics with complications.

(*iv*) Diabetic coma and precoma.

(*v*) Primary or secondary failure of sulphonylurea therapy.

(*vi*) During pregnancy to avoid the possible embryopathic activity of oral hypoglycaemic agents.

(*vii*) Diabetics undergoing surgery.

DIABETIC COMA

Diabetic coma is precipitated in patients of DM due to a marked deficiency of insulin in the system.

Due to the lack of insulin there is a mobilization of fatty acids leading to formation of ketone bodies and acidosis (*ketoacidosis*). There is a **hyperglycaemia** and **glycosuria** resulting in **dehydration** and **hypovolaemia**, which further aggravates acidosis **(Fig. 7.4.2)**. The urine is loaded with **ketone bodies** and **glucose**. The blood glucose is raised to 600–800 mg%. The blood pH is lowered and the carbon dioxide combining power of blood is markedly reduced. During diabetic ketoacidosis an acute but temporary state of insulin resistance develops. **Therefore, high doses of Regular Insulin are needed.**

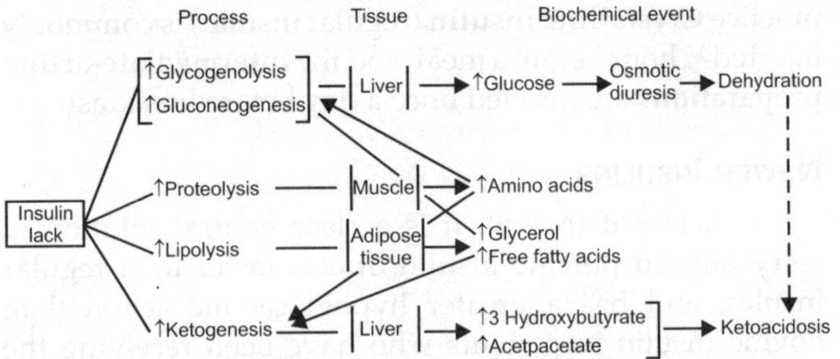

Fig. 7.4.2: Biochemical abnormalities resulting from insulin lack.

HYPOGLYCAEMIC COMA

In diabetics dangerous hypoglycaemia may occur due to missed meals, violent exercise or due to an overdose of insulin. Symptoms are of two types: (a) **Cerebral**, due to low blood glucose level there is *confusion*, *depression*, *convulsions* and *visual disturbances*. There may be cerebral oedema and damage; and (b) **Sympathetic activation**, due to adrenaline liberation there may be *vasoconstriction*, *tachycardia*, *palpitation*, *tremors*, *pallor*, *sweating* and *piloerection*. With fast-acting insulins sympathetic symptoms predominate, and with intermediate-acting insulins hypoglycaemia occurs during sleep, there are nightmares, sweating and headache on waking up.

Management

The guidelines for management are:

(*i*) **Glucose** given orally can relieve symptoms, if given early.

(*ii*) If the patient is comatosed give 50 ml of 50 percent glucose intravenously. Consciousness soon returns.

(*iii*) Injection glucagon 1 mg IM rapidly awakens the patient.

(*iv*) If coma persists administer 50 ml of 50 percent **mannitol** intravenously to relieve cerebral oedema and hypoxia, which are usually responsible for prolonged coma.

GLUCAGON

Glucagon is a single chain polypeptide with 29 amino acids and a molecular weight of 2852. It is synthesized stored and secreted by the alpha-cells of the islets of Langerhans. *Glucose* is the major regulator of glucagon secretion. Hyperglycaemia inhibits, while hypoglycaemia stimulates the release of glucagon.

Mode of Action

Glucagon promotes glucose production (glycogenolysis) from liver glycogen *via* the stimulation the adenyl cyclase cell wall system, formation of c-AMP and activation of hepatic phosphorylase **(Fig. 7.4.3)**.

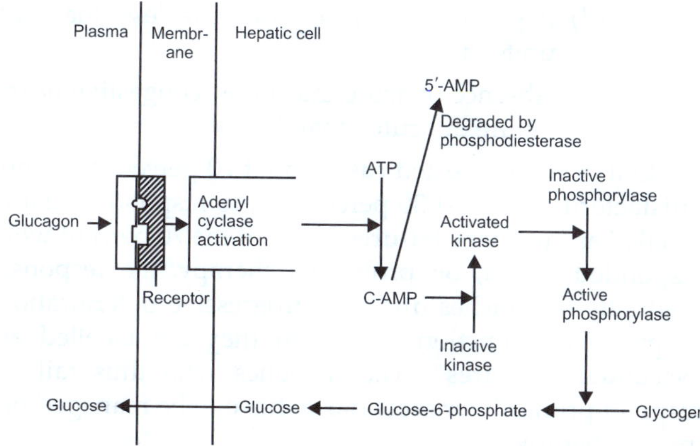

Fig. 7.4.3: The mode of action of glucagon.

Activated phosphorylase breaks down glycogen to glucose which is released into the blood leading to a prompt hyperglycaemia. Glucagon increases hepatic gluconeogenesis and ketogenesis, and stimulates protein catabolism. **Thus, it has classical anti-insulin activity. Glucagon also stimulates the liberation of catecholamines from the adrenal medulla.** It increases the contractility of the myocardium, causing a rise in blood pressure. It is effective parenterally only.

Therapeutic Uses

1. **Insulin hypoglycaemia.**

2. Used with dextrose to cut short insulin induced hypoglycaemic coma.

3. It has been tried in **cardiogenic shock** and refractory heart failure with limited success.

4. Used in the **diagnosis** of insulinomas and pheochromocytomas. A precaution is that it may provoke severe hypertension in patients with pheochromocytomas.

5. **Diagnosis** of the hepatic form of glycogen storage disease, where glucagon fails to elevate blood glucose levels.

6. May be used in the treatment of beta-blocker (propranolol) poisoning.

Adverse reactions. There may be slight nausea after large doses, and hypersensitivity reactions may occur.

Dose. Glucagon hydrochloride 1 mg IM, IV or SC.

Somatostatin

Somatostatin (Growth hormone release inhibiting hormone) is a **tetradecapeptide** which has been isolated from the **hypothalamus, pancreas** and the **upper GI tract**. In the pancreatic islets, the somatostatin-secreting delta (D) cells are situated between the alpha (A) cells and the beta (B) cells. Somatostatin *inhibits* the secretion of *both* glucagon and insulin, and can reduce fasting hyperglycaemia in Type I diabetics. Both natural and synthetic somatostatin have similar biological actions.

The precise role of somatostatin remains unclear, but several endocrine and non-endocrine activities have been attributed to this hormone. **Endocrine:** Inhibition of secretion of growth hormone, thyrotrophin (TSH), glucagon, insulin, gastrin, secretin, and renin. **Non-endocrine**: Inhibition of gastric acid secretion, pancreatic enzyme release, gall bladder contraction, splanchnic blood flow, platelet aggregation, electrical activity of CNS neurones, and acetylcholine release from peripheral nerves.

ORAL HYPOGLYCAEMIC AGENTS

Oral hypoglycaemic agents are divided into two classes: (*i*) **Sulphonylureas**; and (*ii*) **Biguanides (Table 7.4-3).**

SULPHONYLUREAS

The sulphonylureas are chemically related to the sulphonamides but they have no antibacterial activity. The oral hypoglycaemics do not prevent the cardiovascular complications of DM.

Table 7.4-3. *Prescribing details of oral hypoglycaemic agents*

Drug and Class	*Half-life (hours)*	*Duration of action (hours)*	*Tablet strength (mg)*	*Daily dose range*	*Dosage frequency*
Sulphonylureas					
Tolbutamide	4-6	6-12	250, 500	0.5-3.0 g	Divided
Acetohexamide	6-18	12-24	250, 500	0.25-1.5 g	Single/Divided
Tolazamide	7	10-14	100, 250	0.1-1.0 g	Single/Divided
Chlorpropamide	30-36	60	100, 250, 500	0.1-0.5 g	Single
Glibenclamide	5	10-15	5	2.5-15 mg	Single/Divided
Glipizide*	2-4	24	5,10	5-40 mg	Single/Divided
Glyburide*	10	24	1.25, 2.5,5	2.5-20 mg	Single/Divided
Biguanides					
Phenformin	3	4-6	25	50-200 mg	Divided
Phenformin Timed disintegration	3	8-14	50	50-200 mg	Single/Divided
Metformin	3	5-6	500	1-1.5 g	Divided

Pharmacological Actions

The sulphonylureas are readily absorbed from the gastrointestinal tract, appear in the blood within 1–2 hours and peak levels are attained within 4–6 hours. They are partially protein bound and metabolized in the liver.

Sulphonylureas **lower blood glucose level** in non-diabetic and Type II diabetics. Almost simultaneously they **lower the plasma free fatty acid levels**. They are effective only in the presence of a functioning pancreas. They normalize the metabolic status of the diabetic, and like insulin the patients tend to gain weight.

Mode of Action

The sulphonylureas stimulate the beta-cell islet tissue to secrete insulin, i.e., they have an islet **betacytotropic** activity. Evidence is provided by the finding that they cause **degranulation** of the beta-cells. They also probably directly **inhibit hepatic glycogenolysis**. The sulphonylureas are ineffective in patients of Type I diabetes as the pancreas has almost completely lost its capacity to synthesize and secrete insulin. The basic mode of action of all sulphonylureas is similar.

Toxicity

The toxicity of these compounds is remarkably low in properly managed patients. The following reactions have been observed:

(*i*) **Hypoglycaemia.** This may occur due to an excess dose, missed meals, vomiting or associated liver and kidney damage. *Alcohol* may induce severe hypoglycaemia.

(*ii*) Allergic skin reactions.

(*iii*) **Bone marrow depression.** Leucopenia, thrombocytopenia and agranulocytosis may occur.

(*iv*) Chlorpropamide is reported to induce cholestatic jaundice.

(*v*) There is a likelihood of their inducing **embryopathy**. Thus for diabetic women insulin is the drug of choice during pregnancy.

(*vi*) They are **goitrogenic** as they inhibit the iodide uptake by the thyroid gland.

(*vii*) Chlorpropamide may induce severe *intolerance* to alcohol, similar to that caused by disulfiram (Antabuse).

Therapeutic Uses

(*i*) **Maturity-onset diabetes mellitus**. Sulphonylureas are indicated in patients who cannot be controlled on diet alone. The criteria for selection of patients are:

- (a) Obese subjects, aged 40 years or more.
- (b) Diabetics of less than 10 years duration, without significant ketonuria or other acute complications.
- (c) Fasting blood glucose level less than 300 mg/dl.
- (d) Regular insulin requirement less than 40 units/day.
- (e) Absence of acute infections, congestive heart failure or acute renal disease.

Out of these selected cases about 70 percent respond satisfactorily. The rest 30 percent fail to respond, and are labelled as "**primary failures**". Out of the 70 percent who responded earlier, on prolonged therapy, the response gradually diminishes due to a progressive deterioration of pancreatic function, and then they are labelled as "**secondary failures**". The diabetics who thus fail to respond primarily or secondarily have to be managed on insulin therapy.

(*ii*) *Insulin-resistant diabetes mellitus.*

(*iii*) Chlorpropamide has been used in some cases of *diabetes insipidus*.

Precautions

Transfer of patients from insulin to oral hypoglycaemic agents should be done under close supervision, and the patients should be preferably hospitalized. Sulphonylureas are contraindicated in patients with severe renal, cardiac or heptic insufficiency.

Biguanides

The biguanides differ from the sulphonylureas in their action. **The biguanides do not lower blood glucose levels in normal non-diabetic persons but do so in diabetics, and in the absence of a functioning pancreas.** Thus, they lower blood glucose in both types of diabetes mellitus. *It must be emphasized that the biguanides do not induce clinical hypoglycaemia, but potentiate the hypoglycaemic action of insulin and sulphonylureas.* They increase the plasma fibrinolytic activity.

Mode of Action

In contrast to the sulphonylureas, the action of the biguanides is **extrapancreatic**, and does not depend on the presence of endogenous or exogenous insulin in the body. They **stimulate the peripheral utilization of glucose**. They increase the sensitivity of the muscle to insulin action. The biguanides **reduce the intestinal absorption of glucose**. The exact mode of action is illunderstood.

Toxicity

Phenformin induces a metallic taste, nausea, anorexia and diarrhoea. It causes lethargy, muscle weakness and weight loss. Anaphylactoid reactions may occur. **Phenformin may cause ketonuria and lactic acidosis.** This is more common in patients with Type I diabetes being treated with a combination of insulin and phenformin. Phenformin is contraindicated in patients with ketoacidosis, liver, heart and kidney disease. Its administration during pregnancy is not recommended.

Therapeutic Uses

(*i*) Phenformin is used for the treatment of **maturity-onset diabetes mellitus** according to the criteria laid down for the use of sulphonylureas.

(*ii*) Phenformin may be combined with sulphonylureas in case of a primary or secondary failure.

(*iii*) Phenformin may be combined with insulin in the management of juvenile-diabetes, whereby the hypoglycaemic effect is smoother and the dose of insulin can be reduced.

Newer Oral Hypoglycaemic Agents

Thiazolidinedione Derivatives

The *thiazolidinediones*, **pioglitazone** and **rosiglitazone** reduce peripheral insulin resistance, leading to a reduction in blood glucose levels. Either drug can be used alone or in combination with a biguanide like metformin or a sulphonylurea, particularly for obese patients suffering from NIDDM. Their mode of action appears to be by *enhancing the target tissue sensitivity to insulin, lowering insulin resistance* and improving fasting and postprandial hyperglycaemia in patients with NIDDM. These agents should not be used in patients with *coronary artery disease* or *a history of heart failure*. *Side effects* include GI disturbances weight gain, dizziness, arthalgia, and less commonly hypoglycaemia. *Dosage*: Pioglitazone, initially 15-30 mg OD, up to 45 mg OD according to response; Rosiglitazone, initially 4 mg daily, may be increased up to 8 mg daily. The older agent **troglitazone** was approved for use by the US FCA, but on surveillance it was found to cause serious *drug-induced hepatitis* and liver failure. Consequently it was withdrawn from the market in USA, UK, and Japan (the country where it was developed). Other agents under study are **ciglitazone** and **englitazone**.

Alpha-Glucosidase Inhibitor

Acarbose

Acarbose inhibits *intestinal alpha-glucosidases*, and inhibits the digestion and absorption of starch and sucrose from the gut

Postprandial hyperglycaemia in type 1 diadbetes can be reduced. It can also be used in patients with NIDDM insufficiently controlled be diet and exercise. It can be used as an adjunct in patients with NIDDM on oral hypoglyceamics. *Dosage:* Initially 50mg OD in the first week, then 50 mg bid in the *second* and *third weeks*. The dose is to be taken with the first mouthful of the meal. Adverse reactions include abdominal pain, nausea, vomiting, diarrhoea, and stool discolouration, and rarely *hepatitis* and *jaundice*.

Guar Gum

Guar gum is a soluble dietary fibre obtained from Indian cluster beans (Guar), available in granular from. On oral administration it froms a viscous gel in the intestines and decreases carbohydrate absorption, thereby reducing blood glucose levels. It is used in patients of DM as an adjunct to insulin or oral hypoglycaemic therapy. It reduces both fasting and postprandial blood glucose levels. It is given with or immediately before meals initially in a low dose 2.5 g/day, and gradually increased to 5 g stirred well in 150 ml of water tid. It is also used to slow gastric emptying in patients with *dumping syndrome*. It can also be given a trial in patients of *hypercholesterolaemia*.

Glucomannan

Glucomannan, a powdered extract from the tubers of *Amorphophallus konjac* is used to reduce food intake by inducing early satiety. It reduces the absorption of lipids and sugars. Clinically there is a *reduction in blood glucose and cholesterol levels*. It is mainly used as an adjunct in obese patients with NIDDM, in a dose of 1 g stirred well in a glass of water till it is fully dissolved, and taken half an hour before meals upto 3 times a day. It has also been promoted as a *slimming aid*. Adverse reactions include nausea, vomiting, and diarrhoea. Long-term use can cause vitamin deficiencies. **Caution:** It should never be ingested in dry form, as it can cause an *oesophageal obstruction*.

Lately, the USFDA has approved **Exubera**, a fast-acting powdered form of human insulin. It is administered by *inhalation* through the mouth to reach the lungs and the blood stream. It is approved for treating both *type I and II diabetes mellitus*.

Drug Interactions

Insulin and oral hypoglycaemic agents are likely to interact with a number of drugs. Some of them are enumerated in **Table 7.4-4.**

Table 7.4-4. *Drug interactions with insulin and oral hypoglycaemic agents*

Drug (a)	*Drug (b)*	*Effect of b on a*
Insulin	Glucocorticoids	hypoglycaemia –
	ACTH	hypoglycaemia –
	Sulphonamides	hypoglycaemia +
	MAO inhibitors	hypoglycaemia +
	Beta-blockers	hypoglycaemia +
Tolbutamide and	Phenylbutazone	duration +
Chlorpropamide	Salicylates	potency +
	MAO inhibitors	potency +
	Propranolol	potency +
	Thiazides	potency +

+ = increased; – = diminished

During the drug management of diabetes mellitus such interactions are likely to occur. With proper pharmacotherapy of DM with *insulin, oral hypoglycaemics* and *antibiotics*, in addition to *exercise* and *diet regulation*, a diabetic can enjoy almost a normal life.

7.5 ADRENAL CORTICOSTEROIDS

The adrenal corticosteroids are amongst the most widely employed therapeutic agents. However, they do not prevent the progress of the underlying disease, and only offer a symptomatic relief. In addition, prolonged administration of corticosteroids necessarily leads to adverse effects, and the most dreaded of them is an **adrenocortical insufficiency** leading to **adrenocortical failure.**

The corticosteroids are used either: (*i*) in **physiologic doses** as a replacement therapy to correct a deficiency like chronic adrenocortical insufficiency (Addison's disease), or hypopituitarism leading to an insufficiency; or (*ii*) in supraphysiologic or **pharmacologic doses** to treat inflammatory conditions, allergic states, collagen disorders and several other diseases.

Physiologic Consideration

The cells of the adrenal cortex are arranged in three zones: (*i*) the outer **zona glomerulosa**, which secretes aldosterone, (*ii*) the middle **zona fasciculata**; and (*iii*) the inner **zona reticularis**. In man, the cells of the zona fasciculata and zona reticularis function as a single unit and secrete **cortisol, corticosterone,** and small quantities of **male** and **female sex hormones**. The adrenal medulla is composed of dark brown chromaffin cells which secrete catecholamines (adrenaline and noradrenaline) which are mainly autonomic adrenergic agents **(Chap. 3.4)**.

The natural steroid hormones produced and secreted by the adrenal cortex are divided into *three* main groups:

1. **Glucocorticoids.** These are **cortisol** (hydrocortisone) and **corticosterone**. They mainly affect carbohydrate metabolism, and to a lesser extent protein and fat metabolism.

2. **Mineralocorticoids.** These are **aldosterone** and **deoxycorticosterone**. They primarily have sodium-retaining and potassium-depleting actions, and thereby influence salt and water metabolism.

3. **Sex hormones.** The **androgen** (dehydroepiandrosterone) secreted has weaker masculinizing activity compared to testosterone. **Progesterone** is formed as an intermediary in the synthesis of gluco- and mineralocorticoids, and only a **trace of oestrogen** is secreted.

The daily basal secretion of adrenocorticosteroids isolated from adrenal venous blood of normal human adults is shown in **Table 7.5-1.**

Table 7.5-1. *The basal secretion of adrenocorticosteroids in normal human adults.*

Groups	*Natural hormone*	*Mean daily secretion*
Glucorticoids	Cortisol	5-30 mg
	Corticosterone	2-5 mg
Mineralocorticoids	Aldosterone	5-150 mcg
	11-deoxycorticosterone	trace
Sex hormones		
Androgen	Dehydroepiandrosterone	15-30 mg
Progestogen	Progesterone	0.4-0.8 mg
Oestrogen	Oestradiol	trace

The glucocorticoids and mineralocorticoids play an important role in helping the body to adjust in relation to changes in the external environment, i.e., **homeostasis**.

Biosynthesis of Adrenocorticosteroids

All steroid hormones are derived from **cholesterol**, which itself may be derived from acetate or dietary source (animal fats). Cholesterol is converted into **pregnenolone**, the precursor of all steroid hormones. *Four* major classes of steroids are derived from pregnenolone-the **oestrogens**, the **progestogens**, the **androgens** and the **corticosteroids**. The first three classes are regarded as sex steroids.

The steroid hormones can be divided into **three** major groups on the basis of the number of carbon atoms in their structure:

(*i*) The C-21 steroids (progesterone, glucocorticoids and mineralocorticoids);

(*ii*) The C-19 steroids (androgens); and

(*iii*) The C-18 steroids (oestrogens).

In the natural adrenocorticoids there is a certain overlapping of mineralo-and glucocorticoid activity.

The synthesis of cortisol is controlled by ACTH. Aldosterone is modulated by sodium-potassium balance, and the osmolarity of the extracellular fluid, which in turn is regulated by the renal tubule, also involving angiotensin. In a complex manner the renin-angiotensin-aldosterone system is involved in the water and mineral metabolism in the body. From acetate through cholesterol the pathways for synthesis of cortisol, corticosterone and aldosterone are shown in **Fig. 7.5.1.** In man the important hormones are **cortisol** (a glucocorticoid) and **aldosterone** (a mineralocorticoid).

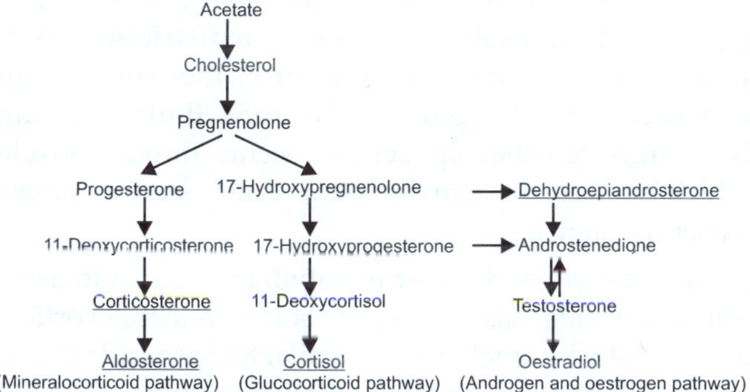

Fig. 7.5.1: Major pathways in the biosynthesis of adrenocortical hormones. The main secretory products (cortisol, corticosterone, aldosterone and dehydroepiandrosterone) are underlined. Dehydroepiandrosterone and androstenedione are very weak androgens.

An enzyme 3-β-dehydrogenase is involved in the conversion of pregnenolone to progesterone, and 17-hydroxypregnenolone to 17-hydroxyprogesterone. Further progressive hydroxylations produce the modifications at carbon atoms 17, 21 and 11, which give the final product *cortisol*. The enzyme β-hydroxylase catalyses the change from 11-deoxycortisol to cortisol, and 11-deoxycorticosterone (DOC) to corticosterone and to aldosterone. The major interconversions involved in steroidogenesis are accomplished by hydroxylases which use NADPH and molecular oxygen.

Regulation of Secretion

The biosynthesis and secretion of glucocorticoids is regulated by the hypothalamo-pituitary-adrenal axis. ACTH is released from the anterior pituitary into the circulation in response to the corticotrophin-releasing hormone (CRH), a neurohormone from the hypothalamus. Released ACTH stimulates the adrenal cortex to increase the production of mainly glucocorticoids, and the sex hormones to some extent **(Chap 7.1)**. The released glucocorticoids (cortisol) exert a **negative feedback** effect on the hypothalamus, thereby regulating the further release of CRH, which regulates the synthesis and release of ACTH from the anterior pituitary.

Circadian Rhythm of Plasma Cortisol

The secretion of adrenal gland (cortisol) and anterior pituitary (ACTH) hormone, does not occur at a steady rate, but varies at different times of the day. It follows a **diurnal** or **circadian** rhythm, which is a 24-hour cycle. The human anterior pituitary in the usual sleep/wakefulness cycle starts producing larger amounts of ACTH after midnight (at this time the hypothalamus gets the drive for diurnal rhythm from the higher CNS to release more CRH). The plasma ACTH reaches its peak at about 6:00 AM. This, in turn, induces the adrenal cortex to secrete large amounts of glucocorticoids between 6.00 and 9.00 AM **(Fig. 7.5.2)**. This high level of circulating corticosteroids in the morning hours cuts off further ACTH production. This cut off effect is by the **negative feedback** exerted by cortisol through the hypothalamus.

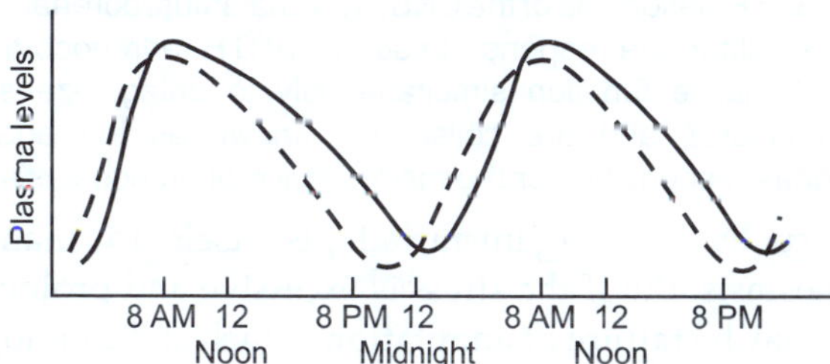

Fig. 7.5.2: Diurnal variations in plasma ACTH (dotted curve) and cortisol (solid curve) levels.

During the day, the glucocorticoids secreted are used up and metabolized, and the **blood steroid level is the lowest in the late evenings**. This operates the hypothalamopituitary mechanism by a negative feedback and once again by midnight the anterior pituitary begins producing more of ACTH.

Stress and Adrenal Steroidogenesis

The circadian rhythm of ACTH and glucocorticoid secretion may be disrupted or masked by **stress** (physical or emotional), or by the administration of **supraphysiologic doses of glucocorticoids**.

Hans Selye elaborated the concept of stress. He defined it as "the nonspecific response of the body to any demand". A **stressor** is an agent which attempts to alter the internal environment, e.g., physical injury, infection, high or low temperature, radiation injury, neuromuscular fatigue, emotions, noise, environmental pollutants and so on. Stressors generally induce two types of syndromes: (*i*) the **local adaptation syndrome** (LAS) which is a local response and would depend on the nature of the agency, like intense heat would cause burns of the exposed part; and (*ii*) the **general adaptation syndrome** (GAS) which would be a response to stressors when their action is prolonged, and irrespective of the agency the response would be the same involving the whole organism. The GAS consists of three phases: (a) the **alarm** reaction, (b) the stage of **resistance**, and (c) the stage of **exhaustion**. The stages of adaptation are shown in **Fig. 7.5.3.**

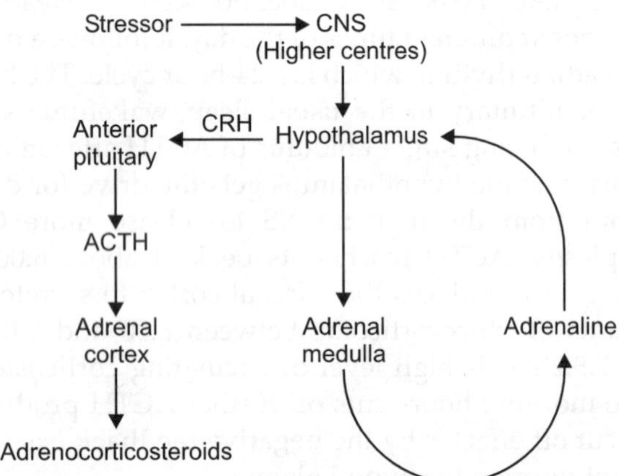

Fig. 7.5.3: Relationship of the CNS, hypothalamus, adrenal cortex and medulla in the response to stress. ACTH, adrenocorticoids and adrenaline function simultaneously to antagonize stress (antistressors), and are collectively known as the adaptive hormones responsible for the maintenance of homeostasis.

Usually the organism adapts itself to maintain homeostasis. But if the stress is excessive and prolonged, there may be **failure of adaptation**, which at the biological level would mean the incapacity of the body to antagonize stress. At this stage the **diseases of adaptation** or **stress-induced diseases** set in. They include a large number of *psychosomatic diseases, allergies, immunological disorders* (autoimmune disease) and *inflammatory disorders*. These diseases respond to glucocorticoid therapy.

Under stressful conditions, excitatory stimuli within the CNS counteract the negative feedback effect of the circulating steroids on the hypothalamus, i.e., **the negative feedback mechanism fails**. Under severe stress the cortisol secretion may be raised up to ten-fold of the normal daily output.

Glucocorticoids

Physiological Actions

In man **cortisol** (hydrocortisone) is responsible for the physiological actions. Cortisol and synthetic glucocorticoids have effects mainly on *carbohydrate, protein* and *lipid metabolism*.

Carbohydrate metabolism. The glucocorticoids increase the production of glycogen, mainly from non-carbohydrate sources, i.e., they promote **gluconeogenesis** or new glucose formation. Cortisol inhibits glucose uptake by tissue leading to **hyperglycaemia** and **glycosuria**, i.e., it has an **anti-insulin action**. Glycogenolysis is inhibited, which is also responsible for the increase in muscle and liver glycogen. Excess of cortisol may lead to "**steroid diabetes**".

Protein metabolism. The glucocorticoids affect protein metabolism in two ways: (*i*) by **catabolic** action they increase the rate of protein breakdown to amino acids; and (*ii*) by an **antianabolic** effect they decrease the rate of dietary amino acid incorporation into new protein molecules. Thus, excess of cortisol leads to a **negative nitrogen balance**. There is *muscle wasting, weakness, osteoporosis, thinning of skin* and *retardation of growth*. The lymphoid tissue is reduced and leads to an increase in uric acid excretion via the urine.

Lipid metabolism. They act directly to breakdown triglycerides to fatty acids (*lipolysis*). However, they also indirectly increase the formation and storage of fat (*lipogenesis*). Cortisol excess causes a **redistribution of fat** in the body—the fat is withdrawn from the extremites and increased deposits occur on the trunk **(buffalo hump)**. It is suggested that lipogenesis occurs through insulin, which is released in extra amounts due to steroid-induced hyperglycaemia.

Electrolyte and water metabolism. The endogenous glucocorticoids also possess some mineralocorticoid activity, which is qualitatively similar to that of aldosterone. Cortisol promotes **sodium retention** and **potassium excretion** by the kidneys. Hydrocortisone administered in supraphysiologic doses may lead to hypopotassaemia, and sodium and water retention leading to oedema, *i.e.*, it has **appreciable mineralocorticoid activity** responsible for side effects.

Pharmacological Actions

The glucocorticoids in small doses are almost exclusively employed as a **replacement therapy** in adrenocortical insufficiency. However, for most of the other clinical indications for natural or synthetic steroid therapy, they have to be employed in supraphysiologic or **pharmacologic doses**. Hydrocortisone (cortisol) is a **prototype** glucocorticoid. The pharmacologic effects of exogenous hydrocortisone are mainly on body metabolism similar to those produced by endogenous cortisol, as discussed earlier. In addition, in pharmacologic doses, they exert **anti-inflammatory, antiallergic**, and **immunosuppressive actions**. The *natural* and *synthetic* corticosteroids resemble each other in their pharmacological profile qualitatively. However, the synthetic corticosteroids offer the advantage that they exert relatively **less of mineralocorticoid activity** and the **anti-inflammatory potency** is higher than hydrocortisone.

Anti-inflammatory activity. The corticosteroids (natural and synthetic) inhibit the inflammatory responses of body tissues to all kinds of noxious stimuli regardless of the cause, i.e., they exert a **non-specific anti-inflammatory action**. Both the early and late phases of inflammation are inhibited. Corticosteroids have been likened to an "asbestos suit against fire" which protects the tissues from damages, but does not extinguish the fire, i.e., they do not treat the cause and only offer a symptomatic relief.

Antiallergic activity. The corticosteroids alter the course of disease in which hypersensitivity (allergy) has a possible role to play. They **suppress immediate hypersensitivity reactions** by interfering with the steps in the process of release of histamine and kinin. **The delayed hypersensitivity reactions may be suppressed by corticosteroids through their ability to inhibit the immune response**. The activity of the cellular mediators of immune reactions like macrophages, monocytes and lymphocytes is suppressed. In part the anti-inflammatory activity is also responsible for the antiallergic action of corticosteroids.

Immunosuppressant activity. It is believed that the corticosteroids **inhibit antibody formation** and **antibody reactions**. However, the corticosteroids have no significant effect on the titre of circulating antibodies, either IgG or IgE, which play a role in certain allergic and immune diseases. In spite of this the symptoms are relieved. Presently the glucocorticoids are also used to prevent the consequences of cell mediated immune reactions like the **graft rejection reaction**. The glucocorticoids cause an involution of the thymus and other lymphatic tissue. They depress the synthesis of DNA and DNA-dependent RNA polymerase in lymphocytes. There is a drammatic destruction of lymphocytes (**lympholysis**), and the lymphocytes are unable to play their role in the immune reactions. The anti-inflammatory activity of these steroids also appears to play an important role in immunosuppression. The major physiological and pharmacological actions of glucocorticoids are summarized in **Fig. 7.5.4.**

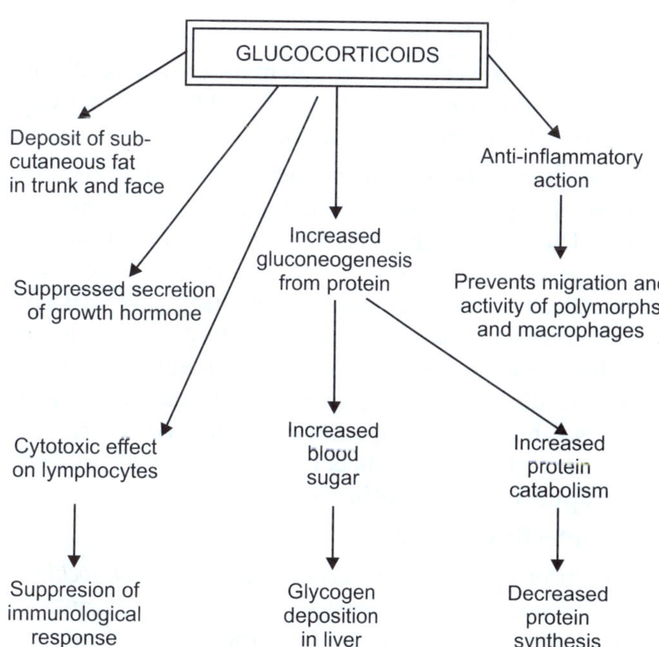

Fig. 7.5.4: The major actions of glucocorticoids.

Effect on Metabolism and Electrolytes

The glucocorticoids maintain the metabolic integrity of the smooth endoplasmic reticulum of the liver. The synthesis and activity of the drug-metabolizing enzymes is also promoted. This is probably due to the increased RNA synthesis. The effects on carbohydrate metabolism are reflected in **hyperglycaemia, glucosuria** and a **diabetic type of glucose tolerance curve**. This effect is associated with **catabolism of proteins** and **lipids**. Cortisol therefore aggravates diabetes mellitus but nevertheless increases the deposition of glycogen in the liver. Protein catabolism is increased, the protein osteoid matrix of the bones atrophies, bone calcium is lost and oesteoporosis occurs. This is further augmented by the **anti-vitamin D action** of glucocorticoids, and an increased calcium excretion by the kidneys. Glucocorticoids have an appreciable **antianabolic** effect and thereby **inhibit wound healing**. The effects on the lipid metabolism are manifested as a lipolysis with mobilization of depot fat. Glucocorticoids cause retention of sodium, chloride, and water, and loss of potassium occurs.

Effect On Organ Systems

Cardiovascular System

The corticosteroids exert a **positive inotropic effect**, and shorten the P–R interval. They increase the reduced responsivity of the vascular smooth muscle to adrenaline and noradrenaline, and capillary dilatation is antagonized. The *blood volume is increased* secondary to electrolyte and water retention. Prolonged corticosteroid administration is likely to cause **steroid-induced hypertension**, as a result of excessive sodium retention, arteriolar oedema and an increased peripheral vascular resistance.

Central Nervous System

They exert **indirect** effects through maintenance of plasma glucose and electrolyte balance essential for CNS activity. The **direct** effects are poorly defined.

The glucocorticoids are required for the maintenance of normal alpha rhythm in the electroencephalogram (EEG). They lower the threshold of nervous tissue to excitation, and the increased CNS excitability may result in convulsions. In both hypocorticism and hypercorticism the EEG reveals a characteristic slow activity, much slower than the alpha rhythm. The abnormal EEG pattern of Addison's disease (adrenal insufficiency) can be reversed by cortisol, but not by deoxycorticosterone. With excessive amounts of glucocorticoids behavioural changes ranging from **euphoria** to **psychosis** can occur.

Gastrointestinal System

Glucocorticoids increase the secretion of gastric hydrochloric acid, pepsinogen and pancreatic trypsinogen. They also facilitate the absorption of fat from the intestines into the lymph. In man they decrease the resistance of the gastric mucosa to the irritant action of the gastric secretions, and produce or aggravate gastric ulceration, i.e., they are *ulcerogenic.*

Urinary System

Cortisol increases plasma volume and filtration pressure, thereby increasing the glomerular filtration rate. There is evidence that cortisol has a direct action on the permeability of the distal and collecting tubular cells, decreasing their permeability to water. This sequence of events leads to **water diuresis**.

Blood and Haemopoietic Tissue

Haematologic effects of glucocorticoids include decrease in lymphatic tissue and in circulating lymphocytes, eosinophils and basophils, but there is an increase in the neutrophils, platelets and erythrocytes. The reduction in lymphatic tissue, and lymphopenia is due to decreased lymphatic mitotic activity (lymphoregression), and destruction of lymphocytes (lympholysis). **Eosinophils are sequestered** in the spleen and lungs under the influence of glucocorticoids. The polymorphonuclear neutrophils are increased in number but their **phagocytic ability is decreased**. The **clotting time is shortened** presumably due to the increased platelets.

Skeletal Muscle

The skeletal muscle needs glucocorticoids for the maintenance of its normal function. Excess of corticoids leads to **muscle wasting** due to catabolism. In Addison's disease the skeletal muscles are weak and fatigue rapidly.

Body Growth

Large doses of glucocorticoids *retard or interrupt the growth of children,* and involves the musculoskeletal system, teeth and other body organs. The cellular activity at the epiphyseal cartilage suffers. Inhibition of growth is widespread. Glucocorticoids inhibit cell division (fibroblasts), and *delay the process of healing.* The *gastric muscosa is devitalized.*

Metabolism and Excretion

In the plasma, cortisol is reversibly bound (95%) to an alpha-globulin called **transcortin** or **corticosteroid binding protein** (CBG). Only free or unbound cortisol (5%) is biologically active. Corticosterone is similarly bound by plasma proteins. The **half-life** of cortisol in the blood is 90–110 minutes. Cortisol is taken up by the liver, where it is **reduced and conjugated** to form water soluble compounds which are excreted in the urine. Most of the cortisol is reduced to **dihydrocortisol** and then to **tetrahydrocortisol**. These tetrahydro-derivatives are conjugated with glucuronic acid, and the highly water soluble glucuronides are excreted by the kidney. A part of cortisol is metabolized and excreted in the urine as **17-ketosteroids**. Corticosterone has a similar metabolism and excretion pathway. **Aldosterone** is mainly bound to albumin. It is broken down in the liver, and its conjugated products (glucuronides) are excreted in the urine.

The **synthetic corticosteroids** are rapidly and almost completely absorbed from the gut on oral administration. They are transported and metabolized in the same manner as endogenous steroids, except that there are **slight differences in their degree of protein binding, stability of the side chain, the rate of reduction and end product formation.**

SYNTHETIC ADRENOCORTICOSTEROIDS

In an attempt to increase the desirable anti-inflammatory action and eliminate the other undesirable pharmacologic effects, the organic chemists have tried to alter and modify the naturally-occurring steroid molecules. Such a molecular manipulation has met with appreciable success, and new synthetic compounds are available in which the *therapeutically useful anti-inflammatory activity has been intensified, and the sodium retaining or mineralocorticoid activity has been minimized.*

Presently, although the natural corticosteroids can be obtained as such from adrenals of animals, they are mostly synthesized from cholic acid, obtained from cattle, or from *steroid sapogenins* like diosgenin found in plants of the *Liliaceae* and *Dioscoreaceae* families. Further modification of these steroids, at various carbon position (1, 2, 6, 9, 16) has resulted in a large group of synthetic glucocorticoids with special pharmacologic characteristics of therapeutic importance. The first synthetic glucocorticoids were **prednisone** and **prednisolone**. They are 4 or 5 times more potent anti-inflammatory agents compared to cortisone and hydrocortisone, and the sodium-retaining activity is much less. Further research resulted in the synthesis of compounds like **dexamethasone** and **betamethasone** in which the anti-inflammatory activity was selectively increased and the salt retaining effect was almost entirely eliminated **(Table 7.5-2).**

Table 7.5-2. *Comparison of the pharmacological profile of commonly used natural and synthetic glucocorticoids*

Glucocorticoid	*Relative Anti-inflammatory potency**	*Relative mineralocorticoid activity***	*Equivalent dose (oral)*	*Routes of Administration****
Short-acting ($t_{1/2}$ <12 hrs)				
Hydrocortisone	1	Strong (2+)	20 mg	PO, IM, IV, IA
Cortisone	0.8	Strong (2+)	25 mg	PO, IM
Intermediate-acting ($t_{1/2}$ 12 to 36 hrs)				
Prednisone	3.5	Moderate (1+)	5 mg	PO
Prednisolone	4	Moderate (1+)	5 mg	PO, IM, IV, IA
Methylprednisolone	5	Little (0)	4 mg	PO, IM, IV, IA
Triamcinolone	5	Little (0)	4 mg	PO, IM, IA
Fluprednisolone	10	Little (0)	1.5 mg	PO
Long-acting ($t_{1/2}$>48 hrs)				
Paramethasone	10	Little (0)	2 mg	PO
Dexamethasone	30	Little (0)	0.75 mg	PO, IM, IA
Betamethasone	30	Little (0)	0.60 mg	PO, IM, IA

* Compared to hydrocortisone, with an arbitrary value of 1.
** Compared to mineralocorticoid fludrocortisone with activity as (5+).
*** PO, oral; IM, intramuscular; IV, intravenous; IA, intra-articular.

Topically applied corticosteroids. When a local effect is desired, corticosteroids may be applied topically in various dosage forms (e.g., ointment, cream, lotion, aerosol, nasal spray, ophthalamic drops), or by intra-articular injection. Their relative potency depends on factors like *concentration of the drug, characteristics of the drug molecule, and the type of vehicle used*. Fluorinated derivatives (betamethasone, fluocinonide, halcinonide) are more potent than non-fluorinated agents (hydrocortisone, desonide), and are also less likely to cause sodium retention, but may exhibit a higher incidence of local adverse effects.

Some important topical glucocorticoids (in alphabetic order) are: alcolometasone, amcinonide, beclomethasone, betamethasone, clobetasol, clocortolone, desonide, desoximetasone, diflorasone, flunisolide, fluocinolone, fluocinonide, fluorometholone, halcinonide, medrysone, mometasone, prednicarbate, and triamcinolone.

To **summarize**, modification of the structure of natural corticosteroids has produced compounds with the following properties:

(1) Mainly glucocorticoid activity with significant mineralocorticoid actions-*Prednisone, Prednisolone, Cortisone.*

(2) Glucocorticoid activity, high anti-inflammatory potency with insignificant mineralocorticoid actions–*Dexamethasone, Betamethasone.*

(3) Mineralocorticoid activity with insignificant glucocorticoid actions–*Fludrocortisone.*

Mode of Action

The natural and synthetic glucocorticoids like other steroid hormones bind to **specific intracellular receptors** located in the cyptoplasm of the target cells. Specific receptors have been clearly demonstrated for **cortisol, aldosterone, testosterone and oestradiol**. The steroids being non-polar, enter the target cells readily by a process of diffusion, and combine with the **cytoplasmic steroid receptors** to form the **steroid–receptor** complex. This is the first obligatory step. The steroid–receptor complex is then transferred (translocated) to the nucleus where it is bound to the chromatin, which functions as the **nuclear acceptor site**. In the nucleus the steroid–receptor complex interacts with DNA and stimulates the transcription of **new messenger-RNA** (m-RNA). This new m-RNA increases the synthesis of the steroid–induced proteins (enzymes), which are responsible for the **glucocorticoid response** in the cells. Thus, there is the steroid–receptor complex formation in the cytoplasm, translocated and bound to nuclear chromatin, leading to transcription of new m-RNA which produces specific steroid-induced enzymes responsible for the glucocorticoid effect **(Fig. 7.5.5)**.

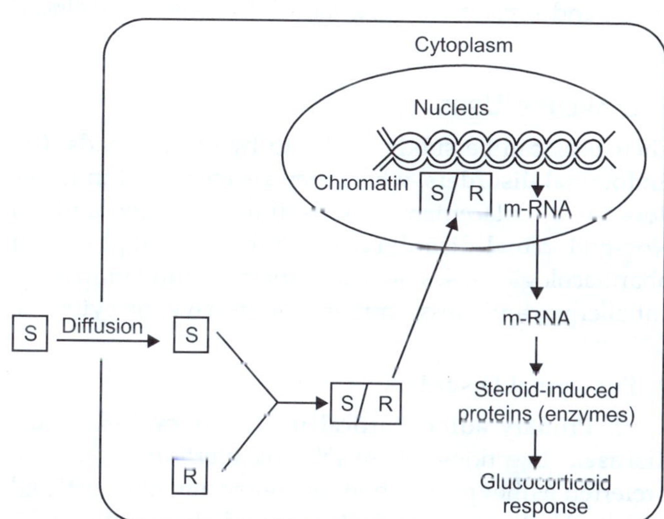

Fig. 7.5.5: A scheme of interaction of the steroid hormone (S) with the cytoplasmic steroid receptor (R), forming the steroid–receptor complex (S/R). Its translocation and binding to nuclear chromatin, transcription of new m-RNA, leading to synthesis of steroid-induced proteins, which are responsible for the glucocorticoid response.

The corticosteroids exert a **non-specific anti-inflammatory action.** The mechanism is incompletely understood. **They decrease hyperaemia, capillary permeability** and **leucocytic infiltration**, resulting in a **decreased fibrinous exudation**. The corticosteroids also **stabilize the lysosomal membranes** in the cells preventing the release of kinins and lytic enzymes. The growth of new capillaries and fibroblastic activity at the site is inhibited, and **healing is delayed**.

The **immunosuppressive action** is possibly due to the cytolytic action of glucocorticoids on the **lymphocytes** and **thymocytes.** In large doses they inhibit antibody formation, and delayed hypersensitivity is also inhibited. The corticosteroids **inhibit homograft rejection reactions** by reducing the amount of antigen liberated by the grafted tissue, as they delay revascularization, and interfere with the sensitization of antibody forming cells.

To **summarize**, the main biologic effects are: enhancement of gluconeogenesis; protein catabolic and antianabolic effect; increased collagen breakdown; anti-inflammatory action due to inhibition of fibroblast proliferation; lysosomal stabilization; reduced capillary permeability and leucocytic infiltration; reduction in lymphoid tissue, circulating lymphocytes and eosinophils; stimulation of erthropoiesis and platelet production; maintenance of muscle strength with physiologic amounts and muscle weakness with supraphysiologic doses; lowered excitation threshold of brain; gastric mucosal atrophy and increased acid secretion; inhibition of bone matrix formation and calcification; reduction of calcium absorption from the gut and promotion of calcium excretion by the kidney; immunosuppression in large doses; and *suppression of the hypothalamo-pituitary adrenal axis*.

THERAPEUTIC USES

Their uses can be subdivided into two main heads: (A) **Endocrinal disorders,** where they are employed in lower doses as a replacement or substitution therapy; and (B) **Non-endocrinal disorders,** where they are employed in pharmacologic doses to exert their anti-inflammatory, antiallergic, antistress, immunosuppressive, or cytotoxic activity.

A. Endocrinal Disorders

1. **Primary adrenocortical insufficiency (Addison's disease).** Injections of *soluble hydrocortisone salts* are preferred, as they possess both gluco- and mineralocorticoid activity. Hydrocortisone 20 to 30 mg daily orally may be administered. It may be supplemented by *fludrocortisone* 0.1 to 0.2 mg daily orally for mineralocorticoid action.

2. **Secondary and tertiary adrenocortical insufficiency**. Secondary adrenocortical insufficiency is due to inadequate ACTH secretion from the pituitary as a result of pituitary disease, surgical ablation, or prolonged administration of pharmacologic doses of glucocorticoids for non-endocrine disorders (iatrogenic; doctor-induced). In tertiary adrenocortical insufficiency there is an inadequate secretion of corticotrophin releasing hormone (CRH) from the hypothalamus. Replacement therapy for both the types of insufficiency is the same, and *cortisol, cortisone* or *prednisone* is commonly used.

3. **Acute adrenocortical insufficiency (Addisonian crisis).** It is characterized by extreme weakness, dehydration, hypotension and gastrointestinal symptoms. It is an emergency, and treated by **hydrocortisone hemisuccinate** 100 mg IV rapidly, followed by **hydrocortisone hemisuccinate** 100 mg IV infusion slowly in 1000 ml of 0.9 percent sodium chloride solution every 8 hourly.

4. **Congenital adrenal hyperplasia syndromes.** In these disorders the synthesis of cortisol and sometimes also aldosterone is interrupted due to certain inherent enzyme deficiency. Due to the lack of the negative feedback, excessive ACTH is released from the pituitary causing an adrenal hyperplasia, and hypersecretion of steroids also occurs from alternate pathways. The symptoms are either of hormone deficiency or excess. The aim of therapy is to suppress ACTH hypersecretion, and usually glucocorticoids (**cortisol, prednisone**) have to be administered throughout life.

5. **Adrenocortical hyperfunction.** In conditions like Cushing's syndrome, adrenogenital syndrome and adrenal virilism, the aim of therapy is to suppress pituitary ACTH production. **Prednisone** and **fludrocortisone** have been tried but the therapy is not effective. Surgical resection of the hyperplastic adrenals has to be done, followed by corticosteroid replacement therapy.

6. **Diagnostic use.** Glucocorticoids (*dexamethasone or betamethasone*) are employed to test the integrity of the hypothalamo-pituitary-adrenal system.

B. Non-endocrinal Disorders

1. **Rheumatic and other joint disorders.** These drugs are used in rheumatoid arthritis, *rheumatoid spondylitis* and *related inflammatory diseases* of the joints, when no response is obtained by conservative treatment with salicylates and other non-steroid anti-inflammatory drugs (NSAID). Arthritic patients do not respond very well to alternate day therapy (ADT), as joint symptoms are severe on the "off" day. Sometimes corticosteroids may have to be injected **intra-articularly**, i.e., directly into the involved joints. Sterile aqueous suspensions of **triamcinolone** often provide relief for 2–4 weeks after each injection. Intra-articular injection of one joint repeatedly should be avoided, as it may lead to joint destruction. Corticosteroids are used in **acute** and **chronic gout** and gouty arthritis.

2. **Collagen diseases.** These diseases are marked by defects in the connective tissue protein (collagen) in the joints, various organs, and deeper layers of the skin. In addition to *rheumatoid arthritis*, they include *disseminated lupus erythermatosus, acute rheumatic fever* and *carditis, periarteritis nodosa, scleroderma* and *pemphigus vulgaris*.

3. **Allergic disorders.** Used in the emergency management of *anaphylactic shock, blood transfusion reactions, Stevens-Johnson syndrome, atopic* and *contact dermatitis, allergic rhinitis, allergic conjunctivitis, hay fever* and *angioneurotic oedema*. For these conditions generally a *short-term therapy is required*, and steroids such as **prednisone** or **methylprednisolone** may be used according to the *stepdown* or *countdown dosage schedule*–a large loading dose is given on the first day, followed by a series of diminishing doses during the next five days. Corticosteroids are employed as immunosuppressants to avoid and control **homograft rejection reactions**.

4. **Dermatologic disorders.** In addition to the above mentioned allergic skin conditions corticosteroids are effective in *psoriasis, seborrheic dermatitis, pruritus vulvi* or *ani, dermatitis herpetiformis* and *pemphigus*. They may be applied topically or taken internally.

5. **Ophthalmic diseases.** These include *irtis, iridocyclitis, choroditis, keratitis, uveitis, corneal ulcers* and *secondary glaucoma*.

6. **Respiratory diseases.** These include *bronchial asthma* and *status asthmatics* and *aspiration pneumonitis*.

7. **Haematologic disorders.** Used in the management of *blood dyscrasias including acquired* or *autoimmune haemolytic anaemia* and *idiopathic thrombocytopenia* or *drug-induced thrombocytopenia, agranulocytosis* and *aplastic anaemia*.

8. **Neoplastic diseases.** Employed as part of the multiple drug regime for acute *lymphatic leukaemia in children, chronic lymphatic leukaemia* in adults, and to control *hypercalcaemia* in cancer including metastatic mammary carcinoma. Also used in *Hodgkin's disease* and other *lymphomatous neoplasms*.

9. **Gastrointestinal diseases.** Employed in cases of *ulcerative colitis, regional enteritis* and *intractable sprue*. Used in liver disorders like *chronic hepatitis, cirrhosis of liver with ascites* which is refractory to diuretic therapy alone.

10. **Acute infectious diseases.** Massive doses of steroids may be employed in acute phases of infections for their *antistress* and *antitoxic* effects, despite their tendency to spread infection. Used in cases of *Gram-negative septicaemia* and *endotoxic shock*, and to control complications of *tuberculous meningitis, tuberculous laryngitis, acute miliary tuberculosis, acute caseous pneumonia, viral infections, mumps orchitis, measles, encephalitis* and so on. Appropriate anti-infective chemotherapy must be administered together with the corticosteroids.

11. **Miscellaneous disorders.** The corticosteroids are used in many other conditions (varied in their aetiology, and have not been included in the above groups). These disorders include *sarcoidosis, berylliosis, Loffler's syndrome, dermatomyositis, myasthenia gravis, infectious mononucleosis, haemorrhagic shock, Bell's palsy, neuritis* and *subacute thyroiditis*.

Contraindications

Corticosteroids must be used with great caution in the following conditions:

1. **Peptic ulcer.** In *active peptic ulcer* these agents may cause haemorrhage and perforation. They may even activate a healed ulcer.

2. **Infections.** Corticosteroids should be avoided in *healed* or *latent tuberculosis, herpes simplex keratitis, fungal* and *exanthematous diseases like chicken pox*.

3. **Hypertension with congestive heart failure.** Fluid retention and potassium loss may complicate the management.

4. **Psychosis.** It may be seriously aggravated. Convulsive disorders may be aggravated.

5. **Diabetes mellitus.** Since corticosteroids are diabetogenic they may aggravate this condition.

6. **Oesteoporosis.** This condition may be worsened due to further demineralization of the bone.

7. **Glaucoma.** The intraocular tension may be further raised.

8. **Pregnancy.** Corticosteroids should be avoided, specially in the first trimester.

Absolute contraindications include *psychoses, severe psychoneuroses, active peptic ulcer, herpes simplex keratitis*, and *infections that cannot be effectively controlled by chemotherapy*.

Adverse Reactions

The adverse reactions of these drugs may be grouped under *five* heads: *metabolic, behavioural, ocular toxicity, adrenal suppression*, and *other complications*.

Metabolic toxicity. Most patients receiving hydrocortisone 100 mg, or an equivalent amount of another glucocorticoid for longer than 2 weeks develop changes termed as **iatrogenic Cushing's syndrome**, and develop "Cushingoid" features. There is a rounding of the face (moon face), the facial skin become flushed, acne-like eruptions develop, and excess of hair growth occurs. Fat deposits at the back of the neck and between the shoulder girdles (**buffalo hump**). The arms and legs thin out as the fat is withdrawn and centripetally deposited on the face and trunk. **Hyperglycaemia**, **glycosuria** and **diabetes** may be unmasked, developed or aggravated. There is an increase in appetite and **weight** gain. **Myopathy** may develop as a result of a negative nitrogen balance. **Osteoporosis** occurs due to demineralization of the bones, as a result of loss of bony matrix. **Avascular aseptic necrosis of bone** can occur. **Peptic ulcers** develop. **Body growth in children is retarded**. The patients may develop **hypertension, oedema,** and **congestive heart failure**. Effect on mineral metabolism may lead to **sodium retention, hypopotassaemia,** and **hypochloraemic alkalosis**.

Behavioural toxicity. Patients develop a **euphoria**, and on prolonged administration they may cause **psychological** and **physical dependence**, leading to a **steroid withdrawal syndrome**. Corticosteroids may induce a **psychotic reaction**. *Cranial nerve palsies* may occur.

Ocular toxicity. Corticosteroids may raise the intraocular pressure, and cause a **steroid-induced glaucoma**. **Posterior subcapsular cataracts** develop, most commonly seen in patients of rheumatoid arthritis on long-term steroid therapy.

Adrenal suppression. When patients are maintained on long-term corticosteroid therapy for chronic disorders there is an appreciable **suppression of the pituitary-adrenal axis** due to the feedback mechanism. The adrenal cortex may become ultimately atrophied leading to a severe adrenal insufficiency, and stoppage of corticosteroids may precipitate an **acute adrenal crisis**. The incidence and severity of adrenal suppression can be minimized by adopting an intermittent dosage schedule, discussed later in this Chapter.

Other complications. Corticosteroids may cause *superinfection* due to resistant microorganisms and fungi *(Candida albicans), exacerbation of infection, accelerated blood coagulation, delayed wound healing,* and *rarely hypersensitivity reactions*. Steroid *arthropathy* may develop on repeated intra-articular injections of corticosteroids.

In general, to minimize steroid-induced adverse effects, patients treated with corticosteroids should be on a *high protein diet*, and *extra potassium* to make up for the loss. *Anabolic steroids* may be used, if required, but not routinely.

PRECAUTIONS

Pharmacologic doses of glucocorticoids may **suppress diagnostic signs** and symptoms of disease due to their anti-inflammatory and immunosuppressive actions. A **peptic ulcer** may perforate with minimal pain and septicaemia may progress without fever. The *two* major aspects to be taken care of are *infection*, and **hypothalamo-pituitary-adrenal** (HPA) axis suppression.

Infection. Glucocorticoid therapy predisposes the patient to infection of all types (becterial, viral, fungal, parasitic). This is largely due to the decreased resistance of the body to infections.

Hypothalamo-pituitary-adrenal axis (HPA) suppression. Exogenous glucocorticoid administration, due to a negative feedback to the HPA, results in some degree of suppression of the HPA axis, depending on the dose and duration of therapy.

INTERMITTENT DOSAGE SCHEDULES

These dosage schedules are **tuned to the circadian rhythm** followed by the HPA axis (discussed earlier in this Chapter), and the **single dose** is administered in the morning, when the pituitary-adrenal axis is least amenable to damage.

Single daily dose schedule. Instead of administration of several small doses during the day, the total daily steroid dose is administered to the patient in the morning at about 8.00 AM.

Alternate Day Therapy (ADT). This dosage regimen is *never* used right from the start of steroid therapy. It is started after the symptoms have been controlled by daily administration of steroids, and then the patient is switched on gradually to this ADT regimen. Some chronic diseases respond equally well to administration of intermediate-acting glucocorticoids *(prednisone, prednisolone, methylprednisolone)* on alternate days.

The ADT regimen consists of administration of a 48-hours dose of an intermediate-acting glucocorticoid between 7.00 to 8.00 AM every other morning. This **simulates the natural circadian rhythm** of glucocorticoid secretion on the "on" day, and the HPA axis is allowed to function physiologically on the "off" day, i.e., when the morning dose is withheld. The ADT is preferred for maintenance whenever possible.

The ADT regimen is useful in the treatment of *asthma, uveitis, nephrotic syndrome* and *disseminated lupus erythematosus*, whereas some patients of *rheumatoid arthritis* and *ulcerative colitis* may develop symptoms on the "off" day when medication is withheld. Such patients may be managed on the single daily dose (24-hour dose) each morning.

STEROID WITHDRAWAL

Once the patient is put on long-term steroid therapy, withdrawal of the drug becomes difficult on two scores: (*i*) the withdrawal may set up an **acute exacerbation** of the underlying disorder, and (*ii*) a **steroid withdrawal syndrome** may develop as the patient craves to take the steroid for the euphoria it produces. Steroids are capable of producing both **psychological** and **physical** dependence, and the withdrawal syndrome is characterized by a feeling of *fatigue, muscle weakness, aches* and *pains, lethargy, anorexia* and *even fever*. The use of ACTH to hasten the recovery of the adrenal gland to produce more endogenous corticosteroids is suggested but debatable.

GUIDELINES FOR CORTICOSTEROID THERAPY

Patients receiving systemic therapy for *non-endocrine disorders* are at risk to develop cushingoid side effects,

Table 7.5-3. *Comparative potency of various mineralocorticoids (compared with cortisone)*

Compound	*Mode of administration*	*Glucocorticoid*	*Mineralocorticoid activity*
Cortisone	Oral	1	1
Adosterone	Injection	None	500
Fludrocortisone	Oral	10-20	150
Deoxycorticosterone	Sublingual	Negligible	50

infections, and suppression of the hypothalamo- pituitary-adrenal (HPA) axis. Following are the main guidelines:

1. **Accurate diagnosis** should be made.

2. Corticosteroid therapy is started only after alternative therapy has failed.

3. The dosage should be determined according to the severity of the disease, and the *smallest dose* that controls the symptoms should be used.

4. Systemic administration of a **single large dose** is usually without adverse effects. With prolonged use of large doses the risk of adverse reactions rises. Intensive therapy must not preferably exceed 72 hours.

5. When possible, **administer corticosteroids locally** (topical, intra-articular) in order to concentrate the therapeutic effect on the diseased part.

6. Pharmacologic doses of **glucocorticoids should not be abruptly stopped**, as an adrenal crisis is likely to develop during the period of recovery of the HPA axis responsiveness, i.e., cessation of prolonged therapy should be very gradual.

MINERALOCORTICOIDS

Aldosterone is the major physiological mineralocorticoid in man, but it is unsuitable for routine medical use as it is inactivated when given orally. **Deoxycorticosterone** (DOC) is also formed and released by the adrenal cortex, although the amount is physiologically insignificant. It also serves as a precursor of aldosterone. **Fludrocortisone,** a synthetic corticosteroid, is the most often used compound when long-term mineralocorticoid treatment is required. Thus out of the *three* mineralocorticoids, only fludrocortisone is clinically useful, and their comparative potency is presented in **Table 7.5-3.**

ALDOSTERONE

Aldosterone is synthesized mainly in the **zona glomerulosa** of the adrenal cortex. ACTH produces only a moderate stimulation of its release. Changes in **plasma potassium** have a marked effect on aldosterone output. A rise in plasma potassium promotes release of aldosterone, which acts on the distal renal tubule, causing an increased output of potassium in urine. **But the most important stimulus to aldosterone secretion is a reduction in blood volume, leading to a fall in mean renal arterial pressure, which results in the release of renin from the juxtaglomerular apparatus of the kidney.** Renin acts upon a circulating alpha$_2$ glubulin (renin substrate), releasing angiotensin I, which is converted to angiotensin II, commonly designated as angiotensin. Angiotensin is a powerful stimulant of aldosterone production by the adrenal cortex **(Fig. 7.5.6)**. Released aldosterone induces the **reabsorption of sodium,** and **loss of potassium with hydrogen ions** in the urine.

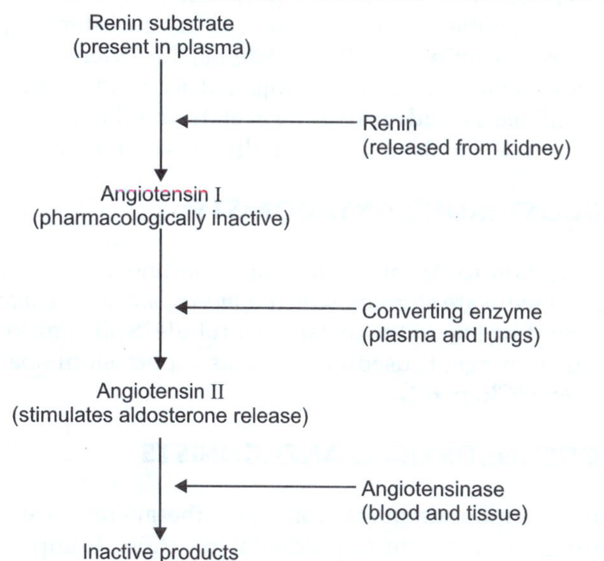

Fig. 7.5.6: The renin-angiotensin-aldosterone system.

Hyperaldosteronism is of two varieties. **Primary hyperaldosteronism** (Conn's disease) is usually due to an adrenal adenoma, or sometimes a carcinoma. It is a rare cause of hypertension. **Secondary hyperaldosteronism** occurs much more commonly, and is associated with disorders like **congestive heart failure, nephrotic syndrome, cirrhosis with ascites, renal artery stenosis, sodium deprivation and potassium excess.**

DEOXYCORTICOSTERONE (DOC)

DOC is a mineralocorticoid with almost no glucocorticoid activity. It is available for parenteral administration as **replacement therapy in chronic primary adrenocortical insufficiency,** and in certain forms of congenital adrenal hyperplasia. **Subcutaneous pellet implantation** maintains the mineralocorticoid effect for 2 to 3 months. Adverse reactions include sodium and water retention, hypokalaemia, hypertension, cardiac enlargement and congestive heart failure.

Fludrocortisone

Fludrocortisone is a halogenated form of cortisol. It has very high mineralocorticoid and moderate glucocorticoid activity. **It is the most often used mineralocorticoid**, as it is the only compound available for oral use, and is employed for the management of **chronic primary adrenocortical insufficiency** and **salt-losing forms of congenital adrenal hyperplasia**. Fludrocortisone is also suitable for use as an anti-inflammatory agent. **Adverse reactions** include oedema, hypertension, and hypokalaemia. Salt intake is adjusted according to need. It is available as **fludrocortisone acetate** and the *dose* ranges between 0.05 to 0.5 mg daily orally for several months.

ALDOSTERONE ANTAGONISTS

In addition to Amphenone B (aldosterone anti-secretory agent) there are steroids which *compete with aldosterone* for the binding site in the distal renal tubule. **Spironolactone** is such an agent, used clinically as a potassium-sparing diuretic **(Chap. 6.2)**.

ADRENOCORTICAL ANTAGONISTS

Such compounds apart from their therapeutic uses can be employed for testing adrenal function. Compounds of clinical importance include **mitotane, metyrapone, aminoglutethimide, and trilostane.**

Mitotane

Mitotane is a derivative of the insecticide chlorphenothane (DDT), and interferes with the corticosteroid biosynthetic pathways, and inhibits steroidogenesis. It may be administered to patients with inoperable adrenal carcinoma in doses upto 10 g daily. Severe toxic effects like tremors, CNS depression, gastrointestinal upset, orthostatic hypotension, retinopathy, and hypersensitivity reaction limit its use. It is available as 500 mg tablets.

Metyrapone

Metyrapone blocks the biosynthesis of corticosteroids by **inhibiting the enzyme 11-β-hydroxylase**. It decreases the synthesis of hydrocortisone, corticosterone and aldosterone.

Metyrapone may be used as a **diuretic** in cases of **resistant oedema associated with aldosterone excess. It is also used to test the capacity of the hypothalamo-pituitary mechanism to produce ACTH**. Metyrapone is available as 250 mg tablets, and also in injectable form.

Aminoglutethimide

Aminoglutethimide *blocks the conversion of cholesterol to pregnenolone*, and thus causes a reduction in the synthesis of all adrenocorticosteroids. *It has been employed with dexamethasone in patients of carcinoma breast to produce a medical adrenalectomy*. Aminoglutethimide is usually administered in a *dose* of 1 g daily. In higher doses it induces extreme lethargy. It may be tried in cases of *adrenocortical malignancy* to inhibit steroid synthesis and secretion.

Trilostane

Trilostane is a synthetic steroid which is a **competitive inhibitor of the 3-β-hydroxysteroid dehydrogenase enzyme system**. There is a corresponding increase in urinary 17-ketosteroids. It has no intrinsic hormonal activity. This agent is available for the treatment of **Cushing's disease**. Trilostane (Modastrane) is available as 30 and 60 mg capsules. The initial dose is 30 mg qid, which may be increased upto 360 mg/day for adequate control. It at best offers temporary relief. **Adverse effects** include GI disturbances, headache, suppression of gonadal function, and hypocortisolism.

DRUG INTERACTIONS

The metabolism of adrenocorticosteroids in the body is increased by drugs that induce the hepatic microsomal enzymes, e.g., *phenobarbitone, phenytoin,* and *rifampicin*. Corticosteroids have a hyperglycaemic effect, and the dose of **hypoglycaemic agents** in the diabetic patients may require an increase. Corticosteroids **increase the clearance of salicylates**, and **decrease the effectiveness of anticoagulants**, which asks for an adjustment of the dose.

7.6 FEMALE SEX HORMONES AND ORAL CONTRACEPTIVES

There are three types of sex hormones: **androgens, oestrogens** and **progestogens**. Both the sexes produce all the three types, but androgens predominate in males, oestrogens and progestogens in females. In the ovaries oestrogens are secreted by the **Graafian follicle**; and progesterone is secreted by the **corpus luteum.**

Physiologic Consideration

The oestrogens and progesterone are responsible for the **cyclic** changes occurring in the endometrium (menstrual cycle). The oestrogens are synthesized in the ovaries, adrenals, placenta and testes. In women the ovaries are the main source of oestrogens. At **puberty** the ovary begins a 30 to 40 years period of cyclic function, under the influence of pituitary gonadotrophins, the most obvious manifestation being **cyclic uterine bleeding**. Ultimately the uterus fails to respond to pituitary gonadotrophins, and there is a cessation of cyclic bleeding termed **menopause**.

The anterior pituitary stimulates the ovary mainly through two gonadotrophic hormones, namely, **follicle stimulating (FSH) and luteinizing (LH) hormone**. The FSH is responsible for the normal growth of the ovarian follicle. Additionally the LH in precise balance with the FSH causes the maturation of the follicle, ovulation, and formation of the corpus luteum. A third hormone, **luteotropic hormone** (LTH, prolactin, lactogenic hormone) then maintains the secretory activity of the corpus luteum to release progesterone. The gonadotrophins therefore initiate pubertal changes in girls and regulate the menstrual cycle in women. **Prolactin** also initiates mammary gland proliferation and secretion of milk. The placenta produces a **chorionic gonadotrophin**, which can be extracted and purified from the urine of pregnant women. It acts like LH plus LTH. Oestrogens and progesterone can inhibit the formation of FSH and LH, respectively, by a **negative feedback mechanism** and prevent ovulation.

At the beginning of each cycle, FSH secretion by the anterior pituitary increases, causing an increase in the oestrogen secretion by the ovarian follicle. This causes proliferation of the endometrium (**proliferative phase**). The oestrogen secretion reaches its peak just before midcycle and synchronized with the brief surge in LH and FSH, precedes ovulation. Thus, under the influence of LH, about day 14 of the cycle, the follicle ruptures and the ovum is released. **Ovulation** is associated with a **rise in basal body temperature** (BBT). After this under the continuing influence of LH, the corpus luteum secretes progesterone **(Fig. 7.6.1)**. Under progesterone effect the uterine glands become coiled and secretory (**secretory phase**). If the ovum is not fertilized, the corpus luteum regresses and the endometrium is shed, i.e., **menstruation** occurs. If fertilization occurs, the corpus luteum continues to secrete oestrogen and progesterone during the early weeks of pregnancy. By the end of the second month of pregnancy the placenta becomes the major source of oestrogen and progesterone for the duration of the pregnancy.

To **summarize**, the main properties of *natural oestrogens* (17-β-Oestradiol, Oestriol, Oestrone; relative potency 100, 10, 1 percent respectively) are to:

1. Stimulate **secondary sex characters** in female.
2. Stimulate the **growth and activity of the mammary gland and endometrium**.
3. Prepare the endometrium for progestogen action (**oestrogen priming**).
4. Prepare the uterus for **spermatozoal transport**.
5. Regulate secretion of gonadotrophins.

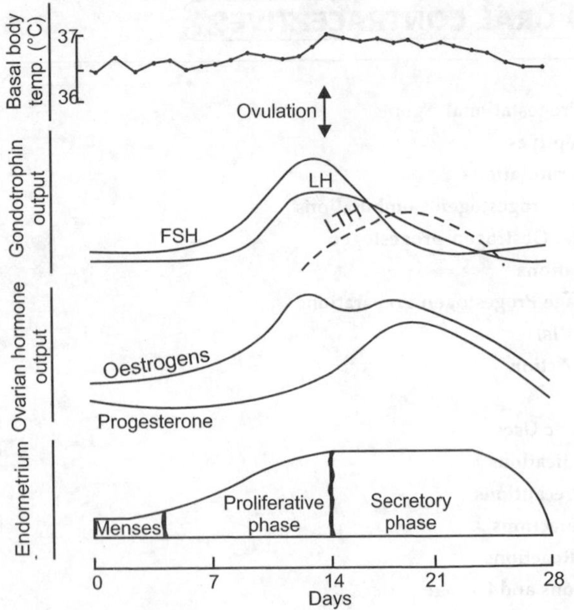

Fig. 7.6.1: The menstrual cycle, showing graphically the pituitary and ovarian hormone output, and the basal body temperature record.

6. Induce mild **anabolism**.
7. Increase vascular permeability and tissue oedema.

The main properties of natural progestogens (Progesterone, 17α-Hydroxyprogesterone, 20α-Hydroxyprogesterone; relative potency 100, 60, 5 percent respectively) are to:

1. Prepare the uterus to receive the embryo.
2. Maintain uterus during pregnancy.
3. Stimulate the growth of mammary glands, but suppress milk secretion.
4. Regulate secretion of gonadotrophins.
5. Induce mild *catabolic* effect.

Oestrogens

The natural oestrogens are steroids, however oestrogenic activity is also shown by non-steroidal compounds. Hence, the term "oestrogen" is used as a **generic** term including all compounds having oestrogenic activity.

Biosynthesis, Metabolism and Excretion

The major natural oestrogens produced by women are **oestradiol**, **oestrone** and **oestriol**. The follicular synthesis of oestradiol is regulated by the pituitary gonadotrophins (LH and FSH) acting together. The gonadotrophins promote the synthesis of enzymes which catalyse the various steps in steroidal biosynthesis. In the first trimester of pregnancy, the **human chorionic gonadotrophin** (HCG) promotes the steroidogenic activity of the corpus luteum. The steps in the synthesis of **androstenedione** are the same in the testes, ovaries and the adrenal cortex.

The initial step in the synthesis of oestrogens is the conversion of acetate to cholesterol. Cholesterol is then converted to **pregnenolone** and **progesterone**. The main stimulatory action of FSH and LH is exerted on the step between cholesterol and pregnenolone. The further steps of synthesis from pregnenolone to androstenedione in the **follicular phase** and **luteal phase** of secretion slightly differ from each other **(Fig. 7.6.2).**

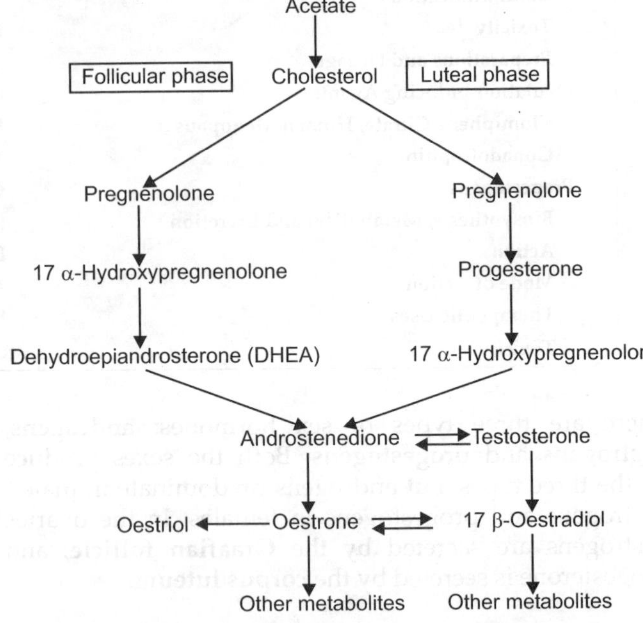

Fig. 7.6.2: Biosynthesis and metabolism of oestrogens.

Androstenedione is either converted directly to oestrone, or may form testosterone which is converted to oestradiol. Testosterone in females is formed in the ovary and adrenal cortex. **Plasma testosterone levels in males are about 10 times higher than in females.**

Oestrogens are secreted at the rate of 200–500 mcg/day at the time of ovulation. About 60 percent of circulating oestrogens are protein-bound, the levels depending on the phase of the menstrual cycle. They are metabolized by the liver, **conjugated** to glucuronide and sulphate, and excreted in the urine and bile. **Urinary excretion levels provide a measure of normal secretion, placental function, and effects of FSH and LH administration in subfertility.**

Actions

Oestrogens are responsible for the **development of the female sexual organs at puberty and the development and maintenance of secondary sexual characteristics.** The oestrogenic effect is exerted on the uterus and adnexa, vagina, clitoris and breast. They cause a thickening and **cornification of the vaginal mucosa**; proliferation of the endometrium of the uterus (proliferative phase); and **ductal growth in the breast**. Their effects are exerted in conjunction with progesterone during the normal menstrual cycle. They contribute to the growth of axillary and pubic hair, and alter the distribution of body fat to produce a **female body contour**. They induce the typical feminine psychological get up and voice. They have **antiandrogenic** actions.

The metabolic actions of oestrogens affect physical growth and plasma proteins. They **promote osteoblastic activity** and **maturation of epiphyses** *in bones*. They decrease the rate of bone resorption in hypogonadal females. They maintain the normal structure of the skin and blood vessels in women. Oestrogens stimulate uterine growth, and reduce the motility of the bowels. They have a growth-promoting activity by stimulating mRNA synthesis, and also act as cofactors in transhydrogenation of NADPH to NAD which promotes **energy production**. Oestrogens have a **hypocholesterolaemic effect**. They enhance blood coagulability, increase plasma fibrinogen levels, and decrease platelet adhesiveness. They promote salt and water retention producing oedema.

Mode of Action

Oestrogens are bound in the target organs to a specific macromolecule–the **oestrogen receptor**. This hormone-receptor complex is transferred to the nucleus where it increases RNA synthesis followed by increased protein synthesis. Oestrogens have a **weak anabolic action**. Physiologically, oestrogens exert either a positive or negative feedback action on the pituitary gonadotrophins, but pharmacologic amounts of oestrogens always lead to an inhibition of the secretion of FSH and LH. *The hypothalamic oestrogen receptors* are more sensitive to oestrogens, than the receptors in the anterior pituitary.

Therapeutic Uses

Oestrogens are used for replacement therapy in oestrogen-deficient patients. For this purpose small doses are adequate. As prolonged therapy leads to endometrial hyperplasia, oestrogens are administered *cyclically*.

1. **Menopausal syndrome.** They provide a relief from vasomotor phenomena, atrophic vaginitis, pruritus vulvae and osteoporosis.
2. **Ovarian dysgenesis**. This condition requires long-term oestrogen administration.
3. **Primary amenorrhoea**. They are administred with or without progestogens.
4. **Carcinoma of the prostate** in the male, and certain breast cancers in postmenopausal women.
5. **Vulvo-vaginitis** in children.
6. Functional uterine bleeding and **endometriosis**.
7. **Acne** and **hirsutism**.
8. **Dysmenorrhoea** (usually combined with progestogens).
9. **Suppression of lactation**.
10. **Postpartum breast engorgement**.
11. For **oral contraception** in combination with progestogens.

The dosages and guidelines vary widely depending on the severity of the specific endocrine disorder.

Contraindications

Oestrogens are not to be used in **oestrogen-dependent neoplasms** of the endometrium or breast. They are contraindicated in patients with **premenopausal carcinomas**, particularly of the breast or uterus, uterine fibroids, renal and hepatic disease, **hypertension** and **thromboembolic diseases**. They should be avoided in undiagnosed genital bleeding. Diethylstilboestrol and related compounds are contraindicated during **pregnancy**.

Toxicity

Anorexia, nausea and *vomiting* is observed frequently specially with the synthetic compounds. Nausea and **breast tenderness** commonly occur, and can be minimized by using the smallest effective dose of oestrogens. Oestrogens are **feminizing**, causing gynaecomastia in males. Salt and water retention leads to weight gain, oedema and cardiac failure. There is an **increased frequency of migraine** headaches. **Hypertension** may develop on prolonged use. Prolonged oestrogen therapy increases the incidence of **thromboembolic disorders** and **hepatic dysfunction**. Calcium retention may occur and lead to renal damage from **nephrocalcinosis**. Despite earlier suggestions of a carcinogenic liability with oestrogen use, in fact, they do not increase the incidence of cervical and breast carcinoma in humans. This possible relationship is a subject of intensive further investigation. *A relationship between the maternal ingestion of diethylstilboestrol during pregnancy and the occurrence of vaginal adenocarcinoma in the offspring has been demonstrated.*

Preparations and Dosage

Three types of oestrogens are available: (*i*) the **naturally occurring** steroid oestrogens; (*ii*) **semisynthetic steroid oestrogens**; and (*iii*) the *synthetic non steroidal oestrogens*. Their specifications are summarized in **Table 7.6-1.**

Oestradiol, oestrone, and oestriol are important naturally occurring oestrogens. **Only oestradiol is the hormone used therapeutically**. Semisynthetic oestrogens like *ethinyloestradiol* are orally effective. *Esterification delays their absorption and prolongs the biologic half-life.* Non-steroidal oestrogens are orally active, and can also be administered parenterally as they are water soluble. *Diethylstilboestrol is possibly the most widely used oestrogen.*

OVULATION INDUCING AGENTS

Certain agents have been employed to induce ovulation, and have been tried in some types of infertility. They

Table 7.6-1. *The three types of common oestrogen preparations available, and their mode of administration*

Classification	*Preparation*	*Usual route of administration*	*Dose range (mg)*
Naturally occurring oestrogen	Oestradiol 17-β	IM	0.22-1.5
Semisynthetic steroidal oestrogens	Oestradiol benzoate (prototype)	Oral	0.1-1.0
	Ethinyloestradiol	Oral	0.05-0.1
	Mestranol	Oral	0.1-0.2
	Quinestrol	Oral	0.05-0.1
	Oestradiol valerate	IM	10-20
	Oestradiol cypionate	IM	5-10
Synthetic non-steroidal oestrogens	Diethylstilboestrol (prototype)	Oral	0.2-1
	Benzoestrol	Oral	3-6
	Hexoestrol	Oral	3-6
	Methallenoestrol	Oral	3-6
	Chlorotrianisene	Oral	10-20

are of no use in women with primary ovarian failure. Representative agents are: *Clomiphene, Human menopausal gonadotrophin, Urofollitrophin,* and *Human chorionic gonadotrophin*.

Clomiphene Citrate

Clomiphene is structurally related to chlorotrianisene. It has an **antioestrogenic** action. Thus through the hypothalamic mechanism, it increases pituitary gonadotrophin (FSH and LH) secretion and stimulates ovulation. The ovaries are enlarged, ovulation and sustained functioning of the corpus luteum are induced. Clomiphene binds to oestrogen receptors, thereby decreasing the number of receptors available for oestrogen action. This is sensed by the hypothalamus and pituitary that the oestrogen level is low, and FSH and LH secretion rises. These responses may be due to the removal of the normal check on gonadotrophin secretion by oestrogens. In proper doses clomiphene is useful in certain cases of **infertility, amenorrhoea** and **functional uterine bleeding**.

Side effects include hot flushes, ovarian enlargement, skin rashes, breast soreness, weight gain, urinary frequency, and heavy menses. Some of the symptoms resemble the menopausal syndrome. Large doses may lead to the formation of **ovarian cysts.**

Dosage

Clomiphene 50 mg orally (beginning on day 5 of the cycle) is administered daily for 5 days. If this dose provokes ovulation it is continued in 5-day course at monthly intervals until pregnancy is established. If there is no response the dose may be increased to 100 mg/day (the duration and interval between courses remaining the same). Treatment beyond three courses is not recommended.

Human Menopausal Gonadotrophins

Human menopausal gonadotrophins (HMG) or **menotrophins** is a purified preparation of gonadotrophins extracted from the urine of postmenopausal women. HMG is biologically standardized for FSH and LH activity, and is an exogenous source of pituitary gonadotrophins. Unlike clomiphere it does not require functional pituitary gonadotrophins for its activity. Treatment with HMG results *only* in follicular growth and maturation; but proper ovulation is induced by subsequent administration of human chorionic gonadotrophin (HCG).

In males, HMG given with HCG for at least 3 months induces **spermatogenesis** in men with primary or secondary pituitary hypofunction.

Menotrophins is used to treat infertility in women with **primary** or **secondary amenorrhoea, polycystic ovary syndrome, anovulatory cycles,** or **irregular menses**. It is used with HCG to stimulate spermatogenesis in men who have **primary** or **secondary hypogonadotrophic hypogonadism**.

Dosage. Menotrophins is available as a powder for injection with 75 U FSH activity, and 75 U LH activity per 2 ml ampoule, or 150 U FSH and 150 U LH activity per 2 ml ampoule. The contents of the ampoule are dissolved in 2 ml of sterile saline and administered IM. In **women,** usually 1 ampoule per day (75 U each of FSH and LH) is given IM for 9–12 days, followed by HCG, 10,000 U IM one day after the last dose of menotrophins. If ovulation occurs without pregnancy, repeat course with same dosage at monthly intervals. If ovulation does not occur, repeat treatment with 1 ampoule/day (150 U each of FSH and LH) for 9–12 days, followed by HCG 10,000 U IM.

Adverse effects of menotrophins include ovarian enlargement with or without abdominal pain, ovarian hyperstimulation syndrome (abdominal pain, ascites, pleural effusion, ovarian enlargement), haemoperitoneum, ovarian cysts, and rarely arterial thromboembolism. Multiple births occur with HMG-HCG treatment in about 15 percent of pregnancies. In men, gynaecomastia occurs.

Urofollitrophin

Urofollitrophin is a purified preparation of gonadotrophin (FSH) extracted from urine of postmenopausal women. It stimulates ovarian follicular growth in women who do not have primary ovarian failure. Treatment results in follicular growth and maturation only; ovulation occurs on subsequent administration of HCG.

Urofollitrophin is available as powder for injection containing 0.83 mg (75 U FSH activity) per ampoule. The recommended initial dose is 75 U/day IM for 7–12 days, followed by HCG 5,000–10,000 U IM one day after the last urofollitrophin dose.

Adverse reactions are of the same type as observed with menotrophins (described above).

Human Chorionic Gonadotrophin

HCG is a purified polypeptide hormone, produced by the human placenta, and extracted from the urine of women during the *first trimester of pregnancy*. The effect of HCG is primarily due to its LH-activity, although it also has some FSH-activity. HCG stimulates the corpus luteum to produce progesterone, and triggers ovulation from FSH-primed follicles. In males, it stimulates the testicular interstitial cells to produce androgens, thereby promoting the development of secondary sex characteristics, and descent of the testes.

HCG is used for **induction of ovulation** in anovulatory women who have been pretreated with HMG or urofollitrophin. HCG is also used to treat **cryptorchidism** (undescended testes) where there is no anatomical obstruction, and for the treatment of **male hypogonadism** secondary to pituitary hypofunction.

Dosage. HCG is available as a powder for injection containing 200 U/ml, 500 U/ml, 1000 U/ml, and 2000 U/ml, after reconstitution. HCG is given IM and the dosage is highly individualized.

Adverse reactions include ovarian hyperstimulation, rupture of ovarian cysts with haemoperitoneum, multiple births, arterial thromboembolism, depression, and gynaecomastia in males. HCG is *contraindicated* in prostatic carcinoma, other androgen-dependent neoplasms, and in the presence of precocious puberty.

Progestogens

Progesterone, a steroid derivative of pregnane, is the main natural progestogen. It is secreted by the **ovary, placenta, testes** and **adrenals**. In addition to its hormonal effects, it serves as a precursor of oestrogens, androgens and adrenocorticosteroids.

Biosynthesis, Metabolism and Excretion

The biosynthesis of progesterone mainly occurs in the **corpus luteum** and the **placenta**. It is synthesized from acetate, cholesterol and pregnenolone **(Fig. 7.6.2)**. The rate of secretion varies, but during the luteal phase the corpus luteum secretes about 10–20 mg/day (males secrete 1 to 5 mg/day). Progesterone is rapidly absorbed following administration by any route. It has a short plasma half-life of 5 minutes. It is **rapidly metabolized in its first passage through the liver** to pregnanediol, which is further metabolized and excreted in the urine as sulphate and glucuronide conjugates. For this reason it is **ineffective orally**. Progesterone is not very effective pharmacologically. Chemical modification of its structure has resulted in derivatives which are orally active and have a much longer half-life.

Actions

Just prior to ovulation, there is an elevation in FSH and LH levels, and the secretion of progesterone is initiated at this time **(Fig. 7.6.1)**. The LH facilitates the transformation of a follicle to a corpus luteum, which secretes progesterone and oestrogen. **Thus progesterone is secreted by the corpus luteum mainly in the second half of the menstrual cycle (luteal phase). Progesterone elevates the basal body temperature shortly after ovulation**. This elevation may be used to detect ovulation in women and is the basis of the "rhythm method" of birth control.

The actions of progesterone on the nonpregnant uterus are evident only after priming by oestrogens, and it induces the secretory phase in the endometrium. **Thus, the actions of oestrogen and progesterone on the uterus are synergistic**. If the ovum is not fertilized, progesterone secretion from the corpus luteum abruptly terminates at the end of the cycle, and this is responsible for the onset of menstruation.

If fertilization of the ovum occurs, the corpus luteum continues to secrete progesterone for upto the third month, and later it is produced in increasing amounts by the placenta. Progesterone prepares the endometrium for the **implantation of the ovum** (nidation). It promotes **aleveolar (acinar) growth in the oestrogen-primed breast**. In addition, the growth hormone and prolactin are also essential for the development of the breast for lactation. **Progesterone renders the uterus less sensitive to oxytocin and ergonovine**. During the third month of pregnancy the developing placenta starts secreting enough of oestrogen and progesterone, and the corpus lutem is no longer required for further gestation. *Progesterone from the placenta inhibits the FSH and LH release, which in turn leads to suppression of ovulation during gestation. In late pregnancy the uterus shifts from the progesterone-dominated state to an oestrogen-dominated state and uterine excitability is increased.*

Mode of Action

Recent studies support the presence of **progesterone receptors**, which are macromolecules located in the cytoplasm and nucleus of the target organs, including the hypothalamus and the anterior pituitary. Progesterone on entering the target cells binds with the cytoplasmic receptors, which is an essential prerequisite for nuclear binding with acidic proteins associated with chromatin. As a result of this, progesterone increases the metabolic activity and growth of the female reproductive organs (uterus, fallopian tubes, breast). It also is partly responsible for inhibiting the pituitary gonadotrophins (FSH, LH).

Therapeutic Uses

Progestogens are mainly used with oestrogens as **oral contraceptives**. They may be tried in **threatened or habitual abortion**, but their efficacy is uncertain. They are used in cases of **dysmenorrhoea, premenstrual tension, menstrual irregularities**, and **functional uterine bleeding**. In **endometriosis** they suppress the symptoms by inhibiting ovulation. The use for diagnosis of pregnancy is reported to be hazardous. A technical report of the WHO which appeared in 1981 has strongly recommended that *hormonal pregnancy tests should be discontinued*, as in case pregnancy is detected the foetus could develop congential defects in the heart and limbs. **Alternative chemical pregnancy tests to detect "human chorionic gonadotrophins" in urine may be used.**

Toxicity

Sodium and water retention may occur. Progesterone and progestational agents administered early in pregnancy, may lead to **masculinization of the external genitalia in the female foetus**. Increased incidence of **congenital abnormalities** has been reported following the use of progestogen-containing hormonal pregnancy tests. **Hence, the use in pregnancy tests is forbidden.**

Dosage

Many synthetic progestogens are available, and have been detailed later in this Chapter. Progesterone (20–60 mg IM daily) may be given in an oily solution. Progesterone suppositories or pellets for subcutaneous implantation are available.

Synthetic Progestational Agents

Many synthetic progestogens, mainly of three types: (*i*) **progesterone derivatives**; (*ii*) **testosterone derivatives**; and (*iii*) **19-nortestosterone derivatives** are available today (**Table 7.6-2**). They possess optimal progestational activity, and have the advantage of being *orally active with a longer duration of action*.

Progesterone and its derivatives are mainly used for **gynaecological disorders**, and in contrast, the 19-nortestosterone derivatives are commonly used with oestrogens (combination/sequential preparations) **for oral contraception in women**. The progestogens related to 19-nortestosterone are more likely to produce virilizing side effects.

Oral Contraceptives

Contraception can be accomplished by intercepting the birth process at any point from gametogenesis in the gonads to endometrial implantation of the fertilized ovum: **oral contraceptives** prevent ovulation; oral agents to *suppress spermatogenesis* are being developed; sperms may be destroyed by **vaginal spermicides**; and union of sperm and ovum may be mechanically prevented. Development of a **vaccine to neutralize human chorionic gonadotrophin** is the latest immunologic approach to contraception.

There are at least **nine** methods of birth control which have been proved to be at least 97 percent effective, i.e.,

Table 7.6-2. *The synthetic progestational agents and their hormonal profile*

Type		Hormonal activities				Duration of action (days)
		Progestogenic	Oestrogenic	Androgenic	Anabolic	
I.	*Progesterone and derivatives*					
	Progesterone	+	–		–	1
	Dydrogesterone	+	–	–	–	1 to 3
	Hydroxyprogesterone caprote	+	–	Slight	–	9 to 17
	Medroxyprogesterone acetate	+	–	+	–	Tab: 1 to 3 days Inj 4 to 12 weeks
II.	*Testosterone derivative*					
	Dimethisterone	Slight	–	–	–	1 to 3
III.	*19-nortestosterone derivatives*					
	Norethynodrel	Slight	+	–	–	1 to 3
	Lynestrenol	Slight	+	+	+	1 to 3
	Norethindrone	+	Slight	+	+	1 to 3
	Ethynodiol diacetate	+	Slight	+	–	1 to 3
	d-Norgestrel	+	–	+	+	1 to 3

* Activities have been worked out on animal species; + = active; – = inactive

only 3 pregnancies occur per 100 women per year in couples who use them strictly according to instructions. They are: the **pill** (combined), the **minipills** (progestogen only), **intrauterine devices** (IUDs), **diaphragms, condoms, condoms plus foam, foam, natural family planning** (basal body temperature method, cervical mucus method), and **sterilization** (tubal ligation for women, or vasectomy for men). The other methods including **calender rhythm, vaginal suppositories** and **tablets** have a much lower effectiveness. The comparative estimates of effectiveness reported in literature are shown in **Table 7.6-3**.

Table 7.6-3. *Comparison of contraceptive efficacy of various contraceptive methods*

Method	*Pregnancy rate per year (%)*	
	Theoretical effectiveness	*Use effectiveness*
The Pill (combined)	0.1	4-7
The "Minipill" (Progestogen only)	2.5	4
Intrauterine Devices (IUDs)	1-3	4-9
Vaginal spermicides	3	2-30
Foam	3	22
Condom and Foam	1	5
Condoms, Diaphragm	3	3-20
Rhythm	13	25-30
No contraception	Pregnancy would occur in 80 to 85% of women	

Family planning aims at the limitation and spacing of childbirths in the best interest of the mother, the child, and the rest of the family. Such a planning is **needed to counter population explosion**. It requires a combined and ceaseless effort by **sociologists, educators, biologists** and the **medical profession**.

Types of Formulations

Three types of oral contraceptive formulations are available: (*i*) Oestrogen-progestogen combinations (*combination pills*); (*ii*) Sequential oestrogen-progestogen preparations (*sequential pills*); and (*iii*) Continuous low-dosage progestogen preparations (*minipills*).

Oestrogen–progestogen combinations. The combination pill is administered as a single daily dose from **day 5 to day 25** of the menstrual cycle (21 days), counting the first day of menses as day 1. Withdrawal bleeding occurs within 3 to 4 days on completion of the course. *In* between there are 7 **pill-free days**, and the course is restarted on day 5 of the next cycle. On repeating this schedule the cycle becomes anovulatory with regular cyclic bleeding. The combination pills are almost 100 percent effective in preventing conception.

Sequential oestrogen-progestogen preparations. In the sequential regime also pills are administered from **day 5 to day 25** of the menstrual cycle (21 days). From day 5 to day 20, a single pill daily containing oestrogen alone is administered, followed by single oestrogen–progestogen combination pill from day 21 to day 25 (16+ 5 = 21). **There are 7 pill-free days** during which withdrawal bleeding occurs. Serial packs are available, containing 16 oestrogen pills, 5 oestrogen–progestogen pills, and 7 placebo pills. **The woman is just instructed to take one pill a day in serial order**. Such packs ensure proper administration and convenience. Inhibition of ovulation is mainly due to oestrogen alone, the progestogen is added to ensure satisfactory bleeding. There can be small variation in the above two pill administration schedules. *This schedule also is highly effective*.

Low-dosage progestogen preparations. The minipills are preparations containing a progestogen alone (norethindrone; norgestrel). These progestogens in low dosage are to be taken daily continually to control fertility. *This schedule is less effective than the combination or sequential contraceptive schedules*.

Mode of Action

The oestrogen-progestogen combination contraceptives suppress ovulation by an interference with the hypothalamic-pituitary mechanisms. The hypothalamic gonadotrophin releasing hormone (FSH-LH-RH) is inhibited, which leads to a **suppression of FSH and LH release** from the anterior pituitary **(Fig. 7.6.3)**. A *direct* inhibiting effect on the pituitary secretion of gonadotrophins is also likely. The follicular FSH, and the midcycle FSH and LH peaks are not seen. In the **combination pills**, the suppression of FSH and LH caused by the oestrogen is enhanced by the progestogen. In contrast, the **sequential pills** depend on oestrogen alone to suppress FSH and LH release. The addition of

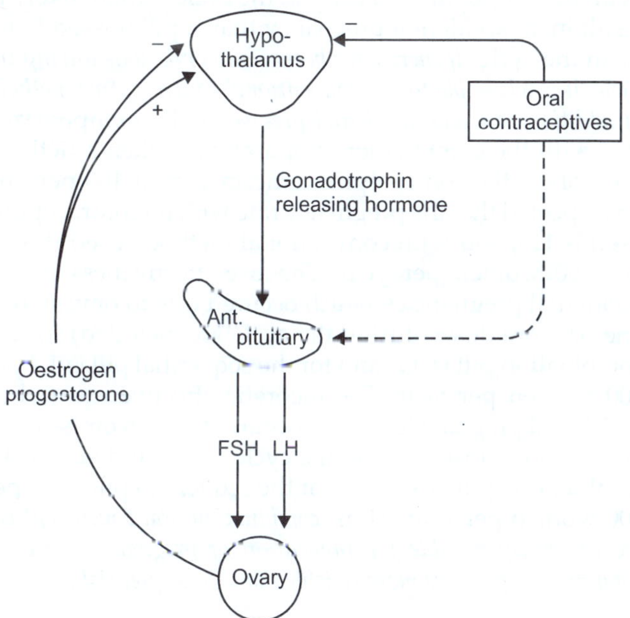

Fig. 7.6.3: The hypothalamo-pituitary-ovarian axis (left). Inhibition of the hypothalamic gonadotrophin releasing hormone by oral contraceptives exerts antiovulatory effect (right). They may exert a direct inhibiting effect on the pituitary secretion of gonadotrophins. (+ = stimulation; – = inhibition).

the progestogen later in the cycle ensures endometrial shedding. Thus, it is reasonable to believe that for the combined preparations, the **inhibition of ovulation is mainly due to the oestrogenic component** of the pill, and progestogens serve to ensure prompt **withdrawal bleeding**.

In addition, these preparations **increase the viscosity of the cervical mucus**, and the secretion is less copious rendering it hostile to penetration by sperms. There is a stromal deciduation of the uterus towards the end of the cycle, and there are certain **changes in the motility and secretions of the fallopian tubes**, which presumably interfere with fertilization. The combination pills offer a better contraceptive control, as with the sequential pills the incidence of breakthrough bleeding is greater and the menstrual flow may be heavy.

The **low dose progestogen preparations** given continually alter the endometrium and put it out of phase with ovulation. There is no disruption of the cycle and **ovulation continues**. The **viscosity of the cervical mucus is increased**. Thus, the "minipill" action is by alteration of the cervical mucus and endometrium, without interfering with ovulation.

Efficacy

The first report on the successful use of orally administered norethynodrel–mestranol combination for inhibition of ovulation appeared in 1956. Now the oral contraceptives have been in use for the past about 55 years.

Forgetting to take a single pill during the 21-day course of the combinations or sequentials rarely leads to ovulation. A pill missed early in the cycle is more likely to result in an accidental pregnancy than a pill missed latter on in the cycle. *If there have been many omissions during the cycle, it is advisable to use conventional contraceptive methods in addition to avoid accidental pregnancy.* It is emphasized that with the combination preparations, taken strictly as prescribed, the contraceptive efficacy is near 100 percent. It is reported that the pregnancy rate with no contraceptive used is 115, and with conventional methods used it is 19 per 100 women per year. The use-effectiveness (when accidental pregnancies which occured due to omission of one or more doses during the cycle are included) for the combination pill is 0.7, and for the sequential pill is 1.4 per 100 women per year. The theoretic effectiveness (when accidental pregnancies which occurred due to omission of one or more doses during the cycle are excluded) for the combination pill is 0.1, and for the sequential pill is 0.5 per 100 women per year. Thus, *combination oral contraceptives are extremely reliable for prevention of pregnancy; and the combination pills are more reliable than the sequential pills.*

Therapeutic Uses

1. **As oral contraceptives.** It is advisable that additional contraceptive means be employed during the first two months of medication, as suppression of ovulation may not be complete. Normal ovulatory cycle follows within 1 to 3 months of stoppage of medication. Thus, they offer a safe and **reversible** contraception.
2. The combination products have been employed in **endometriosis**, when severe dysmenorrhoea is the major symptom. Suppression of ovulation is followed by painless periods. They have been used in certain cases of **premenstrual tension** and **menstrual irregularities**. In cases of **functional sterility** suppression of ovulation for 3 to 6 months may increase the chances of conception (rebound effect).

Contraindications

The *absolute* contraindications are *thromboembolic or arterial disease, diabetes mellitus, hyperlipidaemia, liver disease, breast and uterine carcinoma, undiagnosed vaginal bleeding, migraine* and *pregnancy*. The *relative* contraindications are *hypertension, epilepsy* and *depression*.

Special Precautions

Each woman before oral contraceptive medication must be subjected to a **gynaecologic examination, evaluation of the cardiovascular, and liver function**. Care must be observed in women with a history of asthma, diabetes, endocrine disorders, epilepsy and migraine. Discontinuation of medication is advised on the occurrence of migraine-type headache, acute visual disturbances, and first signs of thrombophelebitis, or embolism. Oral contraceptives may precipitate attacks of porphyria.

Drug Interactions

It is very likely that co-administration of other drugs may cause a failure of contraception in women taking the contraceptive pill. In 1971 it was first reported that **rifampicin**, an antituberculous drug, caused a failure of contraception and pregnancies resulted. Breakthrough bleeding and failure of contraception was noted in patients on anticonvulsant drugs. **Phenobarbitone, phenytoin, primidone** and **carbamazepine** are potent inducers of hepatic microsomal enzymes in humans, and hence are expected to increase the rate of metabolism of the contraceptive steroids. Antibiotics like **ampicillin** and **tetracycline** have also been reported to lead to failure of oral contraception. With these interactions in view, it is advisable for all women taking **broad spectrum antibiotics, anticonvulsants** or **rifampicin**, to use alternative contraceptive methods. Oral contraceptive steroids also interfere with a number of investigative laboratory tests.

Adverse Reactions

Incidence of serious side effects associated with the use of oral contraceptives is low.

Table 7.6-4. *Side effects of oral contraceptives, categorized according to the hormonal defect (excess/deficiency).*

Oestrogen component	*Progestogen component*
Excess*	**Excess***
Nausea, bloating	Increased appetite, weight gain
Hypermenorrhoea	Hypomenorrhoea
Uterine or leg cramps	Acne, hair loss, hirsutism
Chloasma	Depression
Breast fullness or tenderness	Breast regression
Cervical mucorrhoea, polyposis	Monilial vaginitis
Migraine, headache	Changes in libido
Thrombophlebitis	Cholestatic jaundice
Cerebrovascular accidents	Hypertension (?)
Dizziness, vertigo	
Hypertension (?)	**Deficiency***
Deficiency*	Late breakthough bleeding
Irritability, nervousness,	Amenorrhoea
Hot flushes	Hypermenorrhoea
Early/midcycle spotting	Clotting
Decreased libido	
Hypomenorrhoea	

* When these side effects occur, a correction may be attempted by adjusting the oestrogen-progestogen balance or dosage.

Mild side effects include *nausea, vomiting*, headache, lethargy, *breast discomfort* (mastalgia), *breakthrough bleeding* (spotting), oedema, and mild *depression*. Libido is often increased because the fear of pregnancy is removed.

More serious side effects may be *profuse breakthrough bleeding, oligomenorrhoea or amenorrhoea, weight gain, increased skin pigmentation, acne, hirsutism* and *vaginal infection (mainly candidiasis).*

Very serious side effects include the increased risk of deep vein thrombosis, and pulmonary embolism. There is a 5-to 10-fold increase in the incidence of **thromboembolic disorders**. Cerebral or coronary thrombosis may occur. *Severe* **hypertension, decreased glucose tolerance** and **secondary diabetes mellitus** may develop. **Liver damage** and **cholestatic jaundice** with an increased incidence of **hepatic adenomas**, gall bladder diseases including cholecystitis and cholangitis have been reported. **Severe depression** may occur which requires immediate cessation of therapy. **Antenatal exposure to oral contraceptives appreciably increases the incidence of birth defects**, which may be remembered by the acronym "VACTOL" (anomalies of the vertebrae, anus, cardiac function, trachea, oesophagus and limbs). *However, the benefit-risk ratio justifies their use for reversible contraception.* The liability of these agents to induce breast carcinoma is under scrutiny.

The side effects produced by oral contraceptives can be categorized according to the hormonal defect produced **(Table 7.6-4)**. Their incidence can be minimized by choosing the appropriate combination formulation from the large range of preparations available.

Preparations and Dosage

Currently a number of oral contraceptive preparations are available. Some representative agents are listed in Table **7.6-5.**

Many contraceptive preparations are available in *calendar like containers*, which help the user to count the days. A pill is to be taken every day regardless of when menses start or stop.

Intrauterine Progesterone Contraceptive System

This system is a T-shaped intrauterine device (IUD) containing **38 mg of progesterone dispersed in silicone oil.** On its insertion into the uterine cavity, progesterone is continuously released at an average rate of 65 mcg/day. Its effectiveness is about the same as that of progestogen-only tablet for 1 year, after which the system has to be replaced. The system supresses the proliferation of endometrial tissue, creating an environment unfavourable for implantation. It also **decreases sperm survival time** by altering the cervical mucus, but does not prevent ovulation.

Adverse reactions include dysmenorrhoea, amenorrhoea, cervical erosion, vaginitis, endometritis, spotting, prolonged menstrual flow, uterine perforation, ecotopic pregnancy and pain. The device should be inserted immediately after menstruation to ensure absence of pregnancy. The risk of pelvic inflammatory disease (PID) is increased with the use of intrauterine devices.

Table 7.6-5. *The composition of some oral contraceptive preparations*

Trade name	*Progestogen (mg)*	*Oestrogen (mg)*
The combination pills*		
Hemovulen	Ethynodiol diacetate (1.0)	Ethinyloestradiol (0.05)
Ovulen 50	Ethynodiol diacetate (1.0)	Ethinyloestradiol (0.05)
Lyndiol 1 mg	Lynestrenol (1.0)	Ethinyloestradiol (0.05)
Noracyclin	Lynestrenol (1.0)	Ethinyloestradiol (0.05)
Minovlar ED	Norethisterone acetate (1.0)	Ethinyloestradiol (0.05)
Orlest 28	Norethisterone acetate (1.0)	Ethinyloestradiol (0.05)
Ortho-novin	Norethisterone acetate (1.0)	Mestranol (0.05)
Ovral	Norgestrel (0.5)	Ethinyloestradiol (0.03)
Ovral-L	Norgestrel (0.3)	Ethinyloestradiol (0.03)
Primovlar 30	Norgestrel (0.5)	Ethinyloestradiol (0.05)
Primovlar 50	Norgestrel (0.5)	Ethinyloestradiol (0.05)
Primovlar 50 ED	Norgestrel (0.5)	Ethinyloestradiol (0.05)
The sequential pills**		
Oracon	Dimethisterone (25)	Ethinyloestradiol (0.1)
Norquen	Norethindrone (2.0)	Mestranol (0.08)
Ortho-novum SQ	Norethindrone (2.0)	Mestranol (0.08)
The minipills***		
Orvette	Norgestrel (0.075)	—
Micronor	Norethindrone (0.35)	—

* Combinations: for 21 days, and 7 off days.
** Sequentials: only oestrogen for 14 to 16 days, then combination for 5 or 6 days, and 7 or 8 off days.
*** Minipills: Taken daily continuously.

Postcoital Contraception

When coitus has occurred without contraceptive protection, and pregnancy is not desired, large doses of oestrogens may be administered during the preimplantation stage to avoid the unwanted pregnancy. Such interceptive postcoital measures are referred to as "morning after" contraception. Large doses of the oestrogens (diethylstilboestrol is claimed to be most effective) are administered **within 72 hours after unprotected midcycle sexual exposure**. Various regimens may be used **(Table 7.6-6)**.

These high doses of oestrogens disturb the passage of the ovum through the fallopian tubes. They also alter the endometrium and interfere with nidation.

To **summarize,** the oral contraceptives do provide a reliable means for reversible contraception, but the directions for their use and precautions must be strictly observed. The long-term (5 years) implantable contraceptive **Levonorgestrel** in a dose of 1.5 mg as a single dose is effective if taken within 72 hours of unprotected intercourse.

Table 7.6-6. *The various postcoital contraceptive oestrogen regimens*

Oestrogen	*Mode of administration (oral)*
Diethylstilboestrol	25 mg twice daily for 5 days
Ethinyloestradiol	2.5 mg twice daily for 5 days
Oestrone	5 mg thrice daily for 5 days
Ethinyloestradiol and Norgestrel (Ovral)	100 mcg ethinyloestradiol and 1 mg norgestrel (2 Ovral tablets) taken twice 12 hours apart.

7.7 MALE SEX HORMONES, ANABOLIC STEROIDS, MALE ANTIFERTILITY AGENTS AND ANTI-IMPOTENCY DRUGS

The male sex harmones or **androgens** are mainly secreted by the **testes**, and to a lesser extent by the **adrenal cortex** and the **ovary**. The most potent natural androgen is **testosterone**, and is secreted by the testicular **interstitial cells of Leydig**.

ANDROGENS

PHYSIOLOGIC CONSIDERATION

At puberty there is an increased secretion of pituitary gonadotrophins, follicle-stimulating hormone (FSH), and the luteinizing hormone (LH, same as interstitial- cell-stimulating hormone, ICSH in males). The FSH and ICSH have interdependent as well as independent actions. The FSH stimulates the metabolic activity of the **Sertoli cells** in the seminiferous tubules, and promotes spermatogenesis. The ICSH promotes the deveopment of the **interstitial cells of Leydig**, which synthesize and secrete testosterone. The secretion is regulated by a hypothalamic-pituitary servomechanism. **Physiological levels of testosterone are necessary for the maintenance of spermatogenesis, development of accessory sex organs and the secondary sexual characters**. The less potent androgens like **androstenedione** and **dehydroepiandrosterone** are secreted by the adrenal cortex and the ovary, which are biotransformed in liver and kidney to testosterone. The androgens are concerned with sexual maturation in the male, and the development of the male physical characters: **muscularity, facial hair, lower-pitched voice, baldness, texture of the skin** and so on. Testosterone is also responsible for the emotional make up of the male. Under-production leads to **male hypogonadism**.

To summarize the main properties of natural androgens 5-α-dihydrotestosterone, testosterone, androstenedione dehydroepiandrosterone; relative potency 100, 50, 8, 4 percent respectively), are to :

1. Induce secondary sex characters of males (body hair, deep voice, penile growth), and body hair of females.
2. Induce and *maintain secondary sex characters of males* (accessory sex organs).
3. Support *spermatogenesis*.
4. Influence *sexual* and *aggressive behaviour* in males and females.
5. Induce *protein anabolism, somatic growth*, and *ossification*.
6. Regulate *secretion of gonadotrophins*.

BIOSYNTHESIS, METABOLISM AND EXCRETION

The enzymes required for the synthesis of androgens are found in the testes, ovary, adrenal cortex and placenta. Testosterone blood levels in men (0.4–1 mcg/100 ml) are much higher than in women (0.1 mcg/100 ml). Testicular sterioidogenesis mainly occurs in the interstitial cells (**Leydig cells**) and also in the sustentacular cells (**Sertoli cells**). The *Sertoli cell androgens additionally stimulate spermatogenesis*. The interstitial cells contain cholesterol ester from which the natural androgen, testosterone is synthesized **(Fig. 7.7-1)**.

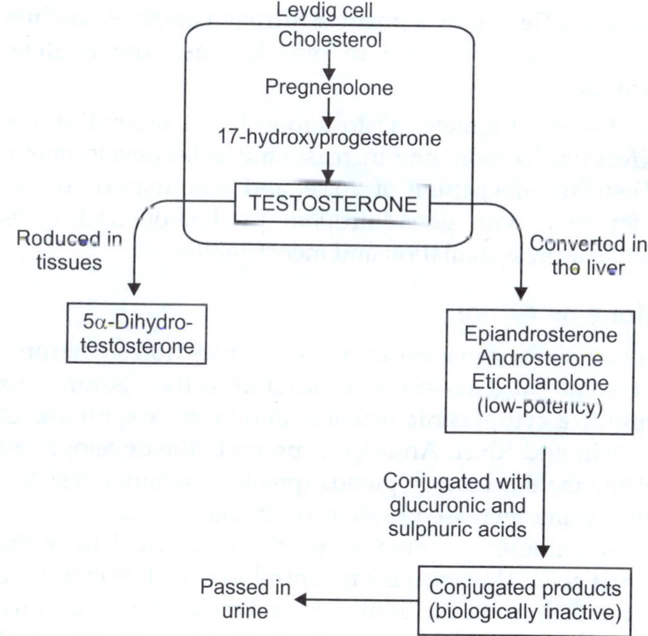

Fig. 7.7.1: The biosynthesis and fate of testosterone.

The Leydig cell testosterone readily enters systemic circulation, is bound to a specific protein carrier, and transported to the tissues where it is reduced to 5-α-*dihydrotestosterone*, which is the active intracellular androgen.

In man, testosterone is inactivited in the liver to *androsterone, epiandrosterone*, and *etiocholanolone*, which are conjugated with sulphate and glucuronic acid. These inactive conjugates are passed in the urine. These can be estimated (as 17-ketosteroids) over 24–48 hours urinary excretion, providing a measure of androgen production.

Testosterone cannot be given orally as it is rapidly inactivated in the liver. The oral preparation methyltestosterone is rapidly absorbed and slowly inactivated by the liver.

ACTIONS

Androgens are responsible for the development of the **primary** and **secondary sex characters in the males at puberty**, and are necessry for **spermatogenesis**. At puberty ICSH induces testosterone production and release, causing growth of the sex organs, the development of pubic hair and male hair distribution, rapid growth of the skeleton and musculature, and deepening of the voice. There is an increase in body weight, thickening and increased oiliness of the skin (acne), growth of the beard, fusion of epiphyses and later on a development of the male pattern of baldness. **Androgens have a weak mineralocorticoid activity. Oestrogens have appreciable antiandrogen activity.**

All the above mentioned effects are dependent on the **androgenic** and **anabolic** effects of testosterone exerted primarily on the reproductive and the musculo-skeletal systems, and the skin and hair. **Anabolic effects are mainly reflected by a positive nitrogen balance, calcium retention and increase in muscle mass and skeletal growth.**

Given to females testosterone has a **masculinizing effect** (virilization) and increases muscular development. Hirsutism, deepening of voice, and acne may occur. By interfering with gonadotrophin production androgens may suppress ovulation and menstruation.

MODE OF ACTION

The active form of testosterone is **5-α-dihydrotestosterone**. At some sites testosterone itself is active. Androgens bind to a **cytoplasmic receptor**, and increase synthesis of protein and RNA. Androgens promote the development of the male accessory glands (prostate, seminal vesicles) by causing increased protein synthesis *via* stimulation of RNA and RNA polymerase activity in the nucleus of the target cells. They also exert control over cell growth by a **direct** action on DNA synthesis, and on the mitotic cycle of the cells. Recent evidence is suggestive of the involvement of cyclic-adenosine monophosphate (c-AMP) as an intermediary in androgen action.

THERAPEUTIC USES

Androgens are employed for their *masculinzing, antioestrogenic* or *protein anabolic actions*. Testosterone has a combined androgenic–anabolic pharmocologic profile.

1. In the male androgens are used in **cryptorchidism**, and as replacement therapy in **hypogonadism** or castration. Their use in impotency is equivocal. Also used for *induction of delayed puberty* and *eunachoidism* at puberty when gonadotrophins are ineffective. May be used in *male climacteric*.
2. In the female they are used in **inoperable breast cancer** and **chronic cystic mastitis**.
3. In both sexes they can be used as **anabolic agents** to reverse protein loss after trauma, surgery, prolonged immobilization, or in debilitating disease. May be used in **senile osteoporosis**.
4. Testosterone is capable of stimulating haemopoiesis and may be used in **refractory** and **aplastic anaemia**, certain **leukaemias**, and in **thrombocytopenia**.

CONTRAINDICATIONS

The contraindications are *pregnancy and lactation; carcinoma of the prostate and male breast, cardiac and renal disease*. Caution must be observed in cases of *hypertension* and *liver disease*. Androgens should be used with great caution in infants and young children.

TOXICITY

Androgens can lead to **sodium retention, hypertension, oedema** and **congestive heart failure**. **Hypercalcaemia, premature closure of epiphyses and stoppage of linear growth** may result. Masculinization or virilization, clitoral enlargement, deepening of voice, baldness and hirsutism may occur in females. **Precocious puberty** (priapism and excessive libido) and acne occur. Hepatic dysfunction and *cholestatic jaundice* has been reported. Large doses in adult males lead to **suppression of spermatogenesis, degeneration of seminiferous tubules, oligospermia and decreased ejaculatory volume**. Certain drug interactions are noteworthy. Androgens increase the action of *coumarin* and *indandione anticoagulants* when given concurrently and increase the risk of haemorrhage. They *decrease the metabolism of oxyphenbutazone*, increasing its intensity and duration of action whereby the response becomes unpredictable.

PREPARATIONS AND DOSAGE

The main use of the natural hormone is in the replacement therapy in **male hypogonadism**. Testosterone preparations have an androgenic: anabolic ratio of 1 : 1. The preparations are:

1. **Testosterone injection.** Usually administered as 50 mg IM three times weekly.
2. **Testoterone pellets.** Pellets of 100 mg are available and are *implanted subcutaneously* into the medial side of the thigh. They dissolve slowly and a dose of 600 mg is sufficient for about 6 months.
3. **Testosterone propionate.** 5 to 25 mg in oil, given IM two to four times weekly. Other preparations (testosterone isobutyrate, enanthate, phenylpropionate) differ only in their duration of action.
4. **Methyltestosterone.** It is a natural androgen which is active when given in a dose of 20 to 50 mg daily *sublingually* or *orally*.
5. **Fluoxymesterone.** For androgen deficiency 10 to 20 mg orally daily, and for anabolic effects 4 to 10 mg orally daily.

Antiandrogens

Oestrogens and some **progestogens** have antiandrogenic actions, but cannot be used practically, as on prolonged use they lead to castration-like actions.

Cyproterone acetate is a synthetic compound with antiandrogenic action. **It possibly acts by preventing the binding of dihydrotestosterone to its receptor in the target cells.** It is a potent **competitive antagonist** of testosterone. In addition it suppresses LH and FSH secretion. *It may be used to decrease sexual drive.* Cyproterone is being evaluated for the treatment of hirsutism in women, and **benign prostatic hyperplasia. Flutamide**, and **finazteride** are newer antiandrogens under evaluation.

Anabolic Steroids

Testosterone has potent anabolic activity, but because of its associated androgenic activity it cannot be used freely, as it causes **virilization**. Steroids have been synthesized with an aim to dissociate the anabolic and androgenic activites. Chemically they are derivatives of testosterone. **Fluoxymesterone** has appreciable anabolic activity. These drugs are predominently anabolic but *retain weak androgenic activity*. When given in proper doses, with an appropriate diet, in patients with cachexia and debilitating disease, they produce anabolic effects without signs of virilism.

Actions

In therapeutic doses the **protein anabolic action is predominant**. The androgenic effects are manifested on prolonged therapy, specially in females. These steroids induce a **positive nitrogen balance**, *i.e.*, the nitrogen taken in is greater than the nitrogen lost from the body. This retained N is incorporated into amino acids and protein leading to **growth, regeneration and hypertrophy of body tissue**. This is clinically manifested by **increase in muscle mass and body weight**. The mechanism of action is illunderstood. The anabolic androgens are not effective in the acute phases of diseases marked by protein catabolism. **They only promote protein synthesis and tissue repair. They antagonize the protein wasting effects of prolonged glucocorticoid therapy**. They prevent the resorption of bone.

Preparations and Dosage

The anabolic: androgenic ratio reliably indicates the anabolic potency of these compounds, and for testostrone this ratio is 1 : 1. All agents except nandrolone are active orally. The preparations and dosage information is summarized in **Table 7.7-1.**

Table 7.7-1 *Pharmacologic profile and dosage of anabolic steroids*

Compound	*Anabolic: Androgenic ratio**	*Usual dosage*
Methandienone	3:1	5-15 mg orally/day
Nandrolone phenylpropionate	6:1	25-50 mg IM every week
Nandrolone decanoate	4:1	25-50 mg IM every 3 weeks
Oxymetholone	3:1	5-10 mg IM orally/day
Stanozolol	6:1	6 mg orally/day
Ethylestrenol	8:1	8-16 mg orally/day
Oxandrolone	13:1	5-10 mg orally/day
Fluoxymesterone	2:1	5-10 mg orally /day

* the ratio for testosterone propionate is 1.1

Therapeutic Uses

These compounds have been used in the treatment of **osteoporosis, chronic renal failure, wasting due to prolonged immobilization, radiotherapy, cancer (except carcinoma prostate) or severe illness.** They may be used in high doses in patients with **metastatic carcinoma of the breast**. They have been used in **growth retardation, refractory** and **aplastic anaemia** and to **antagonize glucocorticoid-induced osteoporosis**

The use of **anabolic steroids** to promote muscle growth and increase performance in athletes has attracted much attention. These drugs may be abused by athletes to improve their performance. Hence their use by athletes is officially banned.

Contraindications

As these agents are related to testosterone they are *contraindicated in prostatic cancer, severe liver insufficiency, severe nephrosis, pregnancy* and *lactation*, and *in male breast cancer*.

Toxicity

As the anabolic steroids have mild androgenic activity, on prolonged use they may lead to side effects like testosterone. **Salt and water retention** leading to oedema may occur. **Hepatoma** may develop in patients on long-term therapy. If used during pregnancy they may lead to *virilization of the foetus* (contraindicated in pregnancy). **They should not be continuously used for periods exceeding 4 weeks**. High doses in women may produce **menstrual disorders, deepening of the voice, and hirsutism**. In children they may lead to **premature closure of epiphyses and virilization**.

Dissociation of the anabolic : androgenic properties is appreciable in many compounds, but serious side effects like **virilization** and **hepatotoxicity** are seen in patients on high doses on prolonged therapy. The anabolic steroids have a place in the treatment of **advanced metastatic breast cancer** in females, **aplastic anaemia** and **wasting disease** in the elderly. They may be useful in **osteoporosis** for which they are suitably combined with calcium supplements.

Danazol

Danazol is a synthetic derivative of 17-α-ethinyltestosterone, and inhibits the release of FSH and LH from the anterior pituitary (*antigonadotrophic action*). It also has a **weak androgenic effect**. It also inhibits enzymes involved in the biosynthesis of gonadal hormones. It **competitively** interferes with the binding of sex steroids to the cytoplasmic receptors.

Danazol is used to treat **endometriosis, fibrocystic breast disease, hereditary angioedema, gynaecomastia, infertility,** and **menorrhagia**. Danazol is used as 50, 100, 200 mg capsules. Therapy is started during menstruation to rule out pregnancy. The usual *dosage* ranges between 100 to 400 mg/day in 2 or 3 divided doses for 3 to 9 months, depending on the disease. **Adverse reactions** include flushing, sweating, vaginitis, oedema, hirsutism, acne, oily skin, weight gain, voice deepening, decreased breast size, and clitoral hypertrophy. Vaginal bleeding, nervousness, and hepatic dysfunction have also been reported.

Male Antifertility Agents

In spite of the continuing need, no safe and reversible chemical agent is known that can adequately control male fertility without producing toxic effects.

Anti-Impotency Drugs

Impotency or ***erectile dysfunction*** (ED) is the inability of a man to achieve satisfactory erection of the penis for sexual intercourse. Normally, erection is induced by ***parasympathetic stimulation*** initiated by the CNS and facilitated by sensory stimuli from the penis. This dilates penile arteries and relaxes *trabecular* smooth muscles through ***nitric oxide*** (NO), functioning as a second messenger. This favours flow of blood into the *corpora cavernosa* leading to tumescence. The increased pressure compresses the venules against the fibrous tissue layer called the *tunica albuginea*, which prevents the outflow of blood from the penis causing an erection. The causes of impotence may be *psychological, organic* (hypogonadism, neurological dysfunction, diabetes mellitus, peripheral vascular disease), or drug-induced or a mixture of the above factors. For psychological factors, behavioural therapy is helpful. The organic causes have to be treated. The under mentioned vasodilators are used in the management of ED:

Phentolamine and Papaverine

The combination of the alpha-adrenoceptor blocker *phentolamine* (2 mg) and the nonspecific vasodilator *papaverine* (12–40 mg) when injected into the *corpora cavernosa* of the penis causes erection in men suffering from ED. Long-term efficacy of this therapy is not fully known. Likely *adverse effects* include priapism, othostatic hypotension, and local fibrotic reactions.

Alprostadil (PGE1)

Intracavernosal injection of the vasodilator *alprostadil* (PGE1) is used to produce penile erection in men with ED. Doses of 0.2 to 140 mcg are used. Penile pain occurs frequently as PGE has an algesic affect. Lately, *triple therapy* combining papaverine, phenotolaime and alprostadil has been tried with a lower incidence of adverse effects.

Sildenafil Citrate (Viagra)

Viagra was the first oral "pill" to treat erectile dysfunction (ED). According to the USFDA sildenafil does not directly cause erection, but effects the response to sexual stimulation. It enhances the smooth muscle relaxant effect of *nitric oxide* (NO), the 'critical' *second messenger* released in the *corpora cavernosa* in response to sexual stimulation. Sildenafil is a potent inhibitor of cyclic-GMP specific phosphodiesterase type 5 (PDE5), the isoenzyme responsible for breakdown of cyclic GMP in the *corpora cavernosa*. Thus the conserved cylic-GMP, and sexual stimulation give a more "natural" erectile response. *Dose*: One Viagra pill is best taken about an hour before sexual activity. *Adverse effects* include headache, flushing, and GI disturbances. A warning has been issued that "pill" *may cause serious side effects in patients suffering from diabetes mellitus* or *cardiac problems*.

Two newer phospodiesterase5 (PDE5) inhibitors used for treating ED are **tadalafil** (Cialis) and **vardenafil** (Levitra). Some other agents are also under trial for the management of ED.

8

THE VITAMINS

Classification
Fat-soluble Vitamins
 Vitamin A
 Vitamin D
 Vitamin E
 Vitamin K
Water-soluble Vitamins
 Vitamin B Complex
 Thiamine, Riboflavine, Nicotinic Acid, Pyridoxine, Folic Acid, Cyanocobalamin, Pantothenic Acid, Biotin, Choline and Inositol, Para-aminobenzoic Acid
 Vitamin C (Ascorbic acid)
 Multivitamin Preparations

The vitamins are essential microconstituents of diet, which do not give energy but are necessary for the normal metabolism of the body. They are organic compounds and were thought to be "vital amines" and named by Funk as **vitamine**. This term today is retained as **vitamin**. Most of the vitamins can be synthesized today. Adequate amounts reach the body *via* a well balanced diet. Deficiencies may occur on restricted diets, malabsorption syndromes, or in states where the body need increases, e.g., during body growth, pregnancy and lactation. Thus, vitamin deficiency states can develop due to: **inadequate diet, impaired absorption, inefficient utilization, increased requirement, and increased rate of excretion**. Efforts should be made to avoid indiscriminate vitamin therapy. *All the vitamins are not harmless.*

CLASSIFICATION

The vitamins may be categorized into two: (*i*) the **fat-soluble** vitamins; and (*ii*) the **water-soluble** vitamins. They are further detailed in **Table 8.1.**

FAT-SOLUBLE VITAMINS

Vitamin A

The *dietary source* of vitamin A includes vegetables, butter, eggs, milk, and fish liver oils. The **carotenes** (α, β, γ) and **cryptoxanthin**, which are fat-soluble **lipochromes** found in plants are converted into vitamin A (active form) in the intestinal mucosa or liver.

Mode of action. Vitamin A plays many essential roles in the body: (*i*) it maintains the **functional and structural integrity of epithelial cells** throughout the body by preventing its metaplasia to stratified squamons type. This vitamin A probably does by stabilizing the -SH groups in proteins, maintaining the normal amounts of mucoprotein, glycoprotein and keratoprotein in epithelial structures; (*ii*) it **stimulates the synthesis of nuclear RNA**, suggesting its role in genetic transcription and cells differentiation; and (*iii*) it is essential for vision in dim light **(dark adaptation)**. The **rods** are particularly sensitive to light of low intensity, and the **cones** to light of high intensity, and to colour. Vitamin A promotes resynthesis of visual purple (rhodopsin), which at the cellular level is responsible for dark adaptation. Vitamin A is enzymatically converted to **retinaldehyde**, which reacts with the protein **opsin**, to form **rhodopsin**. By light rhodopsin is converted to **retinene**, which initiates the nerve impulse. In the absence of light and presence of vitamin A, rhodopsin in regenerated from **retinene. Thus, vitamin A deficiency would suppress the resynthesis of rhodopsin, leading to night blindness**.

Deficiency states. One of the earliest manifestations of vitamin A deficiency is **night blindness (nyctalopia)**, i.e., inability to see in poor light. The growth is retarded, and the susceptibility to infections is increased. Hyperkeratosis may occur, in which the skin becomes horny and rough, specially around the hair follicles. There may be **xerophthalmia**, in which there is a metaplasia of the cornea and conjunctiva with subsequent ulceration and necrosis.

Therapeutic Uses

1. Prevention or cure of vitamin A deficiency states, e.g., **hyperkeratosis, xerophthalmia** and **night blindness**.
2. Vitamin A supplements may be administered during infancy, pregnancy or lactation. Overenthusiastic therapy should be avoided.
3. In **kwashiorkar** and severe forms of vitamin A deficiency, **retinol** (water miscible palmitate) in a dose of 30,000 mcg IM may be administered as a single dose.

Toxicity. Prolonged overdosage leads to **hypervitaminosis A**. The children are more liable to this syndrome, although it has been detected in adults also. Excess of vitamin E is likely to protect against hypervitaminosis A. Hypervitaminosis A is characterized by anorexia, irritability, periosteal thickening, dry skin, pruritus with desquamation, fatigue, myalgia, nystagmus and hepatosplenomegaly. The intracranial pressure may be increased with neurological symptoms.

Preparations

Vitamin A and related compounds: Vitamin A; Water-miscible vitamin A (Aquasol A), Tretinoin.

Preparations containing vitamins A and D. Cod liver oil; Halibut liver oil—these preparations are better absorbed from the gut when administered in emulsion form.

Vitamin D

Certain sterols are capable of preventing the development of rickets, while others attain this quality when exposed to ultraviolet radiation. Vitamin D_1 which was the older product containing a mixture of sterols has limited activity. The two sterols of greater therapeutic importance are **ergocalciferol** vitamin D_2 and **cholecalciferol** (Vitamin D_3).

Vitamin D occurs in fatty fish, fish liver oils, eggs and butter. Small amounts are found in cheese, meat and milk. **Vitamin D in food requires bile and fatty acids for its proper absorption from the small intestines.**

Mode of action. Plasma calcium levels are maintained within narrow limits by the interaction of **vitamin D, parathormone** and **calcitonin** in the body. *Vitamin D* itself is inactive. In the body it is converted by hydroxylation to **calcifediol** and **1,2,5-dihydroxycholecalciferol.** These two products are the active forms of vitamin D.

The *primary action* of vitamin D is to increase the absorption of calcium and phosphorus from the intestines, and also to reciprocally increase the renal excretion of phosphorus. Such an action is needed for proper mineralization of bone, and for the regulation of normal plasma calcium levels. It is known that **large doses of vitamin D cause decalcification of bone.**

Deficiency States

Rickets. In infants and children there is a failure of mineralization of newly formed osteoid tissue and cartilage, causing a defective bone growth. Due to lack of calcification the bones are soft and weak, which results in various forms of body deformities.

Osteomalasia. It is also known as **adult rickets,** which mostly occurs in times of increased calcium need, e.g., pregnancy and lactation. There is a generalized decrease in the bone density.

Therapeutic Uses

1. **For the prevention and treatment of rickets.** It may be noted that vitamin D is ineffective in cases of renal rickets and hypophosphataemic rickets.
2. **Osteomalasia** (adult rickets) responds favourably to vitamin D therapy.
3. **Hypoparathyroidism.** In this condition **dihydrotachysterol** is probably the agent of choice as it has a rapid onset of action, and a shorter duration of action compared to vitamin D. In addition, dihydrotachysterol may be used to raise and maintain serum calcium level in hypocalcaemic tetany.

Toxicity. Acute or chronic administration of large amounts of vitamin D leads to hypervitaminosis D, which is the result of a deranged calcium metabolism. Initially there is hypercalcaemia, fatigue, vomiting and diarrhoea. With prolonged hypercalcaemia there is metastatic calcification, i.e., deposition of calcium in soft tissues. There may be calcium deposition in kidneys—**nephrocalcinosis.** There is associated **generalized osteoporosis** due to withdrawal of calcium from the bones.

Vitamin E

Vitamin E has been isolated from wheat germ oil and named **alpha-tocopherol.** In vitamin E deficient animals (rats) there is an increased oxidation of polyunsaturated fatty acids, with muscle weakness and degeneration. Vitamin E is supposed to maintain the germinal epithelium. Based on these features vitamin E therapy is tried in cases of **infertility in women, habitual abortion, progressive muscular dystrophy, peripheral vascular disease, refractory anaemias** and **haemolytic anaemias.**

Preparations. **See Table 8-1.**

Vitamin K

Vitamin K is a fat soluble substance present in hog liver fat, and in alfalfa. This vitamin is concentrated in the chloroplasts of plant leaves and in many vegetables. The natural vitamin K and menadione are lipid-soluble, but it is possible to make active water soluble derivatives of menadione.

Mode of action. Vitamin K *promotes* the hepatic synthesis of prothrombin, factors II, VII, IX and X. The role of these factors in blood coagulation has been disussed in **Chapter 5.2.**

Deficiency state. The chief manifestation of vitamin K deficiency is an increased bleeding tendency. Epistaxis, haematuria, ecchymoses, gastrointestinal bleeding, postoperative haemorrhage, and intracranial haemorrhage are common.

Therapeutic Uses

1. In cases of **vitamin K deficiency** due to inadequate intake (hypoprothrombinaemia in newborn); inadequate absorption (biliary obstruction or fistula, malabsorption syndromes); or inadequate utilization (hypoprothrombinaemia due to heptatocellular disease) of vitamin K.
2. As an **antidote to hypoprothrombinaemia induced by oral anticoagulants (Chap 5.2).**

Toxicity. In man menadione is irritating to the skin and respiratory tract. It may led to vesication. Menadione can induce **haemolytic anaemia, hyperbilirubinaemia,** and **kernicterus** in the newborn. The haemolytic tendency increases in individuals with a deficiency of glucose-6-phosphate dehydrogenase (G-6-PD) deficiency in the erythrocytes.

Preparations. **See Table 8-1**

WATER-SOLUBLE VITAMINS

Vitamin B Complex

Thiamine (Vitamin B_1)

Long back Eijkman, a Dutch physician demonstrated that by eating polished rice individuals developed **beriberi,** and this disease could be cured by adding rice polishings (rice bran) to the diet. Later a crystalline substance was isolated from **rice polishings** and **yeast,** and this antiberiberi factor was designated as vitamin B_1. The main *dietary sources* are yeast, whole grains (germ and outer layers of seeds, nuts, legumes), pork, meats, eggs and milk.

Mode of action. In the body thiamine functions in the form of the coenzyme thiamine pyrophosphate in which adenosine triphosphate (ATP) acts as the pyrophosphate donor:

Thiamine + ATP → Thiamine pyrophosphate + AMP

Thiamine is devoid of any pharmacodynamic actions of its own. When given intravenously in large doses, there might be a **slight fall in blood pressure due to vasodilation.** The body requirement of thiamine is related to the metabolic rate, and is highest when carbohydrate is the main source of energy. This is of significance in serious patients maintained on parenteral alimentation, receiving practically all their calories in the form of dextrose.

Deficiency state. Severe thiamine deficiency leads to **beriberi,** characterized by weakness, polyneuritis, oedema and heart failure. Mild thiamine deficiency may manifest as muscle weakness, anorexia, pain and paresthesias in extremities. Thiamine deficiency develops fast, as it is scantily stored in the body.

Therapeutic Uses

1. In the prevention and cure of beriberi or other thiamine deficiency states.
2. **Peripheral neuritis, alcoholic neuritis, diabetic neuritis and neuritis of pregnancy**.
3. May be used on an empirical basis for the relief of vague gastrointestinal complaints.

Toxicity. Thiamine can lead to toxic reactions on parenteral administration. Hypersensitivity reactions can occur rarely.

Preparations. Thiamine hydrochloride, thiamine mononitrate.

Riboflavine (Vitamin B_2)

It was identified as a **yellow pigment in milk.** The *dietary sources* include yeast, wheat germ, liver, milk, green vegetables, cheese and eggs.

Mode of action. Riboflavine functions in the body in *two coenzyme forms:* **riboflavine phosphate** and **flavine adenine dinucleotide.** These two physiologically active forms function as coenzymes for the metabolism of many respiratory proteins. They have no pharmacodynamic actions of their own. Riboflavine is a component of **flavoprotein enzymes,** which are necessary for the oxidation of carbohydrates and amino acids.

Table 8-1. *The Vitamins, their recommended dietary allowances (RDAs), and therapeutic doses*

Vitamin	*Major dietary sources*	*Recommended dietary allowances (RDAs)*			*Main deficiency disorder*	*Therapeutic Dose*	
		Children	*Adults*			*Oral*	*Parenteral*
			Males	*Females*			
I. FAT-SOLUBLE VITAMINS							
Vitamin A	Fish liver oils, egg yolk, milk, butter, green and yellow vegetables, tomatoes, yellow fruits	2000-3500 IU	5000 IU	4000 IU	Night bindness, xerophthalmia, hyperkeratosis of the skin, increased susceptibility to colds, influenza and infections, karatinization of epithelial tissues	25,000-100,000 IU	50,000 IU IM
Vitamin D	Fish liver oils, egg yolk, milk, butter margarine, salmon, sardines	400 IU	200-400 IU	200-400 IU	Rickets, Osteomalacia, infantile tetany	*Ergocalciferol* 50,000-500,000IU	50,000-200,000 IU IM
						Cholicalciferol 400-1000 IU	—
						Calcitriol 0.5-1.0 mcg/day	1-2 mg IM
						Calcifediol 300-350 mcg/week	—
						Dihydrotachysterol 0.8-2.4 mg/day	—
Vitamin E	Wheat germ, vegetable oils, green leafy vegetables, nuts, cereals eggs, dairy products	7-10 IU	12-15 IU	12 IU	Deficiency in animals produces sterility, loss of embryo, muscular dystrophy, paralysis. Deficiency state not established in humans, possibly haemolytic anaemia, muscular lesions, creatinuria	*d-alpha-Toopherol*	10-200 mg
						Tocopherols, mixed concentrate 10-200 mg	10-200 mg IM
						d-alpha-Tocopheryl acetate concentrate 10-200 mg	10-200 mg IM
						d-alpha-Tocopheryl acetate 10-200 mg	10-200 mg IM
						d-alpha-Tocopheryl acid succinate 10-200mg	—
Vitamin K	Green leafy vegatables, liver, cheese, egg yolk, tomatoes, meats, cereals	Extremely small	—	—	Hypoprothrombinaemia, haemorrhage	*Menadiol sodium diphosphate (K4)* 5 mg	5-75 mg IM or SC
						Menadione 1 mg	—
						Menadione sodium bisulfite 2.5 mg	2-5 mg IM or SC
						Phytonadione (K_1) 5 mg	1-100 mg IV

(*Contd.*)

(Table 8.1 Contd.)

Vitamin	Major dietary sources	Recommended dietary allowances (RDAs)			Main deficiency disorder	Therapeutic Dose	
		Children	Adults			Oral	Parenteral
			Males	Females			
II. Water -Soluble Vitamins **Vitamin B Complex**							
Thiamine (B_1)	Liver, whole grain, enriched bread, cereals, pork, egg yolk, rice polishings	0.7-1.2 mg	1.2-1.4 mg	1.0-1.1 mg	Beriberi, anorexia, peripheral neuritis, constipation	5-100 mg	5-100 mg LM, IV
Riboflavine (B_2)	Organ meats, milk, eggs, green vegetables enriched bread	0.8-1.4 mg	1.4-1.7 mg	1.2-1.3 mg	Stomatitis, glossitis, facial dermatitis, photopobia, cheilosis, corneal vascularization	1-5 mg	1-10 mg parenteral
Nicotinic acid (B_3) (Niacin)	Liver, fish, poultry, red meat, enriched bread and cereals, rice polishings, bran	9.16 mg	16-19 mg	13-15 mg	Pellagra (nervousness iinsomnia, dermatitis, diarrhoea dementia, delusions, confusion)	20-50 mg	20-50 mg parenteral
Pantothenic acid (B_5)	Organ meats, egg yolk, peanuts, whole grains, cauliflower, rice polishings	*	*	*	"Burning foot" syndrome weakness, fatigue, mood changes, dizziness	20-100 mg	250-500 mg IM, every 6 hrs for 2-3 days for postoperative abdominal distension and paralytic ileus
Pyridoxine (B_6)	Yeast, red meat liver,whole grains, soya beans, green vegetables	0.9-1.6 mg	1.8-2.2 mg	1.8-2.0 mg	Anaemia, CNS lesions, epileptiform convulsions in children, glossitis, stomatitis, cheilosis	5-100 mg	5-100 mg parenteral
Cyanocobalamin (B_{12})	Liver, red meat, milk, egg yolk, oysters, clams	2-3 mcg	3 mcg	3 mcg	Pernicious anaemia, glossitis, confusion, muscle incoordination, paresthesias	10 mcg-1 mg	10 mcg-1 mg parenteral
Vitamin C *Ascorbic acid*	Citrus fruits (oranges, lemons, limes) tomatoes, green vegetables, potatoes, onion, turnips, grape fruits, green peppers. straw berries	45 mg	50-60 mg	50-60 mg	Scurvy (petichiae, bleeding gums, bruising, impaired wound healing, loosened teeth)	100 mg-1 g	100 mg-1g parenteral

Deficiency state. Early deficiency in man is manifested as *sore throat, angular stomatitis (cheilosis).* Later *glossitis* and *seborrheic dermatitis* on the face, and dermatitis on the extremities might occur. The cornea becomes vascularized and *cataract formation* occurs. A *normocytic normochronic anaemia* also develops.

Therapeutic uses. It is used as a replacement therapy in riboflavine deficiency states and in general vitamin B complex deficiencies. **Ariboflavinosis seldom occurs alone, and may be associated with pellagra.**

Toxicity. There is no apparent toxicity of riboflavine.

Preparations. Riboflavine; riboflavine injection.

Nicotinic acid (Niacin)

Goldberger was able to produce a condition known as "black tongue" in dogs by feeding them a diet deficient in the `**PP factor**' (Pellegra Preventing factor). PP factor is found in yeast. This black tongue of dogs was analogous to pellagra in man. It was later identified as nicotinic acid which functioned as the **pellagra-preventing vitamin.** *Dietary sources* include yeast, wheat germ, green vegetables, legumes, kidney, liver, meat, milk and fish.

Mode of action. Nicotinic acid functions in the body as its amide. Nicotinic acid has a **vasodilator activity,** which is lacked by nicotinamide. Nicotinic acid in the body is converted into **diphosphopyridine nucleotide** (DPN) or **triphosphopyridine nucleotide** (TPN), and they (DPN, TPN) function as hydrogen acceptors and donors in the **oxidation-reduction reactions of the citric acid cycle,** and in the carbodydrate, fat and protein metabolisms. Nicotinic acid has a **cholesterol-lowering effect.**

Deficiency state. Deficiency of nicotinic acid causes **pellagra,** characterized by **glossitis, dermatitis** and **encephalophathy.** The tongue is red, swollen and ulcerated. A milder degree of deficiency has been termed as **subclinical pellagra.** Usually an associated deficiency of other vitamin B complex members exists.

Therapeutic Uses

1. In the prevention and treatment of **pellagra**. This is the only established use of nicotinic acid and nicotinamide.
2. In **atherosclerosis** as a hypolipidaemic agent **(Chap. 5.4).**
3. In *migraine, Meniere's disease* and *angina pectoris* nicotinic acid may be employed as a vasodilator.

Toxicity. Nicotinic acid may produce *flushing, pruritus, gastrointestinal distress, activation of peptic ulcer and hepatotoxicity.*

Preparations. **See Table 8-1.**

Pyridoxine (Vitamin B_6)

It was shown by Gyorgy that pyridoxine deficiency produces dermatitis in rats. *Dietary sources* include yeast, rice bran, wheat germ, crude cane molasses and liver.

Mode of action. The name pyridoxine (vitamin B_6) is given to three closely related substances **pyridoxol, pyridoxal** and **pyridoxamine** — their phosphates are active. All three forms are converted to pyridoxal phsophate by the enzyme pyridoxal kinase, as shown below:

Pyridoxal + ATP → Pyridoxal phosphate + ADP

The antitubercular drug, **isoniazid,** inhibits the enzyme pyridoxal kinase, and thus acts **as anti-vitamin B_6.** Pyridoxal phosphate is involved in the metabolic transformation of amino acids. It also facilitates the transport of amino acids across membranes; the synthesis of unsaturated fatty acids; and the conversion of tryptophan to nicotinic acid.

Deficiency state. The clinical syndrome of pyridoxine deficiency is not well defined. In animals (rats, dogs) the deficiency causes dermatitis, convulsive seizures and anaemia.

Therapeutic uses: Pyridoxine is given prophylactically to patients on **isoniazid therapy** to prevent the development of peripheral neuritis.

Toxicity. No definite toxic manifestations are described.

Preparations. **See Table 8-1.**

Folic Acid and Cyanocobalamin (Vitamin B_{12})

See Table 8-1, and Chapter 5.1.

Carnitine

Carnitine, a nitrogenous constituent of muscle, plays a role in the **oxidation of long-chain fatty acids in mammals.** It also facilitates the **aerobic metabolism of carbohydrates, enhances the rate of oxidative phosphorylation,** and **promotes the excretion of organic acids.** This is brought about by carnitine involving complex enzyme systems.

Pharmacologically, L-carnitine is well tolerated by man (upto 15 g/day orally). In contrast, DL-carnitine produces a **myasthenia gravis-like syndrome.** It is because of the likely inhibitory effects of D-carnitine on the transport and function and L-carnitine.

The **dietary sources** for carnitine are *meat* and *dairy products.* For the synthesis of carnitine in the body four microconstituents are required for the various enzymatic steps – **ascorbic acid, niacin, pyridoxine,** and **iron.**

Primary carnitine deficiency is manifested as **myopathic disease,** characterized by marked muscle weakness. **Secondary carnitine deficiency** is manifested as *renal tubular disorder*. For both the above deficiency states, carnitine 1-2 g per day in divided doses is administered orally. It is available as **Levocarnitine** (Carnitor) as enteral liquid (100 mg/ml), and in capsules and tablets. It is also used in some selected cases of **primary cardiomyopathy** and **ischaemic cerebrovascular disease.**

Pantothenic Acid

There is no definite evidence of a disease entity developing from the lack of pantothenic acid in man. It is widely distributed in natural foodstuffs (see **Table 8-1**).

Biotin

There is no established therapeutic indication for biotin in man.

Choline and Inositol

These two agents have a **lipotropic action,** i.e., they decrease the fat content of the liver. Choline has been employed in man to **prevent fatty infiltration** and **cirrhosis of the liver,** with some favourable reports. Inositol does not produce any convincing therapeutic effects.

Para-aminobenzoic Acid

Para-aminobenzoic acid (PABA) has been included in the vitamin B complex group. PABA is an essential metabolite for the growth of the certain bacteria, but there is no evidence that PABA is a dietary essential for man.

Ascorbic acid (Vitamin C)

Lind in 1757 wrote an exhaustive treatise on **scurvy,** which is the first scientificially described deficiency disease. He further showed that when oranges and lemons were included in the diet, scurvy could be prevented. **Dietary sources** of vitamin C include oranges, lemons, limes, tomatoes, grape fruit, cabbage and other vegetables.

Mode of action. Vitamin C is a **strong reducing agent** and probably helps in **oxidation-reduction reactions** induced by various enzymes in the body. It is involved in the maintenance of the **integrity of collagen in mesenchymal tissues,** specially in the blood vessels. Ascorbic acid is involved in the **carbohydrate metabolism.** It also occurs in high concentrations in the adrenal cortex and medulla. In the cortex it is possibly concerned intimately with the **synthesis of adrenocorticosteroids,** and in the medulla it prevents the oxidation of adrenaline. Vitamin C promotes the process of **healing of wounds.** It is probably also required for the **metabolism of tyrosine.**

Deficiency state. A deficient vitamin C intake leads to scurvy. The basic defect is that vitamin C lack results in a **disintegration of the intercellular ground substance.** This, scurvy is characterized by weakening of the intercellular cement substances specially of the capillaries, connective tissue and bone. The gums become spongy and bleed easily. **Haemorrhagic patches** occur on the skin due to increased capillary permeability, and there is associated anaemia.

Therapeutic Uses

1. Prophylaxis and treatment of **scurvy**.
2. **Idiopathic methaemoglobinaemia** – used as a reducing agent.
3. It is used in the treatment of **dental caries, pyorrhoea** and **gum infection**.
4. For the **prevention of upper respiratory infection** it is used in very high doses (1 to 3 g per day).

Toxicity. Serious toxicity due to vitamin C is uncommon, but *diarrhoea* may occur with high dosage. On prolonged therapy *acidification of urine* is likely to lead to the *formation of oxalate stones in the urinary tract.*

Preparations. **See Table 8-1.**

Multivitamin Preparations

Oral dosage forms (usually capsules) containing varying quantities of many vitamins are available in the market, and are in wide use. Now it is generally agreed that in most cases such a multivitamin therapy is **irrational and is a waste of expensive drugs**. There may be a few indications for multivitamin therapy like in persons on a **reducing diet** and in cases of **pellagra** where there is a multiple vitamin deficiency, but in such cases also the specifically needed vitamins in proper doses should be administered separately.

❑❑❑

9

SYSTEMIC ANTI-INFECTIVE AGENTS

9.1 Development of chemotherapy

Chemicals have been used to treat infectious diseases for many centuries, and the occasional curative properties of soils, plants and other material containing living moulds and bacteria also were recognized by primitive people. However, anti-infective drug treatment of systemic infections was put on a rational basis only with the work of the famous German Chemist, **Paul Ehrlich** (1854-1915). Before the pioneer researches of Ehrlich many chemicals were known which eradicated infections when applied topically as **antiseptics** and **disinfectants**, but these were too toxic for internal administration for systemic infections, because of their unfavourable therapeutic index. Paul Ehrlich enunciated the **"Therapia Sterilizans Magna"** in 1906, which offered a challenge to chemists for their quest for singularly nontoxic synthetic antibacterial chemicals. In other words, the control of infections with a single dose of a nontoxic chemical (a magic bullet).

In the pursuit of his goal, Ehrlich synthesized hundreds of chemicals and tested them on laboratory animals injected with pathogenic organisms. His first synthetic anti-infective compound proved to be as toxic to the tissues of the animals, as it was to infecting organisms responsible for **trypanosomiasis** and **syphilis**. Here Ehrlich reasoned out that it might be possible to prepare synthetic compounds that act selectively on parasitic cells without injuring the host cells, and this originated the concept of **selective toxicity**. In the course of his work with organic arsenicals, the 606th compound of this class, **arsphenamine**, finally proved safe enough for treating patients of syphilis, and later the 909th compound, **neoarsphenamine**, was a further improvement. Thus Ehrlich's work laid down the foundation for the use of chemicals to fight systemic infections, and he was acknowledged as the **"Father of Chemotherapy"**.

Other scientists employing Ehrlich's concepts and methods developed drugs for treating **malaria, amoebiasis** and **other protozoal diseases**. Finally, in 1935, **Gerhard Domagk** from Germany reported that the red azo dye **Prontosil** was capable of protecting mice against streptococcal infection. **Sulphanilamide** introduced in the following year proved effective against systemic infections caused by **streptococci, staphylococci, pneumococci** and **meningococci**. The modern era of chemotherapy began with sulphanilamide in 1936. The "golden age" of antimicrobial therapy started with the production of the antibiotic **penicillin** in 1941, when it first became available for limited clinical trials.

Chemotherapeutic Index

Ehrlich believe that desirable anti-infective substances are those which exhibit greater effects on the parasites, i.e., they are **"maximally parasitotropic"**, and have minimal effects on the host cells and tissues, i.e., they are

"minimally organotropic". The **chemotherapeutic index** (Cl), was represented as:

$$CI = \frac{\text{Maximum tolerated dose}}{\text{Minimum curative dose}}$$

But the chemotherapeutic index, as defined by Ehrlich, of certain compounds varies considerably according to the route of administration, as well as in different hosts similarly infected. For this reason the older formula has been replaced by the following:

$$CI = \frac{LD\ 0.1}{CD\ 99.9}$$

where LD 0.1 is the dose which *kills* all animals except 0.1 percent, and CD 99.9 is the dose which *cures* all the animals except 0.1 percent. This index gives a better idea about the **margin of safety** of the compound.

Terms and Concepts

Chemotherapy is a term that applies to the use of both *natural* and *synthetic chemicals* to interfere with the functioning of foreign cell populations. Originally, according to Ehrlich, this term was applied only to the use of synthetic chemicals employed to treat infectious diseases. Current usage makes no distinction between **chemotherapeutic agents of synthetic origin** and the **antibiotics**. This term has been further broadened to include **antineoplastic drugs** used to treat cancer and leukaemia.

Antibiotics are chemical compounds produced by living microorganisms (bacteria, fungi, actinomycetes), which at high dilutions are capable of **inhibiting** or **killing** bacteria and other microorganisms.

Synthetic anti-infective drugs differ from the naturally derived antibiotics only in their origin, in that they are synthetic. Synthetic anti-infective drugs are also designated as **chemotherapeutic agents**. The term **antimicrobial agent** includes both types (antibiotics and synthetic chemotherapeutic agents), and covers all **antibacterial, antifungal, antiprotozoal,** and **antiviral drugs**.

Selective toxicity refers to the ability of chemicals to strike selectively at foreign cells in ways that harm them, without **causing significant damage to the host cells.**

Potency, or activity per milligram, of a chemotherapeutic agent is usually expressed on the basis of **"minimum inhibitory concentration"** (MIC) at which it is capable of inhibiting the multiplication of one of the susceptible microorganisms.

Bacteriostatic activity refers to the ability of a compound to inhibit the growth and multiplication of microorganisms, i.e., inhibited growth in time results in death of the organism. **Bactericidal activity** means an actual killing effect on the microorganisms. Both these terms are based on the *in vitro* testing of antimicrobial drugs **(Table 9.1-1)**. The terms **fungistatic, fungicidal, amoebistatic, amoebicidal** etc. are self-explanatory.

Antibacterial spectrum, also known as antimicrobial spectrum, refers to the range of activity of the compound. Antibiotics are often classified as **broad** or **narrow-spectrum**, depending upon the range of activity **(Table 9.1-2)**. Thus, **penicillin G has a narrow-spectrum** since it primarily affects only gram-positive organisms and neisseria, whereas, the **tetracyclines are broad-spectrum antibiotics**, since they depress not only gram-positive and gram-negative bacteria, but also depress obligate intracellular bacteria like rickettsiae and chlamydiae.

Modes of Action of Anti-infective Agents

Most of the commonly used antibacterial chemotherapeutic agents act by one of the following basic mechanisms: (i) *inhibition of bacterial cell wall synthesis;* (ii) *inhibition of cytoplasmic membrane function;* (iii) *inhibition of nucleic acid synthesis;* (iv) *inhibition of protein synthesis;* (v) *control of microbial enzymes;* and (vi) *substrate competition with an essential metabolite.*

Table 9.1-1. *Examples of bactericidal and bacteriostatic antimicrobials*

Bactericidal	*Bacteriostatic*
Penicillins	Chloramphenicol
Cephalosporins	Erythromycin
Aminoglycosides	Tetracyclines
Cycloserine	Lincomycin
Vancomycin	Clindamycin
Bacitracin	Sulphonamides
Polymyxins	Trimethoprim
Isoniazid	Para-aminosalicylic acid
Co-trimoxazole	

Table 9.1-2. Examples of broad-spectrum and narrow-spectrum antibiotics

Broad-spectrum	*Narrow-spectrum*
Tetracyclines	Penicillin
Chloramphenicol	Streptomycin
Kanamycin	Erythromycin
Cephalosporins	Lincomycin
Ampicillin	Vancomycin

1. **Inhibition of bacterial cell wall synthesis.** Bacterial cell walls differ from those of their mammalian hosts in their content of the pentapeptide **murein**, which is an essential component of their common ground substance, **peptidoglycan**. The latter adds strength and

acts as a skeleton to protect the underlying cytoplasmic membrane from osmotic disruption **(Fig. 9.1.1)**. Thus the bacteria have a rigid cell wall, which is essential to protect the bacterial cell which has a high internal osmotic pressure (about 3 to 5 times greater than the environmental osmotic pressure in gram-positive and gram-negative bacteria). Inhibition of bacterial cell wall synthesis or injury to the cell wall diminishes this protection. Without the protection, in the relatively hypotonic environment of the body, such bacterial cells would explode. Antibiotics which interfere with cell wall synthesis include *penicillins, cephalosporins, cycloserine, bacitracin* and *vancomycin*.

2. **Inhibition of cytoplasmic membrane function.** The cytoplasmic membrane which encloses a cell, functions as a very selective and active filter to keep certain proteins and nucleotides within the cell, and allow other substances to enter the cell for metabolism. The bacterial cell membrane is a semipermeable, triple layered, lipoprotein structure, located between the cytoplasm and the cell wall **(Fig. 9.1.1)**. It poses as an osmotic barrier between the interior and exterior of the cell. Increased permeability of cytoplasmic membrane results in the rapid release of small molecules from the interior of the bacterium, leading to a **disorganization of membrane function**. Drugs which have such an action include *polymyxins, gramicidin, colistin* and *novobiocin. Ampotericin B* and *nystatin* also affect cytoplasmic membranes particularly those which contain sterols.

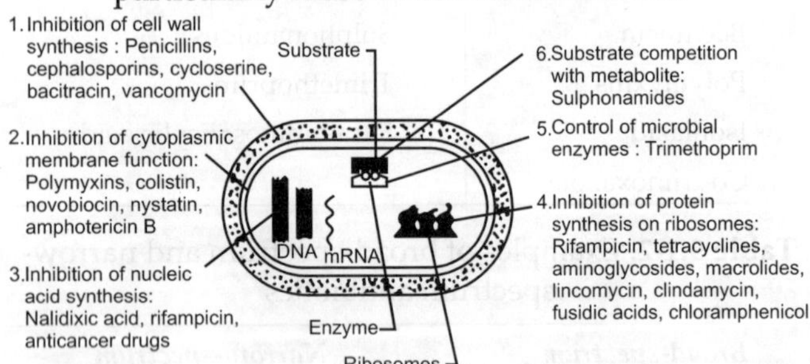

Fig. 9.1.1: The modes of action of some anti-infective and anticancer agents (see text).

3. **Inhibition of nucleic acid synthesis.** Bacterial multiplication and subsequent survival is dependent upon the replication of DNA, since the latter carries encoded information essential to cellular function. Several antimicrobial and anticancer drugs interfere with nucleic acid synthesis in **three** general ways: inhibition of nucleotide metabolism; inhibition of nucleotide interconversions, and inhibition of nucleotide utilization **(Chap. 9.10)**. Certain antibiotics attach to the DNA strands and block further DNA replication, or formation of messenger RNA. Examples include **nalidixic acid**, and various **anticancer agents (Fig. 9.1.1)**.

4. **Inhibition of protein synthesis.** Synthesis of bacterial protein occurs on the ribosomes by an interaction of transfer RNA and messenger RNA **(Fig. 9.1.1)**. Several antibacterial compounds act by disturbing protein synthesis in one of the following ways: (i) **Messenger RNA** formation on the DNA template can be altered by **rifampicin**, which is achieved by the inhibition of the enzyme transcriptase; (ii) **Transfer RNA** is responsible for carrying the appropriate amino acid to the ribosomes where they are assembled into a correct sequence. The transfer RNA function is affected by the **tetracyclines**. In addition the tetracyclines may also affect ribosomal function and chelate calcium within the cell; (iii) **Ribosomal function** may be affected by certain antibacterial agents by binding to one or other of the subunits (two ribosomal subunits occur within the bacterial cell, a smaller 30S and a 50S subunit), which reduces their capacity for protein synthesis. Examples include the **aminoglycosides** (streptomycin and gentamicin) which specifically bind to the 30S subunit, and **chloramphenicol** binds to the 50S subunit; and (iv) **Translocation** can be interfered with by **erythromycin**.

5. **Control of microbial enzymes.** The formation of nucleotides within the bacterial cells is controlled by certain co-factors for which **folinic acid** is essential. The formation of folinic acid from folic acid is controlled by enzyme activity, which can be inhibited by **trimethoprim** (see **Fig. 9.2.2**).

6. **Substrate competition with essential metabolite.** The **sulphonamides** compete with the natural substrate, para-aminobenzoic acid (PABA) which is an essential metabolite for the synthesis of folic acid in certain bacteria. The sulphonamides prevent this synthesis by **substrate competition**. The bacteriostatic action of sulphonamides can be reversed by an excess of PABA.

Classification of Antimicrobial Drugs

The antimicrobial agents can be classified in several ways, according to their: (i) chemical structure; (ii) mechanism of action; and (iii) antimicrobial spectrum. From the clinical standpoint and its functional utility, they may be classified according to their antimicrobial activity as under:

1. **Narrow-spectrum drugs** (effective against gram-positive cocci and bacilli). *Penicillin G*, the *semisynthetic penicillinase-resistant penicillins*, the *macrolides*, the *lincomycins*, *vancomycin* and *bacitracin*.

2. **Narrow-spectrum drugs** (primarily effective against the aerobic gram-negative bacilli). The *aminoglycosides* and *polymyxins*.
3. **Broad-spectrum drugs** (effective against both gram-positive and gram-negative bacteria and chlamydiae and rickettsiae): The *broad-spectrum penicillins (ampicillin and carbenicillin),* the *cephalosporins,* the *tetracyclines, chloramphenicol, trimethoprim,* and the *sulphonamides.*

Bacterial Sensitivity Testing

Sensitivity testing *in vitro* is the most certain way to select the right drug against the organism responsible for the infection. However, such tests are not always necessary, and the doctor often orders the drug, which by experience has proved to be effective against a certain pathogan. For sensitivity and resistance (S and R) studies two microbiologic methods are used.

The **Kirbey-Bauer technique** is now a standard test for determining the infecting organism's susceptibility to drugs. It utilizes paper discs containing known quantities of various antibiotics. These **drug-impregnated discs** are placed on the surface of an agar plate that has been streaked or swabbed with bacteria obtained from the patient. The plate is then **incubated** overnight and read after about 12 to 18 hours. During this time the bacterial colonies continue to grow, except where they come in contact with a growth-inhibiting drug. Thus drugs effective against the pathogen produce a **clear zone of inhibition** around the disc, whereas organisms that resist treatment tend to grow right upto the disc. By this test the organism is graded as **sensitive, resistant** or of **intermediate sensitivity** to each of the tested drugs.

In the **second method**, the isolated organism is inoculated into tubes, or onto plates of the culture medium containing sequentially diminishing drug concentrations. Following suitable incubation, the minimum inhibitory concentration (MIC) of the drug is determined. Bactericidal activity usually occurs at drug concentrations 2 to 10 times greater than the MIC.

Antibiotic Levels in Tissue Fluid

The distribution of antibiotics is an important factor in therapy. Distribution is usually thought of in terms of "blood" or "serum levels", but except in cases of septicaemia the blood antibacterial concentrations are not directly important. What is more important is the concentration achieved and maintained in the infected tissue. This depends on many factors like *site of infection,* the *causative organism,* the *presence of tissue fluid* or *an abscess cavity,* and the *dose* and *route of administration* and *protein binding* of the antimicrobial agent. Antimicrobial agents with a prolonged low peak may achieve satisfactory tissue distribution.

An important factor affecting the **bioavailability** of a drug is the degree to which it is protein-bound. The antibiotics to a large extent are bound to albumins in plasma and tissue fluids **(Table 9.1-3).** Only *free, unbound* antimicrobial agents are able to penetrate tissues and exert desired effects.

Bacterial Resistance to Antimicrobial Drugs

Considered by species, bacteria are **susceptible** to some antibacterial drugs and **resistant** to others. But strains may develop that are resistant to drugs which are supposed to be normally effective against that species. Such a change is particularly true in *staphylococci, gram-negative bacilli,* and *Mycobacterium tuberculosis,* but it may occur with any organism. Bacterial resistance is a major medical problem.

Cross Resistance

Cross resistance is the term applied to a phenomenon in which bacteria, resistant to one drug are found to be resistant to a second drug without having been exposed to the latter. It is commonest among **closely chemically related drugs,** and may be seen between drugs which **share the same mechanism of action** or **attachment.** Examples of cross resistance among closely chemically related antibiotics are (e.g., polymyxin-B-colistin; erythromycin-oleandomycin; neomycin-kanamycin). Occasionally cross resistance may develop between chemically unrelated drugs (e.g., erythromycin-lincomycin; chloramphenicol-tetracycline). The position is more complex with the aminoglycosides, where resistance to gentamicin leads to resistance to kanamycin, neomycin and streptomycin, but resistance to the last three agents does not necessarily extend to gentamicin. This is designated as 'one-way' or **partial cross resistance (Fig. 9.1.2).**

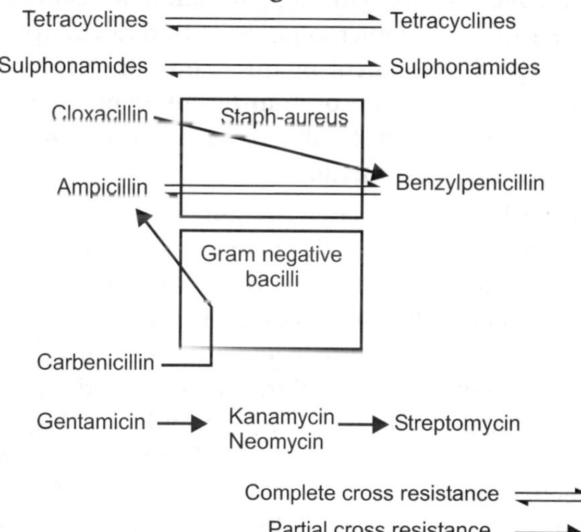

Fig. 9.1.2: Some examples of cross resistance among antimicrobial agents.

Types of Bacterial Resistance

Bacterial resistance to antimicrobial drugs is either **natural** or **acquired**. A related phenomenon is **dependence** which occurs rarely.

Natural resistance. This type of resistance is *genetically* determined, and depends upon the absence of a metabolic process or pathway in a bacterium, which is affected by the antibiotic in question. Natural resistance usually is a characteristic of an entire species, but sometimes as in the case of **penicillin-resistant staphylococci**, the resistance is confined to particular strains within that species.

Acquired resistance. Acquired resistance refers to resistance developing in a previously sensitive bacterial species. This kind of resistance poses a serious clinical problem.

Table 9.1-3. *The extent of protein binding of some antimicrobial agents*

Protein-binding%	*Antimicrobial Agents*
10	Cephalexin, Cephradine, Cycloserine, Kanamycin
11-25	Ampicillin, Amoxycillin, Cephaloridine, Clindamycin
26-50	Carbenicillin, Erythromycin, Gentamicin, Sulphadiazine, Tetracycline, Methicillin
51-65	Benzylpenicillin, Caphalothin, Polymyxin B, Chloramphenicol, Nitrofurantoin
66-85	Griseofulvin, Cephazolin, Rifampicin, Sulphamethoxazole, Sulphadimidine
86-97	Cloxacillin, Flucloxacillin, Fusidic acid, Nalidixic acid

The development of acquired resistance involves a *stable genetic change, heritable from generation to generation.* Antimicrobial drugs are now known to act in several ways that favour the emergence of resistant strains. The most common mechanism is through **mutation**. Resistance may also be acquired by microorganisms through **adaptation**, or through development of **infectious (multiple) drug resistance** as a result of transfer of genetic material from one bacterium to the other by **transformation, transduction** or **conjugation**.

Mutation. Any large population of antibiotic-susceptible bacteria is likely to contain some mutants that are **relatively resistant** to the drug. As the drug acts to eliminate most of the sensitive members of the species, the few bacterial cells that are congenitally resistant to the drug multiply freely (as their brethren are destroyed) until they become a majority of the bacterial population **(Fig. 9.1.3).** Drugs do not cause such mutations, but a drug may act as a **selective force** that favours the emergence of mutants until this **once resistant minority gradually becomes the dominant strain**. In therapeutics a noteworthy point is that if susceptible bacteria are exposed to **subinhibitory** concentrations of antibacterial drugs, drug resistant mutants may develop (induced mutation), either in **one step** (streptomycin-type), or in a **series of steps** (penicillin type).

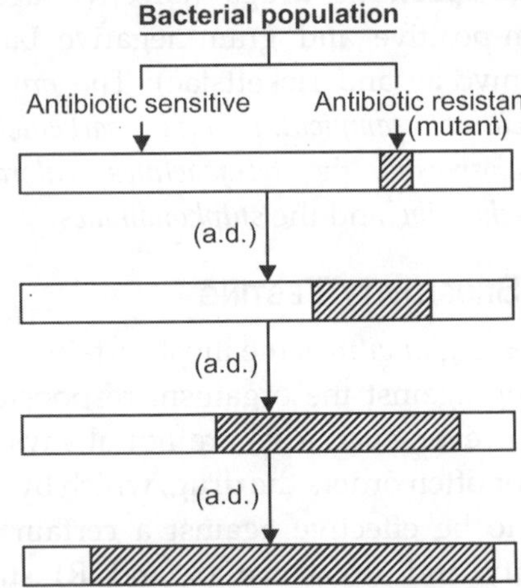

Fig. 9.1.3: Scheme showing how repeated exposure to an antibacterial durg (a.d.) progressively reduces the sensitive organisms in the population, due to a selective force provided by the drug, until the resistant mutants dominate the population (see text).

Adaptation. Adaptation presupposes that organisms contain low concentrations of drug destroying enzymes, or the potential for synthesizing such enzymes, and that lethal enzyme concentrations are "triggered" through enzyme induction following antibiotic exposure, e.g., **penicillinase induction** following semisynthetic penicillin exposure in some strains of staphylococci.

Infectious (multiple) drug resistance is the transfer *in vivo* or *in vitro* of genetic material (R factors) coding for resistance (e.g., beta-lactamase production) from a resistant bacterium to a sensitive bacterium. The origin of R factors remains unknown.

Genes for drug resistance may be associated with either *chromosomal* or *plasmid* DNA. Additionally plasmids may affect bacteria in a number of ways (phage typing, toxin production, fermentation reactions etc.). All plasmids contain genes (R factors) coding for resistance, but gram-negative bacteria possess in addition an RTF (resistance transfer factor: sex factor) that determines replication and transfer. The R factors may be transferred by one of the three following processes.

Transformation involves incorporation by a sensitive bacterium of free (naked) genes from a drug resistant cell. It occurs rarely and is of little clinical significance **(Fig. 9.1.4).**

Transduction refers to the transfer of an R factor carrying plasmid by a bacterial virus (*bacteriophage*) vector along with its own genes. Transduction is particularly important in the transfer of antibiotic resistance among strains of **Staph. aureus,** where some phages can carry plasmids that code for penicillinase, while others transfer information for resistance to erythromycin, tetracycline or chloramphenicol **(Fig. 9.1.4).**

Conjugation refers to the passage of resistant genes (R factors) from cell to cell by direct contact through a **sex pilus** or **bridge**. This is now recognized as an extremely important mechanism for spread of antibiotic resistance, since DNA that codes for resistance to multiple drugs may be so transferred. Resistance transfer factors have been determined in *E. coli, Shigella flexneri, Salmonella typhimurium, Vibrio cholerae, Pseudomonas aeruginosa* and some other species.

In the transfer of R factors the donor and recipient strains may belong to different species, or even to different genera, and transfer can also occur between pathogenic and nonpathogenic organisms indiscriminately. This kind of *infectious multiple drug resistance* has raised the threat, that diseases like **bacillary dysentery, typhoid** and **cholera** might become uncontrollable by any of the available drugs.

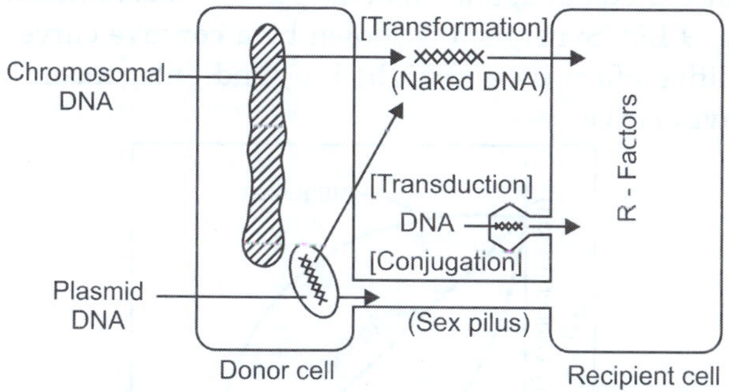

Fig. 9.1.4: Diagrammatic representation of the modes of genetic transfer (Transformation; Transduction; Conjugation) of R factors between bacterial cells. In transduction the DNA is carried in bacteriophage (see text).

Dependence. Organisms can become dependent on an antibacterial drug. Clinically this has been seen occasionally in the treatment of tuberculosis, where **M. tuberculosis** become dependent on streptomycin **(Chap. 9.3).**

Mechanisms of Resistance to Antimicrobial Drugs

There are many different mechanisms through which microorganisms may develop resistance to antimicrobial agents. The following are fairly well supported by evidence:

1. **Increased destruction of drug.** Staphylococci resistant to penicillin G produce a *beta-lactamase* which destroys penicillin. Gram-negative bacteria resistant to aminoglycosides produce *phosphorylating* or *acetylating enzymes* which destroy the drug.
2. **Decreased intracellular drug levels.** Tetracyclines accumulate in susceptible bacteria, but not in resistant bacteria. Resistant bacteria do not bind tetracyclines and produce an *inhibitor of tetracycline transport*.
3. **Altered structural target for the drug.** Chromosomal resistance to *aminoglycosides* occurs due to loss or alteration of a specific protein on the 30S subunit of the bacterial ribosome which serves as the binding site in the susceptible organisms. *Erythromycin-resistant organisms* have an altered protein on 50S subunit of the bacterial ribosome.
4. **Altered metabolic pathway.** This altered pathway bypasses the reaction inhibited by the drug. Some *sulphonamide-resistant bacteria* do not require extracellular PABA, but like mammalian cells they utilize preformed folic acid.
5. **Development of an altered enzyme.** This altered enzyme can still perform its metabolic function, but is much less affected by the drug than the enzyme in the susceptible organisms. In sulphonamide-susceptible bacteria, the *tetrahydropteroic acid synthetase* has a much higher affinity for sulphonamide than for PABA, whereas in sulphonamide-resistant mutants, it is just the opposite.

Prevention of Resistance

Unnecessary exposure to antimicrobial drugs tends to favour the development of resistance. Hence, the steps to be followed in antimicrobial therapy are: (*i*) **identification of the pathogen;** (*ii*) **sensitivity and resistance testing;** and (*iii*) **selection of the proper drug or drug combination,** if rationally indicated. Once the drug has been selected it should be used in **high enough doses** for **long enough periods** to eradicate even the more resistant pathogenic mutants that may be present.

Adverse Reactions to Anti-infective Agents

Antimicrobial drugs are capable of causing adverse effects which fall into the following *three* general classes:

1. **Direct toxic effects** upon such organs as the *gastrointestinal tract, liver, kidneys* or the *auditory, optic* and *other peripheral nerves.*
2. **Allergic reactions** and other types of hypersensitivity reactions affecting the *skin, bone marrow, circulating blood* and *other structures.*
3. **Superinfections** are a result of drug-induced *overgrowths by resistant bacterial strains or fungal organisms.*

Direct tissue toxicity is the result of the drug's pharmacologic effects upon the tissues. **Nephrotoxicity** is a particularly dangerous form of direct toxicity. Antibiotics including *polymyxins, amphotericin B, cephaloridine,* and the *aminoglycosides* may exert nephrotoxic effects. **Neurotoxicity** may occur, specially with *streptomycin* which damages the vestibular branch function of the eighth cranial nerve causing dizziness and vertigo.

Kanamycin and *neomycin* have an ototoxic effect and cause hearing impairment. **Hepatotoxicity** may be caused by the tetracyclines. *Chloramphenicol, lincomycin* and *erythromycin* are metabolized in the liver, and should be administered with caution in hepatic insufficiency.

Allergic reactions of the immediate and delayed types have been reported in atopic and other individuals who have become hypersensitive to a particular agent. These are particularly seen with **penicillin-type antibiotics. Aplastic anaemia** may occur due to chloramphenicol therapy. **Haemolytic anaemia** sometimes develops in patients during sulphonamide therapy who have an inherited deficiency of the enzyme glucose-6-phosphate dehydrogenase (G-6-PD) in their red blood cells.

Superinfections (suprainfections) may be the result of an indiscriminate use of antibiotics which induces dangerous changes in the patients own bacterial flora, by eliminating the susceptible organisms in the *intestinal, respiratory* or *genitourinary tract.* As a result an overgrowth of **resistant staphylococci, yeasts** and **fungi,** or strains of **proteus** and **pseudomonas** occurs, which may be far more serious than the original infection. Superinfections are most common with **broad-spectrum antibiotics** like the tetracyclines, and may also occur in debilitated individuals on *long-term therapy with corticosteroids, cytotoxic* and *immunosuppressive drugs.*

Prophylactic Use of Antimicrobial Drugs

Antimicrobial drugs have drastically altered the natural history of bacterial disease by reducing the morbidity and mortality from infections. In some situations chemoprophylaxis has proved quite effective, and is recommended as a rational procedure **(Table 9.1-4).**

Combination of Antimicrobial Drugs

The combined use of two or more effective antimicrobial agents is sometimes superior to treatment with a single drug. On the other hand, two drugs given together may not be more effective than one drug alone, particularly when the drugs are combined in a fixed-dosage mixture. Occasionally the therapeutic effectiveness of a combination of drugs may actually prove inferior to that of a single drug. *Thus, the use of antibiotics in fixed dosage combinations is to be deprecated.* The administration of antimicrobial drug combinations is best limited to a few clinical situations in which combination therapy has undoubtedly proved to be superior.

Dynamics of Combined Antibiotic Action

The interaction of two antimicrobial drugs may result in **addition** (indifference), **synergism,** or **antagonism.** Simply speaking, usually the interaction of two antimicrobial drugs is evaluated from the plot of drug activity in an **isobologram**. This method essentially determines whether the **minimum inhibitory concentration** (MIC) of one drug is reduced (synergism), unchanged (addition), or increased (antagonism) in the presence of another drug **(Fig. 9.1.5)**. Synergism is shown by a **concave** curve, the additive effect by a **straight** line, and antagonism by a **convex** curve.

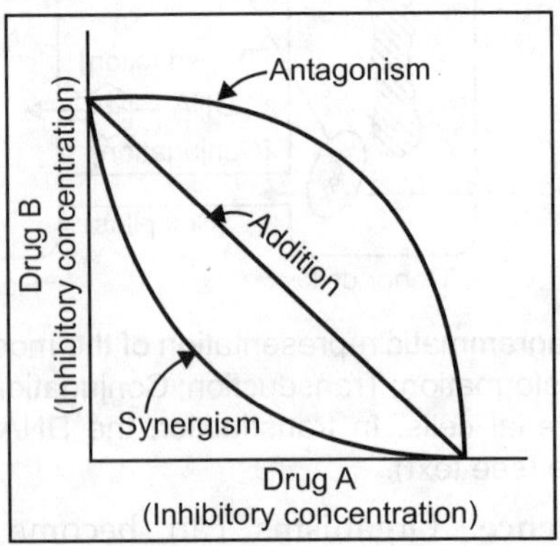

Fig. 9.1.5: Isobologram(s) showing the interaction of two antimicrobial agents A and B (diagrammatic).

Synergism between antibiotics is said to occur when inhibition results from a combination of **one-fourth** or less of the MIC of each drug. If **one-half** of the inhibitory

Table 9.1-4 *Some indications for chemoprophylaxis with antimicrobial drugs*

Antimicrobial Drug	*Indication*
Penicillin G	Prior to oral surgery to prevent the development of subacute bacterial endocarditis in patients with rheumatic endocarditis, congenital heart disease, or a valvular prosthesis; prevention of gas-gangrene in high lower-limb amputations or following major trauma; prevention of recurrent infection with Group A streptococci in patients with reheumatic fever
Ampicillin	Children with cystic fibrosis
Chloroquine	Prevention of malaria
Co-trimoxazole	Prophylaxis of recurrent urinary tract infections
Sulphonamides	Prophylaxis of rheumatic fever
Isoniazid	Prevention of tuberculosis in susceptible close contacts
Doxycycline	Prevention of "traveller's diarrhoea"
Rifampicin or minocycline	Prophylaxis of meningococcal meningitis

concentration of each drugs is required to produce the inhibition, the result is **addition**. If more than **one-half** of the MIC of each drug is necessary to produce the inhibitory effect, the result is **antagonism**.

Addition (indifference). The most common effect of combining two antimicrobial drugs is indifference, i.e., the combined effect of drugs A and B is equal to the arithmetic sum of the effects of the individual drugs in their chosen doses. The same effect could be obtained by the use of a single drug in a dose equivalent to that of the mixture.

Synergism. Sometimes the simultaneous action of two drugs results in an effect (A+B) which is far greater than that of either A alone, or B alone in much larger doses, and also greater than could be expected from simple addition of individual drug effects.

At least *three* types of antimicrobial synergism is fairly well understood: (*i*) **Blockade of successive steps in a metabolic pathway** of the bacterium, e.g., *sulphamethoxazole* and *trimethoprim*; (*ii*) **one drug inhibits an enzyme capable of destroying the second drug,** e.g., Penicillins susceptible to hydrolysis by beta lactamases are inactive against organisms which produce such lactamases. Some lactamase-resistant penicillins and cephalosporins have a much higher affinity for beta-lactamases produced by certain gram-negative bacteria, compared to hydrolysable penicillins. *Methicillin, cloxacillin,* or *cephalosporin* can bind beta-lactamases, and yet be resistant to their action; and (*iii*) **one drug promotes the penetration of the second drug through the bacterial cell envelope,** e.g., Enterococci exhibit a relative permeability barrier to aminoglycosides. If penicillins (which are inhibitors of cell wall synthesis) are administered simultaneously, the aminoglycosides penetrate and exert a bactericidal effect.

To obtain a synergistic combination for the treatment of a given patient, the drugs have to be fitted specifically to the organism isolated from the infection. **(Table 9.1-5)**.

Antagonism. *Antagonism is most marked when a barely active amount of a bacteriostatic drug is added to a minimal amount of a second bactericidal drug.*

Antagonism has been demonstrated between chloramphenicol and ampicillin in the treatment of bacterial meningitis; tetracycline and penicillin in group A haemolytic streptococcal pharyngitis.

It has been suggested that combined antimicrobial action can be predicted, depending on whether the component drugs are bactericidal (penicillins, cephalosporins, aminoglycosides) or *bacteriostatic* (tetracyclines, chloramphenicol, erythromycin) as follows:

Bactericidal + bactericidal = Synergistic effect
Bacteriostatic + bacteriostatic = Additive effect
Bactericidal + bacteriostatic = Antagonistic effect

Drugs of Choice for Common Infections

In practice an antimicrobial agent can be considered the drug of choice only: (*i*) when laboratory susceptibility tests have proved that the strain of the invading pathogen is actually sensitive to it; and (*ii*) the patient who is to be treated is shown not to be hypersensitive or otherwise unable to tolerate the first-line drug.

Table 9.1-5 *Some useful antimicrobial combinations*

Combination	*Infection*	
1. Penicillin + streptomycin	Endocarditis	(*Str. faecalis*)
2. Chloramphenicol + Streptomycin or gentamicin	Pneumonia	(*K. pnemoniae*)
3. Penicillin G + Cloxacillin	Septicaemia Endocarditis Bone infection	(*Staph. aureus*)
4. Carbenicillin + Gentamicin	Septicaemia Pneumonia	(*Ps. aeruginosa*)
5. Tetracycline + Streptomycin	Brucellosis	
6. Streptomycin + Aminosalicylic acid (PAS) + Isoniazid (INAH) 7. Rifampicin + (INAH) 8. Ethambutol + INAH	Tuberculosis (*M. tuberculosis*)	
9. Gentamicin or Ampicillin + Chloramphenicol 10. Gentamicin + Carbenicillin	Mixed intra-abdominal infections	

Table 9.1-6 *Drugs of first choice and alternative drugs for the treatment of common infections*

Microorganism	*Diseases*	*Drug of First Choice*	*Alternative Drugs*
1. GRAM-POSITIVE COCI			
Staphylococcus aureus Penicillin G sensitive strain	Abscesses; bacteraemia; endocarditis; pneumonia; meningitis; osteomyelitis; cellulitis	Penicillin G,	A cephalosporin; clindamycin; erythromycin; vancomycin; amoxycillin + clavulanic acid
Penicillinase-producing strains	As above	A penicillinase resistant penicillin (cloxacillin or dicloxacillin orally, or methicillin and oxacillin parenterally); ciprofloxacin, imipenum	A cephalosporin; vancomycin
Methicillin-resistant strains	As above	Vancomycin	A cephalosporin + kanamycin; erythromycin + rifampicin
Streptococcus pyogenes	Pharyngitis; scarlet fever; otitis media; sinusitis; cellulitis; erysipelas; pneumonia; bacteraemia	Penicillin G parenterally; penicillin V orally; ampicillin	A cephalosporin; vancomycin; amoxycillin; ampicillin; lincomycin; erythromycin; imipenum
Streptococcus viridans group	Endocarditis; meningitis; bacteraemia; urinary tract infections	Penicillin G with or without streptomycin or gentamicin	A cephalosporin; erythromycin; vancomycin; norfloxacin; clindamycin
Streptococcus bovis	Endocarditis; meningitis; bacteraemia; urinary tract infections	Penicillin G with or without gentamicin	A cephalosporin; erythromycin; vancomycin
Streptococcus faecalis	Endocarditis	Penicillin G + an Aminoglycoside	Vancomycin + an Aminoglycoside; imipenum
	Urinary tract infections	Ampicillin; Penicillin G + an aminoglycoside; amoxycillin	A tetracycline; vancomycin; co-trimoxazole; nitrofurantoin
Streptococcus pneumoniae (pneumococcus)	Pneumonia; meningitis; otitis; endocarditis; arthritis	Penicillin G or penicillin V	A cephalosporin; erythromycin chloramphenicol; clindamycin; ciprofloxacin
Streptococcus (anaerobic species)	Bacteraemia; endocarditis; peritonitis; brain abscess	Penicillin G (large doses)	A cephalosporin; erythromycin; clindamycin; chloramphenicol

Table 9.1-6 Contd...

Microorganism	*Diseases*	*Drug of First Choice*	*Alternative Drugs*
II. GRAM-NEGATIVE COCCI			
Neisseria gonorrhoeae (gonococcus)	Gonococcal urethritis; salpingitis; vaginitis; endocarditis or arthritis	Penicillin G alone or combined with probenecid	Ampicillin alone or combined with probenecid; a cephalosporin; co-trimoxazole; cefoxitin
Neisseria meningitidis (meningococcus)	Meningitis; bacteraemia	Penicillin G	Chloramphenicol; moxalactam; cefotaxime; a sulphonamide
	Carrier state	Rifampicin	Minocycline; a sulphonamide
III. GRAM-POSITIVE BACILLI			
Bacillus anthracis (anthrax)	Pneumonia; malignant pustule; meningitis	Penicillin G	A cephalosporin; erythromycin; chloramphenicol; a tetracycline
Corynebacterium diphtheriae	Pharyngitis; laryngitis; tracheitis; pneumonia	Penicillin G	A cephalosporin; erythromycin; clindamycin; lincomycin; rifampicin
	Carrier state	*Erythromycin*	Penicillin G
Clostridium perfringens and others	Gas gangrene	Penicillin G	Chloramphenicol; a cephalosporin; erythromycin; clindamycin; metronidazole
Clostridium tetani	Tetanus	Penicillin G	A tetracycline; erythromycin; a cephalosporin
Listeria monocytogenes	Meningitis; endocarditis; bacteraemia; recurrent abortion	Ampicillin or penicillin G with or without an aminoglycoside	Erythromycin; chloramphenicol; a tetracycline
Corynebacterium species - aerobic and anaerobic (diphtheroids)	Endocarditis; infected foreign bodies	Penicillin G with or without an aminoglycoside; vancomycin	Rifampicin with or without penicillin G; a cephalosporin
IV. GRAM-NEGATIVE BACILLI			
Escherichia coli	Urinary tract infection	Gentamicin; mezlocillin, a sulphonamide; co-trimoxazole	A cephalosporin; ampicillin; a tetracycline; aztreonam; nitrofurantoin; norfloxacin; ciprofloxacin
	Other infections; bacteraemia; meningitis	Ampicillin; gentamicin	A cephalosporin; chloramphenicol; co-trimoxazole

Table 9.1-6 Contd...

Microorganism	*Diseases*	*Drug of First Choice*	*Alternative Drugs*
Enterobacter aerogenes	Urinary tract and other infections; bacteraemia	Gentamicin; tobramycin; azlocillin	Kanamycin; amikacin; carbenicillin; netilmicin; chloramphenicol; ciprofloxacin; cefonicid
Proteus mirabilis	Urinary tract and other infections	Ampicillin; gentamicin; tobramycin	A cephalosporin; chloramphenicol; norfloxacin; a tetracycline; ciprofloxacin
Other Proteus species	Urinary tract and other infections	Gentamicin; tobramycin; a third generation cephalosporin	Carbenicillin; ticarcillin; chloramphenicol; ciprofloxacin; kanamycin; cefoxitin
Pseudomonas aeruginosa	Urinary tract infections bacteraemia; respiratory and skin infections	Carbenicillin or gentamicin alone or in combination; mezlocillin; piperacillin	Colistimethate; imipenum; tobramycin; cefotaxime; moxalactam
Klebsiella pneumoniae	Urinary tract, biliary tract, and bone infections; pneumonia,	A cephalosporin with or without gentamicin; kanamycin or tobramycin	Chloramphenicol; colistimethate; amikacin; netilmicin; a tetracycline; ciprofloxacin
Salmonella typhosa	Typhoid fever	Chloramphenicol	Amoxycillin; ampicillin; cefoperazone; co-trimoxazole
Other Salmonella species	Paratyphoid fever; acute gastroenteritis	Ampicillin; amoxycillin	Chloramphenicol; co-trimoxazole
Shigella species	Acute gastroenteritis (bacillary dysentery; shigellosis)	Co-trimoxazole	Chloramphenicol; ampicillin; a tetracycline
Serratia species	Various systemic infections	Gentamicin; amikacin; cefotaxime	Carbenicillin; imipenum; chloramphenicol; aztreonam; azlocillin
Haemophilus influenzae	Respiratory infection; meningitis; other infections	Ampicillin; amoxycillin or chloramphenicol	A sulphonamide; a tetracycline; co-trimoxazole; cefonicid; cefamandole; ciprofloxacin
Haemophilus ducreyi	Chancroid	Co-trimoxazole	A sulphonamide; erythromycin; cephalothin; streptomycin; tetracycline
Brucella species	Brucellosis	A tetracycline with or without streptomycin	Chloramphenicol with or without streptomycin; co-trimoxazole
Yersinia (Pasturella) pestis	Bubonic plague	Streptomycin with or without a tetracycline	Chloramphenicol; a sulphonamide
Franciscella tularensis	Tularaemia	Streptomycin	Chloramphenicol; a tetracycline
Vibrio cholerae (comma)	Cholera	A tetracycline	Co-trimoxazole; chloramphenicol; erythromycin
Streptobacillus moniliformis	Rat-bite fever; bacteraemia; abscesses	Penicillin G	Streptomycin; a tetracycline; a cephalosporin

Table 9.1-6 Contd...

Microorganism	*Diseases*	*Drug of First Choice*	*Alternative Drugs*
Spirillum minus	Rat-bite fever	Penicillin G	Streptomycin; a tetracycline
Leptotrichia buccalis	Vincent's infection	Penicillin G	Erythromycin; a tetracycline
Bordetella pertusis	Whooping cough	Erythromycin	A tetracycline; ampicillin; co-trimoxazole
V. ACID-FAST BACILLI			
Mycobacterium tuberculosis	Pulmonary tuberculosis	Isoniazid+ethambutol Isoniazid+rifampicin	Aminosalicylic acid (PAS); capreomycin; cycloserine; ethionamide; viomycin; pyrazinamide
	Miliary, renal, meningeal and other infections	Isoniazid+ rifampicin+ streptomycin or ethambutol	
Mycobacterium leprae	Leprosy	Dapsone with or without rifampicin	Amithiozone; clofazimine; ethionamide
VI. SPIROCHETES			
Treponema pallidum	Syphilis	Penicillin G	A tetracycline; erythromycin
Treponema pertenue	Yaws	Penicillin G	A tetracycline
Leptospira	Weil's disease	Penicillin G	A tetracycline
Borrelia recurrentis	Relapsing fever	A tetracycline	Penicillin G
VII. CHLAMYDIA			
Chlamydia psittaci	Psittacosis (ornithosis)	A tetracycline	Chloramphenicol
Chlamydia trachomatis	Trachoma	A tetracycline applied locally	Erythromycin; chloramphenicol; a tetracycline; a sulphonamide
	Lymphogranuloma venereum	A tetracycline	Chloramphenicol; a sulphonamide
	Inclusion conjunctivitis (blennorrhoea)	A tetracycline	Chloramphenicol
	Nonspecific urethritis	A tetracycline	A sulphonamide; erythromycin
VIII. RICKETTSIA	Typhus fever; murine typhus; Rocky Mountain spotted fever; Brill's disease; Q fever; rickettsia pox	A tetracycline	Chloramphenicol
IX. MYCOPLASMA			
Mycoplasma pneumoniae	"Atypical pneumonia"	Erythromycin or a tetracycline	—
Mycoplasma hominis	"Nonspecific urethritis"	Clindamycin or a tetracycline	Chloramphenicol; erythromycin; gentamicin; streptomycin
X. ACTINOMYCETES			
Actinomyces israelii	Actinomycosis	Penicillin G	A cephalosporin; clindamycin; lincomycin; cephalosporin; a tetracycline

Table 9.1-6 Contd...

Microorganism	*Diseases*	*Drug of First Choice*	*Alternative Drugs*
Nocardia asteroides	Nocardiosis	A sulphonamide alone or with ampicillin	Minocycline alone or with cycloserine; co-trimoxazole
XI. FUNGI **(a) Superficial infections** *Candida albicans*	Candidiasis of the skin and mucous membranes	Amphotericin B or nystatin; flucytosine; clotrimazole	Flucytosine; candicidin
Dermatophytes e.g., *Microsporum, Trichophyton,* and *Epidermophyton*	Tinea infection of skin, hair and nails	Griseofulvin orally; or local application of clotrimazole, miconazole, or tolnaftate	—
(b) **Systemic infections** *Aspergillus, Candida albicans, Cryptococcus neoformans*	Aspergillosis candidiasis; cryptococcosis	Amphotericin B with or without flucytosine	Flucytosine
Blastomyces dermatitidis	North American blastomycosis	Amphotericin B	Hydroxystilbamidine; ketoconazole
Blastomyces braziliensis	South American blastomycosis	Amphotericin B	A sulphonamide
Coccidioides immitis	Coccidioidomycosis	Amphotericin B	Miconazole; ketoconazole
Histoplasma capsulatum	Histoplasmosis	Amphotericin B	Ketoconazole
Mucor	Mucormycosis	Amphotericin B	—
Sporothrix schenckii	Sporotrichosis	Amphotericin B	Potassium iodide
Fonsecaea	Chromomycosis	Amphotericin B	
XII. VIRUSES *Herpes simplex virus*	Keratoconjuctivitis	Acyclovir; trifluridine	Idoxuridine; vidarabine
	Encephalitis	Vidarabine	Acyclovir
Influenza virus A	Influenza	Amantadine (for prophylaxis)	—
Vaccinia	Smallpox vaccine complications like vaccinia gangrenosa	Methisazone with or without immune globulin	—

The list of drugs presented in **Table 9.1-6** is only a rough guide to therapy based upon authentic current opinions, and should not be taken as absolute. *For a very rational application of chemotherapy susceptibility tests are mandatory.*

Causes of Failure of Chemotherapy

Usually a 7-day treatment is sufficient to cause a resolution of a susceptible infection. If the patient's condition does not improve, the following possibilities should be considered:

1. Failure due to a wrong diagnosis, wrong choice of drug, and wrong dose, and inadequate duration of therapy.

2. Failure to deliver active antimicrobials to the site of infection because of faulty route of administration, or altered pharmacokinetic parameters in the patient.

3. Failure of the host defences to aid eradication of the infection, which may be due to the location of the infection (e.g. endocarditis), or an impairment in the host's defence mechanisms.

4. Failure due to serious toxicity, necessitating discontinuation of therapy.

5. Failure due to development of **antimicrobial resistance.**

6. Failure due to the presence of pus and **associated disease.**

7. Failure due to **superinfection**, and drug fever.

8. Failure of the patient to **comply** with the therapeutic regimen.

Opportunistic Infections

Opportunistic infections are infections developing as a result of: (*i*) the predisposition caused by other diseases like systemic disease of the lympho-reticular system, leukaemias, chronic anaemia, and metabolic disorders; or (*ii*) use of immunosuppressive or cytotoxic agents in therapeutics. The therapy of such infections (bacterial, protozoal, fungal or viral) is summarized in **Table 9.1-7.**

Table 9.1-7 *The therapy for opportunistic infections*

Organism(s)	*Antimicrobial Drug*
Bacterial infections *Listeria monocytogenes* Atypical mycobacteriae	Penicillin/erythromycin. Depends on sensitivity to antituberculous drugs
Protozoal infections *Toxoplasma gondii* *Pneumocystis carinii*	Spiramycin, pyrimethamine Pentamidine isethionate
Fungal infections *Nocardia asteroides* *Aspergillus neoformans* Candidiasis *Cryptococcus neoformans* *Mucormycosis*	Sulphadiazine Amphotericin B 5-Fluorocytosine Amphotericin B, 5-fluorocytosine Amphotericin B
Viral infections *Herpes simplex* *Cytomegalovirus*	Vidarabine Idoxuridine

Drug Interactions

Some important interactions are listed in **Table 9.1-8.**

Antibiotic Abuse

A certain degree of misuse of antibiotics is unavoidable. However, it is a consequence of three main factors: (*i*) the **availability** of a wide selection of drugs; (*ii*) **limitation on physician's time;** and (*iii*) the **demand from the patient** who cannot fully appreciate the dangerous consequences of antibiotic use. The physician is constantly under pressure to prescribe these wonder drugs, and unnecessary use follows. Sometimes antibiotics are used to "cure" fever using them as "twentieth-century antipyretics", when aspirin might have been a more logical choice.

Table 9.1-8 *Interaction of antimicrobial agents with other drugs*

Antimicrobial Drug	*Interacting Drug*	*Effect of Interaction*
Aminoglycosides	Frusemide Ethacrynic acid Skeletal muscle relaxants	Increased ototoxicity Increased ototoxicity Enhanced neuromuscular blockade
Tetracyclines	Antacids Ferrous sulphate	Diminished absorption due to chelation (lower blood levels)
Sulphonamides	Oral hypoglycaemics Oral anticoagulants Methotrexate	Increased hypoglycaemia Increased anticoagulation Increased methotrexate toxicity
Chloramphenicol	Oral hypoglycaemics Oral anticoagulants	Enhanced hypoglycaemia Enhanced anticoagulation
Ampicillin Cephaloridine Rifampicin	Contraceptive pill Frusemide Warfarin Corticosteroids Contraceptive pill	Failure of contraception is likely Enhanced nephrotoxicity Warfarin metabolism stimulated Cortisol metabolism induced Enzyme induction of oestrogen metabolism, and consequent failure of contraception
Metronidazole	Alcohol Oral anticoagulants	Disulfiram-like syndrome Inhibition of warfarin metabolism
Nalidixic acid Griseofulvin Ampotericin B	Oral anticoagulants Barbiturates Digoxin	Enhanced anticoagulation Reduced griseofulvin effect Amphotericin-induced hypokalaemia increases digitalis toxicity

9.2 SYNTHETIC ANTIMICROBIALS
(Sulphonamides, Trimethoprim: Sulphamethoxazole, and Quinolones)

Historically, the sulphonamides were the first effective chemotherapeutic agents employed systemically for the prevention and cure of bacterial infections in man. Gelmo in 1908 synthesized the intermediary dye **sulphanilamide** for use in the dye industry. Subsequently sulphanilamide and a variety of other azo dyes were used as *urinary antiseptics*. In 1935 **Gerhard Domagk** from Elberfeld, Germany, while working on azo dyes, reported that one of them, the red dye **prontosil** (Prontosil rubrum) protected mice from streptococcal infection, a discovery for which he was awarded the Nobel Prize in Medicine for 1938. Other workers showed that the dye was broken down in the body to aminobenzene sulphonamide, or **sulphanilamide**. Later, sulphanilamide was found to be effective in **puerperal sepsis** and **meningococcal infection**. The term sulphonamide (sulpha drug) is commonly used as a **generic name** for all the derivatives of sulphanilamide.

SULPHONAMIDES

The sulphonamides as a class of *bacteriostatic* agents, had a short period of clinical use, because of the introduction of antibiotics with a broader and more certain action against microorganisms. Much later, in the mid-1970s the combination of **trimethoprim** and **sulphamethoxazole** again resulted in an increased use of sulphonamides.

CHEMISTRY

The sulphonamides may be considered as substituted derivatives of sulphanilamide. As a group they have a basic chemical resemblance to **para-aminobenzoic acid** (PABA). They are white crystalline powders mostly poorly soluble in water. However, soluble sodium salts can be prepared for intravenous use.

The minimal chemical requirements for antibacterial action are contained in sulphanilamide. The para-NH_2 group is essential for maximal antibacterial activity, and can only be replaced by chemical groupings which are converted to free amino group in the host, as is contained in prontosil **(Fig. 9.2.1)**.

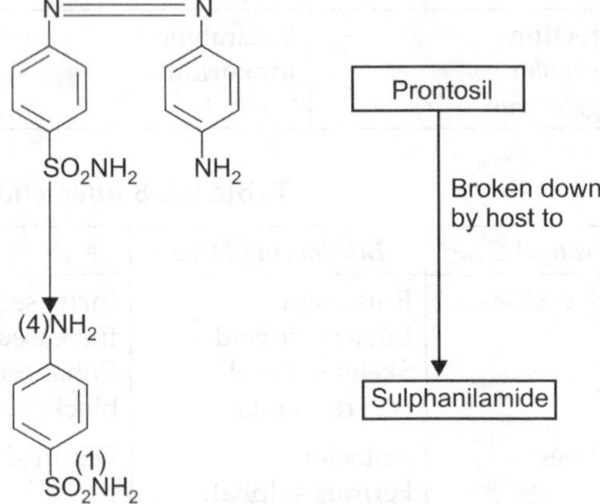

Fig. 9.2.1: The chemical pattern of sulphonamides. The N of the amide NH_2 in all sulphonamides is designated as N^1, and the N of the para-NH_2 as N^4. The majority of effective sulphonamides are N^1 substituted sulphanilamide derivatives (see text).

The sulphamoyl (-SO_2NH_2) group is not essential for antibacterial activity as such, but the sulphur atom should be directly linked to the benzene ring. This sulphamoyl group in sulphanilamide is responsible for the production of metabolic acidosis, and thereby **diuresis**. Subsequently chemical manipulation of sulphanilamide led to the development of sulphamoyl diuretics like carbonic anhydrase inhibitors (acetazolamide), the thiazides and frusemide. Direct benzene ring substitution yields totally inactive compounds.

CLASSIFICATION

Based on the absorption/excretion patterns, and uses, the sulphonamides can be grouped as under:

I. Systemic use

1. **Short-acting agents**
   - Sulphadiazine
   - Sulfisoxazole
   - Sulphamethizole
   - Sulphasalazine
   - Sulfacytine

2. **Intermediate-acting agents**
   Sulphamethoxazole
   Sulphapyridine
3. **Long-acting agent**
   Sulphadoxine

II. Local use

1. **Ophthalmic**
   Sulphacetamide
2. **Topical**
   Mafenide
   Silver sulphadiazine

Antibacterial Spectrum

Sulphonamides are effective against many *gram-positive organisms, some gram-negative diplococci* and *bacilli, actinomyces, nocardia, chlamydia,* and *some protozoa.* Highly sensitive *in vitro* are the majority of the group A streptococci, *Haemophilus influenzae, Haemophilus ducreyi, pneumococci, Escherichia coli; Brucellae, Pasturella pestis, Bacillus anthracis, Corynebacterium diphtheriae, cholera vibrio, nocardiae, actinomycetes, and chlamydia trachomatis.* The gonococci, meningococci and shigellae are variably sensitive, while some strains of *Klebsiella, Enterobacter* and *Proteus* may be sensitive to very high concentrations, such as might be obtained in the urine. *Several species of staphylococci, enterococci, clostridia* and *pseudomonas are highly resistant.* Regarding protozoal infections, the sulphonamides are an effective adjunct to pyrimethamine in treating *toxoplasmosis;* and to quinine and other antimalarials to treat *chloroquine-resistant cases of malaria.*

Mechanism of Action

The sulphonamides are **antimetabolites** of PABA. They inhibit the synthesis of DNA and therefore prevent certain bacteria from replicating. They have no effect on resting bacteria. The sulphonamides are primarily **bacteriostatic** agents, and intact cellular and humoral defence mechanisms of the host are required for their antibacterial effect. **Exceptionally** some sulphonamides may reach bactericidal concentrations *in vivo*, as in the urinary tract following therapy with soluble sulphas (sulfisoxazole, sulphamethizole), and in ocular tissues following topical application of sulphacetamide.

The action of sulphonamides is a good example of **competitive antagonism**. They are structural analogues and competitive antagonists of PABA, and thus prevent the normal bacterial utilization of PABA for the synthesis of folic acid **(Fig. 9.2.2).** Folic acid derivatives are essential for purine and ultimately DNA synthesis in bacteria. **Specifically the sulphonamides competitively inhibit the enzyme dihydrofolic acid synthetase, and thereby prevent dihydrofolic acid formation (PABA is the normal substrate for the enzyme).** This reaction is closely related to the concentration of the sulphonamide and PABA-like substances, so that a high concentration of the latter, as is present in pus and infected tissue antagonizes the antibacterial effect of the sulphonamides.

Sulphonamide-sensitive organisms are those that must synthesize their own folic acid. Bacteria that do not require folic acid or can utilize *preformed* folic acid are insensitive to sulphonamides.

Acquired Resistance to Sulphonamides

Resistance to sulphonamides possibly originates from **random mutation** and **selection**, or by **transfer of resistance by plasmids** (see Chap. 9.1). Once such resistance is maximally developed, it is usually **persistent** and **irreversible**, specially when produced *in vivo*. The mechanism involved in the development of this resistance is an **altered enzymatic constitution** of the bacterial cell characterized by: (*i*) an alteration in the enzyme that utilizes PABA; (*ii*) an increased capacity to destroy the drug; (*iii*) an alternative metabolic pathway for synthesis of essential metabolites, or (*iv*) an increased production of an essential metabolite. Many strains of previously susceptible microorganisms are now resistant to the sulphonamides.

Pharmacokinetics

The sulphonamides are well absorbed from the gastrointestinal tract. Most absorption occurs in the small intestine, but some takes place in the stomach. Approximately 70 to 100 percent of an oral dose is rapidly absorbed, and appears in the urine within 30 minutes of ingestion. After absorption, the sulphonamides become **bound to protein**, and to some extent are **acetylated**, and are excreted chiefly by the kidneys. There are wide variations in the behaviour of different sulphonamides in these three aspects.

Protein binding. All sulphonamides are bound in varying degrees to plasma proteins, particularly to *albumin*. This is determined by the hydrophilicity of the drug, and its pKa. At physiological pH, drugs with a high pKa exhibit low protein binding and *vice versa*. The protein binding is decreased in patients with renal failure. **The acetylated form is protein bound to a greater extent than the free form**. The soluble sulphonamides readily enter pleural, peritoneal, synovial and ocular fluids. **Sulphadiazine** and **sulfisoxazole** attain effective concentrations in the cerebrospinal fluid.

Acetylation. In the liver each sulphonamide is acetylated to a different extent. *The acetylated products have no antibacterial activity, but retain their toxic potential.* They are poorly soluble in urine and are likely to produce *crystalluria*.

Excretion. Excretion of systemically absorbed sulphonamides is almost entirely renal. In bile the concentration is usually low. Sulphonamides in the free form, and their acetylated conjugates are *excreted by glomerular filtration mainly* and also by *tubular secretion*. Later, a part of the secreted drug is reabsorbed. *Sulphonamide clearance is increased in alkaline urine, possibly due to a reduced tubular reabsorption*. Urine concentrations are high, and this has led to the use of sulphonamides in *urinary tract infection*. Complications like *crystalluria* and *ureteric blockage* can occur, but are less likely when the fluid intake is high and the urine is kept alkaline.

Mode of Administration and Dosage

The recommended doses of currently used agents are summarized in **Table 9.2-1**.

Therapeutic Uses

1. Urinary tract infections (UTI). The sulphonamides still have an important place in the treatment of acute infections caused by susceptible *gram-negative uropathogens*. Most acute uncomplicated bladder infections are caused by sulpha-sensitive strains of *E. coli*. The sulphonamides preferred for treating acute UTI are short-acting agents like *sulfisoxazole* (Gantrisin) and *sulphamethizole* (Urolucosil).

2. Ulcerative colitis. Patients of ulcerative colitis are benefited by oral administration of *sulphasalazine* (Salazopyrine), which is converted in the colon to *sulphapyridine* and *aminosalicylic acid*.

3. Respiratory tract infections. The sulphonamides have been used for the treatment of *pneumococcal pneumonia*, and *lower respiratory tract bacterial infections*, but safer and more effective agents are now available.

4. Meningococcal meningitis. Formely sulphonamides were extensively used for the treatment of meningococcal meningitis and septicaemia. However, they can no longer be relied upon now as most strains of meningococci are now resistant to sulphas.

Table 9.2-1 *The recommended dosage schedule of some sulphonamides*

Non-Proprietary Name	*Usual Dosage*		Comments
	Initial	*Maintenance*	
1. Sulphadiazine	4 g orally	1 g 4 hourly	Low solubility requires forcing of fluids; available in combination with other sulphonamides
Sulphadiazine sodium	100 mg/kg IV or SC upto a total dose of 5 g	30-50 mg/kg IV or SC every 6-8 hours	Parenteral form for use in very severe susceptible infections (meningococcal meningitis caused by group A strains of meningococci)
2. Sulfisoxazole	4 g orally	1 g 4 to 6 times daily	Used in acute, chronic and recurrent urinary tract infections caused by *E. coli* and *Proteus species*
Acetyl sulfisoxazole	270-1010 mg orally	270-1010 mg twice daily	Slowly absorbed form for use in paediatrics
Sulfisoxazole diolamide	IV or SC 100 mg/kg initially and same for 24 hours maintenance		This form is used in treating meningitis caused by susceptible strains of meningococci and *H. influenzae*
3. Sulphamethizole	2-3 g orally	0.5 g 4 to 6 times daily	Rapidly excreted; highly soluble in urine
4. Sulphasalazine	4 g orally	1 g 4 times daily	Poorly absorbed agent; used in ulcerative colitis
5. Sulfacytine	500 mg orally	250 mg qid for 10 days	Only used for treating urinary tract infections
6. Sulphamethoxazole	2 g orally	1 g bid or tid	Used in combination with trimethoprim as co-trimoxazole
7. Sulphapyridine	500 mg qid with sufficient fluids		Used to treat dermatitis herpetiformis
8. Sulfadoxine	Available as 0.5 g tablets, and also as a solution for injection (1 g/4 ml); Adult dose is 1-2 g once weekly		Also available in combination with pyrimethamine for prophylaxis and treatment of chloroquine-resistant malaria (Sulfadoxine 500 mg + Pyrimethamine 25 mg; Fansidar)
9. Sulphacetamide sodium	Ophthalmic solution available in 10, 20 and 30% strengths		Used locally in eye infections
10. Mafenide	Applied topically as a 11.2% cream, once or twice daily, as a 1/16 inch thick layer over the burned area.		Used in second- or third-degree burns to prevent infection. Active against many *gram-positive* and *gram-negative* organisms including *Ps. aeruginosa*
11. Silver sulpha-diazine	0.1% ointment for topical application		Used on burn surfaces to control sepsis by gram-negative and gram-positive organisms

5. Venereal diseases. Many strains of the gonococcus are now resistant to sulphonamides. However, some patients allergic to penicillin have been treated successfully with a *combination of trimethoprim and sulphamethoxazole. Chancroid* often responds to sulphonamide therapy, and so also does *lymphogranuloma venereum*.

6. Other chlamydial infections. Eye diseases like *trachoma* and *inclusion conjunctivitis* respond to sulphonamide therapy, particularly when these drugs are administered orally with *tetracycline. Sulphacetamide sodium* and *sulfisoxazole diolamine* are also effective when applied topically in these and other eye infections.

7. Systemic mycoses. Sulphonamides were employed in the past to treat *blastomycosis* and *histoplasmosis*. But these diseases now are treated and cured by *amphotericin B*. However, the sulphonamides even now are often life saving in *nocardiosis*. *Co-trimoxazole* may also work satisfactorily.

8. Protozoal infections. *Malaria* caused by *P. falciparum* strains resistant to chloroquine may be controlled with quinine and pyrimethamine combined with *sulphadiazine* or *sulfadoxine*. *Toxoplasmosis* caused by the protozoan *Toxoplasma gondii* has been effectively controlled by a *combination of sulphadiazine with pyrimethamine*. Combination of *sulphadoxine* and *pyrimethamine* may be used for prophylasis of *Pneumocystis carinii* pneumonia in patients of AIDS.

9. Burns and skin disorders. *Mafenide* may be used for topical therapy of war wounds and burns. The wound is not covered by a dressing, but is kept exposed except the 1/6 inch layer of the cream until the burn eschar separates. *Silver sulphadiazine* has an advantage over mafenide as it does not cause stinging pain which occurs with mafenide cream.

Adverse Reactions

Most patients receiving sulphonamides suffer only a transient headache, nausea, vomiting and abdominal discomfort. However, serious side effects may occur in patients *hypersensitive* to these drugs

1. Hypersensitivity reactions. Allergic skin rashes are frequent complications of sulpha therapy. Serious vascular lesions resembling *periarteritis nodosa* may occur. *Sulfisoxazole* has been associated with the activation of quiescent *systemic lupus erythematosus*. *Exfoliative dermatitis* or rarely *Stevens-Johnson syndrome* (erythema multiforme exudativum) may occur. A syndrome similar to serum sickness or immediate reactions of the *anaphylactoid* type may also occur. *Hepatitis* with focal or diffuse necrosis may occur.

2. Renal damage. Crystalluria can occur causing blockade in the kidney tubules, ureters, or bladder due to the deposition of crystalline aggregates of the sulpha drugs or their insoluble metabolites. Due to local irritation by the deposited crystals haematuria, oliguria, anuria and fatal uraemia may occur. The incidence of crystalluria is low when the soluble sulphonamides are used, e.g., *sulfisoxazole*, and *sulphamethizole*. *Toxic nephrosis* may occur rarely.

3. Blood dyscrasias. Blood dyscrasias are rare, but are potentially fatal. *Haemolytic anaemia* may occur either as a sensitization phenomenon, or from red cell deficiency of glucose-6-phosphate dehydrogenase (G-6-PD). The latter reaction is not dose related, and can occur early in the course of therapy. *Acute haemolytic anaemia* usually develops within the first 2-7 days of therapy. *Agranulocytosis*, *thrombocytopenia*, or *aplastic anaemia* may occur.

4. Effects on the foetus and neonate. The sulphonamides may produce *kernicterus* in the foetus and neonate, as these drugs displace bilirubin from plasma proteins causing *hyperbilirubinaemia* leading to kernicterus in premature infants. These agents are *teratogenic* in some laboratory animals.

5. Miscellaneous reactions. Other adverse reactions which may follow sulphonamide therapy include *goitre* and *hypothyroidism, arthritis, cardiomyopathy, psychiatric disturbances, drug fever, peripheral neuritis, insomnia and nightmares.*

Cautions and Contraindications

The sulphonamides are contraindicated in patients with a history of *sulpha hypersensitivity* and *advanced kidney disease* with an elevated blood urea nitrogen. Caution is required in patients with *liver disease, blood dyscrasias*, and *impaired kidney function*. Pregnant women near term should not receive sulphonamides because of possible placental transmission to the foetus and *danger of kernicterus*.

Drug Interactions

Sulphonamides increase the effect of *oral anticoagulants* and *methotrexate*, probably by displacing these drugs from their binding sites on plasma albumin. They also potentiate the action of *oral sulphonylurea hypoglycaemic agents, thiazides* and the *uricosuric agents*. On the other hand, *indomethacin, probenecid*, and *salicylates* may displace sulphonamides from their binding sites increasing their concentration in the plasma.

Trimethoprim-Sulphamethoxazole (Co-trimoxazole)

Originally *trimethoprim* (a diaminopyrimidine) was tried alone in the treatment of malaria, but later it was marketed in combination with sulphamethoxazole as **co-trimoxazole**. Trimethoprim is chemically related to pyrimethamine. The introduction of the combination of trimethoprim with sulphamethoxazole is an important advance in the practical application of antimicrobial agents, as the two drugs act on *sequential steps* leading to a folate deficiency in the susceptible organisms, thereby having a *synergistic* effect. Most of the commercial preparations contain a mixture of *sulphamethoxazole and trimethoprim in a fixed ratio of 5:1*, and the generic name of **co-trimoxazole** is used for this drug combination (sulphamethoxazole 400 mg and trimethoprim 80 mg per tablet). *Sulphamethoxazole* was chosen from amongst the sulphonamides, because it is absorbed and excreted at about the same rate as trimethoprim. *Double strength tablets* (sulphamethoxazole 800 mg and trimethoprim 160 mg) are also available.

Antibacterial Spectrum

The antibacterial spectrum of trimethoprim is similar to that of sulphamethoxazole, although the former is 20 to 100 times more potent than the latter. The spectrum includes gram-negative species like *E. coli*, salmonellae, *Haemophilis influenzae* and proteus species, also the common gram-positive cocci, *Streptococcus pyogenes* and staphylococci (including penicillin-resistant ones) are usually sensitive. There is no activity against *Pseudomonas aeruginosa, Mycobacterium tuberculosis* and *Treponema pallidum*. Maximal degree of synergism occurs when the organisms are sensitive to both the components. *Malarial parasites* are sensitive to trimethoprim. *Cross-resistance with other agents has not been described.*

Mechanism of Action

The antimicrobial activity of trimethoprim and sulphamethoxazole results from the action on **two sequential steps** of the enzymatic pathway for the synthesis of tetrahydrofolic acid (folinic acid). The sulphonamides being structurally related to para-aminobenzoic acid (PABA) act by competitive blockage of the enzyme **dihydrofolic acid synthetase**, necessary for the conversion of PABA to dihydrofolic acid **(Fig. 9.2.2).**

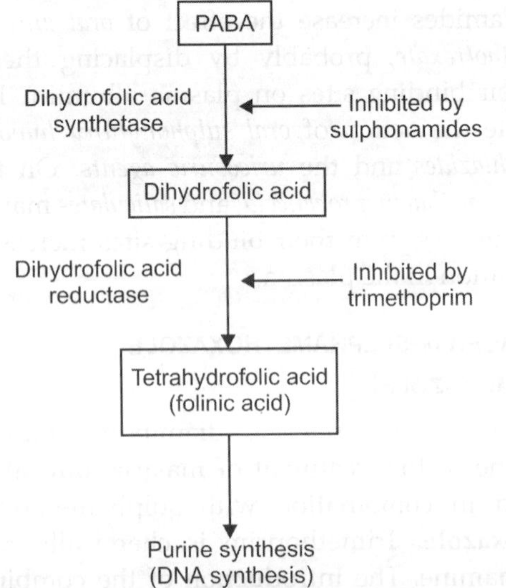

Fig. 9.2.2: Sequential blockade of folinic acid production by sulphonamides and trimethoprim (see text).

Trimethoprim interferes with the action of **dihydrofolic acid reductase**, an enzyme which converts dihydrofolic to tetrahydrofolic acid, an essential stage in the bacterial purine, and DNA synthesis. This sequential action of sulphonamides and trimethoprim explains the **synergistic action** of this combination against sensitive bacteria. The two components of co-trimoxazole (trimethoprim and sulphamethoxazole) separately have **bacteriostatic** activity in clinically achievable concentrations, but their combination is **bactericidal** when synergy is achieved. For the above synergism the critical ratio of 1:5 between trimethoprim (1 part) and sulphamethoxazole (5 parts) is required.

Pharmacokinetics

Absorption of co-trimoxazole by the oral route in rapid; peak plasma levels occur between 2 to 4 hours after administration; persist upto 7 hours; and detectable amounts have been found after 24 hours. Tissue concentrations are high, particularly in the lungs and kidneys.

Following a single dose of 2 tablets of co-trimoxazole (trimethoprim 160 mg plus sulphamethoxazole 800 mg), plasma levels peak between 1-2 mcg/ml and 40-60 mcg/ml respectively, within 2-4 hours: equivalent steady-state plasma levels are achieved after 2-3 days of similar doses twice daily; they are plasma protein bound about 40 percent and 70 percent respectively. The sulphamethoxazole binding to protein is reduced in uraemic patients. Both agents are mainly excreted in the urine, in the free and metabolized form.

Adverse Reactions

The most commonly seen side effects are nausea, vomiting, rash, and mild thrombocytopenia. Other adverse reactions include headache, tinnitus, vertigo, fatigue, peripheral neuritis, abdominal pain, glossitis and stomatitis. Allergic reactions like pruritus, urticaria, periorbital oedema, generalized skin eruptions, photosensitivity, anaphylactic reactions, serum sickness, Stevens-Johnson syndrome and epidermal necrolysis can occur. Blood dyscrasias, purpura, haemolytic anaemia, hypoprothrombinaemia and methaemoglobinaemia have been reported. Co-trimoxazole use should be avoided during pregnancy, particularly during the first trimester, and in children under 12 years of age.

Therapeutic Uses

1. Urinary tract infections. Co-trimoxazole has been extensively used in *acute, chronic,* or *recurrent* urinary tract infections. It has been used with good effect in children and in bacteriuria of pregnancy. It has also higher cure rates than cephalexin and nitrofurantoin **(Chap. 9.11).**

2. Respiratory tract infections. Acute and chronic *bronchitis* may be treated with co-trimoxazole. It has been used as long-term treatment in the prophylaxis of episodes of bronchitis. Pneumonia due to *Str. pneumoniae* or *H. influenzae* responds well to co-trimoxazole, whereas, *P. aeruginosa* is an exception. It can be used to treat pneumocystis pneumonia in immunosuppressed patients, and patients suffering from AIDS.

3. Gastrointestinal infections. Co-trimoxazole is useful in the treatment of *shigellosis*, specially for those strains which are resistant to ampicillin. It has been used with varying degree of success in the treatment of **typhoid fever.**

4. Septicaemia. Co-trimoxazole is useful for the treatment of septicaemias and serious infections due to gram-negative bacilli. Alone or in combination with polymyxin, it is also effective for hospital acquired infections.

5. Plague. Some studies have suggested that a 5-17 days course of co-trimoxazole may be effective in the treatment of bubonic plague.

6. Venereal disease. Gonorrhoea in both men and women may be treated with co-trimoxazole. Large doses for short periods are most effective.

7. Meningitis. Co-trimoxazole has been successfully used in causes of neonatal meningitis due to *E. coli.*

8. Miscellaneous infections. Co-trimoxazole has been used in the treatment of **cholera, brucellosis,** and **melioidosis** with varying degree of success. It has also been used to successfully treat **nocardiosis, histoplasmosis, chloroquine-resistant falciparum malaria,** and prophylaxis of traveller's diarrhoea.

Preparations and Dosage

Tablets each containing 80 mg trimethoprim and 400 mg sulphamethoxazole (Bactrim; Septran; Septrin) are available. The usual dosage of this combination is 1 to 2 tablets twice daily. Double strength tablets containing double amounts of each ingredient are also available (Bactrim D.S. Septrin Forte). A paediatric suspension with each 5 ml containing 50 mg trimethoprim and 200 mg sulphamethoxazole is also available. For intravenous use 5 ml ampoules containing trimethoprim 80 mg and sulphamethoxazole 40 mg (Septrin for infusion) in a vehicle with 40 percent propylene glycol is available. Trimethoprim (Trimpex) alone as 100 mg tablets is also available.

Quinolones

Nalidixic acid, a 4-quinolone, synthesized in 1962, and other chemically related compounds exert antimicrobial action by inhibiting DNA synthesis. Older members of this class of synthetic antimicrobials, namely **nalidixic acid, oxolinic acid,** and **cinoxacin** have been in use for treating acute urinary tract infections due to gram-negative pathogens. But with these agents the rapid development of bacterial resistance was a serious limitation **(Chap. 9.11).** This led to the introduction of **fluorinated 4-quinolones (fluoroquinolones) like enoxacin, norfloxacin and ciprofloxacin,** which have an extended spectrum of action including gram-positive organisms, and the more serious gram-negative organisms such as **Pseudomonas aeruginosa** and gram-negative aerobic bacteria. The antimicrobial action is accomplished by a specific action on **DNA gyrase**, the enzyme responsible for the unwinding and supercoiling of bacterial DNA prior to its replication. **Norfloxacin** is used for *severe* or *resistant urinary infections*, whereas **ciprofloxacin** is an extremely *broad-spectrum agent* and is used to treat serious *systemic* infections.

Antibacterial Spectrum

The quinolones exert a *bactericidal* action against susceptible organisms. *Nalidixic acid* inhibits gram-negative organisms, and is used to treat urinary tract infections produced by *E. coli, Klebsiella,* and *Proteus. Cinoxacin* and *oxolinic acid* possesses a spectrum and degree of activity similar to nalidixic acid. The newer agents, in addition, have high activity against *Neisseria gonorrhoeae*, and *Ureaplasma urealyticum*. The fluoroquinolones, such as *enoxacin, norfloxacin*, and *ciprofloxacin* and others are even more potent against gram-negative bacteria, and also active against staphylococci, and *Pseudomonas aeruginosa*. Among the resistant organisms are *Streptococcus fecalis, Mycobacterium turberculosis,* and *Chlamydia trachomatis.*

Pharmacokinetics

Nalidixic acid. Rapidly absorbed orally; peak serum levels in 1 to 2 hours; highly (90-95%) protein bound in plasma; partially metabolized in the liver, and rapidly excreted by the kidneys. Plasma $t_{1/2}$ is 1 to 3 hours, and **hydroxynalidixic acid** is an active metabolite, and is responsible for 85 percent of the biological activity of nalidixic acid in urine.

Oxolinic acid. Moderately well absorbed orally; widely distributed in tissues, although plasma concentrations tend to be low. It is extensively metabolized and only 5 percent of the drug appears in the urine in active form. The remainder is largely excreted as glucuronide.

Cinoxacin. Rapidly absorbed from the GI tract; peak serum concentrations within 1 to 2 hours; detectable levels for 10 to 12 hours. The drug is excreted almost entirely in the urine (60% as unaltered drug). It is 60 to 80 percent protein bound, and the serum $t_{1/2}$ is 1 to 2 hours, but is increased markedly in the presence of renal impairment.

Enoxacin. Rapidly absorbed from the gut; peak serum levels reached in 2 hours; it has a 32 to 43 percent serum protein binding. The drug's $t_{1/2}$ is 3.3 to 6.2 hours, and is excreted in the urine about 60 to 72 percent as unchanged drug.

Norfloxacin. Oral absorption is incomplete (30-40%), but generally rapid following single doses; peak plasma levels occur in 1 hour; plasma $t_{1/2}$ is 3 to 4 hours, and steady-state plasma levels attained within 2 days. Serum protein binding is minimal (10-15%); the unchanged drug and metabolites are excreted in the urine and faeces. Its action is limited to the urinary tract, bile, and gut.

Ciprofloxacin. Oral absorption is rapid and complete; first-pass metabolism is minimal; food delays rate of absorption but not total amount absorbed; peak serum levels attained within 1 to 2 hours; serum protein binding is minimal (20-30%); plasma $t_{1/2}$ is about 4 hours; and urinary excretion is complete within 24 hours. Unlike norfloxacin, it is not only useful in urinary tract infections, but is also effective against respiratory, skin soft tissue, bone and joint infections due to organisms resistant to most other broad-spectrum antibiotics.

Therapeutic Uses

Nalidixic acid, oxolinic acid and **cinoxacin** are useful only for urinary tract infections caused by susceptible organisms **(Chap. 9.11)**. Disc susceptibility tests should be performed before drug administration.

Ciprofloxacin has potent activity against gram-negative bacteria including *P. aeruginosa*, which has resulted in its extensive use. It is effective in resistant **urinary tract infections** and **prostatitis. Intraabdominal** and **biliary infections** have been treated satisfactorily. It is also useful in the treatment of **osteomyelitis, cystic fibrosis** complicated by **P. aeruginosa** lung infection, all forms of **gonorrhoea** and against bacterial bowel infections caused by **Shigella, Salmonella**, and **Campylobacter**. Use of ciprofloxacin in the treatment of **traveller's diarrhoea** also has been suggested. Ciprofloxacin may be combined with rifampicin for treatment of **serious staphylococcal infection**.

Norfloxacin is used to treat **uncomplicated urinary tract infections** including those caused by gram-negative rods and gram-positive cocci.

Enoxacin is used to treat gonorrhoea, urinary tract infections, and chronic bronchitis. Fluoroquinolones are *ineffective* against infections caused by anaerobes.

Adverse Reactions

Quinolones and fluoroquinolones are well tolerated drugs. Common adverse reactions are nausea, headache, dizziness, abdominal discomfort, photosensitivity and skin rash. Hypersensitivity reactions can occur. *Nalidixic acid* may cause cholestasis, polyarthiritis, paresthesias, metabolic acidosis and blood dyscrasias. *Ciprofloxacin* has been known to cause palpitation, ventricular ectopy, hypertension and angina. There is no absolute contraindication, but a caution must be observed in young children, and in pregnant or nursing mothers.

Preparations and Dosage

Nalidixic acid (Gramoneg) is available as 250, 500 or 1000 mg tablets, and an oral suspension containing 250 mg/5 ml. The dosage for adults is 1 g qid for 1-2 weeks, and then 2 g/day.

Cinoxacin (Cinobac) is available as 250 or 500 mg capsules. Usual dosage is 1 g daily bid or qid for 7-14 days.

Norfloxacin (Negaflox) is available as 400 mg tablets. The usual dosage is 400 mg bid for 7-10 days.

Ciprofloxacin (Ciproflox) is available as 250, 500 or 750 mg tablets. The usual dosage is 250 to 750 mg every 12 hours for 7-14 days.

9.3 ANTIBIOTICS

Microorganisms are subject to either *favourable* or *antagonistic* reactions owing to the presence of other living organisms. **Symbiosis** is the process by which the association of microorganisms exerts **mutually favourable** influences on each other's growth and multiplication. If the association is **unfavourable** (*antagonistic*), the process is designated as **antibiosis**. A substance elaborated by a growing microorganism which exhibits such an antagonistic influence is termed as an **antibiotic** (life against life).

Definition

Antibiotics are chemical substances produced by microorganisms (**fungi, actinomycetes, bacteria**) that suppress the growth of other microorganisms, and may eventually destroy them. **Waksman and Woodruff in 1942 formally defined an antibiotic as a chemical substance produced by a microorganism, which at a high dilution can inhibit the growth and/or multiplication, or kill another microorganism.**

Classification

Antibiotics may be classified according to their (1) *source;* (2) *mode of action;* and (3) *antibacterial spectrum.* The principle underlying their chemotherapeutic action is **selective toxicity**, i.e., the agents should be toxic for pathogenic microorganisms, but non-toxic to the host cells.

1. According to the Source

Antibiotics have been isolated from *three* types of microorganisms:

(*i*) **Antibiotics from fungi.** Penicillin from *Penicillium notatum* and *Penicillium chrysogenum;* griseofulvin from *Penicillium griseofulvum;* fumagillin from *Aspergillus fumigatus;* and others.

(*ii*) **Antibiotics from actinomycetes.** Streptomycin from *Streptomyces griseus;* chlortetracycline from *Streptomyces aureofaciens;* oxytetracycline from *Streptomyces rimosus;* chloramphenicol from *Streptomyces venezuelae;* erythromycin from *Streptomyces erythreus;* and others.

(*iii*) **Antibiotics from bacteria.** Tyrothricin from *Bacillus brevis;* bacitracin from *Bacillus subtilis;* polymyxins from *Bacillus polymyxa;* and others.

2. According to the Mode of Action

(*i*) **Inhibitors of bacterial cell wall synthesis.** Penicillins, cephalosporins, bacitracin, cycloserine, and others.

(*ii*) **Inhibitors of protein synthesis.** Aminoglycosides, tetracyclines, chloramphenicol, macrolides, lincosamides.

(*iii*) **Inhibitors of bacterial cell membrane function.** Polymyxins, nystatin, amphotericin B.

(*iv*) **Inhibitors of nucleic acid metabolism.** Griseofulvin, actinomycin.

3. According to the Antibacterial Spectrum

(*i*) **Narrow-spectrum antibiotics.** Penicillins, streptomycin, erythromycin, lincomycin, polymyxin B, vancomycin, and others.

(*ii*) **Broad-spectrum antibiotics.** Chloramphenicol, tetracyclines, kanamycin, cephalosporins, ampicillin, and others.

The above listing of agents is not complete, and is only representative of the particular class.

Inhibitors of Bacterial Cell Wall Synthesis

Several antibiotics interfere with the biosynthesis of the bacterial cell wall. Of these, the most important are the **penicillins** and the **cephalosporins,** designated as the **Beta-lactam antibiotics.** They have a *bactericidal* action, and their action is very likely to be antagonized on combination with bacteriostatic antibiotics **(Chap. 9.1).**

Penicillins

The penicillins comprise a large group of substances some of which are **natural** products of moulds, while others are **semisynthetic** compounds. They have a common chemical nucleus, **6-aminopenicillanic acid** (6-APA), and a common mode of antibacterial action, i..e, by the inhibition of cell wall mucopeptide synthesis.

Introduction of Penicillin G

Penicillin, the first antibiotic used in man, marks the start of the antibiotic era, which revolutionized the treatment of infections. In 1928, **Alexander Fleming** (later Sir Alexander Fleming), while working in St. Mary's Hospital, London, noted that some colonies of staphylococci were *lysed* when the medium was contaminated by a mould, latter classified as **Penicillium notatum**. This mould growth in broth culture was bactericidal *in vitro* against a variety of organisms, and Fleming named the antibacterial principle **penicillin**. At this stage it was not available in quantities sufficient for clinical trials. Research continued on penicillin until 1939, when under the stimulus of World War II, **Howard Walter Florey** (later Sir Howard Florey) and **Ernst Boris Chain** at Oxford, England started intensive work on this problem. Crude penicillin G became available for limited therapeutic trials in 1941. The supplies were so scanty that the antibiotic was recovered from the recipient patient's urine, and re-used. In 1942 various centres in the USA undertook mass production of penicillin, and by 1943 sufficient quantities of the antibiotic were being produced to serve the allied forces, and in 1944 it became available for limited civilian use. The biosynthesis of penicillins upto 1958-59 depended upon the growth of **Penicillium notatum** and **P. chrysogenum** (gives a higher yield) in deep vat cultures.

The penicillin used by early investigators was an amorphous compound containing impurities, and was a mixture of several penicillin compounds, designated as F, G, K, X, O etc. Only penicillin G has survived, as it was found to be most satisfactory. Thus, **penicillin G is the penicillin prototype** and on a weight basis, provided an organism is susceptible, it is still the most potent penicillin.

The natural compound pencillin G has several shortcomings: (*i*) It is acid labile and is destroyed on oral administration; (*ii*) it is destroyed by beta-lactamase(s); (*iii*) it has a relatively narrow antibacterial spectrum; (*iv*) it is rapidly excreted from the body; (*v*) it poorly penetrates into tissue compartments like the cerebrospinal fluid; and (*vi*) it is antigenic. These factors led to search for better compounds, and in 1958 the basic penicillin nucleus, **6-aminopenicillanic** acid was isolated and it became possible to synthetically add side chains, producing a range of penicillins that collectively overcome the first four shortcomings of penicillin G.

Source

Commercial penicillin is extracted from **P. notatum** and **P. chrysogenum**. Current production of penicillin utilizes the 6-APA nucleus, obtained through the action of bacterial amidases on regular penicillin, with subsequent chemical manipulations. Total chemical synthesis of penicillin has also been achieved. The generic term penicillin is used to include the **natural,** and the **semisynthetic** penicillins.

Chemistry

The basic structure of all penicillins is a sulphur containing **thiazolidine ring,** fused to a **beta-lactam ring,** forming 6-aminopenicillanic acid (6-APA), the so-called penicillin nucleus, upon which the antibacterial activity depends. The side chain determines the individual penicillin characteristics. Bacterial beta-lactamase (penicillinase) and acids, such as gastric acid hydrolyse penicillin to **penicilloic acid** by breaking the beta-lactam ring. Penicilloic acid has no antibacterial activity, but is allergenic.

The first compound in general use was penicillin G, which has a **benzyl** side chain, and subsequently it was found that substituting **phenoxymethyl** or **phenoxyethyl** groups greatly increased acid stability (acid-resistance) and the first "oral" penicillins came into use **(Fig. 9.3.1)**.

The addition of an alpha-NH_3 group led to the production of the first "broad-spectrum" penicillin, **ampicillin** and its derivative **amoxycillin. Carbenicillin** is another broad-spectrum penicillin active against gram-negative species and used to treat infections caused by **Pseudomonas aeruginosa** and proteus species.

The International Unit of penicillin is the specific penicillin activity contained in 0.6 mcg of the crystalline sodium salt of penicillin G (International Penicillin Master Standard). The semisynthetic penicillins derived from 6-APA are measured in milligrams. One milligram of pure sodium penicillin G is equivalent to 1667 units. One million units of penicillin is usually referred to as one megaunit (1,000,000 International Units).

Mode of Action

A distinction between mammalian and bacterial cells is the possession of a thick cell wall by the latter. Bacteria

Table 9.3-1 *Antibacterial spectrum of the penicillins*

NATURAL PENICILLINS*
(Pencillin G, Pencillin V)
Gram-positive cocci
Staphylococcus aureus (nonpenicillinase-producing strains)
Streptococcus pyogenes (groups A, B, C and G)
Streptococcus viridans group
Streptococcus faecalis (enterococcus)
Streptococcus bovis
Streptococcus (Diplococcus) pneumoniae
Gram-negative cocci
Neisseria gonorrhoeae (gonococcus)
Neisseria meningitidis (meningococcus)
Gram-positive bacilli
Bacillus anthracis (anthrax)
Clostridium perfringens (gas gangrene)
Clostridium tetani (tetanus)
Corynebacterium diphtheriae (diphtheria)
Listeria monocytogenes
Gram-negative bacilli
Bacteroides (all species except many strains of *B. fragilis*)
Fusobacterium nucleatum (fusiform bacillus)
Pasturella multocida, *Spirillum minus*, *Streptobacillus moniliformis* } aetiologic agents of rat-bite fevers
Spirochetes
Treponema pallidum (syphilis)
Treponema pertenue (yaws)
Borrelia recurrentis (relapsing fever)
Leptospira (Weil's disease)
Actinomycetes
Actinomyces israelli
PENICILLINASE-RESISTANT PENICILLINS**
(Cloxacillin, Methicillin, Oxacillin and others)
Staphylococcus aureus (penicillinase-producing)
BROAD-SPECTRUM PENICILLINS***
(Ampicillin, Amoxycillin, Hetacillin)
Gram-negative bacilli, including
Bordetella pertussis (whooping cough)
Escherichia coli
Haemophilus influenzae
Proteus mirabilis
Salmonella typhosa and other Salmonella species
Shigella
EXTENDED-SPECTRUM PENICILLINS****
(Carbenicillin disodium, Carbenicillin indanyl sodium, Mezlocillin, Ticarcillin)
Pseudomonas aeruginosa
Proteus species (indole positive)

* Pencillin G, specially in its parenteral forms, is the most effective of these penicillins, and is preferred for severe infections caused by susceptible strains. Penicillin V is used only for oral treatment of less severe infections.

** Penicillins of this type are also effective against the nonpenicillinase-producing gram-positive cocci and other organisms, but a penicillin G preparation is usually preferred. Cloxacillin and dicloxacillin are preferred for oral use; while for parenteral use, methicillin, nafcillin, and oxacillin are preferred.

*** These penicillins are also effective against the same organisms as penicillin G and V, but they are ordinarily reserved for infections in which the latter penicillins are ineffective, in order to avoid development of resistant strains.

**** These penicillins are specially effective against many gram-negative organisms including *P. aeruginosa, Proteus, Salmonella, Acinetobacter, Escherichia* and *Enterobacter*.

are capable of concentrating solutes so that the interior of the bacterial cell has a higher tonicity or osmolality than the surrounding environment. Therefore the integrity of the bacterial cell depends on a fairly rigid cell wall structure, which in gram-positive cocci is capable of withstanding pressures upto 20 atmospheres. In **gram-positive organisms** the cell wall is relatively simple, and is composed of a mixture of sugars, amino sugars, polyols and amino acids. In these organisms the major portion of the cell wall consists of a **mucopeptide layer** known as **murein** or **peptidoglycan,** which supports the lipoprotein cell membrane. **Gram-negative bacteria** have a complex cell wall structure consisting of four layers. Inability to penetrate the various layers of the complex envelope, is the explanation for the intrinsic resistance of gram-negative bacteria to antibiotics.

The **beta-lactam antibiotics** (penicillins, cephalosporins) prevent the normal synthesis of the bacterial cell wall by **selectively inhibiting the synthesis of mucopeptide in the bacterial wall** of susceptible multiplying bacteria. The bacterial cell wall construction and cell division continues, and the progeny after cell division have defective cells walls, which are subject to lysis as a result of osmotic forces.

Thus, **penicillins** and **cephalosporins** exert their **bactericidal** activity, acting maximally during the **logarithmic phase** of bacterial cell growth. Penicillin does not kill bacteria rapidly on contact, but by causing defective cell wall formation it makes them more susceptible to disruption and death. The bacterial cell with an incomplete wall is a very fragile "L-form", or protoplast, that then swells and bursts open due to a hypotonic environment.

Antibacterial Spectrum

Apart from the "broad-spectrum" penicillins introduced lately, penicillin has a **relatively narrow spectrum of activity**. In patients who are not allergic to these drugs, penicillin G (benzyl penicillin) remains the drug of choice to treat infections caused by susceptible **gram-positive** and **gram-negative cocci**. It is highly effective against such **gram-positive cocci** as the streptococcus and the pneumococcus. Although many resistant staphylococcal strains (e.g., hospital-acquired staphylococcal infection) have emerged, it is active against non-penicillinase-producing **Staphylococcus aureus. (Table 9.3-1).**

Bacterial Resistance

Bacterial resistance to penicillins is usually due to the elaboration of beta-lactamases (penicillinases) by the bacteria, which split the beta-lactam ring, rendering penicillin inactive. With the penicillinase-resistant penicillins, the bacterial resistance is due to failure of antibiotic penetration. Acquired penicillin resistance develops in a **stepwise** manner, and may be delayed by administration of sufficiently large doses to overcome the emergence of first step mutants.

Resistance to penicillinase in penicillinase-resistant penicillins (methicillin and others) depends upon the side chain additions **(Fig. 9.3.1).**

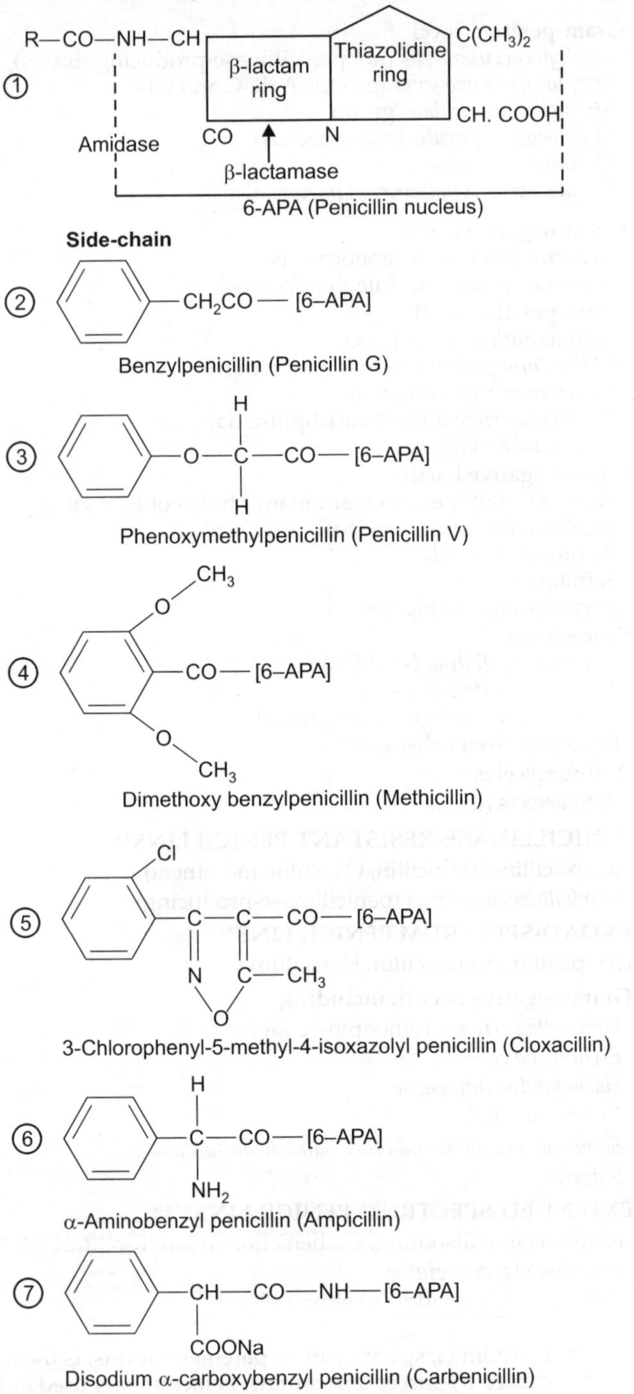

Fig. 9.3.1: The structure of 6-aminopenicillanic acid (6-APA) and some penicillins.

Penicillin Preparations and Dosage

Penicillin G as such is rather unstable, and currently relatively stable *sodium* and *potassium salts* are used clinically. The term "Crystalline penicillin G" or "Crystalline penicillin" is often used as a synonym for either sodium penicillin G (sodium benzylpenicillin) or potassium penicillin G. **(Table 9.3-2).**

Penicillin G Preparations

Absorption, Distribution, Metabolism and Excretion

Absorption

Three main types of penicillin G are available: (*i*) penicillin G for **oral use;** (*ii*) aqueous penicillin G for **parenteral use;** and (*iii*) depot preparations as suspensions for **parenteral** use, also known as "repository", "slow release", or "long-acting" preparations of penicillin G.

Penicillin G is erratically absorbed (15-20%) from the gastrointestinal tract, because much of the oral dose is destroyed by acidic gastric juice before it reaches the duodenum, which is the site of maximal absorption. Other oral penicillins (phenoxypenicillins) are more completely absorbed than penicillin G. To minimize the inactivation of penicillin G by gastric acid, and prevent delay in absorption, the penicillin G tablets are taken on an empty stomach.

Parenteral administration of penicillin G is either by subcutaneous, or *preferably* by IM injection. On SC or IM administration it is rapidly absorbed from the site of injection, and peak plasma levels are attained in about 20 minutes. Intravenous injection may occasionally be required in life-threatening infections, and it has to be infused continuously to maintain high tissue concentrations, because of its rapid elimination by the kidneys.

The **repository forms** of penicillin G are suspensions of poorly soluble salts of penicillin G in water, oil, or other vehicles, e.g., procaine penicillin G suspension, benzathine penicillin G suspension and others **(Table 9.3-2)**. They are injected deep into the muscle—*never intravenously* or *subcutaneously*—to form a depot from which the drug is only slowly absorbed into the blood.

Distribution, Metabolism and Excretion

As penicillin G is absorbed into the blood, a large part of it is bound to plasma proteins. It is distributed widely in the body, and tissue concentrations usually are about 20 percent of simultaneous plasma levels. The antibiotic concentrations in the kidney and urinary tract are high. Penicillin G passes very slowly into the cerebrospinal fluid through normal meninges. When the meninges are inflamed, the levels are higher but are still unreliable.

Penicillin G is only partially broken down in the body by unknown mechanisms. About 90 percent of the drug is excreted unchanged by the kidney; some excreted in the bile, from where it may undergo **enterohepatic recirculation;** also excreted in the milk. The excretion is both by **glomerular filtration** (10-15%), and **tubular secretion** (80-85%). The tubular secretion of penicillin is reduced by the excretion of other natural organic acids (pantothenic acid, uric acid), and by certain drugs e.g., **probenecid, aspirin, indomethacin, phenylbutazone** and some **sulphonamides**. Renal insufficiency may increase the plasma half-life of penicillin G from about 30 minutes to 10 to 15 hours.

Table 9.3-2 *Penicillin preparations and their dosage*

Drug	*Preparations*	*Dosage*	*Remarks*
A. NATURAL PRODUCTS			
I. Penicillin G Preparations (Penicillinase-sensitive penicillins)			
1. *Penicillin G, Potassium* or *Sodium*	*Tablets*-200,000 U, 250,000 U 400,000 U, 500,000 U, 800,000 U *Powder for oral solution*- 200,000 U/5 ml, 400,000 U/5 ml *Powder for injection*- 200,000 500,000 U/vial, 1, 5, 10, 20 million U/vial N.B. 400,000 U = 250 mg,	*Adults: Oral*- 200,000 U to 500,000 U every 6-8 hours for 10 days *IM, IV*- 300,00 U to 8 million U daily. Severe infection may require 20-30 milion U/day *Children below 12 years:* *Oral*- 25000 U to 90,000 U/kg/day in 3 to 6 divided doses. *IM, IV*- 300,000 U to 1.2 million U/day in divided doses (upto 10 million U/day may be required).	Inexpensive, rapid-acting,, and very effective against many organisms, but destroyed by gastric acid and penicillinase, administer orally on an empty stomach; maximal plasma concentrations attained within 30-60 minutes; doses exceeding 10 million U/day must be given by IV infusion only; $t_{1/2}$ normally 30 minutes but may increase to 10 hours in patients with anuria; periodic electrolyte determinations advisable.

Table 9.3-2 Contd...

Drug	*Preparations*	*Dosage*	*Remarks*
2. *Penicillin G, benzathine*	*Tablets*-200,000 U *Injection*-300,000 U/ml, 1,200,000 U/dose, 2,400,000 U/dose	*Adults: Oral*- 400,000 U to 600,000 U every 4-6 hours. *IM*-1,200,00 U as a single injection. *Children below 12 years: Oral*- 25,000 U to 90,000 U/kg/day in 3 to 6 divided doses. *IM*-600,000 U to 1,200,000 U depending on weight. *Prophylaxis of rheumatic fever:* 200,000 U orally bid; or 1.2 million U IM once a month; or 600,000 U IM every 2 weeks.	Benzathine salt of penicillin G is a long- acting dosage form; oral preparations are less effective than IM forms due to unpredictable GI absorption; inject deeply into a large muscle and use a large gauge needle, and do not massage injection site; in small children divide dose between two injection sites.
3. *Penicillin G, procaine*	*Injection*-300,000 U/ml, 500,000 U/ml *Injection*-300,000 U, 600,000 U, 1.2, 2.4 million U per dose	600,000 U to 1.2 million U every day. *Gonorrhoeal infections:* 1 g probenecid followed by 4.8 million U divided into 2 doses and injected at different sites.	Long-acting form of penicillin G, similar to benzathine penicillin G in many respects; indicated in moderately severe susceptible infections; procaine imparts a local anaesthetic effect, making injection less painful than benzathine penicillin G.
4. *Penicillin G, benzathine and procaine penicillin G combined*	*Injection*-150,000 U/150,000 U; 300,000 U/300,000 U, and 900,000 U/300,000 U per ml each, respectively, of benzathine and procaine penicillin G	*Streptococcal infections:* *Adults:* 2.4 million U IM *Children: 30-60 lb*: 900,000-1.2 million U IM. 1.2 million U IM *Children below 30 lb*: 600,000 U IM	Combination of long-acting forms of penicillin G, used to treat moderate to severe streptococcal and pneumococcal infections of the upper respiratory tract, skin and soft tissues, not effective against streptococcal group D infection; for prophylaxis of rheumatic fever administer once a month or every 2 weeks.
B. SEMISYNTHETIC DERIVATIVES **II Acid-Resistant Penicillin**			
1. *Penicillin V, Penicillin V Potassium*	*Tablets*-125, 250, 500 mg *Powder for oral suspension*-125 mg/5 ml, 250 mg/5 ml *Powder for oral solution*-(Potassium salt)-125 mg/5 ml, 250 mg/5 ml	*Adults:* 125-250 mg every 6-8 hours. *Children:* 25-50 mg/kg/day in 3 to 6 divided doses.	Phenoxymethyl derivative of penicillin, with identical range of activity, but more resistant to inactivation by gastric acid; the potassium salt is better absorbed from the GIT; only used for mild infections of the throat, upper respiratory tract, or soft tissues due to streptococci, pneumococci, and susceptible staphylococci; also used to prevent bacterial endocarditis in patients with rheumatic or acquired valvular heart disease.

Table 9.3-2 Contd...

Drug	*Preparations*	*Dosage*	*Remarks*
III.Penicillinase - Resistant Penicillins (Antistaphylococcal penicillins)			
1. *Cloxacillin*	*Capsules*-250, 500 mg *Powder for oral solution*-125 mg/5 ml	*Adults:* 250 mg to 1 g every 6 hours. *Children:* 50-100 mg/kg/day in divided doses every hour.	Mainly used to treat penicillinase-producing staphylococcal infections; best absorbed on empty stomach; highly protein-bound.
2. *Dicloxacillin*	*Capsules*-125, 250, 500 mg *Powder for oral suspension*-62.5 mg/5 ml	*Adults:*125-250 mg 6 hourly (maximum 4 g/day). *Children under 40 kg*: 12.5 mg to 25 mg/kg/day in divided doses 6 hourly.	Similar to cloxacillin and oxacillin, but produces slightly higher plasma levels; do not use in neonates.
3. *Methicillin*	*Powder for injection*-1 g, 4 g, 6 g, 10 g vials	*Adults:* *IM/IV-infusions*-4 to 12 g/day in divided doses every 4-6 hrs. *Children:* 100 to 300 mg/kg/day in divided doses every 4-6 hrs. *Infants:* 50-150 mg/kg/day in divided doses every 6-12 hours.	Indications similar to cloxacillin, but used by injection only; less active than penicillin G against streptococci and pneumococci; can produce interstitial nephritis; achieves high levels in CSF; do not mix with other drugs, but administer separately.
4. *Nafcillin*	*Capsule*-250 mg *Tablets*-500 mg *Powder for oral solution*-250 mg/5 ml *Powder for injection* 500 mg, 1 g, 2 g, 4 g, 10 g, vials	*Adults:* *Oral*-250 mg to 1 g every 4-6 hours. *IM*-500 mg every 4-6 hours. *IV*-500 mg to 1 g every 4 hours. *Children:* *Oral*-50 mg/kg/day in 4 divided doses. *Neonates*-10 mg/kg twice daily.	Same indications as cloxacillin; oral absorption inferior to other similar penicillins; major elimination route is *via* the bile; less active than penicillin G against non-penicillinase-producing organisms.
5. *Oxacillin*	*Capsules*-250, 500 mg *Powder for oral solution*-250 mg/5 ml *Powder for injection*-250 mg, 500 mg, 1 g, 2 g, 5 g, 10 g vials	*Adults:* *Oral*-500 mg to 1 g every 4-6 hours for 7 days. *IM, IV* 250 mg to 1 g every 4-6 hours. *Children under 40 kg:* *Oral* 50-100 mg/kg/day in divided doses. *IM, IV* 50-100 mg/kg/day in divided doses.	Similar to cloxacillin and dicloxacillin in most respects, but slightly less potent orally; highly protein bound; elevation in serum enzymes (SGOT, SGPT, LDH) may occur; high doses may causes transient haematuria, proteinuria, and azotaemia in infants.
IV. Broad-Spectrum Penicillins			
1. *Amoxycillin*	*Capsules*-250, 500 mg *Chewable tablets*-125, 250 mg *Powder for oral suspension*-125 mg/5 ml, 250 mg/5 ml *Drops*-50 mg/ml	*Adults:* 250-500 mg every 8 hrs. *Uncomplicated gonorrhoea*- 3 g with 1 g oral probenecid as a single dose. *Disseminated gonococcal infection*-As above, followed by 500 mg orally qid for 7-10 days.	Broad-spectrum, acid-stable penicillin, rapidly absorbed from the GIT; activity similar to ampicillin, but less effective against *Shigella*; less likely to disturb GI flora compared to ampicillin; available in combination with *potassium clavulanate*, a beta-lactamase inhibitor.

Table 9.3-2 Contd...

Drug	*Preparations*	*Dosage*	*Remarks*
2. *Ampicillin*	*Capsules*-250, 500 mg *Capsules with probenecid*- 389 mg/111 mg *Powder for oral suspension*-125 mg/5 ml, 250 mg/5 ml, 500 mg/5 ml *Drops*-100 mg/ml *Oral suspension with probenecid*-3.5 g/1 g per bottle *Powder for injection (Sodium salt)*-125, 250 mg, 1, 2, 10 g/vial	*Adults:* *Oral*-250 mg every 6 hours. *IM-IV* 250-500 mg every 6 hours. *Children under 40 kg*: *Oral* 50 mg/kg/day in divided doses. *IM, IV*-25-50 mg/kg/day in divided doses.	Broad-spectrum penicillin widely used in respiratory, GI, urinary and soft tissue infections by susceptible organisms; continue treatment for 48-72 hours after symptoms have disappeared; administer on empty stomach to enhance absorption; available in combination with *sulbactam*, a beta-lactamase inhibitor.
3. *Bacampacillin*	*Tablets*-400 mg *Powder for oral suspension*-125 mg/5 ml	*Adults*-400-800 mg every 12 hours. *Gonorrhoea*: 1.6 g with 1 g probenecid as a single dose. *Children*-25-50 mg/kg/day in two equally divided doses.	Rapidly hydrolyzed to ampicillin during GI absorption; each tablet is equivalent to 280 mg ampicillin; more completely absorbed than ampicillin producing effective serum levels upto 12 hours; much more costly than ampicillin.
4. *Cyclacillin*	*Tablets*-250, 500 mg *Powder for oral suspension* 125 mg/ml, 250 mg/5 ml	*Adults*-250-500 mg qid in equally spaced doses. *Children*-125-250 mg tid or qid in equally spaced doses.	Rapidly and completely absorbed on oral administration, yielding peak serum levels within 30 min; rapidly excreted *via* the urine; spectrum of action identical to ampicillin.
V. Extended-Spectrum Penicillins (Antipseudomonal penicillins)			
1. *Azlocillin*	*Powder for injection*-2, 3, 4 g vials	*Urinary infections*: *IV only* 100-200 mg/kg/day (2-3 g every 6 hours) *Serious systemic infections:* 200-300 mg/kg/day in 4-6 divided doses (upto 350 mg/kg/day).	Used either by slow IV injection over 5-10 min, or by IV infusions; effective against *Pseudomonas*, *Proteus*, *Salmonella*, and *Acinetobacter*; synergistic with aminoglycosides, but must be administered by separate syringes.
2. *Carbenicillin disodium*	*Powder for injection*-1, 2, 5 g vials; 10, 20, 30 g bulk packages	*Urinary infections*: *Adults*-200 mg/kg/day IV drip or 1-2 g 1M or IV every 6 hrs. *Children*- 50-200 mg/kg/day IM or IV in divided doses. *Soft tissue infections, septicaemia*: *Adults*- 15-40 g daily IV in divided doses or by IV drip. *Children*-250-500 mg/kg/day IV or IM in divided doses (max. dose 40 g/day).	Specially effective against *Pseudomonas*, *Proteus*, *Acinetobacter*, *Escherichia*, *Salmonella*, and *Enterobacter*; attains very high levels in urine when given IV or IM; fairly high sodium content, hence monitor serum electrolytes on extended use.

Table 9.3-2 Contd...

Drug	Preparations	Dosage	Remarks
3. *Carbenicillin indanyl sodium*	*Tablets*-382 mg	382-764 mg qid	Indanyl ester of carbenicillin is suitable for oral use (acid-stable) in chronic upper and lower urinary tract infections and prostatitis; rapidly excreted in urine; it is a carbenicillin prodrug.
4. *Mezlocillin*	*Powder for injection*-1, 2, 3, 4 g vials or infusion bottles	*Adults*: *IV*-1.5-4 g every 4-6 hours. *IM*- 1.5-2 g every 6 hours. *Children*: *IV, IM*- 75 mg/kg every 6-8 hrs.	Similar to piperacillin, but less effective against *Pseudomonas;* may be combined with an aminoglycoside or cephalosporin.
5. *Piperacillin*	*Powder for injection*-2, 3, 4 g vials or infusion bottles; 40 g bulk vials	3-4 g every 4-6 hours over 20-30 min (max. dose 24 g/day).	Synergistic with aminoglycosides against *Pseudomonas aeruginosa*, but not to be mixed in the same bottle.
6. *Ticarcillin*	*Powder for injection*-1, 3, 6 g vials; 20, 30 g bulk vials	*IV infusion*-150-300 mg/kg/day in divided doses every 3-6 hrs. *IV, IM*-1 g every 6 hours.	Similar in activity to carbenicillin, but more active against *Pseudomonas;* synergistic with gentamicin and tobramycin; monitor serum electrolytes; available in combination with *potassium clavulanate*, a beta-lactamase inhibitor.
VI. Amidinopenicillin			
1. *Amidinocillin*	*Powder for injection*-500 mg, 1 g vials	*Adults:* 60 mg/kg/day in doses by IM injection or IV infusion over 15-20 minutes.	Specially useful in serious urinary tract infections due to *E. coli, Klebsiella* sp., and *Enterobacter;* synergistic with other beta-lactam antibiotics.

Probenecid (Benemid) is a drug which was developed to delay the rapid renal excretion of penicillin, when administered with it. Probenecid **competes** with penicillin for the tubular transport system that transfers the antibiotic from the blood to the tubular fluid. *As a result penicillin remains in the blood and tissues at a higher level for longer periods. Such a combined probenecid-penicillin therapy has proved useful for potentiating penicillin activity in treating infections requiring high penicillin concentrations, e.g., subacute bacterial endocarditis* and *acute gonorrhoea.*The *usual dose* of probenecid to augment penicillin livels is 0.5 g 6 hourly. It is rarely used in the routine patient.

Therapeutic Uses of Penicillin G and Phenoxypenicillins

On the basis of *in vitro* efficacy, and lack of toxicity, penicillin G is considered to be the *drug of choice* to treat infections caused by sensitive organisms, in patients who are not allergic to the drug. For **minor infections**, one of the phenoxypenicillins (acid-resistant) administered orally can provide reliable concentrations of the drug in blood. For **serious infections** parenteral therapy with penicillin G is indicated.

1. Pneumococcal infections. Penicillin G remains the drug of choice for the treatment of infections of all types caused by *Strep. pneumoniae.* For *pneumococcal pneumonia* (lobar pneumonia) a number of dose schedules have been employed. For parenteral therapy of uncomplicated cases penicillin G or procaine penicillin G (300,000 to 600,000 units IM, 12 hourly) are employed. Therapy should be continued for 7-10 days. If *pneumococcal empyema* develops as a complication of lobar pneumonia the dose of penicillin should be increased to 10 to 20 million units per day, with adequate drainage. In **pnenumococcal** *meningitis* penicillin has reduced the death rate from nearly 100 percent to between 8 and 25 percent. Other pneumococcal infections including *suppurative arthritis, osteomyelitis, acute suppurative mastoiditis, endocarditis, peritonitis* and *pericarditis* also respond optimally to penicillin G therapy.

2. Streptococcal infections. Streptococci are pyogenic pathogens that cause acute *pharyngitis* and *tonsillitis, scarlet fever,* and *endocarditis. Streptococcal pneumonia, arthritis, meningitis* and *endocarditis* caused by *Strep. pyogenes,* are treated by daily doses of penicillin G, 10 to 20 million units IV for 2 to 4 weeks.

3. Staphylococcal infections. The majority of staphylococcal infections (60 to 80%) are caused by penicillinase-producing organisms, and are resistant to therapy by most penicillins. A patient with staphylococcal infection requiring antibiotic therapy should receive one of the penicillinase-resistant penicillins, e.g., **nafcillin, oxacillin,** or **methicillin.**

Several reports have appeared about the so-called **hospital staphylococcus,** which is resistant to penicillin G, methicillin and all the other penicillinase-resistant penicillins, and cephalosporins. For such resistant infections **vancomycin** appears to be the drug of choice. **Rifampicin** may sometimes be used concurrently.

4. Meningococcal infections. Penicillin G is the drug of choice for meningococcal disease. Patients should be treated with high doses of penicillin G given intravenously, as described for pneumococcal meningitis.

5. Infections with anaerobes. Many anaerobic infections are caused by mixtures of microorganisms. The majority are sensitive to penicillin G (except *Bacteroides fragilis*, where 20 to 50 percent of strains are resistant to even high doses of penicillin G). **Clindamycin** or **chloramphenicol** may be used to treat infections caused by *B. fragilis*.

6. Clostridial infections. Penicillin G is the drug of choice for **gas gangrene**, for which 10 to 20 million units daily are administreted parenterally. Adequate debridement of the infected area is essential. Penicillin G administration has little effect, if any, on the ultimate outcome of *tetanus*.

7. Other infections. Penicillin G is also effective in treating **diphtheria** (in conjunction with diphtheria antitoxin), **anthrax, actinomycosis, rat-bite fever,** and infections due to **Listeria monocytogenes.**

8. Gram-negative infections. Infections caused by *Escherichia coli, salmonella, shigella, proteus and pseudomonas* cannot be treated by penicillin G in conventional doses. However, administration of penicillin G in high doses of the order of 20 to 60 mega units intravenously daily, giving plasma concentrations from 30 to 500 units per ml, controls severe infections caused by some of these organisms. The newly introduced *antipseudomonal penicillins* (carbenicillin, ticarcillin, carfecillin, mezlocillin) are effective against *Ps. aeruginosa* and *Proteus* species.

9. Venereal Diseases (Gonorrhoea and Syphilis). The management of venereal disease is an important public health problem.

Gonorrhoea. Benzylpenicillin is the most active drug against sensitive strains of **Neisseria gonorrhoeae** minimal inhibitory concentration (MIC) in serum for sensitive strains 0.007 units/ml; for relatively resistant and penicillinase-producing gonococci greater than 1.0 units/ml).

I. Uncomplicated gonococcal infections in adult men and women. (*a*) **Aqueous procaine penicillin** 4.8 mega units (4.8 million units) as a single-dose, injected intramuscularly at two sites, with 1 g of probenecid orally; or (*b*) **tetracycline hydrochloride** 0.5 g orally four times daily for 7 days (total dosage, 14 g); or (*c*) **ampicillin** 3.5 g, **amoxycillin** 3 g, either with 1 g of probenecid orally. The first two (*a, b*) regimens are more effective than the later (*c*) regimen.

Patients who are allergic to penicillins and probenecid should be treated with oral tetracycline; and those who cannot tolerate tetracycline may be treated with **spectinomycin hydrochloride** 2 g in one intramuscular injection, which gives consistent cure rates approaching 100 percent.

II. Penicillinase-producing gonococcal infections. New strains of gonococcus, capable of producing penicillinase (beta-lactamase) have been reported, and they are resistant to all concentrations of penicillin. Patients and their sexual contacts with uncomplicated penicillinase-producing gonococcal infection should be treated with *spectinomycin* 2 g IM in a single injection.

III. Treatment during pregnancy. Drug regimens of choice are *aqueous procaine penicillin G, ampicillin,* or *amoxycillin*, each with probenecid as described above.

IV. Neonatal gonococcal infection. Babies born to mothers with symptomatic gonorrhoea are at a high risk of infection, and require treatment with a single intravenous or intramuscular injection of *aqueous crystalline penicillin* G 50,000 units to full-term babies, or 20,000 units to low-birth weight babies.

V. Disseminated gonococcal infection. One of the following equally effective schedules may be employed to treat the arthritis-dermatitis syndrome: (*i*) **ampicillin** 3.5 g or **amoxycillin** 3 g orally, each with probenecid 1 g orally, followed by **ampicillin** 0.5 g or **amoxycillin** 0.5 g orally four times a day for 7 days; (*ii*) **tetracycline** 0.5 g orally four times a day for 7 days; (*iii*) **spectinomycin** 2 g IM twice a day for 3 days, specially if infection is caused by penicillinase-producing gonococci; (*iv*) **erythromycin** 0.5 g orally four times a day for 7 days; or **aqueous crystalline penicillin G** 10 million units intravenously daily till improvement occurs, and then **ampicillin** 0.5 g four times a day to complete 7 days' treatment.

VI. Complicated infection. *Gonococcal meningitis* and *endocarditis, acute epididymitis* and *salpingitis* require high-dose intravenous penicillin therapy, and the patient should preferably be hospitalized. *Chloramphenicol* may be used in penicillin-allergic patients with meningitis.

The various regimens for the treatment of gonococcal infections are summarized in **Table 9.3-3.**

Table 9.3-3 *Curative regimens for gonococcal infection*

Regimen	*Drug(s)**
Uncomplicated gonorrhoea	
First choice	Penicillin G (Intramuscular)
Alternative	Amoxycillin,, Ampicillin
For cure failures	Spectinomycin
Penicillin allergy	Oxytetracycline, Tetracycline, Chlortetracycline, Co-trimoxazole, Minocycline, Doxycycline
For patients with penicillinase-producing gonococcal infection and their sexual contacts	Spectinomycin, Tetracycline
Complicated gonorrhoea	
Pelvic inflammatory disease (acute salpingitis)	Penicillin G, Tetracycline
Epididymo-orchitis	Penicillin G, Tetracycline
Disseminated gonococcal infection (gonococcal arthritis)	Penicillin G, Amoxycillin, Ampicillin
Penicillin allergy	Tetracycline, Co-trimoxazole, Erythromycin
For patients with penicillinase-producing gonococcal infection	Spectinomycin, Tetracycline

* There are gross differences between the dosage schedules for the treatment of uncomplicated and complicated gonorrhoea cases (see text).

Syphilis

Syphilis, caused by **Treponema pallidum** is a potentially lethal and crippling disease, specially to the foctus, and to those who later develop tertiary symptoms. Penicillin is still the drug of choice for the treatment of syphilis, and in contrast to the gonococcus no increased resistance of the treponeme has been proved. A serum level of only 0.03 units/ml of penicillin is treponemacidal, but the antibiotic levels must be continuously extended and maintained over a period of 8 or 10 to 14 days in infectious syphilis, and 21 days in late and latent cases.

I. Primary, secondary and latent syphilis (less than 1 year duration). Benzathine penicillin G 2.4 million units (2.4 mega units) intramuscularly as a single dose (1.2 million units in each buttock); or **aqueous procaine penicillin** G 600,000 units IM daily for 8 days to a total of 4.8 million units (4.8 mega units). Benzathine penicillin G is the drug of choice as it provides effective treatment in a single visit.

II. Syphilis of more than one year's duration (latent, cardiovascular, late benign, or neurosyphilis). Benzathine penicillin G 2.4 million units (2.4 mega units) IM, injected weekly for 3 successive weeks to a total dose of 7.2 million units (7.2 mega units); or **aqueous procaine penicillin** G 600,000 units IM daily for 15 days to a toal of 9 million units (9 mega units).

III. Syphilis during pregnancy. If there is clinical or serologic evidence of syphilis, or syphilis cannot be excluded with certainty, and the pregnant woman is not allergic to penicillin, she can be treated as outlined above.

IV. Congenital syphilis. If the CSF is normal **benzathine penicillin G** 50,000 units/kg of body weight is given intramuscularly as a single dose; and children with abnormal CSF should be given **aqueous crystalline penicillin G** IM or IV in dose of 50,000 units/kg daily in two divided doses for a minimum of 10 days; or **aqueous procaine penicillin** G 50,000 units/kg once daily 1M for a minimum of 10 days.

10. Chemoprophylaxis of rheumatic fever. Benzathine penicillin G 600,000 to 1200,000 units IM, once, a month may be used successfully. Penicillin V may also be used.

11. Whipple's disease. Bacterial infection with atypical beta-haemolytic enterococci may be involved in this disease. For this reason a 2-week course of crystalline penicillin G followed by oral penicillin V for 3 months has been advocated.

12. Botulism. Penicillin G therapy has been suggested as an adjunct to other treatment for the prevention of clostridium spore germination and release of more toxin in the bowel.

Guidelines for Penicillin G Administration

Intramuscular injection. This is the most commonly employed route of administration for penicillin G. For an adult 0.5 to 1 mega unit 6 hourly is sufficient to cure most infections, caused by sensitive organisms.

Intravenous injection. This route may be justified when a very high concentration in the blood is desired.

Intravenous infusion. For the treatment of serious invasive infections like **meningitis, septicaemia, occasionally pneumonia or endocarditis,** intravenous infusion may be justified. Continuous infusion is not recommended. However, infusion by bolus may be given by dissolving the required dose in 100 to 200 ml of

Table 9.3-4 *Some important hyersensitivity reactions to penicillin*

Type of reaction	*Incidence*	*Time after penicillin exposure*	*Antigenic determinants*	*Type of antibody*	*Manifestations*
Type I (immediate)	0.02 to 0.2%	0-30 minutes	Minor (Major?)	IgE	Urticaria, angioedema, anaphylaxis, rhinitis, asthma, laryngeal oedema, anaphylactic shock and hypotension.
Type I (Accelerated)	1 to 3%	1-72 hours	Major (Minor?)	IgE (IgM?)	Urticaria, angioedema, serum sickness; severe anaphylaxis and death is rare.
Type II	?	Upto 72 hours	Major (Minor?)	IgG of IgM (cytotoxic)	Coomb's positive haemolytic anaemia.
Type III	?	Upto 72 hours	Major (Minor?)	IgG to IgM	Interstitial nephritis, vasculitis, serum sickness, urticaria.
Type IV (Delayed)	?	Over 72 hours	Major (Minor?)	Mediated by T lymphocytes	Fixed drug eruptions, contact dermatitis, Stevens-Johnson syndrome, serum sickness, haemolytic anaemia, lymphadenopathy, recurrent arthralgia, azotaemia, proteinuria, and haematuria.

physiological saline, and run this into an existing infusion apparatus over a period of 15 to 20 minutes.

Toxicity

The untoward effects are chiefly of three kinds: (*i*) **hypersensitivity reactions,** which are common; (*ii*) **direct toxicity,** which is rare; and (*iii*) **miscellaneous reactions**.

1. Hypersensitivity reactions. The incidence of hypersensitivity to the penicillins is between 1 to 5 percent. The outstanding feature of penicillin hypersensitivity is its unpredictability.

Penicillin antigens. The penicillin molecule itself has no free groups to covalently link with carrier proteins to produce an antigen, and the actual **haptenes** are the various **penicillin derivatives** or **breakdown products**. About 95 percent forms the **penicilloyl derivative,** which combines with body proteins and this **penicilloyl protein conjugate** is referred to as the "major antigenic determinant", others constitute the "minor antigenic determinants".

Penicillins may cause hypersensitivity reactions by any of the four immune mechanisms. The types of antibodies produced, and the reactions are summarized in **Table 9.3-4**. Atopic individuals have a 3 to 4-fold increased risk of developing IgE antibodies compared to normal subjects.

Clinically penicillin hypersensitivity reactions are either **immediate, accelerated** or **delayed,** and manifest as anaphylactic reactions, serum sickness, contact dermatitis or local reactions.

Diagnosis of hypersensitivity. No really safe and reliable diagnostic test for penicillin sensitivity is available.

Skin **scratch** and **intradermal** testing with dilute penicillin G, or a mixture of major and minor determinants, or the major antigenic determinant penicilloyl reacted with polylysine (**penicilloyl-polylysine, PPL**) have been used.

Treatment of Hypersensitivity Reactions

In **acute anaphylactic reactions** the following regimen may be followed:

1. **Adrenaline** (subcutaneously or intramuscularly for mild reactions, and intravenously for serious reactions) can be life saving. Usually, adrenaline 1 ml (1 : 1000) subcutaneously repeated in 15 minutes if necessary, is given.

2. **Antihistamines** like promethazine 50 mg or chlorpheniramine 10 mg given intravenously may be helpful.

3. In addition, prompt administration of **oxygen, endotracheal intubation, or tracheostomy** (if laryngeal oedema occurs) is indicated.

4. **Corticosteroids.** After the immediate reaction is controlled, a corticosteroid (e.g., *hydrocortisone* 100 mg intravenously) may be administered to prevent a relapse, and it may be useful in more prolonged reactions like serum sickness. Corticosteroids are not useful in immediate reactions.

5. Positive pressure oxygen administration and treatment of cardiac arrhythmias may be required.

6. A rapid infusion of saline or plasma volume expanders may be necessary to combat shock. If hypotension persists intravenous **metaraminol** (Aramine) should be tried.

Penicillinase has little, if any, place in the treatment of anaphylactic reactions. It has no effect on preformed antigen-antibody complexes.

2. Direct toxicity. Direct toxicity due to penicillin G in humans is very rare, and only occurs with massive doses (100 million units daily) given intravenously, leading to *CNS irritation with convulsions and coma.*

Pain and **sterile inflammation** may occur at the site of intramuscular injection. **Thrombophlebitis** sometimes occurs on intravenous administration of penicillin. Accidental intravenous injection of procaine penicillin may cause micro-embolization, acute psychotic episodes, convulsions, abrupt hypotension and cardio-respiratory arrest.

3. Miscellaneous reactions. Superinfections occurs in about 1 percent of patients. Serious superinfection with resistant gram-negative bacteria (*Pseudomonas, Proteus*) and candida may occur following long-term therapy with a broad-spectrum penicillin like ampicillin.

Jarisch-Herxheimer reaction may develop within a few hours of primary penicillin G exposure of patients with secondary syphilis, and it appears to be due to the release of endotoxins (lipopolysaccharides) from the large number of killed treponemes. Features of this reaction include fever, sore throat, myalgia, tachycardia, and exacerbation of existing syphilitic lesions.

Nephropathy, a sensitivity reaction manifested as interstitial nephritis can occur with large doses of penicillin G. Kidney damage is accompanied by **proteinuria, haematuria** and **acute renal failure**.

Cation intoxication. Massive intravenous doses of penicillin G potassium (1.6 mEq of potassium/mega unit) may cause **hyperkalaemia, convulsions** and **impaired renal function**, thus leading to **potassium intoxication**. The sodium salt (1.7 mEq of sodium/mega unit) is unlikely to cause complications.

Haemolytic anaemia induced by massive intravenous doses of penicillin G may occur in some patients uncommonly. Several semisynthetic penicillins (*carbenicillin, methicillin, ticarcillin*) and even penicillin itself may induce platelet dysfunction leading to bleeding.

Semisynthetic Penicillins

By "semisynthetic penicillin" is meant any congener produced by the incorporation of specific precursors in mould cultures, or made by **chemical modification of penicillin G** (other than salt formation), or made by *chemical modification of* 6-amino-penicillanic acid (6-APA). The compounds included are the acid-resistant penicillins; penicillinase-resistant penicillins; broad-spectrum penicillins; and antipseudomonal penicillins **(Table 9.3-2)**.

Cephalosporins

Cephalosporins are structurally and pharmacologically related to penicillins. They are **water soluble, broad-spectrum, semisynthetic, bactericidal** antibiotics derived from **7-aminocephalosporanic acid (7-ACA)**. Their classification according to "generations" is useful, and is based on the general features of their antimicrobial activity. **Cefoxitin** and **cefotetan** (Cephamycins) and **moxalactam** (a beta-lactam) are included due to their similarity.

Antibacterial Spectrum

Cephalosporins and related compounds are divided into **first, second** and **third** generation agents **(Table 9.3-5)**. Within each group differentiation is primarily based on their pharmacokinetics and antibacterial spectrum. In general, progression from the first to third generation exhibits broadening gram-negative spectrum, loss of efficacy against gram-positive organisms, greater efficacy against resistant organisms, and increased cost. The *first-generation* cephalosporins (*cephalothin, cefazolin*) have appreciable activity against gram-positive bacteria, and relatively modest activity against gram-negative organisms. The **second-generation** agents exhibit increased activity against gram-negative microorganisms, but much less than the third-generation agents. **Third-generation** cephalosporins are less active than first-generation agents against gram-positive cocci, but they are much more active against the *Enterobacteriaceae*, including penicillinase-producing strains. A sub-group of the third-generation agents (cephoperazone, ceftizoxime, ceftriaxone, caftazidime) is also active against *Ps. aeruginosa*.

Mode of action. Cephalosporins and cephamycins have a penicillin-like action. They **inhibit mucopeptide** *synthesis in the bacterial cell wall*, rendering it defective and osmotically unstable. These drugs are usually **bactericidal**, and are more effective against rapidly growing organisms.

Pharmacokinetics. Cephalexin, cepharadine, cefadroxil and cefaclor are well absorbed from the gut. Absorption may be delayed by food, but the absolute amount of the drug absorbed is not affected. Some selected pharmacokinetic data about these agents are summarized in **Table 9.3-5**.

Cephalosporins are widely distributed in most tissues and fluids, with maximum concentrations in liver and kidneys. **First** and **second** generation agents do not readily enter the CSF, except cefuroxime, even when the meninges are inflamed. **Third** generation compounds and cefuroxime readily diffuse into the CSF in patients with inflamed meninges. Cefotaxime, cephalothin and cephapirin are metabolized to less active compounds. Most cephalosporins and their metabolites are mainly excreted via the kidneys.

Beta-lactamase resistance. First generation cephalosporins are inactivated by beta-lactamase producing organisms. Newer agents offer an increased resistance to beta-lactamase inactivation: **Cefoxitin, cefuroxime, ceftriaxone, cefotaxime, ceftizoxime, cefotetan** and **moxalactam** exhibit a high stability in the presence of both penicillinases and cephalosporinases produced by gram-negative and gram-positive bacteria. **Cefoperazone** and **ceftazidime** are also highly stable in the presence of beta-lactamases produced by most gram-negative organisms, and are active against organisms that

Table 9.3-5 *Pharmacokinetic data of some cephalosporins and related compounds*

Compounds	*Protein binding (%)*	*Half-life (min)*	*Peak serum level (Ig IV dose (mcg/ml)*	*Routes*	*Dose (Adults)*
First Generation					
Cefaclor	22-25	36-54	—	Oral	0.25 g 8 hourly
Cephalexin	5-15	30-70	—	Oral	1.0 g 6 hourly
Cafadroxil	20	70-80	—	Oral	1.0 g 12 hourly
Cephradine	8-17	45-120	86	Oral IM/IV	Oral: 1 g 6 hourly I: 2 g 6 hourly
Cephalothin	65-80	25-60	30-64	IM/IV	I: 1-2 g 4 hourly
Cephapirin	40-54	20-40	40-73	IM/IV	I: 1-2 g 4 hourly
Cefazolin	70-86	90-130	185-189	IM/IV	I: 1-1.5 g 6 hourly
Second Generation					
Cefamandole	56-78	30-60	88-139	IM/IV	I: 2 g 4 hourly
Cefoxitin*	65-79	40-60	56-110	IM/IV	I: 2 g 4 hourly or 3 g 6 hourly
Cefuroxime	33-50	60-114	43-98	IM/IV	I: 3 g 8 hourly
Cefonicid	98	210-294	221.3	IM/IV	I: 2 g 24 hourly
Ceforanide	80	150-210	125	IM/IV	I: 1 g 12 hourly
Third Generation					
Cefotaxime	30-51	60	81-102	IM/IV	I: 2 g 4 hourly
Moxalactam	40-57	114-210	71-94	IM/IV	I: 4 g 8 hourly
Ceftizoxime	30	66-133	46-136	IM/IV	I: 3-4 g 8 hourly
Ceftriaxone	85-95	348-522	151	IM/IV	I: 2 g 12 to 24 hourly
Cefoperazone	82-93	102-156	73-153	IM/IV	I: 1.5-4 g 6, 8 or 12 hourly
Cefotetan*	78-91	180-276	158	IM/IV	I: 1 or 2 g 12 hourly
Ceftazidime	10-17	114-120	69-90	IM/IV	I: 1 g 8 hourly

I = injection, IM = intramuscular, IV = intravenous, *cephamycin

are resistant to other beta-lactam antibiotics.

Therapeutic uses. The majority of *gram-positive cocci* and *gram-negative bacteria* are susceptible, but effectiveness is variable, and culture/sensitivity tests must be performed when possible. Cephalosporins are indicated for **preoperative, intraoperative,** and **postoperative prophylaxis** to reduce the incidence of infection in patients undergoing surgery which is likely to be contaminated, e.g., gastrointestinal surgery, cesarean section, vaginal hysterectomy or cholecystectomy.

Some of the third-generation cephalosporins are currently drugs of choice for meningitis caused by gram-negative enteric bacteria because of their favourable antimicrobial activity and good penetration into the CSF. **Nosocomial infections** (hospital infections) are usually caused by organisms which are resistant to many commonly used antimicrobials like ampicillin, aminoglycosides or even first-generation cephalosporins. Third-generation cephalosporins are helpful in such situations.

Adverse reactions. Gastrointestinal disturbances and **hypersensitivity** can occur. Cephalosporins should be administered cautiously to penicillin-sensitive patients, as there is evidence of **partial cross-sensitivity** between the two groups.

Eosinopenia, transient neutropenia, leucopenia, thrombocytopenia, agranulosytosis and **haemolytic anaemia** may occur. Elevated SGOT, SGPT, alkaline phosphatase and LDH have been reported with cephalosporin use. Jaundice may occur with cefamandole and cephapirin. Cephalosporins are nephrotoxic and may cause acute tubular necrosis. Generalized *tonic-clonic convulsions* may occur. **Pseudomembranous colitis** has been reported with the use of cephalosporins. **Superinfection** (bacterial or fungal overgrowth) may occur.

Drug interactions. Bacteriostatic agents interfere with the bactericidal action of cephalosporins, thus concurrent administration must be avoided. **Probenecid** administered concurrently with cephalosporins increases and prolongs plasma levels by competitively inhibiting renal tubular secretion. Probenecid does not significantly effect the elimination of **moxalactam**. The **loop diuretics** increase the nephrotoxicity of cephalosporins. **Alcoholic beverages** may produce acute alcohol intolerance (disulfiram-like reaction), as cafamandole, cefaperazone, moxalactam, and cefotetan inhibit the enzyme alcohol dehydrogenase. Concomitant use of **aminoglycosides** increases nephrotoxicity.

Other Beta-Lactam Antibiotics

Imipenem-Cilastatin

Imipenem (a carbopenem) is a beta-lactam that is structurally different from penicillins and cephalosporins, but has a similar mode of action. it is effective against a wide range or *gram-positive, gram-negative*, and *anaerobic organisms*. It is useful in treating infections resistant to other antimicrobials.

Mode of action. Imipenem penetrates the bacterial cell wall, binds to the penicillin-binding protein 1B and 2, interfering with synthesis of peptidoglycan and subsequent cell wall formation.

Dosage. Imipenem-Cilastatin (Primaxin) contains equivalent amounts of the two drugs. The usual dose of imipenem is 500 mg to 1 g every 6 to 8 hours by IV infusion; maximum daily dose is 4 g.

Adverse reactions include vomiting, abdominal pain, colitis, glossitis, tachycardia, hypotension, pruritus, candidiasis, tinnitus and transient hearing loss.

Aztreonam

Aztreonam is a monocyclic beta-lactam compound (a monobactam) isolated from **Chromobacterium violaceum**. It has a wide-spectrum of action against **gram-negative aerobic pathogens** but is inactive against gram-positive organisms or anaerobes. Aztreonam interacts with penicillin-binding protein 3, and inhibits cell wall synthesis.

Aztreonam is usually given initially with another antimicrobial in seriously ill patients, because it is ineffective against gram-positive and anaerobic organisms.

Dosage. For *urinary tract infections:* 500 mg to 1 g IV or IM every 8 to 12 hours. *Other infections:* 1 g to 2 g IV or IM every 6 to 12 hours.

Adverse reactions include vomiting, confusion, insomnia, hypotension, tinnitus, altered taste, breast tenderness, blood dyscrasias, jaundice and hepatitis.

Other Inhibitors of Bacterial Cell Wall Synthesis

Apart from *penicillins, cephalosporins* and *cephamycins,* other agents like **bacitracin, cycloserine,** and **vancomycin,** also inhibit the synthesis of bacterial cell wall.

Bacitracin

Bacitracin is the generic name for a group of at least four separate bactericidal polypeptide antibiotics, originally isolated from **Bacillus subtilis** contaminating a compound fracture in a girl named Margaret Tracy (hence the name). It is **bactericidal** against gram-positive organisms, specially common skin pathogens like staphylococci, streptococci and Neisseria. It is inactive against most gram-negative bacteria. Bacitracin *interferes with bacterial cell wall synthesis* by preventing the formation of the peptidoglycan chains that are cross-linked to form the rigid bacterial cell wall.

Parenteral use of bacitracin has been stopped because of its *nephrotoxicity*. It is safe when used topically, but hypersensitivity reactions like allergic dermatitis may occur.

For topical use, combination of *bacitracin* with *neomycin* or *polymyxin B* widens the spectrum of activity. Such combinations are effective in the treatment of *ulcers, sycosis, external otitis, pyodermas, infected traumatic* and *surgical wounds*, and *impetigo*. Ophthalmic preparations are useful in treating superficial eye infections like *suppurative conjunctivitis* and infected corneal ulcers.

Cycloserine

Cycloserine is a broad-spectrum *bactericidal* antibiotic produced by **Streptomyces orchidaceous**. Its use should ordinarily be restricted to the treatment of **tuberculosis**, provided it is tolerated. It has also been used in problem cases of **urinary tract tuberculosis (Chap. 9.4)**. The limiting factor in the use of cycloserine is its potential **central nervous system toxicity**, including both neurological and psychic disturbances. **Cycloserine** (Seromycin) is initially given in doses of 15 mg/kg body weight orally, increased by increments of 250 mg every few days (if tolerated) till therapeutic serum levels (15-35 mcg/ml) are produced.

Vancomycin

Vancomycin is a *bactericidal* glycopeptide antibiotic obtained from **Streptomyces orientalis**, primarily effective against gram-positive organisms. It is possibly the most potent antibiotic against staphylococci, but because of its toxicity, its use should be reserved for cases where less toxic antibiotics have failed to control infection. It is a relatively dangerous drug, allergic skin rashes, thrombophlebitis on IV administration, and anaphylactoid reactions may occur. **Superinfection** with gram-negative bacteria and fungi occurs during long-term therapy. Most serious reactions involve the kidney and the eight cranial nerve (cochlea). It may cause **fatal uraemia** and **permanent deafness**. In therapeutics vancomycin is reserved for infections with resistant gram-positive organisms.

Vancomycin (Vancocin) is administered in doses of 1 g IV, to adults twice daily. Oral vancomycin 3-4 g daily may be of value in the treatment of staphylococcal enterocolitis and pseudomembranous colitis, notoriously caused by the lincomycins (see later).

Beta-lactamase Inhibitors

Some molecules can bind to *beta-lactamases* and inactivate them, preventing the destruction of beta-lactams which are substrates for these enzymes. Two such compounds are *clavulanic acid* and *sulbactam*.

Clavulanic acid is produced by **Streptomyces clavuligerus**. It is well absorbed orally and can also be given parenterally. It has been combined with *amoxycillin* (Augmentin) for oral administration; and with *ticarcillin* (Timentin) for parenteral administration.

Sulbactam is another beta-lactamase inhibitor structurally resembling clavulanic acid. It is used orally or parenterally along with beta-lactams. It is available for IM or IV use combined with ampicillin (Unasyn). The usual dose is 1 to 2 g of ampicillin with 0.5 to 1 g sulbactam every 6 hours. This combination has been used effectively for the treatment of mixed intra-abdominal and pelvic infections.

Inhibitors of Protein Synthesis

The antibiotics which inhibit bacterial protein synthesis are a heterogeneous group and include the **aminoglycosides, tetracyclines, chloramphenicol, macrolides,** and the **lincosamides.**

Aminoglycosides

Most aminoglycosides are prepared by natural fermentation from various species of *Streptomyces*. The exceptions are **gentamicin,** which is fermented from *Micromonospora purpurea*, and **amikacin,** which is the first semisynthetic aminoglycoside, obtained by chemical modification of kanamycin. Other aminoglycosides include **streptomycin, kanamycin, neomycin, tobramycin, sisomicin, paromomycin, netilmicin,** and **framycetin.**

Antibacterial Spectrum

All the aminoglycosides are **bactericidal,** and active against gram-positive and mainly gram-negative organisms. *Streptomycin* and *kanamycin* are also active against *Mycobacterium tuberculosis*, while *amikacin, gentamicin* and *tobramycin* have activity against *Streptococcus faecalis* and *Ps. aeruginosa*. The gram-negative cocci *Neisseria gonorrhoeae* and *N meningitidis* are also susceptible to some aminoglycosides, but these drugs are not used to treat infections caused by them. Several other organisms like *Salmonella* and *Shigella* are susceptible to the aminoglycosides, but other safer agents are available.

Bacterial Resistance

Bacteria frequently develop permanent resistance to aminoglycosides. In any large population of microorganisms, naturally occurring "single-step" high level resistant mutants appear, and are rapidly selected. With these agents bacterial resistance develops when *extrachromosomal genes (plasmids)* are transmitted by bacterial conjugation **(Chap. 9.1)**. The aminoglycosides are *bactericidal*, but bacterial resistance can be rapidly acquired, and is partly mediated by the **R-factors** transmitted between bacteria. Resistance is more common on prolonged therapy. **Cross-resistance** is usually complete within the group. Low or subinhibitory concentrations of streptomycin may produce dependence in bacteria, specially *Mycobacterium tuberculosis*.

Mode of Action

The aminoglycosides inhibit bacterial protein synthesis and are **bactericidal**. They enter bacteria by transport on the carrier system naturally utilized by spermine.

The aminoglycosides act on the bacterial 30S ribosomal subunits (but not human ribosomes), and distort the messenger ribonucleic acid (mRNA) translation of the genetic code, thereby preventing the formation of the normal complex required to initiate protein synthesis. In addition, the aminoglycosides **by their strong cationic charges**, combine with anionic membrane groups and **damage the bacterial cell membranes;** they may block energy production at the pyruvate-oxalacetic acid step of the Kreb's cycle. It has been observed *in vitro* studies that depending on the antibiotic, there is 10 to 80-fold increase in potency going from pH 5.5 to 8.0. Hence in the treatment of *urinary tract infections* the simultaneous administration of urinary alkalinizers is advisable.

Pharmacokinetics

The aminoglycosides are poorly absorbed following oral administration, as they are charged molecules. Therefore, they have to be given by injection to treat systemic infections.

The aminoglycosides are poorly bound to serum protein (20-30%), but are widely distributed throughout the body, except the *central nervous system* and the *eye* where penetration is inadequate for antibacterial purposes. They are concentrated in the kidney and are excreted unchanged by glomerular filtration; there is negligible tubular reabsorption. Thus in the presence of renal insufficiency they must be given in reduced dosage to avoid toxicity.

Toxicity

The adverse reactions to aminoglycosides are **ototoxicity,** and to a lesser degree, **nephrotoxicity** and **neuromuscular blockade**. These toxic manifestations are dose-related.

(*i*) **Ototoxicity.** Both *auditory* and *vestibular* divisions of the 8th cranial nerve (incidence 1%) are involved. But *streptomycin, tobramycin* and *gentamicin* predominantly affect the vestibular division, while *neomycin, kanamycin* and *amikacin* affect the auditory division. The ototoxic effects are often *reversible,* and are aggravated by simultaneous therapy with potentially ototoxic diuretics like **frusemide** or **ethacrynic acid**. Meniere-like syndrome may be seen.

(*ii*) **Nephrotoxicity.** The aminoglycosides (except streptomycin) affect upto 15 percent of patients, but the nephrotoxicity is usually *mild* and *reversible.* It is dose-related and tends to develop after the first week of therapy. The lesions occur in the proximal tubule with rises in serum urea and creatinine, and the passage of casts in urine. Dosage adjustment is necessary in impaired renal function. Neomycin is the most nephrotoxic of the group.

(*iii*) **Neuromuscular blockade.** The aminoglycosides have a **curare-like action** and may sometimes cause neuromuscular blockade that can lead to paralysis and potentially fatal respiratory arrest.

Allergic and local **hypersensitivity reactions, superinfection** with fungi or other resistant organisms, and **granulocytopenia** have been reported with the aminoglycosides.

Streptomycin

Streptomycin was the first aminoglycoside, isolated from **Streptomyces griseus** by Waksman and others in 1944. It is active against most strains of human and bovine **Mycobacterium tuberculosis**, and a number of *gram-positive* and *gram-negative* organisms.

Mode of Action

Streptomycin may be **bactericidal** or **bacteriostatic** depending on the organisms involved, the concentration of the drug, and the period of contact between the antibiotic and the organism. It acts by *inhibition of protein synthesis* resulting from interference with ribosomal binding in the 30S subunits.

Bacterial resistance and dependence. A high degree of resistance to streptomycin can be developed rapidly by sensitive organisms. This abrupt `one-step' resistance was first demonstrated when streptomycin was used to treat urinary tract infections, and *Haemophilus influenzae* meningitis. *Mycobacterium tuberculosis* may develop resistance to streptomycin, when the drug is used alone. On exposure of sensitive bacteria to subinhibitory (low) concentrations of streptomycin *in vitro,* a paradoxical stimulation of bacterial cell growth may be seen. Ultimately a state of **streptomycin-dependence** develops in which the bacteria require the antibiotic for their growth.

Pharmacokinetics

Streptomycin is usually injected intramuscularly. Following a dose of 1 g peak levels of 25-50 mcg/ml are attained in ½ to $1_{1/2}$ hours, and the plasma $t_{1/2}$ is about $2_{1/2}$ hours. In patients over 40 years the dose of 0.75 g is recommended. Penetration of the blood-brain barrier is poor, some drug may enter the CSF if the meninges are inflamed. Tuberculous cavities, and levels in pleural fluid are the same as in the plasma. The drug is excreted by glomerular filtration, and 30-90 percent appears in the urine over 24 hours. High concentrations of upto 1 mg/ml are present in urine after 1 g IM.

Therapeutic uses. The major indication of streptomycin is in the **multidrug treatment of tuberculosis**, in combination with isoniazid, ethambutol, or rifampicin (**Chap. 9.4**). Streptomycin is also used in conjunction with penicillin G or ampicillin to treat **Streptococcus faecalis** endocarditis, or combined with tetracycline in the management of **brucellosis**. Synergism is frequentlly seen when streptomycin and penicillin G are used together against enterococci. It is sometimes used with chloramphenicol to treat *Klebsiella pneumoniae* infection. Infections due to *P. pestis* (plague) and *P. tularensis* (tularaemia) respond to streptomycin. To treat **mixed urinary tract infections**, streptomycin may be advantageously combined with nitrofurantoin or penicillin.

Toxicity. The most frequent toxic effect of streptomycin is on the 8th cranial nerve. Both vestibular and auditory functions are upset, the former being more vulnerable. **Deafness** can also occur in babies born of mothers given streptomycin during pregnancy as it crosses the placenta. Streptomycin may rarely cause **peripheral neuritis, facial** and **peripheral paraesthesias,** and **optic neuritis** with **scotomas. Lymphadenopathy, hepatosplenomegaly, proteinuria** and **impaired liver functions** may occur sometimes. Excessive intrathecal streptomycin may be followed by **chemical meningitis, myelitis, convulsive seizures** and **encephalopathy**. Streptomycin may induce **curare-like neuromuscular blockade**. In patients with myasthenia gravis, streptomycin may induce a dramatic increase in muscle weakness.

Hypersensitivity to streptomycin is common, and handling of the drug can cause contact dermatitis in nurses, pharmacists or physicians. Rashes and drug fever occur in 5 percent of patients. **Exfoliative dermatitis, stomatitis, eosinophilia, serum sickness** and **anaphylactic shock** may occur. **Granulocytopenia** progressing to **agranulocytosis, aplastic anaemia** and **thrombocytopenic purpura** occur rarely. **Albuminuria** is commonly seen with prolonged therapy, but it is usually reversible. Cross-resistance amongst the aminoglycosides is almost complete. The pharmacotherapeutic profile of kanamycin, gentamicin, tolramycin, amikacin and netilmicin is presented in **Table 9.3-6.**

Table 9.3-6. *The pharmacotherapeutic profile of the aminoglycosides*

Drug	*Special features and antibacterial spectrum*	*Uses*	*Toxicity*	*Dosage (Plasma* $t_{1/2}$*)*
Streptomycin	Bactericidal against a variety of aerobic gram-negative bacilli and *M. tuberculosis*	Not commonly used today. Reserved for treatment of tuberculosis with other anti- tuberculous drugs	Vestibular damage, auditory damage, drug fever, neuromuscular blockade, hypersensitivity	0.5-2.0 g IM/day ($t_{1/2}$ = 2-3 hours)
Kanamycin	Many strains of *E. coli, Enterobacter, Klebsiella, Proteus* and *Mycobacteria*. Less active on a weight basis than gentamicin and tobramycin	Gram-negative infection (*Proteus*); Enterococcal infection; also gut sterilization and topical application	Mainly deafness; also mild nephrotoxicity and neuromuscular blockade	1 g IM/day; 4-8 g/day orally ($t_{1/2}$ = 1.5-3 hours)
Gentamicin	Broad-spectrum bactericidal drug gram-positive and gram-negative organisms (*Proteus* and *Pseudomonas*)	Serious infections caused by susceptible gram-negative organisms; gram-negative septicaemia	Nephrotoxicity; vestibular damage; hypersensitivity; drug fever	3-5 mg/kg/day IM or IV 8-hourly ($t_{1/2}$ = 1-4 hours)
Tobramycin	Active against *Pseudomonas* strains resistant to gentamicin	*Pseudomonas* infections as an alternative to gentamicin	Vestibular damage	3-4 mg/kg/day IM in 3 divided doses ($t_{1/2}$ = 2 hours)
Amikacin	Semisynthetic derivative of kanamycin; active against gentamicin-resistant *Pseudomonas strains*	Resistant gram-negative infection specially *Pseudomonas* and *Klebsiella*; alternative to gentamicin	Mainly high tone deafness	15 mg/kg/day IM, IV in divided doses ($t_{1/2}$ = 2-3 hours)
Netilmicin	Semisynthetic derivative of sisomicin; similar to gentamicin, but less effective against *Pseudomonas*	Staphylococcal infections where penicillin is contraindicated	Renal, auditory and vestibular damage	3-6 mg/kg/day IM/IV every 8-12 hourly ($t_{1/2}$ = 2-3 hours)

NEOMYCIN: FRAMYCETIN: PAROMOMYCIN

These three aminoglycosides are similar, and they have an antibacterial spectrum like kanamycin, and are now considered too toxic for systemic administration. Their use is limited to oral and topical administration. All the three drugs are capable of causing **irreversible deafness.**

Neomycin can only be used for infections of the skin or mucous membranes, or for bowel sterilization prior to surgery, or in hepatic failure. Topical use may lead to **hypersensitivity**, and oral administration to **malabsorption**. **Ototoxicity** may result from topical application to large areas, e.g., burns. For cutaneous application, not more than 1 g per day should be used in adults, and the use should be restricted to 3 days.

Framycetin is almost identical with neomycin in its actions and uses, having similar restricted indications for oral and topical application.

Paromomycin differs from neomycin and framycetin in that it has a direct **amoebicidal action, which is confined to the intestinal lumen**. It is not effective in hepatic amoebiasis. Thus it is used to treat asymptomatic as well as acute and chronic **intestinal amoebiasis**.

TETRACYCLINES

The first member of this family was chlortetracycline (Aureomycin), derived from the soil organism **Streptomyces aureofaciens** and introduced by Benjamin M. Duggar in 1948. This was followed by oxytetracycline (Terramycin) produced from **Streptomyces rimosus**. Molecular modification by removing the chlorine atom from chlortetracycline produced tetracycline (Achromycin) which was introduced in 1952.

Investigation of the mutant strains of **Streptomyces aureofaciens** in 1957, led to the discovery of a new group of antibiotics, the **demethyltetracyclines**, the first member of which was **demethylchlortetracycline** (Ledermycin), and became available for general use in 1959. Recently a number of other tetracyclines, including **rolitetracycline, lymecycline, methacycline, clomocycline, doxycycline** and **minocycline** have become available, and are labelled as `newer' tetracyclines.

ANTIBACTERIAL SPECTRUM

The tetracyclines have a broad antibacterial spectrum which covers **gram-positive** and **gram-negative bacteria, Rickettsiae, Traponema pallidum, mycoplasmas** and the **Chlamydiae**, e.g., the **psittacosis** and **lymphogranuloma venereum** organisms.

MODE OF ACTION

Tetracyclines enter bacterial cells by either passive diffusion through "pores" on by an active transport system. Inside the bacterial cells, they **bind specifically to 30S ribosomes,** thereby blocking binding of transfer RNA to the messenger RNA-ribosome complex, inhibiting protein synthesis. They also **inhibit replication of DNA** on the cell membrane at high doses.

Tetracyclines also bind magnesium, manganese and calcium, and this chelating action is probably related to their antibacterial activity.

BACTERIAL RESISTANCE

An increasing proportion of pathogens is developing resistance to the tetracyclines (particularly coliforms, streptococci, pneumococci and staphylococci) which results from diminished permeability to the drugs. This resistance develops slowly in a **step-wise** manner (like the penicillins). **Cross-resistance** develops within the group.

PHARMACOKINETICS

The tetracyclines are usually given orally, but can be given intravenously, intramuscularly, and by local application (to the eye and ear). Absorption from the stomach and intestines is variable and incomplete, partly due to the *low solubility* of the tetracyclines, and partly due to *binding* Ca^{++}, Al^{+++}, Fe^{++} and Mg^{++} in food or drugs, in the gastrointestinal tract. Hence, absorption is depressed by food (except for doxycycline), calcium, aluminium, iron and magnesium salts, and slightly by milk, since the tetracyclines form non-absorbable chelates with heavy metals. Gastrointestinal upset is least with the most completely absorbed members of the group (minocycline, doxycycline). After absorption there is a varying degree of plasma protein binding **(Table 9.3-7)**. The blood levels show a slow rise, a prolonged plateau and a slow fall, due to prolonged absorption, high protein binding, and an enterohepatic circulation of these drugs respectively.

The tetracyclines are laid down in growing bones and teeth, probably because of their chelating action with calcium. Tetracyclines on IV administration are excreted primarily in the urine (upto 50%) by glomerular filtration, and much of the remainder is excreted in the bile and enters an enterohepatic circulation. Partly also excreted in the milk during lactation.

THERAPEUTIC USES

The clinical usefulness of the tetracyclines is largely due to their broad-spectrum of activity.

The tetracyclines are notably effective in infections due to the Rickettsiae, the Chlamydia, Mycoplasmas, Bacteroides, haemolytic streptococci and staphylococci. The gram-negative urinary tract infections are also susceptible. Their mode of action against *Balantidium coli* and *E. histolytica* infections is probably indirect. **Doxycycline** and **minocycline** possess greater activity against some anaerobic bacteria and some staphylococci respectively, compared to other tetracyclines. The main clinical indications are:

I. **First-line choice for:**

1. Acute exacerbation of chronic bronchitis.

Table 9.3-7. *The pharmacokinetic parameters of some commonly used tetracyclines*

Drug	*Source*	*Oral absorption (%)*	*Plasma protein binding (%)*	*Renal clearance (ml/min)*	*Half-life (hours)*
Chlortetracycline	*Streptomyces aureofaciens*	30	40-70	30	4-6
Oxytetracycline	*Streptomyces rimosus*	58	20-35	85	8-10
Tetracycline	Semisynthetic	77	25-60	60	8-10
Demethyl-chlortetracycline	*Streptomyces aureofaciens*	66	40-90	25	10-17
Methacycline	Semisynthetic	low	75-90	30	14-15
Doxycycline	Hydrogenation of methacycline	90-100	25-90	25	15-17
Minocycline	Semisynthetic	90-100	70-75	10	15-20

2. Non-specific urethritis.
3. Primary atypical pneumonia (Mycoplasma pneumonia).
4. Rickettsial infections (e.g. typhus).
5. Brucellosis.
6. Lymphogranuloma venereum.
7. Pustular acne (prolonged treatment).
8. Trachoma and inclusion body conjunctivitis.
9. Cholera.

II. **Second-line choice for:**

1. Syphilis (in penicillin-allergic patient it is the first choice).
2. Actinomycosis.
3. Anthrax.
4. Meningococcal carriers.

The tetracyclines have some nonantibacterial uses also, as they (specially demethylchlortetracycline) have the property of binding to some cancerous tissues, and exhibit a **golden yellow fluorescence** when exposed to ultraviolet light. This property forms the basis for several diagnostic tests for **gastric** and **colonic cancer**. Tetracyclines also have been used to determine the **rate of bone turnover,** utilizing their calcium chelating property.

When tetracyclines are used therapeutically, they depress the bacterial flora in the colon, and **vitamin K** 5 mg orally is a useful adjunct to therapy. **Riboflavin** and **folic acid deficiency** are also possible, and with prolonged tetracycline therapy a *multivitamin preparation* is desirable.

The tetracyclines are usually contraindicated during pregnancy, lactation, peptic ulcer and hepatic disease. In hepatic insufficiency the use may be very dangerous.

Toxicity

The tetracyclines have relatively low toxicity at usual dosage levels. Side effects are related to the dose and length of treatment.

Gastrointestinal upset. *Anorexia, heartburn, nausea, vomiting, flatulence* and most often *diarrhoea* occur in about 10 percent of the patients receiving 2 g or more of a tetracycline. *Cheilosis, black hairy tongue, glossitis, anogenital pruritus, proctitis* and *tenesmus* occur in about 20-30 percent of patients. Diarrhoea in a minority of patients may lead to *staphylococcal enterocolitis.*

Superinfection. The tetracyclines rapidly **depress the normal body flora,** particularly that of the gastrointestinal tract, and after a couple of days of therapy the faeces become soft, unformed and odourless, which makes superinfection likely. The usual superinfecting organisms are **penicillinase producing staphylococci,** various strains of **Proteus** and **Pseudomonas** and **Candida albicans. Necrotizing (pseudomembranous) enterocolitis** may also develop. Simultaneous use of immunosuppressive agents make a good setting for superinfection, and must be avoided.

Hypersensitivity reactions. Skin rashes of all types (morbiliform and urticarial), **exfoliative dermatitis, angioneurotic oedema, exacerbation of systemic lupus erythematosus,** and **anaphylactic shock** may occur. **Cross-sensitization** among the tetracyclines is common.

Photosensitivity reactions (phototoxic dermatitis) are common with demethylchlortetracycline and doxycycline; other tetracyclines produce them rarely. Lightheadedness, Jarisch-Herxheimer-like reactions, pancreatitis, and blood dyscrasias (thrombocytopenic purpura, neutropenia, lymphocytosis and haemolytic anaemia) may occur rarely.

Deposition in tissues. Tetracyclines are deposited in growing teeth and bones, and if treatment is very prolonged the **nails become stained by stored tetracycline**. Children may show **brown staining of teeth** if tetracyclines are administered before the appearance of first teeth, and **pigmentation of permanent teeth** can result if the drugs are given between the ages of two months to 8 years. **Thus damage to both deciduous or permanent teeth occurs.** Deposition of tetracycline in the growing ends of bones can cause stunted growth.

Renal Damage. In patients even with normal renal function, the tetracyclines may impair the urinary concentrating ability. *Demethylchlortetracycline* may induce **nephrogenic diabetes insipidus**. The two degradation products, namely *anhydrotetracycline* and *epianhydrotetracycline,* which accumulate in outdated capsules of a tetracycline preparation are nephrotoxic, and can produce a **Fanconi-like syndrome. albuminuria, glycosuria, aminoaciduria,** and **renal tubular acidosis** are noted. In patients with renal failure most tetracyclines may produce clinical and biochemical deterioration, and therefore should not be used.

Metabolic effects. Tetracyclines in excessive doses can produce **fatty degeneration of the liver**. A total dose of 1 g per day IV should not be exceeded. **Oxytetracycline and tetracycline are the least hepatotoxic.** Except for doxycycline and possibly minocycline the tetracyclines are thought to have **antianabolic** effect, which may produce a negative nitrogen balance and increase blood urea nitrogen levels. The tetracyclines **prolong blood coagulation** either *indirectly* by depressing prothrombin synthesis due to depression of colonic bacterial flora, or *directly* by chelating serum calcium.

Administration and Dosage

The tetracyclines are usually given orally, they may be given IM or IV; they should not be used intrathecally. The usual dose of chlortetracycline, tetracycline, and oxytetracycline is 250 mg 6-hourly; in severe infections this dose may be doubled. The comparable doses for demethyl chlortetracycline, methacycline or lymecycline are 150-300 mg 6-hourly.

Tetracycline and **oxytetracycline** are suitable for the IV route, and for IM injection **lymecycline** is probably the drug of choice. For IM use, oxytetracycline may be given in a dose of 100 mg every 8-12 hours, or 250 mg every 12-24 hours.

CHLORAMPHENICOL

Chloramphenicol was isolated from **Streptomyces venezuelae** (a soil organism) by Burkholder in 1947. Now chloramphenicol is manufactured synthetically. Regarding its current status, chloramphenicol is a potent, potentially toxic, broad-spectrum antibiotic which should be reserved for the treatment of life-threatening infections caused by **Haemophilus influenzae**, or **Klebsiella pneumoniae,** and also for **typhoid fever**. It is also useful for the treatment of **bacterial conjunctivitis**.

Antibacterial spectrum. Chloramphenicol has a broad-spectrum of activity, like the tetracyclines. It is effective against many **gram-positive** and **gram-negative** organisms, and exhibits activity against the **Chlamydiae** and **Rickettsiae**. Because of its toxicity on the bone marrow, the use of chloramphenicol is restricted to salmonelloses and infections due to rickettsiae. **Haemophilus influenzae**, gram-positive organisms resistant to less toxic antibiotics, the Chlamydiae, and anaerobic infections caused by **Bacteroides fragilis**. R factor mediated bacterial resistance slowly develops in a stepwise manner similar to penicillin resistance.

Mode of action. Chloramphenicol is primarily *bacteriostatic,* and inhibits bacterial protein synthesis in susceptible organisms. It binds to the 50S subunit of the bacterial 70S ribosomes inhibiting **peptidyltransferase** thereby blocking protein synthesis. It can also inhibit the function of animal mitochondrial 70S ribosomes.

Pharmacokinetics. The drug is well absorbed from the intestine, but large particle size may impair absorption. After a dose of 1 g orally in an adult, peak levels of 8-13 mcg/ml are reached in 2-5 hours, and the $t_{1/2}$ is 1.5-3 hours. Fine suspensions of chloramphenicol can be given intramuscularly, and the sodium succinate salt can be injected subcutaneously, IM or IV.

Chloramphenicol is 60 percent bound to plasma proteins and penetrates tissues better than any other antibiotic. It enters the **eye, foetus, saliva** and **sputum**. It is mainly metabolized in the liver by reduction, or by conjugation to glucuronide. Chloramphenicol itself *depresses microsomal function.*

Chloramphenicol is mainly (90%) excreted in the urine, and only 10 percent is as unchanged chloramphenicol, although this amount is usually sufficient to be effective in urinary tract infections.

Therapeutic uses. Because of a small but definite incidence of **serious bone marrow depression,** chloramphenicol therapy is restricted to those infections only in which other drugs are not as effective. The accepted indications are **enteric fever** and **H. influenzae meningitis.** In both instances, chloramphenicol is superior to ampicillin, but it is not so in relation to many other gram-positive or gram-negative infections. It is also used topically for **eye infections** (as an ointment), and effectively penetrates the aqueous humour.

Salmonella infections. Against S. *typhi* chloramphenicol is the drug of first choice. In certain circumstances **ampicillin, amoxycillin** or **co-trimoxazole** may be useful. In **typhoid fever** chloramphenicol is best administered orally in capsule form. Children may be given **chloramphenicol palmitate** orally, but absorption of this preparation is less certain than chloramphenicol capsule.

Several *dosage regimens* are available for typhoid fever. A convenient regimen in adults is to give 1 g on the first day, 1.5 g on the second day, 2.0 g on the third day, and 3.0 g thereafter to a total of about 35.0 g. Chloramphenicol may be administered in **combination with ampicillin**. Some physicians add **corticosteroids** with chloramphenicol in serious patients of typhoid fever.

Meningitis. Haemophilus meningitis is most appropriately treated with chloramphenicol, as this drug attains effective CSF concentrations and is extremely well absorbed on oral administration. The dose of chloramphenicol base for *H. influenzae* meningitis is 125 mg/kg/day. The treatment should be continued for 10 to 14 days.

There are few other indications for chloramphenicol therapy, and include **Kl pneumoniae** infection; septicaemia due to gram-negative bacilli when alternative drugs have failed; **anaerobic infections** particularly caused by bacteroides; **resistant urinary tract infections**; and **staphylococcal infections resistant to semisynthetic penicillins** and **cephalosporins**.

TOXICITY

Haematological abnormalities. Chloramphenicol causes two types of haemopoietic abnormalities. The *first* is a true toxic reaction as a result of direct haemotoxicity, manifested by bone marrow depression, is dose related, progressive and **reversible** upon stoppage of therapy. It occurs in every patient, if the antibiotic is given long enough, and in high enough doses. There is **anaemia, reticulocytopenia, elevated serum iron and iron-binding capacity,** and **decreased uptake of iron by the erythrocytes. In this instance the marrow is not aplastic.**

The *second* more serious type of bone marrow depression which may occur after a single dose or following prolonged therapy, is **aplastic anaemia**. This is the main reason for limiting the applications of chloramphenicol, though it occurs rarely (1:2,000 to 1:50,000 patients), it may be *fatal* and *unpredictable*.

Other blood dyscrasias noted, specially following large doses include **thrombocytopenia, leucopenia, neutropenia** and **agranulocytosis.**

Hypersensitivity reactions. Drug fever, various skin rashes, angioedema and urticaria may occur on chloramphenicol administration. Rarely anaphylactic and Jarish-Herxheimer-like reactions have been reported during treatment of typhoid.

Gastrointestinal disturbances. Nausea, vomiting, glossitis, stomatitis, enterocolitis and diarrhoea may occur. Cheilosis and pruritus ani may occur, and worsen by superinfection. **Superinfection** with a wide range of organisms, in particular, **Staph. aureus, Pseudomonas, Proteus** and **Candida** may occur. **Necrotizing (pseudomembranous) enterocolitis** is also seen.

The grey (gray) syndrome. The **neonates** and **premature infants** on large doses of chloramphenicol may readily develop the "grey syndrome", characterized by progressive abdominal distension, vomiting, refusal to suck, dyspnoea, cyanosis and loose greenish stools. Within a day or two the baby develops a greyish colour due to cyanosis, and peripheral vascular collapse; death occurs in about 50 percent of cases within 4-5 days. *The cause of the syndrome is the immature and deficient glucuronic-conjugating mechanism in the liver so that chloramphenicol is not metabolized and high plasma levels persist. In addition, there is inadequate renal excretion of the unconjugated drug.*

Other reactions. Headache, depression, delirium or confusion is not uncommon. Optic neuritis, encephalopathy, or peripheral neuritis occurs infrequently.

Preparations and Dosage

Chloramphenicol (250 mg) capsules are available for oral use. The daily adult dose varies between 1.5 to 3.0 g in divided doses every 6 to 8 hourly. On a weight basis the dose may be calculated as 50 mg/kg/day.

Chloramphenicol palmitate is a less bitter form of the drug and as a suspension is available for *paediatric use* containing 125 mg/5 ml. The dose ranges from 50-100 mg/kg/day.

Chloramphenicol sodium succinate is provided in 1 g vials for parenteral use. The usual dose is 50 mg/kg/day in divided doses.

Ophthalmic preparations are available as *drops* (0.5%), *ointment* (1.0%) and *aplicaps* (1.0%).

Macrolides

The macrolide antibiotics structurally consist of a **large lactone ring** to which **sugars** are attached. These compounds have a complex structure, a molecular weight of more than 700, and unusual nitrogen containing sugars. They include **erythromycin, oleandomycin,** and **triacetyloleandomycin** (troleandomycin). Amongst these members only erythromycin maintains a regular place in therapeutics.

Erythromycin

Erythromycin was isolated from **Streptomyces erythreus** in 1952, and enjoyed wide popularity for several years in the treatment of many infections.

Antibacterial spectrum. Erythromycin has an antibacterial spectrum between that of penicillin G and the tetracyclines. It is primarily effective against gram-positive cocci (most staphylococci, streptococci and pneumococci), neisseriae, listeriae, *Bacteroides fragilis, Corynebacterium diphtheriae, H. influenzae,* brucellae, some rickettsiae, *Chlamydia,* spirochetes, and *Entamoeba histolytica.* It is also highly effective against *Mycoplasma pneumoniae,* but not against yeasts and fungi. Bacterial resistance to erythromycin develops fairly rapidly. Cross-resistance is usually complete between the macrolides, and is plasmid-borne.

Mode of Action

Erythromycin is bound to the 50S subunit of the ribosome, and blocks the execution of instructions coded by mRNA. The macrolides do not attach to human ribosomes. Erythromycin essentially is classed as a `bacteriostatic' drug. but in high concentrations it exerts a bactericidal effect.

Pharmacokinetics

Apart from erythromycin base, various erythromycin salts and esters subsequently became available, which were more acid-resistant. The acid-resistant salts such as *stearate* or *estolate* are well absorbed, and produce effective plasma levels on oral administration. Peak plasma levels are attained 2-4 hours after ingestion, and the drug is distributed to most of the tissues except the brain within 6 hours. CNS penetration is better when the meninges are inflamed. The $t_{1/2}$ is 1.5 to 3.0 hours. Only 20 percent of the drug is excreted by the kidneys; the remainder is metabolized by **demethylation** or appears in the bile, where it is highly concentrated.

Therapeutic uses. Erythromycin is used as an alternative in the penicillin-allergic patient, or in the treatment of penicillin-resistant gram-positive organisms. It is also useful in primary atypical pneumonia caused by **Mycoplasma pneumoniae,** and in syphilis or infections with **Haemophilus influenzae**. To summarize, erythromycin is the **first-line choice** as an alternative to penicillin in the penicillin-sensitive patient (e.g., gonorrhoea, syphilis, gas gangrene, streptococcal and pneumococcal infections, rheumatic fever prophylaxis); alternative to a tetracycline in *Mycoplasma pneumoniae* infection; relapsing fever; pertusis (whooping cough); and diphtheria, specially in the treatment of the carrier state. It is a **second-line choice** in bronchitis, otitis media and sinusitis; penicillin-resistant staphylococcal infections; and chronic prostatitis.

Toxicity. Erythromycin is one of the safer antibiotics. Gastrointestinal disturbances and allergy being the commonest adverse reactions. With oral therapy nausea, anorexia, diarrhoea, glossitis and stomatitis are common. Occasionally **superinfection** with **Candida albicans** may develop on prolonged therapy. It is rarely given IM or IV, as severe pain and induration at injection site and thrombophlebitis respectively may develop.

Hypersensitivity reactions with fever, eosinophilia, lymphocytosis, headache and skin rashes are sometimes seen, and are common in those patients who have received erythromycin repeatedly. A delayed hypersensitivity Type IV reaction is the cause of cholestatic jaundice, caused by erythromycin estolate.

Preparations and Dosage

Erythromycin stearate. The usual dose for erythromycin stearate is between 250-500 mg every 6-hourly. It is also available as a suspension for children, the dose being 4-6 mg/kg 4-6 hourly.

Erythromycin ethyl succinate is available dissolved in polyethylene glycol base for IM use. *Dose:* 100 mg every 4-8 hourly.

Erythromycin lactobionate is a soluble salt suitable for slow IV injection or infusion. *Dose:* 300 mg every 6-hourly, or 600 mg every 8 hourly. For children 30-50 mg/kg/day in divided doses every 6-hourly.

Oleandomycins

Oleandomycin and the related compound triacetyloeleandomycin (troleandomycin) are similar to erythromycin. They have the same antibacterial range, and have similar mechanisms of action. However, erythromycin is twice as active as oleandomycins. The use of oleandomycins is limited to the treatment of very severe susceptible infections. As they are excreted in an active form in the bile and urine, they are of particular use in gram-positive infections of these fluids.

Lincosamides (Lincomycins)

The lincosamide antibiotics, **lincomycin** and **clindamycin,** are similar to the macrolides regarding their antibacterial spectrum, mode of action, and therapeutic applications.

Lincomycin and Clindamycin

Lincomycin is a water-soluble, acid stable, naturally occurring bacteriostatic antibiotic produced by **Streptomyces lincolnensis**. **Clindamycin** (7-chlorodeoxylincomycin) is its semisynthetic derivative.

Antibacterial spectrum. Lincomycin is effective against gram-positive cocci and bacteroides, but less so against *Haemophilus* and *Neisseria infections.* In particular it is effective against most pathogenic streptococci (not *Strep.faecalis*), staphylococci, pneumococci, corynebacteria and most of the anaerobes except *Bacteroides fragilis. Clindamycin* has a similar antibacterial spectrum, but inhibits the sensitive bacteria in considerably lower concentration.

Mode of action. The lincomycins inhibit bacterial protein synthesis in the same way as erythromycin at the level of the ribosome. The binding apparently inhibits peptidyltransferase and may cause premature detachment of ribosomes from mRNA. *Cross-resistance* may occur between the two groups (lincomycins and macrolides) of drugs.

Pharmacokinetics. **Lincomycin** is incompletely (20-30%) absorbed from the gut, and the presence of food further decreases the absorption. With doses of 500 mg peak plasma levels of 2-5 mcg/ml are seen within 1-3 hours, and the antibiotic has a $t_{1/2}$ of 5-6 hours. In contrast, *clindamycin* is rapidly and almost completely absorbed on oral administration, and doses of 300 mg yield plasma levels of 3 mcg/ml within 1 to 2 hours. *Distribution* of both drugs is comparable.

Therapeutic uses. Lincomycin and clindamycin are used in similar situations as erythromycin. Both are **bacteriostatic** against streptococci, penicillinase-producing staphylococci and pneumococci. **Acute** and **chronic osteomyelitis** are sound indications for their use. To summarize, they are *first-line choice* for staphylococcal infections, particularly osteomyelitis, and even methicillin-resistant strains may respond; and bacteroides and other anaerobic infections. Clindamycin currently is the treatment of choice for **staphylococcal bone and joint infection,** and **intra-abdominal sepsis**.

Toxicity. Lincomycin and clindamycin are usually well tolerated, but they may cause **fatal colitis**. This has restricted their use to a few specific, and serious infections in hospitalized patients. They produce **diarrhoea,** and rarely **jaundice** and **granulocytopenia**. The major and dangerous side effect is a severe diarrhoea (both on oral or parenteral therapy), which may progress to **pseudomembranous colitis** with a fatal outcome.

Preparations and Dosage

Lincomycin hydrochloride (Lincocin) is available in 500 mg capsules, and syrup (250 mg in 5 ml) form. The dose is 500 mg 6 to 8 hourly. An injection of 600 mg in 2 ml is available, which may be administered as 600 mg IM every 12 to 24 hourly, or by slow IV infusion as 600 mg every 8 to 12-hourly.

Clindamycin hydrochloride (Cleocin) is available as 75 and 150 mg capsules, and 75 mg in 5 ml syrup. The dose being 150-300 mg every 6-hourly. **Clindamycin phosphate** is marketed for injection (150 mg/ml), and may be administered IM or by slow IV infusion.

Inhibitors of Bacterial Cell Membrane Function

The **bacterial cytoplasmic membrane** is the site of cell

wall synthesis in many organisms. In addition it serves as an **osmotic barrier**, and as an organ for selective intracellular transport of essential cell nutrients. The "surface active" antibiotics like the polymyxins, and some **antifungal drugs** (e.g., nystatin, amphotericin B) damage the bacterial cell membrane by increasing the permeability. The antifungal antibiotics are considered in **Chapter 9.13.**

POLYMYXINS

Polymyxin is a generic name for six strongly basic cyclic polypeptides (polymyxins A, B, C, D, E and M), all differing in their amino acid content, and obtained from various strains of **Bacillus polymyxa**. Only two, *polymyxin B* and *E* are therapeutically useful. Polymyxin E is identical with colistin (see later).

POLYMYXIN B

Polymyxin B has a molecular weight of about 1000, and readily forms water soluble salts with mineral acids. The usual preparation is *polymyxin B sulphate*.

Antibacterial spectrum. Polymyxin B has a narrow spectrum limited to action against gram-negative organisms (excluding *Proteus* and *Neisseria*). It is particularly active against *Ps. aeruginosa*. Other susceptible organisms are *Enterobacter aerogenes, E. coli, H.influenzae, Bordetella pertusis, Klebsiella pneumoniae, salmonella and shigella.*

Mode of action. Polymyxin B is **bactericidal**, and binds with the phospholipid components of the cytoplasmic membrane of susceptible bacteria. It impairs the bacterial cell membrane function, and causes leakage of small molecules (e.g., phosphate, nucleosides) from the bacteria. This increased membrane permeability is the reason for their lethal effect. The bactericidal effect of polymyxin B is reduced by serum and tissue fluids, and by soap and other surface active agents. Bacterial resistance develops slowly and is rare. **Cross-resistance** with colistin occurs.

Pharmacokinetics. It is usually administered topically with almost none being absorbed from the site. *Rarely* oral, IV or intrathecal administration is warranted. On parenteral administration peak blood levels develop in about 1 hour. Polymyxin B does not reach the CSF, and intrathecal administration is necessary in patients with CNS infection. The drug is primarily cleared by the kidneys.

Therapeutic uses. The polymyxins are **second-choice** agents in the treatment of **Pseudomonas aeruginosa** infections, particularly those of the urinary tract, external ear, conjunctiva and meninges, and in **septicaemia** when other drugs like carbenicillin and gentamicin are ineffective.

Toxicity. Serious adverse effects are seen on parenteral therapy. Pain at the IM injection site is marked. Paranasal, circumoral, lingual and "glove and stocking" paraesthesias may occur. Facial flushing, drug fever, and skin rashes including urticaria may occur. **Neuromuscular paralysis resistant to neostigmine or calcium gluconate rarely develops**. Ataxia, diplopia and ptosis have been reported.

Kidney damage, with development of proteinuria and haematuria is the most dreaded adverse reaction in patients on systemic therapy. It is dose dependent, and is easily induced in patients with existing renal insufficiency. *Chemical meningitis* may follow intrathecal therapy.

PREPARATIONS AND DOSAGE

Polymyxin B sulphate (Aerosporin) is available for *local*, *oral* or *systemic* administration. It is frequently combined with other antibiotics (bacitracin and neomycin), and with hydrocortisone for topical administration. The average oral dose is 4.0 mg/kg daily. *Intramuscularly*, or preferably IV the daily dose is 1.5-2.5 mg/kg in 3 or 4 divided doses. A total daily dose of 200 mg should not be exceeded when administered parenterally.

COLISTIN

Colistin, a **bactericidal polypeptide antibiotic**, obtained from **Bacillus colistinus**, is identical with polymyxin E. It is available as **colistin sulphate** for oral use, and **colistin sulphomethate sodium** (*sodium colistimethate*) for parenteral use.

Colistin has an antibacterial spectrum and mode of action similar to that of polymyxin B, but is less potent. It is not antagonized by serum and tissue fluids. Bacterial resistance develops rarely, and *cross-resistance* with polymyxin B is present.

Colistin has therapeutic applications similar to those of polymyxin B. It has been suggested that colistin and polymyxin B be reserved for the treatment of systemic **Pseudomonas aeruginosa** infections, when less toxic antibiotics like carbenicillin and gentamicin have failed. Colistin is sometimes used with framycetin to sterilize the bowels.

The pattern of toxicity with colistin is similar to that of polymyxin. In addition, **peripheral neuritis, nystagmus, amblyopia, transient deafness** and **leucopenia** may occur on systemic use. In general, less side effects are seen with parenteral colistin, compared to parenteral polymyxin B.

PREPARATIONS AND DOSAGE

Colistin sulphate (*Coly-Mycin S*). It is suspended in distilled water (5 mg/ml) immediately before use. The recommended dose is 5-15 mg/kg/day in 3 divided doses. The usual dose for children is 3-5 mg/kg/day in divided doses.

Colistimethate sodium (*Coly-Mycin M*). It is available for IM administration in doses of 150 mg, with the local anaesthetic dibucaine 8 mg; the IV and intrathecal preparations do not contain dibucaine. The usual IM dose is 2.5-5.0 mg/kg/day in divided doses. A total daily dose of 10 mg/kg must not be exceeded.

Miscellaneous Antibiotics

Spectinomycin

Spectinomycin is an aminocyclitol produced by **Streptomyces spectabilis**. It is active against a number of gram-negative bacterial species, and it readily inhibits most strains of **Neisseria gonorrhoeae** (gonococci) at plasma levels of 7 to 20 mcg/ml. It inhibits protein synthesis in the bacteria at the level of the 30S subunit of the ribosome. High level bacterial resistance may develop as a result of mutation. *Spectinomycin* is rapidly absorbed after IM injection, and a single 2 g dose produces peak plasma levels of about 100 mcg/ml by 1 hour. It is not significantly bound to the proteins, and is excreted in a biologically active form in the urine within 48 hours.

Spectinomycin is used to treat **acute genital** and **rectal gonorrhoca**. It has no activity against extragenital and extrarectal gonorrhoea or against syphilitic infections. **Cross-resistance of gonococci between penicillin and spectinomycin has not been reported**. Spectinomycin becomes the drug of first choice in pregnant women with gonorrhoea who are allergic to penicillin or probenecid.

Adverse effects occur infrequently and include pain at the site of injection, nausea, chills, fever, urticaria, insomnia and oliguria. Rarely **haematologic, renal** and **hepatic damage** may occur, with fall in haemoglobin and haematocrit, elevation of alkaline phosphatase, blood urea nitrogen (BUN), and serum glutamic pyruvic transaminase (SGPT).

The recommended dose of spectinomycin dihydrochloride (Trobicin) is 2 g/day in men, and 4 g/day in women as a single deep IM injection.

The antibiotics **rifampicin, capreomycin, cycloserine** and **viomycin** have been discussed in **Chapter 9.4** dealing with chemotherapy of tuberculosis; cytotoxic antibiotics in **Chapter 9.10;** and the antifungal antibiotics **nystatin, amphotericin B, griseofulvin** and **hamycin** are discussed in **Chapter 9.13**.

9.4 CHEMOTHERAPY OF TUBERCULOSIS (ANTITUBERCULOUS DRUGS)

About 60 years ago, tuberculosis was considered a serious health hazard. The mortality rate which had been falling by only about 3 percent per year from 1900 to 1948, fell thereafter by about 15 percent per year. The significance of the year 1948 is that it marks the introduction of **streptomycin**. Since then many other antibiotics and synthetic drugs have followed, and the introduction of **isoniazid** in 1952 was another important landmark. In the 1960s, the introduction of **ethambutol** and **rifampicin** further changed the concepts and practices in the treatment of tuberculosis. However, as the causative microorganisms grow slowly, and the disease is often chronic, there are special problems related to **drug toxicity**, **patient compliance**, and **development of bacterial resistance**.

TUBERCULOUS INFECTIONS

Tuberculosis is a chronic infection caused by **Mycobacterium tuberculosis,** and occasionally **Mycobacterium bovis**. Infections due to **atypical mycobacteria** are clinically indistinguishable from *M. tuberculosis* infections, but they occur infrequently. *M. tuberculosis* can remain dormant in the human host for years.

Infection of the upper lung is the most common form of tuberculosis, and the majority of cases that occur in the middle-aged and elderly patients, usually originate from the reactivation of a dormant lesion. Pulmonary tuberculosis in younger people and acute systemic non-pulmonary forms of the disease like *tuberculous meningitis, pericarditis, peritonitis*, and *osteomyelitis* are encountered in the lower socio-economic groups of society.

CLASSIFICATION

In general, antituberculous drugs are divided into *two* major groups: (*i*) the **primary drugs,** or the "first-line" drugs which are used in standard therapeutic regimens, due to their *high level of efficacy* and *acceptable degree of toxicity*; and (*ii*) the **secondary drugs** or the "second-line" drugs, which are used occasionally because of *bacterial resistance* or certain *patient-related factors*. The individual members of the two groups are listed below:

(*i*) **Primary drugs** (used in standard therapeutic regimens) Isoniazid (INH), Rifampicin, Ethambutol, Streptomycin.

(*ii*) **Secondary drugs** (alternative second-line drugs), Pyrazinamide, Ethionamide, Para-aminosalicylic acid (PAS), Cycloserine, Viomycin, Kanamycin, Amikacin, Capreomycin, Thiacetazone, Ciprofloxacin, Ofloxacin, Rifalritin Thiocarlide.

Usually administration of **rifampicin** with **isoniazid** constitutes optimal therapy for all forms of tuberculosis caused by sensitive strains of *Mycobacterium tuberculosis*.

PRIMARY DRUGS

ISONIAZID (INH, ISONEX)

Isoniazid (isonicotinic acid hydrazide), introduced in 1952, is even now the most effective drug for the treatment of tuberculosis. It is very close to being an *ideal* drug as it is least toxic, most efficacious, and the least expensive of the available primary drugs. Isoniazid closely resembles pyridoxine chemically.

Antibacterial spectrum. Isoniazid is both **tuberculostatic** and **tuberculocidal** *in vitro*. The bactericidal effect is exerted only against actively growing tubercle bacilli. The "resting" organisms can resume multiplication when the drug is stopped. Some **atypical mycobacteria** are also susceptible to isoniazid action. Unlike streptomycin, isoniazid penetrates cells with ease.

Mode of action. The main action being the inhibition of the biosynthesis of mycolic acids, which are important constituents of the mycobacterial cell wall. Exposure to isoniazid leads to the loss of acid fastness by the mycobacteria. Only isoniazid-sensitive tubercle bacilli take up the drug, possibly by an active process, where it combines with certain **intracellular mycobacterial enzymes**, and thereby interferes with the bacterial cell metabolism.

Most strains of *M. tuberculosis* are inhibited by an isoniazid concentration of 0.2 mcg/ml or less. Resistance is readily developed to INH by tubercle bacilli. *There is no cross-resistance between isoniazid and other antituberculous drugs.*

Pharmacokinetics. Isoniazid is readily absorbed from the gut, diffuses well into the body tissues, including the CNS. It also penetrates into macrophages so that it is effective against intracellular tubercle bacilli. It is partly metabolized by acetylation in the liver. People are divided genetically into `slow' and `rapid' acetylators of isoniazid **(Chap. 1.4)**, which depends upon the group's ethnic make-up, a high percentage of fast acetylators being found in the Balck and Eskimo populations. The $t_{1/2}$ in **slow acetylators** is more than 140 minutes, whereas it is less than 80 minutes in **fast acetylators**. Slow acetylating patients should be treated with lower doses administered less frequently, and they are also more susceptible to side effects, specially polyneuritis. Fast acetylators on the contrary require more frequent administration of isoniazid.

Isoniazid is excreted primarily through the kidneys in its free form, and its metabolites. The metabolites have no antituberculous activity.

Therapeutic uses. Isoniazid is used for the treatment of tuberculosis, in combination with other drugs, although it may be used alone for prophylaxis (see later). Regarding its therapeutic status, it is still the most important drug in the treatment of all forms of tuberculosis, and its toxic effects can be minimized by prophylactic use of **pyridoxine** (see later).

Toxicity. Isoniazid is relatively free from side effects in doses not exceeding 300 mg daily. Toxic effects are more frequent in slow acetylators. The commonest effects are **restlessness, insomnia, nausea, vomiting and muscle twitching**. **Hypersensitivity reactions** including rashes may occur. **Peripheral neuritis** may occur with higher doses, which can be reversed or prevented by the use of pyridoxine 10-20 mg daily. About 1 percent of treated patients may develop **hepatitis** leading on to hepatic necrosis. **Convulsions, psychotic episodes** and **agranulocytosis** may occur rarely. There have been reports of isoniazid-induced rheumatoid and lupus syndromes. Isoniazid also inhibitis metabolism of diphenylhydantoin sodium, and may precipitate toxicity.

Dosage. For **pulmonary tuberculosis** upto 300 mg daily (adults 3 mg/kg; children 6 mg/kg), or upto 1 g (14 mg/kg) twice weekly is given orally. For **tuberculous meningitis** it is given in a dose of 10 mg/kg daily orally. For oral use 50 and 100 mg tablets are available. The same doses may be administered by IM injection, for which isoniazid 25 mg/ml is available in 2 ml ampoules.

RIFAMPICIN

The *rifamycins* are a group of structurally related, complex macrocyclic antibiotics obtained from **Streptomyces mediterranei**. The three clinically interesting compounds are rifamycin SV, rifamycin B, and rifampicin. *Rifampicin* (rifampin) is a semisynthetic derivative of rifamycin B, and unlike the other two compounds it is well absorbed on oral administration. It is a **zwitterion** and is soluble in water at an acid pH.

Antibacterial spectrum. Rifampicin has a **broad-spectrum** of activity, and inhibits the growth of many gram-positive cocci (e.g., gonococci and meningococci), and gram-negative bacteria such as **Escherichia coli, Pseudomonas,** indole positive and negative proteus and **Klebsiella**. It is also effective against anaerobes like **Bacteroides fragilis**. However, it is less effective than penicillin G, but more effective than erythromycin, lincomycin, and cephalosporins against gram-positive organisms; and it is inferior to the tetracyclines, chloramphenicol, and aminoglycosides against gram-negative bacilli. It is very active against *Staphylococcus aureus*.

Rifampicin is also highly effective against most strains of *Mycobacterium tuberculosis*, and many atypical mycobacteria. It increases the *in vitro* activity of streptomycin and isoniazid, but not of ethambutol, against *M. tuberculosis*. Rifampicin is also active against *Mycobacterium leprae* **(Chap. 9.8).**

Mode of action. Rifampicin is **bactericidal,** and acts by inhibiting bacterial DNA-dependent RNA polymerase, and thereby interferes with RNA synthesis. It exhibits selective toxicity because mammalian RNA polymerases are not affected by the drug. The bacilli are inhibited well below the concentration of 0.5 mcg/ml. It has a high lipid solubility, and diffuses easily through cell membranes to kill intracellular bacteria. Resistance by mycobacteria and other microorganisms may develop rapidly in one or two steps (streptomycin type). Thus, in the treatment of tuberculosis, the addition of a second drug is essential. However, most wild strains of *M. tuberculosis* have a remarkably low proportion of rifampicin-resistant mutants, i.e., about 1/10th of that encountered with isoniazid.

Pharmacokinetics. Absorption of rifampicin from the gut is almost complete, but is impaired or delayed by food. Absorption is also impaired by concurrent PAS treatment. Peak plasma levels of about 10 mcg/ml are reached 3 hours after a single oral dose of 600 mg, and significant levels persist for 12 hours. The $t_{1/2}$ is 2 to 5 hours, and renal insufficiency does not significantly raise the plasma levels. About 85-90 percent of the drug is protein bound in plasma. Rifampicin penetrates well into most tissues, cavities and exudates, although relatively little enters the brain and the CSF. It also crosses the placental barrier. It is metabolized by **deacetylation** and is excreted mainly in the bile; less than 10 percent appears unchanged in the urine. Rifampicin and its metabolites are actively secreted into the bile and undergo a prolonged **enterohepatic circulation**.

Therapeutic uses. Rifampicin is employed in the **primary treatment of tuberculosis,** at least with one other antituberculous drug (see later). The usual dose is 600 mg orally, given once daily, either 1 hour before or 2 hours after a meal. The dose for children is 10-20 mg/kg, with a daily maximum of 600 mg. Rifampicin may exceptionally be used in the treatment of **nasopharyngeal meningococcal carrier state,** and a 4-7 day course is recommended. Combined with vancomycin or a beta-lactam antibiotic, rifampicin may be useful is cases of **osteomyelitis** or **staphylococcal endocarditis**. It also enhances the antifungal activity of amphotericin B.

Toxicity. On daily treatment regimens, signs of **hepatic toxicity** may appear but are usually transient. The drug should be used with caution in alcoholics and patients with hepatic disease.

On intermittent treatment with rifampicin, **six** toxicity syndromes have been recognized: influenzal, abdominal and respiratory symptoms; shock, renal failure and thrombocytopenic purpura. These six syndromes occur in about 20-30 percent of patients. Serious liver damage is uncommon.

Rifampicin markedly **induces hepatic microsomal activity,** and can accelerate the metabolism of several drugs like oestrogens, corticosteroids, sulphonylureas and anticoagulants. **The effectiveness of oral contraceptives is reduced, and where appropriate the method of contraception should be changed.** The drug should be avoided in pregnancy as the effect on the foetus is unknown. The urine, saliva and other **body secretions are coloured orange-red (pink).** As rifampicin turns the urine pink, this may be a useful guide to patient's compliance with therapy.

ETHAMBUTOL

Ethambutol is used as a **first-line drug** in the treatment of tuberculosis. It is less active than isoniazid and rifampicin, and should never be used alone. It is a **bacteriostatic** agent, possibly depressing RNA synthesis, and about 70-80 percent of strains of human **M. tuberculosis** are inhibited at a concentration of 1 mcg/ml. Mycobacterial resistance develops slowly, and no cross-resistance has been described. It effectively inhibits strains which are resistant to INH or streptomycin.

Ethambutol is well absorbed from the gut, and the absorption is not affected by the presence of food in the stomach. A single dose of 25 mg/kg gives a peak plasma level of 5 mcg/ml at 2-4 hours. The plasma $t_{1/2}$ is 5-6 hours. The drug is concentrated in the red blood cells, which provide a depot for entry into the plasma. About 80 percent of the drug is excreted unchanged in the urine, and 15 percent is excreted as an aldehyde or dicarboxylate. Ethambutol is contraindicated in renal insufficiency, as high blood levels may be attained.

Ethambutol is used in the treatment of tuberculosis, in combination with other drugs, usually rifampicin and isoniazid (see later). The usual adult dose is 15 mg/kg given once a day. It has essentially replaced PAS in the treatment of tuberculosis.

Ethambutol produces very few **adverse reactions** in daily doses of 15 mg/kg. In high doses it may cause **loss of visual acuity due to retrobulbar neuritis,** and **loss of colour vision**. This is not always reversible. The first signs of ocular toxicity may be blurring of vision, and loss of red-green perception. In lower doses ocular complications are rare. Testing of colour vision, and visual fields should precede treatment, and the patient should be regularly examined thereafter for visual disturbances. High doses of ethambutol may also produce **rashes, pruritus, joint pains, nausea, abdominal pain, confusion, hallucinations, peripheral neuropathy,** and **hyperuricaemia** (due to decreased urate excretion from the kidneys). Ethambutol today is one of the main agents used in the primary therapy of tuberculosis, and has virtually replaced PAS.

STREPTOMYCIN

The pharmacology of streptomycin has been discussed in detail in **Chapter 9.3.** Streptomycin is **bactericidal** for the tubercle bacillus *in vitro*. However, *in vivo* it is essentially suppressing the growth of the bacillus. Large populations of all strains of tubercle bacilli become markedly resistant to the antibiotic due to mutation, but primary resistance is met with only in 1 to 2 percent of isolates of *M. tuberculosis*. Streptomycin is used in combination with other primary drugs in the treatment of tuberculosis, specially in patients with impaired liver function. Currently since other effective antituberculous drugs have become available, the use of streptomycin for the treatment of pulmonary tuberculosis has sharply declined. The usual dose is 1 g IM daily (see therapeutic regimens).

SECONDARY DRUGS

Alternative or **second-line drugs** discussed below are **less effective** and **more toxic** than the primary drugs. These drugs are used under the following circumstances: (*i*) in the treatment of patients when the **conventional primary therapy has failed** or is not tolerated; and (*ii*) when the **organism is resistant** to the primary drugs, or in **infection with atypical mycobacteria.**

Pyrazinamide. It is chemically related to nicotinamide and is a **bactericidal** drug active against **M. tuberculosis,** but not against **M. bovis.** It is particularly useful in tuberculous meningitis because of good meningeal penetration. It is readily absorbed from the gut and widely distributed throughout the body tissues. Mycobacteria develop a resistance to this drug fairly rapidly, but no cross-resistance with isoniazid has been reported. **Hepatotoxicity** is the most common untoward effect. Other adverse effects are **arthralgias, anorexia, vomiting, fever, urticaria,** and **diabetes mellitus** may become difficult to control. The usual dose is 20-30 mg/kg/day orally with a maximum of 3 g daily.

Ethionamide. It is a close chemical relative of isoniazid, but there is no cross-resistance between the two drugs. It suppresses the multiplication of human strains of *M. tuberculosis*, and is used for the treatment of tuberculosis resistant to first-line drugs. Ethionamide is rapidly absorbed from the gut, and is widely distributed in the CSF as well. **Adverse reactions** are gastrointestinal disturbances including anorexia, salivation, metallic taste, nausea, vomiting and diarrhoea; mental disturbances, depression, insomnia and convulsions; rashes, gynaecomastia, impotence and menstrual irregularities have also been reported. **Peripheral neuropathy, optic neuritis and hypothyroidism** may occur. Hepatitis may occur in 5 percent of treated cases. Acute rheumatic symptoms have been noted. It is contraindicated in the presence of hepatic disease. The *usual dose* is 0.5-1 g orally daily, in divided doses or as a single dose at night.

Para-aminosalicylic acid (PAS). This is a relatively weak antituberculous drug which has been used in combination therapy to inhibit the development of resistant strains of the tubercle bacillus to other concurrently used drugs. **Earlier this drug was listed among the primary drugs, but now it has been displaced to a secondary status by ethambutol.** PAS is an analogue of p-aminobenzoic acid, and acts in a similar way to the sulphonamides. It is bacteriostatic to most strains of *M. tuberculosis* at a concentration of 1 mcg/ml. It is readily absorbed from the gut, and distributed in tissues and body fluids, with the exception of CSF. At present PAS is infrequently used as better tolerated alternative drugs are available. **Adverse effects** of PAS (sodium aminosalicylate) include interference with iodine metabolism leading to **goitre** and **myxoedema**. **Hypersensitivity reactions** occur in about 10 percent of patients. Nausea, vomiting and abdominal discomfort are common as large amounts of the drug are required. Other serious reactions are **hepatitis, jaundice, haematuria, albuminuria** and **encephalitis. Leucopenia, agranulocytosis,** and an **atypical mononucleosis syndrome** have also been reported. The average daily dose is 8-10 g orally in divided doses.

Cycloserine. It is a broad-spectrum antibiotic originally isolated from **Streptomyces orchidaceus** in 1955, but was later synthesized. It is an analogue of D-alanine, and acts by inhibiting the enzyme alanine racemase, and thereby interferes with the incorporation of D-alanine into the mucopeptides of the bacterial cell wall. This inhibition of cell wall synthesis is responsible for its inhibitory effect on *M. tuberculosis*. There is no cross-resistance between cycloserine and other tuberculostatic agents.

Cycloserine is rapidly absorbed from the gut, is widely distributed, and enters the CSF. Excretion is primarily through the kidneys, and the dose must be reduced in renal impairment. The *untoward reactions* commonly involve the CNS manifesting as tremors, dysarthria, vertigo, confusion, psychotic states with suicidal tendencies, paranoid reactions and grand mal seizures. Pyridoxine 100 mg/day may minimize the CNS effects. **Cycloserine is the most toxic of the second-line drugs**. Cycloserine is contraindicated in epilepsy, depression, psychotic states and alcoholism. The usual dose is 0.5-1 g/day orally in divided doses.

Viomycin. Viomycin is an aminglycoside, and is most active *in vitro* against *M. tuberculosis*. Almost all strains of the tubercle bacillus are inhibited by drug concentrations of 1-10 mcg/ml. Viomycin inhibits protein synthesis in *M. tuberculosis*. Resistance may develop rapidly. **Some cross-resistance to streptomycin, kanamycin and capreomycin exists**. It is not effectively absorbed from the gut, and has to be administered intramuscularly. The absorption and excretion of viomycin is similar to streptomycin, and a large portion of the dose is excreted in urine. Penetration into the CSF is poor. **Toxic effects** are much more severe than streptomycin, and include eighth nerve damage (impaired vestibular function), and kidney damage (proteinuria, haematuria, nitrogen retention, severe electrolyte imbalance). Partial deafness and allergic reactions have also been reported. Renal function usually recovers rapidly on stoppage of therapy. The usual dose is 1 g IM daily.

Kanamycin. Kanamycin is an aminoglycoside **(Chap. 9.3).** It inhibits the growth of *M. tuberculosis* in a concentration of 10 mcg/ml or less *in vitro*. It is administered parenterally when treating tuberculosis, and has shown variable cross-resistance with capreomycin. It is sometimes incorporated into the multiple drug regimens, but has no prominent place in the treatment of human tuberculosis. *Adverse reactions* include severe and permanent deafness, which is sometimes associated with loss of labyrinthine function. It is also nephrotoxic. The usual dose is 1 g IM daily.

Amikacin. Amikacin is also an aminoglycoside (a derivative of kanamycin). It is very active against several mycobacterial species, and may become an important drug in the treatment of infections by atypical mycobacteria. It is usually given IM or IV in a dose of 15 mg/kg in 2 divided doses.

Capreomycin. Capreomycin is a polypeptide antibiotic isolated from **Streptomyces capreolus**. It is chemically and pharmacologically related to viomycin, and has similar potential toxicity. It has marked suppressive effect against **M. tuberculosis** and **M. bovis**. Capreomycin approaches streptomycin in therapeutic efficacy, and there is no cross-resistance between the two. Compared to kanamycin it has greater antimycobacterial activity and lesser toxicity. Capreomycin is toxic to the eighth cranial nerve leading to hearing loss, tinnitus and vertigo. Hypersensitivity reaction, liver and renal damage may occur. Like the aminoglycosides it can cause neuromuscular blockade. **This drug should not be combined with streptomycin or other ototoxic drugs.** The usual dose is 1 g IM daily.

Thiacetazone. Thiacetazone (same as amithiozone) is **bacteriostatic,** and is effective against **M. tuberculosis, M. bovis** and **M. leprae.** Cross-resistance can develop between this agent and ethionamide or prothionamide. *It can be used as a tuberculostatic or antileprotic agent.* It may be used in the primary treatment of pulmonary tuberculosis with isoniazid, but the seriousness of its side effects limits its use as a secondary drug only. Serious *side effects include ototoxicity, haemolytic anaemia, agranulocytosis, erythema multiforme (Stevens-Johnson syndrome), cerebral oedema and hepatic dysfunction.* The usual dose is 150 mg/day orally in divided doses.

Ciprofloxacin and ofloxacin. Both these fluoroquinolones are active against *M. tuberculosis* and **atypical mycobacteria.** They may be combined with one or more of the active antitulercular drugs. Dosage Ciprofloxacin 750 mg tid; ofloxacin 600-800 mg OD. **(chap. 9.2)**

Rifabutin. Rifabutin is a bectericidal drug used in the tcatment of tuberculosis as a first-line drug It is a semi-sythetic derivative of rifamycin S, and blocks the DNA- dependent RNA-polymerase of the bacteria. It is active agaiust highly resistant of mycobacteria like *M. tuberculosis* and *M. leprae*. Dosage is 300 mg/day orally.

Thiocarlide. Thiocarlide is a thiourea used in the treatment of multi-drug resistant (MDR) strains of *M. Tuberculosis* It acts by inhibiting **oleicacid** and **tuberculostearic** acid. The dose regimens are yet to be finalised.

Corticosteroids and Tuberculosis

Status of corticosteroid therapy in tuberculosis remains controversial, but corticosteroids are often useful adjuncts to the primary antituberculous drugs in **fulminating pulmonary tuberculosis (tuberculous pneumonitis), tuberculous meningitis** and **pericarditis.** In these conditions corticosteroids may be life-saving. Corticosteroids decrease interstitial pulmonary inflammation, improve gas exchange, and decrease pleural, pericardial and meningeal fibrosis. They also offer benefit by their **antitoxic, antipyretic** and **antianorectic** properties in the treatment of moribund tuberculous patients. In the unconscious patient large IV doses of **methylprednisolone** (80 to 120 mg/day) may be given initially, followed by 40 mg daily for a short period of time. In conscious patients **prednisone** 30-40 mg/day may be given orally. The treatment should be limited to a maximum of 6 weeks. Corticosteroids are not needed in the management of uncomplicated cases of tuberculosis.

Chemotherapeutic Regimens

Although effective antituberculous drugs have been now available for over 60 years, there is little general agreement on an optimal regimen or duration of treatment in tuberculosis. **Except for prophylaxis and some cases of primary tuberculosis in which a single drug may be used (usually isoniazid), both pulmonary and extrapulmonary disease must always be treated with multiple drugs.**

The treatment of tuberculosis may be divided into *two* phases-an **initial phase** using at least three drugs, and a **continuation phase** with two drugs.

Initial phase. The simultaneous use of at least 3 drugs during this phase is designed to reduce the population of viable bacteria as rapidly as possible to minimize the risk of ineffective treatment in those patients infected by drug-resistant bacteria. Treatment of choice for the initial phase is the daily use of **isoniazid** and **rifampicin**, with **ethambutol** or **streptomycin**. These drugs should be continued for 8 weeks and preferably until the result of drug-sensitivity testing is known.

Continuation phase. After the initial phase, treatment is continued with only 2 drugs, one of which should be **isoniazid,** provided it is not contraindicated. The second drug may be **rifampicin, ethambutol,** or **streptomycin.**

Duration of treatment. Sufficient data are now available on the outcome of treatment in the initial phase (3 drugs), followed by continuation phase with 2 drugs (isoniazid and rifampicin), which confirm that a course of **9 months duration** gives satisfactory results in pulmonary tuberculosis regardless of the extent of the lesion. For extrapulmonary tuberculosis a total treatment period of **12 months** is recommended.

More recently it has been found that constant inhibitory concentrations of drugs are not essential, and single pulses can inhibit bacterial replication for several days. Such an **intermittent schedule** may be employed in a stabilized patient during the continuous phase of treatment, and the **twice-weekly regimens** may be used. Ambulatory treatment of tuberculosis after the initial hospitalization has become an effective method of treating pulmonary tuberculosis. The actual treatment regimens are detailed below:

1. (*a*) **Initial therapy (8 weeks).** Daily triple-drug treatment with *streptomycin* (1 g IM), *INH* (300 mg/day), and *rifampicin* (600 mg/day as a single dose); or *ethambutol* (25 mg/kg), *INH* and *rifampicin*, specially in the older patients. This is carried out in hospital in sputum-positive patients, but with effective treatment these patients rapidly become non-infectious.

(*b*) **Continuation therapy (daily therapy at home for 9 to 18 months).** *INH* and *ethambutol*, or *INH* and *rifampicin* may be used daily for a period of 9, 12 or 18 months. This phase may have to be further extended in cases of extrapulmonary tuberculosis or AIDS-related tuberculosis. However, the powerful bactericidal activity of rifampicin and INH could allow for a shorter course of treatment. An intermittent (twice-weekly) schedule may be used in the continuation phase of treatment.

2. If patients cannot be relied upon to take the drugs regularly, they are treated in hospital or as outpatients. The **twice-weekly supervised outpatient treatment** consists of *streptomycin* 1 g IM with *INH* 1 g in a single oral dose, or *rifampicin* 900 mg orally as a single dose with *INH*.

3. If there is a **relapse** after previous treatment, the drugs of the previous regimen are not used (if resistance has developed). For retreatment of such cases *alternative (second-line) drugs* have to be used, although they are less

effective and more toxic.

Failure of chemotherapy may be due to: (*i*) irregular and inadequate therapy because of **poor patient compliance;** (*ii*) use of a single drug because of **interruption in therapy** necessitated by hypersensitivity or toxicity to the other drug in use; (*iii*) **inadequate initial triple-drug therapy;** and (*iv*) **primary mycobacterial resistance** to the drugs in use.

Tuberculous meningitis. Isoniazid is the most useful agent, as it is highly effective and concentrations inhibitory to the tubercle bacillus are obtained on oral administration. **Streptomycin** penetrates optimally when the meninges are inflamed, and as such is only effective in the initial stages of treatment. **Ethambutol** is somewhat similar to streptomycin in its meningeal penetration pattern. **Rifampicin** penetrates poorly into the CSF, possibly due to high plasma protein-binding. **Pyrazinamide** penetrates fairly well. Although there is no consensus on an optimal regimen, the following is considered satisfactory: **Isoniazid** 400 mg, plus **pyridoxine** 10 mg daily; **streptomycin** 1 g IM daily; and **rifampicin** 10 mg/kg daily. **Ethambutol** 25 mg/kg may be substituted for streptomycin. This treatment is continued for 2 months. Isoniazid and rifampicin are then continued for a further period of 6 months, and lastly isoniazid alone for another 6 months. The total duration of chemotherapy comes to 14 months. **Corticosteroids** are sometimes used in the initial stages of treatment, as discussed earlier.

Short-course therapy. There is substantial evidence, based on studies carried out in East Africa and Hong Kong that antituberculous treatment lasting 1 year or even less is adequate, and that further drug use does not change the outcome significantly.

DOTS: A Tuberculosis Control Strategy

DOTS stands for **"Directly Observed Treatment, Short-course"**, and is the name given to the WHO- recommended gobal plan for tuberculosis control. This technical strategy was developed by Dr. Kerel Styblo in the 1980s in Tanzania. By the end of 1991 this project achieved remarkable results, doubling cure rates among TB patients. DOTS was then adopted globally by respective health authorities.

DOTS strategy combines *five* components: (*i*) *government commitment* to control TB; (*ii*) case *detection by sputum-smear* microscopy; (*iii*) *standardized short-course treatment regimen* directly observed by a community health worker for at least 2 months: (*iv*) a *regular drug supply;* and (*v*) standardized *recording and reporting* system allowing assessment of treatment results including checking for *side effects.* Treatment with properly implemented DOTS has a success rate exceeding 95% and *prevents emergence of multi-drug resistant tuberculosis (MDR-TB).*

A further extension of DOTS programme in 1998 included the treatment of MDR-TB, designated as **"DOTS Plus".** Facility to perform *drug-susceptibility testing,* and availabilty of *second-line drugs* with the DOTS drugs is a pre-requisite. Monthly surveillance is done till the culture becomes negative. **DOTS** and **DOTS-Plus** are WHO Global Plan(s) to control TB.

Probably the most effective experimental short treatment regimen is an **initial intensive phase of 4 drugs-** *streptomycin, INH, rifampicin and pyrazinamide*-for about 8 weeks, followed by **twice-weekly** *streptomycin, INH* and *rifampicin* for the continuation phase, till a total treatment time of 6 months. Daily therapy during the continuation phase may further reduce the total treatment time.

Extrapulmonary tuberculosis. Once the diagnosis is established, treatment is generally similar to that of pulmonary disease, *except* for **tuberculous meningitis** and **genito-urinary tuberculosis.** With meningitis, therapy is designed to include drugs which effectively penetrate the blood-brain barrier to achieve adequate antimycobacterial levels in the CSF, and in addition steroids are used for their anti-inflammatory and antifibroblastic properties (see above). **For the treatment of genito-urinary tuberculosis cycloserine is usually considered a primary drug, because it is selectively concentrated in urine, and may be usefully included in the triple-drug regimen.**

Chemoprophylaxis of Tuberculosis

Prophylactic therapy may be employed effectively to prevent the development of active tuberculosis in certain circumstances. **Isoniazid,** 300 mg daily is very useful for prophylaxis. However, because of its hepatotoxicity its prophylactic use is **reserved** for household contacts of patients with proven tuberculosis; persons exposed to tuberculosis; but have no evidence of infection; culture-negative patients who have had tuberculosis in the past but were never treated; patients undergoing corticosteroid therapy who are tuberculin reactors; tuberculin reactors who are immunosuppressed; and tuberculin reactors who have diabetes mellitus or silicosis. Persons without apparent disease whose skin test has converted from negative to positive within the preceding 2 years should be considered for insoniazid prophylaxis for 12 months, as these patients are possibly "infected". Isoniazid prophylaxis is contraindicated in patients with hepatic disease, or who had reactions with the drug.

To conclude, it is proper to stress that appropriate chemotherapy is the most important single factor in the management of patients with tuberculosis.

9.5 CHEMOTHERAPY OF MALARIA (ANTIMALARIAL DRUGS)

Malaria is a parasitic disease caused by the protozoan of the genus **Plasmodium**. The continued prevalence of malaria warrants a sustained and vigorous attack on the **malarial parasite,** and on its insect vector, the **female Anopheles mosquito.** Strains of mosquitoes have developed resistance to DDT, and other insecticides. Similarly the malarial parasite resistant to antimalarial drugs (chloroquine-resistant malaria) now is the cause of the disease in many parts of the world.

The chief drugs employed in the treatment of malaria are **chloroquine** and its congeners; inhibitor of the enzyme dihydrofolate reductase, e.g., **pyrimethamine;** and **primaquine. Quinine,** the antimalarial of the 1920s remains important, because the plasmodia still lack the ability to develop resistance to quinine. India is included in the list of countries with known risk of chloroquine-resistant **P. falciparum** malaria.

TYPES OF MALARIA

Four species of the genus Plasmodium cause human malaria: (*i*) **Plasmodium falciparum,** causes **malignant tertian** (MT) malaria, which is a fulminating form of the disease, and if untreated, it is rapidly fatal; (*ii*) **Plasmodium vivax,** causes **benign tertian** (BT) malaria, and these parasites are mostly responsible for human infection, and relapses are common. The term **tertian** indicates that the attacks of chills and fever typically tend to recur every *third* day; (*iii*) **Plasmodium malariae,** causes **quartan** (Q) malaria, an infection which is not uncommon, but relapses are rarer than in vivax malaria. The term **quartan** indicates that the spikes of fever come every *fourth* day; and (*iv*) **Plasmodium ovale,** causes a rare form of relapsing malaria (common in West Africa). Its periodicity is similar to vivax malaria i.e., it is tertian in nature (ovale tertian, OT), but it runs a milder course and is more easily treated. Infections caused by **P. vivax, P. malariae,** and **P. ovale** are classified as **"relapsing malarias",** because they have a **secondary exoerythrocytic stage** of development which provides a reservoir of parasites for reinfection of erythrocytes (see later). In contrast, **P. falciparum** has **no exoerythrocytic stage** in its life cycle.

LIFE CYCLE OF THE MALARIAL PARASITE

Broadly speaking, the parasite runs its **asexual cycle** in man, and the **sexual cycle** in the mosquito **(Fig. 9.5.1)**. The human phase begins when an infected **female Anopheles mosquito** bites man and injects **sporozoites** from her salivary glands. The injected sporozoites rapidly leave the circulation, and localize in the liver parenchyma cells, develop into **primary tissue schizonts,** and mature within 8-21 days to form **merozoites**. This constitutes the **preerythrocytic stage** during which the subject remains symptom-free. On maturity, the merozoites of all four species, are liberated from the liver cells and invade the erythrocytes, and begin the **erythrocytic cycle** of asexual development. In all except falciparum malaria, a proportion of merozoites infects more tissue cells, forming **secondary tissue schizonts,** and this constitutes the **exoerythrocytic cycle,** which may continue for several years and accounts for the **relapse** of infection (secondary exoerythrocytic forms do not occur with *P. falciparum*, hence no relapse of infection). At the end of the erythrocytic cycle the infected red cells rupture releasing merozoites (they reinvade other red cells), pigments and other products into the blood. This point of time marks the **clinical attack** of malaria manifested by **chills, fever** and **profound sweating**. After several cycles some erythrocytic parasites differentiate into male and female **gametocytes**. No further development of these forms takes place in man. They may be ingested by a female Anopheles mosquito from the blood stream of the infected individual. In the gut of the mosquito, **exflagellation** of the male gametocyte is followed by **fertilization** of the female gametocyte, forming the **zygote**, which develops in the gut wall as an **oocyst**, eventually giving rise to the infective sporozoites, which on rupture of the oocyst make their way to the mosquito's salivary glands. Hence, the cycle is completed. In man there are two complete cycles (**exoerthrocytic schizogony** and **erythrocytic schizogony**), and one partial cycle (**gametogony**), while in the mosquito there is one partial cycle (**completion of gametogony**), and one complete cycle (**sporogony**).

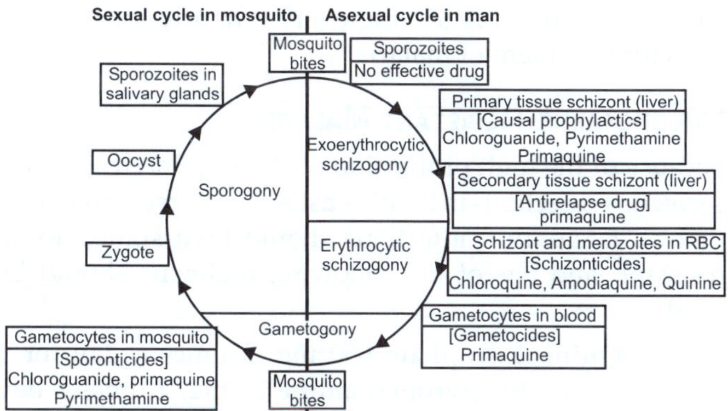

Fig. 9.5.1: The life cycle of the malarial parasite, and the points of action of various categories of antimalarial drugs (diagrammatic).

To control malaria the attack has to be two-fold: (*i*) measures taken against the mosquito vector; and (*ii*) treatment of the disease in man. Drainage of swamps and marshes, and chemical sprays (DDT, and organophosphates) are of importance. Many strains of Anopheles have developed resistance to chemical sprays. In man, it has not been possible to induce *artificial immunity* by the use of vaccine.

Categories of Antimalarial Drug Action

1. **Causal prophylaxis.** A causal prophylactic agent prevents infection by its lethal effect on the plasmodia during their **preerythrocytic stages**. To be effective such therapy should be continued as long as the person remains in an **endemic malarial region**.

Primaquine has causal prophylactic properties, specially against falciparum malaria. **Pyrimethamine** exhibits marked prophylactic effect against falciparum malaria but is weakly active against vivax, malariae and ovale malaria.

2. **Suppressive treatment.** A suppressive drug causes inhibition of the **erythrocytic stage** of development of the parasite, so that the infected subject is kept free of the clinical manifestations of the disease. Three effective suppressives are **chloroquine, pyrimethamine** and **chloroguanide**. Continued suppressive therapy is essential to prevent clinical attacks of vivax malaria, and relapses are very likely to occur on stoppage of therapy.

3. **Clinical cure.** Drugs in this category interrupt **erythrocytic schizogony** of the plasmodia, and thereby terminate the clinical attack. Such agents are called **schizonticides**. The 4-aminoquinolines, **chloroquine** and **amodiaquine** are the drugs of choice. Both vivax and most falciparum malarias respond well. Certain strains of falciparum malaria may be resistant to all synthetic antimalarials. In such cases **quinine** is an effective schizonticide. A noteworthy point is that since *P. falciparum* displays no exoerythrocytic cycle, clinical cure provides radical cure.

4. **Radical cure.** This refers to the eradication of both **exoerythrocytic** and **erythrocytic** phases of the infection. As mentioned above, for falciparum infections clinical cure provides radical cure, and only proper treatment of the clinical attack is required. The drug that accomplishes radical cure in **vivax malaria**, is the 8-aminoquinoline derivative **primaquine**. Usually primaquine is used concurrently with chloroquine, and a high radical cure rate can be expected.

5. **Suppressive cure.** This refers to the complete elimination of the malarial parasite from the body by **continued suppressive therapy**. Continued administration of **pyrimethamine** for 10 weeks after leaving a malarious region is sufficient to cure vivax infections.

6. **Gametocytocidal therapy.** This category of drugs destroys the *sexual forms* of the malarial parasites in human blood. **Pyrimethamine** does not destory gametocytes, but prevents their development in the mosquitoes. **Primaquine** cradicates both vivax and falciparum gametocytes within 3 days.

Classification

Classification Based on Chemical Structure

(*i*) *Cinchona alkaloid:* Quinine.

(*ii*) *4-Aminoquinolines:* Chloroquine, Hydroxychloroquine, Amodiaquine.

(*iii*) *8-Aminoquinolines:* Primaquine.

(*iv*) *Acridine dyes:* Quinacrine.

(*v*) *Diaminopyrimidines:* Pyrimethamine, Trimethoprim.

(*vi*) *4-Quinoline-carbinolamines:* Mefloquine.

(*vii*) *Miscellaneous:* Quinghaosu, Sulphonamides, Sulphones, Tetracyclines, Lincomycins.

Cinchona Alkaloid

Quinine

Quinine is the chief alkaloid obtained from the bark of Cinchona tree. Its d-isomer, quinidine, is used as an antiarrhythmic **(Chap. 4.4)**. Commercially it is produced from natural sources.

Pharmacological actions. Since olden times quinine has been called a "general protoplasmic poison". It has little effect on the cardiac muscle in therapeutic doses, but in higher doses it induces a **quinidine-like** myocardial depression. On the skeletal muscle it has a **curare-like** effect. It induces **bronchoconstriction** which may be severe in asthmatic patients. It has an **oxytocic** effect, which becomes stronger as pregnancy advances. Quinine has a **local anaesthetic action**, and sensory nerves are first stimulated and then paralysed. It has a **local irritant action**, and on oral administration it induces nausea and vomiting. Vascular damage caused by quinine is the basis for its occasional use for **sclerosing varicose veins**. Its very bitter taste is the basis for its use as a **stomachic bitter** to increase gastric juice secretion. By its action on the CNS, quinine produces **analgesia** and mild **antipyresis**.

Antimalarial actions. Quinine has been used for **suppressive prophylaxis** and **clinical cure** in all types of malaria, since it is actively **schizonticidal**. It is also weakly gametocidal for **P. vivax** and **P. malariae**, but not for **P. falciparum**.

Mode of action. Quinine forms a hydrogen-bonded complex with double stranded DNA causing inhibition of protein synthesis, DNA replication, and transcription to RNA. It also interferes with the cellular oxidation of glucose, and depresses many enzyme actions.

Pharmacokinetics. On oral administration, quinine is rapidly and effectively absorbed, mainly from the upper small intestine. Peak levels develop within 1-3 hours, and about 70-80 percent is protein bound. It is degraded in the liver, and only 5-10 percent of the active drug is recoverable in the urine. Quinine is reabsorbed from the renal tubules, but in spite of this cumulation does not usually occur. Subcutaneous or IM administration are not advisable as it is painful, and sterile abscess formation may occur.

Therapeutic uses. The valid use of quinine today is in the treatment of **relapsing vivax malaria** in combination with primaquine; and in the treatment of *malignant tertian malaria* due to strains of *P. falciparum* resistant to chloroquine and cross-resistant to other antimalarials (see later).

Quinine is also used to relieve **nocturnal leg cramps** (night cramps), for which 200-300 mg orally may be administered before retiring. Quinine is *contraindicated* in haemoglobinuria and optic neuritis.

Toxicity. Adverse effects due to quinine include: (*i*) **Cinchonism**, which is a mild toxic state with flushed and wet skin, tinnitus, blurred vision, impaired hearing, dizziness, nausea, vomiting and diarrhoea. In severe cinchonism there may be urticarial skin rashes, deafness, diminished vision or even blindness (quinine amblyopia) due to ischaemic retinal vessels, abdominal pain and cardiac arrhythmias; (*ii*) **Local irritation** is responsible for gastrointestinal discomfort, painful sterile abscesses on SC or IM injection, and thrombophlebitis on IV injection of quinine; (*iii*) **Bone marrow depression** may occur, manifested as leucopenia, thrombocytopenic purpura, and agranulocytosis; (*iv*) **Black-water fever**, due to massive intravascular haemolysis, haemoglobinuria, azotaemia, intravascular sludging and coagulation, and fatal renal failure may be caused by quinine. Haemoglobinuria usually occurs in patients who also have G-6-PD deficiency in their erythrocytes; and (*v*) **Hypersensitivity reactions** including angioneurotic oedema may occur.

Preparations and dosage. Commonly used salts of quinine are: **quinine sulphate** for oral use; and **quinine dihydrochloride** for IV use. The usual oral dose of quinine sulphate (as base) is 650 mg every 8 hourly for 10 or 14 days for treatment of malaria.

CHLOROQUINE-RESISTANT MALARIA

Because of the high proportion of chloroquine-resistant *P. falciparum* infections in South-East Asia, it is recommended that all falciparum infections should be assumed to be resistant, and *one* of the following regimens should be used:

1. **Quinine sulphate** 650 mg, 3 times a day for 3 days, plus **pyrimethamine** 25 mg, 2 times a day for 3 days, plus **sulphadiazine** 500 mg, 4 times a day for 5 days; these three drugs are administered concurrently.
2. **Quinine sulphate** 650 mg, 3 times a day for 3 days, plus **Bactrim Double Strength** (160 mg trimethoprim, and 800 mg sulphamethoxazole), 2 tablets 2 times a day for 5 days, administered concurrently.
3. **Quinine sulphate** 650 mg, 3 times a day for 3 days, plus **tetracycline** 250 mg, 4 times a day for 10 days administered concurrently.
4. Following a course of quinine the patient should be given a single dose of 2 tablets of **Fansidar** (50 mg pyrimethamine, and 1 g sulfadoxine). Alternatively **sulfalene** 1 g may be given with **trimethoprim** 500 mg as a single dose.

For **cerebral malaria**, which occurs in 2 percent of patients suffering from **P. falciparum** malaria occurring in non-immune individuals, first **dexamethasone** 4-6 mg is administered parenterally, and repeated every 4-6 hours, together with **quinine dihydrochloride** 600 mg in 300 ml of 0.9 percent sodium chloride injection infused slowly over a period of at least one hour. This dose of IV quinine is repeated 6-8 hourly (maximum total daily dose, 1.8 g). After clinical response, the patient should be switched on to oral quinine sulphate.

For the **prophylaxis** of chloroquine-resistant falciparum malaria, one of the following regimens may be employed:

1. **Dapsone** 25 mg with *proguanil* 200 mg daily.
2. **Maloprim** (12.5 mg pyrimethamine, and 100 mg dapsone) weekly.
3. **Fansidar** (25 mg pyrimethamine and 0.5 g sulfadoxine) weekly.

Drug treatment must start 2 weeks before entering a malarial region, and continue for 4 weeks afterwards.

4-AMINOQUINOLINES

CHLOROQUINE

Out of the several 4-aminoquinolines, only chloroquine, hydroxychloroquine and amodiaquine and clinically used. **Chloroquine is the most widely used antimalarial.**

Pharmacological actions. Chloroquine was primarily developed as an antimalarial, but in addition it has several other pharmacological actions. Its **anti-inflammatory** properties are well known, and the drug (hydroxychloroquine) is used occasionally in the treatment of **rheumatoid arthritis, discoid lupus erythematosus,** and **systemic lupus erythematosus.** It is active against *extraintestinal* **amoebiasis.** On the cardiovascular system it has a **quinidine-like effect**.

Antimalarial actions. Chloroquine is an excellent *blood schizonticidal drug* for all 4 types of malaria. Chloroquine exerts insignificant activity against the exoerythrocytic stages of plasmodia. *Thus the drug is absolutely ineffective as a causal prophylactic agent.* It has no effect on the secondary tissue schizonts of relapsing malarias, and thus cannot cause a "radical" cure of malaria caused by *P. vivax*, *P. malariae* and *P. ovale*.

Mode of action. Chloroquine and its congeners block the enzymatic synthesis of DNA and RNA. These drugs intercalate with DNA, and prevent DNA from acting as a template for its own replication or transcription to RNA. *Intercalation* may partially explain chloroquine tissue binding, and its plasmodicidal (schizonticidal) action. Parasitized red cells selectively accumulate more chloroquine compared to non-parasitized red cells. Chloroquine has a number of other actions like **stabilization of lysosomes, some anti-inflammatory** and **antihistaminic** activity, and an **increase in the prostaglandin content** of the tissues. It binds to melanin which accounts for its deposition and adverse effects on the retina.

Regarding the mechanism of **chloroquine resistance,** parasites in the presence of increasing amounts of chloroquine over a prolonged period, become partially or completely resistant to the drug. This is probably due to an **impaired mechanism of drug transport across the cell wall of the parasite,** i.e., the concentration of chloroquine in the resistant schizonts never reaches optimal levels to arrest nucleic acid synthesis.

Pharmacokinetics. Chloroquine is rapidly and almost completely absorbed from the intestine, and maximum plasma levels are reached in 1-2 hours. It is rapidly removed from the plasma and concentrated in several tissues, specially **red** and **white blood cells, liver, spleen, skin, kidney, lung** and **retina**. In these tissues the concentration is 200-700 times the plasma concentration. Chloroquine is primarily degraded in the liver and some of the metabolites retain antimalarial activity. It is excreted slowly in the *urine*, and the excretion rate can be increased by acidification of the urine.

As a result of tissue binding, significant **chloroquine cumulation** may develop with long-term therapy, e.g., after prolonged treatment for a collagen disease, the drug may be detected in some tissues upto 5 years after stoppage of the drug.

Therapeutic uses. In human *vivax malaria, chloroquine has neither prophylactic nor radically curative value.* In *falciparum malaria radical cure is possible* as there is no secondary tissue stage.

1. **Acute malarial attacks.** For *P. vivax* infection the recommended total dose of chloroquine (base) is 1.5 g over a 3-day period (600 mg initial dose, 300 mg after 6 hours, and then 300 mg for 2 days). This regimen eliminates parasitaemia and symptoms within 24-72 hours. **Radical curative therapy** has to be administered to eliminate the exoerythrocytic schizonts in the liver. The *two* accepted regimens are:

   (*i*) **Primaquine** 15 mg (base) daily for 14 days. The initial dose should be in association with chloroquine.

   (*ii*) **Primaquine** 45 mg (base) weekly for 8 weeks.

2. **Suppression of malaria.** Chloroquine effectively suppresses all types of malaria, except the resistant strains of *P. falciparum*. For suppressive therapy chloroquine phosphate 500 mg is given on the same day each week, for at least 6 weeks after the last exposure in an endemic area.

3. **Hepatic amoebiasis.** Chloroquine can bring about rapid and complete clinical cure of hepatic amoebiasis **(Chap. 9.6)**.

4. Chloroquine is used as an anti-inflammatory agent in **rheumatoid arthritis** and **discoid lupus erythematosus**. It is also of some value in acute disseminated lupus erythematosus. Prolonged large dose therapy of chloroquine in these conditions is very likely to produce **chloroquine retinopathy**.

5. Chloroquine is the drug of first choice for infestation with **Clonorchis sinensis**, and the drug of second choice for **Fasciola hepatica** and **Paragonimus** infestations. It is also effective in **giardiasis**.

6. In large doses chloroquine is effective in treating *photoallergic reactions*.

Toxicity. When chloroquine is used for chemosuppression of malaria, there are essentially no toxic effects. Occasionally there may be *vertigo, malaise, diarrhoea, blurring of vision* and *urticaria*. After high doses *maculopapular eruptions, exfoliative lesions of the skin, alopecia and graying of the hair* may develop. *Hallucinations, agitation* and *peripheral neuropathies* may occur. Permanent *nerve deafness* in adults has followed high-dose chloroquine therapy. Rarely *psychotic episodes* may occur.

Ocular toxicity of a severe and permanent nature has been reported with high-dose chloroquine therapy. Chloroquine secreted in the tears, is absorbed by the corneal epithelium. The cornea at first becomes insensitive, and diffuse granules appear in the epithelium. These granules then aggregate and form **corneal deposits**. Retinal changes in the form of **chloroquine retinopathy** may occur, characterized by loss of central visual acuity, macular pigmentation and retinal artery constriction. Visual loss is not reversible.

Preparations. Chloroquine phosphate is administered by the oral route, preferably after meals. **Chloroquine hydrochloride** may be employed parenterally, as an IM injection. It has been estimated that chloroquine base 100 mg = chloroquine phosphate 160 mg = chloroquine hydrochloride 125 mg.

The other two 4-aminoquinolines, namely *hydroxychloroquine* (Plaquenil), and *amodiaquine* (Camoquin) are effective for the *prophylaxis* and *treatment of acute attacks* of malaria caused by *P. vivax, P. malariae, P. ovale* and susceptible strains of *P. falciparum*. These agents are similar to chloroquine in their pharmacology, clinical efficacy and adverse effects.

8-Aminoquinolines

Primaquine Phosphate

Primaquine is the most effective and least toxic of the 8-aminoquinolines, having the highest therapeutic index. In this group it is the only agent in current use.

Pharmacological actions. Apart from its antimalarial actions, primaquine does not exert significant pharmacological effects. Its toxicological actions are exerted mainly on the blood.

Antimalarial actions. The 8-aminoquinolines act on the **exoerythrocytic stages** of the plasmodia. Primaquine is highly active against the primary exoerythrocytic forms of **P. vivax** and **P. falciparum**. It also has an effect on the gametocytes; some are destroyed in the blood, and others are unable to mature in the gut of the mosquito. Primaquine therefore is a **"tissue schizonticide"**, and is the only agent available to produce **"radical cures"** in relapsing malarias. Its **gametocidal activity** also makes it the best agent available to check the transmission of malaria from man to mosquito.

Mode of action. In the body primaquine is biotransformed to a more active 5, 6-quinolinequinone metabolite. Primaquine *suppresses the mitochondrial functions of plasmodia in the exoerythrocytic stages*. It may also intercalate into DNA, but the effect on DNA replication and trancription is insignificant. Unfortunately, strains of *P. vivax* have now appeared in South-east Asia that are partially resistant to primaquine.

Pharmacokinetics. Primaquine is never given parenterally, as it can produce ECG changes, and a profound fall in blood pressure. Absorption from the intestine is complete and peak levels are reached in 4-6 hours. Effective clearance of tissue schizonts does not occur until it is biotransformed to its active metabolite (5,6-quinolinequinone). Highest tissue concentrations are found in the liver and lungs. Primaquine and its metabolites are almost completely cleared from the plasma within 24 hours, and only 1 percent of the drug is excreted unchanged in the urine.

Therapeutic uses. Primaquine is highly active against the **primary exoerythrocytic stages** of falciparum and vivax infections, and **secondary exoerythrocytic forms of relapsing malarias** (*P. vivax, P. malariae,* or *P. ovale*). Thus, it is used to induce "radical cures" of relapsing malarias. As it is highly active against the gametocytes of all 4 species of human malaria, it is **used to check transmission of malaria**.

Toxicity. Side effects often seen with larger doses include **nausea, headache, disturbances of visual accommodation, pruritus** and **abdominal cramps**. Severe reactions with high-dose therapy include *lucopenia* and *methaemoglobinaemia* presenting as cyanosis. G-6-PD deficiency in erythrocytes makes the individual sensitive in various degrees to primaquine-induced haemolysis. Such *primaquine sensitivity* must always be watched for in patients on primaquine therapy. The amount of haemolysis is dependent on **three** factors: (*i*) degree of G-6-PD deficiency; (*ii*) age of the red cell population; and (*iii*) the dose size. The haemolysis is dose dependent and self-limiting.

Preparations and dosage. Primaquine phosphate is available in tablet form containing 26.3 mg of the salt, equivalent to 15 mg base. Primaquine is always given orally. **Primaquine** 15 mg (base) daily for 14 days, combined with **standard chloroquine therapy** (1.5 g of base in 3 days) has proved to be the regimen of choice for "radical cure" of vivax malaria (also see **Table 9.5-1**).

Acridine Dyes

Quinacrine

Quinacrine is *obsolete* as an antimalarial drug, but is used in the management of **giardiasis**, as an alternative treatment for which **quinacrine hydrochloride** 100 mg every 8-hourly for 5-8 days is administered.

Diaminopyrimidines

Pyrimethamine was developed and used solely as an antimalarial; and **trimethoprim** was developed as an antibacterial agent **(Chap. 9.2),** and was found later to have antimalarial properties. Both these agents **selectively inhibit dihydrofolate reductase**, and thereby inhibit the conversion of dihydrofolic acid to tetrahydrofolic acid (folinic acid).

Pyrimethamine

Suppressive cure of some vivax infections may be achieved with pyrimethamine administration in prophylactic doses **(see Table 9.5-1)** for 10 weeks after leaving a malarious region. Plasmodial resistance develops rapidly.

Table 9.5-1. *Drugs used for the prophylaxis and treatment of malaria*

Drug	*Prophylaxis**	*Treatment**	*Comments*
Quinine sulphate	—	650 mg orally 8-hourly for 10-14 days	Given with primaquine it may produce a "radical cure" in vivax malaria. *Other uses:* Noctural leg cramps, myotonia congenita, torsion spasms
Quinine dihydrochloride	—	600 mg IV slowly, repeated 6-8 hours, maximum dose 1.8 g per day	Drug of choice for cerebral malaria, but oral therapy should be started as soon as possible
Quinine and urea hydrochloride	—	—	Sclerosing agent for varicose veins
Chloroquine** phosphate	300 mg orally weekly	600 mg initially, then 300 mg at 6, 24 and 48 hours (1.5 g in 3 days)	Drug of choice for treating acute attacks of malaria (clinical cure) *Other uses:* Amoebiasis, giardiasis, rheumatoid arthritis and other collagen diseases
Chloroquine hydrochloride	—	3 mg/kg initially IM or IV, then 3 mg/kg every 6 hours. Max. dose 900 mg/24 hours	Acute attacks of malaria
Hydroxychloro-quine sulphate	300 mg orally weekly	620 mg initially, then 310 mg at 6, 24 and 48 hours	Acute attacks of malaria. Also for giardiasis
Amodiaquine hydrochloride	400 mg orally weekly	600 mg initially, then 400 mg at 6, 24 and 48 hours	No therapeutic advantage over chloroquine
Primaquine phosphate	15 mg orally daily for 14 days after leaving endemic area, or 45 mg weekly for 8 weeks	15 mg orally daily for 14 days	Radical cure for vivax malaria expected in 95% cases treated with primaquine plus chloroquine. Watch for haemolysis and agranulocytosis
Chloroquine and primaquine phosphate	300 mg orally of chloroquine and 45 mg of *primaquine* weekly	—	—
Pyrimethamine	25 mg orally weekly	—	For prophylaxis and suppressive cure
Pyrimethamine sulfadoxine	50 mg *pyrimethamine* and 1 g *sulfadoxine* every other week for 6 weeks	—	For prophylaxis of chloroquine-resistant falciparum malaria
Mefloquine	250 mg weekly for 4 weeks, then 125 mg weekly	1250 mg once	Reserved for prophylaxis and treatment of chloroquine-resistant and multidrug-resistant falciparum malaria

* Slight variations in dosage may exist between this Table and the text.

** Doses of chloroquine are in terms of base: chloroquine base 100 mg = chloroquine phosphate 160 mg = chloroquine hydrochloride 125 mg = chloroquine sulphate 137 mg.

Mode of action. Both the **antifols** or **dihydrofolate reductase inhibitors**, namely **pyrimethamine** and **trimethoprim,** exert a plasmodicidal action by causing a deficiency of tetrahydrofolate, which results in the **inhibition of cell division** and **schizogony**. This interference with folic acid metabolism explains the marked synergy that occurs when any of these drugs is combined with sulphonamides or sulphones causing a **sequential blockade**.

Pharmacokinetics. Pyrimethamine is well absorbed on oral administration. It is eliminated slowly, and the plasma $t_{1/2}$ is about 4 days. Suppressive concentrations remain in the blood for 2 weeks. Its metabolites appear in urine, and it is also excreted in the milk of nursing mothers.

Therapeutic uses. Pyrimethamine administered alone is of little value in the treatment of the acute primary attack of malaria. In combination with a **short-acting sulphonamide** or a **sulphone**, pyrimethamine is useful for the treatment of acute attacks of chloroquine resistant **P. falciparum** malaria.

Pyrimethamine is effective as a **prophylactic** and **suppressive** agent, and has proved useful if given once weekly. Suppressive therapy for 10 weeks after leaving a malarious region provides a *suppressive cure*. The combination of **pyrimethamine** and **sulfadoxine** is useful for prophylaxis. Folinic acid should be given concurrently to avoid haematological toxicity. Pyrimethamine is also of some use in the treatment of **polycythaemia vera**.

Toxicity. With recommended dosage no significant toxic manifestations are seen. Excessive doses may produce a **megaloblastic anaemia** resembling that of folic acid deficiency, and is readily reversible on stoppage of the drug, or administration of *folinic acid*.

Preparations and dosage. Pyrimethamine (Daraprim) marketed in scored tablets containing 25 mg (base). The drug is also available in combination with *dapsone* (Maloprim), which is meant for use as a prophylactic, particularly in areas where multiresistant strains of plasmodia are known. Pyrimethamine in combination with *sulfadoxine* (Fansidar) is available for use in the treatment of multiresistant infections. *Sulfadoxine* is a *sulphonamide* with a long $t_{1/2}$ of 7 to 9 days. The dosages of various antimalarials employed in the prophylaxis and treatment of malaria are summarized in **Table 9.5-1.**

TRIMETHOPRIM

Trimethoprim is mainly used as an antibacterial agent in combination with sulphamethoxaxole (co-trimoxazole). It is used for the treatment of multiresistant strains of plasmodia. Another indication is for **prophylaxis of malaria resistant to pyrimethamine.** For its detailed pharmacology see **Chapter 9.2**.

4-QUINOLINE-CARBINOLAMINES

MEFLOQUINE

Mefloquine is a synthetic 4-quinoline methanol derivative chemically-related to quinine. It can only be given orally, as intense local irritation occurs on parenteral use. It is well absorbed, and peak plasma levels are reached in 2-12 hours. Plasma levels of 200-300 ng/ml achieve chemosuppression in *P. falciparum* infections. Its elimination $t_{1/2}$ varies from 13 to 33 days. The mode of action of mefloquine is unknown.

Mefloquine is used in the prophylaxis and treatment of **chloroquine-resistant** and **multidrug-resistant falciparum malaria**.

Mefloquine is available as 250 mg tablets. A single therapeutic dose (1000 to 1500 mg base) is recommended for multidrug resistant falciparum malaria. **Adverse effects** include vomiting, abdominal pain, disorientation, hallucinations, and depression.

MISCELLANEOUS

QUINGHAOSU (ARTEMISININ)

Quinghaosu (also Quing hao su), a sesquiterpene lactone, has undergone clinical evaluation in cases of resistant **P. falciparum** malaria in China. It is the antimalarial constituent extracted from the plant **Artemisia annua** *L* in 1972 at the Chinese Institute of Materia Medica. Quinghaosu is effective **against asexual blood forms** of the parasite. It lacks activity against tissue stages.

Studies have been reported on over 2000 malaria cases, of which over 1500 were **P. vivax** and over 500 **P. falciparum** infections. In addition, 143 cases of chloroquine-resistant **P. falciparum** and 141 cases of **Cerebral malaria** have been treated with Quinghaosu. The drug was administered in the form of tablets, oil suspension and water suspension. The toal *dose* administered per adult was: tablets 2.5-3.2 g; oil suspension 0.8-1.2 g, and water suspension 1.2 g. It has been concluded that Quinghaosu is a **schizonticide** with **very low toxicity**. It is effective against **P. vivax** and both chloroquine-sensitive and resistant strains of **P. falciparum**. The response is good. The rate of recrudescene (upto 30%) is further reduced when the drug is administered IM in the form of oil suspension.

ARTEMISININ DERIVATIVES

The two commonly used artimisinin derivatives are **artemether** and **artesunate**.

Artemether. It is a potent and rapidly acting **blood scizonticide**, and is highly efficacious in treating **chloroquine-resistant falciparum malaria**, and **complicated falciparum malaria** including **cerebral malaria**. *Adverse reactions* include nausea, vomiting, abdominal pain, bradycardia, first degree heart block, and transient liver dysfunction. *Dose:* A 5-day dose scheme is followed—80 mg (1 ampoule) IM bid on day 1, followed by 80 mg IM OD for the following 4 days.

Artesunate. It also is a potent **blood scizonticide** and is available for oral use in cases of **chloroquine-resistant falciparum malaria**. *Dose:* 100 mg bid orally on day 1, followed by 50 mg bid for 4 days. *Alternatively*, it can also be given parenterally in a dose of 120 mg IM/IV on day 1, followed by 60 mg IM/IV daily for 4 days. *Adverse reactions* Include rash, drug fever, transient first degree heart block, reversible reticulocytopenia, and transient elevation of transaminases.

Sulphonamides and sulphones. The sulphonamides are active against the asexual blood forms of human malarial parasites. *Sulfadoxine* (Fanzil) and *sulfalene* (Kelfizina) have been used for suppression of infection caused by sensitive strains of *P. falciparum*. The use of combinations of pyrimethamine with *dapsone* (Maloprim); and *pyrimethamine* with *sulfadoxine* (Fansidar); have already been discussed (see above).

Tetracyclines. Tetracycline in a dose of 250 mg 6-hourly for 7 days can clear asexual forms of *chloroquine-resistant falciparum infections*, but it has no effect against gametocytes. *Minocycline* may also be used.

Lincomycins. Clindamycin and lincomycin have proved to be effective against resistant *P. falciparum* infections.

Halofantrine

Halofantrine is a phenanthrene methanol derivative related to *quinine* and *mefloquine*. Its suggested mode of action is that it binds to *plasmpesin*, a haemoglobin degrading enzyme in the malarial parasites. Halofantrive is not suitable for the prophylaxis of malaria, or for the treatment of benign malarias. It is only licensed for the treatment of *uncomplicated chloraquine-nesistant malaria* and *vivax malaria* but is used rarely. *Dose*: Three doses of 500 mg orally administered at 6-hourly internals. *Adverse reactions* include nausea, vomiting intravascular haemolytis, and cardiac arrythmias.

Guidelines for use of Antimalarials

Many strains of *P. falciparum*, particularly in South-east Asia are now chloroquine-resistant. In the treatment of resistant strains adjunct therapy with the *sulphonamides*, *sulphones* or the *tetracyclines* is of value (see above).

Treatment of the acute attack. Chloroquine phosphate is the drug of choice. **Hydroxychloroquine** or **amodiaquine** may be used as alternatives, but are considered inferior. **Quinine sulphate** may be used in place of the 4-aminoquinolines if resistance is suspected. The above drugs will lead to radical cure in almost all cases of **P. falciparum** malaria. In **P. vivax**, **P. malariae** and **P. ovale** malarias (relapsing malarias), the addition of a second drug active against the exoerythrocytic phase (tissue phase) of the infection is necessary for radical cure, and *primaquine* is the drug of choice for this purpose.

Treatment of the serious attack. In the treatment of very serious attacks (including cerebral malaria), when heavily parasitized erythrocytes are clogging the arteries, rapid treatment is essential. Parenteral preparations like **chloroquine hydrochloride** (IM, IV), or **quinine dihydrochloride** (IV) may be used, depending on plasmodial resistance. Disseminated intravascular coagulation (defibrination syndrome) may develop rapidly in falciparum malaria, and **heparinization** is needed urgently. *Caution* should be exercised, as the use of heparin may lead to cerebral haemorrhage. **Dexamethasone** is of value to reduce cerebral oedema. **Low molecular weight dextran** given by IV infusion is helpful in reducing red cell "stickness", and improves blood flow through small and vital vessels. Inhalation of 5 percent carbon dioxide for 5-10 minutes every hour improves cerebral blood flow.

Currently, new antimalarial drugs are needed mainly to combat multiresistant strains of **P. falciparum**, and to provide "radical cure" for **P. vivax** malaria.

9.6 CHEMOTHERAPY OF AMOEBIASIS (AMOEBICIDAL DRUGS), AND OTHER PROTOZOAL INFECTIONS

Amoebiasis is an infection caused by *Entamoeba histolytica*. It is an invasion of the gastrointestinal mucosa, liver and other tissues by the *vegetative trophozite forms* of the protozoan. It is widespread in many parts of the world.

Amoebic Disease States

Millions of people harbour **E. histolytica** in their intestines, and manifest no clinical symptoms. These **asymptomatic carriers** of amoebae may spread the infection to other people who are not resistant to the infection. In addition, the carriers who have never had intestinal symptoms, may develop extraintestinal amoebiasis, usually marked by **amoebic liver abscesses.** Amoebiasis in man presents as: (*i*) asymptomatic intestinal infection; (*ii*) mild to moderate intestinal infection; (*iii*) severe intestinal infection (dysentery); (*iv*) amoebic liver abscess; and (*v*) amoeboma or extraintestinal infection.

Life Cycle of the Amoeba

Entamoeba histolytica has a two stage life cycle: (*i*) the **cystic** stage in which the organism can live for long periods, both outside the body and within the human intestine; and (ii) the **trophozoite** (vegetative) stage, which is motile, and occurs under suitable environmental conditions in the intestine (colon). It invades the intestinal mucosa forming multiple ulcers (amoebic dysentery). The trophozoites release a substance that digests mucosal cells, and finally they may find their way to the mesenteric veins to be carried to the liver by portal circulation **(amoebic hepatitis and liver abscess).** The latter is a common complication of invasive intestinal disease. Thus, the trophozoite form is responsible for both the **intestinal** and **extraintestinal** symptoms of amoebiasis.

The disease is transmitted when mature cysts are ingested. Each cyst develops into 8 trophozoites, usually in the ileocaecal region of the intestine. A colony is established in the caecum, which extends throughout the colon **(Fig. 9.6.1).** The trophozoites penetrate the mucosa causing ulceration, diarrhoea and abdominal pain.

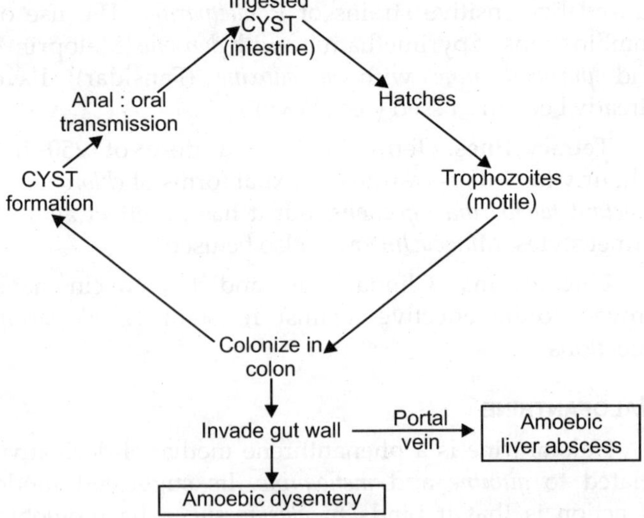

Fig. 9.6.1: Schematic drawing of the life cycle of *E. histolytica* (see text).

Amoebae may gain access to the liver via the portal vein, and cause tissue necrosis forming a bacteriologically `sterile' abscess. Liver is the major site of extraintestinal infection, although amoebic abscesses may also rarely occur in other organs.

Classification

The amoebicidal drugs may be classified according to their site of antiamoebic action as follows:

(*I*) **TISSUE AMOEBICIDES** (drugs primarily acting in the bowel wall, liver and other extraintestinal tissues):

(*a*) Dehydroemetine, Emetine.

(*b*) Chloroquine (mainly active in the liver).

(*II*) **LUMINAL AMOEBICIDES** (Primary action in bowel lumen):

(*a*) **Halogenated hydroxyquinolines.** Iodoquinol (diiodohydroxyquin), Clioquinol (iodochlorohydroxyquin).

(*b*) **Alkaloid.** Emetine

(c) **Amides.** Diloxanide furoate, Teclozan, Etofamide.

(*d*) **Antibiotics.** Tetracyclines, Paromomycin, Erythromycin.

(*III*) **TISSUE AND LUMINAL AMOEBICIDES**

(*a*) **Nitroimidazoles.** Metronidazole, Tinidazole.

The basis of drug therapy is to kill the trophozoite forms in the bowel, as cystic forms cease to be produced if all trophozoites are killed. Treatment of amoebiasis may require the **concomitant** or **sequential** use of several drugs **Table (9.6-1).** No drugs are remommended as safe or effective for chemoprophylaxis.

IPECACUANHA ALKALOIDS

Emetine Hydrochloride

Ipecacuanha is obtained from the dried rhizomes or roots of **Cephaelis ipecacuanha.** Its amoebicidal activity is due to its alalkoid content, mainly *emetine* and *cephaeline*. Emetine is seldom used today, and is of historical interest only.

Amoebicidal action. Emetine has a *direct* lethal action on *E. histolytica*. Emetine in therapeutic doses only acts against trophozoites. At very high doses it may be active against cysts. Emetine inhibits protein synthesis by interfering with attachment of t-RNA to the ribosomes.

In addition, emetine affects almost all tissues. Emetine given parenterally in toxic doses causes cellular damage in the **liver, kidneys, skeletal** and **cardiac muscle**. Cardiac conduction and contraction are depressed, which may lead to arial and ventricular arrhythmias. It also partially blocks transmission at the skeletal neuromuscular junction.

Therapeutic uses. Emetine has a **restricted** use due to its toxicity, and availability of safer drugs. However, it may be cautiously employed in the treatment of severe **amoebic dysentery, amoebic liver abscess, amoebomas** and **extraintestinal amoebiasis (Table 9.6-1).** It has been occassionally used in the treatment of infections with **Balantidium coli, Fasciola hepatica and Paragonimus westermani,** but safer drugs should be used first.

Toxicity. Emetine is **cumulative** in its action. Side effects develop in most patients, but are usually not severe if the dosage does not exceed 60 mg/day for more than 10 days. Hence, emetine must not be administered beyond 10 days.

Gastrointestinal toxicity includes *diarrhoea, nausea* and *vomiting*. Neuromuscular manifestations of toxicity are *muscle weakness; aching tenderness; stiffness of muscles*, specially those of the neck and extremities. It is *cardiotoxic* and the serious manifestations include **hypotension,**

Table 9.6-1 *Drug regimens for the treatment of amoebiasis*

	Pattern of infection	*Drugs of choice*	*Alternative drugs*
1.	Asymptomatic intestinal infection	Diloxanide furoate(1)*	Diiodohydroxyquin(2) *or* Metronidazole(3)
2.	Mild to moderate intestinal infection	Diloxanide(1) *or* Diiodohydroxyquni(2) *plus* A tetracycline(4) *followed by* Chloroquine(5)	Metronidazole(3) *plus* Diloxanide(1) *or* Paromomyin(6) *followed by* Chloroquine(5)
3.	Severe intestinal infection (dysentery)	Metronidazole(3) *plus* Diloxanide(1) *or* Diiodohydroxyquin(2)	A tetracycline(4) plus Diloxaninde(1) *or* Diiodohydroxyquin(2) *or* Dehydroemetine(6) *followed by* Chloroquine(5)
4.	Hepatic abscess	Metronidazole(3) *followed by* Diloxanide(1) *or* diiodohydroxyquin(2) *plus* Chloroquine(5)	Dehydroemetine(6) *plus* Chloroquine(5) *or* Emetine(7) *plus* Chloroquine(5)
5.	Amoeboma or extraintestinal infection	Same as for hepatic abscess, but excluding chloroquine	Same as for hepatic abscess, but excluding chloroquine

* The numerals in parentheses indicate the dosage mentioned below:

(1) Diloxaninde furoate, 500 mg tid for 10 days.

(2) Diiodohydroxyquin (iodoquinol) 650 mg tid for 21 days.

(3) Metronidazole, 750 mg tid for 10 days.

(4) A tetracycline, 250 mg qid for 10 days.

(5) Chloroquine phosphate, 1.0 g (500 mg base) daily for 2 days, then 0.5 g (250 mg base) daily for 2-3 weeks.

(6) Dehydroemetine, 1 mg/kg/day IM or SC for upto 5 days (max. dose 90 mg/day).

(7) Emetine, 1 mg/kg/day IM or SC for upto 5 days (max. dose 65 mg/day).

precordial pain, tachycardia, cardiac arrhythmias, cardiac dilatation, congestive heart failure and **death.**

Preparation and dosage. *Emetine hydrochloride* is administered by deep SC or IM injection. Intravenous use is contraindicated. A dose of 65 mg/day for upto 5 days is recommended.

4-AMINOQUINOLINES

Chloroquine Phosphate

Chloroquine is **amoebicidal**, and is useful in treating **hepatic amoebic infections**. The effectiveness of chloroquine in amoebiasis is almost certainly due to the **quinoline nucleus**. Chloroquine is actively amoebicidal for *extraintestinal* parasites, specially hepatic and pulmonary infection. Chloroquine should always be combined with an intestinal amoebicide **(Table 9.6-1).**

Adverse reactions and precautions to be observed with chloroquine therapy in amoebiasis are the same as detailed for use in malaria **(Chap. 9.5).** Chloroquine phosphate (in terms of salt) is usually given in a dose of 1 g/day orally for 2 days, followed by 0.5 g/day for 2 to 3 weeks to effectively treat hepatic amoebiasis.

Halogenated Hydroxyquinolines

The currently used members of this group are **iodoquinol** and **clioquinol**.

Amoebicidal actions. Iodoquinol (an iodinated 8-hydroxyquinoline) exerts a **direct amoebicidal action** against trophozoites and cysts of **E. histolytica** in the intestines. It is ineffective in extraintestinal amoebiasis.

Pharmacokinetics. On oral administration, a variable but significant portion of the ingested dose is absorbed. Iodoquinol may interfere with certain thyroid function tests by increasing protein-bound serum iodine levels, thereby leading to a decrease in I^{131} uptake.

Therapeutic uses. Iodoquinol is particularly useful for the treatment of **asymptomatic cysts passers** and for **mild to moderate intestinal infection**. Because of the uncertainty about the SMON syndrome, the use of **diloxanide furoate** is probably preferable (see later).

Iodoquinol and clioquinol (iodochlorohydroxyquin) are used to treat superficial fungal infections like **athlete's foot**, and **trichomonal vaginits** for which vaginal inserts are used topically.

Iodoquinol is occasionally used in the treatment of **giardiasis** (and *balantidal dysentery*). It has also been used for the treatment of **acrodermatitis enteropathica** in combination with hydrocortisone.

Toxicity. There is increasing evidence that certain 8-hydroxyquinolines can produce neurotoxicity. The main findings were optic atrophy, visual loss and peripheral neuropathy.

The most important neurologic toxic reaction, particularly due to iodochlorhy droxyquin (clioquinol) is **subacute myelooptic neuropathy** (SMON), the incidence of which has a peculiar geographic distribution. It is a **myelitis-like disease** which was first reported in Japan, where it occurred in epidemic form. SMON syndrome manifests as bilateral sensory disturbances, muscle weakness in legs, pyramidal signs, and sometimes blurred vision and blindness. **Diloxanide furoate** is preferable for the treatment of intestinal amoebiasis.

Other side effects caused by the 8-hydroxyquinolines include *generalized furunculosis, chills, fever, dermatitis, itching, goitre, diarrhoea* and *headache*.

Preparations. Iodoquinol is administered in a dose of 650 mg orally 3 times daily for 21 days. **Clioquinol** is available in the form of an ointment or powder for topical use as an antifungal agent.

AMIDES

Diloxanide Furoate

Diloxanide furoate was introduced in 1957, and has since been used extensively in the treatment of **intestinal amoebiasis.**

Diloxanide is **directly amoebicidal**, and primarily acts against the trophozoite forms of the parasite. It is highly effective in the therapy of **asymptomatic** or **mildly symptomatic cyst-passers**. It is less effective in acute amoebic dysentery.

Diloxanide furoate is **free from serious side effects.** Flatulence is common. Nausea, abdominal cramps, dry mouth, pruritus, urticaria and albuminuria may occur rarely. Since safety of diloxanide in pregnancy is not established, it should not be given to pregnant women, and also children under 2 years. The usual *dose* is 500 mg orally three times daily with meals for 10 days.

Etofamide (Kitnos) and **teclozan** (Falmonox) are newer amides used as intraluminal amoebicides.

Antibiotics

A number of antibiotics are of value in the treatment of intestinal amoebiasis, specially **paromomycin, tetracyclines** and **erythromycin**. Out of them only paromomycin is directly amoebicidal. The tetracyclines and erythromycin eradicate the intestinal bacterial flora which are essential for the proliferation of the trophozoites of *E. histolytica*.

Paromomycin Sulphate

Paromomycin is an aminoglycoside antibiotic **(Chap. 9.3).** It is **directly amoebicidal**, and can be used with other luminal amoebicides to treat mild to moderate intestinal amoebiasis. It also has significant antibacterial activity against the normal and pathogenic microorganisms in the gut. **Side effects** are limited to gastrointestinal upset and diarrhoea. Paromomycin is also effective in the treatment of **tapeworm infection**. The *usual dosage* is 25-35 mg/kg/day orally in three divided doses with meals for 5-10 days. Higer doses upto 66 mg/kg may be used, if needed.

NITROIMIDAZOLES

Metronidazole

Metronidazole is **amoebicidal** at both intestinal and extraintestinal sites, and is currently the preferred drug for all amoebic infections. Metronidazole can be used alone or with other drugs **(Table 9.6-1).** It was originally introduced as a **trichomonacidal** agent, effective orally (see later).

Toxicity. The incidence of adverse effects is low, and serious reactions rarely occur. Frequent reactions are nausea and diarrhoea. Other side effects include *unpleasant taste, furry tongue, glossitis, stomatitis, anorexia, abdominal cramps* and *darkening in the colour of urine.*

When taken with alcoholic beverages, metronidazole may produce a **disulfiram-type reaction** (abdominal distress, nausea, vomiting and headache) caused by accumulation of acetaldehyde in the body.

Superinfection with **Candida albicans** may develop. Metronidazole may cause temporary leucopenia. Agranulocytosis has not been reported. However, as it is a nitroimidazole, its potential for depressing the bone marrow must be kept in mind.

Therapeutic uses. Metronidazole is employed in the treatment of **amoebic dysentery, amoebic liver abscess, amoeboma** and **extraintestinal amoebiasis**. The usual *dose* is 750 mg orally three times daily for 5-10 days. It may be combined with another luminal amoebicide with advantage. A course of metronidazole may be repeated after 2 weeks, if necessary. Metronidazole is also effective against **giardiasis** and **dracunculiasis**, and **anaerobic** bacteria, specially **B. fragilis.**

Tinidazole is a newer nitroimidazole, and is effectively used in the treatment of **amoebiasis, trichomoniasis** and **giardiasis** *Dose*: 2 g single daily dose for 3 days in intestinal amoebiasis.

Guidelines for Amoebicidal Therapy

Success of drug therapy depends upon concomitant or sequential treatment with at least two drug **(Table 9.6-1).** *Metronidazole* (see above) and *niridazole* **(Chap. 9.7)** may ultimately prove effective against both intestinal and extraintestinal infection by the parasite. The ideal treatment for various phases of the disease is summarized below:

1. **Acute amoebic dysentery.** The drug of choice is *metronidazole*, with or without an antibiotic. If this regimen fails, *emetine* is given a trial, with sequential adjunct therapy with either iodoquinol or the antibiotics **(Table 9.6-2).**
2. **Chronic amoebic colitis.** It is best treated with a 3-week course of *diloxanide* plus *chloroquine.* Several courses may be required.
3. **Asymptomatic carrier state.** The asymptomatic carrier (cyst-passer) is best treated with *diloxanide furoate.* Several courses of treatment may be required. A course of *chloroquine* may be given to eradicate any asymptomatic extraintestinal infection.
4. **Extraintestinal amoebiasis.** *Chloroquine* and *emetine* are the drugs of choice for either acute or chronic extraintestinal infection. Open surgical drainage or needle aspiration of abscesses may be required. *Erythromycin* has been recommended as an adjunct drug in the treatment of hepatic amoebiasis since it is selectively concentrated in the liver. *Metronidazole* is also recommended as it possesses activity against both intestinal and extraintestinal infection.

Table 9.6.2 *Site of action of major antiamoebic drugs*

Drug	*Effective against*	
	Intestinal disease	*Hepatic abscess*
Emetine	+	+
Metronidazole	+	+
Iodoquinol	+	–
Diloxanide furoate	+	–
Antibiotics	+	–
Chloroquine	–	+

+ = effective; – = ineffective

Other Protozoal Infections

Apart from malaria and amoebiasis, other important protozoal infections in man are **leishmaniasis, trypanosomiasis, trichomoniasis, giardiasis** and **toxoplasmosis**. Their drug therapy is briefly discussed hereunder.

Leishmaniasis

Leishmaniasis is a term applied to several diseases caused by protozoa of the genus **Leishmania:** kala-azar is caused by **L. donovani**; oriental sore by **L. tropica**; and mucocutaneous leishmaniasis by **L. braziliensis**. In all instances, a **Phlebotomus** sandfly vector is involved in the life cycle of the protozoan. Control of leishmaniasis consists of measures to treat the disease itself, and measures against the vector. A brief mention of the available drugs follows.

Trivalent Antimonials

Tartar emetic (antimony potassium tartrate) has been replaced by pentavalent antimonials in the treatment of leishmaniasis. The trivalent antimonials are of some use in schistosomiasis, chlonorchiasis and filariasis **(Chap. 9.7).**

Pentavalent Antimonials

The pentavalent antimonials are more active, less toxic and more parasticidal in leishmaniasis, but more expensive than the trivalent compounds. **Stibamine glucoside** (Neostam) is a 4 percent solution injected IV in doses of 2.2 mg/kg. **Ethylstibamine (Neostibosan)** is given IV or IM in doses of 200-300 mg every second day. **Sodium stibogluconate** (Pentostam) is given IV or IM in daily doses of 600 mg for 6-10 days.

Adverse effects include nausea, vomiting, diarrhoea, headache, arthralgia, bradycardia and respiratory arrest. Caution should be observed in patients with hepatic and renal disease.

Aromatic Diamidines

There are several compounds in this group, but only **hydroxystilbamidine isethionate,** and **pentamidine isethionate** are used clinically. These drugs are injected IM or IV and this may be followed by rapid development of headache, palpitation, dyspnoea, tachycardia, diarrhoea and abdominal pain. These symptoms are partly due to histamine release.

These drugs are inferior to the pentavalent antimonials in the treatment of leishmaniasis, but may be used in antimony resistant cases. **Hydroxystilbamidine** is sometimes used to treat North American blastomycosis, and **pentamidine** offers dramatic benefit in some cases of **Pneumocystis carinii** pneumonia.

For the treatment of **kala-azar, stibamine glucoside, ethylstibamine** and **sodium stibogluconate** are more effective, than the trivalent antimonials. Pentamidine and hydroxystilbamidine are very effective in cases that do not respond to antimony compounds.

For the treatment of **oriental sore** local measures are more important than antimony compounds. Local intralesion injection of **quinacrine**, or cautery, X-ray irradiation and carbon dioxide snow are of more value. Pentavalent arsenicals or tartar emetic may be used for widespread lesions.

For **mucocutaneous leishmaniasis** intravenous sodium antimony gluconate, trivalent antimonials, amphotericin B, chloroquine, cycloguanil pamoate and aromatic diamidines have been used. **Metronidazole** 250 mg twice daily orally for 15 days has produced good results in Mexican cutaneous leishmaniasis.

Trypanosomiasis

Trypanosomiasis is a term applied to diseases caused by protozoa of the genus *Trypanosoma*. African sleeping sickness is caused by *T. gambiense* and *T. rhodesiense*, and South American sleeping sickness (Chaga's disease) by *T. cruzi*. Following is a brief mention of the drugs used.

Aromatic Diamidines

Pentamidine, stilbamidine and **propamidine** are sufficiently potent as trypanosomicides, with toxicities low enough to be used in the treatment of trypanosomiasis (sleeping sickness). **Pentamidine** is now the drug of choice for treatment and prevention of African sleeping sickness. It clears the organisms from the blood and lymph nodes, but does not, effectively reach the CNS. Thus, other drugs like **suramin or melarsoprol** must be used. **Stilbamidine** and **propamidine** can be used in early trypanosomiasis.

Suramin

Suramin sodium, a benzidine derivative is the drug of choice for the **early stages of trypanosomiasis**. It has also been used in the prophylaxis of trypanosomiasis. Synergistic activity is demonstrable between it and the pentavalent arsenicals or the aromatic diamidines. Suramin is administered intravenously, and adverse reactions are serious. Hypotension and loss of consciousness may follow rapid IV injections.

Arsenicals

Tryparsamide. It is a pentavalent arsenical, and is highly effective in some cases of **trypanosomiasis**, specially if combined with suramin. It is given IV and passes readily into the CSF, a property which is of extreme value in treating trypanosomiasis in its late stages. **Adverse reactions** include ocular symptoms like hemeralopia and transient amblyopia which may progress to total blindness. Hepatitis, skin rashes and gastrointestinal upset are common.

Melarsoprol (Mel B). It is an organic arsenical, and a dimercaprol dervative of melarsen oxide. It probably acts by -SH group inhibition. Small but therapeutically effective trypanocidal CSF levels develop on conventional therapy. Melarsoprol has now replaced tryparsamide as the drug of choice for the treatment of African sleeping sickness (*T. gambiense*). It is given by slow IV infusion in propylene glycol.

Melarsonyl (Mel W). It is a water soluble derivative of Mel B (Melarsoprol), and it resembles the latter in its action. It is administered by IM injection.

The object of treatment in trypanosomiasis is to clear the blood, tissues, and CSF of the parasites. In **T. gambiense** infection either suramin and tryparsamide, or pentamidine and tryparsamide are effective. Early infection with **T. cruzi** may respond to the 8-aminoquinoline antimalarials. For prophylaxis of trypanosomiasis, a single IM injection of pentamidine 250 mg affords adequate protection for 4-6 months. **Nifurtimox** (Lampit), a nitrofuran has been introduced for the treatment of infection by *T. cruzi* (Chaga's disease).

Trichomoniasis

Trichomoniasis is a venereal disease caused by the protozoan **Trichomonas vaginalis**. Out of the many drugs available for topical treatment of the disease, the **pentavalent arsenicals, the 8-hydroxyquinolines, hydrogen peroxide, silver nitrate** and **furazolidone** are popular. These drugs eradicate the infection in many women suffering from Trichomonas vaginalis vaginitis, but often fail when the infection is chronic. **Metronidazole,** a trichomonacidal drug in males and females, marks an important step forward in the drug therapy, since the infection in males which cannot be treated by topical preparations, is often a source of reinfection in the female by sexual contact. **Tinidazole** is the drug of choice for single dose therapy of trichomoniasis.

Giardiasis

Giardiasis (lambliasis) is caused by **Giardia lamblia**, a protozoan which may occur in the gastrointestinal tract. **Quinacrine, iodoquinol, chloroquine** and **hydroxychloroquine** are used. The drug of choice is either **metronidazole** or **tinidazole.**

Balantidiasis

Balantidiasis (ciliate dysentery) is caused by **Balantidium coli**. The tetracyclines, pentavalent arsenicals, diiodohydroxyquin, and emetiine have been used with varying success **(Table 9.6-3).** Probably the **tetracyclines,** specially **oxytetracycline** and **chlortetracycline** are the agents of choice, and are given in doses of 500 mg orally 3 times daily for 10 days.

Toxoplasmosis

Toxoplasmosis is caused by congenital or acquired infection with the protozoan **Toxoplasma gondii**. The treatment of choice is the combination of **sulphadiazine** and **pyrimethamine**, which seem to have synergistic effects. Folinic acid should be administered to prevent the development of megaloblastic anaemia as a result of pyrimethamine administration. **Co-trimoxazole** also is an effective drug. **Glucocorticosteroids** may also be added to the regimen.

Table 9.6-3 *Drugs of choice and alternative drugs for some protozoal infection in man*

Infecting organism	*Drug of choice*	*Alternative drug*
Leishmaniasis		
Leishmania donovani (Kala-azar)	Sodium stibogluconate	Pentamidine
L. topica (Oriental sore)	Sodium stibogluconate	—
L. braziliensis (mucocutaneous leishmaniasis)	Sodium stibogluconate	Amphotericin B, Cycloguanil pamoate
Trypanosomiasis		
Trypanosoma gambiense	Pentamidine	Suramin
T. rhodesiense	Suramin	Pentamidine
T. cruzi (Chaga's disease)	Nifurtimox	Primaquine
Trichomoniasis		
Trichomonas vaginalis	Metronidazole	Topical drugs
Giardiasis		
Giardia lamblia	Quinacrine	Metronidazole
Balantidiasis		
Balantidium coli	Oxytetracycline	Iodoquinol
Toxoplasmosis		
Toxoplasma gondii	Pyrimethamine + trisulfapyrimidines	—

9.7 CHEMOTHERAPY OF HELMINTHIASIS (ANTHELMINTIC DRUGS)

Anthelmintics are drugs used to eradicate parasitic worms (known as helminths) from the human body. It has been estimated that about half of the world's population suffers from helminthiasis, and the number is on the increase. It is not only limited to tropical and subtropical countries, but is also endemic in many regions because of poor sanitation, poor family hygiene, malnutrition, and crowded living conditions.

HELMINTHS INFECTING MAN

Three categories of worms, namely **nematodes** (roundworms), **cestodes** (tapeworms), and **trematodes** (flukes) parasitize man. Infection with more than one type of worm is common. Most anthelmintics in use today are active against *specific* parasites, and some are toxic. Hence, the worms must be identified before treatment is started, usually by finding the **ova**, **parasite**, or **larvae** in the faeces, urine, blood, sputum or tissues of the host.

The anthelmintics used against intestinal helminths (vermifuges), **kill** or **sterilize** the worms, or **paralyse** them so that they lose hold on the intestinal mucosa and are expelled via the faeces. When treating intestinal parasitism, a 12-24 hours fast or light meals, prior to drug administration are advisable.

DRUGS OF CHOICE

The helminths that commonly infect man belong to two different phyla: (*i*) the **Nemathelminthes** composed of the class **Nematoda**, or the roundworms; (*ii*) the **Platyhelminthes** or flatworms which comprise the class **Cestoda** (tapeworms), and the class **Trematoda** (flukes). The drugs of choice and alternative drugs used in the treatment of helminthic infections are listed in **Table 9.7-1.**

ANTHELMINTICS

ALBENDAZOLE

Albendazole is a broad-spectrum oral anthelmintic used for **oxyuriasis, ascariasis, trichuriasis, strongyloidiasis**, and infection with **both hookworm species**. It is also the drug of choice for **hydatid disease**, and alternative drug for **cysticercosis**.

Mode of action. Albendazole blocks glucose uptake by larval and adult stages of susceptible parasites, depleting their glycogen stores, and decreasing formation of ATP. This results in immobilization of the parasite and its death. It has a **larvicidal** effect in necatoriasis, and **ovicidal** effect in ascariasis, ancylostomiasis, and trichuriasis. Albendazole does not have other pharmacologic effects in man in therapeutic doses.

THERAPEUTIC USES AND DOSAGE

1. **Ascariasis, trichuriasis, hookworm and pinworm infections**. In adults and children over 2 years of age a **single** dose of 400 mg orally is administered with a meal. In **pinworm** infection the doses should be repeated in 2 weeks. This achieves 100 percent cure rate in pinworm infection. In **heavy ascariasis, necatoriasis and trichuriasis** a dose of 400 mg/day for 2-3 days may be given.
2. **Strongyloidiasis.** A dose of 400 mg twice daily for 3-7 days, and repeated after one week may be tried.
3. **Hydatid disease.** A dose of 800 mg/day for 30 days is given. This course is repeated 2 or 3 times, with 2 weeks intervals between courses.
4. **Neurocysticercosis.** The treatment schedule is 15 mg/kg/day for 30 days.

Adverse reactions. Headache, diarrhoea, epigastric distress, dizziness, and insomnia have been reported. When used for 1-3 days, albendazole is almost free of adverse effects. In the 3-month treatment for hydatid disease, alopecia, pruritus, leucopenia and eosinophilia has been reported.

ANTIMONY COMPOUNDS

The trivalent antimonials like antimony potassium tartrate (tartar emetic) were used for many years as main drugs for **schistosomiasis** (bilharziasis), but they are no longer used today because of their toxicity, and difficulty in administration.

BITHIONOL

Bithionol is a phenolic derivative, and its possible mode of action is through uncoupling of oxidative phosphorylation. It is active against flukes, including **F. hepatica** (sheep liver fluke) and **P. westermani** (lung fluke). On ingestion, it reaches peak blood levels in 4-8 hours. Absorption is mainly through the intestines. Excretion is via the kidneys.

Therapeutic uses and dosage. Bithionol is the drug of choice for the treatment of **fascioliasis**, and an alternative drug for **pulmonary paragonimiasis**. The dosage of bithionol is 30-50 mg/kg in 2 or 3 divided doses, given orally after meals on alternate days for 10-15 doses.

Adverse reactions occur in upto 40 percent of patients, and occacionally their severity requires interruption of therapy. *Diarrhoea* and *abdominal cramps* are most common. Anorexia, vomiting, dizziness, headache, and pruritic urticarial rashes may occur. Hypersensitivity reactions are rare.

Table 9.7-1 *Drugs for the treatment of helminthic infections*

Infecting Helminth	*Drugs of Choice*	*Alternative Drugs*
NEMATODES (Roundworms)		
Ascaris lumbricoides (roundworm)	Pyrantel pamoate, Mebendazole	Piperazine, Mebendazole, Albendazole
Enterobius (Oxyuris) vermicularis (pinworm)	Pyrantel pamoate, Mebendazole	Albendazole
Trichuris trichuria (whipworm)	Mebendazole	Pyrantel pamoate, Albendazole
Strongyloides stercoralis (threadworm)	Thiabendazole	Mebendazole, Albendazole Ivermectin
Ancylostoma duodenale (hookworm)	Pyrantel pamoate, Mebendazole	Albendazole Tetachloroethylene
Necator americanus (hookworm)	Pyrantel pamoate, Mebendazole	As above
Trichinella spiralis (port roundworm)	Thiabendazole, Mebendazole, plus corticosteroids for severe infection	Albendazole, plus corticosteroids for severe infection
Trychostrongylus orientalis	Pyrantel pamoate	Mebendazole
Filarial worms		
Wuchereria bancrofti, W. malayi *Loa loa*	Diethylcarbamazine	None
Tropical eosinophilia *Dracunculus medinensis* (guinea worm)	Metronidazole	Thiabendazole, Mebendazole
Onichocerca volvulus	Ivermectin	Diethylcarbamazine
CESTODES (Tapeworms)		
Taenia saginate (beef tapeworm)	Niclosamide, Praziquantel	None
Diphyllobothrium Latum (fish tapeworm)	Niclosamide, Praziquantel	None
Hymenolepis nana (dwarf tapeworm)	Praziquantel	Niclosamide
Taenia solium (pork tapeworm)	Niclosamide	Praziquantel
Taenia solium (cysticercosis)	Praziquantel	Albendazole
Echinococcus granulosus (Hydatid disease)	Albendazole	Mebendazole
Echinococcus multilocularis (Alveolar hydatid (disease)	Albendazole	Mebendazole
TREMATODES (Flukes) **Blood flukes**		
Schistosoma haematobium (bilharziasis)	Praziquantel	Mebendazole

Table 9.7-1 Contd...

Infecting Helminth	*Drugs of Choice*	*Alternative Drugs*
Schistosoma mansoni	Praziquantel	Oxamniquine
Schistosoma japonicum	Praziquantel	Niridazole
Liver flukes		
Clonorchis sinensis	Praziquantel	Mebendazole, Albendazole, Chloroquine,
Fasciola hepatica	Bithionol	Emetine, Dehydroemetine, Praziquantel
Lung fluke		
Paragominus westermani	Praziquantel	Bithionol, Cloroquine
Intestinal fluke		
Fasciolepsis buski	Praziquantel, Niclosamide	Tetrachloroethylene, Dichlorophen

DIETHYLCARBAMAZINE CITRATE

Diethylcarbamazine is a piperazine derivative, and is the **drug of choice** for the treatment of filariasis. It causes rapid disappearance of microfilariae of **Wuchereia bancrofti, W. malayi** and **Loa loa** from the blood of man. It possibly sensitizes the microfilariae, and they become susceptible to phagocytosis by the fixed macrophages of the reticuloendothelial system. Diethylcarbamazine also kills adult worms of **W. bancrofti, W. malayi** and **Loa loa.** The mechanism of filaricidal action of diethylcarbamazine is unknown.

Diethylcarbamazine is rapidly absorbed from the gut and peak blood levels are reached within 4 hours. Renal excretion is complete within 48 hours.

Therapeutic uses and dosage. Diethylcarbamazine is used to treat infections with **W. bancrofti, W. malayi, Loa loa** and **O. volvulus.** In the first three radical cure can be achieved by a single or multiple courses of treatment. In the treatment of **tropical eosinophilia** it causes a rapid disappearance of symptoms in a dose of 2 mg/kg tid for 7 days. For treatment of **W. bancrofti** and **W. malayi** infections the usual dose is 2 mg/kg three times daily after meals for 7 days, and for radical cure this dose is continued for 10 to 30 days. For **Loa loa** infection the dose is 4 mg/kg thrice daily after meals for 10 days.

Adverse effects directly due to diethylcarbamazine are mild and include *dizziness, headache, weakness, nausea* and vomiting. Allergic reactions caused by the substances released on destruction of microfilariae, are usually mild in patients with *wuchereiasis*, but may be serious in *loiasis* and *onchocerciasis*, and may include severe pedal oedema, dermatitis, fever, and lymphadenitis.

EMETINE HYDROCHLORIDE

Emetine is an alternative drug for the treatment of **Fasciola hepatica** infection. It is administered by deep subcutaneous injection in doses of 1 mg/kg (maximum 65 mg daily) for 10 days. Its detailed pharmacology is discussed in **Chapter 9.6.**

IVERMECTIN

Ivermectin is a semisynthetic macrocyclic lactone. It is derived form **Streptomyces avermitilis**, a soil actinomycetes. It is the **drug of choice for onchocerciasis.** It acts by increasing the release and binding of gamma-aminobutyric acid (GABA), thereby producing paralysis. It also appears to be highly effective in *strongyloidiasis, ascariasis, trichuriasis*, and *enterobiasis*. It is less effective against hookworms.

For **onchocerciasis** a single oral dose of ivermectin (200 mg/kg) may be as effective as diethylcarbamazine, or more effective in reducing the number of microfilariae. Precisely the dose is by body weight: 3 mg for 15-25 kg body weight; 6 mg for 26-44 kg; 9 mg for 45-64 kg; and 15 mg for 65 kg or more. The dosage ranges between 120-230 mcg/kg.

Adverse reactions are minimal, with pruritus, fever, tender lymph nodes, muscle pain and peripheral oedema. Side effects are considerably less than those observed with diethylcarbamazine use.

MEBENDAZOLE

Mebendazole is the primary drug of choice in **enterobiasis** and **trichuriasis**. Single doses have produced cure rates of 90-100 percent in the former, and after multiple doses, cure rates as high as 94 percent have been reported in the latter. It is particularly useful in the treatment of mixed infections with **whipworms** (trichuriasis), **roundworms** (ascariasis), **hookworms** (ancylostomiasis) and **pinworms** (enterobiasis). *It does not produce satisfactory cures in strongyloidiasis.*

Mode of action. Mebendazole irreversibly blocks the uptake of exogenous glucose by nematodes, leading to glycogen depletion and reduced generation of ATP required for surfival. Due to this the parasites die, or are slowly immobilized and cleared from the gut gradually. It does not affect blood glucose levels in humans. Mebendazole is poorly absorbed from the gut, and peak plasma levels are reached in 2 to 4 hours. The drug is excreted in the urine unchanged or as its metabolites.

Therapeutic uses. Clinically mebendazole is a very useful anthelmintic, and is used for *many conditions enumerated above*. It is *remarkably free of side effects* even in debilitated patients. Mild nausea, vomiting, diarrhoea and abdominal discomfort have been reported infrequently. In children with heavy *Ascaris* infection, abdominal cramps may occur.

Dosage. Mebendazole is available as 100 mg chewable tablets. For the treatment of *ascariasis, trichuriasis* and *hookworm* infections, 100 mg twice daily for 3 days is given. In severe trichuriasis, a longer course of upto 6 days, or a repeat course is necessary. No pre-treatment or post-treatment purging is required. In **strongyloidiasis** the cure rates of 40 to 75 percent are obtained with the standard 3-day duration therapy. This drug is *contraindicated* in pregnant women, and it should be used with caution in children under the age of 2 years.

METRIPHONATE

This is an organophosphorus cholinesterase inhibitor which is effective in the treatment of **Schistosoma haematobium** infections. The cure rate is 90 to 95 percent. It has an added advantage of being cheap in comparison to other anti-schistosomal remedies. The **mode of action** of metrifonate is unknown, but it is assumed that its metabolite dichlorvos acts on both *immature* and *mature* stages of *S. haematobium* by cholinesterase inhibition.

Metrifonate is recommended only for the treatment of **Schistosoma haematobium** infection. Administration of metrifonate shifts the adult worms form the bladder venous plexuses to small arterioles of the lungs, where they are trapped and then die. Metrifonate is available as 100 mg tablets, and the dose is 5 to 15 mg/kg orally 3 times at intervals of 2 weeks. Most **side effects are minimal** and include mild abdominal pain, diarrhoea, weakness, headache, and vertigo.

NICLOSAMIDE

Niclosamide, introduced in 1960, is the *drug of choice* for treating tapeworm infections. It is highly effective, with cure rates greater than 90 percent for *Tinea saginata*, 86 percent for *T. solium*, 97 percent for *Diphyllobothrum latum*, and 80 percent for *Hymenolepis nana*. This agent is conveniently administered orally, and the concomitant use of a laxative is not required, except for *T. solium*. Niclosamide may destroy *T. solium* segments, thereby releasing viable eggs. The laxative administered 1 to 2 hours after the anthelmintic, avoids the possibility of cysticercosis. *No serious side effects have been reported*. This drug should be taken on an empty stomach, and *tablets should be thoroughly chewed*.

Niclosamide is available as 0.5 g chewable tablets. The adult dose is 4 tablets (2g). Pre-and post-treatment purges are not necessary, unless the patient is chronically constipated.

NIRIDAZOLE

Niridazole is the alternative drug for the treatment of **Schistosoma japonicum** infections. Niridazole has some anti-inflammatory properties, and this makes it effective in the treatment and extraction of **Dracunculus medinesis** (guinea worm). Niridazole is also effective against both **intestinal** and **extraintestinal amoebiasis**.

Adverse reactions include gastrointestinal disturbances, vomiting and diarrhoea. Headache, dizziness, and occasionally ECG changes, neuropsychiatric disturbances, insomnia, hallucinations and seizures may develop. Haemolytic anaemia may occur in patients of G-6-PD deficiency. The **usual dose** is 25 mg/kg body weight daily orally in two divided doses, for 5-7 days in schistosomiasis and for 7 to 10 days in dracunculiasis.

OXAMNIQUINE

Oxamniqune is active against both the mature and immature stages of **S. mansoni**. Although the exact mode of action is not known, in experimental animals the drug stops oviposition. In man it induces a shift of the worm from the mesentery to the liver. In the liver the males preferentially concentrate the drug and die. It is ineffective against **S. haematobium** and **S. japonicum**. The **side effects** are dizziness and somnolence, eosinophilia, transient pulmonary infiltration, hallucinations and seizures have been seen. Use of this compound should be avoided in pregnant women. Reddish orange discolouration of the urine may follow treatment. It is usually administered as a **single dose** of 15 mg/kg orally.

PIPERAZINE

Piperazine salts have been drugs of choice earlier in the treatment of **Ascaris** infection. They are not useful in the treatment of ancylostomiasis, trichuriasis, stronglyloidiasis or oxyuriasis infection. **Currently piperazine is an alternative drug for the treatment of ascariasis.** A single dose cures almost 70 percent of infected individuals, and two doses given on successive days increase the cure rate between 90 and 100 percent. The main effect of piperazine on *Ascaris* is to cause **flaccid paralysis** of the worm, which is expelled by peristalsis. It blocks the response of Ascaris muscle to acetylcholine. After therapy Ascaris worms are passed out paralysed and alive, usually 1 to 3 days after treatment. A **laxative** is needed to expel the worms from the intestines.

Piperazine salts are available as tablets, each containing 500 mg, and as syrups and suspensions containing 100 mg/ml. calculated as hexahydrate. All preparations are equally effective. **Piperazine citrate** and **piperazine phosphate** are official preparations. Piperazine preparations are given orally, and it is necessary to supplement treatment with cathartics. In *ascariasis* the usual dose is 3.5 g once daily for 2 consecutive days.

Adverse reactions are uncommon, but may include nausea, vomiting, diarrhoea and allergic reactions. With larger doses muscular incoordination, weakness, vertigo, speech difficulty, confusion and *myoclonic contractions* have been reported. Piperazine may exacerbate *epileptic seizures* in predisposed patients, and for this reason it is contraindicated in epileptic patients.

Praziquantel

Praziquantel is a pyrazinoisoquinoline derivative, and is effective against **schistosome infections** of all species, and most other **trematode** and **cestode infections**. It produces tetanic-like contractions within the muscle system of the fluke, possibly by altering the influx of calcium ions.

Anthelmintic action. Praziquantel is the most effective of the drugs used in the treatment of **schistosomiasis**. It is active against all three major species (*S. haematobium, S. mansoni, S. japonicum*) of schistosomes. It is *not* effective against *Fasciola hepatica* or in hydatid disease. In addition, it is also active against other flukes, and the tapeworms **(D. latum, H. nana, T. saginata, and T. solium)**. Praziquantel is the first drug to be useful in the treatment of **neurocysticercosis**.

Praziquantel is readily absorbed on oral administration, and maximal plasma concentrations occur in 1-2 hours; it has a plasma half-life of 1.5 hours; and is excreted by the kidneys.

Therapeutic uses and dosage. Praziquantel is an extremely active, well tolerated, **broad-spectrum anthelmintic**, and is the drug of choice for treating **schistosomiasis**. Both **S. mansoni** and **S. haematobium** infections respond well to a single oral dose of 40 mg/kg. **S. japonicum** is treated with half this dose, with administration repeated on 3 occasions within a 12-hour period. For **neurocysticercosis** the dosage is 50 mg/kg/day orally in 3 divided doses for 14 to 30 days. For **clonorchiasis** and **paragonimiasis** the dosage is 75 mg/kg/day orally in 3 divided daily doses over a 48-hour period.

Adverse reactions occur in some patients within a few hours of administration and include gastrointestinal intolerance with nausea, vomiting and abdominal discomfort.

Pyrantel Pamoate

Pyrantel pamoate is highly effective for the treatment of **oxyuriasis, ascariasis,** and **Trichostrongylus orientalis** infections. It is moderately active against both species of hookworm (lesser against *N. americanus*). It is ineffective in trichuriasis and strongyloidiasis. **Oxantel**, an analogue of pyrantel is effective in the treatment of **trichuriasis.**

The anthelmintic action of pyrantel is due to the **inhibition of neuromuscular transmission**. It causes a **spastic neuromuscular paralysis** in the worm, which is subsequently expelled from the hosts intestines. Pyrantel in experimental studies shows a typical **depolarizing** neuromuscular blocking effect, and also inhibits the cholinesterases. Pyrantel is poorly and incompletely absorbed from the gastrointestinal tract.

For **roundworms** and **pinworms**, pyrantel is administered orally as a ***single*** dose of 11 mg/kg (pyrantel base) body weight to a maximum of 1 g; for **hookworms** this dose is given for 3 consecutive days. Fasting before treatment is not necessary, and the dosage may be repeated after one month, if needed. **Adverse reactions** include anorexia, nausea, headache, drowsiness, rashes and elevated SGOT levels. It should be used with caution in patients with liver diseases.

Quinacrine

Quinacrine was formerly an effective alternative drug for the *treatment* of tapeworm infections. Because of its toxicity, it is no longer used, unless the drug of choice (niclosamide or praziquantel), is not available. Quinacrine acts on the attachment organ of the worm, thereby expelling it. Treatment is followed by a saline cathartic to facilitate expulsion of the worms which are stained **yellow** by the drug. To reduce nausea and vomiting sodium bicarbonate (500 to 600 mg) may be given prior to each dose, or an antiemetic (e.g. prochlorperazine) may be used, particularly for *T. solium* infection. The usual dose of quinacrine is 800 mg orally given in two divided doses 30 minutes apart.

Tetrachloroethylene

It is useful in the treatment of *hookworm* infections. But since more effective and less toxic agents are available, the drug is now seldom used.

Thiabendazole

Thiabendazole is the drug of choice for the treatment of **Strongyloides stercoralis** infections, and cure rates of almost 100 percent have been achieved. It is also the drug of choice for treating cutaneous **larva migrans** caused by the larvae of **Ancylostoma braziliense**. Common **adverse reactions** include nausea, vomiting and epigastric distress, hypotension, syncope and Stevens-Johnson syndrome. For **stronglyoidiasis, cutaneous larva migrans,** treatment is given for 1 or 2 days. The **usual dose** is 25 mg/kg of body weight (maximum 3 g) twice daily after meals. It is available as 500 mg chewable tablets and suspension containing 500 mg/5 ml.

During the past three decades, many older anthelmintics have been replaced by safer and more effective drugs. Today excellent drugs are available for the treatment of most worm infections.

9.8 CHEMOTHERAPY OF LEPROSY (ANTILEPROTIC DRUGS)

The WHO has estimated that 12 to 20 million people worldwide have leprosy (Hansen's disease). The majority are in India, China and Africa. India alone has about 4 million leprosy patients. Due to the development of effective chemotherapy, most cases can be managed outside the hospitals.

Leprosy is a chronic infectious disease caused by an acid-fast bacillus, **Mycobacterium leprae**, related to the tubercle bacillus. This bacillus multiplies very slowly in the body, and not at all in culture media. Thus, no vaccine is available. It is essentially a disease of **peripheral nerves**, but it also affects the **skin**, and sometimes the **eyes**, the **mucosa of the upper respiratory tract, muscle, bone** and **testes**. The mode of transmission of the disease is not clearly defined.

Forms of Leprosy

Leprosy is classified into four forms: (*i*) **indeterminate;** (*ii*) **tuberculoid;** (*iii*) **lepromatous;** and (*iv*) **dimorphous** (border-line). Indeterminate leprosy is manifested by some localized **hypopigmentation of the skin** and **sensory loss**. When treatment is not given or healing does not occur, the condition may progress to **tuberculoid leprosy** in those with high degree of resistance (Lepromin test positive) to the infection, or to **lepromatous leprosy** with low degree of resistance (Lepromin test negative) to the infection. **Dimorphous** form of the disease has some features of both the tuberculoid and the lepromatous types, with the lepromin test positive and negative respectively. In the Middle Ages when the disease was widespread in Europe, the Church set up special hospitals, or **lazarettos**, to care for lepers. Now no special isolation is required, and patients can be managed outside the hospitals with effective chemotherapy. Chemotherapy is the mainstay in the treatment of leprosy. **Dapsone**, a sulphone, is the drug of choice for all forms of the disease. Some strains of **M. leprae** have become resistant to the sulphones, and occasionally **primary sulphone resistance** has also been encountered.

CLASSIFICATION OF LEPROSTATIC DRUGS

The available drugs may be classed into the *sulphones* and the *nonsulphones* as under:

1. **Sulphones**. *Dapsone, sulfoxone sodium.*
2. **Nonsulphones**
   (*i*) **Antibiotics.** Rifampicin
   (*ii*) **Phenazine dye.** Clofazimine
   (*iii*) **Thioureas.** Thiacetazone (amithiozone)
   (*iv*) **Sulphonamides.** Sulfadoxine
   (*v*) **Anti-inflammatory drugs.** Aspirin, Chloroquine, Thalidomide, Antimonials, Corticosteroids.

SULPHONES

Sulphones were first used in the treatment of leprosy in 1941, and they still remain the most useful drugs. They as a class are derivatives of 4, 4-diaminodiphenylsulphone (dapsone, DDS).

Dapsone (DDS)

Dapsone is the *sulphone of choice* for the treatment of *all forms of leprosy*. The mechanism of action of the sulphones is similar to that of the sulphonamides, as both possess the same range of antibacterial activity, and both are antagonized by paraminobenzoic acid. Dapsone is primarily **bacteriostatic**. Continuous treatment with this drug assures a negative bacterial state in almost all patients of **lepromatous leprosy**, provided it is administered for 5 years or more. Most authorities recommend that administration be continued in lapromatous cases throughout life. Patients with intermediate or **tuberculoid leprosy**, should receive dapsone for 2 years, and those with **dimorphous form**, for 10 years after an "inactive" state has been reached.

Pharmacokinetics. Dapsone is slowly but completely absorbed from the gut. About 50 percent is bound to plasma proteins, and is distributed in total body water. It is concentrated in the liver, muscles, kidney and skin, but passage into the CSF is poor. Concentration in the skin may be 10-15 times greater in the inflamed than in the normal skin. Dapsone is **conjugated** in the liver with glucuronic acid, and excreted in the **urine** and **milk**. Free drug is also excreted in the urine and bile. As an **enterohepatic circulation** follows biliary excretion of the free drug, a single dose of dapsone may be detected in the plasma for upto 12 days.

Toxicity. Adverse reactions developing with sulphone therapy are almost all dose-dependent. **Gastrointestinal upsets** (nausea, vomiting, anorexia, abdominal cramps and diarrhoea) occur in about 10 percent of patients. Headaches, excitement, nervousness, insomnia, **cholestatic jaundice,** drug fever, goiter, haematuria and severe renal failure may develop occasionally. A variety of skin rashes, particularly erythema nodosum, and erythema multiformae, with pruritus and paraesthesias may occur. **Acute psychosis** is rare. A **reversible peripheral neuropathy** has also been reported. The sulphones may induce an exacerbation of lepromatous leprosy, which is thought to be parallel to Jarisch-Herxheimer reaction. This "sulphone syndrome" usually occurs within 5-6 weeks of initiation of therapy, specially in malnourished patients. Use of dapsone in high doses is associated with **methaemoglobinaemia** and **Heinz-body formation**. Dapsone is a potent electron donor and may produce haemolysis in both normal and glucose-6-phosphate dehydrogenase (G-6-PD) deficient red cells. With sulphone therapy the problems of dapsone resistance and microbial persistence have emerged.

Dosage. Dapsone 100 mg daily orally is administered to patients with *lepromatous* and *dimorphous* leprosy, and for *tuberculoid* and *indeterminate* cases 50 mg daily. The duration of the therapy is detailed above. It is advisable to screen patients for G-6-PD deficiency prior to initiation of therapy.

Sulfoxone Sodium

Sulfoxone may be substituted for dapsone in patients who do not tolerate the latter drug well. **It is hydrolysed in the gut to dapsone**, and a 165 mg enteric-coated tablet yields about 25 mg of dapsone. It is seldom used because its absorption is erratic. **Adverse reactions** are similar to those produced by dapsone and other sulphones. Sulfoxone is usually administered in a daily dose of 330 mg orally, which may be increased to 660 mg daily, if necessary.

NONSULPHONES

Rifampicin

The pharmacology of rifampicin (rifampin) with regard to its use in tuberculosis is discussed in **Chapter 9.4.** It may be used as a companion drug to dapsone in certain patients of leprosy. Rifampicin appears to be **bactericidal for M. leprae**, while other drugs are bacteriostatic. In oral doses of 300 to 600 mg daily rifampicin renders bacilli non-infective for the mouse footpad (a method to culture *M. leprae in vivo*), and non-infectious for contacts. This action of rifampicin is more rapid than with dapsone or clofazimine. However, clearance of skin lesions, and reduction in the number of bacilli does not occur as well. To sum up, rifampicin has not proved to be a quick cure for leprosy, although it penetrates cells and nerves well. **Because of the development of resistance to dapsone, the WHO recommends a regimen of multiple drugs, including rifampicin.**

Clofazimine

Clofazimine is a phenazine congener, and is used in patients of leprosy infected with sulphone-resistant *M. leprae.* This **riminophenzine dye** is unique in the sense that it has a **bacteriostatic** action equal to that of dapsone, and also has an **anti-inflammatory** action which is of value in reactional states. Clofazimine interferes with bacterial nucleic acid metabolism by binding to DNA. Many patients of leprosy receiving sulphones develop **erythema nodosum leprosum,** marked by a sudden and acute flare-up of the disease, which is thought to be induced by the therapeutic effect of the sulphones. Painful red lesions occur all over the body, fever, malaise, exacerbation of neuritis, iritis, orchitis and other signs and symptoms of lepromatous leprosy occur (which had subsided earlier). A possibility is that this reaction is an immune reaction. **Clofazimine effectively prevents the development of this reaction.**

Clofazimine is absorbed from the gut and appears to accumulate in the tissues. This makes intermittent therapy possible, with doses separated by 2 or more weeks. Dapsone-sensitive microorganisms are killed immediately, but dapsone-resistant strains do not show appreciable effect until 50 days of clofazimine therapy.

Adverse effects of clofazimine include *nausea, diarrhoea* and *abdominal pain,* and development of *skin pigmentation*. Another drawback is that clofazimine is a costly drug. The dose of clofazimine is 100-300 mg orally daily. When the symptoms have been controlled, 100 mg twice weekly is effective. Sometimes viable bacilli may exist in lepromatous patients even after 6 years of therapy. It may be effectively combined with one or more antileprotic drugs.

Thiacetazone

The tuberculostatic activity of thiosemicarbazones was observed long back in 1946. Thiacetazone exerts a greater effect on the **tuberculoid** than on the lepromatous form of the disease. **M. leprae** develops resistance as treatment is continued, and also develops cross-resistance to thiambutosine. Thiacetazone is more toxic than thiambutosine, but is *much cheaper* and may be useful as a second-line drug. It is given orally in a *dose* of 150 mg daily.

Sulfadoxine

The long-acting sulphonamide, sulfadoxine (0.5 g daily) has been tried in patients not tolerating dapsone.

Management of Reactions in Leprosy

Lepra reaction. The lepromatous lesions become extremely painful. In many patients on sulphones, **lepromatous lepra reactions** manifest in the form of **erythema nodosum leprosum,** as mentioned earlier. When such reactions develop, the sulphones are discontinued (some authorities are not in favour of stopping dapsone therapy), and any of the several undermentioned **anti-inflammatory drugs** are employed to offer symptomatic relief:

Aspirin is still the best and cheapest drug for controlling mild to moderate lepra reactions, for which 600-1200 mg are given 4 to 6 times daily. **Chloroquine,** which has an anti-inflammatory action, may be used for mild reactions in a dose of 150 mg chloroquine base upto 3 times daily.

For severe reactions **thalidomide,** which has potent anti-inflammatory activity may be used in a dose of 400 mg daily, till the reaction is controlled, and then reduced to 50 mg daily. **Thalidomide must never be given to premenopausal women because of its disastrous teratogenic effects.** The schistosomicidal *antimonials* like **stibophen** have also been used for severe reactions. **Corticosteroids** are to be employed in cases of neuritis when a rapid control of inflammation is essential. **Prednisone** or **prednisolone** in a single daily dose of 40-80 mg may be used to control the acute stage, and then taper the dose over a fortnight.

Reversal reaction. This occurs in the **tuberculoid** form of the disease. Cutaneous ulceration, neuritis, and pain occur suddenly. It is controlled with *clofazimine* and *corticosteroids*.

WHO Regimens

According to the WHO Study Group, for treatment purposes leprosy patients are divided into: (*i*) those suffering from **multibacillary leprosy** (lepromatous, borderline-lepromatous, and borderline leprosy); and (*ii*) those suffering from **paucibacillary leprosy** (tuberculoid, borderline-tuberculoid, and indeterminate). A 3-drug regimen is recommended for the former, and a 2-drug regimen for the latter, as detailed below:

Multibacillary leprosy (3-drug regimen)

Rifampicin: 600 mg once-monthly, supervised.
(450 mg for those weighing less than 35 kg)

Dapsone: 100 mg daily, self-administered.

Clofazimine: 300 mg once-monthly, supervised, *and* 50 mg daily, self-administered. (or, if clofazimine is unacceptable, then *ethionamide* 250 mg daily self-administered).

Treatment should be given for **at least 2 years**, and continued, when possible, upto smear negativity. The regimen must be continued even during lepromatous lepra reactions, which if severe should be controlled by *prednisolone* or *increased clofazimine dosage*.

Paucibacillary leprosy (2-drug regimen)

Rifampicin: 600 mg once-monthly, supervised.
(450 mg for those weighing less than 35 kg)

Dapsone: 100 mg daily, self-administered.

Treatment should be given for **6 months**. If treatment is interrupted the regimen should be recommended where it was left off to complete the full course.

Both the above regimens are inadequate to control associated active pulmonary tuberculosis, therefore patients having active pulmonary tuberculosis should receive an appropriate course of antitubercular chemotherapy in addition to the antileprosy regimen.

These WHO regimens are applied worldwide, with minor variations in different countries. In **multibacillary leprosy**, surveillance in the form of yearly follow up (without treatment) for the next 5 years is advisable. No surveillance is routinely done after completion of treatment in cases of **paucibacillary leprosy.** They are advised to report on recurrence of symptoms, if any.

The current recommendations of the WHO are that **all forms of leprosy should be treated with a combination of drugs, rather than relying on therapy with dapsone alone.**

Prophylaxis in Leprosy

To sum up, a simple guide for the treatment of leprosy is to treat until there are no signs of the disease on *clinical* and *bacteriological* assessment. The prognosis for properly treated leprosy patients is good.

9.9 CHEMOTHERAPY OF VIRAL DISEASES (ANTIVIRAL DRUGS)

Types of Viruses
Phases of Viral Infection and Replication
Classification
Antiviral Drugs
  Gamma Globulin, Ribavarin, Idoxuridine, Foscarnet, Vidarabine, Acyclovir, Ganciclovir, Trifluridine, Zidovudine, Interferons, Puromycin, Fluorophenylalanine, Methisazone, Amantadine, Rimantadine, Rifampicin
New Drugs for AIDS and Related Diseases

Infections caused by viruses, which are **obligate intracellular parasites,** present special and difficult problems in chemotherapy. This is so because the viruses require active participation of the metabolic processes of the invaded host cells. In turn, the agents that may inhibit or kill the viruses are also very likely to injure the host cells. This intimate relationship between the virus and the host cell makes the possibility of **selective antiviral action** difficult to achieve. The development of useful antiviral drugs has lagged far behind that of antibacterial agents.

Types of Viruses

Viruses can be divided into: (*i*) the **large viruses** (chlamydia) responsible for molluscum contagiosa, psittacosis/ornithosis, trachoma, inclusion conjunctivitis, lymphogranuloma venereum and the rickettsial infections; and (*ii*) the **true (small) viruses** including the pox viruses, herpes viruses, adenoviruses and picorna viruses. The **large viruses** possess both DNA and RNA, and differ from true viruses both in morphology and in their mode of multiplication. They show varying susceptibility to the penicillins, tetracyclines, chloramphenicol and the sulphonamides **(Chapters 9.1 and 9.2).**

The **true viruses** contain a core of either DNA (smallpox, chickenpox, herpes simplex, herpes zoster), or RNA (poliomyelitis, mumps, measles, rabies), but never both. These viruses can replicate only inside host cells using the host enzyme system. Thus, there are *two* major problems confronting effective antiviral therapy. *First,* since viral replication is intracellular, antiviral drugs must be **highly selective,** and should not interfere with normal cellular functions of the host. *Second,* most viral diseases are of a short duration, and the prodromal phase of viral growth is **asymptomatic.** For these reasons major advances in the treatment of viral diseases have been in the direction of **prevention,** e.g., by control of vectors. Success has been achieved by **active immunization** with either attenuated or killed virus vaccines, and by **passive immunization (Chap. 15). Human gamma globulin** is prepared from pooled blood or from convalescent patients. Antibodies are most effective when used prophylactically in persons who have been exposed to viral diseases like **measles, rubella** (specially in pregnant women), **rabies, infectious hepatitis** and **mumps.** Neither active, nor passive immunization is of value, once the disease has occurred.

Phases of Viral Infection and Replication

The true viruses contain a core or **genome** of nucleic acid (either RNA or DNA) surrounded by a coating of protein subunits or **capsomeres,** the viral antigens. The capsomeres protect the nucleic acid, and may also be responsible for attachment (adsorption) of viruses onto host cells. Further, the reproductive cycle of a virus can be divided into *five* phases:

Phase 1: Attachment and penetration. The virus attaches to *specific receptor sites* on the host cell membrane, and penetrates the membrane by a *phagocytosis-like mechanism.* The virus particle is encapsulated by the host cell cytoplasm, forming a **vacuole** (Inhibitor: e.g. **gamma globulin**).

Phase 2: Uncoating. The protein coat of the virus is dissolved by viral enzymes liberating *free viral DNA* or *RNA,* i.e., the viral **genome** (Inhibitor: e.g. **amantadine**).

Phase 3: Synthesis of viral components. The viral genome is duplicated and the viral proteins are synthesized. Simultaneously, the host synthesis of nucleic acids or protein, or both, is inhibited (Inhibitors: e.g., **vidarabine, zidovudine, ribavirin, idoxuridine, acyclovir**).

Phase 4: Assembly of the virus particle. In this phase the viral components are assembled to form the **mature viral particle.** The viral genome is encapsulated, or not encapsulated in some cases (Inhibitors: e.g., **amantadine, rimantadine**).

Phase 5: Release of the virus. The rapid release of the virus from the host cell is accompanied by **host cell lysis** and cell death. When the virus is released slowly by a process of budding, the host cell may survive.

The antiviral durgs cause interference with any one or more of the above steps. The steps subsequent to the affected steps are also inhibited, although not directly.

Classification

According to their mode of action the antiviral drugs can be classified as under:

I. **Inhibitors of adsorption and penetration**
Gamma globulin.

II. **Inhibitors of intracellular synthesis**
(*i*) Inhibitors of nucleic acid synthesis
Ribavarin, Idoxuridine, Foscarnet, Vidarabine, Acyclovir, Ganciclovir, Desciclovir, Trifluridine, Zidovudine, Zalcitabine, Interferons, Stavudine, Didanosine.
(*ii*) Inhibitor of late protein synthesis
Methisazone.

III. **Inhibitors of assembly or release of virus particles**
Amantadine, Rimantadine, Rifampicin.

Antiviral Drugs

Inhibitors of Adsorption and Penetration

Gamma Globulin

Gamma globulin (IgG) is a fraction obtained from the plasma of normal individuals, and is rich in most of the antibodies found in whole blood. It contains a variety of antibodies against specific viral antigens. Its mode of action is unclear. It probably interferes with the entry of virus particles into cells by **blocking penetration rather than adsorption.**

Therapeutic uses. It is ineffective orally, and has to be administered parenterally. IM injections given during the early infectious stage (incubation period) can partially alleviate the progression of **hepatitis, measles, rabies, poliomyelitis** and probably other viral infections. Protection lasts for 2 to 3 weeks, after a single injection. This procedure confers only a **passive immunity** towards the virus.

Dosage. *Human gamma globulin* (Gamastan) is given in a dose of 0.22 ml/kg IM for prevention of **measles** in non-immune subjects within 6 days of exposure. Persons exposed to **type A infectious hepatitis** should receive 0.02 to 0.04 ml/kg IM of gamma globulin. IV formulations (Gammaimmune, Sandoglobin) are available for patients requiring an immediate increase in immunoglobulin levels. The dosage is 100 mg/kg once monthly. **Adverse reactions** include occasional **anaphylactoid reactions,** and minor allergic manifestations.

Inhibitors of Nucleic Acid Synthesis

Ribaviarin

Ribavarin is a purine nucleoside analogue. It **inhibits the replication** *in vitro* of a wide range of RNA and DNA viruses. Ribavarin appears to interfere with guanidine monophosphate formation, and subsequent nucleic acid synthesis.

Therapeutic uses. It is used to treat infants and young children with severe lower respiratory tract infections (LRTI) due to **respiratory syncytial virus.** Ribavirin aerosol is used to treat **influenza A and B virus** infection; and orally *hepatitis, herpes genitalis, measles,* and *Lassa fever*. Ribavarin also shows transient clinical improvement in cases of AIDS.

Dosage. Ribavarin is available as powder for reconstitution as aerosol containing 20 mg/ml in 100 ml vials. The dose to be delivered to infants is 1.4 mg/kg per hour. Treatment is carried out for 12-18 hours per day for 3-7 days.

Adverse reactions. Ribavarin *aerosols* are generally well tolerated. Conjunctival irritation, rash, wheezing and temporary deterioration in pulmonary function may occur. *Oral* or *IV* ribavarin causes anaemia due to extravascular haemolysis and suppression of bone marrow function. Ribavarin is contraindicated in pregnant women, and in patients on artificial ventilation, as it blocks ventilator circuit by drug deposition.

Idoxuridine

Idoxuridine (IDU) is a structural analogue of thymidine, an essential intermediate in DNA synthesis. As it is rapidly inactivated by enzymes, IDU is used only locally in the eye for the treatment of **herpes simplex keratitis.**The drug is incorporated into viral DNA, producing a faulty molecule incapable of reproduction. Thus the herpes viral cell replication is blocked in the cornea.

Therapeutic use. IDU is used for the treatment of **herpes simplex keratitis.** It controls the infection but has no effect on old scarring or progressive loss of vision. IDU is used either as a 0.5 percent ophthalmic ointment or a 0.1 percent ophthalmic solution. One drop is placed into the infected eye every hour during the day and every 2 hours at night till improvement is noted. The ophthalmic ointment is instilled into the conjunctival sac every 4 hours 5 times a day for at least 5-7 days after healing is complete.

Adverse effects include local irritation, burning, lacrimation, conjunctival hyperaemia. Squamous cell carcinoma may occur at the topical site. Idoxuridine is potentially carcinogenic and is not used systemically.

Foscarnet

Foscarnet sodium is a simple inorganic phosphonate analogue, which **inhibits viral DNA polymerase and reverse transcriptase** by interacting with the pyrophosphate binding sites on these enzymes. These sites are different from the loci of action of acyclovir (DNA polymerase), and zidovudine (reverse transcriptase).

Foscarnet is active against **herpes viruses,** including **cytomegalovirus,** and **HIV (Human Immunodeficiency Virus)** at a concentration of 3 mcg/ml. It is also active against acyclovir-resistant strains of *Herpes simplex*.

Dosage. An initial bolus dose of 20 mg/kg IV is administered over 30 minutes, followed by a continuous infusion of 230 mg/kg per day for 2 to 3 weeks. Foscarnet has been mainly used to treat **retinitis due to cytomegalovirus** in patients with AIDS.

Adverse reactions include reduced renal function, malaise, nausea, vomiting, headache and fatigue. It markedly increases fluid intake and urine output.

Vidarabine (Adenine Arabinoside, Ara-A, Vira-A)

Vidarabine is an analogue of adenosine. It is the least toxic and most effective of the purine analogues. Vidarabine is phosphorylated to the triphosphate derivative in the cell, which **inhibits viral DNA polymerase** much more effectively than mammalian DNA polymerase. *In vivo*, vidarabine is metabolized rapidly by **adenosine deaminase** to less active hypoxanthine arabinoside.

Therapeutic uses. Vidarabine is effective in the treatment of **herpes simplex encephalitis,** but acyclovir is superior. In disseminated lesions, acyclovir is not superior to vidarabine. Vidarabine applied topically is better tolerated and equally effective to idoxuridine for **herpes simplex keratoconjunctivitis**.

Dosage. Vidarabine is available in 5 ml vials containing 200 mg/ml of the monohydrate in suspension (equivalent to 187 mg of vidarabine). It is also available as a 3 percent ophthalmic ointment. The usual daily dose is 15 mg/kg IV over a 12 to 24 hours period, for 10 days. **Adverse reactions** are few, but include rash, weakness, thrombophlebitis, hypokalaemia, psychosis, tremor, and dizziness. Vidarabine is mutagenic and carcinogenic.

Acyclovir

Acyclovir is a guanosine derivative, and has potent antiviral activity essentially against the **herpesviruses,** particularly against **herpes simplex type I virus**. It is more than 100 times more active than vidarabine, and 10 times more active than idoxuridine against herpes simplex type-1 virus.

Mode of action. In order to be effective, acyclovir must be converted to a phosphorylated derivative. Viral thymidine kinase acts on acyclovir to form *acyclovir monophosphate*. The monophosphate is then converted to the diphosphate and triphosphate by host cell enzymes. **Acyclovir triphosphate** (*acyloguanosine triphosphate*) is the active antiviral agent that inhibits the herpes DNA polymerase 10-30 times more than the host cell polymerase, thereby it selectively inhibits herpes virus DNA replication. Acyclovir also has some activity against varicella-zoster virus, cytomegalovirus, and Epstein-Barr virus.

Therapeutic uses. Acyclovir is effective in the treatment of **herpes simplex virus type-1** and **type-2 infections,** primary and secondary **genital herpes, neonatal herpes,** and **herpes simplex encephalitis**. Acyclovir as a topical ointment is effective against **herpes keratoconjunctivitis**. It is also used for the prophylaxis and therapy of herpes simplex virus infections in patients on immunosuppression therapy for leukaemias or after organ transplants.

Adverse reactions are minimal and include headache, nausea and vomiting, skin rash, fever, increased hair loss, and depression. Rarely, reversible renal dysfunction occurs.

Dosage. Acyclovir sodium is available in 200 mg capsules. For genital herpes the usual dose is 200 mg orally every 4 hours for 10 days. Dosage for long-term therapy is 200 mg 3 to 5 times daily for upto 6 months. Acyclovir ointment 5 percent is available for topical treatment.

Ganciclovir

Ganciclovir is mechanistically similar to acyclovir. It is active against all herpes viruses, including cytomegalovirus. It is 100 times more active against cytomegaloviral infections compared to acyclovir.

Mode of action. Ganciclovir enters cells infected with cytomegalovirus and is phosphorylated into a triphosphate which preferentially inhibits cytomegalovirus DNA polymerase. When *ganciclovir triphosphate* is incorporated into cytomegalovirus DNA, it suppresses chain elongation and inhibits virus replication.

Therapeutic uses. The use of ganciclovir is limited to life-threatening infection with cytomegalovirus as it is a toxic agent. In patients with AIDS and **Cytomegalovirus retinitis,** the use of IV doses of 10 mg/kg/day results in clinical improvement. It is also useful in other syndromes in AIDS patients caused by cytomegalovirus like colitis, pneumonia, wasting syndrome and oesophagitis.

Adverse reactions include headache, psychosis, convulsions, and coma. Ganciclovir suppresses the bone marrow leading to leucopenia, neutropenia and thrombocytopenia. Renal function impairment occurs, and its toxicity is increased in renal insufficiency. It is teratogenic and mutagenic in animals.

Dosage. The usual initial daily dose is 10 or 100 mg/kg IV in 2 or 3 divided portions for 14-21 days. Lower doses of 5 mg/kg IV once daily for 5 days are used for suppressive or maintenance therapy.

Trifluridine

Trifluridine is a fluorinated pyrimidine deoxynucleoside which inhibits viral DNA synthesis. **Trifluridine triphosphate** which is synthesized in the body by phosphylation of the parent drug is incorporated into viral, and to a lesser extent, cellular DNA in competition with thymidine triphosphate. This drug is active against **herpes simplex virus types 1 and 2, cytomegalovirus, vaccinia** and some strains of **adenovirus**.

Therapeutic use. Its use is limited to topical treatment of primary and recurrent **keratoconjunctivitis** caused by herpes simplex virus types 1 and 2.

Adverse reactions include local irritation, palpebral oedema, and hypersensitivity reaction. It has exhibited mutagenic and teratogenic activities in animals.

Dosage. Trifluridine is available as a 1 percent aqueous ophthalmic solution. The dose is 1 drop into the conjunctival sac every 2 hours while awake, with a maximum dose of 9 drops per 24 hours.

Zidovudine

Zidovudine was first synthesized in search for anticancer drugs in 1964, and was rediscovered as an antiviral agent in 1974. It is a synthetic pyrimidine deoxynucleoside with a N_3 (azide) group attached to the deoxyribose at 3′ position. It is commonly referred to as AZT.

Mode of action. It is a **phase 3 inhibitor,** which on administration, is converted by a series of kinases to a **triphosphate metabolite,** which is the active inhibitor of the virus. This AZT derivative is incorporated into viral DNA, resulting in inhibition of further synthesis of the viral DNA chain. AZT inhibits the enzyme **reverse transcriptase** in the virus, whose function is to use the viral RNA template to produce single-stranded DNA. This action of the drug is selectively toxic to the virus. Zidovudine is active against HIV-1 and other mammalian retroviruses, but is less effective against HIV-2. It also inhibits human lymphotropic virus type 1 (HTLV-1), associated with T-cell leukaemias.

Therapeutic uses. The efficacy of zidovudine in patients with AIDS (who usually also have **Pneumocystis carinii** pneumonia), and in symptomatic patients with **AIDS-related complex** (ARC) is well established. The drug is effective in reducing opportunistic infections after about 6 weeks of treatment. Zidovudine does not cure HIV infections, but it is helpful in *reducing the viral load, and the degree of severity of AIDS-related infections*.

Adverse reactions. The major adverse effects are granulocytopenia and anaemia, which occur in upto 45 percent of treated patients. Other untoward effects include severe headache, nausea, insomnia, and myalgias. Severe neurotoxicity is also observed. Wernicke's encephalopathy and a polymyositis-like syndrome may occur.

Dosage. Zidovudine is available as 100 mg capsules. The usual dosage is 200 mg orally every 4 hours continuously.

Interferons

The enhanced production of the **antiviral proteins** called **interferons** is one of the body's earliest responses to a viral infection. These interferons are thought to help contain viral infections until the immune system is fully activated. All cells have the capacity to produce interferons.

Interferons are a group of glycoproteins, and possess complex **antiviral, immunomodulating**, and **anti-proliferative** effects. Endogenous production and release of interferon occurs in response to viruses (specially double-standed RNA viruses), bacterial exotoxins, and microorganisms capable of intracellular growth.

There are *three* major types of human interferons, designated as **alpha, beta and gamma**. Interferon alpha and beta are produced by most cells, whereas interferon gamma is restricted to T-lymphocytes. Now exogenous interferons have been produced using recombinant DNA technology whereas earlier the source was the human leucocytes.

Mode of action. Interferons bind to specific cell surface receptors inhibiting viral penetration or uncoating, synthesis of messenger RNA, translation or viral assembly and release. For most viruses the effect is to inhibit viral protein synthesis. Interferons have a relatively broad-spectrum of antiviral activity.

Therapeutic uses. Interferon alpha is currently used for hairly-cell leukaemia, AIDS-related Kaposi's sarcoma, condyloma acuminata (genital warts), and chronic hepatitis.

In cancer patients with *localized herpes zoster*, early treatment with interferon alpha reduces progression of the localized zoster.

Topical administration of interferon alpha with acyclovir or trifluridine is more effective than any single agent in the treatment of **herpes keratoconjunctivitis**. It is also used in infections caused by cytomegalovirus, and colds caused by **rhinoviruses**.

Dosage. *Interferon alpha-2a* is available in solution or as powder for reconstitution, and is administered by the SC or IM route. The usual dose is 36×10^6 IU per day for 5 to 7 days. *Interferon alpha-2b* is also available as powder for reconstitution, and may be administered SC, IM or intralesionally

Adverse reactions include influenza-like illness, headache, myalgia, nausea and diarrhoea. Bone marrow suppression with granulocytopenia and thrombocytopenia may occur. Antibodies to interferons develop over time resulting in its decreased antiviral activity.

Inhibitor of Late Protein Synthesis

Methisazone (a thiosemicarbazone) can block replication of **smallpox virus** in humans, if administered to contacts within 1-2 days of exposure. Methisazone, 2-4 g/day orally for 3-4 days offers protection against clinical smallpox. The availability of methisazone was an important factor in the successful eradication of smallpox.

Inhibitors of Assembly or Release of Virus Particles

Amantadine

Amantadine is a water-soluble, tricyclic symmetric amine. It appears to **block a late stage in the assembly** of the influenza A virus. Some studies indicate that it **inhibits the uncoating** of certain myxoviruses like influenza A virus (not influenza B virus), rubella, and some tumour viruses after entry into susceptible cells.

Therapeutic uses. Amantadine is used for the **prophylaxis** and treatment of **infection with influenza A virus.** Influenza virus vaccine is the preferred method of prophylaxis. It is also useful in the treatment of parkinsonism **(Chap. 2.11).**

Dosage. Amantadine hydrochloride is available as 100 mg capsules and as a syrup (50 mg/5 ml). The usual dose for *adults* is 200 mg once daily, or 100 mg twice daily. For children (1-9 years) the dose is 4.4 to 8.8 mg/kg, to a maximum of 150 mg/day. For those aged over 65 years the dose should be reduced to 100 mg once daily. It is effective only when started within 48 hours of onset of infection.

Adverse reactions include nervousness, hallucinations, confusion, seizures, and coma. Amantadine should not be administered to pregnant women and nursing mothers.

Rimantadine

Rimantadine is an analogue of amantadine, and it has the same antiviral activity, mode of action, and potential for development of resistant strains of the virus.

Rimantadine is as effective as amantadine in the prophylaxis and treatment of influenza A virus infection. It is claimed that the frequency of CNS side effects is lower compared to amantadine.

Rifampicin

Rifampicin prevents the assembly of enveloped mature viral particles. It is not useful in the treatment of human poxvirus infections, but topical application can inhibit *human vaccinia lesions*. It is a primary drug used for the treatment of tuberculosis **(Chap. 9.4).**

Newer Drugs for AIDS and Related Diseases

A number of new drugs are currently under different phases of clinical trials to evaluate their *efficacy* in the therapy of AIDS. They include **dideoxycytidine** (a reverse transcriptase inhibitor); **castanospermine** (inhibits assembly or maturation of viral particles); **pentamidine isethionate** (effective in **Pneumocystic carinii** pneumonia associated with AIDS); and **erythropoietin** effecitve in **anaemia** associated with therapy).

The goal of research in the field of antiviral drugs has been to find drugs capable of destroying the virus invading host cells without damaging the host cell themselves. To achieve such selective toxicity, first the metabolic differences between the *replicative cycles* and *metabolic processes* of viruses and the invaded cells have to be delineated.

9.10 CHEMOTHERAPY OF MALIGNANCY AND IMMUNOSUPPRESSIVE AGENTS (CYTOTOXIC DRUGS)

Next to heart disease, cancer is the major killer of mankind. Irrespective of the aetiology, cancer is basically a disease of cells characterized by the loss of normal cellular growth, maturation and multiplication, and thus homeostasis is disturbed. The main features of cancer are: (*i*) **excessive cell growth**, usually in the form of a tumour; (*ii*) **invasiveness**, i.e., the ability to grow into surrounding tissue; (*iii*) **undifferentiated cells** or **tissues**, more similar to embryonic tissues; (*iv*) **the ability to metastasize** or spread to new sites and establish new growths; (*v*) a **type of acquired heredity** in which the progeny of the cancer cells also retain cancerous properties; and (*vi*) a **shift of cellular metabolism** towards increased production of macromolecules from nucleosides and amino acids, with an increased catabolism of carbohydrates for cellular energy. Such a behaviour of cancer cells leads to illness in the host as a result of : (*i*) **pressure effects** due to local tumour growth; (*ii*) **destruction of the organ involved** by

Table 9.10-1. *Some neoplastic diseases which show a good response to chemotherapy*

	Disease	*Antineoplastic Drugs**
1.	Acute lymphatic leukaemia (child-hood)	*Induction* – vincristine + prednisone ± asparaginase *or* doxorubicin. *Maintenance* – methotexate + 6-mercaptopurine.
2.	Acute myelogenous leukaemia (adult)	Doxorubicin or daunorubicin + cytarabine + thioguanine *or* cytarabine + vincristine + prednisone.
3.	Breast cancer	Oestrogens, progestogens, and tamoxifen. Cyclophosphamide + methotrexate + fluorouracil ± prednisone or Cyclophosphamide + doxorubicin ± fluorouracil
4.	Choriocarcinoma	Methotrexate ± dactinomycin.
5.	Ewing's sarcoma	Cyclophosphamide + doxorubicin + vincristine.
6.	Hodgkin's disease	MOPP [mechlorethamine, vincristine (Oncovin), procarbazine, prednisone] or ABVD [doxorubicin (Adriamycin), bleomycin, vincristine, dacarbazine].
7.	Lung cancer (small cell)	CAV [cyclophosphamide, doxorubicin (Adriamycin), vincristine] *or* etoposide + cisplatin.
8.	Retinoblastoma	Cyclophosphamide.
9.	Testicular cancer	Vinblastine + bleomycin + cisplatin *or* BEP [bleomycin, etoposide, cisplatin (Platinol)]
10.	Wilms' tumour	Dactinomycin + vincristine ± doxorubicin.

* (±) denotes a possible beneficial addition.

the primary growth, or its metastases; and (*iii*) **systemic effects** as a result of the new growths.

The treatment of cancer with drugs was started by Huggins and Hodges in 1941, with the discovery that **oestrogens** palliate prostate cancer. Subsequently the **polyfunctional alkalating agents** were developed during World War II. Since then a number of chemotherapeutic agents have become available for the treatment of cancer.

In the past, due to poor therapeutic response, and a high incidence of adverse reactions, chemotherapy was only considered as a last resort after more successful treatments like **surgery** and **radiotherapy** had failed. The main problem in cancer chemotherapy is the **lack of highly selective drugs**.

Recent progress (particularly with intermittent combination chemotherapeutic schedules) holds considerable promise, and chemotherapy is now the preferred form of treatment for **leukaemias, lymphomas, choriocarcinomas and certain other tumours (Table 9.10-1)**.

Guidelines for Use of Cytotoxic Drugs

The large number of cytotoxic drugs available today has made it possible to use drug combinations. It is possible to combine drugs more logically. An understanding of the **cell-cycle kinetics** is essential for proper use of the available antineoplastic drugs.

The Cell Cycle

Cellular multiplication involves passage of the cell through a **cell cycle**. The various phases of the cell cycle are characterized as: (i) the interval following cell division to the point where DNA synthesis starts, known as the **presynthetic phase** (G_1). The variability in the length of the cell cycle between rapidly and slowly replicating cells is accounted by the differences in the length of G_1 phase; (*ii*) after mitosis some of the daughter cells pass into a resting phase or **non-proliferative phase** (G_0), and do not re-enter the cell cycle phase G_1 immediately. They may enter the G_1 phase later. The G_0 phase is the subphase of G_1; (*iii*) the **DNA synthesis** (S) occurs; (*iv*) the **premitotic or postsynthetic** (G_2) phase follows. In this phase RNA and protein synthesis takes place, and it is shorter than the S phase; and (*v*) lastly **mitotic** (M) phase follows, in which the synthetic activity of the cell is low, the chromosomes separate into two daughter cells through the subphase-**prophase, metaphase, anaphase** and **telophase**. These daughter cells have the option of either entering the G_1 phase or the G_0 subphase of G_1 phase **(Fig. 9.10.1)**.

Most of the antineoplastic drugs act specifically on the processes such as DNA synthesis, transcription, or the mitotic phase, and are labelled as cell cycle **phase specific** drugs (also known as **phase-dependent** drugs). The phase specific drugs do not act on G_0 phase. In contrast, there are certain drugs which kill the cells during all or most phases of the cycle, labelled as cell cycle **phase nonspecific** drugs (also known as **phase-independent** drugs). The phase nonspecific drugs do possess a slight effect on the G_0 phase.

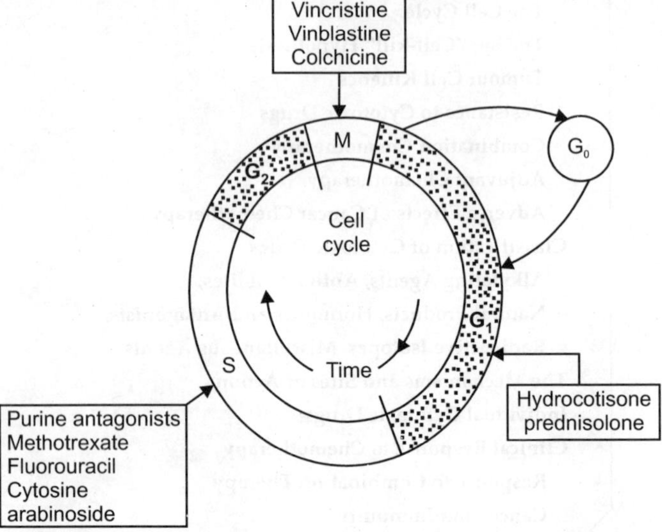

Fig. 9.10.1: The phases of the cell cycle, and the point of action of some predominantly phase specific cytotoxic drugs (diagrammatic). G_1 = presynthetic phase (variable 18 hrs); G_0 = nonproliferative or resting phase; S = DNA synthesis phase (20 hrs); G_2 = premitotic or postsynthetic phase (3 hrs); M = mitotic phase (1 hr). G_1 and G_2 are the first and second "gap periods" respectively (also see text).

In general, the cytotoxic drugs can be classified (Bruce's classification) according to their effect on the cell cycle **(Table 9.10-2)**. Strictly speaking there is overlaping of activity and the drug at best can be classed as either predominantly phase specific or nonspecific. Cell cycle studies have provided a logical basis for high dosage *intermittent combination therapy*, which possibly is the most effective mode of treatment.

Table 9.10-2 *Classification of some cytotoxic drugs according to their predominant effect on the cell cycle*

Phase specific drugs (phase-dependent)	*Phase nonspecific drugs (phase independent)*
Methotrexate	Nitrogen mustard
6-mercaptopurine	Cyclophosphamide
5-fluorouracil	Melphalan
Cytosine arabinoside	Busulphan
Prednisolone	Thio-Tepa
Vincristine	Chlorambucil
Vinblastine	Actinomycin D
Procarbazine	Adriamycin
Hydroxyurea	Daunomycin
Asparaginase	Mitomycin C

The **phase specific drugs** act chiefly on cells in certain phases, and when in experimental studies a tissue culture is treated with these drugs, the percentage of cells surviving falls rapidly at first with increasing doses, but reaches a plateau when further increase in dose produces no further increase in cell death. Therefore, the more rapid the cell turnover, the more effective they are. Their dose-response curve is initially exponential, but at higher doses a maximum response is reached and the curve becomes asymptotic **(Fig. 9.10.2)**. The phase specific drugs have proved effective in haematologic malignancies, and tumours with high rate of proliferation, or *high growth fraction*.

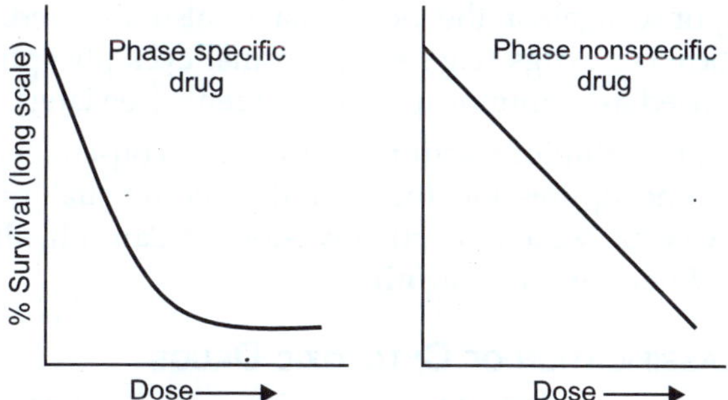

Fig. 9.10.2: The dose-response curve for a phase specific (left), and a phase nonspecific (right) cytotoxic drug.

The **phase nonspecific drugs** act on cells in any phase of the cycle, including a slight action on the G_0 phase. Cell survival in tissue culture falls progressively with increasing doses. Their dose-response curve follows **first-order kinetics**, and the cells are killed exponentially with increasing dosage, and the relationship throughout is linear **(Fig. 9.10.2)**. The phase nonspecific drugs, many of which complex with DNA are useful both in the low growth fraction tumours (or solid tumours), and also in some high growth fraction tumours.

The Log "Cell-kill" Hypothesis

To briefly state, the log cell-kill hypothesis which is based on studies on experimental tumour systems in animals, enunciates that the cell-kill caused by cytotoxic drugs follows **first-order kinetics (Chap 1.5)**. This means that a constant percentage, rather than a constant number of cells is killed by a given dose of a cytotoxic drug. Precisely cytotoxic drugs kill a constant fraction (at best 99 to 99.999% or 2 to 4 log) of the tumour cell population, but never a 100 percent cell-kill. The malignant cells that remain, cause a relapse in the neoplastic disease. A logical derivation to this concept has been to attempt and achieve total cell-kill by the use of several cytotoxic agents simultaneously, or in a rational sequence.

Tumour Cell Kinetics

Cell kinetics of tumours has been extensively studied in animals particularly mouse leukaemia. In a guarded manner this information has been extrapolated from animals to man, and certain guidelines have evolved:

1. The natural history of cancer is much longer than it was thought earlier.
2. The fraction of cells in a tumour which are dividing decreases as the mass of the tumour increases.
3. Cytotoxic drugs given in high doses intermittently produce a higher cell-kill than continuous low dosage schedules.
4. Since every cancer cell has to be eliminated to produce a cure, it is essential to know when this aim has been achieved and therapy must be stopped at this point.

Resistance to Cytotoxic Drugs

Resistance may be **primary** or **acquired**. In the development of resistance by human tumour cells a number of mechanisms may be involved **(Table 9.10-3)**.

Table 9.10-3. *The mechanisms of acquired tumour resistance to cytotoxic drugs*

	Mechanism	*Examples*
(*a*)	Reduced uptake of drug	Methotrexate, Daunorubicin
(*b*)	Absence of enzyme to activate drug	Cytosine arabinoside, 5-fluorouracil
(*c*)	Increased drug detoxification	6-mercaptopurine
(*d*)	Increased concentration of target enzyme	Methotrexate
(*e*)	Decreased requirement for specific metabolic product	Asparaginase
(*f*)	Increased utilization of alternative pathway	Antimetabolites
(*g*)	Decreased number of receptors for drug	Hormones

Combination Chemotherapy

As mentioned earlier, it is possible to devise a combination of drugs which have different mechanisms of action, and provide greater benefit than each agent alone. Such combinations would also be *less toxic*, and the different mechanisms of action may also produce a **greater tumour cell-kill**. They may also allow a more **rapid host recovery**, and **better selectivity** with preferential killing of tumour cells. A common procedure is to first employ phase nonspecific drugs followed by phase specific agents.

Adjuvant Chemotherapy

It has been estimated that about 75 percent of cancer patients die as a result of metastases rather than the primary tumour. These metastases often arise in the pre-clinical course of the disease process. **Adjuvant chemotherapy** is aimed to destroy these **disseminated microfoci** at a time when there is no clinical evidence of residual disease. it is believed that chemotherapy at this stage is more successful because:

1. Fewer cells in small tumours are in G_0 phase, i.e., the growing cell fraction is higher.
2. The total body tumour load is small, and treatment is more likely to be effective.
3. Vascularization of small tumours is better, and thus drug penetration is facilitated.
4. Patients at this stage are less likely to be immunosuppressed, so that host factors may be additionally operative.

In contrast to the above benefits, adjuvant chemotherapy may unnecessarily expose the patient who does not have metastases to the toxic effects of cytotoxic drugs.

Adverse Effects of Cancer Chemotherapy

Immediate side effects with cancer chemotherapy are **nausea** and **vomiting**. These may be relieved by **metoclopramide** (10 mg orally or IV), or other antimetics (**chlorpromazine** 100 mg orally; **prochlorperazine** 12.5 mg IV; domperidone 10 mg IV) The delayed advere effects are briefed below:

(*a*) **Bone marrow depression.** This occurs within 10-14 days after a single dose of a cytotoxic drug, indicated by a fall in circulating leucocytes and platelets.

(*b*) **Gastrointestinal tract**. Bleeding, ulceration and diarrhoea may occur.

(*c*) **Neurotoxicity**. Neuropathy mainly occurs with Vinca alkaloids.

(*d*) **Hepatotoxicity**. This may occur due to the cytotoxic agent itself, or due to its toxic metabolites.

(*e*) **Teratogenecity and fertility**. Cytotoxic drugs impair fertility, increase the incidence of foetal abnormalities, and possibly carcinogenesis. In man these agents can produce a profound reduction in sperm count.

(*f*) **Immunosuppression.** Parallel to bone marrow depression, these agents exert a direct depressant effect on lymphocytes and other immunocytes. Resistance to microbial infections is lowered, and the immunologic response against the neoplasia is also lowered. Many anticancer drugs (e.g., azathioprine, cyclophosphamide) are used as immunosuppressive agents (see later).

(*g*) **Superinfection.** As a consequence of immunosuppression, fungal and other unusual infections may occur, which include invasion by **Candida albicans**, and **Pneumocystis carinii**.

Classification of Cytotoxic Drugs

They may be classed into six major groups: (1) **Alkylating agents**; (2) **Antimetabolites**; (3) **Natural products**; (4) **Hormones and antagontists**; (5) **Radioactive isotopes**; and (6) **Miscellaneous agents**. The individual agents are detailed about their main indications and dosage in **Table 9.10-4.**

Table. 9.10-4. *The available antineoplastic agents for cancer chemotherapy*

CLASS/Type of agent	*Nonproprietary name*	*Major indications*	*Usual dosage*
1. ALKYLATING AGENTS			
(*a*) Nitrogen mustards	Mustine	Hodgkin's disease and other lymphomas; lung, breast and ovarian cancer	200-600 mcg/kg IV in single or divided doses.
	Cyclophosphamide	Acute and chronic lymphocytic leukaemias; Hodgkin's disease; non-Hodgkin's lymphomas; multiple myeloma; Wilms' tumour; breast, lung and ovarian cancer; other solid tumours	30-40 mg/kg IV every 3-4 week; 2-4 mg/kg daily orally
	Chlorambucil	Chronic lymphocytic leukaemia; Hodgkin's disease and other malignant lymphomas	3-10 mg/day orally.
	Melphalan	Multiple myeloma; testicular seminoma; breast and ovarian cancer.	6 mg orally for 2-3 weeks; maintenance 2 mg daily
(*b*) Ethyleneimine derivatives	Thiotepa	Hodgkin's disease; malignant lymphomas; bronchogenic carcinoma; retinoblastoma; breast and ovarian cancer.	0.2 mg/kg IV daily for 5 days every 4 weeks; also by topical instillation.
(*c*) Alkyl sulphonates	Busulphan	Chronic granulocytic leukaemia.	4-8 mg orally per day
(*d*) Triazines	Dacarbazine	Metastatic malignant melanoma.	2-4.5 mg/kg/day IV for 10 days.
(*e*) Nitrosoureas	Carmustine	Brain tumours; Hodgkin's disease and non-Hodgkin's lymphomas; multiple myeloma.	200 mg/m^2 IV every 6 weeks.

Table. 9.10-4. Contd...

CLASS/Type of agent	Nonproprietary name	Major indications	Usual dosage
	Lomustine	Brain tumours; Hodgkin's disease as secondary therapy.	130 mg/m^2 orally every 6 weeks.
	Semustine	Brain tumours; Hodgkin's disease; malignant melanoma; cancer of stomach and colon.	200 mg/m^2 orally every 6 weeks.
	Streptozocin	Malignant pancreatic insulinoma; malignant carcinoid.	1 g/m^2 IV weekly for 4 weeks.
2. ANTIMETABOLITE			
(*a*) Folic acid analogues	Methotrexate	Acute lymphoblastic leukaemia; choriocarcinoma; mycosis fungoides; breast, testes and lung cancer; osteogenic sarcoma.	2.5-5.0 mg/kg/day orally or IM for leukaemia; 15-30 mg orally or IM for 5 days in choriocarcinoma.
(*b*) Pyrimidine analogues	Fluorouracil	Carcinoma of the colon, rectum, breast, stomach and pancreas; topically for solar keratoses.	12 mg/kg IV for 4 days, followed by 6 mg/kg on alternate days through the 12th day.
	Cytarabine	Acute granulocytic leukaemia of adults; other leukaemias of adults and children.	2 mg/kg IV for 10 days.
	Azarabine	Mycosis fungoides; polycythaemia vera; psoriasis.	200 mg/kg orally
(*c*) Purine analogues	6-mercaptopurine	Acute lymphocytic leukaemia; chronic granulocytic leukaemia.	2.5 mg/kg/day orally (50-100 mg for adults and 50 mg for children).
	6-thioguna-nine	Acute leukaemia; chronic granulocytic leukaemia.	2 mg/kg/day orally.
3. NATURAL PRODUCTS			
(*a*) Vinca alkaloids	Vincristine	Acute lymphoblastic leukaemia; lymphosarcoma; Hodgkin's disease reticulum cell sarcoma; neuroblastoma.	2 mg/m^2 IV for children; 1.4 mg/m^2 IV for adults.
	Vinblastine	Hodgkin's disease and other lymphomas; choriocarcinoma; breast, renal cell and testicular carcinoma.	0.1 mg/kg IV increased weekly by 0.05 mg/kg upto 0.5 mg/kg.
(*b*) Antibiotics	Dactinomycin	Choriocarcinoma; Wilms' tumour; osteogenic and other sarcomas.	0.015-0.05 mg/kg IV divided dosage over 1 week; repeat for 3-5 weeks.
	Doxorubicin	Acute lymphoblastic and myelocytic leukaemias; neuroblastoma; Hodgkin's and non-Hodgkin's lymphoma; breast, ovary, bladder and lung carcinoma; cancer thyroid.	65-75 mg/m^2 IV at intervals of 21 days; or 30 mg/m^2 on each day for 3 successive days repeated every 4 weeks
	Daunorubicin	Acute granulocytic and acute lymphocytic leukaemias.	30-60 mg/m^2 IV daily for 3 days or weekly.
	Bleomycin	Squamous cell carcinoma; lymphosarcoma; reticulum cell sarcoma; testicular sarcoma; Hodgkin's disease.	0.25-0.5 units/kg IV, IM or SC, weekly or twice weekly.
	Mithramycin	Various types of testicular tumours; reversal of hypercalcaemia and hypercalciuria.	25-30 mcg/kg/day slowly IV for 8-10 days.
	Mitomycin	Cancer of stomach, cervix, colon, breast, pancreas and bladder.	20 mg/m^2 IV as a single dose, repeated after a drug free interval of 2 days.
(*c*) Enzymes	Asparaginase	Acute lymphocytic leukaemia.	1000 IU/kg/day IV for 10 successive days.

Table. 9.10-4. Contd...

CLASS/Type of agent	Nonproprietary name	Major indications	Usual dosage
4. HORMONES AND ANTAGONISTS			
(*a*) Adrenocorticosteroids	Prednisone (and other equivalent preparations)	Acute and chronic lymphocytic leukaemia; Hodgkin's disease and non-Hodgkin's lymphomas; breast and lung cancer.	10-100 mg orally.
(*b*) Androgens	Testosterone propionate (and its other preparations)	Carcinoma breast.	100 mg IM three times weekly.
(*c*) Oestrogens	Diethylstilboestrol (and other preparations)	Carcinoma prostate; metastatic breast carcinoma in postmenopausal women.	1.5-15 mg orally.
(*d*) Antioestrogen	Tamoxifen	Advanced carcinoma breast	10 mg twice daily.
(*e*) Progestogens	Hydroxyprogesterone caproate (and other preparations)	Endometrial carcinoma recurrences and metastases; cancer breast and prostate.	0.5-1.5 g IM twice weekly.
5. RADIOACTIVE ISOTOPES			
	Sodium phosphate solution (P^{32})	Polycythaemia vera; chronic lymphocytic and granulocytic leukaemia.	6 millicuries orally; 3-5 millicuries intravenously.
	Sodium iodide solution (I^{131})	Thyroid carcinoma; hyperthyroidism.	4-10 millicuries orally for thyrotoxicosis; 50-100 millicuries for thyroid cancer and metastases.
	Radiogold solution (Au^{198})	Malignant pleural and peritoneal effusions.	35-100 millicuries intrapleurally or intraperitoneally.
6. MISCELLANEOUS AGENTS			
	Cisplatin	Ovarian, testicular and bladder carcinoma.	50-80 mg/m^2 IV once every 3 weeks.
	Carboplatin	Same as above	300-400 mg/m^2 IV repeated every 4 to 5 weeks.
	Hydroxyurea	Chronic granulocytic leukaemia; melanoma; ovarian carcinoma.	20-30 mg/kg orally daily, or 80 mg/kg every third day.
	Procarbazine	Hodgkin's disease; metastatic brain tumours; bronchogenic carcinoma.	100-200 mg/day orally, then 300 mg/day until maximal response or toxicity.
	Mitotane	Carcinoma of the adrenal cortex.	8-10 g orally per day.
	Razoxane	Acute granulocytic and lymphocytic leukaemia; Colorectal adrenocarcinoma.	300 mg/m^2 orally.
	Etoposide	Ovarian cancers; lymphomas; lung cancers; acute myelogenous and lymphoblastic leukaemias.	50 mg/m^2 IV daily for 5 days infused slowly.
	Mitoxantrone	Breast cancer; leukaemias; lymphomas.	10-14 mg/m^2 IV every 3 to 4 weeks.
	Interferon alfa-2b	Hairy cell leukaemia; lymphomas; melanoma; ovarian carcinoma.	2 to 3 million IU/m^2 IM or SC daily for several weeks.
	Monoclonal antibodies	Clinical trials on lymphomas, leukaemias; melanoma; and colorectal carcinoma in progress.	A new class of anticancer drugs under study.

The Mechanisms and Sites of Action

The majority of antineoplastic drugs appear to act by affecting either **enzymes** or **substrates** acted upon by enzyme systems. Usually the effects on enzymes or substrates relate to DNA synthesis or function. Drugs which act primarily by inhibiting the enzymes of nucleic acid synthesis are called the **antimetabolites (Fig. 9.10.3).** Another major drug group appears to act primarily by affecting substrates. The usual substrate affected is the DNA macromolecule. These are the **alkylating agents,** which are extremely reactive compounds, and produce effects somewhat similar to those produced by ionizing radiation. For this reason these agents are also known as "radiomimetics". The **antineoplastic antibiotics** produce stable complexes with DNA, thereby inhibiting the synthesis of DNA and RNA. The **Vinca alkaloids** probably bind to microtubular proteins necessary for cell division and dissolve this protein, leading to death of the cell during mitosis **(Fig. 9.10.3).**

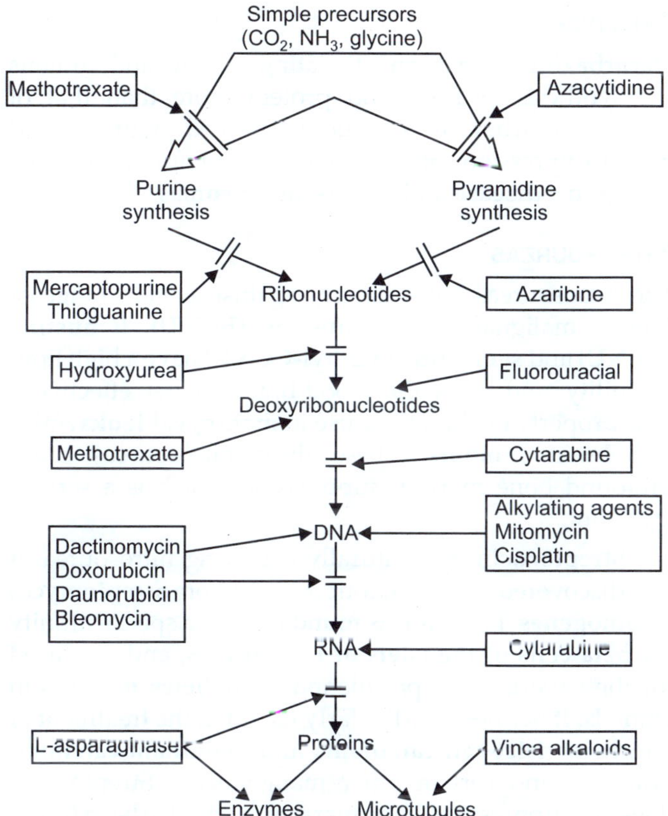

Fig. 9.10.3: The major sites of action of antineoplastic agents (Diagrammatic).

Individual Cytotoxic Drugs

1. Alkylating Agents

The *polyfunctional alkylating agents* were developed from the sulphur mustard vesicant gas dichlorethyl sulphide used in World War I. During World War II, the nitrogen mustards were developed for use as chemical warfare agents. The clinically useful agents are listed in **Table 9.10-4.**

Mode of action. The alkylating agents are highly reactive compounds and form **covalent bonds** between alkyl (C_nH_{2n}+1) groups (positively charged) in their molecule and guanine bases on opposing strands of DNA. In addition they form **covalent bonds** with a variety of nucleophilic groups (negatively charged), and alkylate with groupings like **amino, sulphydryl, hydroxyl** or **phosphate** in physiologically important molecules of cells and render them unavailable for normal metabolic functions. Precisely, all alkylating agents react by forming a **reactive intermediate** which contains a positively charged, carbonium ion or transition complex which forms a covalent link with negatively charged centres. Clinically useful alkylating agents are bi- or poly-functional, containing two or more alkyl end groups that are either unsaturated or cyclic, and react by **cross-linking DNA,** thus preventing it from acting as a template for RNA. **This cross-linking may occur between two DNA molecules; DNA and a protein molecule; or two protein molecules.**

The alkylating agents have a nucleotoxic action similar to X-rays, i.e., radiomimetic action, and thus have a **carcinogenic, mutagenic, teratogenic** and **immunosuppressive** action. In short, the alkylating agents act by damaging DNA, and by interfering with cell replication.

Pharmacokinetics. All alkylating agents have a similar general mode of action, but they differ in their suitability for use against *specific types* of cancer. The main reason for this difference is their widely variable molecular structure. Their physicochemical properties differ, and so also the ways in which they are handled in the body.

Nitrogen Mustards

Mustine hydrochloride. It is the most rapidly acting drug of this class. In solution mustine forms highly reactive **ethyleneimmonium** ions, which make it a very irritant substance. Local reactions thus caused make intravenous administration essential when used clinically.

The **major indications** for this alkylating agent are in the treatment of disseminated **Hodgkin's disease** and other **lymphomas**. It is one of the drugs included in the MVPP regimen-*mustine, vinblastine, procarbazine* and *prednisolone;* and in the MOPP regimen-*mustine, vincristine (Oncovin), procarbazine* and *prednisone*-for the treatment of Hodgkin's disease. It may also be useful in **chronic myelocytic leukaemia, polycythaemia vera, bronchogenic carcinoma** and other solid tumours.

Mustine is administered immediately after preparation of the solution, intravenously via a fast running infusion. Local extravasation causes severe tissue necrosis. *Thrombosis* and **thrombophlebitis** may occur. Severe vomiting is a common side effect which limits its usefulness. The most serious side effect is **myelosuppression**, which usually reaches its maximum 10-14 days after drug administration. It predisposes the patient to superinfection.

Cyclophosphamide. This is a very commonly used alkylating agent, and does not have a vesicant action. It can be administered **orally** or **intravenously**. Cyclophosphamide is not active itself, but is metabolized and activated by the liver microsomal oxidase system to **phosphoramide mustard** which is cytotoxic. The metabolites are excreted in the urine.

The **major indications** for cyclophosphamide are in the treatment of **lymphoproliferative** and **myeloproliferative** diseases. It is a primary drug for induction and maintenance therapy in **non-Hodgkin's lymphoma. Burkitt's lymphoma, acute lymphocytic leukaemia** in children, **multiple myeloma, chronic lymphocytic leukaemia** and solid tumours respond to this drug. It has a marked **immunosuppressive action** and has been used in non-neoplastic diseases like **rheumatoid arthritis**, and **nephrotic syndrome** in children.

Adverse reactions include bone marrow depression and gastrointestinal disturbances. **Alopecia** may occur which is reversible. A dose-limiting toxic effect results from high concentration of active metabolites in the urinary tract leading to **sterile haemorrhagic cystitis.** An increased fluid intake (3-4 litres/day) helps to avoid this complication. **Bladder fibrosis** and **carcinoma of the bladder** have been reported on long-term use. Other toxic effects include hyperpigmentation, amenorrhoea, azospermia, pulmonary fibrosis, myocarditis and congestive heart failure. **Ifosfamide** is related to cyclophosphamide and has similar effects.

Chlorambucil. Chlorambucil is a derivative of mustine, and is the slowest-acting, least toxic nitrogen mustard in clinical use. It is a **phase nonspecific agent** and has a marked **lympholytic action.** It is non-irritant and is well absorbed after oral administration.

Chlorambucil is the drug of choice in **chronic lymphatic leukaemia**, and is also effective in **Hodgkin's disease** and non **Hodgkin's lymphomas**, and **ovarian carcinoma**. It can replace mustine in the MOPP regimen.

Haematologic toxicity is most prominent, and leucopenia develops after the third week of therapy and continues up to 10 days after the last dose. Gastrointestinal, dermatologic and hepatic toxicity may occur. Serum uric acid levels should be monitored frequently to detect hyperuricaemia, which can lead to renal failure.

Melphalan. Its cytotoxic action is similar to other nitrogen mustards, and it is not a vesicant. It is well adsorbed when given orally. Melphalan is used in the treatment of **myelomatosis.** It has also been used as an adjuvant in the treatment of **stage II breast carcinoma. Ovarian carcinoma** and **testicular seminoma** also respond.

Melphalan produces a dose-related depression of bone marrow function resulting in leucopenia, thrombocytopenia and anaemia. Therefore usually it is administered at intervals of 4-6 weeks. It is employed in a multi-drug regime which is probably more effective than a single drug.

ETHYLENEIMINES

Triethylenethiophosphoramide (Thiotepa). Thiotepa may be used by intracavitary instillations in the treatment of **malignant effusions**.

ALKYLSULPHONATES

Busulphan. This agent has a selective depressant action on the bone marrow, and is used in the treatment of **chronic myeloid leukaemia**. Hyperpigmentation of the skin commonly occurs, and a rare but serious toxic effect is **interstitial pulmonary fibrosis.**

TRIAZINES

Dacarbazine. It has an alkylating action, and inhibits the synthesis of RNA and protein more than that of DNA. Dacarbazine produces marked nausea and myelosuppression, and is mainly used for **melanoma, Hodgkin's disease** and **soft tissue sarcomas**.

NITROSOUREAS

The nitrosoureas have activity against a wide range of human malignancies. **Carmustine (BCNU), lomustine (CCNU)** and **semustine (methyl-CCNU)** have a high lipid solubility, and cross the blood-brain barrier effectively. This property enables their use in **meningeal leukaemias** and **brain tumours**. These three nitrosoureas cause profound bone marrow suppression which is a serious limitation.

Streptozocin is a naturally occurring nitrosourea. It was discovered as an antibiotic derived from **Streptomyces acromogenes**. Later, it was found to have a special affinity **for beta-cells of the islets of Langerhans**, and was used for the experimental production of **diabetes mellitus** in animals. It has been particularly useful in the treatment of pancreatic **islet-cell carcinoma** and **malginant carcinoid tumours**, and certain other malignancies. Streptozocin does not suppress the bone marrow. It has also been found to be active in **Hodgkin's disease** and other **lymphomas**.

Some *newer* alkylating agents are: (*i*) **Estramustine** which is a stable combination of an oestrogen with mustine. It has been designed to treat tumours with oestrogen receptors, like **prostatic carcinoma**. It is given orally initially in a dose of 560 mg/day; (*ii*) **Mitobronitol** is used in the treatment of **chronic myeloid leukaemia**; and (*iii*) **Treosulfan** is a bifunctional alkylating agent occasionally used for the treatment of **ovarian carcinoma**.

2. ANTIMETABOLITES

Antimetabolites (analogues) chemically resemble the metabolites normally used by cells. They enter the metabolic system and interfere with the normal biosynthesis by **competing** for important enzymatic reactions in the synthesis of purines, pyrimidines and their precursors. Antimetaboletes with recognized clinical value are **folic acid, pyrimidine** and **purine** analogues. They are phase specific agents, and act primarily during the DNA synthetic phase (S-Phase) of the cell cycle **(Fig. 9.10.1)**.

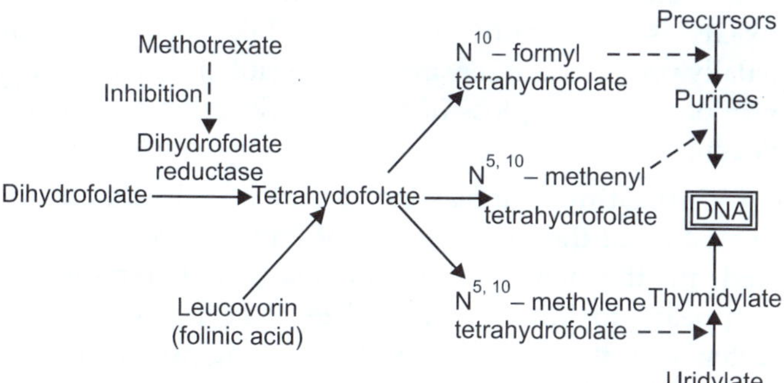

Fig. 9.10.4: Folate metabolism, and the mode of action of methotrexate and leucovorin.

FOLIC ACID ANALOGUES

Methotrexate. Folic acid is required in the synthesis of thymidylic acid and purine nucleotides, and ultimately for the production of DNA **(Fig. 9.10.4)**. Methotrexate resembles folic acid and competes with it for the active site of the enzyme **dihydrofolate reductase**. It binds very tightly to this enzyme as the affinity of methotrexate is 100,000 times greater than that of folic acid, and the binding is **irreversible**. It may be noted in **Fig. 9.10.4** that administration of *leucovorin* (citrovorum factor, folinic acid) bypasses this block and reverses the effect of methotrexate.

With continuous high dose infusions of methotrexate leucovorin "rescue" should be instituted, for which leucovorin is injected in a dose of 15 mg/m^2 every 6 hours for 7 doses. This procedure rescues normals cells, and is expected to prevent toxicity.

Methotrexate can be given orally, IM, IV or intrathecally. After IV injection, it distributes in about 75 percent of body weight. Disappearance from plasma is best described by a three-compartment model, as a **triphasic** decline in plasma concentration is observed. The **initial** phase $t_{1/2}$ is 0.75 hours; the **second** phase $t_{1/2}$ is 2-3.5 hours, and is associated with renal elimination. The **final** phase (which begins 6-24 hours after conventional doses, and 30-48 hours after high doses) is prolonged due to excretion *via* the bile and reabsorption from the gut, and the $t_{1/2}$ is 10-12 hours. Methotrexate enters into cells via an energy-dependent carrier-mediated transport system like folate.

Methotrexate is the drug of choice for **choriocarcinoma** and for intrathecal therapy of malignancy. It induces complete remission in acute **lymphoblastic leukaemia**. It is also used to treat several solid tumours including **osteogenic sarcoma, epidermoid carcinoma of head and neck and some bronchial carcinomas**. It has also been used as an immunosuppressant in **Wegener's granulomatosis, rheumatoid arthritis, sarcoidosis, dermatomyositis**, and occasionally to reduce cellular proliferation in cases of **acute psoriasis.**

Adverse effects include **myelosuppression**, nausea, vomiting, stomatitis and diarrhoea. Prolonged low dose administration may cause hepatic fibrosis, **interstitial pneumonitis** and **osteoporosis**. On intrathecal administration convulsions and symptoms resembling meningitis may occur. **Paraplegia, cranial nerve palsies and cerebellar dysfunction** may occur in addition. The drug acts as an **abortifacient**, and should not be used in the first trimester of pregnancy. **Acquired resistance** to methotrexate action may develop.

PYRIMIDINE ANALOGUES

Fluorouracil (5-FU). This is a fluorinated pyrimidine analogue. Fluorouracil in the body is converted into **ribosyl** and **deoxyribosyl** metabolites. However, its primary action is on DNA synthesis. Regarding its mode of action, fluorouracil is biotransformed to 5-fluoro-deoxyuridylate which **inhibits thymidylate synthetase,** an enzyme that promotes the conversion of deoxyuridine into deoxythymidine **(Fig. 9.10.5)**. Since thymidine is essential for DNA synthesis, its lack halts cell proliferation. In addition fluorouracil is incorporated as the nucleotide into RNA, thereby depressing RNA synthesis directly.

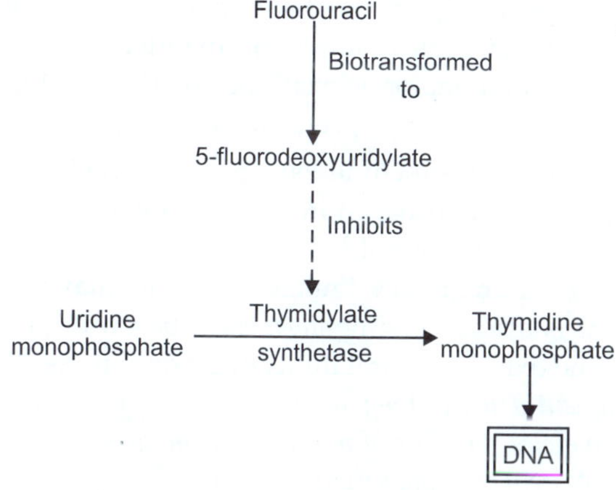

Fig. 9.10.5: The biotransformation and activation of 5-fluorouracil.

Fluorouracil is extensively used in the treatment of **colorectal carcinoma**. It is also effective in **gastric** and **pancreatic adnocarcinoma.** Other responsive tumours are **carcinoma of the breast, bladder, ovary, uterine cervix and hepatoma.**

Fluorouracil is given intravenously, and has a short half-life. Topical fluorouracil (Efudex) is also available as a 1-5 percent cream. It is used for the treatment of multiple **actinic (solar) keratoses** on the head and neck.

Adverse reactions include oral ulceration and diarrhoea; bone marrow suppression which occurs about

14 days after initiation of treatment; and megaloblastic anaemia due to interference with thymidine incorporation into DNA.

Cytarabine. This pyrimidine analogue is a synthetic nucleoside, and it interferes with DNA synthesis by inhibiting DNA polymerase. Thus, it is an S-phase specific antimetabolite. It has a marked **immunosuppressive effect**. Its effectiveness is directly proportional to the duration of exposure of cells to the drug. On intravenous injection cytarabine is metabolized by the widely distributed enzyme **cytidine deaminase** to uracil arabinoside. CSF penetration is not effective, and the drug has to be given intrathecally.

Cytarabine is mainly used for induction or maintenance of remission in **acute leukaemias.** Toxic manifestations include **nausea, vomiting, stomatitis** and **bone marrow depression**.

Azarabine. It is the triacetyl derivative and pro-drug form of azauridine. It was synthesized to achieve better absorption on oral administration. Azarabine has marked therapeutic value in **psoriasis, mycosis fungoides** and **polycythaemia vera**.

Purine Analogues

Mercaptopurine. This agent is the thioanalogue of hypoxanthine, which is part of the synthetic pathway of **adenine** and **guanine**. It interferes with purine synthesis and is a **cell cycle-specific drug** for the S-phase. In addition it has an **immunosuppressant action**. 6-MP is used primarily in the treatment of childhood **acute leukaemia** and as a remission-maintenance agent. Its closely related analogue azathioprine (Imuran) is mainly used as an immunosuppressant (see later).

Toxic effects include leucopenia, thrombocytopenia, haemorrhage, nausea, anorexia, stomatitis and cholestatic jaundice. 6-MP should be avoided during the first trimester of pregnancy. Enhanced toxicity may occur if the patient is also receiving *allopurinol*, because the enzyme xanthine oxidase is vital for its degradation. *As allopurinol is frequently used along with chemotherapy in haematologic malignancies, the dose of mercaptopurine should be reduced to 25-30 percent to avoid serious toxicity.*

Thioguanine. This is an analogue of guanine, and is metabolized along pathways similar to those of mercaptopurine. It is **cell cycle-specific** for the S-phase.

Thioguanine is used solely in the treatment of **acute leukaemias**. It is preferred to mercaptopurine as it causes fewer gastrointestinal reactions. Further, it may be used with allopurinol without an adjustment of the dose.

3. Natural Products

Vinca alkaloids. Th.ese are plant alkaloids extracted from **Vinca rosea**, which cause **metaphase arrest** by interfering with the assembly of microtubules.

Vincristine. It is a major drug in the management of the **leukaemias** and **lymphomas**, particularly for the induction of remission. It is also active against a variety of solid proliferating neoplasms. It is a "spindle poison" and causes arrest of the mitotic cycle. It is very effective in *malignant lymphomas* and the combination of mustine, vincristine, procarbazine and prednisone (MOPP) is considered the treatment of choice in advanced **Hodgkin's disease**.

In contrast to vinblastine, vincristine does not produce bone marrow depression (marrow-sparing). Its main toxicity is **neuropathy** which may take any form, but usually presents as a sensiromotor peripheral neuropathy, with paraesthesias, loss of tendon reflexes and muscular weakness.

Vinblastine. Vinblastine is often substituted for vincristine in the management of **lymphomas**. It is also used in the management of **malignant teratomata**. It appears to bind or crystallize critical microtubular proteins of the mitotic spindle, leading to metaphase arrest. It is **cell cycle specific** for the M-Phase. **Adverse effects** include gastrointestinal disturbances, alopecia and bone marrow depression.

Antibiotics. Many of the antibiotics bind to DNA or fit into the helical lattice (intercalate) between specific bases, and block the transcription of new RNA and DNA and cell replication. The cytotoxic antibiotics include **dactinomycin, the anthracyclines (daunorubicin and doxorubicin), bleomycin, mithramycin and mitomycin**.

Dactinomycin. It is a high molecular weight antineoplastic antibiotic isolated from **Streptomyces parvullus**. It binds to DNA and inhibits mRNA synthesis, and other forms of DNA-dependent RNA synthesis, including the synthesis of ribosomal RNA in the nucleolus. While maximal cell kill is noted in G_1 phase, this drug is still thought to be primarily a phase nonspecific agent. It also has **immunosuppressive activity**.

Dactinomycin is used in combination with surgery and vincristine in the adjuvant treatment of **Wilms' tumour**, with or without radiotherapy. It is also used with methotrexate for **gestational choriocarcinoma**. Adverse reactions include gastrointestinal upset, bone marrow suppression, and alopecia.

Anthracycline Antibiotics

The anthracycline glucoside antibiotics (doxorubicin and daunorubicin) have been isolated from **Streptomyces peucetius var. caesius**. Although they differ only slightly in their chemical structure, doxorubicin is used in the treatment of certain **non-Hodgkin lymphomas, many solid tumours**, and **also acute leukaemias** whereas, daunorubicin is primarily used in **acute myeloid leukaemia**. Regarding their *mode of action*, the anthracyclines intercalate between nucleotide pairs, and the amino sugar binds tightly to DNA. It has been further proposed that these agents have a second mode of binding involving `alkylation' which makes them "**two-hit**" agents. After binding to DNA, these drugs, block DNA-directed RNA synthesis and transcription. The anthracyclines are **phase nonspecific agents**. Major fraction of these drugs and their metabolites are excreted in bile, and about 1/6th in urine. Some metabolites retain antitumour activity. The biliary route of excretion results in **enterohepatic recirculation** of cytotoxic moieties.

Doxorubicin. It is one of the most successful antitumour drugs. it has been used to treat **acute leukaemias**, and many **solid tumours**. It should be given IV into a fast-running infusion, as tissue extravasation causes severe pain and necrosis. **The combination of cisplatin and doxorubicin is very effective in genitourinary tumours, including bladder, prostate, testicular and ovarian carcinoma**.

Doxorubicin should not be given to patients with impaired cardiac function, as the drug itself is cardiotoxic. **Supraventricular arrhythmias** may occur immediately after administration. Progressive **myocardial damage** leading to an irreversible cardiomyopathy is a serious limitation to the use of doxorubicin. It commonly induces **myelosuppression** and **alopecia.**

Daunorubicin. This anthracycline antibiotic was the first agent to be isolated in this class of cytotoxic antibiotics. Its main use is in **acute myeloid leukaemia**, and the toxic manifestations are similar to those with doxorubicin.

Bleomycin. The bleomycins are a series of different cytotoxic glycopeptide antibiotics produced by **Streptomyces verticillus**. Bleomycin sulphate is a mixture of bleomycin A_2 and bleomycin B_2. Regarding the mode of action, bleomycin acts through scission of DNA strands and interference with DNA polymerase, causing damage to DNA. Mitotic arrest occurs as a consequence of this event. Cells are most sensitive to bleomycin during the G_2 and M phases of the cell cycle. Bleomycin is administered by the IM, IV, or subcutaneous route.

Bleomycin is one of the few drugs to show activity in **squamous cell carcinoma**. **Testicular tumours, malignant lymphomas, uterine cervix carcinoma** and **squamous cell carcinomas of the head and neck** are most responsive. *Adverse reactions* include anaphylactoid reactions, fever and pulmonary fibrosis uncommonly. In *Hodgkin's disease* bleomycin has been added to the MOPP regimen.

Mithramycin. It is one of the chromomycin antibiotics isolated from **Streptomyces plicatus**. Its *mode of action* is similar to that of dactinomycin, and it inhibits DNA-dependent synthesis of RNA. It is **phase-specific** for the S-phase. Mithramycin has an effect on calcium metabolism, and probably suppresses osteoclastic activity, and also may block parathormone production. Its primary use is in **embryonal cell carcinoma of the testes**. Currently this agent is rarely used as a cytotoxic agent because it causes marked myelosuppression, and a severe haemorrhagic diathesis. However, it has a place in the **emergency therapy of severe hypercalcaemia** associated with malignant disease, and severe hypercalcaemia refractory to conventional therapy.

Mitomycin. This is a cytotoxic antibiotic isolated from **Streptomyces caespitosus**. It is a cell cycle nonspecific alkylating agent. It has been used predominantly to treat **gastrointestinal tumours**, but because of the myelosuppression it causes and nephrotoxicity in the form of glomerular sclerosis it has not found widespread use.

Enzymes

Asparaginase. Asparaginase (L-asparaginase) is an enzyme derived from the cultures of either **E. coli, or Erwinia carotovora**. Asparagine is a **non-essential amino acid** normally synthesized by the mammalian tissue cells. Asparaginase **inhibits asparagine synthetase**, and catalyses the hydrolysis of asparagine to aspartic acid and ammonia, thus depleting the amount of asparagine in blood and tumour cells. Certain leukaemic cells are unable to synthesize their own asparagine via the asparagine synthetase reaction, and depend upon exogenous sources for the supply of asparagine. Normal cells, however, are able to synthesize asparagine. Thus the asparagine depleting action of asparaginase **interferes with protein, and also DNA and RNA synthesis in tumour cells or leukaemic cells selectively**, thereby killing the malignant cells. The sensitivity of the malignant cells to asparaginase is inversely related to their capacity to synthesize asparagine. In this manner asparaginase has a unique action, and is a **cell cycle specific** agent for the post-mitotic G_1-phase.

Asparaginase is effective in **acute lymphocytic leukaemia** and is most often combined with other chemotherapeutic agents to induce remission in children. It should not be used as a sole induction agent. *Adverse reactions include immunosuppression, hypersensitivity reactions, ranging from urticaria to anaphylactic shock. Neurotoxicity, hepatotoxicity,* and *hyperglycaemia* secondary to decreased insulin production have been reported.

4. Hormones and Antagonists

Although the precise mode of action of the hormones in the treatment of malignant disease is not known, they have been used for decades to treat **endocrine-related tumours** (carcinoma of the breast, prostate, endometrium and ovary), and certain **non-endocrine malignancies** (leukaemia, lymphomas). Recently, **antioestrogens** have been used in patients with advanced carcinoma of the breast.

The most useful hormones and antagonists are as follows:

(i) *Adrenocorticosteroids.* Hydrocortisone acetate, prednisone, prednisolone, dexamethasone.
(ii) *Androgens.* Testosterone propionate, fluoxymesterone.
(iii) *Antiandrogens.* Flutamide.
(iv) *Oestrogens.* Diethylstilboestrol, ethinyloestradiol.
(v) *Antioestrogens.* Tamoxifen, nafoxidine, clomiphene.
(vi) *Progestogens.* Hydroxyprogesterone caproate, medroxyprogesterone, megesterol acetate.
(vii) *Luteinizing hormone-releasing hormone (LH-RH) antagonists.* Buserelin, leuprolide.

Mode of action. The steroid hormones must bind to receptor proteins in the cytoplasm of cancer cells in order to exert their anticancer effects. Highly specific **cytoplasmic receptors** have been identified for **oestradiol, dexamethasone** and **androstenolone**. Evidence further indicates that the steroid hormones form a mobile steroid-receptor complex which binds directly to DNA in the nucleus and **alters the transcription** of structural or regulatory genes **(Fig. 9.10.6)**. Some data indicate that the lethal action on the cancer cell is due to the **steroid-induced rise in free fatty acids** at the nuclear membrane, wich causes dissolution of that membrane and cell death. *Oestrogen receptor positivity predicts responsiveness to endocrine ablation, whereas patients with oestrogen receptor negativity fail to respond to such treatment.*

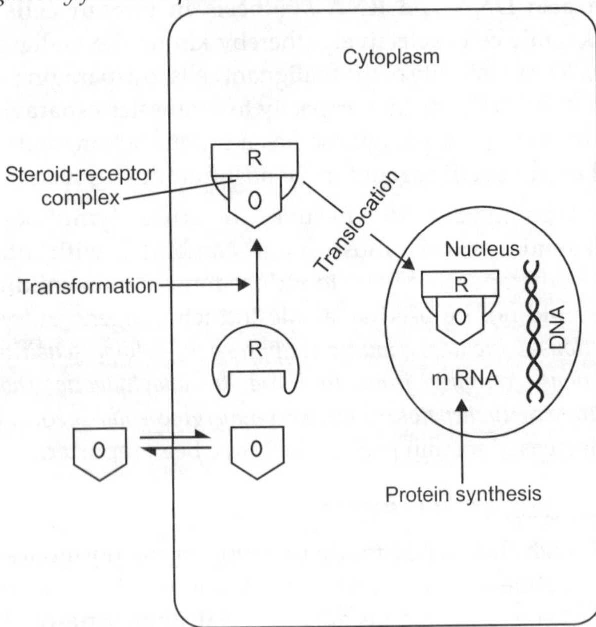

Fig. 9.10.6: A model cancer cell which is oestrogen receptor positive. Oestrogen (O) binds to a 200,000 Mol. Wt. receptor (R), which undergoes two metabolic transformations with reduction in molecular weight, after which it is translocated into the cell's nucleus. This complex is then bound to chromatin, and RNA synthesis and protein synthesis is initiated. A similar process probably applies for *progesterone* or *androgen receptors*. Cells with such steroid hormone receptors respond to hormonal therapy

Adrenocorticosteroids. These agents inhibit RNA and protein synthesis; interfere with lymphoid proliferation; have a lympholytic effect; and cause regression of lymphatic tissue. These steroids inhibit growth of mesenchymal tissues, and have anti-inflammatory and immunosuppressive activities. The corticosteroids are mainly used for **acute** and **chronic lymphatic leukaemia, Hodgkin's disease** and **non-Hodgkin's lymphomas, prostatic carcinoma** and **multiple myeloma.** They are usually combined with other chemotherapeutic agents. **Adverse reactions** include Cushingoid features, sodium retention, oedema, hypertension, muscle weakness, osteoporosis, glycosuria and diabetes mellitus, and proximal myopathy.

Androgens. Large doses of androgens induce a regression of **disseminated carcinoma of the breast**. They may be used in breast cancer in premenopausal women although oophorectomy is more effective. **Adverse effects** include fluid retention, masculinization with clitoral enlargement, hirsutism, deepening of voice, increased libido, acne and alopecia.

Antiandrogens. Flutamide is a nonsteroidal antiandrogen which competes with testosterone for the androgen receptor. It is used to treat **cancer prostate**.

Oestrogens. These agents are effective in the treatment of **metastatic breast carcinoma** in postmenopausal patients, and in **carcinoma of the prostate**. Disseminated prostatic carcinoma can be controlled by orchidectomy or oestrogen therapy. Carcinoma of the male breast is a rare tumour, but it may be controlled by either orchidectomy or the administration of oestrogens.

Antioestrogens. Three antioestrogens, namely **tamoxifen, nafoxidine** and **clomiphene** have been useful in the treatment of human **breast cancer**. These agents are nonsteroidal in nature, and out of them **tamoxifen is preferred** due to its relative lack of toxicity. The antioestrogenic effect of tamoxifen is related to its ability to compete with oestradiol for oestrogen receptor protein. It is useful in the palliative treatment of **advanced breast cancer** in postmenopausal women. It may also be used as an adjunct after surgery for carcinoma breast.

Progestogens. The progestogens have been usefully employed in the management of **endometrial carcinoma, breast cancer, refractory prostatic cancer**, and **rarely carcinoma of the kidney** and **testes**. High dose progestogen therapy may benefit o**varian carcinoma**.

LH-RH antagonists. Buserelin and **leuprolide** are peptide analogues of LH-RH, and decrease oestrogen and testosterone production by gonads. They are both active against **prostatic** and **breast cancers**.

5. Radioactive Isotopes

Mainly *three* radioactive isotopes-**sodium phosphate** (P^{32}), **sodium iodide** ($I1^{31}$) and **radiogold** (Au^{198}), are employed in therapeutics. All emit **beta particles** or "ionizing radiations" in amounts that destroy living tissues in their immediate vicinity. Although beta radiations penetrate only a short distance, they can damage enough erythroid or myeloid cells to produce remissions. With an overdose the bone marrow may be depressed. Radioisotope administration during pregnancy is dangerous due to radiation hazard to the foetus.

Sodium phosphate (P^{32}, Phosphotope). Radioactive phosphorus (P^{32}) accumulates in haemopoietic tissue producing a reduction in red and white cell counts. The half-life is 14.3 days. It is mainly used in the proliferative phase of **polycythaemia vera** and is also effective in **chronic lymphocytic** and **granulocytic leukaemia.** Although usual doses rarely cause radiation sickness, dosage should be adjusted individually. Excessive dosage causes **myelosuppression.**

Sodium iodide (I^{131}, Iodotope). The radioactive isotope of iodine accumulates in the thyroid gland, where its ionizing beta radiations destroy thyroid tissue. I^{131} is used to treat **hyperthyroidism**, and inoperable **thyroid carcinoma.** I^{131} has a half-life of 8 days. Only about 15 percent of thyroid tumours are sufficiently well differentiated to concentrate iodine. Hence, its limited application. **Permanent hypothyroidism** is a common complication of therapy with radioiodine (see Chap. 7.2). Other radioisotopes of iodine (I^{125}, half-life 57 days; I^{132}, half-life 2.3 hours) are employed for diagnostic tests of thyroid function.

Radiogold solution (Au^{198}, Aureotope). This short-lived radioisotope (half-life 2.7 days) emits both beta particles and gamma rays, and is available in the form of colloidal solution. It is used mainly to treat **malignant pleural and peritoneal effusions**, for which it is injected directly into the involved serous cavity

6. Miscellaneous Agents

Cisplatin. It is a heavy metal complex containing a central atom of platinum surrounded by two chloride atoms, and two ammonia molecules in the cis-position. It has **properties like the bifunctional alkylating agents**, and produces cross-links in DNA, exerting a phase nonspecific effect. It is mainly used in the treatment of **metastatic testicular tumours** and **ovarian carcinoma.** Patients with **carcinoma prostate** and **bladder**, also show response. Cisplatin may be combined with bleomycin, vinblastine and doxorubicin with advantage. **Adverse effects** include nephrotoxicity, myelosuppression, nausea and vomiting.

Carboplatin. It is an analogue of cisplatin, but has a lower chemical reactivity and lower risk of toxicity to kidneys, hearing and peripheral nerves. However, it is more **myelosuppressive** than cisplatin. It has the same indications as cisplatin.

Hydroxyurea. Hydroxyurea is an analogue of urea. The exact mode of action is uncertain, but it causes immediate inhibiton of DNA synthesis without altering RNA or protein synthesis. It is a **phase specific agent**, and exerts its lethal effect on cells in S-phase by **inhibiting ribonucleotide reductase**, an enzyme that catalyses the conversion of ribonucleotides to dexyribonucleotide, an important step in the synthesis of DNA **(Fig. 9.10.3).** Hydorxyurea is effective in **chronic granulocytic leukaemia** refractory to busulphn and mercaptopurine. It may be combined with radiation therapy in **squamous cell carcinoma of the head and neck, and uterine cervix. Adverse reactions** include nausea and vomiting, thrombocytopenia, anaemia, disorientation, hallucinations and impairment of renal function with hyperuricaemia and uric acid calculi.

Procarbazine. The mode of action of this methylhydrazine derivative is uncertain. It inhibits synthesis of DNA, RNA and protein by alkylation. It is a phase specific drug for the S-phase. It is effective in **primary** and **metastatic brain tumours, bronchogenic carcinoma** and **Hodgkin's disease.** Bone marrow depression and gastrointestinal disturbances are the primary toxic manifestations.

Mitotane. This drug is a chlorophenothane (DDT) congener. The drug produces selective **atrophy of the zona fasciculata and reticularis of the adrenal cortex.** It interferes with the synthesis of cortisol. It is useful in the treatment of **adrenal carcinoma** (both functional and non-functional inoperable carcinoma). **Adverse reactions** include skin eruptions, diarrhoea and depression.

Razoxane. Razoxane acts by some still unknown mechanism to control cases of **acute granulocytic** and **lymphocytic leukaemia** that are refractory to standard therapy. It has shown some effect in non-Hodgkin lymphoma. There is some evidence that this drug **increases tumour response to radiotherapy.**

Clinical Response to Chemotherapy

Cancer chemotherapy alone as currently employed can be curative in **choriocarcinoma, acute lymphocytic leukaemia**, some **cases of Hodgkin's disease, Burkitt's lymphoma, diffuse histocytic lymphoma, certain testicular tumours, and possibly osteogenic sarcoma.** Enhanced survival has been achieved in acute myelocytic leukaemia, non-Hodgkin's lymphoma, multiple myeloma, chronic leukaemias, and adenocarcinomas of the breast and ovary. **Surgery plus radiotherapy and chemotherapy** have been effective in Wilms' tumour, embryonal rhabdomyosarcoma and Ewing's sarcoma. **Adjuvant chemotherapy** is used in breast cancer and other tumours to achieve total "cell-kill". *Immunotherapy* is under investigation and development, and is expected to play a major role in the treatment of cancer. The current status of chemotherapy of various kinds of cancer is summarized in **Table 9.10-5.**

Table 9.10-5. *Clinical response of various malignancies to chemotherapy*

Type of malignancy	*Primarily preferred regimens*	*Secondary drugs*	*Remarks*
I. HAEMATOLOGIC MALIGNANCIES			
Acute lymphocytic (lymphoblastic) leukaemia	*Induction of remission* Prednisone + Vincristine *For CNS prophylaxis* Methotrexate intrathecally plus cranial irradiation *Maintenance of remission* Mercaptopurine (daily) Methotrexate and Cyclophosphamide intermittently	Daunorubicin Asparaginase Cytarabine Doxorubicin Thioguanine	Initial complete remission induced in upto 90 percent of cases; prolonged survival possible with proper maintenance.
Acute myelocytic (granulocytic) leukaemia	*Induction of remission* Cytarabine + thioguanine or cytarabine + daunorubicin *Maintenance of remission* Same as above, or combination of cytarabine with any of the secondary drugs	Doxorubicin Mercaptopurine Vincristine Azacytidine Carmustine Cyclophosphamide Prednisone Methotrexate Asparaginase	Combination therapy produces remission in 50 percent of cases.
Chronic lymphocytic leukaemia Chronic myelocytic leukaemia	Chlorambucil alone or with prednisone Busulphan	Cyclophosphamide, Triethylenemelamine, Uracil mustard, mercaptopurine, Hydroxyurea, Melphalan	Patients survive 7-10 years or more. Can be controlled for long periods by chemotherapy and splenic irradiation or splenectomy. Treat "blast crisis" as acute form of the disease (see above)
Hodgkin's disease	*MOPP regimen:* Mustine, Vincristine (Oncovin), Procarbazine, Prednisone	*ABVD regimen*: doxorubicin (Adriamycin), bleomycin, vinblastine, dacarbazine. Other drugs are carmustine, lomustine, thiotepa, streptozocin	The MOPP regimen induces complete remissions in advanced (Stage III and IV) cases.
Non-Hodgkin's lymphomas	*COP regimen*: Cyclophosphamide, Vincristine (Oncovin), Prednisone	Various combinations of three or more drugs of the following: Doxorubicin, Prednisone, Bleomycin, Methotrexate, Cytarabine, Cyclophosphamide	Combination therapy produces prolonged remission in upto 70 percent of patients in advanced stages.
Burkitt's lymphoma	Cyclophosphamide	Methotrexate, Cytarabine, Carmustine, Vincristine, Ifosfamide	Can be cured by single-drug therapy if diagnosed early.
Multiple myeloma	Melphalan+prednisone, or cyclophosphamide+ prednisone	Carmustine, Lomustine, Vincristine, Cytarabine, Procarbazine, Chlorambucil, Doxorubicin	Early chemotherapy produces remission and lengthens life.
Polycythaemia vera	Busulphan or Chlorambucil	Radiophosphorus (p^{32}), Cyclophosphamide, Melphalan	Chemotherapy with alkylating agents and irradiation are effective following venesection.
Mycosis fungoides	Mechlorethamine (systemic and topical)	Methotrexate, Cyclophosphamide, Procarbazine, Carmustine, Bleomycin, Doxorubicin	Skin symptoms need drugs for symptomatic relief of pruritus.

Table 9.10-5. Contd...

Type of malignancy	*Primarily preferred regimens*	*Secondary drugs*	*Remarks*
II. SOLID MALIGNANT TUMOURS			
(*a*) **Paediatric types**			
Embryonal rhabdo-myosarcoma	Combinations of dactinomycin, vincristine, and cyclophosphamide	Doxurubicin, Dacarbazine, Lomustine, Methotrexate Fluorouracil, Thiotepa	Chemotherapy with surgery and radiation helps to lengthen survival.
Wilms' tumour	Combination of dactinomycin and vincristine	Doxorubicin	Cure rate has increased by adding chemotheraphy to surgery and radiotherapy.
Neuroblastoma	Combination of cyclophosphamide and vincristine	Doxorubicin, Daunorubicin Dacarbazine	Chemotherapy used as an adjunct to surgery and radiation in advanced cases.
Retinoblastoma	Combination of cyclophosphamide and vincristine	—	Chemotherapy employed following enucleation in patients with poor prognosis.
Osteogenic sarcoma	Doxorubicin	High-dose methotrexate followed by leucovorin, combinations of vincristine, melphalan and cyclophosphamide added to doxorubicin	Chemotherapy following surgery produces prolonged remissions, and possible "cures" in patients without metastases.
(*b*) **Primarily adult types**			
Breast cancer	(*i*) *Nonhormonal chemotherapy* with 3 or 5 of the following drugs: Cyclophosphamide, methotrexate, fluorouracil, vincristine and prednisone; or doxorubicin+ cyclophosphamide.	Combination of drugs which was not used as primary therapy	Combination therapy produces responses in 50-70 percent of cases with metastatic breast cancer. Single agents tested as adjuncts to surgery and radiation.
	(*ii*) *Hormonal therapy*: androgens for premenopausal women and tamoxifen; oestrogens with or without progestogens for postmenopausal women, also tamoxifen		Hormone and antihormone therapy is likely to be useful in patients whose tumour tissue contains oestrogen receptors.
Colorectal carcinoma	Fluorouracil alone or with semustine	Lomustine, Carmustine, Mitomycin, Vincristine	Response rate in recurrent or metastatic case is 15-30 percent. Adjuvant therapy being tried after surgery
Gastric and pancreatic adenocarcinomas	Fluorouracil + semustine or Carmustine, or fluorouracil + doxorubicin+mitomycin	Hydroxyurea, Lomustine	Response rate with new combinations has risen to 40 percent compared to 20 percent with fluorouracil alone.
Bronchogenic carcinoma	Cyclophosphamide + doxorubicin, methotrexate and lomustine	Cisplatin, Vincristine	Response rate with combination chemotherapy better than with single drugs. However, survival time is not significantly improved.
Carcinoma cervix	Mitomycin+bleomycin + Vincristine	Lomustine, Cyclophosphamide, Doxorubicin, Methotrexate	Response to chemotherapy is of a short duration.
Endometrial carcinoma	Doxorubicin + cyclophosphamide	Progestogens, Fluorouracil	Progestogens increase survival time of patients who respond. Results of chemotherapy are inconclusive.
Ovarian carcinoma	Doxorubicin, Cyclophosphamide, and Cisplatin	Melphalan, Fluorouracil, Vincristine, Bleomycin	Alkylating agents produce initial responses in more than 50 percent cases.

Table 9.10-5. Contd...

Type of malignancy	*Primarily preferred regimens*	*Secondary drugs*	*Remarks*
Testicular carcinoma	Combination of Cisplatin, Vinblastine and bleomycin	Methotrexate, Dactinomycin, Doxorubicin, Cyclophosphamide	Combination chemotherapy produces complete and prolonged remissions and even cures. Toxic reactions are common.
Choriocarcinoma (trophoblastic tumours)	Methotrexate alone or in combination with vincristine, dactinomycin and chlorambucil in high-risk cases	Vinblastine, Mercaptopurine, Doxorubicin	Complete remissions occur in 90 percent of patients receiving early treatment. Results in cases with metastatic disease are also good
Prostatic carcinoma	Diethylstilboestrol, Ethinyloestradiol and other oestrogens	Doxorubicin, Cyclophosphamide, Fluorouracil, Mustine, Estramustine	Good response initially in 80 percent of cases treated with hormones. Response to non-hormonal chemotherapy between 20 and 40 percent.
Bladder cancer	Doxorubicin	Fluorouracil, Cisplatin, Cyclophosphamide, Thiotepa instillation	Response ratios of about 30 percent have been reported.
Brain tumours	Carmustine or lomustine	Doxorubicin, Procarbazine, Semustine	Primary drugs produce some improvement in a small minority of patients.
Head and neck squamous cell carcinomas	Methotrexate	Bleomycin, Cisplatin, Cyclophosphamide	Tumour size is often reduced by IV or intra-arterial methotrexate.
Adrenocortical carcinoma	Mitotane	Doxorubicin	This drug suppresses hormone secretion in metastatic tumour masses.
Carcinoma thyroid	Radioiodide (I^{131}), doxorubicin	Bleomycin, Fluorouracil Melphalan	—
Carcinoid	Doxorubicin + Cyclophosphamide	Dactinomycin, Methysergide	—
Insulinoma	Streptozocin	Doxorubicin, Fluorouracil Mitomycin	—

Response to Combination Therapy

Regrowth of tumour cells occurs due to either incomplete eradication of cancer cells, or a stepwise induction of biochemical resistance. Combinations of cytotoxic drugs (some of them are mentioned in **Table 9.10-5**), used in treating cancer, are based on certain principles which have already been discussed. There are more than 125 different combination regimens in current use.

Cancer and Immunity

There is evidence that some types of cancer stimulate an immune response. This brings in the hope that malignant cells might be attacked via immune processes. Attempts are being made to treat cancer by immunotherapy. Two methods are under trial: (*i*) **stimulation of nonspecific cellular immunity** by repeated exposure to an antigen, and usually, BCG (Bacillus Calmette Guerin) injections are employed. Direct injection of BCG into the tumours may cause regression and elimination of metastatic cells. Injection at a distant site from the tumour is much less effective; and (*ii*) **killed tumour cells or extracts** of tumour cells, are injected at intervals to induce an immune response. However, reports are conflicting. Immunotherapy of cancer is under development, and holds hope for future.

To conclude, in early days of cancer chemotherapy, a single agent was used in a low dose. **Intermittent high dose chemotherapy** now forms the basis of most modern chemotherapeutic regimens. This is an application of the fractional "cell kill" principle. **Combination chemotherapy** utilizing different drugs is another advancement. Another advance is **adjuvant chemotherapy**, which aims to destroy **micrometastases**, even at a time when there is no clinical evidence of residual disease.

Immunosuppression

Drugs that suppress the immune pathophysiology of certain disease, and drugs that suppress the immune response, play an important role in **tissue** or **organ transplantation procedures** and some disease associated with disorders of immunity.

The Immune Mechanisms

The introduction of a foreign substance (antigen) into the body provokes an immune reaction, and for this it is essential that the body recognizes it as "non-self". Antigens usually have a molecular weight of 5000 or more, and may be proteins or large carbohydrates. Most antigens are first ingested and concentrated by the **macrophages**, and later passed to the nearby **lymphocytes.** The immune response is initiated by the interaction of the antigen with receptors on the surface of the lymphocytes, and the response may be of two types:

1. **Humoral immunity** in which circulating **immunoglobulins** (antibodies) are produced by the plasma cells, derived from lymphocytes arising from the lymphoid tissue of the gut, known as B cells **(Fig. 9.10.7)**. The immunoglobulins react with the antigen in various ways.

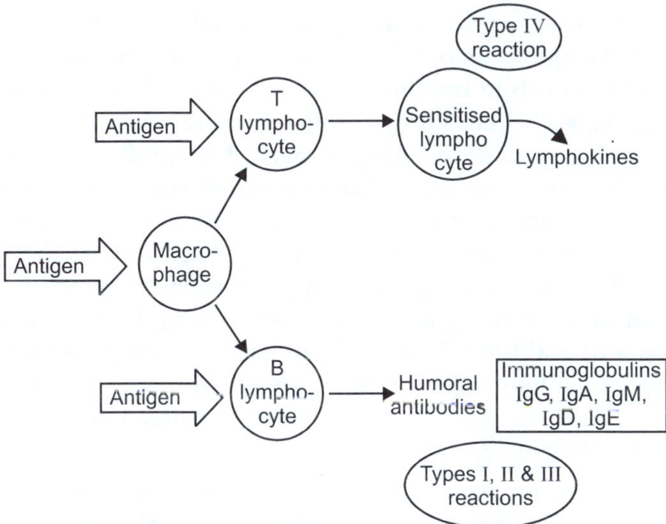

Fig. 9.10.7: The interactions of the immune system.

2. **Cellular immunity** mediated by thymus-derived cells known as T cells, which interact with the antigen to produce lymphokines. The body has the potential to stimulate its immune system to produce antibiodies against itself. Normally such a situation is prevented by a number of suppression mechanisms. But if this suppression mechanism fails, the **autoimmune diseases** result. Deficiencies in the immune system are rarer, but may be congenital or may result from the use of **cytotoxic drugs** and **corticosteroids**. Sometimes the immune reaction to an antigen does not only produce antibodies which damage the antigen, but may also damage body tissues causing hypersensitivity reactions. These reactions are of four types:

Type I (IgE or Reagin-dependent) reaction. In this the antigen antibody combination occurs on the surface of the **mast cells** and **polymorphonuclear leucocytes**, and releases pharmacologically active substances. This reaction is mediated by the IgE antibodies which sensitize the cells (mast cells and polymorphs), and subsequent exposure leads to release of potent chemicals including **histamine, slow reacting substance (SRS-A), eosinophil chemotactic factor (ECF-A), serotonin, bradykinin and other kinins and prostaglandins**. This type of reaction causes **anaphylaxis, allergic asthma, hay fever** and some types of **urticaria**. The onset of type I reaction is within 1-2 minutes, maximal at 15-30 minutes, and lasts $1^{1/2}$ to 2 hours.

Type II (Cytotoxic tissue-specific antibody) reaction. In this the antibody, in the presence of complement, reacts with an antigenic component of a cell or tissue, and results in cell lysis or damage. An *example* of this type of reaction is haemolytic disease in the newborn (**erythroblastosis foetalis**) where antibodies produced by the rhesus-negative mother against the Rh-factor on the red cells of the foetus, cross the placental barrier and cause haemolysis. This reaction is mediated by IgM or IgG antibodies.

Type III (Immune-complex diseases: Arthus reaction) reaction. This is caused by circulating antigen: antibody complexes formed in conditions of slight antigen excess, together with complement which can cause tissue destruction directly and also by attracting polymorphonuclear neutrophils to the site. In a way tissues are damaged as "innocent bystanders". This reaction is delayed and reaches a maximum, hours after exposure to the antigen. **Serum sickness** is a type III reaction. It is mediated by IgM and IgG antibodies.

Type IV (Cell-mediated delayed hypersensitivity) reaction. This immune reaction is mediated by **sensitized circulating lymphocytes of the T-cell type** reacting with the antigen. The immunoglobulins of the type I, II and III reactions are not involved. Most of the manifestations of the reaction are produced by the **lymphokines (Fig. 9.10.7)**, which are soluble factors produced by the sensitized lymphocytes on contact with antigen. These lymphokines cause local inflammation and attract other lymphocytes and macrophages to the site, and enhance phagocytosis. Such a state leads to **vascular thrombosis, granuloma formation and tissue necrosis**. This type of reaction takes 1-2 days to develop after antigen exposure, and reaches its peak at 48-72 hours. *Examples* of this type of reaction are **organ-transplant rejection, contact dermatitis, tuberculous lung reaction,** and **tuberculin skin reaction**.

The most common tissue rejection (allograft rejection) response to an incompatible renal, heart or marrow graft is the development of cytotoxic T lymphocytes. There is consensus of opinion that among the immunosuppressive drugs, the **corticosteroids** are most effective in avoiding the rejection episodes and azathioprine may be helpful. The role of **antilymphocyte globulin (ALG)**, which suppresses the T lymphocyte mediated immune responses is not clear (see later).

The above mentioned immune responses are essential for health. The problem arises when suppression of an unwanted component of an immune reaction is desired. Although such an `ideal' measure is not available, in practice two types of drugs may be used:

(*i*) **Immunosuppressive drugs.** These drugs "damp down" the whole immune system, rendering it less efficient or less competent. These drugs are cytotoxic and attack the lymphocytes, which are reduced in number, and perhaps these agents also interfere with their immune function (see later).

(*ii*) **Antihistamine drugs.** These drugs competitively block the actions of the chemical mediators (mainly histamine) liberated by the type I immune reactions. These agents are discussed in **Chapter 11.1**.

Immunosuppressive Agents

Azathioprine. This drug is a purine analogue (antimetabolite). It is converted in the liver to **6-mercaptopurine** which is its active form. Its immunosuppressive properties and mode of action are similar to those of 6-MP, but it is preferred for immunosuppression in humans, possibly due to its marginally lower toxicity. In fact, it is the most commonly used cytotoxic immunosuppressant. It causes immunosuppression by inhibiting lymphocytes which would otherwise proliferate in response to stimualtion by an antigen. It inhibits delayed hypersensitivity (cell-mediated immunity), and also those aspects of inflammation which depend on cell division.

Clinically azathioprine is used to prevent **transplant rejection** (in a dose of 1-4.0 mg/kg/day orally), and also in the treatment of **autoimmune** and **collagen diseases**. It is partly metabolized in the body by xanthine oxidase, and if **allopurinol** is also prescribed, an equivalent dose reduction is required. **Myelosuppression** is its predominant side effects. Azathioprine sodium is available for IV injection.

Cyclophosphamide. It produces immunosuppression by inhibiting lymphoid cell proliferation. It is most effective if given after an antigenic stimulation, and has some effect if given in large doses before the antigen. Cyclophosphamide combines with the DNA of the lymphocytes, and the cytotoxic action becomes evident when the lymphocytes are stimulated to divide, and are unable to do so. **In fact, it is effective on both (T and B-Lymphocyte) populations of cells when they have been stimulated to divide by the antigen.** It can also reduce antibody production and depress cell-mediated immunity and the associated inflammatory reaction.

Clinically cyclophosphamide can be used to prevent **graft rejection reactions**. It has been used in the treatment of **nephrotic syndrome** resistant to steroids, for which it is superior to azathioprine. In addition, it has been used in nephritis due to **systemic lupus, Wegener's granulomatosis** and **rheumatoid disease**. The usual dose is 3.0 mg/kg/day orally for 8 weeks. Adverse effects include **myelosuppression, alopecia** and **sterility (azospermia) in the male** as a result of prolonged use.

Other cytotoxic agents, including **vincristine, methotrexate, cytarabine** and **chlorambucil** also have immunosuppressive properties, but their use has not been widespread.

Glucocorticosteroids. The corticosteroids are the most widely used immunosuppressive agents, and they were the first to be recognized to have **lympholytic** properties. Administration of a glucocorticoid (prednisone, dexamethasone) reduces the size and lymphoid content of the lymph nodes and spleen, although it has no toxic effect on proliferating myeloid or erythroid stem cells in the bone marrow. **They interfere with the cell cycle of activated lymphoid cells**. The degree of lymphocytopenia is dose-dependent, and high doses reduce lymphocyte counts upto a maximum of 50-75 percent. **A decrease in the absolute number of both T and B lymphocytes occurs, with T cells proportionately more affected**. These steroids, in addition have a marked anti-inflammatory effect, and decrease the release of chemical mediators from mast cells in type I reactions. The release of lytic enzymes from the **lysosomes** of polymorphonuclear leucocytes is also prevented, possibly by **lysosomal membrane stabilization (Chapter 7.5)**. Glucocorticoids also suppress type III and type IV reactions in man. Although steroids do not inhibit the normal humoral immune response in type II reactions, they are effective in treating type II autoimmune diseases.

Based on their potent immunosuppressant activity, the corticosteroids are given **prophylactically** to organ transplant recipients where rejection is a problem, e.g., in renal transplantation. They are also used to treat **rejection episodes**. In addition they are used to treat a wide range of collagen and **autoimmune diseases** like systemic lupus erythematosus, chronic active hepatitis, and autoimmune haemolytic anaemia. Usually when effective immunosuppression is desired, relatively high dosage such as **prednisolone** 60 mg/day is given initially, and then reduced to the lowest maintenance dose. The **adverse reactions** of these agents are potentially hazardous and adrenal suppression is very likely to occur when these agents are used chronically for immunosuppression.

Antilymphocyte globulin (ALG). This antiserum is usually obtained by injecting human lymphocytes or lymphoid cells into large animals (e.g., horses), and raising antibodies. Recently, extremely potent antisera have been obtained by using T lymphocytes from human foetal thymus. Precisely, antihuman lymphocyte globulin (ALG) is an antibody produced in horses by human lymphocytes, and has little effect on antibody production by B-lymphocytes. Regarding its **mode of action**, after injection ALG becomes attached to the lymphocytes and disappears from circulation within 6 hours. The circulating lymphocytes are exposed to a high concentration of ALG. *The lymphocytes that are confined to the tissues around a graft during a rejection crisis are not affected much.* The immunosuppressive effect is thought to be due to the `binding' of ALG around the lymphocyte, which prevents the antigen from reaching its target recognition site. Hence the stimulation for further multiplication is avoided.

Clinically ALG has been used to reduce delayed hypersensitivity and to **prevent graft rejection reaction**. No conclusive controlled trials concerning its efficacy in autoimmune disease have been reported. *Adverse effects* like serum sickness and myelosuppression have been reported. Anaphylactic reactions, urticaria, pruritus and hypotension may occur.

Human Rho (D) immune globulin (Rho GAM). One of the major advances in medicine has been the development of a technique of preventing **Rh haemolytic disease in the newborn** (erythroblastosis foetalis). Sensitization of Rh-negative mothers to the D antigen occurs usually at the time of birth of an Rho (D)-positive infant, when foetal red cells may leak into the mother's blood stream. Sensitization may also occasionally occur with miscarriages or ectopic pregnancies. With subsequent pregnancies in these sensitized mothers, the maternal antibody against Rh-positive cells is transferred to the foetus during the third trimester, leading to the development of **erythroblastosis foetails** or haemolytic disease of the newborn. Thus it is an isoimmune disease.

If an injection of Rho (D) antibody (RhoGAM) is administered (2 ml IM) to the mother within 72 hours after the birth of the baby, the mother's own antibody response to the foreign Rho (D) positive cells is suppressed. When the mother has been treated in this manner, **Rh haemolytic disease of the newborn does not occur in the subsequent pregnancy**. Adverse reactions occur infrequently, and include local discomfort at the injection site with slight fever.

Cyclosporin. This is an immunosuppressive agent used in **human organ transplantation**, and for the treatment of graft-versus host (GVH) syndrome following **bone marrow transplantation**. It is a fat soluble peptide antibiotic which selectively destroys T lymphocytes during their stage of differentiation.

Cyclosporin has been used orally in a dose of 10-25 mg/kg daily. **Adverse reactions** include nephrotoxicity, higher incidence of viral infections, transient liver dysfunction, and very little myelosuppression. It has been used with success as the sole immunosuppressant for **cadaveric transplants of the kidney, pancreas, and liver.**

To conclude, the immunosuppressive agents currently have three clinical indications: (*i*) **organ transplantation**; (*ii*) **autoimmune diseases**, and (*iii*) **isoimmune disorders** like Rh haemolytic disease of the newborn.

Immunostimulating Agents

A new field in pharmacology is the development of agents that stimulate the immune response. The major potential uses of these drugs are: (*i*) **immunodeficiency disorders**; (*ii*) **chronic infections**; and (*iii*) **cancer**.

Thymosin. This is a relatively crude low molecular weight hormone obtained from bovine thymus extracts. Thymosin is under trial for various immunodeficiencies, in patients with T lymphocyte mediated immune diseases (systemic lupus erythematosus, rheumatoid arthritis), and for cancer.

Interferons and interferon-inducers. These agents were first described as antiviral proteins produced by host cells. Later, attempts were made to use them as antiviral drugs **(Chap. 9.9).** Their use in infections, certain forms of cancer, particularly myelomas and lymphomas is under evaluation.

Interleukin-2 (rIL-2) is under trial in patients of AIDS as an immunostimulant.

Immune globulin. When the roles of B and T lymphocytes were elucidated, a clinical classification of immunodeficiency states became possible.

It is now evident that certain types of bacterial infection are associated with true B lymphocyte deficiencies. It is now also possible to quantify immunoglobulins. Thus an appropriate use of immune globulin is in the treatment of *immunodeficiency states due to impaired or absent antibody synthesis*.

The above immunostimulating agents are under investigation for their clinical efficacy. They definitely open a new possibility for the treatment of immunodeficiency states.

9.11 CHEMOTHERAPY OF URINARY TRACT INFECTIONS (UTI)

Acute urinary tract infections are second in frequency only to respiratory tract infections, and particularly women of child-bearing age, are subject to frequent bladder and kidney infections. **Acute pyelonephritis** in the absence of any organic abnormality of the urinary tract, ordinarily does not lead to widespread kidney damage. However, recurrent acute infections in patients with abnormalities that block urine flow can cause kidney damage. The resulting **chronic pyelonephritis** can lead to renal insufficiency and renal failure. Tubercular infection of the urinary tract is considered in **Chapter 9.3.**

Definitions and Terms

A urinary tract infection is defined as a condition characterized by the persistence of actively multiplying bacteria in bladder urine. It occurs when 100,000 or more organisms are present in 1 ml of urine in two separate clean voided samples of urine. When infection is present white blood cells usually accompany the bacteria.

In **acute pyelonephritis** there is loin pain, fever, rigors and frequency of micturition. In this condition it is presumed that there is a bacterial involvement of the renal parenchyma. **Chronic pyelonephritis** is usually associated with asymptomatic bacteriuria. **Asymptomatic bacteriuria** is a laboratory finding and not a clinical condition, and is said to be significant only when 100,000 or more organisms are present in 1 ml of clean voided urine. **Cystitis** is a condition marked by frequency of micturition, fever and tenderness over the suprapubic region. Urine culture indicates infection. In cystitis renal involvement cannot be ruled out.

Causative Organisms

The majority of urinary tract infections are caused by **Escherichia coli**. In domiciliary practice a high proportion of these are sensitive to sulphonamides, but in hospital practice many strains of **Esch. coli** are resistant to **sulphonamides**, and also to antibiotics. It has been demonstrated by serotyping that the strains present in the urinary tract are same as those present in the patient's intestines. Other bowel-derived organisms which cause urinary infections are **Streptococcus faecalis, Proteus mirabilis**, and **Klebsiella aerogenes**. In chronic infections specially when there has been instrumentation of the urethra, or when there is neurological abnormality **Pseudomonas aeruginosa** and sometimes **Staphylococcus aureus** are the causative organisms.

Urinary pH

The pH of urine fluctuates normally, rising after meals and falling at night. Infections caused by urea-splitting organisms (e.g., *Proteus species*) result in the production of alkaline urine. Deliberate alteration of urinary pH influences the action of some urinary chemotherapeutic agents, which may be taken advantage of clinically **(Table 9.11-1)**.

Table 9.11-1. *The influence of urinary pH on the action of some drugs used to treat urinary tract infections*

	Acid Urine		*Alkaline Urine*
Essential:	Hexamine	*Enhanced:*	Sulphonamides
	Mandelic acid		Aminoglycosides
	Mandelamine		Penicillin G
Enhanced:	Nitrofurantoin		

Urine may be made **acidic** by the administration of **ammonium chloride** (6-12 g/day orally), **methionine** (3-10 g/day orally), or **ascorbic acid** (4 g/day orally). **Alkalinization** can be produced by administering **sodium bicarbonate** or **acetazolamide.**

Drugs for Urinary Tract Infection

These drugs may be divided into two groups:

1. **Urinary tract antiseptics**
   Methenamine mandelate
   Quinolones: Nalidixic acid, Clinoxacin, Enoxacin, Norfloxacin, Ciprofloxacin, Nitrofurantoin
   Co-trimoxazole, Trimethoprim, Methylene blue

2. **Antibiotics**
   Ampicillin
   Carbenicillin
   Cephalosporins
   Aminoglycosides: Streptomycin, Kanamycin, Gentamicin,
   Aminosidin sujplhate, Cycloserine

Urinary Tract Antiseptics

Methenamine Mandelate (Mandelamine)

Methenamine mandelate is the salt of **methenamine** and **mandelic acid**, two old urinary antiseptics which are not used individually today. Methenamine is a condensation product of formaldehyde and ammonia from which at a pH of 5.6 or lower the active bactericidal agent formaldehyde is liberated as follows:

$$N_4(CH_2)_6 + 6H_2O \xrightarrow{(H^+)} 4\,NH_3 + 6HCHO$$

Methenamine mandelate is primarily effective against gram-negative bacteria including **Esch. coli**. Microorganisms do not develop resistance or cross-resistance to formaldehyde. Urea-splitting organisms (e.g. **Proteus** species) tend to raise the urinary pH and inhibit the relase of formaldehyde.

Methenamine mandelate is rapidly absorbed on oral administration and concentrated in the urine. Almost no drug is detected in the serum. Since about 20-30 percent of the drug can be prematurely converted into formaldehyde by the gastric acid, the drug is often given in **enteric-coated** tablets. Even though the drug acidifies the urine, simultaneous administration of a urinary acidifying agent like ammonium chloride or sodium acid phosphate is recommended, specially when infection caused by ammonia-producing organisms like **Proteus vulgaris** have to be treated.

Adverse reactions are minimal. Excessive formaldehyde liberated by gastric acid can produce **gastrointestinal upset. Bladder irritation, urinary frequency, burning pain** may occur due to the formaldehyde, and larger doses may cause mild proteinuria or haematuria. The drug is **contraindicated in renal insufficiency** Sulphonamides should not be given simultaneously as they precipitate out in the kidneys in acid urine, and some are directly precipitated by formaldehyde. **Reversible eighth cranial nerve damage** has been reported.

Methenamine mandelate (Mandelamine) is available as tablets and oral suspension. The usual dose for adults is 3-6 g orally in divided doses daily. Mandelamine usually clears the urine within a week provided organisms are susceptible and urinary pH is maintained acid.

Quinolones

The antibacterial 4-quinolones are agents that inhibit DNA synthesis by inhibiting the action of DNA gyrase, the enzyme that is responsible for the **unwinding** and **supercoiling** of DNA in the bacteria prior to replication **(Chap. 9.2)**. Plasmid-mediated resistance does not occur. However, cross-resistance between the 4-quinolones can occur.

Nalidixic Acid

Nalidixic acid is active against some strains of **Esch. coli, Enterobacter aerogenes, Klebsiella** species, and **Proteus** species. Generally **Pseudomonas aeruginosa** is highly resistant. It is a bactericidal agent, but its activity is reduced by tissue fluids.

Nalidixic acid is rapidly and completely absorbed following oral administration. It is rapidly concentrated in the urine both as free drug (20%), and as glucuronated metabolites (80%), and both forms retain their antibacterial activity. There is no likelihood of crystalluria.

Adverse reactions are common and may be serious. Gastrointestinal upsets may be minimized by administering the drug after meals. Transient fever, myalgia, polyarthritis, eosinophilia, vertigo, sleepiness and amblyopia may occur. *Convulsions* may be precipitated. Hepatic damage and blood dyscrasias may occur. Superinfection is rare. Administration during pregnancy should be avoided. It is transferable in breast milk, and should not be given to nursing mothers. Long-term therapy for pyelonephritis is inadvisable because of the high likelihood of **cumulative neurotoxicity**.

Nalidixic acid (Gramoneg) is available in tablets of 250 and 500 mg. The usual dose is 1 g four times daily for 2 weeks, followed by 1 g twice daily for a further 2 weeks. The dose for children is 55 mg/kg daily. It is also available as a suspension 50 mg/ml. No control of urinary pH is necessary, bacterial culture and sensitivity (C/S studies) tests must be done before commencing therapy.

Oxilinic Acid

Oxilinic acid is similar to nalidixic acid, and is suitablefro **acute** and **chronic urinary tract infection** but has an advantage that only a twice-dalily medication is required, and the **adverse reactions are milder**. The recommended dose for adults is 750 mg orally twice daily.

Cinoxacin Acid

Cinoxacin is active against most of the **Enterobacteriaceae** which commonly cause UTI. It produces fewer side effects than nalidixic acid, and is about as effective as co-trimoxazole. The usual dose is 500 mg every 12 hours.

Enoxacin, Norfloxacin, Ciprofloxacin

These three quinolones-*enoxacin, norfloxacin, ciprofloxacin* are more potent than the older agents (nalidixic acid, cinoxacin) against gram-negative bacteria, and are also active against **staphylococci** and **Pseudomonas aeruginosa**. The antipseudomonal activity of ciprofloxacin and norfloxacin is due to their piperazine moiety. Most clinical experience has been gained with ciprofloxacin. The usual doses are - **enoxacin** 200 mg bid for 3 days, and 400 mg bid for 7-14 days for complicated infections; **norfloxacin**, 400 mg bid for 7-10 days; and **ciprofloxacin**, 250 mg bid orally, or 100 mg twice daily IV over 30-60 minutes for 7 days.

Adverse reactions include nausea, diarrhoea, allergic reactions, headache and dizziness. Convulsions and toxic psychosis has been reported. Arthralgia, myalgia, hallucinations, confusion, and disturbances in vision, taste and smell may occur.

Nitrofurantoin

Several **nitrofurans** exhibit mild **antibacterial**, and **antiprotozoal** activity, probably by depressing the formation of acetyl coenzyme A. The three clinically useful compounds are **nitrofurantoin, nitrofurazone** and **furazolidone**. Cross-resistance is complete within this group. The nitrofurans may produce **haemolytic anaemia** in patients with glucose-6-phosphate dehydrogenase (G-6-PD) deficiency.

Nitrofurantoin is a urinary antiseptic, and it is effective against most urinary pathogens. It is effective against many gram-positive and gram-negative organisms, but many strains of *Proteus, Esch. coli, Enterobacter aerogenes, neisseriae, staphylococci, streptococci* and *Pseudomonas aeruginosa* may exhibit resistance. It is primarily a **bacteriostatic** agent and blood plasma reduces its activity. The antibacterial activity is higher in acidic urine.

Nitrofurantoin readily passes the placental barrier, but the concentration in the foetus is too low to be toxic. About 30-50 percent of the dose is cleared by the kidney within 6 hours. The plasma half-life is about 20 minutes. Most of the remainder of the drug is excreted as inactive brown metabolites. There is some tubular reabsorption of nitrofurantoin, which helps to concentrate the drug locally in the renal parenchyma. **Greater tubular reabsorption takes place from acidic urine**. No crystalluria occurs, and nitrofurantoin produces a bright yellow fluorescence in urine.

Adverse reactions. Apart from **hypersensitivity reactions, polyneuropathy** and allergic pneumonitis, the reactions occurring with nitrofurantoin are dose-dependent. **Gastrointestinal upsets** are common and predictable, and to avoid this alterations in particle size and the coating of the drug with liquorice have been attempted. **Haemolytic anaemia** may develop in the G-6 PD deficient patient. A folic acid dependent **megaloblastic anaemia** may develop in patients receiving repeated courses of therapy. Nitrofurantoin causes **ascending sensorimotor neuropathy**. Occurrence of **Loffler's syndrome** or pulmonary eosinophilia has also been reported. It is contraindicated in cases of renal failure.

Nitrofurantoin is **approved only for urinary tract infections** caused by microorganisms known to be sensitive to the drug. It may be effectively used for recurrent infections and for the prevention of bacteriuria after prostatectomy. The three clinically useful nitrofurans are further detailed in **(Table 9.11-2)**.

Trimethoprim-Sulphamethoxazole (Co-Trimoxazole)

Trimethoprim, a nonsulphonamide, together with **sulphamethoxazole**, an intermediate acting sulphonamide, exert a **synergistic bactericidal action against** a wide range of bacteria. This combination is used in the treatment of acute, chronic and **recurrent UTI**, and also in **bacteriuria** of pregnancy. For further detail see **Chapter 9.2.**

Trimethoprim alone in a dose of 100 mg every 12 hours for 10 days can be used for the treatment of uncomplicated UTI due to susceptible strains (*E. coli, P. mirabilis, Klebsiella pneumoniae, Enterobacter* species) of microorganisms.

Table 9.11-2. *The clinically useful 5-nitrofuran compounds*

Drug	*Primary use, Preparations and Dosage*
Nitrofurantoin	Used as an alternative urinary tract antiseptic. Available in tablets of 50 or 100 mg, and as an oral suspension (25 mg/5ml). *Adult dose* is 5-10 mg/kg/day in divided doses with meals for 2 weeks. Between 2 courses, a 1-2 weeks rest period should be observed.
Nitrofurazone	Used for the topical treatment of mixed bacterial skin infections. Antibacterial activity is not reduced by pus, blood or tissue fluids, and it does not depress wound healing. It may induce hypersensitivity rarely. In a 0.2% concentration it is available as an *ointment, cream, solution and dressing*.
Furazolidone	This agent has antibacterial and antiprotozoal actions. Used in the treatment of bacterial enteritis, food poisoning, diarrhoeas, bacillary dysentery and giardiasis. *Usual dose* is 100 mg qid for 2-5 days.

Phenazopyridine Hydrochloride

Phenazopyridine is not an effective urinary antiseptic, although in the past it was used for this purpose. It is of value, however, as a **urinary tract analgesic** to relieve the pain, burning, urgency and frequency associated with cystitis, prostatitis, and urethritis, whether caused by infection or other related disorders. Phenazopyridine is an **azo dye**, and it is absorbed from the gut, and excreted in urine where it exerts its **mild topical analgesic effect** on the urinary tract mucosa. It is available as 100 and 200 mg tablets, and the usual dose is 200 mg three times daily after meals. **Adverse reactions** include gastrointestinal disturbances, headache, haemolytic anaemia, hyperpigmentation, hepatitis, and acute renal failure. It *colours the urine red* or orange and clothing is likely to be stained, of which the patient should be pre-informed to avoid anxiety.

Methylene blue. It is a dye with weak germicidal activity, and is used as a mild genitourinary antiseptic for **cystitis** and **urethritis**. In addition, it is an antidote for **cyanide poisoning**. The usual dose is 65-130 mg tid after meals with a full glass of water. It colours the stool and urine blue-green, and may cause haemolysis in G-6-PD deficient patients.

Antibiotics

Ampicillin. This agent was the first broad-spectrum penicillin, and is active against many urinary pathogens. It may be administered orally or parenterally. It is often effective, but some strains of **Esch. coli** may be resistant. If used repeatedly, ampicillin encourages infection with resistant strains of *Klebsiellae*.

Carbenicillin. This agent is a broad-spectrum penicillin with particular activity against **Ps. aeruginosa** and **Proteus species**. Carbenicillin is not absorbed on oral administration, and is given parenterally, usually by intravenous route. it achieves high concentrations in urine. Infections caused by **Ps. aeruginosa** and **Proteus** species are most difficult to treat, and for this carbenicillin may be beneficially combined with **gentamicin**, an aminoglycoside.

Cephalosporins. Both **cephalothin** (given intravenously), and **cephaloridine** (given intramuscularly) have a place in the treatment of urinary tract infections, specially if accompanied by septicaemia. **Cephalexin** and **cephradine** are two orally absorbed cephalosporins and they have some place in the treatment of UTI due to sensitive strains of **Esch. coli** and **Proteus species (Chap. 9.3)**.

Aminoglycosides. *Gentamicin and kanamycin* are two aminoglycosides that are extremely useful in treating acute UTI, specially when accompanied by septicaemia. Streptomycin is an older agent but may be used in suitably selected cases of UTI. Alkalinization of the urine increases the efficacy of the aminoglycosides in UTI. *They are not drugs of first choice unless the infection is recurrent and resistant to other agents.* While using the aminoglycosides caution has to be observed in renal insufficiency and vestibular lesions **(Chap. 9.3)**.

Cycloserine. Cycloserine is known for its antituberculous action, but some authorities use it for UTI. It inhibits *in vitro* growth of **Esch. coli**, enterococci and staphylococci by inhibiting cell wall synthesis. For **acute** infections (250 mg orally thrice daily), and for **long-term** management (250 mg orally on alternate days) cycloserine may be used. Full doses produce toxic effects, mainly involving the CNS, in the form of neuropsychiatric fits and depression. **It is not a routine drug** for treatment of UTI.

Therapeutic Regimen for UTI

The treatment of UTI may be considered under the following *four* heads:

(*i*) **Removal of predisposing causes.** The precipitating factors like renal calculi, major anatomical abnormalities-congenital, traumatic or disease induced-must be detected and appropriately treated.

(*ii*) **Initial therapy.** The patients selected for initial therapy are those with acute symptomatic pyelonephritis; those with asymptomatic bacteriuria of pregnancy; and those with an anatomical abnormality awaiting correction.

Chemotherapy will be dictated by the results of **urine culture** and **sensitivity tests**.

For very seriously ill patients with invasion of the blood stream, **ampicillin, kanamycin, gentamicin** or **cephalosporins** should be given parenterally. This treatment should continue for at least 10 days, and with the absence of symptoms and sterile urine the treatment is considered successful.

(*iii*) **Long-term therapy**. When initial therapy and surgical measures have not been curative, long-term treatment may offer relief of symptoms. A choice of the drug may be made from: **ampicillin** 500 mg/day; **nitrofurantoin** 100 mg/day; **co-trimoxazole** 1 tab twice daily; and **cycloserine** 250 mg/day. Treatment may continue from 6 weeks to 6 months to eradicate the infection.

(*iv*) **Chemoprophylaxis.** An important measure in the prevention of UTI is the avoidance of catheterization and instrumentation. Cultures should be done and sensitivity determined. *Prophylactic antibacterial agents should not be used routinely.* The conventional sulphonamides are no longer used in the treatment of UTI. **Co-trimoxazole, a quinolone, gentamicin** or a **cephalosporin** are the preferred drugs.

9.12 CHEMOTHERAPY OF SEXUALLY TRANSMITTED DISEASES (STD)

Gonorrhoea	**Vaginitides**
Syphilis	**Trichomoniasis**
Non-gonococcal Urethritis	**Candidiasis**
Genital Herpes	**Chancroid**
Genital and Anorectal Warts	**Lymphogranuloma Venereum**
Mollusca Contagiosa	**Granuloma Inguinale**
Acquired Immunodeficiency Syndrome (AIDS)	

After being nearly controlled in the early 1950s, the sexually transmitted diseases have staged a comeback. The STD have increased dramatically over the past 50 years, specially **gonorrhoea** and **non-gonococcal urethritis**, and more recently the two viral conditions **genital herpes** and **genital warts**. The primary reasons for this are largely social, and not medical. Pre- and extramarital sex, a proportion of which is promiscuous, and the decline in the popularity of the condom as a contraceptive with the advent of the oral contraceptives (the `pill') have probably facilitated the spread of these diseases.

The five main venereal diseases are **gonorrhoea, syphilis, chancroid, lymphogranuloma venereum** and **granuloma inguinale. Non-gonococcal urethritis** is also spread by sexual activity. Other diseases in the STD group are the four viral infections (**herpes genitalis, genital warts, molluscum contagiosum** and AIDS); and two vaginitides (**trichomoniasis** and **candidiasis**).

GONORRHOEA

Over the past 50 years there has been a gradual increase in the prevalence of strains of **Neisseria gonorrhoeae** with mild resistance to the penicillins. However, no other antibacterial drug is as active as benzylpenicillin (penicillin G) against the sensitive strains of gonococci. The treatment schedules for gonococcal infections are detailed in **Chapter 9.3. Ampicillin** and **amoxycillin** are effective alternatives to penicillin G. Penicillin V and the penicillinase-resistant penicillins are less active against *N. gonorrhoeae*. Single dose therapy with any of the penicillins is inadequate for ascending genital infection in women (**pelvic inflammatory disease**); this complication is usually treated with 7-10 day courses of parenteral penicillin G and /or oral ampicillin.

The *drug of first choice* for penicillinase-producing gonococcal infection is **ceftriaxone**; and for penicillin-sensitive infections is **ampicillin plus probenecid**, or **amoxycillin plus probenecid** or **penicillin G plus probenecid**. The aminocyclitol, **spectinomycin dihydrochloride** in a single dose of 2.0 g IM cures 94.8 percent of patients with uncomplicated anogenital infection. In patients allergic to penicillin, the older tetracyclines, or the newer tetracyclines (minocycline or doxycycline), or co-trimoxaxole may be used.

SYPHILIS

Penicillin G is still the drug of choice for the treatment of syphilis, and in contrast to the gonococcus no increased resistance in **Treponema pallidum** has been proved. A serum level of penicillin of only 0.03 units/ml is **treponemacidal**, whereas, to treat gonorrhoea serum levels upto 1000 times higher are required. The drug schedules for the treatment of syphilis are detailed in **Chapter 9.3.** It must be emphasized that **tetracyclines** and **erythromycin** as alternatives to penicillin, are much less efficient antitreponemal drugs. They should be used only when penicillin is contraindicated. Cephalosoprins are promising agents, and **ceftriaxone** has shown good results.

NON-GONOCOCCAL URETHRITIS

Non-gonococcal urethritis is almost as frequent as gonococcal urethritis among the STD. It is diagnosed by the exclusion of the gonococcus from the gram-stained smear of the urethral discharge. The parasite **Chlamydia trachomatis**, of the family which causes lymphogranuloma venereum, and trachoma inclusion conjunctivitis (TRIC) has been shown to be the causative organism in approximately 50 percent of cases. The causative organism for the rest of the cases is indefinite.

The **tetracyclines** are the **drugs of choice** for the treatment of non-gonococcal urethritis. A minimum course should be 8 to 10 days on full dosage (e.g., tetracycline 500 mg 6-hourly), the maximum being 3 weeks therapy. A long-term (1 to 2 months) maintenance course of tetracycline 250 mg 3 times daily often prevents recurrences. Alternatively **doxycycline** (200 mg initially followed by 100 mg daily); or **minocycline** (200 mg initially followed by 100 mg 12 hourly) may be administered for 8 to 10 days.

Second line drugs shown to be effective in treating non-gonococcal urethritis are **erythromycin** in doses of 250 to 500 mg 6-hourly for 8 to 10 days, and **spiramycin** in doses of 500 mg 6-hourly for 8 to 10 days. **Sulphonamides** may be given a trial.

VIRAL INFECTIONS

GENITAL HERPES

Genital ulcers in women and blisters or ulcers in men due to the **Herpes simplex** virus are becoming increasingly common, as the **Herpesvirus hominis** (type I and II) are widespread among young sexually active adults. Genital herpes is a complex infection, due to its recurrent nature, and its probable aetiologic association with **squamous cells carcinoma of the cervix**.

Gentamicin or neomycin are first choice antibiotics for this purpose. The antiviral drug, **idoxuridine**, which is active against the herpes simplex virus may be painted as a 0.5 percent solution at frequent intervals on the part. Such an application may be helpful to avoid recurrences. Idoxuridine (5 to 35%) in dimethylsulphoxide, painted 5 times daily for not more than 3 days, may modify the course of the disease. **Acyclovir**, an antiviral drug, has shown good results. The usual dose is 200 mg orally qid for 5 days, or 5 mg/kg every 8 hourly.

Genital and Anorectal Warts (Condylomata acuminata)

Genital warts is a condition which is sexually transmitted in about 60 percent of cases. It is caused by **human papilloma virus** (HPV). It has a long incubation period of about 1 to 3 months. The treatment is best done by chemical destruction of the lesions by the use of 25 percent **podophyllin** in 90 percent alcohol. This paint is rubbed well into the wart structure. An **anaesthetic ointment** is applied to counter pain the next day, and the lesions should be retreated every 5 to 7 days. **Cryotherapy** (application of liquid nitrogen with a swab, or a slush of acetone and carbon dioxide snow) can be successful, specially in the treatment of hard warts.

Mollusca Contagiosa

The pearly papules, with an umbilicated centre of molluscum contagiosum on the lower abdomen and thighs can be controlled by application of **phenol** by a stick, by **cautery** or **cryotherapy**, or by **canthridin**.

Acquired Immunodeficiency Syndrome (AIDS)

AIDS is caused by a retrovirus referred to as the human immunodeficiency virus (HIV). The drug clinically used is *zindovudine* **(Chapter 9.9)**.

Vaginitides

A pale, cloudy or mucoid vaginal discharge occurs due to an overproduction of cervical mucus, i.e., mucorrhoea. The contraceptive `pill' is often the cause. Vaginitis can occasionally be due to a severe cervical erosion or possibly an infection with **Corynebacterium vaginale (Haemophilus vaginalis)**, a sexually transmissible organism of unknown pathogenicity. **Metronidazole** is effective for the treatment. **Trichomoniasis** and **candidiasis** account for a large number of cases of vaginitis.

Trichomoniasis

Vaginitis due to infection with the flagellate protozoan **Trichomonas vaginalis**, is always a sexually transmitted disease by the asymptomatic male sex partner. It frequently co-exists with gonorrhoea. This organism frequently produces upper vaginitis, unlike *Candida* which involves the lower vagina.

The standard treatment is **metronidazole** 200 mg orally 3 times daily for 7 to 10 days for both patient and partner. A single dose of 2 or 2.5 g orally is also recommended, and the cure rate is comparable. The treatment of choice is probably the newer imidazole analogue **tinidazole** in a single 2 g oral dose for both patient and partner. The cure rates are higher than metronidazole. **Alternative regimens** like metronidazole 400 mg 4 times daily for 2 days, and 3 doses of 1 g **nimorazole** or **tinidazole** 12 hours apart, or a single 1.5 g dose of **ornidazole** orally have been tried. Local treatment is only necessary in those patients who do not tolerate oral therapy, or possibly during early pregnancy.

Candidiasis

The fungus **Candida albicans** is often present in the female genital tract without causing infection. Clinical infection usually occurs when a suitable environment is produced hormonally (in pregnancy, by oral contraceptives, or premenstrually), or in diabetic patients, or following elimination of normal bacterial flora by antibiotic treatment, designated as **superinfection**. Vaginal candidiasis presents as pruritus vulvae, discharge, white `cheesy' deposits, or a combination of these.

Drug treatment of this common and recurring infection is far from satisfactory. The standard treatment has been **nystatin**, administered vaginally in the form of a *cream, pessary or foaming vaginal tablet*. The recommended regimen is one applicatorful of cream twice daily, or 2 vaginal tablets (200,000 units) inserted at night for 7 to 14 days. Oral tablets (500,000 units) 3 or 4 times daily are administered simultaneously to prevent reinfection from the bowel.

The imidazole derivatives may be used and the cure rates are comparable with nystatin. **Miconazole** cream (2%) is applied into the vagina at night for 7 days. **Clotrimazole** or **econazole** may be used as pessaries.

Chancroid

Chancroid, also known as soft chancre or Ducrey's infection, is an acute, localized sexually transmitted disease characterized clinically by multiple, painful, nonindurated genital ulcerations that usually develop within one week following the infecting contact. It is caused by a gram-negative bacillus **Haemophilus ducreyi**. Concurrent infection with another STD specially primary syphilis must be ruled out.

Sulfisoxazole, 1 g 4 times a day is perhaps the safest drug. Alternatively, **sulphamethoxazole** 800 mg in combination with **trimethoprim** 160 mg may be given 12-hourly for 4 days. The next drug of choice is **tetracycline** 500 mg orally 4 times a day for 1-2 weeks. If the infecting strains are unresponsive, erythromycin 500 mg orally 4 times a day is usually effective. In resistant cases **kanamycin sulphate** 500 mg IM every 12 hours for 5 to 14 days may be administered.

Lymphogranuloma Venereum

Lymphogranuloma venereum is an acute systemic sexually transmitted disease caused by **Chlamydia trachomatis** types L_1-L_3. After the genital lesion disappears, the infection spreads to lymph channels and lymph nodes of the genital and rectal area. The incubation period is 5-21 days.

Drug treatment consists of administration of **minocycline**, an improved tetracycline, in an initial dose of 200 mg followed by 100 mg twice daily for 21 days. Other **tetracyclines, erythromycin**, and **oleandomycin** may also be effective. **Trimethoprim-sulphamethoxazole** (Septran) combination is considered to be the drug of choice by some authorities, and is given as 2 tablets twice daily for 2 to 3 weeks. **Sulphadiazine** or **sulphamethoxazole** in an initial dose of 4 g, then 1 g 4 times daily may be given for 2 to 3 weeks. Local treatment of adenopathy, and administration of analgesics are required additionally.

Granuloma Inguinale

Granuloma inguinale is a chronic, relapsing, granulomatous anogenital infection, caused by **Calymmatobacterium granulomatis**, which is related to *Klebsiella* and occurs intracellularly. The incubation period is 8 days to 12 weeks. The lesions occur on the skin or mucous membranes of the genitalia or perineal region.

Drug therapy includes administration of **streptomycin** 1 g IM twice daily for 1 to 3 weeks. **Tetracyclines** are often effective in doses of 500 mg 4 times daily for 3 weeks. **Erythromycin** may be administered in the same dosage. **Trimethoprim-sulphamethoxazole** (Septran) combination is effective in doses of 2 tablets twice daily for 2 weeks. The use of **gentamicin** or **chloramphenicol**, because of their higher toxicity, is reserved for patients who fail to respond to other medication or who relapse.

Effective control of STD can be accomplished by **contact tracing, screening, education and social awareness, accurate diagnosis, specific and curative treatment schedules, and regular post-treatment surveillance**.

9.13 CHEMOTHERAPY OF FUNGAL DISEASES (ANTIFUNGAL DRUGS)

The fungi, like mammalian cells, are **eukaryotic** and possess nuclei, mitochondria and cell membrances containing sterols. None of these structures occur in the bacteria, which is one reason why antibacterial agents can exhibit **selective toxicity**. In contrast, the similarity between fungal and mammalian cells works **against** selective toxicity, and the antifungal drugs are in general more toxic than the antibacterial agents. The success of antibacterial therapy has created ecological stituations in which **opportunistic fungal infections** can occur readily.

Mycotic Infections

Mycotic infections in man can be divided into *two* main groups: (*i*) **superficial mycoses** confined to the epidermis, the hair and the nails; and (*ii*) **deep (systemic) mycoses** involving the dermis, bones and viscera. Apart from these, actimomycetes are a heterogenous group of filamentous organisms, resembling fungi, which grow as mycelia and break into fragments. **Actinomyces bovis produces actionomycosis**. **Nocardia asteroides** and related species of aerobic actinomyces can either cause a localized granuloma of subcutaneous tissues or bones (Madura foot), or systemic infection involving lungs, brain, meninges and other organs.

Superficial Mycoses

Superficial fungal disease is caused by a variety of fungi. Ringworm (e.g., tinea capitis, tinea corporis, tinea cruris, tinea unguium) is caused by the dermatophytes, classified into three genera—*Epidermophyton, Microsporum* and *Tricophyton*—which infect the superficial keratinized tissues, chiefly hair, skin and nails. Other superficial infections include tinea versicolor by *Malassezia furfur*; superficial and intestinal candidiasis by *Candida albicans*; and tinea nigra by *Cladosporium werneckii* and *C.mansoni*.

Deep Mycoses

Deep fungal disease can be caused by **Candida albicans (Monilia albicans)** which is an oval budding yeast-like fungus normally present in the mouth and the gut. It can infect the skin, mucous membranes of the mouth, gut, lungs and the genital tract.

Other mycoses causing systemic involvement include **Cryptococcus neoformans** (*Torula histolytica*), *Histoplasma capsulatum, Blastomyces dermatitidis, Coccidioides immitis and Aspergillus fumigatus.*

CLASSIFICATION OF ANTIFUNGAL AGENTS

The antifungal drugs may be classified as under:

1. **Antifungal Antibiotics**

   Griseofulvin

   Polyenes: Nystatin, Natamycin, Hamycin, Amphotericin B

2. **Synthetic Antifungal Agents**

   Flucytosine (5-fluorocytosine)

   Co-trimoxazole (sulphamathoxazole-trimethoprim)

   Dapsone

   Haloprogin

   Imidazoles: Clotrimazole, Miconazole, Econazole, Ketoconazole, Isoconazole, Sulconazole, Tioconazole

   Triazoles: Fluconazole, Itraconazole.

3. **Miscellaneous Antifungal Agents**

   Hydroxystilbamidine

   Potassium iodide

   Tolnaftate

   Undecylenic acid

   Clioquinol

   Terbinafine

   Ciclopirox

   Triacetin

   Benzoic and salicylic acid

Antifungal Antibiotics

Griseofulvin

Griseofulvin was first isolated from **Penicillium griseofulvum** in 1939. But as it was ineffective against bacteria it received no further attention. Much later in 1959 it was introduced as an antifungal agent.

Antifungal spectrum. Griseofulvin is a systemic agent for treating superficial mycoses, and is effective orally against species of **Epidermophyton, Microsporum** and **Tricophyton** that cause dermatophytic infections. It is ineffective against bacteria, deep mycoses, and *Candida* species.

Mode of action. Griseofulvin is **fungicidal** for growing cells and **fungistatic** for older dormant cells. It somewhat resembles clochicine in structure and blocks dividing cells in metaphase. It possibly interferes with fungal DNA replication resulting in *distorted* hyphal growth. **It rapidly binds to keratin precursor cells and makes them resistant to fungal infection**. Thus new skin, hair and nails are the first to become free of fungal elements. Therapy must be continued until the infected keratin is replaced by keratin containing griseofulvin. This usually takes *3-10 weeks* for skin and hair mycoses, and upto *18 months* for nail mycoses.

Pharmacokinetics. Griseofulvin is erratically absorbed on oral administration, mainly because of its poor solubility. Small-sized (micronized) particles and a fatty meal facilitate absorption. Particles of 2.7 μ diameter are absorbed 2-3 times as rapidly as those of 10.0 μ diameter. The drug is slow in action because it must first be taken up by keratinized structures, which grow slowly to reach the site of infection. The **cell turnover time** thus determines the efficacy of treatment. Griseofulvin is metabolized in the liver to an inactive metabolite **6-demethylgriseofulvin**, which is excreted in the urine.

Therapeutic uses. Griseofulvin is the treatment of choice for **ringworm** infection of hair, skin and nails due to **Epidermophyton, Microsporum** and **Tricophyton**. Epidermophytosis, one variety of athlete's foot, is usually markedly improved, but mycological cure is difficult.

Toxicity. Serious adverse reactions to griseofulvin are few. A minority of patients report headaches, forgetfulness, mental dullness or inattention, which restricts its use in some patients with demanding occupations. Gastrointestinal upsets, fever, thirst (xerostomia), frequency of micturition, headache and serum sickness may develop in upto 5 percent of patients. A variety of skin lesions (lupus erythematosus-like eruptions, urticaria, lichen planus, erythema multiformae, and photodermatitis) may occur. *Cross-sensitivity* has not been described in patients sensitive to penicillin. Griseofulvin may precipitate porphyria. Temporary leucopenia, granulocytopenia, punctate basophilia, and monocytosis may occur rarely. Peripheral neuritis, impaired and perverted sense of taste (dysgeusia), stomatitis, and albminuria have also been reported. Some children may develop gynaecomastia and hyperpigmentation of the nipples and areola and external genitalia. **Superinfection** with *Candida albicans* has been reported occasionally.

Preparations and dosages. Griseofulvin was originally marketed in a macrocrystalline (coarse particle) form which required large doses to achieve effective concentrations. Later a **microcrystalline** (fine particle) form, and recently an **ultramicrocrystalline** form have been marketed which have replaced the coarse particle form, and effective blood levels can be achieved with lower doses.

Griseofulvin (microcrystalline form) 500 mg daily in single or divided doses is administered after meals; 1 g or more daily in divided doses is recommended for obstinate infections. In children 10 mg/kg/day is administered in divided doses after meals. For griseofulvin (ultramicrocrystalline form) the dosage is halved, and administered in the same manner as above.

POLYENES

The polyenes are complex molecules with a large conjugated double bond (–CH=CH–) system in a lactone ring linked to an amino sugar. These large **cyclic lactones** have **lipophilic** and **lipophobic** portions making solubility in water difficult.

NYSTATIN

Nystatin discovered in 1951, is a polyene antibiotic obtained from **Streptomyces noursei**.

Antifungal spectrum. Nystatin is active against a number of yeasts and filamentous fungi, but is mainly used for **Candida albicans** infections of the skin and mucous membranes. *C. albicans* is invariably sensitive, but occasinally a **slow step-wise resistance** may develop. Its high toxicity limits its use to cutaneous and mucocutaneous infections by **Candida** species.

Mode of action. Nystatin may act by altering fungal cell membrane permeability, probably by **complexing with membrane sterols**. Its lack of antibacterial activity is possibly related to the relative absence of sterols in bacterial cell membranes. Nystatin exhibits both **fungistatic** and **fungicidal** activity, depending on the drug concentration; the susceptibility of the fungus; and the presence of blood, pus or tissue fluid which reduce its activity. It is measured in milligrams or units (1 mg = 3500 units).

Pharmacokinetics. Nystatin is usually applied topically or given orally for its local effect in the bowel lumen. Very little nystatin is absorbed from the gut on oral administration, and practically the entire amount is excreted in the faeces.

Therapeutic uses. Nystatin is mainly used in the treatment of **candidiasis of the skin, mouth. intestine** and **vagina**. The typical lesions of thrush and vaginitis usually respond well. Intestinal and pulmonary candidiasis present problems. Pulmonary candidasis and aspergillosis may be treated with nystatin suspension administered as an *aerosol*.

Toxicity. Nystatin, even in large doses, is relatively non- toxic when applied topically. Cutaneous irritation may develop on repeated application. Contact sensitivity is rare.

Preparations and dosage. Nystatin is available in tablets (500,000 units); oral suspension (100,000 units/ml); vaginal cream (100,000 units/4g), and as pessaries (100,000 units) for insertion into the vagina. The usual oral dose is 500,000 units every 6 hourly, doubled in severe infections; by vagina 100,000-200,000 units for 14 nights or more. Suspensions for topical administration are usually applied thrice daily.

AMPHOTERICIN B

Of the two amphotericins, A and B, isolated from **Streptomyces nodosus**, only amphotericin B is used in therapeutics. It is the most important drug for the treatment of **systemic fungal infections**, and is active against most fungi and yeasts. However, it is a toxic drug and side effects are common.

Antifungal spectrum. The effective antifungal spectrum of amphotericin B is the widest of all antifungal agents. It includes, **Histoplasma capsulatum** (histoplasmosis); **Cryptococcus neoformans** (cryptococcosis); **Blastomyces dermatitidis** (blastomycosis); **Candida species** (local and systemic candidiasis); **Coccidioides immitis** (coccidioidomycosis); and **Sporatrichum schenckii** (sporotrichosis). The fungi **Nocardia** and **Aspergillus** are usually resistant. Some forms of infection, like blastomycosis often relapse, and coccidiodomycosis is frequently impossible to cure.

Mode of action. The antifungal activity of amphotericin B is similar to nystatin. **It binds with the sterols in the cell membrane of sensitive fungi and alters membrane permeability**, thereby depressing phosphate uptake, and allowing leakage and loss of small molecules like glucose and essential ions like potassium resulting in depression of metabolism. It is either **fungistatic** or **fungicidal** depending on the concentration of the drug, and the sensitivity of the fungus. The antifungal effects are maximal between pH 6.0 to 7.5. Resistance *in vivo* is rare. *Cross-resistance* with nystatin may develop, but very rarely.

Pharmacokinetics. Amphotericin B is poorly absorbed on oral or IM administration; therefore for systemic mycoses it **must be given intravenously** or **intrathecally**. Even when given IV it distributes very unevenly throughout the body, and the levels in the CSF are 1/40th of the plasma levels. There may be selective concentration of the drug in the reticuloendothelial system. The drug is over 90 percent protein bound which explains its poor penetration. Only 5 percent is excreted in the urine, and elimination is unaffected by renal failure.

Therapeutic uses. Amphotericin B is a toxic drug, but represents an important therapeutic advance, as no other drug is available for the treatment of systemic mycotic infections. **Histoplasmosis, cryptococcosis, coccidioidomycosis, blastomycosis** and **systemic candidiasis** are indications for intravenous amphotericin B therapy. In treating **cryptococcal meningitis** a combination of **amphotericin B** and **fluorocytosine** is used. Effective treatment of systemic mycoses requires several courses, and in spite of toxicity, adequate treatment must be given.

Toxicity. It is a toxic drug and with systemic therapy, adverse reactions develop in almost all patients. Common side effects during IV infusion are fever, chills, headache, nausea, vomiting and malaise. Gastrointestinal upsets with bleeding, hypotension and vertigo may develop. Premedication with sedatives and antihistamines may reduce these reactions. Thrombophlebitis is common and may be reduced by combining it with hydrocortisone and heparin.

Nephrotoxicity almost invariably occurs due to vasoconstriction, impaired acid excretion (renal tubular acidosis), **nephrocalcinosis** and **acute renal failure**. **Normochromic normocytic anaemia** may develop, but is self-limited and reversible, being due to temporary **bone marrow suppression. Hypokalaemia** and **Hypomagnesaemia** have been reported. Intrathecal administration may cause **chemical meningitis, paraesthesias, radiculitis** and **difficulty in micturition. Convulsions, ventricular fibrillation** and **cardiac arrest** may follow too rapid an infusion.

Preparations and dosage. Amphotericin B is available in the microcrystalline form (Fungilin), as tablets, lozenges, suspension, or pessaries for topical application in candidiasis. The usual oral dose of amphotericin B is upto 200 mg every 6-hourly, and by vagina 50-100 mg for 14 nights. A cream, lotion and ointment containing 3 percent of amphotericin B is also marketed.

Amphotericin B (Fungizone) is available for injection. The lyophilized powder contains 50 mg of amphotericin B plus 41 mg of sodium deoxycholate and sodium phosphate buffer per vial. The contents of the vial are dissolved in 10 ml of sterile water, and then added to 5 percent dextrose in water. The usual dose for IV infusion is 250 mcg/kg/day, gradually increased if tolerated to 1 mg/kg/day, to a maximum of 1.5 mg/kg/day, or on alternate days in the severely ill patients. The solution for IV infusion should be freshly prepared and protected from light even during the infusion. Addition of 25 to 50 mg of hydrocortisone to the solution markedly reduces the incidence of chills and thrombophlebitis. The infusion time for each dose should not be less than *6 hours*. Renal toxicity is reduced by keeping the patient hydrated, prolonging the infusion time, alkalinizing the urine, and giving the drug on alternate days.

Intrathecal infusion of amphotericin B may be used in cases of **fungal meningitis;** 0.5 mg of the drug is dissolved in at least 5 ml of spinal fluid and given 2 to 3 times a week. A total of 15 mg by this route is thought to be enough. For **chromoblastomycosis**, injection of amphotericin B into the lesion is often the treatment of choice.

Amphotericin B encapsulated in **liposomes** has become available. It is less toxic than the parent compound, and is recommended for systemic mycoses. The usual dose is 1 mg/kg/day as a single dose.

NATAMYCIN

Natamycin (pimaricin) is a polyene antibiotic produced by **Streptomyces natalensis**. It is related to nystatin and amphotericin B, and has a wide antifungal spectrum. It is active against most **Candida** species, **Aspergillus fumigatus** and **Trichomonas vaginalis**. Natamycin is poorly absorbed orally and is usually administered topically. It has been locally used in the treatment of **candidiasis** and **trichomoniasis**. It has also been used in **pulmonary aspergillosis** and **fungal keratitis**. **Side effects** include nausea, vomiting, diarrhoea on oral administration, and local irritation on topical use. It is available as a 2 percent cream; 1 percent sterile aqueous suspension for oral use and 2.5 percent for inhalation as an aerosol; and vaginal tablets containing 25 mg of the drug. The usual dose by mouth is 10 drops of a 1 percent oral suspension after meals; by inhalation 2.5 mg every 8-hourly; and by vagina 25 mg (1 tab.) for 21 nights.

HAMYCIN

Hamycin is another polyene antifungal agent, obtained from **Streptomyces pimprina** recovered from the local soil, and developed by the Research Laboratories of Hindustan Antibiotics, Pimpri, Pune. It is identical with trichomycin. The drug is well absorbed on oral administration and possesses activity against a variety of fungi, particularly **Candida albicans, Blastomyces dermatitidis, Histoplasma capsulatum, Aspergillus fumigatus,** and **Cryptococcus neoformans**. It is more active than nystatin against *Candida*. Hamycin has anti-inflammatory properties.

Hamycin is used topically and by mouth in a variety of fungal infections including **candidiasis, tinea, blastomycosis,** and **madura foot**. It is available as hamycin pessaries each containing 100,000 units in lactose; and hamycin suspension (oral) containing 40,000 units/ml. **Adverse reactions** on oral use involve the gastrointestinal tract, and the drug is nephrotoxic. Hamycin may be applied topically in the treatment of vaginal candidiasis.

SYNTHETIC ANTIFUNGAL AGENTS

FLUCYTOSINE

Flucytosine (5-fluorocytosine) is a fluorinated pyrimidine, originally synthesized as an antimetabolite, but proved of little value as a cytotoxic agent. Its antifungal spectrum is restricted to **Crytococcus neoformans, Candida albicans** and some other **Candida** species, **Torulopsis glabrata** and **Cladosporum** species. The precise *mode of action* is unknown, but it is deaminated to *5-fluorouracil*, a known antimetabolite which inhibits thymidylate synthetase thereby depressing DNA synthesis, and is incorporated into RNA. Its specificity is due to the presence of cytosine deaminase in fungi. Flucytosine enters the fungus actively by permease enzymes. **Amphotericin B acts synergistically, and presumably facilitates its entry.**

Pharmacokinetics. Unlike amphotericin B flucytosine is well absorbed from the gut, peak levels of 75-90 mcg/ml are attained on a dose of 50 mg/kg 6-hourly. It penetrates adequately into the CSF and lung. It is largely excreted unchanged by glomerular filtration via the kidneys. The $t_{1/2}$ is 6 hours, and is increased by renal failure.

Therapeutic uses. Flucytosine is probably the **drug of first choice for systemic candidiasis** and **cryptococcosis,** provided the strains are sensitive. The optimal oral dose is 150 mg/kg/day in 5-hourly divided doses. For very ill patients an IV preparation is available. It has also been used successfully as **single drug therapy of urinary tract infections** and **fungaemia due to Candida**, and in the treatment of **cryptococcal meningitis**. In seriously ill patients with invasive fungal infection the combined use of **flucytosine** and **amphotericin** *B* is recommended which may have several advantages: (*i*) there may be a more potent antifungal effect than either drug alone i.e., a **synergistic** effect; (*ii*) it may permit a **lower dose of amphotericin B** which is a potentially toxic agent; and (*iii*) the rate of emergence of **acquired resistance to therapy would be lower** than with flucytosine alone.

Toxicity. In contrast to amphotericin B, flucytosine is a drug of relatively low toxicity. The main adverse reactions are gastrointestinal upsets, skin rashes, eosinophilia and **reversible hepatic dysfunction.** Occasionally there may be confusion, hallucinations, headache and vertigo due to the drug. **Thrombocytopenia, leucopenia and sometimes irreversible bone marrow depression** may occur.

Preparations and dosage. Flucytosine is available as 500 mg scored tablets, and 10 mg/ml in 250 ml infusion bottles. The usual dose by mouth or IV infusion is 150-200 mg/kg/day in divided doses. In renal impairment dosage must be reduced.

CO-TRIMOXAZOLE AND DAPSONE

The treatment of **nocardiosis** has traditionally involved prolonged courses of sulphonamides. Lately the sulphonamides have been combined with other agents like **tetracycline, chloramphenicol,** and **cycloserine**.

If the infection is due to *N. caviae* or *N. brasiliensis* (and not *N. asteroides*), *dapsone* may be more effective than co-trimoxazole.

HALOPROGIN

Haloprogin is a synthetic topical antifungal agent, used in the treatment of superficial fungal infections of the skin caused by several species of **Trichophyton, Microsporum** and **Epidermophyton**. It also has some activity against cutaneous candidal infections. The cure rate is slightly higher, and relapses are less frequent with haloprogin than with tolnaftate. **Adverse reactions** include local irritation and vesicle formation. If sensitization is noted therapy should be discontinued. Contact with eyes must be avoided. A 1 percent cream is available which is applied liberally to the affected area twice daily for 2-3 weeks.

Imidazoles

At least three drugs of the imidazole family are useful antifungal agents. **Clotrimazole, miconazole nitrate** and **econazole nitrate** are active against almost all pathogenic fungi, and primary resistance is rare.

The **antifungal imidazoles** have a *broad* antifungal spectrum which includes **Histoplasma capsulatum, Blastomyces dermatitidis, Cryptococcus neoformans, C. immitis** and species of **Aspergillus** and **Candida**. They are also active against the pathogenic dermatophytes (**Epidermophyton, Microsporum** and **Trichophyton** species). The biochemical *mode of action* of the imidazoles is not well understood. At low concentration they are **fungistatic** and at higher concentrations **fungicidal**. There is leakage of ions, amino acids and other molecules from the cells due to drug-induced changes in cell permeability. This probably is responsible for their antifungal activity. Primary resistance is rare.

Clotrimazole is used to treat **candidiasis, trichomoniasis** and **dermatophyte infections of the skin** and **vagina**. *Side effects* include local irritation, pruritus, oedema and burning. The usual dose by vagina is 200 mg for 3 nights, or 100 mg for 6 nights. It is available as a 1 percent cream for skin infection; and vaginal tablets of 100 and 200 mg with applicator.

Miconazole nitrate is used to treat **systemic fungal infections, candidiasis** and **dermatophyte infections**. *Adverse reactions* on topical application are irritation, burning, or maceration. *Hypersensitivity reactions* may occur. IV injection may cause *thrombophlebitis*, pruritus, nausea, diarrhoea, anaemia, thrombocytopenia, hyperlipidaemia and bronchospasm. The usual dose by mouth is 250 mg every 6-hourly; by vagina 200 mg for 7 nights, or 100 mg morning and night for 7 days; and by IV infusion 25 to 30 mg/kg/day in 2 or 3 divided doses at 8 or 12-hour intervals. **Ketocanazole** has an antifungal activity profile similar to that of miconazole.

Econazole nitrate is used to treat **candidiasis** and **dermatophyte** infections. *Side effects* include local irritation, erythema, burning and pruritus. The *usual dose* by vagina is 150 mg for 3 nights for candidal vaginitis. It is also available as a 1 percent cream to treat infections caused by dermatophytes, yeasts, moulds and other fungi.

The other imidazoles–**isoconazole, sulconzole, tioconazole**–are used for local treatment of dermatophyte infection and candidiasis.

Triazoles

Fluconazole

Fluconazole is an oral triazole antifungal effective against *local* and *systemic candidiasis*, and *cryptococcosis* (including meningitis).

Fluconazole is available as 50 mg capsules, oral suspension, and intravenous infusion. The usual dose for **mucosal candidiasis** (except vaginal infection) is 50 mg daily for 7-14 days, or longer in cases of *oesophageal candidiasis* or *candiuria*. For acute or recurrent *vaginal candidiasis* a single dose of 150 mg is given.

For **systemic candidiasis** and **cryptococcosis** it is given by *mouth* or *intravenously*, in a dose of 400 mg initially then 200 mg daily, increased if necessary to 400 mg daily for 6-8 weeks. It is also used for the treatment and prophylaxis of **cryptococcosis in patients of AIDS**, where relapse is common and long-term prophylaxis with amphotericin B is impractical.

Adverse reactions include nausea, abdominal discomfort, flatulence, rashes, and elevation of hepatic enzymes in some patients.

Itraconazole

Itraconazole is an orally effective agent, active against **oropharyngeal** and **vulvovaginal candidiasis, pityriasis versicolor,** and other **dermatophyte** infections.

It is available as 100 mg capsules. The usual dose is 100-200 mg daily for 15-30 days. For AIDS associated oropharyngeal candidiasis it is given in a dose of 200 mg daily for 15 days. *Side effects* include dyspepsia, headache, nausea and abdominal discomfort.

Miscellaneous Antifungal Agents

Hydroxystilbamidine

Hydroxystilbamidine is a valuable drug for many deep fungal diseases. It may be administered intravenously to treat **blastomycosis**, and may even be usefully **combined with amphotericin B** in the treatment of this disease. Hydroxystilbamidine is also a minor alternative drug in the treatment of **leishmaniasis**. *Adverse reactions* include hypotension and tachycardia during or immediately following IV administration. Nausea, malaise, hepatotoxicity, paraesthesias and rashes may occur. Hepatic insufficiency is a relative contraindication to the use of this drug. A total dose of 8 g is given in daily doses of 225 mg in 200 ml of 5 percent dextrose by slow IV infusion. IM administration is painful.

Potassium Iodide

Potassium iodide has a limited ability to resolve chronic granulomas. This property has been usefully employed in the treatment of syphilis and some deep fungal infections. It is of particular value in **cutaneous** and **lymphatic sporotrichosis**, but should be used with caution in pulmonary and disseminated disease. Use of potassium iodide interferes with thyroid function tests, and **iodism** may develop, which is manifested as a metallic taste in the mouth, coryza, parotitis and acneiform skin rashes. The starting dose is 1 g 3 times daily, and may be gradually increased to 12 g daily in severe cases. Therapy should be continued for 4-6 weeks.

Tolnaftate

Tolnaftate is effective topically against **dermatophytic infections**. It is also effective in the treatment of **Trichophyton rubrum** infection which is often resistant to griseofulvin. Tolnaftate may be applied with griseofulvin for local benefit. It may cause local irritation, but no confirmed adverse reactions have been reported. It is available as a 1 percent cream or powder, which is to be rubbed into the lesion twice daily for 2 to 3 weeks.

Undecylenic Acid

Undecylenic acid has been employed topically for the treatment of **dermatophytic infections**, and sometimes in addition to nystatin. It is available as a powder or an ointment, in a strength of 10 percent for the skin, or 1 percent for mucous membranes. It is claimed to be specially useful in the treatment of **tinea pedis (athlete's foot).**

Clioquinol

Clioquinol (iodochlorhydroxyquin) is useful for the localized **dermatophytoses**, specially if the bacteria also are present, as the drug has both antifungal and antibacterial activity. Contact with the eyes should be avoided. It infrequently causes irritation of the skin. Clioquinol is available as a *3 percent cream* and *ointment* to be applied topically several times daily.

Terbinafine

Terbinafine is an allylamine antifungal, which has been recently introduced for the oral treatment of **ringworm** infections. It is ineffective against pityriasis versicolor. The usual dose is 250 mg daily for 2-6 weeks in **tinea pedis**; 2-4 weeks in **tinea cruris**; and 4 weeks in **tinea corporis**. Side effects include nausea, anorexia, diarrhoea, rash, urticaria and abdominal discomfort.

Ciclopirox

Ciclopirox olamine is a **broad-spectrum antifungal** used for **tinea pedis, tinea cruris, tinea corporis, candidiasis,** and **tinea versicolor** due to **Malassezia furfur**. It disrupts the fungal cell membrane, causing leakage and cell death. It penetrates hair, hair follicles, sebaceous glands and dermis.

Ciclopirox olamine is available as a 1 percent cream to be applied locally twice daily. It has a low incidence of side effects which include local irritation, sensitization and photosensitivity. Also available in solution (10 mg/ml) dosage form.

Triacetin

Triacetin is indicated for milder superficial fungal infections e.g., **athlete's foot**. It is available as a cream (25%), ointment (25%), and liquid (25% with cetylpyridium and chloroxylenol) to be applied twice daily for 1 week even after symptoms have subsided.

Benzoic and Salicylic Acid

Benzoic acid (6%) and salicylic acid (3%) ointment called **Whitfield's ointment** combines the mild **fungistatic** action of benzoate with the **keratolytic** action of salicylate. It is used mainly in the treatment of **tinea pedis**. As benzoic acid is only fungistatic, eradication of infection occurs only when the stratum corneum is shed. Hence continuous medication is needed for several weeks to months.

Pharmacotherapy of Mycotic Infections

There are many preparations available for topical use in the treatment of **superficial** fungal disease, but most of them have become obsolete with the introduction of **grisefulvin**. Chemotherapy of **deep** fungal disease is unsatisfactory, and their use is associated with severe toxicity. The drugs of choice employed in the treatment of selected fungal infections are listed in **Table 9.13-1**. The antifungal agents are also briefly discussed in **Chapter 10** as local anti-infective agents.

Table 9.13-1 *Drugs employed in the treatment of some superficial and deep fungal infections*

Disease	*Infecting fungus*	*Drugs of choice*	*Alternatives*
SUPERFICIAL INFECTIONS			
Dermatomycosis (tinea, ringworm)	*Dermatophytes* Epidermophyton Microsporum, Trichophyton	*Topical agents* Miconazole Clotrimazole	*Topical agents* Tolnaftate Undecylenic acid *Oral therapy* Griseofulvin
Candidiasis	*Candida albicans* Superficial Intestinal	Miconazole or Clotrimazole (topical) Nystatin (oral)	Nystatin (topical) Itraconazole
DEEP (SYSTEMIC) INFECTIONS			
Candidiasis Cryptococcosis	*Candida albicans* *Cryptococcus neoformans*	Amphotericin B (with or without Flucytosine)	Flucytosine Potassium iodide Fluconazole
Aspergillosis Histoplasmosis Coccidioidomycosis Phycomycosis	*Aspergillus* *Histoplasma capsulatum* *Coccidioides immitis* *Mucor*	Amphotericin B	Potassium iodide Hydroxystilbamidine *Sulphonamides*
Blastomycosis	*Blastomyces dermatitidis* (North American) *Sporothrix schenkii* *Madurella mycetomi*	Amphotericin B	Hydroxystilbamidine
Sporotrichosis Maduromycosis	*Sporothrix schenkii* *Madurella mycetomic*	Potassium iodide Sulphonamides	Amphotericin B Tetracyclines Amphotericin B
Rhinosporidiosis	*Rhinosporidium seeberi*	Amphotericin B	—
Nocardiosis	*Nocardia asteroides**	Sulphonamides Co-trimoxazole	Tetracyclines Erythromycin
Actinomycosis	*Actinomyces israeli**	Penicillin Erythromycin	Sulphonamides Cephalosporins

* Not a true fungus

To summarize, the **polyene antibiotics** (nystatin and natamycin), and both **clotrimazole** and **miconazole** act locally on skin and mucous membranes against a wide range of fungi, except *nystatin* which is only active against *Candida*. **Amphotericin** *B* is given by intravenous infusion in systemic mycoses, but its toxic effects necessitate caution. **Clotrimazole** and **miconazole** have also been used systemically with occasional success. **Flucytosine** by mouth is active against systemic yeast infections, although resistance can develop rapidly. In severe ringworm infections, oral **griseofulvin** is effective, however, treatment may have to continue for many months.

10

LOCAL ANTI-INFECTIVE AGENTS

Antiseptics and **disinfectants** are a widely used group of drugs. Most of these locally effective drugs have a **low therapeutic index** making them unsuitable for systemic use. They are used for various purposes, e.g., sterilization of skin and surgical instruments prior to operation; disinfection of wounds and ulcers; against certain fungal and parasitic infestations of the skin and hair; and for disinfection of rooms and other articles. Collectively the antiseptics and disinfectants may be termed as **local anti-infective agents.**

Historically the importance of cleansing the hands with chlorine-containing solutions for the prevention of puerperal fever was demonstrated by a Viennese physician **Ignaz Sammelweis** in 1844. He insisted on this procedure to avoid "childbirth fever" or puerperal fever as it is now known. Later **Joseph Lister** in 1867 announced his method for sterilization of wounds, bandages and surgical instruments by using **phenol (carbolic acid).** It was stressed by Lister that **"surgical sterility is not necessarily absolute sterility".** The use of alcohol was rather delayed because **Robert Koch** in 1881 reported that it failed to kill anthrax spores. The superior germicidal properties of 70 percent alcohol were established by Beyer in 1912.

DEFINITIONS

Antiseptics are drugs that are applied to **living** tissues for the purpose of killing bacteria or inhibiting their growth. **Disinfectants** are bactericidal drugs that are applied to **inanimate** objects (surgical dressings and instruments, dishes, bed pans, rooms, wards, lavatories etc.) to destroy microorganisms and prevent infection. These agents destroy harmful microorganisms, including viruses, but may not necessarily destroy bacterial spores. **Disinfection** implies the killing of harmful microorganisms by the direct application of physical or chemical agents. The term **germicide** is frequently used to cover both antiseptics and disinfectants. The three terms (antiseptic, disinfectant, and germicide) are often used interchangeably. **Sterilization** is the process of total destruction of all microbial life, including vegetative bacteria, spores, fungi and viruses.

A **sanitizer** is a chemical agent used to reduce the number of bacterial contaminants to a safe level in items like the utensils and cutlery used in cafes, public eating houses and restaurants, as prescribed by the public health authorities. A **preservative** is an agent that prevents decomposition by either chemical or physical means.

Potency of Local Anti-Infectives

The germicidal potency of a drug can be assessed by various tests. Of these, determination of the **Rideal-Walker Coefficient** or **phenol coefficient** is a simple *in vitro* test. Phenol coefficient is expressed as the ratio between the degree of dilution of the *unknown* agent that kills a 24-hour old culture of **B. typhosus** at 37°C in 7.5 minutes, and the degree of dilution of phenol that kills a 24-hour old culture of **B. typhosus** at 37°C in 7.5 minutes.

Ideally, local anti-infective agents should have the following qualities: (*i*) they should have a rapid and selective action, i.e., they should be maximally parasitotropic and minimally organotropic; (*ii*) they should not interfere with the healing process; (*iii*) they should be minimally absorbed from the site of application; (*iv*) they should be chemically stable and water soluble; and (*v*) their potency should not be affected by the presence of pus, tissue fluid, blood, and the pH of tissues. An "ideal" preparation with all the above qualities is yet to be found.

Mechanisms of Action

Germicidal or local anti-infective activity depends on three basic mechanisms of action: (*i*) **Coagulation of bacterial proteins** leading to destruction of microorganisms. The "protoplasmic poisons" act by this mechanism, and this may also be the main action of moist-heat sterilization; (*ii*) **Surface activity** by the surfactants damages the normal permeability characteristics of the bacterial cell membrane, adversely affecting the bacterial metabolism; and (*iii*) **Poisoning of the enzyme systems** in the bacterial cells is possibly the mode of action of most germicides, and as a result the bacterium is either killed (bactericidal), or is unable to grow and divide (bacteriostatic) further.

Classification

The local anti-infective drugs may be subdivided into: **antibacterial anti-infectives; ectoparasiticides; and antifungal agents.** The anti-bacterial anti-infectives are popularly designated as antiseptics and disinfectants. They are further subdivided into:

I. **Physical Agents.** Heat, ultraviolet light.

II. **Chemical Agents**

- (*i*) *Acids:* Boric acid, benzoic acid, mandelic acid, salicylic acid.
- (*ii*) *Oxidizing agents:* Potassium permanganate, hydrogen peroxide, sodium perborate.
- (*iii*) *Phenolic compounds:* Phenol, cresol, resorcinol, hexylresorcinol, thymol, hexachlorophene.
- (*iv*) *Surface-active agents (Surfactants)*
  - (*a*) *Anionic surfactants:* Soaps.
  - (*b*) *Cationic surfactants:* Benzalkonium chloride, benzethonium chloride, cetylpyridinium chloride, cetrimide.
  - (*c*) *Nonionic surfactants:* Nonoxynol-9.
- (*v*) *Alcohols:* Ethyl alcohol, isopropyl alcohol.
- (*vi*) *Halogens:* Iodine, iodophores, chlorine and chlorine-releasing preparations (chlorinated lime, Dakin's solution, Eusol, chloramine T, halazone, chloroazodin).
- (*vii*) *Aldehydes:* Formaldehyde, glutaraldehyde.
- (*viii*) *Antiseptic dyes:*
  - (*a*) *Acridine dyes:* Acriflavine, proflavine.
  - (*b*) *Triphenylmethane dyes:* Crystal violet, brilliant green.
- (*ix*) *Heavy metals*
  - (*a*) *Mercury compounds:* Mercuric chloride, thimerosal (Merthiolate).
  - (*b*) *Silver compounds:* Silver nitrate, silver proteinate.
  - (*c*) *Zinc salts:* Zinc oxide, zinc sulphate.
- (*x*) *Antibiotics:* Bacitracin, neomycin, polymyxin B, framycetin.
- (*xi*) *Miscellaneous:* Nitrofurazone, ichthammol, dequalinium acetate and chloride, marfanil, chlorhexidine.

The above is a partial list of antiseptics and disinfectants available for clinical use.

COMMONLY USED LOCAL ANTI-INFECTIVES

Physical Agents

Heat

Saturated steam (120°C) at 2 atmospheres pressure is the most important agent for destroying microorganisms. Both the **vegetative** and **spore forms** of most bacteria are killed after an exposure for 20 minutes. Dry heat is much less efficacious, and 3 hours exposure at 140°C may be needed. Simple boiling at normal atmospheric pressure is inadequate to destroy organisms like those for infectious hepatitis. In office practice it is advisable to use disposable syringes and needles.

Ultraviolet Light

The maximum antibacterial effect of light energy is exerted around a wave length of 2700 Å. Microorganisms vary considerably in their resistance to ultraviolet light, and gram-negative non-sporing organisms are most susceptible. Staphylococci, streptococci and viruses are resistant. This method of disinfection is too expensive for general use. Ultraviolet light sterilization is employed to prevent **airborne cross infection in burn units** by creating a light screen between patients. Such techniques have found greatest applicability in burn wards and premature baby units.

CHEMICAL AGENTS

Acids

Boric acid. It is a **weak bacteriostatic** agent. Once boric acid was a popular antiseptic agent in the form of ointments, lotions, or irrigating solutions because of its non-irritating nature. But because of its systemic absorption through abraded and broken skin and toxicity, at present the use is restrited. The usual strength of boric acid in various dosage forms ranges between 1 to 5 percent.

Benzoic acid. It is a relatively non-toxic agent and can be applied on the skin in a fairly high concentration. It is a **bacteriostatic** agent used extensively as a preservative in food and drinks in a concentration of 0.1 percent. In addition benzoic acid has **antifungal** action and is used in the treatment of ringworm infection of the skin as compound Benzoic acid or **Whitfield's ointment** (benzoic acid 6 percent, salicylic acid 3 percent in emulsifying ointment base).

Mandelic acid. This agent is used for urinary tract infections **(Chap. 9.11).** For maximal urinary antiseptic effect the urine pH should be maintained less than 5.5 by administering ammonium chloride. The oral dose of mandelic acid as its sodium salt is between 8 to 12 g daily.

Salicylic acid. It has *weak bacteriostatic* and *antifungal* action. Externally it may be applied as a 1 to 5 percent ointment or dusting powder. In addition 10 percent salicylic acid acts as a **keratolytic** agents, and in collodion base (10-12%) it is an effective application for the removal of corns or warts.

Oxidizing Agents

Potassium permanganate. It is soluble in 16 parts of water forming a purple solution. It acts as a powerful **oxidizing agent**, and oxidizes toxins and bacteria to make them inert. It is used as a **disinfectant** and **deodorant,** but as soon as the oxygen is liberated it loses its germicidal activity. In solid form it is an irritant and caustic. **Its germicidal activity is lost when it comes in contact with organic matter.** It is also used to disinfect ponds and wells. To disinfect bed pans and septic discharges, it is used in a strength of 1:100 to 1:500. Solutions of 1:4,000 to 1:1,000 are used as gargle or mouthwash in **stomatitis,** and to wash **infected ulcers** as well as for irrigating serous cavities. More dilute solutions 1:10,000 to 1:5,000 are used as a bladder or urethral wash. A 0.02 percent solution is used as gastric lavage in the treatment of poisoning after ingestion of organic compounds like **opium** and **strychnine. Pure crystals** are applied locally promptly in cases of snake-bite. To squeeze out the venom the part is incised and potassium permanganate crystals are rubbed in.

Hydrogen peroxide. As a 3 percent solution, this agent has been extensively used for cleaning wounds. The compound is unstable and nascent oxygen is released, particularly on contact with organic matter. The evolution of oxygen mechanically loosens pus and tissue debris, and also kills the bacteria. **The action is weak, short-lived, and the agent has poor penetrating power.** It is widely used for cleansing wounds and discharging ulceres. A dilute solution (5%) can be used as a **mouthwash** and **deodorant** in aphthous stomatitis, tonsillitis, and diphtheria. In dentistry, it is used as a cleanser and helps to remove stains from teeth and debris from septic pockets in the gums. It should never be used in a closed or hollow cavity which has no exit for the liberated oxygen.

Sodium perborate. This agent, like hydrogen peroxide, produces its germicidal effect by liberating oxygen, and has similar uses.

Phenolic Compounds

Phenol was introduced as an antiseptic by Lord Lister in the 1860s, and marked the beginning of modern antiseptic technique. Subsequently phenol became the standard agent against which other compounds were assessed, and the "phenol coefficient" was worked out. A large number of **phenolic derivatives** have been prepared and used as germicides. **These agents are effective against non-sporing pathogens, but are inactive against bacterial spores.**

Phenol. The antimicrobial activity of phenol (carbolic acid) is possibly due to the presence of the phenolic-OH group. Introduction of alkyl or halogen into the benzene ring increases the activity of the compound, e.g., **hexylresorcinol, hexachlorophene.** Phenol reacts with proteins to form insoluble proteinates, coagulates cell protein, destroys cell membrane and acts as a protoplasmic poison. On the skin and mucous membrane, phenol crystals or liquefied phenol causes severe irritation and pain, followed by redness and slough formation. Phenol is used as a local antiseptic and disinfectant against gram-positive and gram-negative bacteria. It is also effective against fungus and many viruses. **It is ineffective against spores or acid-fast organisms.** The disadvantage of phenol is its relatively weak activity and high tissue toxicity. Sometimes even today phenol 5 percent in almond oil is injected around internal haemorrhoids (piles) as a **sclerosing agent.**

Dettol is a liquid germicide containing 4.8 percent **chloroxylenol** (chlorinated phenol). A 5 percent solution is used for cleansing wounds, and a 5 percent solution in 70 percent alcohol is used for disinfection of surgical instruments.

Cresol. It is obtained by distillation of coal tar, and consists of a mixture of ortho-, meta- and para-cresols. **This compound (cresol) is about 10 times more active than phenol, with about the same toxicity.** It is not too soluble in water and is used as a soapy emulsion referred to as **Lysol.** Cresol is commonly used as a commercial disinfectant.

Resorcinol. This agent is less potent than phenol as an antiseptic, but has substantial **keratolytic** and **antipuritic** activity. Hence it is used in skin affections like pruritus, eczema, ringworm and psoriasis. Resorcinol is generally used as an ointment with zinc oxide and salicylic acid. Application over large areas should be avoided, as systemic absorption may give rise to CNS stimulation. Prolonged use may lead to thyroid enlargement (goitrogenic effect).

Hexylresorcinol. Its action in ascariasis and oxyuriasis makes hexylresorcinol a useful *anthelmintic*. It may also be used in *throat lozenges* because of its spreading and penetrating properties.

Thymol. This agent has a weak **fungicidal** and **anthelmintic** activity. A mixture of the iodides of thymol (mainly thymol diiodide) has been employed as a dusting powder.

Hexachlorophene. Hexachlorophene (G_{11}) is a halogenated phenol. It is mainly active against gram-positive and some gram-negative organisms in a concentration of 2 to 5 percent. **Staphylococcus aureus** is sensitive to it even in high dilutions. It is incorporated in a variety of **soaps** meant for scrubbing, and it effectively lowers the incidence of staphylococcal skin infection. It is also useful for the treatment of **acne, impetigo, furuncles, carbuncle,** and **fungal infection** of the skin. Hypersensitivity reactions may occur in some individuals, and keratitis can follow introduction into the eye. Hexachlorophene may also be used as a preservative (upto 0.1%) in cosmetic preparations.

Surface-active Agents (Surfactants)

Surface-active agents are also called **detergents** or wetting agents. They contain in their molecular structure **one hydrophobic group** having affinity for organic matter, which is balanced by **one or more hydrophilic groups** having affinity for water. *Soaps are anionic, and organic quaternary ammonium-compounds are cationic surface-active agents.* Both classes of detergents emulsify sebaceous material which is then removed together with the dirt and the microbes. The mild desquamating effect of the quaternary ammonium compounds aids this cleansing action. The antimicrobial action of detergents is ascribed to alteration of microbial membrane permeability.

Anionic Surfactants

Soaps. These compounds ionize with the **hydrophobic moiety in the anion**. Soaps are active against gram-positive organisms only. The mode of action of soaps is a physical one, and by **emulsification** of the lipoidal secretions of the skin in which bacteria reside, they have a cleansing action. They are not very satisfactory germicides against the common pathogenic microorganisms lodged on the skin. The germicidal activity of the soaps may be enhanced by the addition of other antiseptics like hexachlorophene.

Cationic Surfactants

In the cationic surfactants the **hydrophobic moiety is in the cation,** i.e., they have positively charged hydrophobic groups. These agents are generally more effective than the anionic compounds. They can be used in more dilute solutions (1:5,000 to 1:20,000) and their antimicrobial activity covers a wider range of organisms including some gram-negative bacteria and fungi. Solutions upto 0.1 percent are used as **mouthwash** or on denuded skin as an antiseptic. In strengths of 0.1 to 1.0 percent they are used for **preoperative skin preparation.** These agents may produce **hypersensitivity reactions** when applied to the skin. Commonly used agents are **benzalkonium chloride** (Zephiran); **benzethonium chloride** (Phemerol), and **cetylpyridinium chloride** (Ceepryn). These agents are usually employed as 10 percent solutions or 0.1 percent tinctures. **Methylbenzethonium chloride** (Diaparene) is commonly employed as a rinse for diapers and for bed linen and under clothes of patients suffering from urinary incontinence to prevent dermatitis.

Cetrimide (Cetavlon). Cetrimide is a **cationic detergent** with **bactericidal** activity. In higher dilutions it is **bacteriostatic**. A 0.5 to 1.0 percent solution is used for disinfecting and cleansing wounds, and for preoperative **preparation of the skin.** It is also useful for disinfecting utensils and to **sterilize surgical instruments.** Repeated use on the skin may cause **hypersensitivity reactions.**

Nonionic Surfactants

Nonoxynol-9 is a nonionic detergent used as a **spermicide.** It is incorporated also into antimicrobial hand soap preparations.

Alcohols

Ethyl alcohol (Ethanol). Ethyl alcohol is extensively used for cleaning the skin prior to parenteral injections. **It is ineffective against spores and viruses responsible for serum hepatitis.** Maximum antiseptic effect is possessed by 70 percent ethanol by weight (78% by volume). Solutions of greater or lesser dilutions have lesser antiseptic action. Ethanol may be rubbed on the skin to prevent **bed sores,** as it has a local antiseptic, vasodilator, and anhydrotic action. **It is unsuitable for disinfection of surgical instruments as it is ineffective against spores.**

Dehydrated ethanol may be injected close to a nerve trunk to induce a temporary and reversible **conduction block** for temporary relief of pain, e.g., trigeminal neuralgia. It may also be injected to destroy the lumbar sympathetic ganglia, which leads to vasodilation and provides relief from pain in patients of **vasospastic diseases** involving the lower extremities.

Isopropyl alcohol. Its germicidal potency is the same as that of ethanol, and it is useful as a skin disinfectant. It is active in solutions ranging from 30-90 percent, and the effectiveness is not so sensitive to changes in strength as is the case with ethyl alcohol.

Halogens

Iodine. It is one of the oldest antiseptics. Solutions containing elemental iodine are **antiseptics,** and are **lethal to bacteria and other spore-bearing organisms.** It also possesses high **fungicidal** and **virucidal** activity. A 1:20,000 solution kills most bacteria within one minute; the fungi and viruses are killed by higher concentrations in a longer period of time. The germicidal activity is slowed down in the presence of organic matter.

Many preparations of iodine are available; (*i*) **Iodine tincture** is a 2.5 percent solution of elemental iodine with 2.5 percent potassium iodide in water and 44 to 50 percent ethyl alcohol. It is preferred to the older 7 percent iodine tincture for decontamination of intact skin; (*ii*) **Iodine solution** contains approximately 2.5 percent iodine, and 2.5 percent potassium iodide in water. This preparation is preferred for superficial lacerations to prevent microbial infections, since it is effective and non-irritating; (*iii*) **Strong iodine solution** (Lugol's solution) contains 5 percent iodine, and 10 percent potassium iodide. It is used in the treatment of iodine deficiency, thyroid disease and thyrotoxicosis; and (*iv*) **Compound paint of Iodine (Mandl's throat paint)** contains 1.25 percent iodine, and 2.5 percent potassium iodide in alcohol, and glycerine. This paint is applied over the mucous membrane of the throat and tonsils in pharyngitis and tonsillitis.

Iodine stains the skin and is locally **dermatotoxic.** Topical application may give rise to local hypersensitivity reactions, and rarely generalized reactions. Ingestion of iodine or iodides in therapeutic doses may produce nasal catarrh, conjunctivitis, lacrimation, bronchitis and skin rashes. Hypersensitivity reactions are known as **iodism.** Iodides taken during pregnancy may cause goitre and mental retardation in the offspring. Iodine compounds are also used orally in the treatment of amoebiasis **(Chap. 9.5).**

Iodophores. They are large organic molecules carrying loosely bound iodine which is liberated slowly. They are expensive and more effective than elemental iodine solutions. A popular preparation is **Povidone-Iodine** (Isodin). This iodophore is prepared by the interaction of **iodine** and **polyvinylpyrrolidone.** It is water soluble and slowly releases iodine on contact with the skin or mucous membrane.

Chlorine. It is a potent germicidal agent, and is effective against gram-negative and gram-positive bacteria, some viruses, fungi and many protozoa when used in higher concentrations. Acid-fast microorganisms and spores are more resistant to chlorine. It is most active in acid or neutral medium. **Alkalinity and presence of organic matter reduces its potency.** Chlorine even at very low concentrations suppresses the enzymes associated with glucose metabolism. **Hypochlorous acid** is formed on reaction with water, and this is the basis for the use of chlorine in the disinfection of drinking water and swimming pools.

Chlorinated lime (Bleaching powder) contains not less than 30 percent w/w of available chlorine. When it comes in contact with water and air, chlorine is liberated. The onset of action is quick but short-lasting. It is used as a **disinfectant** and **deodorant,** and is a useful disinfectant for water-closets, faeces, urine, drains, ponds and tanks specially during epidemics of cholera and gastroenteritis.

Because of difficulties in handling chlorine in the form of gas and instability of chlorine water, chlorine-releasing substances like **chlorinated lime,** surgical **chlorinated soda solution** (Dakin's solution), **strong sodium hypochlorite solution, calcium hypochlorite solution** (Eusol), **Chloramine T, halazone** and **chloroazodin** may be used. Free hypochlorous acid is responsible for their bactericidal effect, which is due to the penetration of chlorine into the bacterial cells and chlorination of their enzymes.

Aldehydes

Formaldehyde. Solution of formaldehyde (Formalin) is an aqueous solution (40%) of formaldehyde containing methyl alcohol as a stabilizing agent. Formaldehyde precipitates protein and hardens skins and other tissues. Therefore it is used for **preserving pathological specimens.** It is an effective germicide in a concentration of 1:200, which kills both spore forming and non-spore forming organisms. It has valuable detoxicating properties and can convert diphtheria toxin into a toxoid. **Formaldehyde solution can be used as a disinfectant against bacteria, fungi and viruses, but acts slowly on spores and acid-fast bacteria.** As a mouthwash or gargle it is used in a strength 1:500 for hardening the gums. It is extensively used for disinfecting surgical instruments and excreta. As it is devoid of bleaching effects, linen, woollens, silk and books can be safely disinfected with formalin. As a disinfectant it is used in concentrations of 2 to 8 percent. Formaldehyde also has an **anhidrotic action** when applied to the palms and soles, but not axillae.

Glutaraldehyde (Glutaral). It is a potent dialdehyde with a wide range of germicidal activity. It is rapidly **sporicidal** and possesses **tuberculocidal** activity. A 2 percent aqueous solution buffered with sodium carbonate (0.3%) to a pH of 7.5 to 8.5 may be used to disinfect and sterilize surgical and endoscopic instruments, and plastic and rubber apparatus. Glutaral loses activity within 2 weeks of its preparation. Like formaldehyde it has **anhidrotic** action when applied to palms and soles.

Acridine Dyes

Acriflavine hydrochloride, Proflavine hemisulphate. These acridine dyes are yellow in colour, and act as **bacteriostatic** agents. Gram-negative organisms are much less sensitive, compared to the gram-positive organisms. **Pseudomonas aeruginosa, Proteus vulgaris and acid-fast bacteria are resistant to the acridines.** These agents have a very low toxicity, and do not cause local irritation. They may produce hypersensitive skin reactions rarely. **These dyestuffs do not lose potency in the presence of pus, serum or tissue fluids; and are used for the treatment of wounds, burns and other infections of the skin and mucous membranes.** They may be applied in the form of lotion, cream or ointment. Prolonged treatment is not recommended, as it may delay healing. Acriflavine is usually employed in a strength of 1:1000 in isotonic saline; and proflavine in a strength of 1:100 in isotonic saline.

Triphenylmethane Dyes

Gentian violet. It is also known as **crystal violet** and is toxic to gram-positive organisms. It is specially effective against **Staphylococci, C. diphtheriae** and **P. pyocyanenus.** Acid-fast bacteria and gram-negative organisms are resistant to this dye. In the form of jelly or lotion (0.5%) it is used as an application for burns. Often it is combined with **brilliant green and proflavine hemisulphate (triple dye)** as a first aid treatment for burns. Equal parts of crystal violet and brilliant green are used for disinfection of the skin, in gynaecological practice, and in the treatment of ringworm, infectious eczema, impetigo contagiosa and other superficial pyogenic infections of the skin. It should not be applied over ulcerated areas. Gentian violet is also effective in **oxyuriasis** and **strongyloidosis** on oral administration.

Brilliant green. Like gentian violet, this agent is also an antiseptic and disinfectant. It is used as a 0.05 to 0.1 percent solution in water or hypertonic saline in infected wounds, and may be usefully combined with gentian violet and proflavine in the treatment of burns.

HEAVY METALS

Mercury Compounds

Both inorganic and organic compounds of mercury have now been largely replaced by more potent and less toxic agents. Mercury compounds are **bacteriostatic,** but are ineffective against spores. Mercuric ions precipitate proteins. The antiseptic property depends on the dissociated mercuric ions which combine with and inactivate the **sulphydryl enzymes** of the bacteria and also of the tissues. Except for the phenylmercuric salts, serum and tissue proteins reduce their antimicrobial activity. Skin sensitization is common.

Mercuric chloride. This agent may be used as a hand sterilizing agent on the unbroken skin as a 1:2000 solution. Stronger solutions should be avoided.

Thimerosal (Merthiolate). This is an organic complex containing about 50 percent mercury. A 1:1000 solution is used for sterilizing the skin and mucous membranes, but may lead to sensitivity reactions. For application to wounds or denuded skin a 1:10,000 aqueous solution is used.

Silver Compounds

Two types of silver compounds, the **inorganic** and the **colloidal silver preparations** are used as antiseptics. The inorganic salts like silver nitrate readily ionize in solution and precipitate proteins. Silver nitrate exerts immediate **bactericidal** action, and is irritant to the skin. The colloidal silver compounds in solution slowly dissociate and are non-irritant.

Silver nitrate. A few drops of a 1 percent solution of silver nitrate are instilled into the conjunctival sac of infants as a prophylaxis against **gonococcal ophthalmia neonatorum.**

Colloidal silver preparations (strong silver protein, mild silver protein, and silver halide) are used in the form of microsuspension (solution). A 1 to 5 percent solution of mild silver protein with ephedrine is used as drops for nasal infection, and 10 to 20 percent solutions have been used as antiseptic eye drops.

Zinc Salts

Zinc salts are mild *antiseptics.* They are also **astringents** and **corrosives.** The antiseptic action is probably due to the precipitation of proteins by zinc ions. They are used as antiseptics and astringents on mucous membrances and skin. **Zinc oxide ointment** (10%) can be used in skin diseases like **eczema, impetigo, varicose ulcers** and **psoriasis.** Zinc oxide as calamine is astringent, antiseptic and antipruritic. Solution of **zinc sulphate** (0.1 to 1.0%) is used as antiseptic eye drops. Zinc chloride is used in dentistry as an astringent and a local analgesic.

Antibiotics

The antibiotics that are poorly absorbed by oral route, or produce severe systemic toxic effects, are specially useful preparations for topical use on mucous membranes and skin to produce anti-infective effects. **Bacitracin, polymyxin B, neomycin, framycetin** and **tyrothricin** are some antibiotics used for their local effects **(Chap. 9.2).**

Chlorhexidine (Savlon)

Chlorhexidine salts (acetate, hydrochloride, gluconate) have their primary effect on the bacterial cell membrane. They are used for disinfection of skin pre-operatively, and in obstetrics and wound cleansing. Occasional hypersensitivity reactions may occur.

Ectoparasiticides

Ectoparasiticides are drugs which eradicate or kill the parasites infesting the external surface of the body. This section includes drugs used in the treatment of scabies (caused by *Sarcoptes scabiei,* the itch mite) and pediculosis (infestation with *Pediculus humanus* and *Pediculus capitis,* varieties of lice).

Scabicides are drugs used to eradicate the infestation of the skin caused by the itch mite. The drugs commonly used are benzyl benzoate application, crotamiton, precipitated sulphur, and gamma benzene hexachloride. **Pediculicides** are drugs used to eradicate body infestation by lice.

Benzyl benzoate application. This dosage form contains benzyl benzoate 25 percent w/v with emulsifying wax and purified water. It is also available as a lotion with or without dicophane (DDT). Benzyl benzoate is an effective **scabicide.** The patient is first scrubbed with soap in a hot bath to open up the burrows, and immediately after drying benzyl benzoate application is applied over the whole body surface below the neck. A second application is made on the following day. Alternatively three applications may be made at 12-hourly intervals. Clothing and bedding should be changed to prevent reinfestation. Benzyl benzoate can also be used as a **pediculicide** and an insect repellent. Benzyl benzoate ocassionally causes skin eruptions in sensitized persons. It must not be allowed to come in contact with eyes. Benzyl benzoate 25 percent emulsion (Ascabiol) is also available for use in scabies and pediculosis.

Crotamiton (Crotorax). Crotamiton is a very effective scabicide, and is applied as a 10 percent cream or lotion over whole of the body surface below the neck. Preliminary bathing of the skin is not essential, but if done the skin should be absolutely dry before applying crotamiton. A second application is made 24 hours later. A third application usually is sufficient for complete cure.

Crotamiton is a potent **antipruritic** agent, and local application gives rapid relief from itching. It is used for the relief of pruritus ani, vulvae and scroti, and senile pruritus or itch associated with various dermatoses. One application is usually effective for 6 to 10 hours. Locally crotamiton sometimes may cause transient erythema and a sensation of warmth or irritant contact dermatitis. It should not be applied near the eyes.

Precipitated sulphur. This compound may be applied topically as a 6 percent (range 5% to 10%) ointment in petrolatum to treat **scabies.** It is applied by friction on three consecutive nights, followed by soap water bath on the fourth day. The clothings are boiled to avoid reinfestation. Sulphur is an **antiseptic** and **fungicide** as well, and its action is attributed to the formation of **hydrogen sulphide** and **pentathionic acid,** the latter product appears to be more germicidal and miticidal than the former. Sulphur ointment has staining properties and an unpleasant odour. Rarely it causes irritation and dermatitis if used frequently.

Sulphur dioxide obtained by burning sulphur is used to disinfect rooms, furniture and books. If taken by mouth, sulphur is a mild purgative.

Dicophane (DDT, Dichlorodiphenyl trichloroethane, Chlorophenothane). It is an effective insecticide and larvicide, and is used in the prevention and treatment of arthopod infestation. Mosquitoes and their larvae, flies, bed bugs, fleas and lice are susceptible to this agent. It is used as a watery suspension, solution or dust. DDT has the ability to penetrate the chitinous exoskeleton of insects, and acts on the neuronal membrane to render it unstable. It stimulates the **campaniform organs** (peripheral sensory structures peculiar to arthropods) and results in a convulsive state and ultimately death. It is thus a contact poison.

For **pediculosis,** a single application of 2 percent DDT is highly effective. It may be combined with benzyl benzoate for the treatment of scabies. It is also effective against various insects and arthropods, and is used in the malaria control programme.

DDT is relatively non-toxic in man. However, when swallowed in large amounts for suicidal purposes, it causes stimulation of the supraspinal structures, characterized by tremors, convulsions and hypothermia. The respiration may fail leading to death. Hepatic damage due to prolonged ingestion of contaminated vegetables may occur.

Gamma-benzene hexachloride (Gammexane, Gamma-BHC, Lindane). This agent is effective in all forms of scabies and **pediculosis.** It is irritating to the skin, eyes and mucosa. Allergic contact dermatitis may occur. It is absorbed through intact skin, and systemic toxicity is usually manifested as CNS stimulation and convulsions. Diazepam or the barbiturates are effective in controlling convulsions. Gamma-benzene hexachloride is also an effective **insecticide.** In insects it produces convulsions similar to those produced by DDT.

In the treatment of scabies gama-benzene hexachloride (1%) in vanishing cream base is applied all over the skin below the face, as a thin film. Preliminary bath is not required, and the application is removed after 24 hours, followed by a soap bath. One application is sufficient to cure most of the cases of scabies. A few cases may require a second or a third application, which may be given at an interval of one week.

Other insecticides, insect repellants and larvicides include **dibutylphthalate, pyrethrum, copperacetoarsenite, derris** and **organophosphorus cholinesterase inhibitors like parathion, malathion,** *TEPP* (tetraethylpyrophosphate) and *OMPA* (octamethylpyrophosphoramide). Some other chlorinated hydrocarbons used as insecticides are **chlordane, aldrin** and **dieldrin.**

ANTIFUNGAL AGENTS

Antifungal agents are drugs used to kill or inhibit the growth of common mycotic infestations (local and systemic). An **ideal** antifungal agent, specially for the skin should: (*i*) be fungicidal rather than fungistatic; (*ii*) be non-staining and non-irritating to the skin and free from sensitization reactions; (*iii*) be able to penetrate into the hair, nails, and horny layers of the skin to come in direct contact with the fungus; and (*iv*) have some antibacterial activity, as associated secondary bacterial infections are quite common. From the therapeutic standpoint, fungal infections may be divided into there categories: **dermatophytic, systemic** and **candidal**.

The **dermatophytic** infections involve the skin, hair and nails. About 20 species of **Epidermophyton, Trichophyton** and **Microsporum** are known to cause these infestations. They are treated orally with **griseofulvin,** or topically by the application of **tolnaftate, haloprogin, clotrimazole** or **miconazole.**

The **systemic** fungal infections may be subdivided into *two* groups. The first group of infections is caused by **opportunistic organisms** which occur commonly in immunosuppressed patients, or in those patients in whom the bacterial flora are modified by prolonged antibiotic therapy, e.g., **cryptococcosis, aspergillosis and zygomycosis.** The *second* group of infections includes **histoplasmosis, blastomycosis, coccidioidomycosis, para coccidioidomycosis,** and **sporotrichosis.** The systemic mycotic infections are a serious problem, chronic in nature, and difficult to diagnose. Drugs used in their treatment include **amphotericin B, flucytosine** and **hydroxystibamidine.**

The **candidal** infections are caused in man usually by **Candida albicans,** but rarely by **C. tropicalis** and **C. paropsilosis.** Candidiasis usually affects moist skin or mucous membranes, including the gastrointestinal tract, and may cause systemic disease. Candidiasis only rarely involves the intact skin or nails or normal individuals. Patients with intertrigo, diabetes mellitus, or those on immunosuppressive therapy, antibacterial agents, or oral contraceptives are most susceptible to candidal infections. Drugs effective in mucocutaneous candidosis are **nystatin, hamycin, clotrimazole, miconazole and amphotericin B.** Systemic candidosis is treated by intravenous **amphotericin B** alone or with **flucytosine.** The pharmacological profile of the commonly used antifungal agents is summarized in **Table 10-1.**

Table 10-1. *Commonly used antifungal agents*

Drug	*Antifungal spectrum*	*Adverse reactions/precautions*	*Mode of administration*
1. Dermatophytic infections Griseofulvin	Only drug effective orally against species of *Epidermophyton, Microsporum* and *Trichophyton*. Ineffective against bacteria, other fungi and candida	May cause hepatotoxicity. Contraindicated in acute intermittent porphyrias, and hepatocellular failure.	500 mg daily in single or divided doses orally, after meals.
Tolnaftate	Effective topically against species of *Epidermophyton Microsporum* and *Trichophyton*	May cause local irritation No other confirmed reactions reported.	1% solution, cream or powder is rubbed into the lesion twice daily for 4 to 6 weeks.
Haloprogin	Same as above. Cure rate higher than tolnaftate	Local irritation, burning and vesicle formation. Avoid contact with eyes.	1% cream applied thrice daily for 2 to 3 weeks.
Clotrimazole	Applied topically to the skin and vaginal mucosa for infections cause by pathogenic dermatophytes. Also active against *Histoplasma capsulatum, Blastomyces neoformans, Aspergillus* and *Candida*	Erythema, blistering, peeling of skin. Oedema, pruritus and urticaria may occur.	Topically 1% cream applied twice daily. One tablet (100 mg) inserted into the vagina nightly for 7 to 14 days.
Miconazole nitrate	Chemically relatd to clotrimazole. Effective against pathogenic dermatophytes. Also is trichomonicidal and active against gram-positive bacteria and Candida	Irritation, burning and hypersensitivity reactions. IV injection causes thrombophlebitis and bronchospasm.	Topically a 2% cream applied to cover the part twice daily. Intravenously 25-30 mg/kg in 2 or 3 equally divided doses at 8-12 hours intervals.
2. Systemic fungal infections			
Amphotericin B	Must be injected IV for systemic fungal infections, and intrathecally for fungal meningitis. Topical application effective for condidosis of skin and mucous membranes. Life saving for almost all systemic fungal infections	IV administration may cause chills, fever, headache and azotemia. Polyneuropathy, convulsions, and anaphylactic reactions may occur. Nephrotoxicity occasionally.	Slow intravenous infusion given over a period of 2-6 hours. Initial dose should not exceed 0.25 mg/kg of body weight. Total dose 30 mg/kg administered over 6 to 10 weeks.
Flucytosine	Given orally for the treatment of *Candida* species, *Cryptococcus neoformans* and *Torulopsis*	Less toxic than amphotericin B. Blood dycrasias, renal impairment and hepatotoxicity may occur.	150-200 mg/kg orally daily in divided doses at 6 hour intervals.
Hydroxystilbamidine isethionate	Administered IV to treat blastomycosis. Most effective in patient with dermal or noncavitary pulmonary disease	Hypotension and tachycardia. Paraesthesias and urinary incontinence. Hepatic disease is a relative contraindication.	Intravenously a total dose of 8 g is iven in daily doses of 225 mg in 5% dextrose injection.
3. Candidal infections			
Nystatin	Active *in vitro* against a variety of fungi, including all *Candida* species. Clinical use limited to candidal infections of skin, mucous membrances, gastrointestinal tract and vagina	Nausea and diarrhoea on oral administration. Irritation on topical application.	**Oral:** 500,000 to 1,000,000 units three times daily. **Vaginal:** 100,000 to 200,000 units daily for 2 weeks or longer.

(Contd.)

Table 10-1. Contd...

Drug	*Antifungal spectrum*	*Adverse reactions/precautions*	*Mode of administration*
Hamycin	Active against pathogenic fungi and yeasts including *Aspergillus*, *Candida*, *Trichophyton species*, and *Trichomonas vaginalis*, Clinically used for candidiasis and trichomoniasis. Also blastomycosis and madura foot	May cause some local irritation	Available in the form of pessaries 100,000 units; or oral suspension 40,000 units/ml.
Clotrimazole and Miconazole	These agents are also effective against *Candida* species (see above).		
Amphotericin B and Flucytosine	Systemic candidosis responds to intravenous amphotericin B alone or with flucytosine. The use is justified only if *in vitro* sensititvity tests indicate susceptibility of the organism to both the agents.		

Certain other agents used for the treatment of fungal infections are: (*i*) **Acrisorcin** for chromophytosis, a chronic skin infection; (*ii*) **Iodochlorhydroxyquin** (Clioquinol) for dermatophytoses specially when there is associated bacterial infection; (*iii*) **Gentian violet** is effective against intertriginous candidosis, although it stains the skin; (*iv*) **Potassium iodide** for chronic cutaneous lymphatic sporotrichosis; (*v*) **Selenium sulphide** for chromophytosis and seborrhoeic dermatitis of the scalp; (*vi*) **Undecylenic acid** for localized mild dermatophytic infections, specially in combination with zinc undecylenate; and (*vii*) **Benzoic (6%) and salicylic (3%) acid** ointment has no significant antifungal activity, but is an effective keratolytic agent. Thus, when used, it exposes the deeper layers of the skin to more potent antifungal agents. Various other combinations of antifungal agents are available with antibiotics, corticosteroids, local anaesthetics and local anti-infectives.

❑❑❑

11

AUTACOIDS

11.1 HISTAMINE AND ANTIHISTAMINES

A number of substances, designated as **autacoids,** are formed in various tissues of the body and are believed to function as **local hormones.** These compounds differ from the hormones which are secreted from endocrine glands. They have a local regulatory function to perform in the body. The term autacoid is derived from Greek *autos* (self) and *akos* (remedy). The important autacoids include **histamine, 5-hydroxytryptamine** (serotonin), **prostaglandins** and the **kinins.**

HISTAMINE

Histamine is a biogenic amine, and as the name implies (*Hist*=tissue) it occurs in many tissues in almost all forms of life. In nature it occurs in an inactive form, but is released in a *free* active state in response to injury or to antigen/antibody reactions. Histamine plays a role in the regulation of gastric secretion, in the body's protective mechanism at the site of injury (triple response, acute inflammation), and as a mediator in allergic and anaphylactic conditions.

SYNTHESIS, STORAGE AND METABOLISM

Histamine is synthesized from the amino acid **histidine** by the action of **histidine decarboxylase.** It is present in many mammalian tissues with high concentrations in **lung, skin** and **intestine.** In man about 5 mg of histamine are formed daily. In the brain histamine has a distribution pattern similar to that of serotonin, i.e., it occurs in high concentration in the **hypothalamus,** and low concentration in the white matter and the cerebral cortex. Dietary histamine or histamine synthesized in the gut lumen by bacteria contributes insignificantly to the endogenous tissue **histamine pool.**

Histamine in the body is stored through electrostatic forces in storage granules in at least 3 pools or types of storage sites: (*i*) in the granules of **mast cells** and of **basophils** (the equivalent cells to the mast cells in peripheral blood). **In the mast cells histamine is bound to heparin and serotonin in an inactive form and cannot be metabolized.** The mast cells can be degranulated releasing histamine by the antigen/antibody complex formed in an **immediate allergic reaction.** Histamine releasing drugs can also degranulate mast cells and release active histamine; (*ii*) in the **mucosal cells of the gastrointestinal tract** (not in the mast cells) which cannot be depleted by histamine releasers; and (*iii*) in the cells of the **hypothalamus** and the **area postrema,** where histamine reacts differently and is depleted by reserpine.

Histamine is also present in some nerves, nerve endings and synaptic vesicles. **Non-mast cell histamine** has a more rapid turnover than mast cell histamine and is probably of greater physiological significance.

The metabolism of histamine is shown in **Fig. 11.1.1.** The activity of histamine is terminated within 5 to 15 minutes mainly by **methylation** followed by **deamination** by monoamine oxidase (MAO). Another histaminase (diamine oxidase) also deaminates histamine. The various metabolites of histamine possess little or no pharmacologic activity, and are excreted in the urine.

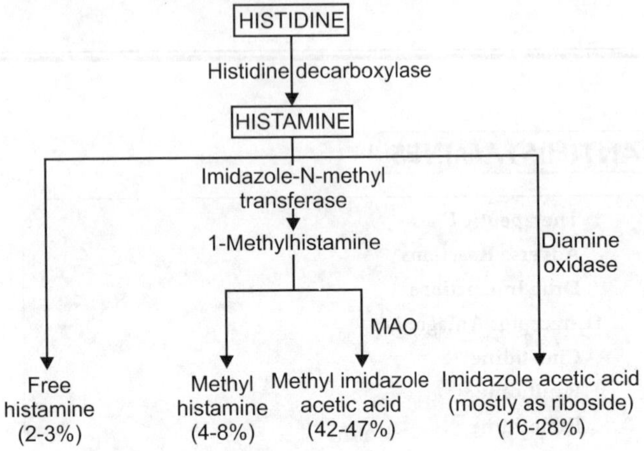

Fig. 11.1.1: The synthesis, metabolism and the urinary metabolites of histamine.

Mode of Action

Histamine acts on two separate and distinct postsynaptic receptors, termed H_1- and H_2-receptors. Contraction of the smooth muscle of the **bronchi** and the **intestine,** and most of the **depressor effects on blood pressure** (BP) are mediated by H_1-receptors, and antagonized by classical antihistamines like **mepyramine** and **diphenhydramine (Table 11.1-1).** In contrast, the **H_2-receptors** mediate the actions of histamine on the **gastric secretion, cardiac acceleration** and **inhibition of the rat uterus.** These actions are antagonized by the new type of antihistamines like **cimetidine** and **ranitidine.** Both, the classical and th new type of antihistamines act as **selective** competitive antagonists to the actions of histamine on the H_1- and H_2-receptors respectively.

Pharmacological Actions

The main actions of histamine are exerted on the **cardiovascular system, smooth muscles and gastric secretion.** The degree and the direction of these actions vary from species to species.

Cardiovascular System

The most important effect of histamine in most species, including man is to markedly and sharply lower BP. This depressor response is attributed to the dilatation of the small terminal arterioles (direct effect on smooth muscle) with subsequent **passive postcapillary venular dilatation, and constriction of the larger veins.** All the small vessels in the body are involved, but in man following an intravenous injection, vasodilatation is most marked over the face (blush area), and upper trunk. Histamine produces dilatation of the cerebral vessels, and in man produces severe **throbbing headache,** due to stretch of the dural pain receptors. In man histamine may induce **postural hypotension** due to venous pooling of blood. This hypotension leads to a sympatho-adrenal activation and tachycardia. With large doses, the combined venous pooling and arteriolar constriction lead to shock. The permeability of the capillaries and small venules is increased and fluid is passed into the extravascular space, leading to **tissue oedema, haemoconcentration** and **elevation of the haematocrit**. Such a tissue oedema is the cause for urticarial lesions.

When histamine is injected into the skin (or the skin is vigorously scratched liberating endogenous histamine), the well known **triple response** is seen, comprising of: (*i*) a circumscribed **"erythematous zone"** over several millimetres of skin at and around the injection site. This area becomes bluish later due to relative deoxygenation; (*ii*) a wider, irregular area of erythema or **"flare"** which develops over several minutes due to local arteriolar dilatation mediated by the axon reflexes (antidromic vasodilator impulses); and (*iii*) localized oedema **"wheal"** at the site of initial erythema due to the increased permeability of the postcapillary bed. The triple response is accompanied by transient pain and itching.

Table 11.1-1. *Distribution and the effects mediated by the histamine receptors in the body*

H_1-receptors	*H_2-receptors*
Effects mediated	**Effects mediated**
Contraction of the smooth muscles of:	Stimulation of gastric secretion
Intestines	Stimulation of the heart (acceleration)
Bronchioles	Inhibition of antigenic histamine relase from basophils
Most of the depressor effects on BP	Rest of depressor effects on BP
Selective competitive antagonists	**Selective competitive antagonists**
Mepyramine	Cimetidine
Diphenhydramine	Ranitidine

Smooth Muscle

Histamine is a powerful, direct stimulant of the **nonvascular** smooth muscles. **Bronchiolar constriction** and **intestinal hypermotility** are the important manifestations of the generalized smooth muscle stimulation.

Gastric Secretion

Histamine causes maximal secretion of **acid** and **pepsin** by the stomach. It is present in high concentration in the gastric mucosa and appears in gastric secretion. Histamine exerts its effect on the **parietal cells of the oxyntic gland area** of the stomach. After vagotomy the secretory response in man falls by about two-thirds. This role of the parasympathetic nervous system may account for the partial antagonism of the secretory effects of histamine by anticholinergic agents. It appears that histamine is the "final common step" in the stimulation of parietal cells leading to acid secretion. H_2-receptor antagonists (cimetidine and ranidine) antagonize the stimulant action of histamine on gastric secretion. Histamine has some stimulant effect on the **lacrimal, salivary, bronchial** and **pancreatic** exocrine glands.

The pain and pruritus associated with insect stings and venoms, are partly due to endogenous histamine release. The adrenal medullary chromaffin cells are stimulated by histamine directly, and indirectly via the splanchnic nerves, causing **release of catecholamines** (adrenaline and noradrenaline) into circulation. Normally the response is insignificant, but in patients with a pheochromocytoma a large amount of catecholamines is released and the blood pressure sharply rises (see later).

Anaphylactic Shock

The similarity between anaphylactic shock and the actions of histamine prompted Laidlow in 1910 to suggest that histamine may be a **mediator of anaphylactic shock.** In addition, other autacoids like **bradykinin, prostaglandins, 5-hydroxytryptamine** (serotonin) and an unsaturated fatty acid called **slow reacting substance of anaphylaxis** (SRS-A) are liberated in varying amounts. Lately, an **eosinophil chemotactic factor of anaphylaxis** (ECF-A) has been described. In anaphylaxis the antigen reacts with the mast cell membrane-bound antibody, and histamine storage granules undergo **exocytosis.** This released **free histamine** is responsible for the various cellular and tissue manifestations of anaphylactic shock. The **catecholamines** may be inhibiting histamine release in addition to their well known antagonism of histamine action in anaphylaxis.

It has been suggested that histamine also plays a role in **inflammatory reactions, regulation of microcirculation, tissue repair** and **growth.** It functions as a neurotransmitter at certain synapses.

Histamine Releasing Drugs

Endogenous histamine may be released by certain drugs, chemicals and physical agents. The major source of the histamine liberated are the mast cells, from which heparin, SRS-A and vasoactive kinins are also released in varying amounts. Such a histamine release may be of a magnitude to precipitate an **anaphylactic reaction.** The most active compound known to release histamine is compound 48/80 **(Table 11.1-2).** A feature of drug/chemical-induced histamine release is the development of *tachyphylaxis.*

Table 11.1-2. *Chemical and physical agents releasing endogenous histamine*

Chemical agents	*Physical agents*
Chymotrypsin	Mechanical trauma
Compound 48/80	Radiant energy
Atropine	Thermal energy
Dextran	
Codeine	
Polymyxin B	
Polyvinylpyrrolidone	
Resepine	
Tubocurarine	
Toxins and Venoms	

Clinical Uses

1. Gastric Analysis

Histamine is useful for the **differential diagnosis of pernicious anaemia** from other stomach diseases on the basis of achlorhydria. This test measures the total number of functioning parietal cells (parietal cell mass) present and identifies patients with **true achlorhydria,** defined as the failure to lower the gastric pH below 6 to maximal histamine stimulation. **True achlorhydria (histamine-fast achlorhydria) is pathognomic of pernicious anaemia.**

Betazole hydrochloride (Histalog), an isomer of histamine, may be used as an alternative to histamine for gastric analysis, in a dose of 0.5 mg/kg SC. Betazole is being replaced by **gastrin** for this test. A **"tubeless" method** of gastric analysis by using the dye **azuresin** (Diagnex blue) orally has also been developed.

2. Diagnosis of Pheochromocytoma

Histamine (3 mcg/kg, IV) **tyramine** (1.0 mg IV), **glucagon** (0.5-1.0 mg IV) or **phentolamine** (5 mg, IV) may be employed for the diagnosis of pheochromocytoma. These tests have to be carried out cautiously **(Chap. 3.5)**

Preparation. Histamine phosphate is available as a solution for injection containing 100 mcg, 200 mcg or 1 mg/ml. Doses of histamine are expressed conventionally in terms of base and 2.75 mg of the phosphate salt are equivalent to 1 mg of histamine base.

Antihistamines

The actions of histamine can be antagonized in three ways: (*i*) **by preventing or reducing histamine release,** e.g., **glucocorticoids** can suppress the tissue effects of antigen/antibody reactions **(Chap. 7.5)** and **cromolyn sodium** (see later) stabilizes the mast cell membranes; (*ii*) by **receptor antagonism,** e.g., by antihistamines; and (*iii*) by using *physiological antagonists* which oppose the actions of histamine, e.g., **adrenaline (Chap 3.4).**

All the antihistamines are *competitive antagonists* at the histamine receptors, and can be divided into two groups: *H_1-receptor antagonists,* which comprise the large group of older classic agents; and the *H_2-receptor antagonists* namely cimetidine and ranitidine, which are newer agents.

Allergic Disorders

The term "allergy" refers to an exaggerated susceptibility to a substance which may be attributable to some underlying **antigen/antibody reaction.** The provoking substance or **allergen** may come from diverse sources including inhalants, foods, and drugs. An antigen is a large molecule, usually a protein capable of stimulating the formation of specific antibodies. Most drug molecules **(hapten)** are too small to be antigenic, but they may combine with a body protein (carrier) to form a **drug-protein complex** which is antigenic. When the antigen is introduced into the body for the first time, antibodies are formed and the body becomes **sensitized** to the antigen. This protein antibody may circulate in the plasma or be fixed in tissues. On *re-exposure* to the specific antigen, an antigen/antibody reaction occurs, resulting in the release of many **mediator substances** which are responsible for the allergic symptoms and resultant cellular damage **(Fig. 11.1.2).**

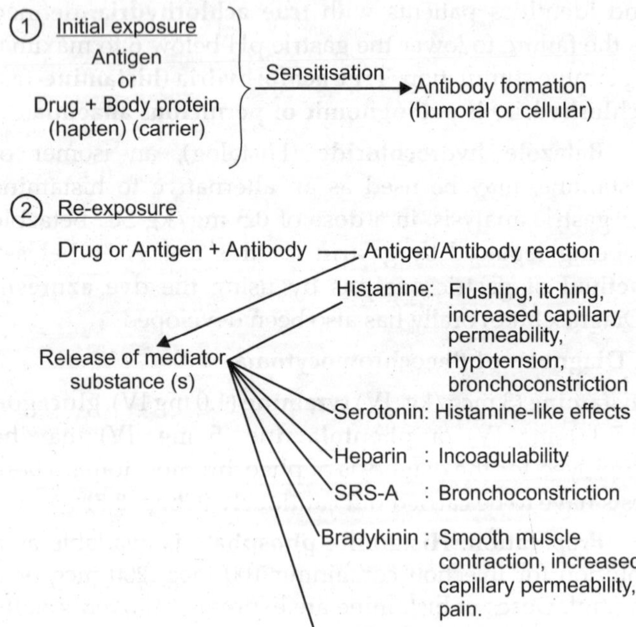

Fig. 11.1.2: Mechanism of allergic reactions.

In humans, SRS-A is generally considered to be an important mediator. Allergic reactions are often categorized as being either **immediate** or **delayed.** Immediate reactions such as anaphylactic shock, occur within minutes. In delayed hypersensitivity reactions, there is a slowly developing cellular response independent of formation of antibody. The sensitized mononuclear cells infiltrate the target area causing chronic inflammation and tissue damage. Histamine is not involved in the delayed reactions.

Mode of Action

Both H_1- and H_2-receptor antagonists do not influence the formation or release of histamine, but **selectively and competitively antagonize its actions presumably at specific receptor sites.** The effectiveness of antihistamines in blocking the actions of injected histamine is greater than in combating the various manifestations of anaphylaxis and allergy.

The antihistamines effectively block the actions of **exogenously** administered histamine in animals and man. The effects mediated through H_2-receptors are only antagonized by cimetidine and related drugs. However, the H_1-receptor antagonists are minimally effective against the symptoms of anaphylaxis or histamine release by histamine releasing chemicals, or drugs, or other conditions which release **endogenous** histamine. The gastric acid hypersecretion induced by endogenous histamine is unaffected by H_1-receptor antagonists.

H_1-Receptor Antagonists (Antihistamines)

Bovet and Staub in 1937 introduced the compound 929F, which protected guinea pigs against five lethal doses of histamine. Antergan, introduced in France in 1942, was the first compound successfully used clinically as an antihistamine. Later, dozens of histamine antagonists have been made available.

Classification

1. **Alkylamines.** Chlorpheniramine, triprolidine, pheniramine, dimethindine, dexchlorpheniramine, brompheniramine.
2. **Phenothiazines.** Promethazine, mequitazine, dimethothiazine, trimeprazine.
3. **Piperazines.** Cyclizine, chlorcyclizine, meclozine, buclizine, cinnarizine.
4. **Ethylenediamines.** Tripelennamine, mepyramine, pyrilamine, methapyrilene, antazoline.
5. **Ethanolamines.** Diphenhydramine, dimenhydrinate, carbinoxamine.
6. **Miscellaneous.** Cyproheptadine, cetirizine, levocetirizine, Fexofenadine.

Pharmacological Actions

Antihistamines prevent the effects of histamine by competing with if for the receptor sites. They give palliative relief from allergic symptoms, but are not as potent and prompt in their action as adrenaline, which is a **physiological antagonist** of histamine.

Central Nervous System

In usual therapeutic doses the antihistamines produce **depression** and **sedation** of the central nervous system like the antipsychotic tranquillizers. Some antihistamines (see later) suppress nausea and vomiting resulting from labyrinthine disturbances, without producing sedation. Motion sickness is also suppressed. The agents **diphenhydramine phenindamine** and **orphenadrine** improve spontaneous movement and speech in patients of **Parkinson's disease,** and related drug-induced extrapyramidal disorders. Their atropine-like activity may be playing an additional role.

Peripheral Nervous System

The antihistamines have **anticholinergic, local anaesthetic** and **antiserotonin** actions in different measures. The anticholinergic activity may be related to their usefulness in motion sickness. The local anaesthetic action may contribute to the relief of pruritus on topical application. The compound cyproheptadine has significant antiserotonin activity in addition to its antihistamine action.

Absorption, Metabolism and Excretion

The antihistamines are readily absorbed on oral or parenteral administration. The actions are manifested within 30 minutes, but their potency, duration of action and sedative effect varies with different agents **(Table 11.1-3).** They are metabolized in the liver by *hydroxylation*, and may stimulate the hepatic microsomal enzymes.

Therapeutic Uses

The antihistamines have a widespread popularity in the symptomatic treatment of many **hypersensitivity states, parkinsonism, insomnia,** and **motion sickness.**

Hypersensitivity states. Antihistamines are used to treat allergic symptoms produced by the release of histamine, e.g., increased capillary permeability, oedema, pruritus, smooth muscle contraction and urticaria.

Antihistamines are effective in the management of **hay fever, vasomotor rhinitis, acute and chronic urticaria, atopic and contact dermatitis, and for treating the pruritus, erythema and oedema of insect bites,** but

Table 11.1-3. *Pharmacologial pofile and dosage of some commonly used antihistamines*

Group and generic name	*Patency*	*Sedative effect*	*Anticholinergic effects*	*Single adult dose (mg)*	*Duration of action (hours)*
Alkylamines					
Chlorpheniramine	++	++	++	4	4-6
Triprolidine	++	+++	++	2-5	8-12
Pheniramine	++	++	+	40	3-4
Phenothiazines					
Promethazine*	+++	+++	+++	25-50	4-6
Mepyramine	++	++	+	50-100	3-4
Piperazines					
Cyclizine*	++	+	+	50-100	6-8
Meclozine*	++	+	+	25-50	8-16
Chlorcyclizine*	++	+	+	50	8-12
Ethylenediamines					
Tripelennamine	++	++	+	50	4-6
Pyrilamine	+	++	+	25-50	4-6
Methapyrilene	+	+	+	25-50	4-5
Ethanolamines					
Diphenhydramine*	+++	+++	+++	50	4-6
Dimenhydrinate	++	++	++	50	4-6
Miscellaneous					
Cyproheptadine	++	++	++	4	2-4
SECOND-GENERATION ANTIHISTAMINES					
Astemizole	++ to +++	±	±	10	24
Terfenadine	++ to +++	±	±	60	12
Loratadine	++ to +++	±	±	10	24
Cetirizine	++ to +++	±	±	10	12-24

+++ = marked; ++ = moderate; + = mild; *= agents with antiemetic effects.

are of little value in erythema multiforme and exfolitive dermatitis.

The antihistamines play only a secondary role in the therapy of **anaphylactic shock, angioneurotic oedema, serum sickness and bronchial asthma.**

Antihistamines like diphenhydramine have been used in the treatment of **parkinsonism** and drug-induced extrapyramidal reactions. The piperazines (cyclizine and others), **promethazine and diphenhydramine** are useful in the prevention of motion sickness, and nausea and vomiting following radiation exposure. *They may be used to manage mild blood transfusion reactions.* Antihistamines are ineffective in the treatment of migraine, but may be of some use in **Meniere's disease** and other types of vertigo. There is little evidence that the antihistamines influence the course of common cold, although some symptomatic benefit may be obtained. **Cyproheptadine accelerates weight gain and stimulates linear growth in children.** However, most patients lose weight when the drug is discontinued.

Adverse Reactions

The incidence and severity of untoward effects varies with the preparation and the individual. Thus it is advisable to determine by trial and error, the preparation tolerated best by the patient. Usually, depression of the CNS, **dizziness, tinnitus, incoordination, diplopia** and **fatigue** develop. Very rarely central excitement, **euphoria, insomnia** and **tremors** may occur. Sedation is by far the most common adverse effect. Hence the patient using antihistamines should be **warned not to drive a vehicle or operate machinery,** as accidents may occur.

Some antihistamines (diphenhydramine, promethazine) possess appreciable anticholinergic activity and produce **xerostomia, dysuria, blurring of vision, impotence** and **constipation. Depression of bone marrow, leucopenia and agranulocytosis occur rarely.** Since some antihistamines have been found to be teratogenic in animals, the use of these agents is contraindicated during pregnancy. Topical use leads to hypersensitivity.

Drug Interactions

Alcohol and certain CNS depressants can potentiate the sedative effect of antihistamines, and the patients should be warned about concomitant use of **alcoholic beverages.**

H_2-Receptor Antagonists

The H_1-receptor antagonists (classical antihistamines) do not block the gastric secretory effect of histamine. To explain this it was proposed that histamine acts on two types of receptors **(Table 11.1-4).** Later, Black and his co-workers in 1972 introduced the first antagonist, **burimamide,** which competitively antagonized the effects of histamine on parietal cells of the stomach and guinea pig atria. These histamine receptors were called H_2-receptors. In 1975 *cimetidine*, a non-thiourea H_2-receptor antagonist was introduced. In contrast to the H_1-antagonists, the H_2-receptors antagonists are less lipid-soluble compounds, and do not cross the blood-brain barrier, and as such do not cause sedation.

Cimetidine

Cimetidine is the first safe H_2-receptor antagonist available for clinical use. It is chemically related to histamine and is a **potent inhibitor of gastric acid secretion.** It counters the action of histamine on H_2-receptors by **selective competitive antagonism.** Cimetidine is employed in the treatment of **gastric** and **duodenal ulcers (Chap. 12).** It also promotes healing of the ulcer. In higher doses cimetidine is also used to treat **oesophagitis** (400 mg orally four times daily). Intravenous administration of cimetidine 200 mg every 4 to 6 hours) is helpful in the treatment of *severe* **haemorrhagic gastritis** or **stress ulceration.** Cimetidine was also found to be effective in **Zollinger-Ellison syndrome. Ranitidine, nizatidine and famotidine** are newer H_2-receptor antagonists, with activity similar to that of cimetidine.

Adverse effects of cimetidine include **drowsiness, itchy skin rashes, gynaecomastia** and impotence. In renal failure caution has to be observed, as it has a renal pathway for elimination. In severe renal impairment cimetidine may be readily removed by haemodialysis.

CROMOLYN SODIUM

Cromolyn sodium (disodium cromoglycate, Ifiral, Intal) was introduced in 1968 as an adjunct for the management of **severe perennial bronchial asthma.** It is administered in the form of a dry powder by means of an oral inhaler. Chemically it is a water soluble synthetic analogue of khellin (the spasmolytic agent extracted from seeds of *Ammi visnaga*).

Table 11.1-4 *Actions of histamine mediated by H_1-and H_2-receptors**

H_1 actions	H_2 actions
1. Contraction of smooth muscle of gut	1. Stimulation of gastric acid secretion
2. Contraction of smooth muscle of bronchi	2. Stimulation of cardiac atrial rate
3. Relaxation of smooth muscle of vascular resistance vessels	3. Relaxation of smooth muscle of vascular resistance vessels
4. Increase in permeability of postcapillary venules	4. Inhibition of contraction of uterus

* The fall in blood pressure produced by histamine involves both H_1- and H_2-receptors, thus both H_1- and H_2-blockers have to be used to abolish this response.

Cromolyn sodium appears to "stabilize" the membrane of the sensitized mast cells, **preventing the release of histamine, serotonin, bradykinin, SRS-A, acetylcholine and other mediators of hypersensitivity reactions.** It is ineffective once these agents have been released from cells.

Cromolyn sodium is **poorly absorbed on oral administration,** and has to be **inhaled** by means of a device known as "spinhaler". Only about 10 percent of the total dose inhaled is absorbed, and is rapidly excreted. It has a half-life of about 80 minutes.

Cromolyn sodium is most useful in the control or prevention of **exercise-induced asthma** and "extrinsic" asthma. It is almost ineffective in "intrinsic" asthma **(Chap. 13).** It is used in a dose of 20 mg (micronized form) every 4 to 6 hours by inhalation. In the management of asthma, as a **prophylactic,** cromolyn sodium is worth a trial, as it reduces the need for bronchodilators and glucocorticosteroids.

Adverse effects are not common. Inhalations may occasionally cause **transient bronchoconstriction** and irritation in the throat. **Urticarial rashes** and **eosinopenic pneumonia** have been reported. The safety of cromolyn sodium in pregnancy is yet to be determined.

11.2 SEROTONIN AND SEROTONIN ANTAGONISTS

Serotonin (5-hydroxytryptamine, 5-HT, enteramine) is not a therapeutic agent itself, but it is important with respect to the action of certain other drugs and diseases.

Occurrence, Biosynthesis and Metabolism

Serotonin, an indoleethylamine, is widely distributed throughout the body, being concentrated in the **enterochromaffin cells** of the gut (90%), and the rest mainly in the **brain** and **platelets.** Some fruits like **bananas** contain high concentration of 5-HT, but there is no threat of poisoning as it is not well absorbed from the gut and is rapidly metabolized. However, ingestion of such fruits may increase the urinary excretion of 5-HT metabolites, giving a false positive test in the diagnosis of carcinoid tumours.

The amino acid **tryptophan** is hydroxylated to 5-hydroxytryptophan by tryptophan hydroxylase, which is then decarboxylated to 5-HT by aromatic L-amino acid decarboxylase **(Fig. 11.2.1).** 5-HT is stored in association with ATP in intracellular storage particles within the **intestinal chromaffin cells, platelets** and the **specific 5-HT containing (serotonergic) neurones** of the brain. The amount of 5-HT in the CNS runs parallel to that of noradrenaline, i.e., it is highest in the **hypothalamus** and **mesencephalon.**

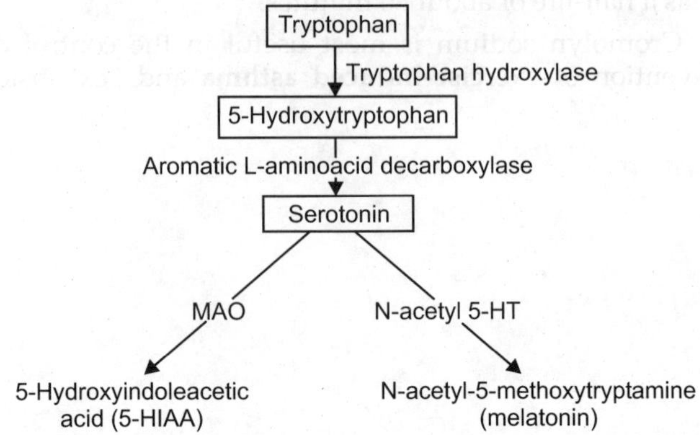

Fig. 11.2.1: The biosynthesis and metabolism of serotonin.

Serotonin is oxidatively deaminated to 5-HIAA. No alternative methylation pathway comparable to catecholamines is available. However, in the pineal gland N-acetylation and 5-methylation produce **melatonin.** The daily excretion of 5-HIAA in the urine is 3 to 10 mg in a normal adult.

Table 11.2-1. *Subtypes of 5-HT receptors*

Receptor subtype	*Distribution*	*Partial agonists*	*Partial antagonists*
5-HT_{1a}	Raphe muclei, hippocampus	Ipsapirone	—
5-HT^*_{1b}	Substantia nigra, globus pallidus, basal ganglia	Sumatriptan	—
5-HT_{1c}	Choroid plexus	Alpha-Methyl-5-HT	Ritanserin, mesulergine
5-HT_{1d}	Substantia nigra, globus pallidus, basal ganglia	Sumatriptan	—
Receptor subtype	*Distribution*	*Partial agonists*	*Partial antagonists*
5-HT_2	Platelets, smooth muscle, cerebral cortex	Alpha-Methyl-5-HT	Ketanserin, spiperone, mesulergine
5-HT_3	Area postrema, sensory and enteric nerves	2-Methyl-5-HT	Ondansetron
5-HT_4	HIppocampus, enteric nerves	—	—

* 5-HT_{1b} receptors occur in rodents only.

The biosynthesis of 5-HT can be blocked by **p-chlorophenylalanine** (PCPA) which inhibits the enzyme tryptophan hydroxylase, the **rate limiting enzyme.** Degradation of 5-HT is also blocked by MAO inhibitors (MAOIs). The turnover of serotonin in the CNS and the intestines is quite rapid. The MAOIs can double the brain content of 5-HT in less than one hour, and the excretion of 5-HIAA is simultaneously decreased. Tumours of the enterochromaffin cells, known as **carcinoid tumours,** produce excess of 5-HT which is responsible in part for the clinical picture of the disease.

Mode of Action

Serotonin has multiple actions, and like histamine, species differences are marked. Based on studies with **selective antagonists,** it is evident that these actions are mediated through a variety of receptors located **intracellularly,** or on the surface of target cells **(Table 11.2-1).**

Pharmacological Actions

The actions of 5-HT are exerted on the **cardiovascular system,** the **gut,** and on the **nervous system.**

Cardiovascular system. 5-HT has complex cardiovascular actions. It acts directly to constrict the arteries and increases the peripheral vascular resistance. An IV injection of a few micrograms of serotonin in animals produces a **triphasic** response: (*i*) a **transient fall** of blood pressure; (*ii*) a **brief rise** of blood pressure; and (*iii*) a more **prolonged** blood pressure fall. The early depressor phase is due to stimulation of chemoreceptors (Bezold-Jarisch effect). The middle pressor phase is due to vasoconstriction. The late and final depressor phase is due to vasodilator action on the skeletal muscle.

Gastrointestinal tract and nervous system. 5-HT stimulates *intestinal, bronchial* and *uterine* muscles, the *adrenal medulla* and *ganglia* of the *ANS*. It is a potent stimulant of the sensory nerve endings and induces *pain* when applied to an exposed blister base. On the gut 5-HT exerts both direct effects and also through ganglion cells. The direct effects are blocked by the serotonin antagonist **lysergic acid diethylamide** (LSD), and the ganglionic action is blocked by morphine. The bronchial stimulant action is marked in asthmatics. 5-HT does not cross the blood-brain barrier, but if injected into the lateral ventricles in cats, it induces **sleep, catatonia** and **fever.**

Role in Physiology and Pathophysiology

The localization of 5-HT in platelets and its vasoconstrictor action are suggestive of its role in blood clotting. The role of 5-HT in mood and behaviour disorders is supported by various evidences. The strongest evidence being that LSD exerts a powerful psychotomimetic effect, i.e., it produces hallucinations. 5-HT also possibly plays a role in intestinal motility. **Carcinoid tumours** may develop in the gastrointestinal or respiratory tracts, and secrete excessive amounts of 5-HT, and possibly also prostaglandins. 5-HT also appears to be involved in the causation of **migraine** and **vascular headaches.** It is involved in inflammatory reactions, allergic and anaphylactic reactions. Serotonin has no clinical application as a drug.

Serotonin Agonists

Serotonin has no clinical uses itself, but several selective subtype-receptor agonists have found clinical application: **Buspirone** is a 5-HT_{1a} agonist, and is an effective *anxiolytic;* **Sumatriptan** is a 5-HT_{1d} agonist, effective in the treatment of *acute migraine* and *cluster headaches.* It is given in a dose of 25 mg orally, or 6mg (sumatriptan succinate) subcutaneouly. Its efficacy is equal to or greatr than other conventional antimigraine drugs. *Adverse effects* are mild and include dizziness, muscle weakness, tingling sensations, neck pain, and chest discomfort. It is *contraindicated* in patients of coronary artery disease and Prinzmetal's angina; and **Cisapride,** a $5HT_4$ agonist is used in the treatment of *gastroesophageal reflux.* In addition selective serotonin reuptake inhibitions (SSRIs) like **fluoxetine** and **paroxetine** are used as *antidepressants.* They modulate serotonergic transmission in the brain.

Serotonin Antagonists (Antiserotonins)

1. **Methysergide.** This compound is a congenor of LSD and is a potent 5-HT receptor blocking agent (it also has moderate agonistic action on serotonin receptors). It is used in the symptomatic treatment of the **carcinoid syndrome,** and in the **prophylaxis of migraine (Chap. 3.5).** Methysergide is active orally, and the side effects include vomiting, abdominal cramps and peripheral vasoconstriction. Serious side effects like retroperitoneal fibrosis may occur on prolonged therapy.
2. **Cyproheptadine.** Cyproheptadine has equal potency at both H_1-histamine receptors and 5-HT receptors as an **antagonist.** Probably this is an added advantage in the treatment of various **allergies** where both histamine and 5-HT are involved. It **increases the appetite** and promotes weight gain and linear growth in children **(Chap. 11.1).** In addition, it may be used for the symptomatic treatment of **carcinoid syndrome,** and for **prophylaxis of migraine** (less effective than methysergide). Drowsiness commonly occurs and it may precipitate glaucoma or urinary retention in predisposed patients due to its anticholinergic activity.
3. **Lysergic acid diethylamide (LSD).** LSD has potent antiserotonin activity and this action was thought to be related to its hallucinogenic effect, by which it caused a toxic phychosis (model psychosis). However the antiserotonin action is not responsible for its hallucinogenic activity,

as 2-bromo-LSD is a more potent serotonin antagonist but lacks the behavioural effects in man. LSD because of its high dependence liability is not a useful therapeutic agent.

4. **Phenothiazines** (chlorpromazine) and the *sympatholytics* (phenoxybenzamine and phentolamine) in addition to their alpha-adrenoceptor blocking activity also block responses to 5-HT.

5. **Ondansetron.** It is a 5-HT_3 antagonist, and approved for use in the prevention of nausea and vomiting associated with cancer chemotherapy. It is also being evaluated for its **anxiolytic** and **antipsychotic** activity.

6. **Ketanserin and Ritanserin.** These two agents are experimental drugs, and possess 5-HT receptor blocking activity. Ketanserin is under trial for the treatment of hypertension.

11.3 PROSTAGLANDINS AND OTHER EICOSANOIDS (THROMBOXANES, LEUKOTRIENES, & RELATED COMPOUNDS)

Prostaglandins	**Pharmacological Actions**
Occurrence, Biosynthesis and Metabolism	**Mode of Action**
Role in Physiology and Pathophysiology	**Therapeutic Uses and Their Basis**

The *prostaglandins* are a group of 20-carbon essential fatty acids. In addition, the other structurally related lipids include the **thromboxanes (TXs),** the **hydroperoxyeicosatetraenoic acids (HPETTEs), the hydroxyeicosatetraenoic acids (HETEs), the leukotrienes (LTs), the lipoxins (LXs), and epoxyeicosatetraenoic acids (EETEs).** These agents are potent naturally occurring autacoids. The term "eicosanoids" (Greek = twenty) is used to indicate that they can all be derived from polyunsaturated fatty acids with 18-, 20-, and 22-carbon skeletons.

The **prostaglandins** were so named by von Euler in 1935, because they were first isolated from the seminal fluid. They are present in greatest amounts in human and sheep seminal plasma. Their widespread occurrence in tissues, including the nervous system, is suggestive of their regulatory function, which may be exerted *via* the basic control system related to **adenylcyclase.**

Occurrence, Biosynthesis and Metabolism

The term prostaglandin (PG) is a generic name for a family of closely related cyclic, oxygenated, 20-carbon unsaturated fatty acids. The basic 20-carbon skeleton of prostaglandins is named as **prostanoic acid.**

Prostaglandins are widely distributed throughout the body, and exert effects on most organs and tissues. They are synthesized from **arachidonic acid** by the action of prostaglandin synthetase (cyclooxygenase), an enzyme which is almost universally distributed in the body (prostate, seminal vesicle, lung, intestine, uterus, heart, thymus, liver, kidney, pancreas, brain, stomach and iris). This step forms the cyclic endoperoxides (PGG_2 PGH_2) and can be blocked by non-steroidal anti-inflammatory agents like **aspirin, indomethacin** and **phenylbutazone** by inhibiting the enzyme prostaglandin synthetase **(Fig. 11.3.1).** The endoperoxides have a short half-life and further synthesis may follow three different paths forming several **prostaglandins, thromboxanes** and **prostacyclin.**

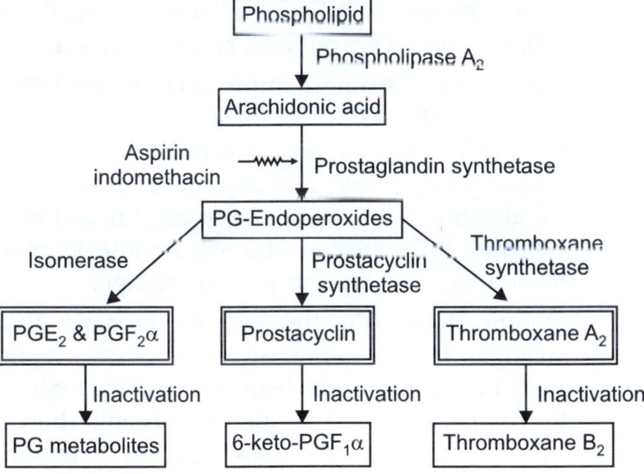

Fig. 11.3.1: The biosynthesis and metabolism of prostaglandins.

On the basis of their chemical structure the prostaglandins have been divided into six groups: A, B, C, D, E and F. The prostaglandins are virtually synthesized by every tissue, and since there is no evidence for their storage (except in the seminal fluid), the rate of release equals the rate of biosynthesis. A wide variety of stimuli can release prostaglandins. They are destroyed by metabolic degradation in many tissues.

Leukotriene biosynthesis. Leukotrienes (LTs) are potent biologically active compounds synthesized by the 5-lipooxygenase in neutrophils, monocytes, mast cells, macrophages, and keratinocytes, and also in the lung, spleen, brain, and heart. Before their structure was known, they were called **slow-reacting substances of anaphylaxis** (*SRS-A*), which are released after immunologic reactions.

Role in Physiology and Pathophysiology

The PGs are involved in many physiological processes, the most interesting being their possible role in **reproductive physiology.** In the **male** they have been implicated in erection, ejaculation, sperm motility and steroidogenesis; and in the **female** in uterine and fallopian tube contractility, luteolysis (except in humans), ovulation, menstruation and labour. There is evidence that PGs play a role in **gastric secretion** and maintenance of **spontaneous smooth muscle tone.**

The PGs are involved in many pathological processes, like **acute inflammation, fever** and various female reproductive disorders including **dysmenorrhoea, anovulation, habitual abortion, toxaemia of pregnancy** and **premature labour.** Their role in male infertility is yet unknown.

Pharmacological Actions

PGs have effects on a variety of tissues, and possibly they modulate hormonal, neurohormonal and other stimuli. Their actions may be considered under four heads: (*i*) smooth muscle; (*ii*) platelets; (*iii*) reproductive organs; and (*iv*) nervous system.

Smooth muscle. The human *arteriolar smooth muscle* is relaxed by PGE_2 and PGI_2. PGs promote vasodilation by activating adenylcyclase. In contrast, TXA_2 and PGF_2 alpha act as vasoconstrictors, specially on veins. The effect on the **gastrointestinal smooth muscle** is complex.

The longitudinal muscle is contracted by PGE_2 and PGF_2 alpha, while the circular muscle is contracted by PGI_2 and PGF_2 alpha, and relaxed by PGE_2. The **respiratory smooth muscle** is relaxed by PGE_1, PGE_2 and PGI_2, while it is contracted by TXA_2 and PGF_2 alpha. The **genitourinary smooth muscle** (specially the gravid uterus at term) is contracted by PGE_2 and PGF_2 alpha. **(Table 11.3-1)**

Platelets. PGE_1 and PGI_2 effectively inhibit platelet aggregation, while TXA_2 markedly facilitates aggregation.

Reproductive organs. PGE_2 and PGF_2 alpha have marked **oxytoxic action;** and when administered intravenously, they produce abortion in about 80 percent of cases. The role of PGs in semen is conjectural. The major source of these PGs is the seminal vesicle. Semen of fertile men contains about 400 mcg/ml of PGE and PGF, and their 19-hydroxy metabolites. There is about 20 times more PGE than PGF in fertile semen, though the ratio varies among individuals. Men with low seminal concentration of PGs are relatively infertile. Aspirin in large doses reduces the PG content of semen.

Table 11.3-1: *Comparison of the actions of PGE_2 and PGF_2 alpha*

Tissue/Parameter	*PGE_2 activity*	*PGF_2 alpha activity*
Blood pressure	Decreased	Increased
Blood vessels	Dilated	Constricted
Capillary permeability	Increased	Little effect
Gastric secretion	Decreated	Little effect
Intestinal muscle	Contracted*	Contracted
Bronchiolar muscle	Relaxed	Contracted
Uterine muscle	Contracted*	Contracted
Sensory fibres	Sensitized*	?

* The responses produced are complex.

Nervous system. PGE_1 and PGE_2 increase body **temperature,** more so when administered intracerebroventricularly. Pyrogens release interleukin-1, which promotes the synthesis and release of PGE_2. This synthesis is blocked by aspirin, and aspirin-like antipyretics. PGD_2 administered intracerbroventicularly **induces natural sleep.** The PGE compounds *inhibit the release of noradrenaline* (NA) from adrenergic presynatic nerve endings. The NSAIDs (aspirin) promote NA release. The PGE compounds **promote release of growth hormone, prolactin, TSH, ACTH, FSH and LH.** However, these effects are not marked in patients receiving PGE compounds.

Mode of Action

PGs have marked effects on the function of cyclic mononucleotides (c-AMP, c-GMP) in cells, and these may function as mediators of PG action. The PGs lead to stimulation of c-AMP production and calcium utilization by various cells. It has been suggested that c-AMP and c-GMP are opposing limbs of a bidirectional intracellular control mechanism. Thus the PGs act directly on smooth muscle and not through neural mechanisms. Specially PGE_2 causes bronchodilation by stimulation of adenylcyclase, causing an increase in c-AMP within the cell **(Fig. 11.3.2).** This increase in c-AMP is not affected by beta-blockers in asthmatics. The effect of PGF is not well understood. If is suggested that the PGF effect is mediated *via* c-GMP system, since c-GMP is thought to produce effects opposing c-AMP. Both **aspirin** and **indomethacin** inhibit the synthesis and release of PGs. Inhibition of PGE_2 in the lung may lead to bronchoconstriction, thus implicating PGs in the mechanisms of aspirin-sensitive asthma.

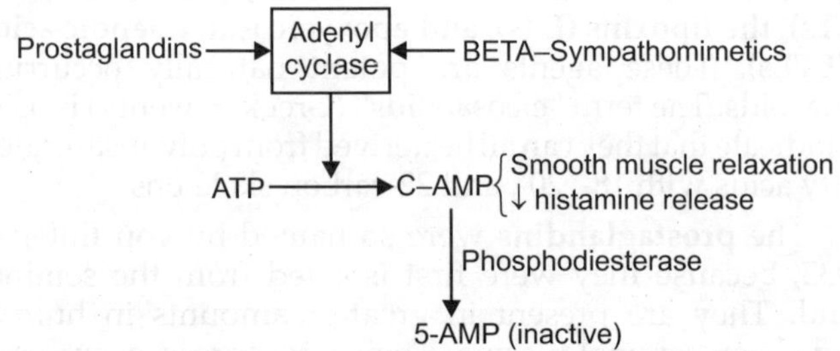

Fig. 11.3.2: Pathway by which prostaglandins increase intracellular c-AMP levels. Beta-blockade does not inhibit PGE_2 induced rise in c-AMP

Therapeutic Uses and Their Basis

The clinical uses of PGs are based on either their physiological action on exogenous application, or in pathological states by preventing their synthesis.

1. **Therapeutic abortion.** PGE_1 and PGF_2 alpha have strong oxytocic action, and can terminate pregnancy at any stage. They are usually employed for *first* and *second* trimester abortion and for ripening the cervix before abortion. Currently intra-amniotic, IM, or intravaginal administration is common.

   Intra-amniotic administration of PGF_2 alpha has about 100 percent success rate with fewer adverse effects than IV usage. **Dinoprost tromethamine (Prostin F_2 alpha)** is given as a single 40 mg intra-amniotic injection. The abortion is usually completed within 20 hours. **Adverse effects** are circulatory collapse and severe pulmonary hypertension.

   Carboprost tromethamine (15-methyl-PGF_2 alpha, Prostin/15 M) 250 mcg IM initially, repeat at 1½ to 3½ hour interval; may increase to 500 mcg IM per dose, if necessary (maximum dose 12 mg) for abortion. This agent is also used in a dose of 250 mcg IM, repeated at 15-90 minute intervals for refractory postpartum haemorrhage.

   Dinoprostone (Prostin E_2), a synthetic PGE_2 analogue may be administered as 20 mg vaginal suppositories. One suppository is inserted high into the vagina; repeat at 3-5 hour intervals until abortion occurs. Adverse reactions include vomiting, diarrhoea, headache, chills and hypotension.

Abortion pill. Recently the antioestrogen, **mifepristone** *(RU-486)* in combination with PGE_2 has been found to produce effective early abortion.

2. **Induction of labour.** The two drugs, PGE_2 and PGF_2 alpha, effectively initiate and stimulate labour. On IV use PGF_2 alpha is one-tenth as potent as PGE_2. Oral PGE_2 (0.5-1.5 mg/hour) has been found to be superior to IV oxytocin for induction of labour.
3. **Dysmenorrhoea.** This disorder is attributed to increased endometrial synthesis of PGE_2 and PGF_2 alpha during menstruation, with uterine contractions leading to ischaemic pain. NSAIDS (aspirin, indomethacin) effectively inhibit the formation of these PGs, and offer relief in 75-85 percent of cases.
4. **Hypertension and vasospastic disease.** PGE and PGA compounds have been used in **hypertensive patients**. These compounds also promote sodium diuresis. Prostacyclin lowers peripheral and coronary resistance. It has been used to treat pulmonary hypertension. PGE and PGI_2 compounds have been tried for treating **Raynaud's disease** and **peripheral atherosclerosis**.
5. **Thrombosis.** TXA_2 promotes platelet aggregation, and PGI_2 inhibits it. Aspirin inhibits TXA_2 by irreversible acetylation of cyclooxygenase. Decrease in platelet TXA_2 production was achieved by a single 200 mg dose of aspirin, followed by daily doses of 20-25 mg. Prostacyclin (PGI_2) inhibits platelet aggregation, and high doses of aspirin may nullify the beneficial effect by inhibiting PGI_2 production from the vascular endothelium. Thus low dose aspirin therapy is recommended. Exogenous form of prostacyclin (epoprostenol) has been used as an antithrombotic in dialysis procedures, and during extracorporeal circulation.
6. **Patent ductus arteriosus.** Patency of the fetal ductus arteriosus is dependent on PGE_2 and PGI_2 synthesis. For palliative therapy of neonates with congenital heart disease (e.g., pulmonary stenosis, tricuspid atresia, tetralogy of Fallot, aortic coarctation) the patency of the ductus arteriosus has to be maintained till surgery. This is maintained by **alprostadil** (PGE_1), which is continuously infused in an initial dose of 0.05-0.1 mcg/kg/min, which may be increased to 0.4 mcg/kg/min. Prolonged treatment is associated with ductal fragility and rupture.
7. **Respiration.** PGF_2 alpha and TXA_2 are strong bronchoconstrictors, and were thought to be primary mediators in asthma. PGE_2 is a strong bronchodilator, but promotes coughing, which is its major limitation. Other analogues are under study.
8. **Gastrointestinal system.** The term "cytoprotection" was used for the protective effect of the E prostaglandins, (specially PGE_1) against gastric ulcers in animals at doses that do not reduce acid secretion. These PGs also inhibit gastric acid secretion. **Misoprostal** (a synthetic analogue of PGE_1) is used as an antiulcer agent. It is also approved for treatment of NSAID-induced gastric ulcers. **Misoprostal** and *other PGE analogues* (e.g., Enprostil) are cytoprotective at low doses and inhibit gastric acid secretion at higher doses.
9. **Immune system.** Monocyte-macrophages are the main cells of the immune system which can synthesize all the eicosanoids. T and B lymphocytes are an exception to the general rule, that all nucleated cells produce eicosanoids. The arachidonic acid released from the lymphocyte cell membranes is used by the monocyte-macrophages for eicosanoid synthesis. The eicosanoids in turn modulate the effects of the immune system.

Acute organ transplant rejection is a cell mediated immune response. PGI_2 given to renal transplant patients reverses the rejection reaction in some cases.

Till date, PGs have limited clinical applications, although their potential in the treatment of variety of pathologic states is enormous. The main limiting factors are their **short duration of action**, and their wide range of side effects. Their approved therapeutic applications are for the induction of **therapeutic abortion,** and for therapy of neonates with **congenital heart detects.** In addition PGE analogues are being investigated for their **antiulcer action, bronchodilator action,** and **vasodilating action** for the treatment of peripheral vascular disease. PGE_2 and PGF_2 alpha may be useful for **inducing labour** at term. PGI_2 has been reported to **limit ischaemic myocardial damage** following coronary artery ligation in animal studies.

11.4 THE KININS

Kinins (Bradykinin and Kallidin)
Occurrence, Biosynthesis and Metabolism
Role in Physiology and Pathophysiology
Pharmacological Actions
Aprotinin

The *kinins* are **vasodilator polypeptides.** Among them the plasmakinins, bradykinin and kallidin, are of greatest importance.

Occurrence, Biosynthesis and Metabolism

The kinins have effects somewhat similar to those of histamine on **vascular smooth muscle, capillary permeability, bronchial** and **intestinal smooth muscle.** Numerous related kinins occur widely distributed in nature such as wasp venom and in the skin of amphibia.

The important kinins are **bradykinin** (a nonapeptide), **kallidin** (lysyl bradykinin, a decapeptide), and related vasodilator peptides. Both bradykinin and kallidin are formed from the same circulating alpha$_2$ globulins (kininogens) by the action of specific proteolytic enzymes (kallikreins). The **kallikreins** are found in many organs and in the saliva, urine, lymph, pancreatic secretion, blood, sweat and tears. The plasma kallikrein exists as an inactive precursor (prekallikrein), but when the plasma equilibrium is disturbed (like change in pH and temperature) various activators including the **Hageman factor** (Factor XII) of blood clotting, convert prekallikrein to its active form **(Fig. 11.4.1),** leading, to the formation of kinins from kininogen. Glandular tissues, such as salivary glands, and pancreas, and also urine are among the rich sources of kallikrein.

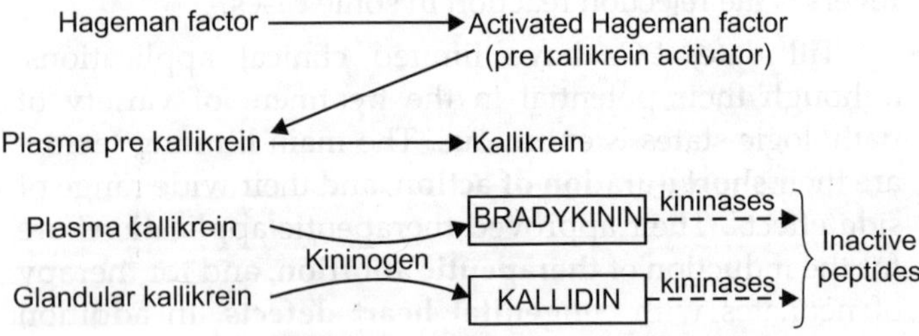

Fig. 11.4.1: The biosynthesis and metabolism of kinins in the body

The kinins are rapidly destroyed in blood t½ less than 1 minute) by kininases which remove one or two amino acids from bradykinin and kallidin, yielding **inactive peptides.**

Role in Physiology and Pathophysiology

Kinins have been implicated in many physiological functions including **reactive hyperaemia, regulation of tissue blood flow, blood pressure control** and **neonatal circulatory changes.** Kininogen has a role to play in **blood clotting,** and the liberated kallikrein activates factor XII by a positive feedback.

Kinins may be involved in many pathological states like **shock, allergy, inflammation, pancreatitis** and the **methysergide-resistant flushing** and **bronchoconstriction associated with carcinoid tumours.**

Pharmacological Actions

An interesting relationship seems to exist between **bradykinin** and **angiotensin.** Both are polypeptides split from plasma proteins. Angiotensin is a potent vasoconstrictor, while bradykinin is a vasodilator. The converting enzyme in the angiotensin system is a strong inactivator of bradykinin. Converting enzyme inhibitors are being tested for their effect on the destruction of bradykinin.

On the cardiovascular system bradykinin has a potent **relaxant effect on the vascular smooth muscles,** causing a fall in blood pressure and increase in capillary permeability. It contracts smooth muscles of the intestines, bronchioles and uterus. It stimulates the adrenal medulla, sympathetic ganglia and sensory nerve endings, causing pain. No clinically effective selective antagonist of bradykinin is available. Clinical studies are suggestive of the application of kallikrein as an adjunct in the treatment of **male infertility** and the treatment of **diabetes.**

Aprotinin, a peptide obtained from bovine lung, inhibits kallikrein, plasmin and other proteases. Aprotinin is used in patients at high risk of blood loss during and after **open heart surgery,** and life-threatening **haemorrhage due to hyperplasminaemia** (occurring during removal of malignant tumours, acute promyelocytic leukaemia, and following thrombolytic therapy).

Aprotinin (Trasylol) is administered by slow IV injection, with a loading dose of 2000,000 units, and maintenance dose of 500,000 units until the end of the operation.

12

DRUGS ACTING ON THE GASTROINTESTINAL SYSTEM

The drugs acting on the gastrointestinal tract exert their effect on its muscular and glandular tissues, either *directly* or *indirectly* through the autonomic nervous system.

Appetite Stimulants (Appetizers, Bitters)

Bitters (stomachics) are substances which stimulate the taste buds of the tongue, and reflexly through the vagus cause secretion of gastric juice. They are used to stimulate or restore the appetite when it has been impaired by illness. Bitters are divided into **simple** and **aromatic** bitters. The former are simple solutions, containing bitter alkaloids, e.g., **strychnine** mixture, **quinine, gentian** and **tincture nux vomica.** Aromatic bitters are preparations containing volatile oils like **tinctures of orange** and **lemon.** Alcoholic drinks and **spices** also function as appetizers. They simply act by their bitter taste or a mild irritant property. **Cyproheptadine,** an antihistamine antiserotonin compound, also has been employed to stimulate appetite and promote growth **(Chap. 11.1).** It has been used to increase the **appetite** of underweight patients with tuberculosis and in some cases of anorexia nervosa. The usual dose is 2-4 mg 3 or 4 times a day.

Appetite Suppressants (Anorexiants)

Anorexiants or **anorectic** drugs are used as adjuncts in the management of **obesity** due to excessive food intake. These agents in general elevate the mood of the patients and make them more tolerant to dietary restrictions. The **amphetamines** and related drugs are used for this purpose. They stimulate the **"satiety centre"** in the medial hypothalamus and block the impulses reaching the **"eating centre"** in the lateral hypothalamus. In addition these agents elevate the plasma free fatty acid (FFA) levels which depress the eating centre. The commonly used anorexiants include the amphetamines and other synthetic sympathomimetics like **diethylpropion hydrochloride** (Tennate), **phenmetrazine hydrochloride** (Preludin) and **fenfluramine hydrochloride**. (Ponderax). These drugs are ineffective over long periods of time, have side effect, and are of no value without strict food restriction **(Chap. 3.4).**

CARMINATIVES

Carminatives are volatile oils which mildly irritate the gastric mucosa and relieve the feeling of discomfort and distension after meals. This they do by causing eructation or movement of gas from the stomach. Carminatives used clinically include tincture of **cardamom, compound tincture of cardamom** and **tincture of ginger.** Other agents like **camphor, peppermint, spearmint, aniseed, corriander, cloves, fennel** and **nutmeg** may also be used. The value of carminatives is doubtful, but some studies on the response of the gastroesophageal sphincter provide support.

ANTIFLATULENTS

Antiflatulents reduce the symptoms of excess gas production in the gastrointestinal tract.

Simethicone (Mylicon) is a silicone derivative possessing **defoaming action** which helps relieve flatulence by dispersing gas pockets trapped in the GI tract. It alters the surface tension of gas bubbles, facilitating their coalescence. The gas is then expelled by belching or by flatus. The pain of dyspepsia, spastic colon, diverticulitis, and postoperative atony is relieved. Usual dosage is 40-125 mg qid. It is available in combination with antacids.

Charcoal (Charcocaps) is an inert **adsorbent** and can adsorb toxins and gas onto the surface of its particles, thereby reducing the volume of intestinal gas, and provides relief from cramping and flatulence. Other uses of charcoal are as an antidote in poisoning **(Chap 1.7).** The usual dose is 520-975 mg after meals. It should not be used for more than 3 days, as it can also adsorb nutrients and digestive enzymes.

DEMULCENTS

Demulcents are compounds of high molecular weight, which form aqueous solutions with the ability of soothing the irritated mucous membranes or abraded surfaces. This they cause by coating the irritated surface, and protecting the underlying cells from irritant stimuli. The demulcents may be applied to the gastrointestinal tract in the form of **demulcent drinks** or enemas; and to the throat in the form of gargles or lozenges. They may also be used to mask the bad taste of certain drugs. Some of the better known demulcents are **acacia, tragacanth, glycyrrhiza, carboxymethylcellulose sodium, diluted glycerine** and **propylene glycol.**

PROTECTIVES AND ADSORBENTS

A number of chemically inert powders are used internally as **protectives** and **adsorbents.** Insoluble salts like **bismuth subnitrate** and **subcarbonate** and **magnesium trisilicate** are employed as protectives in the management of ulcers of the stomach and intestines. The mechanical protection which these agents are expected to offer is doubtful. **Adsorbents** are agents which adsorb noxious gases, toxins and bacteria. They may be employed in cases of diarrhoea as non-specific remedies. The main gastrointestinal adsorbents are **pectin, kaolin, aluminium hydroxide** and **magnesium trisilicate.** The last two agents also function as gastric antacids.

ASTRINGENTS

Astringents are locally acting agents that precipitate the proteins, but as they have very little penetrability, only the surface cells are affected. The precipitated protein layer offers protection to the underlying cells. Metallic ions like **zinc** and **aluminium** have an astringent quality.

DIGESTANTS

The digestants promote the process of digestion in the gastrointestinal tract. They are useful in conditions marked by a lack of one or more substances in the gut which are responsible for the digestion of food. The agents employed are **hydrochloric acid, pepsin, pancreatic enzymes** (pancreatin) and **bile salts.**

EMETICS AND ANTIEMETICS

Nausea and vomiting may be symptoms of serious organic disturbances involving any of the viscera of the chest or abdomen; or produced by **drugs, radiation, movement, infections, metabolic and emotional disturbances, neoplasms or painful stimuli.**

MECHANISMS OF VOMITING

Emesis (vomiting) is a **complex reflex** that is coordinated by the vomiting centre in the medulla. Wang and Borison over 30 years ago proposed that vomiting involves the **"vomiting centre"** located in the lateral reticular formation, ventral to the nucleus and tractus solitarius. The stimulus to vomit may be directed to this centre along a number of **excitatory** pathways. Emetic stimuli **directly** related to the vomiting centre include **tactile pharyngeal stimulation, distention of viscera, rotation or unequal stimulation of the labyrinths, increased intracranial pressure, pain and psychologic factors like sight, memory and smell.** On the contrary blood borne emetic substances first act upon the **chemoreceptor trigger zone** (CTZ) in the ventral surface of the fourth ventricle. The CTZ alone cannot induce vomiting but does so indirectly through the vomiting centre **(Fig. 12.1).** In addition the **vasomotor, cough** and **respiratory centres** also participate in this complex act. The vomiting centre coordinates information from the **labyrinths,** the **proprioceptive system,** and the **cerebellum.** Associated with the vomiting centre is the CTZ which responds to emetic drugs. There is evidence that at least in part this mechanism is dopaminergic, the main mechanism being cholinergic.

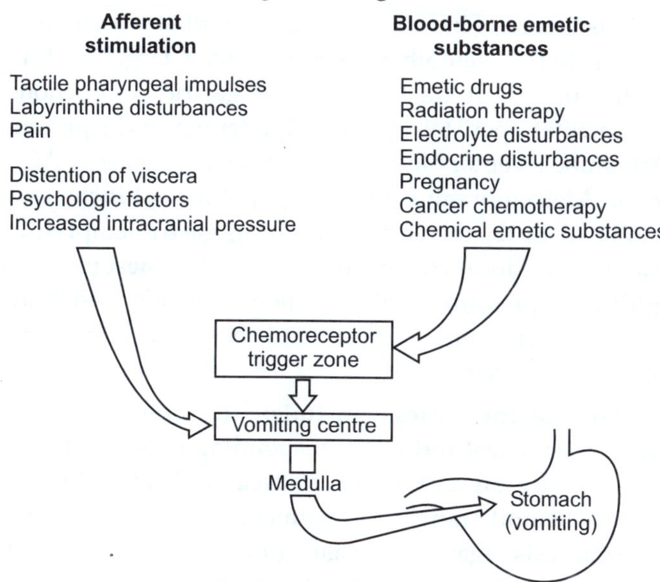

Fig. 12.1: Mechanisms of vomiting.

Emetics

The *two* drugs that are recommended for the induction of vomiting in cases of poisoning are **apomorphine** and **ipecac syrup.**

Apomorphine Hydrochloride

Apomorphine acts directly on the CTZ and induces vomiting within 10 minutes of intramuscular or subcutaneous injection. Apomorphine-induced vomiting is forceful, and the expelled contents may contain reflux from the upper intestinal tract in addition to the gastric contents. Its action is more efficient if 200 to 300 ml of water is given by mouth before the injection. Apomorphine usually produces some degree of **depression of the CNS,** and the patient becomes drowsy afterwards. Like all emetics, apomorphine is **contraindicated** in the unconscious patient, advanced age, or when caustic substances have been ingested. It is also contraindicated in patients with morphine sensitivity or poisoning by CNS depressants (opiates, alcohol or barbiturates).

Apomorphine hydrochloride is available as 6 mg soluble tablets which must be mixed with water just prior to administration. The usual dose is 6 mg in adults or 0.06 mg/kg in children IM or SC injection.

Ipecac Syrup

Ipecac is sometimes preferred in young patients because it produced less of CNS depression compared to apomorphine. Ipecac alkaloids are obtained from the dried root of *Cephaelis ipecacuanha.* Ipecac syrup acts both **reflexly** on the gastric mucosa as an **irritant,** and after absorption **stimulates the CTZ** centrally and induces vomiting within 20 to 30 minutes. The emetic action is increased if 200 to 300 ml of water is taken immediately after the ingestion of the syrup. Like apomorphine, ipecac also induces vomiting of the reflux material from the upper intestines and the gastric contents. Its primary action is as a gastric irritant. *In adults,* ipecac syrup 20 ml orally, followed by 200 to 300 ml of water is given. *In children,* the dose may be halved. If vomiting does not occur within 30 minutes, a gastric lavage should be performed. Absorption of ipecac may cause *myocardial conduction disturbances.*

Antiemetics

Antiemetics are employed in the treatment of nausea and vomiting. Vomiting which result from local irritation is self-limiting. A demulcent drink like **milk,** supplemented by an **adsorbent antacid** may be administered for their soothing effect when severe vomiting has stopped.

The main group of agents used as antiemetics are: (*i*) the **anticholinergics;** (*ii*) the **antihistamines;** (*iii*) the **phenothiazines;** and (*iv*) **miscellaneous drugs,** including cannabinoids. Some antiemetics have antivertigo effects in addition (see later).

Anticholinergics

Scopolamine (Hyoscine)

Scopolamine is a natural alkaloid related to atropine. Its anticholinergic action possibly blocks afferent impulses to the vomiting centre. It may also reduce conduction at the labyrinthine receptors and vestibular pathways, which accounts for its use since World War II in the treatment of **motion sickness.** It is a depressant of the CNS and produces drowsiness, confusion, fatigue and at higher doses may produce **euphoria, excitement** and **hallucinations.** Because of its anticholinergic activity it leads to **blurred vision, xerostomia, tachycardia, amnesia** and **raised intraocular pressure.** It is contraindicated in patients of **glaucoma** and caution is to be observed in patients with prostatic hypertrophy. Because of these side effects now the *antihistaminic antiemetics are preferred* for the treatment of motion sickness. **Scopolamine hydrobromide** may be used in a dose of 0.6 to 1.0 mg SC. **Transdermal scopolamine** in the form of circular flat discs is also available. It adheres to the skin behind the ear, and provides a continuous steady rate of drug release (0.5 mg over 3 days) with minimal side effects.

Antihistamines

The antiemetic activity amongst the antihistamines is almost restricted to the **ethanolamines** (diphenhydramine, dimenhydrinate) and the **piperazines** (cyclizine, meclozine, buclizine). They are specially effective in preventing motion sickness **(Chap. 11.1).**

The antihistamines are not effective against apomorphine-induced vomiting. Their antiemetic action is the result of depression of neural functioning at the labyrinthine receptors, which makes them specially effective in **motion sickness, Meniere's disease, and vestilubar disturbances.** They may have some use in hyperemesis gravidarum, but as they have some likely **teratogenic** activity in animals, they are not recommended. These drugs should not be used to treat vomiting during pregnancy unless absolutely necessary.

The antihistamines are contraindicated in epileptics as they provoke seizures, and in patients of glaucoma and prostatic hypertrophy owing to their anticholinergic effects. In therapeutic doses they are relatively safe. Side effects include **drowsiness** and **xerostomia.** In higher doses excitement, convulsions, dilated pupils, flushed face and fever may occur.

PHENOTHIAZINES

Certain phenothiazines **(Table 12-1)** are of proven value in controlling the nausea and vomiting due to **drug toxicity, radiation sickness, carcinomatosis, gastrointestinal disturbances** and **operative procedures.** Their antiemetic action is exerted at the CTZ, evidenced by their **ability to block apomorphine-induced vomiting.** They essentially have an antidopaminergic action. The phenothiazines are ineffective in controlling motion sickness, except promethazine which probably acts by virtue of its antihistamine activity.

The most common *side effect* of phenothiazines at therapeutic doses is sedation. The incidence of **hypotension** is greater with the aliphatic phenothiazines, while **extrapyramidal reactions** occur more often with the piperazines.

Other side effects include **obstructive jaundice, agranulocytosis, photosensitivity** and **dryness of mouth**. Phenothiazines are **contraindicated** in patients with bone marrow depression, hypotension, pregnancy with preeclampsia and patients with a history of hypersensitivity to phenothiazines.

Miscellaneous Antiemetics

METOCLOPRAMIDE

Metoclopramide (a benzamide) is a **dopamine receptor antagonist** with a dual action, i.e., it sedates the CTZ, and inhibits vomiting induced by copper sulphate (peripheral action). It is a smooth muscle stimulant largely acting on the upper GI tract to increase gastric contractions and facilitate peristalsis in the duodenum and jejunum. Dopamine receptor blockade sensitizes the tissues to ACh action. Metoclopramide **relaxes the pyloric sphincter and duodenal bulb,** thereby **accelerating gastric emptying.** There is a dose-related increase in the **oesophageal sphincter pressure.** Other actions include sedation, increased prolactin release, and elevated circulating aldosterone levels.

Therapeutic uses include: (*i*) treatment of **gastroesophageal reflux** not responding to conventional therapy; (*ii*) prevention of **nausea and vomiting of cancer chemotherapy;** (*iii*) treatment of **acute** or **chronic gastroparesis** (gastric stasis); (*iv*) for facilitation of *small bowel intubation*; and (*v*) investigational uses are **facilitation of lactation, anorexia nervosa,** and **nausea** and **vomiting of pregnancy.**

Dosage. Metoclopramide is available as tablets (5, 10 mg), syrup (5 mg/5 ml), and injection (5 mg/ml). The usual dosage for **gastroesophageal reflux** is 10-15 mg orally upto qid, 30 minutes before meals and at bedtime. For **cytotoxic chemotherapy-induced vomiting,** initially 1-2 mg/kg by slow IV infusions is given 30 minutes before starting chemotherapy. Dose may be repeated every 2 hours for 2 doses, and every 3 hours for 3 doses. Higher dose should be given when highly emetogenic drugs like cisplatin are used. **Side effects** noted at high parenteral doses are drowsiness, fatigue, restlessness, and diarrhoea. Less frequently parkinsonism, akathisia, insomnia, anxiety and rarely depression may occur.

Table 12.1. *Side effects of phenothiazine antiemetics*

Phenothiazine	*Aniemetic dose (mg)*	*Sedation*	*Hypotension*	*Extrapyramidal symptoms*
Aliphatics				
Chlorpromazine (Largactil)	10-25	+++	++	++
Promethazine (Phenargan)	10-20	+	++	++
Triflupromazine (Vesprin)	5-10	+++	+	+++
Piperazines				
Fluphenazine (Prolixin)	1-2	++	+	+++
Perphenazine (Trilafon)	2-5	+	+	+++
Prochlorperazine (Compazine)	5-10	++	+	+++
Thiethylperazine (Torecan)	10	+	++	++

+ = slight; ++ = moderate; +++ = severe.

Cisapride

Cisapride, a benzamide, is a potent stimulant of gastric emptying. It acts by **facilitating the release of acetylcholine** from the myenteric plexus. It has no antiadrenergic, antidopaminergic, or cholinergic side effects. Patients of **gastroparesis** who have failed to respond to metoclopramide frequently respond to cisapride. It also improves the motility of the small intestines and colon in cases of **chronic constipation** (unlike metoclopramide and domperidone). Cisapride is a 5-HT_4 agonist used in the treatment of ***gastroesophageal reflux.***

Domperidone

Domperidone (a benzimidazole) is another drug used to accelerate gastric emptying. It is primarily a **peripheral dopamine antagonist.** Hence it has the advantage over metoclopramide and phenothiazines in that it causes less of sedation and dystonic reactions as it does not readily cross the blood-brain barrier.

Therapeutic uses. It is used for *levodopa* and *bromocriptine induced vomiting* in parkinsonism in a dose of 10-20 mg every 4-8 hours. Also used for nausea and vomiting following **cytotoxic therapy** or **radiotherapy** in a dose of 200-400 mcg/kg every 4-8 hours. *Side effects* include raised prolactin concentrations leading to galactorrhoea and gynaecomastia. Dystonic reactions may occur rarely. Extrapyramidal reactions have not been noted with domperidone.

Butyrophenones

Haloperidol and **droperidol** may be used as alternatives to phenothiazines as antiemetics for patients receiving cancer chemotherapy. They cause less sedation and hypotension compared to chlorpromazine and triflupromazine.

Cannabinoids

Dronabinol

Nabilone

Dronabinol is delta-9-tetrahydrocannabinol (THC), the main psychoactive substance found in **Cannabis sativa** or marijuana. *Nabilone* is a synthetic cannabinoid. They are effective antiemetics, specially in **controlling vomiting due to cancer chemotherapy.** Their use should be reserved for patients not responding to conventional therapy, as they produce profound CNS effects.

Dronabinol is given in a dose of 5-7.5 mg/m^2 orally 1-3 hours before, and every 2-4 hours after chemotherapy. **Nabilone** is given in a dose of 1-2 mg 1-3 hours before, and every 8-12 hours after chemotherapy.

Adverse reactions to cannabinoids include drowsiness, elation, dizziness, impaired thinking ability, altered perception, irritability, euphoria, memory impairment, nightmares, and ataxia.

Cinnarizine

Cinnarizine is used for vestibular disorders, like vertigo, tinnitus, nausea and vomiting in **Meniere's disease,** and motion sickness. It is also used in **peripheral vascular disease,** and **Raynaud's syndrome.** Dose: 15-30 mg orally bid or tid.

Betahistine

Betahistine is a vasodilator like histamine. It improves microcirculation. It is used to relieve vertigo, tinnitus, nausea and vomiting and hearing loss in **Meniere's disease.** Dose: Initially 16 mg tid with food; maintenance 24-48 mg daily.

Ondansetron, a 5-HT_3 inhibitor, has been approved for use in the prevention of **chemotherapy-induced nausea and vomiting.** The *benzodiazepines* may be used to control anticipatory nausea and vomiting.

To **summarize,** for **motion sickness** scopolamine, or scopolamine with dextroamphetamine, or antihistamines (cyclizine, meclozine, dimenhydrirate) may be used. For **postoperative vomiting** piperazine phenothiazines **(perphenazine, prochlorperazine).** For nausea and vomiting during the first trimester of pregnancy drug therapy must be discouraged.

Prokinetic Agents

Cholinergic mechanisms modulate motor activity of the gastrointestinal (GI) tract. Agents which specifically ***promote gastroduodenal peristalsis*** and ***accelerate gastric emptying*** are termed as prokinetic agents.

Metoclopramide and ***cisapride*** (see above) are promoted as selective GI motility stimulants, or *prokinetic agents*. Both these drugs release ACh from cholinergic neurones in the myenteric plexus, and also sensitize intestinal smooth muscle to the action of ACh. They have no effect on gastric or pancreatic secretion. These agents hasten oesophageal clearance, raise lower oesophageal sphincter pressure, accelerate gastric emptying, and shorten the small intestine transit time. Metoclopramide in addition has a central antidopamine effect. Both these agents exert an antiemetic effect.

Domperidone (see above) also accelerates gastric emptying and has a *prokinetic* **effect** on the gut. ***Erythromycin,*** a macrolide antibiotic **(Chap 9.3),** interestingly has a prokinetic effect in the stomach as a *motilin agonist*. To revise, motilin is a GI peptide which stimulates gastric emptying and postprandial gastric contraction. Erythromycin has been found to be effective in patients of *diabetic gastroparesis* and *intestinal pseudo-obstruction.*

Gastric Antacids

Antacids are weak bases that react with gastric hydrochloric acid to form salt and water. They are employed in the treatment of **hyperchlorhydria** and **peptic ulcer,** collectively known as **acid-peptic disease.** Peptic ulceration can occur at the outlet of the stomach (pyloric ulcer), or in the duodenal bulb, where it is usually single. Gastric ulcer is becoming more common as the population lives longer, or "stress" like brain injury, trauma, burns, drugs, and severe infections may cause peptic ulceration. Multiple ulcers can occur farther down in the gastrointestinal tract as in the **Zollinger-Ellison syndrome,** or in the **Meckel's diverticulum.**

Administration of adequate antacids remains the basis of management of acid-peptic disease. Newer approaches to the medical management include the use of **anticholinergic drugs, H_2-receptor antagonists, carbenoxolone sodium, tricyclic antidepressants, the substituted prostaglandins (PGE_2 compounds), proton pump inhibitors, and eradication of Helicobacter pylori infection.**

Mechanisms and Control of Acid Production

Gastric acid secretion is divided into **two** periods: (*i*) **interprandial** (basal secretion); and (*ii*) **postprandial** (stimulated secretion during and after meals). Three phases of acid output are recognized in the postprandial secretion, namely **cephalic, gastric** and **intestinal.** This division is arbitrary, as all of them occur almost simultaneously. The cephalic phase is mediated by the vagus nerve. Vagal influences release pepsin and increase acid production by gastrin release from the antrum. In addition, the vagal effects sensitize parietal cells to the action of gastrin. In the **gastric** phase release of gastrin is promoted by the distention of the pyloric antrum by food. Secretion of gastrin is also pH dependent; high pH levels stimulate release, whereas release is inhibited below pH 1.5. In the **intestinal** phase the duodenum controls secretion of gastric acid. Once the pH of its contents falls below 2.5, or hyperosmolar substances, or emulsified fats reach the duodenum, the gastric acid secretion is suppressed through humoral pathways.

The final common pathway for both vagal effects and effects of gastrin, involve the release of **histamine,** which acts on H_2-receptors, and the parietal cells are stimulated to release acid. **Prostaglandins** (E series) appear to modulate the release of histamine.

Pepsinogen, the inactive precursor of the proteolytic enzyme **pepsin,** is synthesized and stored in the chief cells of the **oxyntic gland** area. It is composed of pepsin and peptide moieties; the terminal moiety is an inhibitor of proteolytic activity. The pepsin-inhibitor comoplex dissociates at about pH 5.4, but optimal peptic activity occurs at pH 4.0. Histamine, vagal stimulation and gastrin promote pepsin secretion.

Gastric antacids partially neutralize the acid gastric secretion. If they elevate the pH above 4.0 to 4.5 they also inhibit the activity of pepsin, and peptic digestion of food suffers.

Mode of Action

The antacids diminish the quantity of free hydrochloric acid in the stomach by three mechanisms: (*i*) **direct neutralization of preformed acid,** thereby elevating the gastric pH to about 4.0 which is not strong enough to damage the mucosal surface, e.g., sodium bicarbonate and magnesium oxide; (*ii*) **buffering of preformed acid,** by agents like magnesium trisilicate and sodium citrate and (*iii*) **adsorption of hydrogen ions plus adsorption and inactivation of pepsin** as brought about by aluminium antacids and anion exchange resins. In addition there are some formulations of antacids in colloidal suspension which form a protective coating over the gastric mucosa and the ulcer crater.

Classification

Antacids are divided into **two** classes: (*i*) **systemic** antacids of which **sodium bicarbonate** is the only example; and (*ii*) **non-systemic** antacids, which either form insoluble products in the small intestine or contain a non-absorbable cation, e.g., **calcium carbonate, magnesium hydroxide, magnesium trisilicate,** and **aluminium hydroxide.** This category of antacids is preferred as the cationic portion is not absorbed from the intestine and the pH is raised to only about 4, whereby peptic digestion continues normally. They are often referred to a **non-systemic buffer antacids.**

SYSTEMIC ANTACID

Sodium Bicarbonate

Sodium bicarbonate (baking soda) is the only systemic antacid that has been used clinically. It has a rapid onset and short duration of action since it is highly soluble, and offers rapid relief of pain. Sodium bicarbonate 1.0 g neutralizes 120 ml 0.1 N HCl:

$$NaHCO_3 + HCl \rightarrow NaCl + H_2O + CO_2$$

It is not recommended for long-term use because it produces **systemic alkalosis.** This leads to excretion of alkaline urine, which disturbs the excretion of some drugs and calcium. If large quantities of milk or a calcium-containing antacid are taken simultaneously, hypercalcaemia and renal calcinosis may occur **(milk-alkali syndrome).** It makes the pH almost neutral or alkaline and thus interferes with the peptic digestion of food, and moreover later due to gastrin release there is a compensatory increased secretion of acid gastric juice known as **"acid rebound". Thus due to the acid rebound, systemic alkalosis, gastric distention, disordered peptic digestion of food and danger of metastatic calcinosis sodium bicarbonate is not much used now.** *Dose* 1 to 5 g.

NON-SYSTEMIC ANTACIDS

Calcium Carbonate

Calcium carbonate is a non-systemic antacid, and its reaction with HCl in the stomach is not as rapid as of sodium bicarbonate, and for this reason it produces a

more prolonged reduction in gastric acidity. It reacts in the stomach, and 1 g neutralizes 200 ml 0.1 N HCl:

$$CaCO_3 + 2HCl \rightarrow CaCl_2 + H_2O + CO_2$$

The calcium chloride is converted in the intestine to insoluble salts (carbonate and phosphate) and calcium soaps. Calcium absorption is limited to only 30 percent of the ingested dose, and a minor degree of hypercalcaemia may occur. But if the kidneys are normal an alkalosis does not develop. As calcium carbonate acts slowly **rebound acid secretion is minimal.** The disadvantage is that it has a chalky taste, and frequent use causes constipation. Dose 1 to 5 g.

MAGNESIUM HYDROXIDE

Powdered magnesium oxide in a water suspension is hydrated to magnesium hydroxide. Magnesium hydroxide mixture **(milk of magnesia)** is used primarily as an antacid-laxative mixture in young children. In the stomach it reacts with HCl, and 1 g neutralizes 500 ml of 0.1 N HCl:

$$Mg(OH)_2 + 2HCl \rightarrow MgCl_2 + 2H_2O$$

Magnesium chloride is soluble, but the magnesium ion is poorly absorbed from the gut. It acts as an **osmotic purgative.** Magnesium retention occurs in patients with chronic renal disease and in dialysis patients. Hence, magnesium antacids are *contraindicated* in these patients. The dose for milk of magnesia is 5 to 10 ml as an antacid, and 25 to 50 ml as a laxative.

MAGNESIUM TRISILICATE

Magnesium trisilicate is a hydrated magnesium silicate. It acts both as an **antacid** and **adsorbent,** and 1 g neutralizes 100 ml of 0.1 N HCl:

$$2MgO_3\ SiO_2 \times H_2O + 4HCl \rightarrow MgCl_2 + 3SiO_2 + (x + 2)\ H_2O$$

This reaction is slow and prolonged. Magnesium chloride and hydrated silicic acid are formed. Silicic acid is gelatinous in consistency and has good adsorbent property. Hence, this agent acts both as an antacid and adsorbent.

The magnesium chloride formed reacts with the bicarbonate in the intestine as under:

$$MgCl_2 + 2NaHCO_3 \rightarrow MgCO_3 + 2NaCl + H_2O + CO_2$$

The magnesium carbonate formed is eliminated in the faeces. With magnesium trisilicate the contents of the stomach are not completely neutralized but are buffered at pH 4 to 6. It has a laxative effect and hypermagnesaemia may occur. Dose 0.5 to 2 g depending on the patient's need.

ALUMINIUM HYDROXIDE

Aluminium hydroxide is the prototype aluminium compound, and is the most commonly used agent of this group. In the gel form it is a **nonabsorbable buffer antacid,** with slow onset of action, and a low neutralizing capacity—1 g neutralizes between 12.5 to 25.0 ml of 0.1 N HCl:

$$Al\ (OH)_3 + 3HCl \rightarrow AlCl_3 + 3H_2O$$

In the intestine aluminium chloride is converted to the hydroxide or to other basic salts. The gastric contents are not completely neutralized and the pH is maintained between 3.5 to 4.0. Thus aluminium hydroxide neutralizes and adsorbs HCl, precipitates and inactivates pepsin, increases gastric mucus production, is a mild astringent and a demulcent. This agent produces **constipation,** as the aluminium phosphate formed relaxes the intestinal smooth muscles. As phosphate ions are bound as insoluble salts in the intestine, **hypophosphataemia** may be produced. Gastrointestinal absorption of the **tetracyclines, barbiturates, warfarin, quinidine** and **chlorpromazine** is depresed due to chelation and formation of insoluble complexes. Neurologic toxicity may occur in uraemic patients on long-term dialysis.

The **advantages** of aluminium hydroxide are its relative palatability and its lack of serious toxic effects. The most common side effect is **constipation** which can be countered by combining with a magnesium based antacid. Aluminium hydroxide gel is used in a dose of 7.5 to 15 ml, depending on the patient's need. (Dose range 5 to 30 ml).

Other aluminium compounds used as antacids include **aluminium glycinate, aluminium phosphate gel, dihydroxyaluminium aminoacetate and aluminium carbonate.**

Dihydroxyaluminium sodium carbonate. It is converted to aluminium hydroxide in the presence of gastric hydrochloric acid, releasing carbon dioxide. It gives a rapid but transient neutralizing effect, and because of its sodium content caution must be observed in sodium restricted patients. *Chewable tablets* (334 mg) are available, and the dose is 1-2 tablets tid to six times a day.

Hydroxymagnesium aluminate. It is a synthetic combination of aluminium and magnesium hydroxides and sulphuric acid, equivalent to 28-39 percent magnesium oxide and 17-25 percent aluminium oxide. It does not produce acid rebound, and has a low incidence of diarrhoea and constipation. It is available in the form of a suspension 540 mg/5 ml; tablets 480 mg; chewable tablets 480 mg. The usual dose is 180-1080 mg tid to six times daily between meals and at bedtime.

OTHER AGENTS

MILK

Milk is a weak antacid and also possesses some protective action, and a "milk drip" containing **aluminium hydroxide gel** administered through a Ryle's tube into the stomach may promote healing of the ulcer.

ANION EXCHANGE RESINS

Anion exchange resins are poor antacids, but are effective **acid adsorbents.** They are rarely used as they are costly, bulky, possess an offensive odour and taste.

Gastric Mucin

Gastric mucin is an alcoholic precipitate of hog stomach. It is an **inefficient** acid neutralizer. It possibly can offer protection to the damaged gastric mucosa.

Anticholinergic Drugs

Anticholinergic drugs like **propantheline (Probanthine)** reduce the inter and postprandial secretion of gastric juice, since these phases are partly under cholinergic control. They **reduce basal acid secretion by about 50 percent, and histamine or gastrin-induced secretion by 40 percent.** They do not reduce food stimulated secretion. In peptic ulcer patients, where gastric hypermotility and muscle spasm are marked, anticholinergics may be useful. They are useful as adjuncts to H_2-receptor antagonists. *Adverse reactions* to anticholinergic drugs include xerostomia, constipation, blurred vision, retention of urine and precipitation of glaucoma **(Chap. 3.3).**

Sedatives and **tranquillizers** have also been employed in the treatment of duodenal ulcers. They reduce emotional tension but have little effect on acid secretion.

Drugs Promoting Ulcer Healing

The following drugs promote ulcer healing:

H_2-Receptor Antagonists

Cimetidine

Cimetidine was the first *histamine H_2-receptor antagonist* available for clinical use, and contains an *imidazole ring.* **It reduces fasting and stimulated acid and pepsin secretion by competitively antagonizing the action of histamine on H_2-receptors (Chap. 11.1).** It is very effective in promoting healing of gastric and peptic ulcers.

Cimetidine given in tablet form (200 mg three times daily and 400 mg each evening) for 4 weeks heals **duodenal ulcers** in about 60 percent of patients, and after 8 weeks therapy the healing occurs in more than 80 percent of patients. When healing has occurred therapy is continued for upto one year in a reduced dose (400 mg twice daily). Duodenal ulcers usually recur in most patients. Cimetidine is also effective in promoting the healing of **gastric ulcers** and in treating **oesophagitis.** The dosage is the same as for duodenal ulcers. Intravenous administration of cimetidine is found to be helpful in the treatment of **haemorrhagic gastritis** or stress ulceration.

Side effects include drowsiness, itchy skin rashes, **gynaecomastia,** interstitial nephritis, acute pancreatitis, cardiac arrhythmias, and **impotence.** The half-life of cimetidine is 90 minutes. Renal failure increases the half-life and dialysis shortens it, as the drug is excreted through the kidneys.

Ranitidine. It has a **thiazole ring.** The elimination half-life is 2.5 to 3.0 hours. Like cimetidine, it has a low incidence of toxicity. **Side effects** include confusion, anicteric hepatitis, and cardiac arrhythmias on IV dosing.

Dose: Ranitidine hydrochloride is available as tablets (150, 300 mg) and as an injectable. The oral dose is 150 mg bid or 300 mg before bedtime. The IV dose is 50 mg every 8 hours. With renal or hepatic dysfunction the dose should be reduced.

Famotidine. It contains a **furan ring** structure. On oral administration the onset of effect is within 1 hour, and inhibition of gastric secretion is upto 10-12 hours. **Side effects** are similar to those as with other H_2-receptor antagonists. Gynaecomastia has not been reported. The **usual oral dose** is 20 mg bid or 40 mg at bedtime. The IV dose is 20 mg every 12 hours. Dose should be reduced by 50 percent if the creatinine clearance is less than 10 ml/min.

Nizatidine. It is the newest H_2-receptor antagonist. It has a **thiazole ring** and a side chain identical to rantidine. The elimination half-life is 1-2 hours. *Side effects* are as with other H_2-receptor antagonists. Gynaecomastia may occur rarely. The **usual dose** for gastric and duodenal ulceration is 300 mg at night, or 150 mg bid for 4-8 weeks; maintenance, 150 mg at night upto 1 year. For gastro-esophageal reflux disease, the dose is 150-300 mg bid for upto 12 weeks.

Roxatidine. It is a new H_2-receptor antagonist, 4 times more potent than cimetidine. The usual **dose** is 150 mg twice daily, or 300 mg at bedtime; maintenance 150 mg at bedtime.

Carbenoxolone Sodium

Carbenoxolone is a derivative of glycyrrhizinic acid, a constituent of liquorice root. It **accelerates the healing of gastric ulcers,** but the mode of action is controversial. An increased production of gastric mucus, and prolongation of the life span of gastric epithelial cells is the possible mechanism involved in the healing. It does not alter the gastric acid or pepsin secretion. It has a **local anti-inflammatory action** and systemic effects like aldosterone, i.e., sodium and water retention and potassium loss leading to oedema, hypertension and hypokalaemia. Carbenoxolone does not appear to accelerate the healing of duodenal ulcers, perhaps because it is rapidly absorbed from the stomach, and the ulcer healing effect is a direct local effect on the mucosa. Carbenoxolone is given in a dose of 100 mg two or three times daily for 4-8 weeks. **Duogastrone** is a "position release" form of carbenoxolone formulated in specical gelatin capsules. These capsules release the active ingredient in the pyloric antrum for discharge into the duodenum for the treatment of duodenal ulcers.

Side effects like **oedema** and **mild hypertension** can be controlled by thiazide diuretics. Aldosterone antagonists should not be used, as they antagonize the ulcer healing effect of the drug.

Pirenzepine. It is an antimuscarinic agent with relative **selectivity for gastric M_1 muscarinic receptors.** It inhibits gastric acid and pepsin secretion with fewer peripheral side effects. It does not cross the blood-brain barrier and is as effective as H_2-receptor antagonists in **healing gastric** and **duodenal ulcers,** and is useful in maintenance therapy. Pirenzepine is also used in conjunction with H_2-receptor antagonists in resistant cases.

Dose: 50 mg bid, increased if necessary to a maximum of 150 mg/day in 3 divided doses before meals for 4-6 weeks, and in resistant cases upto 3 months. *Side effects* include dry mouth, visual disturbances, agranulocytosis and thrombocytopenia. Later studies indicate that pirenzepine is of limited value in the treatment of acid-peptic disease.

Prostaglandins

Prostaglandins of the A, E and I type inhibit gastric acid secretion **(Chap. 11.3).** They have a **cytoprotective action,** and stimulate mucus and bicarbonate secretion by the gastric mucosa.

Misoprostol. It is a synthetic analogue of PGE_1 (alprostadil), and **inhibits gastric acid secretion promoting gastric and duodenal ulcer healing.** It can protect against **NSAID-induced gastric ulcers.** It is also used for the treatment of *peptic ulcer disease.* The recommended dosage for peptic ulceration and NSAID-induced ulceration is 800 mcg daily in 2-4 divided doses, with breakfast or main meals, and at bedtime, for 4-8 weeks. For **prophylaxis** of NSAID-induced ulcers 200 mcg bid or qid is administered. **Side effects** include diarrhoea, abdominal pain, flatulence and menstrual irregularities (menorrhagia, intermenstrual bleeding, and postmenopausal bleeding).

Proton Pump Inhibitors

Omeprazole. It inhibits gastric acid secretion by blocking the H^+-K^+-adenosine triphosphatase (ATPase) enzyme system (the "proton pump") of the gastric parietal cells. It is used to treat **gastric and duodenal ulcers, and erosive oesophagitis.**

Dosage: For **gastric and duodenal ulcers, reflux oesophagitis,** and **ulcers complicating NSAID therapy** 20 mg daily for 4 weeks. In severe cases the dose may be increased to 40 mg daily. Long-term use is not recommended. For **Zollinger Ellison syndrome,** initially 60 mg once daily; usual dose range 20-120 mg daily. Doses above 80 mg are given in 2 divided doses. *Side effects* include diarrhoea, headache, flatulence, skin reactions, and photosensitivity.

Never "proton pump inhibitors" include **lansoprazole, pantoprazole,** and **rabiprazole.**

Sucralfate. It is an aluminium hydroxide sulphated sucrose complex which is only minimally absorbed from the GI tract. It probably acts by selectively binding to necrotic ulcer tissue, where it acts as a barrier to acid, pepsin and bile. Sucralfate is used for **gastric and duodenal ulceration** and **chronic gastritis.** The usual dose is 2 g twice daily on rising and at bedtime, or 1 g 4 times daily 1 hour before meals and at bedtime, for 6-12 weeks. **Side effects** include constipation, diarrhoea, indigestion; dry mouth, pruritus, insomnia, vertigo and dizziness.

Colloidal Bismuth

Colloidal bismuth promotes healing of duodenal ulcers. The **antipepsin activity** may be partly responsible, but in addition bismuth may react with necrotic tissue in the ulcer crater, denaturing the protein, and creating a physical barrier protecting the viable tissue. Healing may thus be promoted.

The tricyclic antidepressant **doxepin** also is claimed to have an ulcer healing effect. Surgery is indicated, if simpler treatment fails, and dangerous complications like continued or recurrent haemorrhage develop. *Vagotomy* may be tried in selected cases.

Purgatives

Purgatives are drugs used to promote the evacuation of faeces from the bowel. The terms **cathartic, laxative, aperient, evacuant,** and **purgative** should be regarded as synonyms to avoid confusion. On the other hand sometimes the terms aperient, laxative, purgative and drastic cathartic are used to describe the magnitude of purgative action.

As a group, the purgatives are used in the treatment of **constipation,** which is a functional disturbance of the gastrointestinal tract, and a symptom of many underlying diseases. They are one of the much **abused drugs** by the laity, particularly by the elderly, who in fact become habituated to the daily dose of a purgative. Sometimes regular diet habit and dietary modification to a high residue diet (more roughage) and adequate intake of water is all that is needed to treat constipation, and drugging is entirely unnecessary.

Classification

According to their **mode of action** the purgatives may be divided into *three* main groups:

1. **Bulk purgatives.** These agents act by increasing the bulk of the intestinal contents and thereby promoting peristalsis and defaecation.
   - (*i*) **Osmotic purgatives.** These salts have a non-absorbable ion which retains water in the intestinal lumen, e.g., *magnesium sulphate, magnesium hydroxide, sodium sulphate, sodium potassium tartrate,* and *lactulose.*
   - (*ii*) **Hydrophilic colloids.** *Methylcellulose,* agar, psyllium are indigestible plant residues, and provide bulk to the faeces.
   - (*iii*) **Vegetable fibres.** *Ispaghula husk* and *Bran* are indigestible and provide bulk. They are not colloidal.

2. **Irritant purgatives.** They produce irritation of the intestines and stimulate the Auerbach's plexus in the bowel wall.
   (*i*) **Anthraquinone (emodin) purgatives.** Rhubarb, Senna, Cascara sagrada and aloes.
   (*ii*) Castor oil.
   (*iii*) Phenolphthalein.
   (*iv*) Bisacodyl
   (*v*) Danthron
   (*vi*) Sodium picosulphate
3. **Lubricant purgatives.** These agents lubricate and soften the faecal matter in the colon and rectum.
   (i) Liquid paraffin.
   (*ii*) Dioctyl sodium sulphosuccinate.
   (*iii*) Glycerine suppositories and soap water enema.
4. **Prebiotics and probiotics**

Osmotic Purgatives (Saline Purgatives)

Certain inorganic salts on ingestion are *minimally* absorbed from the intestines, and by virtue of their osmotic effect retain water in the intestinal lumen. This leads to the production of a soft or even a fluid stool.

Magnesium sulphate (Epsom salts). It is a potent osmotic purgative as both magnesium and sulphate ions are minimally absorbed by the small intestine. It has a bitter taste and rapid action, and may cause considerable loss of water from the body. It provides an almost complete evacuation of the small and large intestine. **Dose:** 5 to 20 g.

Magnesium hydroxide (Milk of magnesia). It acts like magnesium sulphate, but is less potent. In addition it is an **antacid** and may be used to counter the tendency to constipation produced by other antacids. **Dose:** 10 ml of magnesium hydroxide mixture.

Sodium sulphate and sodium potassium tartrate may also be used as saline purgatives in a dose of 15 g and 10 g orally respectively. The **Seidlitz powder** contains sodium potassium tartrate 7.5 g with sodium bicarbonate 2.5 g (in blue paper), and tartaric acid 2.5 g (in white paper). The contents of the blue paper are dissolved in water and the contents of the white paper are added. This results in an effervescing drink.

Hydrophilic Colloids

Methylcellulose. Methycellulose is a partially depolymerized form of cellulose. It is not absorbed in the intestine. It absorbs water and swells to form a gel, so that the faecal bulk is increased. It produces a bulky, moist, well formed stool and should be taken with a substantial volume of water. Rarely intestinal obstruction may occur. **Dose:** 1 to 3 g.

Agar is derived from seaweeds, and has a similar action as methylcellulose. **Dose:** 4 to 12 g.

Psyllium seeds. They are dried ripe seeds of **Plantago psyllium.** They contain a lot of muscilage which swells in the bowel to form a soft, bulky muscilagenous mass. It imbibes about 20 times its weight of water. It increases persistalsis and a soft formed stool is passed. **Dose:** 5 to 15 g.

Vegetable Fibre

Ispagula husk (Isogel). Ispagula husk obtained from **Indian Plantago seed** has similar properties to those of psyllium, and is used as a bulk purgative in the treatment of chronic constipation. **Dose:** 3 to 5 g.

Bran (Fybranta). Bran is the residue of husks after the milling of wheat. It contains about 20 percent of its total weight as fibre, which acts as roughage and promotes intestinal motility. It has to be taken in large amounts to be effective. The usual way of taking bran is in the form of a breakfast cereal. Fybranta tablets contain bran 2 g and calcium phosphate 100 mg, and 6 to 12 tablets daily are to be chewed and swallowed with liquid.

Irritant Purgatives

Anthraquinone (emodin) purgatives. The well known and widely used group of anthraquinone purgatives includes **senna, cascara, rhubarb** and **aloes.** The active principles **(emodin and chrysophanic acid)** are liberated by hydrolysis of parent glycosides in the small intestine. These are absorbed and re-excreted into the colon, where they stimulate the myenteric plexus and induce colonic contractions. Therapeutically they are administered late in the evening, and they exert their action next morning. **Repeated use of anthraquinone purgatives may cause degeneration of the myenteric plexus and impair normal colonic propulsive activity.** Thus, they are *not* recommended for long-term use, though for occasional use they are safe and effective. Senna pod 600 mg per tablet, administered as 2 tablets at bedtime.

Castor oil. Castor oil is a fixed oil obtained from the castor bean **Ricinus communis.** It is hydrolysed in the small intestine liberating **ricinoleic acid.** This mildly irritates the intestine and peristalsis is increased. The hydrolysis requires the presence of bile. The unchanged oil acts as a lubricant. Castor oil produces almost complete emptying of the bowel with a semi-fluid stool, but its use may be followed by prolonged constipation. Sometimes it causes severe griping, and it has an unpleasant taste and smell. Castor oil now has little use as a purgative. **Dose:** 15 to 60 ml orally.

Phenolphthalein. Phenolphthalein is a synthetic purgative. It irritates the mucosa of the small intestine and colon. Some of it is absorbed in the small intestine and is then excreted in the bile (enterohepatic circulation). Purgative effect is produced in 6 to 12 hours. Excretion of absorbed phenolphthalein in the urine produces a pink colouration if the pH is alkaline. The drug may also produce skin rashes and diarrhoea. **Dose:** 60-180 mg. Tablet taken before retiring.

Bisacodyl. Bisacodyl is a synthetic substance and a derivative of pyridine. It **resembles phenolphthalein** in its action, but is not absorbed from the intestine. It stimulates reflex peristalsis by mucosal irritation. Formed faeces are passed 1 hour after inserting a suppository or 8 to 12 hours after oral administration. The **dose** is 15 mg orally and 10 mg by suppository.

Danthron. It is a synthetic irriant purgative that stimulates colonic peristalsis. Onset of action is 6-10 hours. *Dose:* 75-100 mg with the evening meal.

Sodium Picosulphate. It is a new stimulant laxative belonging to the *phenyl methane group*, and acts with in 10-14 hours. *Dose* 5-15 mg orally as a single dose at bed time.

LUBRICANT PURGATIVES

Liquid paraffin. Liquid paraffin is a mineral oil, which is minimally absorbed by the alimentary tract. It mixes with and coats the intestinal contents, leading to the formation of soft oily faeces. It has no other action. The oil may trickle down to the anal sphincter, and leakage occurs which is messy and embarassing to the patient.

Dioctyl sodium sulphosuccinate. It is an **anionic surface-active emulsifying and wetting agent,** and softens the stool by lowering surface tension. It increases the water content of the stool. It is safe, effective and useful in the treatment of painful anal lesions like fissures or following haemorrhoidectomy. **Dose:** 50 to 360 mg daily. It is available in tablet and syrup form.

Glycerine. It can be introduced into the rectum as a suppository, and defaecation usually occurs within 30 minutes.

PREBIOTICS AND PROBIOTICS

A common problem among stressed and working people is *constipation*. **Prebiotic fibres** and **probiotic foods** must be included in the diet to regulate and normalise intestinal motility.

Prebiotics are non-digestable fibres that serve as food source for 'good bacteria' called *probiotics* is the gut. Some prebiotic foods like *oats, bran, suji (semolina)*, and *dalia* also have a cholesterol lowering effects. Fruits and vegetable apart from fibre are a rich source for vitamins and minerals. Fruits like *banana, guava, apples*, and *ripe papaya* contain *pectin*, vitamins A and C.

Probiotics are functional foods which have live 'good bacteria' like *Lactobacillus sporogenes* beneficial to humans. These are contained in fermented dairy products like 'curd'.

Enemas. Enemas evacuate faeces from the bowel by providing the distention stimulus, and by simple lavage. Water alone may be used, but traditionally slightly soapy water is used. The fluid (200-250 ml) is instilled into the rectum, and evacuation generally occurs within a few minutes.

THERAPEUTIC USES

There is a wide individual variation in the normal frequency of bowel evacuation. The nature of the stool passed is probably a better index, and passage of hard faecal masses (scybala) are indicative of constipation. In any case regular use of purgatives is to be avoided. The purgatives are used in the following conditions: (*i*) the treatment of **helminthic infestations** of the bowel; (*ii*) in bowel disease accompanied by chronic constipation, e.g., **megacolon** without aganglionosis; (*iii*) **before surgery on the large bowel** and the rectum; (*iv*) **before proctoscopy or sigmoidoscopy or radiology** of the bowel, although an enema is more effective; (*v*) in local disease of the anus and rectum like **haemorrhoids** or **anal fissure.** Liquid paraffin can be used for this purpose; (*vi*) in cases of **poisoning;** (*vii*) treatment of **hepatic precoma** and **coma;** (*viii*) to relieve constipation produced by drugs; (*ix*) during **convalescence from myocardial infarction, pulmonary embolism and cerebral haemorrhage;** and (*x*) to relieve **cerebral oedema** hypertonic magnesium sulphate is used.

Most of the **irritant purgatives** are slow to act, and should be administered at night before retiring. When rapid purgation is required, as after ingestion of poisons, the **osmotic purgatives** should be employed.

CONTRAINDICATIONS

Purgatives should not be used in cases of **undiagnosed abdominal pain,** for they can precipitate complications like burst appendix. Purgatives are contraindicated in cases of **intestinal obstruction** or **faecal impaction.** Magnesium salts should not be used if renal insufficiency is present. The emodin alkaloids can be transmitted by the nursing mother to the baby. Purgation should be avoided during the later stages of pregnancy.

ADVERSE EFFECTS

Occasional use of purgatives is relatively safe, but on continued use they induce habituation, which is not easy to break. With **habituation** the normal reflex mechanisms initiating defaecation are lost, which further necessitates the continued use of purgatives. Withdrawal may lead to **anorexia, irritability, myalgia, occipital headache, malaise** and **insomnia.** Other effects are colicky abdominal pain, diarrhoea leading to dehydration, and electrolyte imbalance. The anthraquinone purgatives on prolonged use are likely to **damage the myenteric plexus** of the colon, and normal colonic activity is lost.

ANTIDIARRHOEAL DRUGS

Diarrhoea is a symptom marked by a rapid passage of faecal material through the gastrointestinal tract and a frequent passage of semisolid or liquid faeces. Prolonged diarrhoea, whatever the cause, leads to **electrolyte loss,** the correction of which is of utmost importance. The use of antidiarrhoeal drugs only offers a **symptomatic relief,** and specific treatment for the cause must be simultaneously administered.

The Opiates. They have been used for many years for the symptomatic control of diarrhoea. **Paregoric** (comphorated tincture of opium) 4 ml; **laudanum** (tincture of opium) 0.3 to 0.6 ml; and **codeine sulphate** 16 to 32 mg reduce the propulsive movements of the colonic muscle, permitting the faeces to remain longer in the lumen, and water is reabsorbed. **Morphine** acts in a similar manner. The opiates are potent antidiarrhoeal agents, but it must be remembered that addiction and tolerance may develop rapidly.

Diphenoxylate hydrochloride. Diphenoxylate is related to **pethidine,** and acts like the opiates. It may be combined with atropine. The usual dose is 5 mg three times daily. A newer agent is **loperamide** (Imodium) which is related to diphenoxylate. The usual dose is 4 mg, followed by 3 mg after each stool is passed to a maximum of 16 mg/day.

Antispasmodic agents. Anticholinergic agents like **propatheline bromide** (Probanthine) and **dicyclomine hydrochloride** (Merbentyl) may be used to diminish intestinal motility, and frequently the associated abdominal cramps also subside.

Hydrophilic agents. Agents like **methylcellulose, isogel and psyllium seed** may be used as they absorb water forming a gelatinous mass. Such an action reduces the free water content of the stool. These agents have already been described under purgatives, but they are of value both in constipation and diarrhoea because of their hydrophilic nature.

Demulcents, Bismuth subcarbonate, 2 g orally; **calcium carbonate,** 2 g orally; and magnesium oxide, 1 g orally may be used as demulcents to provide a soothing effect to the irritated intestinal/colonic mucosa.

Adsorbents. Many adsorbents have been used, but their value is doubtful. They supposedly adsorb irritants, bind water and reduce mucus secretion. **Activated characoal,** 1 to 6 g orally; *Kaolin* 3 g orally; and **Kaopectate** (mixture of Kaolin and Pectin) 15 ml orally may be used. Kaopectate has both demulcent and adsorbent property.

Oral Rehydration Therapy (ORT)

Oral rehydration therapy (ORT) is today recognized as the **first line** treatment in most cases of acute diarrhoea. Antibacterial agents are required only in infectious diarrhoea where pathogens have been identified. The oral rehydration salts (ORS) solution recommended by the WHO contains *glucose* (20.0 g) and three salts—*sodium chloride* (3.5 g), *trisodium citrate dihydrate* (2.9 g), *or sodium bicarbonate* (2.5 g), and potassium chloride (1.5 g) to be mixed in 1 litre of water (WHO Technical Report Series No. 615, 1977; 641, 1979; 685, 1983; and 722, 1985). It supplies glucose 111, Na^+ 90, HCO_3 30, and K^+20 mmol/litre. The composition of this ORS formulation is optimum for the rehydration of patients of all ages—*infants, children* and *adults*—with *dehydration due to acute diarrhoea of any aetiology.* Its efficacy rests in the fact that *glucose linked sodium reabsorption mechanism* in the small intestine remains largely intact during acute diarrhoeal states and serves to promote sodium entry into the body.

The ORT has been described as "potentially the most important medical advance of this century". The reasons for this are: (*i*) ORT can be used *alone* to successfully rehydrate 90 percent of patients with dehydration due to acute diarrhoea who earlier received intravenous therapy; (*ii*) ORT reduces hospital case-mortality rates by 40-50 percent (*iii*) ORT reduces diarrhoeal disease hospital admission rates by 50-60 percent, and the costs of treatment of diarrhoea are reduced upto 80 percent; (*iv*) ORT used at home in the early stages of the diarrhoeal illness prevents dehydration; (*v*) ORT is cheap and simple, and can easily be administered by mothers and other family members. An *improved ORS formulation* made available in this country lately contains *glycine* in addition to glucose (glycine fortified ORS), which offers the benefits of a **double transport mechanism for sodium.** With this formulation it is claimed that the stool output is lowered by 50 percent, the duration of diarrhoea is shortened by 30 percent, and the amount of ORS required to control diarrhoea is lessened by 43 percent.

OTHER THERAPEUTIC AGENTS

Chenodeoxycholic Acid

Chenodeoxycholic acid is one of the three common bile acids found in humans. Given by mouth for periods of six months or longer, it has been shown to **dissolve or reduce the size** of radiolucent cholesterol gallstones. It presumably alters the composition and properties of bile secreted by the liver, which prevents the precipitation of cholesterol, and increases its capacity to dissolve cholesterol. Prolonged use may lead to **diarrhoea** and **hepatotoxicity.** It is employed in a dose totalling 10-15 mg/kg body weight per 24 hours orally.

Ursodeoxycholic acid a bile acid, may also be used to dissolve cholesterol gallstones. The dose is 8-12 mg/kg daily at bedtime for upto 2 years.

Lactulose

Lactulose is a disaccharide which is not hydrolysed by the pancreatic and intestinal secretions. Taken orally, it passes unchanged to the lower alimentary tract, where it is hydrolysed by *carbohydrate-fermenting bacteria,* and thus provides nutrition to them. The growth of these organisms lowers the faecal pH, and thereby lactulose exerts a **mild laxative effect**. Lactulose is of value in the treatment of **hepatic encephalopathy**. It is available as a 50 percent w/w solution and 50 ml is given orally twice or thrice daily. It may be used in the treatment of **chronic constipation** in a dose of 10 to 20 g after breakfast, but it may take 2 to 3 day to exert a purgative effect.

Cholestyramine

Cholestyramine is an ion exchange resin which adsorbs bile salts. Taken orally, it prevents the reabsorption of bile salts by the distal ileum thereby facilitating the depletion of the bile salt pool. It is of value in **cholestatic syndromes,** and the itching associated with high serum concentration of bile salts is relieved. Cholestyramine is the treatment of choice for **type II hyperlipidaemia,** and it is prescribed with a diet low in animal fat. It is likely to interfere with the absorption of some acidic drugs, and caution should be observed.

Drug Treatment of Traveller's Diarrhoea

Upto 50 percent of travellers or tourists to the tropics develop diarrhoeal illness. It is characterized by an abrupt-onset illness within the first week after arrival, consisting of **abdominal cramp, watery diarrhoea, flatulence** and **fatigue.** Symptoms resolve spontaneously, but in some cases may persist for weeks. The major pathogen is enterotoxigenic **E. coli.** Others include **Shigella sp., Salmonella sp., G. lamblia, E. histolytica, Campylobacter sp. and rotavirus.**

Rationale for chemoprophylaxis remains controversial. One of the following drugs may be used prophylactically. (*i*) **doxycycline** 100 mg qid for periods upto 3 weeks; or (*ii*) **trimethoprim/sulphamethaxazole** (co-trimoxazole) 160/800 mg (1 double-strength tablet) bid for 21 day;s or (*iii*) **bismuth subsalicylate** (not recommended for under 12 years age) 60 ml qid daily for 21 days. **Lactobacillus** preparations may also offer protection. Doxycycline and co-trimoxazole are about 90 percent effective: while bismuth subsalicylate is about 60 percent effective.

The first measure in the treatment is **oral rehydration** of the patient. Milk, dairy products and beverages should be avoided. Effective early treatment regimens include: (*i*) **doxycycline** 1000 mg qid for 48 hours; or (*ii*) **trimethoprim/sulphamethoxazole,** one regular strength tablet bid for 5 days; or trimethoprim 200 mg bid for 5 days; or (*iii*) **bicozamycin** 500 mg orally qid for 3 days; or (*iv*) **bismuth subsalicylate** 30 to 60 ml every half hour for eight doses. Bismuth subsalicylate should not be used in children, as it may cause salicylate intoxication; or (norfloxacin 400 mg plus tinidazole 600 mg tablet) 1 tablet bid for 5 days, is effective in diarrhoea or dysentery of bacterial, amoebic, or mixed origin. Synthetic narcotic analogues like **loperamide** (*lmodium*) and **diphenoxylate** (Lomotil) may be useful as antimotility agents for symptomatic relief.

❑❑❑

13 DRUGS ACTING ON THE RESPIRATORY SYSTEM

Chronic obstructive pulmonary (COPD) diseases include **bronchial asthma, chronic bronchitis** and **emphysema.** These **three** disorders differ in their aetiology but have one common characteristic, i.e., airway obstruction which blocks effective pulmonary ventilation. **Coughing, wheezing** and **dyspnoea** are the symptoms, and become progressively worse, leading to acidosis and electrolyte imbalances. Proneness to frequent respiratory infections can precipitate acute pulmonary failure, congestive heart failure, and even cardiac arrest. The **bronchodilator drugs** are the mainstay in the drug management. The other drugs employed are the **expectorants** and **mucolytic agents, antibacterials, anti-inflammatory agents** and **antitussives.**

BRONCHODILATOR DRUGS

The *tone* of the bronchial muscle is controlled by **humoral factors** and by the **autonomic nervous system**. In health the bronchial calibre is mainly controlled by the **balance** between the parasympathetic and sympathetic nervous systems (**Table 13-1).**

Table 13.1 *Control of the bronchial smooth muscle*

Factor	*Constriction*	*Dilatation*
Neurogenic (ANS)		
Parasympathetic	+	
Sympathetic		+
Autonomic receptors		
Cholinergic (muscarinic)	+	
Adrenergic alpha	+	
$beta_2$		+
Humoral		
Histamine	+	
Serotonin (S-HT)	+	
Bradykinin	+	
SRS-A	+	+
Prostaglandins	(PGF_2 alpha)	(PGE_2)

The parasympathetic system causes **bronchoconstriction** mediated by acetylcholine. The sympathetic stimulation mediated by noradrenaline causes increased pulmonary blood flow, **bronchodilatation,** and vasodilatation of the pulmonary circulation. The *humoral* factors are mainly operative in diseased states.

Classification

The bronchodilators may be classified as under:

I. Anticholinergic agents
- Atropine
- Ipratropium

II. Sympathomimetic amines

(*a*) *Drugs stimulating alpha- and beta-receptors*
- Adrenaline
- Epherdrine

(*b*) *Drugs stimulating beta$_1$-, and beta$_2$-receptors*
- Isoprenaline
- Orciprenaline

(*c*) *Drug stimulating beta$_2$-receptors*
- Salbutamol
- Terbutaline
- Isoetharine
- Rimiterol

III. Theophylline derivatives (Methylxanthines)
- Aminophylline
- Choline theophyllinate
- Diprophylline

Mode of Action

Ahlquist (1948) introduced the concepts of alpha- and beta-adrenergic receptors to account for the excitatory and inhibitory actions of sympathomimetic amines at different sites. Later, Lands (1967) further subdivided the beta-receptors into beta$_1$ responsible for cardiac stimulation and lipolysis, and beta$_2$ responsible for bronchodilatation and vasodepression **(Chaps. 3.1, 3.4). Isoprenaline** is an agent with mixed beta$_1$ and beta$_2$ agonistic action, and the cardiac **stimulation** thus caused is a serious limitation when used for bronchial asthma. Now specific beta$_2$ stimulants like salbutamol are available, which produce bronchodilatation with minimal cardiac side effects.

Beta-adrenoceptor activity is mediated by c-AMP. The beta-adrenergic drugs increase adenylcylase activity, which promotes the conversion of ATP to active c-AMP, and this in turn relaxes the bronchial muscle **(Fig. 13.1). Cyclic-AMP also inhibits the secretion of SRS-A, histamine, and the eosinophil chemotactic factor (ECF-A) from the mast cells.** Cyclic-AMP is broken down by the enzyme phosphodiesterase. The methylaxanthines inhibit this enzyme, thereby conserving c-AMP in the bronchial muscle cell. **Thus, the adrenergic agonists cause bronchodilatation by promoting the formation of c-AMP, and the methylaxanthines act by inhibiting the destruction of c-AMP.**

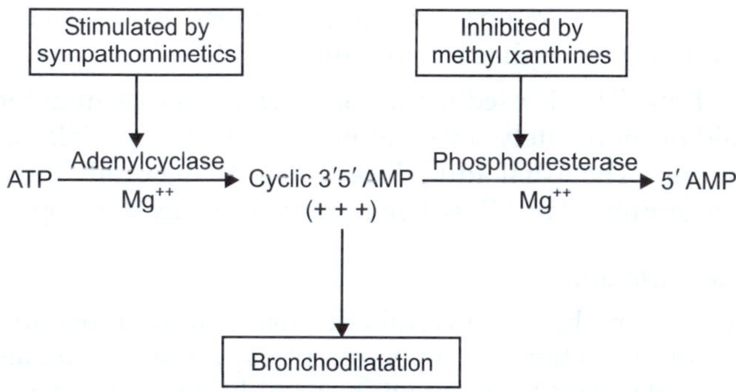

Fig. 13.1: Mode of action of sympathomimetics and methylxanthines as bronchodilators.

Cellular **cyclic guanosine monophosphate (c-GMP)** is under control of the parasympathetic nervous system. Its concentration is increased by vagal stimulation or by cholinergic drugs like carbechol and methacholine. Cyclie-GMP causes constriction of the bronchial muscle. **The resting state of the bronchial muscle is probably regulated by a balance between c-AMP and c-GMP, and thus between sympathetic and parasympathetic stimuli.** The anticholinergic agents may be acting by reducing the concentration of c-GMP in the bronchial muscle.

Anticholinergics

Atropine

Atropine relaxes the bronchial smooth muscle and reduces the secretions in the respiratory tract. Because of the side effects and slow onset of action, atropine today has no place in the management of bronchial asthma.

Ipratropium

Ipratropium is a new synthetic anticholinergic agent. It prevents the increase in c-GMP resulting from parasympathetic activation. It is claimed that ipratropium has some **bronchoselectivity,** producing bronchodilation without unwanted anticholinergic side effects. Ipratropium is available in a **metered dose inhaler** delivering 0.02 mg per inhalation. The usual dosage is one or two puffs three or four times daily.

SYMPATHOMIMETICS

Adrenaline

The detailed pharmacology of the sympathomimetic bronchodilators is discussed in **Chapter 3.4.** Adrenaline has powerful bronchodilator action. It has been **superseded by selective beta$_2$-receptor stimulants.** Adrenaline is still valuable in the treatment of **anaphylactic shock.**

Ephedrine

Ephedrine resembles adrenaline, and stimulates both alpha- and beta-receptors. In addition, it stimulates the release of noradrenaline from the sympathetic nerve endings. It is readily and completely absorbed after oral or parenteral administration. **Side effects** include CNS stimulation, vomiting, sweating, tremors, nervousness, insomnia and cardiac irregularities.

Ephedrine is used mainly as a **chronic** medication for mild or moderately severe bronchial asthma, specially in children. The **usual adult dose** is 30 to 60 mg orally three or four times daily. Resistance (tolerance) may develop.

ISOPRENALINE

Isoprenaline has a powerful effect on beta-receptors and almost no action on alpha-receptors. As it stimulates both **beta$_1$- and beta$_2$-receptors,** in addition to producing bronchodilatation, it increases the heart rate and cardiac output. The major toxic effects are due to beta$_1$ (cardiac) stimulant activity, producing **tachycardia, cardiac arrhythmias including ventricular fibrillation.**

Between 1959 and 1966 when isoprenaline inhalers were in wide use in Great Britain, there was an increased death rate from bronchial asthma. **It has been replaced by the more specific beta$_2$ stimulant drugs.**

ORCIPRENALINE

Orciprenaline is a long-acting derivative of isoprenaline. It stimulates both **beta$_1$- and beta$_2$-receptors.** It is claimed that is has little effect on the heart muscle. It is not inactivated by catechol-O-methyl transferase (COMT), and is more stable in the body. Orciprenaline given orally reduces the frequency and severity of asthmatic attacks. Inhaled as an **aerosol,** it acts promptly and the action lasts for 3 to 6 hours. Orally it is given in a dose of 20 mg every 6 hours. The metered aerosol produces 0.75 mg per dose, and adults may take upto 12 doses in 24 hours.

BETA$_2$ AGONISTS

Salbutamol

Salbutamol is probably the most widely used **beta$_2$-receptor stimulant.** It is effective by **oral, intravenous** and **aerosol** inhalation routes of administration, and has a much longer duration of action than isoprenaline. It is virtually devoid of cardiovascular effects in usual doses. The **oral** dose in the treatment of bronchial asthma is 2 to 4 mg three times daily. For **inhalation** 100 to 200 mcg may be repeated 4 hourly with a maximum of 8 inhalations in 24 hours. Salbutamol may be used by **slow intravenous infusion** (10 to 45 mcg/ minute) to inhibit uterine contractions in premature labour.

TERBUTALINE

Terbutaline is closely related chemically to orciprenaline, but is reputedly **more beta$_2$-selective.** Its pharmacological actions and therapeutic uses resemble those of salbutamol. **Orally** it is given in a dose of 2.5 to 5 mg two or three times daily. It may be administered **subcutaneously** (250 to 500 mcg) or by **inhalation** (200 or 250 mcg metered dose).

ISOETHARINE

Isoetharine is a **selective beta$_2$-receptor stimulant** and is effective by mouth, but its duration of action is short due to rapid inactivation in the body mainly by COMT. **Orally** it may be given in a dose of 10 mg **delayed release tablets,** with an effective duration of action of 4 to 6 hours. **Aerosol** preparation (350 mcg metered dose) is also available.

RIMITEROL

Rimiterol is a short acting **beta$_2$-receptor stimulant,** not active by mouth, but produces potent bronchodilator effect of rapid onset and short duration on inhalation. Its activity is similar to that of salbutamol and terbutaline. Plasma half-life is less than 5 minutes. The **dose** is 0.2 to 0.6 mg (one to three inhalations from a metered aerosol) with not more than 8 inhalations in 24 hours.

Other beta$_2$ stimulants used as bronchodilators are **fenoterol, reproterol** and **tulobuterol.**

METHYLXANTHINES

The methylxanthines act by **inhibiting the enzyme phosphodiesterase,** and hence have actions which resemble the sympathomimetics. They cause bronchodilatation, myocardial stimulation and CNS stimulation.

AMINOPHYLLINE

Aminophylline is a combination of theophylline and ethylenediamine, and has useful bronchodilator properties in conditions like **bronchial asthma** and **pulmonary oedema.** It is often used by **slow intravenous injection** (250 to 500 mg) as a first line treatment in patients with severe asthmatic attacks. When a large intravenous dose of aminophylline is given rapidly, **convulsions, arrhythmias** or **cardiac arrest** may occur. **Aminophylline suppositories** in strengths of 50, 100, 150 and 360 mg may be used to avoid gastric irritation and nausea caused by oral aminophylline.

CHOLINE THEOPHYLLINATE

Choline theophyllinate is used for the relief and prophylaxis of mild to moderate bronchospasm. **The adult oral dose** is 400 to 1600 mg daily in divided doses. It has been observed that when a maximal bronchodilator effect has been achieved by a beta$_2$-receptor stimultant, an additional effect can be obtained by administration of aminophylline or choline theophyllinate.

DIPROPHYLLINE

Diprophylline is a theophylline derivative which is used like aminophylline. It causes less of nausea and gastric irritation. It is better tolerated by mouth and by injection. The usual dose is upto 15 mg/kg every 6 hourly.

DISODIUM CROMOGLYCATE

Disodium cromoglycate (DSCG, Intal, Cromolyn sodium, sodium cromoglycate) is not a bronchodilator; it does not antagonize the mediators like histamine, serotonin, SRS-A and ECF-A involved in bronchial asthma; it has no anti-inflammatory acitivity; but is commonly used in the management of bronchial asthma. Its main action is **prophylactic,** reducing the incidence and severity of allergic asthmatic attacks. DSCG administration permits the **reduction in the dosage of corticosteroids** and **bronchodilators** being used in asthmatic patients. It is of little value in the treatment of acute attacks of asthma.

DSCG inhibits the release of histamine and SRS-A from the sensitized mast cells, possibly by stabilizing the mast cell membrane, and thereby preventing exocytosis. It also prevents exercise-induced bronchoconstriction in normal and asthmatic patients, possibly by **inhibiting the local release of prostaglandins.**

DSCG is very poorly absorbed from the gut. It has to be administered by **inhalation** from a special dispenser, the **spinhaler,** in which a propeller activated by suction creates a cloud of powder from the punctured capsule, which is inhaled. About 5 to 10 percent of the inhalation reaches the lungs, the remainder is deposited in the mouth and oropharynx and is swallowed. DSCG is rapidly absorbed from the lungs, and is excreted unchanged in the urine and bile. It has **no serious toxic effects,** but may cause irritation of the throat and coughing. Isolated cases of **hypersensitivity** have been reported.

DSCG is used in the **prophylaxis of allergic bronchial asthma.** The initial dose is 20 mg four times daily. DSCG has also been tried in other disorders with an allergic basis including **hay fever, allergic rhinitis, food allergy, allergic conjunctivitis** and **ulcerative colitis.**

Ketotifen

Ketotifen has actions similar to cromolyn sodium, and acts primarily by inhibition of mediator release. It also has antihistamine properties. It is used in the **proplylaxis of bronchial asthma** (*Dose:* 2 mg bid orally).

Drug Therapy of Bronchial Asthma

Bronchial asthma is a **bronchial hypersensitivity disorder** characterized by variable dyspnoea due to widespread airway obstruction, which is reversible spontaneously or as a result of treatment.

Based on clinical grounds, and the measurement of IgE, there are **two** major types of asthma: (*i*) **Extrinsic asthma** (reagin-mediated), in which symptoms develop only on exposure to a specific allergen; (*ii*) **intrinsic asthma** (perennial asthma), in which the symptoms are often precipitated by infection, the frequency of status asthmaticus is higher, and no allergic aetiology is detectable. Both these types behave differently to antiasthmatic drugs **(Table 13.2).**

Table 13.2 *Charateristics of extrinsic and intrinsic asthma*

Parameter	*Extrinsic type*	*Intrinsic type*
External allergens	Yes	No
Positive skin test	Yes	No
Serum IgE	Raised in 60%	Normal or low
Age group affected	Children and youth	Older adults
Pattern of asthma	Intermittent	Continuous
Family history of allergy	Common	Uncommon
Drug response to:		
Beta-sympathomimetics	Yes	Poor
Corticosteroids	Yes	Yes
DSCG	Yes	Poor

Three factors contribute to the reduction in airway calibre irrespective of the type of bronchial asthma-**smooth muscle constriction, mucosal congestion** and **exudation (Fig. 13.2).** The therapy is primarily directed at reversing bronchoconstriction by using bronchodilators, which are of three main types—**anticholinergics, sympathomimetics** and **methylxanthines.**

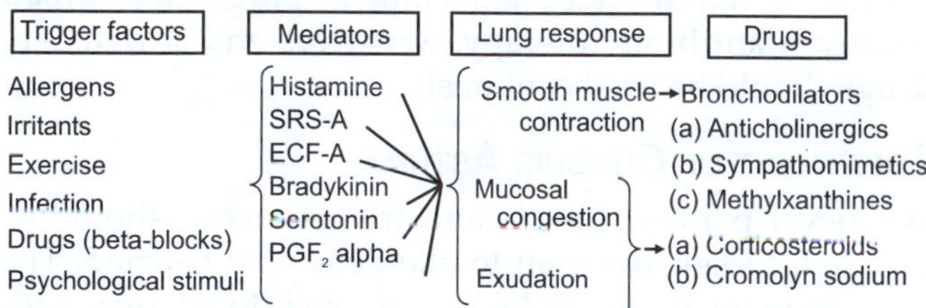

Fig. 13.2: Factors involved in the causation of bronchial asthma, and their drug management.

Prophylaxis

The incidence and severity of attacks may be reduced by regular administration of: (*i*) **disodium cromoglycate** which inhibits the release of mediators from the mast cells; (*ii*) **bronchodilators** like ephedrine orally, orciprenaline orally or by aerosol, or salbutamol orally or by aerosol. Oral aminophylline may be given, and the serum levels adjusted between 9 to 18 mcg/ml to obtain safe bronchodilator effect; (*iii*) **corticosteroids** like prednisolone may be administered orally, but there is a risk of adrenocortical suppression. **Beclomethasone** may be administered by aerosol as a prophylactic without producing significant adrenocortical suppression, and (*iv*) **Desensitization** to an allergen is sometimes feasible.

Treatment of Acute Attack

In the treatment of the acute attack some authorities still advocate the use of subcutaneous **adrenaline,** while others advocate **salbutamol** inhalation. Respiratory infection is to be treated by **antibiotics.** An advocated regimen is outlined below:

(*a*) **Adrenaline** (1: 1000) 0.2 to 0.5 ml subcutaneously. May be repeated every 1 to 2 hours.

(*b*) **Aminophylline** 0.25 g in 10 to 20 ml of saline slowly IV may be used.

(c) **Nebulized drugs** like isoetharine, isoprenaline or salbutamol may be given.

(d) **Corticosteroids.** In a moderate to severe attack hydrocortisone sodium succinate 100 to 200 mg IV may be effective.

(e) **Other drugs.** Methylxanthines may be tried. Sedation should be avoided in severe asthma. In mild to moderate attacks **phenobarbital** (30 mg), or **diazepam** (5 mg) may be useful. **Fluids** are administered to avoid dehydration and to liquefy secretions. **Oxygen inhalations** by mask or by intermittent positive pressure breathing (IPPB) is indicated if symptoms are severe.

Status Asthmaticus

Aminophylline may be administered by intravenous infusion spread over 8 hours. **Hydrocortisone sodium succinate** 100 mg or **methyl prednisolone sodium succinate** 80 mg may be given IV every hour. Beta$_2$-adrenoceptor stimulants may be given by mouth, aerosol or injection. Other measures include IPPB and **bronchial lavage** to remove tenacious mucus plugs; and **broad spectrum antibiotic therapy. Sedatives** and **antianxiety drugs** should be used cautiously.

Treatment of Chronic Asthma

Whenever possible the obvious trigger factors should be avoided. **Desensitization** to allergens may be tried. The main drug treatment of chronic asthma is to interfere with the immune mechanisms, which can be achieved by (*i*) sympathomimetics; (*ii*) disodium cromoglycate; and (*iii*) corticosteroids.

Corticosteroids in Bronchial Asthma

The glucocorticoids and their synthetic analogues have an established place in the treatment of bronchial asthma. They are **life-saving** in an acute attack or status asthmaticus. It is not known exactly as to how the glucocorticoids affect the major components of reversible airway obstruction in asthma, namely bronchospasm, congestion and exudation. Probably they function as **non-specific anti-inflammatory agents** to provide relief from congestion and exudation **(Chap. 7.5).**

Beclomethasone dipropionate is a chlorinated analogue of betamethasone. It acts **locally** on the respiratory mucosa, and the metered-dose inhaler delivers 42 or 50 mcg/puff. Two or three puffs a day are sufficient in mild asthma. Baclomethasone inhalation allows `topical' treatment without major adverse effects like the suppression of the pituitary adrenal axis. It is highly effective locally but **poorly absorbed,** and the amount swallowed is largely inactivated during passage through the liver. However, topical corticosteroids may lead to **local atrophy** of the pharyngeal mucosa and **superinfection** with candida.

Regarding the mode of action of glucocorticoids in bronchial asthma, the views put forward are that: (*i*) they **augment the responsiveness** of the tissues (including the bronchial tissue) to catecholamine action; (*ii*) they **overcome or partially reverse the beta-adrenoceptor blockade** (which is supposed to progressively occur in an asthmatic patient in the natural course of the disease); and (*iii*) they **slow the rate of catecholamine metabolism** by COMT, thus facilitating the activation of adenylcyclase. These three factors tend to increase the levels of c-AMP in the catecholamine sensitive bronchial tissue thereby antagonizing bronchoconstriction. In addition it has been shown that the corticosteroids **inhibit the re-accumulation of histamine in the mast cells.**

Other corticosteroids for inhalation (aerosol) treatment of steroid-dependent bronchial asthma are **dexamethasone, flunisolide,** and **triamcinolone.**

Antihistamines in Bronchial Asthma

The antihistamines are almost ineffective in the treatment of bronchial asthma. This is probably because histamine is released from the sensitized mast cells in very high concentrations near the target cells, and the competitive blockade produced by mepyramine and other antihistamines is ineffective.

Antitussive Drugs

Coughing is a **protective reflex** which may be initiated by irritation in the pharnyx or in the deepest level of the respiratory tract. The **cough receptors** (chemo-and mechano-receptors) lie in the mucosa of the bronchial tree, from the nose to the distal bronchi. The impulses from these receptors are transmitted through the **vagus** and the **glossopharyngeal nerve** to the cough centre in the medulla. The cough centre has a **coordinating network with the respiratory** and **vomiting centres.** The different pathway involves the nerves supplying the abdomen, thoracic muscles, diaphragm and the glottis. It is often not advisible to completely suppress cough in cases of **chronic bronchitis** or **bronchiectasis,** as it may result in the retention of secretions in the tracheobronchial tree.

Classification

Antitussive agents can be divided into **two** groups: (*i*) the **centrally-acting** drugs which suppress the cough centre, and increase the cough threshold; and (*ii*) the **peripherally-acting** drugs which increase the threshold of the cough receptors, or act by relieving the irritation.

I. Centrally-acting-antitussives

(*i*) *Narcotic antitussives*

Codeine, hydrocodone, ethylmorphine, oxycodone.

(*ii*) *Non-narcotic antitussives*

Dextromethorphan, noscapine, propoxyphene, caramiphen.

II. Peripherally-acting antitussives

(*i*) *Mucosal anaesthetics*
Benzonatate, chlophedianol.

(*ii*) *Bronchodilators*
Ephedrine.

(*iii*) *Hydrating agents*
Steam, aerosols, fluids

(*iv*) *Miscellaneous*
Bromhexine, candy, syrup

The *central* antitussives are clinically more popular, compared to the *peripheral* antitussives, which only have a local soothing and demulcent effect and are employed as lozenges and syrups.

Narcotic Antitussives

Codeine

Codeine is an opium alkaloid, available both as sulphate and phosphate in **tablet, elixir** or **syrup** form. It is a very effective antitussive agent and **depresses the cough centre** in the medulla, resulting in an elevation of the cough threshold. When large doses are used **respiratory depression** may occur. Codeine has a potential for the development of dependence like the opioids, and should be used with caution. Codeine causes lesser analgesia, euphoria, hypnosis, respiratory depression, constipation, nausea and vomiting compared to morphine. **(Chap 2.6).** Its antitussive effect equals that of morphine. Thus morphine is hardly ever employed as an antitussive. The **usual adult dose** is 10 to 15 mg orally every 4 to 6 hours. The side effects include nausea and vomiting, constipation, drowsiness, pruritus and respiratory depression. It is **contraindicated** in bronchial asthma as it induces bronchospasm.

Hydrocodone bitartrate is similar to codeine in its action, but possesses a *greater* dependence liability. The dose is 5 to 10 mg every 4 to 6 hours, and the side effects are the same as those of codeine.

Ethylmorphine and **oxycodone** have codeine-like antitussive actions, but do not appear to have an advantage over codeine.

Non-narcotic Antitussives

Dextromethorphan

Dextromethorphan is a synthetic morphine derivative, and a very useful antitussive agent. It is devoid of an analgesic and sedative effect. Dextromethorphan (10 mg) is comparable to 15 mg of codeine in its antitussive activity. It has a very **low addiction liability.** The usual adult dose is 10 to 30 mg every 4 to 6 hours. The **side effects** include slight drowsiness, nausea and dizziness. It is a widely used antitussive.

Noscapine

Noscapine (narcotine) is an opium alkaloid and belongs to the benzylisoquinoline fraction. It has a **potent antitussive action,** almost equalling that of codeine. Although it is derived from opium, noscapine has no narcotic or analgesic effect. It is well absorbed from the gut. The usual adult dose is 15 to 30 mg three or four times daily. It has a wide margin of safety. **Side effects** include drowsiness, headache, nausea and allergic rhinitis.

Propoxyphene Napsylate

Propoxyphene is separable into its l-form and d-form. **The laevoform has antitussive properties, while the dextroform has analgesic action.** The antitussive action of 1-propoxyphene (50 mg) was found to be equivalent to 15 mg of codeine. It does not depress the CNS and respiration. The usual **adult dose** is 50 to 100 mg every 4 hours. The **side effects** include nausea, epigastric discomfort, skin rashes, urticaria, drowsiness and dizziness.

Caramiphen Ethanedisulfonate

Caramiphen raises the threshold of the cough reflex, and is less active than an equal dose of codeine. It has an **atropine like action** and exerts antisecretory and mydriatic effects. The **oral dose** is 10 to 20 mg three or four times daily. The **side effects** include nausea, dizziness and drowsiness.

The **peripherally-acting antitussives** are mucosal anaesthetics, bronchodilators, hydrating agents or demulcents. They provide a soothing effect by correcting the irritation to the cough receptors. In the treatment of cough the first step is to determine the cause and institute specific treatment. The antitussive agents are usually ineffective against cough associated with bronchial asthma.

Expectorants and Mucolytic Agents (Mucokinetic Agents)

Expectrorants and **mucolytic agents** alter the viscosity of the sputum, and promote the removal of secretions from the bronchial tree. A normal person is estimated to secrete almost 100 ml of mucus from the bronchial tree daily. In acute **non-bacterial bronchitis,** the secretions remain relatively thin, and the disease process is self-limited. In **infections** such as bacterial bronchitis, pneumonia, chronic bronchitis or bronchiectasis, the secretion is usually **thick, tenacious and frequently mucopurulent.** If it remains in the lungs, it becomes thicker and obstructs the airways. Blockade of larger airways may produce **segmental** or **lobar atelectasis.** It is in these situations that expectorants and mucolytic agents (collectively named as mucokinetic agents) play an important role. The mucokinetic agents are classified as under:

I. Inhalational agents (also effective orally)

(*i*) *Water*

(*ii*) *Saline solutions* - hypotonic, isotonic, hypertonic.

(*iii*) *Hygroscopic agents* - Glycerol guaiacolate, propylene glycol.

(*iv*) *True mucolytic agent* - Acetylcysteine, pancreatic dornase, trypsin, chymotrypsin, streptodornase and streptokinase.

(*v*) *Volatile agents* - Balsams and other volatile oils.

II. Oral agents

(*i*) *Vagal stimulants* - Creosote derivatives, terpenes, ipecacuanha.

(*ii*) *Direct mucokinetics* - Potassium iodide, ammonium chloride, bromhexine.

Glycerol guaiacolate is the most commonly used expectorant. It is used singly or in combination with dextromethorphan. The usual **adult dose** is 100 to 200 mg three or four times daily. **Side effects** are rare, but nausea, gastrointestinal discomfort and drowsiness may occur.

Propylene glycol is a **hygroscopic** agent with a sweet taste and demulcent properties. It potentiates the mucolytic actions of other mucokinetic agents. A 2 percent solution in water is isosmotic with serum, and is therefore non-irritating to the airways.

Acetylcysteine is a mucolytic agent, both effective *in vivo* and *in vitro*. It acts by opening the disulphide linkages in mucus, thereby lowering the viscosity. Acetylcysteine can be given by means of a **nebulizer** or **instilled** directly into the trachea. When given as an aerosol, it has a **bronchoconstrictive action,** and should be used with a bronchodilator. The **usual dosage** is 3 to 5 ml of 20 percent solution with a bronchodilator and saline when nebulized. It may be repeated three or four times daily. One to 2 ml of a 10 or 20 percent solution can be instilled directly into the trachea. **Side effects** include stomatitis, nausea, rhinorrhoea and sensitization to the drug.

Pancreatic dornase hydrolyses the deoxyribonucleoprotein of purulent sputum and thereby reduces its viscosity. The efficacy of the other enzymes listed above is doubtful.

Creosote derivatives. Hard woods such as beech are used as a source of creosote, which is a mixture of phenols having a characteristic odour. The most important components are **creosol** and **guaiacol. Creosote** is an antiseptic with an expectorant quality. When given orally it acts as a mucokinetic agent, both indirectly, by stimulating the gastric mucosa, and directly when the absorbed drug is secreted into the tracheobronchial tree.

Guaifenesin is a guaiacol derivative, which has replaced creosate as a mucokinetic agent. It is less irritating to the bowel and is absorbed more reliably. The usual **adult dose** is 100 to 200 mg every 3 to 4 hours.

Terpenes are volatile oils related to turpentine and are used in many cough remedies for their expectorant action. Such drugs include **anise oil, eucalyptus oil, lemon oil, pine oil, terpin hydrate** and **thymol.**

Terpin hydrate is the most popular agent. It is usually employed in combination with other agents in a dose of 125 to 300 mg every 6 hours.

Ipecacuanha. The extract of ipecacuanha (ipecac) is primarily used as an emetic **(Chap. 12).** In subemetic doses it is a potent stimulator of the **gastropulmonary mucokinetic vagal reflex,** and it promotes respiratory glandular secretion.

As an expectorant Ipecac syrup (ipecac, glycerine and syrup) is given in a dose of 0.5 to 2 ml orally three to four times daily.

Potassium iodide increases bronchial secretions by **reflex stimulation of the gastric mucosa.** It also increases the volume and decreases the viscosity of salivary, nasal and lacrimal secretions. The use of potassium iodide may lead to unpleasant hypersecretion in the eyes, nose and mouth. **Sneezing, conjunctival irritation, parotid swelling, thyroid enlargement** and **brassy taste** may be troublesome. The usual dosage is 0.3 g as plain or enteric coated tablets 3 to 4 times daily.

Ammonium chloride and other ammonium salts are active expectorants, but less potent than potassium iodide.

Bromhexine is an oral mucokinetic agent. It is obtained from the plant **Adhatoda vasica.** It has been used in this country as Vasaka for many years as a remedy for cough and asthma. The active constituents were found to be **adhatodic acid** and the alkaloid **vasicine,** from which benzylamine bromhexine was obtained. It acts by **depolymerization of the mucopolysaccharides** in the mucus, thereby lowering the viscosity. In addition, it also directly acts on the bronchial glands **liberating lysosomal enzymes** which digest the mucopolysaccharide fibres. The **usual dose** is 8 to 16 mg orally three times a day.

The use of expectorants in the treatment of chronic bronchitis and emphysema is probably beneficial. **Adequate hydration, postural drainage** and **chest physiotherapy** are usually quite effective in acute and chronic conditions to mobilize bronchial secretions.

Oxygen Therapy

Supplemental oxygen is widely used in ptients with **acute respiratory distress.** Mechanical ventilatory assistance may be needed in addition when the neural drive, muscle power or thoracic mechanics is disturbed or lost. There are many situations in which simultaneous mechanical assistance and oxygen is required, e.g., **central respiratory depression** due to narcotic drugs, **severe shock, acute** and **chronic pulmonary disease.** The pre-requisites for oxygen administration are, a patent and adequate airway, maintained if necessary by tracheal intubation or tracheostomy, and a positive pressure device and masks.

Technique of Oxygen Administration

The method of administration selected depends on the concentration of oxygen to be delivered to the lungs, and the need for ventilatory assistance. Oxygen from the cylinder should preferably be **bubbled through water** to humidify it before it is delivered to the patient's airway.

(*i*) **Oxygen tent.** Concentration of 25-50 percent oxygen can be reached, depending on the rate of inflow of oxygen.

(*ii*) **Head tents or hoods.** Concentrations from 50-80 percent can be reached, as they are smaller than tents.

(*iii*) **Nasal catheter or cannula (Prongs).** Concentrations from 40-60 percent can be reached, and this technique is **adequate for most purposes** and more acceptable to the patient.

(*iv*) **Endotracheal tube or facial masks.** 80 to 100 percent concentrations can be delivered by these methods.

(*v*) **Hyperbaric oxygen.** Oxygen can be administered under pressures greater than 1 atmosphere, and as high as 3 atmospheres in **special pressurized chambers.**

Mode of Action

Atmospheric air contains 20.9 percent oxygen, which exerts a partial pressure (PO_2) of 159 mm Hg in the inspired air. The PO_2 in the alveoli is about 100 mm Hg, and there is a gradient across the alveolar membrane, and the PO_2 in arterial blood is about 90 mm Hg. **Under usual conditions, haemoglobin is almost completely (96%) saturated with oxygen (except in anoxic anoxia).** Oxygen administration can act through the increase in dissolved oxygen which is from 0.3 to 2 ml/100 ml.

Therapeutic Uses

Oxygen administration is indicated in cases of anoxia: (*i*) **anoxic anoxia** due to inadequate ventilation, interference with diffusion, right-to-left shunts and ventilation-perfusionabnormalities;(*ii*)**anaemicanoxia,**whentheblood haemoglobin content is low or in cases of carbon monoxide poisoning; (*iii*) **stagnant anoxia** as in cases of shock; and (*iv*) **histotoxic anoxia** as occurs in cases of cyanide poisoning which exerts its lethal effect due to inactivation of cytochrome oxidase.

The chief clinical indications for oxygen therapy are: **acute respiratory failure** or **arrest; arterial hypoxia** due to **acute or chronic respiratory disease; congestive heart failure** or **vascular insufficiency; severe anaemia** or **haemolysis;** and certain **poisons like cyanide and carbon monoxide.** Mixed venous PO_2 values are the best guide for adequate whole-body tissue oxygenation. Such a monitoring is advisable to avoid or recognize the adverse effects of oxygen excess.

Oxygen Toxicity

Adverse reactions induced by oxygen administration are: (*i*) **respiratory tract irritation** involving the nose, pharynx and the trachea; (*ii*) **respiratory depression** due to a carbon dioxide wash out; and (*iii*) **retrolental fibroplasia** in premature infants who are administered oxygen in high concentrations.

Preparation

Medical oxygen is available in cylinders which are painted **white at the valve and down to the shoulder,** and the **remainder is painted black** (white shoulder, black body) according to British convention. The chemical symbol O_2 is clearly stamped on the cylinder valve. According to American convention oxygen cylinders are painted green. Commercial oxygen or welding oxygen is equally pure and may be used, if necessary.

Hyperbaric oxygen. (Oxygen administration between 2 and 3 atmospheres but never more that 4 atmospheres) administered in pressure chambers is effective in the treatment of **carbon monoxide poisoning** and of **gas gangrene** of a diffuse type with spreading muscle necrosis. At 3 atmospheres pressure and 100 percent oxygen, enough oxygen is dissolved in the blood (6 ml/100 ml) to meet the tissue needs, without haemoglobin desaturation. **Oxygen toxicity is increased at higher pressures.** Other applications (like in peripheral vascular disease, cerebrovascular accidents, coronary thrombosis, tumour therapy, preservation of organs and tissues for transplantation) are under evaluation. The value of hyperbaric oxygen in clinical practice is due to three biologic effects: the **relief of hypoxia and anoxia; the potentiation of ionizing radiation effect (radiosensitization);** and the **inhibition of bacterial growth** and **toxin production.**

RESPIRATORY STIMULANTS

The use of drugs to act as respiratory stimulants has been disappointing, as drugs which have a specific stimulant effect on the respiratory drive are not available.

The term "analeptic" is derived from the Greek work "analepticos" which means restorative or strengthening. Essentially analeptics are CNS stimulants, and some of them stimulate the respiratory centre in the medulla. They do not have a specific action on this area, and stimulate the cerebrospinal axis at all levels causing general arousal, and in larger doses produce convulsions **(Chap. 2.9).** The commonly employed analeptics are **nikethamide ethamivan** and **doxapram.**

Nikethamide stimulates the **carotid** and **aortic chemoreceptors** and increase the sensitivity of the respiratory centre to carbon dioxide. It has a stronger action on a depressed respiratory centre compared to a normally functioning centre. The *usual dose* is 2 ml of a 25 percent solution administered IM. It can be given intravenously.

Ethamivan has similar properties to nikethamide, but it has a shorter duration of action, and the effect of an intravenous dose lasts for about 10 minutes. It is given in doses of 150-400 mg IV, or by intravenous infusion at a rate of 20 mg/minute.

Doxapram is a **non-specific analeptic agent** used to stimulate respiration. Its therapeutic index expressed as convulsant dose 50/respiratory stimulant dose 50, is as high as 25. Thus it has a **wider margin of safety** compound to nikethamide and ethamivan. **Side effects** include tachycardia, cardiac arrhythmias, hypertension and vomiting. Doxapram is **administered by intravenous infusion** at an initial rate of 5 mg/minute. reduced to 2 mg/minute later. It may be administered by intravenous injection in a dose of 1 to 1.5 mg/kg body weight. It is **contraindicated** in hypertension, coronary artery disease, thyrotoxicosis, status asthmaticus and cerebrovascular accidents.

Doxapram, and caffeine sodium benzoate may be used as **temporary** measures to correct acute respiratory insufficiency in chronic obstructive lung disease, and to hasten recovery from anaesthesia. According to current opinion analeptics have no place in the management of poisioning by CNS depressant drugs (sedative-hypnotic drugs). **Mechanical assistance** to antagonize drug-induced respiratory depression is safer, better and more reliable.

❑❑❑

14

HEAVY METALS AND CHELATING AGENTS

The heavy metals occupied a prominent place in therapeutics, but now they have been replaced by safer agents. However, they are employed in industrial processes and a large number of workers are at risk of poisoning.

HEAVY METALS

The heavy metals produce their toxic effects by combining with chemical groups known as **ligands** (e.g., -SH, $-NH_2$, -OH), and by doing so they interfere with the functioning of cell constituents which require free ligands as their 'active sites'. They have a special affinity for **sulphydryl groups,** which are essential for the activity of many enzyme systems.

ARSENIC

Arsenic is a transition element or **metalloid.** Arsenicals containing trivalent arsenic were widely used in the treatment of **syphilis** in the past. Organic arsenicals are used in the treatment of **trypanosomiasis,** but they are not converted to free arsenic in the body. Certain arsenicals used as **pesticides, fungicides** and **rodenticides,** or used in **glass, electroplating, dyestuff, paint** and **cosmetic** industries can cause poisoning. Arsenicals are absorbed through mucous membrances. **Organic arsenicals are less toxic. In acute intoxication** there is widespread damage to the capillaries. There may be severe gastroenteritis, dysphagia, epigastric and abdominal pain, vomiting and watery or bloody diarrhoea. Jaundice, Oliguria, muscle cramps and irritability may occur. In **chronic intoxication,** the manifestations include peripheral or optic neuritis, conjunctivitis, diarrhoea, pigmentation of the skin, cirrhosis and dependent oedema. Arsenic has long been associated with palmer and planter keratoses and subsequent carcinomas. The **arsenical gas leuisite** is lipid-soluble and penetrates the skin, causing vesication. Arsenic poisoning is treated with **dimercaprol.**

ANTIMONY

Antimonials such as antimony potassium tartrate (tartar emetic) and stibophen (trivalent compound) are used in the treatment of **schistosomiasis**. The pentavalent compounds are used in the treatment of **leishmaniasis**. The toxicity is similar to that of arsenic, and the treatment is the same.

MERCURY

The organic mercurials are now *rarely* used as diuretics. Compounds containing mercury continue to be used as **antiseptics** and **germicides.** Mercury is also used in the manufacture of **herbicides, fungicides** and **scientific instruments**. Poisoning can occur due to the inhalation of the vaporized metal, or by absorption through the skin. **Acute poisoning** causes haemorrhagic gastroenteritis, shock, renal failure and liver damage. **Chronic poisoning** causes anorexia, stomatitis, colitis, anaemia, hypertension, renal failure and multiple neurological disorders. Treatment is by chelation with **dimercaprol.**

BISMUTH

Insoluble bismuth salts are used in the treatment of peptic ulcer. Soluble bismuth salts are a rare cause of chronic intoxication. The toxic effects are similar to those of mercury. Treatment is by chelation with **dimercaprol.**

GOLD

Gold compounds are now sometimes used in the treatment of **rheumatoid arthritis.** The available preparations contain gold in the **aurous** form, combined with sulphur. They are water soluble and are rapidly absorbed on intramuscular injection. In the blood they are strongly bound to alpha globulin. Gold is excreted by the kidneys slowly, and can be detected in urine upto one year after administration. **Sodium aurothiomalate** is the most commonly used preparation.

Untoward reactions of gold salts include pruritus, dermatitis, glossitis, stomatitis, peripheral neuritis and encephalopathy. Blood dyscrasias, hepatic and renal damage may occur. Treatment of poisoning is with **dimercaprol**.

LEAD

Lead has many industrial uses, and poisoning can occur during the manufacture of **paints, batteries, rubber** and **glazed pottery.** Tetraethyl lead is an `anti-knock' agent added to petrol, and released in **car exhaust fumes,** and can be absorbed through the skin and lung mucosa. Inhalation of lead is a hazard in industry when metals or painted metals are cut or burned. Lead from water pipes can contaminate water and food.

About 10 percent of ingested lead is absorbed. The half-life of lead in the body is 700 to 800 days. The usual intake (diet and air) is about 300 mcg/day. Toxicity occurs if the intake reaches 1000 mcg/day. The toxic level of lead in the serum is 1.3 mg/litre.

Acute intoxication is characterized by **lead encephalopathy** or abdominal pain. In chronic intoxication anaemia is usually present, as lead inhibits the synthesis of heme; protoporphyrin is not converted to heme and haemoglobin. Its immediate precursor, protoporphyrin IX appears in the urine in large amounts. Due to an increased turnover of red blood cells there is **reticulocytosis** and **stippling of erythrocytes.** Hypermotility of the intestinal muscles causes **"lead colic".** In addition there may be a **lead palsy or myopathy, lead line on the gingival margins, and radipaque "lead lines" at the body metaphyses.** Lead poisoning is a chronic occupational hazard. Treatment is by chelation of lead with **calcium disodium edetate** and **dimercaprol.**

SILVER

Silver compounds are used only for their local actions. **Silver nitrate** sticks are used for their caustic (corrosive) action to prevent the formation of granulation tissue. Topical **silver sulphadiazine** is used to prevent the infection of burns. Soluble silver salts are corrosive and ingestion leads to **haemorrhagic gastroenteritis** and **shock.** Chronic silver poisoning can lead to slate-grey pigmentation of the skin, eyes and mucous membranes (argyria). **Sodium thiosulphate solution** injected into the affected areas may reduce the discolouration. **Chelating agents are ineffective in the treatment as silver is present mainly in the free form.**

CHELATING AGENTS

Chelating agents are metal-binding **antidotal chemicals** which bind the ions of heavy metals by incorporating them into an **inner ring structure** in the molecule and rendering them biologically inactive. This is brought about by chemical groups called **ligands.** The chemical complex thus formed is called a **chelate,** is stable and nontoxic, and is excreted by the kidneys. This process of complex formation is known as **chelation,** and the term is derived from the Greek word "chele" which means "claw". The chelating agents are also designated as **heavy metal antagonists.**

Ideally, the chelating agents should be water-soluble, non-toxic and capable of distribution throughout the body. Their major disadvantage is that **none of them is entirely specific** for a given metallic ion, and are capable of removing important ions like calcium and enzyme cofactors. These compounds have flexible molecules with two or more electronegative groups, and thus are classed as: **bidentate** (dimercaprol, penicillamine); or **polydentate** (disodium edetate, calcium disodium edetate, desferrioxamine, and trientine).

DIMERCAPROL (BAL, BRITISH ANTI-LEUISITE)

Dimercaprol was developed during World War II in Great Britain. It was synthesized during a systematic study of possible antidotes against arsenic-containing vesicant war gases like **Leuisite** (hence the name BAL). It was known that arsenicals combine with sulphydryl (-SH) groups, and each atom of the metal combines with two of thiol groups **(Fig. 14.1).** Thus dimercaprol was synthesized which is a **dithiol.** It forms very stable 1 : 1 chelates with **arsenic, mercury** and **lead.** The chelates formed with gold, bismuth, antimony and nickel are less stable.

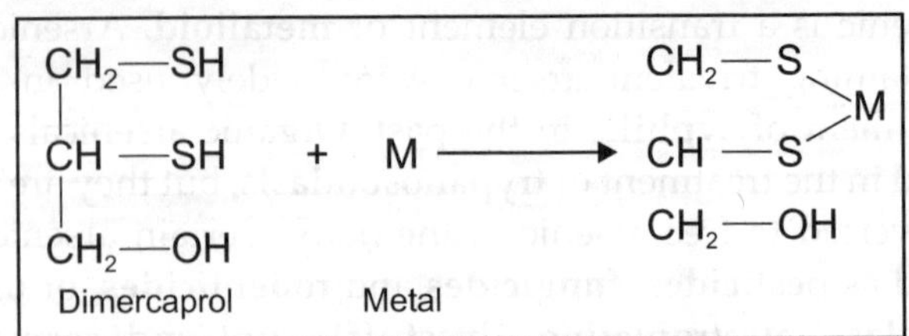

Fig. 14.1: Dimercaprol: Metal complex.

After intramuscular injection dimercaprol plasma levels peak in 30 minutes, and the drug has a very short half-life. Non-complexed drug is excreted rapidly in the urine following its hepatic conjugation to glucuronide. **The chelate is excreted in urine.** Liver damage increases the half-life of the drug.

Therapeutic Uses

Dimercaprol is still the primary agent used in the treatment or arsenic and mercury poisoning. It forms complexes immediately with free metals in tissue fluids, thus causing dissociation of bound metal from tissues by the *Law of Mass Action*. The therapeutic objectives in using dimercaprol are: **firstly**, to protect the essential tissue enzymes from the circulating metallic ions; and **secondly**, to promote the excretion of the metal in the non-toxic chelate form via the kidneys, thereby decreasing the quantity of the poison in the body.

Toxicity

Dimercaprol is a toxic drug, and side effects develop in about half of the patients. Side effects include pain at the site of injection, **hypertension, tachycardia, nausea, vomiting, chest tightness, sweating, abdominal pain, burning** and **tingling sensations, lacrimation, salivation** and **rhinorrhoea.** In high doses it causes convulsions, coma, hyperglycaemia, and metabolic acidosis. Alkalinization of the urine is claimed to protect against the dissociation of the dimercaprol-metal complex and nephrotoxicity.

Dose. Dimercaprol (BAL) is available in peanut oil (100 mg/ml) for injection. Dosage ranges from 3 to 5 mg/kg body weight by deep intramuscular injection, and repeated 1 to 4 times daily depending on the severity of the poisoning.

DMSA (2,3 dimercaptosuccinic acid) is structurally similar to dimercaprol, but is effective when given orally in the treatment of lead poisoning. It also promotes urinary excretion of copper.

Penicillamine

Penicillamine (Dimethylcysteine) is a synthetic sulphydryl compound, and is an inactive degradation product of penicillin. It combines with **copper, iron, mercury, lead** and **arsenic** to form soluble complexes that are excreted by the kidney. It does not chelate calcium or strontium.

Penicillamine is well absorbed from the gut, and is partly oxidized to its disulphide derivative and excreted by the kidney. The **N-acetyl derivative of penicillamine** is more stable, and used in mercury poisoning.

Therapeutic Uses

Penicillamine is used for the removal of copper in **hepatolenticular degeneration (Wilson's disease).** In this condition, copper is deposited in the tissue leading to hepatic cirrhosis and extrapyramidal neurological damage. It is also used in **cystinuria** where it promotes the excretion of cystine as penicillamine-cystine disulphide, which is about 50 times more soluble than cystine. Penicillamine has also been tried in cases of **rheumatoid arthritis,** where it interferes with the formation of the rheumatoid factor, and increases the ratio of "soluble" to "insoluble" collagen in connective tissue.

Toxicity

Side effects include **nausea, anorexia, vomiting, rashes, fever, thrombocytopenia,** and **rarely agranulocytosis** and **nephrotic syndrome.** It may also cause eosinophilia and a decrease in serum iron levels.

Dose. Penicillamine (Cuprimine) is available in 250 mg capsules. The dose for adults is 250 mg four times daily, with gradual increase not to exceed 5 g per day. Pyridoxine replacement (50 mg weekly) should be done simultaneously.

EDTA (Ethylene Diamine Tetra-acetic Acid) and Derivatives

EDTA is a powerful chelating agent. Its affinity for metallic ions increases in the written order: **Ca, Mn, Fe, Co, Zn, Cu, Ni, Cd** and **Pb.** It has been estimated that its affinity for lead (Pb) is 10^7 times that for calcium (Ca). It is insoluble in water and is not used therapeutically.

Disodium edetate (Endrate) is dangerous when injected intravenously, since it chelates calcium, and may lead to **hypocalcaemic tetany, coagulation abnormalities** or even **fatal hypocalcaemia.** Its main use is for the topical treatment of lime burns in the eye.

Calcium disodium edetate (Calcium disodium versenate) is used primarily to treat **lead poisoning (plumbism).** The chelated forms are stable, water-soluble and readily excreted by the kidneys. **Calcium disodium edetate does not produce a negative calcium balance, i.e., it does not induce hypocalcaemia.** It is capable of binding and excreting zinc and copper, but the action is insignificant. It is ineffective in binding metals like gold, nickel, manganese, mercury or arsenic.

Absorption of calcium disodium edetate after oral administration is poor. It is given by intravenous or intramuscular injection, and its plasma half-life is 60 minutes. It is not metabolized in the body and does not enter body cells or the cerebrospinal fluid, and is eliminated by the kidney, unaffected by urinary pH. **Side effects** are common and include thrombophlebitis, hypotension, lacrimation, muscle pain, sneezing and chills. Renal damage and transient bone marrow depression may occur.

Dose. Calcium disodium edetate is available as a solution (200 mg/ml) in 5 ml containers, to be diluted for intravenous infusion. The daily dose should not be exceed 50 mg/kg/day in adults, or 30 mg/kg/day in children.

DTPA (Diethylene Triamine Penta-acetic Acid) is similar to EDTA, but has a greater affinity for all metal ions. Its main use is in the treatment of **poisoning with radioactive metals,** where the object is to remove the metal as fast as possible. However, it is unable to mobilize radium and strontium from the body.

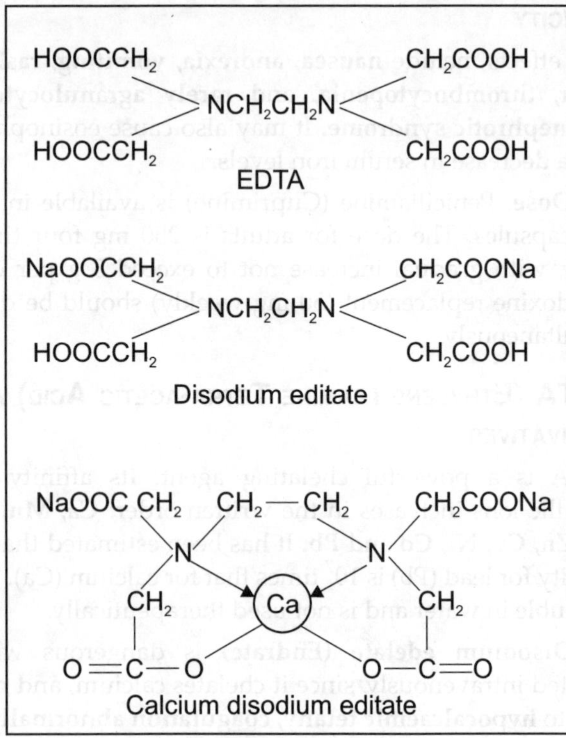

Fig. 14.2: Calcium disodium edetate.

Desferrioxamine Mesylate

Desferroxamine (Deferoxamine) obtained from *Streptomyces pilosus,* is a chelating agent used in the treatment of **iron poisoning.** It forms stable 1 : 1 complexes with inorganic iron, and **can remove iron from ferritin** and **transferrin, but not from haemoglobin** or **cytochromes.** Its affinity for iron is 30 times that for calcium, and forms a stable non-toxic complex excreted in the urine. It is used in the management of **secondary haemochromatosis** and **thalassaemia** to promote iron excretion.

Toxicity

If desferrioxamine is administered intravenously rapidly, it may cause **hypotension, urticaria** and **tachycardia.** The site of intramuscular or subcutaneous injection is painful. Long-term treatment may cause **blurred vision, diarrhoea, leg cramps** and **cataracts.**

Dose. For the treatment of **iron intoxication** desferrioxamine may be infused intravenously at a rate of not more than 15 mg/kg body weight per hour to a maximal dose of 80 mg/kg in 24 hours. Or, it may be administered in a dose of 2 g 1M every 12 hours until the clinical condition is satisfactory and the serum iron level is less than 500 mcg/100 ml.

Trientine

Trientine (triethylenetetramine) is a polydendate copper chelating agent, used in the treatment of **Wilson's disease** (hepatolentricular degeneration). But unlike penicillamine it is **not** useful in cystinuria and rheumatoid arthritis. It is claimed to be less toxic than penicillamine. The **adult dose** in 750-1250 mg/day orally in 2 or 4 divided doses on an empty stomach (1 hour before, or 2 hours after meals). **Side effect** include iron deficiency, dermatitis, heartburn, cramps, muscle pain, and systemic lupus-like syndrome.

To **summarize,** the principal uses of the chelating agents are: **dimercaprol** for arsenic, mercury and gold; **calcium disodium edetate** for lead; **penicillamine** for copper and lead; and **desferrioxamine** for iron poisoning **(Table 14-1). Trientine** is a newer copper chelating agent. These agents have to be used with extreme care and caution.

Table 14-1 *Chelating agents for heavy metal poisoning*

Chelating agent	*Antidote for poisoning*	*Mode of administration (usual regimen)*	
Dimercaprol (BAL)	Arsenic Mercury Gold	IM:	2.5 mg/kg at 4 to 6 hour intervals on the first 2 days. Then reduced to two injections daily for a total of 10 days.
Penicillamine N-acetyl-D, L penicillamine	Copper Lead Iron Mercury	Orally: IV:	250 mg four times a day. 1 g in 250 to 500 ml of 5% dextrose solution by intravenous drip over 1 hr twice daily for 5 days.
Calcium disodium edetate (Calcium disodium Versenate)	Lead		
Desferrioxamine	Iron	IV:	400 to 600 mg once or twice daily. In acute poisoning, 8 to 12 g by gastric tube plus 2 g IM or IV.
Trientine	Copper	Orally:	750-1250 mg/day in 2-4 divided doses on an empty stomach.

15

VACCINES AND ANTISERA

Edward Jenner (1749-1823), the discoverer of vaccine against smallpox, got the idea from a dairy maid who asserted that she would never get smallpox as she had already had cowpox. Jenner's observation that an attack of cowpox conferred immunity against smallpox was the beginning of therapy with vaccines and sera. These biological products are potentially dangerous and are under stricter drug control. They are manufactured and sold under strict surveillance of the Government Health authorities. To make them safe for use, each package of these biologicals bears on its label the date of manufacture, expiry **date, official potency in terms of units, and a certificate that the product identified by the batch number, has passed the official toxicity tests.** Proper storage of this biological material is essential for maintenance of their potency.

Immunity

The vaccines and antisera are employed to produce immunity or resistance in the body to infection. Immunity is a state of relative resistance to disease, which develops after exposure to the specific agent responsible for infection. Immunity may be of two kinds: (*i*) Active immunity; and (*ii*) Passive immunity.

Active Immunity

Active immunity may be acquired naturally by a person due to a previous attack by the same organism, as in the case of smallpox. **Artificial active immunity** is acquired by graded doses of **vaccines, toxins** or **toxoids** that act as antigens, and stimulate the gradual formation of **immune antibodies** by the reticuloendothelial and lymphoid tissues. These antibodies then **circulate in the blood,** particularly in its **gamma globulin fraction.** After immunization whenever the antigen enters the body, the antibodies neutralize it, and avoid tissue damage. Active immunity may be acquired by administering: (*i*) **living organisms;** (*ii*) **attenuated or treated organisms,** e.g., smallpox and rabies; (*iii*) **dead or killed organisms,** e.g., enteric fever and whooping cough; (*iv*) **separated exotoxins,** e.g., scarlet fever; and (*v*) **the toxoid** *or* **modified toxins,** e.g., diphtheria and tetanus.

The term *vaccination* interpreted today includes all the above measures for active immunization. **The most significant achievemnet of active immunization is the global eradication of smallpox from the World.**

Passive Immunity

Passive immunity is conferred by administering immune sera containing **preformed antibodies** or **antitoxins** (prepared from animals or humans who have been actively immunized), to individuals who have either not been previously exposed to the pathogen, or are not immunized adequately. Passive immunization is therefore indicated in cases of actual infection with a specific organism. **Obviously, passive immunization is inferior to active immunication, and the effect is short-lived.** But it is of *immediate* value, as the borrowed antibodies/antitoxins attack the invaders or neutralize the toxins exactly as if they were formed by the patients own tissues.

If the animals used as sources for immune sera are actively immunized by bacterial cells, the sera contain antibodies which kill, lyse, agglutinate or clump the organisms, making them inocuous. Such a serum is called an **antibacterial serum.** On the other hand, if toxins are used to actively immunize animals, the antiserum produced neutralizes the toxins rendering them inocuous. Such a serum is called **antitoxic serum.** Sometimes serum of patients recovering from viral diseases like measles or poliomyelitis is used to confer passive immunity. Such a serum is called **convalescent antiviral serum.**

PRODUCTS FOR ACTIVE IMMUNITY

Antigenic products employed for confering active immunity are mainly of *two* types: **Vaccines made from microorganisms** - viruses, bacteria, and rickettsia— responsible for various diseases, and **toxoids** prepared from the exotoxins of bacteria by treatment with formaldehyde followed by purification. By this process the material loses its toxic property, but maintains its antigenic specificity for the active toxin. Antitoxins formed against these toxoids will neutralize the avtive toxins. Some of the available varieties of vaccines are listed below :

1. **Inactivated (killed) vaccines**
   - (*i*) **Bacterial inactivated vaccines**
     Pertussis (Whooping Cough), Plague, Cholera, Typhoid.
   - (*ii*) **Rickettsial inactivated vaccines**
     Epidemic typhus, Rocky Mountain Spotted Fever, Q fever, Scrub typhus.
   - (*iii*) **Viral inactivated vaccines**
     Influenza, Measles, Mumps, Polimyelitis, Rabies.
2. **Live attenuated vaccines**
   - (*i*) **Bacterial live vaccines**
     Plague, tuberculosis.
   - (*ii*) **Viral live vaccines**
     Smallpox, Polimyelitis, Measles, German measles, Mumps, Yellow fever, Rabies.
3. **Toxoids**

   Diphtheria and Tetanus, often used together (DT), and sometimes combined with pertussis (DTP) vaccine.

PRODUCTS FOR PASSIVE IMMUNITY

These products are more or less purified and concentrated antibody solutions derived either from man or animals (usually horses) who have been exposed to infectious organisms, or to their exotoxins. These immune sera (antisera) may contain **antitoxins, antivenins, antibacterial** or **antiviral antibodies.** Hypersensitivity reactions are very likely if the antibodies are derived from animal sera.

Human blood serum also serves as a source of immune globulins containing antibodies against various bacterial and viral infections. Such homologous sera have the advantage of being free of foreign allergenic proteins that are responsible for horse serum reactions. **Immune serum globulin,** a product obtained from pooled plasma of human donors, contains antibodies against various common diseases like **measles, German measles, poliomyclitis** and **infectious hepatitis**. Other specific **hyperimmune gamma** globulins against specific diseases are also available. Some of the available products are listed below :

1. **Human Gamma Globulin**

   Immune serum globulin is derived from pools of human plasma by low-temperature ethanol fractionation. It can be injected IM or SC, but not intravenously. It has been employed clinically for the management of **hypogammaglobulinaemia, viral hepatitis, measles** and **German measles.**
2. **Specific Hyperimmune Human Gamma Globulins**

   Tetanus, Rabies, Vaccinia, Chickenpox, Rh sensitization, Pertussis.
3. **Antitoxins and Antisera from Animals**

   Diphtheria antitoxin, Botulism antitoxin, Tetanus antitoxin, Antivenins, Gas gangrene antitoxin, Rabies antiserum. Some important immunization schedules are listed in **Table 15-1.**

Table 15.1 *Some important immunization schedules*

Disease	*Organism*	*Active immunization*	*Passive immunization*
Botulism	*Clostridium botulinum*	—	*Botulism Antitoxin:* IM or IV: Prophylactic 2500 U; Therapeutic 10,000 to 50,000 U.
Cholera	*Vibrio comma*	*Cholera Vaccine:* SC or IM 0.5 ml; then 1 ml at least 7 days later. Repeat 0.5 ml dose every 6 months, if necessary.	—
Diphtheria	*Corynebacterium diphtheriae*	*Diphtheria Toxid:* SC injections of 0.5 to 1.0 ml, atleast 4 weeks apart. *Adsorbed Diphtheria Toxoid:* SC or IM: 2 injections of 0.5 to 1.0 ml at least 4 weeks apart, a third reinforcing dose 6 to 12 months later.	*Diphtheria Antitoxin:* IM or IV; Prophylactic 1000 to 10,000 U; Therapeutic 10,000 to 80,000 U.

Table 15.1 Contd...

Disease	*Organism*	*Active immunization*	*Passive immunization*
		Diagnostic Diphtheria Toxin: for Schick test, 0.1 ml intradermal.	
Hepatitis	Hepatitis B virus	—	*Hepatitis B Immune Globulin Human:* 0.06 ml/kg body weight (adult dose 3.0 to 5.0 ml) as soon as possible after exposure, preferably within 7 days. Administer IM in the gluteal or deltoid region and take care to avoid IV injection.
Influenza	Various strains of influenza virus	*Influenza Virus Vaccine:* SC two injection of 1.0 ml, at least 2 months apart.	—
Measles	Various strains of rubeola virus	*Meales Virus Vaccine, Live, Attenuated:* SC, 0.5 ml. *Mealses Virus Vaccine, Inactivated:* IM, 0.5 to 1 ml in 3 doses at montly intervals.	*Measles Immune Globulin* Prophylactic IM 0.22 ml/kg body weight. *Immune Serum Globulin:* Prophylactic IM 0.22 ml/kg; modification of measles 0.045 ml/kg.
Mumps	Various strains of epidemic parotitis virus	*Mumps Virus Vaccine, Live Attenuated:* SC, a single dose of not less than 5000 $TCID_{50}$ for active prophylaxis. *Mumps Vaccine, Inactivated Virus:* SC or IM, 2 injections of 1 ml each administered at intervals of 1-4 weeks.	*Mumps Immune Globulin* Human IM, 1.5 to 4.5 ml depending on body weight.
Pertussis	*Bordetella pertussis*	*Pertussis Vaccine:* SC, 3 injections, usually 0.5 ml at least 4 weeks apart.	*Pertussis Immune Globulin:* Prophylactic 1 or 2 IM injections at 1 week interval in amounts recommended by manufacturer. Therapeutc 2 IM injections at 1 day interval.
Plague	*Pasturella pestis*	*Plagua Vaccine:* SC, 2 injections of 0.5 to 1 ml at least 7 days apart.	—
Pneumonia	Pneumococus	*Pneumococcal Vaccine, Polyvalent:* SC or IM, 0.5 ml in the deltoid or lateral thigh.	—
Poliomyelitis	Various strains of polio virus	*Poliomyelitis Vaccine (Salk Vaccine):* SC, 2 injetions of 1 ml, 4 to 6 weeks apart, then 1 ml at least 7 months later. *Live Oral Poliovirus Vaccine, Monovalent:* Each of the monovalent vaccines is given separately at intervals of 6 to 8 weeks. *Live Oral Poliovirus Vaccine, trivalent (O.P.V.):* Two drops to 2 ml depending on the concentration used, are administered for primary immunization in 3 doses at intervals of 8 weeks.	—
Rabies	Various strains or rabies virus	*Rabies Vaccine:* SC, 2 ml of a 5% suspension, or its equivalent daily for 14 to 21 days for post-exposure immunoprophylaxis.	*Antirabies Serum:* IM, 20 U/lb of body weight.
Smallpox	Variola virus	*Smallpox Vaccine:* Percutaneous injection of the contents of one capillary tube by the multiple puncture method.	—
Tetanus	*Clostridium tetani*	*Tetanus Toxoid (T.T).* SC, 3 injection of 0.5 ml at least 4 weeks apart. *Adsorbed Tetanus Toxoid:* IM or SC, 2 injections of 0.5 ml at least 4 weeks apart.	*Tetanus Antitoxin:* IM or SC, Prophylactic 1500 to 10,000 U; Therapeutic 10,000 to 100,000 U. *Tetanus Immune Globulin: IM* Prophylactic 250 U; Therapeutic 1500 U or more.
Tuberculosis	*Mycobacterium tuberculosis*	*BCG Vaccine:* Intradermal, 0.1 ml; Percutaneous 1 drop on surface of skin, administered by multiple puncture method. Old *Tuberculin (Diagnostic aid):* Intradermal 0.00001 to 0.001 ml. *Purified Protein Derivative of tuberculin (Diagnostic aid):* intradermal 0.02 to 5.0 mcg.	—

Table 15.1 Contd...

Disease	*Organism*	*Active immunization*	*Passive immunization*
Typhoid	*Salmonella typhosa*	*Typhoid Vaccine:* SC, 3 injections of 0.5 ml at least 7 days apart. *Typhoid and Paratyphoid Vaccine:* SC, 3 injections of 0.5 ml at least 7 days apart.	—
Typhus	*Rickettsia prowazekii*	*Typhoid Vaccine:* SC, 2 injections of 1 ml at least 7 days apart.	—
Yellow fever	Virus	*Yellow Fever Vaccine:* SC, 0.5 ml.	—

Triple Antigen (DPT)

Diphtheria toxoid is the type of preparation preferred for long term prophylactic immunization against diphtheria. It is available alone or combined with **tetanus toxoid** (DT), or with **tetanus toxoid** and **pertussis vaccine** (DPT). This "triple antigen" is used for active immunization against **diphtheria, tetanus** *and* **pertussis (whooping cough).** Each 0.5 ml of DPT contains Diphtheria Toxoid 25 Lf, Tetanus Toxoid 5 Lf and *B. pertussis* 20,000 million, adsorbed on aluminium phosphate with thiomersal 0.013 percent as preservative. It is suitable for immunization of young children. **Three doses** of 0.5 ml IM at intervals of 4-8 weeks are administered. A **fourth booster dose** of 0.5 ml IM is given about 1 year later, and **another booster dose** may be given at the school entry age of 5 years.

Antivenins

Antivenins are concentrated globulin fraction of sera of animals (horse) immunized with the **venoms of poisonous snakes (rattlesnakes, vipers, cobras and others), spiders and scropions.**

Haffkine Bio-pharmaceuticals, Mumbai manufacture **antivenine-lyophilized polyvalent anti-snake venom serum** injection for use in the emergency treatment of poisonous snakebite. Kasauli in India manufactures antisera against cobra and Russell's viper (venom of Rusell's viper has strong coagulant activity). The pseudoglobulin fraction of the immune serum contains the concentrated antitoxin. Vials of 10 ml are standardized to neutralize 2 mg of cobra venom and 4 mg of viper venom per ml. **For dosage and route of administration the manufacturer's directions must be followed, and testing for hypersensitivity must be done prior to administration.**

The steps in the management of poisonous snakebite are:

(*i*) Slow down the spread of venom by applying a **tourniquet** and **cold compacts.** Immobilize the part, in addition.

(*ii*) Remove as much venom as possible from the site of the bite by **incision** and **suction.**

(*iii*) Neutralize the venom with **antivenin** administered systemically, and also by regional limb perfusion.

(*iv*) **General supportive therapy:** administer corticosteroids, blood, antibiotics, fluid and electrolytes; tetanus and gas gangrene prophylaxis, and cardiorespiratory support should be instituted, if necessary.

National Immunization Schedule

The National Immunization Schedule remommended by the Government of India to protect pregnant women from **tetanus,** and children from six disabling diseases, namely, **tuberculosis, diphtheria, whooping cough, tetanus, poliomyelitis** and **measles** is as under:

For the Pregnant Woman	
Early in pregnancy	– T.T.-1 or T.T. Booster (injection)
One month after T.T-1	– T.T.-2 (injection)
For the Infant	
After 1½ months	– B.C.G. (injection) – D.P.T.-1 (injection) and – O.P.V.-1 (dose)
After 2½ months	– D.P.T.-2 (injection) and – O.P.V.-2 (dose)
After 3½ months	– D.P.T.-3 (injection) and – O.P.V.-3 (dose)
After 9 months	– Measles (injection)
After 16 to 24 months	– D.P.T. Booster (injection and – O.P.V. Booster (dose)

If the infant has been delivered in a hospital or clinic, the BCG injection and OPV dose should be given at birth. Adherence to the above schedule significantly reduces the risk of the mentioned diseases.

Some Special Vaccines

Rabies Vaccine

Active immunization against rabies is primarily an emergency measure used together with hyperimmune globulin to protect individuals bitten by rabid animals (post-exposure immunization). Sometimes immunization has to be routinely carried out in persons with high-risk (pre-exposure immunization). Both in post and pre-exposure treatment, the vaccine of choice is the **human diploid cell rabies vaccine** which is **more potent** and significantly less reactogenic than older vaccines.

Human Diploid Cell Rabies Vaccine (HDCV), is a freeze-dried preparation containing the inactivated Wistar PM strain of fixed rabies virus. It is supplied as 1 ml single dose vials of liophilized vaccine with accompanying diluent. The HDCV has almost entirely replaced the nerve tissue and duck embryo vaccines because: (*i*) it requires a **lower number of doses;** (*ii*) it elicits a **more rapid and higher antibody response;** (*iii*) it does *not* cause serious adverse reactions or complications; and (*iv*) it has proved clinically effective in controlled studies.

For **post-exposure immunization** the complete series consists of six 1 ml IM injections given on days 0-3-7-14-30-90 (WHO recommendation, 1977). **Specific antirabies hyperimmune globulin** *(RIG)* is given only once at the beginning of treatment with the first dose of the vaccine or upto 7-8 days after, if it was not immediately possible. From the 8th day on, passive antibody administration is needless because an active antibody response to HDCV starts by this time. For **pre-exposure immunization** the primary series consists of three 1 ml doses of HDCV given IM on day 0-7-28. A **booster** is then given every 2 years.

Small local reactions like pain, erythema, and swelling may occur at the site of HDCV injection. Very infrequently mild general reactions like malaise and headache have been reported.

HDCV today is the ideal antirabies vaccine. If it is not available the **Purified check-embryo cell (PCEC) rabies vaccine** may be used. A complete course after exposure consist of a total of six 1 ml IM injections: one injection on each of the days 0-3-7-14-30-90. RIG may be given with the 1st injection as described above. For protective preexposure vaccination the course consists of 3 injections, one injection on each of days 0-28-56, or if immediate prophylaxis is necessary one injection is given on days 0-7-21. **Booster** vaccination is given after 1 year and then after 2 to 5 years.

Measles Virus Vaccine

Active immunization against measles is **recommended for all children**. In developing countries where malnutrition is common and immunization incomplete, the course of illness and secondary bacterial infection is more severe with the mortality as high as 25 percent.

Measles vaccine is a freeze-dried preparation containing live attenuated measles virus. For vaccine production the virus is grown on a *chick embryo cell culture*. Measles vaccine is available as a monovalent (measles only), bivalent (measles-rubella) and trivalent (measles-mumps-rubella) preparation. The live virus content in each immunizing dose is not less than 1000 $TCID_{50}$ (dose infecting 50 percent of tissue cultures calculated according to the Reed and Muench of Kaerbers method). The dried vaccine is reconstituted before use with diluent and is given by the subcutaneous or IM route. It can be given concurrently with the DPT (Diphtheria and Tetanus toxoid and Pertussis Vaccine) and/or OPV (Oral Polio Vaccine) administration. Measles vaccine is recommended for use between 9 to 15 months.

The measles virus enters the respiratory tract and in a short time is carried into the blood (viremia) and other body tissues. Protection is achieved by post-vaccinal circulating antibodies which can neutralize the virus locally or during the primary viremic phase. Effective antibody levels can be detected in blood for *more than 10 years after vaccination. Booster doses are not required* when the initial vaccination is performed at the proper age. Local reactions like urticaria at the injection site are rare and trivial.

Oral Polio Vaccine

For active immunization against poliomyelitis the **trivalent oral polio vaccine** *(OPV)* is the vaccine of choice for infants, children and adolescents (upto 18 years). Poliovirus has three serological types—called type 1, type 2 and type 3—which possess specific antigens and do not induce reciprocal immunity. Thus, the trivalent vaccine is used. Each dose of trivalent vaccine contains about 1,400,000 $TCID_{50}$ (1,000,000 type 1; 100,000 type 2; 300,000 type 3). These doses are usually contained in a volume of 0.1 ml (2 or 3 drop). Ordinary OPV must be stored frozen at -20°C or less, since thawed non-stabilized vaccine maintains its potency for about 3 months at 0-4°C, and for only a few hours at room temperature. Addition of stabilizers like magnesium chloride or sucrose markedly improves the stability of OPV at higher temperatures.

Primary immunization (commenced at 2 or 3 months of age) with trivalent OPV consists of 3 doses, two administered 6-8 weeks apart, and the third 8-12 months after the second dose. A fourth reinforcing dose is then administered before entering school (3 years). Breast feeding dose not interfere with the immunizing power of OPV, but some experts recommend water instead of the breast feeds before and after the administration of the vaccine in infants. OPV does not produce any significant untoward effects.

Meningococcal Polysaccharide Vaccine

Active immunization against *N. meningitidis* of groups, A, C, Y and W-135 is recommended in the control of epidemics of cerebrospinal meningitis, and as a preventive measure in closed communities. Immunization is also indicated for travellers to endemic areas, and in the chemoprophylaxis for contacts of acute cases.

Four types of meningococcal vaccine are currently available, i.e., two monovalent A or C vaccines, a bivalent A/C vaccine, and a quadrivalent A/C/Y/W-135 vaccine. Vaccine consist of capsular polysaccharide precipitated from the bacterial culture.

One 0.5 ml dose of any one of the four mentioned vaccines is injected subcutaneously. In infants immunized with A vaccine two doses 3 to 4 months apart may be required. The precise duration of post-vaccinal immunity is not definite, but it is generally accepted that the group A and group C vaccines give **protection for 3 years and one year** respectively. **Adverse reactions** are infrequent and mainly consist of local erythema which lasts for 1 or 2 days. The effectiveness of this vaccine against the carrier state is uncertain.

Hypersensitivity Reactions

Many persons are hypersensitive to animal protein and drugs. If such material is injected they are likely to develop anaphylaxis. To safeguard against anaphylactic reactions the following steps must be observed:

1. **Intradermal test.** Diluted (1:10) test material is injected intradermally in an amount of 0.1 ml, which raises a bleb. The site is observed for 15 minutes. The appearance of **erythema** and **oedema** with **wheal** formation within 15 minutes is suggestive of specific hypersensitivity.
2. **Conjunctival test.** May be done as an alternative to the intradermal test. One drop of 1:10 dilution of the test material is instilled into a normal conjunctival sac. Itching, lacrimation and redness within 5 minutes is indicative of hypersensitivity. One drop of sterile physiologic saline is instilled into the other eye to serve as control.
3. Past history of any food or drug allergy must be obtained.
4. A syringe containing 1 ml **adrenaline** (1:1000) must be readily available. Other drugs like corticosteroids, and an antihistamine like **diphenhydramine** for injection, and **oxygen** for inhalation must also be at hand, in case an anaphylactic reaction occurs. A **tourniquet** and an intratracheal tube should be readily available, in case needed.

In case hypersensitivity to the specifically indicated material is detected by the above tests, **desensitization** may be cautiously attempted, or an alternative preparation be used.

In this chapter a brief overview of the many active and passive immunizing agents used for prevention and treatment of various infections has been presented. Since many of these diseases, particularly those caused by viruses, can not yet be effectively treated with chemotherapeutic agents and antibiotics, active immunoprophylaxis with viral vaccines and bacterial toxoids is still very valuable.

❑❑❑

16

DIAGNOSTIC AGENTS, HYPERBARIC OXYGEN AND ENZYMES IN THERAPY

Many drugs are used as diagnostic agents to reveal the presence of disease or determine the degree of damage existing in certain organs. Some of them have already been mentioned in the earlier Chapters. Drugs like **edrophonium** for the diagnosis of myasthenia gravis **(Chap 3.2): phentolamine, histamine** or **tyramine** for the diagnosis of pheochromocytoma **(Chap. 3.5);** and **histamine, betazole hydrochloride** (Histalog) or **azuresin** (Diagnex blue) may be used to test gastric acid secretion **(Chap. 11.1).**

TESTS FOR HEPATIC FUNCTION

(*i*) **To test metabolic function**

Laevulose: In normal individuals if 50 g of laevulose is administered orally, the blood levels do not rise above 12 mg/100 ml, and the levels fall below 6.0 mg after 2½ hours. A maximum rise above 14 mg or failure to fall below 7.0 mg by 2½ hours indicates liver damage. The principle of the test is that only the liver and intestine utilize laevulose.

(*ii*) **To test capacity for detoxification**

Sodium benzoate: It is used in the intravenous hippuric acid test. If liver function is normal benzoic acid is excreted as hippuric acid. After emptying the bladder, 20 ml of sodium benzoate solution containing 1.77 g of salt (equivalent to 1.5 g of benzoic acid) is injected intravenously over 5 minutes. The urine is collected exactly 1 hour later, and its hippuric acid content is estimated. Normally at least 1 g of hippuric acid (equal to 0.68 g of benzoic acid) is excreted in the first hour. In the absence of dehydration, nephritis or obstruction of the urinary tract, this test is informative of liver damage.

(*iii*) **To test excretory function**

Phenoltetrachlorophthalein is excreted by the liver. The disodium salt is injected intravenously, and excretion takes place exclusively through the biliary passages. The excretion is diminished in proportion to the amount of liver tissue damage. **Bromsulphalein** (BSP) is a similar compound used for testing liver function. In this test 5 mg/kg of the dye is injected intravenously, and specimens of blood are collected after 5 and 45 minutes. The value of the dye in blood exceeding 10 percent at 45 minutes indicates liver damage.

TESTS FOR RENAL FUNCTION

Renal efficiency tests are based on the capacity of the kidney to excrete certain substances. Excretion of dyes like **indigo carmine, methylene blue** and **phenol red** can be recorded as an index of kidney function. The patient forces fluid for about an hour before the test, and then empties the urinary bladder. Then **indigo carmine** is injected intravenously, or **methylene blue** or **phenol red** may be injected intramuscularly. Urine samples are collected at specified intervals, and the amount of dye that appears in each sample is measured **colorimetrically**.

Mannitol and **inulin** are carbohydrates which are filtered by the glomeruli, and are minimally reabsorbed by the tubules. Mannitol and inulin clearance rates give the measure of glomerular function.

Sodium-p-aminohippurate is a substance secreted by the kidney tubules, and is used to determine the capacity of the tubules to perform their excretory function. **Diodrast**, and organic iodine compound, or **sodium-p-aminohippurate** may be employed to measure renal blood flow. The later compound is preferred due to its low toxicity.

Tests for Glandular Function

Certain drugs are employed to test the functional status of endocrine glands like the anterior pituitary, thyroid, pancreas, and the adrenal cortex and medulla.

Metyrapone (Metopirone) is employed to test anterior pituitary function. Ordinarily when a person is subjected to stress, the anterior pituitary increases its output of ACTH **(Chap. 7.1)**, which in turn stimulates the adrenal cortex to secrete more corticosterioids. Metyrapone inhibits corticosteriod synthesis and secretion, and in the normal person would lead to an increased release of ACTH from the anterior pituitary. But in patients with poor pituitary function this response (increased release of ACTH) to the administration of metyrapone is markedly reduced. This is indicative of **hypopituitarism.**

Corticotrophin (ACTH) itself may be used to test adrenocortical function. Normally, an IM injection of ACTH is followed by a marked increase in the blood level of adrenocorticoids. This does not occur in patients with adrenal insufficiency. Based on similar grounds, ACTH may be infused intravenously slowly, and the urine is tested for increased corticosteroid levels. If no increase occurs; the patient in all likelihood is suffering from **Addison's disease.**

Thyrotrophin (TSH) and **radioactive sodium iodide** are employed in the diagnosis of thyroid malfunction in hypothyroidism and hyperthyroidism. **Tolbutamide sodium** is used intravenously as a diagnostic test for diabetes mellitus (see later). Drugs including **phentolamine** (Regitine), **histamine** or **tyramine** used in the diagnosis of pheochromocytoma have been referred to earlier in this chapter.

Tests for Circulatory Function

Dyes and other drugs are injected directly into the blood stream to determine certain aspects of circulatory function, e.g., blood volume and cardiac output.

Evans blue is injected intravenously to determine plasma volume in patients of heart failure, shock or other

Table 16.1 *Contrast media used for radiographic diagnosis*

Compound	*Use*	*Dosage*
Barium sulphate	Outlining viscera of the gut	300 g orally or 400 g rectally in a suitable suspension.
Calcium ipodate	Cholecystography Cholecystography	3 g as a single dose 10 to 12 hrs before radiographic exam.
Ethiodized oil	Hysterosalpingography	0.5 to 20 ml intracavitary.
Iodized oil injection	Lymphangiograpy Bronchography	10 ml by special injection.
Iodopyracet Injection	Ascending urethrography Hysterosalpingography	20 ml.
Iopanic acid	Cholecystography	3 g orally.
Iophendylate Injection	Myelography	6 ml by special injection, or intrathecally.
Meglumine diatriozoate Injection	Urography Cerebral angiography Angiocardiography Translumbar aortography	25 ml IV of a 60% solution.
Meglumine iodipamide Injection	Cholecystography Cholecystography	20 ml of a 52% solution.
Meglumine iothalamate Injection	Urography Cerebral angiography Aortography Angiocardiography Splenography Venography	30 ml of a 60% solution IV.
Propyliodone, sterile suspension	Bronchography	0.2 ml/kg body weight intratracheal to a maximum of 18 ml.
Sodium diatrizoate Injection	Intravenous urography Retrograde pyelography	30 ml of a 50% solution IV.
Sodium methiodal Injection	IV and retrograde urography	20 g IV in 50 ml.

circulatory abnormalities. The degree to which the dye is diluted in the plasma is measured colorimetrically. **Indocyanine green** (Cardio-Green) is a dye used mainly to determine cardiac output, but it may also be used to determine blood flow through the liver. **Fluorescein sodium** administered intravenously is used to determine circulation time. The time required for the dye to move from the arm vein to various other blood vessels is measured by detecting fluorescence at the second site under ultraviolet light. This drug is excreted in the bile, and may be used for outlining the bile ducts and gall bladder. Occasionally nausea and vomiting may occur. Fluorescein sodium in a 2 percent aqueous solution is applied topically to the cornea to detect minute foreign bodies or **abrasions on the cornea**. It is readily detected because of its marked fluorescence. It does not stain the normal cornea, but produces a deep colouration of ulcers or other defects in the cornea and conjunctiva. **Sodium dehydrocholate** (Decholin sodium) is a bile salt, and is used for determining circulation time, and in the diagnosis and treatment of biliary track disorders. This drug is not a dye, instead the time it takes to travel from the arm-to-tongue is measured when the patient reports a **bitter taste**. It produces serious adverse reactions like nausea, vomiting, diarrhoea and sometimes even fatal anaphylactoid reactions. Hence, its routine use is not recommended.

Radiopaque Media for Radiographic Diagnosis

Radiopaque substances are employed as contrast media for visualization of various internal organs including the **gall bladder** and **gastrointestinal tract, kidneys** and the **urinary tract, lungs** and **other organs (Table 16-1).** Except for barium sulphate, all the contrast media are iodinated organic chemicals. Iodine is a heavy atom (atomic weight, 132), is radiopaque and hence of value in **roentgenography**. Some of the contrast media are taken by mouth for local radiopaque effects in the gut, or are absorbed and excreted into organs like gall baldder. Other media are introduced directly into the organ to be visualized like the **bronchial tree, uterus** or the **spinal tract**. Recently developed contrast media are safe enough to be cautiously injected intravenously or even intra-arterially.

Above is the list of compounds employed for radiographic diagnostic procedures like **cholecystography, urography, arteriography, bronchography, myelography** and various **other special procedures**. The contrast media are substances of low direct issue toxicity, but parenteral administration of any of the organic iodine compounds may lead to untoward reactions, and occasionally fatalities. The deaths may be immediate due to hypersensitivity reactions, or delayed due to renal or liver disease. *These agents should not be used in the presence of serious liver and kidney damage*. As a precautionary measure iodine hypersensitivity testing (ocular, intradermal or oral test) must be carried out in every patient undergoing the radiographic procedure.

Diagnosis by Radioactive Isotopes

Radioactive isotopes are often used for diagnostic purposes. For this only beta radiation, which consists of high speed negatively charged electrons, and gamma radiation, similar to X-rays are of importance. Beta-emiting isotopes have low penetration power (upto 7 mm of water), and are used for the determination of substances contained in body fluids or excretion which can be readily removed from the patient. **Gamma radiation** has a very high penetrating power, and can pass through water or the human body tissues with little loss of energy. Even extremely low concentrations of isotopically labelled chemicals can be detected externally by instruments that pick up gamma rays emitted from organs in which the isotope is concentrated.

Radioactive iodine is used to diagnose thyroid disorders. **Radioactive phosphorus** is employed for localizing brain tumours. Some useful radioisotopes employed in either elemental from (P^{32}); bound to protein (I^{131} human serum albumin, IHSA); or chemically incorporated into organic molecules (L-triiodothyronine I^{131}) are listed in **Table 16-2.**

When radioactive material is used, due care must be taken to avoid exposure of the patients and personnel to radiation.

DIAGNOSTIC TEST FOR DIABETES MELLITUS

Tolbutamide Tolerance Test

Tolbutamide sodium powder 1.0 g (0.081 g as sodium salt) is freshly dissolved in 20 ml of sterile water for injection. This solution is administered intravenously over 2 to 3 minutes to the patient, and blood glucose levels after 20 and 30 minutes are compared with the pre-injection fasting level. In the normal (non-diabetic) person, tolbutamide causes fast and progressive fall in blood glucose approximately 50 percent of the control value within 30 minutes. In diabetic patients, the glucose level usually falls only by 10 percent. This **tolbutamide tolerance test** is also useful in diagnosing **hyperinsulinism** due to pancreatic islet cell tumours. This test should be concluded by oral administration of glucose to restore the blood sugar level.

Hyperbaric Oxygen

Hyperbaric oxygen therapy involves the administration of oxygen to subjects at pressures between 2 and 3 atmospheres, but never more than 4 atmospheres. Hyperbaric oxygenation is usually accomplished in **"pressure chambers"** in which the ambient gas is oxygen under pressure. The duration of safe exposure depends on the oxygen pressure, and is limited by the susceptibility of the retinal cells to oxygen toxicity. It has been observed that visual acuity and fields of vision are reduced after 2 hours of oxygen exposure at 3 atmospheres pressure.

Mode of action. The therapeutic value of hyperbaric oxygen is possibly due to its three biologic effects: (*i*)

Table 16.2 *Some radioisotopes used for diagnostic studies*

Diagnostic study	*Radioisotope used*
Thyroid Function	
Radio-iodine uptake and thyroid scintigram pattern	I^{131}, I^{131} L-triiodothyronine
Cardiovascular function	
Blood volume	I^{131} human serun albumin (IHSA)
Red cell mass	Cr^{51}
Circulation time	Na^{24}, IHSA
Cardiac output	IHSA, I^{131} Hippuran
Renal function	
Renogram	I^{131} Hippuran, Hg^{203} Neohydrin
Renal scintigram pattern	Hg^{197}, Hg^{203} Chlormerodrin
Intestinal absorption	
Vitamin B_{12} absorption study (Schilling test)	$Cobalt^{57}$ or $Cobalt^{60}$ labelled cyanocobalamin
Radioiron absorption study	Fe^{59} citrate
Organ scanning and localization	
Brain scanning	Hg^{197}, IHSA, Cu^{64}, P^{32}
Liver scanning	Au^{98}, I^{131} Rose Bengal
Spleen scanning	Cr^{51}-tagged red cells (heated)
Bone scanning	Ca^{47}, Sr^{89}, Ca^{45}
Lung scanning	Heat-denatured IHSA

relief of hypoxia and anoxia; (*ii*) potentiation of ionizing radiations, i.e., a radiosensitizing effect; and (*iii*) inhibition of bacterial growth and toxin production.

Therapeutic Uses

1. **Relief of hypoxia and anoxia.** In cardiovascular surgery specially before inflow occlusion; for the prevention of traumatic ischaemia; treatment of carbon monoxide and cyanide poisoning; and treatment of decompression shock in divers and aviators, hyperbaric oxygenation may be tried. Other indications are **peripheral vascular disease, coronary thrombosis** and **cerebrovascular accidents**. It may also be used to combat hypoxia due to **acute pulmonary oedema** and **hyaline membrane disease**.
2. **Radiosensitization.** During radiotherapy hyperbaric oxygen may be employed to potentiate the effect of radiation, leading to a reduction in the total dose needed for therapeutic effect.
3. **Inhibition of bacterial growth and toxin production.** It is employed in the control of anaerobic infections like gas gangrene (*Clostridium welchii*) and tetanus. In the management of extensive burns, hyperbaric oxyen therapy exerts a bacteriostatic effect and promotes healing.
4. It may also be employed for the preservation of organs and tissues to be transplanted.

Enzymes in Therapy

An enzyme is a biochemical catalyst produced by living cells, but capable of acting independently of the cells producing it. The substance acted upon by an enzyme is called the **substrate**. Many enzymes have been isolated in pure crystalline form, and are protein in nature. Enzymes sometimes require an additional substance to activate them. Such nonspecific substances are called activators, e.g., hydrochloric acid for pepsin; specific substances which act selectively with certain enzymes only are called **coenzymes**, e.g., enterokinase for trypsinogen. Enzymes of many types are present in the body for catalysing a number of chemical reactions. More than 650 enzymes have been described.

Enzymes used in therapeutics are mainly derived from three sources: (*i*) **Mammalian enzymes**, viz., hyaluronidase, trypsin, chymotrypsin, alpha chymotrypsin, pancreatic dornase, fibrinolysin; (*ii*) **Bacterial enzymes**, viz., streptokinase-streptodornase; and (*iii*) **Plant enzymes**, viz., papain and chymopapain.

Mammalian Enzymes

Hyaluronidase for injection (Hyalase, Wydase). It is a sterile, dry, soluble product obtained from mammalian testes. It depolymerizes hyaluronic acid, the cement substance of connective tissue, and increases the rate of absorption of fluids given subcutaneously. It is a *spreading factor* which increases the diffusion of fluid in the connective tissue.

Therapeutic uses. Hyaluronidase effect increases the dispersion and absorption of fluids and other drugs. Hyaluronidase injection is used: (*i*) **hypodermoclysis**; (*ii*) with **local anaesthetics**; (*iii*) as an adjunct in **subcutaneous urography**, for improving the absorption of the radiopaque agent; (*iv*) to aid **reabsorption of haematomas**; and (*v*) to minimize tumefaction during surgery, and for reducing postoperative oedema.

Dosage. Hyaluronidase is available in a dry, lyophilized form, and is to be freshly dissolved in physiological saline. Commercial preparations contain 150 and 1500 U.S.P. hyaluronidase units. The prepared solution is injected into the tubing at the beginning of hypodermoclysis (subcutaneous infusion of fluids), or added to the solution for infusion.

Trypsin crystallized (Tryptar, Parenzyme). This is a proteolytic enzyme obtained from bovine pancreas. It acts directly and hydrolyses naturally occurring proteins. A freshly prepared solution is used for rapid and safe **debridement of surfaces covered with necrotic tissue** *and* **abscesses**, or for **irrigation of pleural and nasal cavities**. It is used for the liquefaction of coagulated blood and exudates, and less frequently for the digestion of fibrous tissue. It is administered intramuscularly, or dissolved beneath the tongue for the treatment of thrombophlebitis, contusions with ecchymosis, varicose and other skin ulcers, and bronchopulmonary disease. **Trypsin digests only non-viable cells, their debris and bacteria**. Side effects include local histamine-like effects. Used topically in wounds, it may cause a burning sensation. IM injections are painful. Anaphylactic shock may occur in patients previously treated with trypsin. It is contraindicated in patients with hepatic dysfunction, and should never be administered intravenously.

Dosage. Trypsin is administered **topically, sublingually** and **intramuscularly**. Wet dressings and irrigations should be repeated every 3 hours. Intramuscularly 2.5 to 5 mg doses are given 4 times daily. Trypsin in oil is stable (5 mg/ml), and is injected deeply into the gluteal muscle. **Buccal tablets** (5 mg each) are available for sublingual administration. Trypsin crystallized for aerosol 250, 000 N.F. units per ml is available for inhalations of 1 ml aerosols 3 to 6 times daily. Trypsin is also available with chymotrypsin as a tablet.

Chymotrypsin (Chymar). Crystallized chymotrypsin obtained from the bovine pancreas, is an **endopeptidase** that hydrolyses ester and peptide bonds. Its mechanism of action is similar to that of trypsin, but it differs from the latter in that its spectrum of hydrolytic activity is much broader; both IM and oral administrations give measurable blood levels; and it is relatively stable in human intestinal juice for about half an hour. Chymotrypsin in high doses has shown some **anti-inflammatory** activity in animals only, when administered prior to the production of inflammation. Thus, its systemic clinical usefulness for its anti-inflammatory action is **questionable**. Chymotrypsin is a foreign protein and sensitivity reactions may develop on repeated use.

Therapeutic uses. It is reported to be useful in a number of skin conditions, ulceration, and infections in the external ear canal. Its usefulness in inflammatory states secondary to surgical or physical trauma is unproven.

Dosage. Chymotrypsin is marketed as a powder in vials (300 to 750 U.S.P. units), and as tablets (50,000 to 100,000 U.S.P. units). The usual oral dose is 1 to 2 tablets 4 times daily. Combination tablets (chymoral) or trypsin and chymotrypsin in the ratio of 6:1 are available, and used for acute inflammatory oedema.

Alpha-chymotrypsin (Alpha-Chymar). This agent has similar proteolytic activity as chymotrypsin. It is used in **cataract** operations to loosen the lens after the incision of the cornea, termed as **"enzymatic zonulolysis"**. It is possible to remove the lens within its capsule, and with greater ease. Alpha-chymotrypsin injections contain 750 units to be dissolved in 5 ml of sterile saline. For zonulolysis the posterior chamber is irrigated with 2 ml of enzyme solution (150 units/ml).

Desoxyribonuclease (Pancreatic Dornase, Dornavac). This is an enzyme obtained from the aqueous extracts of beef pancreas. It splits desoxyribonucleic acid (DNA) into many smaller molecules, and also digests desoxyribonucleoprotein, which comprises between 30 and 70 percent of the sediment of purulent material of the bronchopulmonary tree. The discharge is converted from a viscous exudate to a thinner material which is readily expectorated when an aerosol of this agent is inhalded. Sensitivity reactions may be encountered rarely.

Dosage. Pancreatic dornase is freshly prepared in sterile isotonic saline (100,000 units in 2 ml), and administered by an aerosolizing apparatus. One or 2 ml may be inhaled once to three times daily for 2 to 6 weeks.

Fibrinolysin (Actase, Thrombolysin). Human fibrinolysin (Plasmin) is derived from the activation of human plasminogen by purified streptokinase. Fibrinolysin dissolves fresh clots, and may be employed as a **thrombolytic agent** in the treatment of **thrombophlebitis, phlebitis** and **pulmonary embolism**. It is given by IV infusion. It may be used as an adjunct to anticoagulant therapy.

Fibrinuclease (Elase) is a combination of **fibrinolysin** and **desoxyribonuclease** used to lyse fibrin and liquefy pus. It helps the **removal of necrotic debris associated with vaginitis and cervicitis**; and for the removal of exudates from wounds, ulcers and burns. Fresh solutions are applied topically, or by irrigation. Hyperaemia of the part may occur.

Bacterial Enzymes

Streptokinase-Streptodornase (Varidase). It is a mixture of proteolytic enzymes derived from cultures of *Streptococcus haemolyticus*. Streptokinase rapidly activates plasminogen to form plasmin, which dissolves fibrin; streptodornase is active against desoxyribonucleic acid, which is a component of pus, and produces liquefaction of the viscous material. These enzymes are used together in solution.

Therapeutic uses. Streptokinase-streptodornase is used to: (*i*) liquefy clotted blood or fibrinous and purulent material caused by injury or inflammation; (*ii*) aid anti-infective drugs; and (*iii*) stimulate healing of wounds. This preparation is used as an adjunct in the treatment of empyema, haemothorax, chronic suppuration, infected wounds and osteomyelitis. It does not act on living cells, and can be injected directly into body cavities or applied locally.

Dosage. Vials are available containing streptokinase 100,000 units and streptodornase 25,000 units as powder for preparing solutions for topical use, and instillation into closed body cavities. It is also available in tablet form.

Two other bacterial proteolytic enzymes are **Collagenase** derived from *Clostridium histolyticum*; and **Sutilains** derived from *Bacillus subtilis*.

Plant Enzymes

Papain (Papase) and Chymopapain (Discase). These potent proteolytic enzymes, or proteases, are isolated from the latex of *Carica papaya*. They are available as aids to digestion, in which they may substitute pepsin in the gastric juice. They may be used topically as papain powder for digesting fibrinoid and purulent discharges in wounds. **Chymopapain is under trial for the removal of nucleus pulposus of prolapsed intervertebral discs.**

Radionuclide Imaging

Radionuclide imaging is the general term used to describe those external counting procedures in nuclear medicine which detect and display the distribution of administered radioactive material in the human body. Depending on the problem, a particular radioactive tracer, termed a **radiopharmaceutical**, is selected and administered to the patient, and an imaging procedure is performed.

Radionuclide imaging, also known as **radioisotope scanning**, includes a number of procedures useful in the study of both localized and systemic disease processes. Its use in assessing function makes it an important procedure in monitoring treatment. Depending upon the radiopharmaceutical administered, regional pathology like metastatic or primary bone tumour, pulmonary emboli, liver metastases, renal function, brain tumour or thyroid pathology can be studied. Today imaging procedures are available for the study of the **skeleton, thyroid, lungs, heart, kidney** and **several other organs** and **tissues**. Regarding the instrumentation involved, the two basic types of imaging systems for most of the external counting procedures are: (*i*) the **rectilinear scanner**; and (*ii*) the **single** or **multiple crystal scintillation camera** to provide two- or three-dimensional images or the distribution of radioactivity.

The important properties of radiopharmaceuticals can be described in *five* major areas: (*i*) **chemistry of the carrier molecules, and the radiopharmaceutical, (*ii*) biological localization, (*iii*) kinetics, (*iv*) pharmacological properties, and (*v*) absorbed radiation dose.**

As a general rule, it is preferable to use radionuclides which deposit only small amounts of energy in the patient, while providing high photon yields within the energy range suitable for imaging, i.e, radionuclides with a high photon yield to radiation dose ratio. Radionuclides which best approach these requiements are those which decay by isomeric transition, or electron capture. The radionuclide most requently used for diagnostic imaging is **technetium-99 m ($^{99m}T_C$)**, and decays by isomeric transition. It serves as the radioactive component in majority of imaging procedures, and has a half-life of 6.03 hours. **Gallium-67 (67Ga)** citrate is used for the localization of inflammatory processes and tumours. It decays by electron capture and releases three different gamma photons. Further, apart from having an efficient supply of photons, the half-life of the radionuclide must be sufficient to allow localization and imaging in the tissue under study, without giving an unnecessary radiation dose to the patient.

The pharmacological properties of radiopharmaceuticals must fulfill the requirements placed on unlabelled material used for diagnosis or treatment. Administered intravenously or by other routes, these materials must be sterile, pyrogen-free and at a suitable pH. Short-life radionuclides like ^{11}C (t½ = 20.3 min), ^{13}N (t½ = 10.0 min), ^{15}O (t½ = 124 sec), 81 m kr (t½ = 130.0 sec) and others are expected to play a role in nuclear medicine imaging in the future.

❑❑❑

17

NEWER DRUG'S DIGEST

Alemtuzumab

Alemtuzumab is a monoclonal antibody mainly used in the treatment of *chronic lymphocytic leukaemia* (CLL), and *T-cell lymphoma.* It targets CD52 protein on the surface of mature lymphocytes, and is used as second line therapy for CLL. Alemtuzumab has been found to be effective in cases of CLL who have failed to respond to combinations of cyclophosphamide, fludarabine, or rituximab. Other uses include therapeutic regimens for *marrow* and *kidney transplantation.* Alemtuzumab also provides some relief in autoimmune diseases like *multiple sclerosis* (MS). In trials, it reduced the number of attacks in patients of MS helping them to recover lost functions. Perhaps it leads to repair of damaged brain tissue.

Adverse reactions include post-infusion hypotension, rigors, fever and bronchospasm. Common side effects are muscle aches, fatigue, headache, dizziness, angioedema and skin rashes. It is *contra-indicated* in patients with active infection, immunodeficiency, and Type I hypersensitivity. Dosage regimens are yet to be finalized based on clinical studies.

ANASTROZOLE

Anastrozole is a drug used to treat *breast cancer after surgery,* and for *metastases* in postmenopausal women. *Mode of action:* In postmenopausal women, the main supply of oestrogen is through the conversion of androgens produced by the adrenal glands into oestrogens. This is carried out by the enzyme *aromatase* by a process of *aromatization.* Anastrozole is an *aromatase inhibitor.* Others in the group are *letrozole* and *exemestane.* It is known that elevated oestrogen levels increase the severity of breast cancer. **Anastrozoie** reversibly binds to the aromatase enzyme, and by *competitive inhibition* the levels of oestrogens in the body are lowered. Anastrozole is preferred for treating postmenopausal women who are *oestrogen* receptor positive. But even receptor negative patients are benefited. It can be used alone or in combination with agents like tamoxifen. *Uses:* Anastrozole is used in postmenopausal women to treat *early* and *advanced breast cancer. Side effects* include hot flushes, vaginal dryness and bleeding, anorexia, nausea, vomiting, diarrhoea, headache, thinning of hair, arthralgia, osteoporosis, and bone fractures. *Dose*: 0.5 mg to 1 mg daily. The length of treatment depends on the individual patient.

AVANAFIL

Avanafil is a new orally active *phosphodiesterase type* 5 (PDE5) inhibitor for the treatment of *erectile dysfunction* (ED). It has demonstrated greater specificity combined with a more rapid onset of action, compared to available agents (sildenafil, vardenafil, tadalafil). Avanafil with nitroglycerin causes smaller changes in blood pressure for a shorter duration. Thus avanafil is safer for patients using drugs for heart problems.

Avanafil starts working within 15 minutes, and the effect ends within one and a half hours. In comparison, Viagra starts working in 30 minutes, and the effect wears off in about 8 hours. Currently trials with avanafil are being carried out with 100, 200 and 300 mg doses. The new pill is less likely to cause the classic Viagra headaches and similar problems.

AZELASTINE

Azelastine is a potent, second generation, selective histamine-H_1-receptor antagonist. *Mode of action:* It has a triple mode of action: (*i*) antihistamine effect; (*ii*) mast cell stabilization; and (*iii*) mild-to-moderate anti-inflammatory effect. *Indications:* Azelastine *nasal spray* (0.1% and 0.15% solution) is used for the treatment of seasonal and perennial *allergic rhinitis, vasomotor rhinitis, rhinorrhoea,* and *sneezing* in adults and children over 5 years of age. Usually one spray/nostril twice daily is effective. Azelastine *eye drops* (0.05%) are effective against *seasonal* and *perennial allergic conjunctivitis,* relieving itching, lacrimation and redness. Usually one drop in each eye is administered bid or tid. It has a fairly rapid onset of action, and the effect lasts for 12 hours. A combination of nasal spray and eye drops is effective in *rhinoconjunctivitis. Adverse effects* include brief eye burning/stinging, bitter taste, headache, nasal burning, and drowsiness.

BENDAMUSTINE

Bendamustine is a *cytotoxic* drug belonging to the *nitrogen mustard* sub-class of *alkylating* agents. *Mode of action:* It is an alkylating agent causing *infra-strand* and *inter-strand cross-links* between DNA bases. On IV infusion it is mainly metabolised by liver *cytochrome* P450, and about 95% of it is bound to albumin. Only free bendamustine is active having a half-life of 6-10 minutes, and a terminal half-life of 30 minutes. It is excreted primarily by the kidneys. *Uses:* It is used in the treatment of *chronic lymphatic leukaemias* (CLL), and *lymphomas* (B-cell non-Hodgkin's lymphomas). It is also being tried as "salvage therapy" in *breast cancer,* and for treatment of sarcoma. It is used as a *monotherapy* or in combination with cytotoxics like etoposide, methotrexate, prednisone, rituximab, and vincristine. *Side effects* include nausea, vomiting, diarrhoea, fatigue, loss of appetite, cough, weight loss, rashes, stomatitis, immunosuppression, anaemia, and thrombocytopenia. *Dose*: It is administered intravenously in a dose of 100 mg/m2 over 30 minutes on day 1 and 2 of a 28-day cycle, up to six cycles.

BREMELANOTIDE

Melanocortinergic agents are currently being investigated for their possible therapeutic role in *male* and *female sexual dysfunction.* These agents affect many physiological responses, including *sexual behaviour.* Several *melanocortins* including HP-228, THIQ, and bremelanotide (PT-141) have shown *erectogenic* properties, thought to be due to their binding to *melanocortin receptors* in the CNS, specially the *hypothalamus.* Bremelanotide, a *nasally* administered synthetic peptide is the only agent that has been clinically studied in both males and females. *Mode of action:* Bremelanotide is a synthetic analog of *alpha-melanocyte stimulating hormone,* and it is an *agonist* at the melanocortin receptors MC3R and MC4R. *Uses:* In clinical trials intranasal dose of bremelanotide has been studied for its potential effects on *sexual arousal* and *desire in premenopausal women* with a sexual disorder. Change in *vaginal pulse amplitude* and *vaginal photoplathysmography* was used to monitor vaginal *vasocongestion.* Many women reported moderate or high sexual desire following intranasal bremelanotide treatment versus placebo in double-blind studies.

Bremelanotide, a *melanocortin agonist,* is also being evaluated for its effect on *erectile dysfunction(ED)* in males. Results show that bremelanotide is well tolerated, and is not associated with hypotension observed with phosphodiesterase-5 (PDE-5) inhibitors like sildenafil. Current researches validate the use of *melanocortinergic agents* for the treatment of both *male* and *female sexual dysfunction.* Different dosages and treatment regimens for intranasally administered bremelanotide are being worked out.

Calcipotriol

Calcipotriol is a synthetic derivative of calcitriol, and is used in the treatment of *psoriasis.* The exact *mode of action* in relieving psoriasis is unknown. Calcipotriol and calcitriol have comparable affinity for the *vitamin D receptor* (VDR), but Calcipotriol is less active in regulating calcium metabolism. The VDR belongs to the *steroid/thyroid receptor* family, and is located in many tissues including the thyroid, bone, kidney and T-cells. The T-cells are known to play a role in psoriasis, and calcipotriol binds to the VDR and modulates T-cell function. Calcipotriol has shown an excellent safety profile in clinical trials, and hypercalcaemia occurs only rarely. *Use:* Available as a cream, ointment, or scalp solution (50 meg/ml). It is to be applied twice daily to *plaque psoriasis,* sparing the face for 2 weeks. Calcipotriol is also available in combination with *betamethasone* for use in severe cases.

Cefpodoxime

Cefpodoxime proxetil is an oral *third-generation cephalosporin.* It is active against most *Gram positive* and *Gram negative* bacteria, but is ineffective against *Pseudomonas aeruginosa, Enterococcus* and *Bacterioides faragilis.* It is used to treat *acute otitis media, pharyngitis,* and *sinusitis.* Caution is to be observed in patients with renal impairment, penicillin sensitivity, pregnancy and breast feeding. It is *contra-indicated* in cephalosporin hypersensitivity and porphyria. *Side effects* include headache, nausea, vomiting, abdominal discomfort, sleep disturbances, and confusion. *Dose*: 250 mg every 8-hourly, doubled for severe infections. Maximum dose is 4 g daily.

Clenbuterol

Clenbuterol is a *beta-2 adrenergic agonist with* ephedrine-like actions. But the effects are more potent and longer-lasting, it increases aerobic capacity, raises blood pressure, stimulates the CNS, and is a smooth muscle relaxant. *Uses.* it is used in breathing disorders as a *decongestant* and *bronchodilator* in asthma. It has also been used as a *slimming aid* despite lack of sufficient supportive evidence. *Side effects* include tachycardia, rise in blood pressure, and loss of appetite. *Dose*: 20-60 mcg/day. Maximum dose is 150 mcg daily.

Dapoxetine

Dapoxetine is a short-acting SSRI (Selective Serotonin Reuptake Inhibitor), an antidepressant, currently being considered for treatment of *premature ejaculation* in men. A single dose of 60 mg has been selected for ongoing large-scale studies. *Side effects* like headache, nausea, and diarrhoea have been reported in about 6% of cases.

Donepezil, Galantamine, Rivastigmine

Symptoms of Alzheimer's disease are divided into two categories: ***(i)* Cognitive symptoms** affecting memory, language, thought and attention; and ***(ii)* Behavioural** and **psychiatric symptoms** marked by depression, delusions, and hostility.

Two types of drugs are available for treating cognitive symptoms: *(i)* **Cholinesterase inhibitors** (donepezil, *galantamine, rivastigmine,* and the older agents *tacrine* & *velnacrine);* and *(ii)* **Glutamate regulator** *(memantine).*

Cholinesterase Inhibitors

Donepezil, galantamine, and rivastigmine are *centrally-acting* reversible cholinesterase inhibitors. *Side effects* with these agents include nausea, vomiting, diarrhoea, dizziness, headache, sweating, insomnia, and urinary tract infections.

Donepezil: Its main therapeutic use is in the treatment of *all stages* of Alzheimer's disease (AD). It increases cortical acetylcholine and facilitates cortical function. Oral bioavailablity is 100%, and it easily crosses the blood-brain barrier (BBB). It has a half-life of 70 hours, and can be combined with memantine for better control of AD. *Dose*: Initial dose is 5 mg/day at bedtime, which can be increased to 10 mg/day.

Galantamine: It is used to treat *mild to moderate* AD in a dose of 4 mg bid for 4 weeks, increased to 8 mg bid for further 4 weeks. *Maintenance dose* is 8-12 mg bid. Galantamine is also being tried in cases of *vascular dementia* as a *nootropic* (memory enhancing) agent.

Rivastigmine: It is used to treat *mild to moderate* AD. *Dose*: Initially 1.5 mg bid, increased in steps of 1.5 mg bid at intervals of 2 weeks. Maximum dose is 6 mg bid.

Tacrine and **velnacrine** are two older agents used to treat AD. However, the cholinesterase inhibitors are unable to reverse the degenerative changes occurring in AD.

Glutamate Regulator

Memantine: In neurodegenerative disorders overstimulation of the *N-methyl-D-aspartate* (NMDA) receptor has been reported. Memantine is a *NMDA receptor antagonist* and offers *neuroprotection.* Thus memantine regulates glutamate activity, and is used to treat *moderate to severe AD. Dose:* Initially 5mg/day. The dose is increased weekly in 5 mg steps up to 20mg daily.

Depression and potential to harm themselves suffered by AD patients is managed by *antidepressants* like *trazodone, sertraline, fluoxetine,* and *citalopram.*

Anxiety: Antianxiety drugs like *lorazepam* and *oxazepam* are used.

Psychosis: Symptoms like hallucinations, hostility, delusions, aggression, and uncooperativeness is controlled by drugs like *clozapine, haloperidol, olanzepine,* and *risperidone.*

ENTACAPONE

Entacapone is a catecho!-O-methyitransferase (COMT) inhibitor, used as an adjunct in the treatment of *Parkinson's disease.* Entacapone prevents the peripheral breakdown of levodopa by inhibiting COMT, thereby allowing more levodopa to reach the brain. *Indication:* Entacaopne is used as an adjunct to levodopa plus a dopa decarboxylase inhibitor (carbidopa or benzserazide) in *Parkinson's disease,* specially to control 'end-of-dose' motor fluctuations. *Side effects* include headache, nausea, vomiting, abdominal pain, diarrhoea, dizziness, confusion, insomnia, muscle pain, dyskinesia, mood changes, hallucinations, and rarely hepatic dysfunction. *Dose*: 200 mg with each dose of levodopa + a dopa decarboxylase inhibitor. Maximum dose 2 g daily.

EPTIFIBATIDE

Eptifibatide reversibiy *inhibits platelet aggregation* by preventing the binding of fibrinogen, von Willebrand factor, and other adhesive ligands to *platelet receptor glycoprotein* (GP) llb/Illa of human platelets. The antiplatelet aggregation effect ends on dissociation of eptifibatide from the platelet receptor GP. Eptifibatide is approved for use with *heparin* or *aspirin* to *prevent myocardial infarction* in patients with *unstable angina.* This drug should be used by specialists only. *Contra-indications* are haemorrhagic diathesis, haemorrhagic stroke, severe hypertension, thrombocytopenia, hepatic and renal insufficiency. *Side effects* include bleeding manifestations, hypotension, rash and rarely anaphylactic reactions. *Dose*: Initially 180 mcg/kg by IV injection over 1 or 2 minutes, then IV infusion in a dose of 2 mcg/kg/minute up to 72 hours.

ESOMEPRAZOSE

Esomeprazole is one of the newer 'proton pump' inhibitors, which suppress gastric acid secretion by blocking the hydrogen-potassium-adenosine triphosphatase (ATPase) enzyme system (proton pump) of the gastric parietal cells. Esomeprazole is the S-enantiomer of omperazole, and is claimed to have an improved efficacy over the racemic mixture of omeprazole. It is used in the treatment of *dyspepsia, gastroesophageal reflux disease (GERD), peptic ulcer disease,* and *Zollinger-Ellison syndrome.* It is also prescribed with amoxicillin and clarithromycin for ulcers caused by *Helicobacter pylori* infections. *Side effects* include headache, diarrhoea, abdominal pain, respiratory infection, confusion, gynaecomastia, hypersensitivity reactions, and blood dyscrasias. *Dose*: 20-40 mg a day, one hour before a meal. For severe GERD it is given intravenously 40 mg once a day over 3 minutes, and continued until oral administration (20 mg) is possible.

EXENATIDE

Exenatide is one of a new class of antidiabetic medications known as incretin-mimetics. The incretin concept is based on the physiologic phenomenon that involves an increased release of insulin from the beta-cells in response to the rise in blood glucose after oral glucose (or meal) ingestion, compared to that following the same rise in glucose after parenteral administration. The gut hormones responsible for this Incretin-effect are two long-chain polypeptides: **GLP-1** and **GIP.** Both stimulate insulin release in a glucose dependent manner. However, GLP-1 has an additional effect by *suppressing glucagon release* from the alpha-cells, it reduces postprandial hyperglycaemia. GLP-1 also *slows gastric emptying* via the CNS. In animal models GLP-1 has also been shown to *reduce beta-cell apoptosis* (cell deletion by fragmentation and phagocytosis), thereby prolonging their survival. However, these agents (GLP-1 & GIP) are rapidly degraded within minutes to inactive compounds by the enzyme *dipeptidyl peptidase-4* (DPP-4). Agents resistant to inactivation by DPP-4 are being developed, and *exenatide* is one of them approved for the treatment of type-2 diabetes mellitus.

Exenatide is the synthetic version of GLP-1 found in human intestines, and in the saliva of Gila monster *Heloderma suspectum*, a venomous lizard found in the arid regions of Southwest USA, and Western Mexico. It is a 39- amino acid peptide and functions as an insulin secretogogue with glucoregulatory effects. It is approved as *adjunctive therapy to* improve glycaemic control in patients with type 2 diabetes taking metformin and/or a sulphonylurea, but have not achieved adequate control. *Mode of action:* Exenatide *augments pancreatic insulin release* in response to meals; it also suppresses release of glucagon in response to meals, and *reduces hepatic glycogenolysis;* slows down gastric emptying and *suppresses glucose absorption* from the gut; *promotes satiety* via hypothalamic receptors; and lastly it *reduces liver fat.* It is not a substitute for insulin in patients who need insulin treatment. *Side effects* include nausea, vomiting, diarrhoea, dyspepsia, hypoglycaemia, increased sweating, rarely anaphylactic reactions, angioedema, and pancreatitis. *Dose*: Exenatide is available as a prefilled fixed dosage injection pen with a small needle for subcutaneous injection on the thigh, abdomen or arm 30 to 60 minutes before the first and last meal of the day. Initially the dose is 5 mcg bid before two main meals (at least 6 hours apart). The dose may be raised to 10 mcg for good glycaemic control with significant reduction in HbA1c levels.

To summarise, exenatide is an incretin-mimetic, suppresses glucagon secretion, slows gastric emptying, and induces satiety via the CNS, It is given by subcutaneous injection as adjunctive treatment for type 2 diabetes mellitus in combination with metformin and/ or a sulphonylurea in patients exhibiting inadequate glycaemic control with conventional oral antidiabetics.

Ezetimide

Ezetimide is a unique *hypolipidaemic agent,* it acts by decreasing cholesterol absorption from the intestine by *localizing over the brush border of the intestinal mucosa.* It can be used alone, or in combination with other hypolipidaemic drugs like the *statins* (e.g. atorvastatin). Ezetimide is used as an adjunct to dietary measures in the management of *hypercholesterolaemia. Side effects* include headache, diarrhoea, and myalgia. Rarely extreme tiredness, and myopathy may occur. *Dose*: 10 mg once a day with or without food. It should preferably be taken around the same time every day.

Febuxostat

Febuxostat is a *xanthine oxidase inhibitor,* and is used in the treatment of *hyperuricaemia* and *gout.* It is a novel *non-purine selective* inhibitor of xanthine oxidase, and acts *non-competitively* by blocking the channel on an active site on the enzyme. As we know xanthine oxidase is needed for successive oxidation of *hypoxanthine* and *xanthine* to *uric acid.* Thus, febuxostat reduces uric acid production in the body. Febuxostat is a potential alternative to allopurinal for patients with hyperuricaemia and gout. *Side effects* include nausea, vomiting, rashes, and Gl disturbances. *Dose*: usual dose is 80 mg or 120 mg daily.

Fexofenadine

Fexofenadine is a *third-generation antihistamine* used for the treatment of *allergic disorders.* It competitively antagonises histamine at the *H_1-receptor sites.* It readily crosses the blood-brain barrier (BBB), and causes minimal drowsiness. Its half-life is 14.4 hours. *Uses:* For symptomatic relief from *seasonal allergic rhinitis]* and for relief from skin manifestations for *chronic idiopathic urticaria. Side effects* include headache, fatigue, drowsiness, nervousness, and sleep disorders. *Dose*: For *seasonal allergies* and *chronic urticaria* the dose is 60 mg bid daily, or 180 mg once daily.

Flutamide, Bicalutamide & Nilutamide

Flutamide is an oral *nonsteroidal antiandrogen* used to treat *prostate cancer. Mode of action:* It competes with *testosterone* and its metabolite *dihydrotestosterone* (DHT), and binds to the *androgen receptor.* Thus, it prevents the stimulus to the prostate to grow under the influence of testosterone. *Uses:* To treat prostate cancer; and to treat excess androgen levels in women. Flutamide is prescribed with a leuteinizing hormone-releasing hormone (LHRH) so as to inhibit the pituitary and block the chain for testosterone production. *Side effects* include gynaecomastia, galactorrhoea, sore throat, nausea, diarrhoea, decreased libido, increased appetite, hypertension, cholestatic jaundice, and hepatic necrosis. *Dose*: 250 mg tid. Total daily dose must be at least 750 mg for optimal effect. **Bicalutamide** is another *antiandrogen* with a profile similar to flutamide, but with milder side effects. *Dose*: 50 mg once daily. **Nilutamide** also is a nonsteroidal *antiandrogen* with an affinity for *androgen receptors.* It is used in the treatment of *advanced* prostate cancer. *Dose*: 300 mg daily, reduced to 150 mg daily after 30 days.

Formoterol

Formoterol is a *long-acting beta-2 agonist,* with a duration of action of up to 12 hours, compared to short-acting beta-2 agonists like salbutamol, which is effective only for 4-6 hours. Formoterol diffuses into the plasma membrane of the lungs, and then is slowly released back, which results in a long (12 hours) duration of action. *Uses:* It is used as a *bronchodilator* in the management of *bronchial asthma, chronic obstructive pulmonary disease* (COPD), and to *prevent exercise-induced bronchospasm. Side effects* include headache, nervousness, tremors, dry mouth, muscle cramps, tiredness, and sore throat. *Dose*: Formoterol is used in *four* forms: metered dose inhaler; dry powder inhaler; oral tablets; and as an inhalation solution. A 12 mcg dose of formoterol is equivalent to 50 mcg of salbutamol. It is also available with inhaled steroids like *beclomethasone dipropionate,* and *budesonide.*

Fosinopril

Fosinopril is an *angiotensin converting enzyme* (ACE) inhibitor used for the treatment of hypertension, and some types of *chronic heart failure.* Fosinopril is a prodrug converted *in vivo* to *fosinoprilat,* its active form. *Side effects* include cough, dizziness, vomiting, fatigue, swelling of face and ankles, lightheadedness, and sore throat. *Dose*: For *hypertension,* initially 10 mg daily, increased *if* necessary after 4 weeks (usual dose range 10-40 mg). For *heart failure* 10 mg daily under close supervision. It may be combined with a *diuretic* for better control.

Fosphenytom

Fosphenytoin is a phenytoin *prodrug* approved for use only in hospitals for short-term (5 days) treatment of *epileptic seizures, status epilepticus,* and for control of *seizures during neurosurgery. Side effects are* similar to those of phenytoin, and include pruritus, nystagmus, *ataxia, somnolence, tinnitus,* and *hypotension.* In addition, it can cause *hyperphosphataemia* in end-stage renal failure. *Dose*: For *status epilepticus,* 20-30 mg/kg is administered IV at a rate of 100-150 mg per minute. For nonemergent therapy 15-30 mg/kg can be administered IV or IM as a loading dose, with maintenance as 6-12 mg/kg. An effective oral dosage form is not available.

Gaboxadol

Gaboxadol is an investigational agent for the treatment of sleep disorders. It is a *direct-acting gamma-amino butyric acid-A* (GABA-A) agonist. Its action is different from the benzodiazepines as it causes its effect *directly via* the GABA-A receptors. Whereas, the benzodiazepines *modulate* the action of GABA receptors. Gaboxadol is being evaluated in multi-centric, randomized, and double-blind phase 3 trials. Gaboxadol affects NREM and REM sleep, and causes a physiological increase in sleep need. GABA-A receptors are directly involved in *homeostatic sleep regulation.* It is believed that the benzodiazepines produce sleep of subjective poor quality, whereas, gaboxadol enhances the quality of sleep. *Uses:* Its use is being evaluated in *early primary insomnia,* and *chronic primary insomnia.*

GEMCITABINE

Gemcitabine is a *nucleoside analogue* (antimetabolite) used as a *cytotoxic* chemotherapeutic agent. As with *fluorouracil* and other pyramidine analogues, gemcitabine replaces building blocks of nucleic acid *cytidine* during DNA replication. Tumour growth is arrested as new nucleosides are unable to attach to the "faulty" nucleoside, resulting in *apoptosis. Uses:* Gemcitabine is used for *non-small cell lung cancer, pancreatic cancer, bladder cancer, soft tissue sarcoma,* and *metastatic breast cancer.* Gemcitabine is considered to be a definite advance in *pancreatic cancer care. Side effects* include fever, fatigue, Flu-like symptoms, nausea, vomiting, anorexia, numbness of arms and legs, skin rash, low blood counts, bleeding, increased risk of infection, insomnia, mouth sores and hair loss. *Dose*: Gemcitabine is given by IV infusion (no oral form is available). The dose calculation is based on height and weight, general health, type of cancer, and other health problems. The exact dosage schedule is decided by the chemotherapist.

GLUCOSAMINE & CHONDROITIN SULPHATE

Glucosamine is an amino sugar, found naturally in the body, made from glucose and the amino acid *glutamine.* Glucosamine is needed in the body to produce *Glucosaminoglycan,* a molecule needed for the formation of *cartilage* and other body tissues. Its production slows with age. It is available as a *nutritional supplement* in the form of health food. Glucosamine is often combined with *chondroitin sulphate,* another molecule naturally present in cartilage. It provides *elasticity to cartilage* by preventing its enzymatic destruction. Glucosamine in patients of osteoarthritis provides an *anti-inflammatory action,* stimulates synthesis of *proteoglycans,* and *decreases the catabolic activity of chondrocytes* by inhibiting the synthesis of proteolytic enzymes that are responsible for damaging the cartilage matrix. Clinical trials on glucosamine in patients of osteoarthritis have generated conflicting results. Glucosamine is mainly derived from shellfish, and shells of other sea animals. An alternative source is by fungal fermentation of corn.

Chondroitin sulphate is a *glycosaminoglycan* composed of chains of alternating sugars. It is an important structural component of cartilage, and provides *resistance to compression strain* to the joint, and maintains the structural integrity of the joint cartilage. Glucosamine with chondroitin have been used as *dietary supplements* for the treatment of *osteoarthritis.*

Glucosamine sulphate (up to 1500 mg/day) plus chondroitin sulphate (up to 1200 mg/day) have been used for treating *osteoarthritis,* a degenerative disease of the joints. They stimulate the production of *proteoglycans* and *glycogen,* restore cartilage matrix, normalize cartilage metabolism, and promote synthesis of synovial fluid. Both these agents have a *synergistic* effect. It is claimed that the combination halts the disease process in osteoarthritis. Though the beneficial effect is not well substantiated, and further studies are in progress. This class of agents has been labeled as *nutraceuticals* or dietary supplements.

ITOPRIDE

Itopride is a novel prokinetic *benzamide derivative,* different from the available prokinetics like metoclopramide, cisapride, mosapride, and domperidone. *Mode of action:* Itopride has *anticholinesterase* (AChE) *activity,* and *dopamine D2 receptor antagonistic* activity. Thus, by a dual mechanism it increases *acetylcholine* (ACh) concentration by its AChE activity, and dopamine D2 receptor antagonism. Higher ACh levels increase GI peristalsis, increase the lower oesophageal sphincter pressure, stimulate gastric motility, and improve gastro-duodenal coordination. *Uses*: It is used in non-ulcer dyspepsia (NUD), gastro-oesophageal reflux disease (GERD), gastritis, diabetic gastroparesis, bloating, and functional dyspepsia. *Side effects* include diarrhoea, giddiness, exhaustion, rash, increased salivation, abdominal pain, headache, sleeping disorders, galactorrhoea, gynaecomastia, and rarely leucopenia. *Dose*: Usual dose is 50 mg of itopride HCI orally in 3 divided doses before each meal.

LAPATINIB

Lapatinib is an orally active chemotherapeutic agent for solid tumours like *breast cancer.* Pharmacologically, lapatinib is a *dual tyrosine kinase inhibitor,* and *interrupts cancer-causing cellular signals* by preventing self-phosphorylation and subsequent activation of the signal mechanism. *Uses'.* For the treatment of *advancèd breast cancer* in HER2-positive women, not responding to other drugs. Phase (II) clinical trials are on for assessing lapatinib as a first-line therapy for HER2-positive breast cancer patients. *Side effects* include fatigue, diarrhoea, nausea, rashes, and rarely reversible toxic hepatitis. *Dose*: Yet to be standardized.

LEVETRIACETAM

Levetriacetam is an *anticonvulsant* used as monotherapy or as an adjunctive treatment for *partial seizures, myoclonic seizures,* and *primary generalized tonic-clonic seizures.* Combined with gabapentin it can be used to treat *neuropathic pain.* Structurally it is related to the *nootropic* drug piracetam. *Mode of action:* It combines with a *synaptic vesicle protein SV2A,* and impedes nerve conduction across synapses. *Side effects* include dyspepsia, nausea, vomiting, diarrhoea, abdominal pain, anorexia, drowsiness, asthenia, rash, pancreatitis, hepatic dysfunction, pancytopenia, and alopecia. *Dose*: Initially 250 mg bid, increased according to the response in steps of 250 mg bid every 2 weeks. Maximum dose is 1.5 g twice daily.

Levocetirizine

Levocetirizine is a *third-generation non-sedative antihistamine,* developed from the second-generation antihistamine cetirizine. It acts by *competitively blocking H_1-histamine receptors. Uses:* It is used to control allergic disorders, and has been shown to *reduce asthma attacks* in children. It is claimed to be more effective with fewer side effects compared to second-generation antihistamines. *Side effects:* Drowsiness, dry mouth, headache, blurred vision, sore throat, and fatigue. *Dose*: 5 mg once daily.

Liraglutide

Incretins are gut hormones which step up insulin secretion from the pancreas even before blood glucose levels rise. This therapy has certain advantages, though not necessarily more potent than the existing ones. There are *two* types of *incretin-based* therapies: (*a*) *incretin-mimetics* like exenatide and liraglutide; and (*b*) those that reduce incretin breakdown (gliptins). Incretin-mimetics lower blood glucose levels, but never to dangerous levels, and the added benefit is *weight loss* with exenatide and liraglutide, and thus are useful in type 2 diabetes where weight loss plays a critical role.

Liraglutide is a long-acting *glucagon-like peptide-1* (GLP-1) analogue approved for the treatment of type 2 diabetes. *Mode of action:* Liraglutide is an acylated *human GLP-1 receptor agonist* GLP-1 receptor is a membrane receptor coupled to *adenylyl* cyclase, which on stimulation *increases intracellular cyclic AMP (cAMP)* leading to insulin release from the pancreatic beta-cells. This insulin secretion subsides when the blood glucose level approaches euglyacemia. Liraglutide is stable against metabolism by peptidases, and has a plasma half-life of 13 hours on subcutaneous injection, and is suitable for *once daily* administration. *Use:* It is used in *adult type 2 diabetes* either as monotherapy or in combination with oral antidiabetics like metformin. This new treatment is carried out in conjunction with diet control and exercise. In addition weight loss is also recorded, specially in obese type 2 diabetics. Liraglutide caused a significant fall in *glycosylated haemoglobin* (HbA1c) levels. In some controlled studies liraglutide once daily provided a better glycaemic control than with twice daily exenatide. *Side effects* include headache, nausea, diarrhoea, and rarely *anti liraglutide-antibody* formation is observed. *Dose*: It is administered in a dose of 1.2 mg or 1.8 mg subcutaneously once daily.

Lopinavir

Lopinavir is an antiretroviral agent belonging to the *protease inhibitor* class. It is available as a combination formulation with *sub-therapeutic* doses of *ritonavir* It is used as a component of combination (lopinavir/ritonavir) therapy to treat HIV/AIDS. At times it may also be used as monotherapy. *Side effects* observed with the combination are nausea, abdominal pain, diarrhoea, asthenia, headache, and hyperlipidaemia. *Dose*: Available as lopinavir 100 mg plus ritonavir 25 mg tablets. The dose is 2-3 tablets twice daily depending on the body-surface area.

Lornoxicam

Lornoxicam is a *non-steroidal anti-inflammatory drug* (NSAID) of the *oxicam* class, with analgesic, anti-inflammatory, and antipyretic properties. It is a new potent NSAID with an improved tolerability profile. *Mode of action:* Like other NSAIDs, lornoxicam *inhibits prostaglandin biosynthesis* by blocking the enzyme cycloxygenase. *It inhibits both COX-1 and COX-2 forms* of the enzyme, and readily penetrates into the synovial fluid. *Uses:* To treat *rheumatoid arthritis, osteoarthritis, postoperative pain, sciatica, soft tissue injuries, gout,* and *non-articular conditions* (bursitis, tendonitis, backache). *Side effects* include dizziness, abdominal pain, diarrhoea, vomiting, stomatitis, and indigestion. Rarely lornoxicam injections may cause palpitation, hypertension, shivering, unusual sweating, leucopenia, and thrombocytopenia. *Dose*: Orally 8 mg to 16 mg in 2 or 3 divided doses. Max. dose 16 mg daily. Parenterally, 8 mg OD or bid by IM/IV injection. Max. dose 24 mg daily.

Maraviroc

Maraviroc is a viral *entry inhibitor.* It blocks HIV from entering human helper T-cells. It has been approved for treatment of *CCR5-tropic HIV-1* infections, and can be combined with other antiretroviral agents. Maraviroc does not cure HIV infection or AIDS, and also does not reduce the risk of passing on the virus to others. *Side effects* include cough, fever, dizziness, headache, lowered blood pressure, nausea, infection, hypercholesterolaemia, and bladder irritation. *Dose*: Maraviroc is available as 150 mg and 300 mg tablets. In most patients 300 mg bid is administered. The dose has to be reduced in patients with associated kidney failure. Phase III and extended studies are on to assess the efficacy and safety of maraviroc.

Moxifloxacin

Moxifloxacin is a synthetic fluoroquinolone with a *broad-spectrum* of antibacterial activity. *Mode of action:* It inhibits bacterial topoisomerases, which are the essential enzymes for replication and repair of bacterial DNA. Moxifloxacin (oral or intravenous) is found in high concentrations in body fluids, skin, bone, and intraocular tissues. But it does *not* reach effective levels in the kidney or urinary tract. *Uses:* It is used to treat respiratory, intra-abdominal, and eye infections. It is also used as a *second-line agent* in the combination therapy of *tuberculosis,* and the duration of antitubercular treatment can be safely reduced from 6 months to 4 months. *Side effects* include gastrointestinal disturbances like abdominal pain, diarrhoea, and pseudomembranous colitis. Rarely skin reactions, hepatotoxicity, and seizures may occur. *Dose*: It is available as 400 mg tablets, and flexibags containing 400 mg in 0.8% sodium chloride aqueous solution. The usual dosage is 400 mg daily orally, or by IV infusion over 1 hour. The duration of treatment depends on the severity of the disease, and the tissue involved. Further clinical studies are in progress.

Newer Insulins

Recombinant human insulin analogues

Short-acting Insulins

Insulin lispro is *a short-acting recombinant human insulin analogue*. It has a *faster onset* and *shorter duration* of action than soluble insulin. Insulin lispro provides better *postprandial glucose control*. It is similar in its action to *insulin aspart*. Both of them can be used for *diabetic emergencies*. *Side effects* include local reaction and fat hypertrophy at injection site, transient oedema, rarely hypersensitivity reactions, and overdose may cause hypoglycaemia. It is administered by *subcutaneous* injection shortly before meals or shortly after meals, according to the requirement. It can also be given by *intravenous injection* or *infusion*.

Insulin aspart is another *short-acting recombinant human insulin analogue*. The *onset* of action is 15 minutes, *peaks* at 45-90 minutes, and *duration* of action is 3-5 hours. Indications and mode of use is the same as with insulin lispro.

Intermediate & long-acting Insulins

Insulin detemir is a *long-acting recombinant human insulin analogue*, for maintaining basal levels of insulin. It is an insulin analogue in which a fatty acid (myristic acid) is bound to the lysine amino acid at position B29. It binds to albumin through the fatty acid at B29, and then slowly dissociates from the complex. On *subcutaneous* injection it has an *onset* of action about 1-2 hours, *maximal effect* 4-12 hours, and *duration* 16-35 hours. Some diabetics have to be given twice daily dose *with a short-acting insulin*, while others receive a once daily depending on the response. *Caution:* Soluble insulin can be mixed with long-acting Insulins (except insulin detemir and insulin glargine) in the same syringe.

Insulin glargine is a *long-acting recombinant human insulin analogue*, given once daily to control basal blood sugar levels in diabetics. It has a duration of action of 18-26 hours, and has a "peakless" profile. Its pharamcokinetics resembles basal insulin secretion of non-diabetic pancreatic beta-cells. *Uses*: In *type 2 diabetes* insulin glargine can be combined with a *sulphonylurea* to control serum glucose levels. In *type 1 diabetes* insulin glargine has to be combined with a fast-acting insulin. *Dose*: It is given subcutaneously once daily, according to need.

Inhalabie Insulin

Exubera is a powdered form of *recombinant human insulin*, delivered through an inhaler into the lungs from where it is absorbed, and begins working in the body. Over the years with the development of technology, this inhalable insulin formulation was approved by the USFDA in January 2006. Exubera is the brand name for the first inhalable insulin. A review concludes that Exubera, the inhaled insulin formulation is effective, but not better than an injected short-acting insulin. The additional cost is much higher and is unlikely to be cost effective.

Exubera is a short-acting insulin and can be used to treat both Type l and type 2 diabetes. Traditionally insulin dose is prescribed in 'International units', but Exubera is prescribed in milligrams (1 mg = 3 units of insulin), but 3 mg of Exubera is equivalent to 8 units and not 9 units as expected. Thus, one should refer to the conversion table provided before prescribing the dose. Type 1 and type 2 diabetics still need and injection of a long-acting insulin to maintain a basal level of insulin over 24 hours. Exubera is approved for use only in non-smoking adults free from any lung disease. Lung function may be temporarily decreased on Exubera administration. Further evaluation for its safety and efficacy is in progress.

Oxcarbazepine

Oxcarbazepine, an antiepileptic, is used in the treatment of *partial seizures*, with or without *generalized tonic-clonic seizures*. It may also be used to treat *trigeminal neuralgia*. It has fewer side effects compared to carbamazepine. *Side effects* include nausea, vomiting, abdominal pain, dizziness, headache, agitation, amnesia, tremors, depression, diplopia, hypersensttivrty reactions, and Stevens-Johnson syndrome. *Dose*: Initially 300 mg bid, can be increased in steps up to 600 mg daily at weekly intervals. Dose range is 0.6-2.4 g daily in divided doses.

Paroxetine

Paroxetine is one of the *selective serotonin reuptake inhibitors* (SSRIs), used as an *antidepressantm* cases of obsessive-compulsive neuroses, depression, panic, social anxiety, and generalized anxiety disorders. *Side effects* include headache, yawning, changes in sex drive, raised cholesterol, and rarely cardiac arrhythmias, confusion, urinary incontinence, and paradoxical anxiety. *Dose*: 20 mg each morning. Max. Dose: 50 mg daily. It starts working in about 10 days.

Perindopril

Perindopril is one of the newer *angiotensin-converting enzyme* (ACE) inhibitors, and inhibits the conversion of angiotensin I to angiotensin II. It is used in the management of hypertension, symptomatic heart failure, for prophylaxis of cardiac irregularities following myocardial infarction, and for revascularization in coronary artery disease. *Side effects* include persistent dry cough, angioedema, rash, constipation/diarrhea, photosensitivity, asthenia, mood and steep disturbances. *Dose*: 4 mg daily in the morning adjusted according to response. Max. dose is 8 mg once daily. **Ramipril** is another ACE-inhibitor having similar actions, uses, and side effects. *Dose*: Initially 1.25 mg once daily, increased at intervals of 1-2 weeks. Maximum dose is 10 mg daily

PREGABALIN

Pregabalin is an *anticonvulsant* and *pain reliever*. The exact mode of action is unknown. It *does not* bind or affect the GABA-receptors. it binds to the tissues of the CNS where there is high flow of calcium, limits calcium flow into the CNS cells, and exerts its *pain-relieving* and *antiseizure* effects. It is used to control central and peripheral *neuropathic pain associated* with *diabetes mellitus*, pain of *herpes zoster*, and as adjunctive therapy for *partial seizures. Side effects* include dry mouth, constipation, flatulence, oedema, fatigue, weight again, and changes in sexual function. *Dose*: 50-200 mg tid, depending on the severity of the condition. Lower the dose for patients with reduced kidney function.

RABEPRAZOLE

Rabeprazone is a newer *proton upmp inhibitor*. It inhibits gastic acid secretion by blocking the hydrogen potassium adenosine triphosphatase (ATPase) enzyme system, also known as the "proton pump", located in the gastric *parietal cells*. Proton pump inhibitors are effective short-term treatment for *gastric* and *duodenal* ulcers in combination with antibacterials for eradication of *Helicobacter pylori* infection. Rabeprazole is also used to control excessive gastric acid secretion in Zollinger-Ellison syndrome. *Side effects* include cough, flu-like syndrome, rhinitis, chest pain, gastrointestinal disturbances, peripheral oedema, arthralgia, Stevens-Johnson syndrome, and nervousness. *Dose:* For duodenal, and gastric ulcers, and gastro-oesophageal reflux disease 20 mg once daily is administered for 4-8 weeks. For Zollinger-Ellison syndrome initially 60 mg OD, adjusted according to response.

RAMIPRIL

Ramipril is an *angiotensin converting enzyme* (ACE) inhibitor. ACE inhibitors lower the production of angiotensin II, thereby relaxing arterial muscles, leading to arteriolar dilatation. This allows the heart to pump blood easily, increasing the blood flow through the circulatory system. Ramipril is a *prodrug* and is converted to its active metabolite *ramiprilat* by liver enzymes. Its half-life is variable (3-16 hours), and is further prolonged by heart, liver or kidney failure. *Uses:* It is used to treat *hypertension*, and *congestive heart failure* (CHF). Also used for prevention of heart failure, stroke, diabetic nephropathy with microalbuminuria, stroke, and cardiovascular accidents which need revascularization of tissues. *Side effects* include dizziness, dry cough, light-headedness, hypotension, decreased libido, fatigue, muscle cramps, and mouth dryness. *Dose:* Patients are started at the lowest dose and titrated every 3-4 weeks (1.25 mg, 2.5 mg, 5 mg, 10 mg) as required.

REPAGLINIDE

Repaglinide lowers blood sugar levels by stimulating the release of insulin from the pancreas. *Mode of action:* Repaglinide increases the release of insulin from the beta-cells of the pancreas. It achieves this by *closing ATP-dependent potassium channels* in the beta-cell membrane. This *depolarizes the beta-cells,* opening the calcium channels, and the resulting *calcium influx* induces insulin secretion. It needs functional beta-cells to exert its action. It is the *first insulin secretagogue* which targets *postprandial hyperglycaemia.* Its rapid onset of action, and short-lived hypoglycaemic effects makes it an *ideal agent for controlling postprandial hyperglycaemia.* A related newer agent is *nateglinide. Uses:* It is used in type 2 (non-insulin dependent) diabetes, specially for *postprandial hyperglycaemia* either alone or in combination with other antibiabetics. *Side effects* include abdominal pain, diarrhoea or constipation, headache, itching, rash, dizziness, breathing trouble, rarely hypoglycaemia, and visual disturbances. *Dose*: Initially 500 mcg is given before main meals. Adjusted according to the response at interval of 1 2 weeks; up to 4 mg may be given as a single dose.

ROSIGLITAZONE

Rosiglitazone is a newer *thiazolidinedione,* used in the treatment of *Type 2 diabetes mellitus,* alone or in combination with a *sulphonylurea* or *metformin.* It reduces peripheral insulin resistance, and lowers blood glucose levels. Long-term benefits of thiazolidinediones are under scrutiny. *Side effects* include gastrointestinal disturbances, cardiac ischaemia, headache, anaemia, oedema, hypoglycaemia, increased appetite, and alopecia. *Dose*: Initially 4 mg OD, increased after 8 weeks to 8 mg daily in 2 divided doses.

SAQUINAVIR

Saquivanir is a *protease inhibitor,* and is used in combination with other *antiretroviral* drugs for HIV infection. *Side effects* include gastrointestinal disturbances, hepatic dysfunction, pancreatitis, anaemia, thrombocytopenia, Stevens-Johnson syndrome, hypersensitivity reactions, peripheral neuropathy, changes in libido, and alopecia. *Dose*: 1 g every 12 hours with sub-therapeutic doses of *ritonavir.*

TAMSULOSIN, ALFUZOSIN, FINASTERIDE & DUTASTERIDE

Agents available for the drug therapy of *benign prostatic hyperplasia* (*i*) Alpha 1-blockers; *Tamsulosin, Alfuzosin* (*ii*) 5-alpha-reductase inhibitors (5-ARI): *Finasteride, Dutasteride* (*iii*) Combination therapy: *Alpha1-blocker+ 5-ARI*

TAMSUIOSIN

Tamsuiosin is an *alpha1-receptor antagonist* with preferential selectivity for the *alpha 1a-receptor* in the prostate in comparison to the alpha 1b-receptor in the blood vessels, i.e., it has uroselective action. Thus, it is used in the symptomatic treatment of *benign prostatic hyperplasia* (BPH). It relieves difficulty in urination (hesitation, dribbling, weak stream & incomplete bladder emptying), dysuria, urinary frequency and urgency. It relaxes the muscles in the prostate and bladder, improving urinary flow. *Adverse effects* include headache, dizziness, hypotension, palpitation, and nasal congestion. In some males it may cause priapism and retrograde ejaculation (redirecting the ejaculate to the urinary bladder). *Dose*: 400 mcg OD half-hour after the same meal each day.

ALFUZOSIN

Alfuzosin is another *alpha 1a-receptor* antagonist used to treat BPH, and acts like tamsulosin, making it easier to urinate. *Side effects* include nausea, loss of appetite, dizziness, hypotension, and priapism. However, the severity of side effects is lesser. Hence alfuzosin is preferred over tamsulosin in sexually active men. Uroselective alpha-blockers (tamsulosin & alfuzosin) are preferred over other alpha-blockers like terazosin and doxazosin. Usual dose is 10 mg OD immediately after the same meal each day.

FINASTERIDE

Finasteride is a synthetic antiandrogen, and acts by inhibiting type II *5-alpha-reductase,* the enzyme which converts testosterone to dihydrotestosterone (DHT). *Indications:* It is used in the treatment of *BPH,* and *androgenic* alopecia (male pattern baldness). *Side effects*: abnormal ejaculation, decreased ejaculatory volume, gynaecomastia, erectile dysfunction, and testicular pain. *Dose*: 5 mg OD for BPH; I mg OD for alopecia.

DUTASTERIAE

Dutasteride is another *5-alpha-reductase inhibitor,* and acts like finasteride. It is used for the treatment of BPH, and *male pattern baldness.* Side effects are similar to those of finasteride. Use of antiandrogens is banned by sports organizations, as they can be used to mask steroid abuse. *Dose*: 500 mcg OD, and it may require 6 months treatment for any evidence of benefit.

Combination therapy (alpha-blocker + 5-ARI) provides greater benefit than tamsulosin or finasteride as monotherapy.

TERIPARATIDE

Teriparatide is a recombinant fraction of the parathyroid hormone. It is used in the treatment of *osteoporosis in postmenopausal women,* and *in men prone to bone fractures,* Also used in the treatment of *corticosteroid-induced osteoporosis. Side effects* include gastrointestinal disorders, palpitation, dyspnoea, headache, fatigue, depression, vertigo, myalgia, and irritation at injection-site. *Dose*: 20 mcg daily by subcutaneous injection for 12 to 18 months.

TRASTUZUMAB

Trastuzumab is a recombinant DNA-derived humanized *monoclonal antibody* which selectively binds with high affinity to *human epidermal growth factor receptor-2* (HER2). It inhibits the proliferation of human tumour cells that overexpress HER2 protein, and thereby exert a cytotoxic effect. *Uses:* For the treatment of *metastatic breast* cancer which overexpresses HER2 protein, and shows an unsatisfactory response to other chemotherapeutic regimens. It is also used as *adjuvant treatment* with *doxorubicin, cyclophosphamide,* and *paclitaxel* regimen in patients who are HER2 positive. *Side effects* include fever, infection, rash, breathlessness, unexplained cough, swelling on arms and legs, anorexia, vomiting, diarrhoea, and weakness. *Dose*: Initial *loading dose* is 4 mg/kg infused IV over 90 minutes. The *weekly maintenance dose* is 2 mg/kg IV infused over 30 minutes. *Precaution:* It should never be administered as an IV push or bolus. It should *not* be coadministered with *doxorubicin* or *cyclophosphamide.* However, trastuzumab can be coadministered with *paclitaxel.*

VITAMIN K2

Vitamin K is a fat-soluble vitamin, and has different forms: **Vitamin K1** *(phylloquinone)* is found in green leafy vegetables, and vegetable oils like soya bean and canola oils. *Phytonadione* is identical to K1, and is synthesized commercially. In the last decade most work has been done on *menaquinones* or **Vitamin K2.** This group is further divided into MK-4 and MK-7 and many others depending on the number of repeating 5-carbon units. Vitamin K2 production by intestinal bacteria provides us only with a small fraction of our daily needs, since it is mostly made in the large intestines, where it is poorly absorbed. **Vitamin K3** *(menadione)* is a potent synthetic form of vitamin K. The role of vitamin K is in *three* physiological processes: (*a*) In blood coagulation (factors II, VII, IX and X); (*b*) In bone metabolism (osteocalcin/bone gla-protein); and (*c*) In vascular smooth muscle (matrix gla-protein, MGP) which inhibits calcification of blood vessels.

Vitamin K2 is a collective term for a group of vitamin K compounds called *menaquinones.* The most commonly found menequinones in food are MK-4, MK-7, MK-8 and MK-9. Vitamin K2 exerts a powerful influence on bone building, specially in *osteoporosis,* and has the most potent gamma-carboxylation activity. The best natural source of vitamin K2 is derived from an ancient Japanese food called *natto,* which is a traditional fermented mixture of soya and rice. MK-7 is the most worked upon compound among the menaquinones. *Mode of action:* Vitamin K2 has a dual role in maintaining *bone homeostasis.* It *promotes osteotrophic processes,* and *slows osteoclastic processes* via calcium binding. Japan was the first country which recognized the role of vitamin K2 in osteoporosis. Vitamin K2 through "carboxylation" induces the osteoblasts to produce the protein *osteocalcin,* which function as a kind of glue that helps in "laying down" of calcium in the bones. *Uses:* The main use is in *osteoporosis,* where it helps to attain and retain bone mass, and the rate of bone loss due to ageing is slowed down. Vitamin K2 also plays a beneficial role in *coronary artery disease* (CAD) by clearing calcium deposits in the vessels. Vitamin K2 supplemntation is also under study for *Alzheimer's disease. Side effects:* Even high doses of vitamin K2 do not cause abnormal clotting. *Dose*: Most vitamin K2 supplements offer 45-150 mcg per day. Further studies are in progress.

VOGIIDOSE

Voglibose is an *alpha-glucosidase inhibitor used* for lowering postprandial blood glucose levels in patients of diabetes mellitus (DM). *Postprandial hyperglycaemia* (PPHG) is due to the first phase insulin secretion, and in type-2 DM this feature of glycaemic control is faulty. Alpha-glucosidase inhibitors delay glucose absorption from the intestines, and prevent a sudden rise in blood glucose levels after meals. There are *three* drugs in this class, namely, *acarbose, miglitol,* and *voglibose* is the latest. Voglibose scores over acarbose and miglitol with lesser side effects. But acarbose scores over voglibose in terms of efficacy offering better control over PPHG and HbA1c levels. *Miglitol* is another alpha-glucosidase inhibitor primarily used in type-2 DM. It lowers the degree of PPHG, and has to be taken at the start of main meals to have maximal effect. *Indications:* Voglibose is used in the management of PPHG, which in turn reduces the risk of vascular complications of DM. *Adverse effects* include nausea, vomiting, flatulence, GI disturbances, and rarely intestinal obstruction-like symptoms. *Dose*: Voglibose 0.2 mg is to be taken immediately before a meal or with the first mouthful of food. It can also be combined with metformin 500 mg for a better overall control of type-2 DM.

ZANAMIVIR

Zanamivir is a *neuraminidase inhibitor used* for the prophylaxis and treatment of Influenza virus A and influenza Virus B Infections. Zanamivir was the first of the neuraminidase inhibitors, used as an *inhalation,* and oseltamivir soon followed as an oral *tablet* formulation. Influenza (flu) is caused by a virus which targets the respiratory cells, and damages the lining of the respiratory tract. It spreads rapidly by replicating itself inside the host cells damaging the respiratory tract causing swelling and inflammation. For some people flu and its complications can be serious and even fatal. *Mode of action:* Zanamivir binds to the active site of the neuraminidase protein, rendering the influenza virus unable to escape the host ceil and infect other cells. It is also an inhibitor of virus replication *in vitro* and *in vivo.* In clinical trials it was found to reduce time to symptom resolution by 1.5 days, provided the therapy was started within 48 hours of onset of symptoms. Influenza virus subtype for *Avian flu* is A/H5N1 subtype, and for *Swine flu* is A/H1N1 subtype. It has been recently reported that even oseltamivir-resistant H5N1 (Avian flu) infection responds to zanamivir administration, and thus has some advantage over oseltamivir. *Side effects* include dizziness, nasal irritation, joint pain, shortness of breath, wheezing, rash, itching, hypersensitivity, swelling of the face, and hoarseness. *Dose*: Zanamivir in powder form comes with a *plastic inhaler and rotadisks.* It has to be inhaled by mouth. Usual dose is 2 inhalations twice daily for 5 days. A *warning* is that respiratory problems may follow in patients with *asthma* or other *chronic obstructive pulmonary disease* (COPD), as it could induce bronchospasm.

A vaccine against H1N1 influenza virus infection (Swine flu) has been developed as the first *indigenous intra-nasal vaccine* by an Indian pharmaceutical firm. This H1N1 vaccine (Nasovac) is delivered directly into the nasal cavity in a dose of 0.5 ml. This vaccine has been developed from the "donor virus" obtained from the WHO. It would guard the person against Swine flu infection for a period of over a year. It is safe and easy to administer, and is meant for children over 3 years of age and the elderly people. Here it may be mentioned that Swine flu is a dangerous disease and it killed over 1000 people across our country in May 2009. Further human clinical studies are in progress.

ZOLEDRONIC ACID

Zoledronic acid is a biphosphonic acid which inhibits *osteoclastic bone resorption.* It is used in the treatment of *Paget's disease* of bones, and *osteoporosis in postmenopausal women.* In addition, it is used to treat *hypercalcaemia of malignancy, multiple myeloma,* and *bone metastases from solid tumours. Side effects* include hypophophataemia, hypercalcaemia, anaemia, flu-like syndrome, bone pains, myalgia, rigors, fever, asthenia, and blood counts. *Dose*: For Paget's disease 5 mg is given as a single dose by IV infusion over 15 minutes. Following the infusion at least 500 mg of elemental calcium should be given twice daily with vitamin D.

ZOPICLONE

Zopiclone, chemically a *cyclopyrrolone,* is a *non-benzodiazepine hypnotic* agent. The other two related agents are *zolpidem* and *zaleplon.* All the three agents have a high affinity for CNS binding sites of the *GABA macromolecule receptor complex.* They have a short duration of action, and are meant for short-term use (up to 4 weeks) for treating *insomnia.* Zopiclone induces sleep without reduction in total REM sleep, and preserves the normal slow-wave sleep. *Uses:* Short-term treatment of insomnia, nocturnal awakening, sttuational or chronic insomnia, and insomnia secondary to psychiatric disturbances. *Side effects* include metallic after-taste, nausea, vomiting, and urticaria. *Dose*: 7.5 to 15 mg shortly before retiring. Reduced doses are administered to the elderly.

I APPENDIX

Weights And Measures

The term **"metrology"** is derived from the Greek word `metron', meaning measure. Metrology is the science of weights and measures. The term weight signifies the force with which a body is attracted towards the earth by gravity. There are two systems of weighing and measuring drugs: (*i*) the **Metric System;** and (*ii*) the **Apothecaries' System.**

The Metric System

The **metric** or **decimal** system of weights and measures has been accepted all over the world for mainly two merits: (*i*) its tables are simple, because they are based upon the decimal system of notation; and (*ii*) its tables of **weights, volume** and **length** are correlated, and the **metre** is the fundamental unit of this system.

The metric system is based on the decimal system, using multiples or fractions of 10. The primary units in this system are **metre** (m) for length, litre (l) for volume, and **gram** (g) for weight. Internationally the abbreviation for gram is recognized as `g'. In UK the gram is abbreviated as `G'. The unit of weight, the gram is defined as the weight of 1 ml of distilled water at 4°C , *in vacuo* i.e., at standard temperature and pressure (STP). Under these conditions 1 g of water and 1 ml of water are equal (1 g H_2O = 1 ml H_2O at STP). Fractional parts of these primary units are expressed by adding Latin prefixes for sizes smaller than the primary unit, and Greek prefixes for multiples, i.e., for sizes larger than the primary unit.

Decreasing prefixes (Latin)

micro = 1/1,000,000

milli = 1/1,000

centi = 1/100

deci = 1/10

Increasing prefixes (Greek)

deca = 10

hecto = 100

kilo = 1,000

myria = 10,000

In ordinary usage the abbreviations are more commonly employed than the full names of the units. In actual practice the prefixes myria-, hecto-, deca-, and deci- are rarely used. On the other hand the prefixes kilo-, centi-, and milli- are commonly used (**Table I-1**).

Table I-1. *The Metric system of weights and measures (capacity and length)*

TABLE OF WEIGHT		
1000 micrograms (mcg)	=	1 milligram (mg)
10 milligrams	=	1 centigram (cg)
10 centigrams	=	1 decigram (dg)
10 decigrams	=	1 gram (g)
10 grams	=	1 decagram (Dg)
10 decagrams	=	1 hectogram (Hg)
10 hectograms	=	1 kilogram (Kg)
10 kilograms	=	1 myriagram (Mg)
10 myriagrams	=	1 quintal (Ql)
10 quintals	=	1 tonne (T)

TABLE OF SMALL WEIGHT			
1 gram (g)	=	1/1000 of	1 kilogram
1 milligram (mg)	=	1/1000 of	1 gram
1 microgram (mcg)	=	1/1000 of	1 milligram
1 nanogram (ng)	=	1/1000 of	1 microgram

TABLE OF CAPACITY (VOLUME)		
10 millilitres (ml)	=	1 centilitre (cl)
10 centilitres	=	1 decilitre (dl)
10 decilitres	=	1 litre (l)
10 litres	=	1 decalitre (Dl)
10 decalitres	=	1 hectolitre (Hl)
10 hectolitres	=	1 kilolitre (Kl)
10 kilolitres	=	1 myrialitre (Ml)

TABLE OF SMALL VOLUMES		
1 litre (l)	=	1000 Cm^3
1 millilitre (ml)	=	1/1000 of 1 litre
1 microlitre (µl)	=	1/1000 of 1 millilitre

TABLE OF LENGTH		
10 millimetres (mm)	=	1 centimetre (cm)
10 centimetres	=	1 decimetre (dm)
10 decimetres	=	1 metre (m)
10 metres	=	1 decametre (Dm)
10 decametres	=	1 hectometre (Hm)
10 hectometres	=	1 kilometre (Km)

TABLE OF SMALL LENGTH		
1 centimetre (cm)	=	1/100 of 1 metre
1 millimetre (mm)	=	1/1000 of 1 metre
1 micrometre (µm)	=	1/1000 of 1 millimetre
1 nanometre (nm)	=	1/1000 of 1 micrometre

The Apothecaries' System

The Apothecaries' system of weights and measures is no longer used in prescription writing. However, the physician must know its basic units and their metric equivalents. The basic unit of weight is the **grain,** and that of capacity is the **minim.** The commonly employed equivalents are shown in **Table I-2.**

Table I-2 *The metric weights and volume with approximate Apothecary equivalents*

1 milligram (mg)	=	1/60 grain
1 gram (g)	=	15 grains
1 kilogram (kg)	=	2.2 pounds (avoirdupois)
1 millilitre (ml)	=	1.5 minims
1 grain	=	60 mg
1 ounce	=	30 g
1 fluid ounce	=	30 ml
1 pint	=	500 ml

Household Measures

Most of the drugs prescribed are usually measured by the patient using kitchen utensils. The approximate contents of these measures are listed in **Table I-3.**

Table I-3. *Household measures*

Measure		Approximate metric equivalent
1 drop	=	0.1 ml
1 teaspoonful	=	5.0 ml
1 dessertspoonful	=	8.0 ml
1 tablespoonful	=	15.0 ml
1 water glass	=	250 ml

The International System of Units (SI Units)

The International System of Units (Systeme Internationale d' Unites) was finally evolved in 1960. It is intended to be used universally. **SI units are all based on the metric system,** i.e, the **kilogram,** the **metre,** and the **second.** The SI units are of three types: **basic** units; **derived** units; and **supplementary** units. Only two supplementary units are at present defined, the **radian** and the **steradian,** which are units for plane and solid angles respectively. Certain units which are not a part of the SI unit system continue to be used **(Table I-4). In April 1977, the World Health Organization recommended the adoption of SI units by the medical community throughout the world.**

The **Calorie** is not included in the SI units, and has been replaced by kJ × 4.186. The commonly used multiples and submultiples of the units are denoted by the following prefixes:

Prefix	*Symbol*	*Multiplication factor*
tera	T	10^{12} = 1000 000 000 000
giga	G	10^{9} = 1 000 000 000
mega	M	10^{6} = 1 000 000
kilo	k	10^{3} = 1 000
hecta	h	10^{2} = 1 00
deca	da	10^{1} = 1 0
deci	d	10^{-1} = 0.1
centi	c	10^{-2} = 0.01
milli	m	10^{-3} = 0.001
micro	µ	10^{-6} = 0.000 001
nano	n	10^{-9} = 0.000 000 001
pico	p	10^{-12} = 0.000 000 000 001
femto	f	10^{-15} = 0.000 000 000 000 001
atto	a	10^{-18} = 0.000 000 000 000 000 001

Millimoles and Milliequivalents

The SI unit of quantity, the **mole,** is used for quantification in pharmacological work. The basis of the unit is the atomic weight of carbon, which is 12. Thus the **mole** is the amount of a substance which contains the same number of elementary units (atoms, molecules, ions, electrons etc.), as there are in 12 g of carbon-12. A **millimole** (mmol) is one thousandth of this amount, and for ions is the ionic weight (the sum of the atomic weights of the elements of an ion) expressed in milligrams. A **milliequivalent** (mEq) is this quantity divided by the valency of the ion. The valency is important in determining a mole of an ion, e.g., a millimole per litre of Ca^{++} is 40 mg/l, whereas a mEq/l is 20 mg/l, as the valency of calcium is 2. **A solution which contains 1 mol/l of a substance is a molar solution (M); if it contains 1 mol/kg of solvent it is a molal solution.** One mole of some important drugs can be determined from the molecular weights, which are readily available in the **British Pharmacopoeia** or the **Pharmaceutical Codex** or the **Extra Pharmacopoeia**. In medical and pharmaceutical practice molar concentration is currently used for expressing the strength of parenteral electrolyte infusion and dialysis solutions. Drug doses are in terms of mass concentration. In the SI units, the concentration is expressed as mass concentration (e.g., g/l, mg/l, mcg/l), or as molar concentration (e.g., mol/l, mmol/l, µ mol/l). Mass concentration is also used to express the concentration of mixtures of substances with indefinite or known, molecular weights.

Preparation of Solutions

A solution contains a **solute** which is dissolved in a **solvent** giving a homogeneous mixture. Most solutions used in the practice of medicine are unsaturated solutions, i.e., the solute to be dissolved is usually well below the capacity of the volume of solvent employed. The strengths of pharmaceutical preparations are usually expressed in terms of **percent strength,** and for very dilute solutions, expressions of **ratio strength** or **mg%** may be used **(Table I-5).**

Table I-4 *SI Units and examples of units derived from the SI units*

Quantity measurement	*Name of SI unit*	*Symbol*
Basic Units		
Length	metre	m
Mass	kilogram	kg
Time	second	s
Electric current	ampere	A
Thermodynamic temperature	kelvin	K
Luminous intensity	candela	cd
Amount of substance	mole	mol
Derived units (examples)		
Frequency	hertz	Hz
Force	newton	N
Pressure	pascal	Pa
Work energy, quantity of heat	joule	J
Power	watt	W
Electric potential difference	volt	V
Not SI units but continue to be used (examples)		
Time	minute	min
hour	h	
day	d	
Volume	litre	l
Temperature	degree Celsius	°C
Length	angstrom	Å

The calculation of percentage strengths of solutions either by weight of a drug in grams, or by volume of a drug in millilitres, and taking percentages of grams to millilitres is based on the following equation:

1 g of water = 1 ml of water at STP

Conversion Formulae

Temperature

To convert *Fahrenheit to Centigrade*, subtract 32 from °F, multiply by 5/9.

To convert C*entigrade to Fahrenheit multiply* °C by 9/5, and add 32.

Weight

1 Kg = 2.2 lb 1 lb = 0.45 Kg

1 Gm = 15.43 grains 1 grain = 0.065 grams

mg% to mEq/L

In case of solids

$$\frac{\text{mg \%} \times \text{valance} \times 10}{\text{atomic wt.}} = \text{mEq/L}$$

In cae of gases

$$\frac{\text{vol \%} \times 10}{22.4} = \text{mM/L}$$

(For CO_2 use 22.26 instead of 22.4).

Table I-5 *Methods of expressing the strengths of solutions*

Expression	*Abbreviation*	*Meaning (example)*
Percent weight-in-volume	% w/v	Number of grams of a constituent in 100 ml of preparation (e.g., 1% w/v = 1 g of constituent in 100 ml of preparation).
Percent volume-in-volume	% v/v	Number of ml of constituent in 100 ml of preparation (e.g., 1% v/v = 1 ml of constituent in 100 ml of preparation).
Percent weight-in-weight	% w/w	Number of grams of a constituent in 100 g of preparation (e.g., 1% w/w = 1 g of constituent in 100 g of preparation).
Ratio strength, weight-in-volume	– : – w/v	Number of grams of constituent in stated number of ml of preparation (e.g. 1:1000 w/v = 1 g of constituent in 1000 ml of preparation).
Ratio strength, volume-in-volume	– : – v/v	Number of ml of constituent in stated number of ml of preparation (e.g., 1:1000 v/v = 1 ml of constituent in 1000 ml of preparation).
Ratio strength, weight-in-weight	– : – w/w	Number of grams of constituent in stated number of grams of preparation (e.g., 1:1000 w/w = 1 g of constituent in 1000 g of preparation).
Milligram percent	mg%	Number of mg of constituent in 100 ml of preparation (e.g., 5 mg% = 5 mg of constituent in 100 ml preparation).

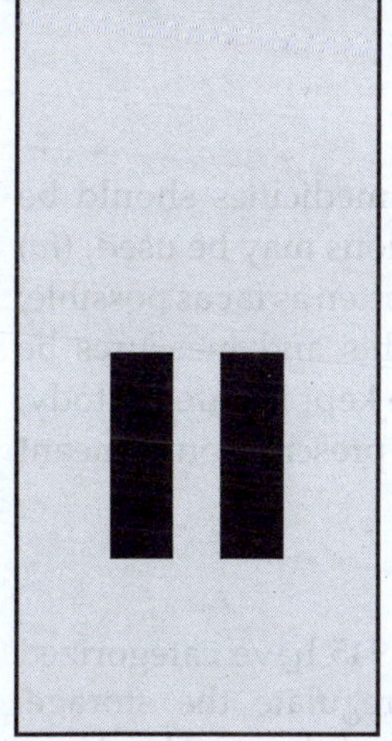

APPENDIX

Prescription Writing and Drug Compendia

The prescription is the focal point in the **physician-patient-pharmacist relationship**. It serves as a communication between the physician and pharmacist, both of whom share the responsibility of safeguarding the patient. It is the **legal method** for dispensing the drugs to the patient.

A **prescription** is defined as a written order of a registered physician to the pharmacist with directions for the preparation of the prescribed drugs, and their use by the patient. A valid prescription should invariably be written and signed by the prescriber.

Parts of a Prescription

Traditionally, a prescription order follows a definite pattern, which facilitates its interpretation. It consits of the following parts:

1. **Name and address of the physician,** and his or her telephone number. This part is usually printed on a prepared pad of blanks.
2. **Patient's name and address,** his or her **age,** and the **date.**
3. **Superscription.** This consists of the symbol Rx, the abbreviation for "receipe", which means "take thou". This symbol has also been considered to be an invocation to Horus, Egyptian God of the Sun and Jupiter, the father of the Gods whose help is wished to make the prescription effective.
4. **Inscription.** This part forms the **body of the prescription** order. It contains the name and the amount of each ingredient. The metric system of weights and measures must be used. Many physicians use a vertical line for decimal points, known as the **"decimal line"**. Above this line one may place "g or ml". This may be printed on the prescription order pad (see model prescription). The inscription consists of four subdivisions: (*i*) **Basis:** This is the main drug which is responsible for the chief action of the prescription; (*ii*) **Adjuvant:** It is the helping drug which promotes the action of the main drug; (*iii*) **Corrective:** It modifies or eliminates the undesirable effects of the basis and adjuvant; and (*iv*) **Vehicle:** This is the agent used as a solvent or carrier of the drugs into the human system.
5. **Subscription.** Right under the body of the prescription are written the directions to the pharmacist regarding the compounding and dispensing of the prescription. These directions form the subscription.
6. **Signature or Signatura.** This includes the directions for the patient. Some physicians prefer the term **label,** as these directions are written by the pharmacist on the label of the container in which the preparation is dispensed.
7. **Prescriber's signature and Registration number.** It is required by law that the physician's signature and registration number must appear on every prescription order.

The following is a model prescription order (the Arabic numerals on the extreme left correspond with the above mentioned parts of the order):

1. Dr. A.B.C. Address:
   Telephone:
2. Patient's name: Data
   Address: Sex Age:
3. Rx
4.

	g or ml		(alternative)
(Basis) Theophylline	3	6	3.6 g
(Adjuvant) Ephedrine sulphate		7	0.7 g
(Corrective) Phenobarbital		7	0.7 g
Wild Cherry Syrup	90		90.0 ml
(Vehicle) Distilled water q.s ad	180		180.0 ml

5. Mix and make the mixture.
6. *Label:* One teaspoonful every 4 hours, as needed
7. Signature

Regn. No.

Let us go through another model prescription (the parts 1, 2, and 7 have been excluded):

Rx

Ammonium bicarbonate	0.2 g
Ipecacuanha tincture	0.3 ml
Liquorice liquid extract	0.6 ml
Anise water	4 ml
Camphor water	8 ml
Water to make	15 ml

Mix to make a mixture. Send such 6 doses.

Label: One tablespoonful to be taken three times a day.

Although it is not desirable to use Latin in an English prescription, conventionally a lot of Latin abbreviations are used by physicians, perhaps to save time. Thus, some commonly used **abbreviations** must be known to the physician and are listed in **Table II-1.**

In the interest of the patient the following features in prescription writing must be observed: (*i*) it should be legible, complete and writen in ink; (*ii*) there should be no overwriting; (*iii*) full names of medicines should be written. However, official abbreviations may be used; (*iv*) generic names of drugs should be written as far as possible; (*v*) official abbreviations for weights and measures be used; (*vi*) prescription pads must be kept in safe custody; and (*vii*) the duration for which the prescription is meant must be clearly indicated.

Categories of Drugs

The Drugs and Cosmetics Rules, 1945 have categorized drugs into various schedules to regulate the storage, sale, **compounding** and **dispensing** of drugs. **The drugs included in Schedule H and L should be dispensed only on the prescription of a registered medical practitioner.** Drugs other than those included in Schedule H and L may be dispensed without prescription. However, it is much better and safer to give a prescription for every category of drug.

Modern Prescription Writing

The use of complicated mixtures for the treatment of disease is on the decline, except by the old and orthodox

Table II-1 *Some commonly used Latin abbreviations*

Abbreviation	*Latin derivation*	*English meaning*
aa	ana	of each
a.c	ante cibum	before meals
ad	ad	to, up to
ad lib.	ad libitum	at pleasure (as desired)
Aq.	aqua	water
b.i.d.	bis in die	twice a day
C̄	cum	with
Caps.	capsula	capsule
Comp.	compositus	compound
dil.	dilutus	dilute
et	et	and
ft.	fiat	make, let be made
g,, G or gm	Gramma	a gram
h.	hora	hour
h.s.	hora somni	at bedtime
inj	injectio	injection
M.	misce	mix
o.h.	omni hora	every hour
p.c.	post cibum	after meals
p.r.n.	pro re nata	as needed
pulv.	pulvis	powder
q.i.d.	quater in die	four times a day
q.s.	quantum sufficit	a sufficient amount
s̄	sine	without
s.o.s.	si opus sit	if needed
Sig.	signa	write on the label
sol.	solution	solution
ss.	semis	half
stat.	statim	at once
tab.	tabella	tablet
t.i.d.	ter in die	three times a day
t.d.s.	ter die sumendum	three times a day
Tr.	tinctura	tincture
ung.	unguentum	ointment

physicians. Modern prescription writing is generally simple. Prescriptions for antibiotics, psychotropic drugs, analgesics and vitamins are written most frequently. Prescriptions today are commonly for **proprietary remedies**, although the cost to the patient is comparatively higher. A prescription for a proprietary remedy must have the **name of the manufacturer** written on it.

Drug Compendia

Drug compendia are concise and comprehensive books which provide authoritative information on drugs. The **pharmacopoeias** are a class of drug compendia, which are **official** or **semi-official** publications giving accounts of preparations of drugs used therapeutically. The objective of a pharmacopoeia is to select from among the available therapeutic substances, those substances the utility of which is fully established and understood, and to form from them preparations and compositions which can be used with maximum therapeutic efficacy and advantage. A pharmacopoeia is periodically revised and kept up-to-date, and for a drug to the included in it there must be good evidence for its **therapeutic merit** or its **pharmaceutic necessity**. The **National Formulary** compiled by the respective pharmaceutical associations is also revised periodically, and includes drugs and formulations of demonstrated therapeutic value. It is a smaller and much more handy book compared to the pharmacopoeia. Quite a few countries in the world have compiled their own pharmacopoeia and National Formulary. The main body of the pharmacopoeia is occupied by various **pharmacopoeal monographs** on drugs (Official) and ancilliary substances. A monograph includes the structural and chemical formulae, solubility information, description, identification, purity data, directions for storage, dosage and dose range of a particular agent. Apart from this, these books contain details of methods for biological standardization and quality control of drugs. It is advisable to have a look through a pharmacopoeia available in the library, and find for yourself the enormous amount of information it contains about drugs.

The **International Pharmacopoeia** (Pharmacopoeia Internationalis) is published by the World Health Organization, Geneva. The First Edition was published in two volumes (1951 and 1955 respectively). The Second Edition in 1967, followed by a supplement in 1971. It is published in many languages (English, French, Russian, Spanish) The Third Edition is under publication. Volume 1 was published in 1979, containing the description of general methods of analysis; it will be followed by volumes containing the monographs, i.e., quality specifications for individual drugs, primarily for those most widely used in general health care. This pharmacopoeia is meant for use and adoption all over the World.

The **European Pharmacopoeia** (Vol. I, 1969; Vol. II, 1971) was published under the direction of the Council of Europe (Partial Agreement) in accordance with the Convention on the Elaboration of a European Pharmacopoeia. It was prepared by the Public Health Committee and the European Pharmacopoeia Commission. Official texts are available in the English and French language, for use mainly in Europe. In addition to the pharmacopoeias and the national formularies, in many countries there are other authentic compilations available for consultation by pharmacists, chemists and physicians **(Chap 1.1)**.

❑❑❑

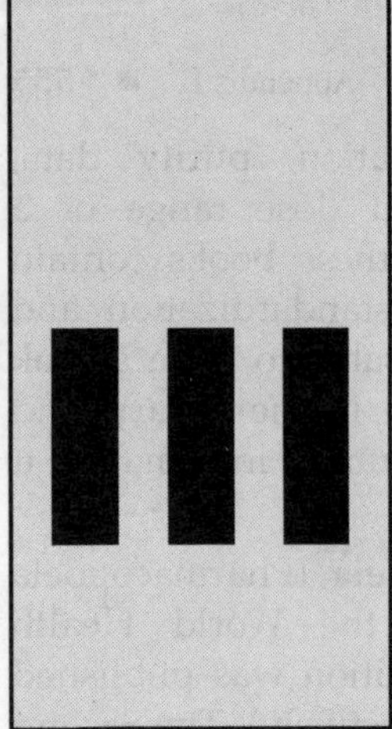

APPENDIX

REFERENCES FOR GENERAL READING

— Brunton LL, Chabner BA, Knollmann BC, eds. *Godman* and *Gilman's* ; *The Phramacological Basis of Therapeutics*, 12th ed. The McGraw-Hill Companies, 2011.

— *British Natijonal Formulary (BNF 61)*. London: British Medical Association and Royal Pharmaceutical Society of Great Britain, No. 61, March 2011.

— Caruthers SJ, Hoffmann BB, Melmon KL, Nierenberg DW et al. eds. *Melmon and Morrelli's Clinical Pharmacology (Paperback)*, 4th ed. McGraw-Hill Medical 2000.

— Craig CR, Stitzel RE, eds. *Modern Phamacology with Clinical Applications*, 6th ed. Lippincott William and Wilkins, 2004.

— *Drug Facts and Comparisons 2011*, Facts and Comparisons, 65th ed. Lippincott William and Wilkins, 2010.

— Grahame-Smith D, Jeffery KA. *Oxford Textbook of Clinical Pharmacology and drug Therapy (Paperback)*. 3rd Oxford University Press, USA.

— Katzung BG, Masters SB, Trever AJ, eds. *Basic and Clinical Phramacology*, 11th ed. The McGraw-Hill Companies, Lange Educational Libraray, 2009.

— Laurence DR, Bennett PN, Brown MJ. *Clinical Pharmacology*. 8th ed. Edinburgh: Churchill Livingstone, 1997.

— Rang HP, Dale MM, Ritter JM, Flower RJ, Henderson G, eds. *Rang and Dale's Pharmacology*, 7th ed. US Elsivier Health, 2011.

— Reynolds JEF, Kathleen P, eds. *Martindale The Extra Pharmacopoeia*. 31st ed. London: The Royal Pharmaceutical Society, 1996.

— **Websites:**

a. *www.nlm.nih.gov/medicine/print/druginfo*

b. *www.netdoctor.co.uk/medicines*

c. *www.rxlist.com/cgi/generic*

d. *www.healthresource.com/library*

e. *www.mentalhealth.com/drug*

f. *www.medclik.com*

❑❑❑

INDEX

Q

R

❑❑❑